Tax Planning for Owner-Managed Companies

2011/12

Tax Planning for Family and Owner-Managed Companies

2011/12

By Peter Rayney FCA CTA(Fellow) TEP
Peter Rayney Tax Consulting Ltd

Bloomsbury Professional

Bloomsbury Professional
Maxwelton House
41–43 Boltro Road
Haywards Heath
West Sussex
RH16 1BJ

© Bloomsbury Professional Ltd 2011

Bloomsbury Professional is an imprint of Bloomsbury Publishing plc

British Library Cataloguing-in-Publication Data

A CIP Catalogue record for this book is available from the British Library.

ISBN   978 1 84766 765 6

Typeset by Phoenix Photosetting, Chatham, Kent
Printed and bound in Great Britain by Hobbs the Printers Ltd, Totton, Hampshire

Preface

There are few areas of taxation that do not impact on family or owner-managed companies and their shareholders. Consequently, this book covers a wide variety of tax planning matters. The book continues to grow in size with each new edition and this year's is fully up-to-date with the *FA 2011* changes.

For most 'fiscal mortals' like me, we do have to seriously question whether we can ever be fully up-to-date at any point in time, such is the speed with which new legislation tends to be introduced. This edition also reflects new practical insights and experiences, together with emerging case law and HMRC practice.

In this book I have taken a slightly unique approach of summarising the key planning points from the separate viewpoints of the company itself, the shareholders who work for the company (usually as directors), the non-working shareholders and in some instances the employees. Only by taking that approach can the complete picture be seen – the planning checklists appear at the end of all relevant chapters. Many worked examples are also provided to illustrate the practical tax and commercial implications for a host of typical situations (all references to characters and companies in the examples are, of course, entirely fictitious!).

Clearly there will be occasions when what is tax efficient for the company itself will not necessarily be effective for the shareholders in their capacity as individual taxpayers. This conflict need not always present a major problem, but proper regard must be had to the interests of all parties before embarking upon any tax planning exercise.

It is intended that this book will provide the complete picture on family/owner-managed company tax planning for professional advisers such as tax consultants, accountants and solicitors, and to the owners and financial directors of these types of company themselves. This book has been extensively updated since it was first published in 1995 and draws heavily on my extensive practical experience in dealing with owner-managed companies.

The book naturally enough starts with consideration of the family/owner-managed company, its structure and its operation (I have assumed that the (private) limited company is the most appropriate vehicle for the business.) Consideration is then given to the corporate structure, followed by an overview of appropriate tax strategy. The book also provides a brief guide to the computation of a company's corporation tax liability for both trading and investment companies (with fully-updated references to the new *Corporation Tax Acts 2009* and *2010*) and the impact of HMRC's new penalty regime.

I then look at specific areas affecting the family/owner-managed company, including:

- the ways in which funds can be extracted from the company;

- key remuneration strategies (including the *FA 2011* 'disguised remuneration' legislation;

- the treatment of benefits and expenses, including the company car regime; and

- full consideration of the fast-changing pension regime as it affects owner-managers and helpful planning strategies.

The main employee share schemes and arrangements are also discussed, with full coverage of Enterprise Management Incentive (EMI) share option schemes. I also consider the ways in which extra shares can be found to eventually pass to employees who are not members of the family. Detailed practical consideration is given to the potential impact of the 'restricted securities' regime in the context of relatively straightforward unapproved share awards and options. In many cases, 'standard' private company shareholdings should not be 'restricted securities', but it may still prudent to make a protective election to ensure that any future share gains remain fully within the beneficial CGT regime.

It is true to say that for any size of company the individual circumstances and mode of operation must be fully considered. With a family or owner-managed company, there is more to it than that and in particular the various methods of rewarding key executives are fully considered with reference to all factors.

I have analysed the impact of the IR 35 rules for those individuals providing services through their 'personal service company'. Subsequent attempts to circumvent the IR 35 legislation through the use of so-called 'Personal Service Companies or 'Composites' were blocked by the *Finance Act 2007* – these provisions are covered in Chapter 6.

Succession planning is a vital issue for a long established family or owner-managed companies and I therefore cover the relevant tax and commercial angles extensively in Chapter 17 (Succession Planning and Passing on the Family Company). It must be recognised that the next generation may not have the desire or, possibly, the ability to take over the running of the business. In such cases, a sale of the company or a management buy-out (perhaps through a purchase of own shares) must be contemplated.

Most owner managers will subsequently benefit from the improved Entrepreneurs' relief (ER) regime, which provides them with a 10% CGT rate on exit. The ER regime for share sales and related planning issues in relation to different deal structures is reviewed extensively in Chapter 15. Valuing a family company is a minefield when either passing on a family/owner-managed company or selling it to outsiders. The principles of commercial and fiscal share valuations are therefore discussed in some detail.

This book also covers other important tax aspects of family and owner-managed companies. These include financing issues, expanding the business by way of acquisitions, corporate reconstructions where a separation of shareholders is required, and how to wind-up the company in a tax-efficient manner as well as securing the best possible relief for any shareholder losses.

A family or owner-managed company can be an invigorating environment, and it is one which has a major role to play in the UK business world. This is evidenced by the many tax breaks that have been given to the owner-managed business sector in recent years.

The successful company will have seen a number of changes (e.g. the growing use of non-executive directors and the increase in demands for a specialised service or product). With proper tax planning strategies being adopted, the family or owner-managed company can look forward to continuing success. It is hoped that this book will be an indispensable guide for those involved in advising and running family and owner-managed companies.

This book went to press before the Chancellor's Autumn Tax update but I have tried to bring in some of the key prospective '6 April 2012' changes where appropriate.

I must give special thanks to my partner, Patricia Caputo, and my friends, Alison Conley, Sarah Gain and Partha Ray for their support with the final editing process of this book.

As ever, I also owe a considerable debt of gratitude to the commitment and professionalism of the team at Bloomsbury Professional and their encouragement, with particular thanks to Jane Bradford for her sterling work. Finally, I must express my sincere appreciation for the loving support and encouragement provided by Patricia who keeps me sane and on track!

Preface

I am always pleased to receive any comments or suggestions for future editions – please email me (peter@prtaxconsulting.co.uk).

Peter Rayney

November 2011

Whilst every care has been taken to ensure the accuracy of the contents of this work, no responsibility for loss occasioned to any person acting or refraining from action as a result of any statement in it can be accepted by the authors or the publisher.

'For Patricia '

Contents

Contents

Table of Statutes

Table of Statutory Instruments

Table of Cases

Z

Chapter 1

The Family and Owner-Managed Company and Tax Planning

IMPORTANCE OF FAMILY AND OWNER-MANAGED COMPANIES

1.1   Many empirical studies show that family-owned businesses are still the dominant form of business organisation, accounting for about two-thirds of all UK companies. It is estimated that family firms represent around 3 million of the total 4.6 million private sector businesses in the UK. According to research conducted by the *Institute for Family Business*, family enterprises produce about 38% of the turnover in the private sector and account for around 38% of the UK's Gross Domestic Product (GDP) in the private sector (31% of GDP in the overall economy). Some 85% of family businesses are run by owner-managers.

Apart from their vital contribution to the UK economy, the family business sector provides an important platform for developing entrepreneurial talent and start-ups.

Many family businesses are household names, such as Bestway Group, JC Bamford (commonly known as JCB), Laing O'Rourke and Clarks Shoes. Even many prominent public companies, such as Sainsbury, retain a strong family connection through substantial shareholdings or representation at board level. Many other private companies are the product of management buy-outs, management buy-ins and 'public to private' transactions.

DEFINING A FAMILY OR OWNER-MANAGED COMPANY

1.2   Perhaps the most important feature of family and owner-managed companies is that control of the company (both at shareholder and board levels) is concentrated in the hands of just a few individuals or a single 'dominant' chief executive. This book is aimed at the complete spectrum of family and owner-managed businesses and it would be disingenuous to attempt a rigid definition.

1

A family company could be broadly defined as one in which a single family holds more than 50% of the voting shares and effectively controls the business by occupying the key positions in the senior management/executive team. More importantly perhaps, this working definition will also include companies that are themselves acknowledged to be family businesses (for example in promotional literature and even in advertising campaigns).

In many cases, family companies will be characterised by more than one generation being involved in the business. While many families are involved in the day-to-day running of the business, many others take a more 'hands-off' approach by involving professional 'non-family' managers.

Many of the tax planning techniques covered in this book will apply to companies where there are family connections which are not sufficient to give voting control.

The 'owner-managed company' nomenclature represents a much wider class of private company. Generally, it will be a company controlled by a small group of individuals (who are not necessarily *family* members), often originating from management buy-out or buy-in transactions. That said, many of the issues faced by firms that consider themselves 'non-family' companies, such as ownership, succession and business strategy tend to be the same as those faced by any other business.

CLOSE COMPANIES

1.3   There is an important term used in the tax legislation which effectively covers family and owner-managed companies and that is the term 'close company'. There are a number of special tax provisions which only apply to a 'close company' and these are covered in this book. Essentially, a close company is one which is controlled by its directors or by five or fewer participators (shareholders). This means that the vast majority of family or owner-managed companies will be close companies, but not all close companies will be family or owner-managed companies [*CTA 2010, s 439 (ICTA 1988, s 414)*].

KEY CHARACTERISTICS AND DYNAMICS OF FAMILY AND OWNER-MANAGED COMPANIES

1.4   The family or owner-managed company has considerable flexibility since it is free from the scrutiny of investment analysts and the shareholder accountability of 'plcs'. That said, if a private company has institutional or 'third party' shareholding or venture capital finance, the consequential shareholder or loan agreements are likely to place certain (sometimes significant) restrictions on the owner manager's operation of the business.

The decision making process in family and owner-managed companies is generally much quicker, which brings many operational benefits and enhances relationships with employees.

Many family companies succeed because they foster a unique sense of belonging and enhanced common purpose across the whole workforce. Indeed, family companies are particularly pre-eminent in the service sector, notably within hotels, retail stores, restaurants and similar businesses, where the 'personal touch' is essential.

Almost all family businesses have grown from the vision and 'hard graft' of the founder and in many cases the employees will have a very special loyalty to the business and the family owner managers. The inherent strengths of family businesses are commitment, culture and pride that often combine to produce a competitive edge.

1.5 On the other hand family businesses are often introspective and steeped in tradition. Many believe they have cornered a 'niche' and are best placed to defend their position as they have been making the same product(s) for long enough to know their market 'inside-out'. However, such attitudes can make the family business particularly vulnerable since they fail to make the necessary adjustments demanded by a rapidly changing technological and economic environment. In many cases, reluctance to embrace change is due to the perceived adverse effects that it may have on individual family members.

It follows that tax planning for the family or owner-managed company and their proprietorial shareholders should always be based on a clear understanding of, and be compatible with, the particular family dynamics and the culture of the business.

SUCCESSION PLANNING

1.6 Probably the most significant (and often *heated*) issue facing many family companies is succession. The failure rate is very high. Recent statistics indicate that around only 30% and 15% make it to the second and third generations respectively. There are possibly many explanations for this – for example, the 'current' generation have more job opportunities, greater geographic job mobility or may value 'life beyond work' (especially if they have seen the family work very hard for little reward!).

According to recent research, less than one in five UK family firms continue to 'reserve' managerial positions for members of the family. This perhaps removes the common perception that all family businesses tend to be suspicious of outsiders. In the author's view, 'outsiders' and non-executive directors can inject considerable fresh thinking, objectivity and professionalism into what is often an inward-looking environment.

Succession planning has to be managed very carefully indeed and may involve making some tough decisions. The key issues for the owner manager are:

- Whether members of the family have the necessary acumen and skills to develop and run the business (and do they want to)?

- Can the existing family members achieve the true potential of the business?

- Would it be better to bring in an 'outsider' to take over the company (perhaps under a 'management buy-in')?

1.7   Sometimes succession issues may create friction between the various family members which, in turn, can have an adverse effect on the business. Succession planning should start many years before the owner manager plans to retire – it is a process rather than an event. This should be clearly communicated to those family members involved in the business as well as the shareholders. In some cases it may be appropriate for family members to work in another business to ensure they have the right skills and knowledge before (re)joining the family firm. Much of the emotional 'heat' can be taken out of this 'succession' process by using relevant business advisers or, possibly, the company's own independent 'non-executive' directors.

The owner manager should produce a written succession plan, specifying their 'retirement date', and adhere to it! – this would avoid the frustration and demotivation of many 'next-in-line' successors caused by the incumbent owner manager's (often) frequent deferral of their retirement from the business. The relevant tax issues involved in passing on the company to the next generation, etc are fully dealt with in Chapter 17.

The vast majority of owner managers are able to benefit from the generous Entrepreneurs' relief (which gives a CGT tax rate of 10% (currently) on qualifying gains up to £10 million). In many cases, they will tend to seek an exit from their business rather than take a chance that their children will be able to carry on the business. In the author's experience, relatively few people now follow their parents into the family business.

The general strategy for the majority of owner-managed companies today seems to be to grow the business for a successful trade sale or management buy-out 'exit'.

FINANCIAL MANAGEMENT AND CASH FLOW

1.8   All companies must constantly plan and monitor their financial position. The development of the business is invariably dictated by the availability of finance and the budgeting and control of cash flow is essential. Especially in the early phase of a business, the ability to 'keep the bank manager happy' will often be critical to its survival. Consequently, cash flow will often be a key driver in evaluating the efficacy of any business tax planning exercise.

Many family and owner-managed companies in the 'start-up' phase will need to be especially vigilant to the danger of growing too fast, since they will not usually have the necessary borrowing facilities in place or capital base to provide the requisite level of working capital.

TAX PLANNING STRATEGIES

Interaction with family dynamics

1.9 This book particularly concentrates on tax planning strategies for the family and owner-managed company. It must be appreciated that there are a number of special factors that apply to such companies where any plan of action is being proposed – whether the plan is related to tax or any other topic. The special features, relationships, and 'emotional' interests within a family company should never be overlooked when giving tax advice to the company and its owners. Otherwise, putting forward what might seem to be sound tax planning techniques could sooner or later create resistance or major problems.

It is always true to say, no matter who the taxpayer may be, that the 'tax tail should not wag the commercial dog'. Whilst tax is an important factor in the decision-making processes it should never be considered in isolation.

Some planning techniques will centre on the structure of the company and its shareholders. Other strategies will be brought about by that company's activity. Broadly speaking a family or owner-managed company can carry out either a 'trading' or 'investment' activity. Various tax reliefs will be available depending on the nature of these activities.

Owner managers of trading companies will invariably benefit from a 10% CGT Entrepreneurs' Relief (ER) rate on their share disposal gains (up to a lifetime limit of £10 million). Amongst other things, the ER rules impose a minimum voting 5% shareholding requirement, and thus many small minority shareholdings are unlikely to qualify and are likely to pay CGT at 18%/28% (See Chapter 15 for detailed coverage of ER.) On the other hand, investment company shareholders will generally incur a 28% CGT rate on significant share sales.

Various reliefs and incentives are given to *all* companies but will be of particular interest to family or owner-managed companies where there is an in-built facility to match reward with ownership.

Tax planning and the 'Ramsay' doctrine

1.10   The ability to make appropriate tax planning arrangements was first 'blessed' by the courts way back in 1935. In *Duke of Westminster v CIR* (1935) 19 TC 490, Lord Tomlin had firmly established that: 'Every man is entitled if he can to order his tax affairs so that the tax attaching under the appropriate Acts is less than it would otherwise be.'

The clear principle arising from this 'watershed' case was that taxpayers were entitled to organise their tax affairs so as to minimise their tax liabilities. This meant that the courts would look at the legal form of the relevant transactions as opposed to their substance, unless the documents were effectively a 'sham'.

In broad terms, tax avoidance schemes are arrangements or plans to avoid the payment of tax which include artificial steps for which there is no commercial justification. In *CIR v Willoughby* [1997] STC 995 (at page 1003h), Lord Nolan said that:

'The hallmark of tax avoidance is that the taxpayer reduces his liability to tax without incurring the economic consequences that Parliament intended to be suffered by any taxpayer qualifying for such reduction in his tax liability'. He distinguished this from tax mitigation, which is evidenced by the taxpayer taking advantage of a fiscally attractive option afforded to him by the legislation so that he 'genuinely suffers the economic consequences that Parliament intended to be suffered by those taking the option'.

1.11   With tax avoidance, the taxpayer's objective is to have a taxable event without paying the relevant tax and without (technically) breaking the law. The high tax rates during the 1960s and 1970s encouraged the growth of a sophisticated tax avoidance industry, which relied on the principles that had been established in the *Duke of Westminster* case. However, the House of Lord's landmark decision in *WT Ramsay v CIR* [1981] STC 174 marked the death knell for these types of tax avoidance arrangements. In essence, *Ramsay* applied to pre-arranged tax avoidance schemes that were largely of a 'circular' or 'self-cancelling' nature where the parties ended up in the same economic position from which they started, apart from the intended tax saving and professional costs. In *Ramsay* the taxpayer created a non-taxable gain which was matched by an allowable CGT loss. If each step in the scheme was viewed separately, the taxpayer had created a deductible loss that sheltered the CGT on the gain. However, if the scheme was looked at as a 'whole', there was no loss since it was matched by a (non-taxable) contrived gain and on this basis the loss claim failed. Thus, under the so-called *Ramsay* approach, the courts could tax the relevant parties according to the real economic substance of the transaction. By looking at the scheme as a whole rather than its individual steps, the courts are able to negate the purported tax advantage.

1.12   The so-called *Ramsay* doctrine was further extended in *Furniss v Dawson* [1984] STC 153 and *Craven v White* [1988] STC 476 (and other cases) to tax avoidance transactions where the parties ended up in a different position from that in which they started. In *Furniss v Dawson*, Lord Brightman defined the relevant principles as follows:

'First, there must be a pre-ordained series of transactions ...

Secondly, there must be steps inserted which have no other commercial (business) purpose apart from the avoidance of a liability to tax ...

If those two ingredients exist, the inserted steps are to be disregarded for fiscal purposes.'

The courts also placed some important limitations on the application of the doctrine so that it could only be applied to tax planning steps that are implemented at a time when there was a near certainty of the end result. This is important since if tax planning is undertaken where there are uncertain elements as to the final result, it should succeed.

Subsequent major cases, including *MacNiven v Westmoreland Investments Ltd* [2001] STC 237, have placed further technical refinements on the *Ramsay* principle, with some contending that they contradict the formulation laid down by Lord Brightman in *Furniss v Dawson*. In *Westmoreland Investments*, the end result of the scheme was that nothing had changed. However, their Lordships were not prepared to allow a statute to be interpreted artificially by the Revenue, merely because the taxpayer gained a tax advantage. In deciding whether a particular form of tax avoidance is acceptable or unacceptable, Lord Hoffmann opined that you have to apply '... the statutory language to the facts of the case. The court must therefore interpret the relevant statute and apply it to the particular circumstances of the case'.

The courts have clearly shown a disapproval of contrived and aggressive tax schemes, such as demonstrated by the recent decisions in *Drummond v HMRC* [2008] STC 2707 and *Underwood v HMRC* [2009] STC 239.

1.13   An important emerging principle is the need to look at the purpose of the legislation rather than taking a literal approach to its interpretation. In recent years, the courts have repeatedly decided to construe a particular taxing statute in such a way so as to 'tease-out' the wishes or intention of Parliament in the context of the relevant transactions. For example, in *Barclays Mercantile Finance Ltd v Mawson* [2005] STC 1, the House of Lords said 'The present case ... illustrates the need for a close analysis of what, on a purposive construction, the statute actually requires'. More recently, the Court of Appeal adapted a purposive approach in *Prizedome Ltd, Limitgood Ltd v The Commissioners of Her Majesty's Revenue and Customs* [2009] EWCA Civ 177. The case involved an elaborate attempt to circumvent the corporate 'pre-entry loss provisions. In finding for HMRC, Lord Justice Mummery observed: 'This interpretation makes no sense and cannot have been intended by Parliament.' Ascertaining the intention of Parliament brings its own problems.

In cases of ambiguity, *Pepper v Hart* [1992] STC 898 held that reference can be made to Parliamentary debate (Hansard) provided a clear statement was made by a relevant minister addressing the point under consideration when the legislation was introduced. (This principle might also extend to the explanatory notes produced by on new legislation HM Treasury.) However, in many cases there are no clear ministerial statements – for example, the particular 'fact pattern' under consideration may not have been contemplated by Parliament/ HM Treasury. In such cases, the judges may then end up having to 'second-guess' the intention of Parliament!

More recently, the Courts have continued to adopt a purposive approach. For example, in *PA Holdings Ltd v HMRC* [2010] STC 2343, the Upper Tribunal confirmed that payments of dividends through a special tax avoidance structure could be treated as earnings. Interestingly, it held that the *Ramsay* principle could apply to determine whether a payment represented earnings and hence taxed as employment income. However, since the payments were also properly declared dividends, the 'dividend' priority rule (in what was *ICTA 1988, s 20(2)*) had to be applied and thus the amounts were taxed as dividends. However, since there was no equivalent NIC rule, the amounts were treated as earnings for NIC purposes (see 5.3).

SCHEMES INVOLVING FINANCIAL INSTRUMENTS

1.13A There have been a number of cases involving linked financial instruments designed to achieve a tax advantage on the basis that each instrument should be taxed under its own separate tax rules (which would typically give rise to a tax-relievable loss). The decision in *Scottish Provident Institution v HMRC* [2004] UKHL 52 demonstrates that such highly-linked instruments would be treated as a single transaction under *Ramsay*, thus nullifying any purported tax loss. This principle was followed in *Peter Schofield v HMRC* [2010] UKFTT 196 (TC), which involved the artificial creation of a capital loss using four linked option contracts.

The First Tier Tribunal had little difficulty in concluding that the four options should be viewed as a composite transaction and thus no actual capital loss arose.

Many avoidance cases tend to rely on the creation of an 'artificial' term in the legal documentation which provides there is a remote chance of the scheme not being implemented as planned. In *Astall v HMRC* [2010] STC 137 the taxpayer attempted to bring a loan note within the relevant discounted security rules by inserting a clause permitting its early redemption. The taxpayer's contended that since the amount payable on an early redemption would have involved a deep gain, it should be treated as a relevant discounted security. However, since the exercise of this option was very unlikely, HMRC argued that it should be ignored when construing the terms of the loan note. The Special Commissioner agreed, concluding that the position should be viewed realistically and it was practically certain in this case that the redemption right would not be exercised.

The High Court also agreed with the Special Commissioner's findings confirming that the *Ramsay* and *Barclays Mercantile* dicta required all relevant possibilities to be viewed in such a way as to restrict them to the 'real ones'.

Although this can often be a very subjective issue, the courts usually tend to lack sympathy when looking at tax avoidance cases such as this!

PROPOSALS FOR A GENERAL ANTI-AVOIDANCE RULE (GAAR)

1.13B In the June 2010 Budget, the Government announced that it was considering the introduction of a general anti-avoidance rule or GAAR. On 21 November 2011, Graham Aaronson QC published his commissioned report on the merits of introducing a GAAR. The main conclusion is that a narrowly-targeted GAAR would be desirable and it should be aimed at blocking the most 'egregious' tax avoidance arrangements – ie those which are highly abusive and artificial – "which are widely regarded as intolerable". The study concluded that the GAAR should contain important safeguards for taxpayers who sought to structure their tax affairs on a reasonable commercial basis. Whilst this report is broadly welcomed, it remains to be seen how far its proposals will be adopted by Government.

HIGH-RISK AREAS PERCEIVED BY HMRC

1.14 HMRC's Anti-Avoidance Group (see 1.20 below) have identified a number of common attributes ('signposts') that, in *their* view, indicate unacceptable forms of tax avoidance. These include transactions/arrangements:

- involving little or no economic substance (such as in *Ramsay* – see 1.11).
- producing little or no pre-tax profit that rely wholly or substantially on the anticipated tax reduction for the significant post-tax profit.
- that result in a mismatch such as, for example, between the legal form or accounting treatment and the economic substance (eg the *Dextra* case – see 8.8A).
- showing little or no business/commercial or driver.
- involving contrived, artificial, transitory, pre-ordained or commercially unnecessary steps or transactions.
- where the income, gains, expenditure, or losses falling within the UK tax net are not proportionate to the economic activity taking place or value added in the UK.
- which seek to sidestep the effect of specific anti-avoidance legislation.

DISCLOSURE OF TAX AVOIDANCE SCHEMES (DOTAS) REGIME

Background to the DOTAS rules

1.15 Prior to the introduction of DOTAS (sometimes also referred to as Tax Avoidance Disclosure or 'TAD') there had been a growing trend in the 'marketing' of innovative aggressive tax planning schemes. During 2003 alone, HM Revenue and Customs ('HMRC') effectively 'closed' down a number of fairly artificial schemes, including those creating tax deductions through the use of gilt strips, capital redemption policies and life-insurance policies. Such schemes were regarded as particularly 'unpalatable' and were closed as soon as they became known to HMRC.

However, there was a considerable delay between the wide implementation of such schemes and HMRC finding out about them. Under the normal self-assessment return processes, HMRC would not normally have received information about tax avoidance schemes until a long time after they had been implemented. HMRC also explained that large amounts of tax were lost simply because such arrangements were not 'picked-up' during their review of income and corporate tax returns (due to inadequate disclosure and so on).

Notifiable arrangements

1.16   As a result of these developments, the *Finance Act 2004, ss 306 to 319* (together with supplementary sets of regulations) introduced the Tax Avoidance Disclosure ('DOTAS') regime. The intention behind DOTAS was to provide HMRC with an 'early-warning' system for new and innovative tax planning schemes, enabling the Government to block those which it deemed to be unacceptable. Furthermore, DOTAS increases the risk of a disclosed tax avoidance scheme being 'blocked' by swift legislation during the course of its implementation, which is likely to dissuade most potential users of 'aggressive schemes'. It is probably fair to say that the DOTAS rules have proved to be a very effective weapon in stamping out aggressive tax avoidance schemes.

Furthermore, the requirement for schemes to be given a scheme reference number (SRN) which must be reported on the tax returns of those using the relevant scheme enables HMRC to make a prompt enquiry into the case rather than rely on the more uncertain discovery assessment rules (see 4.55).

The original 2004 DOTAS rules applied to tax arrangements concerning employment or certain financial products, which were identified as high-risk areas for HMRC. Since then they have been substantially widened. The revised DOTAS rules now apply to the whole of income tax, corporation tax and capital gains tax, National Insurance Contributions ('NICs'), and (since 6 April 2011) schemes that seek to avoid an Inheritance Tax (IHT) charge on transfers of assets into trusts (see 1.22A). As a general rule, schemes that were generally available before the relevant DOTAS commencement date for the particular tax are not required to be disclosed.

Special DOTA rules also apply for both VAT and SDLT (which are covered in 1.25 and 1.26).The DOTAS rules seek to ensure that a tax/NIC saving arrangement is disclosed where:

- it will, or might be expected to, enable someone to obtain a tax/NIC advantage (*FA 2004, s 318*);

- the tax/NIC advantage is (or might be expected to be) the main benefit/ one of the main benefits of that arrangement [*FA 2004, s 306(1)(c)*]; and

- the relevant scheme falls within at least one of the presented 'hallmarks' set out in the legislation (see 1.18 to 1.22 below).

The broad effect of the 'hallmark' tests (see 1.18 to 1.22 below) is to limit disclosure to those tax and NIC avoidance schemes that are highly innovative in the way they produce a tax/NIC saving. HMRC have confirmed that the DOTAS rules also operate for 'tax benefits' that are intended to be obtained in relation to legislation that has yet to be implemented.

Relevant disclosures must be made by the 'scheme promoter or introducer' (widely defined) within five days of the scheme being 'made available'. Because HMRC felt that many promoters were delaying their disclosure notification until the scheme was almost about to be implemented, an earlier trigger point was introduced from 8 April 2010. This requires the promoter/ introducer to notify HMRC within five days of the date the scheme is first marketed (even in general terms) to clients or potential clients. (In the case of 'in-house' schemes, where the person using the scheme has designed and implemented it themselves, the scheme must be disclosed within 30 days of it being implemented.)

A large number of firms tend to adopt a prudent approach here. Thus, if a client *could* be advised about a particular scheme/arrangement (because sufficient detailed research or analysis has been done), then it is likely to be considered 'disclosable'.

Promoters are broadly defined as those who design, implement, or are involved in the organisation and management of, relevant tax schemes or arrangements made available to taxpayers [*FA 2004, s 307*]. Many promoters will be responsible for designing a tax avoidance scheme or making firm approaches to taxpayers with the view to making such schemes available for their use. Both UK and overseas based promoters are subject to the DOTAS rules but only to the extent that the scheme is expected to provide a UK tax advantage.

FA 2010 also added the concept of an 'introducer', who generally 'market' tax schemes or products (see also 1.17).

Promoters and introducers are generally required to register such schemes with HMRC's Anti-Avoidance Group (AAG) on the declaration form AAG1 within the period specified above. (The AAG is responsible for the development, maintenance and delivery of HMRC's anti-avoidance strategy.)

The registration on form AAG1 must provide brief details of the scheme, the type of transactions involved, the expected tax consequences and the statutory tax rules that are being relied upon. HMRC will then issue a scheme registration number (SRN) for the 'scheme' (generally) to the promoter.

FA 2004, s 312 broadly requires the promoter to pass the SRN to the users of the relevant tax scheme or arrangement (and any other parties that may benefit from it). In many cases, this must be done within 30 days of the receipt of the SRN from HMRC. The SRN must be disclosed by taxpayers using the scheme on their relevant income tax, corporation tax, or IHT returns or form AAG4.

FA 2010 introduced a new requirement for promoters to give HMRC details of those clients provided with an SRN (see 1.17).

There is a penalty of up to £5,000 (to be determined by the First-tier Tribunal Commissioners) for failing to disclose, which can be increased by £600 for each day the failure continues after that determination. HMRC generally seek to enforce penalties unless the promoter has exercised reasonable judgement in deciding that no disclosure is required or where the promoter can demonstrate a 'reasonable excuse'.

HMRC have the necessary power to investigate compliance under the DOTAS provisions, such as to make enquires into whether a scheme is fully disclosable [*FA 2004, s 313A*] or to request more detailed disclosure [*FA 2004, s 308A*].

Providing details of clients ('client lists')

1.16A   From 1 January 2011, promoters must provide HMRC with quarterly details of clients that have been issued with an SRN within 30 days of the end of the relevant quarterly return period. (The first quarterly return is due for the calendar quarter ended 31 March 2011).

The requirement to provide client lists was introduced to address HMRC's concerns that they are not generally able to assess the extent to which a particular tax scheme has been used until they receive disclosures of SRNs provided with individual tax returns. Since promoters now have to submit details of clients 'receiving' SRNs, HMRC can quantify the take-up' of a particular scheme more quickly, enabling it to take swift counter-action where appropriate.

Introducer obligations

1.17   Some accountants, tax advisers and other financial advisers sell tax schemes to their clients as introducers (see 1.16 above). In many cases, they will have been provided with details of a particular tax scheme by a promoter. HMRC have the power to require 'introducers' (such as accountants etc) to provide the names and addresses of those who have provided them with details of a proposed or actual scheme. *FA 2004, s 213C* makes it clear that HMRC must first serve a notice on the introducer to provide the information. Failing to comply with the notice will give rise to a penalty of up to £5,000 (with daily penalties up to £600).

Summary of 'hallmarks'

Confidentiality

1.18   This hallmark applies where an element of the arrangements gives rise to an expected tax advantage, and a promoter might reasonably expect the mechanics of that 'tax advantage' to be kept confidential from other promoters. This hallmark also applies if the way in which the tax advantage arises should be kept confidential from HMRC (so that the relevant element of the arrangements could be reused in future).

For example, the use of a confidentiality letter would usually 'trigger' this hallmark, except where the scheme in question is reasonably well known in the tax profession.

This hallmark does not apply to small or medium-sized businesses where there is no 'promoter' of the scheme.

Premium fee

1.19   A scheme falls under this hallmark if it might reasonably be expected that a promoter *would be able to* obtain a premium fee from someone reasonably experienced in receiving services of the type being provided. This is a hypothetical test, so that it does not depend on whether such a fee is actually received. A premium fee would be one that is *significantly* attributable to obtaining the relevant tax advantage – this would therefore catch success-based fees and contingent fees. It is not meant to relate to fees generated simply by those taking up a tax-saving scheme.

New sub-categories have been added to deal with bespoke arrangements (subject to a £1 million minimum fee threshold) and certain collective investment schemes.

Standardised tax products

1.20   This hallmark is designed to capture what HMRC refer to as 'mass marketed schemes'. These are 'shrink-wrapped' or 'plug and play' tax schemes (giving rise to a 'main tax benefit') that are easily replicated and require little modification to suit individual client circumstances. The scope of this particular 'hallmark', such as whether there is a tax product that is made available generally, is determined by various tests. The hallmark does not apply to arrangements first made available before 1 August 2006. Certain 'products' are also exempt from disclosure, such as EIS or VCT schemes or approved share incentive plans (see *SI 2006/1543, regs 10* and *11*).

Certain tax shelters

Loss schemes

1.21   The 'loss schemes' hallmark captures schemes designed to generate trading losses for individuals (who can then offset the losses against their income tax and capital gains tax liabilities). This hallmark will apply where more than one individual is expected to implement the arrangements, and the main benefit of such arrangements is to generate a loss for potential use against income tax or CGT liabilities. This was extended in 2010 to also cover schemes designed to generate corporate losses.

Leasing arrangements

1.22   This hallmark broadly applies to arrangements which include a 'short-term' plant or machinery lease for a term of two years or less, where the value of any leased asset is at least £10,000,000 (or where the value of all of the leased assets is at least £25,000,000). This is a complex hallmark, and the relevant detailed rules are set out in *SI 2006/1543, regs 13 to 17.*

Extension of DOTAS to Inheritance Tax on transfers into trust.

1.22A   Since 6 April 2011, the DOTAS reporting rules also apply to arrangements that are designed to avoid Inheritance Tax (IHT) on transfers into trusts (but no other aspect of IHT charges).

Broadly, the IHT DOTAS rules are aimed at lifetime transfers into trust that are structured to avoid an IHT charge. Planning that was generally made available before 6 April 2011 is 'grandfathered' and thus falls outside the scope of the IHT DOTAS rules. This would, for example, include the normal use of reliefs and exemptions, such as Business Property Relief, Agricultural Property Relief, the 'normal expenditure out of income' exemption, and the creation of 'pilot' trusts.

Similarly, HMRC have confirmed that 'plain vanilla' IHT planning arrangements are also excluded from the IHT DOTAS rules.

Working with the DOTAS regime

1.23   Given the tax authorities' wish to ensure that everyday tax advice and arrangements do not trigger a disclosure obligation, the relevant hallmarks included in the updated version of the regulations are now more tightly targeted at innovative or sophisticated avoidance schemes. The 'early notification' of such schemes generally means they are likely to have a short 'shelf-life'. Furthermore, the very existence of the DOTAS regime is likely to have the desired effect of dissuading more risk-averse taxpayers from considering aggressive tax-saving schemes.

Where a particular arrangement has been disclosed under DOTAS and given an HMRC scheme reference number or SRN. This does not imply any form of acceptance or clearance by HMRC – so HMRC does not necessarily approve the relevant scheme or accept that it works. HMRC have said in their guidance notes that: 'on its own the disclosure of a tax arrangement has no effect on the tax position of any person who uses it. However, a disclosed tax arrangement may be rendered ineffective by Parliament, possibly with retrospective effect'.

Based on recent experience with HMRC, it would appear that to avoid a 'discovery' (ie an enquiry outside the normal time limit), full details of the relevant scheme or arrangement must be given on the tax return. In HMRC's view, following *Langham v Veltema* it is *not* sufficient just to enter the scheme reference disclosure number.

Legal professional privilege

1.24   There has been considerable debate on the extent to which disclosure is prevented on the grounds of legal professional privilege, which applies to confidential communications between solicitors and their clients for the purpose of obtaining legal advice. The House of Lords has recognised legal professional privilege as a fundamental human right.

The disclosure rules were designed to provide details about the relevant tax scheme and not the identity of the particular taxpayer or their circumstances. Nevertheless, in July 2004, the Law Society indicated that they would not be able to comply with the disclosure regime on the grounds of legal professional privilege.

HMRC's legislative response to this has been that if a particular disclosure would be covered by 'legal professional privilege', then the responsibility for disclosing the arrangements falls on the client/taxpayer. The client/taxpayer also has the option of (unambiguously) waiving privilege to enable the (solicitor) promoter to make the appropriate disclosure.

VAT and stamp duty land tax disclosure regimes

Notifiable VAT schemes

1.25   A separate DOTAS regime applies for VAT purposes. In contrast to the 'direct tax' system, under the VAT rules the disclosure obligation primarily rests with businesses:

- companies with an annual turnover of at least £600,000 must disclose the use of certain 'listed' schemes. The specified schemes are those considered to be abusive and include the first grant of a major interest in an occupied building to recover VAT on refurbishment costs, credit card or cash handling services, and so on (see *VAT (Disclosure of Avoidance*

Schemes) (Designations) Order 2004 (SI 2004/1933) for details). Penalties of up to 15% of the VAT avoided are levied for non-disclosure, subject to a 'reasonable excuse' defence; and

● companies with an annual turnover of more than £10 million that engage in so-called 'hallmark' schemes must provide relevant details of any scheme where the main or one of the main purposes is to obtain a VAT advantage, which is broadly anything that reduces the VAT payable. These disclosure rules apply to any scheme that involves one or more of 'the (seven) hallmarks of tax avoidance' – these are defined in the *VAT (Disclosure of Avoidance Schemes) (Designations) Order 2004* as follows:

1   Confidentiality conditions laid down in an agreement.

2   The sharing of the VAT advantage with another party.

3   The promoter's fees being contingent on the tax saving.

4   Prepayments between connected companies.

5   Funding by share subscriptions or loans.

6   Offshore loops.

7   Construction work connected with a property transaction between connected persons.

Details of the relevant scheme must be provided to HMRC broadly within 30 days of the due date for filing a VAT return. There is a penalty of £5,000 for failing to disclose a 'hallmark' scheme [*VAT (Disclosure of Avoidance Schemes) Regulations 2004 (SI 2004/1929)*].

Stamp duty land tax DOTAS rules

1.26   Special DOTAS rules have applied since 2005 to stamp duty land tax (SDLT) schemes which involve *commercial* property with a market value of at least £5 million. The scope of the SDLT DOTAS rules widened from 1 April 2010 (under SI 2010/No 407) to also include residential property of £1 million or more (or mixed use property where the residential or non residential part exceeds the £1 million/£5 million threshold.

SDLT disclosures are made where there is a substantial risk of tax avoidance and broadly follow the normal direct tax disclosure rules.

The SDLT rules are effectively 'bolted-on' to the existing primary 'disclosure regime' legislation for direct tax (outlined in 1.20). Thus, the main benefit of the SDLT scheme (or one of them) must be to obtain a tax advantage. However, the direct tax disclosure regime's 'hallmark' criteria (see 1.18 to 1.22) do *not* apply to SDLT schemes.

No disclosure is required where the SDLT scheme incorporates one or more of the main steps listed in the Appendix to the SDLT regulations, *unless* the scheme depends on *combinations* of steps or *multiple* use of the same step. These steps include the use of Special Purpose Vehicles, claiming SDLT reliefs, and transferring businesses as a going concern [*Stamp Duty Land Tax Avoidance Schemes (Prescribed Descriptions of Arrangements) Regulations 2005 (SI 2005/1868)*].

Although HMRC will issue a reference number for notified SDLT schemes, this is to aid identification and prevent the same scheme being disclosed again. The reference number does *not* have to be entered on the SDLT return and indeed HMRC recommend that the reference number is not passed on to the user.

Chapter 2

Extracting Funds from the Company

SHOULD SURPLUS PROFITS BE RETAINED OR EXTRACTED?

Main issues

2.1   Family and owner-managed companies can freely decide how much of their profits should be returned to the shareholders or retained within the business. The 'working' shareholders will need to extract a basic level of income from the company to satisfy their personal requirements. Hitherto, the comparatively lower income tax rates tended to encourage companies to extract surplus profits. Companies that relied on bank borrowings or institutional finance may, however, have been prescribed financial limits on the amount of dividends and other payments which can be made to the owner-manager shareholders.

From a commercial perspective, the company's cash flow and working capital requirements must be considered when determining the timing and amount of funds to be taken out. Given that the extraction of funds (see 2.5) gives rise to a tax charge, which will be particularly expensive where large sums are involved, there is little point in taking them out by bonus, dividend, etc unless they are required by the owner-manager for their personal/family's needs. The post-5 April 2010 'super' income tax rate is likely to change owner-managers' behaviour and will probably lead to an increased retention of profits within their companies. Owner managers will now have to carefully monitor their income levels to ensure that the ravages of the 'super' tax rate is minimised or avoided. Within these constraints, some owner-managers may still wish to regularly remove 'surplus' cash from the business so as to remove it from any further business risk (subject to the requirements of the *Insolvency Act 1986*, for example, the 'two year' look-back period for 'preferential' or 'under-value' transactions under *IA 1986, ss 238* and *239*).

A further factor to consider is the potential double charge to tax, which arises where profits retained in the company are invested in appreciating assets. The appreciation in asset values could potentially be taxed both in the company and when the value is realised by the shareholders, perhaps on a sale or liquidation of the company. However, if the company is eventually sold for a price based on a multiple of earnings, the value of the shares may bear little relationship to the level of retained profits. Furthermore, the 'double charge' effect would not be a problem where the company's shares are to be passed down as a family heirloom on death. Owners of personal service companies are effectively forced to extract 'tainted' income and additional factors will come into play (see Chapter 6).

Entrepreneurs' Relief

2.2   Owner managers of trading companies enjoy particularly favourable CGT treatment, with a current 'exit' ER CGT rate of 10% (up to a cumulative lifetime gains, limit of £10 million). (The detailed ER rules are examined in 15.33–15.42.) However, all other 'non-ER' significant gains become taxable at 28%.

Retention of profits

2.3   With a current ER limit of £10 million, the overall tax costs of realising retained profits as a capital gain (for example, by liquidation or sale – see 2.4) have remained identical to the pre-6 April 2008 taper regime (assuming the (cumulative) gains are below £10 million).

Retained profits only suffer corporation tax at the company's marginal tax rate and may ultimately be realised at low CGT rates.

The ability to reinvest profits within the company at a relatively low tax rate (especially with the post-6 April 2010 50% 'super' income tax rate) is likely to encourage many sole traders and partnerships to incorporate their businesses.

For 2011/12, unincorporated businesses earning substantial profits will generally suffer a marginal 52% combined income tax/Class 4 NIC rate on their profits, regardless of whether the profits are 'ploughed-back' within the business or extracted.

If a company pays tax at the current small profits rate of 20% , the total effective rate of taking profits as a capital sum is 28% (ignoring the impact of any base cost, etc) calculated as follows:

	£
Profit	100
Corporation tax at 20%	(20)
Retained profit = chargeable gain	80
CGT @ 10% (assuming ER)	(8)
Net realisation	72
Total effective tax rate	28%

If ER is not available at the time the retained profits are taken as a 'capital distribution', the overall effective rate increases to 42.4% (assuming a 28% CGT rate). The rates on retained profits compare very favourably with the post-6 April 2010 top rate of income tax.

Taking profits as capital gains

2.4 Unless the owner-manager is making a complete or almost complete 'exit' from the company, it may be difficult to find an effective method of converting profits into a capital sum. Taking the profits as a capital distribution on a subsequent winding-up is not a realistic option if the business is continuing (see also 16.27–16.30). This means that the individual will have to sell their shares either back to the company or by way of an external sale, with a watchful eye on the Transaction in Securities provisions of *ITA 2007, s 684* .

Given the relatively wide gap between CGT and dividend tax rates, HMRC are likely to use their *s 684* weapon where shares in close companies are sold to a commonly controlled company, Employee Benefit Trust, pension fund, etc but not normally on commercially driven sales to third parties. However, unless there is *complete certainty* that transaction will satisfy the post-sale 'no-connection' test (introduced by the *Finance Act 2010*), it is recommended that the advance clearance procedure in *ITA 2007, s 701* is used to obtain assurance that HMRC is happy with the bona fide commercial purposes of the sale (see 15.77).

If the company is likely to be sold, the level of its *retained* profits will not normally influence its sale price, which is normally based on a multiple of its post-tax earnings. With the relatively low rates of CGT, however, it is tempting to 'gross up' the price for the retained earnings rather than strip them out as a pre-sale dividend.

Taking all the above factors into account, a balanced approach between retention and extraction of profits will generally be required in practice. Ultimately, the decision must depend on whether the shareholders need the money for their personal requirements and whether they are able to obtain a better 'return' on the funds than the company.

Extracting funds or value from the company

2.5 It is possible to extract funds or value from the company in a number of ways, although (*a*) to (*c*) below are usually available only for those shareholders who work in the company as a director or employee. The most important methods of extracting value are listed below (the references indicate where a detailed discussion of the topic may be found in this book):

(*a*) directors' remuneration or bonuses and paying salaries to other family members (see 2.9–2.44 and Chapter 5);

(*b*)   provision of benefits in kind and company shares (see Chapters 7 and 8);

(*c*)   pension contributions (see Chapter 10);

(*d*)   dividends (see 2.12–2.18, 2.25–2.27 and Chapter 9);

(*e*)   charging rent on personally owned property which is used in the company's trade (see 2.45–2.49);

(*f*)   selling assets to the company for value (see 2.50–2.52);

(*g*)   charging interest on loans to the company (see 2.53–2.55, 11.9–11.15);

(*h*)   loans or advances from the company (see 2.56–2.61);

(*i*)   purchase of own shares (see 13.41–13.56); and

(*j*)   liquidation of the company (see Chapter 16).

The overall tax cost of the various methods of extraction will vary and it is important to determine the tax efficiency for each method of extracting funds/value.

2.6   On an ongoing basis, the working shareholders may well, in addition to drawing a normal salary, decide whether to extract surplus profits by means of a bonus or dividend. This aspect is considered in further detail at 2.9–2.43. In addition, owner-managers will often ensure that adequate provision is made for their future pension and that tax efficacious benefits in kind are provided. Owner-managers may also consider extracting funds through a loan account, but this too involves a tax cost.

CAPITAL RECEIPTS VERSUS INCOME RECEIPTS

Basic planning techniques

2.7   A purchase of the company's own shares, liquidation or sale of a company tend to be the most common 'exit-routes' for shareholders when they wish to leave the company, retire or realise capital value.

In the context of a purchase by the company of its own shares, it is usually possible to structure the transaction either as a capital gains receipt within *CTA 2010, s 1033* , or as a distribution. Similarly, if the company is about to be wound up, value can be extracted by means of an income dividend if the amount is paid prior to liquidation. Any amount distributed during the winding up would be a capital distribution (liable to CGT) for the shareholder. On the sale of the company, it may be possible to substitute dividend income for sale proceeds by means of a pre-sale dividend.

Comparing income and capital gain positions

2.8   It is particularly important to compare the tax liabilities under the income and capital route *well in advance* of these transactions in order to determine the most tax-efficient route.

For individual shareholders, an income distribution in 2011/12 carries an effective tax charge of 25% for a higher rate taxpayer or, to the extent that the recipient's taxable income exceeds £150,000, 36.1%. The tax efficiency of taking a capital gain will therefore depend on the shareholder's potential effective CGT rate (maximum of 28% with reduction to 10% if ER is available).

Any planning steps which are then necessary, for example, to characterise the transaction as income, can then be implemented with minimal risk of an HMRC attack under the *Furniss v Dawson* doctrine (*Furniss v Dawson* [1984] STC 153).

BONUS VERSUS DIVIDENDS

Impact of National Insurance Contributions (NIC)

2.9   Although the working shareholders can reward themselves in a number of ways, the main choice often lies between whether to pay a bonus or a dividend. The recent hike in NIC rates has meant that more owner-managers tend to draw a substantial part of their profits in the form of dividends. Profits extracted as 'remuneration' (ie salary or bonus) are now subject to significant NIC charges. For 2011/12 , the first £136 per week (or if remuneration is calculated on an annual basis, £7,072 per year) does not suffer employers' NIC. Above this 'secondary threshold', the company pays NIC on all earnings and most P11D benefits in kind at the rate of 13.8%.

For 2011/12 , directors and employees suffer NIC at the rate of 12% on their earnings and benefits between £139 and £817 per week (or if earnings are calculated on an annual basis, £7,225 and £42,475). An additional employee NIC charge of 2% is levied where the individual's total earnings/benefits exceed the 2011/12 upper earnings limit of £42,475. This means that a 2% employees' NIC charge arises on all earnings, etc above the £42,475 threshold with no restrictions.

For those owner-managers with the 'work till you drop' ethos, it is perhaps worth noting that employees' NIC ceases to be payable on their earnings after they have reached 'pensionable age'. This is currently 65 years old for men, 60 years old for women born before 6 April 1950, and 65 for women born after 5 April 1955 (with a sliding scale operating between those dates). However, employers' (ie secondary) NICs continue to be paid on an individual's earnings beyond their pensionable age.

An employer's NIC charge under Class 1A applies to the majority of benefits in kind, including company cars and private fuel. The Class 1A NIC charge is based on the total benefits taxed as 'employment income' under the *ITEPA 2003* rules.

National Minimum Wage Regulations

2.10   Owner-managers will need to consider the implications of the *National Minimum Wage Act 1998* and the *National Minimum Wage Regulations 1999*.

This legislation only applies where an individual has a contract of employment. In law, the directors' rights and duties are defined by that office. They can be removed from office by a simple majority of the votes cast at a general meeting of the company. Clearly, if the director *actively* works in the business, receives a salary, and enjoys other rights accorded to employees, an employer/employee relationship will be established.

In contrast, an employee's rights and duties are expressed in a contract of employment, which need not be in writing and can be an implied or oral contract. Due to the informal nature of the arrangements in many small companies, there may be some uncertainty as to whether an employment contract exists between the company and its controlling director. The question of whether an office holder is employed will clearly depend on the facts of each case. Where there is no explicit contract it is generally accepted that the national minimum wage rules will not apply even if the director carries out a wide range of activities, which might include 'working in the company's shop'. In such cases, the work would be regarded as done in the director's capacity as an office holder. Indeed, the Department for Business, Innovation and Skills (BIS) confirmed that if there is no written employment contract or other evidence of an intention to create an employer/worker relationship, it will not seek to contend that there is an unwritten or implied employment relationship between a director and his company.

A prudent course of action would be for owner-managerial directors to pay themselves (and of course their staff) sufficient remuneration to satisfy the minimum wage requirements – £6.08 for each hour 'worked' from 1 October 2011 (previously £5.93 for the 12 months to 30 September 2011) .

Dividends cannot be treated as remuneration for this purpose nor can benefits in kind other than the provision of living accommodation. HMRC are responsible for policing the minimum wage legislation. There is a daily penalty of £12.16 per underpaid worker per day for non-compliance after an enforcement notice has been served. The company must keep sufficient records to demonstrate that it has complied with the rules, otherwise it may be liable to a fine of up to £5,000. The impact of the legislation on directors is explained in greater detail in the ICAEW Tax Faculty Tax Guide 7/00.

Determining appropriate amount to extract from company

2.11 Most discussions about profit extraction usually start by focusing on the amount available to be paid out to the owner-manager(s). This is generally influenced by one or more of the following factors:

- the amount required for future retention in the business (to satisfy future working capital or capital investment purposes);

- the level of the company's distributable reserves and 'free' cash flow;

- any provisions or restrictions laid down in Shareholder Agreements or a company's Articles, particularly where venture capital finance has been used;

- the desire to 'de-risk' part of the 'surplus cash' generated by the business by taking it out of the company;

- the shareholders personal 'income' requirements and tax position (and the impact of the 'super' income tax rate!);

- 'one-man-band' type service companies may be affected by IR35 (see Chapter 6) and 'spousal' settlement considerations in fixing the level of 'remuneration' to be paid out, although the House of Lords decision in the *Arctic Systems* case gives potentially vulnerable taxpayers greater comfort in this area (see 9.26–9.29).

Having broadly determined the appropriate level of profits that can be 'extracted' by the owner-manager(s), attention then usually shifts to deciding whether the amount should be paid out as a bonus and/or dividend.

Comparison between bonus and dividends

2.12 If the company pays tax at the small profits' rate it is nearly always beneficial to extract surplus funds by means of a dividend as the now relatively high cost of NICs is avoided. The substitution of dividends for remuneration is not regarded as an abnormal pay practice for NIC purposes (*Social Security and Benefits Act 1992, Sch 1, para 4(c)*). It is possible, however, that the National Insurance Contributions Office (NICO) may seek to challenge dividends which have not been declared in accordance with the relevant *Companies Act* formalities. If the correct legal procedures are not followed, it can be asserted that a payment is not a 'valid' dividend and hence must be 'NIC-able' earnings (see 9.2).

Since 6 April 2010, dividends can be taxed at one of three rates (or a combination of them), as follows:

Total taxable income (including dividend)	Tax rate applied to dividend
Below basic rate income threshold – £37,400	10% (covered by 10% tax credit)
Between basic rate threshold and £150,000	32.5% (less 10% tax credit) Effective rate = 25% of net cash amount received
Above £150,000	42.5% (less 10% tax credit) Effective rate = 36.1% of net cash amount received

Dividend taxation is extensively covered in 9.11.

Some owner-managers may be tempted to extract their income entirely in the form of dividends, but it is often sensible to extract a reasonable level of salary. In any event, if the owner-manager has no other taxable income, it is better to pay at least a sufficient salary to use up the personal allowance (since no 10% tax credit is available to the extent to which dividends are covered by personal allowances).

Various tax comparisons between extracting surplus profits as a bonus or a dividend for 2011/12 are shown in the worked examples below. The various factors listed at 2.26 may also influence the decision, depending on the relevant circumstances of each case.

Bonus versus dividend comparison – 2011/12 (company taxed at small profits rate)

2.13   Example 1 (assuming a marginal income tax rate of 40%) and Example 2 (assuming a marginal income tax rate of 50%) below illustrate that it is beneficial to extract surplus profits as a dividend where the company is paying tax at the small profits rate (20% % for 2011/12). However, this is subject to the other factors cited at 2.26.

It should be noted that where a company pays a bonus, there is an additional NIC cost but corporate tax relief is given on the total cost of the bonus and related NIC, ie the company does not pay corporation tax on this part of its profits. On the other hand, a dividend is not tax deductible and hence profits earmarked for a dividend suffer corporation tax.

Example 1

2011/12 Bonus versus dividend comparison (Owner manager's marginal tax rate of 40% and CT at 20%)

Greaves Limited is likely to have surplus profits available of £100,000 for the year ended 31 March 2012, which could be paid to its sole shareholder, Mr

Jimmy, as a bonus or dividend. Mr Jimmy already draws a monthly salary of £3,600 (ie in excess of the basic rate threshold upper earnings limit), and therefore his marginal tax rate is 40%. Greaves Limited is subject to corporation tax at 20% .

The relevant tax and NIC effects are compared below.

	£	*Bonus* £	£	*Dividend* £
Available profits		100,000		100,000
Less Employer's NIC –		(12,127)		
£88,873 @ 13.8%				
Corporation tax @ 20%				(20,000)
		87,873		80,000
Income tax and NIC thereon				
Bonus	87,873 @ 40%	(35,149)		
Employees' NIC @ 2% (rate on earnings above upper limit)	87,873 @ 2%	(1,758)		

	£	*Bonus* £	£	*Dividend* £
Dividend:				
Cash	80,000			
Tax credit				
(10/90)	8,889			
Gross	88,889 @ 32.5%		(28,889)	
Less Tax credit			8,889	(20,000)
Net cash available		£50,966		£60,000
Tax and NIC liabilities				
Employer's NIC		12,127		
Corporation tax				20,000
PAYE and NIC (£35,149 + £1,758)		36,907		
Higher rate tax liability				20,000
		49,034		40,000
Effective overall tax rate		49%		40.0%

Tax saved by dividend = £9,034 (£49,034 less £40,000).

Example 2

2011/12 Bonus versus dividend comparison (Owner Manager's marginal tax rate of 50% and CT at 20%)

Bonds Limited is likely to have surplus profits available of £100,000 for the year ended 31 March 2012, which could be paid to its sole shareholder, Mr Billy, as a bonus or dividend. Mr Billy has already drawn a monthly salary of £14,000 and therefore his marginal tax rate is 50%. Bonds Ltd is subject to corporation tax at 20%.

The relevant tax and NIC effects are compared below.

	£		Bonus £	£	Dividend £
Available profits			100,000		100,000
Less Employer's NIC –	£87,873	@ 13.8%	(12,127)		
Corporation tax @ 20%					(20,000)
			87,873		80,000
Income tax and NIC thereon					
Bonus	87,873	@ 50%	(43,937)		
Employees' NIC @ 2% (rate on earnings above upper limit)	87,873	@ 2%	(1,758)		
Dividend:					
Cash	80,000				
Tax credit					
(10/90)	8,889				
Gross	88,889	@ 42.5%		(37,778)	
Less Tax credit				8,889	(28,889)
Net cash available			£42,178		£51,111
Tax and NIC liabilities					
Employer's NIC			12,127		

	Bonus		Dividend
£	£	£	£
Corporation tax			20,000
PAYE and NIC			
(£43,937 + £1,758)	45,695		
Higher rate tax liability			28,889
	57,822		48,889
Effective overall tax rate	57.8%		48.9%

Tax saved by dividend = £8,933 (£57,822 less £48,889).

Bonus versus dividend comparison – 2011/12 (company paying tax at full rate)

2.14   Example 3 (assuming a marginal income tax rate of 40%) and Example 4 (assuming a marginal income tax rate of 50%), show that where the company's profit suffers tax at the main rate of 26% , there is still a tax advantage in favour of dividends. (The additional NIC costs outweigh the benefit of the higher corporation tax relief for the bonus (and employer's NIC). When the timing of the relevant tax cash flows is taken into account, dividends become even more attractive, given the earlier PAYE and NIC payments on bonuses.

Example 3

2011/12 Bonus versus dividend comparison (Owner manager's marginal tax rate of 40% and CT at 26%)

Assume the same facts as in *Example 1*, except that Greaves Limited pays corporation tax at the main rate of 26% .

		Bonus		Dividend
	£	£	£	£
Available profits		100,000		100,000
Less Employer's NIC –				
£87,873 @ 13.8%		(12.127)		
Corporation tax @ 28%				(26,000)
		87,873		74,000

29

			Bonus			Dividend
	£		£	£		£
Income tax thereon						
Bonus	87,873	@ 40%	(35,149)			
Employees' NIC @ 2% (rate on earnings above upper limit)	87,873	@ 12%	(1,758)			
Dividend:						
Cash	74,000					
Tax credit						
(10/90)	8,222					
Gross	82,222	@ 32.5%		(26,722)		
Less Tax credit				8,222		(18,500)
Tax						
Net cash available			50,966			55,500
Tax and NIC liabilities						
Employer's NIC			12,127			
Corporation tax						26,000
PAYE and NIC						
(£35,149 + £1,758)			36,907			
Higher rate tax liability						18,500
			49,034			44,500
Effective overall tax rate			49.0%			44.5%

Tax saved by paying a dividend = £4,534 (£49,034 less £44,500).

Example 4

2011/12 Bonus versus dividend comparison (Owner manager's marginal tax rate of 50% and CT at 26%)

Assume the same facts as in *Example 2*, except that Bonds Ltd pays corporation tax at the main rate of 26% .

	£	Bonus £	£	Dividend £
Available profits		100,000		100,000
Less Employer's NIC –				
£87,873 @ 13.8%		(12,127)		
Corporation tax @ 26%				(26,000)
		87,873		74,000
Income tax thereon				
Bonus	87,873 @ 50%	(43,937)		
Employees' NIC @ 1% (rate on earnings above upper limit)	87,873 @ 2%	(1,758)		
Dividend				
Cash	74,000			
Tax credit				
(10/90)	8,222			
Gross	82,222 @ 42.5%		(34,944)	
Less Tax credit			8,222	(26,722)
Net cash available		42,178		47,278
Tax and NIC liabilities		12,127		
Employer's NIC				
Corporation tax				26,000
PAYE and NIC				
(£43,937 + £1,758)		45,695		
Higher rate tax liability				26,722
		57,822		52,722
Effective overall tax rate		57.8%		52.7%

Tax saved by paying a dividend = £5,100 (£57,822 less £52,722).

Bonus versus dividend comparison – 2011/12 (company paying tax at marginal rate)

2.15   If the company pays tax at the '2011/12' marginal corporate tax rate of 27.5% (for example, in the case of a singleton company with no associated companies having taxable profits between £300,001 and £1,500,000), the balance of advantage is still marginally in favour of dividends.

Where the owner-manager's marginal tax rate is 40%, the effective combined tax/NIC rate for profits taken as a bonus is still 49% (as in Examples 1 and 3), whereas if the entire bonus is taxed at the super tax rate of 50%, the combined rate would be 57.8% (as in Examples 2 and 4).

The corresponding overall rates for a dividend would 45.68% (40% marginal rate) and 53.68% (50% marginal rate), which could be (quickly) derived as follows:

	£	%
Total income below £150,000		
Profits before tax (say)	100.00	
Less: Corporation tax @ 27.5%	27.50	27.50
Post tax profit = cash dividend	72.50	
Income tax @ effective rate of 25%	18.13	18.13
Net post-tax receipt	54.37	
Effective tax rate		45.63%
Total income above £150,000	£	%
Profits before tax (say)	100.00	
Less: Corporation tax @ 27.5%	27.50	27.50
Post tax profit = cash dividend	72.50	
Income tax @ effective rate of 36.1%	26.18	26.18
Net post-tax receipt	46.32	
Effective tax rate		53.68%

Shareholders paying tax at the lower/basic rates

2.16   Where the shareholder only pays tax at the basic rate, their dividend income would be subject to income tax at 10% in their hands. However, because the tax liability is fully offset by the 10% tax credit no additional tax liability arises, as shown below:

	£
Cash dividend (say)	90
Add: Tax credit (1/9th of £90)	10
Taxable gross dividend	100
Income tax at 10%	10
Less: Tax credit	(10)
Income tax payable	–

2.17 'Basic rate' shareholders would therefore generally prefer dividends (irrespective of the corporate tax rate). They do not suffer any income tax on the dividend income – the only 'indirect' tax suffered is the corporate tax on the profits from which the dividend is paid.

This conclusion is reinforced by the following table which compares 'bonuses and dividends' in terms of the combined effective tax rates (including 12% NICs for bonuses) for 2011/12 :

Marginal corporation tax rate	Bonus	Dividend
	Effective tax rate	*Effective tax rate*
20%	40.3%	20.0%
27.5%	40.3%	27.5%
26%	40.3%	26%

Avoiding the super tax rate

2.18 Examples 2 and 4 above illustrate how severe the super tax rate can be when the owner manager needs to extract substantial cash from the business. The new penal income tax rates are likely to encourage owner managers to retain more of the company's profits within the business, which may cause some to reflect on lifestyle changes!

Many well-advised owner managers will have paid a large dividend before April 2010 and lent all or part of it back. Having a healthy (credit) loan account is likely to prove useful as a means of supplementing their income from the company (which can therefore be drawn at levels below the £150,000 super tax rate trigger).

The above examples have been simplified to show the relevant tax that would be payable at relevant marginal rates. There will, of course, be many cases where tax/NIC is payable over two or more rate bands and detailed calculations will be required, but dividends will generally be preferred.

As a result of the increasingly large 'gap' between individual and corporate tax rates, companies will become increasingly attractive as a vehicle to earn and retain income. It follows that many highly profitable sole traders, partnerships and LLPs are likely to consider incorporation in the near future.

COMPANIES WITH TAX LOSSES

2.19   If the company has tax losses, the payment of a bonus will increase the tax-adjusted trading loss. If there is scope to carry back the loss against the previous year, corporation tax relief is effectively obtained. The rate of relief would depend on the level of the prior year's profits. If there is no scope to relieve the bonus by loss carry-back (or group relief), then it will be included as part of the company's carried forward trading losses and the tax relief is effectively deferred until the losses are offset against future trading profits.

Repayment interest would accrue on tax repaid for the previous year, from nine months after the end of that period.

In contrast, a dividend would not create an additional loss.

The 'bonus versus dividend' equation therefore depends, amongst other things, on the effective rate of company tax relief and the amount of any repayment interest.

WHEN SHOULD COMPARISON BE MADE?

2.20   It is generally preferable for the computational 'bonus versus dividend' profit extraction comparison to be made *before* the year end. From the owner-manager's viewpoint, there may of course be a timing point regarding the particular tax year into which the bonus/dividend should fall (particularly if there is a need to avoid the 'super tax rate).

The position with bonuses is more flexible since it is also possible to make a provision in the year end statutory accounts and obtain tax relief in that period, provided the bonus is paid within nine months of the year end (see 2.22). Such a provision must comply with Financial Reporting Standard 12, which requires a legal or constructive obligation to pay the bonus to exist at the balance sheet date (see 4.5). In practical terms, this means that the anticipated results should be considered before the year end, and an agreement should be in place for any required bonuses. It may also be preferable to look at the anticipated results of the company for other reasons. For example, this would enable the directors to consider the amount of any pension contributions which must be paid before the year end to ensure tax relief is obtained in the current period. This means that reliable management accounting figures should be available.

DETAILED IMPLICATIONS OF PAYING A BONUS

Corporation tax relief

2.21   In the case of a trading company, the remuneration or bonus should be deductible against profits. It is very rare for an Inspector to challenge the level of remuneration paid to working director shareholders. The amounts paid to owner-managers will generally stand up to scrutiny as being a commercial rate, given their role in the company and the responsibility involved. In contrast, HMRC often seek to limit the tax deduction for directors' fees paid by investment companies to a very modest amount (see 4.43 note (*i*)). In such cases, extracting funds via a dividend is likely to be more tax efficient.

If the Inspector challenges the corporation tax deduction for the remuneration and denies relief for the amount considered to be excessive, this amount will still be subject to PAYE tax and NICs. However, by concession, HMRC are prepared to refund the PAYE tax paid on this amount, provided the excess amount is formally waived by the director and the amount is actually reimbursed to the company (see *ICAEW Tax Faculty Technical Release TAX 11/93*). However, any NIC liability will still stand as the NICO does not apply this concession.

Relief for accrued remuneration

2.22   A special rule applies to remuneration which is accrued or unpaid at the end of a company's accounting period, such as a provision for a bonus. Such remuneration can only be deducted against the company's taxable profits for that period if it is paid within nine months after the period end [*CTA 2009, ss 1288 and 1289*]. The date when remuneration is deemed to be paid is defined in *ITEPA 2003, s 18* (this rule also applies for PAYE purposes (see 5.5)).

In the case of directors, the date of payment will often be the time when payment is actually made or when the director becomes legally entitled to the amount (although the statutory definition also includes other events). Unless a director has a service agreement, his remuneration can only be determined when it is approved by the shareholders at the company's AGM, which will normally be the date on which the company's annual accounts are signed. However, where appropriate, reliance can be placed on the decision in *Re Duomatic* [1969] 1 All ER 161 (applied more recently in *Cane v Jones* [1981] 1 All ER 533). This case decided that where the directors agree in their capacity as shareholders the amount to be paid to them as directors' remuneration, this agreement will have the same effect as a resolution passed at the AGM. Consequently, where the AGM is likely to occur after the end of the nine-month period, it should still be possible to trigger a 'payment' of the bonus within the nine-month period by agreement of the director shareholders, which should be formally minuted.

It will be appreciated that bonuses provide a convenient way of reducing a company's taxable profits after the year end.

2.23   If the shareholder director is fortunate enough to have a healthy credit balance on their loan/current account, they can draw amounts from the account during the accounting period without attracting any PAYE or NIC charges. The loan/current account can then be 'topped up' by a bonus following the year end and the exercise repeated next year.

The tax deduction rules for accrued bonus/remuneration may be used to obtain earlier corporation tax relief for amounts to be paid within the nine months following the year end. Provided the statutory accounts have not been signed-off, a provision can be made for bonuses paid (or to be paid) within nine months of the year end. Care must be taken that any such provision is FRS 12 compliant. This would require there to be a 'present obligation' at the balance sheet date to pay a bonus. This could be evidenced by minutes of a board meeting held prior to the year end, or even by the fact that such bonuses are regularly made. A provision written into the accounts after the year end (which does not satisfy FRS 12) would be open to challenge from HMRC, who would seek to disallow the deduction in the year. HMRC are increasingly looking at accounting and accounting standards as part of their enquiries.

When providing for accrued directors' remuneration in the accounts, it is normal practice to provide also for the PAYE and NIC (including employer's NIC) liabilities in the accounts to which the remuneration relates. If this practice is not adopted the amount would be provided gross and when the directors' final remuneration is approved (at the AGM, if not earlier), the net remuneration would then be credited to the relevant director's accounts. At that date, the PAYE and NICs must then be accounted for (*ICAEW Tax Faculty Guidance Note TAX 11/93*).

PAYE and cash flow

2.24   The payment of the bonus will, of course, attract a PAYE/NIC liability. PAYE at the basic rate (and higher rate, if applicable) and Class 1 NICs are normally payable 14 days after the end of the month in which the bonus is 'paid' or 'made available' [*SI 2003 No 2682, reg 69*]. If the director receives a relatively low monthly salary and a high bonus payment once a year, further NICs are likely to become due on the annual re-calculation (this is because the NICs accounted for will have been subject to the monthly 'upper earnings limit', as shown in 5.16 – Example 4).

If the tax due on the bonus was incorrect (for example, if the PAYE code was wrong), there may be additional tax to pay when the individual submits their tax return (at the latest by 31 January following the relevant tax year). However, provided the unpaid amount is less than £3,000 (from 2011/12) and the tax return is submitted early (say by 30 December after the tax year),

HMRC will adjust the PAYE code for the following tax year enabling that tax to be collected on a gradual basis over the next tax year.

With a bonus, the owner-manager only receives the net amount after deducting PAYE and NIC. In contrast, where a dividend is paid, the owner-manager receives the full cash amount and does not have to pay the higher rate tax until a later date. Payments of tax on the dividend are made in accordance with the normal self-assessment rules. This requires interim tax payments to be made on 31 January in the tax year and on 31 July following the tax year (based on the previous year's tax liability) with a final payment being due on the following 31 January. Where a regular payment of dividends is established, the tax may become factored into the interim payments. Some owner-managers alternate between bonuses and dividends to prevent tax on dividends being factored into their payments of accounts.

In some cases, it may be beneficial to defer the payment of a dividend from say March to 6 April or later, as this may defer the higher rate liability (particularly if the director/shareholder's interim tax payments are based on a low prior year tax liability).

The tax cash flow implications therefore need to be considered, which will vary according to the individual circumstances of each case. When interest costs have been taken into account, this may affect the 'bonus v dividend' comparisons considered above.

PAYMENT OF DIVIDENDS

2.25 In the context of a family or owner-managed company, the company's directors decide on the maximum level of the annual dividend that should be paid, based on the company's annual accounts and general financial position. Their proposed dividend is then put forward to the shareholders (in many cases, the same or largely the same individuals as the directors) who vote (by ordinary resolution) whether to pay the suggested figure or a *lower* amount. Dividends are paid proportionately to the number of shares held (of the same class), although it is possible for shareholders to waive all or some of their dividend entitlement. Some companies have different classes of shares enabling them to alter the level of dividend paid on each separate class. It is only possible to pay dissimilar levels of dividend on different classes of shares. Once the vote has been passed, the dividend becomes 'declared' when it is then strictly regarded as having been made for tax purposes (see 9.29).

Directors usually have the power to make interim dividends before the final dividend is made. It is therefore possible to pay dividends on a regular basis. However, many owner-managers find it easier just to pay one 'large' dividend, which is then credited to their current account with the company upon which they can draw through the year. In practice, HMRC treat the 'crediting' of a dividend to a loan/current account as having been paid for tax purposes.

Further detailed coverage of the procedures for paying and taxing dividends is given in Chapter 9.

BONUS VERSUS DIVIDEND – OTHER FACTORS

2.26 The 'bonus versus dividend' decision will often be influenced by a number of other factors, the main ones being set out below:

(a) *Pension provision* –In the past, owner-managers often enjoyed considerable flexibility regarding the level of contributions they were able to make. However, from 6 April 2011, they will only be able to enjoy tax relief on pension contributions of up to £50,000 in the relevant tax year (plus any unused 'allowance' brought forward from the three previous years). The £50,000 'annual allowance' limit applies to both personal and company contributions. It cannot therefore be side-stepped by routing pension contributions through the company. The introduction of a 'lower' £50,000 annual allowance from 2011/12 does not affect the existing rules governing pension contributions. Personal contributions only rank for income tax relief if the payer has sufficient 'relevant earnings' since relief is available on up to 100% of their relevant earnings for the tax year. However, if they have little or no earnings, relief is always given on gross contributions of up to a maximum of £3,600. Thus, where the owner-manager decides to draw little or no salary, they will still be able to fund a personal pension scheme at a rate of up to £3,600 (gross) per year. It should be noted that dividend income does not count as relevant earnings. Owner-managers will need to have a reasonable level of salary/bonuses/ benefits to make worthwhile (tax relievable) pension contributions. Thus, where additional pension provision is required, it will often be necessary to pay appropriate bonuses. The bonus would not attract any income tax if it can be sheltered by a matching pension contribution (made within the relevant limit). However, a personal pension payment would *not* shelter the employers' and employees' NIC liability on the bonus. These NIC costs can be avoided where the company undertakes to pay the individual's pension contributions (instead of the bonus). Although the company is discharging a pecuniary benefit of the individual, this does not currently give rise to a taxable benefit. Detailed commentary of the post-5 April 2011 pension contributions relief system is provided in Chapter 10.

(b) *Protecting social security and basic state retirement benefits* – Dividends do not attract NICs and therefore a certain level of remuneration is required to secure certain earnings-related social security benefits and the National Insurance Retirement Pension ('NIRP'). It is only necessary for an individual's earnings to be above the lower earnings limit (£102 per week for 2011/12) to qualify and, therefore, a small salary should always be paid (also possibly to satisfy the National Minimum Wage requirements – see 2.10). In fact, provided the earnings exceed the lower earnings limit but are below the primary earnings threshold (£139 per week for 2011/12), basic state retirement benefits can be protected without incurring any NIC liability.

(c) **Share valuations** – A history of dividend payments might increase the value of minority shareholdings for tax purposes. This is because the valuation of a minority shareholding may be determined by the expectation of dividend income. Share valuations for controlling shareholders are unlikely to be affected (see 14.38–14.39 and 14.50– 14.53).

(d) **Spread of shareholdings** – as shareholders receive dividends in proportion to their holdings, the amount of dividends received by each shareholder may not provide a fair reward for the working shareholders and may prove too generous for the non-working or 'passive' shareholders. On the other hand a bonus can, therefore, be a problem where the company's shareholdings have become widely spread over time. A 'dividend waiver' may be the answer here, provided it does not create any 'settlement' problems (see 9.16–9.21). Use of a separate class of shares for the non-working shareholders might be a more elegant solution on a long term basis (see 9.22).

(e) **Personal borrowing and other issues** – some lenders may not understand the methodology of profit extraction used by owner-managed companies and only focus on 'remuneration/salary' (as opposed to bonuses and dividends) when providing mortgages, loans, etc. Remuneration is also used to calculate redundancy pay and remains important for income protection plans. PHI cover can be provided to take salary/bonus as well as dividends into account.

EXTRACTING SURPLUS PROFITS – SOME CONCLUSIONS

2.27 The various worked examples in this chapter largely concentrate on the extraction of 'surplus' profits where a reasonable level of salary has already been paid. It is often considered beneficial to pay a modest level of salary. However, where tax-efficiency is paramount, there is no substitute for doing the relative computations to compare the combined effective tax rates (for the company and its owner-manager(s)).

Where the company is paying tax at the small profits rate it is now clearly beneficial to pay *surplus* profits out as dividends, particularly if there is a long delay before the higher rate tax has to be paid. Where the company pays tax at the main 26% rate, the current high NIC rates mean that dividends become marginally better (in terms of effective tax rates). Dividends also offer the added potential of a longer deferment in the payment of income tax.

If the company's profits are likely to fall in the 27.5% marginal rate band, a bonus could be paid to reduce the profits to the small profits rate level (thus taking relief for the bonus at the marginal rate) and the remainder can be paid as a dividend. Again, however, the position swings back in favour of dividends once the main rate of corporation tax falls to 26%.

Where shareholders only pay tax at the lower or basic rates, dividends will invariably be more tax efficient.

However, the above broad generalisations may be overturned by various other factors. Thus, a relatively high bonus payment might be required to enable the owner-manager to augment their personal pension fund with tax allowable contributions (subject to the anti-forestalling rules for abnormal contributions made after 21 April 2009 and the new limit from 6 April 2011). In certain situations, the payment of a bonus may provide a useful way of keeping a company outside the quarterly instalment regime for corporation tax.

In summary, family and owner-managed companies should consider a sensible combination of bonuses and dividends and, in appropriate cases, pension contributions. The precise mix would depend on the particular circumstances of each company and its shareholders.

REMUNERATION PAID TO OTHER MEMBERS OF THE FAMILY

2.28   As a general rule, tax will be saved if income can be paid to other members of the owner-manager's family in order to use their annual personal allowances and benefit from their lower marginal tax rates. Inspectors are likely to scrutinise salaries paid to members of the family to see whether they are paid at or above the market rate for the duties performed. Where the amount clearly exceeds the commercial rate, the Inspector will seek to disallow the 'excess' element on the grounds that it has *not* been incurred wholly and exclusively for the purposes of the company's trade. In practice, the agreement of an 'allowable' amount is likely to be negotiated.

TRANSFERRING INCOME TO THE SPOUSE

Income tax for spouse (or civil partner)

2.29   For the sake of brevity, but at the risk of appearing sexist(!), the following commentary (in particular) is couched exclusively in terms of the husband being the one who owns and runs the company and puts income into his wife's hands. However, the comments below apply equally to those situations where the wife owns the company and the roles are reversed. (The same considerations also apply to single-sex couples who have registered as civil partners.)

Under independent taxation, each spouse has their own personal allowance and personal basic rate bands. It is generally beneficial to bring the spouse in as a director or employee and pay them a salary, provided the following conditions are met:

(*a*)   the salary is taxable at a lower rate of tax (than that suffered by the owner-manager on his income);

(*b*)   this income tax saving is not exceeded by the additional NIC liability (see 2.39); and

(*c*)   the company is able to obtain a tax deduction for the salary (see 2.46).

In all such cases, it is recommended that the remuneration (or dividend – see 2.43) should not be paid into a joint bank account, but one in the spouse's sole name. The same benefits may also apply to bringing in a civil partner as an employee/director.

Many spouses only work on a 'part-time' basis. However, part-time workers also fall within the minimum wage legislation. Hence, the amount paid to the spouse must not be lower than the (minimum) £6.08 (from 1 October 2011, previously £5.93) per hour requirement. However, if the spouse works for the company without any remuneration at all, she may well not be an employee, and hence the minimum wage legislation will not apply as the relationship may be explained by a desire to assist the company voluntarily (*ICAEW Tax Guide 7/00*).

Working tax credit (WTC) and child tax credit (CTC) regime

Background

2.30   In the past some owner managed companies have regulated the amount of income extracted from the company to generate a Working Tax Credit (WTC) and possibly also child tax credit (CTC). However, the Budget 2011 marked a change in Government policy to target these benefits to those at the lower end of the income scale. Consequently, there is much less scope for exploiting these benefits and very few owner managers are likely to be concerned with them. Only the basic WTC and CTC rules are therefore summarised here.

Working Tax Credit (WTC)

2.31   WTC is available to UK residents (aged 16 or over) working (or in the case of couples, one of whom works) at least 16 hours per week. The claimant (or, in the case of a couple, one of the claimants) must broadly have dependent children (or a mental or physical disability which puts them at a disadvantage in getting a job) *or* be at least 25 years old and work for at least 30 hours a week.

A WTC may comprise:

- A basic element of £1,920 (for 2011/12);

- A second adult element (for a cohabiting couple or a lone parent with a dependent child) – £1,950 for 2011/12);

- A 30 hour element where the claimant (or, for a cohabiting couple, one of the claimants) works for at least 30 hours per week *or*, if the couple have a dependent child or young person, and one of them works at least 16 hours per week and they together work for at least 30 hours per week – £790 for 2011/12

- A childcare element equal to 70% (for 2011/12) of eligible childcare costs up to a maximum of £175 a week for one child or £300 for two or more children.

There are disability, severe disability, and 50 + elements for certain claimants aged at least 50.

These benefits are subject to a tapering reduction, based on the level of the claimant's relevant income (see 2.35 below)

Child Tax Credit (CTC)

2.32   CTC is entirely separate from child benefit. CTC is generally paid to those who are responsible for at least one child. CTC is *not* conditional on the claimant's employment. It provides support for a child until 1 September following their 16th birthday (and may continue to a child's 19th birthday if they remain in full-time education of a 'non-advanced' manner). CTC is generally paid into the bank account of the main carer and is made either weekly or every four weeks.

Child element

The child element of CTC (£2,555 for 2011/12) is paid for *each* child the claimant is responsible for. A child is someone under the age of 16 years. In the year that the child reaches their 16th birthday, the CTC will still be paid until the following 1 September after their 16th birthday. The child element is extended until their 19th birthday, if they are in full-time education.

If the child is disabled, a disability or severe disability element is paid in addition to the child element.

Family element

The *family* element is paid to all people entitled to the CTC. For the 2011/12 tax year, the amount is £545 (unchanged since 2007/08) but where the family has a child under the age of one year, this amount is increased to £1,090, for the first year only. 'First year' refers to the calendar year, not the tax year (ie 12 months from the date of birth).

Both the child and family elements are tapered down according to the level of the claimant's relevant income (see 2.35 below)

Claims procedure

2.33   CTC and WTC must be claimed on the complex HMRC form TC600 (online claims are no longer permitted) and are geared to the level of a couple's joint gross taxable income ('relevant income'). Thus, couples (whether married or not, including single-sex couples) will need to provide details of their joint income on the return. Claimants must be physically present and ordinarily resident in the UK to be eligible to claim credits. If the claimant is a lone parent, tax credits will be based on their taxable 'relevant income' (*which would be reduced by trading losses, charitable donations and pension contributions and would exclude any maintenance payments or student loans*). The amount of CTC and WTC is not restricted by the level of the claimant's capital.

Protective claims

2.34   Tax credit awards are usually based provisionally on a claimant's income for the preceding tax year. Consequently, where a claimant's income decreases, they may have unsuspectingly qualified for tax credits for the year. To take advantage of this, a protective claim must be in place at the start of the year. If the claimant leaves it until later on in the year when their circumstances change, the award can normally only be backdated by up to three months.

The entitlement to credits accrues on a daily basis over the tax year. Therefore someone earning £30,000 a year in the first six months of the year, and earning nothing in the remaining last six months, can be awarded tax credits for the first six months at a rate appropriate to someone earning £15,000 a year.

Protective claims should be considered where income levels are uncertain, for example where increased pension contributions are likely to be made, or where large self employment/property business losses are expected, whether these are trading or property business losses. Whilst employees will know their employment income for the year on receipt of their P60s, their levels of relevant income may be uncertain where for example they have losses arising from other activities.

Claimants should be aware that by submitting a form and receiving a nil award, they are still subject to all of the CTC rules, eg notifying the HMRC of any changes in circumstance, such as a change in income levels or the birth of a child. However, HMRC has confirmed that it will not seek to charge penalties for failure to notify where a nil award is received. Failure to notify will result in the claim being backdated to only three months.

Calculation of CTC/WTC

2.35 WTCs and CTCs are subject to tapering if the couples' or a single claimant's relevant gross income exceeds specified thresholds.

Claimant entitled to	For 2011/12 Maximum credits are withdrawn at the rate of
WTC or WTC and CTC *(excluding family element)*	41p for every £1 of the excess of relevant income over £6,420
CTC only *(excluding family element)*	41p for every £1 of the excess of relevant income over £15,860
Family element of CTC	41p for every £1 of the excess of relevant income over £40,000.

The family element is only now available to those on lower incomes since, from April 2011, the withdrawal rate was increased from 6.67p (for every £1 of income over £50,000) to 41p (for every £1 of income over £40,000). The 'withdrawal taper' is first applied to the non-childcare elements of WTC, then to the childcare element of WTC, and lastly CTC.

2.37 The amount of tax credits actually received depends on the level of the claimant's income. However, certain deductions are available to reduce the level of relevant income, which are as follows:

(a) For tax credit purposes, trading losses are set off primarily against any other joint income of the tax year, regardless of the actual trading loss claim made. Any unutilised losses are carried forward to be offset against future profits from the same trade. (Trading losses are therefore treated differently for tax credit purposes compared to their income tax treatment.)

(b) The gross amount of any pension contributions and charitable payments paid during the year.

(c) IR35 income – HMRC do not regard the deemed employment income under the IR35 legislation as income for tax credit purposes, and therefore any deemed income arising under IR35 can be disregarded (see Chapter 6). The income reported on the tax credit form should therefore only include any dividends and salary actually paid.

Contributions to a registered pension scheme are deductible in working out the joint household income and may provide useful tax-saving opportunities. Large pension contributions may therefore trigger an unexpected entitlement to credits and a claim might be beneficial in such cases.

HMRC initially work out the amount of CTC and WTC payable by reference to the income of the previous tax year. The final award is made after a comparison of the previous year's income with 'claim year' income. The revision of the tax credit may confirm the initial award, or may result in an underpayment or overpayment of credit.

If the 'claim year' income is greater than the previous year's income, the award will only be amended where there has been a material change (ie a difference in income of more than £10,000 for 2011/12) unless the claimant specifically requests that the claim is updated. Claims cannot be backdated for more than three months.

Example 5 illustrates the computation of relevant income for the purposes of Tax Credit claims and Example 6 provides an illustrative calculation of a WTC/CTC claim for a married couple.

Example 5

Wayne and Coleen live together (unmarried) and have three children. Their income for 2010/11 is made up as follows:

	Wayne	Coleen
	£	£
Gross salary	35,000	
Car benefit	3,600	
Trading loss from self employment		(500)
UK bank interest (paid gross)		1,200
Child benefit		2,412
Pension contributions paid	2,800	
Gift aid donations	1,000	

Calculation of income for tax credit purposes:	£
Bank interest (gross)	1,200
Deduct first £300 of investment income (Note 1)	(300)
Employment income including benefits	38,600
	39,500
Deductions:	
Trading losses	(500)
Gift aid payment × 100/80	(1,250)
Pension contribution × 100/80	(3,500)
Income for tax credit purposes	**34,250**

Notes

1   The first £300 of investment income is excluded for tax credit purposes. If investment income exceeds £300, only the excess is included.

2   Child benefit is exempt income for tax credit purposes.

Example 6

Cheryl and Ashley have three children, who are 9, 12, and 14 years old. Ashley is the managing director and sole shareholder of Cole Ltd, and receives a salary of £30,000 a year. Ashley currently pays £150 a month into the company's registered pension scheme.

Cheryl also works part time for Cole Ltd (19 hours), providing secretarial and administrative services for which she is paid an annual salary of £7,000.

Ashley's income tax computation for the year ended 5 April 2012 is as follows:

	£
Salary	30,000
Less: pension contributions (£150 × 12)	(1,800)
Employment income	28,200
Less: Personal allowance	(7,475)
Taxable income	20,725
Tax thereon:	
£20,725 @ 20%	4,145

Cheryl and Ashley's joint income for tax credit purposes is Ashley and Cheryl's employment income, less pension contributions paid ie £35,200 (£30,000 + £7,000 – £1,800).

Cheryl and Ashley are entitled to the following tax credits for the year ended 5 April 2012:

Child Tax Credit:	
Family element	545
Child element (£2,555 × 3)	7,665
Working Tax Credit:	
Basic element	1,920
Couple's element	1,950
30 hour element (as Ashley works full time)	790
Maximum credits:	12,870
Less: restriction	
(Joint income of £35,200 – £6,420) × 41%	(11,800)
Total credits available	1,070

Spouse's NIC liabilities

2.39   The income tax benefits of giving a salary to a spouse are often reduced by the NIC cost. In 2011/12 , if the spouse earns £139 or more per week (or more than £7,225 on an annual basis), *employees'* NICs are payable at 12% on earnings between £139 and £817 per week (£7,225 –£42,475 per year). The first £139 per week is free of NICs. The rate of employees' NIC for contracted out schemes is 10.4% . When the spouse's total annual earnings (including benefits) reach the upper earnings limit of £42,475, a 2% NIC 'surcharge' is levied on any amount exceeding the limit.

For 2011/12 , *employer's* NICs are levied at the standard rate of 13.8% for earnings exceeding £136 per week with no maximum limit. (The first £136 per week (£7,072 per year) is NIC free). Employers in contracted out schemes pay NICs at lower rates on earnings between £136 and £817 per week (10.1% for salary related pension schemes and 12.4% for money purchase pension schemes).

Following the near harmonisation of income tax and NIC thresholds, an annual salary of up to £7,072 can therefore be paid in 2011/12 without any income tax or NIC liability.

TAX DEDUCTION FOR REMUNERATION PAID TO SPOUSE

2.40   The optimum amount to be paid to the spouse must therefore be carefully considered. Unless the spouse works for the company on a full-time basis, HMRC will require the amount to be substantiated in relation to the duties performed. Inspectors often critically assess the amount of remuneration paid to a wife in relation to the work she performs. It may be helpful to draw up a job specification listing all the wife's duties (for example, secretarial, certain administrative duties, etc) together with some indication of the time commitment. There must also be some evidence of payment to the spouse. Unsurprisingly, in *Moschi v Kelly [1952]* 33 TC 442, tax relief for the wife's wages was denied since they were charged to the owner's own drawings account!

If the wife is appointed as a director, then the legal obligations and responsibilities assumed in that position alone should justify a reasonable level of remuneration. Provided the amount paid to the wife reflects the work she *actually* carries out, the company should have no difficulty in obtaining a tax deduction. (Similar considerations apply to remuneration paid to a civil partner, etc.)

A further advantage of paying remuneration to the wife is that it can be used to support company pension contributions to provide her with a pension in her own right, subject to the spouse's overall package meeting the 'wholly and exclusively' requirement (and the pension payment being within the annual allowance – see 10.0).

A spouse could also pay tax-deductible personal pension contributions up to 100% of her salary.

The Copeman v William Flood & Sons Ltd case

2.41   Where HMRC consider the level of remuneration to be excessive, they will challenge it using the decision in *Copeman v William Flood & Sons Ltd* (1940) 24 TC 53. (Similar issues apply to the tax deductibility of company pension contributions – see 10.25.) This case enables them to disallow the 'excess' part of the remuneration charged in the accounts on the grounds that this element was not paid wholly and exclusively for the purposes of the company's trade (the rule which is now contained in *CTA 2009, s 54*).

In the *Copeman* case, the Revenue contested the deduction for remuneration of £2,600 paid in 1938 to a pig dealer's daughter, for dealing with telephone queries. This would be equivalent to remuneration of well over £75,000 in current day values! The case was remitted to the Commissioners to determine the amount which should be disallowed.

Waiving 'disallowed' remuneration

2.42   If HMRC succeed in substituting a lower figure for the tax deductible remuneration, the wife would strictly be taxable on the *full amount* of the remuneration. However, provided the 'excess' element is formally waived and paid back to the company, HMRC will generally restrict the income tax charge to the *deductible* element of the remuneration (*para 42730, Employment Income Manual*).

If the spouse is also a shareholder, the Inspector may treat any non-waived 'disallowed' amount as a distribution, which should not increase the tax liability. However, HMRC will still retain any NIC liability.

Paying dividends to a spouse

2.43   If the wife does little or no work for the company, no relief can really be justified. In these cases, it is generally better to structure the shareholdings so that the spouse receives dividend income instead. Provided fully-fledged ordinary shares are provided to the spouse, HMRC is unlikely to challenge it now, following its defeat in *Garnett v Jones* [2007] STC 1536 – the so-called *Arctic Systems* case. On the other hand, if the shares issued only contain dividend rights (such as non-voting preference shares), HMRC will probably be able to counter the relevant arrangements, as they successfully did in *Young v Pearce* [1996] STC 743 (see 9.10).

Dividend-splitting is now likely to be considered by those 'owner-managers affected by the 'super' dividend tax rate of 36.1%. In many cases, owner-managers will seek to pay their spouses part of 'their' dividend entitlement to avoid paying this 'draconian' super tax rate on their dividends.

HMRC were very keen to introduce legislation to negate these types of income-shifting/income splitting arrangements as soon as the *Arctic Systems* ruling went against it. However, the Treasury seems to have lost the appetite to introduce appropriate new legislation to counter income splitting between married couples. (The initial draft income-splitting legislation issued in December 2007 was fiercely criticised by the various professional bodies and industry groups as being entirely unworkable and impractical!). Recent statements subsequently issued in the Pre-Budget 2008 and Budget 2009 reports indicate that the introduction of income-splitting rules have been firmly moved onto the 'back-burner'.

For 2011/12 , it is possible to receive a cash dividend of up to, say, £38,200 (in the absence of any other taxable income) without attracting a tax liability, calculated as follows:

		£
Cash dividend		38,200
Tax credit (10/90)		4,244
Gross dividend		42,444
Personal allowance		(7,475)
Taxable		34,969
Tax liability (within 'basic rate' band)		
£34,969 × 10%		3,497
Less Tax credit		(3,497)
		Nil

Under *ITTOIA 2005, s 397(2)*, the deductible dividend tax credit is restricted to 10% of the taxable dividend (for example, after offsetting the individual's personal allowance). The balance of the tax credit is therefore lost. It cannot be used to cover any higher rate tax liability on paying a (slightly) higher dividend.

If there is no other income, the part of the dividend covered by the personal allowance does not obtain the benefit of the 10% tax credit. The tax position could be improved if the wife has sufficient other income to 'soak-up' her personal allowance. Consequently, a small salary should be paid to the wife provided this can be justified on the grounds of her duties and/or directorship, as illustrated (for 2011/12) below:

	£	£
Salary		7,475
Cash dividend (say)	31,500	
Tax credit (10/90)	3,500	35,000
Total income		42,475
Personal allowance		(7,475)
Taxable		35,000
Tax liability		
Less Tax credit		3,500
£35,000 × 10%		(3,500)
		Nil

In this case, the total amount received would be £38,975 (ie £31,500 + £7,475), which is £775 more than the dividend of £38,200 in the first example. In the second example, the part of the dividend tax credit covered by the personal allowance has not been lost (being 10% × £7,475).

Where the spouse takes dividends, they would have little or no relevant earnings for pension purposes. However, it is still possible for her to make annual tax-deductible *gross* pension contributions of up to £3,600 gross (£2,880 net of basic rate tax relief relieved at source).

Example 7

Salary or dividend for spouse

Mr Astle is the controlling shareholder of Astle Ltd. His wife holds 20% of the ordinary shares in Astle Ltd.

Mr Astle is deciding whether to pay £18,000 to his wife as a salary (before NICs) or dividend for the year to 31 March 2012. She has no other income. Mrs Astle performs secretarial and administrative duties for the company which should be sufficient to justify corporation tax relief for the salary.

Astle Ltd expects to pay corporation tax at 20% in the year to 31 March 2012.

		Salary	Dividend
	£	£	£
Available Profits		18,000	18,000
Less Employer's NIC (13.8% on £16,675 – £7,072)		(1,325)	
Gross pay		16,675	
Less Employees' NIC 12% × (£16,675 – £7,225)		(1,134)	
Corporation tax at 20%			(3,600)
		15,541	14,400
Less Income tax thereon			
On Salary			
Salary	16,675		
Less PA	(7,475)		
Taxable	9,200		
Income tax (£9,200 at 20%)	(1,840)		(1,840)

On Dividend			
Cash	14,400		
Tax credit (10/90)	1,600		
	16,000		
Less PA	(7,475)		
Taxable	8,525		
£8,525 × 10%	853		
Tax credit	(1,600)		
Refund	(Nil)		–
Post-tax receipt		13,701	14,400

Note: There is no refund of tax credit on dividends.

EMPLOYING THE CHILDREN

2.44 The owner-manager's children may also work for the company at weekends or in their school/college/university holidays. The company will need to comply with the appropriate legislation and by-laws for employing children aged under 16. Children cannot be employed in a factory and those under 13 cannot be employed except for light duties in limited circumstances. The National Minimum Wage (NMW) rules must be adhered to for children aged 21 or over (see 2.10). From October 2011, a minimum wage of £4.98 applies to those aged 18 to 20 inclusive and and 3.68 per hour applies to those aged 16 or 17 (other than those in full-time education) .

If the children have taken out student loans, then the company may be liable to make appropriate deductions from their salary towards repayment of their loan. No student loan deductions are currently required where the salary is less than £15,000 per year.

The wages received by the children can be paid tax free up to their personal allowance, with any excess being liable at the basic rate or higher rate, as appropriate. Once again, HMRC will seek to establish the commercial justification for the payment in relation to the work done by the children. Payments made to the owner-manager's children which constitute 'disguised pocket money' will be disallowed (see *Dollar v Lyon* [1981] STC 333). There will, of course, be cases where a fairly reasonable amount can be substantiated as a genuine trading expense of the company. For example, the author is aware of a case where a teenage son of an owner-manager was paid a justifiable commercial wage for trial testing computer games that had been developed by the business. In such cases, such amounts will clearly be allowable as a trading expense.

Under the current pension regime, pension contributions of up to £3,600 gross (£2,880 net of the basic rate tax relief contributed at source by HMRC) can be made for each child, even in the absence of any relevant earnings (see 10.23).

CHARGING RENT ON PERSONALLY OWNED ASSETS USED BY THE COMPANY

Rationale for holding property personally and tax treatment of rent

2.45 A number of owner-managers leave the trading property outside the company to mitigate the effect of the potential 'double-tax' charge and to create wealth outside the company (free from the claims of its creditors (subject to personal guarantees), etc).

In such cases, the owner-manager can extract funds from the company by charging the company a market rent for the use of the property. The rent may be paid under a formal lease agreement between the owner-manager and the company. If the property is jointly-owned, for example, by the owner-manager and their spouse, then the rent would be paid to both in the appropriate shares.

SDLT of 1% is payable where (and to the extent that) the chargeable consideration for the lease exceeds the relevant exemption of £150,000 (for commercial property). In broad terms, the chargeable consideration represents the net present value of the future rental income, with special rules applying to variable and/or contingent rents (see 12.28). It is not possible to mitigate the SDLT charge by charging a low rent, since a deemed market rental value applies where the property is let to a 'connected company' (as will generally be the case). If the SDLT charge is prohibitive, it may be worth considering granting a simple 'licence to occupy' the property since this is an *exempt* interest in land for SDLT purposes. In broad terms, a licence to occupy represents a non-exclusive right of occupation so it is important that any documentation does not grant the company the sole exclusive right to occupy the property [*FA 2003, s 48(2) (b)*].

The rent paid by the company would be deductible against its profits (provided it represents a market rent) and the rent received would be taxable in the owner-manager's hands as property income (but no NIC liability would arise). The owner-manager can deduct, as property business expenses, the normal expenses of running the let property, including repairs (not capital improvements), service expenses, insurance, security costs and relevant professional fees, as well as any interest paid on a loan to purchase or improve the property. Indeed, where the owner-manager has borrowed money to purchase the property, he would normally charge rent to secure immediate tax relief for the interest [*ITTOIA 2005, s 272*]. Clearly, if only part of the building is let, then only a corresponding part of the costs can be deducted as property business expenses.

Where personally held property is subsequently sold alongside a disposal of the owner-manager's shares, it may be possible to claim Entrepreneurs' Relief (ER) on the property gain under the associated disposal rules. Provided the owner-manager has 'ER capacity' after relief has been claimed against the share sale, a 10% ER CGT rate can be applied to the property gain. However, in such cases, the gain qualifying for ER would be denied or restricted where the owner-manager has previously charged a rent for the use of the property(see 2.45 and 15.41).

2.46   In some cases, the owner-manager may not charge a rent, but will arrange for the company to pay the interest on their personal borrowings that were taken out to purchase or improve the property. Such 'interest' would be deductible in computing the company's trading profits as it represents consideration for occupying the property for trading purposes. Following normal accountancy principles, the company's interest payment on the owner-manager's behalf is counted as a property business receipt in the owner-manager's hands, but this would be offset by the owner-manager's actual obligation to pay the interest. (If the company does not pay rent or interest, the owner-manager cannot secure any income tax relief for the interest.)

Other allowable deductions include capital allowances on integral features and plant attached to the building.

VAT issues

2.47   Provided the property is used for normal commercial (non-residential) purposes, the owner-manager can elect to opt to tax it. Where the owner-manager is VAT registered, VAT would be added to the rent charged to the company (as well as on any service charges). An option to tax would almost certainly be required where VAT was charged on the purchase price paid for the property (or on any substantial improvements). Provided the election is in place, this will enable the owner-manager to recover VAT on any expenses incurred in relation to the property in their capacity as a landlord. However, it also means that if the property is sold, VAT would have to be charged on the sale proceeds.

Provided the company is fully taxable (for VAT purposes), the VAT would be fully recovered. Thus, overall, charging VAT on the rent is likely to be cash neutral whilst enabling VAT to be reclaimed on property improvements and running expenses. Where the owner-manager is only likely to suffer minimal VAT costs, it may not be worthwhile to opt to tax (unless of course VAT was charged on the original purchase cost which needs to be recovered).

Extraction of profits via rent

2.48 The tax effect of extracting profits via a rent is similar to the payment of remuneration, except that no PAYE or NIC is payable.

Example 8

Rent charged to company for use of owner-manager's property

Mr Tevez owns the entire share capital of The Tevez Scoring Company Ltd. The factory used by the company was, however, purchased by Mr and Mrs Tevez in equal shares many years ago.

For the year ended 31 March 2012 the company was charged a rent of £30,000. Mr and Mrs Tevez's claim for allowable property expenses were £3,000 each.

Assuming that, for the year ended 31 March 2012, the company's taxable profits *before* charging the rent were £260,000, the tax consequences are as follows:

	Company	*Mr Tevez*	*Mrs Tevez*
	£	£	£
Taxable profits before rent	260,000		
Less: Rent charged	(30,000)	15,000	15,000
Taxable profit (after rent charge)	230,000		
Less: Corporation tax @ 20%%	(46,000)		
Post-tax profit	184,000		
Less: Allowable property expenses		(3,000)	(3,000)
Taxable rent		12,000	12,000
Company tax saving on rent			
£30,000 @ 20%	6,000		
Income tax payable:			
Marginal tax rate @ 40%		4,800	
Marginal tax rate @ 20%			2,400

Subsequent sale of property

2.49 If the owner manager subsequently sells the property, any capital gain will generally be taxed at the main current CGT rate of 28%. Where the property is being sold along with an ER-eligible disposal of shares in the company, the owner manager may be able to obtain a 10% rate on any unused ER entitlement against the property gain under the 'associated disposal' rules (see 2.45 and 15.41).

SELLING AN ASSET TO THE COMPANY FOR VALUE

Background

2.50   The controlling shareholder may personally own the company's trading premises. This means that the property should not be exposed to the company's creditors on a winding up, although in many cases, banks or other lenders will secure a charge on the property. Consequently, as far as the commercial risk is concerned, there may be little difference whether the property is owned by the company or shareholder.

Owner-managers might consider extracting a capital sum from their company by selling the (personally-owned) property to the company. The disposal would generate a capital gain in their hands, which will generally be taxed at 28% . (Indexation relief ceased to be available to individuals from 6 April 2008 and associated disposal ER relief is not available for 'separate property sales – see 15.41.)

SDLT may be payable on the purchase by the company (see 12.23 for current SDLT rates) In such cases, SDLT would normally be levied on the market value of the property irrespective of the actual sale price paid by the company (see 2.52). The transfer of the property to the company may also improve the owner-manager's business property relief for IHT purposes (see 17.106).

Care is necessary to ensure that the property is not sold at an over-value, since the excess amount could be taxed as employment income (or as a shareholder distribution) [*CTA 2010, s 1000 (ICTA 1988, s 209(4))*].

CGT treatment

2.51   An immediate chargeable gain can be avoided by selling the property to the company at its *original base cost* (which will be the March 1982 value where the property was held by the owner-manager at that date). Although the disposal computed by reference to market value, the 'unrealised element' of the gain can be held over under the business asset gift relief provisions in *TCGA 1992, s 165* (which must be claimed on form IR295). This relief is not affected by any previous rent charges. By concession, it is not necessary to agree the market value of the gifted asset with HMRC. The 'transferor' owner-manager and the company must request this treatment in writing (SP8/92).

Where the owner-manager sells the asset at its original base cost/March 1982 value, the company will effectively acquire it at that amount (see 13.14–13.23 for the operation of CGT hold-over relief).

Where the asset is sold to the company at its original base cost or a lower amount, this will be the acquisition cost on the company's balance sheet. However, it is possible to bolster the company's balance sheet by subsequently revaluing the asset. The uplift in valuation would be credited to a revaluation surplus account within shareholders' funds.

VAT and SDLT

2.52   The owner-manager will normally be connected with the company within *CTA 2010, s 1122 (ICTA 1988, s 839)*, since they either control it in their own right or together with their family members. Consequently, the 'deemed market value' rule in *FA 2003, s 53* will apply for SDLT purposes, irrespective of the actual consideration paid by the company. The amount of SDLT payable on the acquisition of the property by the company will therefore depend on its market value (which is treated as the 'chargeable consideration' – see 12.23). (The SDLT chargeable consideration normally includes any VAT chargeable on the sale and it appears that HMRC require any potential VAT to be added to the 'deemed' market value consideration for these purposes.)

Where the property is subject to a VAT option to tax (see 2.47), the owner-manager will need to charge VAT on the purchase price (which is normally recoverable by the company). Some care is required over the timing of the transaction to ensure that the company is able to recover the input VAT before it is paid over by the owner-manager. Although the property may have been previously let to the company at a commercial rent, the sale cannot be treated as a transfer of a going concern since the same letting business would not be carried on by the company (the property would then become 'owner-occupied').

CHARGING INTEREST ON LOANS TO THE COMPANY

Commercial implications

2.53   Where owner-managers make a loan to the company or have a credit balance on their current account, there is nothing to stop them charging the company with interest on the loan. The interest rate charged should be at a commercial rate, which (depending on the company's financial position and creditworthiness) could be several base points above the bank base lending rate. This would recognise the 'risk' element of non-recovery if the company gets into financial difficulty, although it may be possible to secure the lending (for example) against the company's property. If the interest charged by a shareholder-director materially exceeds a commercial rate, HMRC may seek to treat the 'excess' amount as a salary (seeking PAYE and NIC) or dividend distribution.

Company's tax deduction for interest

2.54   Under the 'loan relationship' rules, the company normally obtains relief for interest charged in its accounts on an accruals basis, ie on the amount charged against its profits. However, any loan to a *close company* from a shareholder (or an associate of a shareholder) is subject to the 'late interest' rule (see 3.12 for definition of a close company). Loans made by a company that is controlled by a shareholder of the borrowing company (or in which the shareholder has a 'major' 40% interest) are also caught by these provisions. This means that the corporate tax deduction for any interest that remains unpaid more than 12 months after the accounting period end, is deferred until the interest is actually paid [*CTA 2009, ss 373 and 375*].

A close company therefore only gets relief for the interest on a loan from its owner-manager on an accruals basis provided it is paid in, or within 12 months after the end of, the relevant accounting period.

If the period of the loan exceeds (or can be extended beyond) one year, the interest would be 'annual interest'. Since the interest is paid to an individual, the company must deduct lower rate tax (of 20%) at source when the interest is paid. This interest is reported and paid over to HMRC on Form CT 61. The recipient shareholder-director is taxed on the gross interest *received* (with credit being given for any tax deducted at source). The interest does not constitute earnings and therefore no NICs are payable.

In some cases, it may be possible to secure a timing advantage by exploiting the late interest rule within the constraints of the rules. For example, a company could accrue interest on an owner-manager's loan account in its accounting period ended 31 March 2012 with the interest being paid in (say) June 2012. Thus, the interest would still be deductible against the company's profits for the year ended 31 March 2012 (with the benefit of the tax reduction being obtained on 1 January 2013). On the other hand, the recipient would be taxed on a 'received' basis in 2012/13 , with the income tax liability being payable on 31 January 2014.

Example 9

Charging interest on a director's loan account

2.55   Mr Wayne is a 75% shareholder of Wayne's Red Card Company Ltd. Over the years, he has ploughed back most of his dividend income to provide additional working capital for the company.

During the year ended 31 March 2012, the balance outstanding on his loan account with the company was £300,000 on which he charged interest at 8% per year.

The company's taxable profits (*before* charging interest on Mr Wayne's shareholder loan account) for the year ended 31 March 2012 were £780,000 (Mr Wayne has a controlling interest in three other companies and thus there are four associated companies for corporation tax purposes (see 3.20)).

The tax position for the company and Mr Wayne is as follows:

Year ended 31 March 2012	
Company	£
Taxable profits before interest	780,000
Less: Interest charge	
£300,000 × 8% =	(24,000)
Taxable profit after interest charge	756,000)
Corporation tax @ 26%	(196,560)
Profit after tax	559,440
Company tax saving on interest	
£24,000 @ 26%	6,240

The company will only obtain tax relief in the year ended 31 March 2012 provided the interest is actually paid to Mr Wayne by 31 March 2013.Relief will not be given if the interest is simply 'rolled-up' as a credit to his loan account and remains outstanding at 31 March 2013.

Mr Wayne	
Interest received net of tax deducted by company	
£24,000 less £4,800 (ie 20% × £24,000)	19,200
Less: Income tax payable	
£24,000 @ (say) 40% = £9,600 less £4,800 (tax deducted at source by company	(4,800)
Net amount received	14,400

LOANS FROM THE COMPANY

Companies Act restriction

2.56 Since 1 October 2007 private companies have been able to make loans to directors (provided they have been approved by shareholders) [*CA 2006, s 197*]. Loans to those connected with the director are also subject to the same 'shareholder approval' rules. (Connected persons under the Companies Act 2006 include spouses, minor and adult children, parents, and so on.)

The Companies Act 2006 does not require any approval for small loans/quasi-loans (£10,000) and minor credit transactions (£15,000).

If the company fails to obtain the required resolution of its shareholders, the loan is voidable under *CA 2006, s 213*. This means that the company could rescind the loan and recoup its money. However, such a remedy is unlikely to be exercised by an owner-managed company given that its owners and directors invariably are one and the same!

Scope of CTA 2010, s 455 charge

2.57   A number of tax consequences arise where loans are made to a director shareholder. First, *CTA 2010, s455 (ICTA 1988, s 419)* applies to any loan made to a participator (ie shareholder or loan creditor) of a close company (see 3.12 for definition of a close company). The charge can also apply where a loan is made to an 'associate' of the shareholder, such as a spouse, parent, grandparent, child, grandchild, brother or sister, as well as a business partner [*CTA 2010, s 448(2)*].

Partners are also deemed to be an associate of the participator under *CTA 2010, s 448(1) (ICTA 1988, s 417(3) (a))*. This means that *s 455* can also be triggered where a company makes a loan to an (English) partnership ,in which one of its shareholders is a partner (Note that all partners are 'associated' with each other for this purpose (see CTA 2010, s448(1)(a) and the special exemption in CTA 2010, s27 does not apply here). An *English* partnership is not a separate legal entity and therefore the loan falls within *s 455*. HMRC seem to take the same view in relation to loans made to Limited Liability Partnerships. Presumably this is because *ICTA 1988, s 118ZA* will generally apply to treat such the LLP as 'transparent' for corporation tax purposes – and thus the loan would be regarded as having been made to the individual LLP members.

Scottish partnerships are treated as a separate legal entity but there is no statutory rule that deems them to be transparent for tax purposes (HMRC Corporation Tax Manual para 61515). Thus, HMRC accepts that a loan to a Scottish partnership cannot be caught by *s 455* (since it is being made to the partnership 'entity' itself and not the individual partners).

There is a separate rule which deems a *CTA 2010, s 455* liability to arise where a participator (or associate) incurs a debt to the company – for example, where the shareholder buys a 'personal' asset on credit in the company's name [*CTA 2010, s 455(4) (ICTA 1988, s 419(2))*]. This particular trap can also occur with management charges which remain due to a partnership service company (for longer than six months (see exemption (*b*) below)). (In such case, at least one participator of the company would also be a partner of the partnership.) Any debt incurred by the partnership would fall within *CTA 2010, s 455(4) [ICTA*

1988, s 419] (see *Grant v Watton; Andrew Grant Services Ltd v Watton* [1999] STC 330).

There are various exemptions from the *s 455* tax liability, but they are of little assistance to most family and owner-managed companies:

(*a*)　loans up to £15,000 in total are exempt where the borrower works full time for the company and does not own more than 5% of the ordinary share capital [*CTA 2010, s456(4) (ICTA 1988, s 420(2))*];

(*b*)　indirect loans involving the supply of goods on credit by the close company are exempt provided this is made in the normal course of trade (except where the credit given exceeds six months) [*CTA 2010, s 456(2) (ICTA 1988, s 420(1))*];

(*c*)　the tax charge does not apply where the company is a lending institution which makes the loan or advance in the ordinary course of its business [*CTA 2010, s 456(1) (ICTA 1988, s 419(1))*]. HMRC only regard this exemption as being available where the company is carrying on the business of money lending and this is part of its general business activities.

Shareholder directors will also suffer an employment income benefits charge under the beneficial loan provisions to the extent that they do not pay a commercial rate of interest on the loan [*ITEPA 2003, s 175*]. These provisions are fully explained at 7.54.

Mechanics of CTA 2010, s 455 charge

2.58　　The aim of this legislation is to levy tax on what would otherwise be an easy method of extracting cash from the close company on a tax-free basis. *CTA 2010, s 455* (previously *ICTA 1988, s 419*) requires the company to account for tax at the rate of 25% of the loan advanced (there has been no change to this rate following the introduction of the post-5 April 2010 super tax rate).

The *s 455* tax therefore represents a standalone charge which is deposited with HMRC. If the loan or overdrawn account is repaid in whole or in part (or is released (see 2.64)), the appropriate portion of the *s 455* tax is discharged or refunded [*CTA 2010, s 458(2) (ICTA 1988, s 419(4))*]. Any repayment from HMRC must be claimed within four years from the end of the financial year in which the loan is repaid/released.

For companies that are not subject to the Quarterly Instalment Payment (QIP) regime, the *CTA 2010, s455 (ICTA 1988, s 419)* liability falls due nine months after the end of their company's accounting period (in line with their normal due date for payment of tax). However, if the company pays its tax under the QIP regime, any (undischarged) *s 455* liability must be factored into its instalment payments (see 4.48–4.81).

Some owner-managers may wish to consider extracting funds from company by making a substantial loan to mitigate their income tax liabilities. There will be a one-off *s 455* charge (equal to 25% of the loan) and an annual employment benefit charge based on the official rate of interest. Thus, the *s 455* charge on a £100,000 loan in 2011/12 would be £25,000 and the tax on the 'interest' benefit would be just £1,600 for a 40% taxpayer (ie £100,000 × 4% × 40%). However, care should be exercised where loans are regularly advanced since HMRC may seek to tax these amounts as earnings under PAYE (see 2.60). It is generally recommended that such loans are evidenced by appropriate loan documentation and board minutes.

2.59　If the loan is repaid before the *s 455* tax is due for payment, the liability is discharged and the tax does not have to be paid over. However, if the loan remains outstanding after the nine month due date, HMRC will seek the *s 455* tax and charge interest from the due date until the tax is paid.

When the loan is subsequently repaid, the repayment of the *s 455* tax is deferred until nine months after the *end of the CTAP in which the loan is repaid or reduced,* with repayment interest arising on any delayed repayment. Given this lead time for repayment of the *s 455* tax, owner managers should always try to avoid triggering a *s 455* liability by repaying their loans within nine months of the balance sheet date.

Director's overdrawn loan accounts

2.60　In practice, there is usually a potential *s 455* exposure on overdrawn director-shareholder's current or loan accounts. In many cases, an overdrawn loan account may not be established until some time after the balance sheet date, eg when the accounts are completed or following certain audit adjustments. It is therefore important to establish the proper balance before the 'nine month' due date for the *s 455* tax. This will enable the owner-manager to decide whether to clear the balance by voting an additional bonus or declaring an appropriate dividend. Dividends must be properly declared and documented to demonstrate that the debt due to the company has been repaid (see 9.2 and 9.14). Repayment via cheque to the company is the most robust way of demonstrating repayment.

If an overdrawn balance remains after the 'nine month' due date, the *s 455* tax falls due and interest will begin to accrue. Where regular advances/loans are made to a company's shareholder director, HMRC will often contend that these have the character of 'earnings' and seek to apply PAYE and NIC on the relevant amounts. Proper loan documentation will help to rebut such challenges. To avoid HMRC seeking (unexpected) PAYE and NIC liabilities on regular withdrawals, where the owner-manager wishes to extract regular amounts from the company, it may be better for them to pay regular 'quarterly' dividends instead.

In cases where frequent advances have been accepted as loans under an HMRC enquiry, there may be insufficient evidence as to the amounts that have been cleared by subsequent repayment(s). Inspectors normally seek to apply the rule in *Clayton's* case (1816 MR Ch Vol 1, 572), which provides that repayments are set against the oldest debts first.

HMRC will often seek to challenge 'bed and breakfast' arrangements where advances/loans are made during an accounting period and then (consistently) repaid (say) shortly before the balance sheet date only for a similar loan to be taken from the company soon after. Where HMRC successfully challenge these 'rolling loans', it will seek penalties.

Inspectors will not accept that separate 'director's' accounts can be aggregated or netted off each other since the *s 455* charge arises where a close company 'makes any loan or advances any money' to a shareholder. HMRC seem to accept that genuine book entries (with supporting documentation) can be made where a credit balance is used to repay a debit balance. However, the *ICAEW Tax Faculty Guidance Note TAX 11/93* recommends that a company should draw a cheque to pay off the whole or part of the credit balance with another cheque being paid into the company to clear the debit balance. This will therefore provide firm evidence of the date the loan is repaid.

CTSA reporting obligations

2.61   Under corporation tax self-assessment, the *s 455* tax must be reported on the corporation tax return form CT600 and various details of loans made to participators, etc must be given on the supplementary page CT600A (even if the *s 455* liability has been discharged by repayment or waiver). Companies that are liable to pay their corporation tax in instalments must include any anticipated or actual *s 455* tax in their instalment liabilities (see 4.48).

The CT600 return form must normally be submitted within 12 months from the end of the company's accounting period. Late returns attract a flat rate penalty of £100 increasing to £200 if the return is more than three months late. (These penalties become £500 and £1,000 respectively, if the company was subject to a flat penalty charge in each of its two preceding accounting periods.)

Companies must take care to ensure they report all *s 455* loans correctly since they are now potentially exposed to tougher HMRC penalties (which can apply to CT600 returns submitted after 31 March 2009 – so this can cover year-ends as early as 30 April 2008.) Under the current regime, penalties are charged according to the underlying taxpayer behaviour that gave rise to the error. Thus, HMRC will charge a greater penalty where it can show that the understatement of the tax liability was deliberate (as opposed to an innocent error).

Penalties are based on the relevant amount of tax that has been understated, the nature of the taxpayer's behaviour and the extent of disclosure. For example, a penalty of

- *up to 30%* will arise on any understated *s 455* tax due to lack of reasonable care: or

- *up to 70%* on any *deliberately* understated *s 455* tax.

For these purposes, in arriving at the understated *s 455* tax *no* reduction is made for any offset under *s 458(2)* (where the loan has been subsequently repaid (see 2.59).

The relevant penalty would be substantially reduced where the taxpayer makes full disclosure or takes active steps to correct the mistake. No penalty should arise where the taxpayer makes a genuine mistake. See 4.57–4.62 for full details of penalty regime.

Example 10

Section 455 tax and interest on overdrawn director's loan

Mr Nolan, a shareholder in a Claret Captain Ltd (a close company), overdrew his director's loan account by £20,000 in November 2011. This amount was still outstanding at the end of the company's accounting period on 31 December 2011, although it was entirely cleared by the payment of a bonus on 30 June 2012.

The company's accounts, corporation tax computations and return form CT600 for the year ended 31 December 2011 were submitted to HMRC in September 2012.

Under corporation tax self-assessment, the company must complete the supplementary page CT600A and submit it with the return. In Part 1, the company must show the loan of £20,000 made to Mr Nolan during the period, but would also claim relief from the *s 455* liability (in Part 2) as the loan was repaid by 30 September 2012 – ie within nine months of the end of the accounting period –.

Mr Nolan would also be subject to an employment income charge on the benefit of the interest-free loan.

WAIVER OF LOANS TO SHAREHOLDERS

Income tax charge on shareholder

2.62 An income tax charge arises if the company releases or simply writes off a loan to a shareholder (or an associate of a shareholder) [*ITTOIA 2005, s 415*]. The loan must be formally waived or written-off, as opposed to merely not being collected by the company. In such cases, the amount of the loan released or waived is 'grossed-up' at the dividend ordinary rate for income tax purposes, which is presently 10%.

Loans released or written off are taxed as dividend income under *ITA 2007, s 19*. For 'basic rate' taxpayers the 10% 'franked' tax liability on the 'gross' waiver is deemed to be satisfied, so there is no further tax liability.

However, in the majority of cases , the recipient is liable to higher and/or top rate income tax, depending on the level of their overall income (and the deemed 'dividend income' is treated as the top slice of their total income). Thus, the grossed-up amount of the release is taxed at the following rate(s):

Total income (including gross amount of the loan released)	Tax rate applied	Effective rate on the actual loan released (ignoring 10% gross-up)
Up to £150,000	32.5% less 10% = 22.5%	25%
More than £150,000	42.5% less 10% = 32.5%	36.1%

Loans released before 5 April 2011 are only subject to the dividend higher rate tax of 22.5% (32.5% less 10%) (where applicable).

It is fairly clear that if a waiver or release was in contemplation at the time the original 'loan' was made, then it is unlikely to be treated as a loan in the first place – there would be strong arguments for treating the payment as 'income' which would be characterised according to the underlying facts!

Where the shareholder is a director (or an employee), the *ITTOIA 2005, s 415* charge also takes priority over any employment income tax charge on the waiver under *ITEPA 2003, s 188* (due to the statutory priority rule in *ITEPA 2003, s 188*). Although the *s 415* charge takes precedence, any such release is almost certain to be treated as 'earnings' for NIC purposes. It could be argued that since the 'shareholder link' takes precedence for income tax purposes, this should displace any potential NIC charge, but this is not the view taken by HMRC. Earnings is widely defined for NIC purposes to include 'any remuneration or profit derived from the employment' (*s 3(1)(a) SSCBA 1992*). HMRC's view is that given this wide coverage, the release of debt would be seen as rewarding the director for services rendered and would thus be liable to Class 1 NICs. This reasoning was followed by the Upper Tribunal in PA Holdings Ltd v HMRC UT [2010] STC 2343.

Clearly, if the shareholder is neither a director nor an employee, there can be no question of an NIC charge being levied on the release

Novation of loans

2.63 The case of *Collins v Addies* [1992] STC 746 held that the novation of a shareholder loan gives rise to a release. The company had advanced a loan to its two director shareholders and the company was subsequently sold. As part of the sale, the purchaser of the company agreed to take over these debts.

Thus, the shareholder loan were novated so that the target company released the shareholders from their debts and the purchaser agreed to take them over. The Court held that novation of the £68,000 debt constituted a taxable release under what is now *ITTOIA 2005, s 415*. As illustrated by this case, the debtor (borrower) cannot assign the debt. A novation takes place under which the existing debtor is released from the debt and the new debtor takes on a new debt. *Section 415* will therefore catch situations where loans are assigned to someone else.

Recovery of s 455 tax

2.64   Where a loan is released or waived, the company can recover from HMRC any tax paid under *CTA 2010, s 455 (ICTA 1988, s 419)*. The amount is due for repayment nine months after the accounting period in which the loan is waived (see 2.59).

Corporation tax treatment of loan waiver

2.65   A properly executed release of a loan (provided it is properly accounted for under GAAP) would reduce the amount of debt that is due to be paid which would be written-off against the company's profits. However, the *FA 2010* introduced legislation preventing almost all owner-managed companies from claiming a loan relationship (non-trading) tax deduction for the release or write-off of a loan made to a *shareholder (or associate thereof)* (CTA 2009, s321A). This rule (which applies to close companies) affects amounts that are written-off after 23 March 2010. Nevertheless, despite these changes, it remains possible for companies to deduct amounts written-off in respect of other loans (where the borrower is *not* a shareholder or one of their 'associates').

Before 24 March 2010, the loan relationship legislation [*CTA 2009, s 324(1)*] contained an apparent loophole, since it permitted relief to be claimed on the write-off of shareholder loans as well as other 'third party' loans.

All loan relationship debits are, however, subject to the overriding 'unallowable' purpose test in *CTA 2009, s 421* which enables HMRC to deny relief for a non-trading debit where the transaction is *not* carried out for the business purposes of the company. Thus, relief could be denied where it is evident that the loan has *not* been released for the benefit of the company's business.

Example 11

Section 415 tax liability on release of shareholder loan

In June 2010, Hotspur Ltd (which is a close company) advanced an interest-free loan of £90,000 to Mr Lennon, who is a 30% shareholder of the company. He does *not* work for Hotspur Ltd.

The loan remained outstanding nine months after the 31 December 2010 year end and therefore *s 455* tax of £22,500 (25% × £90,000) was paid to HMRC on 1 October 2011.

In November 2011, the company decided to waive the £90,000 loan due from Mr Lennon and both Mr Lennon and Hotspur entered into a formal deed to release the debt.

Hotspur Ltd

Since the company is 'close' and Mr Lennon is a shareholder ('participator'), the CTA 2009, s321A restriction applies to the amount written-off (which occurred after 23 March 2010). Thus, the consequent loan relationship debit of £90,000 is not deductible for corporation tax purposes.

The *s 455* tax of £22,500 also becomes repayable (which must be claimed), being due for repayment on 1 October 2012, ie nine months after the end of the accounting period in which the loan is waived – the year ended 31 December 2011.

Mr Lennon

Assuming Mr Lennon's total income (including the gross amount of the waiver) exceeds £150,000, his *ITTOIA 2005, s 415* charge in 2011/12 will be as follows:

	£
Amount waived	90,000
Gross-up at dividend lower rate (10/90)	10,000
Gross waiver	100,000
Tax at 42.5%	42,500
Less: Lower rate tax satisfied	(10,000)
	32,500

It is important to note that if Mr Lennon were a *director or employee* of Hotspur Ltd, the *ITTOIA 2005, s 415* charge would still prevail, but HMRC would also seek to impose a Class 1 NIC charge.

BENEFITS IN KIND TO NON-WORKING SHAREHOLDERS

2.66   Certain expenses or benefits provided to a close company shareholder (or an associate of a shareholder) are treated as a distribution under *CTA 2010, s 1064 (ICTA 1988, s 418)*. Without these special provisions it would be possible to provide benefits to a non-working shareholder on a tax-free basis.

This 'deemed distribution' treatment does not apply where the expense or benefit is already taxed under the employment income rules in *ITEPA 2003*. Consequently, in practice, these rules would effectively apply to *non-working* shareholders being provided with living accommodation and other benefits or services (to the extent that they are not made good by the shareholder or their associate). These rules do not include pensions or lump sums payable on death or retirement.

The value of the distribution is taken to be the same amount that would have applied if the amount had been treated as an employment-related benefit (see Chapter 7). The recipient shareholder would be taxed on this amount in accordance with the relevant 'dividend taxation' rules (see Chapter 9).

The amount of the 'distribution' cannot be deducted against profits for corporation tax purposes

If a non-working shareholder was provided with a car, the distribution would be based on the scale benefit charge computed under the rules in 7.8 to 7.10. This would not be the same figure as the depreciation and running costs that would have to be disallowed in calculating the company's taxable profits (since being incurred for a *non-working* shareholder, they would not generally be for the purposes of the trade).

PLANNING CHECKLIST – STRATEGIES FOR EXTRACTING FUNDS FROM THE COMPANY

Company

- The extraction of funds is often influenced by the company's cash flow and working capital position.

- Where appropriate, shareholders can loan funds back to the company to restore liquidity and provide working capital.

- Dividend payments can easily be timed for optimum income tax efficiency in the hands of the shareholder(s).

- Corporate tax relief for bonuses can be effectively back-dated by making provision in the statutory accounts under the nine-month rule. However, care must be taken to ensure such provisions also comply with FRS 12.

Working shareholders

- Generally require a sensible mix of remuneration/bonuses and dividends. However, dividends are becoming increasingly attractive, particularly in view of the (increasing) NIC costs levied on remuneration.

- Some owner-managers wish to extract surplus cash funds from the company to remove them from any further business risk.

- Those owner-managers who created loan accounts (by introducing all or part of their large dividend payments in contemplation of the super tax rates) should consider making repayments of the loan to supplement their income under the post-6 April 2010 so as to avoid having to pay the top tax rate(s).

- Owner managers could consider providing 'cheap' loans from the company, which will only suffer employment tax at 1.6%/12% (ie official rate 4% × 40%/50%) for a complete tax year, rather than taking substantial amounts of salary/bonus. The loans can be repaid when appropriate, although a *CTA 2010, s 455 [ICTA 1988, s 419]* charge will arise if the loans are not repaid within nine months of the company year-end in which they were made.

- Dividends are very attractive for shareholders who are only liable to lower or basic rate income tax. A small salary is usually worthwhile to ensure full use is made of personal allowances.

- Owner-managers can mitigate income tax on their earnings to the extent that they are paid out as pension contributions. From 2011/12 income tax relief for pension contributions is subject to the annual £50,000 'annual allowance' restriction (also taking into account any potential unused relief from the previous three years).

- Where the company's trading premises are personally owned by the controlling shareholder, it may be desirable to sell them to the company to obtain a tax-efficient extraction of cash.

Other employees

- Employees generally look for good remuneration packages with tax-efficient benefits (although there is now an increasing preference for cash).

- In appropriate cases, an incentive-based bonus scheme should be considered.

Non-working shareholders

- Dividends are much more tax-efficient as the company cannot claim tax relief for 'remuneration', particularly for non-working spouses. However, some care must be exercised to avoid the dividend being taxed on the owner-manager(s) under the settlement legislation.

- Consider paying pension contributions of up to £2,808 net (tax relief of up to £792 is added at source by HMRC) for non-working shareholders.

Chapter 3

Shareholding and Corporate Structures

SHARES VERSUS DEBT

Overview

3.1   This chapter reviews the issues involved in deciding how a family or owner-managed company's shareholding should be split and the way in which its trading activities may be structured.

The owner-managers and other parties can inject funds into the company in two ways:

(*a*)   by a subscription for shares; and/or

(*b*)   by lending money to the company.

It is far easier to obtain repayment of funds injected on loan account. Cash paid for shares can normally only be returned on a winding up, a company's purchase of its own shares or under the Companies Act 2006 share capital reduction provisions (via a special resolution supported by a solvency statement). The company may, of course, issue redeemable preference shares provided that it is authorised to do so by its Articles and the company already has non-redeemable shares in existence.

The relevant tax/commercial considerations involved in choosing the mix between shares and debt are considered in Chapter 11.

Shareholder's rights

3.2   In essence, shares give the holder various membership rights in the company. These rights spring from the *Companies Act 1985* and the *Companies Act 2006* and the company's own Articles or shareholder's agreement, etc. They would include the right to attend and vote at general meetings, receive dividends and a return of their capital on liquidation. The shareholder enjoys these benefits in return for their lack of security. Minority shareholders generally have little say in the management of the company's affairs – their main protection is the potential to bring an 'unfair prejudice' action before the court. The court has the power to impose a variety of remedies, including a purchase of the aggrieved member's shares or a winding-up order.

Lender's rights

3.3   Money can be loaned to the company in various ways. Where the loan is unsecured, the lender has a contract with the company for the debt. Contract law and the terms of any loan agreement will govern the lender's rights and remedies (for example, the return of the loan and the right to interest payments). In some cases, an unsecured lender may request a personal guarantee, possibly from one or more directors. Thus, if the company fails to repay the loan, the lender can claim against the guarantor. Many 'owner-manager' loans are interest-free, although the payment of interest on a loan should be considered where there are other 'outside' shareholders and as a way of extracting profits without any NIC cost.

Where a loan is secured, the lender has additional 'security' rights in addition to their contractual ones. Where the lender takes a fixed charge over (invariably) land and buildings, the borrowing company cannot deal with these assets in any way until the loan is fully repaid. On the other hand, a floating charge generally covers the borrowing company's fixed assets (other than land and buildings), debts, and trading stock. Consequently, the company has the ability to deal freely with these assets unless and until the floating charge crystallises. If the lender's security becomes threatened, the debenture/loan agreement will enable them to appoint an administrator/receiver who will then be able to realise the relevant underlying assets for satisfying the loan (and accrued interest). A lender can petition the court to put the company into compulsory liquidation. However, following the *Enterprise Act 2002*, a company in financial difficulty is more likely to appoint an administrator (out of court) to rescue the company as a going concern or achieve a better realisation of its assets (than a liquidation).

STRUCTURING THE SHAREHOLDINGS

Formation of company

3.4   The shareholding structure of the company is best decided on its formation. Typically, the shares will be subscribed for at par when the company has little value. Subsequent changes can of course be made to the shareholding structure.

If the company has been profitable, its shares will have increased in value. Although transfers between shareholdings in a family or owner-managed company can often be made without incurring an immediate IHT or CGT liability, there may be other risks. For example, if an individual shareholder dies within seven years of gifting shares, an IHT liability may arise (see 17.10 and 17.11). Similarly, the ability to hold-over the capital gain is dependent on the company qualifying as a 'trading company' and may also be restricted where the company has some 'chargeable' investment assets (see 13.20).

Given the recent tightening of the 'employee share' legislation (see Chapter 8) and, in particular, the much wider definition of when shares are deemed to be acquired by reason of a directorship or employment, it would appear that the vast majority of share issues must now be reported on HMRC Form 42. Where a Form 42 has been issued to the company, this must be submitted by 6 July following the end of the relevant tax year (see 8.84). A simplified form can be used to report share acquisitions on the incorporation of a company – this form can be downloaded from the HMRC website.

Inheritance tax issues

3.5   In a typical family or owner-managed company, the proprietor will often hold the majority of the issued share capital. The current 100% IHT exemption on private trading company shareholdings means that retention of the shares will often be a sensible policy, as the shares will be fully exempt from IHT on death and will also benefit from a tax-free uplift in value for CGT purposes (see 17.17 and 17.18).

The 100% IHT business property (BPR) exemption looks set to remain intact for the foreseeable future and is unlikely to be changed by the current coalition Government wishing to provide a favourable climate for entrepreneurs. However, IHT should not be the only consideration here. If the proprietor's children or other close family members play an active part in the business, it may be necessary for the owner manager to pass some shares to them during their lifetime. This will motivate them and perhaps reward their contribution to the increase in the company's value created by their efforts. This will also aid the 'succession planning' process and, of course, the psychological impact can be a significant factor.

In most cases, it should be possible to transfer the shares directly to the intended family recipients or an 'intermediate' family trust with CGT deferral (under an appropriate hold-over election) and without incurring any immediate IHT liability due to the BPR exemption. Where shares are issued or gifted to close family members, there should be no employment income tax charge due to the exemption in *ITEPA 2003, s 421B* for 'shares made available in the 'normal course of domestic, family, or personal relationships'.

The owner-manager will usually require a substantial holding or perhaps a separate class of shares to satisfy their personal financial needs (through dividends). In many cases, the shares must provide the owner-manager adequate control over the company but effective control need not be relinquished if an appropriate trust is used. These issues are considered further in Chapter 17.

FACTORS THAT MAY INFLUENCE SHAREHOLDING STRUCTURE

Level of control required

3.6 Owner-managers should consider whether it is necessary for them to own all the shares. From a capital tax viewpoint, they may consider that this is the best course, given the complete exemption from IHT on death coupled with a tax-free uplift in the share values for CGT.

Owner-managers can, in fact, obtain absolute control by holding at least 75% of the voting rights, since they would then be able to pass special resolutions, sell the business, vary its constitution and put it into liquidation. For effective day-to-day control, such as the appointment and removal of directors, determination of remuneration and dividend policy, it is only necessary to hold more than 50% of the shares.

The owner-manager may be prepared to share effective 'control' with their spouse and family trusts, of which he would be 'first named' trustee (see 17.53).

Based on many practical experiences, it is always advisable for owner-managers to keep the company's shares tightly held between 'trusted' family members and possibly key management team members. In many cases, proprietors regret their (or their parents') decision to issue shares to certain family members (usually to satisfy some emotional obligation!). This is especially problematic when the level of such shareholdings increases following other shares being repurchased by the company, etc.

Particular care should be taken to ensure that the company's Articles of Association provide appropriate protection against shares being transferred outside a 'closely defined' shareholder group.

Financial security and likelihood of a future sale

3.7 Many owner-managers view the business as a way of building up their financial security. When the time comes for them to step down and hand over control, the company should have provided them with sufficient funds for their future requirements. For many, this equates to maximising the amount of shares held. However, even where the company is to pass to the next generation, the owner-manager (with perhaps their spouse) only needs to control the company, ie by having shares carrying more than 50% of the votes. As explained in 17.40, 'value' can be built up by taking sufficient remuneration, dividends, and ensuring appropriate pension provision is made.

If the owner-manager's main objective is to build up the company for a future sale or indeed flotation, they should ensure they have sufficient shares to achieve the desired level of the future sale proceeds.

Providing dividends to the spouse and other family members

3.8   Where the owner-manager's spouse (or civil partner) has little income of their own, it will often be beneficial for the spouse/civil partner to hold some shares to obtain an appropriate level of dividend. This is best done by issuing the appropriate number of ordinary shares to the spouse/civil partner on formation of the company or the owner-manager subsequently gifting some ordinary shares to them. In some cases, their shares can be re-categorised as a separate class (whilst retaining the same rights). This will provide greater flexibility with future dividend payments.

Spousal dividends are typically used to provide the spouse with a 'tax-free' dividend (the dividend would fall within the spouse's basic rate band and thus the 10% tax liability would be completely satisfied by the 10% tax credit).

However, some owner managers are also using spousal dividends to counter the effect of the 'super-tax' dividend rate 42.5% (36.1% on the net dividend) (see 9.1). The basic strategy here is to reduce the owner-manager's dividend (so as to avoid the top rate tax band) with a suitable increase in the spouse's dividend (so as to maximise the amount taxed at the 25% effective rate).

HMRC are now likely to accept spousal dividends following the House of Lords important ruling in the *Arctic Systems* case. Although such arrangements are likely to create a settlement for income tax purposes, the Law Lords held that the spousal dividends could not be taxed in the *transferor* spouse's hands under the settlements legislation, since the 'inter-spousal' outright gifts exemption in (what is now) *ITTOIA 2005, s 626* applied to fully-fledged ordinary shares (see 9.23–9.29). Based on statements issued in the Pre-Budget Report 2008 and Budget 2009, the Treasury seems to have given up (at least for now) in attempting to introduce specific legislation to block so-called 'income-shifting' arrangements.

The *Arctic Systems* case effectively provides a template for risk-free spousal dividend arrangements. The owner-manager should ensure that they provide the spouse with ordinary shares which carry substantive rights in addition to the right to a dividend. The rights attaching to the shares (which could be of a separate class of ordinary shares) would include the right to vote at company meetings and to participate in the distribution of assets on a winding up of the company. (The same tax analysis would apply for a civil partner.)

On the other hand, the use of non-voting *preference* shares is likely to be a 'non-starter'. As demonstrated in *Young v Pearce* [1996] STC 743, the provision of such shares would be regarded as a settlement but would not be exempted under the outright gifts exemption in *ITTOIA 2005, s 626* since typically the shares would effectively represent a right to income (see 9.31).

Shares can also be provided to other family members to provide dividend income to them. However, the payment of dividends to minor children of the owner-manager (settlor) or trusts set up for their benefit are likely to be caught by the parental settlement rules in *ITTOIA 2005*. Importantly, in such cases, there is no equivalent of the 'outright gifts' exemption available to married couples/civil partners. It is considered unlikely that HMRC could invoke the settlement legislation in other cases (see 9.36 and 9.34–9.38 for further discussion of this area).

CGT ENTREPRENEURS' RELIEF ('ER')

3.9   The Finance Act 2008 introduced a new Entrepreneurs' Relief effective from 6 April 2008. ER replaced the more beneficial business asset taper relief.

Under the current ER legislation, owner-managers can sell their companies/ businesses with the first £10 million of 'qualifying business gains' being taxed at10%, with any excess gains being taxed at 28%. To be eligible for ER, the owner-manager and their fellow shareholders must ensure they own at least five per cent of the ordinary share capital (carrying at least five per cent of the voting rights) in the 12 months before the share sale/cessation of trade (see 15.33 to 15.42).

INHERITANCE TAX PLANNING

3.10   Some proprietors are only willing to pass 'control' of the company down to the next generation on their death. In such cases, they are likely to maximise their shareholding (and perhaps their spouse's). This would enable them to take full advantage of the 100% IHT Business Property Relief (BPR) exemption (see 3.5 and 17.4–17.17) and the CGT free 'step-up' in base cost on death. In contrast, loans held by shareholders do not attract any BPR and, therefore, will be liable to IHT.

EMPLOYEE SHARE SCHEMES

3.11   The proprietor may want to provide shares for his key managers or employees (possibly through an approved share scheme) to foster a true sense of ownership and involvement in the company.

The proportion of shares issued to employees is usually nominal to avoid disturbing the balance of power. It is often possible and desirable for employee shares to be a separate class of shares – this often gives the appropriate flexibility to pay different rates of dividend to separate groups of shareholders. The principal aim is to give employees shareholder status. The detailed considerations are set out in Chapter 8.

CLOSE COMPANY LEGISLATION

Definition of a close company

3.12   The vast majority of typical family or owner-managed companies will be 'close companies' for tax purposes. Put simply, a company will be close if it is under the control of:

- five or fewer shareholders; or

- any number of shareholders who are also directors of the company, ie controlled by director-shareholders [*CTA 2010, s 439 (ICTA 1988, s 414(1))*].

For these purposes, any shares held by any associate of an individual shareholder must be attributed to that shareholder [*CTA 2010, s 451(4), ICTA 1988, s416(6)*]. This means that any shares held by a business partner or by relatives of a shareholder, such as his parents, spouse or civil partner, children (both minor and adult), brothers and sisters would be treated as held by them [*CTA 2010, s 448(1)(a)(2) (ICTA 1988, s 417(3)(a), (4))*]. Similarly, shares held by the trustees of a trust created by the participator (or one of his relatives) or a trust in which the participator has an interest are treated as held by an associate [*CTA 2010, s 448(1)(b)(c) (ICTA 1988, s 417(3)(b), (c))*]. Shares held by a nominee are also counted [*CTA 2010, s 451(3) (ICTA 1988, s 416(5))*].

One or more people would be taken as having control if they have or are entitled to have more than 50% of the issued share capital, voting power, or company's assets on a winding up. This would catch any arrangements, such as options, to acquire shares at a future date – these are counted at the current date in determining whether the relevant controlling interest is held [*CTA 2010, s 451(4)(5) (ICTA 1988, s 416(2)–(4))*].

The Newfields Developments Ltd case

3.13   In *R v CIR, ex p Newfields Developments Ltd* (2001) STC 901, the House of Lords found that the wide definition of 'control' in (what was) *ICTA 1988, s 416* was capable of applying to people who had no real control over a company's affairs. Lord Hoffmann concluded that the attribution of associates' holdings to the 'relevant' individual must be made irrespective of whether that individual was an *actual* participator (shareholder) in the company. Indeed, it may be necessary to attribute the rights and powers of persons over whom the relevant individual 'may in real life have little or no power of control'.

Given this wide definition, particularly the attribution of a relative's shareholdings, a family or owner-managed company will find it difficult, if not impractical, to structure its shareholdings so as to fall outside the close company definition. However, the consequences of being a close company are not as serious as they once were.

Disadvantages of close company status

3.14   Currently, the principal tax disadvantages of being a close company are as follows:

(*a*)   the 25% tax charge which arises under *CTA 2010, s 455 (ICTA 1988, s 419)* when any loan or advance is made to a shareholder of the company (see 2.56–2.65);

(*b*)   where the company incurs any expense or provides any benefit to a non-working shareholder or 'associate', this will be treated as a distribution (ie the same as a dividend), upon which the recipient will be taxed. The company is therefore denied a tax deduction for the relevant cost [*CTA 2010, ss 1000(2)* and *1064 (ICTA 1988, s 418)*] (see 2.62);

(*c*)   if the company is a close *investment* holding company, it will be subject to corporation tax at the full rate, regardless of the level of its profits (see 4.44–4.47) [*CTA 2010, s 18(b) (ICTA 1988, s 13(1)(b))*]. Shareholders may be unable to obtain interest relief on their personal borrowings to acquire shares in the company, although relief is available for close *trading* or *property rental* companies [*ITA 2007, s 392*] (see 11.11).

CORPORATE TAX RATES AND ASSOCIATED COMPANIES

Corporate tax rates

3.15   Corporation tax is levied by reference to financial years ('FY') – a financial year represents a 12-month period to 31 March. For example, the financial year 2011 represents the 12 months to 31 March 2012.

If a company's profits do not exceed the lower limit (currently £300,000 per year), it is entitled to the lower small profits rate of tax. The full or main rate of corporation tax applies where profits exceed the upper limit. Marginal relief is given where profits fall between the lower and upper limits. Where a company is 'associated' with other active trading companies during the relevant accounting period or the accounting period is less than 12 months, the relevant limits are reduced on a pro-rata basis (see 3.20 and 3.23).

Small profits rate

3.16   The small profits rate for FY 2011 is 20% (see Table in 3.17 for previous rates) These rates apply to all profits where they do not exceed £300,000. The £300,000 limit is apportioned amongst 'associated companies' (see 3.20) and reduced on a pro rata basis for periods of less than 12 months. The small profits rate is *not* available to close investment holding companies (see 4.38–4.41).

Summary of other corporate tax rates

3.17   The other corporate tax rates and limits for the financial years 2007 to 2011 (inclusive) are given below:

	FY2008	*FY2009*	*FY2010*	*FY2011*
Main rate	28%	28%	28%	26%
Small profits' rate (previously small companies' rate)	21%	21%	21%	20%
Lower limit*	£300,000	£300,000	£300,000	£300,000
Upper limit*	£1,500,000	£1,500,000	£1,500,000	£1,500,000

*Apportioned between total number of associated companies

Note: The March 2011 Budget announced that the main rate of corporation tax will reduce by 1% each year from the 26% rate in FY 2011 to 23% by FY 2014.

Small profits marginal relief

3.18   Small profits marginal relief will apply where a company's taxable profits fall between the lower and upper limit. The company's profits are taxed at the main rate and the small profits marginal relief is then deducted.

For FY 2011 (ie year ended 31 March 2012, the marginal relief formula (under the CTA 2010) is:

$$F \times (U - A) \times \frac{N}{A}$$

where:

F   = standard marginal fraction (3/200 for FY 2011)
U   = upper limit (see Table at 3.17)

A   = augmented profits, which are:
        the company's total taxable profit plus
        grossed-up dividend income (Franked Investment Income) but
        excluding dividends from 51% subsidiaries. (Note – This includes
        exempt dividends/distributions received from non-51% group
        companies from 1 July 2009)

N   = total taxable profits

A useful short-cut method of computation is to look at the effective marginal rate on the profits exceeding the lower limit. For example, in respect of the FY 2011, this is found as follows:

	Profits	*Tax*
	£	£
26% × upper limit profits of	1,500,000	390,000
20% × lower limit profits of	(300,000)	60,000
Therefore tax on marginal band of	1,200,000	330,000

The marginal rate is therefore normally 27.5% (ie 330,000/1,200,000 × 100%).

This will vary if the company receives franked investment income (excluding dividends from subsidiaries).

CT600 reporting and corporation tax payment

3.19   Under *CTA 2010*, the small profits rate is given (and does not require a formal claim). However, the company must give the number of active 'associated companies' which the company had during the accounting period or confirmation that there was none. In many cases, the details of the related parties shown in the company accounts is likely to be a good starting point but HMRC expect companies to carry out a diligent review and analysis to determine the number of active associated companies (including non-resident companies).

If the company pays tax at the small profits rate or enjoys marginal relief, it pays its tax within nine months after the end of its corporation tax accounting period (CTAP). Companies subject to tax at the main rate are normally required to pay their tax in four equal quarterly instalments (see 4.42–4.44).

Impact of associated companies

3.20   Where the owner manager (and/or members of their family) have interests in other companies, it is necessary to bear in mind the 'associated company' rule. This rule is designed to prevent a company from splitting its business between several companies to secure the maximum benefit from the small profits rate of corporation tax.

If the company is associated with another company or companies, then both the upper and lower corporation tax rate limits must be apportioned (equally) between them – i.e. by the number of associated companies and the company itself (see 3.23 for definition of associated company) [*CTA 2010, s 24 ICTA 1988, s 13(3)*]. It is not possible to transfer any unused relief between the associated companies.

Where a family or owner-managed business carries on a number of separate activities, this rule can be an important factor in determining the appropriate operating structure. If the activities are of an investment nature (for example, property letting), consideration should be given to keeping them in personal ownership or in a separate company to avoid prejudicing the shareholder's entrepreneurs' relief on the trading business or businesses.

If the company can regularly benefit from the small profit's rate of corporation tax, it can save significant amounts of tax over a number of years (although when the main rate reaches 23% by FY 2014, the savings will inevitably be much less!). It is therefore often best to keep the number of associated companies to a minimum, although commercial requirements (such as the protection of limited liability) may dictate that certain trades or activities should run through a separate company (see 3.29).

A regular review should be taken to determine whether virtually inactive companies are unnecessarily reducing the availability of the small profits' limit.

Example 1

Apportioning limits for tax rate calculations

Allen Ltd (which is wholly owned by Mr Allen) has taxable profits of £263,000 for the year ended 31 March 2012. During the period, Mr Allen also held controlling interests in five other trading companies.

The relevant upper and lower limits for the company would be:

Lower limit $^{£300,000}/6 = £50,000$

Upper limit $^{£1,500,000}/6 = £250,000$

Allen Ltd's taxable profits exceed the upper limit of £250,000 and therefore the liability will be at the full rate, ie:

£263,000 × 26% = £68,380

As the limits are apportioned equally between the associated companies, this rule is particularly disadvantageous where the taxable profits arise unevenly between them.

Example 2

Small profits relief

Sinclair Ltd's tax-adjusted profits for the year ended 31 December 2011 were £140,000. Sinclair Ltd was wholly owned by Trevor who also had a controlling stake in Leftwing Ltd.

The existence of the associated company means that the lower limits applicable to Sinclair Ltd for corporation tax purposes are halved and apportioned (*working in months*) between the relevant financial years as follows:

	FY 2010	FY 2011
Lower limits	$\frac{3}{12}$ × (£300,000/2) = £37,500	$\frac{9}{12}$ × (£300,000/2) = £112,500
Taxable profits	$\frac{3}{12}$ × £140,000 = £35,000	$\frac{9}{12}$ × £140,000 = £105,000

As the taxable profits fall below the apportioned lower limits for each financial year, they are taxed at the small profits rates as follows:

Corporation tax liability for the year ended 31 December 2011	£
FY 2010 – £35,000 × 21%	7,350
FY 2011 – £105,000 × 20%	21,000
Total CT liability	28,350

3.21   Where there is a change in the lower limit between financial years and a CTAP straddles 31 March, the relevant part of each financial year is treated as a separate CTAP for the purpose of this calculation.

Upper and lower limits – periods less than 12 months

3.22   The upper and lower limits are proportionally reduced where the CTAP is less than 12 months [*CTA 2010, s 24(4) (ICTA 1988, s 13(6)*]. Two apportionments will therefore be required where the company has associated companies and has a CTAP of less than 12 months.

Determining number of 'associated companies'

3.23   Broadly speaking, associated companies are those carrying on a business under common control. A company is associated with another company if one of them has control of the other or if both are under the control of the same person or persons [*CTA 2010, s 25 (ICTA 1988 13(4)*]. The 'associated company' definition would catch companies which are controlled by the same individual or group of individuals, as well as by a parent company. Associated companies that are not resident in the UK for tax purposes will also be counted (as was recently confirmed in *Jansen Nielsen Pilkes Ltd v Tomlinson* [2004] STC (SSCD) 226).

The important requirement that an 'associated company' must be carrying on a business at some time within the relevant CTAP is covered in 3.27 and 3.28.

Control for the purposes of determining whether companies are 'associated' is widely defined in *CTA 2010, s 450 (ICTA 1988, s 416)*. It can include cases where a person has (or persons have) control over the company's affairs (this is at shareholder or general meeting level as confirmed in *Steele v EVC International NV 69 TC 88*). The 'control' test can be satisfied where a group of two or more people exercise control. In practice, HMRC apply a 'minimum controlling combination' rule to determine whether the (same) person or group of people have 'control' – see 3.24.

Furthermore, someone will also be considered to have control where they hold more than 50% of the share capital, voting power, distributable income or net assets on a notional winding up. Although the legislation provides that shares held held by an individual's associates are attributed to them for the purpose of the control test in *CTA 2010, s 450 (ICTA 1988, s 416* – which means that they are counted as part of that individual's holding). However, this practical impact of this rule for shares held by family members was 'watered-down' by ESC C9 and, for accounting periods ending after 31 March 2011, by legislation introduced by FA 2011. In essence, the FA 2011 'relaxation' now only requires associates' holdings to be attributed where there is 'substantial commercial interdependence' between the relevant companies (see 3.25 for detailed FA 2011 rules and 3.26 for ESC C9 regime). In *R v CIR, ex p Newfields Developments Ltd* (2001) STC 901, it was held that the rights of an 'identified' individual's associates could be attributed to them even where the 'identified' individual did not hold shares in the relevant company (ie was not a participator). Furthermore, the Revenue did not have any power of discretion when deciding whether to treat companies as 'associated' with each other (see 3.13A).

There are additional rules which require shares held by a nominee on an individual's behalf to be treated as their holding *(CTA 2010, s 451(3))*. Any future entitlement to shares, for example, options, is deemed to be held currently for this purpose [*CTA 2010, s 450(2)*].

The minimum controlling combination

3.24   In determining whether companies are under the control of the same person or persons for these purposes, HMRC seek to determine whether the companies are under the control of the 'minimum controlling combination'. A 'minimum controlling combination' means a group of persons that has control of the company, but would not have control if any one of them were excluded (see *IR Company Taxation Manual*, CT 3730). In this context, each company's shareholdings would need to be analysed (possibly including associates' holdings where appropriate (see 3.23 and 3.26)) to find the *smallest* possible number that can control the company. Clearly, depending on the spread of the shareholdings, there may be more than one minimum controlling combination. HMRC can look at whether there is 'control' under any of the tests in *CTA 2010, s 450*, such as shareholdings, voting power, and any rights under the articles or entitlement to assets on a winding up.

However, to establish control, HMRC consider that dicta in *Newfields Developments Ltd* (see 3.23 above) on the use of the word 'may' in the context of their power to make 'associate' attributions gives wide flexibility. HMRC can thus make all possible 'associate' attributions, some of the attributions or even none at all (*IR Company Taxation Manual*, CT 3750). This means that additional combinations could be made.

If the *same* (minimum) group of shareholders has control of two (or more) companies, those companies would each be associated with the other.

Example 3

Determining various minimum controlling combinations

The shares in Loftus Favourites Ltd were held as follows (none of the shareholders are related to each other):

	Number of shares	Minimum controlling combinations		
		1	2	3
Mr Bowles	300	300	300	–
Mr Givens	300	300	–	300
Mr Francis	200	–	200	200
Mr Parkes	200	–	200	200
	1,000	600	700	700
		60%	70%	70%

This shows that Loftus Favourites Ltd has three minimum controlling combinations. If an identical 'minimum' group also had control of another company, that company would be associated with Loftus Favourites Ltd.

Example 4

Control by the minimum controlling combination

The shareholdings of Stoke Ltd and Hammers Ltd are summarised as follows:

	Stoke Ltd	*Hammers Ltd*
	%	%
Mr Hurst	60	40
Mr Peters	20	30
Various others	20	30

Mr Hurst and Mr Peters together control both Stoke Ltd and Hammers Ltd.

However, Mr Hurst can control Stoke Ltd on his own. Mr Hurst is therefore 'the minimum controlling combination' in Stoke Ltd. As he does not control Hammers Ltd on his own, the two companies will *not* be treated as associated.

Applying 'associates attribution' rules (for CTAPs ending after 31 March 2011)

Basic rules

3.25   Following extensive prior consultation, FA 2011, s55 amended CTA 2010, s27 which made important changes to the associates' attribution rules. These changes, which apply for CTAPS ending after 31 March 2011, operate only when determining whether companies are 'associated' with each other so that the lower and upper corporation tax profits limits can be apportioned (see 3.6, 3.7 and 3.20).

Under the 'revised' CTA 2010, s27 provisions, the following process is now applied when determining whether companies are associated with each other:

(1)   How many companies are under the control of a person or persons (ignoring any associates' holdings/rights)?

(2)   Are any companies in a 'substantial commercial interdependence' relationship (see below)?

If no 'substantial commercial interdependence' exists between the relevant companies, the number of associated companies is simply found at stage (1). This would mean, for example, that any companies that were controlled by the associate(s) of a shareholder would be ignored. One important change under the FA 2011 regime is that two companies that are separately controlled by a husband and wife would no longer necessarily be associated with each other (see 3.26 for pre-FA 2011 attribution rules under ESC C9).

Where 'substantial commercial interdependence' exists between two or more companies, then it is necessary to include associates' holdings in determining whether they are under 'common control' by the same person or group of persons.

For these purposes, an 'associate' will mainly include:

- Any relative (ie spouse, civil partner, parent or grandparent, children or grandchildren, or brother/sister);

- A business partner (see 3.25A for further commentary);

- The trustees of a settlement

  - created by an individual or their relative (living or dead);or

  - in which the individual has an interest where the settlement holds shares in the company.

Substantial commercial interdependence

The Corporation Tax Act 2010 (Factors Determining Substantial Commercial Interdependence) Order (SI 2011/1784) sets out the relevant factors that should be taken into account in assessing whether a companies is substantially commercially interdependent with another (which have been 'borrowed' from the VAT disaggregation provisions!).

Only one of three types of linkage is required for companies to meet this condition:

- *Financial interdependence* – This reflects the extent to which one company gives financial support (directly or indirectly) to another. However, the provision of a loan from a family member may cause a company to be 'associated' under the 'loan creditor' rules since they may be entitled to share than more than half the assets of that company on a notional winding-up for the purposes of CTA 2010 s450(3) and s454(2)(b).

- *Economically interdependent* – Two companies would be 'economically interdependent' if (in particular) they seek to realise the same economic objective, the activities of one benefit the other, or they have common customers.

- *Organisational interdependence* – This will be the case where the businesses of the companies have common management/employees, common premises, or common equipment.

Unfortunately, the term 'substantial' is not defined. HMRC's considers that both the degree of interdependence and the period during which it exists during a particular CTAP should be taken into account (see HMRC CTM03780). CTM03770 also implies that a 10% test should be used in relation to the specified indicators set out above but the overall 'picture' should be assessed rather than looking at these indicators in isolation. HMRC also provide a wide selection of scenarios together with its 'associated company' analysis in HMRC CTM03750 to CTM03800.

Many feel that HMRC have glossed-over the strict meaning of the term 'interdependence', which applies that each company must be dependent in some way on the other and vice versa (rather than dependency being 'one-way' only!)

Ultimately the application of the 'substantial commercial interdependence' is a subjective one and will invariably depend on the particular facts and circumstances of each case.

When reviewing such cases, it is also worth bearing in mind HMRC's objective behind the relaxation of the 'associated company' rules. They were revamped to ensure that companies are not treated as 'associated' simply by accident of 'circumstance' (under the 'associate attribution provisions) where there is *no* material business relationship between them.

Example 5

Application of 'substantial commercial interdependence' test

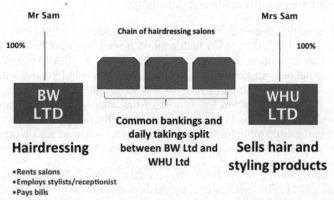

BW Ltd runs a chain of hairdressing salons and is 100% owned by Mr Sam. BW Ltd rents the salons, employs the stylists and receptionist as well as paying all the bills.

Mr Sam's wife owns 100% of the share capital of WHU Ltd, which sells hairdressing products.

Based on the facts, there is 'substantial commercial interdependence' between BW Ltd and WHU Ltd (they both share the same employees, premises and the same customers). Consequently, since Mr Sam would be deemed to 'control' both companies (his wife's holding in WHU Ltd would be attributed to him) they would be associated companies for corporation tax rate purposes.

When the complete 'picture' is viewed, it appears that effectively one business has been 'split' into two to access the benefit of two £300,000 small profits' rate bands.

Attributing shares held by 'business partners'

3.25A For CTAPs ending after 31 March 2011, the attribution of shares held by fellow partners of a partnership (or LLP) are dealt with in the same way as other 'associate' holdings – see 3.25.

However, for earlier CTAPs, specific legislation was already in place for partners (which was introduced by the FA 2008). The original definition of 'associate' included business partners but HMRC tended to operate a fairly 'light' touch in this area until the so-called 'Wick' letters were send to partners of film partnerships in late 2006 – (they were colloquially called 'Wick' letters since they emanated from the tax office in Wick, Scotland!).

The 'Wick' letters broadly explained the strict implications of the 'partner' associate rules and asked the 'partner' to enquire about the existence of other companies that were 'controlled' by their fellow partners. This letter sparked off representations from the leading professional bodies, particularly since the strict enforcement of these rules would impose an unfair compliance burden on shareholders who also had other business interests through partnerships.

HMRC accepted these submissions which culminated in a 'quick-fix' piece of legislation in *FA 2008, s 35,* which applied from 1 April 2008. This provided a complete exemption from the 'associate' attribution rules (for small profits and marginal rate purposes only) in relation to rights held by those with whom the relevant person is in partnership except where 'tax planning arrangements' existed to (broadly) exploit the benefit of the small profits rate (or marginal relief) rules in *CTA 2010, ss 18* and *19.* Consequently, film partnerships and other similar partnership vehicles that engaged in tax shelter/deferral arrangements would not generally have expected to be caught by the post-*FA 2008* legislation.

As indicated above, the *FA 2008* rules ceased to apply for CTAPS ending after 31 March 2011. Thus, shares held by partners would now be 'attributed' under the associate rules if substantial commercial interdependence exists between the relevant companies. This is likely to mean that 'corporate partners' in many partnerships would now be treated as associated with each other (since they would each be treated as carrying on the same 'underlying' partnership business).

HMRC accept that some companies might be disadvantaged under the *FA 2011* associated company provisions and hence it is possible to 'elect' to disregard them for a CTAPs beginning before 1 April 2011 *(CTA 2010, s27(3)).* This election to be taxed under the old rules (mentioned above) must be made within one year from the end of the relevant CTAP.

HMRC take the view that 'members' of a limited liability partnership (LLP) would also be treated as a 'partner' for *CTA 2010, s 448(1)(a)* purposes, but there is no clear statutory authority for this.

ESC C9 concession for relatives shareholdings

3.26   For CTAPs ending before 1 April 2011, the strict application of the 'associates' rule was relaxed by ESC C9. Under this concession, shares held by an individual's close relatives (*except those of their spouse/civil partner and minor children*) would *not* be attributed to them when determining whether they exercised 'control' within *CTA 2010, s 450* provided there was no substantial commercial interdependence between the relevant companies.

The pre-*FA 2011* position was therefore very similar to the current rules with the important exception that the previous ESC C9 treatment always required shares held by spouses, civil partners and minor children to be attributed (regardless of whether substantial commercial interdependence existed). However, they generally removed what might otherwise have been an impractical or even impossible burden of obtaining detailed information about companies controlled by 'distant' relatives.

Associated companies' 'carrying on a business' requirement

3.27   The associated companies' legislation disregards any company that is not carrying on a trade or business at any point in the CTAP. In the vast majority of cases, it will be very clear that a company is carrying on a business or trade. However, in certain situations, careful consideration may be required to determine whether a company is 'carrying on a business', which has a wider meaning than trading. Although some earlier case law debated the point (see, for example, *CIR v The Korean Syndicate Ltd* 12 TC 181), it seems that the concept of 'carrying on a business' implies some activity being actively carried on. As a general rule, where a company earns an income return from its assets, this indicates that it is carrying on a business and would be therefore be counted as an associated company for the purposes of the relevant corporation tax limits.

On the other hand, dormant associated companies which have not carried on any trade or business at any time during the relevant CTAP are disregarded [*CTA 2010, s 25(3)*] – the rationale for this is that such companies would not be able to benefit from their share of the lower limit. Interestingly, following *Jowett v O'Neill and Brennan Construction Ltd* [1998] STC 482, where a company only receives bank deposit interest in the CTAP, it should not be counted as an 'associated company' as this does not constitute the carrying on of an investment business..

This approach was followed in *HMRC v Salaried Persons Postal Loans Ltd* [2006] STC 1315, where a company received rent from a property it had previously occupied for its trade. It was held that the company was not an associated company as it had not carried on a business – the letting was merely a continuation of the letting of the former trading premises and was not actively managed.

On the other hand, in *Land Management Ltd v Fox* [2002] STC (SSCD) 152, a company that let property and made and held investments, advanced an interest-bearing loan to a connected company, and placed funds on deposit at the bank, was held to be carrying on a business and thus an associated company.

Non-trading holding company exemption

3.28   In fairly restricted cases, *CTA 2010, s 26* (which enacts the previous SP4/94) exempts certain 'non-trading holding' companies from being 'associated companies' by deeming them not to carry on a trade or business. Such holding companies are exempted provided they:

(a)   do not carry on a trade

(b)   have one or more 51% subsidiaries

(c)   are passive

Broadly speaking, a holding company would be regarded as 'passive' for the relevant CTAP where

● it has no assets

● any dividends received from its subsidiaries have been fully re-distributed to its own shareholders

● it has no chargeable gains, management expenses or qualifying charitable donations.

In practice, it is unlikely that many holding companies would satisfy all the relevant conditions for the *CTA 2010, s 26* exemption. However, this does necessarily prevent the group from arguing, on the facts, that the holding company is not carrying on a business and is effectively dormant. This would include cases where the holding company does not carry on any business activity and simply 'passively' holds shares in one or more subsidiaries. However, if it incurs significant costs and/or investment income, HMRC will often (successfully) argue that the company is carrying on a business.

CHOOSING AN APPROPRIATE CORPORATE STRUCTURE

Main types of corporate structure

3.29   Where various members of the family or owner-managers carry on a number of trades or ventures, which is the case for many medium or large-sized businesses, it is necessary to choose the most appropriate and efficient operating structure from both the tax and commercial point of view.

Many medium and large-sized family and owner-managed businesses enjoy varying degrees of diversification by carrying on a number of different trades or activities. Over time, such additional activities may need to be bolted-on, either by organic growth or by acquiring existing businesses. The commercial rationale might be to increase market share, gain economies of scale, acquire different channels of distribution or simply add value by entering into a new area.

The choice of corporate structure for a diversified family and owner-managed business often lies between the following:

● single divisionalised company (see 3.30);

- parallel companies (see 3.33);
- corporate group structure (see 3.35).

Given its importance to the shareholders 'exit' planning, entrepreneurs' relief considerations are likely to have a major influence on the ultimate choice of structure. For example, any 'investment-type' activity that could prejudice a shareholder's entrepreneurs' relief should be carried on through a separate company (see Chapter 15). In the case of a divisionalised company, it may be necessary to keep out or extract any high-risk activity that could potentially dissipate the assets of the entire company and lead to its demise.

Diversified owner-managed businesses must continually review their legal structures to see whether these remain appropriate for their various operations. This can only be done by a systematic and rational appraisal of the main commercial, legal and tax implications associated with each type of structure.

The three main legal corporate structures are illustrated in Example 6 below. The main commercial, legal and tax implications for each structure are dealt with in 3.38 and 3.39, which includes a detailed checklist.

Example 6

Illustration of different operating structures

John and Paul Barnes have decided to incorporate their existing transport and haulage businesses. John manages the warehousing operation and Paul manages the haulage side of the business.

The main types of operating structure are illustrated below:

Divisionalised structure

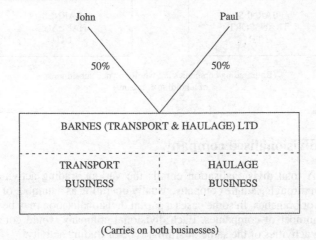

(Carries on both businesses)

Parallel company structure

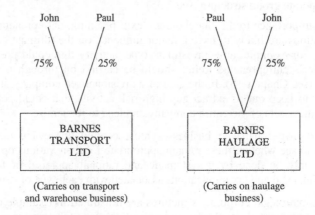

(Carries on transport   (Carries on haulage
and warehouse business)   business)

Corporate group structure

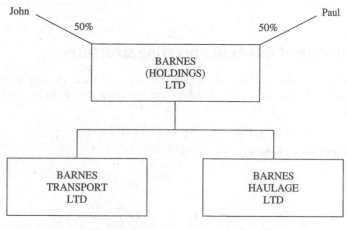

(Both trading companies are wholly owned subsidiaries
of a holding company)

Single divisionalised company

3.30   A total divisionalisation entails the various trading activities being carried on through a single company, usually operating as a number of separate divisions or branches. In some cases a partial divisionalisation may be required using a number of companies. Each divisional company would combine the operating activities of the same or similar type of trading activity.

Divisionalisation should bring administration cost savings through streamlining, etc. However, high risk businesses should usually be excluded from the divisionalised company and retained in a separate subsidiary company. This will prevent the assets of the divisionalised company being exposed to potential claims from creditors of the high-risk business in the event of its collapse. The writer has witnessed the difficulties encountered where one of the divisionalised businesses (of a single company) made substantial losses and its closure was being contemplated. The divisionalised company had no choice but to meet all its liabilities and commitments.

Before the *FA 2011*, divisionalised structures at a clear tax disadvantage as compared with a typical corporate group structure (see 3.35). The sale of a profitable trading division would have often produced a capital gains charge (on the sale of goodwill, etc) whereas if the trade had been carried on through a separate subsidiary company, the gain would generally be tax-free under the Substantial Shareholding Exemption (SSE) (see 3.40).

However, the radical *FA 2011* changes to corporate group gains will frequently mean that a divisionalised company will now be able to obtain effective exemption for any degrouping charge. This would be achieved by first hiving-down the relevant trade and assets to a new company (Newco) which would then be sold with the benefit of the SSE applying to any gain on the sale of Newco's shares *and* the degrouping gain. Whilst Newco would not normally have been held by the 'divisionalised' company for the minimum 12 month 'substantial shareholding' period for SSE (see 3.40), *TCGA 1992, Sch 7AC, para 15A* (introduced by *FA 2011, Sch 10*, para 6) deems the 'seller (ie the divisionalised company) to have satisfied this 'holding' requirement whilst the 'hived-down' assets were used for trading purposes by the group. Furthermore, Newco would also be deemed to have been a trading company for the minimum 12 month 'SSE' period before the sale. Consequently, since degrouping gains are generally added to the seller's capital gains consideration under the *FA 2011* regime, they would normally be exempted under the SSE (see 3.43A). However, such planning is only effective for the (pre-1 April 2002) goodwill since there has been no change in the degrouping rules for *CTA 2009, Part 8* regime intangibles and goodwill (created or acquired after 31 March 2002 – see 12.46 to 12.48).

Switching a corporate group to a divisionalised structure

3.31   If a diversified business is currently operating within a corporate group structure, it is usually possible to restructure it on a divisionalised basis without any material tax costs. The trade, assets and liabilities of each subsidiary would be transferred up to the parent company (which becomes the divisionalised company).

Each subsidiary will usually transfer its net assets at book value for a cash consideration, which is frequently left outstanding as an inter-company loan because the then dormant subsidiary has no requirement for cash. The assets are normally transferred at their book values (Provided the transferring subsidiary has positive reserves, a transfer at its carrying book value does not create a distribution for *Companies Act 2006* purposes – see 13.72).

CTA 2010, Part 22, Chapter 1 ensures that no capital allowance clawbacks occur (the assets being transferred at their tax written down values). Furthermore, provided all the relevant liabilities are transferred to the new divisionalised company, any unused trading losses would automatically be transferred with the trade offset in the divisionalised company against the future profits of that *same* trading activity.

No capital gains would arise on the assets transferred as they would be transferred under the no gain/no loss rule under *TGCA 1992, s 171*. The capital gains 'no gain/no loss' still applies to goodwill and other intellectual property (IP) held by the group at 1 April 2002 which continue to rank as 'capital gains' assets in the hands of the (related) transferee company (since this falls outside the scope of *CTA 2009, s 882(1)(a)(3)*).

Goodwill and other IP assets acquired (from third parties) or created by the group after 31 March 2002 are transferred on a 'tax-neutral' basis under the *CTA 2009, Part 8* intangibles regime [*CTA 2009, ss 775, 776, and 848*].

The 'hive-up' transfer of assets should not produce any stamp duty land tax or VAT costs [*FA 2003, Sch 7, para 1* and *VATA 1994, s 43* or *VAT (Special Provisions) Order 1995, art 5*].

The proposed divisionalisation may affect the confidence of the employees, customers, suppliers and bankers. It will therefore be important to give advance notification to all interested parties setting out the particular reasons in each case. A number of important commercial issues will also need to be addressed. For example, borrowing arrangements will have to be re-negotiated and various trading contracts may need to be signed, re-negotiated or novated.

Protection of valuable trading names

3.32   It is possible that well-known and highly valued trade names may be attached to the subsidiary companies which become dormant as a result of the divisionalisation. However, the valuable trading names of subsidiaries can be protected by the divisionalised company entering into 'undisclosed agency' agreements with dormant subsidiaries.

Each dormant subsidiary would act as an agent for an undisclosed principal, ie the divisionalised company. In this way, the valuable name of the dormant subsidiary is retained. The trading results would still be reflected in the divisionalised company (as principal), although the 'outside world' would still believe that it is dealing with the subsidiaries (for example, sales invoices would still be raised in the name of the dormant subsidiary).

Parallel companies

3.33   In a parallel company structure, each trade is run through a separate company. The shareholdings in each company reflect the management responsibility of each underlying business. Typically, the separate companies may together be owned by a group of individuals. This structure also offers more scope for some shares to be owned by senior management.

Probably the main benefit of a parallel company structure arises if one of the companies is sold off. The sale proceeds will be paid directly to the individual shareholders and the shareholders will often be able to secure a 10% ER CGT rate on (currently) their first £10 million of qualifying gains (see 15.33 to 15.42).

Direct ownership of the shares also tend to give the shareholders greater flexibility in mitigating their CGT liabilities which might include ER claims, potential emigration, EIS CGT deferral relief, and so on (see Chapter 15).

By way of contrast, the overall tax charge is likely to be higher where a company is sold as a subsidiary in a corporate group structure. Although the sale of the subsidiary itself would often be free of tax (assuming the relevant conditions for the SSE applied (see 3.40)), the sale proceeds are 'locked in' the parent company. If the sale proceeds are required by the shareholders, these are likely to be extracted as a dividend which would incur an income tax charge generally at an effective rate of 25%/36.1% (see 2.13–2.15 and 9.11).

A *continuing* shareholder cannot extract value as a capital gain since *ITA 2007, s 684* would almost certainly be invoked by HMRC to tax the amount as a quasi-dividend. In such cases, the only available routes would be a capital distribution on winding up the parent company or a 'capital gains' structured buy-back of shares (not available unless the shareholder 'retires' – see Chapters 13 and 15).

Companies controlled by the same individual or group of individuals will normally be *associated* for corporation tax purposes (see 3.24). In such cases, the upper and lower profit limits must be split equally between them.

Where 'parallel' companies owned by different members of the same family are shown *not* to be associated with each other, each company can generate up to £300,000 of taxable profits at the small profits' rate.

Converting parallel companies to a corporate group structure

3.34   If it becomes necessary to switch from a parallel company to a corporate group structure, this can normally be done using a share for share exchange. The shareholders of each parallel company will transfer their shares to a new company (or an existing parallel company) in exchange for shares.

Provided this reorganisation is undertaken for commercial reasons, the share exchange will avoid CGT under *TCGA 1992, ss 127* and *135*. This means that the new shares are treated as being acquired at the same time and at the same base cost as the shareholders' old shares in the parallel company.

However, a stamp duty liability may arise (equal to ½% of the value of each parallel company 'sold') *unless* the strict conditions of *FA 1986, s 77* can be satisfied. This requires the new acquiring company's share capital to 'mirror' precisely that of each acquired parallel company, with the proportions held by *each* shareholder being the same as they were before the transfer. Where there are different shareholdings, it may be possible save stamp duty on the first share exchange by arranging for the new 'holding' company to acquire the most valuable company. The shares of the new company will be a 'mirror-image' of the acquired company and should therefore qualify for the *FA 1986, s 77* exemption.

It is not possible to transfer unlisted shares in a trading company to another company under the protection of a *TCGA 1992, s 165* business asset hold-over claim (see 13.14)

Corporate group structure

3.35 In a conventional corporate group structure, the individual shareholders will own the shares in the parent company, which in turn will hold the shares in the various trading subsidiaries. The corporate group structure has particular operational tax advantages over the parallel company structure. The combined effect of the various 'group' tax reliefs effectively enables the group to be treated as a single entity for tax purposes, although there are some limitations to this principle.

A further attraction is a group's ability to dispose of its subsidiaries tax-free under the SSE (see 3.40). On the other hand, the tax compliance and administration for a sizeable group can involve considerable costs; a single divisionalised company tends to be more tax efficient.

The availability of the various tax reliefs for groups generally depends on the percentage of the subsidiary's ordinary shares held by the parent. In many cases, the subsidiaries will be wholly owned and hence can benefit from the full range of reliefs. If there are outside minority or joint-venture interests, the availability of certain reliefs will depend on whether the parent has:

- more than 50% of the subsidiary's shares (*a 51% subsidiary*);

- at least 75% of the subsidiary's ordinary shares (*a 75% subsidiary*).

A checklist of the main group tax reliefs, showing those available with a 51% and 75% subsidiary, is provided at 3.45.

Entrepreneurs' relief status – holding company of a trading group

Key tests

3.36 It is important to confirm that the holding company qualifies as a 'holding company of a trading group' to ensure that entrepreneurs' relief is available to the shareholders. To qualify, a two-stage test must be satisfied:

- the company must be a holding company, ie its business must consist wholly or mainly (more than 50%) of the holding of shares in one or more 51% subsidiaries (ignoring any trade actually carried on by it);

- the group must be a trading group, ie when looking at all the activities actually carried on by the group, they must be of a 'trading' nature – for these purposes, any investment/non-trading activities are ignored provided they are not 'substantial' in relation to the group's total activities [*TCGA 1992, s 165A*].

The ER group test is virtually the same as the one that previously applied for business asset taper relief and is therefore relatively stringent [*TCGA 1992, s 165A*]. Broadly, the relevant company/group must be wholly engaged in carrying on trading activities, subject to the *de minimis* rule for 'substantial' non-trading activities (see also 15.36 to 15.39 for further detailed commentary).

HMRC's practice is to interpret 'substantial' as meaning 'more than 20%'. There is no definitive measure of this and therefore various indicative measures could be examined when reviewing a company's qualifying ER status, with each case being judged on its own facts.

Thus, if there are non-trading activities, such as property letting to *non-group* members, holding share investments, and so on, these must represent less than 20% of whatever measure is appropriate in each case. The possible measures used may include the turnover from non-trading activities, the value of non-trading investments, the underlying costs, or the time spent by the company's directors and employees on non-trading activities.

Since the legislation requires all of the group's activities to be 'taken together', any intra-group transactions, such as where a holding company lets property to a (51%) subsidiary, would be ignored.

Given the subjective nature of these tests, it is probably better to keep 'tainted' activities in a separate company outside the group.

Beneficial treatment of joint venture interests

3.37 A qualifying equity investment in a joint venture trading company (which would otherwise be treated as an investment) is treated as an appropriate part of the trading activities of a trading company/holding company of a trading group.

The holding company's shareholding in a joint venture company (JVC) qualifies for 'trading' treatment provided:

- it holds *at least 10%* of the JVC's ordinary shares;

- the JVC is a trading company or holding company of a trading group; and

- at least 75% of the JVC's equity share capital is held by five or fewer *companies*.

It must be appreciated that the ER rules lay down an 'all or nothing' test. The holding company either meets the 'joint venture' conditions or it does not – there is no proportionate relief! For further commentary, see 15.39.

TAX AND COMMERCIAL FACTORS AFFECTING CHOICE OF STRUCTURE

3.38 The selection of a suitable structure depends upon the relative importance of a number of commercial, tax and legal factors.

The commercial consideration of limited liability may outweigh all other considerations, particularly in relation to certain types of trading activity, which are vulnerable to large claims and liabilities. This would point to the use of separate parallel companies or a group structure. However, many banks and other lenders will wish to protect their position by entering into cross-guarantee and personal guarantee arrangements.

Conventional corporate group structures may be attractive given that disposals of subsidiaries are often tax-free under the SSE (see 3.40). However, where the owner-managers wish to extract the sale proceeds from the holding company, an income tax charge would be incurred. If one or more of the companies are likely to be sold, the availability of ER (on the first £10 million of gains) giving a CGT charge of 10% on disposal, gives considerable impetus to a 'parallel company' arrangement.

If one or more trades are making substantial losses, it is normally advisable to ensure their immediate offset, which would point towards a group or divisionalised structure.

In many cases, the optimum shareholding structure may be a 'hybrid' arrangement using a combination of the main structures outlined above. The detailed tax reliefs available to groups are considered further at 3.44 and 3.45. The main tax and commercial considerations are summarised in the checklist – see 3.39 below.

OPERATING STRUCTURE CHECKLIST

3.39

	Single company (divisionalised structure)	*Parallel companies*	*Corporate group*
Commercial liability	Risks and liabilities of any one trade may threaten the viability of the other trades (eg the entire company may be forced into receivership as a result of a major claim or liability in one division).	Limited liability for each company subject to any loan cross-guarantee arrangements (collapse of one company does not bring others down).	Limited liability for each company (subject to any cross-guarantee arrangements for borrowings, etc). Parent company is not legally obliged to support an insolvent subsidiary, although may need to do so to avoid adverse commercial publicity.
Audit and administration	Single audit fee for one company. Minimum audit fees, secretarial and legal compliance costs.	Each company requires an audit. Duplication of administrative costs, etc.	Each company requires an audit. Duplication of administrative costs.
	Detailed results of each trade can be hidden within one set of 'combined' accounts, which prevents competitors and potential predators obtaining detailed information about each trade.	Each company needs to prepare accounts.	Need to prepare consolidated accounts.

	Single company (divisionalised structure)	*Parallel companies*	*Corporate group*
	Divisionalised accounts may show a much larger-sized business with much greater financial strength (this may assist certain companies in contracts). Brings pressure to harmonise employment terms and conditions, etc for employees and managers of all divisions, which may create problems. Possibility of demotivating key members of management team, eg lower perceived status of divisional manager as compared with company director.		In certain cases, the consolidated accounts create the impression of much greater size and financial backing.
Shareholder control	No direct relationship between shareholdings and management responsibility for each business.	Shareholdings can reflect management responsibility of each business, giving greater control and reward for efforts.	Shares should normally be held in holding company as this enables company to secure a statutory corporate tax deduction for employee shares under *CTA 2009, Part 12, Chapter 2.*

	Single company (divisionalised structure)	Parallel companies	Corporate group
			Where appropriate, subsidiary company employees can be given a special class of shares in the parent company with the required rights over the subsidiary's profits and assets, etc.
Sale of company/trade	Proceeds are received directly by shareholders and subject to CGT with the possible benefit of ER, therefore no element of double taxation.	Proceeds received directly by shareholders, with possible low CGT liability due to the availability of ER (as for single company)	Subsidiaries can often be sold without a tax charge under the Substantial Shareholdings Exemption (SSE) (see 3.40). Generally, no problems where the sale proceeds are reinvested in the group's trading activities, but a tax charge arises on the ultimate shareholders where the sale proceeds are retained as an investment.
	'Following FA 2011, it should now be possible to sell a division on an exempt basis under SSE by first hiving-down the trade and asset to a new subsidiary. However, a tax change will be incurred if the sale proceeds are required to be extracted by the ultimate	Each business can be sold separately through a company.	Group roll-over relief is also available for asset sales (for property and goodwill), although goodwill/IP roll-over is more restrictive (see 15.11).

	Single company (divisionalised structure)	*Parallel companies*	*Corporate group*
	shareholders. This strategy will not apply where the goodwill of the trade started or was acquired after 31 March 2002, since a degrouping charge will arise under the intangibles regime'		Shareholders suffer tax charge if proceeds are extracted from the group.
Tax implications			
Small profits rate	Small profits rate will be available without any need to equalise profits between two or more associates.	If 'common control' can be avoided, this enables the benefits of the small profits rate to be maximised. This is also the case where companies are controlled by various family members *but* there is no substantial inter-company trading. If companies are associated and profits are distributed unevenly, the overall tax liability may be higher as some companies may be taxed at full marginal rate.	May involve some loss of small profits rate, although profits may be equalised by group relief.

	Single company (divisionalised structure)	*Parallel companies*	*Corporate group*
Tax reliefs	Very efficient for tax purposes – maximises available reliefs and provides full matching of payments, receipts and gains. In particular, losses of any trade can be relieved by offset against current year's total profits, and: – offset against total profits of previous year; – carried forward against profits of the same trade.	Within each company, the position is the same as that of a single company. However, trading losses and capital losses cannot be relieved by transfer between the companies.	Trading losses can be surrendered between each member of a 75% group on a current year basis. Various other reliefs are available (see 3.35).
Capital losses	Chargeable gains will also be offset against allowable capital losses.		Disposals of chargeable assets no longer have to be 'routed' through a capital loss company to obtain relief for capital losses. A joint election can be made under *TCGA 1992, s 171A* to *deem* assets to be sold via a 'capital loss' company. This provides a system of group relief for capital losses (it is not possible to use pre-entry capital losses – broadly *pre-acquisition* capital losses of *acquired* subsidiaries).

THE SUBSTANTIAL SHAREHOLDINGS EXEMPTION (SSE)

Background

3.40   Many trading groups and companies are able to obtain a capital gains exemption on selling their trading subsidiaries under the Substantial Shareholdings Exemption (SSE) [*TCGA 1992, Sch 7AC*]. The corollary is that no relief is available for capital losses arising on an SSE-qualifying disposal.

For these purposes, substantial means at least 10% of the ordinary share capital (and other economic rights such as at least a 10% entitlement in profits available for distribution) [*TCGA 1992, Sch 7AC, para 8*]. Thus, the exemption should apply to most sales of trading subsidiary companies as well as equity interests in joint ventures and other affiliated companies. The SSE will apply equally to disposals of UK and overseas resident companies.

As part of a radical revamping of the capital gains degrouping rules in FA 2011, degrouping charges are often now exempt under SSE (see 3.46 for detailed rules). However, such SSE protection is not available for degrouping charges on CTA 2009, Part 8 intangible assets (i.e. goodwill and other intangible assets created or acquired after 31 March 2002) (see 3.48).

Main qualifying conditions

3.41   It is clearly important to ensure that the relevant main conditions for obtaining the SSE will be satisfied. Briefly, these are:

(*a*)   the 'investing company' must be a sole trading company or a member of a trading group (see 3.42) throughout the 'qualifying period' which *begins* at the start of the relevant 12-month 'substantial shareholding' period (see (*b*) below) and *ends* when the substantial shareholding is sold. After the disposal, the investing company must remain a qualifying trading company or a member of a qualifying trading group [*TCGA 1992, Sch 7AC, para 18*];

(*b*)   the relevant shareholding investment must qualify as a 'substantial shareholding' held in the investee company *throughout* a 12-month period starting not more than two years before the shares are disposed of (it is possible to 'look through' any prior no gain/no loss transfer (such as an intra-group transfer) and include the *transferor's* period of ownership for the purpose of satisfying this test) [*TCGA 1992, Sch 7AC, paras 7, 8 and 10*]; and

(*c*)   the investee company in which the shares are held must be a qualifying trading company (see 3.42) or qualifying holding company of a trading (sub-)group from the start of the 12 month 'substantial shareholding' period (in (b) above) and ending with the disposal date. The investee company must also be a qualifying trading company/holding company of a trading sub-group immediately after the disposal [*TCGA 1992, Sch 7AC, para 19*].

In practice, most disposals tend to meet the conditions in (a), (b) and (c) by reference to the 12 months immediately before the disposal date.

'Trading company or trading group member' requirement

3.42   For the purpose of determining whether companies make up a group, the capital gain group rules in *TCGA 1992, s 170* are followed but with 51% subsidiaries being included (rather than the normal 75% subsidiary test). A 'subgroup' represents companies that would form a (51%) group but where the 'sub-holding' company is a 51% subsidiary of another group company.

The key SSE trading company and trading group definitions are identical to those used for CGT ER purposes [*TCGA 1992, Sch 7AC, paras 20* and *21*] (see 15.36–15.39 for further analysis). Also, as with ER, there are special rules that treat certain 10% plus shareholdings in trading joint ventures as being trading activities (rather than investments) [*TCGA 1992, Sch 7AC, para 24*] (see 15.36).

To qualify for SSE, both the investing and investee company must be *trading* in their own right or be part of a trading group. They will not qualify if there are any 'substantial' *non-trading* activities. The legislation does not define 'substantial' which must therefore be taken to be an absolute test. However, HMRC generally seek to apply a relative test using a 20% benchmark (see *IR Tax Bulletin 62* (see 15.36)). This 20% test is likely to be applied by Inspectors when considering whether SSE is likely to apply on a particular transaction. In practice, the HMRC would therefore apply the 20% test to various measures, such as income, assets, and management time. In the writer's view, although these tests are helpful, they merely provide a pragmatic guide. They should not be followed rigidly and (in some cases) one or more of these criteria may not provide a reliable indicator, for example, the disposition of a company's assets might reveal the true nature of the company's main activities – assets are not activities, they are merely the result of the activities.

The holding of cash/income can still be treated as trading if the amounts are earmarked for future trading use. Similarly, the holding of surplus cash which is derived from a previous trading activity should not be counted as a non-trading activity provided it is not actively managed as an investment. If the disposal proceeds are going to be passed to the ultimate shareholders of the parent company, they will be ignored and will not prejudice the group's post-sale trading status.

In *TCGA 1992, Sch 7AC, para 22(2)*, trading activities include those activities carried on 'with a view' to acquiring or starting to carry on a trade or acquiring (at least) a 51% stake in a trading company. (Comments made by Lord Hoffmann in *Dextra Accessories Ltd v MacDonald* [2005] STC 1111 that 'with a view to' means 'at least a realistic possibility' may be helpful here.) Thus, where the group intends to reinvest the proceeds for trading purposes or a future acquisition of a trading company, the proceeds are treated as being held on 'trading account'. Companies and groups should ensure that there is sufficient documentary evidence to support their case (such as notes of management or board meetings and financial budgets/forecasts, etc).

3.43   Similarly, investments which are merely transitory in nature, pending their application towards a 'trading' application, should be disregarded. If HMRC apply an asset test, then the value of a trading company's or group's goodwill (which is essentially trading in character) should be included, even though it may not be on the balance sheet. In broad terms, goodwill represents the amount by which the market value of the company/group exceeds its tangible net asset value.

Groups are effectively viewed as a 'single entity' for SSE purposes, thus intra-group transactions are ignored (even if they are of an investment nature – such as the letting of 'trading' properties to subsidiary companies). Similarly, management time spent on trading subsidiaries would also be disregarded. In dealing with any HMRC challenge in this area, it should always be remembered that these tests do not have any statutory backing and would not necessarily be followed by the courts.

Given the substantial amounts that may be involved in an SSE claim, if there are any potential doubts or concerns about a company's or group's trading status, it is generally prudent to seek an appropriate assurance from HMRC by applying for a non-statutory business clearance. HMRC will accept COP 10 clearance applications where there is a material uncertainty over the SSE status of an impending transaction (see HMRC Business Brief 41/07). The application should cover the various matters on HMRC's checklist (see HMRC website at www.hmrc.gov.uk/cap/annex-a-checklist.pdf.

In the context of an SSE application, this would include the reasons for the transaction, the relevant facts, the company's view of the application of the SSE to the disposal and the issues on which HMRC's opinion is sought. It is worth noting that HMRC may reject or not respond to an SSE clearance application if it does not explain in sufficient detail the genuine uncertainty inherent in the availability of SSE.

Example 7

Exempt disposal under the SSE

3.43A   Terry Holdings Ltd has had three wholly-owned trading subsidiaries for many years as follows:

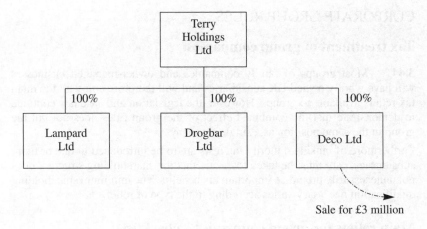

Sale for £3 million

The group is currently valued at some £35 million and has no investment activities.

However, in May 2011, it receives an offer to sell Deco Ltd to Stamford Bridge plc for £3 million. The disposal of Deco Ltd takes place on 1 June 2011, which gives rise to a capital gain of £2.8 million. The £3 million received on the sale is used to repay bank borrowings.

The capital gain of £2.8 million arising on the disposal of the shares in Deco Ltd should be exempt under the SSE because:

- Terry Holdings Ltd (the investing company) qualified as a member of a trading group in the 12 months to 1 June 2011 and would similarly qualify immediately afterwards. Since the £3 million cash has been used to repay group borrowings, it cannot interfere with the group's trading status post-sale. Even if the cash was invested it would be well within the 20% deminimis tolerance for non-trading activities (given the group is worth some £35 million).

- Since Deco Ltd has been wholly-owned by Terry Holdings Ltd for at least the previous 12 months up to 1 June 2011, it satisfies the 'substantial shareholding' test.

- Deco Ltd (the company invested in) has been a trading company for the 12 months to 1 June 2011, and should also satisfy this condition immediately after it is sold. It is generally considered prudent to obtain a warranty from the purchaser that it would not jeopardise the 'post-sale' trading requirement.

CORPORATE GROUP RULES

Tax treatment of group companies

3.44   Most groups of family companies and owner-managed businesses will have wholly owned UK subsidiaries and will therefore enjoy all the main tax reliefs available to groups. However, the legislation and case law continue to demonstrate that the combined effect of the group rules does not put the group in the same position as a single company.

Furthermore, if outside minority interests are to be introduced in one or more subsidiaries, care must be taken to ensure that the shareholding structure does not unnecessarily prejudice important tax benefits. The minimum shareholding qualification necessary varies according to the type of relief.

Main reliefs for group companies – checklist

3.45

Required group structure	Main reliefs
51% + subsidiary	• Substantial Shareholdings Exemption (SSE) is frequently available to exempt sale of trading subsidiaries. (*Note*: the SSE also extends to the sale of a 10% plus equity interest in a trading company, such as a joint venture shareholding – see 3.40.)
	• Intra-group debts can be released on a 'tax-neutral' basis under the loan relationship rules. Although the lending company does not obtain any tax deduction for the amount waived, the borrowing company's credit to profit and loss is tax-free
	• Companies may participate in 'group payment' arrangements to pay corporation tax in quarterly instalments. One payment is made for the participating group companies and the group's tax interest exposure is minimised (see 4.48–4.51).
75% + subsidiary	• Current year tax losses generated by one group member can be surrendered to another by way of group relief (see 4.32) [*CTA 2010, ss 99–106*].
	• Consortium relief may be available for a pro rata share of current losses [*CTA 2010, ss 132, 133* and *143–153*].

Required group structure | **Main reliefs**

- Chargeable assets can be transferred between group companies with the deferral of the relevant tax until the asset is sold outside the group, or a degrouping charge arises on the transferee company leaving the group within six years (although any degrouping may now be exempted under the SSE – see 3.46) [*TCGA 1992, ss 171* and *79*] .

  Similarly, post-1 April 2002 intangible fixed assets are transferred on a 'tax-neutral' basis between 75% group members, thus preventing any taxable profit arising on the transfer [*CTA 2009, ss 775, 776,* and *848*].

- Effective group capital loss relief can be obtained by electing under *TCGA 1992, s 171A*. This deems a third party disposal to have been made via a group member with appropriate capital losses.

- Tax refunds can be surrendered to other group members to minimise the group's net interest on unpaid tax [*CTA 2010, s 963*].

- All group companies are effectively regarded as a single entity for the purposes of roll-over relief. This enables a capital gain realised by one group company to be rolled-over against qualifying assets purchased by another outside the group [*TCGA 1992, s 175*].

- Intangible fixed asset roll-over relief is also available for reinvestment in goodwill and other intangible fixed assets on a group basis [*CTA 2009, ss 754–763*]. (See 12.50–12.51 and 15.11.)

- Trades can be transferred between the group companies without the adverse tax consequences of a cessation. Assets on which capital allowances have been claimed would be transferred at their tax written down values and unused trading losses are carried across into the transferee company (subject only to the restrictions applying where the transferor company is technically insolvent) [*CTA 2010, Part 22, Chapter 1*].

Required group structure   **Main reliefs**

- Land and property (subject to stamp duty land tax (SDLT)) and shares (subject to stamp duty) can normally be transferred between group companies without any SDLT/stamp duty liability. However, the SDLT and stamp duty group relief provisions do not apply where there are arrangements for the transferee company to leave the group or the consideration for the transfer is being provided directly or non-directly by a third party [SDLT – *FA 2003, Sch 7, para 2*; stamp duty – *FA 1930, s 42; FA 1967, s 27* – see SP 3/98].

  However, an SDLT de-grouping charge arises in respect of *land and property* transferred intra-group where the *transferee* company leaves the group within three years of the intra-group transfer and continues to hold the property [*FA 2003, Sch 7, para 3*].

Capital gains' degrouping charges and interaction with SSE

3.46   Companies which are members of the same (75%) group are permitted to transfer chargeable assets between themselves on a nil gain/nil loss basis (under *TCGA 1992, s 171*). This recognises that, although each group company is a separate legal entity, the group companies effectively operate together as a single economic unit.

To ensure that this rule cannot be abused by the so-called 'envelope trick', we have degrouping charge rules in *TCGA 1992, s 179*. Broadly speaking, the degrouping charge rules apply where a chargeable asset has been transferred into a subsidiary within *six years* of it leaving the group (typically via a third party sale). Provided the relevant asset is still held by the subsidiary when it leaves the group, *TCGA 1992, s 179(4)* provides that there is a deemed disposal (and re-acquisition) of that asset. Historically, the degrouping tax charge has arisen in the 'departing' subsidiary although an election could be made to allocate the gain to its fellow (75%) group members. (Similar rules apply to degrouping charges realised under the *CTA 2009, Part 8* intangibles regime)

Whilst the rationale for the degrouping charge is understandable, it has often caused many problems for corporate groups seeking to sell part of their activities some time after a group restructuring exercise. Furthermore, since the introduction of the SSE in 2002, shares in a subsidiary can often be sold 'tax-free' under the SSE (see 3.40 to 3.43A) but that subsidiary could still be exposed to a degrouping tax charge. *FA 2011* addressed these concerns by radically changing the mechanics of the degrouping charge. These changes apply to companies leaving groups after 18 July 2011 (or, where an early commencement election is made under *FA 2011, Sch 10, para 9(6)*, 1 April 2011).

The actual degrouping gain/loss is still calculated on the same basis – i.e. the transferee subsidiary is deemed to sell and reacquire the relevant asset at its market value immediately after the previous intra-group transfer. However, where the transferee leaves the group due to a *sale of its shares* (or shares in another group company) – as will typically be the case – then the degrouping gain is added to the consideration received for the disposal of the shares. On the other hand, if the deemed degrouping disposal gives rise to a capital loss, this is effectively added to the base cost of the shares being sold (*TCGA 1992, s 179(3D)*). The '*FA 2011*' degrouping charge provisions are *not* 'mirrored' under the *CTA 2009, Part 8* intangibles regime (see 3.48).

If the subsidiary leaves the group as a result of more than one 'group' share disposal, the degrouping gains/losses can be allocated between the various disposals as the group sees fit (*TCGA 1992, s 179(F)*).

One very important consequence of these changes is that where the sale of the subsidiary (or other group company) qualifies for the SSE, this will also effectively ensure that the degrouping gain obtains the benefit of the exemption. The interaction between the SSE and revised degrouping rules is illustrated in example 8 below.

The original method for taxing the degrouping charge will continue to apply where a company leaves the group otherwise than as a result of a share disposal by a UK resident company – for example, as a result of a share issue that 'swamps' the existing 75% group connection.

Example 8

SSE protection for degrouping charges (under *FA 2011*)

3.47   Allardyce Holdings Ltd is the parent company of several 100% owned trading subsidiaries.

In September 2011, Allardyce Holdings Ltd sold its 100% shareholding in Scott Ltd for £2.5 million. (The current 'indexed' base cost of the shares is £450,000).

Scott Ltd had acquired its current office premises from a fellow 75% subsidiary, Noble Ltd, in May 2009 at its then market value of £1.2 million, although for tax purposes it was transferred on a nil gain/nil loss basis under TCGA 1992 s171. These office premises had been purchased by Noble Ltd in July 1991 for £500,000.

The sale of Scott Ltd qualifies for exemption under the SSE rules. This means that the degrouping gain in respect of its office premises is also exempted since it is added to the capital gains consideration for the Scott Ltd share sale.

The relevant calculations are as follows:

Sale of 100% holding in Scott Ltd	
	£000
Share sale	2,500
Degrouping gain (see below)	405
Total sale consideration	2,905
Less: Indexed base cost	(450)
Capital gain = Exempt under SSE	2,455
Degrouping charge	
Deemed MV (May 2009) consideration	1,200
Less: Base cost	(500)
Indexation (£500,000 × 0.59)	(295)
Capital gain	405*
*treated as part of consideration for sale of Scott Ltd	

Intangibles degrouping charge

3.48   The intangibles legislation applies to goodwill, intellectual property, and other intangibles created or acquired by a group *after 31 March 2002.* It has similar (but not the same) degrouping charge rules to those used for 'capital gains' assets under *TCGA 1992, s 179.*

Under the intangibles regime, where a (75%) subsidiary company leaves a group

–   holding 'new' goodwill or intangible assets;

–   which it previously acquired within the previous six years from a fellow group company under the 'tax-neutral' rule in *CTA 2009, s 776; CTA 2009, s 780* imposes a degrouping charge on the 'departing' subsidiary. The subsidiary is deemed to have realised and reacquired the asset immediately after the original intra-group transfer at its then market value. Consequently, this will normally give rise to a taxable credit, based on the excess of the market value over any available base cost. (On the other hand, if the base cost exceeds the market value, a tax deductible debit arises). Given that the goodwill/intangible asset is deemed to be re-acquired at market value, the subsidiary's deductible debits would also be subsequently be revised, being based on the market value of the goodwill/intangible asset (at the date of the intra-group transfer) rather than the original 'tax-neutral' cost. The degrouping charge is therefore calculated as a 'combined' net credit (or debit), reflecting:

– the actual degrouping gain (up to the date of the intra-group transfer); and

– the 'net' adjustment to the intangible amortisation amounts between the original intra-group transfer and the date the subsidiary is sold. This 'combined' charge is normally taxed in the relevant 'transferee' subsidiary company as a trading profit immediately before it leaves the group (although it is possible to reallocate the profit/loss to a fellow 75% group company).

Unfortunately, the *FA 2011* changes have not been extended to the corresponding intangibles degrouping charge in *CTA 2009, s 780*. An intangibles degrouping tax charge would therefore still arise in a subsidiary that was sold within six years of a prior transfer of (*post-March 2002*) goodwill to it, even though SSE is likely to be available to the 'disposing' company.

Given the differing tax treatment between capital gains and intangibles degrouping charges, groups will need to carefully identify whether any goodwill subject to the charge arose or was acquired before 31 March 2002 or afterwards.

PLANNING CHECKLIST — SHAREHOLDING AND CORPORATE STRUCTURES

Company

● Keep number of companies to a minimum consistent with commercial objectives.

● Companies that have a number of common shareholders must be carefully reviewed to see whether they are likely to be 'associated' with each other under the widely drawn rules for looking at 'minimum controlling shareholding' combinations.

● Under the post-*FA 2011* 'associate' attribution rules, companies which are separately owned by husband and wife should not be treated as associated companies if there is no material business or economic links between them.

● Activities which carry a high level of commercial risk should be kept in a separate company.

- It should often be possible to sell subsidiaries without a tax charge under the SSE, although a careful check must always be made to ensure that the relevant conditions are satisfied.

- Under the *FA 2011* degrouping charge provisions, it should now often be possible to sell a trading subsidiary with SSE protection for the degrouping gain as well as the 'share disposal' gain. However, this beneficial treatment does *not* apply to degrouping charges arising on (post-March 2002) goodwill or intangible assets.

- The company's 'trading' status for SSE and ER purposes should be kept under review .

- The company must ensure that all chargeable events in connection with shares and share options are reported on form 42, normally by 6 July following the end of the relevant tax year.

Working shareholders

- Owner-manager shareholders should normally be eligible for ER, which provides an a low 10% CGT rate on cumulative qualifying gains up to £10 million. ER is only available if the company satisfies the fairly stringent trading criteria throughout the 12 months prior to any share sale.

- Shares provided to the owner manager's children and other family members should be exempt from any employment income tax charges since they are made available in the 'normal course' of domestic and family relationships.

- The award of new shares or the exercise of share options to employees and key managers may be taxed as employment income where they are acquired at less than market value. If these shares are subject to the standard pre-emption rights, etc applying to all shareholders, they are unlikely to be 'restricted'. However, it is still generally prudent to make a protective *ITEPA 2003, s 431* election to ensure that any future growth in the shares falls within the capital gains regime post-acquisition (see 8.14–8.37).

- Owner-managers will have effective control of their company by owning more than 50% of voting shares – this may include shares held by trusts in which they are (first-named) trustees.

- To obtain the greatest benefit from the 100% IHT business property relief (BPR) exemption, owner-managers should maximise their own/spouse's shareholding – money introduced by way of loan does not qualify for any IHT relief.

- Separate companies enable ownership to be more directly related to management of different businesses.

- Different classes of shares can be used to give flexibility over future dividend payments.

Other employees

- Employee share incentives increase identification with company and offer possibility of a large capital profit on future sale (which might be taxed at a lower rate if the employee has sufficient shares to be eligible for ER).

- Owner-managed groups should aim to issue all shares to their employees (including those employed by subsidiary companies) at 'parent company' level to obtain the statutory corporate tax deduction for shares issued to employees under *CTA 2009, Part 12, Chapter 2*.

Non-working shareholders

- 100% BPR is generally available on any shareholding in a trading company or group. This means that BPR can be obtained on both voting and non-voting shareholdings, including preference shares.

- All capital gains will normally be taxed at 28% (or possibly 18% for those on low income).

Chapter 4

Trading Company versus Investment Company Computations under CTSA

TAX STATUS OF COMPANY

General tax treatment of trading and investment companies

4.1   It is often important to determine whether a company is a trading company or an investment company since this may affect the tax reliefs or exemptions that are available to the company or its shareholders. For example, certain CGT and IHT reliefs may be enjoyed by shareholders of a trading company (or holding company of a trading group – see below), but not by shareholders of an investment company.

In this context, it should be appreciated that the definition of a 'trading company' for CGT Entrepreneurs' relief (ER), CGT business asset hold-over relief and the *corporate* Substantial Shareholdings Exemption (SSE) is markedly different from that used for most other tax purposes, particularly corporation tax.

Where family or owner-managed businesses are operated through a holding/subsidiary company structure, the holding company may be treated as carrying on an investment business even though it does little more than hold shares in its trading subsidiaries. However, the various tax reliefs given to the shareholders of trading companies are extended to situations where the shareholders own shares in a holding company of a trading group. Of course, where a holding company carries on a substantial trading activity in its own right, for example, supplying management and administrative support services to its trading subsidiaries for a management charge, it will often be treated as a trading company for tax purposes.

The computation of the taxable profits for each type of company is computed in a different way for corporation tax (see 4.2 and 4.3). For simplicity, this chapter covers the corporation tax treatment of both trading and investment companies. Although the legislation no longer insists on a company being an investment company to claim certain tax corporation tax reliefs, this chapter retains the 'investment company' nomenclature since, in practice, the vast majority of companies carrying on investment businesses will be colloquially known or identified as 'investment companies'.

This chapter also contains a summary of the corporation tax payment rules and the corporation tax self-assessment (CTSA) return, which is given at 4.48–4.51 and 4.53–4.54, respectively.

Trading companies

4.2   Broadly, for many tax purposes (with the notable exceptions of CGT ER, business asset hold-over relief and the corporate SSE) a trading company is one which exists *wholly or mainly* for the purpose of carrying on a trade.

In many cases, it will be clear that the company exists for trading purposes. In marginal cases, it may be possible to demonstrate that the company is a trading company by applying the 'wholly or mainly' test to the company's turnover, net profits, net assets and management time. Ideally, more than two should 'wholly or mainly' relate to the trading activities. HMRC usually regard the expression 'wholly or mainly' as meaning more than 50%.

4.3   A more stringent definition applies for CGT ER and CGT business asset hold-over relief. Here, the owner manager and the other shareholders only obtain ER if the company exists '*wholly* for the purpose of carrying on one or more trades', although the legislation ignores any *non-trading* activities where they have no substantial (ie 20%) effect on the total business (see 15.36– 15.38). A similar rule applies for corporate SSE (see 3.40 and 3.41).

CORPORATION TAX COMPUTATIONS

Pro-forma computation for trading company

4.4   A detailed pro-forma corporation tax computation for a typical trading company is set out below, together with accompanying notes. For corporation tax purposes, the assessable profits represent the amount of income and gains arising in the accounting period [*CTA 2009, ss 2* and *5(2)*]. The pro-forma computation is comprehensive so all items will not necessarily occur in the same period, for example, if the company claims relief for a current year trading loss, there will not be a trading profit, unless the company is carrying on another trade.

Pro-forma Trading Co Ltd

Corporation tax computation based on the accounting period ended

	£	£	Notes
Tax-adjusted trading profit (after deducting capital allowances) (see 4.71– 4.32)		X	(a)

	£	£	Notes
Less Trading losses brought forward under *CTA 2010, s 45* (see 4.38)	(X)	X	(b)
Property business income (net of allowable expenses)		X	(c)
Non-trading loan relationship profits (including interest receivable)	X		(d)
Less Non-trading loan relationship deficit carried back	(X)	X	
Dividends received from CFC and tax-haven companies		X	(e)/(f)
Other taxable income		X	
Chargeable gains (less allowable capital losses)		X	(g)
		X	
Less Non-trading loan relationship deficit brought forward (against **non-trading** profits only)		(X)	(h)
		X	
Less Current year non-trading loan relationship deficit		(X)	(h)
		X	
Less Current year trading loss offset under *CTA 2010, s 37(3)(a)* (see 4.34)		(X)	(i)
		X	
Less: Charitable donations relief		(X)	(j)
		X	
Less Group relief (see 4.39)		(X)	(k)
		X	
Less Trading losses carried back under *CTA 2010, s 37(3)(b)* (see 4.35)		(X)	(l)
TAXABLE TOTAL PROFITS		X	

Pro-forma computation of corporation tax liability

	£	Notes
Corporation tax on 'profits' @ X%	X	
Less Small profits marginal relief (see 3.15–3.20)	(X)	
	X	
Less Double tax relief	(X)	
	X	
Less Income tax on excess of unfranked investment income	(X)	
CORPORATION TAX LIABILITY	X	(m)

Notes:

(*a*)   All trading related interest and other trading loan relationship (LR) debits and credits are included in the company's tax-adjusted trading results. An allowable trading LR debit is available for 'impaired' debts (which includes bad and irrecoverable debts), unless they are due from 'connected companies'.

All types of interest payments to other UK companies (and UK banks) is now always paid gross (ie without any tax being deducted).

Amortisation or any write-off relating to goodwill and other intangibles is now dealt with under *Part 8* of the *CTA 2009* (previously introduced in *FA 2002, Sch 29* regime). However, this only includes goodwill and other intangibles acquired from third parties or created by the company/group after 31 March 2002. The amortisation and write-off of such goodwill/intangibles are deductible against the trading profits, broadly based on the amounts deducted in the company's accounts under GAAP. Similarly, any credits or profits arising on *post-31 March 2002 goodwill and intangibles* are generally taxed as part of the company's trading profits (see 12.46).

All patent royalties are deducted as a trading expense on an accruals basis, normally based on the amount reflected in the accounts (ie on an 'accruals basis') [*CTA 2009, s 728*]. Patent royalties to UK companies are paid gross.

(*b*)   Unused trading losses brought forward from the previous period can only be offset against trading profits of the *same* trade (see 4.38). Such losses are vulnerable to forfeiture if a major change in the conduct of the company's trade occurs within three years of a sale of the company (or other change in ownership [*CTA 2010, ss 673* and *674 (ICTA 1988, s 768)*] (see 12.56).

(*c*)   The corporation tax treatment of rental and other income from the letting of UK and overseas land and property is taxed as a single property business under *CTA 2009, s 209* (there is no need to keep separate results for each property). Broadly speaking, the profits and losses of the property business are computed on an accruals basis using the same principles for calculating taxable trading profits (see *CTA 2009, ss 210 and 214*). Capital allowances relating to a property business (for example, plant provided in the let property) is deducted as a property business expense. (Relief for a property business loss is examined in 4.43, note (*c*).)

(*d*)   Non-trading loan relationship (LR) profits include all *non-trading* interest receivable, such as bank, building society and intra-group interest and other profits arising from the company's *non-trading* LRs (including non-trading foreign exchange gains). In the case of a trading company, interest is invariably received on *non-trading* account.

However, any non-trading loan interest payable and other non-trading loan relationship/foreign exchange deficits must be deducted in arriving at the (net) 'non-trading' LR income [*CTA 2009, s 301(4)*] – interest on borrowings used to finance investments would be non-trading. A non-trading LR deficit may be carried back against the company's 'non-trade' loan relationship profits of the previous year [*CTA 2009, s 462*] (see also note (h) below and 4.43, note (*e*)).

(*e*) Dividends from *UK* companies are not chargeable to corporation tax [*CTA 2009, s 1285*] (but see note (*f*) below for recent developments).

(*f*) Since *1 July 2009*, the vast majority of dividends from foreign resident companies are exempt from UK corporation tax, although dividends from Controlled Foreign Companies (CFCs) and 'tax-haven' companies remain taxable. Thus, owner-managed companies can generally repatriate dividends from any overseas-resident company free of UK tax. It is therefore important to eliminate or reduce any overseas withholding tax, which can no longer be credited for double tax relief purposes and would therefore be a cost.

This exemption recognises that the UK could no longer continue to tax foreign dividends since this infringed EU legislation, as was confirmed by the decision in the recent *GLO* case (*The FII Group Litigation Order (GLO) (C-446/04)*).The *GLO* case concerned dividends from 'minority' holdings in EU-resident companies and determined that the UK's lack of 'underlying tax' relief for very small minority holdings (see below) infringed the EU treaty.

Under the *pre-1 July 2009* regime, the UK legislation taxed dividends from overseas companies, although in recent years some advisers considered that they were able to exempt them in company tax returns on the basis that this was supported by EU principles.

Before July 2009, the UK taxed foreign source dividends, which were 'grossed-up' for any withholding taxes and (where the company held more than 10% of the voting rights of the overseas company) the 'underlying tax'. The underlying tax represents the overseas tax payable on the profits out of which the dividend was paid [*TIOPA 2010, ss32* and *57–59 (ICTA 1988, ss 795(1)* and *799)*]. Double tax relief is claimed for these amounts up to a maximum limit, representing the UK corporation tax on the grossed-up dividend [*TIOPA 2010, ss 2–6* and *18 (ICTA 1988, ss 788* and *790)*]. These rules also apply to overseas dividends that remain taxable under the post-30 June 2009 regime.

The 'onshore pooling' regime enables the foreign tax borne on *qualifying* overseas dividends to be averaged together so as to represent foreign tax arising on a single 'pooled' dividend. Foreign tax of up to 45% can be included in the averaging calculation in respect of any single dividend.

The onshore pooling rules effectively help companies to obtain greater relief for foreign taxes on high and low taxed overseas dividends. Excess double tax relief can be carried back against the previous three years or against future years (same) foreign income.

(*g*) Chargeable gains are computed in the normal way with relief given for indexation. Roll-over relief may be available for gains arising on most types of fixed assets used in the trade (for example, property occupied for trading purposes and *fixed* plant and machinery). Capital gains arising on the disposal of (pre-*31 March 2002*) goodwill can only be rolled-over against the acquisition of 'new' goodwill and intangibles (see 15.14).

Profits arising on the *sale (realisation)* of *post-31 March 2002* acquired/ generated goodwill and other intangibles are included within the company's trading profits, but may be deferred under the intangibles roll-over regime in *CTA 2009, Chapter 7* (see 12.46–12.47).

Capital gains arising on the sale of trading subsidiaries and other qualifying shareholding investments should normally be exempt under the Substantial Shareholdings Exemption (SSE). Broadly speaking, the SSE applies to the disposal of both UK and overseas resident trading companies which have been (at least) 10% owned throughout the 12 months before the disposal (see 3.40).

(*h*) A non-trading loan relationship (LR) deduction is available for interest payable on loans taken out for non-trading purposes and any losses or deficits arising on non-trading loans (including non-trading foreign exchange losses). The amount eligible for a non-trading deduction must be computed *after* deducting any non-trading interest income and other non-trading loan related profits.

Under *CTA 2009, ss 456* to *463*, a non-trading LR deficit can be relieved in one or more of the following ways:

(i) offset against the company's taxable profits of the same corporation tax accounting period (CTAP)

(ii) surrendered under the group relief provisions for offset against the current year profits of fellow (75%) group members or consortium company claimants

(iii) carried back for offset against the company's *non-trading LR profits* of the previous year; or

(iv) carried forward for offset against the company's total *non-trading* profits of the *next* CTAP (or the following CTAP after that). (The carry-forward relief is fairly restrictive for a *trading* company as it will not normally have much in the way of *non-trading* profits, although it might, for example, have a significant one-off capital gain that can be sheltered.)

(*i*)   A current year trading loss (see 4.34) is deducted against profits *before* deducting charges on income [*CTA 2010, s 189 (ICTA 1988, s 338(1))*].

(*j*)   Under the *CTA 2010*, donations to charities are given as 'charitable donations relief' (they were previously deducted as non-trade charges on income). They are relieved in the CTAP in which they are paid and deducted from the company's total profits after any other relief but before group relief. Qualifying charitable donations broadly comprise payments to charities (which are made 'gross') and the value of assets gifted to a charity [*CTA 2010, Part 6 (ICTA 1988, ss 338–339]*.

(*k*)   Losses claimed from other group companies by way of group relief are deducted in priority to trading losses carried back from a subsequent period [*CTA 2010, s137(4), (5) (ICTA 1988, s 407(1)(a))*].

(*l*)   If trading losses are carried back under *CTA 2010, s 37(3)(b) ICTA 1988, s 393A(1)(b)*, (see 4.35) they are set-off *before* charitable donations relief, which may therefore become unrelieved. If the company is a member of a group, it may be possible to surrender the charitable donations relief by way of group relief.

(*m*)   'Large' companies pay their tax under the quarterly instalment rules. For these purposes, a large company is one whose taxable profits exceed the upper limit of £1,500,000 for the CTAP. This limit is apportioned, where appropriate, to take account of active associated companies (see 3.23) and periods of less than 12 months (see 4.48 for further details).

All other companies (generally those which pay tax at the small profits rate or enjoy small profits marginal relief) pay all their corporation tax nine months after the end of their CTAP.

CALCULATING THE TAX-ADJUSTED TRADING PROFIT

Importance of GAAP

4.5   The principal source of income for a trading company would be its trading profits. The starting point for computing the tax-adjusted trading profit will be the accounting profit, which will have been prepared on generally accepted commercial and accounting principles (eg see *Johnston v Britannia Airways* [1994] STC 763). There is now a statutory requirement for a company's profits to be computed in accordance with generally accepted accounting practice (GAAP), except where this is overridden by legislative provisions [*CA 2006, s 46*].

In recent years, the courts have placed considerable weight on generally accepted accounting principles (GAAP) in determining the way in which an item should be treated for tax purposes (in the absence of a contrary statutory rule). HMRC accept that GAAP determines the period in which income or expenditure is recognised for tax purposes. The tax treatment of year-end provisions which often gave rise to disputes with HMRC has now been codified by Financial Reporting Standard 12 (FRS12), which determines when a provision can be charged in a company's accounts (it does not deal with provisions which adjust the carrying value of assets). (Similar rules are laid down in the Financial Reporting Standard for Smaller Entities.) The basic rule is that a provision can only be made where the company has an obligation (legally or constructively by its actions) to incur expenditure as a result of past events. The provision must be estimated with reasonable accuracy. It is accepted that any provision validly made under FRS12 will be allowed for tax purposes unless the amount relates to disallowable capital expenditure or is treated differently under specific tax legislation (see *IR Press Release dated 20 July 1999*). Consequently, the accounting and tax treatment of various important provisions will be as follows:

- provisions for future repairs and overhauls of plant and machinery will no longer be admitted unless the obligation to incur the expenditure has crystallised at the balance sheet date;

- provisions for restructuring and reorganisation can only be made at the balance sheet date where the company has a detailed plan and has raised a valid expectation among those affected that it will be implemented;

- provision must be made where a contract becomes onerous, for example, where a company vacates leasehold premises and remains responsible for the lease rents.

The principle of allowing relief for future rentals payable on vacated premises was accepted in *Herbert Smith v Honour* [1999] STC 173. The Revenue abandoned their appeal against the decision and they now accept that there is no rule of tax law which prevents provisions for 'anticipated' losses and events. This is confirmed by the Revenue's decision to allow provisions for foreseeable losses on long-term work in progress contracts (*see IR Press Release dated 20 July 1999*).

In the author's experience, HMRC are increasingly looking at provisions in their enquiries and regularly refer provisions (and other items relating to the application of GAAP) to their 'in-house' accountants to comment on their validity under FRS 12.

As the concept of materiality does not exist for corporation tax, this may lead to a mismatch between what the company's auditors have agreed is a true and fair figure in the accounts and what HMRC believes to be the case. It is therefore always advisable to consider such provisions thoroughly from a corporation tax perspective, and document them accordingly. (See 4.9 for the treatment of bad debt provisions generally.)

Adjustments to company's profit and loss account

4.6 The company's profit and loss account will invariably include non-trading and capital items and various adjustments must be made in order to arrive at the assessable trading profit. However, amounts relating to a company's 'loan relationships' (including interest) and intangible fixed assets (within the Intangible fixed assets regime (including patent royalties) are generally reflected within the trading profit. The tax deductible or taxable amounts are usually based on the amounts reflected in the accounts under generally accepted accounting practice (GAAP).

The changes introduced by the *Finance Act 2004* dealing with the application of International Accounting Standards currently only apply to *listed* and AIM companies and are unlikely to affect owner-managed or family companies.

Certain types of expenditure charged in the accounts are not deductible for tax purposes. For example, depreciation on fixed assets must be added back to the profits and replaced by capital allowances, which is the statutory tax relief for capital expenditure (see 4.13–4.32). On the other hand, any amortisation of goodwill or other intangible fixed assets created or acquired by the company (from an unrelated third party) after 31 March 2002 is deducted under *CTA 2009, Part 8* (previously the *FA 2002, Sch 29* regime) (see 12.46–12.47).

Income that is dealt with under a different tax regime or category must be excluded from the accounting profit and dealt with under the relevant rules for that tax regime. Similarly, income that is exempt from tax must be excluded.

A trading loss will arise where the allowable expenses and capital allowances exceed the trading receipts.

Computation of taxable trading profits

4.7 A pro-forma computation for the adjustment of trading profits for tax purposes is given below.

Taxable trading profit computation

	£	£
Net profit on ordinary activities before taxation per accounts		X
Add Depreciation (except on intangible fixed assets created/ acquired *after 31 March 2002*)	X	
Loss on disposal of fixed assets	X	
Capital expenditure (eg alterations, improvements) charged to repairs, etc	X	
Entertaining (client)	X	

	£	£
Non-trading interest payable	X	
Non-trading foreign exchange losses	X	
Legal and professional charges (eg relating to disposals/ purchases of property)	X	
Donations	X	
Increase in general provisions	X	
Pension contributions charged to profit and loss account	X	
Remuneration accrued, but not paid within nine months of end of period	X	
	—	
	X	
Less Relief for employee share awards and share options (see note 8.86 below)	(X)	
Adjustment for qualifying research and development expenditure – (see note 4.32 below)	(X)	
Profit on sale of fixed assets/investments	(X)	
Other capital profits/gains	(X)	
Dividends received from UK companies	(X)	
Income from overseas companies	(X)	
Bank deposit interest	(X)	
Building society interest	(X)	
Other non-trading loan interest receivable	(X)	
Non-trading foreign exchange profits	(X)	
Net property rental income	(X)	
Other investment income	(X)	
Decrease in general provisions	(X)	
Pension contributions paid in period	(X)	
Pension scheme refund	(X)	
Non-taxable income	(X)	
Accrued remuneration paid more than nine months after end of previous period	(X)	
Capital allowances (net of balancing charges)		
– Plant and machinery (see 4.13–4.32)	(X)	
– Industrial buildings	(X)	
– Other	(X)	
		(X)
Tax adjusted trading profit/(loss)		X

'Wholly and exclusively' requirement for trading expenses

4.8   It is well known that a trading company can only obtain relief against its trading profits for those expenses that have been incurred wholly and exclusively for the purposes of its trade [*CTA 2009, s 54* (previously *ICTA 1988, s 74*)].

The *Corporation Tax Act 2009* (which applies for accounting periods ending after 31 March 2009) now makes it clear partial relief can be given where expenditure is incurred for 'mixed' purposes. In such cases, relief can be claimed for 'any identifiable part or identifiable proportion of the expense which is incurred wholly and exclusively for trading purposes' [*CTA 2009, s 54(2)*].

Relief for impaired/bad debts (and debt releases)

Trade debts

4.9   Companies can generally obtain tax relief for 'impaired' trading debts written-off and specific provisions against doubtful trading debts (which are dealt with under the loan relationship (LR) rules) by virtue of *CTA 2009, s 481(1)(3)(d)*. (Trade debts come within the 'non-lending' relationships within *CTA 2009, s 479*.) (Trade debts were brought within the LR regime by the *F(No2)A 2005* – one important practical effect of this change was to deny impairment relief for trade debts between connected companies (see 4.10))

To ensure impairment relief is claimable, it would generally be necessary to demonstrate that the 'bad or doubtful' debt has arisen in the normal course of the company's trade and the relevant transactions had been commercially motivated. In assessing the amount that may need to be treated as an 'impairment loss' (ie bad or doubtful), it is permissible to take account of events and circumstances arising after the balance sheet date (but before the date the accounts are signed off) where they provide further evidence of conditions that existed at the 'balance sheet' date (*IR Tax Bulletin, Issue 12*). Relief can also be claimed where a trade debt is written-off as a result of a formal release by the 'creditor' company.

The *F(No 2)A 2005* changes meant that treatment of released debts between connected companies lacked symmetry. The 'connected' creditor was denied tax relief for the debit under the normal LR restriction for debts between connected companies whilst the 'connected' debtor company was still taxed on the release. This 'anomaly' no longer arises for debts released from 22 April 2009 onwards. *CTA 2009, s 481(1)(3)(f)* now ensures that the release is dealt with under the LR regime, so that it would be 'tax-free' under the normal 'connected companies' LR rules. (*CTA 2009, s 464(1)* gives loan relationships priority over any other taxing provisions, so *CTA 2009, s 94* no longer applies to 'money' trade debts.) However, this rule also means that an 'unconnected' creditor would generally be taxed on the release under normal LR principles.

A special exemption applies where a debt is released under a statutory insolvency arrangement. In such cases, *CTA 2009, s 322 (3)* enables the credit released to profit and loss account to be 'tax-free'.

Funding loans

4.10   Funding or finance loans are dealt with under the LR regime and therefore follow the same principles as in 4.9. Thus, impairment relief is generally available on doubtful and irrecoverable loans. Similarly, debits arising from 'releases' are tax-deductible.

However, no LR relief is available for the impairment write-off or 'debit release' of a 'connected' company debt [*CTA 2009, s 354*]. This rule applies where a company is connected at any time in the accounting period.

In broad terms, a company is 'connected' with another company where one of the companies controls the other or where they are both under the control of the same company [*CTA 2009, s 466 (2)*]. (For these purposes, control would be exercised by a company where it is able conduct another company's affairs according to its wishes (whether through the holding of shares, voting power or by powers contained in the articles of association).)

An allowable LR debit is given where a debt is released as part of a qualifying 'debt/equity' swap even where the relevant companies become connected in the accounting period in which the swap takes place (see 11.22 to 11.24 for detailed analysis).

TRANSFER PRICING REGIME

Overview

4.11   CT600 self-assessment returns must apply arm's-length transfer prices on all transactions with 'connected persons'. Broadly speaking, the transfer pricing rules normally only apply where a UK company is 'large' (or is part of a 'large' group) as defined under EU guidelines. The transfer pricing rules are contained in *TIOPA 2010, ss 147–217* (*ICTA 1988, Sch 28AA*).

A 'large' owner managed company must therefore apply 'arm's length' transfer pricing on all transactions with any fellow-group or 'sister' companies – irrespective of whether they are UK or non-UK resident for tax purposes. Examples where arm's length transfer pricing would be used may include:

- The sale of goods to an overseas subsidiary that acts as a sales distributor in the overseas country. The goods might be sold to the overseas company on a 're-sale' price basis after making appropriate deductions for the overseas company's sale and marketing costs and their resale 'profit margin'. An alternative approach would be to apply a cost-plus method – such as cost to UK company plus (say) 20% to 25%.

- Provision of management and administrative support to all group companies – a management charge would be rendered to each company on a 'fair and justifiable' basis, bearing in mind the time spent and the salary/staff costs and attributable overheads. The company may devise a standard costing model to arrive at a reasonable hourly rate for management and administrative support services.

- The licensing of intellectual property (IP) to other group companies – a charge may be made on (say) a 'royalty' rate basis on sales or by a 'profit-split' method which allocates the profit from using the IP to each company on a reasonable basis.

- Loans made to overseas companies – the company must charge a commercial rate of interest on the loans – which might, for example, be LIBOR + 6% to 10%, depending on lending risk.

Large companies within the scope of the UK transfer pricing rules must be vigilant and ensure they identify all services that are provided to their fellow 'group' companies, ensuring that a commensurate commercial price is charged to them. This exercise may not always be straightforward as some services may be of an indirect nature or 'hidden'.

There is a limited exemption for companies that were dormant at 31 March 2004 (the 'start-date' for the revised UK transfer pricing regime), with the exception of an intra-group balance. In such cases, provided the company was dormant for at least three months up to 31 March 2004, it will stay outside the scope of the transfer pricing rules so long as it remains dormant. Thus, interest will need to be charged on intra-group balances with companies that became dormant from 1 April 2004. It is accepted that establishing an appropriate 'arm's length' price sometimes involves a degree of judgement and HMRC is generally prepared to discuss particular transfer pricing issues before a CT600 return is made or before the transactions take place.

Companies may wish to avoid reporting commercial transfer pricing in their accounts. This is acceptable to HMRC provided the company makes appropriate transfer pricing adjustments in its tax computation and CT600.

Under CTSA, companies have a statutory obligation to keep and retain appropriate records and support documentation to back up their transfer pricing policies and implementation. This would include the primary accounting records, details of transactions with 'connected companies' and any appropriate tax adjustments to ensure the computations reflect 'arm's length' transfer-pricing. There are stringent penalties for non-compliance – see 4.56.

Whenever a transfer pricing adjustment is made in the tax computation of the company providing the goods/services, the UK legislation enables the 'counterpart' UK company to claim a corresponding adjustment (eg an increase in the relevant expenses) to its taxable profits/income in its own tax return [*TIOPA 2010, ss 174–176 (ICTA 1988, Sch 28AA, para 6)*]. The counterpart UK resident company must make their corresponding adjustment within two years from the date the 'provider' UK company makes its adjustment. HMRC cannot, of course, require an overseas tax jurisdiction to make a 'corresponding adjustment' in an *overseas* company's tax return, but double taxation would result if no relief were granted. Consequently, most of the UK's double tax treaties allow a 'mutual agreement' procedure, under which the overseas tax authority (known as the 'competent authority') is required to consider granting corresponding relief. If the case cannot be resolved by the overseas tax authority unilaterally, both HMRC and the overseas tax authority can consult to resolve the case by mutual agreement, but this cannot be guaranteed. The general time limit for seeking 'competent authority' are often based on Article 25 of the OECD Model Treaty, which provides a three year period from the notification of the 'double tax' issue. Cases involving connected EU companies are decided under the European Arbitration Convention.

UK groups may be affected by transfer pricing adjustments made by an overseas tax jurisdiction. This might be the case where, for example, an overseas company provides support services to a 'connected' UK resident company. In this case, the UK company would have to seek relief by making a competent authority claim (see *TIOPA 2010, ss 214* and *215 (ICTA 1988, s 815AA)*). Small and medium-sized companies are generally exempt from the UK's transfer pricing rules – see 4.12 below).

4.12   Small and medium-sized enterprises (SMEs) do *not* have to apply statutory transfer pricing principles on their dealings with 'connected' UK companies or on the vast majority of cross-border transactions with their 'connected' overseas companies. The exemption to overseas companies applies where the overseas jurisdiction's double tax treaty with the UK contains a non-discrimination article [*TIOPA 2010, ss 166* and *167 (ICTA 1988, Sch 28AA, para 5B)*].

This exemption would cover EU countries, Australia, Canada, Japan and the USA and many other developed countries (see HMRC website for full details). In practice, this means that SMEs would apply transfer pricing on transactions with 'connected' companies based in tax-havens [*TIOPA 2010, s 167(3) (ICTA 1988, Sch 28AA, para 5B(4))*].

An SME company can also elect to 'disapply' its exemption from the transfer pricing rules for a particular CTAP. Where the election is made, all its relevant transactions will be subject to arm's length transfer pricing [*TIOPA 2010, s 167(2) ICTA 1988, Sch 28AA, para 5B(3)*].

SMEs are defined under special EU regulations (*CTA 2010, s 172 (ICTA 1988, Sch 28AA, para 5D* and the *Annex* to the *Commission Recommendation 2003/361/EC* of 6 May 2003). It is important to appreciate that the relevant economic/financial criteria are tested on a (consolidated) group basis:

	Small Company	*Medium-sized Company*
Employees	Less than 50	Less than 250
AND EITHER		
Turnover	*Less than* €10 (approx £9) million	*Less than* €50 (approx £44) million
OR		
Balance sheet total (ie Gross Asset value)	*Less than* €10 (approx £9) million	*Less than* €43 (approx £38) million

Notes:

1   The above criteria can apply to any form of business enterprise, but only companies are covered here.

2   The test are considered separately for each period - .to satisfy either the 'small' or 'medium' sized criteria, the company must meet the 'employee headcount' condition *and either* the 'turnover' *or* 'balance sheet' conditions.

3   Translations to sterling (£) should be done at the average rate for the period.

4   The *appropriate pro-rata share* of employees/turnover/gross assets of linked enterprises and relevant partnership interests must be included.

In broad terms, a linked enterprise is one which can be controlled through shareholding, voting or contractual rights. A relevant partnership interest is one where at least 25% of a partnership's capital or voting rights are held.

In the case of medium-sized enterprises only, HMRC also have the power to apply the transfer pricing rules. Where this power is invoked, the UK company would receive a 'transfer pricing' notice for the relevant CTAP requiring appropriate adjustments to its UK profits. Any right of appeal against the notice can only be made on the basis that the company is a 'small enterprise'. It is expected that this power would only be exercised where there is blatant manipulation leading to a significant loss of UK tax.

Capital allowances

4.13   Capital expenditure incurred cannot be deducted against the taxable trading profit. Expenditure charged to fixed assets in the accounts will invariably be treated as capital expenditure. The periodic write-off of fixed asset expenditure through depreciation charges will be disallowed (although the amortisation of intangibles and goodwill (acquired or created after 31 March 2002 is allowable under *CTA 2009, Part 8*). Certain capital expenditure may also be charged directly against profits and, for tax purposes, this must also be disallowed. However, provided the capital expenditure falls into one of the defined categories, tax relief will be given through the capital allowances system.

There has been a considerable amount of tinkering with capital allowances over recent years – hardly giving business a stable framework to plan their capital investment. A major change occurred from April 2008 when an Annual Investment Allowance (AIA) for plant and machinery expenditure of up to £50,000 for each year was introduced. AIA-eligible expenditure is immediately written off for tax purposes. The AIA limit increased to £100,000 from 1 April 2009 but the June 2010 Budget announced that it will be cut to £25,000 from April 2012. Expenditure in excess of the £50,000/£100,000 AIA limit (which may be lower for separate group companies) then qualifies for WDAs or FYAs depending on the rules for that period. A temporary first year allowance (FYA) of 40% on plant and machinery was introduced in the Budget 2009, but only on expenditure in the 12 months to 31 March 2010. This temporary 40% FYA was given to all companies, irrespective of their size! (see 4.21).

Plant and machinery acquired between 1 April 2010 and 31 March 2012, will therefore attract a 100% AIA on the first £100,000 of qualifying expenditure with any balance being eligible for the normal 20% annual WDAs. From April 2012, the WDA rate reduces to 18% pa.

Industrial Buildings allowances were completely abolished on 1 April 2011 .

The main types of capital allowances and the current rates obtainable for each class of expenditure are set out below. Capital allowances must be claimed on the company's tax return [*CAA 2001, s 3*].

Current main rates of capital allowances

4.14

	Note	Initial/ first-year allowance (FYA) and AIA	Writing-down allowance (WDA) and AIA
Plant and machinery (see also (standard rate) 4.15–4.18)	(*a*) (*b*)	40%	20%/18%
		10%/8% (reduced rate)	
Annual Investment Allowance (AIA) (see 4.20)	(*c*)	(100% on first £100,000/ £25,000	

132

	Note	Initial/ first-year allowance (FYA) and AIA	Writing-down allowance (WDA) and AIA
Enhanced capital allowances			
Low-emission (up to 110 g/km CO_2 emission) cars (see 4.23)	*(d)*	100%	
Natural gas/hydrogen refuelling equipment	*(d)*	100%	
Designated energy efficient or water saving plant (see 4.23)	*(e)*	100%	
Environmentally beneficial plant and machinery (see 4.23)	*(f)*	100%	
Other cars			
Cars – 100g/km to 160 g/km CO_2 emissions (see 4.25)			20% (main pool)
Cars – over 160 g/km CO_2 emissions (see 4.25)			10% (special rate pool)
'Long-life' plant and machinery (see also 12.45)	*(g)*		10%
Renovation of business premises in disadvantaged areas	*(h)*	100%	
Enterprise zone buildings		100%	
Research and development		100%	
Qualifying 'flat-conversions' above shops	*(i)*	100%	
Industrial buildings and hotels (see also 12.39)	*(j)*		1% (2010/11) 2% (2009/10)
Agricultural works and buildings	*(j)*		1% (2010/11) 2% (2009/10)

Notes:

(a) A temporary FYA of 40% is available to all companies for eligible plant and machinery expenditure incurred in the 12 months to 31 March 2010.

Between 1 April 2005 and 1 April 2008, 40% FYAs used to be generally available to small or medium-sized companies only, with a special 50%

FYA being given to small companies between 1 April 2006 and 31 March 2008 (and between 1 April 2004 and 31 March 2005).

From 1 April 2012 the annual WDA rate is 18% (a hybrid rate is computed for accounting periods straddling this date (see 4.30)). Between 1 April 2008 and 31 March 2011, the WDA rate is 20% (25% before 1 April 2008).

Since 2004. a company will be small or medium-sized where at least two of the three thresholds are satisfied for the current or previous financial year:

	Small	**Medium**
	Not more than:	*Not more than:*
Turnover	£5.6 million	£22.8 million
Balance sheet – total Assets	£2.8 million	£11.4 million
Number of employees	50	250

Where a company is a member of a group (including a group owned by an overseas parent) the *consolidated* group must be small or medium-sized by reference to the above criteria. These definitions follow *Companies Act 2006, ss 382* and *465, [CAA 2001, ss 47(2) and 49]*.

FYAs *cannot* generally be claimed on cars (other than taxis and certain low-emission or electrically propelled cars (see note (*d*) below)), plant and machinery used in a leasing trade, and plant acquired from a 'connected' person.

(*b*) Expenditure included in the special rate pool attracts a lower WDA of 8% (10% before 1 April 2012).

The Finance Act 2008 introduced the special rate pool which includes integral features (see 4.24 for details), thermal insulation (such as roof lining, double glazing and cavity wall insulation), long life assets (see (d) below and 4.25) and (since April 2009) cars with CO_2 emissions of 160k/km or more.

(*c*) The Annual Investment Allowance (AIA) is available on the first £100,000 of qualifying plant and machinery expenditure in a 12 month CTAP. This AIA expenditure limit reduces to £25,000 from 1 April 2012. Where an accounting period straddles 1 April 2012, there are transitional rules which deal with the amount of AIA that may be claimed (see 4.00).

AIAs were first introduced from 1 April 2008 and the pre-1 April 2010 annual limit was £50,000 (see 4.20).

(*d*) Low-emission cars (that emit no more than 110g/km of CO_2), electric cars, or (from April 2010) zero emission goods vehicles qualify for 100% FYAs (regardless of the company's size)

100% FYAs can also be claimed on expenditure on natural gas/hydrogen refuelling equipment, such as storage tanks, pumps, controls, etc. These types of 100% FYAs are available to all companies irrespective of their size.

(*e*)   Since April 2001, *any company* can claim 100% FYAs on expenditure on designated energy-saving plant and equipment specified on the 'Energy Technology List'. This list is highly prescriptive, specifying the individual items of plant, etc made by each manufacturer that meets the required energy efficiency criteria. Products that qualify are contained on the Energy Technology list (www.eca.gov.uk) which is continuously updated.

Eligible categories of energy saving plant and equipment include:

- boilers;
- combined heat and power systems;
- compressed-air equipment;
- heat pumps;
- radiant and warm air heaters;
- refrigeration display cabinets;
- solar thermal systems; and
- thermal screens.

(*f*)   Any company can claim 100% FYAs on *designated energy efficient or water saving* plant . Such plant must meet strict water saving or efficiency criteria. Current eligible items include specified meters and monitoring equipment, flow controllers, leakage detection systems and efficient toilets and taps.

(*g*)   Since 1 April 2008, expenditure on 'long life' plant is included in the 'special rate' pool (see (b) above). The annual WDA rate on long life plant is therefore 8% (10% between 1 April 2008 to 31 March 2012 and 6% before 1 April 2008)

The long-life asset rules apply to certain types of plant with a working life of 25 years or more, provided the company spends more than the annual *de minimis* limit of £100,000 (apportioned amongst associated companies) for the accounting period.

Plant and machinery which is a fixture in or provided for use in a retail shop, showroom, hotel or office is specifically excluded from 'long-life' asset treatment and is therefore eligible for 'normal' allowances.

(*h*)   A 100% Business Premises Renovation Allowance (BPRA) is given for capital expenditure incurred on the conversion or renovation of qualifying business premises situated in a 'designated' disadvantaged area. The premises must be situated in a 'disadvantaged' area and must not have been used for at least one year before the renovation work begins – its last use being as office accommodation or for general trading purposes (but *not* as a dwelling). The 100% allowance is particularly attractive for renovated shops and commercial offices (since they would typically attract little or no relief under the capital allowances legislation).

Only conversion work qualifies for the 100% BPRA (ie it does not include (for example) expenditure on buying the building, extending it (other than to provide access), or on plant and machinery (other than fixtures)). No balancing charge/allowance is made if the renovated building continues to be used (or suitable and available for letting) for at least seven years after the remedial work [*CAA 2001, ss 360A to 360Z4*].

(*i*)   100% FYAs are given on the capital cost of a qualifying 'flat-conversion' above a pre-1980 shop and are primarily deductible against the property rental business income from the flat.

(*j*)   Writing down allowances on industrial buildings and hotels, and agricultural works/buildings were gradually phased out from April 2008 and finally abolished on 1 April 2011.

PLANT AND MACHINERY ALLOWANCES

Main conditions

4.15   A company qualifies for plant and machinery allowances provided it carries on a 'qualifying activity' (the most common category being a trade) and incurs 'qualifying expenditure' [*CAA 2001, s 11*]. To qualify:

● a company's expenditure must be of a capital nature on the provision of plant or machinery (wholly or partly) for its qualifying activity; and

● the company must own the asset as a result of incurring the expenditure.

It is a fundamental requirement that capital expenditure must be incurred. Sometimes, there may be problems in determining whether loose tools, utensils and other 'short life' items should be treated as capital or revenue. Based on the ruling in *Hinton v Maden and Ireland Ltd* [1959] 38 TC 391, if the anticipated life of the relevant item is less than two years, the expenditure may normally be written off as a trading expense. If the plant's useful life is likely to exceed two years then it will normally be considered a capital asset on which capital allowances can usually be claimed [*CTA 2009, s 53 (ICTA 1988, s 74(1)(d))*].

Meaning of 'plant'

4.16   The tax legislation does not define the meaning of 'plant' although it does specify items that are deemed to be 'plant' (for example, alterations to an existing building incidental to the installation of plant or machinery [*CAA 2001, s 25*]). It has been left to the courts to establish those items that qualify as plant and as companies have tried to extend the scope of the meaning of plant, there has been a plethora of tax cases on this particular subject.

The leading case of *Yarmouth v France* (1887) 19 QBD 647 established three important conditions for an item to qualify as plant, namely:

(*a*)   it must be apparatus;

(*b*)   it must be used for the carrying on of the business;

(*c*)   it must be kept for permanent use in the business.

Subsequent cases introduced a further qualification that the item must not form part of the premises in or upon which the business is conducted. This fundamental distinction between 'setting' and 'apparatus' is central to most of the cases on the identification of plant. The courts have invariably applied the 'apparatus' test in determining whether the relevant item fulfils a functional role (either active or passive) in the carrying on of a particular trade. For example, those items accepted as plant include office partitioning (moved frequently to meet trading conditions) (*Jarrold v John Good & Sons Ltd* (1962) 40 TC 681) and decorative articles contributing to the atmosphere in a hotel (*CIR v Scottish and Newcastle Breweries Ltd* [1982] STC 296).

Following the ruling in *Scottish and Newcastle Breweries Ltd*, HMRC will generally accept that expenditure on 'ambience' or 'decorative' plant is eligible for capital allowances where they are provided for the enjoyment of the public in a hotel, restaurant or similar trades. Typically, the trade would involve the creating an appropriate 'ambience' for its customer and the plant would be specially chosen to achieve that.

In *Wimpy International Ltd v Warland* [1989] STC 273, Lord Justice Fox re-affirmed the well established 'premises' test. Items will not qualify as plant where they are part of the premises or place in which the business is conducted, as opposed to being an asset with which the business is conducted.

Some important guidance with regard to fitting-out costs of existing premises is provided in the First Tier Tribunal ruling in *JD Wetherspoon v HMRC* [2009] UKFTT 374 (TC). This case involved a £33 million refurbishment project undertaken by Weatherspoon. Importantly, capital allowance claims were upheld on a wide range of items on the grounds they were 'incidental' building alterations to permit the installation of plant or machinery. Based on the precise facts, these included the replacement of various floors, drainage installations, kitchen and toilet walls, lighting to toilets, toilet cubicles and a reinforced kitchen floor. The Tribunal also confirmed the approach normally adopted in practice in relation to the allocation of preliminary costs (such as overheads and professional fees), stating that these costs can usually be apportioned on an appropriate 'pro-rata' basis.

Items that have been held not to be plant under the premises test include:

- a metal canopy over petrol pumps at a petrol filling station (*Dixon v Fitch's Garage Ltd* [1975] STC 480); and

- false ceilings concealing piping and wiring (*Hampton v Fortes Autogrill Ltd* [1980] STC 80).

Restrictions for buildings and structures

4.17   Case law and HMRC practice have established that, in certain circumstances, structural and other items included in buildings qualify as 'plant' for capital allowance purposes. However, HMRC attempted to restrict any further extension in this area by introducing a statutory code in the *Finance Act 1994* (mainly due to a number of cases brought to the Commissioners by certain large supermarket chains). Broadly, expenditure on buildings (including any assets forming part of a building), structures and on land alterations will *not* qualify as plant unless it falls into one of the various categories specified in List C [*CAA 2001, s 23*].

List C (see 4.18) attempts to codify those items that case law or HMRC practice has previously treated as plant.

The legislation first specifies those buildings (including assets incorporated within buildings), structures or any works involving land alterations which are deemed *not* to be plant (but may, of course, qualify for industrial buildings allowances and so on). These items are listed in Lists A and B (*CAA 2001, ss 21* and *22*) which are fully reproduced below.

List A

Assets treated as buildings

1.   Walls, floors, ceilings, doors, gates, shutters, windows and stairs.

2.   Mains services, and systems, for water, electricity and gas.

3.   Waste disposal systems.

4.   Sewerage and drainage systems.

5.   Shafts or other structures in which lifts, hoists, escalators and moving walkways are installed.

6.   Fire safety systems.

List B

Excluded structures and other assets

1.   A tunnel, bridge, viaduct, aqueduct, embankment or cutting.

2.   A way, hard standing (such as a pavement), road, railway, tramway, a park for vehicles or containers, or an airstrip or runway.

3.   An inland navigation, including a canal or basin or a navigable river.

4.   A dam, reservoir or barrage, including any sluices, gates, generators and other equipment associated with the dam, reservoir or barrage.

5.   A dock, harbour, wharf, pier, marina or jetty or any other structure in or at which vessels may be kept, or merchandise or passengers may be shipped or unshipped.

6.   A dike, sea wall, weir or drainage ditch.

7.   Any structure not within items 1 to 6 other than —

    (*a*)   a structure (but not a building) within *Chapter 2* of *Part 3* (meaning of 'industrial building'),

    (*b*)   a structure in use for the purposes of an undertaking for the extraction, production, processing or distribution of gas, and

    (*c*)   a structure in use for the purposes of a trade which consists in the provision of telecommunication, television or radio services.

Items unaffected by deemed 'non-plant' treatment

4.18   Numerous categories of expenditure are not affected by the deemed 'non-plant' treatment. First, expenditure on thermal insulation, fire safety, etc are statutorily treated as plant (see *CAA 2001, ss 28–32*). List C (reproduced below) also 'carves out' 33 important generic headings from the deemed 'non-plant' rules in Lists A and B above and may therefore be plant (depending on the facts of the case and case law precedent) [*CAA 2001, s 23*].

This list was also amended from 1 April 2008 as a result of the new rules for integral features, which now only qualify for a lower WDA of 8% per annum (10% per annum before 1 April 2012). (The various items listed in 4.24 were deleted from list C from 1 April 2008).

List C

Expenditure unaffected by sections 21 and 22

1. Machinery (including devices for providing motive power) not within any other item in this list.

2. Gas and sewerage systems provided mainly —

    (*a*) to meet the particular requirements of the qualifying activity, or

    (*b*) to serve particular plant or machinery used for the purposes of the qualifying activity.

3. ...

4. Manufacturing or processing equipment; storage equipment (including cold rooms); display equipment; and counters, checkouts and similar equipment.

5. Cookers, washing machines, dishwashers, refrigerators and similar equipment; washbasins, sinks, baths, showers, sanitary ware and similar equipment; and furniture and furnishings.

6. Hoists.

7. Sound insulation provided mainly to meet the particular requirement of the qualifying activity.

8. Computer, telecommunication and surveillance systems (including their wiring or other links).

9. Refrigeration or cooling equipment.

10. Fire alarm systems; sprinkler and other equipment for extinguishing or containing fires.

11. Burglar alarm systems.

12. Strong rooms in bank or building society premises; safes.

13. Partition walls, where moveable and intended to be moved in the course of the qualifying activity.

14. Decorative assets provided for the enjoyment of the public in hotel, restaurant or similar trades.

15. Advertising hoardings; signs, displays and similar assets.

16. Swimming pools (including diving boards, slides and structures on which such boards or slides are mounted).

17. Any glasshouse constructed so that the required environment (namely, air, heat, light, irrigation and temperature) for the growing of plants is provided automatically by means of devices forming an integral part of its structure.

18.   Cold stores.

19.   Caravans provided mainly for holiday lettings.

20.   Buildings provided for testing aircraft engines run within the buildings.

21.   Moveable buildings intended to be moved in the course of the qualifying activity.

22.   The alteration of land for the purpose only of installing plant or machinery.

23.   The provision of dry docks.

24.   The provision of any jetty or similar structure provided mainly to carry plant or machinery.

25.   The provision of pipelines or underground ducts or tunnels with a primary purpose of carrying utility conduits.

26.   The provision of towers to support floodlights.

27.   The provision of —

   (*a*)   any reservoir incorporated into a water treatment works, or

   (*b*)   any service reservoir of treated water for supply within any housing estate or other particular locality.

28.   The provision of —

   (*a*)   silos provided for temporary storage, or

   (*b*)   storage tanks.

29.   The provision of slurry pits or silage clamps.

30.   The provision of fish tanks or fish ponds.

31.   The provision of rails, sleepers and ballast for a railway or tramway.

32.   The provision of structures and other assets for providing the setting for any ride at an amusement park or exhibition.

33.   The provision of fixed zoo cages.

Note: Items 1 to 16 do not include any asset 'whose principal purpose is to insulate or enclose the interior of a building or to provide an interior wall, floor or ceiling which (in each case) is intended to remain permanently in place' [*CAA 2001, s 23(4)*].

Timing of Annual Investment Allowance (AIAs) and other capital allowances

4.19 Plant and machinery may qualify for the annual investment allowance (AIA), temporary first year allowances ('FYAs') (until 31 March 2010) or writing down allowances ('WDAs') in the corporation tax accounting period ('CTAP') in which the expenditure is incurred.

As a general rule, capital expenditure is deemed to be incurred for (all) capital allowance purposes on 'the date the obligation to pay becomes unconditional', regardless of whether there is a later date by which payment should be made. This would be determined by reference to the terms of the purchase contract. In some cases, the relevant date may be the date the relevant expenditure is invoiced. However, in many cases, the company may be required to pay for plant or machinery within a certain period after delivery. In such cases, the Revenue considers that the obligation to pay becomes unconditional when the asset is delivered (see *IR Tax Bulletin, Issue 9, November 1993, page 97*).

However, the 'unconditional obligation to pay' date rule does *not* apply if:

- the purchase agreement provides for a credit period exceeding four months after the payment obligation becomes unconditional; or

- the payment obligation occurs earlier than under normal commercial practice and this was solely or mainly designed to accelerate the timing of capital allowances [*CAA 2001, s 5*].

ANNUAL INVESTMENT ALLOWANCES (AIAS)

Basic rules for claiming AIA

4.20 The annual investment allowance (AIA) was introduced on 1 April 2008 and is available to all companies (irrespective of size). The AIA provides 100% relief on most plant and machinery expenditure up to a specified annual limit (*CAA 2001, s 38A*), which has changed frequently (!). The AIA is available on most plant and machinery expenditure with the notable exception of cars.

Qualifying AIA expenditure also *excludes* expenditure incurred:

- in the CTAP during which the qualifying activity is permanently discontinued;

- in connection with a change in the nature or conduct of the trade carried on by someone other than the person incurring the expenditure, where obtaining the AIA is one of the main benefits resulting from the change.

The company can only claim the AIA in the same CTAP in which the expenditure is incurred and must have owned the asset at some point during that CTAP (*CAA 2001, s 51A*).

The *annual* AIA expenditure limit is calculated on a pro-rata basis where the CTAP is less than 12 months.

The relevant annual limits (see *CAA 2001, s 51A (5)*) are as follows:

1 April 2008 to 31 March 2010	£50,000
1 April 2010 to 31 March 2012	£100,000
From 1 April 2012	£25,000

Thus, expenditure on plant and machinery in a particular CTAP (excluding plant qualifying for special 100% FYAs and cars) will qualify for 100% AIAs up to the relevant limit, with any balance qualifying for standard or special rate pool WDAs. It is possible to make a partial AIA claim but any unused allowance cannot be carried forward and is therefore lost.

Companies may allocate the AIA to any qualifying expenditure as they see fit [*CAA 2001, s 51B(2)*]. This provides flexibility, allowing the company to set the AIA against the expenditure which secures the most beneficial advantage. For example, a company may allocate the allowance first against any expenditure which would otherwise attract the lowest rates of relief, such as 'integral features' or long life assets (which attract 10%/8% WDAs) (see 4.24).

Special transitional rules apply for CTAPs straddling 1 April 2012

Where a company's CTAP straddles 31 March 2012, transitional rules regulate the maximum AIA limit for the entire period as follows:

Period to 31 March 2012

£100,000 × n/12 (where n = number of months in period to 31 March 2012) = A

April 2012 to end of CTAP

£25,000 × n/12 (where n = number of months in period to CTAP end) = B

The AIA limit for the entire period is the amount calculated at A + B, but the expenditure limit from 1 April 2012 to the end of the CTAP is also limited to the amount calculated in B.

Example 1

AIA in transitional CTAP for the year ended 31 December 2012

Nolan Ltd spent £80,000 on qualifying plant and equipment in the year ended 31 December 2012 which was broken down as follows:

1 January 2012 to 31 March 2012		£15,000
1 April 2012 to 31 December 2012		£65,000

The relevant AIA limits for the accounting period were:

		£
1 January 2012 to 31 March 2012	3/12 × £100,000 =	25,000
1 April 2012 to 31 December 2012	9/12 × £25,000 =	18,750
AIA limit for CTAP		£43,750

While the AIA limit overall for the CTAP is £43,750, there is also another AIA expenditure restriction of £18,750 for the nine month period to 31 December 2012.

Thus, Nolan Ltd's AIA claim for the year ended 31 December 2012 would be:

		£
1 April 2012 to 31 December 2012	£65,000 restricted to	18,750
1 April 2012 to 31 December 2012	Amount spent	15,000
AIA limit for CTAP		£33,750

Thus, of the £80,000 qualifying expenditure, only £33,750 would rank for AIAs with the balance of £46,250 being eligible for WDAs.

Special rules for group companies and certain related companies

Each company has its own AIA allowance. However, only a single AIA is given for a group of companies [*CAA 2001, ss 51C* and *51D*]. In practice, the anti-fragmentation provisions severely limit the application of the AIA for groups. For these purposes a group of companies exists if one company is a 'parent undertaking' of another company. The term 'parent undertaking' [*Companies Act 2006, s 1162*] essentially applies to a company which holds the majority in the voting rights of another company (ie > 50%), or a company which has a right to exercise a dominant influence over another company either through a 'control' contract or a provision in that company's articles.

The same rules apply where *similar* 'qualifying activities' are carried by two or more 'commonly controlled' companies. For these purposes, the similar activities condition applies if at the end of the accounting period for *either* company more than 50% of its turnover is broadly derived from a similar economic activity (broadly under the same NACE qualification, which is the first level of EU statistical classification under *EU Regulation (EC) 1893/2006* of the European Parliament). However, in practice, such cases are likely to be relatively rare.

Thus, most AIA claims by commonly controlled companies should not be restricted, so that each company would be able to claim its full AIA entitlement.

FIRST YEAR ALLOWANCES (FYAS)

Temporary 40% FYAs for 12 months to 31 March 2010

4.21   The Budget 2009 introduced *temporary* FYAs of 40% for most types of plant and machinery expenditure allocated to the main pool (known as 'first year qualifying expenditure) during the 12 month period to 31 March 2010. Temporary 40% FYAs are not given on assets qualifying for the special 100% FYA rate (see 4.23 or 4.24) or on integral features (which are allocated to a special rate pool – see 4.24)

Furthermore, FYAs are *not* available for certain assets or in some special circumstances, which are set out as 'general exclusions' in *CAA 2001, s 46(2)*. The 'general exclusions' are summarised as follows:

- the CTAP in which the qualifying activity, such as the trade, permanently ceases;

- expenditure on the purchase of a car (this *excludes* goods vehicles, those of a type not commonly used as a private vehicle and *low emission* or electrical cars (see 4.234.24 below)) [*CAA 2001, s 81*];

- expenditure on ships, etc [*CAA 2001, s 94*] and on various 'railway assets' as defined in *CAA 2001, s 95(2)* including trains, rolling stock, and station apparatus, etc;

- long life assets (see 4.27);

- plant or machinery leased (under an operating or finance lease) in the course of a leasing trade or otherwise. In this context, it should be noted that the letting of any asset on hire would be regarded as leasing. ('Long funding leases' finalised on or after 1 April 2006, allow for capital allowances to be claimed by the lessee. Consequently, the lessor's expenditure on plant or machinery will *not* qualify for capital allowances [*CAA 2001, s 70A*].)

  Exceptionally, FYAs are permitted on certain *leased* assets eligible for 100% FYAs such as low emission/electrically propelled cars, natural gas/hydrogen refuelling equipment and other energy saving equipment and environmentally beneficial plant or machinery (see 4.23–4.24) ;

- where the provision of the plant is connected with a change in the conduct of a trade by another party and the obtaining of an FYA is the main benefit or one of the main benefits reasonably expected to arise from that change;

- where plant is allocated to a qualifying activity, such as a trade (having previously been used for a non-qualifying activity) or where plant is received as a gift (as a deemed 'market value' acquisition).

Anti-avoidance rules for FYAs

4.22   There are also various 'anti-avoidance' rules that are designed to prevent FYAs being given (*CAA 2001, s 217*) where:

- plant is purchased from a 'connected person' [*CAA 2001, s 214*];

- the sole or main benefit of the transaction is to claim capital allowances [*CAA 2001, s 215*]; and

- plant is acquired in a sale and leaseback transaction [*CAA 2001, s 216*].

If the expenditure on plant or machinery does *not* qualify for FYAs, it will be allocated to one of the relevant pools (see below). The majority of such expenditure will flow through to the main pool and attract annual WDAs of 20% [*CAA 2001, s 56(1)*].

Special 100% FYAs for low emission cars and environmentally-friendly plant

4.23   The following main categories of expenditure are eligible for 100% FYAs (known as 'first year qualifying expenditure') irrespective of the company's size:

- low-emission cars. From 1 April 2008, cars with emissions not exceeding 110g/km qualify as 'low emission' cars for FYA purposes (prior to 1 April 2008 the relevant rate was 120g/km) (see 4.25 and for related employee scale charge rules – see 7.19).

- Zero emission cars and vans (ie those powered entirely be electricity or hydrogen fuel cell. Electric cars and vans are completely exempt from employee scale benefit charge for a five year period ending 31 March 2015 – see 7.12).)

- natural gas/hydrogen refuelling equipment;

- designated energy-saving plant and equipment;

- environmentally beneficial *new* plant or machinery designated as meeting specified water saving or efficiency standards.

146

SPECIAL CAPITAL ALLOWANCE RULES

Integral features

4.24   The concept of 'integral features' (broadly certain fixtures embedded within buildings) was introduced on 1 April 2008. The policy intention is that such items have a reasonably long life and should not therefore attract an accelerated form of tax relief (through normal WDAs etc). However, the more cynical view is that was simply a further way of restricting capital allowances claimed on items of plant included in buildings.

The following items of expenditure are classified as expenditure on integral features:

(i)   electrical systems (including lighting systems) and cold water;

(ii)   space or water heating systems; powered systems of ventilation, air cooling or air purification; and any floor or ceiling comprised in such systems; and

(iii)   lifts, escalators and moving walkways

(iv)   external solar shading

Post-31 March 2008 expenditure on integral features must be included in a new special rate pool (see 4.29) and will only attract WDAs at the lower rate of 8 per year (reducing balance basis) – 10% before 1 April 2012 (see 4.20 for transitional period calculations).

For accounting periods straddling 1 April 2008, expenditure on integral features must be analysed into pre-1 April 2008 and post-31 March 2008 elements. Pre-April 2008 expenditure attracts normal WDAs and only the post-March 2008 element is allocated to the special rate pool and ranks for the restricted 10% WDA.

Repair and replacement expenditure on integral feature items is generally allowable as a 'revenue' deduction. However, the legislation deems any repairs/ replacements of integral features to be capital expenditure if the amount spent over a 12-month period exceeds 50% of the replacement cost of the relevant integral feature. If this 50% limit is exceeded, then the entire repair/replacement expenditure will be added to the special rate pool and only attracts the 10% WDA (as opposed to an immediate 'revenue' deduction). Although HMRC have indicated that they will take a reasonably relaxed approach to operating this rule, it seems fairly mean! Thus, where companies anticipate that they might exceed the '50% rule', they might consider deferring some of the repair costs so as to fall outside the relevant 12-month period.

Capital allowances on cars

Emissions-based regime from 1 April 2009

4.25 The capital allowances regime for cars changed radically on 1 April 2009, with the view to encouraging businesses towards more eco-friendly cars. Cars held by the business at 1 April 2009 continue to be dealt with under the 'old' regime for a transitional period (see 4.26 below).

Companies still qualify for 100% FYAs on cars provided their CO_2 emissions limit does not exceed 110g/km. Electric cars and vans also attract 100% FYAs (see 4.23).

The full cost of 'eco-friendly' cars can therefore be written-off against the company's taxable profits in the year of purchase. (Currently, there are not many cars on the market with CO2 ratings not exceeding 110g/km – among the few that would qualify are the Mini Cooper 1.6 (104g/km), Toyota Aygo 1.0 WT-j (108g/km) and the Peugeot 107 1.0 Urban (109g/km.)

For other cars (ie those exceeding the critical 110g/km 100% FYA threshold), the capital allowances depends entirely on their emissions rating (the purchase cost becomes irrelevant).

The treatment is summarised as follows:

CO_2 emissions	Capital Allowances treatment
111g/km to 160g/km	20% WDAs within the normal 'plant and machinery' pool
Over 160k/km	10% WDAs within the 'special rate' capital allowances' pool

These rules do *not* apply to vans, black-cabs, and motorcycles – they can (usually) be allocated to the main plant and machinery pool (attracting 20%/18% WDAs – see 4.14) or 100% AIAs (see 44.20), as appropriate. In most cases, *rental payments* on *leased cars* will be deductible for tax purposes in accordance with the amount charged to profit and loss under GAAP, subject to a restriction for less eco-efficient cars (but see 7.32 for further details).

It is worth remembering that company cars with relatively low emission rates tend to be more tax-efficient for the employees, since they attract relatively smaller taxable benefit charges (and commensurately lower Class 1A NICs) (see 7.30). Electric cars are extremely beneficial from this point of view since they are now completely exempt from any employee scale benefit charge until 31 March 2015 (see 7.12).

An up-to-date guide to the 'top' green cars can be found at www.green-car-guide.com, which also provides other useful data, including CO2 ratings and fuel consumption.

Pre-1 April 2009 regime

4.26   The capital allowances treatment for *existing cars* (ie cars purchased before April 2009) – which distinguishes between *expensive* cars (ie those costing more than £12,000) and non-expensive cars – still continues subject to transitional rules

Non-expensive cars remain within the main 'plant and machinery' capital allowances pool. Broadly they will have lost their separate identity on acquisition and be subsumed within the general pool (which qualifies for 18% (20% before 1 April 2012) WDAs).

Each expensive car will still have its own separate pool, upon which 18% (20% before 1 April 2012) annual WDAs are claimable, subject to a cap of £3,000. Thus, the WDA on such cars will be £3,000 per year until the balance brought forward on the pool is less than £12,000. If the car is disposed of by 1 April 2014, a balancing adjustment will arise in the normal way. However, if the car remains held at that date, it will be transferred to the main plant and machinery pool at its then TWDV.

Long life assets

4.27   Where the plant is treated as 'long life', it will only be entitled to WDA at the rate of 8% (10% before 1 April 2012) each year (increased from 6% for expenditure incurred after 31 March 2008). Long life plant is added to the special rate pool, which gives 8%/10% WDAs on a reducing balance basis) [*CAA 2001, s 102(1), (4)*].

Plant is treated as 'long life' if it is reasonable to expect that its useful economic life is 25 years or more *when new* [*CAA 2001, s 91(1)*]. However, it is important to note that the 'long life' asset rules do not apply where the company's *total* expenditure on plant is less than £100,000 in the (12-month) accounting period – this £100,000 limit is split equally amongst associated companies [*CAA 2001, ss 97–99*]. Similarly the long life asset rules do not apply where the relevant plant is a fixture used in a retail shop, showroom, office or hotel [*CAA 2001, s 93*]. In all such cases, the plant will remain eligible for WDAs at the normal rates.

Short-life assets

4.28   Short-life asset elections are typically made for assets which are likely to be sold or scrapped by the eighth anniversary of the end of the CTAP in which they were acquired, such as computer equipment, tooling, etc. The 'short life asset' cut off was increased to eight years for expenditure incurred after 31 March 2011. For earlier expenditure the short life asset period was four years. Each short-life asset or annual group of 'similar' short-life assets (see *IR Statement of Practice SP1/86*) is included in a separate pool, which often enables a beneficial balancing allowance to be claimed on disposal. The increase in the short life 'cut-off' period from four to eight years should bring capital allowances more into line with the asset's economic depreciation. The legislation does not stipulate an eight (four) year asset life requirement at the outset, but no tax benefit would arise from making a short life asset election if the plant or machinery is ultimately used for more than eight (four) years. This is because, if the asset is still retained at the eighth anniversary of the end of the accounting period of its acquisition, it is transferred back to the main capital allowances pool and loses its separate identity.

Since we now have an 'eight year' short life asset window and the main WDA rate of capital allowances reduces to 18% pa from 1 April 2012, more short life asset claims are likely to be made as a means of accelerating tax relief for most plant and machinery assets.

Example 2

Short life v main pool treatment

Baldock Ltd incurred £100,000 on 'short life' plant on 1 April 2012. The finance director, Mr Sam, prepared the following calculations to determine whether a short life asset election would be worthwhile (assuming that the plant would be sold in year seven for 10% of its original cost).

Year	Main Pool £'000	Short life asset £'000
Cost	100.00	100.00
WDA – 1	(18.00)	(18.00)
WDA – 2	(14.76)	(14.76)
WDA – 3	(12.10)	(12.10)
WDA – 4	(9.92)	(9.92)
WDA – 5	(8.14)	(8.14)
WDA – 6	(6.67)	(6.67)
Disposal – 7	(10.00)	(10.00)
BA –7	–	(20.41)
WDA – 7	(3.67)	
TWDV c/fwd	16.73	
Total allowances	83.26	100.00

The above calculations show that, with a short life asset election, the plant would be fully written off for tax purposes in year seven. In contrast, with no election, the plant (within the main pool) only about 83% of the plant's cost would have been written off, with about 17% still to be relieved over a relatively long period.

COMPUTATIONAL PROCEDURE

Allocation to relevant pools

4.29 A capital allowance computation is prepared for each corporation tax accounting period (CTAP). To claim the allowances, a company must first allocate its qualifying expenditure to one of the relevant pools [*CAA 2001, s 58*]. (Strictly, the residue of first year qualifying expenditure (ie after any FYAs have been claimed) would normally be allocated to a pool in the *next* CTAP.)

A company's qualifying capital expenditure on plant and machinery for a CTAP is allocated to a relevant 'pool' being either:

● a single asset pool;

● a special rate pool; or

● the main pool.

A *single asset* pool only includes expenditure relating to *one* single asset, the main categories of single asset pool being 'elected' short life assets (see 4.28) and pre-1 April 2009 expensive motor cars (cars costing more than £12,000 – see 4.26) [*CAA 2001, s 54(2), (3)*]. The *special rate pool* is used to capture the *total* expenditure relating to integral features, (see 4.24), (from 1 April 2009) cars with CO2 emissions of more 160 g/km (see 4.25), thermal insulation of an existing building used in a qualifying trade, and 'long life' assets (see 4.27). Up to 1 April 2008, the class pool/special rate pool included expenditure on assets leased overseas (under 'non-protected' leasing transactions).The overseas leasing rules were effectively abolished by FA 2006 [*CAA 2001, ss 54(4), (5) and 105(2A)*].

The annual WDA for expenditure in the special rate pool is 8% (*10% before 1 April 2012*) .

All other plant and machinery expenditure is allocated to the *main pool*. The main pool therefore collects and aggregates the vast majority of expenditure. Thus, after allocating the first £25,000/£100,000 eligible for AIAs, the remaining amount attracts the 18% WDAs (20% for expenditure incurred between 1 April 2008 and 31 March 2012), which are calculated on a reducing balance basis.

Where the tax written down value of the main and special pools (before the WDA for the period) is £1,000 or less, it can be fully written off as the WDA for the period. (The £1,000 de minimis amount is computed on a pro-rata basis for CTAPs of less than 12 months.)

Plant and machinery included in the main pool effectively loses its identity and is written down along with the other assets in the pool. Assuming no FYAs, with a WDA of 18% calculated on a reducing balance basis, it can take about ten years to write off 90% of the relevant expenditure. Thus, if it is likely that the plant will be used for less than eight years, it will be advantageous to make a short-life asset election to place the asset (or group of similar assets) in a separate pool (see 4.28). The potential advantage is that a balancing allowance would be triggered on disposal, thus ensuring that the plant (less its scrap/disposal value) is fully written off for tax purposes over its working life in the business (see 4.21).

Calculation of writing down allowances on the main pool

4.30 The main steps for calculating capital allowances are set out below:

(*a*) the unrelieved TWDV of qualifying expenditure on the main pool (ie the tax written-down value (TWDV) brought forward) is brought forward from the previous CTAP;

(*b*) expenditure on plant and machinery, etc for the CTAP *(excluding expenditure qualifying for annual investment allowance (AIAs))* is allocated to the main pool. Broadly, when added to the opening TWDV, this gives the 'available qualifying expenditure' (AQE). (Where companies claim FYAs/AIAs on their plant and machinery expenditure, this expenditure is not allocated to a pool for that period.);

(*c*) the total of any disposal receipts (TDR) for the CTAP is then calculated. The company brings in the disposal receipts for all assets that have triggered a 'disposal event'. Typically, a disposal receipt will represent the sale proceeds arising on the sale of an asset, although the amount is limited (where appropriate) to the original cost of the asset [*CAA 2001, ss 55, 61, and 62*];

(*d*) WDAs at the rate of 20% for a (12-month) CTAP are then calculated on the amount by which the AQE exceeds the TDR. (The WDA is given in the year of purchase, regardless of the date on which the asset is acquired.) *However, if AQE exceeds TDR by £1,000 or less the balance (ie the amount by which AQE exceeds TDR) can be taken as the WDA for the period [CAA 2001, s 56A(2)]*. No WDAs are available for the period in which the company ceases to trade [*CAA 2001, s 55(2), (4)*];

If a company's accounting period straddles 1 April 2012 (when the WDA changes from 20% to 18%) a hybrid rate applies. The WDA rate is arrived at by calculating the number of days before and after the charge of the WDA rate. Thus, if a company has a 31 December 2012 year-end, the relevant WDA would be 18.4973%, calculated as follows:

		Number of days:
1/1/12 – 31/3/12	before change	91
1/4/12 – 31/12/12	after change	275
		366
91/366 × 20%		4.9727%
275/366 × 18%		13.5246%
Hybrid WDA rate		18.4973%

(*e*) if the TDR exceeds the AQE, a balancing charge will arise [*CAA 2001, s 55(3)*];

(*f*) a balancing allowance on the main pool (ie where the AQE exceeds the TDR) only occurs on the permanent cessation of the company's trade or any other qualifying activity [*CAA 2001, ss 55(1)* and *55(2), (4)*].

4.31   In contrast to the main pool or class pool, a disposal event on a single asset pool will always result in a balancing allowance or balancing charge:

- a balancing allowance arises where AQE exceeds TDR;

- a balancing charge arises where TDR exceeds AQE.

Plant and machinery allowances computation

4.32   Example 3 illustrates how plant and machinery allowances are calculated.

Example 3

Gerrard Engineering Ltd (which is a singleton company) incurred the following capital expenditure during the year ended 31 March 2012.

	AIA qualifying expenditure	Qualifying for WDAs	Special rate pool	Total
	£	£	£	£
5 Dart 750 Machining centres (see note below)	100,000	78,000		178,000

	AIA qualifying expenditure	Qualifying for WDAs	Special rate pool	Total
	£	£	£	£
Clicker press		4,580		4,580
Dell PCs and autocad software –		10,900		10,900
Hyundai i10 car (including extras) – 139 g/km		7,430		7,430
Works delivery van		18,200		18,200
Volvo S80 2.0f Se premium (including extras) – 199g/km				22,975
	100,000	119,110	22,975	242,085

Note – Only the first £100,000 out of the £178,000 spent on the Machining centres attracts AIAs – with the balance of £78,000 being eligible for WDAs.

During the period, the company sold one of its test rigs for £5,800 and the Saab car for £12,000.

The company's capital allowance computation for the year ended 31 March 2012 is as follows:

	Main pool	Special rate pool	Expensive car (Saab)	Total	Total allowances
	£	£	£	£	£
TWDV b/fwd	150,180	–	22,560	172,740	
Additions	119,110	22,975		142,085	
AQE	269,290	22,975	22,560	314,825	
TDR – Disposal proceeds	(5,800)		(12,000)	(17,800)	
	263,490	22,975	10,560	297,025	

154

	Main pool	Special rate pool	Expensive car (Saab)	Total	Total allowances
	£	£	£	£	£
WDA – 20% /10%	(52,698)	(2,297)		(54,995)	54,995
Balancing allowance			(10,560)	(10,560)	10,560
AIA Qualifying Expenditure	100,000		100,000		
AIA	(100,000)			(100,000)	100,000
TWDV c/fwd	210,792	20,678		231,470	
Total allowances					**165,555**

RELIEF FOR COMPANY TRADING LOSSES

4.33   The basic reliefs available for trading losses are summarised below; their order of offset is shown in the pro-forma computation in 4.4 above.

Current year offset against total profits

4.34   Trading losses arising in a corporation tax accounting period (CTAP) can be offset against the company's other profits of the same period (calculated before charitable donations relief, but *after* deducting any current/prior year non-trading loan relationship deficit). Relief is only available if the trade is operated on a 'commercial' basis with the view to making a profit. The claim (which is made on the CT600 return) must be made within two years after the end of the loss-making CTAP, although HMRC can extend this period [*CTA 2010, s37(3)(a) ICTA 1988, s 393A(1)(a)*].

'Three-year' carry-back against total profits

4.35   Where the current year *trading* losses cannot be fully deducted against the profits of the current period, any remaining loss can generally be carried back under *CTA 2010, s 37(3)(b) (ICTA 1988, s 393A(2))* against the company's total profits of the CTAP(s) of the previous 12 months (subject to the extended 'three year' carry back rule that was temporarily introduced in the *Finance Act 2009*, albeit limited to a total offset of £50,000 for the earliest two years – see below). Although a careful review of losses is often required to ensure their most beneficial use, companies often find that carrying back losses provides beneficial tax repayments (with interest).

If a CTAP straddles the previous 12-month period, then the profits are apportioned and the loss can only be set-off against the part falling within the previous 12 months.

If a trading loss arises in any CTAP which *ends* in the period between 24 November 2008 and 23 November 2010, a company may carry back up to £50,000 of its tax loss against the 'second' and 'third' previous year (ie the earliest two years of the extended three year loss carry-back period), with the loss being offset against the most recent years in priority to later years.

Thus, if a company makes a trading loss (say) in its accounting period ended 31 December 2009, then if it has losses remaining after a full offset against the previous year (ending 31 December 2008), it can carry back up losses of up to *£50,000* against the year ended 31 December 2007 (1st) and then any residual amount against the year ended 31 December 2006. The ability to carry back losses for up to three years (albeit restricted to £50,000 for the earliest two years) recognises that many businesses are likely to make trading losses in 2008 to 2010. However, the extension is not particularly generous since the maximum additional tax saving for two consecutive loss offsets is only worth around £30,000 (max). The one year loss carry back against the immediately preceding year remains unrestricted.

Losses of an earlier CTAP must be relieved before later ones [*CTA 2010, s 37(8) (ICTA 1988, s 393A(1))*], as shown below.

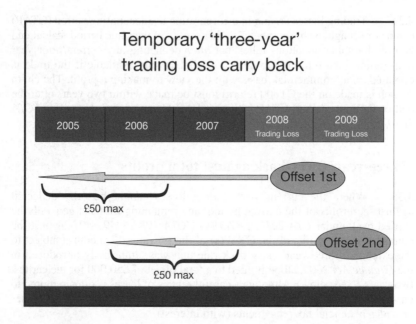

In a number of cases, losses may have been generated in two consecutive years. However, the earliest loss must be offset first, which will often restrict the 'carry-back' capacity for the later year, as shown in Example 2 below.

Example 4

Temporary 'three-year' trading loss carryback

McAvennie Ltd incurred trading losses of £77,400 and £102,560 in its accounting periods ending 30 September 2009 and 2010 respectively. The losses can be relieved under the 'temporary' three year loss carry-back rules as shown below:

	Year ended 30 September				
	2006	2007	2008	2009	2010
	£	£	£	£	£
Taxable trading profits	75,380	86,590	48,100		
2008 loss offset under s 393A(1)(b)		(29,300)	(48,100)	(77,400)	
2009 loss offset under s 393A(1)(b) – max		(50,000)			(102,560)
Corporation tax profits	75,380	7,290	–	–	–

The loss of £77,400 for the year ended 30 September 2009 is fully offset. However, only £50,000 of the £102,560 loss for the year ended 30 September 2010 can be relieved against the taxable profits of the year ended 30 September 2007, leaving £52,560 trading losses to carry forward under *CTA 2010, s 45)*.

4.36 The trading losses can only be offset if the company was carrying on the same trade in which the loss arose in the previous CTAP. The loss carry-back relief is subject to the same two-year time limit and 'commercial basis' test as the current year offset in 4.34 above.

The loss carry-back claim must be for the full amount of the loss (or if less the relievable profits). It is not possible to make a partial claim. A carried back loss is offset against a company's profits *after* deducting group relief but *before* charitable donations relief. This means that charitable donations (including covenanted donations and charitable gifts of assets) may become permanently 'disallowed' . An extended 'three' carry-back can be made where the company ceases to trade. In such cases, trading losses incurred in the 12 months prior to cessation may be carried back against the profits of the CTAPs of the previous *three years* on an unrestricted basis (ie they are not subject to the £50,000 restriction for losses carried back by 'continuing' companies) (see 16.6).

The detailed mechanics of the loss carry back relief under *CTA 2010, s 37(3)(b)* (for a CTAP for the year ended 31 December 2011) are illustrated in Example 5 below.

Trading loss relief

4.37

Example 5

Hurst Hatricks Ltd incurred a trading loss of £280,600 in its accounting period for the 12 months ended 31 December 2011. It makes up accounts for calendar years.

The 2011 loss of £280,600 can be mainly relieved as follows:

	2008	*2009*	*20109*	*2011*	*2011 Loss utilisation*
	£	£	£	£	£
Tax-adjusted trading profit	193,500	135,500	189,700	–	(280,600)
Net property rental income	10,700	12,400	13,100	14,300	
Chargeable gain			–	6,800	
Non-trading loan relationship deficit	(31,300)	(34,700)	(56,900)	(50,200)	
	172,900	113,200	145,900	29,100	
Less CTA 2010, s 37(3) (a) current loss offset				(29,100)	29,100
Less CTA 2010, s 37(3) (b) loss offset vs 2010			(145,900)		145,900
Less Charge on income/qualifying charitable donation	(1,500)	(1,500)	–*		
Corporation tax profits	171,400	111,700	–	–	
Loss carried forward under *CTA 2010, s 45*					(105,600)

* Qualifying charitable donations of £1,500 in 2010 become unrelieved.

Since the loss arose in an accounting period ending after 28 November 2010, it is not possible to use the extended temporary loss carry back facility of up to £50,000 (see 4.35).

Carry-forward against future trading profits

4.38   Unused trading losses can be carried forward for offset against the first available taxable *profits of the same trade* [*CTA 2010, s 45 (ICTA 1988, s 393(1))*]. It follows that if the company's trading activity ceases, any excess losses are effectively forfeited.

GROUP RELIEF

4.39   Trading losses (as well as certain other items of relief including non-trading loan relationship deficits, property rental business losses and management expenses) can be surrendered by a member of the group in whole or in part to another group member for offset against the claimant's total profits of its current CTAP (*CTA 2010, Part 5 (ICTA 1988, ss 402–413)*).

For this purpose, all group companies must be part of a 75% corporate group. From 1 April 2000, it is possible to trace the required 75% ownership through any company, irrespective of its tax residence.

Historically, only 75% of UK-resident companies (or UK branches of non-resident companies) could participate in group relief claims. However, there was an important extension of the UK group relief rules in the Finance Act 2006, following the European Court of Justice ruling in *Marks & Spencer plc v Halsey* [2005] Case C-446/03. Under these new rules losses arising in a foreign subsidiary may be surrendered to a UK group company by way of group relief, but only in restricted circumstances. Overseas losses can now only be group relieved where the foreign subsidiary has fully exhausted all possible methods of relieving the loss in its 'local' jurisdiction (including carrying the losses forward for offset against future profits). In practical terms, this means that overseas losses (computed on a UK tax basis) may be relieved where the foreign subsidiary has ceased trading (as was the case in *Marks & Spencer*).

Group relief can only be offset against the total profits of a corresponding CTAP of the claimant company.

INVESTMENT COMPANIES AND COMPANIES WITH INVESTMENT BUSINESSES

Investment businesses

4.40   In practice, the tax rules giving relief for management expenses will generally apply to investment companies, ie those companies that mainly carry on investment activities, such as holding a portfolio of investments in shares or property investment.

It is no longer necessary for a company to be an 'investment company' to claim corporation tax relief for its management expenses and capital allowances. *FA 2004* substantially relaxed the legislation in this area. From 1 April 2004, management expenses and any associated capital allowances relating to an *investment business* can now be deducted against the income/ profits of that investment business (see 4.41). This means, for example, that holding companies that carry on a trading activity can claim relief for their management expenses relating to their investment business.

An investment business is any business consisting wholly or partly of making investments [*CTA 2009, s 1218*]. Existing case law has interpreted this to mean simply holding investments rather than making them and also includes making a single investment.

In contrast, an investment dealing company, whose object is to make a profit from buying and selling investments would be treated as carrying on an investment dealing trade and would therefore be a trading company. The receipt of any investment income from its investments would be incidental to its main activity.

It is also unlikely that a company in liquidation would be treated as carrying on an investment business. Only rarely will a liquidator carry on a business existing wholly or mainly in the making of investments. The liquidator's main objective is to realise the company's assets to the best advantage.

Tax relief for management expenses

4.41   Any company carrying on an investment business can claim corporate tax relief for the management expenses (and capital allowances) relating to that business. Thus, for example, a company that carries on a trade and makes investments will now be entitled to relieve any management expenses incurred in relation to its investment business.

Under *CTA 2009, ss 1219* and *1225*, management expenses are now deductible on an 'accruals' basis, based on the amount debited to the company's profit and loss account (or the statement of total recognised gains and losses) in accordance with generally accepted accounting practice (GAAP). For further details, see also 4.43 notes (*h*) to (*j*).

Where the corporation tax accounting period does not coincide with the period for which the statutory accounts are drawn up, the debits are apportioned on a time basis (some other method can be used if that is more just and reasonable). Subsequent credits or 'reversals' relating to management expenses are 'credited' against the management expenses for that period, with any 'excess' amount being taxed [*CTA 2009, s 1229*].

Unallowable purposes

4.42   Management expenses are disallowed if they relate to investments held for an 'unallowable purpose' [*CTA 2009, s 1220*]. In the main, this relates to investments that are not held for a business or other commercial purpose, which in practice should be very rare.

The Revenue's 2004 guidance notes gives as an example expenditure relating to shares in a football club supported by one of the company's directors. However, where the investment was motivated (at least) partly as a way of promoting the company's business, only part of the cost would be disallowed as relating to an 'unallowable purpose'.

The 'unallowable purpose' exclusion also extends to expenditure relating to investment activities run on a mutual basis or by members clubs.

INVESTMENT COMPANIES AND COMPANIES WITH INVESTMENT BUSINESSES – PRO-FORMA TAX COMPUTATION

4.43   Where a company is an investment company or carrying on one or more investment activities, its corporate tax computation will bring together the assessable income and gains from all sources and then deducts from its total profits its management expenses and charges on income, etc.

A pro-forma corporation tax computation is provided below, together with accompanying notes.

Pro-forma Investment Co Ltd

Corporation tax computation based on the accounting period ended

	£	£	Notes
Property business income	X		
Rents receivable			(a)
Less Allowable letting expenses	(X)		
Capital allowances on let property	(X)		(b)
		(X)	
		X	(c)
Non-trading forex/loan relationship profits and interest (net of any non-trading debits)	X		(d)

	£	£	Notes
Less Non-trading forex/loan relationship deficit carried back	(X)	X	(*e*)
Unfranked investment income		X	
		X	
Less Share loss relief on disposals of shares in unquoted trading companies		(X)	(*f*)
Income		X	
Chargeable gains		X	
Total profits		X	
Less Capital allowances re investment business		(X)	(*g*)
Less Management expenses			
Excess management expenses b/fwd	X		
Amount incurred for period	X		(*h*) (*i*)
	X		
Offset against profits	(X)	(X)	
Excess management expenses c/fwd	X		(*j*)
		X	
Less Current non-trading forex/loan relationship deficit (net of any non-trading loan relationship profits) arising in period		(X)	(*k*)
		(X)	
		X	
Less Charitable donations relief (being qualifying charitable donations and gifts of assets to charities)		(X)	(*l*)
Total profits before group relief		X	
Less Group relief		(X)	
TAXABLE TOTAL PROFITS		X	

Notes:

(*a*)   *Property business income* – The receipt of rental income, such as in the case of a property investment company, is taxed on an accruals basis in accordance with generally accepted accounting principles (GAAP) [*CTA 2009, ss 203–206*]. Expenses wholly and exclusively incurred for the rental business are deductible against the rental income (applying the

162

same principles used for calculating taxable trading profits) [*CTA 2009, s 209*]. Similarly, any debit and credit amounts relating to intangible fixed assets within a property rental business are reflected in its taxable results [*CTA 2009, s 748*].

The company must split its expenses between those incurred in managing its investment properties and those of managing the company itself. This may also necessitate an apportionment of expenditure such as directors' remuneration (see note (*i*) below). The property management expenses are deducted against property income. The expenses of managing the company are deductible as management expenses (see note (*h*) below).

(*b*)   *Capital allowances relating to let property* – Capital allowances relating to let property are deductible as a property business expense (which may increase or create a property business loss). Industrial buildings allowances may be claimed (up to 31 March 2011) if the lessee is using the building for a qualifying industrial purpose.

(*c*)   *Property rental business losses* – If a property rental business loss arises, this is offset against the company's current year profits. Any unrelieved loss can be carried forward and set-off against future *total* profits (provided the rental business continues). If the rental business ceases, an investment company can carry forward any unrelieved losses as a management expense.

It is also possible to surrender a property rental business loss by way of group relief to the extent that it (together with any *current period* management expenses and charges on income) exceeds the surrendering company's *gross* profits. Where an 'excess' amount is available for surrender, the order of offset is charges, then property business losses, then management expenses.

(*d*)   *Non-trading loan relationship profits* – The non-trading loan relationship profits include all *non-trading* interest receivable, such as bank, building society and intra-group interest and other profits arising from the company's *non-trading* loan relationships (including non-trading foreign exchange gains).

However, any *non-trading* loan interest payable (and other non-trading loan relationship/foreign exchange deficits) must be deducted in arriving at the 'non-trade' loan relationship income [*CTA 2006, s 301(4)*]. (All interest payable to UK companies/UK banks is paid gross (ie without deducting 20% income tax).)

(*e*)   *Carry-back of non-trading loan relationship deficit* – A claim can be made under *CTA 2006, s 462* to carry back all or part of a non-trading deficit (including foreign exchange losses) against the company's 'non-trade' loan relationship profits of the previous year. This relief is deducted after *all other reliefs* except group relief for trading losses [*CTA 2009, s 463(5)*].

(*f*) Share loss relief – Where an 'investment company' realises a capital loss on a disposal of an unquoted trading company's shares, it may elect to offset that loss against its income of the same period and then the previous period. A capital loss arising from a 'negligible value' claim (see 16.38) can also be relieved under these rules. A number of conditions must be satisfied to obtain relief.

For these purposes, the company must be an 'investment company' as defined in *CTA 2009, s 1218 (ICTA 1988, s 130)*. An investment company is defined as 'any company whose business consists wholly or mainly in the making of investments and the principal part of whose income is derived therefrom'. In *FPH Finance Trust Ltd v CIR* (1944) 26 TC 131, it was held that these tests should be applied over a representative period rather than the accounting period under review. Clearly, the company's main activity must be to hold investments for the receipt of income in the form of interest, dividends and rents (see *Casey v Monteagle Estate Co* [1962] IR 406). In *Jowett v O'Neill and Brennan Construction Ltd* [1998] STC 482, it was held that the simple placing of funds on deposit in a bank account is unlikely to constitute a business or investment activity.

Relief can only be claimed if the investment company originally *subscribed* for the shares (ie it is not available for 'second-hand' shareholdings). The shares must be in an unquoted company which was either trading at the date of the disposal or has ceased to trade within three years of the disposal date (and has not since become an investment company or engaged in certain excluded activities, such as dealing in shares, land or commodities). Broadly speaking, relief is only available to shares in companies that would qualify for EIS relief (see 11.26–11.46). In all cases, the investee company must *not* be an 'associated company', such as a 51% subsidiary [*CTA 2010, s 68–90 (ICTA 1988, s 573)*].

(*g*) *Capital allowances* – Capital allowances can be claimed on plant and machinery purchased for the purpose of a company's investments business in the same way as a trading company. This would include, for example, the purchase of office furniture, office equipment, computers, cars, etc [*CAA 2001, ss 11* and *15(1)(g)*]. If the capital allowances exceed the company's income for a period, the excess is added to the company's management expenses for general offset against its total profits. Any unrelieved capital allowances are treated in the same way as excess management expenses.

(*h*) *Management expenses* – Any company carrying on an investment business can obtain relief for its relevant management expenses against its total profits (see 4.40 and 4.41). Under *CTA 2009, s 1225*, management expenses are generally based on the amount reflected in the accounts in accordance with GAAP (see 4.34).

Generally, management expenses are those incurred in managing the investments and would therefore include normal office running costs and reasonable directors' remuneration. Capital' expenditure is not deductible as a management expense [*CTA 2009, s 1219(3*], although HMRC accept that it may often be difficult to draw the dividing line on costs relating to the acquisition of investments (see below).

Certain statutory 'management expense' deductions are available which includes the relief for shares awarded to or share options exercised by directors and employees [*CTA 2009, ss 1221, 1013(3) and 1021(3)*] (see Chapter 8 for detailed coverage of relief for employee shares).

The scope of expenses allowed by the definition is often unclear, particularly in relation to research and the appraisal of potential 'target' companies for investment. The company will not necessarily obtain relief for every expense and positively has to show that an expense falls to be treated as an expense of management. In practice, difficulties often arise in obtaining relief for directors' remuneration (see note (*i*) below) and expenses relating to seeking and changing investments.

For example, brokerage and stamp duties on the purchase or sale of investments are considered to be part of the cost of purchasing or selling an investment and would therefore not be allowed as a management expense (*Capital and National Trust Ltd v Golder* (1949) 31 TC 265). HMRC's guidance notes take the view that expenditure on appraising and investigating investments, such as obtaining preliminary reports for a number of possible investment options, are not regarded as capital and hence would qualify for relief. On the other hand, HMRC has generally taken the view that once a decision has been taken to acquire a particular investment, any costs incurred from that point are capital. Case law suggests that this may not always be the case. For example, professional fees incurred in evaluating and preparing for the purchase of a company that was subsequently *aborted* were allowed by the Court of Appeal in *Camas plc v Atkinson* [2003] STC 968.

(*i*)   *Directors' remuneration* – Inspectors often seek to limit the 'management expenses' deduction to the amount they consider reasonable, having regard to the duties performed (in contrast, directors of trading companies generally have no difficulty in voting themselves significant levels of remuneration).

In the case of an investment business, HMRC typically argue that only a modest amount relates to the cost of managing the company's investments and the company itself. Where there are likely to be difficulties in obtaining relief for directors' remuneration, the use of dividends should be considered as a means of extracting funds from a company (see 2.7–2.11). If the Inspector disallows excess remuneration, it is possible to eliminate the employment income tax liability (but not the NIC liability) by formally waiving the remuneration and reimbursing the amounts to the company (see 2.21).

In the case of a property investment company, a higher level of remuneration can be justified on the basis that it relates to the management of the properties, which would require a greater degree of management time. In practice, directors' remuneration of between 7.5% and 15% of a company's rental income might be allowed, although a higher amount could be substantiated where the directors are personally involved in collecting rent, supervising maintenance and improvements and negotiating rent reviews, etc. This would be relieved as a property rental business expense rather than a management expense (see note (*a*) above).

The 'nine-month rule' for accrued remuneration also applies to directors' remuneration deductible as a management expense [*CTA 2009, s 1249*] (see 2.22 and 5.14). This restriction on the level of allowable remuneration an 'investment company' can pay also means that the directors can only make modest provision for pensions.

(*j*) *Surplus management expenses* – If the company's management expenses exceed its profit (ie effectively, the company has a loss), the surplus management expenses are carried forward to the next CTAP. They will then be treated as management expenses of the next period (and offset against total profits) [*CTA 2009, s 1223(3)*]. Excess management expenses can be carried forward indefinitely, unless the company ceases to carry on its investment business or where there is a major change in the conduct of the company's business, etc within three years either side of a change in ownership [*CTA 2010, ss 677 and 678 (ICTA 1988, s 768B)*].

(*k*) *Current year offset of non-trading loan relationship deficit* – A claim can be made to relieve a non-trading deficit against the company's taxable profits of the same CTAP (known as the 'deficit period') [*CTA 2009, s 461*]. In the case of most investment companies, all interest payable and losses or deficits arising on loans (including foreign exchange losses) will normally be 'non-trading'. The amount eligible for a non-trading deduction must be computed after deducting any non-trading interest *income* and other non-trading loan related profits (see note (*d*) above).

(*l*) *Charitable donations relief* – This relief is given on qualifying donations to a charity (within *CTA 2010, s 191 (ICTA 1988, s 339)*) and the market value of assets gifted to a charity (under *CTA 2010, s203 (ICTA 1988, s 587B)*). Charitable donations relief is also available where assets are sold to a charity below their market value – in this case the relief is based on the amount by which the market value exceeds the sale price. Relief is given in the period in which the payments/asset transfer is made.

Annual payments or annuities are claimed as a management expense provided they are incurred for business purposes, subject to the 'unallowable purpose' rule (see 4.42).

CLOSE INVESTMENT HOLDING COMPANIES ('CICS')

Consequences of being a CIC

4.44   A CIC is a special category of company which cannot obtain the benefit of the small profits rate or small profits marginal relief [*CTA 2010, s 18(b) (ICTA 1988, s 13(1))*]. Interest relief is also unavailable on borrowings to purchase shares in a CIC [*ITA 2007, s 392(2)*].

Scope of CIC definition

4.45   First of all, the company must be a *close* company, which broadly means that it is controlled by five or fewer shareholders *or* by shareholders (of any number) who are directors of the company (see also 3.12) [*CTA 2010, s 439 (ICTA 1988, s 414(2))*].

4.46   Secondly, *CTA 2010, s 34(1)* treats a close company as being a CIC for a CTAP *unless* it exists wholly or mainly for one or more of the purposes listed below:

●   carrying on a trade or trades on a commercial basis – this will include land dealing and share dealing companies);

●   making investments in land, such as the letting of property to non-connected persons (a company would therefore be a CIC if it mainly lets property to a person/persons connected with the company);

●   the holding of shares in or making loans to companies which are not CICs; or

●   companies whose business is mainly managing subsidiaries (which are not themselves CICs).

Treatment where company is wound up

4.47   Where a trading company is wound up, it is unlikely to satisfy one of the above qualifying purposes. However, there is a let-out in that it will not be treated as a CIC in the accounting period following the start of the winding up provided it was not a CIC for the last period [*CTA 2010, s 34(5) (ICTA 1988, s 13A(4))*]. If the company ceases to trade before the start of the winding up, the Revenue consider that it will become a CIC immediately before it goes into liquidation and the relief in *s 34(5)* will not apply (*IR Tax Bulletin*, Issue 3, May 1992). If there is sufficient tax at stake and it is practicable, the company should trade up to the date it is wound up.

PAYMENT OF CORPORATION TAX

Quarterly instalment payment (QIP) rules

4.48 Large companies pay their tax under the quarterly instalment payment (QIP) system. The detailed rules are found in the *Corporation Tax (Instalment Payments) Regulations 1998 (SI 1998 No 3175)*.

For QIP purposes, a large company is a company whose profits exceed the corporation tax upper limit (in force at the end of the relevant accounting period) (see 3.15). The current limit of £1,500,000 must be apportioned by reference to the number of associated companies (at the end of the *last* CTAP) and reduced where the CTAP is less than 12 months. Although HMRC will do their best to issue reminders and payslips to those companies they believe to fall within the QIP regime, the responsibility to make QIPs still falls on each company.

To assist growing companies, a company which becomes 'large' will not have to pay tax in instalments for that period (only) provided its profits are less than £10 million (again reduced for any associated companies). If profits are hovering around the £1,500,000 threshold, there may be a case for providing an additional bonus to the proprietor to avoid the instalment rules!

All other (ie non-large) companies pay their corporation tax liability nine months after the end of the corporation tax accounting period.

QIP timetable

4.49 Large companies pay their corporation tax in four equal quarterly instalments. The tax instalment payments for a 12-month accounting period are made as follows:

First instalment	25% —	six months and 13 days after the start of the accounting period
Second instalment	25% —	three months after the first instalment
Third instalment	25% —	three months after the second instalment
Final instalment	25% —	three months and 14 days after the *end* of the accounting period

Thus, if the company has a 31 December year-end, its QIPs will fall due on 14 July, 14 October, 14 January and 14 April.

If the corporation tax accounting period lasts less than 12 months, the *last* instalment falls due three months and 14 days from the end of the accounting period. The *other* instalments would be due every three months starting six months and 13 days from the start of the relevant accounting period.

Estimating potential corporation tax liability

4.50   To minimise the company's interest exposure, appropriate revisions to the quarterly instalments (and, where appropriate, 'top-up' payments) would be made as the company's view of its *estimated* tax liability for the relevant year changes.

The requirement to estimate the tax liability for the entire period some six months into it requires companies to establish reliable forecasts. However, there may be an unforeseen change in trading patterns or unpredictable events, such as the sale of an investment towards the end of the period or unplanned capital expenditure and so on. Such variations are likely to create material interest costs where the actual liability turns out to be greater. A penalty may be charged where a company fraudulently or deliberately fails to pay the appropriate instalments.

Comparing quarterly instalments with actual tax liability

4.51   Once the company has calculated its final tax liability for the period, the tax instalments and balancing payment that it should have made are compared with its QIPs. Interest on underpaid and overpaid amounts can then be calculated. The QIP regime requires companies continually to review their expected tax liabilities and make 'top-up' payments where necessary to reduce their interest costs. Similarly, if the company considers that too much tax has been paid to date (for example, as a result of reduced profits or an anticipated loss), it may make an appropriate reduction in the next instalment or claim a repayment.

Interest will accrue from the first QIP date to the 'nine-month' due date at the base rate plus 1% for *unpaid* tax and base rate less 0.25% for overpaid tax. After the nine-month normal due date, the interest increases to base rate plus 2.5% for underpayments and base rate less 1% for overpayments. The interest payments will be worked out on a last in first out basis. Thus, for example, any repayment will generally consist of the latter payments made by the company.

HMRC's temporary 'Time To Pay' (TTP) regime

4.52   A large number of companies have been struggling to pay their tax liabilities in the current economic downturn. This was recognised in the Pre-Budget Report 2008, which introduced temporary measures aimed at businesses facing cash flow difficulties. Although HMRC is continuing to operate the TTP scheme, anecdotal evidence suggests that it businesses are finding that there has been a tightening-up with tougher questions being raised and more applications being turned down. However, there has been a substantial take-up

˙in TTP arrangements with many companies benefiting from the ability to defer their tax payments – indeed for the six months to June 2011, HMRC approved around 48,500 TTP agreements covering tax of some £860m.

Under the 'Time To Pay' (TTP) initiative, such companies can apply to HMRC's dedicated Business Payment Support Service (BPSS) to defer their tax payments over an appropriate suitable pre-agreed period. This facility applies to *all* their tax liabilities, including corporation tax, PAYE, National Insurance, Construction Industry Scheme tax deductions, and VAT. Companies must contact HMRC as soon as it as appears likely that they anticipate a problem in paying their tax.

HMRC will often grant companies a deferred period over which to pay their taxes provided they are satisfied that the company cannot pay them on the due date(s). The TTP arrangements are negotiated on a 'case-by-case' basis taking into account the company's cash flow profile, and can vary from a few months to a longer period (although cases lasting over a year are only agreed in exceptional circumstances). HMRC stress that the same principles are applied to all taxpayers, although the precise arrangements would be tailored to reflect the risk/return associated with different tax liabilities. For higher risk cases, HMRC will demand more supporting information for TTP applications.

HMRC expect the company to put forward a realistic payment proposal and they will allow viable companies to pay over a period they can afford. Currently, HMRC appears to be requesting an 'up-front' lump sum with fairly tight monthly repayment schedules.

Where a company's financial position improves, HMRC must be contacted since the company is likely to be asked to increase or clear their tax payments.

HMRC emphasise the need to contact the BPSS before tax payments become overdue – otherwise the local office handling the collection of overdue tax will need to be contacted and surcharges are likely to apply.

The advantage of deferring tax payments through the BPSS is that surcharges and penalties will not apply to deferred payments, though interest will be charged for the period that tax payments remain outstanding.

Companies applying for the 'time to pay' concession must contact the BPSS (0845 302 1435). They must be able to provide their tax reference number, details of the relevant tax that it is seeking to defer and basic details of its cash inflows and outflows. Anecdotal evidence suggests that HMRC are able to give a reasonably prompt decision over the phone. However larger deferrals or complex cases may require more time and further information is generally required before payment arrangements can be agreed.

CORPORATION TAX SELF-ASSESSMENT (CTSA) RETURN

CT600 return

4.53   All companies are subject to the corporation tax self-assessment (CTSA) regime which evolved from Pay and File and incorporates much the same rules for filing the return, claims and late filing penalties.

The return form CT600 must normally be filed, together with the accounts and tax computations, within 12 months from the end of the relevant corporation tax accounting period (CTAP). (Non-corporate distribution tax (see 9.9) was also required to be reported on the return.)

Most *trading* companies can use the short version of the computational return.

The detailed version of the return must be used where special claims are made (such as group relief), where any entry is £10 million or more, and by investment companies. Loans to shareholders of close companies during the period must be summarised on supplementary page CT600A. Group relief claims and surrenders are detailed on supplementary page CT600C.

The penalty for late filing is £100, rising to £200 where the return is more than three months late. The penalty rates rise to £500 and £1,000 for persistent offenders (where the return is filed late for a third consecutive period).

The CTSA system

4.54   The CT600 return is a true self-assessment. The onus is on the company to ensure that its tax return is correct and complete. No assessment or determination is issued by HMRC to agree the tax result. The returns are subject to a 'process now, check later' system, with any obvious mistakes arising from the processing of the returns being corrected by HMRC.

However, the tax profit or loss is automatically treated as final after 12 months from the filing date (ie usually two years from the end of the relevant corporation tax accounting period CTAP), unless HMRC initiate an enquiry leading to an amendment of the return within the 12-month period.

Where the return is submitted early, the 12-month enquiry 'window' now starts from when the return is submitted (so the window will close sooner). However, this rule does not apply to large and medium sized groups (under the Companies Act 2006). HMRC will therefore still be able to open an enquiry into the company tax return of any member of a large or medium-sized group within the 12-month period of the statutory filing date, however early the return is delivered. However, HMRC is keen to encourage these larger companies to file early where it is possible for them to do so. Therefore, where it is practical to do so, HMRC's policy is to open all enquiries into a group's returns within 12 months of the delivery of the last individual company tax return from any member of that group. HMRC's operational note states that whilst this procedural change will apply to those companies dealt with by either HMRC's Large Business Services or Local Compliance (Large and Complex) offices. This is because HMRC is unlikely to have sufficient resources to extent this treatment to other large or medium-sized corporate taxpayers dealt with outside of these two units (mainly medium sized companies).

Companies can generally adjust their returns (post-submission) within the 12-month period following the statutory filing date.

The majority of cases selected for enquiry are chosen on an objective basis, ie that there may be something wrong in the return following various checks made by HMRC on the return information. Also, a small number of cases will be selected at random. For further details of HMRC's procedures and practice for enquiries, see *IR Code of Practice 14*.

HMRC's Discovery powers

4.55   To ensure finality under CTSA, HMRC's ability to 'open-up' previous years CT returns is generally restricted to the '12-month' enquiry window discussed in 4.54 above. From April 2010, HMRC can only raise 'discovery' assessments within *four* years of the end of the relevant CTAP where it can show that tax has been under-stated on a CT return as a result of a mistake with *insufficient disclosure* on that return. Before April 2010, the time limit was six years from the end of the CTAP.

However, the time limit for raising discovery assessments is extended in more 'serious' cases involving failure to take reasonable care (six years from the end of the CTAP) or where there has been a deliberate understatement (20 years from the end of the CTAP).

As mentioned above, discovery assessments can be raised where the company fails to provide sufficient information for the inspector to realise (within the enquiry period) that the 'self assessment' is inadequate. The relevant principles for determining whether sufficient disclosure has been made are covered in *Langham v Veltema* [2004] STC 544 and the Special Commissioners ruling in *Corbally-Stourton v HMRC* [2008] SpC 692.

The *Langham v Veltema* makes it clear that the information provided by the taxpayer must make the inspector aware of an *actual* insufficiency in the self assessment. It is not sufficient to prompt HMRC into making further enquiries that would reveal the under-assessment of tax.

This principle was refined in *Corbally-Stourton,* in which the taxpayer had purchased a capital-loss scheme. It seems clear that HMRC will be prevented from making a 'discovery' where at the end of the normal 12-month enquiry window, the inspector 'could not have been reasonably expected, on the basis of the information made available to him before that time, to be aware of the [circumstances giving rise to the loss of tax]'.However, the case also had to consider the level of disclosure that was required in the return. The Special Commissioner accepted that the test should be whether a reasonable officer would conclude that it was more probable than not that there had been a loss of tax, as expressed below

'Thus in my view it is not required that the officer be aware that there was in truth an insufficiency or that he be aware that it was beyond all reasonable doubt that there was an insufficiency, but merely that the information should enable him to conclude on balance that there was an insufficiency. Again a mere suspicion would not be enough, but, a conclusion in relation to which he had some residual doubt may well be sufficient. If he could reasonably have been expected to have come to such a conclusion before (*the end of the normal enquiry period*) he is precluded from making a discovery assessment'.

However, in this case, although a reasonable level of disclosure had been given on the tax return, it was not enough to satisfy the Special Commissioner that it was 'probably wrong'!

Assessing the correct level of disclosure is likely to be difficult in many cases. However, some comfort can be obtained from the later Special Commissioners ruling in *Mr & Mrs Bird v HMRC* [2008] (SpC 720). In this case, HMRC was unable to make 'out-of-time' discovery assessments under the parental settlement rules. The Special Commissioner ruled that the taxpayer had *not* been negligent ('negligence' is replaced by carelessness for discovery assessments made from April 2010). He held that the taxpayer could not have realised that the arrangements for allowing his (minor) children to subscribe for shares in his company constituted a settlement for income tax purposes – 'this would demand a sophistication that is beyond what is expected of the assumed reasonable competent taxpayer'.

Record retention requirements

4.56 The self-assessment regime requires specific accounting records, documents, vouchers, etc to be retained to enable a complete and correct return. Where companies are within the scope of the transfer pricing regime (see 4.11), documentation must also be retained to demonstrate that transfer pricing on goods and services, etc supplied to and from overseas and UK affiliates as well as between UK and UK affiliates have been conducted on an arm's length basis (see 4.11 and 4.12).

All supporting records and documents must be kept for six years from the end of the return period or longer if an HMRC enquiry is still in progress. Penalties of up to £3,000 will be levied for failure to comply.

PENALTIES UNDER CTSA

Circumstances giving rise to a penalty

4.57   As a simplification measure, *FA 2007, Sch 24* introduced a common regime for penalties for all the main taxes, and includes corporation tax. For corporation tax, the *Sch 24* penalty regime will apply to all CTAPs starting *after 31 March 2008* for CT returns due to be filed *after 31 March 2009*.

The old penalty CTSA penalty regime still generally applies to CT returns filed before April 2009, but it is likely that HMRC are still likely to follow the principles of the *Sch 24* regime to those cases.

A penalty can be charged where there is either an error in a document *or* an under-assessment by HMRC. In the context of CTSA, *FA 2007, Sch 24, para 1* states that a penalty will be payable where a company provides a CT600 return or accounts (or *any other* document relied on for determining its liability to corporation tax, which might be a document submitted in correspondence with HMRC *after* the submission of a CT600) provided two conditions are satisfied:

> *Condition 1* – the return, accounts or relevant document contains an *inaccuracy* leading to either an understatement of a liability to tax, a false or inflated loss, or a false or inflated claim to a tax repayment; and

> *Condition 2* – the accuracy is *careless* or *deliberate*.

Penalties can arise if a company is careless and fails to take 'reasonable care' (although it is possible for such penalties to be suspended – see 4.61 below). The test of what is 'reasonable' will vary from company to company, and depends on their particular circumstances. Every company is expected to maintain sufficient records to provide a complete and accurate return. Where a company is involved in an unfamiliar transaction or area, HMRC stress that it is reasonable to expect the tax implications to be checked out and/or appropriate advice to be taken.

The legislation also extends to the company's tax agent(s) [*FA 2007, Sch 24, para 18*]. However, penalties should not be levied provided reasonable care is taken by the 'agent'. Penalties can also be applied to managers, secretaries or any other persons managing the company's affairs.

Calculation of penalties

4.58   With the introduction of these fixed penalties, there is likely to be less scope for negotiating the penalties with HMRC. Penalties are applied to the 'potential lost revenue' (PLR). PLR broadly represents the additional tax due or payable to HMRC as a result of correcting an inaccuracy or understatement. Group relief and repayments of *CTA 2010, s 455 (ICTA 1988, s 419)* tax are ignored in calculating the PLR. This means that groups of companies cannot reduce any tax understatements by making group relief claims.

The fixed penalty rates are based on the taxpayer's behaviour that gives rise to an error. These are distinguished into three types of culpability – a careless mistake (ie failing to take 'reasonable care'), a deliberate but not concealed inaccuracy, and a deliberate and concealed inaccuracy. Clearly penalties can be avoided or minimised by providing correct tax returns, keeping appropriate records to provide complete and accurate returns, taking appropriate tax advice, and promptly disclosing any problems or errors on returns that have already been submitted.

The relevant maximum penalty rates are as follows:

Culpability	Maximum penalty
Careless error	30%
Deliberate error (without concealment)	70%
Deliberate *and* concealed error	100%

Determining reduction in penalty

4.59   A penalty can be reduced where the error is disclosed to HMRC since varying percentage reductions are applied to the relevant penalty rate for 'prompted' and 'unprompted' disclosures. Thus, lower penalties will be levied for less serious taxpayer behaviour and higher penalties for more serious types of behaviour. Thus, for example, where a company informs HMRC about an error in a tax return on an *unprompted* basis (ie where the company has no reason to believe HMRC are about to discover it) then it may be possible for the penalty to be completely eliminated. Penalties will be reduced where HMRC is informed about any errors and the company assists it in working out the additional tax with access to the relevant figures. However, a lower reduction in penalty applies where HMRC effectively 'prompts' the relevant disclosure.

Disclosure is defined in *FA 2007, Sch 24, para 9 (1)* as

(a)   telling HMRC about it;

(b)   giving HMRC reasonable help in quantifying the item; and

(c)   allowing HMRC access to the records to ensure that the error is fully corrected.

The 'quality' of a disclosure includes consideration of the timing, nature and extent of that disclosure [*FA 2007, Sch 24, para 9(3)*]. Effective management of any enquiry or voluntary disclosures will therefore be crucial in reducing any penalty due.

FA 2007, Sch 24, para 10 provides for a potential reduction in penalties and lays down a minimum penalty for each case, as follows:

Culpability	Maximum penalty	Minimum penalty	
		for unprompted disclosure	*for prompted disclosure*
Careless error	30%	0%	15%
Deliberate error (without concealment)	70%	20%	35%
Deliberate <u>and</u> concealed error	100%	30%	50%

This can be shown diagrammatically as follows:

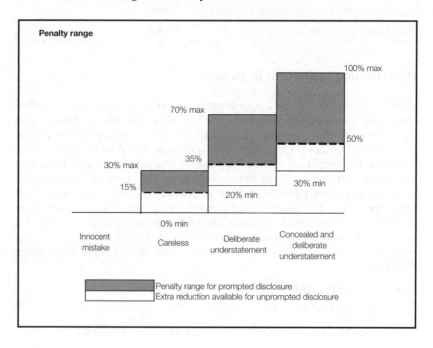

Penalty computation check-list

4.60   The following computational steps should be used for each *separate* error

1.	Compute taxable profits, income or capital gain for relevant error	
2.	Calculate Potential Lost Revenue on those taxable profits, income, or gains =	PLR
3.	Determine relevant behaviour category • Innocent – (so ignore = nil penalty) • Careless • Deliberate but not concealed • Deliberate and concealed	
4.	If *not* an innocent error, identify the highest % penalty for relevant error =	H%
5.	Is the disclosure voluntary/unprompted *or* prompted?	
6.	Identify lowest % penalty for the behaviour =	L%
7.	Maximum disclosure reduction= H less L =	MDR%
8.	Assess quality of disclosure that was made	
9.	Negotiate with HMRC, the % reduction for 'disclosure' =	NR%
10.	The actual reduction in the penalty = MDR% × NR% =	AR%
11.	The applied penalty %=H% less AR%	P%
12.	Actual penalty applied to error = PLR × P%	

Suspension of penalties

4.61   Where a penalty has been charged for failing to take '*reasonable care*' (careless inaccuracy), HMRC may suspend all or part of the penalty for up to two years [*FA 2007, Sch 24, para 14*]. HMRC must issue a written 'penalty suspension' notice which will provide certain conditions for the suspension of the penalty, which may include action to be taken by the company.

Provided all the suspension conditions have been met during the suspension period, HMRC will cancel the penalty. A suspended penalty will become payable if the company breaks one of the suspension conditions or incurs another tax penalty.

Penalty for failing to notify an under-assessment by HMRC

4.62   Penalties can also be charged where an assessment issued by HMRC understates a liability to tax and reasonable steps are not taken to notify HMRC within 30 days from the date of the assessment in question. In considering whether the steps are reasonable, account is taken of whether the taxpayer knew of the underassessment or ought to have known. In such cases, the penalty loading is 30% (with the same reduction percentage as for careless errors).

PLANNING CHECKLIST - TRADING COMPANY AND INVESTMENT COMPANIES - SUMMARY OF TAX TREATMENT AND MAIN TAX RELIEFS

	TRADING COMPANY	**INVESTMENT COMPANY**
Corporation tax small profits rate available (if profits below relevant limits)	Yes.	Yes, but not if company is a CIC ('close investment holding company').
Relief for expenses	Trading expenses deductible against trading profits, provided incurred wholly and exclusively for the purposes of the trade.	Management expenses (basically all costs of managing company's investments are deducted against total profits on an 'accruals' basis (including capital gains)). (There is no statutory 'wholly and exclusively' restriction, but in practice HMRC tend to apply one.)
Relief for directors' remuneration	Usually no problem in practice for proprietorial directors (although strictly subject to the 'wholly and exclusively' test).	Level of deduction frequently challenged – remuneration generally limited to a (much lower) justifiable figure.
Relief for interest costs	All interest deductible on an accruals basis as a trading or non-trading deduction, depending on the purpose of the borrowing.	All interest will normally be deductible on an accruals basis as a non-trading loan relationship debit.
Relief for capital expenditure	Relief given under the capital allowances system.	Relief given under capital allowances system (on same basis as trading company).

	TRADING COMPANY	**INVESTMENT COMPANY**
Relief for losses	Trading losses can be carried back against total profits for previous year(s) and/or carried forward against future *trading* profits of the same trade.	Excess management expenses (effectively an investment company's 'loss') can be carried forward against total profits (but not carried back).
Roll-over relief	Available on certain categories of asset (such as property, fixed plant) used for trading purposes.	Not available for investment property.
	Gains or profits on the sale of goodwill and other intangible fixed assets may be rolled-over against the purchase of goodwill/ intangible fixed assets.	Gains or profits from the sale of intangible fixed assets used within a property rental or other 'investment' business may be rolled-over against goodwill/ intangible fixed assets.
Share loss relief for capital losses on unquoted shares	No relief.	Can elect to offset loss against income subject to certain conditions.
Availability of shareholder reliefs: **– Entrepreneurs' relief (ER) (from 6 April 2008)**	CGT rate of 10% for cumulative qualifying gains up to (currently) £15 million. Since 23 June 2010, excess gains taxed at 28%	ER not available – since 23 June 2010, significant gains are likely to be taxed at 28%.
– CGT hold-over relief for gifts or undervalue sales of business assets	Relief normally available, but note 'narrow' trading company definition applies. Relief is restricted where company holds investment property.	Relief not given unless company is a 'holding company of a trading group'.

	TRADING COMPANY	INVESTMENT COMPANY
– **Capital treatment for purchase of own shares, IHT business property relief**	Relief available (but in most cases reliefs are restricted where company holds investment property).	No relief, unless company qualifies as a holding company of a trading group.
– **Substantial Shareholdings Exemption**	Can generally be claimed by a trading investor company.	Only available if the 'investment' holding company qualifies as a member of a trading group.
– **Interest relief on loan to buy shares in company**	Yes.	Yes, unless company is a CIC (close investment holding company).

Chapter 5

Remuneration Strategies

BACKGROUND

Factors influencing levels of remuneration

5.1 Many family or owner-managed companies do not follow any particular remuneration strategy and simply leave matters to market forces. Whilst a rigid set of rules may well be inappropriate, remuneration planning can be to everyone's advantage.

For owner managers and other working shareholders the level of remuneration will generally be determined by a number of factors:

(*a*) dividend strategies as a means of mitigating the impact of costly NICs (see 2.9–2.18 and Chapter 9);

(*b*) the need to make a suitable pension provision – personal pension contributions are still dependent on sufficient remuneration being taken to 'frank' the tax-relievable contribution, but the attraction of making substantial additional pension contributions has been reduced in recent years. From 6 April 2011, pension contributions relief is limited to the annual allowance of £50,000 (with rules to carry forward unused relief for the previous three years) (see Chapter 10);

(*c*) the anti-avoidance IR 35 rules for taxing income of personal service companies (see Chapter 6);

(*d*) the possible commercial need to retain a specific level of profits;

(*e*) meeting the national minimum wage (NMW) requirements (where there is an underlying employment contract) of £6.08 per hour (from 1 October 2011) (see 2.10 for the impact of the NMW on family and owner-managed companies);

(*f*) the requirements of a shareholders' agreement, for example, with a venture capitalist investor;

(*g*) the possible need to keep directors' remuneration within the limits imposed by a lending bank; and

(*h*) the working shareholders' personal spending requirements.

Most owner managers will also wish to avoid the ravages of the 50% super tax rate, preferring to keep their combined salary/bonuses/dividends below the £150,000 income threshold.

Furthermore, owner managers often seek to minimise the current high levels of NICs (see 5.4). For the working shareholders, this is likely to involve 'payment' in the form of dividends (see 2.9) and perhaps the payment of company pension contributions for their benefit. The use of salary sacrifices and tax-efficient benefits (see Chapter 7) may also be useful.

The interests of non-working shareholders may often be different, but they will be keen to see the adoption of a properly formulated and consistent strategy. The general staff of the business will have their own agendas too: their first concern will be an appropriate level of basic remuneration, but they will also be interested in fringe benefits and performance-related bonuses.

EBT AND EFRBS ARRANGEMENTS

5.2   Over the past decade, a number of owner managers have been tempted to use employee benefit trusts (EBTs) and, more recently, employer funded retirement benefit schemes (EFRBSs) as a means of side-stepping substantial income tax and NIC costs on their remuneration packages. HMRC's response was to introduce 'wide-ranging' anti-avoidance legislation in *FA 2011* – 'Employment income provided through third parties' – to negate the purported tax/NIC advantages of such schemes (see **5.00**). This legislation is not retrospective but HMRC are continuing to vigorously challenge (pre-10 December 2010) arrangements and have obtained tax settlements in many cases (see **5.0**)

ALPHABET SHARE ARRANGEMENTS

5.3   A number of companies have been substituting dividends for bonuses by using so-called 'alphabet share' arrangements for their employees. Broadly, these involve issuing employees with A, B, C, etc shares carrying an entitlement to such dividends as may be declared by the ordinary shareholders/directors, but with minimal other rights. In such cases, HMRC are likely to contend that the dividends constitute employment income under the special benefits from securities rules in *ITEPA 2003, Chapter 4* and *s 447*. HMRC may seek to apply this legislation where they can show that tax avoidance is involved, which would enable the dividend to be treated as a 'benefit' derived from the shares acquired by virtue of employment. HMRC are also likely to press for NICs on the basis that they constitute earnings. Alphabet share arrangements are used by 'umbrella companies' which have been subject to anti-avoidance legislation since 2007 (see **6.37**).

However, pro-rata dividends paid on fully-fledged ordinary shares are unlikely to be caught by these rules (even where the shares are employment related). In particular, these rules should not apply to different classes of shares issued on incorporation, where the subscribers subsequently become employees/ directors. Furthermore, there can be no problem where different classes of shares are used to provide flexibility in making different levels of dividends, avoiding the need for waivers. However, the position appears less clear where the employees receive ordinary shares carrying full rights with the shares being designated into different classes to enable different levels of dividend to be paid to particular employees or groups of employees, presumably because HMRC will seek to establish an underlying 'tax avoidance' motive (see *ICAEW Tax Faculty Taxline*, March 2005).

In this context, it is worth noting that some eminent tax barristers have expressed the view that the 'dividend' priority rule in *ITEPA 2003, s 716A* ensures that such income should still be treated as dividend income. Indeed, this line of reasoning has received judicial approval in *PA Holdings Ltd v HMRC* [2009] UKFTT 95 (TC) which involved an EBT plan that effectively converted 'bonuses' into dividends. The EBT established preference shares in a captive company, with the employees receiving dividends in line with their bonus expectation. The Tribunal found that the amounts were emoluments since the main purpose of the payment was to motivate the employees. However, this did not displace the fact that the amounts were also legally declared dividends. Consequently, by applying the 'dividend' priority rule in what was *ICTA 1988, s 20*, they were taxed as dividends. However, the 'dividends' were treated as earnings for NIC purposes (since there was no comparable 'priority ' provision). The Tribunal found that this was not an 'off the shelf' scheme and their decision may have been different if it were. An important factor was that the trustees of the EBT had acted independently. The case underlies the importance of establishing substance to be safe from a 'tax avoidance' attack.

(There is also a decent argument that dividends paid on the shares of the same class are *not* special benefits – only benefits accruing to a shareholder outside their normal share rights but by virtue of their shareholding should be caught under *ITEPA 2003, Chapter 4.*)

NATIONAL INSURANCE CONTRIBUTIONS (NICS)

Scope of NICs

5.4   Directors and employees are usually liable to primary Class 1 National Insurance Contributions (NICs) on their earnings, which include payments of money and money's worth. (For NIC purposes, earnings includes remuneration or profit derived from employment *–SSCBA 1992, s 3.*) This would cover payments in respect of contracts made personally by the director or employee which are paid for by the employing company (for example, 'personal' private healthcare or mobile phone contracts).

A simple but effective NIC saving idea is to move contracts into the company's name, such as a telephone contract for the private home phone line. Where a contract is in the individual's name but reimbursed by the company, both Class 1 primary and secondary contributions are due. In contrast, if the contract is directly with the third party and in the company's name, the benefit is reported on the employee's P11D form (where earnings exceed £8,500). This arrangement will only be liable to Class 1A NICs, providing a potential NI saving.

Non-cash vouchers (which can be surrendered for goods and service) are also subject to NICs (subject to certain special exemptions, for example, the popular childcare vouchers). Special rules apply to ensure that NICs are applied to readily convertible assets (see 13.36). In certain cases, tips should not count as earnings for NIC purposes provided they are received directly from the customer (and have not been distributed/allocated first by the employer).

NIC RATES

5.4A   For the year ending 5 April 2012, NIC on directors' and employees' earnings (including benefits) are calculated as follows:

- employees' NICs are levied at the rate of 12% on earnings falling between the primary threshold (£7,225 per year) and upper earnings limit (£42,475 per year), with a 2% NIC charge being levied on earnings above the upper earnings limit (without any 'ceiling');

- employer's NICs of 12.8% are charged on earnings above the annual secondary threshold of £7,072.

The basic calculation of Class 1 NICs for directors is covered at 5.16. The lower earnings limit and earnings threshold are applied in relation to each separate employment/office – rather than per earner. It is therefore likely that employees/directors with a number of concurrent employments/directorships will pay a lower amount of NICs (as compared with the NICs that would have been payable had the earnings come from a single employment/directorship). However, there are special rules which are designed to counter any artificial fragmentation arrangements using 'connected' companies etc [*Social Security (Contributions) Regulations 2001, reg 15*].

It should also be noted that NICs are effectively 'credited' for state benefits once they reach the lower earnings limit (£5,304 per year) whereas (employees') NICs do not become payable until they reach the primary earnings threshold (£7,225 per year). In appropriate cases (eg part-time workers and owner-managers), remuneration levels could be 'fixed' to take advantage of these rules ensuring that employees/directors maintain their entitlement to state benefits.

Given the relatively high levels of NICs, many owner-managers have tended to reduce their normal salary/bonuses and pay themselves larger dividends instead (see 2.9).

TEMPORARY REGIONAL EMPLOYER NICS HOLIDAY FOR NEW BUSINESSES

5.4B   The June 2010 Budget also announced a temporary exemption for employer's NIC for new businesses which start up in targeted areas outside London, the South East and the East of England. These new businesses are exempt from the £5,000 of employer NICs that would otherwise be due in the first 12 months of employment. This exemption applies for each of the first ten employees hired in the first year of business. (There are special rules that prevent a business being treated as 'new' where the owner has carried on another business within the previous six months consisting mostly of the same activities.)

The measure will apply in Scotland, Northern Ireland and Wales, and the following English regions: the North West, North East, Yorkshire and Humber, West Midlands, East Midlands and South West. The scheme applies to any new business set up from 22 June 2010 and lasts until 5 September 2013.

TAXATION OF EARNINGS

Basic position for employees and directors

5.5   Tax is charged on the full amount of employment income received during the tax year. For employees (who are resident, ordinarily resident and domiciled in the UK), earnings are treated as received on the *earlier* of:

(*a*)   actual payment of earnings or on account of earnings; or

(*b*)   entitlement to payment of earnings or to payment on account of earnings.

These timing rules do not necessarily apply to benefits in kind (see Chapter 7).

The basic rules may sound reasonably straightforward, but not surprisingly there are further provisions where *directors* (who are resident, ordinarily resident and domiciled in the UK) are concerned. For this purpose, a 'director' means:

(i)   in relation to a company whose affairs are managed by a board of directors or similar body, a member of that body;

(ii)   in relation to a company whose affairs are managed by a single director or similar person, that director or person; and

(iii)   in relation to a company whose affairs are managed by the members themselves, a member of the company [*ITEPA 2003, s 18(3)*].

Furthermore, a director includes any person in accordance with whose directions or instructions the company's directors are accustomed to act, often referred to as a 'shadow director'. Someone giving advice in a professional capacity is ignored [*ITEPA 2003, s 18(3)*].

Directors earnings are treated as received on the *earliest* of:

(*a*)   actual payment of (or on account of) earnings;

(*b*)   entitlement to payment of (or on account of) earnings;

(*c*)   the time at which the sums are credited to the company's accounts or records (any restrictions on the right to draw them are ignored);

(*d*)   the end of a period of account where earnings are determined before the end of that period;

(*e*)   the determination of earnings for a period of account if they are determined after the end of that period [*ITEPA 2003, s 18(1)*].

A director resigning during the tax year does not avoid these special rules for that year [*ITEPA 2003, s 18(2)*].

ADDITIONAL 'TIMING' RULES FOR DIRECTORS

5.6   Earnings are treated as being paid when they are credited to the accounts, even where a legal restriction operates to prevent them being drawn until a later date or event occurs. However, remuneration that enjoys no right of payment unless a pre-determined condition occurs is not treated as paid until the right to payment becomes unequivocal.

When accounts are prepared in readiness for an AGM they will invariably include a provision entry for directors' remuneration (see 5.14 for the corporation tax implications of such a provision). This will not normally constitute pay until the amount has been formally agreed by the Board (when it will become necessary to operate PAYE). However, if the remuneration has been formally agreed and is not credited to an account in the director's name but to another account or record of the company, it will still be deemed to be taxable employment income.

If the shareholders approve the director's remuneration by formal agreement before the AGM, a receipt may be deemed to arise following the decision in *Re Duomatic* [1969] 1 All ER 161. This important rule will often establish a 'taxable' entitlement to director's remuneration before the AGM (see 2.22).

For all payments that are deemed to arise under the rules set out above, PAYE and NIC should be calculated and accounted for as for actual payments.

If the amount of remuneration is determined before the end of the period to which it relates, but by the end of the period some or all of it has not actually been paid, or become due to be paid, or been credited, then payment of the unpaid amount is not regarded as having taken place until the end of the period.

Where the level of remuneration is profit-related, payment thereof is made when all the relevant profit information is known so the amount can be calculated, and not when the actual formula is agreed.

Owner-managers will now pay more attention to the timing of their bonus payments to reduce their exposure to the very high combined PAYE/NIC rates. In some cases, this may mean owner-managers/directors deferring bonus payments to shift them into another tax year (when their marginal tax rates are lower). In some cases, it might be sensible for the company to provide temporary loans to meet their personal cash flow requirements, since the tax cost of the potential benefit-in-kind charge is relatively low (see 2.18 for further commentary and 7.54 for benefit-in-kind rules on beneficial loans)

PERSONAL SERVICE COMPANIES

5.6A If the business of the owner-managed company involves providing a service, some or all of its income may be caught by the IR 35 provisions (now enacted in *ITEPA 2003, Chapter 8*), or the managed service companies rules introduced in the *Finance Act 2007* (see Chapter 6). If this is the case, those provisions will govern the remuneration strategy for the working shareholders and other employees.

CORPORATION TAX RELIEF FOR THE COMPANY

5.7 The remuneration for directors and other employees is generally deductible for the period of account to which it relates, subject to the overriding rule that the amount is commercially justifiable. Where remuneration/bonus remains unpaid at the balance sheet date, *CTA 2009, ss 1288–1289* provides that this may still be deductible for the accounting period ending on that date, provided it is actually 'paid' within nine months of the year-end. A similar rule applies for determining the allowable management expenses of investment businesses [*CTA 2009, ss 1249* and *1250*]. The date of payment is defined fairly widely and is the same as the date of receipt for 'employment' income tax purposes, as set out in 5.5 and 5.6 [*CTA 2009, ss 1289(4)* and *1250(4)*].

However, this is subject to the overriding accounting rule in *CTA 2009, s 46* (previously *FA 1998, s 42*), which requires that profits must be computed in accordance with generally accepted accounting principles ('GAAP'). In this particular context, any provision for bonuses etc. would have to comply with FRS 12 (see 4.5). This means that (amongst other things), the company must have created a current obligation to pay the relevant bonus by the year-end date – for example, by means of an appropriate written agreement or Board minute.

Where the accrued bonus/remuneration is not paid within nine months from the end of the period, the above statutory rules provide that the tax deduction is only given in the (later) period when the amount is paid.

If the company submits its accounts and tax computations before nine months after the end of the period of account, any earnings still unpaid at that time should not be claimed. An adjustment to the tax computations is then made if the remuneration is actually paid within the nine-month period, provided a claim is made under *CTA 2009, s 1289(3)* or *1250(3)* within two years from the end of the period of account concerned.

See 2.22–2.23 for a full discussion of this topic.

THE PAYE SYSTEM AND THE FAMILY OR OWNER-MANAGED COMPANY

Basic position

5.8   The time of payment of earnings for PAYE purposes is specifically defined in *ITEPA 2003, s 686*. The time when payment is made for PAYE purposes is virtually identical to that used in *ITEPA 2003, s 18* (as detailed in 5.5 above).

HMRC APPROACH

5.9   With a family or owner-managed company, HMRC are often particularly keen to check that PAYE is being applied to sums received by directors.

Interest is chargeable on unpaid PAYE from 19 April (extended to 22 April if the return is filed online) following the end of the tax year [*Income Tax (PAYE) Regulations 2003, SI 2003 No 2682, reg 82*].

Under the current employer compliance regime HMRC will often, when finding underpayments of PAYE or benefits not declared (such as company cars) for directors and their families, wish to widen the scope of their enquiries. In such cases, they may launch a formal investigation into the director's personal tax affairs, based on the perceived irregularities they have found within the business. Clearly, this could involve a wide ranging review of the director's tax affairs.

Another weapon available to HMRC which is less commonly used is a *reg 80* determination. This is also under *SI 2003 No 2682* and can be used where the Inspector considers that tax is due under PAYE and has not been remitted to the Collector. In the context of family or owner-managed companies, it is often used to collect tax on directors' remuneration voted in the accounts. The problem with a *reg 80* determination is that it carries interest that runs from 19 April following the tax year to which it relates [*SI 2003 No 2682, reg 82*].

Furthermore, if the determination is not paid within 30 days of the determination notice becoming final, HMRC reserve the right to recover the outstanding PAYE liability due from the employee if they have reason to believe that the employee was aware that the company wilfully failed to deduct PAYE [*SI 2003 No 2682, reg 81*]. The employee is entitled to appeal against the direction notice.

PAYMENT IN ASSETS

5.10   PAYE and NIC have to be accounted for on the provision of a 'readily convertible asset' (RCA) to a director/employee. An RCA means an asset:

(*a*)   which is capable of being realised on a recognised investment exchange, the London Bullion Market, the New York Stock Exchange or on any market specified in PAYE regulations;

(*b*)   that consists in the rights of an assignee, or any other rights, in respect of a money debt due to the employer or any other person;

(*c*)   that consists of property subject to a fiscal warehousing regime;

(*d*)   that represents anything likely (without anything being done by the employee) to give rise to a right to obtain an amount of money that is similar to the cost involved in providing the asset; and

(*e*)   for which trading arrangements exist or are likely to come into existence [*ITEPA 2003, s 702*].

An extended definition of RCAs applies where shares are awarded to or options are exercised by directors or employees. Although in most cases, shares in owner managed companies are not RCAs (since there is no available market to trade the shares), there are special rules which deem shares in a subsidiary (under the control of an unlisted company) to be RCAs and hence subject to PAYE and NIC (see 8.38–8.40).

PAYE also has to be accounted for on:

•   the provision of a cash voucher;

•   the provision of a 'non-cash' voucher capable of being exchanged for goods coming within the RCA definition; and

•   credit tokens to obtain money or such goods [*ITEPA 2003, ss 693–695*].

If the director/employee does not reimburse the employer for the relevant PAYE within 90 days of 'receipt' of the relevant item, this PAYE tax will also be taxed as employment income and entered on the P11D (see Example 1 and 5.10) [*ITEPA 2003, s 222(1)(c), (2)*].

Example 1

Payment in assets

Mr Parker receives a bonus of £5,000 from Scott Ltd paid by way of gold bullion on 1 May 2011.

PAYE due, say £2,500 (50%), is paid to the Collector of Taxes by 19 May 2011.

If Mr Parker does not pay £2,500 to his employer by 29 July 2011 (90 days from 1 May 2011), he will be taxed on £7,500 in 2011/12 with a credit of £2,500 tax.

USE OF EMPLOYEE BENEFIT TRUSTS & EMPLOYER FINANCED RETIREMENT BENEFIT SCHEMES

Pre-FA 2011 EBT arrangements

5.11   Since the mid-1990s, employee benefit trusts ('EBTs') increased in popularity, with many schemes being structured to 're-characterise' payments made to owner managers (and employees) without triggering PAYE or NIC liabilities. However, a severe blow was dealt to the tax efficacy of a large number of EBTs by the House of Lords in *Dextra Accessories Ltd v MacDonald* [2005] STC 1111. Tax relief for the company's contributions to the EBT was denied on the basis that there was a reasonable prospect of the entire funds being paid out by the trust intermediary as employees' remuneration. This meant that they constituted 'potential emoluments' (within what was *FA 1989, s 43(11)*), thus postponing the tax relief until they were actually paid out to (and taxed on) the employees.

The effectiveness of such arrangements was further nullified by the *Finance Act 2003*, which broadly defers corporation tax relief for contributions made to EBTs until the relevant amounts have been subjected to PAYE and NIC or used to meet qualifying expenses of the trust [*CTA 2009, ss 1290–1296 (previously FA 2003, Sch 24)*].

For an interesting analysis relating to an EBT plan that effectively converted bonuses into dividend income, see the decision in *PA Holdings Ltd v HMRC* [2009] UKFTT 95 (TC) (which is discussed at 5.3).

Use of EBTs for share schemes

A large number of EBTs are set up to acquire new or existing shares in the company. Typically, the EBT is a separate trust entity and is funded by contributions from the sponsoring company. The trustees, who should be independent from the company, can decide how to use the trust funds for the beneficiaries, often consulting with the company. The acquisition of shares may be funded by company contributions or borrowing. The trust often holds the shares for a number of years for distribution in due course to employees. The distribution is either direct or via an employee share scheme. The likely advantages of an EBT for a family or owner-managed company include the following:

- shares may be acquired at a low price for distribution to employees;

- it can be used as a 'warehouse' for problem shareholdings such as those acquired from an outgoing shareholder;

- an internal share market is created, enabling employees to buy and sell shares.

The statutory deduction rules for company EBT contributions do not apply where the EBT is awarding or transferring shares to directors and employees (see *CTA 2009, s 1290(4)*. This is because the company obtains it tax deduction under the employee share acquisition relief rules in *CTA 2009, Part 12* (see 8.86 to 8.89).

IHT issues for EBTs

5.11A   The EBT beneficiaries are normally the company's/group's current and previous employees and their families and dependants. In such cases, the EBT should fall within the *IHTA 1984, s 86* exemption (see *IHTA 1984, s 58(1)(b)*) from the normal IHT charges that apply to (discretionary) trusts (see 17.91 to 17.94) The trustees decide which beneficiaries are to benefit and the amount to be made available to them. Benefits are often provided by outright payments to different employees, cheap loans, and the provision of assets as well as shares.

In the context of a close 'owner-managed' company, shareholders (participators) holding 5% or more of the company's shares are generally *excluded* from benefit. This is because *IHTA 1994 s 13* only exempts the company's contributions from being counted as a 'transfer of value' for IHT purposes where the EBT's 'shareholder' beneficiaries do *not* have 5% or more of the voting rights. (A close company's transfer of value is apportioned amongst its (5% plus) shareholders under *IHTA 1984, s 94*.) Even where the 5% plus shareholders are excluded from benefit, HMRC will deny the *s 13* exemption where they have actually received a benefit from the EBT – for example by way of a loan or a sub-trust for their/their family's benefit.

However, there should be *no* need to rely on the protection given by *IHTA 1984, s 13* where the company can deduct the contribution for corporate tax purposes [*IHTA 1984, s 12*] and/or it can be demonstrated that the contribution was not intended to give a gratuitous benefit [*IHTA 1984, s 10*]. HMRC took a further 'swipe' at EBTs in *HMRC Business Brief 61/09*. The view is that reliance cannot be placed on the 'corporation tax deduction' IHT exemption in *IHTA 1984, s 12* where the relief is not available in the accounting period of payment. Thus, assuming reliance cannot be placed on *IHTA 1984, s 13* above, a transfer of value would arise for IHT where the company's tax relief is deferred, because the employees receives their benefits from the EBT more than nine months after the end of the relevant accounting period (see 8.9 below).

Even where the *s 12* 'corporate tax deduction' IHT exemption is not available, it seems that it may not be possible to rely on the 'non-gratuitous' benefit let-out in *IHTA 1984, s 10*. HMRC's view is that 'the possibility of the slightest benefit (from the EBT) suffices to infringe the requirement'. Amongst other things, an EBT is a discretionary trust and HMRC considers that contributions to an EBT will often confer a gratuitous benefit on the shareholders. HMRC conclude that the *possibility* of gratuitous intent when the contribution is made, is all that is necessary for the '*s 10* exemption' to be denied!

It follows that where the trust falls outside the protection of the main EBT exemption in *IHTA 1984, s 13* and the contribution to the trust cannot be deducted in the accounting payment of payment, HMRC will seek a potential IHT charge on the company's shareholders under *IHTA 1984, s 94*.

Nevertheless, many tax advisors disagree with HMRC's stance, contending that an EBT is a commercial arrangement to provide employee bonuses and benefits and cannot therefore be 'gratuitous'. This reasoning received strong judicial approval in *Postlethwaite's Executors v HMRC* [2007] SSCD 81, which held that a £700,000 contribution to an *EFRBS* for the benefit of Mr Postlethwaite and his family was not a transfer of value since it did not confer any gratuitous benefit. HMRC's response in Brief 61/09 is that due to the stringent nature of the non-gratuitous benefit rule in *IHTA 1984, s10*, this decision did not apply to *EBTs*. However, in a subsequent Brief 18/11, HMRC indicated that trading companies could obtain protection from any IHT charge where 100% business property relief is available (see 17.19)

THE SUBSEQUENT USE OF EFRBSs (PRE-FA 2011)

5.11B Following the *FA 2003* (see 5.11A), similar arrangements were structured through Employer Financed Retirement Benefit Schemes (EFRBSs) since payments to an EFRBS qualified as a statutory deduction for a 'qualifying benefit' within (what is now) *CTA 2009, s 1292(5)*.

EFRBSs were originally designed to provide pension benefits for employees (over and above the limits applying to 'registered' pension schemes). Broadly, speaking an EFRBS is a flexible discretionary trust which enables benefits to be provided after retirement to the 'employee' members of the scheme. After an employee's death, the trustees will have the power to provide a pension or other benefits to the employees dependants. EFRBSs are more flexible than registered schemes since they are not restricted by the various constraints imposed on 'registered' pension schemes.

EFRBS can make loans to members (whether before or after retirement). However, pre-retirement loans must carry a market rate of interest. Typical arrangements involved owner managed companies making (purportedly) tax deductible contributions to 'their' EFRBSs. Most of the contributed funds were then 'earmarked' for the principal director-shareholders within the EFRBS as a 'sub-fund'. The (friendly) trustees of the EFRBS then advanced interest-bearing loans to these director-shareholders. However, at the end of each tax year, the interest would be 'made good' by them through the use of further loans from the EFRBS. The basic mechanics of a typical EFRBS 'scheme' are illustrated below:

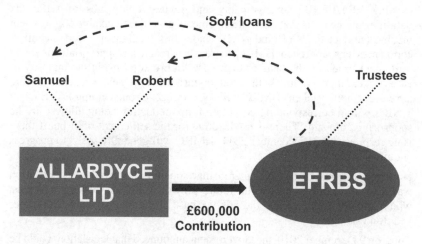

In HMRC's view, these types of EFRBS arrangements were 'unacceptable'. Although the loans made by the EFRBS come within the beneficial loan provisions (being enjoyed by reason of directorship/employment – see 7.54), the interest 'settled' on the loans (which cancels the charge) is immediately lent back as a further loan.

However, loans made by the EFRBS avoid the *CTA 2010, s 455* loan to participator charge. So, in essence, the intended effect of the scheme is to provide corporation tax relief on 'tax-free' loans to owner managers and employees.

Many companies also opt for offshore-based EFRBSs since they are not subject to tax on overseas income and gains (although UK basic rate income tax would be payable on any UK source income).

In early 2010, HMRC issued Spotlight 5, which made it clear that it did not agree that these arrangements achieved their intended tax advantages. HMRC have mounted a strong campaign of attack on these type of arrangements since. In the vast majority of cases, HMRC has sought tax settlements on the basis the appointment on 'sub-trusts' and the onward loans are effectively employment income on which PAYE and NIC is due.

HMRC's contentions were strengthened by its 'success' in *Aberdeen Asset Management v HMRC* [2010] UKFTT 524 (TC) which involved an EBT scheme. The first-tier tribunal found that the 'scheme' involved a series of steps designed to operate together, and was a means of 'channeling' additional remuneration to the company's employees. The EBT trustees were mere ciphers who did what they were told. It was held that these arrangements were capable of being taxed under the *Ramsay* anti-avoidance doctrine (see 1.10 to 1.12). (However, the earlier decisions in *Dextra Accessories Ltd v MacDonald* [2005] STC 1111 and *Sempra Metals v HMRC* [2008] (SpC00698) found otherwise!).

Following this decision, HMRC became very confident that they could defeat existing EBT/EFRBS arrangements and invited companies to settle tax liabilities on the basis that these arrangements gave rise to taxable employment income (subject to PAYE and NIC). Under this 'settlement offer' incentive, companies can approach HMRC to reach a reach an appropriate financial settlement based on the facts of their case. In broad terms, in the majority of cases (where there is a link with employment), if a settlement is reached (before a 'relevant step' is taken) HMRC will seek to recover outstanding PAYE/Class 1 NICs with a corresponding corporation tax deduction being allowed in the sponsoring company. There is no deadline for the settlement offer but if there is no response by 31 December 2011, HMRC will generally seek "to progress enquiries formally".

However, HMRC clearly considered that specific anti-avoidance legislation was also necessary to thwart the future growth in the use of such schemes, which apparently threatened the UK tax base at the rate of some £500m per year (and rising).

Thus, on 9 December 2010, the Government announced that legislation would be introduced to impose a PAYE employment income tax and NIC charge on EBT, EFRBSs and other similar 'disguised remuneration' arrangements (see 5.12).

FA 2011 'EMPLOYMENT INCOME PROVIDED THROUGH THIRD PARTIES' LEGISLATION

Purpose of FA 2011 legislation

5.12   The aim of the *FA 2011* – 'Employment income provided through third parties' contained in *ITEPA 2003, Part 7A* (sometimes referred to as the 'disguised remuneration' rules) – is to impose a PAYE and NIC charge where third-party arrangements are used to provide what is, in substance, 'a reward, recognition or a loan' in connection with the employee's current, former or future employment. In practice, the 'third part' will normally be an EBT or EFRBS. The legislation (which runs to some 68 pages) has an extremely wide-scope and applies from 6 April 2011 but also catches certain 'payments' made between 9 December 2010 and 5 April 2011. Similar NIC regulations are also in force.

BASIC APPLICATION OF THE ITEPA 2003, PART 7A RULES

5.12A The application of the complex *ITEPA 2003, Part 7A* can be broken down into three main stages:

(1)	*Is there a third party?*	The legislation does not apply where an employer provides something directly to an employee (unless the employer is acting as a 'trustee' or has given an undertaken to pay contributions to an EFRBS)
(2)	*Are the ITEPA 2003, s 554A conditions satisfied?*	This involves three questions: • *Is there a 'relevant arrangement' relating to A?* • *'Is it reasonable to suppose that, in essence'… the relevant arrangement … is (wholly or partly) a means of providing … with the provision of rewards or recognition or loans in connection with A's employment with B'?* • *Has a relevant third person taken a <u>relevant step in connection with that arrangement?</u>* Notes: (a) 'A' is a current, former, or prospective employee. (b) 'B' is (normally) the employee's company. (c) For these purposes, a relevant arrangement is widely defined to include 'any agreement, scheme, settlement, transaction, trust or understanding, whether it is legally or enforceable or not' (*ITEPA 2003, s 554Z(3)*).

In most cases, a relevant third person will be the trustees of an EBT or EFRBS, but it can be any other person (which could include an employer acting as trustee).

There are three kinds of relevant step:

(i) *Earmarking* – 'earmarking' is a very broad concept and means earmarking (however informally) of a sum or an asset with the view to taking a later step. Under *ITEPA 2003, s 554B*, it does not matter whether any details of the later step have been worked out, such as the asset or sum in question or whether the employee or a 'linked person' has any legal right to have the step taken.

(A 'linked person' covers anyone connected with the employee or a close company in which the employee is a participator or a 51% subsidiary of that company.)

Chronologically, this is likely to be the earliest charging point. This 'relevant step' is intended to catch those cases where an EBT/EFRBS sets aside a 'sub-fund' for an employee and imposes a charge at that point (even though the employee may never receive it!)

It is considered that a genuine discretionary trust, such as an EFRBS that provides pension benefits based on a final salary arrangements would not be caught by Part 7A – since there is no 'earmarking'.

(ii) *Payment or transfer of an asset* – this refers to the 'payment' to a 'relevant person' (ie A or any other person chosen by A). This also covers other 'benefits' provided to a relevant person, such as a loan, a transfer of an asset, and the grant of a lease (likely to exceed 21 years) (see *ITEPA 2003, s 554C* for details)

Note that this 'relevant step' catches a 'loan' (as well as an absolute payment of money) which triggers a PAYE/NIC charge. Further, other than in limited cases, no relief from the charge is available if the loan is subsequently repaid.

(iii) *Making an asset available* – this applies where the relevant third person

– makes an asset available (without transferring it) to A (i.e. the employee) or 'linked person' (see (e)(ii) above); or

– makes the asset available to A two or more years after A's employment with B (*ITEPA 2003, s 554D*).

For these purposes, it does not matter whether A enjoys any actual benefit (*ITEPA 2003, s 554D(3)(c)*).

(3)	*Do any of the exclusions in ITEPA 2003, Part 7A apply?*	Even though points (1) and (2) above are satisfied, it may still be exempted from an employment income/NIC charge if it falls within one of the numerous exclusions, which limit the scope of the legislation quite considerably.
		These exclusions are very prescriptive and the main types are summarised below:
		A direct issue of shares by fellow group companies (since a group company is not a relevant third person provided there are no tax avoidance motives) and shares acquired for full value (see 8.14 and 13.29).
		Loans made directly by the employing company/group (since there is no relevant third person) (see 7.54).
		EBTs operating with approved share schemes (CSOPs, EMI schemes, SIPs, and SAYE schemes) provided there are no related tax avoidance arrangements (*ITEPA 2003, s 554E) (see 8.48 – 8.78*).

Employee benefits arrangements and shared-car ownership schemes (see chapter 7). A number of benefits are provided by *third parties* (e.g child care vouchers) and would potentially be caught by *ITEPA 2003, Part 7A*. However, exemption is given under ITEPA 2003, S554G provided the (third-party) employee benefits are generally made available to a substantial proportion (eg at least over 50%) of employees *and* do not have a tax avoidance motive.

Deferred bonus arrangements provided the vesting date is within five years and provided there are no tax avoidance arrangements. In such cases, the PAYE/NIC charge is deferred until the bonus is awarded (*ITEPA 2003, s 554H*)

Long Term Incentive Plans (LTIPs) under which a 'reasonable' amount of shares are earmarked for long term awards provided there are no tax avoidance arrangements (*ITEPA 2003, s 554J*).

Exit-based cash or share awards are excluded from an 'earmarking' charge on a similar basis to LTIPs (*ITEPA 2003, s 554K*)

Share options and phantom share scheme arrangements are excluded from an 'earmarking' charge (*ITEPA 2003, s 554L*) (see 8.7).

Payments or assets from pre-6 April 2011 non-registered or unfunded pension schemes or pre-6 April 2006 contributions to EFRBSs (which retain their existing income tax treatment (see 10.37)

While pension schemes generally come within the ambit of the *ITEPA 2003, Part 7A* legislation, no tax charge arises on any relevant step taken by registered pension schemes (subject to the annual and lifetime allowances).

However, there are no special exemptions for qualifying non-UK pension schemes (QNUPs) or qualifying registered overseas pension schemes (QROPs), since they are not 'registered' pension schemes) (see chapter 10).

Where an *ITEPA 2003, Part 7A* charge potentially arises on shares which is also taxable under employment related securities legislation. In such cases, *ITEPA 2003, s 554N* provides that shares are taxed under the employment related securities regime (which takes precedence) (see 8.13 – 8.37).

Thus, even if a transactions satisfies (1) and (2) above, there is no ITEPA Part 7A charge if it falls within one of the 'exclusions' listed in (3)

TRANSITIONAL RULES FOR EBT/EFRBS LOANS

5.12B   Loans made by EBTs and EFRBSs to employees before 9 *December 2010* are not caught by the *ITEPA 2003, Part 7A*, although these schemes may still generally be under HMRC enquiry along the lines discussed in 5.12A above. Such loans may also be taxable under the beneficial loan rules in *ITEPA 2003, s 175* (since they will be provided by reason of the individual's employment or office) (see 7.54). However, if the loan is a qualifying one (ie the interest would have been 'tax-deductible' (or would have been if the loan was interest-bearing), then no *ITEPA 2003, s 175* arises.

HMRC have confirmed that the 'writing-off' of a pre-9 December 2010 loan is not a 'relevant step' under the *ITEPA 2007, Part 7A* rules. It may also be the case that altering the terms of an existing pre-9 December 2010 loan is not a 'relevant step'– for example, the trustees may agree to extend the repayment period of the loan. However, HMRC has indicated that any alteration to the terms of a loan would be assessed on a 'case-by-case' basis

Loans made *after 8 December 2010 and before 6 April 2011* will be subject to a charge under the *ITEPA 2003, Part 7A* provisions, *if they are not repaid by 6 April 2012*. If the loans are not repaid by then, the amount of the loan would be taxed as 'PAYE' employment income (and subject to NICs) in the director's/ employee's hands.

Clearly, loans made after 5 April 2011 would be taxable as a relevant step under *ITEPA 2003, Part 7A* (see 5.12A (2) – note e (ii)).

PAYE AND NIC TAX CHARGES UNDER ITEPA 2003, PART 7A

5.12C   The tax charge under *ITEPA 2003, Part 7A* arises when a relevant step is taken. It will be appreciated that there may be several 'relevant steps' in relation to the same amount (for example, an amount might be first 'earmarked followed by a loan of the same amount). In such cases, the tax charge arises at the first of those relevant steps. However, the tax charge on the first relieves any potential tax on a subsequent relevant step in relation to the same arrangements

PAYE and NIC applies to the value of the relevant step and is payable as part of the monthly PAYE liability. The *ITEPA 2003, Part 7A* charge takes precedence over the normal PAYE rules and is likely to occur at an earlier stage (eg at the 'earmarking' step).

The tax cost of a *Part 7A* charge would increase if the employee concerned does not reimburse the PAYE tax within 90 days. If the PAYE is not reimbursed within the 90 day period, then a further tax charge arises on them under *ITEPA 2003, s 222* (see 8.45). This provision is interpreted strictly and any refund outside the relevant 90 day period will not be prevent a charge arising (*Chilcott v HMRC* [2010] EWCA Civ 1538

As a general rule, the rules are particularly penal in that the Part 7A tax charge is not refundable if the 'relevant step' is unwound – for example if the loan is repaid or the asset is transferred back to the provider. The same problem arises where an employee is subject to a tax charge on 'earmarking', yet actually end-up receiving nothing. However, in this situation, the tax may be refunded provided the arrangements are altered so that the employee is incapable of benefiting from the earmarked amount and no other person becomes able to benefit from it.

Example 3

PAYE/NIC on loan from an EFRBS

Mr Carlton (a UK resident) owns 20% of the entire issued capital of Shoot Ltd, and is also its sales director.

In December 2011, Shoot Ltd set up an EFRBS and paid a contribution of £200,000 to it.

After properly considering a request from the employing company, the trustees of the EFRB made a loan of £80,000 to Mr Carlton in recognition of his work over the past few years.

- The EFRBS would be an arrangement under *ITEPA 2003, s 554A*.

- The trustees of the EFRBS are a 'relevant third person' and the loan is a relevant step within *ITEPA 2003, s 554C*.

- The arrangements therefore meet the necessary conditions in *ITEPA 2003, s 554A*.

The £80,000 loan (the value of the relevant step) is treated as Mr Carlton's employment 'earnings' and hence is subject to PAYE/NIC, with Mr Carlton being liable to reimburse the PAYE tax within 90 days earnings (otherwise an additional tax charge arises under *ITEPA 2003, s 222*.

Example 4

Treatment of existing (pre-9 December 2010) EBT loan

Robert is an employee of the Thames (Iron Works) Ltd. He received an interest-bearing loan of £30,000 from the company's EBT on 12 April 2010.

This loan does not give rise to any *ITEPA 2003, Part 7A* charge since it was made before 9 December 2010. If the loan simply remains unpaid without any further steps being taken, it will remain outside the scope of *ITEPA 2003, Part 7A* . However, it may suffer a beneficial loan charge under *ITEPA 2003, s 175* if and to the extent that the interest is below the official rate of interest for each tax year.

USE OF SHARE OPTIONS

Popularity of share option schemes

5.13   Share option schemes have been used for many years as a method of delivering a performance reward to employees at very low cost to the company. However, the use of unapproved share option schemes has snowballed in recent times as smaller companies seek to use share options as a replacement for the high salaries they cannot afford to pay.

Gains on most unapproved option shares are now taxed at the current CGT rates of 18%/28% unless Entrepreneurs' relief applies (see 8.11)). However, provided the 'up-front' income tax charge can be minimised, unapproved share option arrangements can still be quite attractive (and are still preferable to highly taxed (and NIC-able) remuneration). Where shares represent very small minority holdings, the value agreed with HMRC should in most cases be relatively small (due to the substantial valuation discount applied against the valuation).

Considerable care must be taken to mitigate the sometimes harsh effects of the 'employment-related' restricted securities regime (see Chapter 8). Standard ordinary shares issued by most private companies should not be 'restricted', but it is recommended that protective ITEPA 2003, s431 elections are made to avoid the risk of subsequently incurring an employment income tax charge when the shares are subsequently sold (see 8.32).

Beneficial statutory corporate tax relief is available for shares provided to employees as well as on the exercise of employee share options. The relief is broadly given on the 'value' taxed as employment income in the employees' hands (replacing any charge that may have flowed through the profit and loss account under GAAP). EMI share options are favourably treated since corporate tax relief is still obtained on the market value of shares on exercise (despite the fact that the employee typically only pays the market value at the time the option is granted) (see 8.87).

Unapproved share option schemes can often give rise to obligations to account for PAYE and National Insurance (rather than the normal payment of tax under the self-assessment system) where the shares are readily convertible assets (RCAs). This is unlikely in most cases since there is no ready available market for the shares, although shares in subsidiary companies are caught as deemed RCAs (see 5.10).

PAYE ON SHARE OPTIONS

5.13A   When a director/employee receives shares from their employer or exercises share options granted by their employer, they are taxed on the market value of those shares at the time of receipt or exercise. If the shares are readily convertible assets ('RCAs') (see 5.10), PAYE and NICs must be applied at the time the share option is exercised. The PAYE/NIC is levied on the market value of the relevant shares less any amount paid for them and the option (see Example 2).

It may not be clear that the shares in a private company are RCAs unless the company is about to be sold or listed on a recognised exchange such as OFEX or AIM (see also 13.36).

The amount of PAYE due when the share options are exercised may be considerable and it may not be possible to deduct this from the employee's pay in a single month. If this is the case, the company must recover the excess

PAYE from the employee within 90 days after the date the shares were received or the option exercised (see 5.10 ,Example 1, and 8.45). If the company fails to do this, the unpaid tax is taxed as employment income in the employee's hands. The employee will then be charged tax and NICs on this deemed employment income. The company could grant a formal loan to the employee during this period to cover the PAYE tax – this may then fall to be taxed under the beneficial loan provisions (see 7.54). It is worth noting here that if the company cannot recover all of the PAYE from the employee, the company is still legally obliged to pay over the full amount of PAYE to HMRC.

Unless the PAYE tax has been formalised as a loan, there is no provision for HMRC to extend the recovery period in any circumstances, even if the employee pays the PAYE due shortly after 90 days have elapsed.

NICS ON SHARE OPTIONS

5.14 NICs can arise in a number of cases in relation to shares *that are RCAs* (see 5.10) such as where such shares are acquired through unapproved share option arrangements (or a simple award of shares).

In broad terms, the NIC charge is calculated on the market value of the shares when the option is exercised, after deducting the exercise price and any amount paid for the option. The employing company thus has to account for NICs on the profit realised by its employees on exercise of their share options. Thus, where the shares are RCAs and they increase in value, the NIC cost of the share option scheme spirals upwards.

A solution to this sticky problem is for the liability for the NIC charge to be passed to the employee either by joint NIC election or voluntary agreement [*SSCBA 1992, Sch 1, paras 3A, 3B* as amended by the *National Insurance Contributions and Statutory Payments Act 2004 (NICSPA 2004, s 3)*]. Companies can make provision in their share plan documentation to put employees under a contractual obligation to enter into a joint NIC election or voluntary agreement. Where employees pick-up the employers' NIC in this way, they can get relief for the NICs due on the exercise of the option against the PAYE due on the same event (see 5.10) [*ITEPA 2003, s 481*]. However, it makes the calculation of the net PAYE due rather more complicated.

NICs can also be levied on certain other 'chargeable events' under *ITEPA 2003, Pt 7*. For example, where (in the absence of an *ITEPA 2003, s 431* election) the value of shares (falling within the 'restricted securities' regime) are artificially increased (by the amendment or lifting of restrictions) – the NIC charge generally arises on the relevant increase in value. Following the *NICSPA 2004*, employers can also enter into joint elections or voluntary agreements to pass on NICs arising *after* the acquisition of restricted securities (and on the exercise of an option over such shares). This ability does not extend to all the potential chargeable events under *ITEPA 2003, Pt 7*.

The mechanics of various share option and share incentive schemes are discussed in Chapter 8.

Example 5

Tax on unapproved share option

Mr Dowie has unapproved share options in Rangers Ltd, an unquoted company, with no employment income tax charge on the grant. The exercise price is £2 per share on 20,000 shares. Rangers Ltd draws up accounts to 31 December each year.

Rangers Ltd is seeking a flotation on AIM. Before then, in May 2011, Mr Dowie exercises the share options and acquires the 20,000 shares now worth £16 each. On the exercise he is taxed under *ITEPA 2003, ss 476–478* on:

$(20,000 \times £16) - (20,000 \times £2) = £280,000$

HMRC will argue that PAYE has to be operated on the £280,000 'profit' as the shares are RCAs (since at the date the option is exercised there is an understanding that trading arrangements are likely to come into existence).

Rangers Ltd will be able to claim a corporate tax 'trading' deduction for the 'taxable amount' of £280,000 (see 5.5).

CORPORATE TAX RELIEF FOR SHARE AWARDS AND THE EXERCISE OF SHARE OPTIONS

5.15   Companies can claim corporation tax relief on the issue of shares to, or the exercise of share options by, directors and employees. In broad terms, the relief is based on the amount charged to income tax in the director's/employee's hands (or in the case of shares provided under an approved share scheme, the amount that would have been taxed). Details of the statutory corporate tax rules for employee shares and share option exercises are provided in Chapter 8.

NATIONAL INSURANCE CONTRIBUTIONS FOR DIRECTORS

Earnings periods

5.16   Contributions are payable by reference to the gross earnings for an earnings period (in contrast to the PAYE system, where tax is applied on a cumulative basis). NICs are therefore applied to employees' pay based on their weekly or monthly pay interval. This means that the maximum thresholds are applied on a monthly or weekly basis.

However, special rules apply to directors, who have an 'annual earnings' period even if they are paid at regular or irregular monthly or weekly intervals. This is to avoid a director receiving a large amount of earnings as a single payment thereby restricting the amount of NICs due for that month (as a result of the monthly upper earnings limit). There are no equivalent rules for employees who are not directors.

In terms of the administrative arrangements, broadly an employing company can choose to make NIC payments on account during the tax year based on the actual intervals of payment of earnings in the same way as for other employees. The director's overall NIC liability is then calculated by reference to the complete annual earnings period. Where the director only draws a regular salary, the annual re-calculation exercise is likely to have little impact on the director's/company's total NIC liability. However, if any irregular and/or varying payments have been made, additional NIC will usually be payable.

Where a director is appointed during a tax year, there is a pro rata earnings period. No change is made to the annual earnings period when a director resigns [*Social Security (Contributions) Regulations 2001, reg 8*].

Example 6

NIC calculation for director appointed during the tax year

Mr Franco (a UK resident) is appointed a director of Zola's Irons Ltd when there are 20 weeks left in the tax year 2011/12 . With a primary threshold of £139 per week and an upper earnings limit of £817 per week, Mr Franco's pro rata limits are:

20 × £139 = £2,780

and

20 × £817 = £16,340

Zola's Irons Ltd pays secondary Class 1 NICs above the secondary threshold of £136 per week.

20 × £136 = £2,720

The NIC position for 2011/12 is:

Total earnings	*Mr Franco*
£2,780 or less	Nil
£2,780 to £16,340	12% of earnings between £2,780 and £16,340
Over £16,340	2% of earnings above £16,340

Total earnings	Zola's Irons Ltd
£2,720 or less	Nil
Over £2,720	13.8% of earnings above £2,720

Example 5

Payments on account for a director

Mr Pearson is a director receiving a regular monthly salary of £1,000. His company decides to use a monthly earnings period for 2011/12 as follows:

Monthly secondary (employer) threshold	£589
Monthly primary (employee) threshold	£602
Monthly upper earnings limit	£3,540

He receives a bonus of £10,000, to be paid with his June 2011 salary. The NIC position for 2011/12 is:

	Earnings	*Director's NIC*	*Employer's NIC*
	£	£	£
Month 1 (April)	1,000	47.76	56.72
Month 2 (May)	1,000	47.76	56.72
Month 3 (June)	11,000	501.76	1,436.72
By month 11, totals are:	21,000	979.36	2,003.92

The month 12 calculation must consider the total earnings in the annual earnings period:

	Earnings	*Director's NIC*	*Employer's NIC*
	£	£	£
Month 12 (cumulative total)	22,000	1,773.00	2,060.01
Less paid on account		(979.36)	(2,003.92)
Due for month 12		793.64	56.09

DIRECTORSHIPS HELD BY MEMBERS OF A PARTNERSHIP

5.17   In some cases, fees are received by directors who are also members of a partnership. This does not alter the fact that the fees come from holding office and should therefore be taxed as employment income with consequent PAYE and NIC obligations. However, by concession (ESC A37), HMRC accept that such amounts can be treated as professional income of the partnership provided:

- The directorship is a normal incident of the profession and the relevant firm;

- The fees only represent a small part of the firm's profits; and

- The fees are pooled for division amongst the partners under the partnership agreement

The firm must provide a written undertaking to HMRC that the directors' fees will be included in its gross income. The same practice is also followed for NIC purposes under *Social Security (Contributions) Regulations 2001, reg 27.*

This concession also extends to directors fees which are subjected to corporation tax (for example, where a company has the right to appoint a director to the Board of another company), but not where a director has 'control' of that company under *CTA 2010, s 1124.*

OVERSEAS SECONDMENTS

5.18   A number of owner-managed companies will have extended their business operations overseas, possibly having one or more overseas branches and/or subsidiaries. Sometimes this will involve the secondment of UK-based managers or directors to develop the overseas' business.

As a general rule, where a UK director or employee is sent to work in another EU member state (or Iceland, Liechtenstein, Norway and Switzerland) for up to 24 months, they can continue to remain within the UK NIC regime. Initially, the application to continue paying UK NICs must be made on form E101. After that, by mutual agreement of the competent authorities of the home and host countries, the period of protection can be extended for up to five years. In essence, a director or employee seconded overseas can remain within the UK NIC/social security system for up to five years (and would not be subject to further social security contributions in the host EU country). This period would also count towards entitlement to UK pensions, etc.

In other cases, notably secondments to Canada, the USA and Japan, the potential duplication of UK NICs and host country social security contributions would normally be resolved by a reciprocal agreement/social security treaty. In many cases, the agreement/treaty generally gives five years automatic protection from host country contributions, with the UK secondee remaining subject to UK NICs and pension/benefit entitlements.

NON-EXECUTIVE DIRECTORS

5.19   If there are non-executive directors on the board, then as a general rule PAYE and NIC should be applied to remuneration and fees paid in the normal way. The tax treatment for reimbursed expenses, such as attending board meetings, depends on the manner in which they are paid. If the expenses are paid in cash by the non-executive director and subsequently reimbursed by the company, the payments made by the company are liable to PAYE and NICs. Where the expenses are met directly by the company and paid to the third party, the payments are reportable on the form P11Ds (although the ESC A4 effectively exempts travelling expenses incurred on travelling between companies in the same group and other defined situations).

Many companies are seeking to minimise the current high levels of NICs (see 5.4). For the working shareholders, this is likely to involve 'payment' in the form of dividends (see 2.9) and perhaps the payment of company pension contributions for their benefit. The use of salary sacrifices and tax-efficient benefits (see Chapter 7) may also be useful given the relatively high National Insurance costs.

By concession, HMRC usually accept 'self-employed' status for non-executive directors of small companies. Where the non-executive director's duties are provided as office holder through a limited company that is UK registered (and no other services are provided), HMRC permit the non-executive director to be paid *gross* on the production of an invoice (*Employment Status Manual* at ESM 3268). This concessionary treatment only applies where the fees are subject to corporation tax (as trading income) in the company's hands and the director and his family do not control the paying company. (The IR 35 rules do *not* apply – since *ITEPA 2003, s 49* do not extend to office-holders. Thus, the non-executive's PSC does *not* have to account for PAYE and NIC.) Any travelling and other expenses should be listed on their fees invoice (otherwise the payments are likely to be subject to PAYE).

The 'self-employed' dispensation does not extend to NICs. Thus, where the fees exceed the primary threshold, the company must account for NICs and employees' NICs are deductible from the invoiced amount (see 5.4 and 5.16). However, employees' NICs would not be due where the non-executive director is over the state retirement age (as is often the case!).

SHARE AND OTHER INCENTIVE ARRANGEMENTS

5.20   Approved share option schemes bring many advantages, giving employees a sense of proprietorship thus aligning their interests with those of the owners. Moreover, share schemes can provide employees with the potential to generate tax efficient capital gains provided there is a planned 'exit' strategy.

In some cases shares can be sold to an EBT or it is possible for the company to buy back the shares where someone leaves.

Employee share schemes may provide a cost-effective mechanism for rewarding directors and employees and are often regarded as a key element of their remuneration package. They include Share Incentive Plans (SIPs), Company Share Option Plans (CSOPs) and EMI schemes – all of which are covered in Chapter 8.

5.21 The range of tax-efficient incentive schemes available to employers also include:

- a discretionary bonus scheme, to fund a tax-efficient investment such as an Individual Savings Account (ISA) or pension scheme;

- a flexible benefits programme;

- interest free loans up to £5,000 in total per employee (no income tax charge on the benefit)

TERMINATION PAYMENTS

Exemptions for termination payments

5.22 Termination payments have become a key focus of HMRC. Inspectors seem to be look very closely at any returns where termination payments have been reported, and often seek to challenge the tax-exempt treatment of them.

Where an employee is made redundant, or otherwise has their employment terminated, there may be scope for receiving the first £30,000 of any pay-off tax-free. This relies on taking advantage of the £30,000 exemption in *ITEPA 2003, ss 401–403*, but this only applies where the payment would *not* otherwise be taxable under basic employment taxation rules. In other words, the payment must not represent earnings derived from the office or employment, but must be triggered by its termination. This crucial point is not always easily resolved, as demonstrated by the large body of case law in this area.

Except in the case of a genuine redundancy payment (see 5.23), if the director/employee has a right to the termination payment, then it will invariably be treated as earnings from the office/employment under the general rule in *ITEPA 2003, s 62*. Such rights may be contained in the individual's employment or service contract, letter of appointment, or staff handbook. Similarly, where the director/employee has a reasonable expectation of receiving a termination payment, HMRC always seek to treat this as taxable earnings (see 5.25).

Where the director/employee is also a shareholder, they will often want to sell their shares on ceasing to work (indeed they may be forced to sell them in certain circumstances). Where the size of the director's shareholding is able to exert influence, it is not surprising that Inspectors often attempt to argue that a lump sum 'termination' does not enjoy the *section 403* exemption. Instead, HMRC often seek to treat it as a (non-relievable) distribution by the company or as part of the sale proceeds for the shares.

Termination payments fall into various categories (as outlined below). The nature of the payment will usually have a significant bearing on the tax treatment for the company and director/employee. In practice, it may often be necessary to go behind the actual description of the 'termination' payment and establish the precise reason for and circumstances surrounding it.

There is no 'absolute right' to the £30,000 termination payments or exemption. The relevant documentation (for example, Board minutes, termination agreement) must reflect the reality of the circumstances in which the payment is being made. In the author's experience, Inspectors frequently challenge claims for the tax exemption and each case must be examined carefully on its own facts to determine whether the claim is defensible. In practice, probably the most 'clear-cut' case is where the director/employee receives damages as compensation for loss of their office or employment (see 5.24).

As a general rule, termination payments that are eligible for the £30,000 exemption are recognised for tax purposes when they are received or the recipient becomes entitled to receive them. Non-cash benefits included in a 'termination package' are deemed to be received when they are used or enjoyed [*ITEPA 2003, s 403(3)(b)*]. All payments made from the same employment and employer must be aggregated for the purpose of the £30,000 exemption (together with those made by associated employers) [*ITEPA 2003, s 404*]. Any benefits in excess of the £30,000 exemption would be taxed under the normal benefit rules.

Employer contributions towards the employee's legal fees in relation to their termination of employment are exempt from tax.

It is important to note that a termination payment will be completely exempt (ie not just up to the £30,000 threshold) where it is made on account of the employee's death or injury or disability of the employee [*ITEPA 2003, s 406*].

NICs will normally be due where the employee has a contractual right to receive the payment or where there is an established practice of making such payments. On the other hand, no NIC liability should arise on a genuine termination payment as this does not relate to 'remuneration or profits derived from an employment'. The NIC exemption for termination payments is completely unrestricted so the full amount of any termination payment should escape NIC liability.

REDUNDANCY PAYMENTS

5.23 Under the *Employment Rights Act 1996, s 139* 'redundancy' broadly occurs where an employee's dismissal results from the cessation, relocation or reorganisation of the business.

Statutory redundancy payments made under *the Employment Rights Act 1996, s 167(1) (*or Northern Ireland equivalent) are exempt from income tax under *ITEPA 2003, s 309.*

The exemption in *ITEPA 2003, s 309* also applies to an 'approved contractual payment' under an agreement within the *Employment Rights Act 1996, s 157.*

Both statutory redundancy and relevant approved contractual payments are, however, taken into account in exempting the first £30,000 of any overall termination package [*ITEPA 2003, s 309(3)*]. Consequently, if the total termination payment is in excess of the £30,000 exemption threshold, income tax is charged on the excess amount.

Redundancy payments can be made under 'non-statutory' schemes and arrangements (for example, schemes designed to deal with the specific closure of a business division or the making of 'top-up' payments in addition to statutory payments). Non-statutory redundancy payments are normally treated in the same way as 'statutory' redundancy payments provided there is a genuine redundancy in accordance with Statement of Practice SP1/94. Basically, this situation arises where the Inspector is satisfied that the payment falls within the definition of a 'redundancy payment' under the *Employment Rights Act 1996* and that there has been a genuine redundancy. The payment must not represent a terminal bonus for carrying out additional duties.

In *Colquhoun v HMRC* [2010] UKUT 431 the Upper Tax Tribunal held that a payment received for giving up rights in a redundancy scheme fell within *ITEPA 2003, s 403*, even where the termination occurs some time later. Consequently, the payment qualified for the £30,000 exemption

Application can be made to the Inspector for advance clearance to pay lump sum redundancy payments of up to £30,000 free of tax – the written application should include copies of the scheme documentation and any intended letter to be sent to employees.

COMPENSATION FOR LOSS OF OFFICE OR UNFAIR DISMISSAL AND COMPROMISE AGREEMENTS

5.24   It may be possible to show that the payment to the director validly represents compensation for loss of office. If so, the amount of compensation should be determined properly taking the following factors into account:

(*a*)   the gross future remuneration lost to the director because of the breach of contract;

(*b*)   a discount to reflect the difference in timing between the date the compensation is paid and the date(s) on which the remuneration would actually have been paid under the terms of the contract;

(*c*)   a reduction to reflect the prospect of the director obtaining future employment from which they will derive earnings that would wholly or partly replace the earnings they would have received under the contract;

(*d*)   a reduction to reflect unemployment benefit receivable;

(*e*)   an adjustment to reflect the fact that the entire remuneration payable under the contract would have been taxable in the director's hands whereas only the excess of the compensation payment over £30,000 is actually taxable.

The director or employee will normally be required to sign a 'termination agreement' or 'compromise agreement' where they accept the compensation 'in full and final settlement' of any claims that they may have against the company – as part of these arrangements, the director/employee normally agrees not to litigate against the company. HMRC have previously confirmed that such 'compromise arrangements' will not give rise to a 'restrictive covenant' tax charge under *ITEPA 2003, s 225*. However, HMRC probably will seek to challenge the composition of the 'package' where it looks excessive. On the other hand, where an amount is allocated to a specific 'restrictive' undertaking given by the director/employee (not to compete with the company or solicit its employees, or not to litigate against the company etc), this would be taxed under *ITEPA 2003, s 225* as employment income (subject to PAYE). Such payments would also attract NICs.

Where an employee is awarded compensation by an Employment Tribunal, this will generally benefit from the £30,000 exemption. This is unlikely to be the case where the employee is reinstated by the Tribunal with the employee receiving compensation from the time of their dismissal to the date they were re-instated. However, *Wilson v Clayton* [2005] STC 157 helpfully provides that, following a 'reinstatement' decision, a negotiated compromise payment to compensate for 'unfair dismissal' as a result of the employer withdrawing an essential car user allowance was not taxable (falling within the exemption in what is now *ITEPA 2003, s 401*). This was on the basis that the payment had been made to compensate for unfair dismissal and was therefore made in connection with the termination of the employment.

In some cases, it might be argued that all or part of the payment represents compensation for the injury to the employee's feelings. This was the case in *Walker v Adams* [2004] STC (SCD) 269, where the Special Commissioners decided that part of an Employment Tribunal award relating to 'injury to feelings' was free of tax. If it can be proved that a compensation payment relates to damages paid for unlawful conduct, etc on the part of the employing company, this should not be taxable as earnings. Furthermore, even though compensation receipts (derived from assets) are within the charge to CGT under *TCGA 1992, s 22*, they should be exempted under ESC D33 on the basis that there is no underlying asset in such cases.

PAYMENTS IN LIEU OF NOTICE (PILONS) AND GARDEN LEAVE

5.25   A payment in lieu of notice ('PILON') can be made in a variety of situations. Four possibilities were identified by Lord Browne-Wilkinson in *Delaney v Staples* [1992] 1 AC 687, these being where:

(*a*)   'garden leave' is taken – where notice is given, but not worked, and a salary for the period is paid as a 'lump sum';

(*b*)   a PILON is provided in the employment contract as an alternative to a period of notice;

(*c*)   a PILON is made on the employer and employee agreeing (at the point of 'termination') that the employment is to cease without proper notice;

(*d*)   the contractual arrangements do not provide for a PILON, but the employer terminates the contract and tenders a PILON.

In such cases, it will be necessary to establish whether the PILON would be taxed as employment income under the general rule in *ITEPA 2003, ss 6* and *7(2)*. This would be done by reviewing the relevant provisions in the employee's contract of employment, together with established practices which could create a reasonable expectation that a PILON would be received. Thus, if such payments have always been made in the past, a custom will have been established.

In *SCA Packaging Ltd v HMRC* [2007] EWHC 270 (Ch), the company argued that PILONs should escape tax since they were paid under the terms of a trade union-negotiated memorandum inserted into the employees' contracts. However, Justice Lightman held that even though the PILONs were paid as a result of a collective agreement, they were still received under the terms of the employees' contracts and hence were taxable as earnings. The PILONs were therefore subject to PAYE and NIC in the normal way. On the other hand, if the company had simply terminated the contracts without giving the employees notice, they would have been entitled to damages instead, which would have ranked for the £30,000 exemption in *ITEPA 2003, s 403*. It is unlikely that the right to make a PILON could be implied into a contract that expressly provided for employees to be given specified notice periods (*John Morrish v NTL Group Ltd* [2007] CISH 56).

HMRC will seek to tax any so-called AutoPILONs (which is made by the employer as an *automatic* response to notice being given by either side). Such payments usually equate to the gross pay due for the relevant notice period. In practice, HMRC will invariably seek to tax PILONs, and it is therefore important to ensure that the correct terminology is applied to the payment. It is recommended that employers carry out a 'critical assessment' in each case to assess whether or not the employee works their notice period and, if not, what level of payment should be made.

If it can be shown that the employee is receiving a true damages payment for the early termination of their contract, then it should be eligible for exemption. In such cases, an employer would normally seek to mitigate damages to the minimum level payable. Thus, for example, the PILON should *not* match the gross pay for the notice period but should be reduced to take account of tax and NIC that would have been suffered under the *Gourley* principle (the House of Lords decided in *British Transport Commission v Gourley* [1955] 3 All ER 796 that damages based on loss of income should be reduced to take account of the tax that would have been suffered on the 'lost' income).

Where the employee is on garden leave, they are still employed and remain bound by their contract of employment. HMRC generally take the view that any payment for garden leave is fully taxable as employment income, since it represents the salary for the notice period. This has received judicial blessing in *Richardson v Delaney* [2001] STC 1328 (see also *Ibe v McNally* [2005] STC 1426*)*. Where an employment is terminated within situation (*b*) above, the analysis applied is that the contract is terminated in accordance with its terms. Hence, as the payment is a contractual one, it falls to be taxed as earnings. This reasoning is supported by the Court of Appeal in *EMI Group Electronics Ltd v Coldicott* [1999] STC 803.

On the other hand, where a PILON is made in situation (*c*) above, it would *not* normally be treated as earnings from the employment, provided there is no existing prior understanding which might point to it being a contractual provision. There is also a strong argument that the payment is being made to avoid the risk of a compensation payment being awarded at an Employment Tribunal. Similarly, any PILON made within the circumstances in (*d*) would represent liquidated damages for breach of contract (for failing to give proper notice) and would therefore be eligible for the £30,000 exemption within *ITEPA 2003, s 403* (see *IR Tax Bulletin 24* (August 1996)).

EX GRATIA PAYMENTS

5.26   Where a working shareholder ceases to work for the company, in certain limited circumstances it may be possible to receive a tax-free payment which is of an 'ex gratia' nature. This should be exempt from tax up to the £30,000 exemption threshold limit (see 5.22) provided it is not made by reference to past services. For example, in the recent case of *Barclays Bank Plc v Revenue and Customs Comrs* [2007] STC 747 it was held that benefits received were in reference to past service.

Ex gratia payments are not defined in the legislation and so the meaning of ex gratia for tax purposes derives primarily from case law. In *Mercer v Pearson* [1976] STC 22, an ex gratia payment was defined as one 'which is made voluntarily, that is pursuant to the exercise of a liberty and without the payer acting under the compulsion of a duty'. HMRC contend that genuine ex gratia payments very rarely arise, and will frequently challenge these.

Previously, HMRC's view as stated in Statement of Practice SP13/91 was that ex gratia payments made on retirement or death were receipts from an unapproved retirement benefits scheme and were specifically taxed as employment income under *ITEPA 2003, s 394(1)*. Thus, any ex gratia payment made near or at retirement would not have enjoyed the £30,000 exemption.

SP13/91 has now been withdrawn following the changes to the pension rules from 6 April 2006. Any payments or other benefits made on retirement or death are now considered to be receipts from an Employer-Financed Retirements Benefit Scheme. However, the tax treatment remains largely unchanged – the £30,000 exemption is not applicable, as any ex-gratia lump sum payments made on retirement or death will constitute 'relevant benefits' and so will be counted as employment income under *ITEPA 2003, ss 393B* and *394(1)*.

HMRC is vigilant to the fact that some employers may seek to dress up a 'retirement' as a termination in order to take advantage of the termination payment exemption under *ITEPA 2003, s 401* and are likely to look very closely at the underlying facts see whether the 'termination' payment should be taxed under the above rules.

Severance payments made on redundancy, loss of office or on death or disability due to an accident will generally be exempt and would not be taxed under the above 'retirement' rules.

CONTEMPORANEOUS SALE OF SHARES

5.27   Particular care is required where there are arrangements to make termination payments to directors (particular if they are also controlling shareholders) around the same time as the company is sold or their shares are re-purchased by the company.

In *Allum v Another v Marsh* [2005] STC (SCD) 191 HMRC were able to persuade the Special Commissioner that voluntary payments of £30,000 each(!) made to the shareholders (husband and wife) at the time their shares were re-purchased by the company were taxable as they were made in recognition of services provided. This was probably not helped by the company saying that the payments were made 'following [their] resignation due to retirement ... in appreciation of their services to the company over many years'.

The decision in *Snook (James) & Co Ltd v Blasdale* (1952) 33 TC 244 is also particularly instructive as it provides a further example of how *not* to do things! This case involved an agreement to sell shares, with a provision to pay compensation for loss of office being included in the agreement. It was held that the compensation payments could not be deducted against profits as they were linked to the agreement for the sale of the company.

In such cases, to have any possibility of success, it will be necessary to demonstrate to a (usually 'cynical') Inspector that the termination payment

215

was not linked to the sale of the shares in any way. In such cases, it is important to be able to demonstrate that the termination payment and consideration for the shares were arrived at independently and there was no value shifted to the 'tax-exempt' payment. Where the Inspector succeeds in denying relief, they will often tax the payment as a distribution or as part of the proceeds for the sale of the shares.

EMPLOYER'S PAYE OBLIGATIONS AND PENSION PLANNING

5.28 Where the termination payment is taxable/NIC-able', the company must account for PAYE and employees' NIC/employer's NIC. If the exemption is incorrectly applied to the termination package, the employing company will therefore have to pick up a large PAYE and NIC bill later on, with possible penalties and interest on top! Many companies will wish to protect their position by operating PAYE and NIC where there is any doubt surrounding the availability of the tax exemption. On the other hand, given that the company will then have to pay employer's NIC on the payment, it is important not to be over-prudent in this area and apply PAYE/NIC without proper consideration of the legal principles. In *Norman v Yellow Pages Sales Ltd* [2010] EWCA Civ 1395, the Court of Appeal held that if a termination settlement agreement failed to specify any apportionment between taxable and non-taxable elements (such as injury to feelings – see 5.24), then for the purposes of operating PAYE, the employer company is entitled to apply PAYE on the full amount.

From 6 April 2011, where a termination payment is made *after the employee's P45 has been issued*, companies must deduct the full amount of tax under PAYE (previously, they were only required to deduct basic rate tax on payments made *after* the P45 was issued).

Where there is some doubt about the taxation of a proposed termination payment, the employer should seek an advance ruling from HMRC under the 'non-statutory' clearance procedure.

Where all or part of the intended termination payment would fall to be taxed, it might be beneficial for the company to make a large pension payment instead. The pension payment would be earmarked for the employee's benefit, although care would need to taken to ensure that this fell within the £50,000 annual allowance (also allowing for any unused relief brought forward from the three previous years) (see 10.21). It may also be desirable to obtain specialist pensions advice .

Sometimes, employers may be asked to make the termination payment 'gross' (without any tax or NICs being deducted), on the basis that the employee is giving an indemnity to reimburse any tax and NIC ultimately found to be payable by HMRC. In the writer's experience, it can be difficult to successfully pursue a claim under the indemnity, due to difficulties in tracking down the former employee etc!

The employer must also report details of termination payments (including benefits) that exceed £30,000 in value. The director/employee must report full details of any termination payment or benefits on their tax return.

PLANNING CHECKLIST – REMUNERATION STRATEGIES

Company

- Consider commercial desirability of retaining a level of profits.

- Surplus profits could be distributed as bonuses to selected personnel, or through pension scheme contributions or other benefits.

- Review any share option scheme for PAYE and NIC implications and remember to claim a corporate tax deduction for any shares or share options provided to employees.

- Remuneration properly provided in year-end accounts should be paid within nine months from the end of the accounting period. Any provision for bonuses in the year end must comply with GAAP. Broadly, this means that the obligation to pay the bonus must have crystallised by the year-end.

- Where workers have been re-categorised as employees, the company should seek to obtain 'credit' for the tax/NIC previously paid by the worker in any negotiated PAYE settlement (under the 2008 regulations).

- Carefully determine whether PAYE/NIC must be applied to any (post-5 April 2011) 'relevant steps' taken within an EBT or EFRBS, such as earmarking for or making loans to employees.

- Review all arrangements where employee benefits etc. are provided by third parties to ensure that they are exempted from any PAYE/NIC under the *ITEPA 2003, Part 7A* rules.

- Consider whether the repayment terms of existing (pre-9 December 2010) loans from EBTs/EFRBS can be extended without triggering any 'relevant step' under *ITEPA 2003, Part 7A*.

- Carefully review any proposed termination payment to ensure whether it can be paid without deduction of PAYE or NIC.

Working shareholders

- Dividend strategy may determine the level of profits available for distribution as remuneration.

- Consider whether IR 35 or managed service company provisions apply to any contracts performed through a personal/managed service company.

- Ensure that any PAYE arising under the *ITEPA 2003, Part 7* rules is reimbursed to the company within 90 days to prevent a further employment tax charge arising under *ITEPA 2003, s 222*.

- Consider the required level of earnings for pension funding.

Other employees

- Look for basic remuneration plus performance-related bonus.

- Check that pay received for hours worked is at least as much as the national minimum wage.

Non-working shareholders

- Consider whether any excess remuneration is commercially justifiable or desirable. In such cases, it is generally better for them to take it as a dividend.

Chapter 6

Personal Service and Managed Service Companies

INTRODUCTION

Personal service companies (PSCs)

6.1   The term 'personal service company' (PSC) was not in common use before 9 March 1999, when Gordon Brown slipped his press release, IR 35, into his Spring Budget pack. This infamous press release marked a radical change in tax policy. It enabled the then Inland Revenue to 'look through' an established corporate structure and treat its underlying income as derived from a 'deemed' employment in appropriate cases. This controversial principle is applied where the 'worker' (who owns the company) would have been treated as an employee if they had worked directly for the client, rather than through their 'intermediary' company.

The relevant anti-avoidance legislation, which targets the provision of services through an 'intermediary' was introduced in *FA 2000, Sch 12* (now 'consolidated' into *ITEPA 2003, Pt 2, Ch 8*, although it is generally referred to as 'the IR 35 rules'). The IR 35 regime only bites when the business involves *services* performed by an individual rather than the production or trading of goods. Such personal service companies commonly provided computer or management consultancy, copywriting, designing and construction-type work.

The Budget 2011 notes confirmed that the Government will retain the IR35 rules but will make some administrative improvements.

Managed service companies (MSCs)

6.2   PSCs are typically owned by a single employee/director. Their shareholders would control the company including its finances. However, HMRC considered that the IR 35 rules for PSCs also applied to so-called managed service companies (MSCs).

MSCs tended to be structured so that the 'worker' is unlikely to be controlling the company or its finances. Instead, the MSC would generally be controlled by a provider – often referred to as the scheme provider. HMRC found it difficult to apply the IR 35 rules to MSCs.

By the time HMRC had established that a PAYE/NIC debt existed within an MSC, the company could avoid that liability by winding up or ceasing to trade and moving its 'workers' into a new MSC. Since MSCs tend to have few if any assets, HMRC would be unable to collect any tax liability that they had established. New legislation was therefore introduced in *Finance Act 2007* (*ITEPA 2003, Pt 2, Ch 9*) – these provisions take MSCs out of the existing IR 35 regime and subject them to a separate code (reviewed in 6.39-6.50). Under the *FA 2007*, any debt of an MSC can be collected from certain third parties. Furthermore, the 'workers' may not be able to claim tax relief for their travel costs to and from their end client.

TAX AVOIDANCE

6.3   Individuals working in a wide variety of industries, from IT to door security, find that they are forced to operate through a company rather than as sole traders, in order to gain work. The limited liability company was seen as a convenient vehicle to protect the client from the strict employment tests, which would normally require the client to treat the worker as an employee and apply PAYE and National Insurance to his invoice. A limited company also gives some protection to the assets of the individual from creditors of the business should the venture fail.

The government perceived that businesses which operated as companies for these reasons and paid out a proportion of their profits as dividends rather than remuneration (as described at 2.12) were deliberately avoiding payment of NICs and should be stopped. Such businesses were also viewed as avoiding tax by gaining tax relief for expenses borne by the business which would not be deductible for tax purposes if the work was performed through an employment contract taxed as earnings.

In Autumn 2000, an umbrella body of 'knowledge-based workers', known as the Professional Contractors Group (PCG), demonstrated the strength of opposition to the IR 35 regime by bringing a judicial review action. However, the PCG lost their action in both the UK courts (High Court and Court of Appeal) in Autumn 2001 (*R (on the application of Professional Contractors Group Ltd) v IRC* [2002] STC 165) and the European Court of Justice (2002).

CONSEQUENCES OF IR 35

6.4   The apparent intended effect of the IR 35 rules is to level the playing field between employees and 'contractors' who work alongside them through personal service companies, and who may pay lower NICs on an equivalent amount of income. The anti-avoidance provisions in *ITEPA 2003, ss 48–61* – the IR 35 rules – look through the personal service company and apply PAYE to income caught by the rules (see 6.22).

Similar rules are contained in the *Social Security Contributions (Intermediaries) Regulations 2000 (SI 2000/727),* which also bring the deemed salary within the charge to NIC.

In broad terms, the intermediary 'personal service company' must compute the deemed earnings of its 'owner-manager'. This is done by quantifying the income from the company's clients (net of VAT) and deducting various permitted expenses. The net amount is deemed to be pay received by the owner-manager at the end of the tax year which is then subject to PAYE and NIC.

The IR 35 rules do not apply where the relationship is only that of 'office holder'. Thus, for example, non-executive directors who invoice for their directorships from their PSCs do not have to subject this income to PAYE under the IR 35 regime (see 5.9).

The potential application of IR 35 must be taken seriously. When HMRC successfully uphold the IR 35 status of a company, the amount of back-tax can be substantial as demonstrated in *Dragonfly Consulting* [2008] EWHC 2113 where the taxpayer lost and was liable to a tax bill of nearly £100,000.

What income is caught?

6.5   The IR 35 rules apply to income from 'relevant engagements' performed through a personal service company which fulfil certain conditions (see 6.8). Such income (after making certain deductions) will be treated as 'deemed' earnings subject to PAYE and NIC. It is the money actually received by the personal service company which is considered to be proceeds of the relevant engagement. Any commission which is deducted by an agency before payment of the balance on to the personal service company is outside the scope of the IR 35 rules.

For these purposes, a relevant engagement is one which is:

- performed personally by the 'personal service' worker;
- under a contract arranged between the client and the personal service company;
- in circumstances in which the worker would be classified as an employee of the client if the services had been provided directly to the client [*ITEPA 2003, s 49(1)*].

Thus, the key defence to an IR 35 challenge by HMRC is for the personal service worker to demonstrate that, if the intermediary company had not been interposed, they would have had a 'self-employment' relationship with the ultimate client.

Employed v self-employed

6.6   Individuals who work for a living are classified as either employed or self-employed. Unfortunately there is no statutory definition of either term, so a number of tests drawn from case law have to be applied to each circumstance to determine whether the working conditions are those of employment or self-employment when all the facts are considered.

To fall outside the IR 35 rules it must be shown that the worker would be self-employed and not employed. HMRC provide guidance about the application of IR 35 and helpful information is contained in its booklets *IR175 Supplying services though a limited company or partnership* and *IR56 Employed or self-employed?* – which are available on HMRC's website.

In spite of this detailed guidance, each personal service company must be examined on its own facts based on the points considered below. One of the problems is that each contract undertaken by the personal service company must be looked at separately for tax purposes. If the classification of a particular contract is challenged, the Inspector of Taxes will quote selectively from case law to support his stance, often using older cases which have little bearing on modern working practices.

6.7   It is not therefore surprising that IR 35 has spawned a long line of cases, each of which add further layers of complexity to the 'employed v self-employed' problem. Determining whether someone is employed or self-employed can often be a murky area for small businesses. These difficulties are clearly demonstrated by the case of *Larkstar Data Ltd* [2008] EWHC 3284. The General Commissioners agreed that a contractor was not caught by IR35. However, HMRC appealed to the High Court, which sent the case back to the General Commissioners for a rehearing. The High Court held they had misdirected themselves in law by failing to consider all the evidence put before them by HMRC!

Many remain sceptical about the efficacy of the IR35 regime. The Professional Contractors Group (PCG) requested details of the tax revenue collected under IR 35 from HMRC under *The Freedom of Information Act* in 2009. It found that just £9.2 million of tax/NIC was collected under IR 35 between 2002/03 and 2007/08 - an average of around only £1.5 million per tax year. This is a very long way from the predicted £220 million per year in NICs alone that was expected to be raised under the initial regulatory impact assessment for IR35 in 1999!

On the other hand, HMRC's response is that these statistics demonstrate IR35's success. HMRC contend that the IR 35 rules have 'steered' contractors away from attempting to gain tax benefits from acting through personal service companies when effectively they were employees.

The PCG has also indicated that of the 1,468 IR35 investigations it has been involved with, HMRC only collected additional tax in six cases. However, IR

35 continues to be an arduous burden for those who consider that they may be potentially within its scope. The new coalition Government has promised to consider whether IR35 can be simplified whilst also maintaining its deterrent effect as part of its review of small business taxation.

Conditions for the company

6.8   A personal service company is regarded as a 'relevant intermediary' and thus falls within the IR 35 provisions where the worker:

- has a *material interest* in the company; *or*

- receives a payment from the company that is not employment income, but could reasonably be taken to represent earnings from a relevant engagement, such as a dividend [*ITEPA 2003, s 51(1)*].

A material interest is:

- the beneficial ownership of, or the ability directly or indirectly to control more than 5% of the company's ordinary share capital;

- possession of, or the right to acquire, more than 5% of the company's distributions; or

- entitlement to receive more than 5% of the assets available for distribution among participators in a close company [*ITEPA 2003, s 51(4)*].

The worker's interest in the company includes any shares held by his associates. In this context an associate includes a husband, wife (or civil partner), parent or remoter forebear, child or remoter issue, brother, sister or business partner. Note that for the purposes of the IR 35 rules a 'live-in' girlfriend or boyfriend is treated as a spouse [*ITEPA 2003, s 61(4)*].

The 'second limb' for payments that 'could reasonably be taken to represent remuneration' is likely to catch a 'composite service' company that employs many workers (assuming the other IR 35 conditions are satisfied). In such cases, each employee will normally have a separate class of shares which entitles them to receive dividends based on the amount the company receives from the client for their respective services. Thus, any dividend effectively represents earnings for services provided by the worker to the client.

THE TESTS FOR SELF-EMPLOYMENT

In business on own account

6.9   The overriding fact which the courts have sought to establish is whether an individual is in business on their own account. One of the key distinctions is whether the work is being provided under a:

- 'contract of service' – which implies a master/servant (ie employment) relationship; *or*

- contract for services – in this context the 'services' nomenclature generally contemplates a series of services being provided to different customers by an independent self-employed worker/contractor.

A number of factors must always be considered when reaching a conclusion as to whether someone is engaged in business on their own account (self-employed), as was pointed out by Mummery LJ in *Hall v Lorimer* [1994] STC 23. In *Walls v Sinnett* [1987] STC 236 the judge emphasised that the facts as a whole must be looked at and that something which is compelling in one case may not be so important in another. The case of *Barnett v Brabyn* [1996] STC 716 is interesting because here HMRC argued, unusually but successfully, that the taxpayer was self-employed.

In *Lewis (t/a MAL Scaffolding) and others v HMRC* [2006] (SSCD) 253, the Special Commissioners again adopted this approach, finding that, on the evidence and the balance of probabilities, scaffolders engaged by Mr Lewis were not employees.

An IT contractor was held to be operating under a contract that would have been an employment one but for the interposed IR 35 company in *Island Consultants Ltd v HMRC* [2007] SSCD 700. The IT contractor worked on a customer's five year project under three-month contracts, which were invariably renewed. He was paid a daily rate and did not receive paid holidays, sick pay or pension contributions which might be useful indicators of self-employment (see 6.17). However, the IT contractor had no other customers and the repeated renewal of the contract indicated a longer term relationship with mutual obligations.

In *Datagate Services Ltd v HMRC* [2008] STC (SCD) 453, a computer software consultant (B) was the sole director and shareholder of a company providing computer consultancy services. B's company entered into a contract with another company, TPS, to provide services to a third company, MBDA. The taxpayer B successfully won on appeal. Applying the IR 35 concept, which ignores the two PSCs, the Commissioner found that the taxpayer was 'in business on his own account and was not a person working as an employee in someone else's business'.

The case of *Demibourne Ltd v HMRC* [2005] (SSCD) 667 concerned a hotel maintenance man who retired but continued working in the same capacity, albeit as a self-employed contractor. The Special Commissioner held that there was still an employer-employee relationship and hence PAYE should have been operated by the hotel. The Commissioner said that to change from being an employee to becoming 'self-employed' meant significant changes in practice and working arrangements would have been required .... (In this case, the Commissioner also ruled that the employer would be responsible for all the PAYE/NIC, with no 'set-off' or credit being made for the tax that had already been paid by the worker under self-assessment. This triggered considerable widespread difficulties in 're-categorisation' cases which have now largely been resolved.

6.10   In both *Battersby v Campbell* [2001] (SSCD) 189 and *F s Consulting Ltd v McCaul* [2002] (SSCD) 138, the Special Commissioner decided that the substance of the contractual arrangements largely pointed towards the existence of a contract of service (ie employment relationship).

However, in the case of *Lime-IT Ltd v Justin (Officer of the Board of Inland Revenue)* [2003] (SSCD) 15, the taxpayer (Miss Fernley) succeeded in demonstrating sufficient indicators of 'self-employment' to persuade the Special Commissioner that she was working on her own account. The Special Commissioner made the following findings:

- the client company contracted for specific projects with the contract being terminated when the specified work was completed (in fact, the contract was terminated prematurely) (see 6.17 and 6.19). During the contract Miss Fernley worked for four other clients;

- no significant control was exercised over Miss Fernley's activities (see 6.16);

- monthly invoices were rendered with 30-day terms of payment;

- the personal service company (Lime-IT Ltd) and Miss Fernley had to provide their own computer equipment (see 6.10);

- there was a genuine right of substitution (even though it had not actually been used) (see 6.14);

- there was a large variation in the hours that were actually worked for the client company each week (with no work being carried out in some weeks);

- Miss Fernley was found not to be 'part and parcel' of the client company's organisation (she had a different security pass from employees, her own business cards and could not enjoy employee benefits) (see 6.15).

The *Lime-IT* case illustrates the benefits of having a properly prepared and implemented 'contract for services' and also a taxpayer's passionate determination to uphold it!

In *Larkstar Data Ltd* [2008] EWHC 3284 (see 6.7), HMRC contended that IR 35 applied to a company that provided the computer consultancy services of Mr Brill primarily to one client for about two and a half years. Mr Brill had to work exclusively at the client's office for security reasons and thus had to use the client's equipment.

However, Mr Brill did not have any 'employment-type' benefits such as sick and holiday pay and there was limited control over how he performed his work. Furthermore, there was a substitution clause in his contract, which if genuine, is a strong determinant in favour of self-employment, but there were some doubts as to whether this could ever be enforced due to security issues. Mr Brill was outside the company's structure and he was seen as a professionally independent 'contractor'. He was also able to take on other clients, which was also helpful as an indicator of 'self-employment'.

The Commissioners considered that there was no evidence of mutuality of obligation which indicated 'independent contracting'. However, on appeal, the High Court found that they had misdirected themselves on this issue. There were two significant aspects here:

(a)   Although Mr Brill was a consultant and there was no 'control' by the client how he carried out work, the Commissioners did not properly consider the authorities referred to by HMRC (such as *Cornwall County Council v Prater*) on this aspect.

(b)   One of the findings of fact was that Mr Brill was encouraged to work during the client's core hours, on Mr Brill's own evidence. Had they found that Mr Brill was indeed required to work these hours, the Commissioners' may have concluded this pointed towards employment.

The case was therefore referred back for a second hearing before a different set of Commissioners. However, somewhat surprisingly, it was reported in April 2010 that HMRC has dropped the case with an agreed settlement of £129.79!

Mutuality of obligations

6.11   One of the fundamental attributes of an employment contract is the mutuality of obligation. In *Ansell Computer Services Ltd v Richardson* [2004] (SSCD) 472, the Special Commissioner held that the lack of mutual obligations pointed to self-employment status. Other factors also supported this view.

In *Ansell*, the worker was a specialist defence industry software contractor and his personal service company provided services (via an agency) to Marconi and British Aerospace. These services involved working on specific defence contracts alongside their permanent employees and other freelance contractors. The personal service company's contracts were renewed regularly from one year to the next. However, the worker had complete flexibility over the number of hours worked. Although there was an overriding maximum number of hours for the engagement, there was no minimum requirement and the worker was not obliged to 'put in' a particular number of hours each day or week. Other factors supporting 'self-employed' status were the right to appoint a substitute (although this was unlikely to be exercised in practice) and the various practical differences between the freelance workers and the regular employees (such as lack of sick pay/holiday pay, etc).

Ansell usefully demonstrates that each case must be subjectively judged on its own facts. Although there were few indicators of being 'in business on own account', these facets were not really typical for someone engaged on secret projects in secure premises.

Cornwall County Council v Prater [2006] EWCA Civ 102 involved a home tutor engaged by the Council to teach children at home. The home tutor simply performed whatever engagements the council gave to her, without any guarantee of work. However, Justice Mummery held that this made no difference –

'… once a contract was entered into and while that contract continued, she was under an obligation to teach the pupil and Council was under an obligation to pay her …. That was all that was legally necessary to support the finding that each individual teaching engagement was a contract of service'.

Financial risk

6.12   The degree of financial risk an individual takes with their business is an indication of self-employment. If their own money is invested in the business to buy capital assets or services the business needs there is a risk that the business may not generate the funds to cover the outlay. For example, an individual may undertake a training course in the hope that the cost of the course will be covered by the additional fees they will be able to charge based on their improved knowledge. However, there is no guarantee that they will be able to gain work after the course to repay the investment. Even the issuing of an invoice to secure payment involves a small financial risk as the invoice might not be paid, or there may be some delay in payment.

Profit from sound management

6.13   If an individual is paid by the task they may be able to increase the profit made from that job by completing the task in a shorter time. The power to organise the work and perform tasks more efficiently is an indication of self-employment. If there is a real prospect of making a loss on any particular assignment the indication of self-employment is stronger (*Market Investigations Ltd v Minister of Social Security QB* [1968] 3 All ER 732).

Substitute others

6.14   The issue of substitution is likely to be crucial for many personal service companies. The fact that an individual can choose whether to complete a contract personally or send a substitute is a strong indication of self-employment. It should be stressed that the right to supply a substitute must be a real one which must be agreed by the client.

In the employment tribunal case, *Express and Echo Publications Ltd v Tanton* [1999] IRLR 367, it was enough that the contract allowed the individual to send a substitute to complete the task to conclude that the contract was for services and thus a self-employment rather than an employment. In *First Word Software Ltd v HMRC* [2008] STC (SCD) 389, the individual worked solely for one company for one year on a specified software project, and was still held to be self-employed due to a substitution clause in the contract. Other factors also supported this view. On the other hand, in another employment tribunal case, *Glasgow City Council v Mrs MacFarlane and Mrs Skivington*, the women had a limited right to substitution in their contracts but were still found to be employees.

The Court in *Dragonfly Consultancy Ltd v HMRC* [2008] EWHC 2113 was sceptical about the use of 'substitution' clauses which the end user would not accept. Dragonfly had various consecutive contracts with an agency over a three year period to supply an IT tester (Mr Bessell - its sole director) to an end user client. However, the High Court held that it was unrealistic to suppose that the end user would ever have agreed to an unqualified right of substitution – they 'wanted Mr Bessell'! The taxpayer's case primarily failed because of the lack of effective right of substitution in the contract – Mr Bessell was effectively required to perform the work personally.

The Special Commissioner in *Castle Construction (Chesterfield) v HMRC* [2009] STC (SCD) 97 was even more sceptical when he commented

'it is quite common for advisers to insert 'substitution' clauses into contracts, or into the final contract with the client in IR 35 ('intermediary') cases, obviously in an effort to diminish the impression that the relationship is one of employment … In many cases, the substitution clauses inserted have been qualified by the requirement that the counter-party must consent to the choice of substitute … I consider that in the present case the clause was broadly nonsense, with no attention to reality … it seems to me that the substitution clause was a fiction, designed by an adviser, or the draftsman of some precedent document, to enhance the 'non-employee' case, and that on the facts of this case, that endeavour fails, and is if anything (by suggesting the need to resort to such artificiality) counter-productive'.

Control

6.15   HMRC tend to place a lot of emphasis on this aspect of the working relationship. The Inspector will examine the extent of the client's ability to control the worker. The operation of actual control is largely irrelevant – it is the right to control that is important. If the client can move the worker from task to task and specify how the work is to be done, in addition to where and when the work is to be performed, an extensive right of control is being exercised. Alternatively, if the client has no power to shift the worker on to different tasks but requires regular reports on the task to be submitted, there is only a limited right of control.

Cable & Wireless Plc v Muscat [2006] EWCA Civ 220 was a case begun at the Employment Appeal Tribunal, concerning the unfair dismissal claim of an individual who provided services to Cable & Wireless through a service company. It was held at the Court of Appeal that the essentials of a contract of employment were the obligation to provide work for remuneration and the obligation to perform it, coupled with control by the 'employer'. It did not matter whether the arrangements for payment were made directly or indirectly – there was an implied contract between the worker and the end-user, and they were entitled to rights as an employee.

This could have a fundamental effect on the IR 35 regulations, as implying a contract between the end-user and the worker would bypass any intermediary companies and hence IR 35 could not apply. If an implied contract exists, the worker is an employee and would be subject to PAYE and NIC in the normal way. There is, therefore, currently uncertainty regarding the application of IR 35 in such cases.

Cable & Wireless v Muscat obviously has an impact on both clients and employment agencies. They now face uncertainty as to whether they will be liable for unexpected PAYE and NIC (as well as the possibility of employment rights claims from workers previously supposed to be self-employed).

Provision of equipment or premises

6.16 If a worker provides their own tools and equipment to perform the relevant tasks, they are more likely to be self-employed, particularly if the items provided are large (*Ready Mixed Concrete (South East) Ltd v Minister of Pensions and National Insurance* [1968] 2 QB 497).

If a certain amount of the work is performed at premises controlled by the personal service company rather than the client, the contract has more chance of falling outside the IR 35 provisions. In *Tax Bulletin, Issue 45*, Example 2 shows the fact that an engineer working largely at home using his own computer and office equipment is a strong pointer to self-employment. However, the occasional choice to work at home using one's own equipment will not make an employed worker self-employed.

Basis of payment

6.17 It is normal for employees to have paid holidays, sick pay, maternity pay and long service bonuses. HMRC will view any payment of overtime as an indication of employment. A fixed payment for a particular task is an indication of self-employment. However, piecework or commission payments can apply to both employment and self-employment. The lack of employee benefits such as a company pension does not necessarily mean that the worker is self-employed, as many short-term employments do not carry these advantages.

Intention

6.18   If there was no intention by either of the parties to create an employment, this will be treated as a pointer to self-employment (*Massey v Crown Life Insurance Co* [1978] ICR 590). If all the other factors of the working relationship are neutral, the intention of the parties may be the decisive factor in 'employment status' cases.

Long-term contract

6.19   HMRC place a high degree of significance on the length of a particular engagement when deciding whether it will fall within the IR 35 rules or not. Note that it is the total engagement with the particular client that is normally examined, not the length of each contract. One engagement may be made up of several short contracts, or an initial short contract that is extended.

Standard agency contracts

6.20   Workers who use agencies to obtain contracts for them to work through their own personal service company often rely on standard contracts drawn up by those agencies. These contracts tend to require the contractor to:

(*a*)   perform the work at a location specified by the client;

(*b*)   spend at least a given number of hours per week on the task;

(*c*)   be remunerated at an agreed hourly rate or daily rate;

(*d*)   keep a timesheet checked and authorised by the client; and

(*e*)   be subject to the direction of the client.

The *IR Press Release* dated 7 February 2000 stated that where such a standard contract is used for a period of one month or more the Revenue view is that the contract falls within the IR 35 rules.

The 'employment' cases of *Franks v Reuters Ltd and First Employment Ltd* [2003] EWCA Civ 417 and *Ducas v Brook Street Bureau (UK) Ltd* and *Wandsworth London Borough Council* [2004] EWCA Civ 217– both held that, where a worker 'worked' through an employment agency, an employment relationship had still been established between the worker and the end-user.

In both cases, the worker had worked on a 'long-term' basis for one specific customer and thus had been largely integrated into the end user's business.

This reasoning was followed in *Muscat v Cable & Wireless plc* [2006] EWCA Civ 220, where Mr Muscat's personal service company supplied his services to Cable & Wireless through an agency. Subsequently, Cable & Wireless terminated the contract with the agency. The Court of Appeal upheld Mr Muscat's compensation claim for unfair dismissal ruling that he was an employee and implied contracts were imposed to grant him employment rights.

Following these developments, it is quite possible that where an arrangement falls within IR35, it could now be treated as an actual employment rather than deemed employment. If this is the case, the 'end-user' could well have an obligation to apply PAYE and NIC (rather than the personal service company 'intermediary').

Summary and other factors

6.21   Based on the indicators of 'self-employment v employment' set out in 6.4 to 6.20 above, it is helpful to summarise some of the key determinants that should be considered when determining whether IR 35 will apply in relation to any particular situation.

- How many clients does the 'worker' have?

- What is the intention of the parties?

- How long does the contract last and what are its terms? (eg is there a notice period, specified hours of work, where and how is the work carried out?)

- Does the contract contain an 'employee-type' pay structure, such as hourly rate, fixed pay, holiday pay, and employee-type benefits?

- Is the worker paid an agreed fee for a particular project stage and are there performance deadlines etc?

- Are any benefits provided similar to employees (company car/van, sick pay bonuses etc)?

- What is the degree of the worker's financial risk in the project and do they have to rectify work at their own cost?

- Does the worker provide their own equipment etc. on site?

- Does the worker have a genuine ability to provide a 'substitute' to carry out the work in their place?

- Is the worker integrated into the client's business?

HMRC will also look at factors outside the immediate working relationship to determine the status of a particular contract. It will look at past contracts, if appropriate, and consider the individual's business characteristics, for example, whether they advertise their services or undertake other expenditure to win work.

Deemed salary

6.22   The IR 35 provisions treat the net income arising from the company's relevant engagements (see 6.5) as the employment income of the worker who performed the engagement, subject to the permitted deductions listed at 6.23.

It is the money actually received by the personal service company which is considered to be proceeds of the relevant engagement. Any commission which is deducted by an agency before payment of the balance on to the personal service company is outside the scope of the IR 35 rules.

The permitted deductions include any salary and benefits that were paid to the worker (excluding VAT) during the tax year must be excluded. All these amounts are deducted from the net income from relevant engagements to arrive at the worker's deemed IR 35 salary. This is treated as paid on 5 April (the last day of the relevant tax year), with PAYE and NICs due 14 days later. The value of any taxable benefits provided directly by the final client to the worker is added when calculating the deemed salary.

Permitted deductions

6.23   The permitted deductions are:

(*a*)   a general deduction equal to 5% of the *gross* receipts from relevant engagements (net of VAT) to cover all the other costs of running the company including seeking other work;

(*b*)   normal expenses of employment allowable under *ITEPA 2003, s 336* and other deductions allowed by *ITEPA 2003, Pt 5, Chs 1–5*, such as professional indemnity insurance premiums and professional subscriptions;

(*c*)   capital allowances on equipment which is wholly, exclusively and necessarily purchased for the performance of a relevant engagement [*CAA 2001, s 262*];

(*d*)   employer's contributions paid to an approved pension scheme or personal pension scheme;

(*e*)   employer's NICs (including Class 1A NICs) due on actual remuneration and benefits in kind;

(*f*)   the final amount of employer's NICs due on the deemed salary; and

(*g*)   the total of the payments and benefits received by the worker during the year [*ITEPA 2003, s 54*].

6.24   There is no requirement to demonstrate that the costs covered by the 5% deduction for the general expenses of running the personal service company have actually been incurred. This additional deduction will be allowed in all cases.

The cost of training paid for by the personal service company is not permitted as a separate deduction. Training expenses must be covered by the 5% general deduction, or paid for directly by the customer company (see Statement from the Paymaster General available on HMRC's website – www.hmrc.gov.uk/ ir35/pmgltr.htm).

Capital allowances on equipment which does not meet the 'wholly, exclusively and necessarily' test cannot be deducted for the deemed salary calculation, but they remain deductible for corporation tax purposes. Thus a personal service company that owns a significant amount of equipment may easily make a trading loss (for corporation tax purposes) if all, or most, of its (post-5 April 2000) income is derived from relevant engagements.

Example 1

IR 35 calculations – comprehensive worked example of deemed salary and PAYE/NIC

Henry owns 100% of Thierry Ltd, which makes up its accounts to 5 April each year. All of the income received by the company is from relevant engagements. The company's results for year to 5 April 2012 are:

	£	£
Income (net of VAT)		80,000
Expenses:		
Travelling and subsistence (allowable under *ITEPA 2003, s 336*)	2,999	
Accountancy and company secretarial costs	3,000	
Telephone, internet and stationery	1,500	
Salary paid to Henry	10,000	
Employer's NI on salary (£10,000 – £7,225) × 13.8%	382	
Employer pension contributions	2,500	
Total expenses		20,381
Net profit before tax		59,619

Calculation of deemed salary

	£	£
Receipts in the tax year		80,000
Less:		
Salary + NICs paid in year	10,382	
Employer's pension contribution	2,500	
Employee expenses allowable under *s 198*	2,999	
General expense deduction – 5% × £80,000	4,000	
		19,881
Deemed salary including employer's NIC		60,119

Note: the deemed salary is £500 greater than the net profit of the company because the general costs of running Thierry Ltd (£3,000 + £1,500) exceed the 5% allowance by £500.

Accounting for deemed salary and PAYE/NIC

	£	£
Deemed salary including secondary NICs	60,119	
Employer's NIC (£60,119 × 13.8%/113.8%)	(7,290)	7,290
Deemed gross salary	52,829	
Employee's Class 1 NICs:		
– £42,475 – £10,000 × 12%	3,897	
– £52,829 – £42,475 × 2%	207	4,104
PAYE:		
Basic rate: £35,000 – (£10,000 – £7,475) = £32,475 × 20%	6,495	
Higher rate: (£52,829 – £35,000) = £17,829 × 40%	7,132	13,627
Total payment due to HMRC		25,021

Thierry Ltd's corporation tax computation for the year ended 5 April 2012 (after adjustment for deemed salary):

	£	£
Income		80,000
Expenses:		
Travelling and subsistence	2,999	
Accountancy and company secretarial costs	3,000	
Telephone, internet and stationery	1,500	
Salary paid or due to Henry (£10,000 + £52,829)	62,829	
Employer's NIC on salary (£382 + £7,290)	7,672	
Employer pension contributions	2,500	
		(80,500)
Loss for corporation tax purposes		(500)

PAYE payment

6.25 A director whose personal service company is subject to the IR 35 rules has just two weeks from the end of the tax year to calculate any deemed salary. It is accepted that this timetable is tight, so by concession HMRC will allow personal service companies to submit estimated figures for the amount of PAYE and NICs due on the deemed salary.

However, the employer's annual return must be submitted online by 19 May showing any actual remuneration paid during the year plus the estimated amount of deemed payment, with NICs and PAYE correctly calculated on these figures. The company must also make a provisional payment of the tax and NICs due and tell the Collector of Taxes that it is based on an estimated calculation. A supplementary form P35 must be submitted with the final figures as soon as possible. Given that this is a concessional treatment, no penalty should be levied on the grounds that the original form 35 was 'negligently' incorrect (under HMRC's new practice with supplementary form P35s), and it is expected that HMRC will not seek to collect any penalty under the new penalty regime.

Interest on underpaid PAYE and NICs will run from 19 April, but penalties will not be charged under *TMA 1970, s 98A* if the above procedures have been complied with and the final figures are provided by 31 January following the tax year end.

Deduction for corporation tax

6.26 The deemed salary is treated as paid on 5 April whether or not it is actually paid, so it can only be deducted from the corporation tax profits for the accounting period covering that 5 April [*FA 2000, Sch 12, para 17(2)*]. This could create cash flow problems for companies with a 31 December or 31 March year end. For such companies there can be no deduction in the corporation tax computation for any deemed salary treated as paid on the 5 April following the company year end. For this reason many companies will want to review the date of their year end to ensure a matching corporate tax deduction is available in the same period.

Double taxation trap

6.27 If the deemed salary is actually paid out after 5 April, further PAYE and NICs become due on the actual payment, because paying PAYE and NICs on the deemed salary treated as paid on 5 April does not frank a subsequent salary payment. The same salary is thus subject to PAYE and NICs twice. On the other hand, if the deemed salary is extracted from the company by way of a dividend, the double taxation can be relieved by the company making a claim to reduce the amount of dividend taxed in the shareholder's hands (see 6.31).

Investigation

6.28 The application of the IR 35 rules is monitored by HMRC's PAYE audit teams (known as Employer Compliance Units). HMRC can raise an employment income tax and National Insurance charge on any underpaid PAYE and NICs arising on a deemed salary plus interest and penalties, due from 19 April following the end of the tax year during which the salary was deemed to have been paid. If the company does not meet its obligations to pay over the tax, NICs and penalties due, HMRC can collect the amounts due directly from the employee/shareholder.

VAT

6.29 Any VAT the personal service company charges on relevant engagements is not included in the calculation of the deemed salary of the contractor. If the turnover of the personal service company is above the VAT threshold it must register for VAT and account for VAT on all its supplies, including the amounts invoiced for relevant engagements. The personal service company may well find itself having to keep two sets of accounting records, one for VAT purposes and one for the IR 35 rules, with the latter having a much more restricted range of allowable expenses.

Contractors in the construction industry

6.30 The IR 35 rules can apply to personal service companies operating in the construction industry, who may also be subcontractors themselves subject to the tax deduction system for the construction industry (CIS).

Under the new CIS scheme, the company 'sub-contractor' is paid net of either a 0/20/30 per cent tax by the contractor, depending on the sub-contractor's status. The income from the contract would be included as gross in the deemed earnings payment and hence subject to PAYE and NIC on top of the 'CIS tax' already withheld by the main contractor. However, the pressure on the company's cash flow can be reduced by offsetting the tax withheld from amounts received under the sub-contractors' scheme (taxed as deemed IR 35 earnings) from the company's own tax payments of corporation tax, PAYE, NICs and so on. Clearly, such potential cash flow issues should not arise if a company can ensure that it is paid on a 'gross' basis under the CIS.

PROBLEMS WITH IR 35

Extracting funds

Dividends

6.31   Any dividends paid by a personal service company are ignored in the calculation of the deemed salary under the IR 35 rules. If the dividend is paid out of income from relevant engagements, the income will first be subject to PAYE and NICs before being taxed again in the hands of the shareholder.

This double tax charge is relieved by the personal service company making a claim to reduce the value of the dividend by the amount of the deemed salary [*ITEPA 2003, s 58*].

Other employees

6.32   If the personal service company employs people who are direct fee earners, the full employment costs are deductible for corporation tax purposes, but are not deductible in the calculation of the deemed salary to the extent that those costs exceed the permitted 5% allowance. The personal service company is obliged to pay PAYE and NICs in full on the employee's wages, but such costs will have to be met out of the deemed salary of the contractor, so PAYE and NICs will be charged twice on the same income. There is no relief for this double tax charge.

Other contractors

6.33   Where there are two or more employees who perform relevant engagements within a personal service company, the receipts need to be divided between them on a 'just and reasonable basis' to determine the deemed salary of each worker. If the personal service company apportions the receipts in a way which HMRC believe is not reasonable, the Inspector can reapportion the money and demand tax from the company according to their own apportionment. The company can appeal against HMRC's decision, but this power introduces another level of uncertainty into the calculation of the deemed salary.

Mixture of work

6.34   Personal service companies that receive income from relevant engagements as well as other sources need to apportion their gross receipts and expenses between the sources subject to IR 35 and those sources outside these rules. This may involve keeping records on a project or contract-by-contract basis.

Example 2

Apportionment between IR 35 income and other income

Richard writes software which is marketed through his personal service company, Wright IT Ltd. However, as the sales of the software can be volatile Richard also works as an IT contractor through the same company.

An apportionment of income and expenses is likely to be required between the software receipts (which are not deemed employment income under the IR 35 rules) and the contracting work (which may be subject to the IR 35 regime).

Solutions

Seeking an opinion from HMRC

6.35   Taxpayers who are uncertain about the status of contracts performed through their personal service companies can seek an opinion from HMRC. Such queries should be addressed to the specialised HMRC office:

    IR 35 Unit
    HM Revenue & Customs
    North East Metropolitan Area
    Fountain Court
    119 Grange Road
    Middlesbrough
    TS1 2XA
    Tel: (0845) 303 3535
    Fax: (0845) 302 3535

A copy of the signed contract should be posted or faxed to the above address, together with relevant information such as details of other work performed recently through the same personal service company. The contractor must also supply his own National Insurance number, the tax reference number of his company and the postcode of its registered office. These details may also be submitted by e-mail to *IR35@inlandrevenue.gov.uk*, with the subject line containing the tax reference number of the company followed by the company's postcode.

HMRC aim to provide a reply to requests directed through the IR 35 Unit within 28 days of receiving all the details. Note that HMRC will not give any advice on a proposed contract, so the contract must be signed and agreed by the parties before an Inspector is prepared to examine its terms.

If there is no written contract governing the terms of the worker's engagement, the worker should write to HMRC setting out the terms and conditions that have been agreed with the client. The client will also need to confirm that it has agreed such terms in a separate letter.

Form of contract

6.36   The contract between the personal service company and the client is a vital document when determining the tax treatment of the receipts from that contract. Both legal and tax issues will be relevant, so ideally both a lawyer and a taxation practitioner should review the draft contract. The contract should contain as many attributes providing strong indications of self-employment as possible to escape from the IR 35 rules (see the decision in *Lime-IT Ltd v Justin (Officer of the Board of Inland Revenue)* [2003] (SSCD) 15). These would include:

- fixed term – if the job is not completed within the original term or a further task is found, a separate contract should be drawn up;

- short period of engagement – long-term engagements covering periods of more than six months are taken as an indication of employment;

- fixed price – the personal service company bears the risk of a reduced profit margin if the work is not completed on time;

- the right to send a substitute;

- the use of equipment and premises provided by the personal service company;

- evidence of the intention of the parties not to create an employment;

- no provision for attributes of employment such as sick pay, holiday pay, over-time rates, or benefits such as reserved parking;

- no restrictions on the worker performing other work during or for a period after the term of the contract.

The written contract will be ineffective if the *actual* performance of the work and the relationship between the worker and client tell a different story. This point was confirmed in *Netherlane Ltd v York* [2005] (SSCD) 305. Making the normal IR 35 assumption that the services are being provided directly, it is only possible to determine whether the worker is self-employed or is operating under a contract of service by looking at the entire relationship. See also 6.21 for a review of key indicators of employment and self employment.

Although the actual contractual arrangements are indicative, it is also necessary to look at all the other circumstances in which the services are being performed. In this case, the worker acted as a team leader on the company's premises (for seven days a week) and reported to a named supervisor. There was little evidence that he was in business on his own account (other than by providing his own laptop and mobile phone).

A PAYE audit team investigating a personal service company will normally visit the premises where the work is actually carried out to determine the facts of the working arrangement.

Pension contributions

6.37 Where a worker/contractor has operated for many years through his personal service company drawing large dividends and a small salary, his pension fund may be relatively low. This is because dividends cannot be used as a basis to pay a company pension or personal pension contributions.

The deemed IR 35 salary counts as 'earnings' for pensions purposes, which means the worker can pay personal contributions of up to 100% of their earnings, restricted, where appropriate, to the annual 'input' allowance of £50,000 for 2011/12 (which can be increased by any available carried-forward relief under the 'three-year' rule . Any pension contributions made in excess of this limit will trigger a 'clawback' tax charge.

Any *company* pension contributions can be deducted in calculating the deemed earnings for IR 35 purposes. Similarly, such contributions can be made without any NIC cost. Under the post-5 April 2011 pensions regime, the worker can arrange for pension contributions to be paid by their company, but these are also subject to the £50,000 annual input restriction rules.

For further commentary, see Chapter 10.

Offshore companies

6.38 Working on relevant engagements in the UK through a personal service company registered overseas does not avoid the IR 35 provisions. The place where the work is performed determines if the individual would be subject to UK PAYE and NICs and if the engagement would be treated as an employment, then it will fall within the IR 35 rules.

If an offshore company supplies a contractor to perform a relevant engagement in the UK, but fails to deduct the PAYE and NICs required under the IR 35 rules, HMRC may take action to recover the tax due from the contractor. In addition, any assets of the offshore company located in the UK may be seized as part of an action to recover unpaid tax.

MANAGED SERVICE COMPANIES

Background to FA 2007 legislation

6.39   MSCs are similar to PSCs, in that they are companies through which individuals offer their services to an end client. However, whereas a PSC is likely to have a single shareholder and director, a managed service company (MSC) is likely to act on behalf of a number of individuals and therefore the worker/shareholder is unlikely to be controlling the company or its finances. Typically, workers in an MSC do not exercise any control over the company – control lies in the hands of the provider of the MSC (known as the scheme provider). MSC scheme providers tend to be companies which provide the structure and are responsible for the administration and running of the company.

The *FA 2007* legislation (inserted in *ITEPA 2003, Ch 9*), is HMRC's response to the widespread tax avoidance created through the growth in MSCs – a problem which apparently involves around 240,000 workers including teachers, nurses and train drivers. HMRC estimate that if the new legislation had not been introduced, the potential 'tax revenue' loss in 2007/08 would have been in the region of £350 million.

6.40   MSCs have been used to sidestep the original stringent IR 35 rules. They typically involve a 'provider' who sets the company up and runs it on behalf of the workers. The *FA 2007* targets the 'provider' – in HMRC's view, the relevant 'workers' are only operating through a service company because there is a provider who is willing to run and manage the company (for a decent fee!)

HMRC have declared that using the IR 35 rules to deal with this growing avoidance problem in the service sector would be far too labour-intensive. This would inevitably involve a time consuming 'contract-by-contract' analysis to determine whether there is a disguised employment. Under the new Chapter 9 MSC rules, the countering tax charge is triggered simply by the presence of a provider – without the need to unravel the underlying contracts.

6.41   The legislation therefore aims to identify any companies that are managed by a provider. Although there are a number of different company structures, MSCs often use so called 'alphabet shares' with A shares being issued to worker A, B shares to worker B and so on. This enables the workers net income (after certain deductions) to be channelled to them as tax efficient dividend income. However, where a company falls within the *FA 2007* regime, this dividend income is deemed to be earnings for both PAYE and NIC purposes (see 6.44). HMRC consider this to be a far more efficient approach and, given the growing avoidance problem, justifies the wider-ranging Chapter 9 regime.

In the past, even where HMRC established that an MSC was caught under the IR 35 'intermediaries' legislation, any enforcement action taken to collect the outstanding PAYE/NIC due debt often proved fruitless since these companies generally had few assets. It was also easy for such companies to cease trading and for workers to be moved into a new MSC.

Typical MSC structures

6.42   Various structures have been adopted in practice – but under a typical MSC scheme the workers would obtain their work engagements through an agency (in a similar way to those who operate PSCs). A common 'composite company' structure (which would be targeted by the *FA 2007*) is illustrated below:

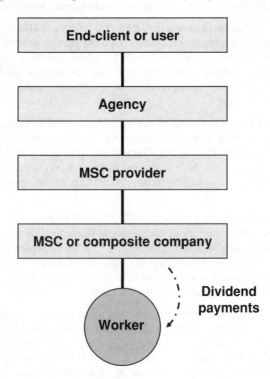

Typical Managed Service Company Structure

Notes:

1.   The agency would typically pay the MSC scheme provider for the work - the contract would be between the agency and the composite company. There would be a separate contract between the scheme provider and the composite company;

2.   In the composite company several otherwise 'unrelated' workers (HMRC estimate they typically number between 10 and 20) are made worker/ shareholders of the company. Each worker would usually be paid the National Minimum Wage and hold a different class of share. This would enable the company to pay different rates of dividends to each worker (which would be linked to the amount paid by each relevant end client in respect of that worker)

3.   The worker is treated as having the employment with the MSC – this enables the worker to claim tax relief for the cost of travel from 'home' to the workplace on the basis that this is a temporary place of work.

4.   The scheme provider would charge a fee for arranging payments to the composite company. The scheme provider would normally also exercise control of the composite company rather than the workers/shareholders.

Offshore MSCs

6.43   The MSC legislation in *ITEPA 2003, Ch 9* also catches offshore MSCs, where both the relevant services are provided in the UK, and the worker is resident in UK. Where these two conditions are met, HMRC consider that the MSC has a place of business in the UK, whether or not it in fact does so.

If an offshore MSC fails to apply the legislation, HMRC can determine the PAYE and NICs that should have been accounted for, and can recover the liability from the third parties listed in 6.49 should the offshore MSC not meet its liability.

Identifying a 'tainted' Managed Service Company

6.44   A MSC company will fall within *ITEPA 2003, Ch 9* where it meets *all* of the following criteria:

●   Its business consists wholly or mainly of providing a worker's services to others

●   More than half of the company's income is paid out to the worker in some form

●   The method used to pay the worker (principally by way of dividend) increases the net amount received by the worker (as compared with the amount that would have been given if every amount was earnings from an employment)

- An MSC provider (or associate) is *involved* with the company – (an MSC provider is defined as a person who carries on a business of promoting or facilitating the use of companies to provide the services of individuals)

6.45   The involvement of an MSC provider is likely to be a very sensitive 'trigger' condition, and for these purposes an MSC (or any associate) will be 'involved' with the relevant company [*ITEPA 2003, s 61B (2)*] if either

- It benefits financially on an ongoing basis from the provision of the individual's services; or

- It influences or controls the provision of those services, or the way in which the payments to the individual (or their associate) are made, or the company's finances, or any of its activities; or

- It gives or promotes an undertaking to make good any tax loss

The meaning of 'associate' for the purposes of *ITEPA 2003, s 61B(2)* is tightly defined as someone who acts in concert with the MSC provider for the purpose of securing that the workers services are provided by a company.

Further recent guidance can be obtained from HMRC's website.

6.46   HMRC have confirmed that it is not their intention to bring accountants and genuine employment agencies within the scope of the *Chapter 9* regime for MSCs – thus there are 'carve-out' exemptions in *ITEPA 2003, s 61B(3)* and *(4)(5)*. The vast majority of firms providing legal or accounting services in a professional capacity will *not* be treated as an MSC provider. HMRC's MSC guidance of July 2007 clarified that 'professional capacity' only applied to persons professionally qualified (or training for a professional qualification), regulated by a regulatory body. Examples of businesses that HMRC consider to be exempt are:

(1)   a firm of accountants carrying on the business of being accountants;

(2)   a tax adviser carrying on the business of being a tax adviser;

(3)   a company formation agent;

(4)   a chartered secretary;

(5)   an employment agency undertaking its core business of placing workers with end clients;

(6)   service companies like insurance companies and payroll bureaux;

(7)   a trade association operating in the service sector.

However, there can be a fine dividing line between accountants giving advice to individuals in the normal course of their business and those that encourage a particular course of behaviour. For example, HMRC indicate that the exemption will *not* apply to 'a firm of accountants carrying on a discernable part of their business specifically to market and/or provide corporate solutions and services to individuals providing their services to end-clients' – this would be an MSC provider.

Deemed employment income

6.47 From 6 April 2007, *ITEPA 2003, s 61D* treats all 'non-employment' income extracted from the company (which will typically be dividends) as earnings from an employment.

The deemed employment payment is calculated by taking the amount of the payment or benefit and then making a deduction for expenses that would have been deductible if the worker had been employed directly by the client. This net figure is deemed to be inclusive of employer's NIC, so a further recalculation is necessary is required to determine the final amount liable to PAYE and employee's NIC (*ITEPA 2003, s 61E*).

NICs will only be due on deemed employment payments received by individuals from 6 August 2007.

Example 3

ITEPA 2003, s 61E calculation of deemed employment payment on dividend received from an MSC

Jose works as a project consultancy manager providing his services through Roman Ltd.

Roman Ltd provides all the relevant administration relating to Jose's work and a number of others. It arranges for all work to be invoiced, collects payment and arranges payment of Jose's salary and dividends through the use of a special class of shares. Roman Ltd falls to be treated as an MSC within *ITEPA 2003, s 61B*.

During the year to 31 March 2011, Jose receives a salary of £6,000 and two dividend payments (in August 2011 and March 2012) totalling £80,000 (after providing for the relevant corporation tax).

During the year, Jose incurred expenses of £8,000 (which would have been deductible 'employment expenses' if he had been directly employed by his clients).

Jose's deemed employment payment for 2011/12 would be calculated as follows:

	£	£
Dividend payments		80,000
Less: Allowable expenses		(8,000)
Net amount		72,000
Therefore:		
Employer's NIC – £72,000 × 13.8/113.8		8,731
Deemed employment payment (subject to PAYE and NIC)		63,269
		72,000

Restriction for travelling and subsistence expenses

6.48   Section 61G(3) places 'tainted' MSCs at a further disadvantage by blocking tax relief for travelling and subsistence expenses (including statutory mileage allowance relief) for its workers.

Transfer of debt provisions

6.49   In the past, HMRC attempted to challenge MSCs under the previous IR 35 legislation. However, once HMRC had successfully established unpaid PAYE and NIC, one of the key practical problems was collecting it.

Many unscrupulous providers side-stepped HMRC's 'clutches' by engaging in 'phoenixism' – they were able to cease trading with few if any assets (so HMRC did not collect the outstanding tax) and the business would be transferred to a new company.

Consequently, under *SI 2007 No 2069*, HMRC have been given fairly widespread powers to collect the relevant unpaid tax from other 'related' parties. If the MSC fails to settle its PAYE/NIC debt and the PAYE debt is incurred after 6 January 2008 this may be collected from these other parties in the following order:

(1)   the MSC director (or other office holder or associate of the MSC);

(2)   the MSC provider (or other office holder or associate of the MSC provider);

(3)   other persons actively involved in the provision of the MSC.

HMRC may not serve a transfer notice on those persons listed under (3) above if the relevant PAYE debt is incurred prior to 6 January 2008.

If HMRC decides that the Exchequer is at risk due to PAYE and NICs debts which have not been recovered within a reasonable period, HMRC can transfer the debt to any of the parties listed above. HMRC has confirmed that it will not approach those in category 3 unless it had attempted to collect the debt from the MSC and those in category 1 and 2 and those attempts had failed. To ensure consistency of treatment, HMRC will use a central team to decide how these provisions will be enforced. See guidance note on HMRC's website for further interpretation of the 'transfer of debt' provisions

6.50 In HMRC's view, an MSC provider would not get a tax deduction for settling the PAYE debt on behalf of the MSC. HMRC have indicated that those who encourage or are actively involved in operating MSCs from outside the UK have a higher risk of having the MSC's PAYE and NIC debt transferred to them!

PLANNING CHECKLIST – PERSONAL SERVICE COMPANIES AND MANAGED SERVICE COMPANIES

Company

- Review all contracts performed by the company to check if the work could be treated as an employment.

- Consider indemnities for PAYE and NIC in contracts. Ensure accounting system can produce timely information to calculate any deemed salary.

- Consider changing company year end to the fiscal year to minimise accounting work.

- Remember where the relevant contract is less than two years, travel and subsistence expenses can be deducted.

- Check that general company expenses can be covered by the 5% allowance for IR35 purposes (the 5% allowance helps to cover such things as accountants' fees).

- Check if the company meets all the relevant conditions to be an MSC. However, if the company provides legal or accounting services in a professional capacity, this would take it outside the MSC rules.

- In the case of an MSC, consider indemnities for PAYE and NIC so that the debts are not transferred to third parties.

Working shareholders (PSCs)

- Wherever possible, ensure legal contracts and actual substance of arrangements support 'self-employment' status.

- Review pricing of contracts which may fall within IR 35 to cover additional tax due.

- Review travel and subsistence expenses to ensure that they would fall to be allowed under the relevant *ITEPA 2003* provisions if incurred in connection with a relevant engagement.

- Deduct any expenses that would have been allowable if the worker could have claimed a deduction against any expenses if the worker had been an employee of the end client. This includes any travelling and subsistence expenses.

- For PSCs pay out 95% of net income from relevant engagements as salary to the worker in the same tax year (and accounting period) as the income is received.

- For PSCs consider transferring ownership of expensive equipment to the individual to avoid disallowance of capital allowances.

- Use pension funding to mitigate income tax liability on deemed IR 35 earnings, subject to £50,000 annual input restriction (subject to any unused relief brought forward from the three previous years)

Non-working shareholders

- Request confirmation from company that a claim has been made to reduce the taxable value of dividends by any amounts taxed as a deemed salary/deemed employment payments.

Chapter 7

Benefits and Expenses

STRATEGY FOR WORKING SHAREHOLDERS

7.1   Most working shareholders will want the company to meet the cost of all expenses which could be said to have a business connection or relationship, no matter how remote that connection may be.

Although the director can claim tax relief under the general rule in *ITEPA 2003, s 336* for those expenses that are 'wholly, exclusively and necessarily incurred in the performance of the duties of the employment', this is notoriously restrictive terminology. From a strategic point of view, it is generally sensible to arrange that the company meets all expenses (directly or by reimbursement) which would not have been incurred but for the existence of the employment in question.

Many working shareholders also want the company to provide them with as many 'fringe' benefits as is possible, provided their personal income tax liability is not of such a magnitude that it would be cheaper for them to purchase the item in question.

This chapter reviews the more important types of benefits and expense payments, including the following.

This chapter also covers various issues relating to structuring remuneration packages, typical transactions with working and non-working shareholders, the relevant P11D compliance obligations and PAYE Settlement Agreements. (The main statutory references are to *Income Tax (Earnings and Pensions) Act 2003 (ITEPA 2003)*.)

Leaving aside the company car and private fuel, there can be advantages in a whole host of goods and services being provided by the company for the employee. There will be an income tax charge on the employee to cover the 'private' element of the benefit, but this is often less than the real value to them of having the benefit. This is especially the case when one considers that (ignoring NICs) a 40% tax-paying employee who wants to purchase goods costing say £900 would need to use £1,500 of gross salary, whereas he would be charged to income tax on £900 (tax = £360) if the company provided the item. Care needs to be taken with this philosophy, however, as there could be no end to the 'private' goods which the employer provides. Instead, the employing company should concentrate on buying those goods which are connected with the 'employment' and which the working shareholder would purchase personally if the company did not do so.

TAX RELIEF FOR THE COMPANY

7.2 The deductibility of the benefit for company tax purposes must always be considered. This is something that HMRC will sometimes question.

If the provision of a benefit constitutes revenue expenditure there should be no problem in obtaining corporate tax relief. This is because it is simply part of the cost of obtaining the director's/employee's services within a 'total' remuneration package and the expense is, therefore, incurred wholly and exclusively for the purposes of the company's trade.

Where the benefit is provided through capital expenditure, however, the position can be more difficult. For the employer to obtain capital allowances on the expenditure it has to be on the provision of machinery or plant for the purposes of the trade. Taking the example of a boat, it is likely that only restricted capital allowances would be claimable to reflect the business aspect. Restricted tax relief for the company (or possibly no relief at all) would *not* necessarily avoid an income tax charge on the director or employee.

POTENTIAL IMPACT OF THE DISGUISED REMUNERATION RULES

7.2A Following *FA 2011's* introduction of *ITEPA 2003, Part 7A* ('Employment Income provided through Third Parties' – often referred to as the 'disguised remuneration' rules'), care must be taken to determine whether any benefits provided by a *third party* (which is an essential component of the regime) are subject to tax under these rules. However, in the vast majority of cases, *ITEPA 2003, s 554G* provides a fairly wide exclusion from the disguised remuneration rules for most employee benefit packages. Benefits provided by the employing (or fellow group) company are not within the scope of the disguised remuneration rules.

'HOBBY' ASSETS

7.2B Experience suggests that HMRC are particularly vigilant to the use of yachts, helicopters, racing cars, race horses and other similar 'toys' purchased by owner-managed companies. Indeed if an HMRC inspector picks up the presence of such assets within a company, a full investigation will inevitably follow. Although such assets are often 'dressed-up' or structured in a way to make them look like a sponsorship, advertising or a separate leasing business activity, HMRC suspect they are really 'hobby' assets and are frequently successful in demonstrating that they are available for private use and are therefore taxable on the owner-manager, and will seek to restrict capital allowance claims on them. Owner-managers who wish to use their company to finance their personal and family pursuits generally regret it after they have been subject to a full-blown HMRC investigation!

STRATEGY FOR OTHER EMPLOYEES

7.3 The strategy is generally likely to be rather different for employees who are not shareholders. Fringe benefits will often be provided as an incentive device, with particular emphasis on those where the income tax charge on the employee is less than the real value to him.

A structured remuneration package could be introduced using the 'cafeteria' system whereby the employing company determines the fixed gross annual cost, with the executive then choosing the components within specified limits. The 'cafeteria' system is illustrated later in this chapter by a comprehensive example (see 7.80).

NATIONAL INSURANCE CONTRIBUTIONS ON EXPENSE AND BENEFITS

Class 1A NICs

7.4 Class 1A National Insurance Contributions (NICs) are now charged on most benefits in kind and expense payments. This would include payments for the employee's benefit (irrespective of whether the liability is the employee's or the company's).

This is generally based on the same amount as the employment income tax charge, although there are a few exceptions.

Class 1A NICs will generally apply unless the benefit is:

- exempt from income tax;
- wholly covered by a deduction under *ITEPA 2003, s 336*;
- covered by a P11D dispensation notice;
- part of a PAYE Settlement Agreement (PSA); or
- received by a lower-paid employee for whom a P11D return is not required.

The Class 1A NIC liability is based on the cash equivalent of the benefit in the same way as the income tax charge and is reported on the form P11D and P11D(b), where the overall NIC liability is calculated. The P11D form is colour-coded to assist with the calculation of the Class 1A liability – the expenses and 'cash equivalents' attracting Class 1A NICs are those entered in the brown boxes with the 'A' indicator (see 7.90). The employer's overall Class 1A liability can be computed on form P11D(b) (Return of Class 1A National Insurance Contributions due) – this calculation is made at the 'employer level' rather than for each employee. This form also contains the employer's declaration that all the required forms have been submitted and the relevant details on those forms have been fully and truly stated.

Class 1A NICs are payable at the current employer's rate of 13.8% (12.8% before 6 April 2011). On the other hand, no employee's contributions are due on benefits that are subject to a Class 1A NIC charge. The payment is due by 19 July 2012 (for 2011/12).

Class 1 NIC charge on earnings

7.5   Transactions made on a company credit card for the supply of goods, money or services for the employee's private use are treated as earnings for NIC purposes. This imposes a Class 1 NIC liability on the value of such transactions and will potentially generate a director's/employee's liability at either 12% or 2% (depending on the level of earnings).

The purchase of private fuel and other motoring expenses on a company credit card will *not* be subject to Class 1 NICs where the amounts are already covered by a Class 1A charge.

USE OF ASSETS

Calculation of taxable benefit

General rules

7.6   Directors and employees are charged to income tax annually for the *use* of an asset (other than a car, van or living accommodation). The taxable benefit is 20% of the market value of the asset when it is first provided or on the rental paid for the asset if that gives a greater taxable benefit [*ITEPA 2003, s 205(1)–(3)*]. A fast-depreciating asset could be provided and the tax charge on the employee could be kept to a minimum in relation to the value enjoyed by him. There would also be a separate income tax charge on any expenses incurred by the employer in providing the asset.

Where the asset is used for a mixture of business and private purposes, the taxable benefit is only calculated on the private use element. However, Class 1A NICs arise on the *full* annual value of mixed-use assets, except where the private use is insubstantial.

The combined taxable benefit and NIC charge on exotic 'hobby' assets over a number of years can be substantial, particularly where there are interest and penalties 'on-top'! Such assets are prime targets for HMRC investigations (see 7.2A).

Taxable benefit on computers

7.6A   Employers should be aware that computers and related IT equipment made available to employees may, in certain circumstances, attract a taxable benefit

Up until 5 April 2006, computer equipment lent to employees was treated as an 'excluded benefit' and did not therefore attract a tax charge. Up to £500 of the annual value of the benefit (ie 20% of £2,500) was tax-free and this exemption was widely used by companies to provide employees with PCs and laptops under the Home Computer Initiative (HCI) scheme. Launched in 2004 by the Department of Trade and Industry (DTI) (now renamed the Department for Business Enterprise & Regulatory Reform (BERR)), the scheme allowed employees to 'sacrifice' part of their gross salary (see 7.78), and in exchange they were loaned a computer for, usually, three years.

At the end of the loan period, the employee would be given the opportunity to purchase the computer for its market value, which would invariably be minimal due to the progress of technology in the intervening period. This effectively allowed employees to purchase a computer out of their gross salary, with three years interest-free credit. Unfortunately, the excluded benefit exemption for computers was removed without warning in the Finance Act 2006, leading to the overnight demise of the HCI scheme. Ironically the DTI (now BERR) was reported to be implementing a scheme for their own employees days before the Chancellor announced the HCI was to be scrapped!

The changes do not affect employees who were in a scheme prior to 6 April 2006. HMRC have also said that where the employer and employee had agreed the terms on which the computer was made available in writing before 6 April 2006 the tax exemption would still apply, even if, due to circumstances beyond their control, the employee wasn't able to take physical possession of the computer equipment by 6 April.

HMRC have stated, 'Section 316 of the Income Tax (Earnings & Pensions) Act 2003 provides that no income tax will arise on accommodation, supplies and services used in employment duties. This includes computer equipment provided for business purposes where any private use made is not significant. Consequently, where employers provide computer equipment to employees solely for them to carry out the duties of the employment at home, HM Revenue and Customs accept it is unlikely that private use of the computer will be significant, when compared with the primary business purpose of providing the computer equipment'.

If significant private use is made of a computer provided for business purposes a tax charge will arise on the private use element based on the value of the computer and the extent of the business and private use. Employers will also be liable to Class 1A National Insurance contributions.

Subsequent transfer of asset

7.7   Where the ownership of the asset 'used' by the employee is subsequently transferred to them, *ITEPA 2003, s 206* states that an income tax charge then arises based on the *greater* of:

- the market value of the asset at the *time of transfer*; and

- the market value when it is first provided by the company *less* the amounts already charged for the use of the asset.

The transfer of previously 'loaned' computers and bicycles is simply based on the market value of the transferred asset [*ITEPA 2003, s 206(6)*].

The transfer of ownership charge can possibly be avoided as follows:

(*a*)   for (say) clothing or computer equipment, by donating it to charity;

(*b*)   the employee continuing to pay rent equivalent to the annual value so that no charge to income tax arises on the use of the asset (ie with no transfer of ownership).

The fast-depreciating assets could be furniture or consumer durables for the director's/employee's home, but the advantage to the company would be less than for business clothing which helps to promote its image. The company may well be able to make special arrangements so that it purchases the clothing at a discount.

COMPANY CARS AND PRIVATE FUEL

Company cars – basic rules

7.8   The calculation of the taxable benefit (for directors and employees earning more than £8,500 per year) on a 'company car' has been based on *the appropriate percentage for the year* applied to the *price of the car.* This percentage is generally based on the CO_2 emission levels of the relevant car (for post-31 December 1997 registrations), otherwise it depends on the engine size of the car. There is no discount for (high) business mileage or for older cars [*ITEPA 2003, ss 120–148*]. (See 7.9 below.)

For the purposes of the company car benefit rules, a car is a mechanically propelled road vehicle *other than* goods vehicles (for example, commercial vehicles such as lorries, trucks or vans), vehicles not commonly used as a private vehicle (for example, buses and coaches), motor cycles and invalid carriages. In applying this definition, the legislation looks at the predominant purpose for which the vehicle was constructed rather than its actual use. For tax treatment of vans provided to employees, see 7.40.

Since 6 April 2010, electric cars are completely exempt from the taxable benefit and Class 1A NIC charge (see 7.12). A special exemption also applies for cars with 'pool car' status – see 7.26.

The price of the car is the sum of the following:

(*a*) the published list price of the car when it was first registered (including the price of any optional extras or accessories supplied with the car) [*ITEPA 2003, ss 122–131*];

(*b*) VAT (plus any other tax which may be charged on a car, but not the cost of the road fund licence) [*ITEPA 2003, s 123(2)*];

(*c*) delivery charges [*ITEPA 2003, s 123(2)*];

(*d*) the published price of accessories or optional extras provided subsequently, unless these amount to less than £100, in which case they can be ignored [*ITEPA 2003, s 126(3)*].

Since the current car benefit rules began, the price of any car was 'capped' at £80,000. However, this 'cap' was removed from 6 April 2011, with the taxable benefits for very expensive cars becoming based on their true 'value'(*ITEPA 2003, s121*). Thus, a car with a list price of (say) £250,000 with the maximum 35% percentage, would have a taxable benefit in 2011/12 of £87,500 (£250,000 × 35%), which would be a substantial increase on the 'capped' 2010/11 charge of £28,000 (£80,000 'cap' × 35%).

All the relevant details (including, for each car, the make and model, date of first registration, CO_2 emission level, dates the car was made available, list price, etc) must be reported on the P11D (section F).

'Made available by reason of employment'

7.8A A taxable benefit only arises if the car is made available by reason by reason of employment and must be available for the director's/employee's private use [*ITEPA 2003, s 118*]. The First-tier Tribunal reached an interesting decision in a case involving a Ferrari owned by an antiques company [*Michael Golding v HMRC* [2011] UKFTT 232. In this case, the judge was persuaded that there had been no private use of the car since, during the relevant period, the car was either being used as a marketing tool or was up for sale. He concluded that "it would be artificial to regard the car, in those circumstances, as 'made available' to the appellant in his capacity as an employee for his use and benefit (whether or not he chose to use it)'. Thus, "even if a director or employee does drive or use a vehicle owned by a company, that is not determinative of whether or not that vehicle has been 'made available' to him by reason of his employment or directorship".

In *A Whitby v HMRC (and related appeal)* FTT [2009] UKFTT 311, it was confirmed that a taxable benefit charge arose on various cars, even though the company provided them on commercial lease terms to certain directors. A taxable benefit was also held to apply where the directors' cars were leased from a third party, with the cost of the lease being charged to the directors' loan accounts (*Stanford Management Services Ltd v HMRC (and related appeals)* FTT [2010] UKFTT 98. In both these cases, the taxable benefit was reduced by payments made by the directors (see 7.8B below).

In *Christensen v Vasili* [2004] STC 935, the High Court held that the 'shared' ownership of a car between an employer and employee did not prevent a taxable benefit arising in respect of the car.

'Private use' payments by directors/employees

7.8B   The company car 'taxable benefit' can be reduced if the director/ employee is required to make a payment as a condition of the car being made available for private use and the payment is only for that purpose. These requirements are interpreted strictly, as evidenced in *Brown v Ware (HMIT)* [1995] SSCD 155. It was held in this case that no relief was available for a 'contribution' made by employee so that he could drive a better car since this was not a payment for private use.

For treatment of 'one-off' capital contributions, see 7.22.

Other related car benefits

7.8C   It is worth noting the additional benefit for the cost of providing a cherished or private number plate. HMRC's view is that most of the cost relates to the right to use the relevant numbers or letters and it is not therefore treated as an 'accessory'. However, the car benefit does not cover the provision of a chauffeur/driver, so the private cost proportion of the cost of providing a chauffeur/driver must be included as a separate taxable benefit.

The Revenue have previously confirmed that company car (and van) drivers who incur a congestion zone charge and have this amount reimbursed by the company will not suffer tax on this amount, even where this is part of their ordinary commuting costs. (The congestion charge effectively attaches to the car as opposed to the driver). Thus, the 'exemption' in *ITEPA 2003, s 239(4), (5)* applies. This broadly states that any benefit in connection with a company car or company van does not give rise to any further taxable benefits under *ITEPA 2003, s 203(1)* other than on the provision of any 'driver'. As the charge is an employer liability (it is the company's car), no NIC liability arises as it is a payment in kind. However, congestion charges reimbursed on *'employee-owned'* cars will attract tax and NIC

CO_2 emissions tables

7.9   For 2011/12 the taxable benefit for cars with petrol engines emitting CO_2 *at or below* a lower threshold of 125 grams per kilometre (g/km) starts at 15% of the car's list price. Each additional 5g/km then increases the appropriate percentage by one point, subject to a maximum of 35% of the list price. Class 1A NICs also apply to the taxable benefit, increasing the overall 'cost' of running company cars (see 7.4). For prospective changes from 2012/13 see 7.14 below.

The Vehicle Certification Agency produces a free indicative guide to the CO_2 emissions figures for all new cars (registered from 1 March 2001) – this can also be found at *www.vcacarfueldata.org.uk*. Relevant details for cars registered between 1 January 1998 and 28 February 2001 can be found on the website of the Society of Motor Manufacturers and Traders – *www.smmt.co.uk*. For cars registered before 1 January 1998, see 7.13.

For all cars registered from (at least) March 2001, the relevant CO_2 emissions figure is stated on the Vehicle Registration Document (V5) (employers supply emissions details on the Form P46 (Car) when a car is changed or first supplied). Thus, the CO_2 emissions figure applying at the date of the first registration is set for the life of the car.

A special reduced rate applies for the most eco-efficient cars – known as 'qualifying low emission cars' or 'QUALECS' – which are non-electrically propelled cars with a CO_2 emissions rating of 120 g/km or less (CO_2 emissions are *not* rounded down for this purposes))[*ITEPA 2003, s139(3A)*]. These environmentally-friendly cars attract a special lower taxable benefit of 10% of the car's list price (13% for a diesel car) (see 7.19). An even lower figure of 5% applies if a car's emissions do not exceed 75g/km, although this is more theoretical than real!

Note that the CO_2 threshold for claiming 100% capital allowances on such cars is currently 110 g/km (not 120 g/km – see 7.12).

The relevant amounts for *2011/12* are shown in the table below.

7.9   *Benefits and Expenses*

Car benefit calculator – 2011–12

CO_2 *emissions rating g/km*	*% of list price*
up to 75	5
75 to 120 (QUALEC)	10
125	15
130	16
135	17
140	18
145	19
150	20
155	21
160	22
165	23
170	24
175	25
180	26
185	27
190	28
195	29
200	30
205	31
210	32
215	33
220	34
≥225	35

Notes:

1   The CO_2 emissions figures for a car are rounded down to the nearest five grams per kilometre (g/km) (apart from determining whether a car falls within the 120g/km QUALEC limit [*ITEPA 2003, s 139*].

2   Where the car is 'not available for part of the year', the relevant scale charge is reduced on a pro-rata basis, subject to the rules mentioned in 7.19 below.

3.   The taxable benefit for *diesel* cars is 3% higher in every case than for petrol engines, up to a maximum of 35% of the list price. Diesel cars generally have lower CO_2 emissions than petrol cars, but the particulates from diesel engines have contributed to increases in respiratory illnesses – the 'simple' flat 3% increase recognises this. The 3% supplement applies even if a diesel car is a qualifying low emission vehicle. It will therefore be charged at 13% (10% QUALEC rate + 3% supplement). Since April 2011, the 3% supplement also applies to diesel cars meeting the Euro IV emission standard (Before April 2011, they were exempted from the 3% diesel supplement).

4   A 2% discount is given for cars run on E85 fuel (which are not QUALECS) .E85 fuel is essentially a biofuel, comprised of ethanol mixed with 15% petrol. Biofuel enabled cars which are currently available on the market include the Saab 9–5 BioPower and the Ford Focus Flexi-Fuel vehicle.

5.   Electric cars are completely exempt from 6 April 2010 (see 7.12)!

6.   Employees of motor dealers often have access to number of different cars. Historically, they have calculated their car benefit using a locally agreed 'average' car. From April 2009, HMRC will permit the representative 'average' car to be calculated on a national or regional basis for the dealership (see *EIM 23656*).

Worked examples of taxable car benefits

7.10

Example 1

Calculation of car benefit

Mr David is the sales director of Specialist Kicks Ltd. He drives around 40,000 business miles a year in a company-provided BMW 318i Manual ES142.

The BMW 318i has a CO_2 emissions rating of 142 g/km and cost £21,145 in June 2009. For the purpose of determining the relevant percentage, the CO_2 emissions rating is rounded down to the nearest 5 grams per kilometre, ie 140 g/km in this case.

Thus, Mr David's taxable benefit for 2011/12 is £3,806 , being 18% × £21,145. (There are no discounts for the high business mileage.)

Example 2

Calculation of company car benefits

The 2011/12 tax and the company's NIC Class 1A charges relating to the cars provided to the directors of Crouch Ltd are calculated (assuming their marginal tax rate is 40%) as follows:

Director	Car	List price	CO_2 g/km	Rel-evant %	Taxable benefit	Tax at 40%	Class 1A NIC @ 13.8%
Mr R Benitez	Vauxhall Corsa	£20,045	115	10%	£2,005	£802	£277
Mr D Kuyt	Landrover Discovery V8I ESDR 7 seat	£34,735	397	35%	£12,157	£4,863	1,678

Alternative fuel vehicles

7.11   Alternative fuel vehicles are generally more environmentally friendly but cost more than 'normal' petrol cars. This is reflected in their 'discounted' scale charges, as shown below:

	2011/12	**2010/11**
Electric car (see 7.12)	Exemption from charge	Exemption from charge
Hybrid electric and petrol car	otherwise normal scale charge	otherwise normal scale charge
Bi-fuel gas and petrol cars	10% charge if CO_2 emission 120 g/km or less	10% charge if CO_2 emission 120 g/km or less

Note also the 2% deduction available from 2008/09 for cars which can run on E85 fuel. (Before April 2011, Hybrid and Bi-fuel cars attracted discounts on the normal scale percentage of 2% and 3% respectively.)

Tax breaks for electric cars

7.12   The Government wishes to embrace the development of the electric car, which now carries a plethora of tax breaks and other benefits.

In particular, electric cars are completely exempt from any taxable benefit for five years from 2010/11, providing valuable tax and NIC savings for employers and employees. They will also attract 100% capital allowances, exemption from car tax, and do not incur any congestion charges. Furthermore, electric cars carry free parking and no expensive fuel bills, so there is no taxable fuel scale charge! The electricity cost is typically 2p per mile!

These cars also qualify for a government grant of 25% of the cost up to a maximum of £5,000.

Employees who drive a large number of business miles during the year may find it cost-effective to 'convert' their company cars to run on LPG instead of petrol or diesel or even consider an electric car!

Pre-1 January 1998 cars and cars with no CO_2 emissions rating

7.13   The taxable benefit scales do not apply to:

- vehicles with no approved CO_2 emissions rating (for example, cars which have been imported from outside the EU); or

- older vehicles registered before January 1998 for which the CO_2 emissions rating is unknown [*ITEPA 2003, ss 140* and *142*].

The taxable benefit in such cases is based on a percentage of the list price as follows:

Engine size	No emissions figure	Pre-January 1998 car
Up to 1,400 cc	15%	15%
1,401–2,000 cc	25%	22%
Over 2,000 cc	35%	32%

The 3% diesel supplement applies to cars with no emissions figures (to a maximum of 35%), but it does not apply to older cars registered before 1 January 1998.

Company car tax – prospective changes from 2012/13

7.14   From 2012/13, the company car tax band will be extended down to a new 10% band, with the 10% scale charge (13% for diesel cars) being applied to company cars with CO_2 emissions up to 99g/km. All CO_2 emissions thresholds will also move down by 5g/km. The current QUALEC category will disappear.

This means that the lower end of the emissions scale percentages for 2012/13 will be as follows:

CO_2 emissions rating g/km	% of list price	
	Petrol	Diesel
Up to 75	5	8
76 to 99	10	13
100–104	11	14
105–109	12	15
110–114	13	16
115–119	14	17
120–124	15	18
125–129	16	19
130–134	17	20

Furthermore, from April 2013, an additional 1% increase is proposed for cars with emissions exceeding 95g/km. The overall effect of these changes will produce some pretty sizeable increases at the lower end of the emissions scale table.

VAT recovery on purchase/lease of car

7.14A   As a general rule, a company cannot recover the input VAT on the purchase cost of a car. Where the car is leased, 50% of the input VAT on lease payments is recoverable (where the car is used partly for business and private purposes by the director/employee).

Where it can be demonstrated that a purchased or leased car is genuinely planned to be used *exclusively* for business purposes, all of the VAT may be recovered (subject to any partial exemption restriction). The test is restrictive since it means that 'it is *not* intended to make the car available for the private use of anyone, save where it is done in the course of a commercial leasing or rental operation'.

Home to work use is regarded as private, unless the employee works from home. In the case of *C&E Comrs v Elm Milk Ltd* [2006] STC 792, the Tribunal, the High Court and the Court of Appeal accepted that a Mercedes E320 provided to the only director of a company was solely intended for business use. A board minute provided that the car was not available for private use and that any such use would represent a breach of the employee's employment contract. The director travelled some 50,000 miles on business each year and the car was garaged overnight near the company's premises (where the keys were kept!), although this was also nearby the director's home. The fact that the director used his wife's Rover for private use probably clinched the decision!

The 'motor car' definition for VAT purposes is similar, but not identical, to that which applies for the employee benefits legislation (see 7.8). Taxis, mini-cabs, self-drive hire cars and cars used for driving tuition will normally qualify for full input recovery.

Where the input VAT has been blocked, no VAT is chargeable on any contributions made by the employee for private use of the car. Where VAT has been fully recovered on a car, output VAT must be charged on a subsequent sale. Similarly, if a 'business' car begins to be used for private purposes, this triggers a 'self-supply' for VAT purposes. Output VAT must then be accounted for on the current price of the car with no recovery of the related input VAT.

Car fuel benefit

7.15   The system for calculating the car fuel scale charge on a *company car* is based on the relevant car's CO_2 percentage. A director's/employee's fuel scale charge for 2011/12 is computed by reference to a base figure of £18,800

(£18,000 for 2010/11) , against which the relevant CO_2 percentage (the same as their company car benefit percentage – see table in 7.9) is applied [*ITEPA 2003, s 150*]. The recent increases to the appropriate percentages for company cars always has an adverse knock-on effect for those paying the fuel scale charge.

The (practical) minimum and maximum charge for 2011/12 is therefore normally £1,880 (£18,800 × 10%) and £6,580 (£18,800 × 35%) respectively (see CO_2 emissions table in 7.9). Where the director or employee starts or stops paying for private fuel during the tax year, the relevant taxable fuel benefit is apportioned.

Based on the prevailing figures, it is difficult to see any circumstances in which it makes sense for the employing company to provide *private* fuel since the tax charge on the benefit is likely to exceed the true cost of the fuel. From the company's point of view, these amounts also attract a significant Class 1A NIC cost.

Taxable benefits for private fuel are not adjusted for any particular level of business mileage. To avoid the fuel scale charge, the employee must reimburse the company with the *full* cost of all the fuel used on 'non-business' journeys during the tax year. A partial reimbursement does not reduce the scale charge [*ITEPA 2003, s 151(2)*].

By concession, HMRC permit reimbursements to be made after the end of the year provided they are made within a reasonable period after the tax year-end (giving companies time to process their final mileage claims and repayments) or within 30 days of discovering an unintentional error (*HMRC EIM para 23782*). However, this treatment is not the law and the Special Commissioner refused to apply it in *Impact Foiling Ltd and others v HMRC* [2006] STC (SCD) 764. In this case, the company had invoiced the directors the full cost of their 2002 to 2004 fuel in January 2005, which was a substantial delay.

Probably the safest way to avoid the fuel scale charge is for the directors and employers to pay for all their fuel initially and then to reclaim genuine business mileage from the company using the advisory fuel rates (see 7.186)

Where fuel is provided for an employee's *own car*, the fuel scale charges above do *not* apply. Instead an income tax and NIC charge will arise on the cost to the employer of providing the fuel.

VAT recovery on fuel

7.16 Where a company provides free or cheap fuel for private use, the input VAT on the fuel is recoverable in full. However, the company must then account for VAT, based on the fixed scale charge (which varies according to the car's CO2 emissions rating).

7.16 *Benefits and Expenses*

Recent quarterly VAT fuel scale rates are shown below. The VAT scale charge figures are *VAT inclusive* and thus, with a current 20% rate, the charge must be multiplied by 20/120 (or 1/6th):

Quarterly VAT scale charge $CO_2 g/km$
From 1 May 2011
£

120 or less	157
125	236
130	252
135	268
140	283
145	299
150	315
155	331
160	346
165	362
170	378
175	394
180	409
185	425
190	441
195	457
200	472
205	488
210	504
215	520
220	536
225 or more	551

Where the CO_2 emissions figure of a vehicle is not a multiple of 5, the figure is rounded down to the next multiple of 5 to determine the level of charge.

Thus, the VAT due on a car with CO_2 emissions of 200 g/km for the VAT quarter ended September 2011 would be calculated as £472 (scale charge) × 20%/120% = £78.67

Opting out of the VAT scale charge and claiming VAT on business fuel

7.17 The VAT fuel scale charges are likely to be beneficial where cars build up high levels of private motoring. However, the fuel scale charges are not compulsory. As an alternative, companies can opt out of the scale charge process by only claiming back the VAT element on fuel that has been used for *business travel*. In such cases, the company can recover VAT on the purchased fuel by reference to the business mileage (as a proportion of the total mileage) for each car.

Detailed mileage records must be kept and in this context it is often incorrectly assumed that 'home to work' travel is business (which will only be in exceptional cases where 'home base' status has been agreed). For example, assume that that an owner-manager's total mileage is 4,290 of which 3,780 can be identified as relating to business journeys, and the total cost of the fuel is £428

This would enable input VAT to be reclaimed on the fuel of £62.85 , calculated as follows:

Business mileage cost – £428 × 3,780/4,290 = £377.12 .

Input tax reclaimed on fuel – £377.12 × 20/120 (or 1/6) = £62.85.

Companies also have the option of not reclaiming any VAT on their fuel spend. This might be helpful where the total mileage is very low so that the VAT on the scale charge gives rise to an excessive VAT cost. However, if the company wishes to opt-out completely, this applies to all their fuel, including that used for vans and lorries etc.

Reimbursement of private fuel for company cars ('Advisory fuel rates')

7.18 HMRC have published 'advisory rates' to be used for the reimbursement of private fuel from directors/employees driving *company cars*, which aim to save time and costs. These advisory rates can be used where the company initially pays for all the fuel and then recovers the 'private' element from the director/employee driver. Where these rates are used to 'recover' the cost of private fuel, no income tax or Class 1 NIC arises.

These rates may also be used to reimburse employees for the cost of fuel on 'business' journeys, thus avoiding the need to keep details of the actual costs. The rates are likely to be reviewed when there is a material change in petrol prices.

HMRC private mileage advisory fuel rates are now reviewed and amended in late February, May, August, and November each year and can be found at www.hmrc.gov.uk/cars/fuel_company_cars.htm.

Recent rates are shown below:

Advisory fuel rates for company cars

From 1 September 2011

	Petrol	Diesel	LPG
Up to 1400 cccc	15p	12p	11p
1401cc–1600 cc	18p	12p	13p
1601cc-2000cc	18p	15p	13p
Over 2000 cc	26p	18p	18p

From 1 June 2011 to 31 August 2011

Up to 1–,400 cc	14p	13p	10p
1401cc–2000cc	16p	13p	12p
Over 2,000 cc	23p	18p	17p

Companies can pay at the current or previous rates in the month following the date the rates changed, and may wish to make supplementary payments.

The above rates are also accepted for VAT purposes. The amount reimbursed by the director/employee is chargeable to VAT at 20% (or 17.5% before 3 January 2011). The company may use other 'reimbursement rates' if they are justifiable. However, if a greater rate is paid that cannot be justified by reference to the actual costs incurred, then the 'excess' amount is subject to income tax.

HOW TO REDUCE THE TAX CHARGE ON A COMPANY CAR

Car not always used

7.19   The car benefit charge is reduced, on a time basis, when the car is incapable of being used at all for at least 30 consecutive days or it is not actually provided throughout the relevant tax year. The car fuel benefit is reduced on the same basis.

Consequently, where employees do not need the car for a certain period, it is recommended that they hand in their keys. The company should prepare a memo confirming the non-availability of the car until the keys are returned to the employee. Provided the period of 'non-availability' is at least 30 consecutive days, there should be a pro-rata reduction in the tax charge [*ITEPA 2003, s 143(2)*].

However, for company cars driven by directors of a family company there may be difficulties in establishing that the car is unavailable for a period, as illustrated in *Taxation*, 15 November 2001. A 'Feedback' contribution referred to a case of a director who had a heart attack and did not use the car for 12 months. He had changed the insurance to 'third party, fire and theft' only and surrendered his driving licence. Somewhat surprisingly on the facts, this case had to be taken to the General Commissioners, who resolved it in the director's favour!

Which cars to buy

7.20 Given that taxable car benefits are based on CO_2 emissions, any decision to purchase a new company car should include consideration of the vehicle's emission rating. Looking at matters from a pure tax perspective, the best way to keep the company car tax bill down will be to choose a cheaper, more fuel-efficient car.

Drivers of automatic cars should be wary of the fact that they tend to have an emissions rating typically three or four tax bands worse than their manual counterparts.

High-mileage company cars do not receive any special discount and will generally suffer a relatively high scale charge. In some cases, they would probably benefit by switching to a cash alternative, having their own car and being compensated for their business mileage under the approved mileage allowance payments (AMAPs) system (discussed in 7.36).

Tax favoured 'low emission' cars (QUALECs)

7.21 A number of very respectable eco-efficient cars can now be purchased and many more companies and their car users are seeking to take advantage of the generous tax breaks which are now available on these cars – technically known as QUALECs (qualifying low emissions cars)

Low emission cars qualify for 100% first year capital allowances, thus enabling the car to be fully written-off for corporate tax purposes in the year of purchase (see 4.00). Similarly, if low-emission cars are leased (rather than purchased outright), their lease rental payments are fully deductible (see 7.31).

Somewhat surprisingly, the CO_2 emissions threshold for 100% capital allowances is 110 g/km (since 1 April 2008) whereas the qualifying CO_2 level for QUALEC is 120g/km or below (up until 5 April 2012). However, from 6 April 2011, the ability to claim the 10% scale rate will require the car to have emissions of less than 100g/km! (see 7.14).

Low-emission cars also attract low taxable benefits for the director/employee. For example, a car costing £10,000 would only suffer a monthly tax charge during 2011/12 of £16.67 in the hands of an employee (paying tax at the basic rate) (see 7.21).

A number qualify for this favourable tax treatment, including the following models:

Model	CO2 emissions (g/km)	Fuel	List Price
Renault Clio Extreme eco2 dCi 86	98	Diesel	£12,690
Lexus CT200h	94	Hybrid	£23,485
Peugeot 3008 HYbrid4	99	Hybrid	£26,995
Honda Jazz hybrid	104	Hybrid	£15,995
Ford Focus 1.6 150PS	109	Petrol	£15,995
Volkswagen Jetta Bluemotion 1.6TDI	109	Diesel	£17,000

All of these cars would produce a car benefit of either 10% or, in the case of diesel models, 13% (10% plus 3% diesel loading) of their list price. Some of these cars may be attractive to employees and will assist in minimising their tax costs.

The company also benefits from first year allowances against its corporate tax liability, lower Class 1A NICs and lower road fund licence costs (and, currently, exemption from congestion charges!).

As 'high-performance' *electric* cars are fast becoming a reality, some 'adventurous' owner-managers may wish to consider the tremendous tax breaks available, including the complete exemption from a taxable benefit charge for five years from 1 April 2010.

Director/employee capital contributions

7.22   Many family or owner-managed companies have a policy on company cars, which allows a group of employees to have the use of a car up to an allotted price level. If an employee then wishes to have a more expensive car, the company may be happy to arrange this provided the employee meets the difference out of their own pocket. There is a reduction in the tax charge where the employee contributes a capital sum to the cost of the car or accessories when the car is first made available to them.

The deductible capital contribution up to a fixed level of £5,000 reduces the list price, on which the taxable benefit is computed [*ITEPA 2003, s 132*]. However, if the employee is entitled to a *full* reimbursement of the contribution when the car is subsequently sold, HMRC considers that no capital contribution has been made – probably because the refundable contribution is really a loan.

On the other hand, if the employee is only entitled to a proportionate reimbursement (usually based on the sale value), the employee can retain the 'deduction' for the full capital contribution and is not subject to any tax on the reimbursed amount (see HMRC leaflet IR 172). Based on this reasoning, it appears possible still to secure a full reduction in list price (up to £5,000) by providing that only a 'small' amount should be refunded to the company (as it would remain *partly-refundable*). In certain cases, the initial contribution towards the cost of the company car may be funded by a non-taxable interest-free loan from the company (using the £5,000 de-minimis exemption – see 7.54).

Under the 'capital contribution' rules, the director/employee only gets the benefit of a reduction at the relevant CO_2 percentage (applied to the reduced list price). The reduction in the taxable benefit will apply for every year 'their' company car is used for private purpose. However, it may be better to arrange for the director's/employee's proposed contribution to be paid over a period rather than as an initial lump-sum. It could then be expressed as a payment made as a condition of the car being made available for their private use. In that way, the legislation allows the annual contribution to be deducted from the actual taxable benefit (see 7.8B).

Taking a lower-value car

7.23   Looking at the other extreme, an employee could choose to take a car below the price range allotted to them by the company. In that case, the company could make a payment of the difference to a pension plan for the employee's benefit. This is tax-neutral where the company structures the payment as an additional voluntary contribution.

Car for spouses and adult children

7.24   Perk cars, such as those provided to spouses or a child at university, fare relatively well under the company car regime. This is because discounts are no longer offered for heavy or average business mileage. The normal taxable benefit arises even where the car is used not by the owner-manager (director) but by a member of their family or household [*ITEPA 2003, ss 114(1)(a)* and *721(5)*]. Without this rule it would, of course, be easy to avoid the tax charge.

269

Example 3

Calculation of car benefit (for spouse)

Mrs Becks is married to Mr Becks, who is managing director of Galaxy Footballs Ltd. Mrs Becks does some administrative work for the company, which provides her with a BMW 7 Series 735i. The list price of her BMW when it was first registered was £28,240. The car has a CO_2 emissions rating of 235 g/km and Mrs Becks has minimal business mileage.

Mrs Becks' taxable benefit for 2011/12 is:

£28,240 × 35% = £9,884.

7.25   In certain cases it may even be possible for the owner-manager's spouse (or civil partner) to be provided with (say) a suitable 'eco-friendly' car with no tax charge arising by ensuring that she does not exceed the £8,500 earnings and benefits limit rule for taxing company car benefits.

Such planning usually relies on the spouse performing limited employment duties for which she receives a modest salary (but she must not be a director). In calculating whether the £8,500 limit is exceeded, the potential car scale charge must be computed [*ITEPA 2003, s 217*], but the assumption is that this would be relatively small for a very environmentally-friendly car. (It is recommended that the company should not provide private fuel since this is likely to take the wife over the £8,500 threshold.) However, such planning would only be efficacious if it can be shown that the car is provided to the wife in her own right as an employee and the provision of the car meets the following other conditions:

- the provision of an 'equivalent' car is normal commercial practice for the job she undertakes; and

- the company can demonstrate that equivalent cars are made available on the same basis to other (unrelated) employees doing similar jobs [*ITEPA 2003, s 169*].

It will be appreciated that these conditions may be pretty difficult to meet in many family company situations, particularly where there are no 'comparable' employee roles. However, for larger companies, it should be possible to implement such arrangements.

If the spouse is either a director or earning at least £8,500 per year (including benefits and expenses), there would be a company car scale charge under the normal rules.

There may also be financial benefits in providing 'environmentally-friendly' cars to other family members, such as children at university, since the car does not have to be used in the business. This means, for example, that a 'student-child' could be provided with a 'green' car (in the environmental sense!)

costing (say) £15,000. In such cases, the car would generally be treated as being provided by reason of the owner-manager's directorship. This would result in a maximum annual tax charge for them of only £600 (10% × £15,000 × (say) 40%), provided the car qualifies as a QUALEC (with an emissions rating not exceeding 120 grams per kilometre. Furthermore, the company should be able to obtain capital allowances on the car and be able to reclaim the VAT on the car's servicing costs.

The 'pool car'

7.26   Instead of having the exclusive use of a car, the employee could be entitled to use a 'pool car'. If this is the case, there would be no income tax charge on them (ITEPA 2003, s167) .

For a car to form part of a 'car pool', various conditions have to be satisfied. In broad terms:

- the car must actually be used by *more than one* employee and not ordinarily be used by any one of them to the exclusion of the others;

- any private use must be merely incidental to business use;

- the car must not normally be kept overnight at or near the residence of the director or employee unless that person happens to live in the vicinity of the employer's premises where the car is garaged [*ITEPA 2003, s 167*].

In HMRC's view, the requirement for private use to be 'merely incidental' to business use imposes a qualitative test rather than a quantitative test. A typical example would be where an employee who is required to undertake a long business journey is allowed to take a pool car home the previous night in readiness for an early morning start. The journey from office to home is, of course, private use, but in this particular context it is subordinate to the lengthy business trip the following day and is undertaken to further the business trip. In such cases, HMRC would regard the private use as being merely incidental to the business use, unless it happened too often.

7.27   Leaflet IR 480 states that a car is treated as not normally kept overnight at or near the homes of employees where the occasions on which it is taken to the employees' homes does not exceed 60% of the year. Where a car is garaged at employees' homes on a large number of occasions (albeit within the 60% limit), HMRC suggests that the private use from home to work would *not* be merely incidental to business use. These are stringent conditions and room for manoeuvre is limited. However, a prestige car kept at the forecourt of the company's premises could fit the bill and help promote the company's image.

Where there is insufficient evidence to demonstrate that the 'pool car' conditions have been met, the tribunal will not allow the 'exemption' to be claimed (for example, see *Yum Yum Ltd v HMRC* [2010] UKFTT 331, *Ryan-Munden v HMRC*

[2011] UKFTT 12 and *McKenna Demolition Ltd v HMRC* [2011] UK FTT 344.)
It is advisable to keep proper records to support any 'car pool' exemption.

HMRC REPORTING REQUIREMENTS

7.28 Where a company car is provide for the first time or where any other
changes occur concerning the provision of a company car, the company must
report the details on form P46 (Car) to HMRC within 28 days of the end of
the quarter (to 5 July, 5 October, 5 January or 5 April) in which the change
occurred. The relevant CO_2 emissions' data is also provided on form P46 (Car).

Directors or employees who are provided with a car for the first time should be
informed of the benefit on which they will be taxed. (Where fuel is provided,
they should keep accurate records of the private business miles driven). The
penalties for not submitting form P46 (Car) or submitting inaccurate forms are
the same as for late submission of forms P11D (see 7.90).

COMPANY CAR VERSUS OWN CAR

7.29 One way to judge whether or not a company car (plus fuel) is worthwhile
for any tax year is to ascertain the cost per private mile in terms of the tax
charge, and then compare that with the actual cost. Examples 4 and 5 below
compare the tax cost for 2011/12 with the estimated running costs of the car.

Example 4

Tax cost per private mile versus actual running cost per mile (1)

	Car	
	Subaru Impreza Sport	
(a)	List price	£15,560
(b)	CO_2 emissions rating	214g/km
(b)	Relevant percentage	32%
(c)	Car benefit	£4,979
(d)	Fuel benefit base	£18,800
(e)	Relevant fuel percentage	32%
(f)	Fuel benefit	£6,016
(g)	Add (c) and (f)	£10,995
(h)	Tax at 20% on (g)	£2,199

	Tax per private mile	
	Miles	*Tax (pence*
	2,000	110p
	4,000	55p
	6,000	37p
	8,000	28p
	10,000	22p
	12,000	18p

Note: Estimated running costs (including fixed costs) per mile (based on petrol at 130p p per litre) for 10,000 and 15,000 miles would range between (say) 81p to 65p respectively. Hence, if the private mileage is high, the tax cost should be acceptable.

Example 5

Tax cost per private mile versus actual running cost per mile (2)

	Car	
	Volvo 70 Series	
(a)	List price	£24,230
(b)	CO_2 emissions rating	240g/km
(b)	Relevant percentage	35%
(c)	Car benefit	£8,481
(d)	Fuel benefit base	£18,800
(e)	Relevant fuel percentage	35%
(f)	Fuel benefit	£6,580
(g)	Add (c) and (f)	£15,061
(h)	Tax at 40% on (g)	£6,024

	Tax per private mile	
	Miles	*Tax (pence)*
	2,000	301p
	4,000	151p
	6,000	100p
	8,000	75p
	10,000	60p
	12,000	50p
	14,000	43p

Note: Estimated running costs (including fixed costs) per mile (based on petrol at 130p per litre) for 10,000 and 15,000 miles would range between (say) 100p to 80p respectively. Where the private mileage is likely to be more than (say) 8,000, the provision of a company car and fuel will probably be beneficial taxwise.

THE COMPANY'S POSITION

Class 1A NIC charge on company car benefits

7.30   There is an extra burden on a company when it provides a car for private use by an employee. This is the Class 1A NIC at a flat rate of 13.8% (12.8% before 5 April 2011) levied on the same taxable benefit figure for the private use of a car and for private fuel.

This Class 1A NIC is often a substantial cost for many family or owner-managed companies. Clearly, a company should be able to secure a reduction in its NIC costs by encouraging its employees to drive low CO_2 emission cars and to opt out of free fuel.

No Class 1A NIC liability applies where:

(*a*)   the employee earns less than £8,500 per annum; or

(*b*)   the car is not available for private use; or

(*c*)   the employee fully reimburses the cost of private motoring.

Car leasing versus purchasing

Capital allowances on outright purchase

7.31   The employment benefit tax charge on the employee is unaffected by the method the employer uses to provide the car. The employing company can claim capital allowances when a car is acquired via:

- outright purchase;

- hire purchase (or any lease contract that provides an option to purchase at the end of the primary lease term).

For the most *new* eco-efficient cars (emissions of less than 110 g/km), the entire cost of the car can be written-off for tax purposes by claiming 100% fist year capital allowances. (100% FYAs apply to 'qualifying low-emission' cars purchased between 17 April 2002 and 31 March 2013) (see 4.25).

Since April 2009, capital allowances on cars are entirely emission-based with cars attracting writing down allowances (WDAs) as follows:

- up to 160g/km : normal 20% annual WDA (within the main pool)

- over 160g/km : the lower WDA rate of 10%.

Thus, all cars *acquired from April 2009* (including those costing more than £12,000) either enter the main '20% WDA' pool or a lower special 10% rate pool (see 4.25).

Before April 2009, cars that did not qualify for 100% allowances, qualified for writing-down allowances of 20% per year (25% per year before April 2008). Their existing tax treatment continues under the new regime.

Similarly, existing (pre-1 April 2009) expensive cars (those costing more than £12,000) are still retained in their own separate capital allowance pool, with the maximum annual WDA being restricted to £3,000. The full cost eventually attracts full tax relief but it takes longer with a restricted WDA of only £3,000 per year. However, these 'transitional' rules end in the company's first accounting period ending after 31 March 2014. If the expensive car is still owned at that point, it will then be transferred into the main capital allowances pool.

Tax treatment of lease rental costs

7.32   For leased cars, tax relief as revenue expenditure is claimable on the lease rental costs when a car is acquired via:

- contract hire;

- finance leasing.

For finance leasing, the tax deductibility of rental payments follows the amount charged under SSAP 21 (as outlined in SP 3/91), although there may be a restriction in the deductible amount for certain cars (see 7.33 below).

SSAP 21 will usually apply for accounting purposes so that part of the capital repayment element is deductible as revenue expenditure through the depreciation charge to the profit and loss account. The finance charge is also deductible. This normally means that no adjustment is necessary for corporation tax purposes with relief being given for the depreciation and finance charge.

For contract hire under a with-maintenance contract, it should be arranged for the maintenance element to be the subject of a separate contract and amount. In that way, the cost of the maintenance element is segregated and fully tax deductible, whereas ordinarily the full amount might be subject to the potential restriction as part of the rental cost (see 7.33 below).

Restriction on deductible leasing costs

7.33 The tax deductible leasing costs on contract hire and finance leasing may be subject to a restriction.

For lease contracts entered into after 31 March 2009, there will be a 15% disallowance where the leased car's emission rating exceeds 160 g/km. More eco-friendly cars (with emissions of 160 g/km or below) are not subject to any restriction (irrespective of whether their original retail price exceeds £12,000). (Where there is a chain of leases, any disallowance will only apply to one lessee in that 'chain'.)

However, the lease rental payment disallowance for *existing* (pre-1 April 2009) leases is still based on the 'expensive car' rules (although there is no restriction for designated qualifying low emission cars). Anti-avoidance rules prevent existing leases being renewed to come within the emissions based regime for post-31 March 2009 leases.

For *existing* leases, the disallowance applies where the car's retail price when new exceeds £12,000. In such cases, the *deductible* rental payment is calculated using the fraction:

$$\frac{12,000 + \text{retail price}}{2 \times \text{retail price}}$$

Example 6

Allowable hire costs

In July 2011, Ronaldo Ltd leases a Land Rover Freelander 2.2 TD4 car for its managing director under a normal contract hire deal. The 'Freelander' has an emissions rating of 194 g/km

The car has a retail price when new of £30,500. The annual lease cost is £11,500.

There is a 15% disallowance of the annual lease rental payments since the emissions rating of the Freelander exceeds 160 g/km.

Thus the annual tax-deductible lease cost is

£11,500 × 85% (being 100% − 15%) = £9,775

CHOICE OF COMPANY CAR OR SALARY

7.34   The company could offer an increased salary to those employees who decide not to accept a company car. The question for the company is how much of a cash alternative to offer. A neutral position for the company would be to offer exactly the same amount as the cost for providing the car. However, the employee may be better or worse off depending on his level of private mileage, as shown in 7.29. Sophisticated modelling techniques can be used to calculate how much employees should receive to allow them to personally own exactly the same car at no additional cost.

PERSONAL OWNERSHIP OF CAR – KEY POINTS

Purchase of own car

7.35   The alternative to the company car is for the director or employee to purchase a car of their own. In the right circumstances, it may be possible for an employee to purchase a company-owned car at market value after the company has suffered the 'heavy' first year's depreciation. A reliable indicator of market value can be found from Glass's Motoring Guide, available at *www. glass.co.uk.* If the car is transferred to the director/employee at an under-value, the consequent benefit is taxable and also subject to Class 1A NICs (or if the car is a readily convertible asset, Class 1 NICs).

Where the director or employee personally owns the car, the company could pay a mileage allowance for their business use.

Approved mileage allowance payments (AMAPs)

7.36   There is a statutory system of mileage rates that can be paid free from income tax and NICs. Where a director or employee uses their own car or van for business travel, the company can pay them a tax/NIC-free mileage allowance up to the approved mileage allowance payments (AMAPs) rates. Payments made in excess of the statutory AMAPs rates are liable to income tax and NICs in the normal way.

Employers can pay employees up to 5p a mile tax-free for each 'fellow employee' passenger carried in their vehicle. It is not possible for employees to claim this tax relief where employers do not actually make this payment.

Having remained unchanged since 2002, the Budget 2011 increased the main AMAP rate from 40p to 45p per mile, to recognise the substantial increases in fuel costs. HMRC indicated it was considering changes to the system of AMAPs to take into account cost and the environmental impact of driving, but there have been no further developments.

7.37 HMRC's approved mileage allowance payments (AMAPs) for business journeys (ie the amounts which may be paid free of income tax and NICs), are as follows:

Approved mileage allowance payments for 2011/12

Rate per mile

Annual business mileage

Up to 10,000 miles	45p
Over 10,000 miles	25p

Note: The rate used for NIC purposes is 45p,
regardless of business mileage

For each passenger making same business trip	5p

Rules for claiming business mileage payments

7.38 Where employers pay less than the statutory rate, employees may claim tax relief on the difference. Claims for tax relief based on the actual 'allowable' expenditure incurred by the director/employee are no longer allowed. This is the case even where the 'actual' basis would result in tax relief greater than that offered by the AMAPs rates.

7.39 In the past, companies could reclaim a pre-agreed VAT element to recover the estimated VAT input tax relating to business fuel. However, since 1 January 2006, HMRC requires the company to hold appropriate VAT invoices to (at least) cover the (pre-agreed) input tax on the business fuel part of the reimbursed mileage allowance.

In practice, companies will only be able to recover the agreed fuel input tax where employees have provided VAT invoices (at least) covering their fuel purchases (made on the employer's behalf). Normally, such VAT invoices will not exceed £250 and can therefore be less detailed – eg they do not need to show the employer's name. Where a reimbursement agreement is in place, HMRC generally accepts that the purchases are being made in the employer's name.

TAXATION OF COMPANY VANS

Definition of van

7.40 Instead of having a car provided by their employer for private use, an employee may be given the use of a van. The tax regime for vans only applies to directors and employees earning more than £8,500 per year.

Broadly, a van is a *goods* vehicle (ie primarily designed to carry goods, etc) with a 'normal' design weight not exceeding 3,500kg [*ITEPA 2003, s 115(1),*

(2)]. (If the design weight of the vehicle exceeds 3,500kg, then it is a 'heavy goods vehicle'.) For some vehicles, it might not always be easy to determine whether they constitute a 'van' or a 'car' (as to which, see 7.8) for employment benefits purposes. In such cases, HMRC will normally look at the pre-dominant purpose for which the vehicle was built (as opposed to its actual use). Clearly, where HMRC accepts that the vehicle can be treated as a van, the employee's tax charge is likely to be reduced significantly or may be avoided completely under the work/commuting exemption (see 7.41).

VAT incurred on the purchase of vans can normally be recovered in full.

Double cab pick-ups can be an especially difficult area – for these purposes, HMRC treat a double cab pick-up with a payload carrying capacity of one tonne (1,000kg) as a van. Where the payload area is fitted with a hard cover, the weight of the cover must be deducted from the payload weight. The 'one tonne' test applies to the net weight. (See HMRC Employment Income Manual EIM 23045.)

Given the recent blurring of the distinction between cars and vans, (the then) HM Customs & Excise issued a list of 'car-derived' vans in its Business Brief 16/2004 (the list was issued for VAT purposes but this could apply for income tax purposes). This lists the vehicles produced or converted by the manufacturers/sole concessionaires that have been notified to Customs and meet the relevant criteria for a 'van'. These include, for example, a Land Rover Freelander (1.8 Petrol and 2.0 Diesel) and Discovery (2.5 Diesel), Rover Commerce (CDV 1.4 and CDV 2.0 TD), and Vauxhall Corsa (Corsavan and Combo) and Astra (Astravan).

Tax exemption on vans provided for work/commuter journeys

7.41 Many employees are now able to take their company vans home without suffering any taxable benefit. Since 6 April 2005, no taxable benefit arises where an employee only uses the van for work journeys (for example, delivering goods and calling on customers) and ordinary commuting between home and their workplace (which is normally regarded as 'private use'). Insignificant private use is also allowed (like HMRC's examples of taking rubbish to the tip once or twice a year or regularly making a slight detour to drop off a child at school!).

Detailed mileage records should be kept to demonstrate that no taxable benefit arises on the employee-user ie private use is restricted to travel between home and work. Further protection should be obtained if the private use of the van is restricted to 'commuting' by formal agreement/under an employment contract.

Tax charge on vans

7.42 Some directors and employees may be happy to have a company van (particularly the more ergonomic type!) for their extensive private use (ie

279

falling outside the 'work/commuter' use exemption above). They may also take the view that any disadvantage is largely outweighed by the significant reduction in the income tax charge.

Where a van is made available for the private use of a director/employee (or member of their family or household) which falls outside the 'work/commuting' exemption in 7.41:

- the taxable 'cash equivalent' of the van for 2011/12 is £3,000 (remaining unchanged since April 2007). An additional charge of £550 is made for the provision of private fuel (£500 between 2007/08 and 2009/10). The 'cash equivalent' also attracts Class 1A NICs.

- if the van is unavailable to the employee for at least 30 consecutive days or it is a 'shared' van for part of the year (see 7.43), the basic cash equivalent is reduced on a pro-rata basis on the same basis as a company car – see 7.19 [*ITEPA 2003, ss 156, 157*]. Where a van is made unavailable for a 'shorter period' (ie less than 30 days), but it is replaced by another van for that period, *ITEPA 2003, s 159* effectively treats the 'replacement van' as taking the place of the normal van, thus avoiding any additional tax charge.

Any cash contribution made by the employee for the private use of the van (as a condition of it being made available for private use) is then deducted to arrive at the final taxable benefit.

The Budget 2010 introduced two major tax breaks for new *electric* vans:

- A 100% first year allowance on post-31 March 2010 expenditure (but not available on second-hand vans)

- A complete exemption from the benefit-in-kind charge for five years from 6 April 2010, thus the employee avoids any tax charge. The exemption also applies for Class 1A NICs

Tax charge on shared vans

7.43 A van is treated as a 'shared van' if it is made available for the *private* use of more than one employee concurrently [*ITEPA 2003, s 157*]. Where a van is part of a 'van pool' (broadly defined in the same way as 'pool' cars), it will not be treated as being available for private use and is therefore exempt from tax [*ITEPA 2003, s 168*].

The cash equivalent of a 'shared van' is first calculated as set out in 7.42. Thus, if the van was unavailable for at least 30 consecutive days, there would be a pro-rata reduction in the benefit (based on the number of days that the van was unavailable). Where an employee's private use of a 'shared' van is restricted to ordinary commuting between home and work (as in 7.41), they would not suffer any taxable benefit in respect of that van.

The tax charge is apportioned between the relevant employees on a 'just and reasonable' basis.

Example 7

Taxable benefits for a shared company van

Zola's Electricals Ltd has three company vans, which are shared between its three service engineers during the year ended 5 April 2012.

The service engineers' shared use of the vans during the year has been calculated as follows:

Van	Service engineer		
	Mr Collins	*Mr Konchesky*	*Mr Gabbidon*
WHU 100	75%	25%	–
WHU 101	25%	50%	25% (but only used for work/commuting)
WHU 102	–	25%	75% (but only used for work/commuting)

The company requires Mr Collins to contribute £1,000 towards his private use of the shared vans during the year.

	Mr Collins		*Mr Konchesky*		*Mr Gabbidon*	
	£	£	£	£	£	£
WHU 100						
Charge	3,000		3,000		–	
Reduction 25% for sharing	(750)	2,250	75% (2,250)	750		
WHU 101						
Charge	3,000		3,000		Commuting Exemption	
Reduction 75% for sharing	(2,250)	750	50% (1,500)	1,500		
WHU 102						
Charge	–		3,000		Commuting Exemption	
Reduction for sharing			75% (2,250)	750		
		3,000		3,000		
Less: Cash		(1,000)		–		
Taxable benefit		2,000		3,000		–

BICYCLES AND MOTORCYCLES

7.44 Often derided, the 'tax-free' company bicycle can be attractive in the right circumstances! The tax and NIC exemption applies to the benefit of a bicycle or related safety equipment lent by an employer to an employee for travel to and from home and work [*ITEPA 2003, s 244*]. Similarly, no tax or NIC arises on workplace parking for bicycles and motorcycles.

These exemptions do not apply unless the benefit is available generally to all employees, but clearly common sense has to be used to see which employees could possibly have use for a company bicycle! Where the bicycle is subsequently purchased by the employee, no tax charge arises provided the amount paid is at least its current market value.

A number of companies (for example, Cyclescheme) offer a comprehensive scheme to provide bikes to employees (in conjunction with a large number of independent bike shops). The bikes are typically provided through a salary sacrifice. Since gross salary is sacrificed for a non-taxable benefit, the employee saves income tax and NIC. The arrangement also reduces the company's NIC. The employee normally has the option to purchase the bike at the end of the 'loan' period.

For business use of an employee's *own* bicycle, tax relief at 20p per mile can be claimed less any amounts paid by the employer. This only covers business use, so excludes travel to and from home and work. Again, if the circumstances fit, this could be a useful claim.Similarly, tax relief can be claimed for the business use of an employee's own motorbike at 24p per mile.

CAR PARKING

7.45 There is no tax charge on a director or employee where the company provides a free parking space for a car or motorcycle at or near the workplace. Facilities for parking bicycles are also tax-exempt [*ITEPA 2003, s 237*].

FREE OR SUBSIDISED WORKS BUSES

7.46 With the general aim of reducing the amount of commuting by car, no employment income tax or NIC charge arises on the 'benefit' of free or subsidised works buses (and on subsidies paid to local bus companies where the employees are carried free or at a reduced rate).

TAXIS AND MINI-CABS FOR LATE NIGHT WORKING

7.47 The Budget 2011 abolished the 'benefit in kind' exemption for the provision of infrequent taxis and mini cabs from work to home as a result of 'late working'!

TRAVEL AND SUBSISTENCE COSTS

Allowable business travel

7.48 Family or owner-managed companies will generally meet all (reasonable) 'business' travel costs incurred by directors and employees. The rules relating to admissible 'business travel' were revised by the *Finance Act 1998* to bring the system into line with modern working practices. The relevant legislation is in *ITEPA 2003, ss 337–340*.

Travelling expenses are allowed where they cover the full cost of necessary travel in the performance of the duties, and the full cost of travel to/from a place where necessary duties are performed. For this purpose, 'in the performance of the duties' covers travel:

(*a*)   to/from a place the employee has to attend; or

(*b*)   to carry out duties at a 'temporary workplace'; or

(*c*)   after duties have commenced (necessary 'on-the-job' travel).

A 'temporary workplace' is a workplace where the employee goes only to perform a task of limited duration or other temporary purpose. This includes attendance for a continuous period likely to last not more than 24 months or where less than 40% of working time is spent. It does not include a permanent workplace under a fixed term appointment of less than 24 months.

A journey which is really 'ordinary commuting' (see 7.49) cannot be made a business journey just by arranging a business appointment on route. The test is necessity to attend the particular place, rather than personal convenience of attending.

Subsistence costs

7.48A The cost of business travel includes subsistence costs related to the journey.

Overnight subsistence expenses (such as accommodation and costs) will normally be exempt provided they are accompanied by receipts, such as a hotel bill. Where a company rents accommodation to save long term hotel costs, HMRC will generally treat the property rent as part of the exempt subsistence payment [see EIM31836].

Any 'personal expenses', such as SKY TV and newspapers etc. will be taxable as a benefit in kind, subject to the £5 (UK) or £10 (overseas) per night exemption for 'Incidental Overnight Expenses' (PIEs), which might cover an employee's telephone calls, dry-cleaning and so on (ITEPA 2003, s240). This useful exemption is granted to cover expenses that would not normally be allowable but are incurred as a result of the 'inconvenience' of working away from home.

Disallowable costs

7.49   On the other hand, costs are disallowed where they represent 'ordinary commuting' travel or travel between employments. 'Ordinary commuting' means any travel between a 'permanent workplace' and home, or any other place that is not a workplace.

A 'permanent workplace' is a workplace (other than a temporary workplace) attended regularly in the performance of the duties of the employment – this is the base from which the director or employee:

- performs their duties; or
- is allocated the tasks to be carried out by them in the performance of their duties.

There is, however, an exception to this rule and travel costs are admissible where there are two employers and both employers are members of the same group (51% subsidiaries). Travel is 'on-the-job' travel between employers for a joint project, or where duties are performed wholly or partly overseas.

'IR 35' cases

7.50   Working shareholders who are caught by the IR 35 rules for personal service companies (see Chapter 6) are still employees of their own companies. Thus, the travel and subsistence rules apply in the same manner to them as to employees of other companies that do not fall under IR 35. The worker can claim tax relief on travel from his company's base, which may be at his home, to the client's premises, plus related subsistence if applicable. The client's premises are treated as a temporary workplace as long as either the 24-month test or the 40% test is not breached.

Worked examples

7.51

Example 8

Necessary 'business' travel – I

Mr Clough lives in Derby. He has no normal place of work as a computer consultant, although he occasionally visits HQ in London. He spends a few days or weeks at the offices, etc, of various clients of his employing company. His travel expenses are reimbursed.

Mr Clough has no tax liability on his reimbursed travel expenses as his journeys are to/from a place where necessary duties are performed and is not ordinary commuting travel.

Example 9

Necessary 'business' travel – II

Nobby lives in Hartlepool and works in Nottingham. He commutes by car every day.

He visits a client's office in Leeds by car, driving there directly and returning home. The cost is reimbursed by his employer.

Mr Stiles does not suffer any tax on the reimbursed cost, as the journey is to/from a place where necessary duties are performed and is not ordinary commuting travel.

Triangular travel

7.52   Where triangular travel is involved, the company may feel it is inappropriate to reimburse more than the additional cost of the trip. In such situations the employee can claim tax relief on the difference between the actual cost and the amount reimbursed.

Example 10

Triangular travel

Nigel normally travels 14 miles to his workplace. To avoid travelling an extra 18 miles to visit a customer, he travels direct to/from home to the customer. This involves a 24 mile trip as shown below:

Nigel could receive tax-free reimbursement for 48 miles. If the employer only reimbursed 20 miles, being only the additional distance travelled (48 miles *less* 28 miles saved by not going to the normal workplace), Nigel could claim tax relief on the cost for 28 miles.

NICs on business travel

7.53   There are no NICs on reasonable business travel and subsistence allowances paid to employees. NICs are charged on payments which more than reimburse the employee for the cost of business travel.

For car mileage allowances there is no NIC liability if they do not exceed HMRC's approved 45p per mile AMAPs rate (see 7.36). (It is impracticable to use the two-tier rates as NICs are calculated in each earnings period during the tax year).

BENEFICIAL LOANS

Calculation of taxable benefit

7.54   A taxable benefit arises on the provision of a beneficial loan which is made available by reason of employment. Such loans are typically interest-free or are 'cheap', carrying less than a market rate of interest.

Broadly, the taxable benefit is equivalent to:

- the amount of interest that would have been paid if the director/employee had paid interest at the 'official rate of interest' (which approximates to a commercial rate); *less*

- any interest actually paid by them.

The benefit is normally calculated using the 'average method'. This takes the average loan for the tax year by averaging the balances on the loan accounts at the beginning and at the end of the tax year. The official interest rate is then applied to this average balance. (If the loan was first made or repaid during the year, the balance is taken on the relevant date of the loan/repayment, as appropriate). It is also possible to elect for the benefit to be calculated precisely on a daily basis.

Since 6 April 2010, the official rate of interest has been 4.00% and the published (average) rates for recent tax years are:

	Official rate
2010/11	4.00%
2009/10	4.75%
2008/09	6.10%

There is no taxable benefit or Class 1A NICs charge on loans made to employees where the total of all loans (at any time in the relevant tax year) to the same employee does not exceed £5,000. This might exempt some 'small' interest-free season ticket-loans!

There is also no taxable benefit on *qualifying* loans (ie where assuming interest had been paid on the loan it would have been deductible for tax purposes). This would include a loan made to a shareholder to buy shares in a close (unlisted) trading company, such as the company they work for [*ITEPA 2003, ss 173–187*]. Such qualifying loans do not need to be reported on the form P11D.

Where a loan is made to a director/shareholder, a corporate tax charge may arise under *CTA 2010, s 455 (ICTA 1988, s 419)* (see 2.57).

Loans to purchase a main residence

7.55 It should be noted that interest paid on a loan to purchase the employee's main residence is *not* tax deductible (although many will remember when it used to be!)

Consequently, any cheap loan facility to purchase a main residence attracts a taxable benefit. However, the company might provide alternative assistance towards the purchase of a house by an employee by making temporary deposits with building societies for preferential mortgage treatment.

The granting of a loan to an employee at a reduced rate of interest for the purchase of a house is a traditional benefit offered by banks and insurance companies. There is no real reason why a family or owner-managed company should not offer the same benefit, but it may not be wise in view of the substantial funds likely to be needed and the level of control required over the use of the loan proceeds.

Example 11

Beneficial loans to employees

Venables Ltd, trading as a sugar refiner, provides house purchase loans of £30,000 to employees to help them purchase their main residence.

The interest rate charged on the employee loans is 2% per annum.

The official rate of interest is 4.0% for 2010/11, so the income tax liability on each employee is based on a benefit of £600 , ie £30,000 × 2.0% (4.0% − 2.0 %).

Tax rate	Income tax liability
20%	£600 @ 20% = £120
40%	£600 @ 40% = £240

Note: Venables Ltd would also be liable for Class 1A NICs on the taxable benefit figure of £600

LIVING ACCOMMODATION

Overview of tax rules

7.56 An employment tax charge arises where living accommodation is provided for an employee/director (or members of their family), subject to certain 'narrow' exemptions (see 7.57 and 7.58).

The provision of living accommodation for an employee/director is subject to two charging provisions which depend on the cost incurred by the company (for these purposes, 'cost' represents the cost of acquiring the property plus any improvements to it) (see 7.59 and 7.60).

The same rules apply to both UK and overseas situs property, although there is an important exemption for individuals who purchase *overseas* property through a company (see 7.65).

Where accommodation is provided, it is probably sensible to make sure that the director/employee does not obtain a protected tenancy. This can be avoided by:

(*a*)   providing a 'service tenancy', linked to the employment and enabling the company to terminate the tenancy on termination of the employment if it can be shown that the accommodation is provided for the better fulfilment (not necessary fulfilment) of the duties of the employment; or

(*b*)   the company showing it requires the accommodation for another employee; or

(*c*)   the tenancy being outside the scope of the protected tenancy legislation.

Accommodation provided for proper performance of duties

7.57   There is no income tax charge where the accommodation is provided for a director or employee in certain circumstances (often referred to as the 'representative occupation' exemption). However, the restrictive nature of this exemption is generally of little use to the vast majority of working shareholders. The exemption in *ITEPA 2003, s 99* applies where either:

(*a*)   it is necessary for the proper performance of the employee's duties that they should reside in the accommodation; or

(*b*)   the accommodation is provided for the better performance of the duties of the employment, and it is customary for employers to provide living accommodation for those engaged in such employment.

Furthermore, these exemptions do *not* apply to *directors* unless they own no more than 5% of the shares *and* they are full-time working directors. If the 'full time' test is not satisfied, the director may still qualify for the exemption where the company is 'non-profit' making (ie it does not carry on a trade and its functions do not consist wholly or mainly in holding investments or other property) *or* it is established for charitable purposes only [*ITEPA 2003, s 99(3)*].

Employees may face difficulty in obtaining exemption following the case of *Vertigan v Brady* [1988] STC 91. The exemption in (*a*) above was held to be directed to a necessity based on the relationship between the proper performance of the taxpayer's duties and the accommodation provided, and not on the personal demands of the employee. The exemption in (*b*) is generally thought to cover the 'flat over the shop' situation for a shop manager or a caretaker's on-site residence. This was held to require identification of three constituent factors in identifying where the employment was 'one of the kinds of employment in the case of which it is customary for employers to provide living accommodation', which are:

- the statistical evidence as to how common the practice was;

- how long the practice has continued; and

- whether it had achieved acceptance generally by the relevant employers.

Accommodation provided as a result of a security threat

7.58 Similarly, the provision of accommodation is also exempt if there is a special threat to the employee's security, so that special security arrangements are in force and the employee resides in the accommodation as part of those arrangements [*ITEPA 2003, s 100)*].

Where cost of accommodation does not exceed £75,000

7.59 Where the accommodation cost does not exceed £75,000, the taxable benefit is:

	£
Rental value of the property	X
Less: Actual rent paid by the employee	(X)
Taxable benefit	X

The rental value is the amount that would have been payable if the employee had paid an annual rent equal to the annual value. For these purposes, the rateable value is taken as an indication of the commercial rent that the tenant might pay. However, in most cases, it will be very much lower than the actual commercial rent as rateable values have not changed in England and Wales since 1973. The gross rateable value can only be used where the provider of the accommodation, usually the employer, owns the property. Sometimes there will be no rateable value (for example the property may be recently built), in which case an estimate is made. If there is a dispute on the amount of the 'annual value', this can be appealed to the First-Tier Tribunal.

If the company rents the premises the tax charge is generally based on the rent payable by the company less any rent paid by the employee. (In such cases, the company's rent is likely to be greater than the gross rateable value.) [*ITEPA 2003, s 105.*]

Any lease premium paid by the company is also taxed as rent (except where the property is being leased for more than 10 years). The taxable lease premium is spread over the period of the lease and added to any annual rent charge in calculating the benefit (subject to any deduction for amounts made good by the employee).

Where cost of accommodation exceeds £75,000

7.60   *ITEPA 2003, s 106* levies a tax charge on such accommodation, which is made up of two elements:

- the basic 'annual rental/value' charge calculated under (*a*) above; plus

- an 'additional yearly rental' charge calculated as follows:

   ORI × (C – £75,000)

Where:

(i)   ORI is the official rate of interest in force on 6 April in the tax year – 4.00% for 2011/12 (see 7.49);

(ii)   C is the cost of the property together with any improvements (less any amount reimbursed by the director/employee or paid by them for the grant of the tenancy).

This is subject to the 'market value' rule, which generally applies where the company acquired their interest in the property more than six years before it was provided to the director/employee. In such cases, C becomes the *open market value* of the property when it was first occupied by the director/employee (as opposed to the original cost) plus the cost of any subsequent improvements.

This higher tax charge means that properties costing over, say, £100,000 might be a less tax-efficient part of a remuneration package.

If the accommodation is only made available for less than a year, the chargeable amount is appropriately reduced. Similarly, if the property is shared by more than one employee, the charge will be scaled down having regard to all the relevant facts (and the total amount charged cannot exceed the amount that would be charged on sole occupation).

Accommodation expenses and assets

7.61   There is a separate tax charge on directors and those earning at least £8,500 per year in respect of ancillary benefits, such as expenditure incurred or reimbursed by the employer on heating, lighting, cleaning, repairs, furnishings, etc.

The provision of assets in the property (such as furniture, television and video, hi-fi equipment, etc) is subject to a special 'annual value' tax charge. This is computed as 20% of the market value of the relevant assets when they were first provided (see 7.56) [*ITEPA 2003, ss 201* and *205*].

There is no tax charge on alterations and additions to the premises of a structural nature or repairs which would be the lessor's obligation if the premises were let under a lease to which *s 11* of the *Landlord and Tenant Act 1985* applied. However, such expenditure must be borne by the employer and not by the employee who is then reimbursed [*ITEPA 2003, s 313*].

If the accommodation itself is exempt as being necessary for the performance of the employee's duties, etc (see 7.57), then this tax charge is restricted to 10% of the employee's net emoluments [*ITEPA 2003, s 315*]. Furthermore, in such cases, there is no tax charge on council tax or water rates/charges.

Example 12

Beneficial occupation of accommodation

Peacock Limited purchases a house for £185,000. An employee occupies the property throughout the tax year 2011/12 and pays rent of £200 per annum. The gross rateable value is £2,000. The employee meets the lighting and heating costs and other normal tenant's running expenses. The accommodation was furnished by Peacock Limited at a total cost of £5,000.

Income tax for 2011/12 on:			£
Accommodation charge –	Step 1	Gross rateable value	2,000
s 104	Step 2/3	4% of (£185,000 –	4,400
		£75,000)	
			6,400
	Step 4	Less: rent paid	(200)
		Accommodation charge	6,200
Provision of assets charge		20% of cost of	1,000
under s 205	–	furnishings of £5,000	
			£7,200

The total income tax charge on this £7,200 deemed income should then be compared with the annual market rent that would otherwise have been paid by the employee. The potential rent might well exceed £2,880 (£7,200 × (say) 40% – say £240 per month, depending on the house value and location.

Main planning points

Restricting availability of the property

7.62   If an employee uses living accommodation provided by their employer for (say) 30 days in a tax year, it is necessary to consider whether the charge is based on the annual value for the complete tax year. The legislation refers to the accommodation provided in any period. Hence, to restrict the tax charge to the actual period of occupation by the employee or member of their family or household, it might be necessary to show that the accommodation could only be occupied by them for that period. Appropriate documentation would need to be in place to demonstrate that this was because of conditions imposed by the employer (rather than through the employee's choice).

If the employer provides living accommodation by acquiring a right to 'time-share' a holiday home for a specific period this would restrict the tax charge on the employees by reference to the period for which the home is available for occupation.

Furnished letting

7.63 With the annual value (gross rateable value) being the measure of the tax charge where the provider of the accommodation owns the property, the tax charge on the employee is invariably less than the commercial rent that would otherwise have been paid. Tax-efficient arrangements include the employer acquiring the freehold or long leasehold of premises and repairing and fitting them up to the standard requirement for furnished lettings.

The employee is then granted a lease (after the repair work has been carried out so that no tax charge is levied thereon). The lease would be on the normal basis of the employer/lessor meeting the cost of exterior repairs, ground rent, etc and the employee/tenant paying the rates, lighting and heating costs, etc.

7.64 For overseas property owned by the employer, the tax charge would normally be based on the market rent obtainable on a letting in the absence of any rateable value. (HMRC have been known to accept using the rateable value of a similar size property in a coastal part of England as a convenience measure.) In such cases, ESC A91 provides that no tax charge will arise under standard tax charging rule in *ITEPA 2003, s 105* (see 7.59).

Certain cases, such as where an individual has structured their purchase of overseas property through a company, may be eligible for the FA 2008 exemption (see 7.65).

As a general rule, the annual tax charge on the furniture and fittings is 20% of the market value when they were first provided (as in 7.61). However, where the provision of the living accommodation is exempt from the tax charge on the basis of *representative* occupation, maximum advantage can be taken of the limitation of the tax charge on ancillary benefits to 10% of net emoluments. The furnishings and fittings can be of the highest quality without any additional tax charge arising, provided they are held to be 'normal for domestic occupation' as required by *ITEPA 2003, s 315(3)(c)*.

Example 13

Exempt accommodation necessary for employment duties – fixtures and fittings

Pearce Limited purchases antique furniture, household appliances, television, hi-fi equipment, etc for £20,000, which are placed in 'exempt' accommodation. This would normally give an annual income tax charge on the director/ employee on the annual benefit of £4,000 (20% of £20,000). The employee's net emoluments are, say:

	£	£
Salary, benefits and expenses		28,600
Less Allowable expenses	(400)	
Pension contributions	(2,200)	(2,600)
Net emoluments		26,000

The tax charge is therefore based on 10% of £26,000 = £2,600, instead of the standard £4,000 benefit charge.

Exemption for overseas property held through an overseas company

7.65 Ownership of overseas property by UK citizens has grown dramatically in recent years. In a substantial number of cases, the properties are acquired through an offshore company. There are a number of reasons for this, including the desire to avoid local rules restricting foreign ownership or forced heirship regimes which require that a significant part of the property must pass on death to the owner's children.

Even though such property owning structures have not been motivated by UK tax planning considerations, HMRC originally took the strict view that a benefit charge arose on the 'individual' owner, which was strengthened by the ruling in *R v Allen* [2001] STC 1537. This was generally because the individual shareholder of the company would fall to be treated as a 'shadow director' – ie someone who provides instructions or directions which are normally followed by the actual directors (see *ITEPA 2003, s 67*).

Because of these potential tax issues, many individuals have used an overseas company to acquire the property as a nominee on their behalf. Provided the legal documents are drawn-up correctly, the individual would be treated as beneficially owning the property for UK tax purposes and therefore no UK benefit charge can be sustained.

In the Budget 2007, HMRC effectively acknowledged that it was inequitable to impose a benefits charge in such cases (after some excellent 'behind the scenes' work by The Chartered Institute of Taxation). Accordingly, legislation has been enacted in the *Finance Act 2008. ITEPA 2003, s 100A* provides an exemption in respect of non-UK living accommodation provided by a company for a director (including any member of his family) or any other officer of the company. However, the exemption is framed in such a way to cover only those cases where a company has been used (only) to hold the overseas property. The relevant conditions are:

- The property is held by a company that is *wholly owned* by individuals (therefore trustee ownership would not count).

- The property is the company's only or main asset and its only activities are those that are incidental to its ownership of the property.

- The property is not funded either directly or indirectly by a 'connected company'.

Where these conditions are satisfied for the relevant tax year, the exemption (which only applies to income tax) will apply retrospectively without any time limit. However, this is a fairly narrow exemption and is therefore unlikely to apply to the vast majority of overseas holiday homes owned or property investments held by owner-managed companies.

Tax-efficient investment

7.66 The provision of holiday accommodation by a family or owner-managed company is not only tax efficient, it can also have the following advantages:

(i) the prospect of capital growth as a purchased investment;

(ii) an incentive to employees if the accommodation is situated in a desirable location – the employer could award varying periods of stay based on predetermined performance targets;

(iii) it can force working shareholders to take a necessary and meaningful break from their work positions, which they might otherwise avoid;

(iv) it may provide an attractive venue for working conventions for salesmen or senior executives.

The tax charge on the provision of a 'holiday' in a company-owned property (not costing over £75,000) is illustrated in Example 14.

While the provision of holiday accommodation can often be tax efficient, it is important to ensure that it does not impact upon the trading status of the company for CGT entrepreneurs' relief or IHT Business Property Relief purposes.

Example 14

Holiday accommodation

Carlos Ltd owns the following two 'holiday' premises, each of which can be used by its employees for holidays once a year (for a maximum stay of two weeks). During the year ended 5 April 2012, Mr Roberto takes up his full allocation and his consequent tax liability is calculated as follows:

	UK property	Overseas property (not eligible for FA 2008 exemption)
Gross rateable value	£520	not applicable
Market rent	£3,120	£8,320
Period of stay	2 weeks	2 weeks
Tax charge on:	2/52 × £520	2/52 × £8,320
	= £20	= £320
Marginal tax rate	40%	40%
Income tax payable	£8	£128

Deductible expenses

7.67 The amount of the charge as a benefit for the provision of living accommodation can be reduced by an expense claim under *ITEPA 2003, s 336*. This enables the director or employee to claim expenses that would have been deductible had the accommodation been paid for out of their employment earnings. Some guidance as to the scope for this reduction in the tax charge is provided by HMRC's booklet IR 480 at sections 21.22 and 21.23:

'If accommodation is provided for an employee, for example in a flat or hotel, while the employee is on business duties away from his or her home and normal place of work, the cost of this may be allowable as a deduction under the expenses rule. For example, a company in Yorkshire may rent a London flat for an employee who has to make frequent business trips to London. The extent of any tax allowance will depend upon the circumstances. If the accommodation is no more than an alternative to hotel accommodation and is not available for private occupation the whole cost of renting and running the flat may be allowed as a deduction. On the other hand if the employee or his or her family also had the use of the flat as a private residence any allowance would be restricted.

If, however, a London flat is provided for an employee whose job is in London and the flat is used by the employee as a *pied à terre* no allowance would be due. Equally if the flat is used by the employee or the employee's family as their only or second home, no deduction for tax purposes would be due.'

RELOCATION PACKAGES AND REMOVAL EXPENSES

Basic rules

7.68 There is an income tax and NIC exemption for directors and employees for qualifying removal benefits and expenses reasonably incurred or provided in connection with a change in the employee's residence [*ITEPA 2003, ss 271–289*]. The exemption is restricted to a maximum of £8,000 of qualifying benefits provided and expenses incurred (see 7.69). To qualify these must be provided or incurred *before* the end of the tax year following that in which the job change takes place or a later time if reasonable [*ITEPA 2003, s 274*].

The change in residence must be made wholly or mainly to allow the employee to reside within a reasonable daily travelling distance of his employment base. Furthermore, the change must result from:

(*a*)   the employee becoming employed by a new employer; or

(*b*)   an alteration of the duties of an existing employment; or

(*c*)   the place of performance of the duties of an existing employment being changed.

Furthermore, the employee's old residence must not be within a reasonable daily travelling distance of the new workplace, but it does not need to be disposed of for the tax exemption to apply. The requirement is to cease to use the old residence as the main residence and instead use the new residence as such [*ITEPA 2003, s 273*].

The £8,000 relocation exemption prevents the removal benefits and expenses being taxed as earnings. They are therefore ignored for all purposes, including the form P11D. Any excess amount over the £8,000 attracts income tax and Class 1A NICs and is returned on the form P11D. Control is largely via a PAYE audit.

Qualifying removal benefits and expenses

7.69 The qualifying removal benefits and expenses are summarised below:

●   *acquisition benefits and expenses* – this covers legal expenses on acquisition, legal expenses on loan raised, loan procurement fees, survey fees, Land Registration fees, stamp duty and public utilities connection charges – the interest acquired by a member of the employee's family or household is included [*ITEPA 2003, s 277*];

- *abortive acquisition benefits and expenses* – this is as for buying/ renting a new home above, provided the interest in the residence fails to be acquired because of circumstances outside the employee's control or because he reasonably declines to proceed [*ITEPA 2003, s 278*];

- *disposal benefits and expenses* – this covers legal expenses of selling the old home, legal expenses on loan redemption, loan redemption penalty, estate agent/auctioneer fees, advertising, public utilities disconnection charges, security, maintenance and insurance costs when unoccupied and rent payable when unoccupied [*ITEPA 2003, s 279*].

Again, the interest disposed of by a member of the employee's family or household is included. HMRC accepts this also covers the interest owned by a co-habitee;

- *transporting belongings* – this covers the removal costs of transporting domestic belongings, insurance cover, temporary storage and detaching/ attaching/adapting domestic fittings from the old residence to the new residence [*ITEPA 2003, s 280*];

- *travelling and subsistence* – this covers a wide range of expenditure:

  (*a*)   travel and subsistence (ie food, drink and temporary living accommodation) of the employee and family/household members on temporary visits to a new area in connection with the residence change;

  (*b*)   employee's travel to/from the former residence and new employment base;

  (*c*)   costs of temporary living accommodation for the *employee* (but not family/household);

  (*d*)   employee's travel to/from the old residence and any temporary accommodation;

  (*e*)   travel of employee and family/household from the old residence in connection with the change in residence;

  (*f*)   subsistence of a child under the age of 19 being a member of employee's family/household, while remaining in living accommodation in the old area for educational continuity after the change or in the new area for educational continuity before the change;

  (*g*)   travel of the child between their living accommodation and the employee's new or old residence as appropriate [*ITEPA 2003, s 281*];

- *replacement of domestic goods* – this covers the cost of replacement of domestic goods used at the old residence but unsuitable for use at the new residence, *less* any sale proceeds of the goods replaced [*ITEPA 2003, s 285*];

- **bridging loan expenses** – this covers interest on a bridging loan where a period elapses between incurring expenditure on acquiring a new residence and receiving the proceeds of sale of the old residence – the loan limit is the market value of the old residence and no account is taken of that part of the loan used to purchase the new residence or to redeem a loan on the old residence [*ITEPA 2003, ss 272(2)(b)* and *284*].

If the bridging loan is a cheap loan provided by the employer, this is excluded from relief under this head. However, if the rest of the relocation package does not exceed £8,000, the balance can be included in this way [*ITEPA 2003, s 288*].

Other issues

7.70 A flat rate allowance may be paid rather than reimbursing specific expenditure, in which case the allowance can be paid gross, provided HMRC are satisfied that it does no more than reimburse eligible costs. The allowance should be included on the form P11D, if not exempt under the specific relief.

The £8,000 limit is unlikely to be reasonable for many UK moves, and is certainly unreasonable for international relocations. Example 15 illustrates a typical case that exceeds the £8,000 limit even where some eligible heads have nil entries.

Example 15

Relocation package

Gary was a senior production manager with Crispgoals Ltd. In September 2011, the company relocated him from its Leicester production plant to its head office based in London.

The following costs were incurred in connection with Gary's relocation:

	£
Expenses on sale (house sold for £100,000)	1,500
Expenses on purchase (house bought for £100,000)	2,000
Abortive acquisition costs	Nil
Removal costs	2,500
Temporary accommodation	3,500
Bridging loan expenses	Nil
Replacement of domestic goods	2,500
	£12,000

PAYE is not applied to the excess of eligible costs over £8,000. Instead, the excess over £8,000 is included on the form P11D (see 7.90).

OTHER COMMON EMPLOYEE BENEFITS

Workplace nurseries and employer-supported childcare

7.71 Many working parents rely on childcare arrangements and so this can be a very attractive benefit to provide for employees. However, employer-supported childcare generally gives rise to a taxable benefit under normal principles, based on the cost to the employer of providing such assistance. However, employee supported childcare arrangements will attract a valuable income tax and Class 1/Class 1A NIC exemption provided they meet certain conditions. These arrangements broadly cover all children of the employee up to the 1 September after their 15th birthday.

There are three separate forms of eligible child-care relief:

- *Employer-provided childcare or workplace nurseries* – This is where the childcare is provided on the company's premises, such as in the form of a nursery or crèche. To qualify as a 'tax-free' benefit, the care must be provided on premises controlled by the company, or the company must play a significant role in managing and financing the care facilities [*ITEPA 2003, s 318*]. This requirement has generally prevented many smaller family companies from providing tax-free childcare for their employees. However, it is possible for the company to enter into 'partnership arrangements' with commercial nursery providers, provided the company is still "wholly or partly responsible for the financing and managing" the child care facility. (The exemption for Class 1A NICs is wider and extends to employers contracting for places in commercial nurseries or for the services of a childminder, as well as to childcare vouchers).

- *Child-care voucher scheme* – This involves the employees receiving 'child-care' vouchers from their employer. Up to a limit of £55 per week per employee, these tax and NIC-free vouchers form a valuable contribution towards the provision of childcare. Payment must be made in vouchers – it is possible for the company to establish its own voucher scheme, rather than outsourcing it. Payments will not be eligible for the 'child-care' exemption where the employee contracts privately for the childcare, which is then settled by the company [*ITEPA 2003, ss 270A and 318A–318D*].

- *Third-party contracted child-care* – A company can provide childcare through a third party. In this case, the first £55 per week of childcare costs per employee is exempt from tax and NICs.

The child-care under the *childcare voucher* and *'third-party' contract* schemes, must be:

- open to all the employees (or, where appropriate, to all the employees working at the location where the scheme operates); and

- provided by a registered child-carer or an approved home child-carer.

The *FA 2011* introduced a concession for companies operating a 'salary sacrifice' scheme for childcare provision, employees. In such cases, employees could not take part in the childcare scheme if it would reduce their remaining earnings below the national minimum wage. Consequently, such employees can be excluded without affecting the availability of tax relief for others employees. Some employees will also need to consider the potential adverse impact on their working tax credit position (see 2.33).

Employees are only entitled to *one* weekly £55 exemption, even if the care is provided to more than one child. The *FA 2011* introduced an important restriction for higher-rate taxpayers. Before 6 April 2011, the £55 per week income tax exemption was applied so that the employee obtained effective relief at their marginal tax rate – thus, for example, a 40% taxpayer obtained relief at 40%. This position is still maintained for those employees already in an employer childcare scheme at 6 April 2011. However, for those joining schemes after 5 April 2011, the income tax exemption is only given at the basic rate of tax.

Thus, the relief available to higher rate taxpayers who join a childcare scheme after 5 April 2011, is restricted to the basic income tax rate (20%) by reducing the weekly exempt amount. The overall effect is to give all employee's tax relief of £11 per week. This means that the relevant weekly exempt amounts would be as follows:

Taxpayer	Weekly exemption
20%	£55
40%	£28
50%	£22

To decide which exempt amount to apply, the employer is responsible for making an assessment of each employee's earnings at the start of the year. Any failure to carry out this assessment will prevent tax relief being available for the employer's scheme.

There is no reason why the proprietorial directors of a family or owner-managed company cannot enjoy the tax-free childcare arrangements. It is worth noting that a husband and wife can each claim a separate exemption in respect of the same child. (Clearly they would both have to be directors/genuine employees.)

Given the valuable tax exemption, employer supported childcare schemes are often incorporated into salary sacrifice arrangements (see 7.78).

Corporate clothing

7.72   Nowadays, HMRC tend to accept that no income tax charge should arise on employee 'uniforms'. This can be extended to more attractive corporate clothing, including a suit, provided there is a prominent company name or logo sewn into the garment. Many companies send samples of the relevant clothing to obtain 'informal clearance' that it meets the necessary criteria for the 'corporate clothing' exemption. The employer's policy should be consistent so that, say, all employees meeting customers/clients or on view to them are able to wear the corporate clothing.

Within a family or owner-managed company, corporate identity through clothing certainly has its place.

Life cover and permanent health insurance

7.73   Life cover for death in service, and sickness and disability insurance, often forms part of a pension scheme and, as such, is tax efficient. The attractiveness of permanent health insurance as part of a benefits programme lies in its ability to provide an income of 75% of salary on disability right up to the normal retirement date. Thus, this ensures the employees' continued participation in the pension scheme instead of having to rely on benefit levels applicable at the enforced early retirement date.

Mobile phones

7.74   The benefit of private use of a mobile phone is exempt from tax [*ITEPA 2003, s 319*]. The provision of a mobile phone must be regarded as attractive, given their increasing importance to business communications. The employer needs to exercise some control over the amount of private use, given the potential costs involved. From 2006/07 the exemption is restricted to one mobile phone per employee.

Provided the mobile phone contract is in the company's name (which is often the case), no Class 1A NIC liability arises. However, if the employing company reimburses the employee's own mobile phone bill, this will be treated as 'NICable' earnings under general principles, except where business calls can be identified.

Top-up cards are 'non-cash vouchers' and prior to 2006/07 attracted Class 1 NICs. From 6 April 2006 such 'vouchers' are exempt from tax and NIC under *ITEPA 2003, s 266(2)* where they are used to facilitate the loan of a mobile phone to an employee for private use, but only where the benefit in kind arising on the loan of the mobile phone would have been exempt if a voucher had not been used.

Prior to the Finance Act 2006, 'Blackberries' were covered by the mobile phone exemption. From 6 April 2006, however, HMRC consider that these have additional functions more typically associated with a computer and so no longer consider them to be primarily a mobile phone. Instead, Blackberries, i-Phones (and similar PDA devices) are treated as computers. Hence, there may be a taxable benefit where there is *significant* private use (see 7.6A for treatment of computers).

Private health insurance and medical check-ups

7.75 This is a valuable benefit to provide, as it can be a cost-effective way for the working and non-working shareholder, and other employees, to obtain access to private medical treatment.

The director or employee is charged to income tax on the cost to the company. However, where the company generally has at least six members within a group scheme, it will be able to obtain a larger 'group' discount than the individual director/employee would have done on a 'personal' basis. The director/ employee is, therefore, charged to income tax on a lower amount (than the cost to the individual). From the company's viewpoint, it is an attractive proposition to arrange for its senior personnel to have access to private healthcare where the service is normally quicker than under the NHS.

The company also has to pay Class 1A NICs on the cash equivalent of the benefit provided.

In contrast, where the company reimburses the cost of medical insurance premiums that have been taken out personally by the director/employee, such amounts are counted as general earnings and subject to Class 1 NICs.

Medical treatment given outside the UK and insurance against such treatment is still free from tax and NICs.

Employer-provided health screening and medical check-ups are exempt from tax provided they are generally available to all employees on similar terms [*Income Tax (Exceptions of Minor Benefits) (Amendment) Regulations 2007, SI 2007/2090*].

Scholarship and apprenticeship schemes

7.76 From time to time, companies send employees on full time/'sandwich' training courses at Universities or technical colleges. Broadly, the employee must be enrolled on a full time course for at least one academic year and attend for at least 20 weeks in that year. The HMRC Statement of Practice, SP4/86, enables 'tax exempt' support to be given to employees for their lodgings, travel and subsistence expenses up to a maximum of £15,480 for each academic year (from 1 September 2007). However, university and other tuition fees paid by the employee are *not* covered by the exemption. If the annual limit is exceeded, the full amount becomes taxable. Such payments are also exempt from NICs (provided they are made under an employment contract). Courses that are run at the company's own training centre cannot benefit from this concessionary exemption.

Subsidised canteens

7.76A Meals provided in a company canteen on a free or subsidised basis will generally be exempt from any benefits charge. However, this facility must be available to all employees (and, if the company operates a hotel or restaurant business, the staff must eat in a designated area).

However, the Budget 2010 prevents this exemption from being abused in salary sacrifice arrangements where employees are given a 'structured contractual entitlement' to the benefit of canteen meals instead of cash salary. In such cases, the normal taxable benefits rules will apply to meals that become taxable under these arrangements.

Minor and trivial benefits

7.77 HMRC are prepared to treat certain benefits as being exempt from tax, on request, on the grounds that the cash equivalent of the benefit taxable on the employee would be so trivial as to be not worth pursuing. These include, for example, small gifts to employees, such as flowers on the occasion of an employee's marriage, or Christmas presents such as a bottle of wine or a box of chocolates. These are not specifically exempted by statute, and therefore if a request for exemption is not made (and agreed by HMRC) they should be included on a form P11D or PAYE Settlement Agreement (see 7.90 and 7.97).

Other minor benefits are specifically exempted by statute. For example, an employer may spend up to £150 per person on an annual function for employees, such as a Christmas party, without the employee incurring a taxable benefit [*ITEPA 2003, s 264*].

SALARY SACRIFICE ARRANGEMENTS

Tax-efficiency of arrangements

7.78 Salary sacrifice arrangements can often provide a useful way of reducing the employers' Class 1 NIC costs, particularly when spread across the workforce. Furthermore, salary sacrifice arrangements can also produce tax savings and cost reductions arising from the bulk purchase of the benefits made available.

This involves an employee agreeing to forgo part of their salary (possibly by not taking up part of a proposed salary increase) in return for receiving one or more additional non-cash benefits from the employer. Typically, this would cover such 'tax (and NIC) free' benefits as childcare vouchers and the provision of childcare (see 7.74), bicycles (see 7.44) , mobile phones (see 7.67) and possibly additional pension contributions (see 10.25).

Salary sacrifices have become even more attractive following the recent hefty increases in the NIC thresholds, increasing the employee's NIC liability. Thus, in some cases, a salary sacrifice can be quite beneficial for employees. In addition, the employer will save NIC at 13.8% It is not uncommon for the employer to use some of this NIC saving to increase, for example, an employee's pension contributions.

The implementation of the arrangements must be handled carefully to ensure they produce the desired tax (and NIC) savings. Under the general principle established in *Heaton v Bell* (1969) 46 TC 11, where an employee could receive an additional amount by surrendering the right to a benefit (such the use of a car, etc), this was 'money's worth' and thus taxable as earnings under what is now *ITEPA 2003, s 62*. (Special provisions prevent this rule applying to cars and living accommodation, unless the employee earns less than £8,500 per year).

Where an employment contract is varied for at least 12 months, HMRC are likely to accept that the conversion of the benefit has no money's worth. However, this minimum period does not apply to childcare vouchers, since they are specifically exempted from tax under any provision (including the general earnings rule in *ITEPA 2003, s 62*).

VAT and other considerations

7.78A Following the European Court of Justice decision in *Astra Zeneca v HMRC* [2010] (C-40/09), HMRC now consider that the provision of benefits in return for a salary sacrifice represents a supply for VAT (see *Revenue & Customs Brief 28/11*). Consequently, where a company provides employees with benefits under a salary sacrifice arrangement, they will (where appropriate) be subject to VAT on the amount of the salary sacrificed (i.e. the consideration for the benefit). HMRC have announced that they intend to operate this VAT treatment from 1 January 2012.

In practice, the *Astra Zeneca* ruling will affect those benefits that are typically made available by way of salary sacrifice arrangements, such as bicycles, cars and mobile telephones. In such cases, companies will account for VAT on the relevant salary forgone (or, if higher, the cost of the benefit), although they will be entitled to reclaim any VAT incurred in supplying the goods or services in question. However, pension contributions and childcare vouchers provided under salary sacrifice arrangements will not be affected since they are exempt from VAT.

Other issues also need to be considered when implementing salary sacrifice arrangements, such as the impact on employees' mortgage applications, the effect on any tax credit claims, the effect on future salary rises (where calculated on a percentage basis) and the National Minimum Wage (see 2.10).

THE REMUNERATION PACKAGE AND FLEXIBLE BENEFITS

Basic approach

7.79   For senior employees who are not shareholders, or who only have a non-influential minority holding, a structured remuneration package could be provided. This is generally easier to provide for a new employee, as otherwise there may be an element of salary sacrifice by the employee which might be effectively negated by reference to the case of *Heaton v Bell* (1969) 46 TC 211.

However, there is no taxable employment income in certain circumstances where there is an offer of cash or benefits. With care, there should be no problem where an existing employee takes fringe benefits at the time of a salary review or on promotion.

Membership of a contribution-free pension scheme is part of the package. The subject of pension schemes is covered in Chapter 10.

Flexible benefits programme

7.80   This is a slightly different way of providing a remuneration package. It offers employees a choice in receiving benefits using the cafeteria or menu system, involving somewhere between 10 to 15 options, although of course this must be dependent upon the particular requirements and mode of operation of the employer concerned.

The aims of a flexible benefits programme include the following:

(*a*)   improving staff motivation;

(*b*)   presenting the employer as a caring employer;

(*c*)   meeting the employee's own preferences via the cafeteria system;

(*d*)   reducing the income tax liability of the employee by selecting some non-taxable benefits (for example, extra holiday, pension contributions, death in service life cover);

(*e*)   reducing the income tax liability of the employee by selecting some benefits which are taxable at cost rather than value (for example, retail vouchers where major retailers give a discount of up to 5%, or private health insurance where a group discount of 30% or more is available, but the employee is taxed on the actual cost to the employer);

(*f*)   reducing the cost to the employee of an item which they would in any event either require or like to have (for example, employer's bulk purchase at a substantial discount of items such as critical illness cover); and

(*g*)   potential savings in NICs.

The annual allowance

7.81   The employer gives the employee an 'annual flexible allowance' with details of the benefit options available. The employee then indicates their preference for the desired levels of benefits and it is made clear exactly what the cost is from the pre-determined annual flexible allowance.

The cost from the allowance will of course vary depending on many circumstances, but as an illustration could involve the following:

- private medical insurance for employee only – £600;

- company car (no private fuel) – £9,000;

- financial counselling – £700;

- personal tax service – £700;

- increasing holiday entitlement by five days – £1,200.

7.82   The options available within a family or owner-managed company are likely to concentrate on those where there is a clear benefit to the company and where the administrative aspects of providing a flexible benefits programme are carefully contained.

Example 16

Structuring a remuneration package

Lancaster Gate Events Ltd is to spend £54,000 per annum on a new executive, Mr Capello, who is offered the cafeteria system of choosing a remuneration package.

Mr Capello decides upon the following:

	Gross cost to Lancaster Gate Ltd (ignoring corporate tax relief) £	Gross 'benefit' to Mr Capello £	Taxable on Mr Capello £
Salary cost	38,832 (a)	35,000	35,000
Pension contribution	2,500	2,500	Nil
Volvo 70 series 2.3 car	5,400 (b)	6,000	8,481 (g)
Petrol	2,700 (c)	1,800	6,580 (h)
Mobile phone	1,000	1,000	Nil (i)
Private health insurance	350 (d)	500	350
Clothing	1,080 (e)	1,200	216
Class 1A NICs	2,156 (f)	Nil	Nil
	54,018	48,000	50,627

Notes:

(a) Salary £35,000 and employer's Class 1 NIC of £3,832 (13.8% on excess over £7,225).

(b) Contract hire £450 per month (net of 10% company discount).

(c) 18,000 total miles including 12,000 private miles @ 15p per mile based on petrol at 130p per litre.

(d) 30% discount on group scheme for health insurance.

(e) 10% discount on clothing, but as it is not corporate clothing, taxable benefit: 20% × £1,080.

(f) 13.8% × £15,627 (£8,481 + £6,580 + £350 + £216).

(g) Original list price of £24,230 and CO_2 emissions rating of 240 g/km. Taxable benefit is 35% × £24,230 = £8,481.

(h) Fuel scale benefit – £18,800 × 35% = £6,580 .

(i) Not subject to Class 1A NICs.

Tax efficiency of benefits

7.83   The tax efficiency of employee benefits depends on a number of factors, including the calculation of the tax charge and the amount the employee would have to spend personally (out of their post-tax income) of providing that benefit personally.

A broad 'benefit efficiency' percentage calculation for the relevant benefit might be calculated as follows:

$$\frac{\text{Cost to employee-taxable benefit}}{\text{Cost to company}} \times 100\%$$

Using this calculation, the greater the 'benefit-efficiency' percentage, the more tax efficient would be the benefit. The cost to the employee would be the amount the employee would have to incur personally to provide the relevant benefit. The 'taxable benefit' would be the amount of the benefit that is subject to tax in the employees' hands.

OTHER TRANSACTIONS BETWEEN THE COMPANY AND ITS SHAREHOLDERS

Working and non-working shareholders

7.84 Where a close company's business involves the provision of goods or services, and the company provides them to a director (or indeed to any employee) at a discounted price there can be an income tax charge.

Where the same arrangement is made for a *non-working* shareholder, this gives rise to a taxable distribution (based on the cash equivalent under employment benefit rules) made by the company under *CTA 2010, s 1064 (ICTA 1988, s 418)*.

Calculation of taxable benefits

7.85 The income tax charge is based on the cost to the company of providing the goods or service *less* so much as is paid by the director [*ITEPA 2003, ss 203, 204*]. For goods, this should mean that the director/employee has no tax liability if they pay at least the wholesale price. For services, there may be a negligible additional cost of providing them to a specific individual given that further expenditure may not be incurred. Indeed, following the case of *Pepper v Hart* [1992] STC 898, in-house benefits are taxed by reference to their 'marginal cost' only.

7.86 From an IR Press Release dated 21 January 1993, the position for a family or owner-managed company and its directors or employees can be summarised as follows:

(*a*)   goods sold at a discount to a director or employee which results in them paying at least the wholesale price involve no or negligible net benefit;

(b)   if the company is running a private school, teachers paying at least 15% of the normal school fees for their children have no tax charge;

(c)   professional services not requiring any additional personnel can be provided free of tax to directors or employees; this covers, for example, legal or financial services provided by in-house personnel (any disbursements would involve a tax charge on the users, if they do not pay for them);

(d)   if an asset is used both for business and private purposes, fixed costs relating thereto are not included in determining the tax charge where the private use is incidental to the business use as they are not *additional* costs (this does not apply to cars or vans where a fixed scale charge applies).

Assets acquired at undervalue

7.87   Where a working shareholder or owner manager acquires or buys an asset, such as a property, from the company, it is advisable to obtain a professional valuation. This will reduce the risk of HMRC seeking to tax it as an unintended distribution or taxable benefit. For example, property may be transferred to the owner manager at a competent value of (say) £400,000 but the company may ultimately agree a figure of £480,000 with HMRC's District Valuer. Assuming a professional valuation was obtained prior to the transaction, HMRC will not seek to tax the 'under-value' element of £80,000 (ie £480,000 less £400,000) as a distribution received by the working-shareholder/owner manager provided they 'repay' the £80,000 to the company.

In such cases, it is recommended that the market value is promptly agreed with HMRC's District Valuer. (Form CG34 can be used (downloaded from the HMRC website) to obtain a post-transaction pre-return 'valuation check'. This will reduce the risk of HMRC seeking to argue that the 'under-value' amount is in effect a loan, which would incur a *CTA 2010, s 455 (ICTA 1988, s 419)* liability (see 2.57) and beneficial loan charge (see 7.54).

In such cases, if the *working* shareholder/owner manager does not pay full market value for the transferred asset or receives it for no consideration, they could be taxed on any 'under-value' element under the distribution [*CTA 2010, s 1000 (ICTA 1988, s 209)*] *or* as earnings (HMRC generally consider the land to be 'money's worth for *ITEPA 2003, s 62* purposes – see also HMRC EIM 08001). Under *ITEPA 2003, s 62* (employment income generally takes precedence over the benefits in kind rules (subject to the items listed at EIM 00530).

A distribution-in-specie (see 9.8) would clearly arise where the company has declared it as a legal distribution, with the appropriate minutes etc.

On the other hand, if the company votes the amount as a bonus to the owner-manager/director and states that the property is being transferred in satisfaction of their bonus entitlement, then it will be taxed as an employment benefit. (Provided the property is not a readily convertible asset (see 5.10 and 8.38), the transaction should not be subject to PAYE but would still need to be reported on the P11D. If the property is received as earnings, Class 1 NICs would be due in the normal way.

In the absence of any paperwork, board minutes or other evidence indicating the reason for the transfer of the property, HMRC will examine the relevant circumstances. However, if the recipient is a director/employee who actively works for the company, HMRC are likely to treat it as earnings rather than a distribution.

Company's tax treatment

7.88   For chargeable assets, the company would have to substitute market value in calculating its chargeable gain on the disposal, and the shareholder would be treated as acquiring the asset at market value (provided the transaction is between connected persons). This applies under *TCGA 1992, s 18*, where the shareholder has control of the company or the shareholder and connected persons have control of it [*TCGA 1992, s 286(6)* and *(7)*].

7.89   The market value rule also applies where an asset is transferred in consideration for services rendered as an employee (as would often be the case) or where it is *not* an arm's length transaction [*TCGA 1992, s 17(1)*].

THE P11D AND P9D FORMS

Introduction

7.90   The P11D form is an extremely important form, being the return of expense payments and benefits. Many companies report their P11D benefits on substitute forms or spreadsheets, which are acceptable to HMRC provided all the relevant details are reported.

The deadline for submission is 6 July after the relevant tax year although HMRC may not charge penalties if the return is filed by 19 July. There is no automatic penalty for a 'late' P11D submission.If HMRC seek a penalty, the company would be notified of HMRC's application to a tax tribunal to charge a penalty of up to £300 per late P11D. If the forms are filed before the tribunal hearing, the penalty is avoided. However, any further delay could mean an additional penalty charge of up to £60 per late P11D per day of continuing failure [*TMA 1970, s 98(1)*] – see 7.94.

HMRC now apply the normal penalty rules for incorrect P11D's (see 4.57–4.61 for further details). This means that the percentage penalty loading (applied to the potential tax lost) varies according to taxpayer behaviour, and the degree of culpability or guilt, as summarised below:

	Penalty loading %
Genuine mistake after taking reasonable care	0%
Careless action	30%
Deliberate but not concealed action	70%
Deliberate and concealed action	100%

Forms P11D must be prepared for all company directors (if they receive benefits and expenses), even if they draw only a very small amount from the company, and all other employees who earn (including benefits, etc) at a rate of at least £8,500 per year and receive benefits or expense payments not covered by a dispensation. Thus a form P11D must be prepared for individuals who are employed for only part of the tax year if their remuneration exceeds £163.46 per week. A common error when preparing P11Ds is to assume that all expenses are either tax deductible or covered by a dispensation (see below).

Expenses and benefits provided to employees earning *less than* £8,500 per year must be returned on a 'simple' P9D form (Class 1A NICs are not payable on expenses/benefits returned on the P9D form). HMRC now provide employers with a CD-ROM which contains forms P9D, P11D, P11D(b) and the various P11D working sheets (see below).

Under the self-assessment provisions, employers must provide each employee with a copy of the completed form P11D or a statement of his benefits by 6 July following the tax year to which it applies, otherwise the penalties listed above can apply.

HMRC produce a number of P11D working sheets to help with the calculation of 'cash equivalents' for various benefits. The following sheets can be downloaded from *www.hmrc.gov.uk/employers/emp-form.htm*:

* living accommodation (P11DWS1);
* cars and fuel benefits (P11DWS2);
* vans for private use (P11DWS3);
* interest-free and low interest loans (P11DWS4);
* relocation expenses (P11DWS5); and
* mileage allowance and 'passenger' payments (P11DWS6).

Looking further ahead, HMRC have announced proposals to abandon P11D reporting by switching to a 'payroll' system of taxing benefits instead. Many consider that this will give rise to many practical problems since it will require certain benefits to be estimated and payroll departments may not have the necessary expertise to do this.

Dispensations

7.91   Expenses payments and benefits covered by a dispensation given by the Inspector of Taxes do not have to be included on the form P11D. This avoids the employer having to report such items and the director/employee then having to claim exemption or making a claim for tax relief for legitimate business expenses.

HMRC has the power to grant a dispensation under *ITEPA 2003, s 65*. The company will apply for an appropriate dispensation by writing to HMRC with details of its arrangements for paying expenses and providing particular benefits. The Inspector will wish to see that expense payments are supported by receipts and independently authorised. Provided the Inspector is satisfied that in all circumstances the item concerned would be fully covered by an exemption, concession or an expenses deduction, so that no income tax charge could arise, a dispensation would normally be granted.

Typical items for which a dispensation is often sought include:

- Annual parties and similar functions (see 7.77)

- Reasonable travel and subsistence expenses

- Certain allowable expenses, such as professional subscriptions, uniforms, business telephone calls of employee's personal phones.

- Non-taxable benefit of parking at or near the employee's work place

- Exempt payments of incidental overnight expenses

- Exempt periodic medical check-ups and eye tests for employees who use computers etc.

- Trivial benefits provided to employees (see 7.77)

With a family company, the Inspector might well look closely at the arrangements for controlling reimbursements to directors and other working shareholders.

HMRC generally permit dispensations to be back-dated to the start of the tax year in which the application is made. Once given, a dispensation will continue indefinitely unless HMRC revokes it. However, the exact wording of the dispensation should be checked each year and the whole document reviewed every few years or following changes in tax rules.

HMRC is currently undertaking a review of P11D dispensations to bring them up to date. Employers are being invited to complete and return a P11DX, which might be sent to them or can be downloaded from the HMRC website. In such cases, HMRC has indicated that unless the relevant information is provided, it will assume that the dispensation is no longer required and withdraw the agreement.

Completing the form

7.92   The HMRC P11D Guide and the accompanying work sheets provide a good deal of information to help the employer through the minefield of benefits and expenses reporting requirements. In the case of any uncertainty, reference should also be made to the relevant chapter of the IR 480 booklet which covers various benefits and expenses [for guidance on Class 1/Class 1A NICs, see CWG5 at the website address above].

Care should be taken to ensure all P11Ds or P11 worksheets are prepared correctly. HMRC has issued a P11D quality standard for forms, which must include:

● employer reference

● employee's name and National Insurance number (or their date of birth and gender)

● the list price of any company car provided

● if box 10 in section F is completed (total cash equivalent of car fuel provided) so must, box 9 (total cash equivalent of cars provided)

● if a beneficial loan is provided and is reported in section H, box 15 (cash equivalent of loans) must be completed.

Submitting the form

7.93   The government is striving to bring all its departments into the electronic age and will now accept forms P11D submitted electronically. This can be via floppy disk, certain magnetic tapes and data cartridges, and over the Internet. Further details of submitting forms electronically can be found at HMRC's website (http://www.hmrc.gov.uk/online).

PAYE AND NIC COMPLIANCE

Key filing dates for 2011/12

7.94   A timetable showing the main PAYE and NIC obligations for 2011/12 is set out below:

19 April 2012 (but see below)	Last date for paying PAYE and NIC.
	– Interest is charged after this date.
19 May 2012	Last date for submission of return forms P35 (see 7.85), P14, CIS 36.
	– There are automatic penalties of £100 for every 50 employees for each month the returns are outstanding.
31 May 2012	Employee should have been provided with P60 by this date.
6 July 2012	Last date for submission of P11D, P9D and P11D(b).
	– Late submission of P11Ds may attract discretionary penalties of up to £300 per return (plus a further £60 per day for continuing failure).
	– Late submission of P11D(b) attracts automatic penalties of £100 for every 50 employees for each month (or part month) the returns are outstanding.
	Employees should be supplied with copies of P11D information.
	Any PAYE Settlement Agreements must be in place.
19 July 2012	Last date for payment of Class 1A NICs on benefits and expenses.
	Interest is charged on late payments.
19 October 2012	Tax and NICs on PAYE Settlement Agreements are due to be paid.
	Interest is charged on late payments.

Electronic filing of PAYE returns

7.95   As part of the government's drive towards greater use of electronic filing, employers will be required to file their year-end PAYE and NIC returns (P14s and P35s) online and make their PAYE and NIC payments electronically. (A small number of employees/employers who operate special 'direct collection' arrangments continue to file on paper.)

PAYE online filing is now compulsory for virtually all businesses. Many companies are using the PAYE online service over the Internet (*www.hmrc. gov.uk/online*).

Large employers (those with at least 250 employees) must also pay their PAYE and NICs online electronically – the due date being the 22nd of the month (as opposed to the 19th). Medium and small employers are also encouraged to pay by electronic means (and can defer payment (i.e. cleared funds) by three days to the 22nd of the month if they do so)

PAYE tax and NIC payments are subject to a penalty where they have been made late. There is no penalty charge where only one PAYE payment is made late in a tax year (unless that payment is over six months late).

Where there are two or more late payments, the penalty will be equal to 1% of the total overdue amount. This figure increases on a sliding scale reaching up to 4% where eleven late payments are made in a tax year.

If a payment remains still remains overdue after six months, a further 5% penalty arises (increased by a further 5% if the amount remains unpaid 12 months).

It may be difficult for HMRC to tell whether a particular payment is late, particularly if the company's PAYE/NIC payments vary from month to month. However, HMRC will clearly be able to see whether the final payment for the year (due the following April 19/22) is late. Given, that HMRC are likely to review late payment history on a 'risk-basis', companies must strive to make their final payment on time.

If an adjustment is made after the end of the tax-year under a special IR 35 arrangements, HMRC will not charge any late payment penalties made under the terms of those arrangements.

For Class 1A and 1B NIC payments, HMRC determinations, or corrections to returns, the 'penalty date' is 30 days after the due date. A 5% penalty is levied if the full amount remains unpaid 30 days after the due date (increasing by an additional 5% or 10% if the full amount is unpaid after 6 months or 12 months of the due date respectively).

The standard penalty regime applies for PAYE returns .. HMRC have indicated that provided 'reasonable care' is taken *no* penalties will be charged on mistakes in returns. For these purposes, 'reasonable care' would include keeping accurate records, seeking advice when unsure about the correct tax treatment and informing HMRC about any errors that are discovered on returns that have already been submitted. On the other hand, errors arising from failing to take reasonable care are likely to have substantial penalty loadings (see 4.57–4.61)

BENEFITS OF PAYE SETTLEMENT AGREEMENTS

7.96   Many companies provide a range of minor or irregular benefits (for example, motivational awards, taxable costs of providing staff parties (where the cost exceeds the £150 per head limit), etc – see 7.77). In most such cases, the company is usually willing to settle the director's/ employee's tax liability.

This can be done under a PAYE Settlement Agreement (PSA) under which the company undertakes to pay the relevant tax and Class 1B NICs on behalf of the appropriate directors and employees (*ITEPA 2003, ss 703–707 (*previously *ICTA 1988, s 206A*)). The tax and NICs must be calculated on a 'grossed-up' basis as settlement of the directors'/employees' personal tax liability would itself give rise to a taxable benefit. The PSA effectively excludes the relevant benefits from the employees' taxable income and there is no need for them to be reported on the forms P11D or P9D.

ALLOWABLE EXPENSES

7.97   When an item appears on a form P11D it does not automatically mean that the employee concerned will suffer income tax on it. Technically what happens is that all items are brought into charge to income tax and some of them can then be covered by an expenses claim.

Such claims can only succeed if the relevant expenditure comes within any one of the following restrictive heads:

(*a*)   travel in the performance of the duties of the employment or travel to/ from a place where necessary duties are performed (see 7.48) [*ITEPA 2003, ss 337–342*];

(*b*)   fees and subscriptions to professional bodies or learned societies which are listed in *ITEPA 2003, s 343(2)* whose activities are relevant to the employment [*ITEPA 2003, s 343*];

(*c*)   any other item of expenditure which is incurred wholly, exclusively and necessarily in the performance of the duties of the employment [*ITEPA 2003, s 336*].

PLANNING CHECKLIST – BENEFITS AND EXPENSES

Company

- As a general rule, the company should generally meet all expenses with a business element.

- Consider the corporation tax deductibility of expenses and benefits, but in the majority of cases relief should be available as an employment cost.

- Do not provide unnecessary goods for private use of directors.

- Consider finance lease or contract hire of company cars.

- Significant tax savings are available on the provision of eco-friendly or 'electric' company cars and in most cases the company will also benefit from 100% capital allowances on them.

- It is possible to claim 50% of the input VAT on lease payments for company cars.

- In many cases, it is not economic for companies to provide their employees with private fuel. It would generally be more efficient for employees to meet their own private fuel costs and reclaim the fuel costs incurred by them for business motoring

- Make full use of P11D dispensations and PAYE Settlement Agreements.

- To avoid expensive penalties, ensure compliance with stringent year-end PAYE/NIC filing deadlines, check returns, and keep accurate underlying records.

- All year-end PAYE returns must be filed online.

Working shareholders

- Maximise claim for income tax relief on business element of expenses and benefits.

- Arrange for company to meet all expenses and benefits that have a justifiable business purpose.

- Consider the CO_2 emissions rate when purchasing or leasing new company cars.

- Compare tax cost of company car against costs of running the same vehicle privately.

Other employees

- Look to fringe benefits as an incentive, where income tax liability is less than the real economic value.

- In appropriate cases, consider 'salary sacrifice' arrangements and tax-free/efficient benefits.

- Check tax cost of company car against costs of running the same vehicle privately.

Non-working shareholders

- Attempt to achieve a balance between commercial acceptability and tax advantages to the recipient of benefits.

Chapter 8

Providing shares to employees

USES AND STRATEGIES FOR EMPLOYEE SHARES

Key practical and tax issues

8.1　　Many enlightened owner-managed companies now provide shares to their managers and employees, despite the natural reluctance of the owner-manager(s) to concede part of their equity share capital. Empirical studies have shown that providing managers and employees with valuable shares or share option rights can be a very powerful incentive and motivator. The employing company invariably benefits from increased commitment and productivity and the retention of its key managers. Broadly, if a share plan is approved by HMRC, the tax consequences for the director/employee should generally be the same (or indeed more favourable) as for shares held in any other company. Typically, under an *approved* scheme there is a capital gains tax (CGT) charge on sale of the shares.

However, when issuing or granting options over employee shares, owner managers should always consider the dilutive impact on them and the other existing shareholders.

HMRC are keen to ensure that any profit or reward element on *unapproved* shares/share options is taxed as employment income. The law in this area has become increasingly complex following the introduction of the employment related securities and restricted securities legislation in 2003.

The employee being offered a small number of shares in a family or owner-managed company might not consider them to be of any real or meaningful value, with future capital growth only being capable of realisation in the event of flotation on the stock market or a take-over. Nevertheless, this lack of marketability in the meantime could, however, be partly alleviated by using an employee share ownership plan or by purchase of own shares.

The June 2010 budget raised CGT to 28% for many employee shareholders and option holder (unless they could benefit from ER). However, employee share arrangements designed to maximise the amount of profit falling within the CGT regime are still attractive when compared with the penal income tax/ NIC charges that arise on most other forms of employee rewards and bonuses.

The statutory references in this chapter are to *ITEPA 2003* which applied from 6 April 2003.

EMI and unapproved schemes

8.1A   Where an Enterprise Management Incentives (EMI) scheme is available, this will very often be the preferred route since it achieves a desirable tax position for the employee. For options granted at full value, there are no income tax or NIC costs yet the company can obtain a corporate tax deduction for (broadly) the value of the EMI shares on exercise.

Since 23 June 2010, capital gains on EMI option shares are likely to incur a maximum CGT rate of 28% (after deducting the annual exemption). The lower 18% CGT rate would only apply if and to the extent the employee has not used their basic rate income tax band. (Small employee 'EMI' shareholdings minority shares are unlikely to benefit from the 10% Entrepreneurs' relief (ER) CGT.) However, an exit rate of 28%/18% is still considerably cheaper than the combined income tax/NIC on a cash-based employee bonus.

However, if shares are given under an *unapproved* scheme the tax charge can be expensive because the shares are received by reason of the office or employment. Under an unapproved scheme an income tax liability and, possibly, an NIC charge may arise before the shares are actually sold. However, if *unapproved* shares can be provided when they are at a relatively low value (with the benefit of a substantial 'minority' valuation discount), this can be much simpler and often works relatively well.

For 'unapproved' arrangements, the main employment income tax charge occurs when a director/employee receives free or cheap shares, whether from a direct share award or on the exercise of a share option. This tax charge is based on the 'benefit' received, which is broadly calculated by reference to the market value of the shares less any consideration paid by the employee.

The *Finance Act 2003* made substantial changes to the tax treatment of shares that are issued subject to restrictions or conditions. In the past, it was often possible to minimise income tax charges on employee shares by making the acquisition conditional or by restricting their rights in some way, thus depressing the value that would be subject to income tax (under the 'money's worth' principle in *Weight v Salmon* (1935) 19 TC 174 (see 8.10)). The *FA 2003* provisions now ensure that employment income tax charges are levied on any 'artificial' increase in value created by the removal or alteration of such restrictions, etc. This legislation is widely drawn and could potentially apply to many types of shares issued to directors and employees (after 15 April 2003). This may include shares acquired under an EMI option. Special vigilance is therefore required to avoid creating any unnecessary income tax charges under these rules. In the vast majority of cases, the income tax exposure can be substantially or completely eliminated by making an appropriate election (see 8.32).

The Supreme Court's recent decision in *Gray's Timber Products Ltd v CIR* [2010] UKSC 4 has attracted widespread concern and underlines the need to introduce enhanced 'exit' rights with care. Based on the rather special facts of the case (and in particular the close link between the terms of a share subscription agreement and the taxpayer's employment rights), the Court ruled that the 'excess' consideration received on a share sale (over the statute-based 'market value' of the shares) fell to be taxed as employment income (rather than subject to CGT) (see 8.36).

HMRC are now taking a more stringent line on the reporting of employee share awards and options and other related chargeable events (see 8.84).

Potential impact of disguised remuneration rules in ITEPA 2003, Part 7A

8.1B The 'Employment income provided through third parties' legislation or so-called 'disguised remuneration' rules in *ITEPA 2003, Part 7A* can impose an immediate PAYE and NIC charge on the transfers of assets (for example, shares) by a 'third party' (such as a trust) to an employee (see 5.12).

This legislation has the potential to catch 'commercial' employee share schemes and, in some cases, could impose a tax charge even if the employee does not ultimately receive the relevant shares. However, *ITEPA 2003, ss 554J to 554M* provides various 'prescriptive' exemptions from the *ITEPA 2003, Part 7A* tax/NIC charges for various share scheme transactions. These legislative exclusions should provide protection in most cases although, of course, 'normal' tax charges can still arise under the employment related securities and other rules. Furthermore, HMRC guidance also confirms that no *ITEPA 2003, Part 7A* charges will be sought in relation to commercially-based employee share arrangements.

Corporate tax deductions for employee shares

8.2 Companies can claim a statutory tax deduction for employee/director share awards or option exercises. The relief is broadly based on the amount that would have been charged to income tax in the recipient's hands. Relief is also available for shares transferred under approved shares on a similar basis, which makes EMI schemes even more attractive (see 8.86–8.89).

EMPLOYEE SHARE SCHEMES – PRACTICAL DESIGN ISSUES

Legal and commercial considerations

8.3 The company will have to consider a number of practical issues in determining the detailed legal and commercial considerations for the provision of shares or share options for its employees. The key issues include the following:

- Which director or employees will participate in the share scheme and are their holdings viewed as quasi-proprietorial in nature or simply a 'stake' to obtain some capital value on 'exit'?

- The potential dilutive effect of any share options or share award

- What price should be paid for the shares or on the exercise of the share options?

- Where share options are used, when will the employees be allowed to exercise their options? This may only be on a subsequent flotation, when the company is sold, or some other 'exit' event.

- What rights would attach to the employee shares? Will they carry the same rights as the existing shares (such as on voting and dividend rights) or will the employee shares be a separate class of shares with perhaps more restricted rights (for example, as to capital and dividends)? This will mainly be driven by the overall objectives for the share scheme.

- Can the employees sell their shares, and if so to whom can they be sold? Is there a need to set up an employee trust to create a 'market' for the employees' shares?

- On what basis are the shares to be valued? For 'unlisted' family and owner-managed companies, a clear valuation model can be helpful to determine the value when the employee sells their shares to an employee share trust or back to the company (on a purchase of own shares).

- If the company is sold (ie there is a 'change of control'), what mechanism should be in place to deal with the employee shares?

- What happens to an individual employee's shares if they leave the company? Should they be treated more favourably if the employee leaves due to disability, death or redundancy?

- Whether the trade carried on by the company prevents an Enterprise Management Incentives (EMI) scheme being used.

There are also a number of other factors that must be considered within a family or owner-managed company environment.

Approved versus unapproved share schemes

8.4   Despite recent CGT changes, the Enterprise Management Incentives (EMI) scheme still remains the most popular vehicle for providing share options to directors and employees of owner-managed companies (see 8.48–8.72).

Many EMI schemes tend to be 'exit' driven, with the share options being exercisable on a sale or flotation of the company (or some other similar 'event'). In such cases, payment for the exercise of the share option can be 'funded' from the employee's share of the sale proceeds.

Exit-based EMI schemes will enable employees to benefit from a share of the sale consideration for the company, typically at the current CGT rate of 28%. (Even if the option shares carry more than 5% of the votes, ER will not apply unless the shares (or a separate '5% holding') have been held for a full 12 months before the sale.)

The EMI rules contain various restrictions that prevent them being used by very large or 'controlled' companies and in relation to certain trading activities (see 8.63 and 8.64).

In some cases, an approved company share option plan (CSOP) (see 8.73–8.76) may provide a suitable alternative. However, the £30,000 limit (based on the market value of the shares at grant) under a CSOP often proves to be unduly restrictive in many cases.

There will be many cases where, for a variety of reasons, a company will only be able to provide shares under an unapproved arrangement. Under an unapproved scheme, an employee may be asked to pay market value for their shares or suffer an income tax charge by reference to market value. Where a reasonably low 'market value' can be agreed for the very small minority shareholding with HMRC, the tax can probably be managed. On the other hand, if the share value is relatively high, the payment of income tax without any concurrent sale proceeds can be a practical problem.

An unapproved share option scheme enables an option to be granted at a lower price than the share price at that time. This gives an immediate value to the option rights as a 'golden hello' to a new executive or as 'golden handcuffs' to a key existing executive. As a general rule, this 'benefit' cannot be taxed at the date the option is granted, irrespective of the period over which the option can be exercised. (This exemption is also available under the EMI scheme (see 8.50).)

An exit-based *unapproved* share option would not offer any real tax benefits, since virtually the entire 'value' would attract income tax and NIC.

Material interest

8.5　HMRC approved share plans are not available to an individual who holds a material interest in the company. Interests of associates must be included in the test, which means that approved plans may be limited to unrelated employees or those with minority holdings.

The size of holding which will constitute a material interest varies as shown below by reference to the ordinary share capital and, for a close company, to the assets which would be distributed in the event of the company being wound-up.

Scheme	*Test for material interest*
Enterprise management incentive (EMI) share options	Over 30%
Company share option plans (CSOP)	Over 25% (over 10% before 9 April 2003)
SAYE share options	Over 25%
SIPs	Over 25%

Dilution of share capital

8.6 Awarding shares to employees often results in the company making a new issue of shares, thereby diluting the value of the existing shareholdings. This may be objected to by non-working shareholders who are less likely than working shareholders to appreciate the overall benefits of allowing certain employees to acquire shares. The existing shareholders (both working and non-working) may also be loath to see a fragmented share ownership with several people owning very small holdings.

The potential impact on dilutive employee options on shareholder's EMI entitlements needs to be monitored and planned for. For example, management shareholders with (say) a 5% stake in the company are likely to be very dissatisfied if the exercise of employee share options before a sale dilute their holdings below the crucial 5% required for ER!

Investor protection committees publish guidelines designed to prevent dilution of shareholders' equity for *quoted* companies. These provide a useful starting point for non-working shareholders' involvement in developing a strategy, albeit that an unquoted company would probably wish to have greater flexibility. A simple strategy is to limit the issued share capital for all employee share schemes to (say) a limit of between 5% and 10% of the ordinary share capital.

Phantom share options

8.7 Phantom share options are essentially a cash-based bonus arrangement. They usually involve a cash bonus being paid where the company's share price increases by a specified amount, or where shares are issued by reference to pre-determined profit targets being met.

For most family or owner-managed companies, such plans are likely to be of limited use. The company's share price will not be readily available (unless, for example, the company is listed on the Alternative Investment Market). Share values are not, therefore, going to be an appropriate measure of performance and a cash bonus scheme linked to profits or sales, etc will generally be preferred.

SIMPLE ISSUE OR GIFT OF SHARES

Employment income tax issues

8.8 Many family or owner-managed companies may not wish to use share options or other means of deferred share ownership, preferring a simple issue or gift of shares to selected employees instead. This will invariably trigger an income tax charge on the employee, with the 'profit' element being taxed as earnings under *ITEPA 2003, s 62* under the principles laid down in *Weight v Salmon* (1935) 19 TC 174. In certain cases, this amount may also be treated as earnings for NIC purposes (see 13.36). However, as the market value is based on a 'money's worth' principle, the tax charge may be reduced to a palatable amount if a 'lowish' discounted minority valuation can be agreed for the shares. For basis of valuation, see 14.38 and 14.39. For transferor's CGT treatment, see 13.39.

Where shares are issued to an employee, *CA 2006, s 588* provides that they are taken to be allotted where the employee acquires the unconditional right to be included in the company's share register (this would be when the beneficial interest in the shares is acquired – see *ITEPA 2003, s 477(4)*). If a private company has only one class of share capital the directors may allot shares without shareholder approval (unless the company's articles expressly prohibit this). In any case, there is no need to obtain shareholder approval for share awards granted under an employee share scheme (as defined in CA 2006, s 1166).

The standard pre-emption rights for share allotments do not apply to employee share schemes [*CA 2006, s 566*].

Special tax rules apply for shares received by a director/employee (after 15 April 2003), where the shares are 'restricted securities' within *ITEPA 2003, s 423* (see 8.14–8.33). Clearly, where shares are subject to 'employee-specific' restrictions or conditions, etc that are sufficiently material so as to reduce their value, they will fall to be treated as 'restricted'. Typical restrictions include the forfeiture of shares if the employee subsequently leaves the company or fails to meet performance targets.

8.9   Where restricted shares are acquired, the tax charge is based on the 'money's worth' principle (the under-value element being treated as earnings under *ITEPA 2003, s 62*). Consequently, the taxable amount would be calculated by reference to the actual value of the shares *taking the inherent restrictions into account*. However, immediate attention must be given to making an election under (normally) *ITEPA 2003, s 431* (see 8.32). Where the election is made, *ITEPA 2003, s 431(1)(a)* alters the basis of the tax charge to one which is based on the market value of the shares ignoring the various restrictions. Special rules apply to shares that are subject to the risk of forfeiture that fall away within five years (see 8.26).

Failure to make the election will mean that part of the value passing to the director/employee on a subsequent chargeable event (such as a future sale of the shares) will also be subject to income tax (and possibly NIC) (see 8.31). By making the election, the director/employee ensures that any income tax exposure at the date of acquisition is limited to the *unrestricted value* of the shares (ie the value of the shares ignoring the relevant restrictions). This ensures that any future growth in value is entirely within the beneficial CGT regime (see 8.32).

8.10   In practice, it may not always be easy to determine whether the restrictions attaching to certain shares are sufficiently substantive to render them 'restricted' within *s 423*. One of the key requirements is that the relevant restrictions have the effect of reducing the value of the shares, which can often be a subjective matter.

Depending on the precise nature of any restrictions, it may be possible to agree with HMRC – Shares & Asset Valuation that there is no discernable difference between the unrestricted and restricted value of the relevant shares – this effectively makes the shares 'unrestricted' (see *ITEPA 2003, s 423(1) (b)*). There is anecdotal evidence that suggests that HMRC may adopt this approach where the shares are simply subject to the usual transfer restrictions and pre-emption rights. Indeed, it is possible to argue that where directors have the usual right to refuse to register shareholders, this may not always be enforceable as a matter of general law. Given the lack of complete certainty in this area, many would argue that a protective *ITEPA 2003, s 431* election should always be made. Indeed, in practice such elections are invariably made, even where the risk of the relevant shares being treated as 'restricted' is remote (see also 8.17 and 8.32).

See 8.84 for HMRC reporting requirements on employee share acquisitions.

As part of the arrangements for providing shares to employees/directors, the company may pay the income tax on the employee's behalf (obviously incurring a further 'grossed-up' tax charge for settling the employee's pecuniary liability).

CGT treatment of employee shares

8.11   When offered shares in their employing company, many directors and employees generally tend to focus on the potential capital gains benefits. Although the shares may incur an income tax charge on acquisition (unless they are offered under an HMRC approved scheme) many employees anticipate the prospect of realising a substantial capital gain on 'exit' (at favourable CGT rates).

Under the post-22 June 2010 CGT regime, the employees will normally pay CGT at 28% (or 18% to the extent they have sufficient 'income tax' basic rate band capacity) on their 'exit' gains. However, some employees' gains will be covered by the annual exemption and would be tax-free.

A relatively small number may be able to benefit from Entrepreneurs' relief (ER). In such cases, they will need to hold at least 5% of the ordinary (voting) shares at least one year before the sale (see 15.33 for detailed conditions). Some senior management/director-shareholders might qualify. With ER, employees and directors will be able to realise gains at the beneficial 10% CGT rate (on gains up to their lifetime ER allowance of £10 million).

As a general rule, EMI shares must be held for at least a year after the option has been exercised to obtain the 10% ER CGT rate (see 15.33). In contrast to the 'old' taper relief rules there is no beneficial provision that treats the shares as being held from the date of grant for ER purposes. However, in some cases, directors and employees might still be able to qualify where they hold at least 5% of the company's ordinary voting shares in their own right (in addition to their EMI option) throughout the year before the sale.

CHECKLIST OF KEY PRACTICAL POINTS

8.12   In establishing any share scheme, each party should consider the following main practical issues:

(*a*)   the identification of the key personnel and shares to be offered;

(*b*)   the planned revision of the company's share capital structure to provide shares subject to options;

(*c*)   the future share capital structure, with the implications of any dilution for existing shareholders;

(*d*)   draft scheme rules;

(*e*)   how the directors/employees will finance the exercise of their options;

(*f*)   determination of the current market value of the relevant shares;

(*g*)   plans for future flotation or sale;

(*h*)   the possibility of the company purchasing its own shares from a scheme member.

UNAPPROVED SHARE SCHEMES – SUMMARY OF KEY TAX CHARGES ON EMPLOYEE SHARES

Main employment income and NIC charging provisions

8.13   An employee/director is subject to an employment income tax charge in the main circumstances summarised below. Clearly, the various income tax charging rules generally only apply where the shares are acquired by reason of the directorship or employment, and the legislation extends this to cover a past or prospective office/employment (see also 13.29). This will normally be the case where shares are awarded or share options are granted to a director or employee. The main exception to this rule is where shares are transferred to a family member, since this would be a personal gift to a family member etc (see 8.15).

Restricted securities regime for share issues or transfers

Background

8.14   The 'restricted securities' regime was introduced by the *FA 2003* to provide a comprehensive framework for taxing employee shares, particularly dealing with shares that were issued subject to restrictions or conditions or were artificially depressed in value. For these purposes, 'securities' are widely defined and includes loan notes, government gilts, warrants, units in a collective investment scheme, and futures, etc as well as shares. In the context of family and owner managed companies we will, of course, invariably be concerned with shares (and this term is generally used here).

Due to their pervasive nature, the introduction of the 'restricted securities' legislation attracted widespread criticism. On a strict statutory interpretation, these provisions appear to potentially catch many 'innocent cases' even where there has been no intention to manipulate the value of the shares by changing or lifting restrictions, etc.

The restricted securities legislation applies to securities issued after 15 April 2003 but its charging provisions only came into effect from 1 September 2003.

Since the legislation was issued, some boundaries have been placed on its practical application, largely through:

- the answers to Frequently Answered Questions (FAQs) on HMRC's website; and

- a series of joint statements, such as 'The Memorandum of Understanding between the BVCA (British Venture Capital Association) and the Inland Revenue on the income tax treatment of managers' equity investments in venture capital and private equity backed companies', issued on 25 July 2003 (see 8.24 and 8.25).

The potential application of the restricted securities legislation to earn-out deals satisfied in shares/loan notes is reviewed at 15.71.

Scope of 'restricted securities' regime

8.15   Broadly speaking, the 'restricted securities' provisions apply to any shares :

- acquired by a current, prospective or past director (*ITEPA 2003, s 5*) or employee by reason of their office or employment [*ITEPA 2003, s 421B*];

- which, at the time of acquisition:

  (i)   are subject to compulsory transfer or forfeiture for less than their market value (for example, when an employee ceases to work for the company). (Based on the legislation, HMRC's view is that if there is a chance that the employee would receive less than market value, then he is not entitled to at least market value within *ITEPA 2003, s 423(2)(c)*.); or

(ii) carry restrictions on disposing or retaining or restrictions on any other rights attaching to the shares; or

(iii) contain other restrictions that make retaining the shares or exercising the rights attaching to them disadvantageous; and

● as a result of which the market value of the shares is less than they would be, but for these restrictions [*ITEPA 2003, s 423*].

HMRC treat restricted securities as if they had two values – an actual market value taking into account all the restrictions (the AMV or 'restricted value') and an 'unrestricted market value' (UMV), assuming all the restrictions and similar provisions were taken out. The difference between the unrestricted and restricted market value of the shares will drive their tax treatment.

The legislation only applies where the shares are acquired by reason of the individual's office or employment. This also extends to cases where some *other* person (such as a family member) acquires the shares by reason of someone else's employment or office. However, shares that are given in the 'normal course of domestic family or personal relationships' are exempted – thus, in a family company, shares transferred to spouses, adult children or other close family members should *not* be subject to any employment income tax charges (see also 13.29 and 13.31).

There is a very important rule that deems a director or founder shareholder receiving shares through a subsequent bonus or rights issue as being within the scope of these provisions, even where their *original* shareholding was acquired before 16 April 2003. However, there would normally be no tax charge on the bonus share issue, etc, since any reduction in value of their existing shareholding is treated as consideration for the new shares (*ITEPA 2003, s 421D*).

Shares are *not* restricted simply because they do not carry the full range of benefits – for example, if they are non-voting or do not carry any dividend rights – provided these limited rights apply to *all* the shares of the same class indefinitely. However, where the shares are only subject to temporary limitations (for example, they are non-voting for a prescribed period and then become voting), they will be restricted (*HMRC Employment Related Securities Manual, para 30310*).

If the shares fall within the 'restricted securities' regime, special tax considerations apply when they are originally acquired (see 8.9, 8.10, 8.23 and 8.32). Unless an *ITEPA 2003, s 431* election is made, the director/employee would be 'exposed' to an income tax charge where subsequent 'chargeable events' (as defined in *ITEPA 2003, s 426*) occur, being where:

- the shares cease to be 'restricted' as a result of a removal of the restrictions or effluxion of time (see 8.31); or

- the restrictions attaching to the shares are varied; or

- the shares are sold whilst they are still restricted.

In those cases where the shares are *readily convertible assets* (see 8.38), the income tax becomes payable under PAYE and NICs become payable by the employee and employer.

Clearly, if it can be demonstrated that the shares are not 'restricted' within the meaning of *ITEPA 2003, s 423* (see above), then any tax charge on acquisition would normally be calculated under general principles. Thus, where free or cheap (non-restricted) shares are awarded, the 'benefit' received is treated as a general earnings, based on *Weight v Salmon* (1935) 19 TC 174.

Founders' shares

8.16   A much stricter stance appears to be taken with 'founders' shares' as HMRC has indicated that such shares would normally be taken to be employment-related securities. However, this does not necessarily mean that an income tax charge will arise. Some value has to pass by using the shares, etc – it is not the intention to tax normal commercial growth (*HMRC Employment Related Securities Manual, para 20240*).

As a general rule, it is no longer possible to argue that shares acquired by managers on a management buy-out are 'founders' shares' (see 8.23).

Shares subject to transfer restrictions and pre-emption rights

8.17   There has been considerable debate as to whether most shareholdings in private companies would be restricted on the grounds they are subject to the standard transfer restrictions and pre-emption rights . There have been suggestions that such conditions may not necessarily make them fall within the restricted securities regime. The standard 'restriction' contained in most articles is that the directors may refuse to register a transfer to any person that they disapprove of. Some have pointed out that the existence of these pre-emption rights can be considered as favourable to the existing shareholders, since it removes the risk of 'undesirable' shareholders etc.

Furthermore, given that compulsory 'fair valuation' is applied to a pre-emption transfer of shares, there is a strongly held view that the shares would not be restricted (since this value is likely to exceed a discounted fiscal valuation of a minority shareholding) – indeed, this point is confirmed in the current version of HMRC's guidance on completion of Form 42 (at example 3 on page 26). In any event, shares with (only) *standard* pre-emption rights are likely to be treated as having the same value with or without those rights. Consequently, in such cases, only the basic 'excess over market value' charge under *Weight v Salmon* would need to be considered.

However, even where it is very unlikely that the shares would be regarded as 'restricted securities' under a legalistic analysis, many advisers assume that HMRC might subsequently treat them as 'restricted'. They therefore adopt a practical 'belt and braces' approach by ensuring that protective *ITEPA 2003, s 431* elections are always made (see 8.32). This approach seems to be justified because there have been a number of reported cases where HMRC now seem to be taking the view that private company shares are 'restricted' because of the presence of pre-emption rights or some other restrictions on shareholders' abilities to freely sell their shares!

Many contend that this point is debatable since 'restrictions' which are inherent characteristics of the shares affecting *all* the shareholders, as opposed to being specific to the employees or directors, should be ignored for this purpose. Furthermore, as explained above, the existence of pre-emption rights also has a potential upside for shareholders. Whilst HMRC may not be readily sympathetic to such arguments, they are worth pursuing in a 'defensive' situation.

Leaver clauses

8.18 Shares issued to directors/employees typically require the shares to be sold if the employee leaves. Different exit rules apply for 'good' and 'bad' leavers:

- *good leavers* are usually those employees who die in service, retire at normal retirement age or are made redundant. Good leavers are usually given the capital growth on their shares up to the point when they leave. Thus, the pre-emption price would generally be the higher of the original price paid for their shares or market value/fair value;

- *bad leavers* would include employees who are fired or leave to join a competitor. A bad leaver would be required to give up their shares at the *lower* of market value and the amount originally paid for their shares.

Under *ITEPA 2003, s 424(1)(b)*, a 'bad leaver' clause requiring an employee to give up their shares if they leave on the ground of misconduct does *not* count as a 'restriction' under the restricted securities regime (misconduct typically involves breaking the company's rules and may also include 'termination for cause' (see *Employment Procedures Manual*, para 30240)).

Where a 'bad leaver' receives the 'bad leaver price', HMRC – Shares & Asset Valuation (SAV) invariably resist attempting to apply the *TCGA 1992, s 17* 'market value' rule for CGT purposes. This is on the basis that the departing employee has received their legal entitlement under the articles.

Valuation issues

8.19   Valuations under the *ITEPA 2003* employee shares regime follow the capital gains methodology. This means that the relative size of the shareholding (and its overall cost) will determine the appropriate information standard. These principles are fully explained in 14.34–14.39. It is perhaps worth noting here that most employee holdings will represent small minority interests. Consequently, the details that would be deemed to be available for the purpose of the valuation would be restricted to signed accounts, press information, company website news, and general industry knowledge (see 14.36).

The statutory CGT basis of valuation requires a willing hypothetical vendor and a prudent hypothetical purchaser, who could be anyone. Where there is a restriction on sale (either in the articles, shareholders' agreement, or employment contract), HMRC's view is that the shares must be valued as if that restriction remains relevant in the purchaser's hands.

On this basis, the hypothetical purchaser looks very much like an employee(!), but this interpretation is not readily supported by share valuation jurisprudence or indeed SAV! The existence of a 'bad leaver' price in the articles could therefore influence the restricted value of the shares, depending on whether the (hypothetical) employee shareholder was more likely to leave before any sale of the company. In practice, such an assessment is likely to be ignored by SAV, especially since the CGT basis clearly contemplates a hypothetical purchaser who could be *anyone* at all. However, it might be possible to argue successfully that the existence of a 'bad leaver' price should not restrict the value of the shares. Where the pre-emption right extends to the same class, the other shareholder(s) stand to gain by acquiring the shares at a favourable 'par' value. So since it is not known which shareholder would leave first (all shareholders being 'hypothetical'), the overall effect would be relatively neutral. On the other hand, where the pre-emption right *first* extends to a different class, the existence of a bad leaver price would restrict the share value.

There is some practical evidence to suggest that there is little consistency in HMRC's approach to valuations. For example, some valuers have agreed Actual Market value (AMV) and the Unrestricted Market value (UMV) (see 8.15) at the same figure while others have insisted on a 10% or more difference between the two figures (without any particular reason). A common approach is to assume that any share valuation is the AMV, which should be increased by an appropriate fixed percentage to give the UMV. However, many argue that this is incorrect since it would produce dissimilar UMVs for *identical* shares subject to different restrictions. It therefore follows that the correct approach would be to treat the share value as the UMV with a suitable reduction being applied to reflect the relevant restrictions.

Impact on approved share schemes

8.20 'Restricted' shares acquired under Enterprise Management Incentives (EMI) options (after 15 April 2003) have always been within the 'restricted securities' legislation. However, a deemed *s 431* election is made when the EMI option is exercised for (at least) their market value at the date of grant (*ITEPA 2003, s 431A*). However, for 'discounted' EMI options (ie where an income tax charge arises on exercise), a *s 431* election is generally recommended (see 8.51).

Since 18 June 2004, any 'post-acquisition' taxable events (see 8.31) on 'restricted' shares issued under HMRC approved schemes, such as company share ownership plans (CSOPs), SAYE schemes and share incentive plans (SIPs), are subject to the 'restricted securities' rules. However, no tax charge arises on the *acquisition or award* of shares under these approved schemes. Before this *FA 2004* amendment, such approved schemes were specifically exempted from the 'restricted securities' regime.

'Narrow' employee-controlled company exemption

8.21 There is a 'narrow' exemption from the relevant income charges under *ITEPA 2003, s 426* for 'employee-controlled' companies under *ITEPA 2003, s 429*. Broadly, in relation to a particular class of shares, an 'employee-controlled' company is one where the majority of the shares of that class are held by or for the benefit of employees who are able to control the company [*ITEPA 2003, s 421H*]. Since 2 December 2004, the exemption is also circumscribed by the requirement to ensure that the avoidance of tax or NICs was not one of the main purposes of the arrangements under which the shares were acquired.

It is important to appreciate that this exemption is fairly limited in scope, since it only applies if *all* the shares are affected by the same relevant chargeable *event*. This exemption would *not* therefore apply where, for example, an employee (not protected by an *ITEPA 2003, s 431* election – see 8.32) subsequently sells their shares without the company being 'sold'.

Special relief for research institution 'spin-out' companies

8.22 Various universities, public-sector research institutions, and similar bodies own intellectual property (IP) created by their employees, mainly from research work undertaken in the pharmaceutical, bioscience, or new technology sectors. In most cases, part of the profits made from the subsequent exploitation of the IP (for example, through licensing or selling it) is passed to the employees who helped to create it under so-called IP sharing policies.

Such arrangements frequently take the form of employee share ownership in what are known as 'spin-out' companies. Such companies are set up to develop the IP to the point where it can be exploited commercially. The value of shares in the spin-out company would clearly be enhanced by the transfer of IP from the relevant university or research establishment (or from any company controlled by it).

As the 'employee' shares in the spin-out company would clearly be 'employment-related', the increase in the value of the shares attributable to the IP transfer would normally be subject to income tax, the main potential categories being as general earnings (under *ITEPA 2003, s 62*), as a 'post-acquisition' benefit under *ITEPA 2003, s 447*, or employment income on the exercise of a share option (under *ITEPA 2003, s 476*).

The impact of an income tax charge at a time when the employees did not have the funds to meet it was seen as a contributory factor to the downturn in the creation of spin-out companies since April 2003. Consequently, a 'concessionary' solution was initially reached between the Revenue and the relevant research sector representatives, which effectively deferred the income tax charge until the relevant shares were sold.

However, the *FA 2005* established a more 'beneficial' solution. Provided the relevant shares are acquired or the IP transfer agreement is made after 1 December 2004, the value of the IP transferred is effectively disregarded when valuing the shares for the purposes of the relevant employees' income tax charges (see above). Thus, no income tax (or, where relevant, NIC) charges arise to the extent that the value of the shares relate to the transferred IP. This relief is not available where the avoidance of tax or NIC is one of the main purposes of the 'spin-out' arrangements [*ITEPA 2003, ss 451–460*].

Employment-related securities and management buy-outs

Implications of shares being treated as restricted securities

8.23   Before the *FA 2003*, it was generally believed that where a management team set up a new company (Newco) to acquire the target company, their Newco shares would *not* be treated as acquired by reason of employment. Now, the management team's Newco shares would be 'employment-related securities' (see 8.16) since the shares are treated as made available by virtue of their previous employment with the target company. Furthermore, the shares issued to managers on the 'majority' of buy-outs are likely to be 'restricted securities'. This is because many managers' shares will be subject to the usual 'good leaver/bad leaver' provisions that require the compulsory transfer of their shares at less than market value if they leave the company within a specified period other than by reason of ill health or disability, etc.

The full implications of *Pt 7* of *ITEPA 2003* must therefore be considered when issuing shares to a manager on an Management Buy-Out (MBO) or Management Buy-in (MBI). In such cases, the shares are likely to be restricted securities and may be acquired at an 'under-value' as compared to the price paid for shares issued to others, such as by venture capital providers.

The same tax issues can arise where managers receive shares in the buy-out company vehicle (Newco) in exchange for their previous shares in their 'old' company ('Oldco'). *ITEPA 2003, s 421D* effectively operates to deem both the old shares and therefore the new 'consideration' shares to be received 'by reason of employment', even where the 'old' shares were acquired before 16 April 2003 (see 8.15).

Although the normal 'share for share' exchange rules should apply for CGT purposes (see 15.44), the consideration given for the Newco shares by the managers for the purposes of the 'employment-related' securities regime is the (relevant proportion) of the deal value placed on Oldco's shares. Given that the value of Oldco's shares would reflect any (material) relevant restrictions in Oldco's articles, the unrestricted market value of the managers' Newco shares could exceed the actual market value of their Oldco's shares. The tax outcome will clearly depend on the relevant valuations in each particular case and it may be possible to argue that there is no real difference between the restricted and unrestricted values of the shares. It may also be possible to argue that the 'consideration' given by the managers for their Newco shares is the same as the amount given by the institutional investors (see 8.24).

As a general rule, the managers will elect under *ITEPA 2003, s 431* to be taxed by reference to the 'unrestricted market value' of the Newco shares. (Indeed, this will be a requirement of the venture capitalist to ensure that the company is not exposed to additional PAYE/NIC liabilities on an 'exit'!) Consequently, if there is a material difference in values, it is possible for an income tax charge to arise on the share exchange.

Memorandum of understanding ('MOU') with BVCA

8.24 The British Venture Capital Association (BVCA) sought to clarify with the Inland Revenue the extent to which shares issued to managers in venture capital and private equity backed companies would be caught under the *FA 2003* 'employment-related securities' regime in *Pt 7 of ITEPA 2003*. Typically, this applies to shares issued to the management team in MBO and MBI transactions.

Some helpful guidance on the issues raised is contained in the 'Memorandum of Understanding' (MOU) that was issued on 25 July 2003. The BVCA Memorandum follows a 'safe harbour' approach for shares issued to managers (provided there are no inherent tax-avoidance arrangements). However, it is still open for taxpayers to argue each case on its own particular circumstances. Where there is uncertainty about the application of the MOU guidelines to a particular 'buy-out', this may be resolved by applying to HMRC for a informal ruling (see 15.40).

Where there are no 'ratchet' arrangements (see 8.25), HMRC will accept that the price paid for the managers' shares is equivalent to:

- their initial unrestricted market value (IUMV), where the shares are 'restricted securities'; or

- their market value, if the shares are *not* restricted;

provided the following conditions are met:

(*a*) the managers' shares are ordinary share capital;

(*b*) any preferred debt or equity capital provided by the venture capitalist is on normal commercial terms;

(*c*) the price paid for the managers' shares is *not less* than the price the venture capitalist pays for their 'equivalent' ordinary shares;

(*d*) the managers acquire their shares at the same time as the venture capital provider acquires its ordinary shares (in practice, HMRC generally appear to accept cases where the shares are acquired within up to 90 days of each other);

(*e*) the managers' shares have no features that give them (or allow them to acquire) rights not available to other holders of ordinary share capital;

(*f*) the managers are fully remunerated through salary and bonuses (where appropriate) under a separate employment/service contract (see paras 3.1 and 4.1 of the Memorandum).

Managers' shares often carry restrictions of the type laid down in *ITEPA 2003, s 423(2)*. For example, the typical requirement in a 'leaver' clause to transfer the managers' shares for less than market value. The managers will be treated as paying a price that is *not* discounted as a result of these restrictions, provided the price paid is the same as that paid by the venture capitalist (see (*d*) above). Thus, in such cases, the price paid would (at least) be equivalent to the IUMV of the shares.

Similarly, the (initial) value of shares would not be depressed where they are subject to the commonly used 'drag-along' and 'tag-along' provisions – 'drag-along' rights force the minority shareholders to sell in cases where the majority wish to sell the company; 'tag-along' rights give the minority shareholders the right to sell their shares where an offer has been made to the controlling shareholders. These provisions are unlikely to reduce the value of the shares since they enable the minority shareholders to obtain market value for their shares on an 'exit'.

Potential impact of ratchet arrangements

8.25   In many MBO and MBI deals the ordinary shares issued to managers are subject to a 'ratchet' mechanism, so that the managers' shares obtain additional rights and value when target rates of return are achieved by the venture capitalist or when pre-determined performance targets are met by the company.

Ratchets are generally designed to achieve a venture capitalist's ('VCs') commercial objectives. The 'ratchet' mechanism laid down in the Articles or Shareholders' Agreement can either increase the interest of the managers' shares or reduce the interests attaching to the other shares (typically held by the VC investor).

For example, the VC investor may start off with (say) 80% of the ordinary shares with management having the other 20%. If the company's performance (normally measured by the investors 'internal rate of return') exceeds the relevant target(s) or 'hurdles', then part of the VCs holding will convert into worthless deferred shares. This would then reduce the investor's economic stake to (say) 75% with management's rising to 25%. Such mechanisms are frequently referred to as 'positive' or 'upward' ratchets.

On the other hand, 'negative' or 'downward' ratchets work by reducing management's equity stake – with their initial stake being set at the maximum possible assuming all relevant performance targets were achieved. Thus, if the target internal rate of return is not achieved, then management's shares convert into worthless deferred shares with a consequent reduction in their equity stake.

There remains a risk, albeit a debatable one, that ratchets may be subject to an income tax charge under *ITEPA 2003, s 447*.

These 'ratchet' mechanisms also provide an incentive for the managers. If the company prospers, the ratchet will increase their shares of the exit proceeds.

The BVCA MOU (July 2003) states that a ratchet should *not* produce any income tax charge under the *ITEPA 2003, Ch 4* 'post-acquisition benefits' regime, provided certain conditions are met:

(a)   there are no personal performance conditions attached to the ratchet;

(b)   the ratchet arrangements are in existence when the venture capitalist acquired their shares; and

(c)   the managers paid a price for shares *reflecting their maximum economic entitlement*.

Following the MOU, many ratchet arrangements were structured as a 'negative' ratchet to give the managers the maximum equity interest on 'day one'.

Under perhaps the more common route of a 'positive ratchet', where managers' shareholding interests can appreciate (as a result of the other (venture capitalists) shares being diluted), it was argued that managers must effectively pay a 'premium' for the 'upside' element.

In June 2004, the Inland Revenue indicated that an income tax charge would arise where the initial price paid by the managers did *not* reflect their full economic entitlement under the ratchet. The increase in value may result from the lifting of restrictions because new rights are acquired or simply as a consequence of the equity holding being increased. In such cases, any additional 'value' passing to the managers under an incremental ratchet based on performance would be taxed as a post-acquisition benefit derived from the shares under *Ch 4* of *ITEPA 2003*. The Revenue's view was that the increase in the value of the managers' holding should be taxed by reference to the valuation of the shareholding at the time of the 'ratcheted' increase in the managers' shareholding. Any such charge would be subject to PAYE and NIC as the shares are deemed to be RCAs for this purpose under *ITEPA 2003, s 698(3)*.

HMRC have now revised their view (following legal advice), which is reflected in revised guidance issued 21 August 2006. In summary, HMRC accepted that a charge under ITEPA 2003, *Ch 4* was not sustainable where the benefit to the manager reflected 'ratchet' rights that already existed in their shares when they were first acquired.

HMRC now advise that where shares are acquired under arrangements consistent with those described in the MOU (see 8.24 (*a*) to (*f*) above) then no *Ch 4* 'post-acquisition benefit' charge will arise on the disposal of the shares or on the operation of the ratchet (if earlier). Furthermore, where the ratchet also meets conditions (*a*) and (*b*) above, any gains realised on exit will only be subject to CGT.

This seems to suggest that condition (*c*) (the managers must pay a price that reflects their maximum economic entitlement under the 'ratchet' arrangement) no longer applies, and hence a 'positive ratchet' would not, in itself, give rise to a *Ch 4* charge. However, it does appear that the price paid for the shares should reflect the future value of the ratchet, albeit with a discount for the risk that the ratchet may not operate. It therefore is prudent to structure ratchet deals with managers paying a price that reflects the 'maximum' amount they may end up with (with appropriate discounts for uncertainty etc.). Furthermore, protective *s 431* elections should also be made in case HMRC do not accept that the full unrestricted value has been paid.

Shares subject to conditions or forfeitable shares

8.26   Shares that are issued on a 'conditional' basis are now taxed as a 'restricted security' and therefore a tax charge would generally arise under *ITEPA 2003, s 426* when the conditions are lifted and the director/employee enjoys the full benefit of the shares (see 8.31). Such shares are commonly used under long-term incentive plans (LTIPs), where shares are usually given to employees or directors at nil or nominal cost, but subject to pre-determined performance conditions being met.

The basic rule is that no *initial* income tax (or, where relevant, NIC) charge on forfeitable shares is made where the terms of the award are such that the forfeiture restriction will cease within five years of acquisition.

However, a joint election (between the employer and employee) can be made to apply the income tax charge at the time of the initial award. Such elections are irrevocable and must be made within 14 days of the share acquisition. The elections do not have to be submitted to HMRC, but must be retained since they may be requested for inspection as part of an HMRC enquiry.

Where an election is made, the tax charge is based on the full market value of the shares ignoring the depreciatory effect of the forfeiture risk [*ITEPA 2003, s 425(3)*]. Where an election is made, all future growth in share value (including the increase caused by the lifting of any forfeiture restriction) is dealt with under the CGT regime. Approved *s 425* election forms can be found on the HMRC website at www.hmrc.gov.uk/shareschemes/s425-1-pe.rtf. A *s 425* election differs from the (more frequent) *s 431* election, the latter being used to being taxed on the full unrestricted value of the shares (rather than the discount relating to forfeiture restrictions) (see 8.32).

Even where there is no immediate charge, an 'acquisition-based' charge could still arise under certain other provisions, such as where shares are acquired 'partly paid' or under a securities option [*ITEPA 2003, s 425(2)*].

Example 1

Tax treatment of forfeitable shares

On 31 January 2011, Mr Mullins purchased 1,000 shares in Hayden Ltd at £1 each, recognising that the shares would be forfeited (at a price of £1 per share) within three years if certain performance targets were not achieved during that period. The value of the shares, ignoring the forfeiture restriction, is £2.50 per share.

Because the 1,000 shares are forfeitable within three years, no tax charge arises in January 2011 under *ITEPA 2003, s 425(1)*.

If the shares are retained after three years (because the performance targets are satisfied), there will be a charge when the restriction is lifted. Thus, if the shares were worth (say) £5 per share in January 2014, Mr Mullins will suffer a tax charge based on £5 per share when the forfeiture 'restriction' is lifted (see 8.31).

However, if a joint *ITEPA 2003, s 425* election were made by 14 February 2011, Mr Mullins would have an initial employment income charge of £1,500 (ie £2,500 less £1,000). (If the market value of the shares when the restrictions are lifted is lower than when they were first acquired, there is no mechanism for relief and no tax refunds are possible.) Once an election has been made, there would be no further income tax charges.

Tax charges on exercise of unapproved share option

8.27   The exercise of an option to acquire employment-related shares or securities is taxed under *ITEPA 2003, s 476*. The income tax charge is based on the excess of the market value of the shares when the option is exercised *over* the amount given for the shares (ie the exercise price) – see 8.34 (Example 3). In an era of 50% super tax rates, directors and employees must consider the timing of any option exercises so as to minimise their income tax liabilities. For example, if may be preferable to exercise an option in a period when the taxable element will only be charged at 40%.

The company must report details of share option exercises to HMRC on Form 42 (see 8.84).

No tax charge arises on the exercise of 'approved' CSOP options [*ITEPA 2003, s 524*] or EMI options (to acquire shares for a price equivalent to their market value when the option is granted) [*ITEPA 2003, s 530*] (see 8.59). Note that the general *CA 2006* rules for share allotments (see 8.10) also apply to the grant of share options.

A UK-resident/ordinarily resident employee does not have any tax charge on the grant of the option itself, irrespective of the option's exercise period [*ITEPA 2003, s 475*]. Where the shares are transferred by an *existing* shareholder, an employment income charge still arises on the director/employee. However, for post-9 April 2003 exercises, *TCGA 1992, s 144ZA* states that the deemed CGT consideration for the transfer (ie both for the transferor and recipient) is the *actual proceeds* (rather than the shares' market value as would normally be the case under *TCGA 1992, s 17* – see 13.10 and 13.39). Any amount subject to an income tax charge on the exercise of the option would then be added to the director's/employee's CGT base cost [*TCGA 1992, s 119A*].

The issues surrounding the base cost for share options exercised before 10 April 2003 is covered in 8.28 below.

Base cost issues arising from Mansworth v Jelley

8.28   Before the decision in *Mansworth v Jelley* [2003] STC 53, the generally accepted treatment for share options was that the *TCGA 1992, s 17* 'market value' rule did not apply to the exercise of the option (see *TCGA 1992, s 149A*). The *transferor shareholder's* CGT consideration and the transferee's deemed acquisition value was the *actual amount paid* for the shares.

The Court of Appeal disagreed with this approach in *Mansworth v Jelley*. In essence, *Mansworth v Jelley* held that the base cost for shares (acquired on the exercise of an option *before* 10 April 2003) is built up as follows:

Market value of shares at date share option was exercised (since it was held that the 'market value' rule in *TCGA 1992, s 17* applied)	X
Add amount charged to income tax (by virtue of the relief given by *TCGA 1992, s 120(4)*)	X
Total base cost	X

The *Mansworth v Jelley* analysis was contrary to the generally accepted position at the time. Before this decision, the Revenue did *not* apply the deemed 'market value' disposal rule to the grantor/transferor of the option when they transferred the shares. It was accepted that the director/employee acquired their shares as the holder of the option (and not in respect of the 'director/ employment' relationship). This meant that the transferor was only taxed on the amount actually received for the shares (on exercise), avoiding the need to make a hold-over election.

Employment income tax charges on the exercise of the option and under the employment-related securities regime would be added to the director's/ employee's CGT base cost [*TCGA 1992, ss 119A, 120, and 149A*].

Many directors and employees have benefited from the *Mansworth v Jelley* ruling, provided they exercised their options before 10 April 2003 (when the previous application of the law was effectively reinstated). The increased CGT base cost under *Mansworth v Jelley* enabled directors/employees to reduce their existing capital gain or realise (additional) capital losses on disposals of shares acquired through the exercise of unapproved share options or approved options that give rise to an income tax charge on exercise – see Example 2 below.

Where tax returns had previously been filed on the basis of the pre-*Mansworth v Jelley* position, it was not always be possible to amend the tax treatment under the prior *TMA 1970, s 33* 'error or mistake' claim legislation. This is because such claims could not be made where the tax return was filed on the basis of the generally accepted understanding of the legislation at that time, as demonstrated in *Monro v HMRC* [2008] STC 1815.

8.29   There is now a further complication. In May 2009, HMRC announced in *Revenue & Customs Brief 30/09*, that it had changed its view of the law in this area, after taking legal advice. HMRC now considers that the base cost of the shares acquired on the exercise of the option is (simply) the market value of the shares. That value is the full measure of their deemed cost of acquisition and it is not further augmented by the relevant amount charged to income tax as was considered to be the case in *Mansworth v Jelley*.

As a result of this revised view, HMRC have indicated that this will affect a number of capital loss claims and those affected by this change 'may' need to make or amend a self assessment return or loss claim (provided they are in time to do so). This change may affect those who acquired shares on the exercise of an option before 10 April 2003 who suffered an income tax charge on acquisition. It does not affect options exercised after 9 April 2003, which are dealt with under the rule in 8.27 above.

HMRC's 'U-turn' has been greeted with considerable criticism from the leading professional bodies. HMRC's potential requirement to amend returns has also caused anxiety. However, most tax advisers take the view that *Mansworth v Jelley*-type capital losses claimed for years in which the enquiry window has closed (and are not otherwise under enquiry) cannot be disturbed. Such losses should therefore be available to set against gains of subsequent years. Arguably, no action should be taken for capital loss claims already made for years potentially, or already, under enquiry, as they would have been completed by reference to the practice prevailing at the time.

Example 2

Impact of *Mansworth v Jelley* adjustments

In 2002/03, Mr Bonds and Mr Goddard exercised their unapproved share options over shares in Boleyn Ltd.

Mr Bonds sold his shares the day after he exercised his option, whereas Mr Goddard sold his shares some ten months later. Following the *Mansworth v Jelley* case, their earlier CGT computations were amended as follows:

	Mr Bonds	*Mr Goddard*
No of shares	1,000	1,000
Exercise date	3 January 2003	3 January 2003
Amount paid on exercise	£1	£1
Value of shares at exercise date	£6	£6
Date shares sold	4 January 2003	31 October 2003
Sale proceeds per share	£6	£10

	Pre-MvJ position £	Post MvJ position £	Pre-MvJ position £	Post-MvJ position £
Amount charged to income tax on exercise				
1,000 × (£6 less £1)	5,000	5,000	5,000	5,000
Capital gain on sale				
Sale proceeds	6,000	6,000	10,000	10,000
Less:				
Amount paid	(1,000)	–	(1,000)	–
Amount charged to income tax	(5,000)	(5,000)	(5,000)	(5,000)
Market value of shares at exercise	N/A	(5,000)	N/A	(5,000)
Capital gain (loss)	Nil	(4,000)	4,000	Nil

Note ; Many taxpayers have filed (or amended their filing) to reflect the *Mansworth v Jelley* analysis with their tax position for the relevant year being 'closed'.

However, in May 2009, HMRC changed its view of the law and now require such CGT computations to be calculated taking *only* the market value of the shares (at the date of exercise) as the base cost of the shares.

Amount received on assignment or release of option

8.30　An employment income tax charge under *ITEPA 2003, s 476* also occurs where the director/employee (see *ITEPA 2003, s 472*) omits to exercise their right to acquire shares under the option or where they grant or assign that right to someone else. The charge is based on the benefit in money or money's worth received in consideration.

The tax charge on any cash received for the assignment or release of an option is collected under the PAYE regime. Otherwise, the application of PAYE depends on whether the relevant shares are a 'readily convertible asset' (see 8.38 and 8.39).

Income tax charges on subsequent chargeable events

Chargeable events

8.31　In broad terms, shares, etc within the 'restricted securities' regime are vulnerable to an income tax charge in the tax year when a subsequent chargeable event occurs, such as where:

- the shares are sold; or
- the restrictions on those shares are lifted or varied [*ITEPA 2003, ss 426, 427*].

This income tax charge only bites if the shares were originally acquired by the director/employee for less than their 'unrestricted' market value – that is the value of the shares ignoring any restrictions attaching to them *or* where a valid *ITEPA 2003, s 431* election is in place to tax them by reference to that value (see 8.32).

If (at least) the unrestricted 'market value' is paid for the shares, then they should just be subject to CGT on their ultimate sale in the usual way.

Such chargeable events must be reported to HMRC on Form 42 (see 8.84).

Section 431 election for initial acquisition to be taxed on unrestricted value

8.32   Where the shares were acquired at less than their 'market value', an election can be made to pay income tax on the difference between *unrestricted market value* of the shares and the amount actually paid for them (see also 8.15 and 8.34 – Example 3). By taking the *unrestricted market value* of the shares, any restrictions are ignored for the purposes of assessing their value, which may produce a higher value than it otherwise would be. This means that the director/employee must either pay:

● an appropriate higher value for their shares; or

● income tax on the 'benefit' received by obtaining the shares for less than that 'unrestricted' amount.

In short, the director/employee must be satisfied that they are either paying the 'unrestricted' market value *or* the tax on the relevant amount. If the valuation is unsound, HMRC could argue that the rules do, in fact, apply.

Clearly, the valuation of a minority shareholding in an unquoted company is a subjective matter, and it is not unusual for the employee/company and HMRC to determine different valuations. The employee may therefore believe that they have paid the proper market price for the shares but HMRC may subsequently succeed in arguing that a higher amount should have been paid for the shares. Provided a *s 431* election has been made, the employee's maximum income tax exposure would be limited to the unrestricted market value of the shares. Without an election, the employee could be exposed to a sizeable income tax liability if the shares have gone up in value significantly (See 8.33).

For example, if the value of the shares on an unrestricted basis is £1 and the employee pays the restricted value of 70p, then in the absence of an election, 30% of all future growth in those shares would be taxed to income tax and not CGT. However, by making a joint election for the director/employee to pay income tax on 30p per share, no further income tax is payable and the entire future growth in the shares would be liable to a lower CGT charge. The election also covers any NIC liability (if the shares are readily convertible assets).

In the majority of cases an election would therefore be beneficial as it removes any future increase in the value of the shares from the (higher) income tax net and into the more favourable CGT regime on their subsequent sale. In turn, this effectively ensures that the normal commercial growth in value of the shares is taxed at the lower effective CGT tax rate. The 'downside' of making the election is that income tax could potentially be paid on acquisition on a value that may never be realised, if the shares subsequently dropped in value.

The *ITEPA 2003, s 431* election needs to be made jointly between the *employer* and *employee* and must be made within 14 days of the acquisition of shares.

Pro-forma elections are available on HMRC's website at http://www.hmrc.gov.uk/shareschemes/s431-1-pe.rtf (a one-part election), or http://www.hmrc.gov.uk/shareschemes/s431-2-pe.rtf (a two-part election).

A copy of HMRC's prescribed joint election under ITEPA 2003, s 431 is reproduced below.

Joint Election under s 431 ITEPA 2003 for full or partial disapplication of Chapter 2 Income Tax (Earnings and Pensions) Act 2003

Two Part Election   *(For this joint election to be valid both Parts A and B must be signed and dated)*

Part A – To be completed by the Employee

1.   Between

the Employee . . . . *[insert name of employee]*

whose National Insurance Number is . . . . *[insert NINO]*

and

the Company (who is the Employee's employer) . . . . *[insert name of company]*

of Company Registration Number . . . . *[insert CRN]*

2.   Purpose of Election

This joint election is made pursuant to section 431(1) or 431(2) Income Tax (Earnings and Pensions) Act 2003 (ITEPA) and applies where employment-related securities, which are restricted securities by reason of section 423 ITEPA, are acquired.

The effect of an election under section 431(1) is that, for the relevant Income Tax and NIC purposes, the employment-related securities and their market value will be treated as if they were not restricted securities and that sections 425 to 430 ITEPA do not apply. An election under section 431(2) will ignore one or more of the restrictions in computing the charge on acquisition. Additional Income Tax will be payable (with PAYE and NIC where the securities are Readily Convertible Assets).

Should the value of the securities fall following the acquisition, it is possible that Income Tax/NIC that would have arisen because of any future chargeable event (in the absence of an election) would have been less than the Income Tax/NIC due by reason of this election. Should this be the case, there is no Income Tax/NIC relief available under Part 7 of ITEPA 2003; nor is it available if the securities acquired are subsequently transferred, forfeited or revert to the original owner.

3. Application

This joint election is made not later than 14 days after the date of acquisition of the securities by the employee and applies to:

Number of securities . . . . *[insert number]*

Description of securities . . . . *[insert description]*

Name of issuer of securities . . . . *[insert name of issuer]*

* acquired by the Employee on . . . . *[insert date]*
* to be acquired by the Employee between *[dd/mm/yyyy]* and *[dd/mm/yyyy]*
* to be acquired by the Employee after *[dd/mm/yyyy]* under the terms of *[insert scheme/plan name]*

(delete as appropriate)*

4. Extent of Application

This election disapplies *(* delete as appropriate)*:

* S.431(1) ITEPA: All restrictions attaching to the securities, or

* S431(2) ITEPA: The following specified restriction : *[details of specified restriction]*

5. Declaration

This election will become irrevocable upon the later of its signing or the acquisition (* and each subsequent acquisition) of employment-related securities to which this election applies.

(delete as appropriate)*

In signing this joint election, I agree to be bound by its terms as stated above.

. . . . /. . . . /. . . . .

Signature of employee   Date

Note: Where the election is in respect of multiple acquisitions, prior to the date of any subsequent acquisition of a security it may be revoked by agreement between the employee and employer in respect of that and any later acquisition.

Joint Election under s 431 for full or partial disapplication of Chapter 2 Income Tax (Earnings and Pensions) Act 2003.

Two Part Election   *(For this joint election to be valid both Parts A and B must be signed and dated)*

Part B – To be completed by the Employer

1.   Between

the Employees, listed on the attached schedule, who have completed **Part A** to this joint election.

and

the Company (who is the Employees' employer) . . . .
[insert name of company]

of Company Registration Number . . . . *[insert CRN]*

2.   Purpose of Election

This joint election is made pursuant to section 431(1) or 431(2) Income Tax (Earnings and Pensions) Act 2003 (ITEPA) and applies where employment-related securities, which are restricted securities by reason of section 423 ITEPA, are acquired.

The effect of an election under section 431(1) is that, for the relevant Income Tax and NIC purposes, the employment-related securities and their market value will be treated as if they were not restricted securities and that sections 425 to 430 ITEPA do not apply. An election under section 431(2) will ignore one or more of the restrictions in computing the charge on acquisition. Additional Income Tax will be payable (with PAYE and NIC where the securities are Readily Convertible Assets).

Should the value of the securities fall following the acquisition, it is possible that Income Tax/NIC that would have arisen because of any future chargeable event (in the absence of an election) would have been less than the Income Tax/NIC due by reason of this election. Should this be the case, there is no Income Tax/NIC relief available under Part 7 of ITEPA 2003; nor is it available if the securities acquired are subsequently transferred, forfeited or revert to the original owner.

---

3. Application

This joint election is made not later than 14 days after the date of acquisition of the securities by the employee and applies to:

Number of securities . . . . *[insert number]*

Description of securities . . . . *[insert description]*

Name of issuer of securities . . . . *[insert name of issuer]*

* acquired by the Employee on . . . . *[insert date]*
* to be acquired by the Employee between *[dd/mm/yyyy]* and *[dd/mm/yyyy]*
* to be acquired by the Employee after *[dd/mm/yyyy]* under the terms of *[insert scheme/plan name]*

(* delete as appropriate)

4. Extent of Application

This election disapplies *(* delete as appropriate)*:

* S.431(1) ITEPA: All restrictions attaching to the securities, or
* S431(2) ITEPA: The following specified restriction :
  [details of specified restriction]

5. Declaration

This election will become irrevocable upon the later of its signing or the acquisition (* and each subsequent acquisition) of employment-related securities to which this election applies.

(* delete as appropriate)

In signing this joint election, we agree to be bound by its terms as stated above.

. . . ./. . . ./. . . . .

Signed for and on behalf of the company . . . . Date

. . . .

Position in company

Note: Where the election is in respect of multiple acquisitions, prior to the date of any subsequent acquisition of a security it may be revoked by agreement between the employee and employer in respect of that and any later acquisition.

Companies normally insist (especially where an 'exit' is envisaged, such as in MBO situations) that an election is always made to avoid any risk of incurring PAYE and NIC liabilities on part of the employees' sale proceeds on a sale of the company (since the shares would become Readily Convertible Assets at that point).

The *s 431* election does not have to be sent to HMRC, but must be carefully retained by the employer in the event of a subsequent HMRC enquiry into the employing company's records. The safe retention by the employer is particularly important given that *s 431* elections may need to be produced at a later date as evidence to resist a potentially large income tax bill.

Calculation of income tax on chargeable event

8.33   If no election is made, an income tax charge would be imposed on the chargeable event under *ITEPA 2003, ss 426–428*, by reference to the following formula:

UMV × (IUP – PCP – OP) – CE

Where:

UMV	=	Unrestricted Market Value at time of chargeable event.
IUP	=	Initial Uncharged Proportion, which is broadly the proportion of the unrestricted market value at the date of acquisition that was *not* charged to income tax.
PCP	=	Previously Charged Proportion, being amounts that have been charged to income tax on a previous chargeable event or events.
OP	=	Outstanding Proportion, being

$$\frac{\text{UMV less AMV}}{\text{UMV}}$$

Where:

UMV is as above and AMV is Actual Market Value *immediately after the chargeable event* taking account of restrictions.

CE	=	Consideration paid by the employee for varying rights, etc and any other expenses.

In the vast majority of cases, the formula will simplify to UMV × IUP. Broadly speaking, this would represent the fractional part of the unrestricted market value that was not charged to income tax (on acquisition) multiplied by the market value of the shares at the time of the event (eg sale proceeds on share sale). Consequently, the amount of sale proceeds, etc that would be subject to income tax would grow in line with any increase in the amount by which the initial unrestricted value of the shares exceeds their restricted value.

A simplified calculation of the tax that would be levied on a chargeable event is given in Example 3 below.

Comprehensive example of option to acquire restricted shares

Example 3

Tax treatment of restricted shares

8.34 On 1 October 2011, Mr Gibson exercises an option to purchase 10,000 £1 B ordinary shares in his employer company, Goalies Ltd, at their par value of £1 each, which represented a 3% equity holding in the company. The B ordinary shares were subject to various restrictions, including the fact that the shares had to be sold back to the company at par on cessation of employment.

Goalies Ltd draws up accounts to 31 December each year.

The value of each B share at 1 October 2011 was as follows:

	Per share
Restricted value	£2
Unrestricted value	£3

No election

Without an *ITEPA 2003, s 431* election, Mr Gibson would have taxable income of £10,000 under *ITEPA 2003, s 476*, being the difference between the restricted market value and the amount actually paid by him, as follows:

	£
Restricted market value – (10,000 × £2)	20,000
Less: Amount paid – (10,000 × £1)	(10,000)
Taxable on exercise of option	10,000

This would mean that Mr Gibson would also suffer an income tax charge based on around a third of the value of the shares on a future 'chargeable event'. Thus, based on the above facts, the amount subject to income tax on a subsequent sale of the shares in (say) December 2012 for £70,000 (when the company was sold and hence the shares become RCAs) would be calculated as follows:

UMV × (IUP – PCP – OP) – CE   Where: UMV $\qquad$ = £ 70,000 (being the sale price)   IUP $\qquad$ = $\dfrac{£30,000 \text{ less } £20,000}{£30,000} = 0.333$ PCP and OP and CE $\qquad$ = 0   Therefore, *ITEPA 2003, s 426* income tax charge: £70,000 × (0.333 – 0 – 0) = £23,334

Thus, assuming Mr Gibson's marginal rate for 2012/13 is 50%, his income tax liability (collected under PAYE) would be £11,667.

He would also incur additional 2% NIC of £233 and the company would suffer NIC of £3,220 (i.e. £23,334 × 13.8%).

Goalies Ltd would be able to claim a corporate tax deduction of £10,000 (during the year ended 31 December 2011 and £23,334 (during the year ended 31 December 2012) (see 8.86 and 8.89).

Mr Gibson's CGT liability on the sale of the shares would be computed as follows:

		£	£
Sale proceeds			70,000
Less:	Cost (October 2011)	(10,000)	
	Amount taxed as income (October 2011)	(10,000)	
	Amount taxed as income (see above)*	(23,334)	(43,334)
Chargeable gain† (subject to annual exemption)			26,666

To prevent 'double taxation', the amount charged as employment income is treated as additional expenditure on the shares for CGT purposes (*TCGA 1992, s 119A*).

† Mr Gibson's 3% holding would not attract any ER.

With election

Mr Gibson could jointly elect with Goalies Ltd (his employer) under *ITEPA 2003, s 431(1)* to be taxed at acquisition on the *unrestricted* value of the shares, as follows:

	£
Unrestricted market value – (10,000 × £3)	30,000
Less: Amount paid – (10,000 × £1)	(10,000)
Taxable on exercise of option	20,000

In this case, Goalies Ltd would be able to claim a corporate tax deduction of £20,000 (during the year ended 31 December 2011).

Although Mr Gibson suffers a higher income tax charge by making the election, any further growth in value of the shares falls completely within the favourable CGT regime. Thus, if the shares were sold for (say) £70,000 in December 2012, his taxable gain would be:

		£	£
Sale proceeds			70,000
Less:	Cost (October 2011)	(10,000)	
	Amount taxed as income (October 2011)	(20,000)	(30,000)
Chargeable gain (subject to annual exemption)			40,000[†]

[†] Mr Gibson's 3% holding would not attract ER.

Sale of shares at more than market value

8.35   Where a director/employee sells their (employment-related) shares, *for more* than market value, *ITEPA 2003, s 446Y (Pt 7, Ch 3D)* imposes an employment income tax charge on the 'excess' amount. For these purposes, the 'market value' concept in *TCGA 1992, s 272* is used – broadly this means the price which the shares might reasonably be expected to fetch on a sale in the open market. Amounts taxed under *ITEPA 2003, s 446X* are treated as a payment of employment income by the company and therefore *subject to PAYE and NIC*.

Implications of the 'Gray's Timber Products' case

8.36   The ambit of these rules have now been considered by the Supreme Court in *Grays Timber Products v HMRC* [2010] UKSC 4.

The main facts were as follows:

- In 1999, Mr Gibson (the managing director of Gray's Timber Products Ltd (Timber)) acquired about 6.5% of the ordinary share capital of Gray's Group Ltd (Group) – Timber's parent company. Group's Articles conferred equal rights on all its ordinary shares.

- At the same time, there was a shareholders agreement (agreed by 83.3% of Company Groups' shareholders) which prevailed over any conflicting provision in its articles of association. Clause 4 of the agreement governed Mr Gibson's share of sale proceeds on any 'sale' of Group. The agreement also specified that Mr Gibson would enter into a service agreement with Group and that he would be appointed director of Timber and Group.

- The agreement provided that, should Group be sold, Mr Gibson's entitlement to the sale consideration would be calculated according to a formula. After two years, Mr Gibson would be entitled to one third of the increase in Group's value since Mr Gibson acquired his shares.

In 2003, Group was sold to a third party with Mr Gibson receiving £1,451,172 (as calculated under the shareholders agreement).

HMRC considered that Mr Gibson was only entitled to a pro-rata share under Group's articles. It followed that he had disposed of his shares for more than their 'market value' (being the (lower) price which the shares would have fetched on a hypothetical sale (under *TCGA 1992, s 272*) as determined under the pro-rata basis laid down in the articles). Consequently, HMRC pressed for income tax under *ITEPA 2003, Pt 7, Ch 3D (s 446X) on the excess of the sale proceeds* on £1,059,687, being the amount by which his actual enhanced proceeds exceeded his pro-rata entitlement of £391,485. (The shares still fell within the employment-related securities regime even though they were acquired in 1999. The Scottish appeal court refused to accept the taxpayer's argument that the market value of the shares was the consideration actually paid by the purchaser. However, there was no evidence for this – for example, the transaction had not attributed any market value to Mr Gibson's shares in particular – and the only evidence was that the entire share capital of Group had been sold for about £6 million. The court therefore concluded that Mr Gibson had sold his shares for more than market value and the excess was taxable as employment income under *ITEPA 2003, s 446X*.

It seems that the Court placed much weight on the link between the terms of the subscription agreement and Mr Gibson's service contract. Nevertheless, the case shows there may be a potential income tax exposure where shareholders receive sale consideration on a disproportionate basis (ie not in proportion to their shareholding ratios).

The Supreme Court upheld the Scottish civil appeal court's decision. Mr Gibson's extra consideration on a sale of their shares, did not increase the 'market value" of their holding. These rights were personal to Mr Gibson and had been granted to him in relation to his service contract. Consequently, the 'personal rights' would not affect the price that a hypothetical purchaser would be willing to pay. They would not be valuable to the 'notional' purchaser and hence those shares were worth the same as the other shares.

Although these rights were contained in a shareholders agreement, the Supreme Court Justices indicated that this would also be the case where these 'personal' rights were enshrined in the Articles. Such rights were 'intrinsic' to the shares and thus income tax was payable on the excess of the (enhanced) sale proceeds over the market value of the shares. The decisive factor was that the rights could not be assigned to the hypothetical purchaser so as to give the enhanced value in their hands. (It was not therefore relevant that the rights were simply contained in a shareholders agreement, as had been concluded by the Special Commissioners and Scottish civil appeal court.)

Arrangements for providing directors with shares giving an enhanced 'exit' value must now be implemented with care. Following the Supreme Court's decision, such enhanced rights must attach to the (class of) shares themselves and should not be personal to the holder of the shares. If the rights attach to the shares then they would be capable of being assigned to a (notional) buyer.

The ruling in the *Grays Timber Products Ltd case* gives a clear warning that any *subsequent* amendments to incorporate changes to a pro-rata apportionment of the sale consideration potentially gives rise to an income tax charge under the post-acquisition benefits rules from employment-related securities in *ITEPA 2003, Pt 7, Ch 3B*. Clearly the treatment of 'excessive' sale consideration will depend on the precise facts of each case. For example, if the excess is a reward for services provided this should be subject to employment income tax via PAYE (with NIC) as a bonus. On the other hand, where the 'excess' is a payment for management taking on any potential claims that could arise from the warranties or indemnities, there might be an argument that this should not be subject to employment income tax.

In *Grays Timber Products Ltd*, the Supreme Court Justices expressed some concern that they were interpreting the 'market value' for *ITEPA 2003 s 446X* purposes in a different manner to the other *ITEPA 2003* provisions relating to restricted securities and shares with artificially depressed values. In such cases personal rights and restrictions *are* factored into the valuation of the shares which leads to some inconsistency in applying the 'market value' provisions for different charging provisions. Lord Wake hoped that 'that Parliament may find time to review the complex and obscure provisions of *Part 7* of *ITEPA 2003*'(!).

Artificial enhancement of shares

8.37 A special income tax charge arises (under *ITEPA 2003, s 446K–P*) where there is a non-commercial increase in the value of 'employment-related' shares. A 'non-commercial' increase includes arrangements motivated by tax or NIC avoidance and non-arm's length transactions between (51%) group members (except a payment for corporate tax group relief).

The employment income tax charge only arises when the market value of the shares at the end of a relevant period (ie the first relevant period being from the date the shares are acquired to the following 5 April and subsequent relevant periods being based on the tax year to 5 April) is at least 10% greater than it would have been but for the 'non-commercial' arrangement. The following formula is used to calculate the tax charge for the relevant tax year.

IMV – MV

Where:

IMV   =   Market value of the shares at the end of the tax year

MV   =   Market value of the shares at the end of the tax year *assuming any non-commercial increase in value of the shares is disregarded*

APPLICATION OF PAYE/NIC ON SHARE SCHEME TAX CHARGES

Readily convertible assets (RCAs)

8.38 Most of the tax charges arising on 'unapproved' share and share option arrangements (as outlined in 8.13–8.35) are based on 'unrealised' gains and the director/employee does not receive any cash to finance the tax liability which often creates difficulties. This can be particularly harsh where the tax has to be paid under the PAYE system (together with National Insurance contributions (NICs). Indeed, since employer's NIC would currently be payable at 12.8% on the chargeable amount (without any restriction), the potential NIC liabilities arising from employee share incentives can be substantial. However, the legislation enables the employing company to pass on the 'employer's NIC' liability on an exercise of a share option (and on other certain chargeable events relating to the shares) – see 8.41–8.44. In most cases, any employee's personal NIC liability should be the relatively modest marginal 2% (given that their other earnings will already have attracted 12% up to the 'upper earnings limit').

A PAYE and NICs charge arises where the relevant shares are subject to an income tax charge and constitute *readily convertible assets*. However, the scope of the *readily convertible assets* definition has been considerably widened for chargeable share transactions occurring after 15 April 2003. Tax charges arising under the 'restricted securities' regime are also subject to PAYE and NIC where the shares are RCAs. The legislation also states that where the shares themselves are not RCAs, but the consideration received for the shares is in the form of an RCA, then the underlying shares will also qualify as RCAs [*ITEPA 2003, s 698*].

8.39   Following *FA 2003*, there are essentially two separate tests for RCA status, only *one* of which needs to be met for the relevant shares to be treated as an RCA. The RCA tests should be reviewed on a regular basis. For example, shares may not be RCAs at the time of an option grant, but circumstances may have changed so that they become RCAs when the shares are acquired on the exercise of the option.

Thus, the shares are treated as RCAs where either:

- **Test 1**: trading arrangements exist (or are likely to come into existence) which can be used to turn the shares into cash. This would include, for example, where an employer has set up a facility to enable employees to sell their unlisted shares to an employee trust or particular individual or where the employee has the benefit of a put option to sell their shares (see 13.36); or

- **Test 2**: the company *cannot* claim a statutory corporation tax deduction for the shares or the relevant chargeable event in relation to the shares (see 8.86–8.89). For *unlisted* owner-managed companies, PAYE and NIC would therefore apply where the director/employee holds shares in a subsidiary company (see 8.88).

8.40   In most cases, PAYE and NIC should *not* therefore have to be accounted for on unlisted shareholdings in private companies. One of the main traps here would be to award employees shares in a subsidiary company, which would cause the shares to be RCAs. In such cases, consideration should be given to providing shares (with special rights only relating to the relevant subsidiary) in the parent company.

Transfer of NIC liability to director/employee

8.41   To avoid a potentially open-ended NIC liability (which must be provided in the accounts under GAAP – see UITF 25), employers and employees can jointly elect to transfer the employer's NIC liability to the employee (see 8.43). In such cases, no NIC liability should appear in the accounts.

Alternatively, the company can enter into a voluntary agreement under which the director/employee agrees to fund all or part of the employer's NICs liability arising on shares. This is less 'clean' from an accounting perspective since a full provision for the liability must still be made in the company's statutory accounts, with the expected NIC reimbursement being included as a separate asset (if the receipt is fairly certain). Only the 'net' charge is shown in the profit and loss account.

Clearly, the company must decide the method of 'passing-on' the employer's NIC before it grants a share option. The transfer of the company's NIC liability to the employee does not affect its corporate tax relief for its share awards and option exercises etc, which can be claimed in the usual way.

8.42 Under the *National Insurance Contributions and Statutory Payments Act 2004 (NICSPA 2004)*, the company can pass under the voluntary agreement any NICs liability on chargeable events arising in relation to share options or on chargeable events arising *after* the director's/employee's acquisition of restricted or convertible securities – for example, on the lifting of a restriction. Principally, these are the charges under *ITEPA 2003, ss 426 and 438*. Model elections can be obtained from HMRC's website.

The company's ability to transfer its NICs does not extend to the charges in *Chapters 3A–Chapter 4* of *ITEPA 2003*. Prior to the passing of *the NICSPA 2004* on 13 May 2004, only NIC charges in relation to share options could be covered by a voluntary agreement.

8.43 Alternatively, both parties may elect (with prior HMRC approval) for part or all of the NIC liability to be transferred to the director/employee. As with a 'voluntary agreement', the election now covers any NIC liability arising from post-acquisition chargeable events in relation to restricted or convertible securities (including the exercise of share options). A model NIC election is available from HMRC.

8.44 In such cases, the individual will be able to set off any additional NICs they pay under such arrangements in calculating the income tax charge arising on the share option gains.

The NIC burden is thus passed on to the director/employee who may need to sell a larger proportion of shares to pay the tax due. The company may also grant options over a greater number of shares to compensate for the additional NIC charge. The cost of the employer's NIC effectively often moves to the shareholders who suffer an additional dilution of the share capital.

Example 4

Tax effect of employer's NIC liability passing to employee

In November 2011, Matthew realised a gain of £250,000 on the exercise of his unapproved share option to acquire 5,000 shares in Etherington Ltd. Matthew had worked for the company for many years as a sales director.

8.45   *Providing shares to employees*

As the option was exercised immediately before the company was sold to Curbishley plc, the shares became RCAs. Thus, the income tax on the share option gain was payable under the PAYE system and also attracted employee's NIC of 2% and employer's NIC of 13.8%.

Matthew had entered into an election with the company to pay the *employer's NIC*. His marginal tax rate for 2011/12 is 50%.

His total tax and NIC liability was calculated as follows:

	£	£
Employer's NIC liability – £250,000 × 13.8%		34,500
Income tax liability (taxed under PAYE)		
Share option gain	250,000	
Less: Employer's NIC	(34,500)	
	215,500 × 50%	107,750
Employee's NIC	250,000 × 2%	5,000
Total PAYE and NIC		147,250

This equates to a combined income tax and NIC charge of 58.9% (£147,250 /£250,000) and illustrates why unapproved share options that are exercised on the sale of a company are not particularly tax efficient, particularly compared with EMI share options (see Example 4 at 8.72).

Reimbursement of PAYE

8.45   A particular tax trap can arise with share options if the amount of PAYE due on the option exercise is high, but the employee's salary is relatively low. There may not be enough monthly salary from which to deduct all the PAYE due, in which case the employer has to account for the tax due. If the employee does not reimburse the employer with the tax due within 90 days, a further tax charge arises under *ITEPA 2003, s 222* when the PAYE tax (not NIC) is treated as additional remuneration. Tax would become due on the 'non-reimbursed' PAYE and interest may also accrue if the tax due under *s 222* is not paid promptly. The employee may be forced to sell at least part of his shareholding to avoid this problem.

The rules of an unapproved share scheme should always provide the employer with the authority to collect tax from participating employees.

The employers' NICs arising on the exercise of share options can be passed to the employee by agreement and deducted against their taxable employment income (see 8.41–8.44 above).

APPROVED SHARE SCHEMES AND PLANS

Overview

8.46   The income tax and NIC charges applied to unapproved share awards and options are generally avoided where employees acquire shares under one of HMRC's approved schemes. Under an approved company share option plan (CSOP), selected 'full-time' employees can only be granted tax-privileged options over up to £30,000 worth of shares, which is relatively modest.

The main benefit of acquiring shares under a CSOP or EMI option (as compared with an unapproved share option/award) is that the tax on the gain between the grant and exercise is deferred until the shares are sold, and is then subject to beneficial CGT rates, typically 28% . Although EMI options are generally restricted to the more risky type of trading companies, EMI share options can be created for significantly higher values (up to the £120,000 market value restriction as compared with £30,000 for a CSOP).

Parent companies

8.47   In the context of a group, it is normal to use the parent company's shares to reward group employees. The legislation only permits shares in a subsidiary to be used, where the parent is *listed*. EMI options can only be granted by a parent company of a qualifying group – no EMI options can be granted in a 51% subsidiary.

Providing employees of subsidiaries with shares in the parent company can cause a conflict, especially where employee relations and involvement are, in the main, the responsibility of the subsidiary company's management. In such a case a 'non-equity' based profit-sharing scheme is likely to be more appropriate as a performance-linked motivation tool.

A group scheme can extend to all companies controlled by the grantor company under an approved share scheme. The legislation also provides that this can include a jointly owned company and any companies controlled by it (see, for example, *ITEPA 2003, Sch 4, para 4* re CSOPs).

ENTERPRISE MANAGEMENT INCENTIVES (EMI) SCHEMES

Background

8.48   The EMI scheme is structured as an option based scheme and is specifically aimed at the smaller 'higher risk' company. It provides greater benefits and is more flexible than a CSOP. In most cases, where directors or employees exercise their EMI options at the market value (on grant), their entire profit on sale will be taxed under the capital gains regime.

EMI options are by far the most popular type of tax-advantaged share scheme. According to recent HMRC Statistics (July 2009), the combined cost to the Treasury of the income tax and NIC relief on EMI option exercises in 2007/08 was £240 million. Over the same period, some 2,830 companies granted EMI options to 26,400 employees.

In a recent survey commissioned by HMRC (reported in February 2008), 92% of employers questioned mentioned that employee retention was the key reason for adopting EMI. Staff motivation and engendering a feeling of ownership were also cited as important benefits. EMI's associated tax advantages were also seen as attractive for employers.

The detailed rules for EMI options are contained in *ITEPA 2003, ss 527–541* and *Sch 5*. However, the *FA 2008* introduced a very important 'total employee restriction from 21 July 2008. This prevents further qualifying EMI options being granted after 20 July 2008 where a company/group has 250 or more employees. However, existing EMI options granted by such companies remain unaffected.

CGT treatment of EMI shares

8.49   The CGT advantages of EMI options were curtailed by the abolition of business taper relief. Under the pre-6 April 2008 regime, there was a beneficial rule that treated EMI option shares as being acquired at the date the option was granted. This generally ensured that gains on EMI shares were taxed at a very beneficial rate of 10%. (For detailed examination of the beneficial CGT treatment of EMI option shares sold before 6 April 2008, please refer to this chapter in the earlier editions of this book.)

Following the *FA 2008* changes, the sale of EMI shares will generally attract CGT at 28% (or 18% to the extent the seller has 'basic rate income tax band' capacity) – most employee shareholders generally hold less than the 5% equity stake required for ER.

However, very small gains will fall within employees' annual CGT exemptions (possibly doubled by arranging for some shares to be transferred through a spouse/civil partner, provided the scheme rules permit).

A number of management/director EMI holdings may carry at least 5% of the voting ordinary shares and may be able to obtain ER. In such cases, they should benefit from the ER CGT 10% rate (up to the £10 million gains threshold). However, they will need to ensure that they are able to hold their shares (post-exercise) for at least for one year before the sale to qualify for the relief. (In contrast to CGT taper relief; there is no equivalent rule that treats the shares as being held from the grant date for ER.) Alternatively, the manager/director may qualify for ER on the basis of holding at least 5% of the voting ordinary shares in their own right (ie separate from their EMI option) for the relevant one year period.

Key advantages of EMI schemes

8.50 Despite the adverse CGT changes, EMI still remains the scheme of choice. In most cases, where directors or employees exercise their EMI options at the market value (at the grant date), their entire profit on sale will be taxed under the capital gains regime. The ability to acquire shares at a later date based on the market value at the earlier grant date without any income tax/ NIC charge still remains a key attraction of EMI (especially since the market value at grant will typically be subject to a significant valuation discount. Technically, ITEPA 2003, s 530 exempts from the normal income tax charging rules the excess of the market value of the shares at the time of exercise over market value at the 'grant' date (sometimes this is referred to as 'EMI relief').

The other key advantages of an EMI scheme for a family or owner-managed company are that:

- the company can obtain a statutory corporation tax deduction on the market value (less any amount paid on exercise) of the shares issued or transferred to satisfy EMI options (even though there is no income tax charge on the employee!). This is a very attractive proposition!;

- the company can choose exactly who receives the options, subject to the 30% 'material interest' barrier;

- the options can be granted conditionally subject to performance criteria;

- the company can decide the exercise price and the option period;

- voting restrictions can be placed over the shares subject to EMI options to protect the owner-managers' position;

- the scheme does not need prior approval from HMRC, but notice of each option grant must be given to HMRC within 92 days of the grant.

A survey on EMI schemes conducted by FDS International Ltd on HMRC's behalf, found that at senior levels and among staff crucial to the company's success, options were considered to be an important commitment valued by the recipient. The potential for a future float or 'exit' was also felt to be an important element in the strategy for implementing an EMI scheme, which reflects my own practical experience. The survey also found that venture capitalists are keen on EMI schemes since they view them as aligning the interests of employees and directors with their own financial ambitions.

According to the survey, implementing an EMI scheme generally involves professional fees of between £5,000 and £10,000. As a general rule, the cost tends to be less economic, the fewer the number of participants.

Example 5

Comparison of EMI share gains under different employee CGT profiles

In January 2008, Red Devils (1958) Ltd granted the following EMI options to three of its key employees:

Employee	Number of Red Devils Ltd shares	Fully diluted % holding
D Edwards	12,000	3%
E Colman	10,000	2.5%
R Byrne	1,000	0.25%

All EMI options were to be exercised on a future sale/flotation of the company (or earlier at the Board's discretion) at their agreed market value of £8 per share (in January 2008).

In September 2011, Red Devils (1958) Ltd was acquired by Matt plc. Immediately before the sale was completed, all three employees exercised their 'January 2008' options.

The agreed sale consideration paid to all the shareholders of Red Devils (1958) Ltd was £15 per share.

The capital gains of the EMI shareholders (assuming they are higher-rate taxpayers) are computed as follows:

	D Edwards £	E Colman £	R Byrne £
Sale proceeds – £15 × 12,000 / 10,000 / 1,000	180,000	150,000	15,000
Less: Cost – £8 × 12,000 / 10,000 / 1,000	(96,000)	(80,000)	(8,000)
Chargeable gain	84,000	70,000	7,000
Less: Annual exemption	(10,600)	(10,600)	(7,000)
Taxable gain	73,400	59,400	–
CGT @ 28%	£20,552	£16,632	

The employees have exercised their EMI options, paying the market value at the date of grant. This means that the entire growth in the value of the shares from grant date falls within the CGT regime. Contrast this with the position if the options had been unapproved. See Example 3 where virtually all the value of the shares at the date of sale is subject to (significantly higher) income tax and NIC.

EMI schemes – summary of main conditions

Purpose and basis of EMI options

8.51   A qualifying option for EMI purposes is one which meets all the requirements of ITEPA 2003, Sch 5.

Options under an EMI scheme will normally be granted by the employing company or its parent company, but existing individual or employee trust shareholders may also offer their shares. No tax charge arises on the grant.

It is possible to build individual performance conditions into each EMI option, which can provide an important incentive tool.

Options can be granted on a conditional basis. Some companies tend to stipulate a period of two or three years before the options can be exercised (under a so-called 'vesting period'), although there is no statutory minimum period.

Individual limit for value of EMI shares under option

8.52   One of the most important requirements is that the value of unexercised EMI option shares (at the date of the option grant) held by any employee cannot exceed £120,000 (£100,000 for options granted before 6 April 2008). Where the EMI option shares are 'restricted', the £120,000 limit is based on the *unrestricted* market value. Thus, when agreeing the market value of (restricted) EMI shares HMRC – Shares & Asset Valuation will seek to agree both the unrestricted market value (UMV) (for this purpose) and the actual market value (AMV) (see 8.62).

It should be noted that where an employee has been granted EMI options worth £120,000 it is not possible to grant any further EMI options within the next three years (even where the initial EMI options have been exercised). Furthermore, the values of any existing CSOP options are also taken into account for the purpose of the £120,000/£100,000 limitation [*ITEPA 2003, Sch 5, para 5*].

However, each director/employee may be awarded a different amount within the £120,000 financial limit. Many EMI option agreements provide that if (following negotiations) the market value of the relevant option shares exceeds the valuation limit (currently £120,000), then it will deem £120,000 worth of option shares as being granted under the EMI regime with the 'excess' amount being *unapproved* share options.

Global £3 million limit for EMI shares under option

8.53   The maximum value of 'unexercised' options over the company's shares must not exceed £3 million. Any option that exceeds this limit when it is granted will not qualify for EMI treatment.

Qualifying ordinary shares and EMI options

8.54   An EMI option must be over (fully paid and irredeemable) ordinary share capital giving a right to a share of profits and must be non-assignable. The shares can be of any class and it is, possible to place restrictions over the shares, for example, limited voting rights to protect the owner-managers' position. It is therefore possible for the EMI shares to be of a separate class, but care must be taken not to make the rights too limited or restricted, given that they must satisfy the 'commercial purpose' test (see 8.58).

Once the EMI options have been granted, ITEPA 2003, s 536(1)(a) provides there must be no alteration to the terms of the option which would cause

- the option to fail one or more of the qualifying EMI conditions in ITEPA 2003, Sch 5 - fairly minor alterations to options would still be caught by this rule (see *CIR v Eurocopy plc* [1991] STC 707); or

- an increase in the market value of the shares under option .

Such alterations would 'trigger' a disqualifying event (see 8.69). Furthermore, where the terms of an option are subsequently altered, there is a risk that this may result in a rescission of the original option with a new 'replacement' one being granted.

Employing companies are completely free to set their own exercise period, but the options must be exercisable (and any relevant conditions must be capable of being satisfied) within ten years to obtain the tax benefits. EMI options are, therefore, more flexible than CSOP options which have a three-year 'waiting period'.

The EMI option agreement must be in writing and specify:

- The date of grant

- A statement that the option qualifies under the EMI rules in ITEPA 2003, Sch 5.

- The number or maximum number of shares that may be acquired under the option

- The price payable or method for determining price

- When and how the option may be exercised

- Any conditions affecting the exercise of the option (such as performance conditions)

- Details of any restrictions that apply to the shares

HMRC accept that the details of restrictions, performance conditions or forfeiture conditions may be contained in another document (such as the articles, share scheme rules, or a shareholders agreement) *attached* to the option agreement and incorporated into it by reference to the document.

An agreement can not be legally binding unless it is entered into for a consideration (even if this is purely nominal). In practice, this issue is overcome by granting the option as a deed which recites all the relevant terms. The option does not qualify as an EMI option unless it is signed and executed.

Employee conditions and material interest test

8.55 Broadly, the employee's 'committed time' (ie spent on the employment) must be at least 25 hours per week or, if less, 75% of his available working time including self-employment. In some business 'start-ups', some EMI option holders will need to be paid at least the national minimum wage to ensure that they are accepted as an employee.

EMI options cannot be granted to an employee if he has (together with associates) at least a 30% equity interest in the company, including unexercised options other than EMI options. Note, that for these purposes, the trustees of most employee benefit trusts are *not* counted as an associate.

Employee headcount restriction

8.56 The *Finance Act 2008* introduced an unpopular restriction which prevented EMI options being granted by a company/group with 250 (equivalent full-time) employees or more. This means that from 21 July 2008 (date of Royal Assent for the *FA 2008*), companies that breach the 250-employee limitation test can no longer grant EMI options. However, any EMI options granted before that date still remain (irrespective of the employee headcount).

Replacement options

8.57 A replacement option granted on a takeover by a qualifying EMI company retains the EMI benefits of the original one (see special rules in *ITEPA 2003, Sch 5, paras 39–43*).

Commercial purpose requirement

8.58   The EMI legislation contains a specific 'commercial purpose' test stating that an option only qualifies if it is granted '… to recruit or retain an employee in a company' and not for tax avoidance [*ITEPA 2003, Sch 5, para 4*]. It appears that, in practice, HMRC accept that almost all EMI schemes have been initiated because of the company's commercial requirements to have some type of equity incentive scheme in place.

Market value versus discounted options

8.59   The company has complete flexibility over the option price set for the EMI option shares. Many companies grant options to acquire the shares at their actual market value *at the date of the grant* (which would reflect the impact of any substantive restrictions). In such cases, there should be no income tax (or NIC) charge when the option is exercised.

It is of course possible for 'discounted options' to be granted under an EMI scheme. The exercise price can therefore be set at a lower amount than market value at the grant date (although it is illegal to issue shares for less than their nominal value) without affecting the qualifying status and tax advantages of the scheme.

8.60   The basic thrust of the EMI regime is to tax the growth in value of the shares from the grant as a capital gain. If the option has been granted at a *discount* to the initial value of the shares, this is taxed as employment income on exercise. If the shares are RCAs, the PAYE and NIC rules outlined above will apply (see 8.38–8.45).

However, the income tax charge on discounted EMI options is based on the amount of the discount, or, if lower, the excess of the market value of the shares at the date of *exercise* over the amount paid for them. This contrasts with the treatment of unapproved share option exercises where the charge is based on the market value at the exercise date. See 8.61 and 8.62 below where shares are 'restricted'.

Restricted EMI shares

8.61   It is possible that the EMI shares may fall within the 'restricted securities' regime. Therefore, the possibility of making a (protective) *ITEPA 2003, s 431* election should still be considered. This would usually avoid any income tax charge arising on the option exercise as a result of any restrictions attaching to the shares and ensure that their future growth in value is entirely within the CGT regime [*ITEPA 2003, ss 476, 530 and 541(2)*].

However, for EMI options exercised after 18 June 2004, the legislation *deems* that an *ITEPA 2003, s 431* election has been made provided no income tax liability arises on the exercise of the option. However, this can only be determined where the value of the shares at the date of grant has been agreed with HMRC – Shares & Asset Valuation and the employee pays that amount on exercise. However, where the valuation has not been agreed, it would be prudent to make an actual *s 431* election when the option is exercised.

Where EMI options were exercised before 14 April 2004, it was necessary to make an actual *s 431* election (as there was no similar 'deeming' provision).

8.62   Where a *discounted* EMI option is granted over 'restricted shares' (see 8.15), they may be vulnerable to a *future* income tax charge on a subsequent sale, etc. However, this risk can be removed by making an *ITEPA 2003, s 431* election to suffer an 'up-front' income tax charge on the exercise (after 15 April 2003) based on the *unrestricted* value of the shares (at the date of grant or, if lower, at the exercise date). The election would also cover any income tax arising on a disqualifying event (see 8.69).

Qualifying company – independence requirement

8.63   A company will only be a qualifying 'EMI company' if it satisfies certain conditions which are designed to ensure that only small independent 'higher risk' companies qualify.

A company will meet the 'independence requirement' provided it is not a '51% subsidiary' of another company *or* under the control of another company *and* persons connected with that company within ITEPA 2003, s 719 and hence ITA 2007, s 995, *s 1124 (ICTA 1988, s 840)*.

For these purposes,

- a company is a 51% subsidiary if more than 50% of its share capital is owned directly or indirectly by another company [*CTA 2010, s 1154 (ICTA 1988, s 838)*];

- control is defined in terms of being able to conduct the affairs of the company through the holding of share capital, voting rights, or other powers contained in the company's articles of association or other document (such as a shareholders' agreement). Connected persons are defined in s993, ITA 2007 by s718, ITEPA 2003.

This rule is extended to cases which prevents valid EMI option grants where there are arrangements in existence for the company to become under the control of another. This can be problematic where a company is seeking to implement EMI scheme and, at around the same time, the directors are about to enter into negotiations for a sale of the company. While it is not always possible to control the timing of these events, the company should ensure its

EMI options are granted (well) before it enters into 'heads of agreement'. Of course, if there is an impending sale, HMRC – Shares and Assets Valuation will argue for a considerably higher value on the EMI shares.

Care should also be taken if a limited partnership controls the company (which is often the case with a private equity structure). In such cases, there is likely to be a corporate partner of the limited partnership (often the general partner) and all partners of a partnership are connected. This means that the independence requirement is frequently failed since the relevant company would normally be under the control of a company (the corporate partner) and other partners (persons connected with that company).

Where the shares in a company are held equally by (say) two joint venture shareholders (on a 50%:50% basis), HMRC will often contend that it fails the 'independence test'. The argument would run that the company's corporate shareholders are 'acting together' and thus the company is under the control of a company and *persons* connected with the company.

Qualifying company – gross assets and 'subsidiary company' tests

8.64   For a singleton company seeking to use the EMI scheme, the gross asset value shown in its balance sheet (according to UK GAAP) must not exceed £30 million (£15 million for options granted before 1 January 2002). In the case of a (51%) group, the £30 million/£15 million tests are tested against the aggregate gross assets for the entire group. This calculation would include purchased goodwill but would exclude any goodwill arising on consolidation. [*ITEPA 2003, Sch 5, paras 9–12*].

An 'EMI company' may have 'qualifying' subsidiary companies. For options granted after 16 March 2004, any subsidiary must be at least 51% (directly or indirectly) owned by the grantor company, subject to an exception for a property management subsidiary which must be 90% owned. (For these purposes, a property management subsidiary is one whose business consists wholly or mainly in the holding of land or property) [*ITEPA 2003, Sch 5, paras 11–11B*].

The 51% qualifying subsidiary requirement may prevent EMI options being available where the issuing company holds shares in a joint venture company which it controls, either on its own or with a connected person (applying the *CTA 2010, s 450* (ICTA 1988 s416) definition of control) but does *not* own more than 50% of its shares.

For pre-17 March 2004 option grants, the legislation requires any subsidiaries to be at least 75% owned.

Qualifying trades

8.65   The grantor company must also carry on a 'qualifying trade'. Most trades should qualify but the definition is defined negatively so as to prevent prohibited 'low-risk' activities in a similar way as for Enterprise Investment Scheme and Venture Capital Trust companies (see 11.28).

The *F(No 2)A 2010* now requires that companies must simply have a permanent establishment in the UK – this broadly means that they must be carrying on a UK trade in the UK. This change was made to bring the EMI legislation in line with EU state aid guidelines. Previously a company had to be carrying on its trade wholly or mainly in the UK. It is therefore possible for an overseas company to grant EMI options where it has a permanent establishment in the UK (although most of its trade is carried on abroad).

Furthermore, the company's activities must *not* consist substantially (ie more than 20%) in the carrying on of 'excluded activities' such as dealing in land or shares, banking, leasing, receiving licence fees or royalties, legal and accountancy, property development, farming, and operating and managing hotels and nursing homes. Shipbuilding, producing coal and producing steel were also excluded by the *FA 2008* (to comply with EU State Aid directives).

High tech and E-commerce companies should be assisted by the special 'let-out' rule that enables a company to be an EMI company where it receives royalties and licence fees from the exploitation of 'internally created' intellectual property.

Groups of companies

8.66   Where the company is a parent company of a group, all its subsidiaries must be at least 50% owned (as to shares, votes, assets and beneficial entitlement to profits). The £30 million (£15 million for pre-1 January 2002 options) gross asset limit is based on the combined balance sheet value of the group's assets (ie ignoring shares in group companies) (see 8.64). Furthermore, the group's business, taken as a whole, must not substantially consist of non-qualifying activities and at least one member of the group must satisfy the 'qualifying trade' test in its own right.

Valuation and notification procedure

8.67   The (unquoted) owner-managed company will clearly need to value the relevant shares at the date of grant to determine whether the £120,000 (£100,000 for pre-6 April 2008 option grants) limit has been met (based on the unrestricted value) and whether any discount element (based on the restricted value) is subsequently liable to tax on exercise.

8.68 *Providing shares to employees*

An unquoted company is often valued on an appropriate multiple of its maintainable (post-tax) earnings with the pro-rata amount attributed to the shares being discounted for their minority status and any inherent restrictions (see Chapter 14). The share value must be agreed with HMRC – Shares & Asset Valuation, which will normally give such cases priority for agreement.

8.68   The EMI option is subject to a 'self-assessment' style notification and declaration process. A notice of each option grant must be submitted on Form EMI 1 within 92 days of the grant for each employee. This contains a signed declaration from a director or secretary of the *employing* company confirming that EMI rules are satisfied and the employee must also 'sign off' on the 'working time' commitment condition. (There is no longer any requirement to submit the relevant option agreement). The Form EMI 1 notification process is very important since failure to give the relevant notice within the 92-day period, will render its qualifying EMI status invalid.

Individual option agreements should contain details of any restrictions attaching to the option – where there is doubt as to whether any particular provision constitutes a restriction it is prudent to include it as HMRC have been known to challenge the validity of options where they do not contain full details of all terms attaching to them. Where the exercisable option shares are subject to a formula (often linked to the value realised for the company/business on a 'exit' event), the option agreement must specify the maximum number of EMI option shares [*ITEPA 2003, Sch 5, para 37 (1)(2)*].

It is still worthwhile devising a standard set of scheme rules governing its operation to demonstrate a level 'playing field' between employees.

HMRC are entitled to make an enquiry into the Form EMI 1 notification within 12 months of the end of the 92-day notice period. If no enquiry notice is issued, it can be assumed that the scheme has met the relevant EMI scheme requirements.

Where HMRC wishes to enquire into the eligibility of the EMI scheme, this will be concluded by a closure notice, which will give HMRC's decision as to whether the relevant EMI requirements have been met. Any 'negative' notice can be appealed within 30 days.

It is possible for companies to seek an informal clearance in advance to obtain comfort that their proposed options satisfy the relevant legislative requirements by writing to

Small Company Enterprise Centre
H M Revenue & Customs
1st floor
Castle Meadow Road
Nottingham NG2 1BB
Email: www.hmrc.gov.uk/shareschemes/to-nottingham.htm

Further ongoing annual EMI reporting (notifying EMI option exercises, disqualifying events, replacement EMI options etc) is made on Form EMI 40, which is due by the 7 July following the end of the relevant tax year.

Impact of disqualifying events

8.69 If one of the relevant EMI conditions is broken (referred to as a 'disqualifying event') during the life of the option, the employee must exercise it within 40 days to retain his EMI benefits (ie no tax charge on the increase over grant value). A disqualifying event will be triggered, for example, if the company ceases to be independent or meet the 'qualifying trade' test or the employee ceases to work for the company, etc.

Some EMI schemes permit employees to exercise their EMI option within the 40 day period, although there are a number which do not, which will normally be disadvantageous to the employee.

Failing to exercise the option within the 40-day period will render the employee liable to an (additional) income tax charge on the growth in value of the shares between the disqualifying event and option exercise [*ITEPA 2003, ss 532–536*].

Example 6

Tax treatment of disqualifying event (on a 'discounted' EMI option)

In December 2006, Eggbertsson Ltd granted a discounted EMI option for 20,000 £1 shares (representing a 4% holding in the company) to one of its key employees, Mr Tevez. The option exercise price was 10p per share and the market value of the option shares at that time was £4 per share. The EMI option could only be exercised on a future sale of Eggbertson Ltd and there were no provisions enabling the option to be exercised as a result of a 'disqualifying event'.

Mr Tevez decided to leave the company in June 2008 (when the option shares were worth £12 each) and the company was sold in December 2009 for £19 per share.

Under the terms of the EMI scheme, Mr Tevez could only exercise his option when the company was sold in December 2009.

His tax position would be as follows:

- Employment income tax on the 'discount' element of the option (*ITEPA s 476; ITEPA 2003*) – £78,00 (being the excess of the market value of his shares in December 2006 (£80,000 less £2,000 (10p × 20,000))

- Employment income tax on £140,000 – £380,000 (£19 × 20,000) less £240,000 (£12 × 20,000). This represents the increase in the value of the

371

shares after the disqualifying event in June 2008 (when he left the company) up to the 'exercise' date in December 2009 (*ITEPA s 476; ITEPA 2003*).

Mr Tevez's capital gain is £160,000 – this reflects the uplift in the value of his shares between the grant date and time of the disqualifying event, being based on the excess of £240,000 (£12 × 20,000) over £80,000 (£4 × 20,000). The capital gain on sale does *not* qualify for ER.

A graphical summary of the amount subject to income tax and CGT *for each share* is illustrated below.

Discounted EMI option – rising share price

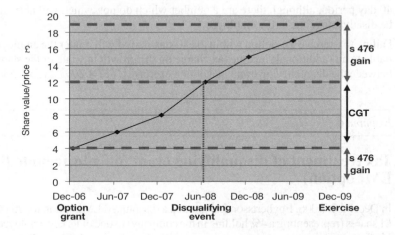

Sale of EMI shares

8.70   Employees are only likely to exercise their options if the value of their 'employing' company or group has increased and they can realise some of that value by exercising their option. Clearly, the employees of a family or owner-managed company would hope to realise substantial value on a sale or flotation. Other available exit routes would be a sale to another shareholder, employee trust, or sale back to the company, but these may be at discounted minority values.

Many EMI options are 'exit-based', which broadly means that they are only exercisable in the event of a company sale or float. Given that the 'value' of the EMI option shares attracts a statutory corporate tax deduction under *CTA 2009, Chapter 12, Part 2* (see 8.86), it is important to recognise that this will enhance the company's net asset value on sale.

One particular trap to watch here is where the company is about to be sold to an *unlisted* company. If the EMI options are exercised immediately after the *unlisted* purchaser obtains control of the company, it will not obtain its tax relief for the EMI options (as it will then become a subsidiary of an unlisted company – see 8.88). Thus, when designing such EMI option agreements, it will normally be preferable (subject to other considerations) for the options to be exercisable just before a 'change in control' of the company – possibly on receipt of the formal offer. This can be a delicate issue since this often means that EMI option holders will need to become privy to the knowledge of an impending takeover.

Graphical overview of EMI tax treatment

8.71 The basic EMI model shows that all the post-grant growth in the value of the shares falls within the CGT regime (and will frequently attract the relatively low CGT rate of 28% (or lower in certain cases, eg where ER is available)), as illustrated in the graph below (assuming the employee exercises their option for an amount based on the market value is of the shares at the date of grant).

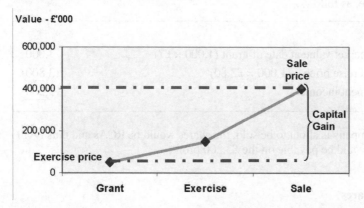

Comprehensive example of 'exit-based' discounted EMI options

8.72 A worked example showing the EMI tax treatment of a 'discounted' exercise and subsequent sale of the shares is given in Example 7 below.

Example 7

EMI share option granted at a discount and sale of company

David is the financial director of Goalkeepers Ltd. On 18 August 2005, he was granted an EMI option to acquire 1,000 £1 ordinary shares (representing a 2% stake) in the company at £3.80 per share exercisable at any time within ten years. The actual market value of the shares at that time was agreed at £7 per share.

In December 2011, assume an offer is made to acquire the entire share capital of Goalkeepers Ltd and David exercises his option. (Since this is a 'discounted' option, David enters into a joint s 431 election when he exercises his option to ensure that all subsequent gains are subject to capital gains tax.)

The company is subsequently sold in January 2012 with David receiving £200,000 for his shares.

Exercise of option

David will have an employment income tax liability when he exercises his EMI option in December 2011 as he acquired the shares at a discount on their grant value, as follows:

	£
Actual market value at date of grant (1,000 × £7)	7,000
Less: Exercise price – (1,000 × £3.80)	(3,800)
Employment income	3,200

As the company is about to be sold, the shares would be RCAs and thus PAYE and NIC would be payable on the £3,200 profit.

Sale of shares

David's capital gain arising on the sale in January 2012 is likely to be calculated as follows:

	£	£
Sale proceeds		200,000
Less: Base cost	(3,800)	
Taxable 'discount' element	(3,200)	(7,000)
Capital gain		193,000
Less: Annual exemption		(10,600)
Taxable gain		182,400
CGT @ 28%		£51,072

Note: If David had been granted an *unapproved* option (on the basis that an *ITEPA 2003, s 431* election was made), he would have been subject to an income tax charge on the *current unrestricted value* of his shares (less £3,800 exercise price) on the December 2011 exercise. Only the small increase to the full January 2012 sale value of £200,000 would be taxed as a capital gain.

COMPANY SHARE OPTION PLANS (CSOPS)

Benefits of CSOPs

8.73   This is commonly known as the company share option plan (CSOP) (also referred to as an executive share option scheme or a discretionary share option scheme). CSOPs are available for use by all companies regardless of type of trade or size. The relevant CSOP legislation is contained in *ITEPA 2003, ss 521–526* and *Sch 4*. (The *FA 2010* contained restrictions preventing CSOP options being granted in subsidiaries of *listed* companies (to prevent the use of 'growth' share schemes). However, these have no impact on owner-managed companies and are not considered further here.)

Given that the CGT rate no longer depends on the period over which shares (or EMI options) have been held, there is some renewed interest in CSOP schemes. CSOP schemes may be a useful method of providing equity for employees (up to the maximum value of £30,000 per employee) where the circumstances do not permit a valid EMI scheme. However, CSOP options can only be exercised after three years from the date of grant. CSOPs that are currently in place may continue alongside an EMI scheme, although the monetary limits of share options per employee will apply across both schemes (see 8.52).

A properly structured CSOP brings a number of benefits to an owner-managed company (particularly if its share ownership is already widely dispersed). Key advantages include:

- enabling employees to enjoy a share of the 'exit' value on sale or flotation;

- attracting key personnel with options granted on a selective basis, where the £30,000 monetary limit is not a problem;

- providing golden-handcuffs on existing key personnel with options granted on a selective basis;

- ensuring flexibility, with participants not being locked in;

- increasing productivity and efficiency;

- creating an awareness that the company's success is closely linked to an employee's personal wealth.

Basic mechanics

8.74   Selected employees are granted an option to purchase shares at a later date, but with the price fixed at the outset – typically at their market value when the option was granted. Any executive owning not more than 25% (10% before 9 April 2003) of the voting rights (with associates) can be granted an option. The 'grant' value of shares under option to each employee cannot exceed £30,000.

To claim CGT treatment on selling the shares, and with no income tax liability on exercising the option, the options must be exercised between three and ten years after the grant. Unapproved CSOP options exercised within three years of their grant date give rise to an income tax liability, based on the *excess* of the market value of the shares less their exercise price. Where the shares constitute a 'readily convertible asset' (see 8.38), income tax would be paid under the PAYE regime along with NICs.

Under current rules, CSOP options can still be exercised on an 'approved' basis (ie without triggering an income tax charge) *within* three years of an earlier 'approved' exercise, provided this is between the third and tenth anniversary of the original grant date. This means that all CSOP options gain 'approved' status after three years. (Before 9 April 2003, approved CSOP options could not be exercised more frequently than once every three years).

'Good leavers' can exercise their CSOP options on an approved basis within three years of the original grant date provided they exercise them within six months of leaving their employment [*ITEPA 2003, s 524*].

Income tax charge on discounted CSOP options

8.75   An income tax and NIC charge can also arise on discounted options, ie where the option price (often fixed at a nominal amount) plus the exercise price are less than the market value on the date the option is granted. This employment income charge arises in the tax year of grant [*ITEPA 2003, s 526*]. Approved CSOPs are now caught by the 'restricted securities' rules (see 8.14).

For example, a tax charge would arise where a CSOP option is granted for £1 per share with the right to exercise at £5 per share and a market value on grant of £8 per share. In this case, an income tax charge arises on £2 per share (ie £8 per share *less* £1 per share plus £5 per share). However, if the option exercise price of £5 per share is regarded as manifestly less than £8, the scheme would not, in any event, be an approved CSOP.

Performance conditions

8.76   The options can be performance related in that they are not able to be exercised unless the company and/or executive has met specified targets (see

CIR v Burton Group plc [1990] STC 242). Measuring this by reference to the share price is clearly a problem with a private company and, in general terms, a performance related trigger may not be appropriate.

SAYE SHARE OPTION SCHEMES

8.77   Sometimes known as 'sharesave', the scheme uses SAYE contracts and is open to all employees. The scheme can be used in conjunction with an EMI scheme (see 8.48–8.72) or share incentive plan (see 8.78).

The scheme can be useful for:

- making regular savings of up to £250 per month with the added attraction of an income tax-free profit if the company is successful (although the cost to the employee comes out of after-tax earnings);

- enabling the company to receive proceeds of SAYE contracts as an injection in the form of additional share capital rather than paying cash out;

- companies who do not mind widely dispersed employee share ownership;

- achieving a bonus after three years to uplift the total profit, and then acquiring shares at a 20% discount.

SHARE INCENTIVE PLANS (SIPS)

Basic workings of an SIP

8.78   Share incentive plans (SIPs) (previously known as All Employee Share Ownership Plans (AESOPs)) have not enjoyed the same level of success as EMI schemes – this is probably because they are quite complex to understand. The amount of free shares that can be given to individual employees is relatively low and they would involve considerable administration for a reasonably sized workforce. SIPs have, therefore, mainly been used by quoted companies.

An SIP must (subject to the 25% 'material interest' prohibition – see 8.5) be open to all employees on the same basis, but the company can impose a qualifying service period of up to 18 months. An SIP would involve the creation of a trust from which shares are appropriated to employees [*ITEPA 2003, ss 488–515 and Sch 2 (FA 2000, Sch 8)*].

8.79   The maximum value of shares that can be appropriated to one employee *in a tax year* is £7,500, split across the following categories:

(*a*)   free shares gifted by the company: £3,000;

(*b*)   partnership shares purchased by employees: £1,500; and

(*c*)   matching shares allocated in proportion to partnership shares: £3,000.

If the shares are held in the trust for five years after appropriation, there is no income tax charge on withdrawal. Withdrawals made within three years of appropriation generate an employment income tax charge based on the market value of the shares at that time. Withdrawals made between three and five years after appropriation create an income tax charge on the lower of the share value at appropriation and the value at the date of withdrawal.

Corporation tax relief is available for the cost of free or matching 'SIP-shares' under *CTA 2009, ss 983–998*. However, the *FA 2010* introduced special anti-avoidance provisions to prevent SIP schemes being created largely with the view to generating large corporation tax deductions. (Where the value of the shares is then artificially reduced rather than being passed to employees.) Broadly, HMRC can deny relief will be denied where the SIP contribution is mainly motivated by tax avoidance arrangements.

Advantages of an SIP

8.80   The potential advantages for a family or owner-managed company of an SIP may include:

- allocation of free shares on the basis of employee performance;

- tax and NIC saving on salary paid as free shares or used to purchase partnership shares;

- golden handcuffs for employees as shares may be forfeited on termination of employment;

- corporation tax deduction for all set-up and operating costs of the scheme plus the market value of all free and matching shares allocated;

- promoting the employees' interest in the company and generating a feeling of involvement in the business.

Administrative issues

8.81–8.83   As noted above, SIPs tend to involve a considerable level of administration for the comparatively small tax benefits offered. Many family and owner-managed companies have found that it is easier to use the Enterprise Management Incentive (EMI) scheme, particularly now that EMI options can be offered to an unlimited number of employees.

A fast-track approval procedure has been set up to allow companies to implement an SIP without delay.

EMPLOYEE SHARE REPORTING TO HMRC

Form 42

8.84   HMRC is now stringently enforcing the annual reporting requirements for unapproved share arrangements for directors and employees. All relevant events must be reported, regardless of whether any tax charge arises. Clearly, HMRC will use this information to ensure that directors/employees report and pay the correct amount of tax under self-assessment. HMRC place significant importance on having a robust reporting procedure for reporting value passing to directors/employees through share-related benefits.

The main events required to be reported on form 42 (pictured below) include:

- the acquisition of shares or securities, including shares/securities acquired on the exercise of an option;

- the grant of an option (including EMI options granted over shares worth more than £120,000);

- chargeable events under the 'restricted securities' regime;

- artificial enhancement of value of shares/securities; and

- assignment or release of an option.

The 'employer' company normally reports the relevant events on IR form 42. However, this obligation also extends to any issuer or provider of the shares (such as an employee share trust). The relevant details can also be submitted to HMRC by letter or spreadsheet, where this is more convenient.

Since 6 April 2005, the acquisition of initial subscriber shares or 'founder shares' in new UK incorporated companies will not need to be reported provided the following conditions are met:

- all the initial subscriber shares are acquired at their nominal value;

- the shares are not acquired by reason of another employment; and

- the shares are acquired by a person who is a director or prospective director of the company (or someone who has a personal family relationship with the director and the right is made available in the normal course of the domestic, family or personal relationship with that director).

There are separate reporting requirements for shares acquired under Revenue approved schemes, such as a CSOP (see 8.73) or an SAYE scheme (see 8.77). Shares acquired on the exercise of a qualifying EMI option are reported on Form EMI 40.

Reporting deadlines and penalties

8.85 The form 42 or spreadsheet/letter alternative must be submitted on 7 July following the end of the relevant tax year (or, if later, within 30 days from the date the form is issued). For example, for the year ended 5 April 2011, the form must normally be submitted by 7 July 2011.

Severe penalties can be levied for unreported events or events reported late. (Each share option grant or exercise could be an 'event' for this purpose.) In the case of unapproved share arrangements, penalties of £300 can be imposed for *each* event not reported with a £60 penalty for *each* day the event is reported 'late'.

CORPORATE TAX DEDUCTION FOR 'DIRECTOR/ EMPLOYEE' SHARE AWARDS OR OPTIONS

Basic rules

8.86 Companies can claim a corporate tax deduction for shares provided to their directors and employees. Broadly speaking, the company obtains relief on the amount charged to income tax in the hands of the recipient director/ employee.

A tax deduction is still available where the legislation specifically exempts the shares from an income tax charge, such as in the case of options exercised under an EMI scheme. In such cases, the relief equates to the amount that would otherwise have attracted income tax. Once the shares or options are relieved under these rules, relief cannot be claimed under any other provision.

Some unlisted companies may apply FRS 20, which requires the 'economic cost' of share awards and share options granted to employees (and others) to be recognised as an expense through the profit and loss account. Those 'smaller' companies adopting the FRSSE (Financial Reporting Standard For Smaller Entities) do not have to apply this treatment.

Where the company adopts FRS 20 and charges the profit and loss account with the value of shares/options provided to employees, the relevant 'accounting' charge will need to be adjusted for and replaced by the relevant statutory tax relief under (what is now) *CTA 2009, Chapter 12, Part 2* .

Before the statutory deduction rules were introduced in *FA 2003*, companies could only obtain relief by making contributions to Employee benefit trusts (EBTs) BTs under so-called 'tax symmetry' arrangements. This was because up until recently a 'share option' gain or a share issue did not produce a profit and loss account charge under normal accounting principles. The EBT then subscribed for the relevant shares, which were subsequently awarded to the employees.

Corporate tax relief can be obtained for expenses involved in running the share scheme under normal 'trading deduction' principles.

Main conditions for corporate tax relief

8.87   Corporate tax relief is given where an individual, by reason of their (or another person's) office or employment:

- is awarded shares or an interest in such shares (for example, as a gift or purchase at under-value); or

- acquires shares by exercising a share option; and

- suffers a charge to income tax charge on the shares [*CTA 2009, s 1007*].

Similarly, relief is given on the amount of any income tax charges that arise under the 'restricted securities' or convertible shares regimes [*CTA 2009, ss 1018, 1019, 1025 and 1030*].

Tax relief can still be claimed where directors/employees do not suffer an income tax charge because either:

- their shares are protected by a statutory exemption from income tax, such as share options granted under CSOPs, an EMI scheme and sharesave option plans; or

- they are not resident and ordinarily resident in the UK.

In the case of an EMI scheme, the corporate tax deduction is given on the full amount of any discount (which would be taxed on the employee) and the amount of tax 'relief' given under the EMI scheme (being the increase in the value of the option shares from the date of the *option grant* to the date of exercise) [*CTA 2009, s 1019(2)(b),(3)(b)*].

Relief is only available where the shares are awarded or options are granted for the purposes of the employing company's business (which must be within the charge to corporation tax). As long as this 'business purpose' test is satisfied it should be possible for relief to be claimed where an employee acquires shares after they have left the employment.

Qualifying shares

8.88   Relief is only available for 'qualifying shares', which must be non-redeemable and fully-paid. For *unlisted* companies, such as owner-managed companies, the shares must be in either:

- an independent company (ie one which is not under the control of another company) (see 8.70 for potential problems with 'exit-based' EMI options); or

- a 'non-close' company that is under the control of a *listed* company [*CTA 2009, s 1008*].

An important practical effect of this restriction is that relief is denied on employee share awards/exercises in a subsidiary of a private company.

There are no restrictions where shares are held in a listed company.

The shares must be issued by the:

(*a*)   employing company; or

(*b*)   its parent company; or

(*c*)   a consortium member that owns either (*a*) or (*b*); or

(*d*)   a fellow 'consortium member' of (*a*) or (*b*) that is part of the same commercial association of companies of the consortium-owned company [*CTA 2009, ss 1008(1)(2)* and *1016 (1)(2)*].

Mechanics of relief

8.89   The relief is broadly calculated as follows:

Market value of shares at time shares are transferred or option exercised	x
Less: Consideration paid by employee	(x)
Corporate tax deduction	x

Clearly, the total tax deduction will be the aggregate of all the above calculations for each employee. The way in which the relief is computed does not require that shares must come from the company – relief can still be claimed, for example, on shares transferred from a controlling shareholder, EBT or an employee share ownership trust.

Example 8

Statutory corporate tax relief for employee shares

Using the figures set out in Example 3 at 8.34, Goalies Ltd can claim corporate tax deductions as shown below.

Accounting period – year ended	Event	Corporate tax relief	
		With no *s 431* election	With *s 431* election
		£	£
31 December 2011	Exercise of option	10,000	20,000
31 December 2012	Sale	23,334	–

Special rules apply to reduce the company's relief for any amount that has been claimed under the previous system, such as where shares have been transferred from an EBT to which tax-deductible contributions had been made (see 8.9A).

In most cases, relief will be claimed as a trading deduction where the shares were awarded or options granted for the purpose of the relevant business. Relief is generally given in the accounting period in which the recipient beneficially acquires the shares or exercises their share option.

The legislation allows the relief to be apportioned on a 'just and reasonable' basis between various businesses where the shares are awarded or options granted for the purposes of those businesses. This rule may apply where, for example, a parent company of a large group of companies grants options over its shares to employees of a subsidiary company with the primary aim of providing incentives to increase shareholder value as well as developing its subsidiary's trade.

Special rules were introduced in the *FA 2010* to counter artificial tax avoidance structures which used SIPs to generate a corporation tax deduction (see 8.79). Typically, this involved a company making a contribution to the SIP to enable it to buy shares from an existing shareholder but with no meaningful provision of shares being made available to its employees. From 22 March 2010, companies will be denied tax relief where this was the main purpose of making the payment to the SIP.

Where, on a takeover, a company's share options are 'rolled-over' into options over the acquiring company's shares, tax relief can still be claimed in the original company for whose business the options were previously granted [*CTA 2009, s 1022*].

PLANNING CHECKLIST – EMPLOYEE SHARE SCHEMES AND PLANS

Company

- Consider limiting shares in employee share schemes to, say, 10% of ordinary share capital.

- Watch out for potential share option exercises diluting existing shareholders below critical tax shareholding requirements, such as the 5% ordinary voting share requirement for ER which is tested throughout the year before a sale.

- Ensure that statutory corporation tax relief is claimed on all shares awarded or share options exercised. Such relief can be claimed on both unapproved and approved (for example, EMI) share schemes.

- In the context of a 'private' corporate group, ensure that employee shares are issued in the parent company to avoid 'loss' of corporate tax relief (and prevent shares being liable to PAYE and NIC as readily convertible assets).

- Consider using an EBT, employee trust or a company purchase of own shares where an 'internal' exit route is required for outgoing employee shareholders.

- Where employee shares are to be provided by an EBT or employee trust, carefully check whether the arrangements are exempted under the 'disguised remuneration' legislation.

- An EMI scheme is likely to be most attractive for key or, in some cases, all employees. A CSOP may prove useful where the company does not have qualifying status for EMI.

- On 'exit-based' EMI options, consider the impact of the enhancement in the company's net asset value as a result of corporate tax relief being claimed on the value of the relevant EMI share option exercises.

- Ensure all relevant share acquisitions and other relevant 'chargeable events' are reported on form 42 (or by letter/spreadsheet format).

Working shareholders

- It is arguable that fairly 'straightforward' shareholdings in private companies are unlikely to be restricted. However, given the uncertainty and the potential income tax exposure that exists with restricted shares, it is normally worth making a protective *s 431* election to ensure that the shares only attract CGT on a future sale.

- Provided there are valid commercial reasons, it may be beneficial to sell some shares to an EBT (subject to the possibility of a *ITA 2007, s 684* challenge).

- Consider advantages offered by EMI share option scheme for favourable capital gains treatment (ensure that 30% 'material interest' test is not breached.

- Where directors/employees hold at least 5% of the (voting) ordinary shares, they should be able to benefit from the lower ER CGT rate of 10% on their gains. However, where they have share options, the options would need to be exercised at least one year before any sale to meet the 'one year' minimum holding period required by the ER legislation. Some employees may find it difficult to fund the purchase consideration far in advance of a sale.

- In the majority of cases, directors/employees will be unable to qualify for ER. Where their gains fall within the annual CGT exemption, they will be tax-free. Larger gains are likely to be taxed at the top 28% CGT rate.

- Take advice on whether to enter into an agreement or election to bear the employer's NIC liability arising on a share option.

Other employees

- Other employees generally have the same issues as working shareholders.

- Look upon a share option scheme as a possible means of obtaining a lump sum on flotation or take-over as a 'bonus' that may or may not occur.

Non-working shareholders

- Balance the advantages of share schemes used as incentive device for employees with the dilution of shareholders' funds.

Chapter 9

Distribution of profits and dividend planning

INTRODUCTION

9.1   Owner-managed companies may need to pay dividends for a number of reasons. Where the company is subject to the small profits' tax rate, dividends are likely to provide a particularly tax-efficient way of extracting profits for the working shareholders, as illustrated at 2.12–2.16. However, since 6 April 2010, dividends for those with taxable income of £150,000 plus, are taxed at 42.5% on the gross dividend (32.5% net of the 10% tax credit), which equates to an effective rate of 36.1% on the cash dividend.

Many owner managers prefer to extract cash which is clearly surplus to the current and future requirements of the business, removing it from future exposure to business risk by way of dividend. Surplus cash might also prejudice a company's trading status for ER purposes but provided the cash has been derived from trading activities and is not actively managed as an investment asset, this should not be the case (see 15.37).

In all cases, owner-managers will need to carefully plan the timing and level of dividends to mitigate their exposure to the penal 36.1% top dividend rate. Assuming this top tax rate is temporary, many will now wish to retain cash in the company until they are able to extract it at more palatable tax rates. The current use of income-shifting techniques (see Example 5 at 9.23A) may enable many owner-managers to avoid or reduce the amount of dividends taxed at the top 36.1% rate.

Dividends may need to be paid to those shareholders who have invested in the company to provide a regular income. For example, where the company was acquired by means of a management buy-out, venture capitalists may hold a significant part of the equity investment, often a preferential class of shares, upon which a dividend must be paid. (Dividends are not taxed in the hands of a corporate shareholder.)

On the other hand, certain shareholders may have invested for capital growth and do not require dividends. In practice, any conflicting requirements of the shareholders can often be satisfied by the use of separate classes of shares, with different rights as to dividends, votes and return of capital.

PROCEDURE FOR PAYING A DIVIDEND AND CONCEPT OF 'DISTRIBUTABLE PROFITS'

Companies Act formalities

9.2   A dividend represents a payment made from a company's distributable profits in respect of a share in a company. A dividend can either be fixed in amount (for example, on a preference share) or a variable amount on an ordinary (equity) share.

For private companies that were incorporated after 30 September 2009, the method of paying dividends is likely to be regulated by the 'Model Articles for Private Companies Limited by Shares (contained in The Companies (Model Articles) Regulations 2008. Otherwise, the procedure is often governed by the company's Articles of Association – companies that were registered before 1 October 2009 will have adopted the standard Table A Articles. In such cases, Articles 102–108 of Table A will apply in the absence of any contrary rules [*Companies (Tables A to F) Regulations 1985 (SI 1985 No 805)*]. A final dividend must be recommended by the directors and approved by the shareholders in a general meeting.

Article 30 of the Model Articles (Article 103 of Table A) authorises the directors (under a Board resolution) to pay interim dividends. A resolution of the Board to pay an interim dividend does not create a debt and may, therefore, be revoked before it is paid – (*Potel v CIR* (1970) 46 TC 658). Reliable up-to-date management accounts should be available to show there are sufficient distributable profits to support the intended interim dividend.

The normal procedure for paying dividends is to calculate the total dividend and then the dividend per share. Unless the articles state otherwise, dividends are payable to those shareholders registered at the time of the declaration. Each 'recipient' shareholder should receive a dividend voucher stating the amount of the dividend, related tax credit, etc.

In the case of an interim dividend, directors' Board minutes must be drawn up approving the payment. In the case of the final dividend, documentation must be prepared for the annual general meeting (AGM) to approve the dividend recommended by the directors. Where elective resolutions have been passed, the dividend payments should be validated by a written resolution of the Board of directors.

In some cases, HMRC may seek to argue that a dividend paid to a director shareholder should be treated as remuneration. However, any such challenge should easily be rebutted where the dividend has been properly declared in accordance with the Companies Act formalities and the company's Articles.

Under FRS 25 'Financial Instruments: Disclosure and Presentation' , the accounts presentation of dividends paid should be reflected in the reserves and reconciliation of movements in shareholders funds (and not in the profit and loss account). Proposed dividends are not proper liabilities of the company (since there is no legal obligation to pay them until they have been formally ratified by the shareholders). Consequently, FRS 25 requires that proposed dividends are simply shown as a note to the accounts, except where they represent a genuine liability of the company at the balance sheet date. Dividends declared after the balance sheet date but before the accounts have been authorised should not be recognised as a liability, following FRS 21 'Events after the Balance Sheet Date'. The *Companies Act 2006* disclosure rules have been brought into line with the requirements of FRS 25 [*Companies Act 1985 (International Accounting Standards and other Accounting Amendments) Regulations 2004 (SI 2004/2947)*].

Preference shares

9.3   Preference shareholders normally have a fixed dividend entitlement (as a percentage of the amount paid up on their shares). Preference dividends are paid in priority to dividends to ordinary shareholders. There is, however, no automatic right to a payment of a preference dividend, since any dividend can only be declared out of distributable profits. Where preference dividends cannot be paid in a particular period (for whatever reason), they are assumed to be cumulative (in the absence of any express provision in the company's Memorandum or Articles of Association). Such dividends accumulate until they can be paid.

Under FRS 25 redeemable preference shares are classified as a liability as a company has an obligation to redeem the shares on a specific date. Dividends on these shares would be recognised as expenses and classified as interest. Despite this presentation in the accounts, the dividends would still not be deductible for corporation tax purposes.

Determination of distributable profits and directors' duties

Calculation of distributable profits

9.4   A company cannot legally pay a dividend unless it has sufficient distributable profits to cover the dividend [*CA 2006, s 830*]. For these purposes, distributable profits represent the company's accumulated realised profits less its accumulated realised losses (and any other amount written off in a reduction or reorganisation of capital). It is not therefore necessary for a company to make a profit for the year in which the dividend is paid but, in this scenario, there must be sufficient retained profits from prior years to cover it.

9.5 *Distribution of profits and dividend planning*

The relevant profits for determining the position are those reported in the company's last audited accounts circulated to its members. If the statutory accounts contain a qualified auditors report, the auditor must indicate (in writing) whether the matters leading to that 'qualification' are material for determining whether the company has sufficient distributable profits.

Where the statutory accounts show insufficient profits, interim accounts must be prepared for the period in which the distribution is intended to be made to enable a proper judgement to be made by the directors. In practice, reliable up-to-date management accounts which make proper provision for all liabilities (including tax) should be adequate in most cases (see *CA 2006, ss 837–839*).

Where assets are distributed in specie, there are now special rules which measure the amount of any legal 'distribution' (see 13.96).

Realised profits

9.5 Profits must be realised and for this purpose, profits are treated as realised in accordance with generally accepted accounting principles ('GAAP'). It is not, therefore, possible to pay a dividend from an unrealised profit, such as a revaluation surplus. Similarly, it is not possible to pay a dividend from a share premium account or any capital redemption reserve. (Public companies and listed investment companies are subject to additional restrictions – see *CA 2006, ss 831* and *832.*)

Financial Reporting Standard (FRS) 18 states that profits would be 'realised' under the *Companies Act* rules only where they are realised in the form of either cash, or of any other asset, where the ultimate cash realisation of that asset can be assessed with reasonable certainty.

These concepts are developed further in *ICAEW: TECH 7/03 – Guidance on the Determination of Realised Profits and Losses in the Context of Distributions Under the Companies Act 1985 and ICAS & ICAEW: TECH 02/07 – Distributable Profits: Implications of Recent Accounting Changes.* These principles apply to companies adopting UK Generally Accepted Accounting Principles (GAAP) or International Financial Reporting Standards (IFRSs)

One of the main concepts is that a profit will be realised on a particular transaction where the company receives 'qualifying consideration', which comprises:

- cash; or

- an asset that is readily convertible into cash ; or

- the release of all or part of a liability of the company (or its settlement or assumption by another party), subject to certain exceptions.

Broadly speaking, an asset is considered to be 'readily convertible into cash' for these purposes when:

- the value at which it can be readily 'converted' into cash can be determined at the relevant date; and

- this value is observable by reference to price/rates by market participants; and

- the company must be able to immediately convert the asset into cash without any material adverse consequences.

Areas that would require special consideration would include, for example, profits on the sale of assets between group companies where no actual payment is received, share for share exchanges, transactions between related parties particularly where they do not appear to be on an arm's length or involving circular cash movements, and the inclusion of unrealised exchange gains on long-term monetary items (such as long term foreign currency loans).

TECH 02/07 also considers when realised profits are created where companies use 'fair value' accounting. (Fair value accounting is not limited to financial instruments but also include commodities, investment property and biological assets.) In broad terms, profits and losses arising from changes in fair values will be recognised as realised where they are readily convertible into cash.

It is important to appreciate that, in a group context, the profits available for distribution in each individual company are those stated in the accounts of the relevant company (as distinct from the consolidated group accounts). Where a subsidiary distributes an asset in specie, this will represent an *unrealised* profit in the parent company's hands, unless the 'distributed' asset meets the definition of qualifying consideration (see above). However, where the 'non-cash' asset is distributed by the parent company to its shareholder(s), *CA 2006, s 846* will apply to treat that 'unrealised profit' as a realised profit for the parent for the purpose of the onward distribution, provided the profit is recorded in the parent's accounts.

The directors must also have the appropriate provisions in the company's Memorandum or Articles of Association. This may require a dividend to be paid to certain classes of preferred shares in preference to the ordinary shares. The Articles may also carry some other restrictions, for example, as to whether capital profits are distributable.

Example 1

Determination of distributable profits

The directors of Boyce Ltd are considering the level of dividend that should be paid out to its shareholders in October 2011.

The statutory accounts for the year ended 30 June 2011 showed the retained earnings (ie the balance on its accumulated profit and loss account) of £1,725,000 which was made up as follows:

		£
Balance at 30 June 2010		1,500,000
Add	Total recognised income and expense for the period	660,000
Less	Currency translation differences on foreign currency net investment	(35,000)
	Dividend paid during the year	(400,000)
Balance at 30 June 2011		1,725,000

The company also had a revaluation surplus on its trading property of £1,200,000 which was not reflected in the above figures (and does not form part of its distributable profits).

As the directors wished to pay a dividend of around £500,000, this should be well within the limits of its distributable profits of around £1,725,000 (subject to any significant realised losses in the period between 30 June 2011 and October 2011). The directors would also need to take the company's cash flow requirements into account.

DIRECTORS' FIDUCIARY AND STATUTORY DUTIES

9.6 In making a distribution, the directors have a fiduciary/legal duty to think about the company's best interests generally. Although this common law jurisprudence is maintained, this is reinforced by the *CA 2006* which lays down a statutory statement of directors' duties. These statutory duties include acting within the company's powers, promoting the success of the company, exercising independent judgement, and applying reasonable care, skill and diligence.

When deciding whether to pay a dividend and, where appropriate, the relevant amount the directors would need to consider the company's solvency. This would require them to look at the company's cash-flow profile and the ability to repay its debts as they fall due. The directors must therefore conduct a full and proper investigation into the accounts.

Where a dividend is paid unlawfully (such as where there are insufficient distributable profits), the directors may be personally liable to make good the loss caused to the company and they may also be in breach of their common law duties. The case of *CIR v Richmond (Re Loquitur Ltd)* [2003] STC 1394 demonstrates the serious consequences for directors who fail to exercise proper judgement in carrying out their fiduciary duties with regard to the payment of a dividend. In this case, the directors authorised and procured a dividend that was subsequently shown to be unlawful. This was because the company failed to provide for the corporation tax liability (around £2.3 million) on the sale of its 'Ronson' product range for £10 million. Although a claim had been made to roll over the gain, it was held that this claim failed. As the directors were in breach of their duties under (what was) *CA 1985, s 270*, they were personally liable to make good the money misapplied as an unlawful dividend (being limited to the full tax liability on the capital gain).

Where the *Companies Act* requirements governing the payment of dividends have been breached, the directors may be granted relief under *CA 2006, s 1157* where it can be shown that they acted honestly and reasonably. The directors may also plead relief under the Statute of Limitations for dividends paid more than six years ago.

LEGAL AND TAX CONSEQUENCES OF AN UNLAWFUL DIVIDEND

9.7   If a company's dividend exceeds its distributable reserves, this will be an unlawful distribution and the company may be able to obtain repayment from the shareholder recipient. Where a shareholder knows or has reasonable grounds for believing that a particular dividend is illegal (due to the lack of sufficient distributable profits), *CA 2006, s 847* provides that they are liable to pay it back to the company. The Court of Appeal held that an unlawful distribution received by the company's holding company (which knew the facts) was liable to be repaid (*Precision Dippings Ltd v Precision Dipping Marketing Ltd* [1986] Ch 447). Consequently, where a shareholder knowingly receives an illegal dividend, it is certainly arguable that they hold the cash received as a 'constructive trustee' for the company since they are liable to repay it (or such part of it that is unlawful). Similar issues can arise where assets are transferred to a 'related' company at an under-value – see 13.71.

The legal analysis of an unlawful distribution is usually followed for tax purposes. HMRC often argue that an 'unlawful dividend' represents a loan to the relevant shareholder(s), which may be subject to a *CTA 2010, s 455 (ICTA 1988, s 419)* charge (see 2.57–2.60). This is likely to be the case for the majority of unlawful distributions made by family and owner-managed companies.

In *It's a Wrap (UK) Ltd v Gula* [2006] EWCA Civ 544, unlawful dividends paid to members as 'quasi-salaries' (on the advice of their accountant to save tax!) were found on appeal to be repayable by the shareholders. Although they were unaware of the illegality, it was held that a shareholder was liable to return a distribution if they knew or should have been aware that it had been paid in circumstances which amounted to a contravention of the restrictions on distributions (irrespective of whether or not they knew of those restrictions) (see 9.5) (*see also Re Paycheck Services 3 Ltd and Other Companies – R & C Commrs v Holland* [2009] STC 1639).

The company's director(s) may also be personally liable for any improper distributions as this may amount to a breach of their common law fiduciary duty and/or their statutory duties imposed by the Companies Act 2006 (see 9.6).

Cash and in specie dividends

9.8   A dividend can either be paid in cash or *in specie*. Generally, dividends can only be paid in cash whereas an *in specie* dividend (which involves the transfer of a specific asset) requires express authority in the Articles (this is given in Article 105 of Table A). It is, of course, possible for the Articles to be amended by a special resolution where the relevant authority is not available (note that the pre-1948 versions of Table A do not contain this power).

An *in specie* distribution of an asset to a shareholder would involve a 'market value' disposal by the company for capital gains purposes [*TCGA 1992, s 17(1)*]. In such cases, *CA 2006, s 846* enables any revaluation surplus actually 'booked' in the accounts in respect of the distributed asset to be treated as distributable. Where no revaluation surplus is 'credited' in the accounts, only the 'carrying cost' (or value) of the asset recorded in the accounts would have to be met from the company's reserves. This principle is particularly important in determining whether the company has sufficient reserves to be able facilitate a statutory demerger, which involves an in-specie distribution of shares in a 75% subsidiary or trade and assets (see 9.5 and 13.96).

Land and property distributed *in specie* to a shareholder is normally exempt from stamp duty land tax (SDLT), since no consideration is given by the recipient shareholder [*FA 2003, Sch 3, para 1*]. Beware of cases, where the property is transferred with a mortgage or loan, since this will constitute consideration for SDLT purposes. However, an SDLT charge based on the market value of the land/property applies where the company making the distribution had previously received the relevant land/property under the SDLT group relief provisions in the past three years. In such cases, it is therefore advisable to move the property to the 'parent' company via a SDLT-free distribution in specie which avoids the need to rely on the SDLT group relief provisions [*FA 2003, Sch 3, para 2*].

Dividend taxation issues

Abolition of ACT

9.9   The *Finance (No 2) Act 1997* and *Finance Act 1998* made fundamental changes to the way in which dividends are taxed.

First, ACT on dividends and other distributions was abolished after 5 April 1999. This gave a significant cash flow benefit to owner-managed companies; particularly for the many companies outside the corporation tax instalment payment rules that pay their full corporation tax liability nine months after the end of their accounting period (see 4.48). Companies with surplus ACT carried forward can still recover it under the Shadow ACT regime (see earlier editions of this book for detailed coverage of Shadow ACT regime).

Secondly, despite the abolition of ACT, shareholders still receive a 'tax credit' on their dividend and distribution income although it cannot be *repaid* to shareholders whose dividend income is not subject to tax (for example, because it is covered by their personal allowance).

Common examples of company distributions

9.10   A distribution may arise, for example:

- where a company pays a cash dividend or distributes an asset in specie (see 9.8) to its shareholder(s);

- on a company purchase of its own shares (see 13.44);

- where assets are transferred to a shareholder for less than full consideration (i.e. at an undervalue) or where a *shareholder* transfers an asset to the company for more than its market value (i.e. at an overvalue) [*CTA 2010, s 1000(1)B (ICTA 1988, s 209)*]; or

- where a *non-working* shareholder obtains a benefit or has personal expenses paid by the company [*CTA 2010, s 1064 (ICTA 1988, s 418)*] (see 2.66).

9.10A   A distribution may also arise where a shareholders sells an asset to the company at an over-value. This might occur, for example, when goodwill is sold to a company by a sole trader on incorporation. Let's assume the goodwill is sold at a market value of £500,000 (backed up by a professional market valuation report), which is credited to the shareholders' loan account. If HMRC – Shares and Assets Valuation were to successfully challenge the goodwill value and it is ultimately agreed at (say) £350,000, there would be a prima-facie distribution of £150,000 (being the excess of the consideration received for the goodwill (£500,000) over its agreed market value of £350,000).

However, provided the goodwill was professionally valued (as in this case), HMRC are prepared for the distribution to be unwound by adjusting the shareholder's loan account. It is usually recommended for the 'consideration' clause in the sale contract to provide sufficient flexibility for it to be adjusted – for example, '£500,000 or such other amount as may ultimately be agreed by HMRC – Shares and Assets Valuation'. If the valuation of the asset has not been backed-up by a professional valuation, then HMRC would treat the £150,000 'excess' as a distribution

Tax treatment for different types of individual shareholder (since 2010/11)

9.11 From 6 April 2010, dividends and other company distributions are taxed at three different tax rates, depending on the level of the shareholder's total taxable income. Dividends/distributions carry a tax credit equal to 10% of the 'gross' dividend (or one-ninth of the 'net' dividend paid), which partially reflects the corporation tax paid on the profits out of which the dividend is paid.

Dividends/distributions are treated as forming the top slice of an individual shareholder's income [*ITA 2007, s 16*].

For tax treatment of dividends received by UK companies, see 9.12A). (See 17.69 and 17.81 for the treatment of dividends received by trusts.)

Thus, for 2011/12, the relevant tax rates applying to dividends/distributions received by *individual* shareholders are as follows

Tax band in which gross dividend falls	Tax rate	Tax payable on gross dividend (net of 10% credit)	Effective tax rate on net cash dividend (see below)
Up to basic rate threshold of £35,000	10%	0%	0%
£35,001 to higher rate limit of £150,000	32.5%	22.5%	25%
Above higher rate limit of £150,000	42.5%	32.5%	36.1%

Calculation of effective rates

		£
Cash dividend		90
Tax credit – 10/90		10
Gross dividend		100
	£	£
Dividend tax @ 32.5%/42.5%	32.5	42.5
Less: Tax credit	(10.0)	(10.0)
Tax liability	22.5	32.5
Effective rate = £22.5/£90 × 100%	25%	
Effective rate = £32.5/£90 × 100%		36.1

Those owner-managers drawing substantial dividends will pay tax at effective rates of 25% and/or 36.1%. Many owner managers will wish to avoid the amount of dividend tax paid at the top rate of 36.1%. Some created substantial credit balances on their loan accounts before 6 April 2010 by ploughing dividend monies back to the company. In such cases, owner-managers should use their loan accounts to supplement their dividend income (so as to avoid the higher rate tax). Income-shifting arrangements, making use of spousal dividends is another possibility (see 9.23A).

Shareholders whose dividend income falls below the higher rate tax threshold pay tax at the ordinary dividend rate of 10% which is completely offset by the 10% tax credit and thus have no further tax to pay. This explains why many owner-managers prefer to provide their spouses with dividend income within the basic rate threshold.

Where a shareholder's dividend income is covered by their personal allowance, the 10% tax credit cannot be reclaimed – it is non-repayable. Similarly pension funds are exempt from tax on their income and cannot reclaim the 10% tax credit.

Example 2

Taxation of dividends for 2011/12

In July 2011, Goalies Ltd paid a dividend of £300,000 to its shareholders, as follows

Shareholder	% holding	Cash dividend £	Tax credit (1/9) £	Gross Dividend £
R Green – Managing director	84%	252,000	28,000	280,000
D Seaman – Sales Director	10%	30,000	3,333	33,333
P Shilton	4.5%	13,500	1,500	15,000
G Banks	1.5%	4,500	500	5,000
		300,000	33,333	333,333

The tax computations for each shareholder, showing the tax treatment of the dividend in their hands is set out below:

9.11 *Distribution of profits and dividend planning*

	G Banks	P Shilton	D Seaman	R Green
	£	£	£	£
Employment Income (inc benefits)	–	20,000	100,000	140,000
Gross dividend (see above)	5,000	15,000	33,333	280,000
	5,000	35,000	133,333	420,000
Less: PA	(7,475)	(7,475)	–*	–*
Taxable income	–	27,525	133,333	420,000

* No personal allowance where total income exceeds £114,950 .

Income tax liability

G Banks	£			Nil
P Shilton				
Salary	12,525	@ 20%		2,505
Dividend	15,000	@ 10%		1,500
	27,525			4,005
D Seaman				
Salary	35,000	@ 20%		7,000
Next	65,000	@ 40%		26,000
	100,000			33,000
Dividend	33,333	@ 32.5%		10,833
	133,333			
R Green				
Salary First	35,000	@ 20%		7,000
Next	105,000	@ 40%		42,000
	140,000			49,000
Dividend	10,000	@ 32.5%		3,250
Next	270,000	@ 42.5%		114,750
	420,000			

	G Banks	P Shilton	D Seaman	R Green
Total liability	Nil	4,005	43,833	167,000
Less: Taxed under PAYE		2,505	(33,000)	(49,000)
Less: Dividend tax credit	–	(1,500)	(3,333)	(28,000)
Additional liability due	Nil**	Nil	7,500	90,000

** Dividend tax credit not repayable

Overseas dividends received by individuals

9.12 Some owner-managers may be able to successfully establish a non-resident company in order to expand their trade in an overseas country. However, unless sufficient care is taken, HMRC will often be able to show that all the (highest-level) decisions affecting the company are taken in the UK, and hence 'central management and control' abides in the UK. This would make the company resident in the UK (under the rule in *De Beers Consolidated Mines Ltd v Howe* 5 TC 198) and therefore any dividends paid will be 'UK-source' and taxed as in 9.11 above.

Where dividends are paid from a genuine non-resident company, they are entitled to the same non-repayable 10% tax credit. This was only available on shareholdings of less than 10% from since 6 April 2008 but was extended to 10% plus shareholdings from 22 April 2009. However, the 10% tax credit will only be available if there is a double taxation treaty between the source country and the UK (with a non-discrimination article).

Overseas dividends are taxed in the same way as dividends from UK resident companies (see 9.11) and the UK tax would be reduced by Double Tax Relief (ie relief for any overseas tax already suffered on them).

Taxation of dividends/distributions received by UK companies

9.12A The corporation tax treatment of dividends received by UK companies changed in July 2009. Under the previous regime, dividends/distributions from UK resident companies were exempt from corporation tax under CTA 2009 s1285. *Dividends* from non-resident companies were taxable, subject to double tax relief for foreign withholding tax and (for 10% plus shareholdings) underlying foreign tax.

The taxation of overseas dividends had been challenged under the rules of the EC Treaty in Test Claimants in the *FII Group Litigation v HMRC* [2010] STC 1251. The European Court of Justice (ECJ) referred the matter to the UK courts which broadly concluded that, for the most part, the UK taxation of foreign dividends was in contravention of the EU treaty. The UK therefore had to do something about it!

The FA 2009 therefore introduced rules to put the corporate tax treatment of UK and non-resident company dividends on to a level-footing. Unfortunately, the rules are fairly complex.

Broadly, CTA 2009 s931A taxes all dividends/distributions (irrespective of their source) and then grants various exemptions. Different rules apply for dividends received by a small company (under EU rules) and medium/large sized companies.

For these purposes, a recipient company is treated as 'small' if it is a 'micro' or small' enterprise as defined in the Annex to the Commission Recommended 2003/361/EC which broadly means that

- it must have fewer than 50 employees *and*

- both its annual turnover and balance sheet value must not exceed €10 million.

Small companies

Small companies are exempt on their dividend/distribution received provided all the *CTA 2009, s 931B* conditions are satisfied:

- The paying company is UK resident or resident in a 'qualifying territory' (i.e. one which has a double tax treaty with the UK containing a non-discrimination provision)

- No tax deduction must have been given for the dividend/distribution in the hands of the paying/distributing company.

- The distribution must not be made 'as part of a tax advantage scheme', where one of the main purposes of the distribution is to obtain a tax advantage.

However, for technical reasons, distributions which represent an 'excessive' commercial return on securities (*CTA 2010, s 1000(1), paragraph E*) *or* interest relating to certain types of securities which fall within *CTA 2010, s 1000(1), paragraph F* are not covered by the exemption. This is because

- 'excessive' interest will generally fall to be dealt with under the transfer pricing rules;

- Other types of interest return on securities falling within *CTA 2010* will generally already be exempted under the rule in *CTA 2010.*

Other companies

Dividends/distributions received by other (i.e. non-small) companies are exempt provided they fall within *one* of the five exempt classes listed in *CTA 2009, ss 931F–9311* (and do not fall within any of the specific anti-avoidance rules):

1   Dividends/distributions made in respect of non-redeemable ordinary shares.

2   For these purposes, an ordinary share is one that does *not* carry ' any present of future preferential right to dividends or to a company's assets on a winding-up. The underlying logic for excluding redeemable shares is probably due to the fact that HMRC regard them more in the nature of debt than equity.

3   Dividends/distributions from a 'controlled company' – which will often be invoked to exempt dividends from UK and overseas group companies

4   'Portfolio-type' dividends/distributions received from a company in which the recipient holds less than 10% of the share capital.

5   Dividends (but not distributions) paid from 'good' profits (ie profits that do not include the results of transactions designed to achieve a UK tax reduction).

6   Dividends (but not distributions) from shares classified as loans under the loan relationship rules.

In complex cases, reference should be made to the anti-avoidance rules in *CTA 2009, ss 931J–931Q*.

Dividend reporting

9.13   Companies no longer have to account for the dividend or the 10% tax credit on the CT61 (which now only reflects income tax accounted for on interest and other annual payments made to individuals, etc). Dividend certificates (showing the cash dividend, tax credit at 10% and the total) must be provided to shareholders in the usual way.

A sample shareholder dividend certificate is shown below:

DIVIDEND TAX VOUCHER

Company name – CAPUTO GARDENING SUPPLIES LTD

Final dividend for the period ended 31 December 2011

Shareholder
Mrs Ruth Black
19 Esther Avenue
Luton
LU3 3OK

Shareholding	2,000 £1 Ordinary Shares	Date paid : 11 June 2012

Dividend	Net: £90,000	Tax credit: £10,000

Sebastian Black

Company Secretary

You have a legal obligation to keep records of dividends and the associated tax credits for tax purposes

---

TIMING PAYMENTS OF DIVIDENDS

Rules for determining when a dividend is paid

9.14 It is well established in company law that the declaration of a dividend creates an immediate debt unless the company specifies a future date for payment. The legal position for a final and interim dividend differs slightly.

A final dividend is due and payable on the date it is declared and approved by shareholders at the AGM, unless the resolution declaring it specifies some later date (*Hurll v IRC* (1922) 8 TC 292). Thus, a debt is created when a final dividend is declared, which can be discharged by a cash payment, a cheque sent to the shareholder, or the company crediting the shareholder's account with the company or third party.

An interim dividend could be rescinded by the directors at any time until it is actually paid out to the shareholders. Consequently, an interim dividend only becomes due when it is *paid*. Thus, under company law, an interim dividend cannot be paid by the 'crediting' of an account. However, HMRC's *Company Tax Manual* (CT 2007a) treats dividends as being paid when 'a right to draw on the dividend exists', such as when they are credited to an account (*Potel v IRC* (1970) 46 TC 658). However, it may be that the relevant credit is not made until a later accounting period, such as when the company's statutory accounts are prepared. For these reasons, it may be desirable to ensure physical payment of the dividend with the subsequent loan-back of those funds to the company (with an appropriate credit to the owner-manager's/shareholder's loan account.

Planning issues

9.15 The directors of the family company will normally have complete flexibility as to the timing and amount of dividend payments (assuming the company has Model Articles or the former Articles of Association follow article 70 in Table A or similar). The directors/shareholders should therefore try to regulate the timing of dividends to ensure they make best use of their personal allowances, dividend lower rate bands and other reliefs. For example, it would not be efficient to pay substantial dividends in one tax year, if the directors/shareholders have little or no other income in an earlier and/or later year. Delaying a dividend until after 5 April can also provide a valuable deferral of the higher rate or super tax liability (depending on the individual's prior year income/self-assessment tax payment position, etc).

It is not possible to 'backdate' a dividend – this is tantamount to fraud. Any backdated dividend (if recognised at all) will be treated as being made on the actual date of payment for tax purposes.

DIVIDEND WAIVERS

Tax effect of dividend waivers

9.16   Dividend waivers are often used for planning purposes. Broadly, a dividend waiver involves a shareholder waiving their entitlement to the dividend before the right to the dividend has accrued. A dividend waiver can therefore be seen as a method of reducing the income the shareholder receives from the company.

A dividend waiver will be effective for income tax purposes if it is made before the right to the dividend has accrued. An interim dividend will not be counted as the shareholder's income provided the waiver is executed before the specified date of payment. Similarly, a waiver of a final dividend must be made before the relevant Board resolution is passed – in practice, it is normal to execute the waiver before the company's AGM (as a final dividend requires the shareholders' approval) (see 9.20). To be legally effective, a dividend waiver must be made by a Deed, but this no longer has to be made under seal.

To prevent a dividend waiver from being treated as a transfer of value for IHT purposes, the shareholder must waive his right to the dividend (every time) by deed within the 12 months before it becomes payable [*IHTA 1984, s 15*].

Application of settlement legislation to dividend waivers

9.17   A dividend waiver could also be used to divert income to one or more of the other shareholders. HMRC may challenge such dividend waivers on the basis that the waiver constitutes a 'settlement' for income tax purposes. *ITTOIA 2005, s 620(1)* defines a settlement as including 'any disposition, trust, covenant, agreement or arrangement' – this wide definition would clearly catch a dividend waiver.

Any income arising from a settlement will be deemed to be the settlor's income where they or their spouse/civil partner has an interest in the settled property [*ITTOIA 2005, ss 624* and *625*]. Similarly, the settlements legislation also deems income paid to an unmarried (under 18) child of the settlor to be the settlor's for income tax purposes, unless the total does not exceed £100 per tax year for each child [*ITTOIA 2005, s 629*]. (See also 9.36 for detailed analysis of parental settlements for 'minor' children.)

Vulnerable situations

9.18   Case law demonstrates that an element of 'bounty' is necessary for the settlement provisions to apply (see, for example, *Bulmer v CIR* (1966) 44 TC 1; *CIR v Plummer* [1979] STC 793).The requirement for the relevant arrangement to be bounteous was reaffirmed by the House of Lords in *Jones v Garnett* [2007]

UKHL 35, although Lord Hoffmann preferred to say that the transaction must involve a benefit that would *not* have been provided at arm's length!

In the context of a dividend waiver, HMRC take the view that 'bounty' is present where the waiver enables one or more of the shareholders (legally) to receive a larger dividend than would have been possible had no waiver been made.

9.19   This was confirmed in the recent case of *Buck v HMRC* [2008] SpC 716, where Sir Stephen Oliver QC, Special Commissioner, held that the settlements legislation was applicable to a dividend waiver (see also 9.34). In this case, Mr Buck (sole director) owned 9,999 out of the issued 10,000 ordinary shares; his then wife owed the other share.

Mr Buck had waived his dividend entitlement for the years ended 31 March 1999 and 31 March 2000, which enabled the company to pay a £35,000 dividend to his wife for each year. The distributable profits at 31 March 1999 and 31 March 2000 were £46,287 and £46,694 respectively, and therefore the dividends paid to Mrs Buck would have been impossible without the dividend waivers

HMRC contended that Mr Buck's dividend waiver was a 'settlement' so that the income represented by the waived dividend was taxable on him. On appeal, Sir Stephen agreed that this was a settlement since the relevant arrangements would not have been entered into had the individuals been acting at arm's length – this followed Lord Hoffmann's approach in *Jones v Garnett* [2007] BTC 476 (see 9.28)). He inferred from the facts that Mr Buck waived his entitlements so that his wife could receive the dividend income. (Had Mr Buck not waived his dividend entitlement, the company would have required around £300 million of reserves to provide his wife with a dividend of £35,000 on her pro-rata share!)

Furthermore, Sir Stephen also held that the inter-spousal outright gifts exemption (see 9.29) did *not* apply in the case of a dividend waiver. There was no outright gift; merely a waiver of dividends (ie a right to income) and the shares were retained by Mr Buck.

Preventing a potential HMRC settlement challenge

9.20   Based on HMRC practice and the ruling in *Buck* above, it should be possible to resist an HMRC attack under the 'settlement' provisions if it can be demonstrated that the dividend declared per share (see 9.2) multiplied by the number of shares in issue does not exceed the amount of the company's distributable reserves. HMRC could only argue that 'bounty' had occurred where the dividend declared could not be satisfied out of the current distributable profits unless a waiver was made ie the waiver would enable the other shareholder(s) to receive a greater dividend than would otherwise have been possible. Under the settlement legislation, this element would be deemed to be the income of the shareholder executing the waiver (ie the settlor) and therefore taxed in their hands.

Example 4

Effect of dividend waiver

Campbell Ltd has an issued share capital of 100 £1 ordinary shares owned as to 20% by Mr Sol and 80% by The Sol Children's Trust (which is a discretionary trust for Mr Sol's minor children).

At 31 March 2011, it has distributable profits of £200,000.

If a dividend of £1,000 per share is declared and Mr Sol waives his entitlement before the right to the dividend accrues, there is no 'bounty'.

On the other hand, if the company declares a dividend of £2,400 per share in the knowledge that Mr Sol is going to waive his dividend, HMRC would argue that 'bounty' had occurred and under the parental settlement provisions, Mr Sol would be taxed on the 'dividend' diverted.

The relevant figures are summarised below:

Dividend declared	£1,000 per share		£2,400 per share	
	£	£	£	£
Distributable profits		200,000		200,000
Less Dividend declared	100,000		240,000	
Amount waived (20%)	(20,000)		(48,000)	
Dividend paid		(80,000)		(192,000)
Retained profits		120,000		8,000

9.21   In practice, HMRC is only likely to take the 'settlement' point where the dividend waiver is considered to create a tax advantage. A dividend waiver diverting income from one higher rate taxpayer to another is unlikely to be challenged, unless there were other circumstances involved. However, dividend waivers are often attacked where they have been used to increase the dividends paid to the proprietor's spouse or children or to the trustees of an accumulation and maintenance trust for his children.

A dividend waiver in favour of a spouse is unlikely to be protected under the 'inter-spousal settlement' exemption [see *ITTOIA 2005, s 626*] as the waiver entirely represents a 'gift' of income. (See also 9.29.)

SEPARATE CLASSES OF SHARES

9.22   Dividend waivers are frequently used to avoid all or part of the declared dividends going to non-passive or 'non-working' shareholders. To avoid the perennial problem of entering into dividend waivers, a more elegant solution would be to sub-divide the company's ordinary share capital into two (or more) classes of shares. This would give the required flexibility to declare (different) dividends on each separate class of shares.

A reorganisation of share capital should normally be tax neutral under the reorganisation provisions in *TCGA 1992, ss 126* and *127*, provided each class of shares retains the same rights. If there is a material variation in a shareholder's rights after the 'reorganisation', HMRC may consider a value shifting charge under *TCGA 1992, s 29(2)*. However, in practice, provided the company is an unquoted trading company or holding company of a trading group, it should normally be possible to make a business asset 'hold-over' election under *TCGA 1992, s 165* (see 13.14–13.23).

PROVIDING DIVIDEND INCOME FOR THE SPOUSE

Income-shifting/income splitting – an overview

9.23   Following the House of Lords ruling for the taxpayer in *Jones v Garnett* (see below) (commonly known as the *Arctic Systems* case), HMRC promptly announced its intention to introduce 'income shifting/income splitting' legislation. ('Income-splitting refers to the arrangements that small businesses use under which the main worker passes part of their dividend income to another person, typically a spouse, who is subject to a lower rate of tax.)

HMRC introduced draft legislative proposals in December 2007 but these were widely condemned as being unworkable and too costly to administer. These would have meant attempting to formally value (and hence self-assess) a person's 'contribution' to a business – which would have been extremely difficult for the very small business, which was the principal target of the proposed legislation.

The Treasury's appetite for tackling income-splitting seems to have dissipated, particularly as the current economic challenges must be its main priority. Furthermore, it would be disingenuous of Government to place further burdens on small businesses experiencing the effects of the economic downturn. In his Budget 2009 report, the Chancellor simply indicated that legislation to counter 'income-splitting' would be indefinitely postponed. It therefore looks likely that any countering legislation would not be introduced at least in the short to medium term.

Owner managers often seek to exploit the tax benefits of paying dividends to their spouses. For example, it is possible to pay a dividend of up to (say) £39,400 to a (non-working) spouse without attracting any tax liability in the year ended 5 April 2011 (see 2.43).

The taxpayer's victory in the landmark case of *Jones v Garnett* [2007] UKHL 35 BTC 476 gives considerable support for the tax-effectiveness of paying dividends to spousal shareholders (see 9.27). Part of these arrangements will involve issuing or gifting shares to the spouse. This will often constitute a 'settlement' for income tax purposes unless the spouse purchases the relevant shares at their full market value.

However, provided the shares transferred or issued to the spouse contain substantive rights to dividends, voting, capital and so on, the dividends paid on those shares would be exempted under the important *inter-spousal* settlement exemption in (what is now) *ITTOIA 2005, s 626* (see 9.29). Shares which give a right to a dividend (with little else) are likely to be ineffective (see 9.31). Thus, provided sufficient care is taken with the implementation of the arrangements, the payment of dividends to spouses should be effective for tax purposes for the foreseeable future. The recent ruling in *Patmore v Revenue and Customs Commissioners* [2010] UKFTT 334 (TC) shows that the courts will take a wide view of the arrangements (see 9.31A).

Using income-shifting to avoid/mitigate the penal 'super' tax rate on dividends

9.23A   Following the introduction of the 'super' tax rate on dividends (falling in the £150,000 plus taxable income bracket), many owner-managers are using income-shifting arrangements to reduce or avoid paying tax at the penal 'top' dividend rate of 36.1% – this is demonstrated in Example 5 below:

Example 5

Dividend income shifting to mitigate effective top rate tax on dividends

Kenny currently holds 100% of the ordinary shares in Logan Recording Studios Ltd. The company provides studio facilities and regularly generates profits over £750,000 each year. Kenny has historically received a dividend of £300,000 each year from the company (having already drawn salary and benefits of £50,000).

Following the introduction of the 'super' tax rate for taxable income over £150,000, he has been advised to transfer some shares to his wife, Gabby. This would enable her to receive some of the dividend income at lower tax rates than the 36.1% that would be payable if it had been received by Kenny. (Gabby does some secretarial work for the company and receives a salary of £10,000).

To achieve this, the company's ordinary shares are reorganised into two separate classes – A Ordinary shares and B Ordinary shares, each having identical rights to votes, dividends and capital on a winding-up. The share reorganisation falls within *TCGA 1992, s 126*, with Kenny's base cost being split between them. No value-shifting charge is appropriate since Kenny still retains both the A and B ordinary shares.

Subsequently some six months later, Kenny transfers the B ordinary shares to Gabby (which is a no gain/no loss disposal within *TCGA 1992, s 58*).

If required, the company is now in a position to declare separate dividends on each class of share.

9.23A *Distribution of profits and dividend planning*

The potential tax savings that would flow from this arrangement, based on a dividend of £300,000 in 2011/12 are illustrated below. It is assumed that both Kenny and Gabby would receive a dividend of £150,000 each:

	Without arrangement			With income-shifting planning		
	Kenny			Kenny		Gabby
	£	£		£	£	£
Salary		50,000		50,000		10,000
Dividend						
Cash	300,000		150,000	150,000		
Tax credit	33,333	333,333	16,667	166,667	16,667	166,667
Taxable income		383,333		216,667		176,667
Income tax liability		£		£		£
Salary £	@ 20%	7,000		7,000		
First 35,000						
Next 15,000	@ 40%	6,000		6,000		
50,000						
First 10,000	@ 20%					2,000
Dividend						
First 100,000	@ 32.5%	32,500				
Next 233,333	@ 42.5%	99,167				
333,333						
First 100,000	@ 32.5%			32,500		
Next 66,667	@ 42.5%			28,334		
166,667						
First 25,000	@ 10%					2,500
Next 115,000	@ 32.5%					37,375
140,000						
Next 36,666	@ 42.5%					11,333
		144,667		73,834		53,208
Less: Dividend tax credit		(33,333)		(16,667)		(16,667)
Income tax liability		111,334		57,167		36,541

This shows that a tax saving of £17,625 (ie £111,334 less £93,708 (£57,167 + £36,541) results from the proposed 'income-shifting' arrangements.

Potential HMRC challenge under settlements legislation

9.24   Before the landmark ruling in the *Arctic Systems* case, HMRC sought to nullify the payment of tax-effective dividends to spouses (and other family members) in what they considered to be 'unacceptable' circumstances under the settlements legislation.

The settlement legislation has been around in various guises since 1938 and is primarily aimed at situations where income has been diverted from the taxpayer to another party who pays little or no tax on that income. (Anyone who makes a settlement is called a 'settlor' and a settlement may be created directly or through an indirect provision of funds.) These rules apply where, amongst other things, the settlor *or their spouse* retains an interest in the property transferred. These provisions now also apply to civil partners in the same manner.

An individual 'settlor' will be treated as creating a 'settlement' for income tax purposes if they make any disposition, trust, covenant, agreement or arrangement or transfer of assets [*ITTOIA 2005, s 620(1)*]. It will be appreciated that the payment of dividends to the wife would normally be facilitated by the creation of a new class of shares or by the husband transferring some of his existing shareholding.

A settlement may be created without any formal (trust) documentation and may therefore potentially apply to many income-splitting arrangements, such as where a 'principal' shareholder has diverted 'income' that they have effectively 'earned' within a corporate structure to another shareholder (typically their spouse!).

If an arrangement is caught by the settlement rules, the relevant income would be treated as the taxpayer's income under *ITTOIA 2005, s 625*. Thus, if HMRC were successful, the hoped for tax advantage would have been completely negated, since the husband ('the settlor') would have been taxed on the dividend instead (at his highest tax rate). However, in the case of spouses (and civil partners), there is an important exemption for inter-spousal gifts, which was held to apply in the *Arctic Systems* case (see 9.29). This important exemption should provide protection for most types of 'income-splitting' arrangements.

9.25   In recent years, HMRC's main area of attack has focused on 'one-man-band' service type companies which have all or most of the following characteristics:

- A small company is owned by a married couple

- One spouse (very often the husband) generates virtually all company's income from their (consultancy) work. The other spouse may perform some administration work.

- Both spouses pay themselves very modest salaries, the salary of the 'main worker' being well-below 'market rate'

- As a result of the low salary costs, the company is able to pay sizeable dividends to both spouses. This often benefits the wife (who has little or no other taxable income). Her dividend will have little or no extra tax (the 10% tax credit will satisfy her dividend tax liability) whereas the husband would have suffered higher rate dividend tax if he had received it. National Insurance Contributions are also avoided.

The above fact pattern is identical to that in the *Arctic Systems* case. For the moment, the *Arctic Systems* ruling by the House of Lords limits quite significantly HMRC's ability to challenge the more vulnerable 'personal service' company scenario where ordinary shares have been given to a spouse in the anticipation of being able to route 'tax advantageous' dividends to them.

The House of Lords ruling in Arctic Systems

House of Lords – key findings

9.26   The recent House of Lords decision in the *Arctic Systems* case (more formally *Jones v Garnett* [2007] UKHL 35 BTC 476) establishes two fundamental points in the area of *inter-spousal* settlements:

- The use of a corporate structure involving the issue/transfer of shares to the intended 'beneficiary' of the planning is likely to form an 'arrangement', thus creating a settlement. The subsequent steps which may be uncertain at the outset, such as the generation of profits to fund the dividend payments, may *not* be part of the arrangement itself but can provide the necessary 'element of bounty'. In other words the mere expectation of the plan coming to fruition is all that is necessary to find there is an arrangement and the Courts can have regard to what subsequently happens in reaching its conclusion, taking a 'broad and realistic view of the matter'.

- However, even though a settlement exists, the issue/transfer of fully-fledged ordinary shares to a spouse will invariably be protected by the exemption for outright gifts between spouses This exemption does not apply where the subject matter of the gift is wholly or substantially a right to income but ordinary shares carry rights above and beyond a right to income (dividends) and so come within the exemption (see 9.29).

Arctic Systems – key facts

9.27   Geoff Jones decided to become a freelance computer consultant after he was made redundant. It was well known that the agencies used by computer consultants need to deal with companies to minimise the risk of creating any 'employer/employee' relationship. So Mr Jones set up his own company, Arctic Systems Ltd, which was acquired 'off the shelf'. Both he and his wife were each issued with one share in the company, which was therefore owned on a 50:50 basis. Mr Jones was the sole director and Mrs Jones was the company secretary.

Mr Jones worked fairly long hours as an Oracle database designer dealing mostly with private sector clients. The company's income was predominantly generated by him, while his wife spent about four to five hours a week dealing with administration at their home office.

Acting on advice from their accountant, they both took low salaries which meant that a substantial part of their post-tax profits could be paid out to them equally in the form of dividends. The Joneses operated on this basis for many years.

Many small owner managed companies structure their financial affairs on a similar basis, clearly to take advantage of the tax efficient treatment of dividends in the hands of a spouse (with little or no other income) (see 2.43)

MAIN CONCLUSIONS ON DEFINING A SETTLEMENT

9.28   In common with most other anti-avoidance legislation, the tentacles of the settlement definition are widely spread. Thus, *ITTOIA 2005, s 620* says that a 'settlement' includes 'any disposition, trust, covenant, agreement, arrangement or transfer of assets'. It has been left to the courts to determine the ambit of this definition and there are a reasonable body of precedents dating back to times when personal income tax rates were exorbitant (at least by today's standards!).

To determine whether a settlement had been created in the *Arctic Systems* case, the Law Lords focused on construing the meaning of an 'arrangement'. They reviewed most of the leading case law authorities. An arrangement only constitutes a settlement if there is an 'element of bounty' (*CIR v Leiner* (1964) 41 TC 589 and *CIR v Plummer* [1979] STC 793). Lord Hoffmann preferred to put it another way – 'the settlor must provide a benefit that would not have been provided in an arm's length transaction'.

This analysis assisted HMRC's position case. Their view was that the transfer of a 50% shareholding to Mrs Jones, 'which enabled her to receive dividends on the shares which were expected to be paid' was such an arrangement. The point was that Mr Jones would not have transferred the shares to a stranger (who undertook to do the same work as Mrs Jones) on the same basis.

Lord Hoffmann found support in *Crossland v Hawkins* [1961] 39 TC 493 which (on similar legislation dealing with parental settlements in favour of their minor children) took a broad and realistic view of the taxpayer's arrangements. The *Hawkins* case involved the legendary actor, Jack Hawkins and involved the use of a company as a vehicle for a settlement. Mr Hawkins agreed to work for the company for a small salary. This enabled dividends to be paid on shares that had been settled in trust for the benefit of his children (by his father-in-law). In this case, it was held that a combination of transactions (including

411

the subsequent creation of a trust) was an 'arrangement' and Mr Hawkins was found to be an 'indirect' settlor of the trust (since the income from *his* services funded the dividend payments).

Further assistance was provided by *Butler v Wildin* [1989] STC 22 which involved an arrangement to benefit the infant children of two brothers. In this case, the children had subscribed for shares in a company set up by their parents (the brothers) using money provided by grandparents. Lord Hoffmann found authority here for saying that the relevant time for determining whether there was an arrangement was when the company was acquired and the shares allotted to the children. However, he would have found it difficult to say that the subsequent events (such as entering into third-party agreements and property development) were *not* part of the arrangements. It was the expectation of such events and the hope of profit that gave the 'element of bounty' to the arrangement.

Based on the existing jurisprudence, their Lordships found that the 'reward' structure set up by the Joneses did in fact create a settlement. Lord Hoffmann concurred with much of HMRC's arguments:

'… It was not a transaction at arms' length because Mr Jones would never have agreed to the transfer of half the issued share capital, carrying with it the expectation of substantial dividends, to a stranger who merely undertook to provide the paid services which Mrs Jones provided. That provided the necessary "element of bounty". The object of the arrangement was to keep the entire income within the family but to gain the benefit of Mrs Jones's lower rates. The dividends paid to Mrs Jones arose under the arrangement. Mr Jones, by working for the company, provided it with the funds which enabled the dividends to be paid. He was therefore a settlor within the meaning of section 660G (2). As Mrs Jones was the spouse of Mr Jones, he was to be treated as having an interest in the income derived from her share and that income was therefore treated as his income'.

In giving his judgment, Lord Neuberger made a notable observation –

'If the parties intended an element of bounty to accrue, and that intended element of bounty does indeed eventuate, then, absent any other good reason to the contrary, there is indeed an "arrangement"'.

THE 'INTER-SPOUSAL' GIFT EXEMPTION

9.29 Married couples (and now civil partners) have an important exemption, which prevents the settlement provisions from applying where:

- there is an *outright gift* of property from one spouse to another, and

- the property is *not* wholly or substantially a right to income

Having concluded there was a settlement, the Law Lords then went on to consider whether it could be *disregarded* under the exemption in (what is now) *ITTOIA 2005, s 626* (formerly *ICTA 1988, s 660A(6)*).

HMRC contended that since Mrs Jones subscribed for her share there was no *gift*, but this point was quickly dismissed by both Lord Hoffmann and Lord Neuberger. HMRC's analysis was too narrow. If there was sufficient bounty to create a settlement then there must be a gift on any normal interpretation of the word. It did not therefore matter that Mrs Jones's share was purchased from the company formation agents rather than being gifted to her by her husband.

It then had to be demonstrated that what Mr Jones had passed to his wife was *not* 'wholly or substantially a right to income'. Their Lordships again had little difficulty with this. They concluded that a 'gift' of ordinary shares would always be covered by the exemption. Ordinary shares contained a bundle of rights, such as voting rights and capital rights on a sale/winding-up, and so on. These rights go beyond a right to a dividend (income) if one is declared.

This was contrasted with the preference shares in the case of *Young v Pearce* [1996] STC 743 (see 9.31). In this case, the controlling shareholders of a trading company arranged for *non-voting* preference shares to be issued to their respective wives at par. The creation of the new preference shares and their allotment to the directors' wives constituted a settlement. However, it was decided that the inter-spousal settlement exemption did *not* apply since, in reality, the preference shares just represented a right to income (as the other rights attaching to the shares were minimal). They had been stripped of all other rights other than the right to dividend income (if the directors declared one).

By contrast, fully-fledged ordinary shares will have many rights including the right to attend and vote at general meetings, to receive dividends, rights to capital growth on a sale, and to obtain a return of capital on a winding-up.

It is always advised that dividends paid to a spouse should be paid/banked into their own separate bank account to avoid any HMRC contention that the 'transferor spouse' has retained an interest in the dividend monies.

MR JONES 'JOURNEY' TO THE HOUSE OF LORDS

9.30 It has to be recognised that the courts found some difficulty in applying the settlement legislation in relation to the facts in the *Arctic Systems case*.

There was effectively a 'penalty shoot out' at the Special Commissioners – the two expert Commissioners completely disagreed in their reasoning but the presiding Commissioner exercised her casting vote in the Revenue's favour.

Mr Justice Park in the High Court ([2005] STC 1667) decided that a settlement had been created (based on his interpretation of the case law precedents). He considered that a bounteous arrangement could include something which is planned and expected, but is not legally binding.

However, all three Court of Appeal judges completely disagreed and found for Mr Jones (at [2006] STC 783). They concluded that the initial shareholding structure and the surrounding arrangements were *not sufficiently certain* to create a settlement. There was no guarantee at the outset that Arctic Systems would earn the profits to pay the dividends even though this was hoped for.

The House of Lords then reverted to Mr Justice Park's logic. Put briefly, their Lordships decided that the Joneses had created an arrangement in the nature of a settlement when they set up Arctic Systems Ltd but then found that the *s 660A(6)* exemption for gifts between spouses also applied so that the dividends paid to Mrs Jones could be treated as her income.

The Jones's tenacity in fighting the case – frequently referred to as a 'David v Goliath' battle – has attracted justifiable admiration in both the professional and national press. When it was decided earlier that HMRC could not serve a £42,000 back tax bill covering six years, the tax at stake was then whittled down to about £6,000 (plus interest) for the year 1999/2000). At that stage, it would have been very easy for Mr Jones to have 'thrown in the towel'. But there was a point of principle at stake and the Joneses (with the valuable assistance of the Professional Contractors Group) continued their fight.

Looking at the totality of the arrangements – Patmore v HMRC

9.30A   The decision in *Young v Pearce* (see 9.31) should be contrasted with the First-tier Tribunal Ruling in Patmore v HMRC [2010]. This case also involved dividends being paid to a spouse on non-voting shares, but when all the relevant transactions were viewed as whole, there was no settlement for tax purposes.

Mr and Mrs Patmore had purchased the shares of an engineering company for £320,000, with the first instalment of £100,000 being funded by a second mortgage on their home. Their accountant advised them to reorganise the company's shares into separate A ordinary voting shares and B 'non-voting' shares. Mrs Patmore ended up with only 2% of the A shares and 10% of the B shares with her husband owning the remaining shares of each class. For a number of years, large dividends were paid to Mrs Patmore on her B 'non-voting' shares, which she then passed to her husband to repay the outstanding debt for the original purchase of the company.

HMRC contended that these arrangements created a settlement (under what is now *ITTOIA 2005, s 620*). It was argued that Mr Patmore used his control of the company to pay these dividends to enable his wife to benefit from a lower tax charge. Mr Patmore was therefore taxed, as the settlor, on the B share dividends received by his wife.

However, the couple's adviser indicated that the A and B share structure simply gave the required flexibility to pay dividends to Mrs Patmore without necessarily paying dividends to her husband. Further, it was stressed this reflected Mrs Patmore's higher risk on the mortgage liability since she had no daily involvement in the company. However, her dividends were used by her husband to repay the outstanding debt.

The judge considered that the tax efficiency of the share structure was not a significant factor since the legislation did not impose a 'motive' test. Following Lord Hoffmann's approach in the *Arctic Systems* case (see 9.26), she concluded that the courts should take "a broad and realistic view" of all the arrangements in settlements cases.

Although HMRC agreed that Mrs Patmore had a joint and equal responsibility for the debt incurred on the purchase of the company, this analysis was not followed to its logical conclusion – this being that Mrs Patmore was entitled to half of the acquired shares and an 'appropriate share of the dividends'. Somewhat helpfully, the judge concluded that there had been an inequitable division of the A ordinary shares between the couple. Mrs Patmore should have had 50% of the A shares but ended up with a very small shareholding, which meant there was a constructive trust in her favour. The shares allocated to Mrs Patmore, did not reflect the amount of her original investment in acquiring the company. There was no bounty from Mr Patmore and hence no settlement had been created for tax purposes. (Interestingly, the judge resolved matters by allocating the dividends declared on all classes of shares between the couple on an 'equal' basis!).

HMRC have decided to appeal against the First Tier Tribunal decision but the case has not been heard at the time of writing.

The Young v Pearce case – non-voting preference shares

9.31   In *Young v Pearce* [1996] STC 743, the controlling shareholders of a trading company arranged for non-voting preference shares to be issued to their wives *at par*. The preference shares carried a coupon of 30% of the company's net profit for each year, if the Board determined that a dividend would be paid for the year. (The ordinary shareholders would receive a dividend equal to the residual profit.)

The preference shares were entitled to a return of the nominal (£25) subscription price on a winding up, but had no right to participate in a surplus.

In the High Court, Sir John Vinelott held that the creation of the new preference shares and their allotment to the directors' wives constituted an 'arrangement or disposition' within the 'settlement' definition. Furthermore, he considered that the relevant criteria for the important 'outright gifts' exemption for spouses had not been satisfied. Although finding that the allotment of the preference shares to each wife was an outright gift from which dividend income arose, the preference shares represented property consisting wholly or substantially of a right to the dividend income. Their other rights were viewed as minimal and the wives were only entitled to a repayment of the nominal subscription price.

Sir John Vinelott said:

> 'As a matter of strict legal principle, the preference shares were assets distinct from the income derived from them, but in reality they could never have been realised. The income was dependent upon the [controlling shareholder-directors] determining to distribute part of the profits of the company.'

The settlement rules therefore applied to treat the preference share dividends as taxable in the hands of the 'settlor-husbands'. The *Young v Pearce* case provides clear authority for countering dividends on non-voting preference shares issued to spouses. However, as subsequently confirmed in *Jones v Garnett* [2007] UKHL 35 (see 9.29), the exemption will invariably protect similar arrangements involving fully-fledged ordinary shares.

Practical issues with spouse shareholdings and disclosure on tax returns

9.32   The House of Lords ruling in the *Arctic Systems* case demonstrates that the 'settlement' legislation can only be used to attack income-splitting arrangements in very small 'personal-service' type companies where the company's income stream solely arises from the efforts of one of the spouses but large dividends are paid to the other. In such cases, there is likely to be a settlement. This means that shareholding structures used to benefit minor children could be vulnerable (since there is no equivalent *ITTOIA 2005, s 626* exemption) (see 9.53).

The question is where should the 'dividing' line be drawn. Even before this case was first heard, the Revenue had expressed the view that larger businesses which had a number of employees, trading premises, capital equipment, and so on, would *not* be caught by these rules (see April 2003 *Tax Bulletin*). Presumably this is on the basis that the profit earning capacity of the company was a 'team effort' and not down to the work of just one person.

Furthermore, where a wife pays full market value for her shares (out of her own resources), it is reasonably clear that the dividends subsequently paid out on those shares would represent a normal commercial return on a proper business transaction with no element of bounty (see 9.31A). HMRC also generally accept that the issue of founder shares at par is also a commercial arrangement where the couple are both *fully involved* in the company. Similarly, there should be no difficulties where the main earner is paid a proper market rate for their services or where the couple's contributions to the company were more or less equal.

Even where the structure of the arrangements fall to be treated as a settlement, the House of Lords decision in the *Arctic Systems* case now confirms that the inter-spousal gifts exemption provides a valuable fall-back position (see 9.29). However, this will only be the case if ordinary shares with the full range of rights are used, including the right to vote and to receive a surplus on a winding up. (Company law also provides rights for members who are unfairly prejudiced and matrimonial law would also recognise the capital value of a wife's share.) Since the settlement rules affect civil partnerships in the same way as married couples, shares transferred between civil partners also attract the 'outright gifts' exemption.

9.33   Taxpayers (and/or their advisors) are required to self-assess any tax liability under the settlement legislation. In practice, there are likely to be shareholding structures and business arrangements that cover the full length of the 'acceptable/unacceptable' tax spectrum. Each case should therefore be considered carefully to determine whether it falls on the 'right side of the line'. Clearly, where cases are on 'all fours' with the circumstances in *Arctic Systems*, the taxpayer will be entitled to the 'outright gifts' exemption (see 9.27). In borderline or uncertain cases, taxpayers would generally give themselves the benefit of any doubt as to whether they report any income tax liability under the settlement provisions.

Following the Court of Appeal decision in *Langham v Veltema* [2004] STC 544, a later discovery assessment can only be avoided where the precise point on which protection from discovery is required is brought to the attention of the Inspector who deals with the taxpayer's affairs ie it is not sufficient to rely on information that may be held elsewhere within HMRC.

Some comfort can perhaps be gleaned from the judgement of Sir Stephen Oliver QC in *Mr & Mrs Bird v HMRC* [2008] Spc 720. Apart from ruling that the relevant arrangements by Mr & Mrs Bird constituted a parental settlement (see also 9.36 for details), Sir Stephen had to decide whether the Birds' failure to report the daughters' dividends on their own tax returns (under the settlement provisions) constituted fraudulent or negligent conduct (as contended by HMRC). If it was, HMRC was entitled to raise discovery assessments outside the (then applicable) five-year and 10-month time limit (as the rule was then) in *TMA 1970, s 34*. However, Sir Stephen rejected the charge of 'fraudulent or negligent conduct' primarily on the grounds that this 'would require a high level of constructive reasoning ... [and] demand a sophistication that is beyond what is expected of the assumed reasonable taxpayer'.

Indeed, the only relevant box in the 1995 tax return was headed 'Income and Capital from settlements for which you have provided funds'. The Special Commissioner also found that HMRC had failed to adduce any positive evidence that the daughters' funds came from the Birds. Thus, the Birds succeeded in escaping from three out of the five years under review.

Shares provided to children, other family members and friends

9.34 It is perhaps worth emphasising that the 'outright gifts' exemption in 9.29 only applies to inter-spousal settlements (and those made between registered civil partners). Such protection is *not* available where shares are transferred to a settlor's unmarried minor child/children or a trust set up for their benefit. The House of Lords ruling in *Arctic Systems* is therefore likely to strengthen arguments by HMRC that shareholdings structures set up in small service-type companies constitute a settlement. Consequently, dividends paid out to (or for the benefit of) the settlor's children are very likely to be taxed on the settlor [*ITTOIA 2005, s 629*].

HMRC appear to take the view that the settlement legislation is capable of applying to cases where the dividend income goes to a 'co-habiting partner', another family member, or a friend, although it has not seemed to press this point in practice. The Revenue certainly considered this to be a possibility in example 2 in its April 2003 *Tax Bulletin* (RI 268) which deals with a case with 'Aunt Jane' holding shares. This is based on the notion that the settlor's earning power is the property being transferred. Thus, the settlor's ability to withhold their services represents a retention of their interest in the settlement and is caught by the basic 'settlor-interested' settlement rule in *ITTOIA 2005, s 625* (previously *ICTA 1988, s 660A*). However, this line of thinking has subsequently been firmly rejected by Mr Justice Park *in Jones v Garnett* [2005] STC 1667. He concluded that if Mr Jones's co-shareholder had been his sister, the settlement rules could *not* have applied.

USE OF JOINTLY-HELD SHARES FOR MARRIED COUPLES

FA 2004 rules for 'close company' joint shareholdings

9.35 Prior to the Budget 2004, it was widely believed that 'jointly-held' shares (with the shares being jointly-owned by husband and wife) could be used to circumvent the application of the settlements legislation. Under the pre-*FA 2004* legislation, it was possible to split the underlying beneficial ownership of shares on a (say) 95% (husband): 5% (wife) basis whilst the dividend income on the shares would be shared equally between the couple. In such cases, there were strong grounds for arguing that any risk of attack under the settlement code (see 9.23) would be confined to the 5% effectively transferred to the wife [*ICTA 1988, s 282A(5)*]. (For detailed treatment of pre-6 April 2004 rules for jointly-held shares, please refer to the earlier editions of this book.)

However, from 6 April 2004, the use of jointly-held *shares in close companies* (see 1.3) no longer achieves these tax advantages, since the dividend income is now taxed in accordance with the underlying beneficial interests. Thus, in the above-mentioned example, the husband and wife would now be taxed on 95% and 5% of the dividend respectively. The same treatment applies to shares jointly held by civil partners.

PROVIDING DIVIDEND INCOME FOR CHILDREN

9.36   From a legal viewpoint, it is perfectly possible for minor children to receive a transfer of shares in a company and be a full member and shareholder of the company (although the company has the power to refuse to register the transfer). A minor can at any time before reaching their 18th birthday repudiate the shares.

Children have their own personal allowances and lower/basic income tax rate bands. However, it is notoriously difficult for parents to exploit these advantages. The 'parental-settlement' provisions in *ITTOIA 2005, s 629* will nullify any transfer of income by a parent to their children (including step-children and adopted children) if they are under 18 and unmarried, subject to the *de minimis* rule allowing £100 for each child every year (see 9.17).

For example, if a parent transfers some shares to their son or daughter, any dividend paid on these shares whilst they are an unmarried minor is taxed in the transferor-parent's hands. On the other hand, it is possible for another member of a family to make a tax-effective transfer of shares to a minor child (provided it is not part of a wider arrangement which would cause the parent to be identified as the 'real' or indirect settlor) (see 9.38). These issues do not arise where shares are held by the owner-manager's adult children (see 9.37).

Adult children

9.37   Once a child reaches their 18th birthday (or marries), the income is taxed on them (ie the parental-settlement rule ceases to bite). A gift of shares to provide dividend income after their 18th birthday therefore offers considerable tax advantages. (It will normally be possible for any capital gain arising on the deemed market value of the gifted shares to be held over under *TCGA 1992, s 165*, or it may fall within the parent's annual CGT exemption – see 13.14–13.23.)

It is possible to pay a dividend of (say) up to £39,500 in 2011/12 tax free to an individual (with no other taxable income). This is because the (10%) dividend tax credit extinguishes the (low) tax liability on that level of income (see 2.33). Parents may find this strategy a less painful way of financing the increasing costs of their children's further education. The dividend income can, of course, be applied by the child for any purpose or simply saved.

Minor children

9.38   The parental settlement rules ensure that parents cannot provide a tax-effective transfer of income to their minor children (see 9.17), even if the arrangements made to 'divert' the income are fairly subtle. This is well illustrated by the recent Special Commissioner's decision in *Mr & Mrs Bird v HMRC [2008] Spc* 720. This was a fairly complex case involving a family company which was initially run by Mr and Mrs Bird, who each held one share in C Ltd. In December 1994, Mr Bird's father died and his estate was left equally to each of the Birds' three daughters upon them reaching the age of 18. When Mr Bird's father died, the oldest daughter was 15 and the other twin daughters were 10.

In 1995 C Ltd wished to expand but had difficulty in raising funds. Consequently, in March 1995, Mr Bird (acting as sole executor of his father's estate) made unsecured (interest-bearing) loans from the estate to C Ltd – £7,000 (March 1995) and £54,364 (May 1995).

In April 1995, C Ltd issued further shares which resulted in each daughter having a 20% shareholding in the company (60% of the company was therefore then held by the daughters). C Ltd remained profitable and in each year paid dividends to all the shareholders (including the daughters) until it ceased trading in 2002.

HMRC argued that the dividends paid to the daughters (until they reached the age of 18) constituted income under a parental settlement within *ICTA 1988, s 660B* (now *ITTOIA 2005, s 629*), and consequently the dividends were taxable on Mr and Mrs Bird. However, the Birds' contended that their daughters' shares were received as repayment of the loan from their grandfather's estate, which was therefore a commercial transaction.

However based on the evidence presented, the Special Commissioner, Sir Stephen Oliver QC, found that the terms of the share issue contained no reference to the 'estate' loan and, even if there was a connection, this did not explain why Mr and Mrs Bird were also recipients of the newly issued shares in April 1995. The daughters had not taken part in making the loan; it was Mr Bird who had arranged to lend the monies to the company. Given the fact that Mr and Mrs Bird decided not to attend the hearing at the last minute, no further evidence was available and Sir Stephen had to discount the Birds' explanation (see also 9.33 for additional point in relation to discovery assessments).

There is, however, nothing to stop another member of the family, for example a grandparent, from transferring income to their grandchildren. In principle, the parental-settlement legislation should not apply provided the transfer of shares cannot in any way be linked to a wider arrangement with the parent (so that the parent is identified as the 'settlor'). For example, a transfer of shares by a parent to a grandparent as part of an arrangement to transfer them on to a grandchild is particularly vulnerable to challenge – HMRC are likely to be able to sustain the argument that the parent was the 'real' settlor in such cases (see *Butler v Wildin* [1989] STC 22 (see 9.28)). It is also important to remember that the HMRC can counteract any pre-ordained series of transactions under the *Furniss v Dawson* doctrine (see 1.10). Furthermore, any reciprocal arrangements are specifically caught as a 'settlement' by *ITTOIA 2005, s 620(3)*. As a general rule, shares transferred to children by other family members or friends (on their own volition) should not be vulnerable to attack under the 'settlement' rules where they have previously held the shares for a lengthy period. This will enable the dividends paid on those shares to be treated as the child's own income (invariably with no further tax liability). However, as a child cannot give a valid receipt, the dividend income will be received by the parents as 'bare trustees', which could be used to pay school fees!

Some owner-managers may wish to consider placing some shares in a discretionary trust for the benefit of their children. Dividend income paid to such trusts is not caught by the parental-settlement rules provided the income is accumulated within the trust. On the other hand, the parent-settlor would be taxed on any income paid out from the trust for their children's benefit (subject to the £100 per child *de minimis* limit). Note, it is not possible to avoid this rule by making capital payments from the trust as they would be matched with any undistributed income and taxed on the settlor under *ITTOIA 2005, s 633*. See Chapter 17 for a full discussion on trusts.

PLANNING CHECKLIST – DISTRIBUTION OF PROFITS AND DIVIDEND PLANNING

Company

- Directors must consider the legal requirements, the company's cash flow and working capital requirements when determining the amount and timing of dividend payments.

- Extraction of funds that are clearly surplus to the current/future trading requirements may be useful to remove them from subsequent commercial risk, but this is subject to the tax costs of extracting them. Surplus cash arising from trading activities should not jeopardize a company's trading company status for ER purposes provided it is not actively managed as an investment.

- The company can time its dividend payments to suit the income tax position of the shareholder(s).

Working shareholders

- Dividends are very tax efficient if the company pays tax at small profits' rate and the shareholders pay tax at the basic rate. In many

---

cases, dividends are usually preferable to bonuses as a mechanism for extracting surplus profits.

- Owner-managers should carefully review their proposed dividend payments each year to reduce their exposure to the penal 36.1% dividend tax rate.

- If the owner manager has 'healthy' loan account available, this can be used to supplement their taxable income (and avoid top rate taxation). Consider also making 'cheap' loans from the company (which only incur a small tax cost under the beneficial loan rules, although the company will incur a *s 455* charge if the loan remains outstanding more than nine months after the year end.

- Shareholder may obtain longer credit period for payment of higher rate tax where additional dividends are paid early in tax year (subject to self-assessment interim payment position).

- Where dividends are used to extract 'bonuses', invite non-working shareholders to waive their dividend entitlement.

- Dividends paid to spouses who undertake significant work for the business should not be caught by the settlement rules (provided the spouse has fully-fledged ordinary shares with substantive rights). Consider making use of spousal dividends to mitigate the impact of the top dividend tax rate of 36.1%.

Other employees

- Not affected by dividend strategies.

Non-working shareholders

- Dividend waivers must be made in writing (by Deed) before the right to dividend vests.

- Those waiving dividends may be taxed on them if the waiver is made late.

- Following the landmark ruling by the House of Lords in the *Arctic Systems* case, tax-efficient dividends paid to a spouse (or civil partner) should be safe from any HMRC challenge, provided these emanate from ordinary shares (and not non-voting preference shares). Government plans to legislate in this area have been put on hold indefinitely!

- Consider potential advantages of paying dividends to adult children (for example, while they are in higher education, etc).

- They may be invited to waive their dividends by working shareholders, but they cannot be compelled to do so.

Chapter 10

Pension Scheme Strategies

THE OWNER-MANAGER'S PERSPECTIVE

10.1   Owner-managers have generally used conventional methods of pension provision. Their fairly special position enables them to take, and 'their' company to obtain, full advantage of the various tax breaks on offer.

However, in recent years, experience has shown that many owner-managers are becoming increasingly sceptical of traditional methods of providing for a future pension. This is largely due to a combination of 'falling' stock markets, the effective reduction in pension fund returns on dividend income (due to the abolition of dividend tax credit repayments in July 1997) and the financial problems that have recently beset many high-profile pension providers. The most attractive pension proposition is where higher rate tax relief is obtained on contributions paid in but only basic rate tax is suffered when the pensions are subsequently taken.

Some owner-managers now prefer other ways of providing for a future pension (such as Individual Savings Accounts (ISAs), property investment, etc) where the assets remain under their control. Many are even prepared to forego the beneficial income tax relief to obtain the greater flexibility afforded by such arrangements.

Various investment projection models suggest that ISAs may prove more attractive for high earners wishing to top up their retirement funds (where they cannot obtain tax relief on their pension contributions can only obtain 20% tax relief on contributions but are likely to pay the highest tax rates in retirement). Although ISAs do not receive any tax relief on funds paid in (currently up to £10,680 for those aged 50 or over), they will grow within a tax-free vehicle and do not attract any tax when withdrawn. Contrastingly, pensions receive tax relief (albeit restricted in some cases) but are largely taxed when the pensions are received in retirement. Other potential opportunities for tax-efficient investment include Enterprise Investment Schemes, Venture Capital Trusts, and offshore Investments. It may also be worth considering investing for capital gains, which are currently taxed at a maximum rate of 28% when realised.

RESTRICTIONS IN PENSIONS TAX RELIEF

10.1A The tendency to look for other forms of retirement saving beyond pension funds has also been driven by the restrictions that have been placed on tax relief for pension contributions over the past few years. The combination of the complexities of the anti-forestalling provisions in 2009/10 and 2010/11 and the substantial reduction in the annual pension input allowance from 6 April 2011, have dissuaded many individuals from making significant contributions to their pension 'pots'

OVERVIEW OF THE CURRENT PENSIONS REGIME

10.2 The current rules are based on the major 'simplification' to the pensions legislation that was introduced on 6 April 2006 (known as 'A day'), based on legislation introduced in the Finance Act 2004 (with many subsequent amendments!). From A-day the previous tax provisions relating to all types of pension schemes were replaced by a single scheme for all tax-privileged pension schemes. All existing approved pension schemes at A-day automatically became registered schemes under the A-day legislation.

The aim was to establish a single 'unified' regime for pensions, sweeping away the complexities and distinctions between the diverse pension systems that were previously in operation. However, whilst the pensions regime as a whole might be considered simpler, many would argue that the constant Government 'tinkering' with the rules in recent years has introduced many other complexities, leaving many to question whether the pensions code is really that much simpler!

In broad terms, UK resident individuals may concurrently belong to more than one pension scheme without any restriction (provided they are under 75). To secure tax relief, individuals must have a commensurate level of taxable earnings (although annual contributions of up to £3,600 are permitted regardless of any earnings)). Pension funds have always enjoyed many tax benefits, including the ability to generally receive investment income and enjoy capital growth in a tax-free environment.

From 6 April 2011, personal tax reliefs for contributions are now generally geared to the amounts paid and the maximum £50,000 annual allowance (subject to any carry forward of unused 'relief' from the previous three years).

10.3 Planning with 'registered pension schemes' involves three main phases:

Funding – Individuals/companies have various rules that regulate the amount that can be contributed to an 'approved' registered pension fund on a 'tax-privileged' basis. This is mainly governed by the Annual Allowance (AA) provisions (see 10.21) which restrict the tax relief on 'pension inputs' to Defined Contribution (DC) or Defined Benefit (DB or 'final salary') schemes. A further limit on the total amount that can be placed in a tax-exempt pension fund is the

Lifetime Allowance (currently £1,800,000, but reducing to £1,500,000 from 6 April 2012 (see 10.21), subject to transitional protection).

Investment – Although the original *FA 2004* simplification proposals removed many of the pre-existing restrictions placed on the choice of pension fund investments, the chancellor subsequently felt that this freedom might be abused. Thus, certain restrictions were placed on those pension funds where the members have control or influence over the scheme's investment choices – known as 'investment regulated' pensions (see 10.11, 10.12 and 10.29).

Benefits – There have been various relaxations to the benefits members can take from their pension funds on 'retirement' and to their dependants in the event of their death and the consequential tax liabilities on them (see 10.33 and 10.34). One of the main attractions is the ability to take a tax free 'lump-sums', which depends on the funds available at the vesting date (although this may be restricted to the lifetime allowance).

For detailed commentary on the pre-6 April 2011 pension rules, see 2009/10 and earlier editions of this book.

OVERVIEW OF PENSION SCHEMES

10.4   Apart from the state scheme, pensions are provided through a personal pension scheme and/or a company (occupational) pension scheme. The pensions legislation and supplementary regulations apply equally to both types of pension scheme. It is not necessary to seek HMRC 'approval' for a pension scheme – instead, the scheme merely has to be registered with a written declaration that all statutory requirements have been met. (All existing 'approved' schemes at A day were deemed to be 'registered' on A day.)

All existing pension schemes at A-day retained their existing nomenclatures even though the relevant tax conditions applying to that particular scheme ceased then. It is still useful to summarise the main features of the arrangements that have traditionally been used by family/owner-managed companies and their directors, which are:

(*a*)   occupational pension schemes ('OPSs') for all employees (see 10.5–10.8)

(*b*)   'top-up' executive schemes for working shareholders and other senior executives (see 10.9);

(*c*)   self-administered schemes for working shareholders (see 10.10–10.14);

(*d*)   personal pension plans ('PPPs') and group personal pension (GPP) schemes (see 10.15);

(*e*)   self-invested pension plans ('SIPPs') (see 10.16);

(*f*)   stakeholder pension plans for all employees (see 10.17–10.18).

The rules for operating company pension schemes are generally set out in guidance provided by HMRC Audit and Pension Schemes Services (APSS).

The relevant practice notes can be found on HMRC's website at www.hmrc. gov.uk/pensionschemes/updates.htm.

Pension scheme members receive regular illustrations of their anticipated pension benefits (in present-day values), which provide a realistic assessment of the value of their pension funds and the extent of any further provision required.

OCCUPATIONAL PENSION SCHEMES

Final salary versus money purchase

10.5   The occupational pension scheme (OPS) traditionally provided benefits based on final salary. In the medium to long term, real investment returns had to cover both inflation and salary growth. Funding in this way, by reference to future liabilities of the pension fund, can create problems in policing the funds. Furthermore, under a final salary (or defined benefit (DB)) scheme, members will not always know the value of their pension benefits at any given time before retirement.

In recent years, 'final salary' schemes are fast becoming a dying species, primarily as a result of weak investment markets. As a result, many companies being required to make substantial contributions to 'make good' the resulting pension fund deficits. Consequently, very few owner managed companies operate final salary schemes. The lack of consistency with defined benefit schemes has resulted in money purchase schemes (defined contribution schemes) becoming the standard choice. With defined contribution schemes, the value of the pension fund for each member is based on the contributions made to it and the investment return achieved.

Many employers also offer access to a group personal pension scheme giving the employees a high degree of portability for their pension fund.

Some companies have made payments to employees in final salary schemes to compensate them for a reduction in benefits or to transfer to a money purchase scheme. HMRC consider such payments to be taxable and 'NIC-able' as employment income.

Exemption from stakeholder pension provisions

10.6   There are two key areas where the employer will not have to provide employees with access to a stakeholder pension scheme (see 10.17):

- if an employer has an OPS, this will exempt the employer provided their employees can join the scheme within 12 months of starting work – membership can be closed to employees under 18 years of age or within five years of retirement;

- employers can also be exempt if membership of a group personal pension (GPP) scheme is offered (see 10.15). In this case, exemption will only be available if the employer contributes at least 3% of basic pay to the scheme, offers GPP membership within three months of joining (except to those under 18 years of age) and allows payroll deduction for employee premiums. In addition, the GPP must not apply any penalties on exit and the employer cannot require the member to pay more than 3% of basic salary as a condition of membership.

A company can apply to the APSS to convert its approved money purchase pension scheme into a stakeholder pension scheme. It will need to change the rules of the pension scheme to comply with the stakeholder regulations and possibly revise its contributions to avoid the scheme becoming overfunded.

Pension benefits

10.7 The benefits that can be taken from an OPS now follow the standardised post-A day rules (see 10.33). The previous complex formulae that applied to benefits taken under defined benefit and defined contribution schemes no longer apply.

Loans and pension mortgages to individual members of an OPS

10.8 Under an insured scheme, insurance companies can offer loans to individual members although this could result in payment charges. Security is required and using the loan to purchase a private residence can be an attractive proposition.

There are no longer any company law restrictions on 'loans' to directors (of private companies) (see 2.57). The personal loans/mortgages available vary considerably.

EXECUTIVE PENSION PLANS

10.9 Usually, executive pension plans ('EPPs') are insured defined contribution occupational schemes which are taken out to provide benefits to a *single* member (although it is possible to have more than one member). The policies are therefore 'earmarked' for the individual member. This differs from other money purchase occupational schemes where typically an individual member's benefits relate to their share of assets held in a common pool of funds.

Since A day, the previous actuarial funding limits cease to apply and the amounts that may be contributed to and held by an EPP are simply subject to the annual and lifetime allowances (see 10.21).

SELF-ADMINISTERED PENSION SCHEMES (SSASS)

Overview

10.10   In a large number of cases, working shareholders of a family or owner-managed company have tended to look upon a pension scheme as a tax-saving vehicle during their working lives, rather than as a means of providing income on retirement. Not surprisingly, HMRC have always been keen to remind everyone that a pension scheme is intended to provide benefits on retirement with the tax provisions providing appropriate encouragement.

Small self-administered schemes ('SSASs') have traditionally provided a tax-efficient pension fund vehicle for many owner-managers. They are particularly appropriate where the company is wholly owned by the working directors. Typically, membership of such schemes is restricted to just a few owner-managers, with a maximum permitted membership of 12. As trustees of the pension fund, they are able to enjoy some control over the investments made by the pension fund (as opposed to leaving it to the pension scheme fund managers or insurance company concerned). This means that the relevant company can (subject to certain restrictions) retain the use of the sums paid into the fund. The trustees of the fund will often include a professional trustee, but it is no longer an HMRC requirement to have a pensioner trustee, and tax reliefs are not conditional on the appointment or continued presence of such a trustee.

All SSASs existing at A-Day were subsumed into the current pensions regime and are deemed to be registered with HMRC. New schemes must be registered with HMRC, but are no longer subject to approval.

There is a reasonable amount of scope for using pension contributions to keep the company within the small companies' rate of corporate tax (see 10.25 for rules relating to corporate tax relief). Where substantial funds are transferred to a SSAS, the share value of the company is reduced for CGT and IHT purposes, with the funds still effectively being available to the company to a certain extent.

From 6 April 2011, company contributions to a SSAS made after 5 April 2011 are subject to the annual allowance (AA) restrictions. Any contribution paid in respect of an individual member exceeding the £50,000 AA (plus any unused relief brought forward) will result in an income tax charge for the relevant individual (see 10.21 – 10.24).

Eligible investments

10.11   A SSAS is able to invest in a fairly wide range of investments, including holding/purchasing the company's trading property (see 10.12) and making loans to the company (see 10.13). Company pension schemes (previously formed under the 'old' Self Administered Pension Scheme (SSAS) rules) can be used to meet the owner-managers' personal pension requirements whilst also providing useful financial benefits for 'their' companies.

It was originally proposed that the types of investments made by a pension fund would be liberalised to include almost any asset. Many individuals were therefore planning to introduce residential property and other exotic assets, such as works of art, vintage cars, fine wines, etc (see 10.30). However, in the pre-Budget report delivered on 5 December 2005, there was a dramatic U-turn which heavily penalised the use of such assets. Those who were advanced in their planning understandably felt resentful to the turnaround in policy. However, the government clearly felt that retaining complete freedom over the choice of 'tax-relievable' investments would have led too many people to make too many imprudent decisions about building for their long term security.

It is permissible for a company to purchase shares in the (sponsoring) company, but this is limited to 5% of the company's share capital. (Pre-A day, the holding of shares in an unlisted company was generally restricted to a more generous 30% of share capital.) Existing (pre-A day) company shareholdings can continue to be held under the post-A day regime. See 10.30 for further details about eligible pension fund investments.

Property investments

10.12   Many SSASs own property which they let to the employer company. The company obtains corporate tax relief on the rent paid and the SSAS receives it tax-free. Any capital growth on the property accrues tax-free within the SSAS.

A SSAS can purchase property from individuals connected with the company (which could *not* be done before A day). Thus, where an owner-manager personally owns property, this can now be sold to 'their' pension fund at market value (enabling cash to be released to them). Generally, it is not possible for the property to be transferred to the fund as an *in specie* contribution (see 10.25). The only circumstance in which it may be possible to transfer a property in specie is if a debt had been created prior to the specie contribution being made. The rules are complicated and most providers are unwilling or cautious about administering such transactions.

The sale of the property will have capital gains implications and is likely to result in an SDLT charge (see 12.22). The effective CGT rate on the transfer is likely to be 28% (Entrepreneurs' Relief would not normally be available in such cases.) The future capital growth in the property would be exempt from tax within the fund.

A SSAS can also invest in commercial property for third party letting.

Loans to company

10.13   Pension fund loans to the company must be secured, not exceed five years in duration (but can be rolled over once) and must be on commercial terms (with equal annual repayments and interest of at least a composite bank base rate plus 1%). Furthermore, such loans must not exceed 50% of the value of the pension fund.

As a general rule, the company no longer has to deduct and withhold 20% income tax on interest paid to pension funds, irrespective of whether the loan is intended to last for more than a year (see *ITA 2007, ss 930(1)* and *936(2)(g)*).

SSAS Borrowing limits

10.14 Pension fund borrowings are restricted to 50% of the funds assets and must be secured. Furthermore, the term of such borrowings must not exceed five years (see 10.31 for further details).

Borrowings for prospective property investment that took place before A day could be carried through into the post-A day regime. Before 6 April 2006, a SSAS could borrow up to 45% of the fund value plus three times the (prior) annual contributions made to the fund by the company and its members. It is still not possible for the fund to make loans to members.

Example 1

Advantages of SSAS owning company's trading premises

A SSAS was established for the three shareholder-directors of Gerrard Ltd in 1995. During 2010, the trustees of the SSAS (which included all three directors) decided to acquire new business premises for the company costing £1,200,000, partly using bank borrowing.

Gerrard Ltd pays a commercial rent of £85,000 per year, which is deductible for corporation tax purposes, but received tax-free in the hands of the SSAS. The rental payments and regular annual contributions are used by the SSAS to repay the bank borrowings. The capital appreciation in the property takes place in a tax-exempt vehicle.

PERSONAL PENSION PLANS (PPPS) AND GROUP PERSONAL PENSION (GPP) SCHEMES

10.15 Personal pension plans can be taken out by directors and employees, which effectively go with them from job to job or indeed from job to self-employment. The benefits are always based on the level of contributions (and not the level of final income on retirement).

Members can obtain tax relief on their personal contributions at their highest marginal tax rate (up to the £50,000 AA (plus any unused relief brought forward) (see 10.21–10.22 for further details).

Currently contributions by members are paid net of basic rate tax (currently 20%) under the relief at source (RAS) rules, with any higher rate relief being given through the self-assessment return. The pension provider reclaims the 20% basic rate tax deducted at source from HMRC, which effectively forms part of the member's contributions.

Some employers run group personal pension (GPP) schemes. Broadly speaking, GPP schemes are a collection of individual personal pension schemes operated by one administrator (normally the pension provider). However, the employer's involvement can be relatively limited as many of the duties imposed on trustees are avoided. The main responsibility of the employing company is to ensure that contributions are paid over to the pension provider within 19 days of the end of the relevant 'contribution' period.

SELF-INVESTED PERSONAL PENSION PLANS (SIPPS)

10.16 A self-invested pension plan or SIPP is effectively a personal pension 'wrapper' into which eligible investments are placed without any capital gains tax charge on profits. Consequently, there is no employer or pension fund involvement. With a SIPP, the individual decides how the funds are invested. They can therefore choose their underlying pension fund investments. Traditionally, these have included quoted stocks and shares (including AIM shares), unit and investment trusts, insurance company managed funds and unit linked funds and commercial property.

In contrast to managed funds, SIPPs give much greater control over investments within the fund. Provided the fund is of a reasonable size, the SIPP can choose a fund manager (agreeing the charging basis) and draw up a suitable asset allocation model. Care should also be taken to agree investment performance criteria and the monitoring of results.

SIPPs are subject to the (post-A day) unified rules that apply to all pension funds. However, owner-managers with a SIPP should note there is *no restriction* on the amount of share capital or loan investment in their 'own' company (since a SIPP does not have any sponsoring employer (see 10.30)).

In the past, SIPPs have generally required a minimum annual contribution of around £4,000 to make them viable. The arrival of online SIPPs (which have far lower charging structures) has made them more suitable for a far wider range of people.

Mortgages against SIPPs are available from third parties such as building societies and banks up to a factor of the annual pension contributions and with a minimum annual pension contribution being required. Such a facility is simply another source of finance (albeit of a greater amount than might be obtainable from traditional sources) with no benefit passing to the SIPP itself. To that extent, for a house purchase, it should be compared to a mortgage on the capital repayment basis or to a mortgage linked with an endowment policy.

STAKEHOLDER PENSION SCHEMES

Main features

10.17   Since October 2001, employers who do not offer an OPS (see 10.5) or a group personal pension scheme (GPP) (see 10.15) *must* provide their employees with access to a stakeholder pension.

Stakeholder pensions are low cost pension arrangements that operate in the same fashion as a personal pension scheme. The charges must be no more than 1.5% of the pension fund for the first ten years, reducing to 1% thereafter. This covers basic advice and information to members. The pension scheme provider can charge an additional fee for further services such as individual financial advice.

Stakeholder pensions were intended to augment the state pension scheme and are principally designed for those earning between £10,000 and £20,000 per year, although they are, of course, open to all. However, when the S2P (the 'Second State Pension Scheme') replaced SERPs on 6 April 2001, individuals were able to contract out of S2P by using a stakeholder pension plan (generating a rebate of NICs into their stakeholder scheme).

The stakeholder pension regime will cease when the proposed Personal Accounts regime comes in (see 10.20A).

Employer obligations

10.18   All companies with five or more employees must provide access to a stakeholder pension scheme, unless the company's pension scheme fulfils the requirements of accessibility for the entire workforce.

The company is *not* obliged to provide access to a stakeholder scheme for employees if it has an OPS that is open to all employees, except those who:

- are within five years of normal pension age;

- have worked for the company for less than 12 months;

- whose earnings have been below the NIC lower earnings limit for at least three months; or

- who cannot join a stakeholder scheme because they are not resident in the UK.

Alternatively, an employer that offers membership of a GPP within three months of employment, and contributes at least 3% of salary (whilst not requiring the employee to contribute more than 3%) is exempted.

Clearly, companies who have fewer than five employees are not obliged to set up a stakeholder pension scheme.

The company does not have to run the stakeholder pension scheme itself. In many cases, companies have chosen their registered stakeholder scheme from a list held by the Pensions Regulator. Details of the scheme must be provided to its workforce.

The company is required to deduct the employee's contributions through the payroll and forward them on to the pension scheme (within 19 days of the end of the relevant 'payment-month'). It is not required to make contributions itself to the stakeholder scheme, although it may choose to do so.

Contribution limits

10.19   The annual tax relievable contribution limits follow the unified pensions rules, broadly being the greater of:

- £3,600 (gross); or

- 100% of the individual's relevant earnings, subject to the relevant AA (see 10.21)

All contributions to a stakeholder pension are paid net of basic rate tax. Higher rate taxpayers can claim the higher rate relief through their self-assessment tax return.

Employees do not have to contribute to any stakeholder pension schemes made available by their employer. However, the company may allow non-working shareholders and relatives of directors or employees to take advantage of the stakeholder pension arranged for the workforce and make contributions to that scheme.

The stakeholder regime will no longer be required when NEST is fully implemented (see 10.20A).

Many owner-managers continue to make use of the ability to pay a gross amount of £3,600 each year into a stakeholder pension scheme for members of their family who have little or no relevant earnings. Thus, for example, up to £3,600 (£2,880 net of basic rate tax relief) can be contributed to a pension scheme each year for 'non-working' spouses, children and grandchildren (see 10.22). Such arrangements are not caught by the settlement provisions (see 9.36).

INDIVIDUAL PENSION ACCOUNT (IPAS)

10.20   Individual pension accounts (IPAs) provide individuals with a degree of control over their pension savings. They represent a basket of investments somewhat like an ISA. The IPA will rest within a certain pension scheme which could be any money purchase scheme, including a stakeholder pension or personal pension.

When the individual changes their job and wishes to join a different pension scheme, they may be able to transfer the value, or the actual investments in their IPA, into a new IPA held within the new pension scheme. Alternatively, the individual may keep their original IPA and start a new IPA. There is no limit to the number of IPAs an individual may hold.

IPAs complement the stakeholder pensions regime and there is no charge for transferring an IPA into or out of a stakeholder scheme. In practice, there are very few providers who offer IPAs.

NATIONAL EMPLOYMENT SAVINGS TRUST (NEST) (FROM OCTOBER 2012 ONWARDS)

10.20A   It is clear that many people currently make little or no provision for their future pension. Furthermore, there is a lack of employer-supported pension provision, particularly in smaller firms.

The Government sought to address this issue in the *Pensions Act 2008* reform. A key part of these proposals is the introduction of good quality pension scheme for those who are not already in a workplace pension scheme. In appropriate cases, employers will be able to set up these schemes within the National Employment Savings Trust (or NEST) which is within the existing tax regime for registered pensions.

The NEST regime is designed to help low-to-medium earners who do not currently have access to a suitable employer pension scheme or pensions product.

The Government has recognised that the implementation of NEST will be complex and costly for many employers. Consequently, auto-enrolment into NEST will take place on a staggered basis between October 2012 (for companies with 120,000 plus employees) to March 2014/Feb 2016 (for those with less than 50 employees).

Under the scheme, all employers (regardless of size) must automatically enrol all their employees (aged over 22) into a (low-cost) pension scheme. New employees must be registered from commencement of employment. It is possible for employees to opt out (but this 'opt-out' must be renewed every three years).

Once an employee has their own pension 'account', it will be completely 'portable' and will remain with them throughout their working life. Through NEST, their personal pension accounts will provide a pension on retirement (including the tax-free lump sum equal to 25% of the fund). Companies with an existing good quality pension schemes can apply for exemption from the NEST scheme.

Companies that do not currently offer pension provision for their workforce (especially many smaller companies) will need to think about the type of pension scheme they wish to introduce and clearly communicate the details to their employees. Many small owner-managed companies are likely to see a rise in their payroll costs on full implementation of the Personal Accounts scheme

Both employers and employees will be obliged to pay a minimum level of contributions based on all the employee's earnings (falling within their basic rate income tax band). Employees will receive an additional 1% through tax relief. Annual contributions paid into employee's NEST accounts may be subject to a maximum limit.

It is likely that the required minimum contribution levels will be phased in as follows:

	Employee (inc 1% tax relief)	Employer	Total
Oct 2012	2%	1%	3%
Oct 2016	4%	2%	6%
Oct 2017	5%	3%	8%

TAX TREATMENT OF PENSION CONTRIBUTIONS

Individual's tax relief and the annual allowance (AA)

10.21 Only cash contributions are eligible for relief – it is not generally possible to make contributions in the form of assets. Exceptionally, shares acquired through an SAYE share option scheme (see 8.77) or share incentive plan (see 8.78) can be contributed *in specie* as a tax deductible contribution.

Income tax relief for contributions to registered pension schemes is given on the *greater* of £3,600 (gross) or 100% of the individual's taxable *earnings*. An owner-manager's taxable earnings broadly include their employment income and benefits – dividends and investment income are *not* included.

Under the post-A day rules, pension contributions tax relief was subject to an overall financial limit, in the form of an annual allowance (AA). The AA was originally very generous – in 2006/07 it was £215,000 and was increased every year with the 2010/11 AA reaching £255,000 (for details of pre-6 April 2011 AAs – see previous editions of this book).

In the current fiscal climate, the government began to view pension tax relief as imposing a massive 'cost' to the Exchequer and sought to restrict it. The previous Labour government planned to limit tax relief for individual's with annual income of over £130,000 (with the pre-6 April 2011 anti-forestalling rules being based on these principles –see 2010/11 edition at 10.24 for details). However, the incoming coalition government rejected this basis, and simply restricted pension contribution relief by reducing the annual allowance to £50,000 from 2011/12 onwards.

The lifetime allowance also provides a further restriction on the total value of pension savings that can benefit from tax relief when the contributions were made. When an individual's pension funds 'crystallises', the value of all their pension funds are totalled and tested against the prevailing lifetime allowance. Any excess will be subject to an penal income tax charge (see 10.28 for details).

Excess AA charge

10.22　From 6 April 2011, if an individual's annual pension contribution exceeds £50,000 (plus any unused relief brought forward – see 10.23A), they are liable to excess AA tax charge. The taxable excess is treated as though it was the 'top slice' of an individual's taxable income, and will therefore typically be at 50%/40% (as appropriate, having regard to the relevant slice/slices of income. (Note – the higher rate and additional rate thresholds are extended by 'grossed-up' gift aid donations and personal pension contributions.)

The excess AA charge is therefore taxed at the marginal tax(s) rate on which the individual claimed tax relief (*FA 2004, s 227 (4) (4A)*). Although the excess is taxed, it is not regarded as taxable income (and cannot therefore be reduced by losses or other reliefs) (*FA 2004, s 227 (5)*). If the excess AA charge for a year is £2,000 or less, it must be paid via self-assessment. Where it exceeds £2,000, it may be possible to pass this to the scheme administrator (see 10.24A).

Pension fund administrators are required to send 'pension statements' (showing details for the current year and three previous years) to those members whose inputs have exceeded the annual allowance.

AA AND PENSION INPUTS

10.23 Pensions tax relief is based on the contributions *made in the tax year* (*FA 2004, s 188*). However, the £50,000 AA is tested against the 'pension input' made in the individual's pension input period (or PIP) *ending in the relevant tax year* for the purposes of calculating the 'excess' AA tax charge.

The concept of PIPs was introduced on A-day, but given the lower AA limit, it is important to understand how PIPs work. When testing the PIPs against the 'pension input', it is necessary to look at all relevant pension contributions – i.e. personal contributions (the input is grossed-up at the basic rate tax added by HMRC), company contributions, and (for those in 'final salary' schemes) the increase in their pension 'promise (see 10.24A).

The rationale for including *company contributions* is that the individual enjoys effective tax relief on them, since they are not counted as a taxable benefit in kind!

For most pension scheme members, the first PIP *started* when the first contribution was paid after 6 April 2011 (i.e. A day) and ended on the first anniversary of its start date (*FA 2004, s 238*). Subsequent PIPs last one year.

However, *for those joining a new pension schemes after 6 April 2011*, the *FA 2011* aligns the PIP with the tax year. This means that the first PIP of a new joiner will end on 5 April each year, unless another date is nominated (*FA 2004, s 238*, as amended by *FA 2011, Sch 17, para 16*).

For those in *final salary* schemes (on A-day), pension rights are deemed to accrue on a daily basis (*FA 2004, s 238(2)*). This means that their first PIP will have begun on 6 April 2006 and ended 6 April 2007, so that their pension accrual during 2006/07 will be tested against the AA for 2007/08, with all future PIPS also being effectively one year out of sync! (see *HMRC Registered Pension Schemes Manual 06100060*). If a final salary scheme member joins after A day, their PIP will start on a different day from existing (pre-A-day) members and they will therefore have different PIPs

Since a PIP will depend on the pension scheme, it is possible for someone in a number of pension schemes to have different PIPs. An individual may therefore have different PIPs for their various schemes.

It is possible to change a PIP, subject to various restrictions. This might be helpful to align an individual's PIP with those of other scheme members or to align it to a tax year. Only one change can be made in a tax year and retrospective changes are no longer possible (*FA 2004, s 238(4A) (6)*). There is no need to notify a change of PIP to HMRC ((see *HMRC Registered Pension Schemes Manual 061000700*).

10.23A   There is no pension input amount for a PIP which ends in the tax year in which a member dies or satisfies the 'severe ill health condition' (within *FA 2004, s 229(3)(a), (4)*). However, payments into a pension scheme where someone takes early retirement for less serious conditions are still counted as pension inputs. (This alters the previous pre-*FA 2011* rule which ignored contributions made in the year benefits were taken – *FA 2004, s 229(3)(a)*).

Example 2

PIPs for defined contribution scheme

Mr Milner has been a member of defined contribution scheme for many years, making quarterly contributions.

His first (post-5 April 2006) pension contribution was made on 30 June 2006.

Consequently, Mr Milner's first PIP would start on 30 June 2006 and end on 30 June 2007. His subsequent PIPs would start on 1 July and end on 30 June each year.

Carry forward of unused relief

10.24   In calculating the AA charge (see 10.22), taxpayers can bring forward any unused relief from the *three* previous years (*FA 2004, s 228A*). Put another way, unused relief for a year can only be used for the next three years.

It is only possible for them to bring forward unused relief from a year provided an individual was a member of a pension scheme in that year (although they did not necessarily have to make a contribution (*FA 2004, s 227A(4)*).

The facility to carry forward unused relief is particularly helpful to those wishing to make contributions from large bonuses and redundancy payments.

Usefully, the carry forward rules includes 'transitional' rules to carry forward unused relief for pre-6 April 2011 periods but for these purposes the AA for 2008/09, 2009/10 and 2010/11 is only deemed to be £50,000 (as opposed to the actual AA for these years).

In calculating whether an excess AA charge is appropriate on pension contributions, the 'available relief' is used as follows:

- The AA for the relevant tax year (used first – *FA 2004, s 228A(3)*); then

- The unused relief from the three previous years (taken on a FIFO basis) is taken.

On 28 November 2011, HMRC confirmed that, due to a defect in the drafting of the 'transitional' unused relief legislation, there will be *no* clawback of the carried-forward relief where any 'transitional' year has pension contributions exceeding the excess over the deemed £50,000 AA.

There is no requirement to show the calculation on unused relief on the SA return, but workings should be retained in the event of an enquiry. It may be useful to record the unused relief on the 'white space'.

Example 3

Pension contributions and the AA

Mr Defoe, owns the entire share capital of 'his' company, Opportunist Strikers Ltd.

He made a single substantial pension contribution of £100,000 in August 2011 and his taxable income (after deducting all reliefs including the pension contribution) is £200,000.

Given that £100,000 contribution exceeds the AA of £50,000, it is necessary to calculate whether any excess AA charge is due for 2011/12.

Mr Defoe's pension contribution history is as follows:

PIP	Contributions in PIP	Tax Year	Annual Allowance
	£		£
1 Dec 2006 to 1 Dec 2007	80,000	2007/08	225,000
2 Dec 2007 to 1 Dec 2008	50,000	2008/09	235,000
2 Dec 2008 to 1 Dec 2009	60,000	2009/10	245,000
2 Dec 2009 to 1 Dec 2010	30,000	2010/11	255,000
2 Dec 2010 to 1 Dec 2011	100,000	2011/12	50,000

His unused relief brought forward is calculated as follows:

Tax Year	Contributions	(Deemed) Maximum AA	Unused relief
	£	£	£
2008/09	40,000	50,000	10,000
2009/10	60,000	50,000	(10,000)
2010/11	30,000	50,000	20,000
2011/12	100,000	50,000	–

This means that Mr Defoe has unused relief of £20,000 to carry forward to 2011/12. (Note – HMRC confirmed on 28 November 2011 that it would not be seeking any 'clawback' in the transitional relief bought forward where any year had premiums exceeding the deemed £50,000 – as in 2009/10 above – this excess is simply ignored.)

Although Mr Defoe would have originally claimed full tax relief on his £100,000 pension contribution in 2011/12, an appropriate part will be 'clawed-back' via an excess AA charge.

This is calculated as follows:

				£
2011/12 Pension contributions				100,000
Less:	AA	2011/12	50,000	
	Deemed AA	2010/11	20,000	
Available relief				(70,000)
Excess				30,000
AA charge @ 50% (marginal rate)				£15,000

Excess charge for 'defined scheme benefit' membeers

10.24A   Measuring the 'pension input' for a *defined benefit* (or 'final salary' scheme) is more complex. The pension scheme member accrues their rights by virtue of continued service. The funding of the scheme has no direct relationship with the increase in their pension rights. This could be done by obtaining full actuarial valuations each year but this would be a costly exercise. Consequently, the legislation provides that the increase in input value is simply based on a flat rate multiplier.

From 6 April 2011, the increase in the value of the 'pension promise' is multiplied by a flat rate of 16. Also, to eliminate the effect of inflation, the value of the opening 'pension promise' is indexed by the Consumer Prices Index over the PIP. See Example 4 below for illustrative 'pension input' calculation for a defined benefit scheme.

In some cases, a high salary increase (say on a promotion) combined with long service may give rise to a substantial input (which might still be protected from an AA charge due to the availability of unused relief from earlier years).

Example 4

Pension input for defined benefit scheme member

Mr Parker is a member of a defined benefit scheme, which provides for a retirement pension of 1/60th of his final salary for each year of service.

On 6 April 2011, Mr Parker's annual salary was £100,000 and he had been a member of the scheme for 15 years.

On 5 April 2012, his annual salary had risen to £120,000 with 16 years service.

The increase in Mr Parker's pension promise (i.e. his 'pension input' for 2011/12) is measured as follows (assuming the CPI increase is 4%):

5/4/12 – £120,000 ×16/60	32,000
6/4/11 – £100,000 × 15/60 × 1.04	(26,000)
Increase	6,000
Pension input (× 16)	£96,000

Mr Parker might have an excess AA charge in 2011/12 on an 'input' of £96,000, unless he has sufficient unused relief carried forward to 'shelter' the £46,000 excess over the 2011/12 AA of £50,000.

'Scheme to settle liability' for an AA charge

10.24B An 'excess' AA charge exceeding £2,000 can be met out of pension scheme funds. *FA 2004, s 237A* (as amended by *FA 2011, Sch 17, para 15*) provides that an individual can elect that the scheme administrator be jointly and severally liable with them for the AA charge. This election must be made by giving notice to the scheme by 31 July in the year following the tax year in which the AA charge arises. (For 2011/12 only, the deadline for giving notice is extended to 31 December 2013.) The 31 July following the tax year in which the charge arose is after the 31 January self-assessment deadline, which gives the individual time to determine their marginal tax rate and thus the charge payable by their pension fund.

Where such an election is made, this will lead to a 'reasonable' commensurate reduction in the individual's pension fund (*FA 2004, ss 237B* and *237E*). HMRC has confirmed that pension schemes are not permitted to make an administration charge for dealing with the AA charge and adjusting the pension benefits

Planning using the £3,600 tax-deductible contribution

10.24C Contributions of up to £3,600 per year can be paid without reference to the level of the individual's earnings. This useful feature enables proprietors of family and owner-managed companies to provide pensions for their 'non-working' spouses, children and grandchildren. Contributions can be made using the 'normal expenditure out of income' exemption for IHT (see 17.9).

Making contributions in this way to a stakeholder pension could well be a useful method for wealthy grandparents to extract money from their estates for inheritance tax purposes. Provided that the payments are regular (for example, are paid by monthly or quarterly direct debit), are paid out of income and do not diminish the normal standard of living of the grandparents, they should fall within the 'gifts out of normal expenditure' exemption [*IHTA 1984, s 21*].

Using this planning arrangement, grandparents could invest £300 gross monthly (£3,600 a year) for each grandchild from birth up until the age of 18 (and then make no further contributions). Contributions are made net of basic rate income tax, so that the actual amount paid by the grandparents is £2,880 a year, to which HMRC would add £720 (£3,600 at the basic rate of 20%). (Where appropriate, the grandchild could claim the higher rate tax relief on the grandparents' contributions.)

Assuming investment growth of 4% a year net of charges, about £95,000 in today's money would be accumulated by the time the child is 18. If this were then left to grow until the grandchild reached the pensionable age , the pension fund would be about £500,000. The actual return would of course depend on the performance of the fund and the level of annuity rates at the time the pension was drawn. Although the flexibility of this planning is significantly limited by the fact that the pension cannot be drawn until the age of 55, this may not matter – a substantial sum invested on behalf of the grandchildren could well free up their own savings to be invested in more flexible ways. In addition, planning of this kind may be particularly helpful where there is concern over an impetuous child and the grandparent wishes to fund an investment for later life.

The £3,600 contribution rule can also be used by UK employees who are seconded overseas. Provided they were a member of a GPP or Stakeholder scheme before leaving the UK and pay no UK tax, it is possible for them to pay a net amount of up to £2,880 a year to the pension scheme. They can do this for a maximum period of five years while overseas with the benefit of a tax credit from HMRC, thus enabling them to gross-up the payment to £3,600.

Migrant workers who come to the UK on secondment will be able to receive tax relief on contributions paid to overseas pension schemes that are recognised as such by HMRC. The relief will be restricted up to the level of their UK earnings.

Company contributions to registered schemes

10.25 Company contributions to a registered pension scheme can be deducted as a trading expense in the period in which they are paid, provided they are made wholly and exclusively for the purposes of the trade (*FA 2004, s 196*). Similar 'management expense' relief can be claimed by investment companies.

The pension rules provide that contributions must be made in cash – *in specie* contributions are not allowed. Under the *FA 2011* regime, it must be remembered that any *company contribution* for an employee/director is added to an individual's total pension inputs for the purposes of determining any excess AA charge (see 10.21 – 10.24). However, a company contribution is *not* restricted by reference to earnings.

It appears that HMRC applies the 'wholly and exclusively' test against the individual's *total* remuneration package. Inspectors must first clear any proposed company contribution 'disallowance' with HMRC's Audit and Pension Schemes Services (APSS) first, which should ensure a degree of consistency.

Many controlling directors (and members of their family) tend to pay themselves substantial dividends and a small salary, which potentially creates difficulties in securing corporate tax relief for pension contributions made for their benefit. HMRC has indicated that the 'wholly and exclusively' test would be judged against the contribution that would have been required to fund the pension provision for a third party employee in comparable circumstances, and that the salary and other benefits including pension contributions should be commensurate with the duties undertaken by the director. It is difficult to determine such a 'market rate' for an owner-managed company director/ participator. In practice, companies should be able to claim relief for fairly substantial contributions (up to the annual allowance), given that owner-managers invariably carry on considerably more onerous and responsible work than ordinary employees. In appropriate cases, the payment should be documented or verified by external supporting evidence (such as from an actuary's report). In such cases, the impact of the anti-forestalling rules would also need to be considered, since they may trigger a special tax charge on the owner manager.

It used to be beneficial to make a large company pension contribution where an an owner-manager was over 55 years old (and started drawing benefits), since this was not treated a pension input. However, the *FA 2011* now requires such contributions to be restricted by the AA (see 10.23A)

The 'wholly and exclusively' requirement is, however, unlikely to be satisfied where the company wishes to pay contributions for those members of the owner-manager's family who do not actively work for the company or only provide limited duties.

In practice, there should be no problems in obtaining tax relief for company pension contributions for the workforce. If the company has an OPS, an employee may be eligible to become a member. However, he may choose to take out his own person pension plan (PPP) instead. Whether or not that is the better option depends partly on the company's policy on contributing to the employee's PPPs. If the employer is prepared to contribute, it is better for it to pay directly to the PPP rather than increase the employee's salary, so as to save employer NICs which are not chargeable on the former arrangement.

In Example 5, the employee gets tax relief on his contribution of £1,000 which cancels his tax liability on the extra salary.

Example 5

Company pension contribution to employee's personal pension scheme

Best Ltd agrees to contribute £1,000 to an employee's PPP in 2011/12. It is willing to do this either directly to the PPP or indirectly by increasing the employee's salary to allow him to make the contribution.

Best Ltd pays corporation tax at the rate of 20%.

Contribution by Best Ltd	£
Gross	1,000
Corporation tax relief @ 20%	(200)
Net cost	800
Extra salary to employee	£
Gross	1,000
NIC (13.8%)	138
	1,138
Corporation tax relief @ 20%	(227)
Net cost	911
The saving is £111 (or about 11% of the contribution)	

10.25A Corporate tax relief for very large 'one-off' contributions will be spread over a maximum of four accounting periods (see below). Spreading only applies where:

- there are contributions in two consecutive years; and

- the second year's contribution is more than 210% of the first year's; and

- the relevant excess contributions (RECs) *exceed* £500,000 (RECs are the difference between the second year's contribution and 110% of the first year's contribution).

REC	*Number of accounting periods*
£500,000 to £999,999	2
£1,000,000 to £1,999,999	3
£2,000,000 or more	4

Planning should enable a gradual step up of the contributions to maximise the 110% allowance and reduce the need for spreading.

Where spreading is applied, this is based on the company contributions actually paid in the period. These should exclude contributions made in respect of funding cost of living increases for current pensioners, and funding future service benefits for employees who join the scheme this year – which are fully deductible. Furthermore, where the company has not paid any contributions in an accounting period (eg where a contribution holiday was taken), contributions for the next period are not subject to spreading.

To get around the 'spreading' rules companies sought to route their payments through another group company. However, the *FA 2008* introduced anti-avoidance rules (effective from 10 October 2007) to counter this type of planning.

Pensions surpluses repaid to employers

10.26 Authorised pension scheme surpluses (based on an actuarial valuation), which are normally only likely to arise in occupational schemes, can be repaid to the employing company provided certain conditions have been satisfied (see *Registered Pension Schemes (Authorised Surplus Payments) Regulations 2006 (SI 2006 No 574)*. Where an 'authorised surplus payment' is made, the scheme administrator must withhold tax at 35% from the payment and account for it to HMRC (*FA 2004, ss 177* and *207*).

Where a surplus payment is not authorised, the employer is liable to the unauthorised payments 'income tax' charge (see 10.27 below).

Where a registered scheme is subject to the 'surplus payments' provisions under the *Pensions Act 1995*, these must also be complied with to ensure the payment can be authorised. In the case of a continuing scheme, the trustees must obtain an actuarial certificate before exercising their power to repay a surplus.

Unauthorised payment charge

10.27 Where a pension scheme makes unauthorised payment, there is a tax charge of up to 55% on the scheme member. (The basic charge is 40% of the payment, with a 15% surcharge applying if certain limits are exceeded.) Furthermore, there is also a scheme sanction charge of 40% (but generally reduced to 15%) on the scheme administrator (which can be increased to 40%) (*FA 2004, ss 208–213*).

The case of *Thorpe v HMRC* SpC 683 provides authority on the treatment of unauthorised payments from a trust scheme (in this case a SIPP). Mr Thorpe was the only beneficiary of the scheme and decided that he could bring the scheme to an end and extract the funds under the rule in *Saunders v Vautier* [1835] 42 All ER Rep 58. However, although he was the only beneficiary at the time, it was possible that other beneficiaries could arise (he might marry or 'acquire' dependants within the meaning of the scheme rules). It was decided that Mr Thorpe was not entitled to the entire beneficial interest of the fund and the payment to him was a *taxable* unauthorised payment. However, the High Court ruled that therefore when, Mr Thorpe, (acting as trustee) sanctioned the unauthorised payment, he committed a breach of trust. Thus, since the money had been wrongly taken from the trust, he held it as a constructive trustee to the fund. He was willing and able to transfer the funds back and therefore no tax charge arose on the payment. A tax liability would have arisen on payments that he could not return.

LIFETIME ALLOWANCE RELATING TO REGISTERED SCHEMES

10.28 The lifetime allowance for 2011/12 is £1,800,000. However, from 6 April 2012, it will reduce to £1,500,000 (the rationale being that, with the 6 April 2011 reduction in the AA to £50,000 (see 10.21), the lifetime allowance need not be so high).

The lifetime allowance represents the eligible amount of pension value that attracts tax relief (i.e. tax-free 'lump sum up to 25% of the pension fund value and the remainder used to supply income by annuity or drawdown)

On A day, the lifetime allowance was set at £1,500,000 (and regularly increased in later years). However, individuals with substantial benefits built up before 6 April 2006 were able to protect their pension rights and benefits by electing for primary and enhanced protection.

As a result of the lifetime allowance being reduced to £1,500,000 from 6 April 2012, there are transitional provisions to deal with those who have pension funds already worth more than £1,500,000. In such cases, they can apply to HMRC for a 'personal' lifetime allowance based on the pre-existing £1,800,000. Similarly, individuals who consider that normal investment growth in their fund will take them above £1,500,000 (provided they make no further inputs) can also elect for a personal lifetime allowance of £1,800,000.

Broadly speaking, the lifetime allowance is tested on drawing benefits, on reaching the age of 75 with unvested funds, or on death. The value of the fund can be easily measured in the case of a defined contribution scheme. However, in the case of a defined benefits scheme, the value is determined by reference to various formulae. These include the conversion of pension income into a capital equivalent (by applying a factor of 20).

Where a member's total capitalised pension wealth exceeds the lifetime allowance, the excess amount is subject to a Lifetime Allowance Charge (LTAC) or 'recovery' charge. The LTAC tax rate charged depends on whether the 'excess capital' is taken as a pension (25%) or a lump sum (55%). The scheme rules may lay down how any 'excess' should be taken and HMRC expects the LTAC to be deducted at source, with the net amount being applied towards the lump sum/pension benefit.

Although pension income only attracts an LATC of 25%, the residual amount is then taxed at the relevant marginal income tax rate in the member's hands, thus generally resulting in a total effective tax charge of 55%. The registered scheme administrator and the member are jointly and severally liable for paying the tax charge.

PENSION FUND INVESTMENTS

10.29   Tax relief is now only available where the pension funds invest in traditional investments and commercial property. It is also possible for commercial property transactions to take place with connected parties on arm's length terms (see also 10.12).

Where property is acquired which is to be developed as commercial property, this may be vulnerable to a tax charge. Whilst capital gains are exempt within a pension fund (see 10.2), trading profits are not. Profits from a property development activity may therefore be taxed.

Pension funds cannot invest in residential properties (such as buy-to-let and second homes) and 'collectable' items (such as vintage cars and works of art). The Treasury justified these restrictions on the grounds that the pension fund tax breaks were only intended for those who were genuinely using the fund to provide themselves with a pension. It clearly wished to avoid leisure pursuits being sheltered from tax as a result of them being channelled through pension funds. The regulations also prohibit 'indirect' investment in residential property, etc – this would include, for example, the purchase of residential property by a company in which a SIPP holds 100% of the shares.

Sections 174A, 185A to 185I, 273ZA of and Schedule 29A to the Finance Act 2004 make provision for tax charges where an investment regulated pension scheme holds investments that are taxable property. Taxable property consists of residential property and most tangible moveable assets.

The provisions apply to taxable property that is held directly and also to indirect holdings of property. Pension funds are, however, able to invest indirectly in such 'prohibited' assets by investing in commercially diverse vehicles that hold residential properties. This would include investing in Real Estate Investment Trusts ('REITs') which hold residential properties.

Where a pension fund invests in a company, any 'chattels' owned by the company (worth less than £6,000 per asset) which are used for the purposes of its trade, management or administration are exempt from the 'private property' charge rules. This would normally cover such items as desks, computers, plant and machinery.

10.30   Furthermore, if a vehicle meets certain conditions, where the pension scheme and associates (broadly, members of the pension scheme and their families) own no more than 10% of the vehicle and have no right to private use of any taxable property, there is no tax charge.

'Arm's length' trading vehicles also qualify as 'commercially diverse', provided that they meet four conditions:

- The vehicle's main activity is the carrying on of a trade, profession or vocation.

- The pension scheme either alone or together with associated persons does not have control of the vehicle

- The pension scheme *member* or a 'connected person' [*CTA 2010, s 1122* is not a controlling director of the vehicle.

- The pension scheme does not hold an interest in the vehicle for the purposes of enabling a member (or connected person) to occupy or use the property.

It will be appreciated that this 'let out' will not be available to the majority of owner-managed companies.

Income and gains from the 'taxable' property would be taxed at 50%. Furthermore, the property would be subject to various unauthorised payment charges on the amount invested (40%) and possibly payment surcharges (15%), as well as a scheme sanction charge of 15% (see 10.27). It would therefore be sensible to hold such assets personally.

Pension funds can lend money to the employing company. However, loans made after 5 April 2006 must be secured, not exceed five years in duration (but can be rolled over once), and must be on commercial terms (with equal annual repayments and an interest charge at least equal to a composite bank base rate plus 1%). Furthermore, such loans must not exceed 50% of the fund. There is no requirement to re-negotiate existing borrowings to comply with the post-A day limits. It is not possible for the fund to make loans to members.

Shares can be purchased in the sponsoring 'employer' company, but only up to a maximum amount of 5% of the pension funds assets. Helpfully, all investments currently held by an existing pension scheme may be maintained after A day.

PENSION FUND BORROWINGS

10.31   Pension fund borrowings are limited to 50% of the fund. Given that it is only possible to 'gear-up' by 50%, if the value of the existing fund is relatively low, fairly large contributions are likely to be needed to make sizeable commercial property investments. However, in some cases it may be possible for the owner-manager's company to make the required contributions (within the rules set out in 10.21 to 10.24).

VESTING OF PENSION FUNDS

Retirement age

10.32 The minimum age for taking retirement benefits moves is now 55 (50 before 6 April 2010). Those with existing entitlements to lower retirement ages retain the right to retire at that age (provided this right was in force before 10 December 2003), although the member's lifetime allowance is proportionately restricted. Benefits from the registered scheme may be taken before age 55 if the member is prevented from continuing their current occupation because of ill health (as confirmed by a registered medical practitioner).

The scheme rules may allow benefits to be taken while the member continues to. Many owner-managers will clearly wish to take advantage of the fact that they can draw pension benefits while continuing to work in the company!

Benefits from a registered scheme

10.33 The tax-privileged pension benefits that can be paid out are purely dependent on the prevailing lifetime allowance (see 10.28)

Pensions must be paid at least on an annual basis (and are subject to PAYE) except where payments are from retirement annuity policies. A tax-free cash sum can be taken of up to 25% of the value of the fund, the maximum amount being limited to 25% of the current lifetime allowance limit. (Since 6 April 2011, lump sum benefits can be taken at any age, whilst in 'drawdown' (see 10.34 and 10.35).)

Pension payments normally stop on death. However, in some cases, the pension can be guaranteed for fixed period which does not stop on death. In such cases, the value of the estate's right to receive the remaining payments should be brought into account for IHT. However, payments made to the surviving spouse or civil partner are *not* included. The pension fund may also be passed down to family members on death (so, for example, children could be nominated pension members on death). IHT may be chargeable on such an event and will depend on the circumstances of the case – for example, the spouse exemption may be available.

The *FA 2006* introduced anti-avoidance rules to prevent the 're-cycling' of tax-free cash sums, whereby a scheme member aged 50 or over draws a lump sum tax-free and reinvests it into the scheme (obtaining tax relief) then withdraws 25% of the newly-invested sum (again tax-free), reinvests it (obtaining tax relief), withdraws 25% of this reinvested sum, etc. Without the *FA 2006* restrictions, the value of the fund could be significantly increased by this method. Post-*FA 2006*, subject to certain conditions, the re-investment will now be treated as an unauthorised payment, with a resulting 40% income tax charge on the member. There is, however, still scope for limited re-cycling to increase the value of the fund, as it will only be caught if the lump sum is more than 1% of the lifetime allowance.

The requirement to use registered pension scheme funds to buy an annuity at age 75 will be scrapped from 2011/12. Pending implementation of the necessary changes, from 22 June 2010, the 'annuity' age threshold rises from 75 to 77. This change also applies for the purposes of inheritance tax (IHT) charges for pension scheme members aged 75 or more. For members of money purchase pension schemes who reach age 75 after 21 June 2010, the strict alternatively secured pension (ASP) income limits will apply from age 77.

10.34   There is much greater flexibility as to how and when pension benefits can be enjoyed and there is no longer any requirement to purchase an annuity by the age of 77. Broadly speaking, benefits can be taken in one of the following ways:

- *scheme pension* – the pension is provided from the registered scheme or appropriate insurance company (see 10.35). For occupational scheme members, this is the only option available although the scheme can offer unsecured income if the rules are amended to allow the scheme to do so;

- *lifetime annuity* – the annuity is secured through an insurance company;

- *'Capped drawdown'* – (from 6 April 2011) a single income drawdown facility is available (irrespective of whether the individual has reached their 77th birthday). Under income drawdown, individuals can choose how much they wish to draw down annually from their pension fund (subject to a capped limit), or whether they wish to take any income at all (see 10.35). (Under the pre-6 April 2011, unsecured pension (USP) arrangements were available until an individual's 77th birthday, with 'alternatively unsecured pensions' (ASPs) being available the age of 77).

Following the *FA 2011* changes, the payment of the tax-free lump sum takes place when drawdown commences.

Where a member of a pension scheme dies *before age 75*, death benefits can either be taken as a tax-free 'lump sum' to a nominated beneficiary (up to the amount of the lifetime allowance) *or* as a pension paid to one or more dependants.

Death benefits after the age of 75 are more restrictive since the funds must be used to provide dependants' pensions. It is not therefore possible to return funds to family members without penal tax charges being applied (see 10.35).

CAPPED DRAWDOWN

10.35   Under the 'drawdown' rules, the member's pension scheme fund remains invested under the control of the scheme trustees, with the member being able to take an annual income based on figures produced by the Government Actuary's Department (GAD). These GAD limits are designed to offer a flexible income stream broadly equivalent to an annuity. However, some individuals may be able to opt for flexible drawdown (see 10.37)

Since 6 April 2011, the drawdown rules have been relaxed considerably. Drawdown is available on the same terms during an individual's retirement. *Regardless of age*, they can take annual income of any amount between nil and 100% of the Government Actuary's Department (GAD) limits (the GAD tables have been recently revised to reflect up-to-date life expectancy levels).

With 'drawdown', there will be an undrawn balance on the member's death. This could be used to provide income benefits to their survivors (e.g. a widow's pension, which is taxed in their hands in the normal way) or paid out as a lump sum death benefit.

The tax position for lump sum death benefits is as follows:

	Tax treatment of death benefit
Death in service (i.e. before taking a Pension Commencement Lump Sum – deadline for taking it is 75th birthday)	Tax-free (up to the lifetime allowance (see 10.28)
Death thereafter	Tax charge at 55%

Flexible drawdown

10.36   The ability to take a 'flexible drawdown' outside the constraints of the GAD 'annuity' limits (in 10.36 above) is available to those who can satisfy the minimum income requirement rules (*FA 2011, Sch 16*). Following consultation, the government permitted a more flexible drawdown facility, subject to the overriding requirement to ensure that individuals did not deplete their funds by excessive income payments.

Flexible drawdown arrangements are available provided an individual satisfies the minimum income requirement for the relevant tax year. The minimum income requirement is £20,000 per year, which must be made up of some combination of:

● A scheme pension from a registered pension scheme (or overseas equivalent)

● A lifetime annuity from a registered pension scheme (or overseas equivalent)

● The State Pension (or overseas equivalent)

Where an individual makes a 'minimum income' declaration to their pension funds trustees, they may take unlimited amounts from 'their' scheme (provided the scheme rules permit it). This is taxed as pension income in the normal way (and does not constitute an unauthorised payment – see 10.27).

The flexible drawdown rules enable individuals to take as much income as they need (even to the extent of exhausting their drawdown 'pot'). Dependants (such as widows and widowers) can also take advantage of drawdown arrangements in respect of a deceased member's pension funds.

Although scheme pensions (see 10.36A) have certain advantages over income drawdown, drawdown may be more suitable where a member has a much younger spouse. If they die with a drawdown, their pension can be passed to their 'younger' spouse who can use it under income drawdown rules (which should give a higher income and greater investment freedom).

Use of scheme pension products

10.35A Schemes are available that allow pension fund members to take control over their retirement funds once they reach the age of 77. These so-called 'scheme pensions' offer an alternative to buying an annuity or taking income drawndown since they enable families to invest their pensions together and pass assets down to other family members. Scheme pension products can be obtained from a number of reputable providers. However, in practice, they are only likely to be suitable for very large pension funds (since they are usually fairly expensive to set-up and involve running costs). Some providers have suggested that the value of the scheme should be at least £200,000.

In a smaller scheme pension (which can be set up for two to 12 members), the actuary will calculate the amount of income to be paid to the member. Here there are no set limits (in contrast with income drawdown – see 10.36) so the amount to be paid out can be more tailored to the beneficiary's age and health. Thus, a scheme pension is likely to pay a higher pension in retirement.

There are no set limits – if the member dies, the remainder of their pension is pooled and shared amongst the other members, which (in the context of an owner managed company) will be other family members. There is some flexibility on the distribution of the growth within the fund – it does not have to be distributed on an equal basis. It is therefore possible for older members to pass some of their fund to the younger members (although the actuary must have a good reason for doing this).

Scheme pension products have the option of guaranteeing the income payouts for ten years. Thus, if a member dies, the remaining family members will continue to receive the income (which is taxed at their income tax rates and is not subject to IHT). Any funds remaining in the scheme are transferred to the other members, although they cannot access them until they reach normal pensionable age. They can of course, decide to take the funds earlier but these would be exposed to a penal tax charge.

FUNDED UNAPPROVED RETIREMENT BENEFIT SCHEMES (FURBS))

Background

10.37   Funded Unapproved Retirement Benefit Schemes (FURBS) have traditionally been used to provide valuable top-up pension benefits to key personnel where the (pre-A day) earnings cap restricted their pension provision.

10.38   FURBS are not normally 'registered schemes' (see 10.4) and (since A-day) have been designated as 'Employer-financed Retirement Benefit Schemes'. Consequently, such schemes do not enjoy any special tax advantages under the pension regime.

Funds accumulated within a FURBS are not included within an individual's lifetime allowance (see 10.28). Similarly, post-5 April 2006 contributions are not included in computing the individual's annual allowance (see 10.21).

Since 6 April 2006, companies do not receive tax relief on their contributions to the scheme until benefits start to be paid to the member (and taxed in their hands). However, payments made by the company are not taxed in the employees' hands.

All benefits paid from the scheme after 5 April 2006 will be taxed. Investment income and capital gains within a FURBS are taxed at the normal trust tax rates (see 17.81). Discretionary trust-based schemes are subject to the normal IHT charges (see 17.88–17.94).

In recent years, FURBS have been promoted and used as a successor to Employee Benefit Trusts in aggressive tax planning schemes. Broadly, such arrangements usually seek to claim a corporation tax deduction for contributions made to an EFRB. The trustees of the EFRB then 'ear-mark' the contributed funds for the benefit of the owner manager(s) and possibly senior management. Typically, the funds are then lent to the owner managers/senior management on a commercial basis with the aim of avoiding any tax charge on their receipt.

However, the purported tax advantages of FURBS have now been blocked by the *FA 2011* 'disguised remuneration' legislation. In such cases, any 'earmarking' of funds or loans made to owner managers or employees will be treated as employment income (subject to PAYE and NIC) (see 5.12). HMRC are also challenging companies who have used EFRBs to avoid paying tax on 'effective' bonus payments, with the view to collecting unpaid PAYE and NIC on the amounts 'lent' to owner managers/employees (see 5.11A).

Special transitional provision

10.39   *Lump sum benefits* from pre-6 April 2006 FURBs can continue to be taken tax-free (see 10.33) provided the employer company has made no further contributions to the scheme after 5 April 2006.

Where such payments have been made, the amount of lump sum that may be taken without a tax charge is restricted to the market value of the scheme's assets at 5 April 2006, as increased by the amount of the RPI at the date of payment (plus any post-5 April 2006 *employee* contributions).

Similarly, where no contributions have been made to the scheme after 5 April 2006, the fund will enjoy pre-A day IHT treatment, including exemption from the 10-year periodic charge (see 10.38). If further contributions have been made after 5 April 2006, beneficial IHT treatment is only given to the 'protected portion' of the fund (ie the pre-A day fund).

STATE PENSION ISSUES

Dealing with the pensions crisis

10.40   Increasing life expectancy coupled with lower investment returns have considerably increased the value of the basic state pension over the last decade or so. For example, a youngster would require a pension fund of around £500,000 at age 65 to provide the (real term) equivalent of the current basic state pension.

The cost of providing state pensions is expected to rise significantly in the medium term. The government accepts that the present system is unsustainable and difficult choices have to be made to deal with the 'cost' of an ageing society.

Faced with a looming pensions crisis, the independent commission headed by Lord Turner announced recommendations for a radical overhaul of the pensions system. The government have produced a White Paper in response, with proposals broadly in line with Lord Turner's recommendations. These include a more generous basic state pension, linked to earnings not prices. This will be partly 'paid for' by an increase in the state pension age, increasing to 68 by 2044. (Under current rules, both men and women would retire at 65 from 2020.)

These proposals will also be supplemented by the new 'mandatory' NEST regime (see 10.21).

CURRENT STATE PENSIONS REGIME

10.41   Directors and employees only need to have earnings above the lower NIC earnings limit to qualify for a basic state pension). It is not necessary to pay any actual contributions, although this will normally be the case.

The rules changed on 6 April 2010 – a NICs 'contribution' record of just 30 years is required to achieve a full state pension (previously it was normally 44 years for men and 39 years for women!). Furthermore, every qualifying NIC year accrues some state pension benefit. Special rules reduce the number of qualifying years for entitlement in certain cases, for example, non-working mothers will qualify for home responsibilities protection where they receive child benefit. These will help to maximise a spouse's pension.

Employees (but not the self-employed) are also entitled to additional state pension or earnings-related pension (also referred to as State Second Pension or S2P. Provided they have earnings just above the lower earnings limit, they are treated as having earnings for additional state pension purposes, for 2011/12, of £14,400. At the current surplus percentage rate of 40% (for those retiring after 2010), this potentially produces an additional pension of £3,638 (£14,400 less £5,304 @ 40%). On the other hand, employees may contract out of the state system and have the benefit paid into a private pension fund. Further information can be obtained on the Department for Work and Pensions website (www.thepensionservice.gov.uk).

PLANNING CHECKLIST – PENSION SCHEME STRATEGIES

Company

- 'Substantial' company pension contributions in respect of owner-managers must be capable of justification (based on the entire reward package, including the contribution).

- Watch the potential annual allowance (AA) charge where total pension inputs (including company contributions) exceed the 2011/12 AA of £50,000 plus any unused relief brought forward).

- Consider company pension (self-administered) scheme for working shareholders to be used as tax saving vehicle.

- Stakeholder pension may provide best value if there are only a small number of employees, or a company (occupational pension) scheme for a larger payroll.

- Those companies that do not offer any form of pension provision for their workforce must think about the impact of the compulsory NEST 'personal pension account' which will require them to contribute to a pension for all their employees (aged over 22). The NEST regime is being introduced on a staggered basis from late 2012 to 2016.

Working shareholders

- From 2012/13 onwards owner-managers will only be able to hold up to £1.5 million (lifetime allowance) in their pension fund on a tax-

---

privileged basis. However, if their fund exceeds £1.5 million but is within the previous £1.8 million lifetime allowance, they can elect to continue with a 'personal' £1.8 million pension fund 'ceiling'.

- Where owner-managers personally own the company's trading property, they can realise cash at a favourable CGT rate by selling the property at market value to 'their' pension fund. This may attract an SDLT charge for the pension fund.

- Since 6 April 2011, owner managers making pension contributions exceeding £50,000 in a year may have to pay an excess AA charge if the total contributions in their pension input period (PIP) *ending in the tax year* exceeds the £50,000 AA (plus any unused relief brought forward). The excess AA chare rules reduce the attraction of a company paying special contributions as part of a pre-sale tax planning arrangement for the owner manager.

- It will be helpful to keep a summary of unused 'AA' relief which can be carried forward for up to three years and can be used to avoid paying an excess AA charge. Unused relief can only be brought forward if the 'worker' was an enrolled member of a pension scheme in that year.

- There is much greater flexibility on the drawing of pension benefits – tax-free lump sums can be taken without the need effectively to draw a pension and there is no longer any need to purchase an annuity at age 77.

- Owner-managers have the ability to draw their pension benefits whilst continuing to work in 'their' company.

Other employees

- Those earning below £10,000 per year may be better off staying in the state pension scheme, but many in the pensions industry think this is true for the vast majority regardless of their earnings.

- Consider the use of 'salary sacrifice' arrangements as a means of securing additional pension contributions.

Non-working shareholders

- Contributions of up to £3,600 per year may be made by an individual to a pension scheme for non-working shareholders, including spouses, children and grandchildren.

Chapter 11

Share Issues and Financing the Company's activities

INTRODUCTION

11.1   Typical 'investment' stages would include: 'seed', start-up, early stage, expansion, management buy-in, MBO and rescue/turnaround situations.

There are also many ways in which a company can improve its finances. These can be internally generated by retaining profits or improving cash flow without any immediate tax consequences. This could include such areas as tighter credit control procedures, careful planning of payments to suppliers, controlling overheads, and managing stock levels.

In the current difficult economic climate, many companies are struggling to pay their tax bills (including corporation tax, PAYE and VAT). This was recognised in the Pre-Budget Report 2008, which gave companies the ability to agree deferred payment terms for their tax liabilities with HMRC under the 'Time To Pay' initiative. HMRC continue to operate the scheme although are taking a tougher stance with companies to ensure that their payment proposals are realistic! (see 4.52)

Externally generated funds may arise from the shareholders or from third parties, such as friends, business associates and so on. Other options would include bank overdrafts and loans, factoring and invoice discounting, regional grants and special loans. Current economic conditions have significantly tightened the availability of bank lending. The recently introduced Enterprise Finance Guarantee Scheme should enable viable businesses to access working capital facilities (backed by Government guarantee) (see 11.3).

Where additional equity investment is needed, the owner-manager may seek finance from a private equity firm/venture capitalist (see 11.4) or a business angel (see 11.4).

The commercial impact and tax consequences can vary tremendously. The best method of raising finance from a tax viewpoint is often not apparent until the trading results have been established over a few years. Tax planning with the benefit of hindsight is of course impossible, but in this particular area there are often other factors which dictate the method of raising funds. The issue should be considered from all angles, with a combination of methods sometimes giving the optimum position.

In some cases, it may be possible to structure equity investments under the Enterprise Investment Scheme (EIS), which currently gives valuable income tax and CGT reliefs (see 11.26–11.51). Great care is required when the EIS is being used to attract investment from outside investors. In such cases, any 'promise' of relief by the company should be carefully explained and given appropriate 'caveats' and disclaimers.

Legal and other specialist input is also vital to ensure adherence with the *Financial Services Act* rules concerning 'investment advertisements' (especially *Financial Services and Markets Act 2000, s 21*). It is a criminal offence to make or assist in the promotion of a share issue unless the communications have been made (or have been approved) by an authorised person (unless one of the exemptions applies). Similarly, a prospectus may be required under the *Public Offer Securities Regulations 1995*.

LONG- VERSUS SHORT-TERM FUNDING

11.2   Long-term funding will be in the form of share capital (equity) or long term loans. The owner-managers will inject equity or share capital finance and often provide 'shareholder loans'.

Short-term funding is generally required to finance the company's varying working capital requirements. Although this will frequently be in the form of a bank overdraft, in recent years we have witnessed a major growth in invoice financing with many 'competitive' products now being available. Provided the company can satisfy certain criteria, invoice discounting can provide more flexibility giving the business the money it needs without having to provide the 'belt and braces' security required by banks. Importantly, it overcomes the problem of the lead time between invoice issue and the payment by the customer.

Many companies make the mistake of funding long-term objectives with short-term borrowings. If funding is required for in excess of 12 months, it may be well to discuss a term loan with the company's bankers and to agree favourable rates and conditions.

GOVERNMENT-BACKED FINANCE SCHEMES

11.3   In the current economic climate, 'small' businesses have generally found it difficult to obtain access to finance as banks have tightened their lending programmes. To support small businesses experiencing such difficulties the Government introduced the Enterprise Finance Guarantee Scheme (EFGS).

The EFGS will generally support bank lending (between three months and ten years maturity), to UK businesses with a turnover of up to £25 million who are currently having difficulties obtaining the finance they need. There are certain restrictions to businesses operating in agriculture, financial, education, forestry, insurance, and transport sectors.

The scheme is fully managed by the participating lenders, including the decision as to whether it should be provided in connection with any specific lending transaction. Under the scheme, 'small' businesses are able to obtain loans of between £1,000 and £1 million backed by the Government guarantee, payable over up to 10 years. (The Government guarantees 75% of the relevant scheme loan with the bank effectively covering the remaining 25%.) The scheme can also be used to refinance existing loans, convert overdrafts into loans, as well as providing overdraft facilities.

Although the scheme was due to finish on 31 March 2011, the coalition Government confirmed that it would continue for the next four years, making about £2bn available.

VENTURE CAPITAL/PRIVATE EQUITY

11.4   In some cases, venture capitalists/private fund managers or so-called 'business angels' may also contribute a 'slice' of equity capital and/or loan finance. Most private equity firms 'target' companies requiring investment of over £100,000, mainly in the early and expansion stages of growth. According to the British Venture Capital Association ('BVCA') (www.bvca.co.uk), most of the companies 'backed' receive amounts of less than £1 million.

Private equity is not suitable for every company, especially for those owner-managers who are independently minded and do not wish to concede any part of their equity to an outsider. Similarly, private equity is unlikely to be suitable for so-called 'life-style' businesses which enable their owners to enjoy a good standard of living and job satisfaction. Private equity firms generally look for entrepreneurial businesses that have potential for realistic growth, backed up by a credible business plan, and an experienced and ambitious management team. Companies are also likely to benefit from the experienced input and commitment of the private equity executives.

Under a typical private equity transaction, the selling shareholders will often have some retained interest in the business (either through equity share capital and/or loan notes). Management will also hold some of the equity interest. The percentage of share capital held by the private equity fund can vary from a large controlling equity stake (for a highly-leveraged buy-out) to less than 50% for 'growth' funding. The funds generated from the private equity deal will generally used to buy the outgoing shareholders shares and to provide growth capital to facilitate future growth. Where a business is in its 'growth stage' the selling shareholders will be expected to remain heavily involved in the running of the business, which can sometimes lead to some tax complications (see, for example, 15.76)

Where venture capital/private equity funding is provided, there will normally be a shareholders' agreement, which regulates the shareholder 'relationship' between the 'management' team and venture capitalist(s), etc, specifying their respective powers and obligations to the company and between themselves.

In some ways, venture capital is a partnership between the investor and owner-manager which focuses almost exclusively on building the capital value of the business for future realisation. A private equity investor will always ensure that there is a mechanism for achieving their 'exit' at an appropriate stage, such as by a company purchase of own shares, selling the shares to another private equity firm, a 'trade' sale of the shares or flotation.

Private equity has come under the spotlight in recent years, with criticism from Trade Unions, amongst others, that private equity firms are acting as 'asset strippers', and that private equity companies tend to be run for short-term gain rather than adopting a long-term approach which would benefit employees and customers.

Although the private equity sector has come under increasing scrutiny, its highly positive contribution to the UK economy must also be recognised – for example:

- Private equity backed companies grow sales, profits, and employment faster than other companies.

- Because of this, returns of private-equity backed companies have consistently outstripped the returns of listed entities

- The private equity industry attracts significant investment into the UK (over 70% of its investors are based overseas).

BUSINESS ANGELS

11.5   Business angels are wealthy individuals (often successful entrepreneurs or senior managers) that wish to invest their own money in return for an equity stake. They typically invest between £10,000 and £100,000 in start-up and other early stage financing in return for a share of the rewards if the company succeeds. They can also bring management expertise to the company.

COMPANY BORROWINGS

Interest

11.6   The tax treatment of interest on company borrowings is governed by the 'loan relationship' rules. The loan giving rise to the interest is a loan relationship, and the interest, usually calculated on an accruals basis, is a 'debit' of that relationship. The relief given for the interest depends on whether or not the loan was taken out for the purposes of the company's trade.

Amounts borrowed to buy fixed assets for use in the trade, for working capital, or an 'asset purchase' of a trade will be treated as trading loan relationships. Borrowing to finance an investment or to purchase shares in a trading company will be non-trading (see also 4.4(*h*) and 4.43(*d*)).

Highly-leveraged private equity deals can often make the borrowing company 'thinly capitalised' and this may lead to a disallowance of some of the interest cost (under the 'transfer pricing' rules (see 4.11)). Withholding taxes may also apply where overseas private equity funds are involved.

Trading loan relationships

11.7   Interest on loans taken out for the purposes of the trade is treated as an expense of the trade and is an allowable deduction in arriving at the profits of the trade.

If the interest augments or creates a trade loss for corporation tax purposes, the trading loss can be carried forward to set against future profits of the same trade [*CTA 2010, s 45 (ICTA 1988, s 393(1))*]. Alternatively, the trading loss can be offset against any profits of the same accounting period [*CTA 2010, s 37(3)(a) (ICTA 1988, s 393A(1)(a))*] and if required then against any profits of the previous 12 months [*CTA 2010, s 37(3)(b) (ICTA 1988, s 393A(1)(b))*]. See 4.35 for details of the 'temporary' extended three year carry back rules for losses arising in accounting periods with year-ends between 24 November 2008 and 23 November 2010.

Non-trading loan relationships

11.8   Interest payable on non-trading loan relationships (ie loan relationships entered into other than for the purposes of the trade) is aggregated with any other non-trading relationship debits and credits (for example, interest receivable, discounts, etc).

If the resultant figure is a net credit (ie total non-trading credits exceed non-trading debits), then this is taxed as a non-trading profit. Similarly, if a net debit arises, this is relieved as a non-trading deficit (see 4.4(*h*)) [*CTA 2009, s 301*].

Under current rules, a non-trading deficit can be relieved in various ways. First, it is possible to surrender all or part of the deficit by way of group relief (without having to offset it against the surrendering company's profits first) [*CTA 2009, s 457(2)(a)*].

Relief for any non-trading deficit is also available under *CTA 2009, s 459*:

- by set-off against the total profits of the same accounting period (which is referred to in the statute as the deficit period)

- by carry-back and set-off against *non-trading loan relationship* profits arising in the previous 12 months.

Failing that, the deficit must broadly be carried forward and offset against the company's future non-trading profits (ie *all profits except trading profits*) [*CTA 2009, s 457*]. Where a company consistently generates non-trading deficits, the limited offset available against future *non-trading profits* is likely to result in 'stranded' deficits that cannot be relieved.

Example 1

Loan relationship – 'accruals' basis of recognition for tax purposes

Brooking Plastics Ltd borrowed £50,000 on 1 January 2011 for a four-year period with a fixed interest rate of 10% per annum. The amount was borrowed to purchase a new plastic moulding machine. Interest is payable every six months from 1 July 2011.

The company's accounting year end is 31 March. The company's accounts have always been drawn up on the accruals basis. The accounts for the year ended 31 March 2011 would include accrued interest for three months of £1,250 (£50,000 @ 10% × 3/12). This amount is deductible as a trading expense in the corporation tax computation for the accounting period to 31 March 2011.

The interest relieved as a trading expense for later periods would be as follows:

		£
Year to	31/3/12	5,000
	31/3/13	5,000
	31/3/14	5,000
	31/3/15	3,750

SHAREHOLDER LOANS TO COMPANY

Tax relief for interest on loans taken out to lend to company

11.9   It is possible for shareholders to borrow the funds themselves and then to lend these to the company. The shareholder can only obtain interest relief where the borrowing company is a qualifying close company within *CTA 2010, s 34* – broadly, a company that is mainly trading or property letting (to third parties).

The company must apply the funds wholly and exclusively for the purposes of its business or that of an associated company [*ITA 2007, s 392*]. Relief from income tax will be available to the shareholder in respect of loan interest paid (but *not* in respect of bank overdraft interest) provided certain conditions are satisfied (see 11.10–11.12).

Allowable interest payments are deducted against total taxable income. For relief to be obtained the borrower must, therefore, have sufficient taxable income to offset it. It is not possible to carry excess interest payments forward or back to set against total income of future or prior years.

If the shareholder has a high level of taxable income it might be considered preferable for them to borrow personally as the tax rates are higher for an individual than for a company. This is, of course, unlikely where the individual needs to extract income from the company to repay their borrowings, as this will create an additional personal tax liability. Relief for personal borrowings can generally be obtained on tax at 40% or 50% whereas on corporate borrowings the *maximum* relief for companies is much lower .

The 'material interest' and 'full time working' conditions

11.10   A shareholder will qualify for interest relief where they possess a 'material interest' in the relevant company, ie the shareholder must control either directly (or indirectly through intermediate companies) over 5% of the ordinary share capital of the company. This ownership can be alone or through associates. Alternatively, a right to acquire more than 5% of the assets on a winding up would also satisfy the 'material interest' test [*ITA 2007, ss 393(4) and 394*].

Ordinary shareholders who do *not* meet the 'material interest' test would also be entitled to relief provided they have worked for the greater part of their time in the actual management or conduct of the company (or 'associated company') [*ITA 2007, s 393(3)*].

IR Tax Bulletin November 1993 sets out the Revenue's views on the meaning of working 'for the greater part of their time in the actual management or conduct of the company', which is strictly construed.

A distinction is drawn between directors and other individuals for the purpose of this test. Clearly, a director would satisfy this test. Failing that, the individual must possess significant managerial or technical responsibilities and must be concerned in the overall running and policy making of the company as a whole. Managerial or technical responsibility for just one particular area will not be sufficient. However, it is accepted that whether an individual satisfies the 'actual management or conduct' test is a question that can only be answered by consideration of the full facts of the particular case. (HMRC interpret 'the greater part of the individual's time' as meaning more than half the working day throughout the period in question).

Members of family or owner-managed companies whose management is divided between several individuals may therefore have difficulty in claiming relief for interest if they do not have a shareholding over 5%.

The 'qualifying close company' condition

11.11   The company concerned must be a qualifying close company within the meaning of *CTA 2010, s 34 (ICTA 1988, s 13A(2))*. Consequently, the company must exist either wholly or mainly to carry on a trade on a commercial basis or to let property to unconnected third parties. Alternatively, the company concerned may own shares in a qualifying company or co-ordinate the activities of two or more qualifying companies – many holding companies would fall into this category.

Conditions to be satisfied when interest is paid

11.12   At the time *when the interest is paid* by the individual, the requirements set out both in 11.10 and 11.11 above must still be met. However, if the company has lost its close company status, for example due to additional equity having been issued to a venture capital fund, relief will still be available provided the company continues to trade (see SP 3/78).

Recovery of capital

11.13   The individual must also be able to demonstrate that, in the period from the application of the proceeds of the loan to the payment of the interest, they have not recovered any capital from the company [*ITA 2007, s 406*]. The events giving rise to a 'recovery of capital' include a sale, gift, or repayment of share capital or the repayment of a loan made to them by the company [*ITA 2007, s 407(1)*], regardless of whether any of the monies have been applied in reducing the actual original loan.

Thus, where a company repays part of the shareholder's loan, the 'repayment' will represent a 'recovery of capital' and is treated as reducing the qualifying loan. The allowable interest would then be based on the deemed *reduced* qualifying loan. If the loan is repaid regularly during the year, HMRC may accept an average of the opening and closing balances as approximating to the deemed qualifying loan for interest relief purposes.

Security issues

11.14   Where an individual makes the borrowing the bank or lending institution will normally insist upon security, for example, the applicant's house or insurance policy. Sometimes shareholders are of the opinion that this can be avoided if the loan is taken out by the company. So often this is not the case and the lending institution will again insist upon personal security being provided by the director shareholders.

Irrecoverable shareholder loans

11.15   In some cases, the shareholder may be unfortunate enough to find that the loan becomes irrecoverable. Provided the company has used the funds only for the purposes of its trade, the individual can claim an allowable loss for CGT purposes on the amount of the loan which is proved to be irrecoverable.

The relief also applies where the loan involves a guarantor who is called on to pay the debt, such as where the individual shareholder personally guarantees the company's bank borrowings. The guarantor then qualifies for the loss for capital gains purposes [*TCGA 1992, s 253*].

Normally, losses in respect of irrecoverable loans are deemed to arise when claimed, but the claim can be backdated to an earlier period within the previous two years [*TCGA 1992, s 253(3A)*]. A similar situation applies to shares that have become worthless [*TCGA 1992, s 24(2)*]. (The detailed treatment of irrecoverable loans and shares which become of 'negligible value' is examined in 16.47–16.52.)

FINANCING WITH SHARE CAPITAL

Basic legal aspects of share issues

11.16   Private companies are not permitted to offer or allot their shares to the 'public'. The directors have the power to issue shares, but it is only possible to issue shares up to the amount of the company's authorised share capital. Since October 2008, companies are not required to specify an authorised share capital on incorporation – instead an initial statement of capital will be required, which must be subsequently updated when required – for example, when a new issue of shares takes place.

If further shares are 'required', then the authorised share capital can be increased by an ordinary resolution of the members. It is always necessary to check the company's articles before a new share issue is made. (Existing companies can now amend their articles to remove any reference to authorised share capital.)

Shares are often issued at a premium, where the price paid to the company exceeds the nominal value of the share(s) issued. The nominal value is the minimum price for which the shares can be issued. Thus, if shares with a nominal value of £1 are issued at a price of (say) £2.50, there is a premium of £1.50 (ie £2.50 less £1).

Where the consideration for the share issue exceeds its nominal value, the excess amount must be credited to a share premium account in the company's books [*CA 2006, s 610*]. Use of the share premium account is restricted. It can only be used to write off expenses incurred in connection with the share issue giving rise to that premium or issuing fully-paid bonus shares.

Companies cannot issue shares at a discount, ie for a consideration that is less than their nominal value.

The directors have a duty to act in the best interests of the company when issuing shares. Thus, if a £1 nominal value share is worth (say) £2.50, they would need to have a good reason for issuing it at a price below £2.50.

A company's shares are deemed to be paid-up where the consideration received is a cash consideration, which is widely defined in *CA 2006, s 583* as a release of a liability of the company for a liquidated sum – *s 583(3)(c)*. A private company can accept virtually any form of valuable consideration, including the provision of services, goodwill and know how [*CA 2006, s 582(1)*].

Private companies with PLC status

11.16A   Some 'private' owner managed companies are keen to have 'PLC' or 'plc' (Public Limited Company) status, which they feel will provide them with greater prestige and 'cudos' in the market place. Companies can use 'PLC' as opposed to 'LIMITED', even where they have no intention of listing their shares on a recognised stock exchange.

However, PLC status carries a number of important requirements and restrictions. A key prerequisite is that they will need to have a minimum allotted share capital of £50,000, with at least £12,500 paid-up. Furthermore, a PLC must have at least two shareholders, two directors, and a minimum of one 'appropriately qualified' company secretary.

PLC's cannot take advantage of many of the exemptions for private companies and must file their accounts within six months of their year-end.

Issue of shares and pre-emption rights

11.17   Where shares are being issued for cash, *CA 2006, s 561* requires that they must first be offered to the existing shareholders in proportion to their existing shareholdings – generally referred to as 'pre-emption rights'. The offer to existing shareholders remains open for 21 days and the shares can only be presented elsewhere if a member declines to take up their offer (*CA 2006, s 562*). It is possible to override these statutory pre-emption rights by special resolution (which must be passed by 75% of the company's members) [*CA 2006, s 569*]. Some private companies' articles *exclude* the statutory pre-emption rights in *CA 2006, s 561*, but will usually contain further pre-emption restrictions.

SH01 (which includes a satement of share capital) must be filed (in paper or online) with the Registrar of Companies within one month of the date on which the shares are allotted. Where the shares are being issued for a non-cash consideration, the form will generally show the proportion that each share is to be taken as being 'paid-up' and a description of the consideration. (If there is no written contract specifying the consideration, then a form 88(3) must be completed.)

Once the board of directors has agreed to issue the shares, the register of members must be written-up and new share certificates issued. The shares are not issued and a person does not become a shareholder until their name has been written-up in the register of members (see also 11.20).

Income tax relief for interest on loans to acquire shares

11.18 The rules for income tax relief on loan interest to buy *ordinary shares* are basically the same as where borrowings are used to pass funds to a qualifying *close* company (see 11.9–11.15). However, in contrast to the relief for shareholder loans (in 11.9), the legislation does not require the proceeds received on a share issue to be applied for the purposes of the company's trade. It is important to note that interest relief is available where the shares are acquired by subscription or purchased from a third party [*ITA 2007, s 392*].

Some couples may take out a joint loan to acquire shares. In such cases, if only one of the spouses meets the conditions for interest relief, that spouse can still claim their share of the interest as a tax deduction (*Tax Bulletin, February 1992*).

In start-up situations the company may not have commenced trading at the time the loan is applied to acquire shares in the company. The ICAEW raised this matter with the Revenue in 1992 since in many cases the company could not start trading until the relevant funds had been invested in the company. The Revenue recognised this and confirmed that interest relief would be allowed provided the trade starts within a 'reasonable period' of time after the loan has been applied to acquire the shares and the company remains close when trading starts (see ICAEW TAX 15/92 – dated 16 November 1992).

Vigilance is also required in the case of MBO transactions, where the management team invariably borrow money to fund the purchase of shares in a new company (Newco). Newco is used to coordinate the various sources of financing, including bank and venture capitalist debt, and then acquires the target company or business. However, following the decision in *Lord v Tustain (1993) STC 755*, HMRC accept a wider interpretation of the qualifying close company condition for interest relief purposes (see 11.9).

However, if the company *ceases to be close* (because the original managers' shares are diluted by private equity investment) before trading commences, HMRC will deny relief.

Although the relevant conditions for relief must also be satisfied when each interest payment is made, HMRC do not insist that the company retains its 'close company' status at that time *(SP3/78)*.

An important bar to obtaining 'loan interest' tax relief is where the ordinary shares qualified for Enterprise Investment Scheme (EIS) relief or for CGT EIS gain deferral relief f[*ITA 2007, s 392(3)*]. The EIS is discussed at 11.26–11.51.

The 'recovery of capital' conditions in *ITA 2007, s 392* also apply (see 11.13). This means that the shareholder's interest relief will be restricted where there has been a recovery of capital – such as on a sale or gift of the shares. In these cases, the qualifying loan for interest relief purposes is reduced by the sale proceeds or the market value of the shares, as appropriate. This restriction could also strictly apply where shares are sold in exchange for shares, perhaps within *TCGA 1992, s 135*. However, *ITA 2007, s 410* (which legislated the former ESC A43) confirms relief will not be restricted. This treatment only applies to those cases where interest relief would have been available had the borrowing been taken out to acquire the 'consideration' shares received. Effectively, this normally means that the acquiring company must be a qualifying close company (see 11.11).

Capital loss on shares

11.19 Where a shareholder suffers a loss on selling the shares, the allowable loss established for CGT purposes may qualify for income tax relief. This relief can also be claimed on a capital distribution received on a liquidation or for shares claimed to be of negligible value under *TCGA 1992, s 24(2)* (see 16.47).

Income tax relief for capital losses on shares (share loss relief)

11.20 Income tax relief can be claimed for capital losses arising on shares under *ITA 2007, ss 25(3)* and *131,* provided:

(*a*)   the individual *subscribed* for the shares and did not acquire them after they had been issued (ie relief is not available where the shares are acquired 'second-hand');

(*b*)   the company qualifies under the EIS rules (although the shares do not have to be shares on which EIS relief was actually given) [*ITA 2007, s 134(2)*] (see 11.40);

(*c*)   the company was a trading company for at least six consecutive years up to the disposal date, or for a shorter period provided that it did not trade beforehand in shares, land, commodities or futures [*ITA 2007, s 134*].

The increased risk of injecting funds by way of shares being issued must be compared with the likely extra tax relief as a deduction from income rather than against chargeable gains. With a new family or owner-managed company, where prospects are encouraging, a balance between share capital and loans is likely to be the solution, particularly as loans can easily be repaid.

VAT treatment of share issue costs

11.21   The case of *Kretztechnic AG* (Case C-465/03) marked an important change in the VAT status of share issues. Before the European Court of Justice (ECJ) ruling, share issues were treated as an exempt supply. However, the ECJ held that share issues were not a supply at all for VAT purposes.

This means that the VAT on the related professional costs became 'residual' overhead VAT and can be recovered (to the extent that the company makes taxable supplies).

UK companies should therefore normally be able to reclaim their VAT on share issues, subject to any partial exemption restrictions.

Even where the company makes other exempt supplies for VAT as part of its business, it may still be able to recover any attributable 'exempt' input tax under the deminimis partial exemption rules.

DEBT FOR EQUITY SWAPS

Commercial rationale for debt-for-equity swaps

11.22   Where a company is in financial difficulties or is suffering from high gearing taken on before the mid-2008/2009 'credit-crunch', its major lender may be prepared to swap its debt for increased equity participation. Furthermore, as loan repayment maturity dates get closer, the existing shareholders may also be prepared to consider re-structuring the company's balance sheet, especially if the chances of re-financing appear slim.

In such cases, some lenders take the view that the company still has the potential of producing a worthwhile return in the future. They may therefore be prepared to discharge some or all of their debt in exchange for an issue of new shares – often known as a debt-for-equity swap. The consequent increase in the company's issued shares will inevitably dilute the stake held by the existing shareholders, sometimes quite substantially.

Using new shares to replace debt will lead to savings in interest payments and give a business a much better chance of returning to profit! Debt-for-equity swaps are therefore driven by the mutual interest of the borrowing company and its lender to ensure the company does not go into insolvency.

The treatment of debt-for-equity swaps (involving funding debt/loans) is largely dealt with under the corporate loan relationship regime, which gives a number of tax breaks for such transactions provided they are correctly structured within the legislation.

Corporate tax treatment for borrower

11.23 In *distressed* debt cases, a debt-for-equity swap is likely to involve part of the relevant debt/loan being discharged in consideration of new shares being issued.

Tax issues arise where part of the debt is released. Where the parties are 'unconnected', any profit element arising in the borrower's accounts (where part of the debt is actually released) would normally be taxable under the loan relationship legislation. However, where all or part of the debt is cancelled as part of a debt-for-equity swap, generally accepted accounting principles have normally required the relevant amount to be credited to the borrowing company's share premium account. In this context, *CTA 2009, s 321* would enable any credit recognised within shareholders' funds to be taxed in the same way as amounts passing directly to the profit and loss account. Thus, although any debt 'release' comprised in the debt-for-equity swap would be potentially taxable, no taxable credit will arise provided the debt/equity swap satisfies the relevant conditions in *CTA 2009, s 322*.

Some complications may arise if the company adopts UITF Abstract 47 – *'Extinguishing Financial Liabilities with Equity Instruments* – which applies for accounting period beginning after 30 June 2010 and applies to UK companies within FRS 26. In cases where a company does not remove the entire debt through the debt-for-equity swap, it states 'that the issue of shares may reflect consideration for both the extinguishment of a financial liability and the modification of the terms of part of the liability that remains outstanding'. Many debt-for-equity swaps will entail the debt being reduced to an appropriate level.

Consequently, if the accounting treatment allocates the consequential 'release credit' between the fair value of the remaining debt and the new shares, it is uncertain whether the entire amount is protected by the *CTA 2009, s 322* exemption (particular as the equity value is likely to be relatively low). In practice, this potential problem is usually avoided by separating the debt and equity elements. The part of the debt which is being extinguished is novated to the holding company which enables a 'clean' debt-for-equity swap to be implemented. The residual debt is left in the 'borrowing' subsidiary company. On this basis, no part of the 'release credit' can be attributed to the residual debt since this is not in the holding company's books.

The release credit *comprised in a debt-for-equity swap* is exempt under *CTA 2009, s 422* provided the following conditions are satisfied:

- The 'amortised cost' basis must have been used in the period in which the loan relationship debt is released [*CTA 2009, s 322(1)*]. Under the amortised cost basis, a loan relationship is reflected in the accounts at cost less any repayment, release, etc [*CTA 2009, s 313(4)*]. The vast majority of companies are required to use this basis for their loan relationships, so this condition should generally be satisfied.

- The release must be made in consideration of, or any entitlement to, *ordinary* shares in the borrowing company [*CTA 2009, s 322(4)*]. For these purposes, 'ordinary shares' broadly includes all shares *except* those paying a fixed dividend coupon. This means that the shares must contain a variable dividend right. Fixed or zero rate preference shares will not therefore qualify for the beneficial tax treatment (Note – under the loan relationship rules, a share in a company must have an entitlement to receive distributions – *CTA 2009, s 476(1)*).

- The requirement for the release to be made 'in consideration' of ordinary shares appears to be construed purposively by HMRC. In HMRC's *Corporate Finance Manual* at CFM 33202, this condition would not be satisfied where almost immediately after the debt-for-equity swap, the (bank) lender sold its newly-acquired shares to the existing shareholders who did not wish to have their equity holdings diluted. In substance, HMRC would argue that the bank's debt had effectively been realised for shares. HMRC would therefore look at the timing of any subsequent sale of the lender's shares although a commercial decision to sell them (after (say) six months) is likely to be acceptable. If there is any uncertainty about whether a proposed debt-for-equity swap would qualify for the tax-free 'release' of debt, it is recommended that a non-statutory clearance is sought.

It is important to ensure that the terms of the debt-for-equity swap agreement reflect that the entire release is comprised in the swap. If, for example, it shows that part of the debt is released for no consideration, the borrower will be taxed on this amount under the general principles discussed above. It is often suggested that where any amount is released separately through the profit and loss account, there is a risk that HMRC may regard this as being a separate release which is *not* 'in consideration' for the new ordinary shares.

The mechanics of a typical debt-for-equity swap are illustrated in the worked example below.

Example 2

Debt-for-equity swap – tax treatment for borrower

Radio Zola (Radio) Ltd is a commercial radio operator. Its current ordinary share ownership and debt structure is as follows:

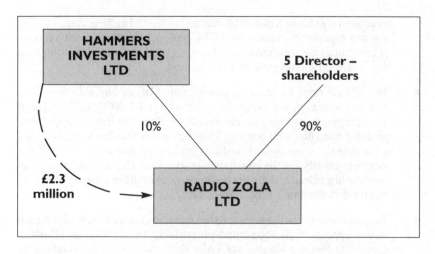

In recent years, Hammers Investments Ltd (Hammers) has also injected interest-bearing loans of £2.3 million to Radio. (Radio accounts for these on an amortised cost basis.) Over the last two years or so, Radio has experienced a substantial decline in its advertising revenues. This fall in revenue, together with the substantial interest payments on the Hammers loan, has generated sizeable trading losses.

Radio's directors have approved with Hammers their plans to re-brand the business which they hope will enable it to return to profit in the medium term. As part of this strategy, Hammers has agreed to cancel £2 million of its interest-bearing loan in return for new ordinary shares in Radio, which would then give it a 49% stake in the company.

To ensure that Radio avoids any tax charge on the debt-for-equity swap, Hammers will therefore enter into an agreement where £2 million of its existing debt of £2.3 million is discharged in consideration for a fresh issue of ordinary shares by Radio.

The following entries would be made in Radio's accounts:

	Dr	Cr
Hammers loan account	£2,000,000	
Ordinary share capital		£20,000
Share premium		£1,980,000

No tax charge arises on any part of the release reflected in the share premium account credit

Other tax issues

11.24   In some cases, the issue of new shares on a 'distressed' debt-for-equity swap will result in the lending company acquiring 'control' of the borrower. The borrowing company may therefore need to consider the impact on such areas as:

- *Tax group reliefs* – If the borrower is part of a tax group, the debt-for-equity swap may dilute the existing group shareholding below critical tax (50% and 75%) thresholds. Thus, for example, if the group's shareholding falls below 75%, the borrowing company will lose its ability to surrender tax losses to its fellow group companies.

  The borrowing company may also become de-grouped for 'capital gains' purposes and stamp duty land tax (SDLT) purposes, which may trigger a capital gains charge (under *TCGA 1992, s 179*) or an SDLT clawback (under *FA 2003, Sch 7, para 9*) (see 13.71).

- *Unused trading losses* – under *CTA 2010, ss 673* and *674 (ICTA 1988 s 768)*, if HMRC can demonstrate there has been a *major change* in the nature or conduct of the (borrowing) company's trade within three years either side of a change in 'control', it can prevent unused trading tax losses being carried forward beyond the date of the debt-for-equity swap (ie where there is a 'change of ownership' within *CTA 2010, ss 719–726 (ICTA 1988, s 769)*. Similar rules apply to companies carrying on investment businesses [*CTA 2010, ss 677–686 (ICTA 1988, s 768B)*] but these are much wider in scope since they can be triggered simply by a 'substantial increase in company's share capital'.

Tax position of the lender

11.25   A 'distressed' debt-for-equity swap may make the lender connected with the borrower for the accounting period (for loan relationship purposes) in which the swap occurs [*CTA 2009, ss 348* and *466*]. (This is because the lender will often acquire 'control' of the borrowing company [*CTA 2007, s 472*].

As a general rule, a connected lender cannot obtain any tax relief for impairment losses or amounts written off on a release of a 'connected' company debt. However, *CTA 2009, s 356* permits the lending company to obtain a tax deduction for any amount written-off where the borrower treats that part of the relevant loan as discharged and this is done in consideration of the issue of *ordinary* shares to it. Broadly speaking, the lender's CGT base cost will be the market value of the shares at the time of the swap (which in such cases is likely to be below the amount treated as subscribed for the shares – see 16.56).

ENTERPRISE INVESTMENT SCHEME (EIS)

Introduction

11.26 The aim of the EIS is to provide a targeted incentive for new equity investment in unquoted trading companies, and of course nearly all family or owner-managed companies are just that. Business angels should be attracted to the EIS as they can be employed by the company and draw reasonable remuneration. This naturally allows them to have a degree of 'hands on' involvement in the company which, in turn, usually gives them greater security over their investment. There are, however, several restrictions which may mean that investors may be difficult to find.

Potentially, the EIS has a major role to play when a family or owner-managed company requires funds. The fact that well over £11.5 billion of equity has been invested under the EIS (and VCT) schemes provides an indication of its success. However, the tighter rules introduced in recent Budgets, which effectively restrict relief to equity investment in the 'smaller' companies, has restricted EIS funding for growing companies, particularly as they seek to raise further finance. The amount invested under the EIS has therefore declined over the past few years. The Rowlands Review (2009) – *'The Provision of Growth Capital to UK Small and Medium Sized Enterprises'* – indentifies an 'equity gap' that now exists between £2 million and £10 million. The Budget 2011 announced a number of measures to increase various investment and employee thresholds to address this problem. These are likely to be introduced from 6 April 2012.

How EIS works

Income tax relief

11.27 Income tax relief is available at 30% on subscription monies of up to £500,000 in each tax year or (if less) the amount that would reduce the taxpayer's liability to nil. The 30% EIS income tax relief is still given to 20% basic-rate taxpayers. (For pre-6 April 2011 EIS share issues, income tax relief was given at 20%.) The Budget 2011 announced proposals to increase the maximum investment limit from £500,000 to £1 million from 6 April 2012.

It is also possible to obtain EIS relief by carrying-back qualifying investments made in the following year (in the period to 5 October) – see 11.28. Where a claim is made to carry back EIS relief to 2010/11 on EIS shares subscribed for in 2011/12, relief is only given at 20% (i.e. the rate applying for the 2010/11 tax year.

For shares issued before 6 April 2008, the maximum investment was limited to £400,000. However, the investor must invest a minimum yearly amount of £500 in any single company to obtain the relief for the relevant year [*ITA 2007, s 157(1), (2)*]. (Note that all *ITA 2007* references have effect as to shares issued after 5 April 2007.) EIS eligible shares also attract an outright CGT exemption (see 11.29) and can be used to hold-over capital gains on other disposals (see 11.30).

The investment must be:

- made by a qualifying investor (see 11.32);

- subscribing wholly in cash (see 11.37);

- for fully paid-up eligible shares (see 11.37);

- issued by a qualifying company (see 11.40).

The *FA 2007* introduced overriding rules on a company's 'tax-privileged' investment limits, which apply from 6 April 2007. For an 'investment' to qualify for relief under the EIS (or CVS – see 11.58), or be treated as a qualifying holding of a VCT (see 11.52), the company (or group of companies) must not have raised more than £2 million under these schemes in the past 12 months ending with the date of the share issue (This 'venture capital' investment threshold is likely to increase to £10 million from 6 April 2012, as announced in the Budget 2011.).

This test is applied on a 'rolling-basis. If the £2 million 'venture capital schemes' limit is exceeded, EIS relief is denied on the *whole* of that investment. For example, if a company raises £1,000,000 under a qualifying EIS share issue on 1 December 2009 and then intends to raise a further £1,200,000 under EIS in May 2010, relief will be denied on the entire £1,200,000. On the other hand, if it restricted the May 2010 EIS issue to (say) £950,000, this would qualify.

The legislation normally gives relief in the tax year in which the shares are *issued* (ie when the shares are entered in the company's Register of Members (*National Westminster Bank plc v CIR (1994) STC 580*)), although the relief may be claimed in the previous year (for pre-22 April 2009 investment, the amount of EIS 'carried-back' was restricted) (see 11.28).

The Court Of Appeal decision in *Blackburn (t/a Alan Blackburn Sports Ltd v HMRC* [2008] EWHC 266 (Ch) shows the potential dangers of advancing monies to the company before the shares are formally issued. There should be a proper share subscription agreement, supported by appropriate Board resolutions and minutes. These should make it clear that the monies are being paid into the company by way of a subscription for the 'EIS' share issue (see 11.37 for detailed analysis of the *Blackburn* case).

For a 'start up' company, EIS relief is not obtained unless and until the company has carried on the qualifying trade for four months.

It should be noted that income tax relief cannot be claimed on interest paid on borrowings taken out to subscribe for a qualifying EIS share issue [*ITA 2007, s 392(3)*] (see 11.18).

The share issue must also be for genuine commercial reasons and not part of a tax avoidance scheme [*ITA 2007, s 178*].

Provided the EIS investment qualified for income tax relief, it can subsequently be realised free of CGT after three years (five years for shares issued before 6 April 2000). Note that the three-year holding period runs from the date that the trade commenced if this was after the issue of the EIS shares.

Carry-back election

11.28   If an EIS investment is made in the first half of a tax year (ie 6 April to 5 October inclusive), from 2009/10 an election can be made to relate back the *entire EIS investment* (ie up to the £500,000 limit) for offset against the investors taxable income of the preceding tax year. Note that EIS relief is obtained at the relevant rate for that year (see 11.27).

For 2008/09 and earlier, the ability to relate back EIS relief was restricted to *half* of the EIS subscription made in the pre-6 October period (subject to a maximum carry-back of £50,000 (£25,000 prior to 6 April 2006) [*ITA 2007, s 158(5)*].

EIS CGT exemption

11.29   Gains made on the sale of EIS-relieved shares are exempt provided they are disposed of after the relevant 'three year' period – normally three years from the date the shares are issued (or if the shares were issued before 6 April 2000, five years from the issue date) [*TCGA 1992, s 150A(2)* and *ITA 2007, ss 159(2)* and *256*] (see 11.50).

If the EIS shares are disposed of within the relevant 'three-year' period, the EIS relief is restricted/withdrawn and a taxable gain arises in the normal way (see 11.50).

EIS CGT deferral relief

11.30   Individuals can also defer their chargeable gains on any disposal where they reinvest in a qualifying company under the CGT EIS deferral relief regime. Indeed, given that EIS CGT deferral relief can be claimed by existing shareholders (irrespective of whether they are 'connected' with the relevant company), this often proves to be a popular way for owner-managers to relieve their capital gains. This was clearly illustrated in the case of *Blackburn (t/a Alan Blackburn Sports Ltd v HMRC* [2008] EWHC 266 (Ch) where Mr Blackburn, who controlled the company with his wife, subscribed £1.19 million for shares to defer his capital gains – see 11.27.

It is worth bearing in mind that any pre-23 June 2010 gains deferred under EIS are likely to be clawed-back at much higher CGT rates. The detailed rules for EIS CGT deferral relief are discussed further at 15.80–15.88.

Debarred arrangements

11.31 There is no EIS relief if arrangements already exist at the time the shares are issued for the disposal of the shares, a disposal of the company's assets, the cessation of its trade or the guaranteeing of the EIS investment [*ITA 2007, s 177*].

Main EIS conditions

Qualifying investor

11.32 A qualifying investor is an individual liable to UK income tax who is *not connected with the company* (see 11.34) at any time in the designated period. The designated period broadly:

- begins two years *before* the issue of the shares; and

- ends immediately before the third anniversary of the share issue (or if the company was not trading when the shares were issued, the third anniversary of the date trading commenced) [*ITA 2007, ss 157(1) and 163 (1)(2)*].

For shares issued before 6 April 2000, the period was seven years instead of five, beginning two years before the share issue and ending five years afterwards.

'The use of the money raised' requirement

11.33 This test was simplified by the Finance Act 2009 and gives companies greater freedom over the timing of the use of the EIS share proceeds. For shares issued *after 21 April 2009*, the legislation requires that *all* of the money raised by the EIS share issue must be *wholly employed* for the purposes of a qualifying trade *or* research and development (R&D)(see 11.42) within *two years* of the share issue (or if later within two years of the company commencing to trade).

For pre-22 April 2009 share issues, at least 80% of the EIS monies raised had to be wholly employed for the trade/R&D within 12 months of the share issue (or, if later, within 12 months of the trade starting) with the balance of 20% being used within 12 months thereafter [*ITA 2007, s 175*]. As a practical measure, it may be helpful to place all EIS subscriptions in a separate bank account – this will make it easier to demonstrate that they have been applied for qualifying purposes.

In *Domain Dynamics (Holdings) Ltd v HMRC* [2008] SpC 701, EIS relief was refused on a share issue that *included* shares being issued in consideration for the provision of a guarantee from a director and for the conversion of loan notes. Other shares were issued for a cash consideration on the same day. However, EIS relief was refused on the entire share issue since some of the shares were not issued for the purpose of a qualifying business activity. However, this was recognised as being unfair and *FA 2004* contained a relaxation enabling *other* shares to be issued contemporaneously without prejudicing the investors' tax relief on valid EIS share issues. The issuing company can therefore make

- a bonus issue to its existing shareholders, or

- an issue of shares to 'non-EIS' investors for a *'non-cash'* consideration

without affecting the eligibility of its *EIS* share issue. Furthermore, there is no restriction on the use of money raised by the issue of non EIS shares.

For post-16 March 2004 EIS issues, the relevant qualifying trade/R&D activity can be carried on by the company issuing the EIS shares or its 90% qualifying subsidiary, thus giving groups flexibility in arranging the company or companies that carry on the activity without prejudicing the investors' EIS reliefs [*ITA 2007, s 175*].

From 6 April 2007, the monies raised must be within the £2 million limit imposed by *FA 2007* for all 'tax-privileged' venture capital schemes (see 11.27).

'No connection with the issuing company' requirement

11.34   The term 'connected with the company' basically means that the 'investor' (together with their associates) must *not* directly or indirectly possess (or be entitled to possess) *over 30%* of:

(*a*)   the issued ordinary share capital of the company or any subsidiary; or

(*b*)   the loan capital and issued share capital of the company or any subsidiary; or

(*c*)   the voting power in the company or any subsidiary [*ITA 2007, ss 163* and *170* – previously *ICTA 1988, s 291B(1)*)].

Test (*b*) will be modified from 6 April 2012 to exclude loan capital completely. Thus, (*b*), the 30% test will be applied to the issued share capital.

In this context, it should be noted that the EIS definition of 'associate' is narrower than the one which normally applies for most other tax purposes – notably, brothers and sisters cannot be treated as associates [*ITA 2007, s 253*]. An investor would be 'associated' with any trust that they created. One particular trap applies to partners – these are 'associated'. Thus, in establishing whether the 30% 'connection' test is breached, all the holdings held by the partners must be aggregated. This normally prevents any qualifying EIS investment being made by the partners of a partnership or members of an LLP

Employees and directors of the issuing company would normally be denied EIS relief since they are deemed to be connected with it under *ITA 2007, s 167*. However, a special provision still enables 'incoming' directors to obtain relief (see 11.35). Certain reciprocal arrangements are also caught under *ITA 2007, s 171*.

Where the size of an individual's investment is likely to breach the 30% connection test, it is worth considering issuing the shares at a premium. This reduces the number of ordinary shares required to be issued to the potential investor(s) and the voting rights they would hold. This may also be a commercial requirement of the existing shareholder(s) who would generally wish to avoid any unnecessary dilution of their interest.

Exceptionally, the 30% connection test does not apply to the period between the incorporation of the company and the earlier of when the company started to prepare for trading or its first share issue (ie *after* the original subscriber shares).

If the investor held one or more of the subscriber shares of the company before it began trading and before any other shares had been issued, they would not be regarded as connected with the company at that time simply by reason of this [*ITA 2007, s 170(5)*].

Potential investors should appreciate the risk element in view of the fact that they cannot hold over 30% of the issued ordinary share capital, nor be entitled to acquire more than 30% of the assets on a winding up [*ITA 2007, s 170(1)*] during their designated period. However, they are likely to obtain greater comfort by working for the company as a director and there is a special exception from the normal 'employee/director' connection test which enables 'incoming' directors to obtain EIS relief (see 11.35 below).

EIS consequences of being a director or employee

11.35　As a general rule, the investor (or any of their associates) must *not* be:

- an employee (for this purpose, a director is not an employee);
- a partner; or
- a director (but see exception below for income directors)

of the investee company or any of its 51% subsidiaries in the five-year period beginning two years *before* the share issue [*ITA 2007, ss 163* and *170*].

The investor would ordinarily be connected with the company if he is a director and therefore debarred from EIS relief. However, if that is the *only* reason for connection, *ITA 2007, s 168* and *169* provide that EIS relief is still available to an 'incoming' *director* provided the following conditions are satisfied:

(*a*)   the director's remuneration is reasonable for the services performed;

(*b*)   when issued with eligible shares, the director-investor was not and had not previously been:

(i) connected with the investee company (see 11.34); or

(ii)   involved in carrying on the trade (or any part of it) now being carried on by the investee company or its subsidiary (this is widely drafted to catch 'involvement' in the capacity as a sole trader, partner, director, or employee).

In summary, an investor who was previously *unconnected* with the company may become a *paid* director and still qualify for EIS relief, provided the remuneration is 'reasonable' in relation to their duties (and it must not be 'linked' to the amount of their investment). The ability to become a 'paid' director will often be an attractive feature to a new investor. It is advisable for their appointment as director to be made *after* the share issue.

However, where the investor is an *existing* director or employee of the investee company or any of its 51% subsidiaries (*before* the share issue), they will not qualify. Members of a management buy-out team would therefore be unable to obtain EIS relief on their share investment in a new company to acquire the shares of their former company. This is because they would previously have been involved in carrying on the trade as an employee or director through (what is now) a subsidiary of the investee company before the share issue.

Investor warranties

11.36   The investor's EIS relief can subsequently be restricted or withdrawn by the investee company's actions. Consequently, where a material amount is being invested, it would often be reasonable for the investor(s) to obtain an appropriate set of EIS-specific warranties and indemnities from the company. These might include the investee company warranting that it will:

● not change the rights attaching to the investor's EIS shares (see 11.34);

● use all reasonable endeavours to carry out a qualifying trade (see 11.42);

● not purchase any non-qualifying subsidiaries or enter into any joint ventures (see 11.45).

Eligible shares

11.37   To be eligible for relief the shares must be subscribed for entirely in cash and must be fully-paid up at the time of issue. This point was considered in *Blackburn (t/a Alan Blackburn Sports Ltd v HMRC* [2008] EWHC 266 (Ch). HMRC contended that certain share issues had not been 'fully paid-up' at the time of issue and therefore failed this test. However, the Special Commissioners firmly rejected this. They found that the shares were not *unconditionally* issued and therefore were issued when subsequent payment was made (a few days later) and HMRC did not appeal on this point (see also 11.39)

The EIS legislation also requires that the shares are new ordinary shares which do not carry any preferential right as to dividends or asset distributions on a winding up, or redemption for three years from issue. If the company starts trading some time after the EIS issue, the three-year period runs from the commencement of trade [*ITA 2007, s 173(2)*].

In some cases, it may be considered desirable for EIS shares to carry certain restrictions and this can be done without breaking their EIS status.

'Value received' rules

11.38   The purpose of the EIS is to encourage fresh equity investment and therefore there are 'receipt of value' rules which deny or restrict relief where there are arrangements that do not result in new money being available to the company. Thus, the investor's original EIS relief is restricted or withdrawn completely where they 'receive value' from the investee company (or any connected person) during the so-called 'period of restriction' – Period C in *ITA 2007, s 159(4)* – normally, the one year before and the three-year period following the EIS share issue).

Where the investor receives value from the company (*ignoring any 'insignificant amount'*), their original EIS relief is reduced on a pro-rata basis. Thus, the reduction in relief is calculated as the 'value received' multiplied by 20%. Where this exceeds the EIS relief (after taking into account any prior reductions), the original EIS relief is completely withdrawn.

Insignificant receipts of value are ignored (broadly, amounts up to £1,000, although greater amounts may qualify where they are insignificant in relation to the total EIS investment). These clawback rules will also be disregarded where the investor returns the amount received without unreasonable delay.

The legislation effectively looks at direct and indirect returns of value. The relevant circumstances identified in *ITA 2007, s 216 (2)* in which value is deemed to be 'received' *include* the investee company:

- repaying, redeeming or repurchasing any of the investor's shares;

- repaying a debt owed to the investor in connection with the arrangements for the EIS share issue (excluding loans made after the shares were issued)

- providing any benefit or facility to the investor;

- disposing of an asset to the investor for no consideration or at an undervalue;

- making any payment *other than* such qualifying payments as reasonable remuneration, permissible reimbursement of expenses, commercial interest, rents or dividends, etc (see *ITA 2007, ss 168(2)(3), 216(2)(h)*).

The *investor's EIS relief* is restricted in a similar way where any company (or any subsidiary) redeems or repays the share capital of *any other shareholder* in the 'period of restriction' [*ITA 2007, s 224*].

Value received by repayment of debt

11.39   For post-16 March 2004 share issues, the 'repayment of debt' return of value rule was relaxed following the Special Commissioners' decision in *Inwards v Williamson* [2003] STC (SCD) 355 (which involved a similar point on the old-style CGT reinvestment relief). This meant that only repayments of loans in the course of arrangements for the EIS issue would be treated as a 'return of value'. The EIS relief should not therefore be prejudiced in such cases, provided the prior repayment of a loan is not made in connection with any arrangements for the acquisition of the shares [*ITA 2007, s 216 (2)(b)*]. This should make it easier for individuals to make short-term loans to the company since the repayment of such loans should not jeopardise their EIS tax relief on qualifying share investments made within the following 12 months

The Court of Appeal in *Blackburn (t/a Alan Blackburn Sports Ltd v HMRC* [2008] EWHC 266 (Ch) adopted a pragmatic approach on the similar 'debt repayment' rule relating to an EIS CGT deferral relief claim under *TCGA 1992, Sch 5B*. HMRC had originally rejected Mr Blackburn's claim for EIS capital gains deferral relief on some £1.19 million which was 'injected' into the company through six separate share issues between September 2008 and January 2001. The Court of Appeal had to consider share issues 1, 5 and 6 where part of the payments was made before the shares were issued. HMRC's contention was that, in the absence of proper applications and allotments, the advance payments were a 'debt' and hence the EIS relief was denied under the 'return of value' rules in *TCGA 1992, Sch 5B*, para 13. The Court of Appeal rejected this argument (as regards issues 5 and 6) on the basis that the advance payments were not 'debts' in the normal sense of the word. However, perhaps surprisingly, relief on the first issue was rejected (on the basis that the company had not established any course of dealings at that point and it was therefore possible to treat the monies as a loan!). (The treatment of issues 2, 3 and 4 is considered in 11.37).

Qualifying company

11.40   A company is a qualifying company for EIS purposes provided:

(*a*)   it is unquoted when the shares are issued – no arrangements must exist for the company to be listed or to become a wholly owned subsidiary of a new holding company if arrangements exist for that company to be listed [*ITA 2007, s 184*];

(*b*)   it is a trading company or parent company of a trading group (see 11.42) carrying on a *qualifying trade or trades or research and development* (see 11.42) for at least three years [*ITA 2007, s 181*];

(*c*)   it has total gross assets of not more than £7 million *before* the relevant EIS issue and no more than £8 million *afterwards* [*ITA 2007, s 186*]. The pre-investment 'gross asset' limit will be increased to £15 million and the 'post-investment' limit will be lifted to £16 million from 6 April 2012 onwards (subject to EU State Aid approval).

Where the company is a holding company of a group, the aggregate of the group's assets (ignoring shareholdings in its subsidiaries) is taken. The company's total 'gross assets' (ie before deducting any liabilities) are measured according to their balance sheet value (at that point) based on generally accepted accounting principles (and on the same basis as prior accounts) [see *IR Statement of Practice SP 2/00*];

(*d*)   the company must have a permanent establishment in the UK – which would generally be met simply by having a trading activity in the UK [*ITA 2007, s 179(1)–(5)*]. This relaxation in *F (No 2) A 2010* now enables companies to expand overseas without adversely affecting their EIS status. Before the law was changed, a company had to be trading '*wholly or mainly*' within the UK, which was always vulnerable to challenge under the evolving principle of non-discrimination under EU law.; and

(*e*)   it has fewer than 50 full time employees (or their equivalents) at the date the relevant shares or securities are issued. From 6 April 2012, the 'employee limit' is to be increased to 250 full time employees (subject to EU State Aid approval).

The employees test applies to a company or group of companies (for EIS shares issued after 19 July 2007). The test is only applied at the point the shares are issued, and hence there may be scope for timing the steps in a transaction to comply with the rules. For example, where a company plans to use the EIS monies to finance a business acquisition (which will increase the number of relevant employees) then the EIS issue should be made some time before the acquisition. It does not matter if the company/group employee 'headcount' exceeds 50 after the EIS issue, since there are no clawback provisions.

Prior to *FA 2004*, when looking at the 'application of EIS share monies' test, the Revenue considered that the purchase of a qualifying subsidiary did not qualify (as this is not a qualifying trade – see (*b*) above), unless the trade was hived up into the acquiring company immediately post acquisition.

The *FA 2004* made subtle changes to the 'qualifying business activity' requirement in what is now *ITA 2007, s 179(1)–(3)*. These changes enabled the qualifying activity to be satisfied by a (90%) subsidiary. The Revenue confirmed that from

17 March 2004, it is no longer necessary to hive up the trade on acquisition by the company issuing the EIS shares. However, it must be ensured that the subsidiary is a direct (90%) qualifying subsidiary of the acquiring company to meet this test. If it is not, then the shares in the subsidiary will need to be 'moved' to the acquiring (issuing) company immediately.

If the issuing company ceases to qualify within the relevant three year period, the investor's EIS relief is completely withdrawn. Similarly, if the company is wound up during the relevant three-year period, it would cease to be a qualifying company. However, it can retain its qualifying status, provided the winding up or dissolution is for genuine commercial reasons and not tax avoidance. A similar rule applies where a company appoints a receiver or administrator [*ITA 2007, s 182)*].

The 'independence' requirement

11.41   A company is only able to issue eligible EIS shares provided it satisfies the so called 'independence' requirement throughout the 'three year' period following the EIS share issue. This means that the issuing company must *neither be;*

(*a*)   a 51% subsidiary of another company; *nor*

(*b*)   under the 'control' of another company

Furthermore, it must not be subject to any arrangements to cause it to be within (a) or (b) above [*ITA 2007, s 185(2)*]. The *CTA 2010, s 1124 (ICTA 1988, s 840)* definition applies for these purposes, which broadly looks at the ability of the other 'investor' company to control the EIS company's affairs, through voting power, a shareholders agreement and so on (see also 8.63).

Qualifying trade

11.42   As a general rule, the broad policy aim of the EIS regime is to prevent 'lower risk'/asset-backed activities from attracting EIS relief. All trades (and research and development activities) qualify with the exception of those activities that fall within the special exclusions mentioned below [*ITA 2007, s 192*] at any time in the three years from the share issue (or if later the three years from commencement of the trade):

(*a*)   dealing in land, commodities, futures, shares, securities or other financial instruments;

(*b*)   dealing in goods otherwise than as wholesale or retail distributors;

(*c*)   banking, insurance, money lending, debt factoring, hire-purchase financing, etc;

(*d*)   leasing (this includes letting pleasure craft ships and letting other assets on hire – see 11.43) or receiving royalties or licence fees (although the exploitation of the company's 'internally' generated intellectual property is permitted – see 11.44);

(*e*)   providing legal or accountancy services;

(*f*)   property development;

(*g*)   farming or market gardening;

(*h*)   forestry activities, woodlands, or timber production;

(*i*)   operating or managing hotels or guest houses, etc;

(*j*)   operating or managing nursing or residential care homes;

(*k*)   providing services or facilities for any trade, profession or vocation substantially falling within (*a*) to (*j*) which is carried on by another person (other than a parent company) where one person has a controlling interest in both trades [*ITA 2007, ss 189 and 192*].

Trades within (*i*) and (*j*) above are only excluded where the company has an estate or interest in, or is in occupation of, the hotel, nursing home, etc.

The excluded list was extended in *FA 2008* to include shipbuilding, producing coal and producing steel.

The *F(No 2)A 2010* denies EIS relief where the company is in financial difficulty – for example, subject to insolvency proceedings. This change was required to bring EIS into line with the EC State Aid Risk Capital Guidelines.

Where the company engages in carrying on one or more excluded activities on a very small scale, this may not be fatal to the shareholder's EIS relief although the position must be carefully monitored. *ITA 2007, s 189(1)* effectively enables the investee company to carry on the above excluded activities to an 'insubstantial' (less than 20%) extent without prejudicing its qualifying EIS status (see 15.37 for further discussion) [*ITA 2007, s 189(1)*].

Reference must always be made to the detailed legislation to determine whether a particular company will qualify for relief. The investee company's trade must also be conducted on a commercial basis with the view to realising profits [*ITA 2007, s 189 (1)(a)*]. In practice, it is always advisable to first seek advance clearance from HMRC that the trade qualifies for EIS purposes.

Leasing activities

11.43   HMRC interprets 'leasing' as covering any trading activity that consists in allowing the customer (lessee/hirer) the use of the company's property and such arrangements would normally prevent EIS relief being claimed (subject to the 20% *de minimis* test) [*ITA 2007, s 192(1)(d)*]. This would include many cases where assets are 'hired' out and the customer is free to use the asset as their own. Common examples would include car hire, television and video rentals, and warehousing facilities.

On the other hand, arrangements where the customer cannot use the asset freely are effectively regarded as the provision of a service and would be treated as an allowable activity. This would include the chauffeured car hire (for example, 'wedding car' hire) and certain storage activities where the customer is denied free access (see *IR Tax Bulletin,* August 1995).

There would seem to be a fine line drawn between (say) a *self storage* warehouse where the customer has reasonable access and (say) a storage facility that is primarily operated by the investee company. In the former case, EIS is unlikely to be available, whereas in the latter case, the customer is paying for a service or facility and therefore EIS should be given. In such cases, it is recommended that an advance EIS ruling is obtained from HMRC (see 11.47).

Royalties and licence fees

11.44 The general EIS prohibition on the receipt of royalties and licence fees (by the investee company) (see 11.42) is relaxed where the income:

- derives from the company's *own* research or development activities – these must be intended to result in a new (innovative) patentable invention or computer program; *or*

- is mainly from the exploitation of intangible assets created by the company. The definition of intangible assets is that used in normal accounting practice and would include intellectual property and industrial know-how. The investee company can therefore create and exploit its own intellectual property (for example, patents, copyrights, designs, computer software, etc). Where some of the royalties or licence fee income relates to 'third-party' intellectual property rights, these can be ignored provided they do not represent a substantial (20%) part of the total income.

HMRC would regard the receipt of licence fees as a 'non-qualifying' activity for EIS purposes. Thus, a car park trade would not attract EIS relief because its income would largely be in the form of licence fees for car parking. On the other hand, where the grant of a right over land is merely incidental to the main 'service' (such as in the case of a cinema provider), then it would be ignored (see *IR Tax Bulletin*, August 1995).

Group situations – parent company of a trading group

11.45 A company can also be a qualifying EIS company if it is a parent company of a trading group that has at least *one* subsidiary. For these purposes:

- *each* of its subsidiaries must be a qualifying 51% subsidiary with the important exception that any subsidiary 'benefiting' from the proceeds of an EIS issue (or whose qualifying activity is being counted in relation to an EIS issue – see 11.40) must be a 90% subsidiary. Furthermore, any property management subsidiary must also be a 90% subsidiary of the investee company (for shares issued before 17 March 2004, each of the investee company's subsidiaries had to be a 75% subsidiary) [*ITA 2007, ss 190* and *191*]; and

- taking all the groups' activities together, the qualifying trade requirements in 11.42 are satisfied, with any non-qualifying activities being below the 20% de minimis limit. For the purpose of the activities test, group shareholdings, intra-group lending or property letting is effectively ignored, ie the group is effectively looked at on a 'con-solidated accounts' basis [*ITA 2007, ss 190* and *191*].

From 6 April 2007, a qualifying trade can be also be carried on by:

- a 90% subsidiary of a wholly-owned subsidiary of the issuing company'; or.

- a 100% subsidiary of a directly-held 90% subsidiary of the issuing company.

Relevant 'subsidiary' requirements

11.46   The relevant subsidiary shareholding requirements (ie 51%, 75% or 90%, as appropriate) must be tested against the normal type of economic ownership measures, such as shares, voting power, entitlement to dividends and assets on a winding-up. Thus, if the investee company subsequently acquires a shareholding in another company, the investment must broadly be at least 51% of its share capital. Similarly, non-controlling shareholdings (ie less than 51% investments) are treated as investments. Consequently, unless their total value is insubstantial (under the 20% *de minimis* rule) compared to the group's total value, the investee company will be a non-qualifying company for EIS purposes.

Thus, if a parent company subsequently acquires investments (which are not qualifying subsidiaries), it may cease to qualify for EIS purposes. The EIS legislation does not have any 'joint venture' provisions that treat investments in certain *trading* joint ventures as effectively being transparent (as is the case with SSE).

HMRC clearance application

11.47   HMRC operate a formal Advance Assurance Application' procedure to confirm whether a potential investee company satisfies the relevant conditions for being a qualifying company and whether the rules for the share issue are met. Informal advice can also be sought about queries relating to whether the trade qualifies, the application of the 'connection rules', and so on. These points can be confirmed by completing the AA1 form, which should be sent to the Small Company Enterprise Centre (SCEC), Ferrers House, Castle Meadow Road, Nottingham NG2 1BB (Tel: 0115 974 1250). Form AA1 requires various details and documents to be sent, such as the company's memorandum and articles and subscription agreement and so on. The Nottingham SCEC office then allocates the case to one of the two dedicated offices in Cardiff or to Maidstone, which will deal with the case going forward. It is important to remember that advance EIS clearances are given on the basis of the information provided and hence failure to disclose material facts may invalidate the clearance given.

Once the company has traded for a period of four months (or longer if involved in certain activities such as R&D), it can then provide the required information relating to the EIS share issue(s) on an EIS 1 form (www.hmrc. gov.uk/forms/eis1.pdf), available on request from the SCEC or from the HMRC website. HMRC will then (if satisfied) issue the authorisation (on form EIS 2) to enable the company partly to complete and issue the form EIS 3 certificate(s) to the relevant investor(s). Each investor must submit their form EIS 3 with the relevant tax returns to their own tax offices in order to claim the EIS relief.

The investor's tax relief

11.48   The relief reduces the investor's income tax liability rather than his income – it is therefore akin to a 'tax credit' style relief. The investor's tax liability for the purposes of determining the EIS relief is calculated ignoring the following:

(*a*)   personal allowances and maintenance payments which attract relief at a reduced rate;

(*b*)   double taxation relief or unilateral relief;

(*c*)   basic rate tax relief deducted at source from certain payments.

Disposal of EIS shares – withdrawal/restriction of EIS relief

11.49   If the EIS shares are disposed of by way of a non-arm's length bargain within three years, the EIS relief is completely withdrawn, based on the rate at which it was originally given (i.e. 20% for pre-6 April 2011 EIS share issues and 30% for EIS shares issued after 5 April 2011 (*ITA 2009, s 209(2)*)). However, relief is not withdrawn where the shares are transferred to a spouse/ civil partner (*ITA 2007, s 209(4)*).

For arm's length disposals within the relevant three-year period, the relief is withdrawn or reduced on a pro-rata basis.

The restriction of the EIS relief is the *lower* of:

(a)   the EIS relief originally claimed on the shares

(b)   the original EIS rate claimed – 30% or 20% (see above) – multiplied by the sale proceeds received on the disposal

This broadly means that where the shares are sold at a profit (ie (a) will be lower than (b), the original EIS relief is completely withdrawn. Where the shares are sold at a loss, the EIS relief will generally be reduced by the amount in (b) above.

In those cases where the original EIS relief was restricted – because the amount subscribed exceeded the relevant EIS limit, the amount at (b) is multiplied by: *reduced relief* EIS at 30% or 20% (as appropriate).

Any disposal of 'EIS-relieved' shares made within the relevant 'three-year' period must be reported to HMRC within 60 days (*ITA 2007, s 240*). Failure to give a notice will attract a penalty.

Example 3

Disposal of eligible shares – EIS relief position

2010/11	Moore claims EIS relief due on £150,000 @ 20% = £30,000
2011/12	Moore sells all the shares (at arm's length) for £90,000

Reduction in EIS relief for 2010/11 = £90,000 × 20% = £18,000

Disposal of EIS shares – CGT treatment

11.50   Where the sale of 'EIS-relieved' shares after the three-year holding period results in a capital gain, this is exempt from CGT. (The original EIS relief is also retained. However, if the shares are sold within the relevant three-year period, the original EIS relief is restricted/withdrawn completely (see 11.49)

However, an allowable capital loss will arise where the shares are sold at a loss (irrespective of whether the disposal is before or after the three-year holding period (see 11.19). In such cases, the loss calculation is adjusted so that the deductible CGT base cost of the shares is reduced by the amount of EIS income tax relief given. Any loss can normally be set against income under the 'share loss relief' rules in the same and/or the previous tax year under *ITA 2007, s 131*.

Example 4

Disposal of eligible shares – income tax and CGT position

Mr Hargreaves subscribed for shares in June 2010 for £100,000. EIS relief of £20,000 (£100,000 × 20%) was obtained in 2010/11.

Subsequently assume that in (say) January 2012, Mr Hargreaves sells the shares for £60,000.

EIS relief position – 2010/11

Withdrawal of relief in 2010/11 = £60,000 @ 20% = £12,000

CGT position – 2011/12

The EIS shares are sold at a loss and therefore the CGT base cost must be reduced by the amount of EIS relief retained – £8,000 (being the original relief of £20,000 less the withdrawn amount of £12,000)

	£	£
Proceeds		60,000
Cost	100,000	
Less EIS relief retained		
(£20,000 – £12,000)	(8,000)	(92,000)
Allowable loss		(32,000)

If the conditions in *ITA 2007, s 131* are met, the loss can be set against Mr Hargreaves' taxable income for 2011/12 and/or 2010/11 (see 11.20).

Disposal of EIS shares for share consideration – income tax and CGT positions

11.51   When an EIS company is sold, part of the consideration for the EIS shares may be in the form of shares issued by the acquiring company. Where the sale takes place *after* the relevant three-year period, *TCGA 1992, s 150A* treats this as a normal CGT disposal (ie the normal CGT share exchange reorganisation rule does not apply). In summary, the tax analysis is as follows:

- Any deferred gains against the EIS shares are brought into charge (see 11.30).

- The capital gain on the EIS shares will be exempt under the normal EIS rules, regardless of whether consideration is received in the form of cash or shares (see 11.50) (subject to the normal CGT rules on EIS disposals (see 11.29)).

- The base cost of the new consideration shares will be their market value at the time of the exchange.

- Any gains on the subsequent disposal of the new consideration shares will not be exempt under the EIS provisions (as they will not be EIS qualifying shares).

There are some important exceptions to this rule. The most important case is where shares are sold (after the requisite holding period) for shares in another qualifying EIS company. (The new shares must not carry any present or future preferential rights to dividends or assets on a winding up, etc) (*TCGA 1992, s 150A(8A)*). In such cases, there is no disposal and the new shares stand in the place of the old EIS shares in all respects and attract the same relief. However, this treatment only applies where HMRC have issued a certificate in relation to the new shares. Furthermore, the normal advance clearance should be obtained from HMRC to confirm that they are satisfied that the exchange is being made for bona fide commercial reasons and does not form part of a tax-avoidance scheme (*TCGA 1992, s 138*).

Similarly, ITA 2007, s 247 permits a new company (which only has subscriber shares) to acquire shares in an existing EIS company without triggering any disposal so that the new shares 'step into the shoes' of the old subscriber share(s) for EIS purposes. This means that the existing EIS shareholders' holdings are treated as continuing for EIS purposes [TCGA 1992, s 150A (8D)]. Prior approval for the arrangement must be obtained from HMRC.

VENTURE CAPITAL TRUSTS

Introduction

11.52   VCT investments are targeted incentives for investing in a range of small to medium-sized unquoted companies carrying on qualifying trades in the UK. They represent a combination of an EIS company and an authorised investment trust company, with the VCT's shares being quoted on the stock market. As part of obtaining EU approval under the 'State Aid' guidelines, the *F (No 2) A 2010* now permits VCTs to be listed on an approved EU/EEA exchange.

Although VCTs are inherently risky, the potential 30% income tax saving currently available on the amount invested can make them relatively attractive investments. In essence, they enable an individual to invest in unquoted (including AIM) companies by buying shares in a (*non-close*) quoted VCT company. In contrast to direct investment in unquoted shares, the VCT shares can be sold in the market.

The VCT structure

11.53   HMRC approval for a VCT is required under *ITA 2007, s 259*. Many of the provisions of *s 259* applying to authorised investment trust companies also apply to an authorised VCT, but one of the exceptions is that there is no requirement that the VCT is resident in the UK. The VCT managers will be responsible for ensuring that the VCT continues to comply with the requirements of *ITA 2007, Part 5, Chapters 3 and 4*.

Currently, at least 70% (by value) of the VCT's investments must be in *shares and securities* which are qualifying 'unquoted' holdings (which do not include 'enterprises in difficulty'). (The *FA 2007* introduced a relaxation to this rule, where a VCT sells a qualifying investment that has been held for at least six months. In such cases, the disposal proceeds will be ignored for the purpose of the 70% test for the next six months, allowing the VCT time to reinvest or distribute the sale proceeds.)

Furthermore, under the *F(No 2)A 2010*, at least 70% (previously 30%)(by value) of the qualifying holdings must comprise eligible shares which are ordinary share capital in qualifying investee companies (see 11.55). These shares must not carry any present or future preferential rights as to dividends or assets on a winding up or redemption.

No holding in any single company may exceed 15% of the VCT's total investments, but that restriction does not apply to investments in unit trusts, government or local authority securities, or investments in other VCTs.

The VCT must also ensure that it retains no more than 15% of its income from investments in shares and securities. The *FA 2006* modified the meaning of 'investments' so that it included money that the VCT holds (or that is held on its behalf).

As with EIS, the *FA 2007* introduced rules on overriding investment limits for venture capital reliefs. For an 'investment' to be treated as a qualifying holding of a VCT, the investee company (or group of companies) must have raised no more than £2 million under any or all of the schemes (EIS and VCT) in the past 12 months. This 'venture capital' investment limit will be increased to £10 million from 6 April 2012 (provided EU State Aid approval is granted).

The 'employees' test (see 11.38) and 90% subsidiaries rules (11.45) also apply to VCTs, .

If the VCT breaks any of the qualifying conditions, the investors lose all their tax benefits (see 11.55).

Qualifying investee companies

11.54   The unquoted companies in which the VCT invests must carry on a qualifying trade. The VCT legislation effectively applies the similar tests and rules as those that operate for the EIS (see 11.42).

A VCT can only invest in 'non-controlling' holdings in investee companies. Each investee company's gross assets must *not* exceed £7 million before the VCT investment and £8 million immediately after the investment is made. These limits will increase to £15 million and £16 million respectively from 6 April 2012.)

Although an investee company can have 51% subsidiaries, any subsidiary company using funds raised through the VCT must be a 90% subsidiary. Similarly, any property management subsidiary of the investee company must be a 90% subsidiary. For VCT shares issued before 17 March 2004, investee companies could only have 75% subsidiaries.

The tax position

11.55 The *FA 2006* amended the income tax incentives for VCT investments. Since 6 April 2006, income tax relief is now given at a *fixed rate* of 30% on new ordinary shares *subscribed* for in a VCT up to an overall investment limit of £200,000 in any tax year. Although investors will typically be higher rate taxpayers, it should be noted that VCT investments made by basic rate taxpayers will still benefit from a 30% tax 'rebate'.

Spouses enjoy their own £200,000 VCT relief, thus enabling married couples to increase their overall VCT investment to £400,000.

The claim(s) must be made within five years of the 31 January following the end of the relevant tax year – in practice, the claim will normally be made by completing the relevant box on the tax return.

The income tax relief is retained provided the VCT shares are held for at least *five* years. After that period, the market quote should help the investor to dispose of their shares if they wish to do so.

When looking at the amount of tax relief available on a VCT investment, it is offset against the individual's tax liability for the tax year concerned in priority to other deductions and reliefs which are given in terms of tax offset. This order of priority means that VCT relief is given before EIS relief.

11.56 Provided the VCT investments fall within the £200,000 limit:

- any dividends paid by the VCT are completely exempt from tax in the investor's hands, which is especially beneficial for higher rate taxpayers (non-taxpayers cannot reclaim the dividend tax credits) [*ITTOIA 2005, Chapter 5*]; and

- there is no CGT on a subsequent sale of the VCT shares (and, similarly, any capital losses are not allowable) [*TCGA 1992, s 151A*].

11.57 Given that VCTs primarily invest for capital growth, investors also indirectly benefit from the VCT's own 'tax-free' capital gains on the realisation of its underlying investments. The 'five-year' rule does not apply to transfers between spouses (or civil couples) but is binding on the 'successor' spouse/ civil partner.

The dividend and capital gains exemptions are also available on the purchase of *existing* VCT shares, but these do not attract any 'up-front' income tax relief on the purchase cost (the lower market prices of existing VCT shares reflect this!).

Unfortunately, the *FA 2004* removed the ability to 'hold-over' *capital gains* against VCT investments made after 5 April 2004. However, investors are more likely to prefer the ability to shelter their income tax liabilities at 30%.

CORPORATE VENTURING SCHEME (ABOLISHED ON 31 MARCH 2010)

Introduction

11.58   The Corporate Venturing Scheme (CVS) introduced in *FA 2000, s 63, Schs 15* and *16* ceased to be available for shares issued after 31 March 2010, but the provisions still operate for shares issued earlier. CVS was intended to give larger companies an incentive to invest in smaller unquoted trading companies, in a similar fashion to investments under EIS. The investment had to be provided by way of subscription for relevant shares paid for in cash, rather than by way of loans or other arrangements (see 11.64).

CVS permits the investing company to have a limited involvement in the company it invests in (the issuing company), but it must *not* hold a material interest in it or control it. A trading company could attract equity funding under EIS and CVS at the same time as long as it continued to meet the requirements for both schemes, which are broadly similar. However, the scheme imposes strict restrictions on transactions between the two companies and with the issuing company's other shareholders which, if breached, risk withdrawal of all the CVS tax relief.

How CVS works

Tax relief

11.59   The investing company can take advantage of three types of tax relief provided the relevant (pre-1 April 2010 issued) shares are held for at least three years:

(*a*)   investment relief;

(*b*)   loss relief;

(*c*)   deferral relief.

494

The three-year holding period runs from the date the shares are issued, or from the date the trade commenced, if later.

The investment relief is given as a reduction in the corporation tax liability of the company of 20% of the amount invested in the issuing company. The relief is limited by the total tax liability for the year.

11.60 Loss relief provides income relief for capital losses subsequently arising on the disposal of a CVS investment.

Deferral relief allows the company to defer capital gains arising on the disposal of relevant shares, by investing in a different company under CVS (before 1 April 2010). In both cases, the relevant shares must first qualify for the investment relief.

The investing company

11.61 The investing company had to be a trading company, or the holding company of a trading group. However, financial trades including leasing, money lending, insurance or share dealing were prohibited. The relevant shares acquired under CVS had to be held as assets and not as trading stock.

For three years after the issue of the relevant shares, the investing company must *not* hold a material interest in, or control, the issuing company. Material interest is defined as acquiring or being entitled to acquire more than 30% of the share capital or 30% of the voting rights. When calculating whether control is achieved, all the shareholdings of the directors and relatives of the directors of the investing company and its subsidiaries must be considered.

The 'employees' and investment limits tests (see 11.40) and 90% subsidiaries rules (11.45) introduced in the *FA 2007* also apply to CVS, investment made after 18 July 2007.

The issuing company

11.62 The issuing company had to be an unquoted trading company or the holding company of an unquoted trading group that carried on a qualifying trade, or was preparing to carry on such a trade when the relevant shares were issued. The qualifying trade is defined as for EIS (see 11.40). A research and development activity can also be a qualifying trade if it is undertaken either for the benefit of the company's qualifying trade or in preparation for carrying on its qualifying trade [*FA 2000, Sch 15, para 26*].

11.63 There was a similar sized restriction for the issuing company as that applying to EIS (see 11.26). Thus, the gross assets of the issuing company could not exceed £7 million before the investment or £8 million afterwards

(£15 million before and £16 million afterwards for shares issued before 6 April 2006). The issuing company also had to be independent (ie not controlled by another company) and at least 20% owned by independent individuals. Those individuals could not be employees or directors, or relatives of an employee or director, of the investing company or any company connected with the investing company.

From 22 April 2009, the issuing company has up to 24 months to apply the (pre-1 April 2010) CVS subscription monies for a qualifying trade, which provides far greater flexibility. The funds raised may be used to prepare to carry on a qualifying trade, and the condition will not be broken if an insignificant amount is used for some other purpose.

For CVS investments made before 22 April 2009, the issuing company had to apply 80% of the CVS subscription monies for a qualifying trade within 12 months of the share issue with the remaining 20% being used within 24 months.

From 6 April 2007, amounts raised under CVS had to be within the £2 million limit for amounts raised under all 'venture capital' schemes within the previous 12 months (see 11.27).

Relevant shares – conditions

11.64   The relevant CVS shares had to be fully paid-up non-redeemable ordinary shares subscribed for in cash. For three years from issue, or three years from the start of the trade if that is later, the shares must not have any present or future preferential rights to dividends or assets on a winding-up.

Pre-arranged exits

11.65   The issuing company must ensure that the issuing arrangements for the relevant shares do not include a provision for its shares to be repurchased, a disposal of its assets, a cessation of its trade or a guarantee for the investing company. All of these arrangements can amount to a pre-arranged exit for the investing company.

Obtaining CVS relief

11.66   The following steps need to be taken to allow the investing company to claim CVS relief:

(*a*)   the issuing company submits a compliance statement to HMRC;

(*b*)   HMRC give permission for the issuing company to send a compliance certificate to the investing company;

(*c*)   on receipt of the compliance certificate, the investing company can make a claim for the relief due to be given in respect of the accounting period in which the shares were issued.

Compliance statement

11.67 The compliance statement must be submitted to HMRC after the qualifying trade has been carried on for four months, and within two years from the end of the accounting period in which the CVS shares were issued. This document must include details of the companies that subscribed for shares under the scheme (before 1 April 2010) and proof that those shares had been subscribed for wholly in cash and were fully paid-up, plus any other details HMRC may require. If the company submits a negligent or fraudulent compliance statement, it can be fined up to £3,000.

Withdrawal of relief

11.68 The investment relief can be withdrawn or reduced if during a period beginning one year before the share issue and ending three years afterwards:

(*a*) the issuing company repays any of its share capital to any of its shareholders or pays them for giving up rights to share capital during the period of restriction; or

(*b*) the investing company receives some significant return of value, which is not replaced, from the issuing company (see 11.38 since similar rules apply as for EIS); or

(*c*) the investing company disposes of or grants options over the relevant shares.

If the CVS conditions are breached by either company, both that company and any connected person who has knowledge of the causal event, must give notice to HMRC within 60 days of the event, or of coming to know of the event. If some relief can continue to be given under the scheme, the issuing company must reapply for permission to issue replacement compliance certificates to its CVS investors.

PLANNING CHECKLIST – SHARE ISSUES AND FINANCING THE COMPANY'S ACTIVITIES

Company

- Borrowing arrangements should ensure corporate tax relief is secured on a prompt basis.

- Companies in financial distress should consider a debt-for-equity swap to improve their balance sheet.

- The company should look to VCTs and EIS investors to obtain equity funds.

- Before making an EIS share issue the company must ensure that the anticipated subscription monies do not breach the £2 million limit (£10 million from 6 April 2012) on 'venture capital relief' investment made during the past 12 months. This £2 million/£10 million limit is tested on a rolling basis and covers prior EIS and CVS share issues (as well as share issues to a VCT).

- The directors should monitor the company's business activities on a regular basis to avoid prejudicing EIS and other 'venture capital' reliefs.

- The company should always obtain advance clearance from HMRC before making an EIS issue on form AA1

Working shareholders

- Consider the advantages of using company borrowings (with perhaps a personal guarantee) to acquire assets, etc given the additional tax costs that normally arise on extracting funds from the company to repay personal borrowing.

- Use capital or borrowings to subscribe for further shares, striking a commercial balance between debt and equity. Shareholders should be aware of the increased financial risk that is involved in subscribing for shares rather than loaning funds. Loan accounts can be repaid more easily and are therefore more flexible.

- *Incoming* directors can make qualifying EIS investments provided care is taken to ensure the relevant conditions are complied with.

- Owner managers with significant CGT liabilities can shelter their gains by subscribing for new equity shares in their company under the EIS CGT deferral relief rules (which do not contain any restriction regarding 'connected' investors).

- EIS investors should try to obtain appropriate warranties and indemnities from the company to reduce the financial risk of subsequently losing their EIS relief.

- Income tax relievable interest cannot be claimed on monies borrowed to finance EIS shares.

- In appropriate cases, consider VCT investments (up to £200,000 per tax year) for saving income tax at 30%.

Non-working shareholders

- The strategy for non-working shareholders is broadly the same as for working shareholders.

- Interest relief is available on their personal borrowings (to inject (non-EIS) share capital or loan finance) provided they have over 5% of the ordinary share capital.

Chapter 12

Expanding the Company's Activities and Structuring Business Acquisitions

MAKING A BUSINESS ACQUISITION

12.1   Companies can expand organically or by acquiring established businesses. The decision to make an acquisition should be based on a definite strategy. The company must have a clear idea of what it needs to achieve from the acquisition, for example, increased capacity and economies of scale, additional market share, new technology or diversification into new products or services. Sensible business acquisitions usually enable a company to grow at a faster rate. The business may also be expanded by the use of franchising (see 12.76–12.78).

The acquiring company must do a considerable amount of homework in identifying suitable targets and approaching selected prospects to draw up a shortlist. A considerable amount of valuable management time can be devoted to this exercise which may be detrimental to the running of the existing business. Management should therefore consider obtaining professional assistance from a reputable corporate finance department or firm.

Typical acquisition process

12.1A   For the vast majority of deals where the acquirer has identified and approached a potential Target company/business, the typical acquisition process can be outlined as follows:

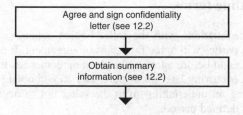

499

A preliminary investigation of the Target company/business should be made. This will enable the purchaser to confirm its reasons and rationale for making the acquisition and assess likely consideration price.

An early review of the Target will enable the purchaser to also identify potentially big issues that would impact on the acquisition, such as major tax irregularities, the recent loss of a large customer, cost rationalisation opportunities. The purchaser will also want to assess any surplus assets and the business's working capital requirements going forward. In some cases, where a deal is agreed in principle, the parties may also wish to frame the scope of the due diligence investigation (see 12.3 and 12.4).

Agreeing outline terms

12.2   After negotiations with the seller (which, again, can be very time consuming), the parties will agree the heads of agreement. It is important that legal advice is sought before agreeing heads of agreement as this may prevent legal difficulties occurring later on. A purchaser should obtain an 'exclusivity agreement', being an undertaking from the seller not to negotiate with any other party for a defined period.

Heads of agreement should be expressed as, to be 'subject to contract' pending preparation of the full sale and purchase agreement. This would normally cover the following areas:

(*a*)   the subject matter of the purchase (ie is it a purchase of shares or assets?);

(*b*)   the consideration for acquisition and the payment terms;

(*c*)   whether the price is to be satisfied by cash or shares/loan notes issued by the purchaser;

(*d*)   conditions;

(*e*)   warranties and indemnities;

(*f*)   consultancy and service agreements.

Agreement should be obtained as to the approach which will be taken on potentially contentious issues at this stage.

Due diligence investigation

12.3   The purchasing company must obtain full details of the financial performance and commercial operations of the target business, including details of its product range, position in the market, management team, customer base, intellectual property, properties, etc. A well-advised seller will require the purchaser to enter into a binding confidentiality agreement in relation to information disclosed during the negotiations.

The purchaser (and/or its lenders) will usually instruct accountants and possibly other experts to undertake a 'due diligence' investigation into the target company (or, where an asset purchase is contemplated, the target company's business). A comprehensive due diligence exercise will review the commercial, financial, tax, legal and environmental aspects of the target company and its business.

The *accountants'* due diligence report would typically cover the target's:

(*a*)   corporate structure;

(*b*)   management and personnel;

(*c*)   trading operations;

(*d*)   accounting and management information systems;

(*e*)   sales, marketing and distribution;

(*f*)   purchasing and raw material supplies;

(*g*)   research and development;

(*h*)   accounting policies; and

(*i*) financial, tax and trading position (the scope of a tax 'due diligence' investigation is detailed in 12.3).

The review would typically examine past performance, current trading and future prospects of the business

A surveyor may also report on the properties owned by the target company and an actuary's report may be required on the target's company pension scheme. An environmental audit may be appropriate if there are potential risks inherent in the nature of the target's business, such as contaminated land.

Tax due diligence

12.4 The tax due diligence will provide the purchaser with a full picture of the target's tax affairs and liabilities and those relating to the proposed transaction.

The tax due diligence would be primarily aimed at those areas that are considered to pose the greatest 'tax risk'. Its scope and coverage will inevitably depend on the precise nature of the target's trade and the industry or business sector in which it operates.

The tax work is likely to cover (to a greater or lesser extent):

- corporate taxes;

- payroll and social security taxes (such as PAYE and NIC);

- sales taxes (such as VAT and Customs duties); and

- transfer taxes (stamp duty land tax ('SDLT') and stamp duty).

A detailed and properly targeted review should identify historical tax risks and issues. Once the scope of the due diligence exercise has been agreed, the purchaser's advisers will determine the relevant documentation they require for review (this would include copies of relevant tax returns, tax computations, correspondence with HMRC and other tax authorities and so on). On the corporate tax side, part of this work usually involves a review of the target's effective corporate tax rates on its accounting profits for recent periods with explanations being sought for material variances from the normal 'expected' tax charge.

The due diligence exercise should reveal any future potential tax exposures and unprovided tax liabilities. The due diligence report should also analyse the tax consequences of the proposed deal structure together with any potential tax charges that would be triggered by a change in the ownership of the target company and how these may be mitigated.

Depending on the nature of such tax (and other) issues, the due diligence report may recommend a reduction in the purchase price, a retention or specific warranties and indemnities.

Post-acquisition integration of target business

12.5   An area often underestimated is the integration of the new business within the purchasing company. In some cases, the seller shareholders may need to be kept on in key managerial or technical positions.

FINAL SALE CONTRACT

Sale and purchase agreement

12.6   The sale and purchase agreement will build on the principles and terms agreed at the heads of agreement stage, the main areas being:

(*a*)   the detailed agreement for the sale;

(*b*)   the price payable, detailing any specific adjustments to it, and how it is to be satisfied;

(*c*)   conditions relating to the completion of the agreement and the completion procedure;

(*d*)   warranties and the deed of indemnity (or tax covenant) (see 12.62–12.75).

Non-compete covenants

12.7   The acquiring company should also obtain a 'non-compete' covenant prohibiting the seller company/shareholder from:

- carrying on the same or similar business;

- within a reasonable geographical area; and

- for a certain number of years.

The purchasing company is entitled to a statutory trading deduction (under *CTA 2009, s 69*) for payments to obtain a 'non-compete' undertaking (where the seller shareholder/director is liable to an employment tax charge on the receipt under *ITEPA 2003, s 225*).

Restrictive covenant payments are only liable to NICs if they are paid to an employee of the paying company. Thus, where an acquiring company makes the payment, this would not incur any NIC charge as no employer/employee relationship exists. However, sellers will now generally be reluctant to agree to allocating part of their share sale consideration to a non-competition covenant, given that (even without the availability of ER) they will enjoy a (much) lower tax rate on their capital gain than on the 'employment income' receipt for the non-competition covenant.

STRUCTURING AN ACQUISITION – ASSETS OR SHARES?

Overview

12.8   A business acquisition can basically be structured either as a purchase of the trade and assets of the target company as a going concern, or the shares of the target company carrying on the business.

The acquiring company now obtains considerable benefits from the tax relief available on goodwill and intellectual property purchases. This may have a significant impact on the way in which businesses are purchased. Furthermore, goodwill and debts are exempt from stamp duty. However, any commercial land and property acquired on a business purchase can attract a significant SDLT cost at rates of up to 4% (see 12.23). One of the key advantages of an asset-based deal, is that the purchaser is generally not at 'risk' in relation to any latent historic tax liabilities within the selling company.

On balance, purchasers now generally find asset-based acquisitions increasingly attractive. This is likely to create a tension with sellers who usually obtain the best tax treatment by selling their shares. However, in the current economic climate, many 'distress' sales (where sellers are desperate to sell to enable their businesses to survive) will often be structured as an asset deal (or a share sale of a new 'hive-down' company) (see 16.5–16.7.)

When negotiating the deal, each party will have their own preferred route in mind. For example, the purchaser may perceive that there are considerable pre-acquisition risks with the target's business and will not want to be hit with any latent liabilities. In such cases, the purchaser may insist the deal being structured as an asset purchase. The relative bargaining strength of the parties normally dictates the ultimate deal structure. However, in tightly negotiated deals, a 'price adjustment' may be struck where one party requires a particular route (say) to benefit from a particular tax relief.

Summary of tax effects – share versus asset purchase

12.9

	Assets	*Shares*
1. Tax relief on assets purchased, for example, goodwill/intangible fixed assets, capital allowance assets and trading stock.	Relief generally based on price paid for individual assets.	Relief continues to be claimed on historic cost in target company.

2.	Tax losses.	Not transferred with the trade and thus normally forfeited.	Transferred for use against post-acquisition profits (subject to anti-avoidance rules).
3.	Degrouping charges.	None.	Potential charges arising from prior intra-group transfers include: – capital gains (although this will often be exempted under the post-FA 2011 SSE rules – see 3.0) – intangibles (*no SSE* protection is available here) – stamp duty land tax and stamp duty.
4.	Stamp duty land tax/stamp duty.	Up to 4% on commercial land and property.	½% on amount paid for shares.
5.	Contingent liabilities.	Not transferred.	Transferred (subject to warranties/indemnities).

OUTLINE OF TRADE AND ASSET PURCHASE

Tax reliefs on acquired assets

12.10   As a general rule, the purchaser will often prefer to acquire the assets on which tax relief can be claimed such as trading stock (which is normally deductible in the first period) and plant and machinery.

A further significant benefit is the ability to obtain trading deductions on goodwill and other intangible fixed assets, such as brands, know-how, trading names, etc. Corporate tax relief is now given on such acquisitions under the rules in *CTA 2009, Part 8* (previously known as the *FA 2002, Sch 29* regime). The tax relief is broadly based on the amount that is written off or amortised in the purchaser's accounts for the relevant period (see 12.46).

The purchaser may also benefit from an uplift in base values for capital allowances and capital gains purposes (ie exceeding the amount that would have been available to the target company).

Forfeiture of target company's tax losses

12.11   On an asset deal, the purchaser would not be entitled to benefit from the target company's unused tax losses. Such losses are effectively lost since the seller company can only use them against the future profits of the same trade, which will disappear after the trade has been sold (see 12.38).

Exceptionally, *CTA 2010, s 944(3) (ICTA 1988, s 343)* allows trading losses to be transferred to the acquirer (on a trade and asset purchase) where the trade effectively remains under the *same* (at least 75%) beneficial ownership, provided certain other conditions are satisfied.

Reduced commercial risk

12.12   An asset based deal is invariably more advantageous for the purchaser. By buying the assets, the purchaser avoids responsibility for past actions of the company and the contingent liabilities such as tax, litigation, etc which remain with the seller. Although the purchaser can minimise these risks by a careful due diligence exercise, warranties and tax indemnities, it is better not to assume any liabilities in the first place rather than be embroiled in pursuing a warranty claim, etc against the seller post-acquisition.

An asset purchase can often be quite complex from a legal and administrative viewpoint (see 12.18), although this also gives the purchaser the ability to 'cherry pick' the desirable assets.

However, responsibilities for the employees' contracts of employment (and hence the accrued entitlements to redundancy pay, etc) are invariably transferred to the purchaser under the *Transfer of Undertakings (Protection of Employment) Regulations 1981.*

Roll over of existing capital gains

12.13   An asset purchase is particularly useful where the acquiring company or group has generated capital gains on the sale of existing 'chargeable' trading assets. However, capital gains on qualifying assets cannot be rolled over against the acquisition of goodwill (which is included in a separate intangibles roll-over regime (see 12.50 – 12.51). Consequently, the main categories of reinvestment expenditure that currently qualifies for *capital gains* roll over relief are:

- property occupied and used for trading purposes; and
- fixed plant and equipment.

Stamp duty land tax versus stamp duty on shares

12.14   Where the trade and asset purchase includes UK land and property, there is likely to be a stamp duty land tax (SDLT) cost. Where a substantial amount is being paid for property, the SDLT costs can be quite significant and often attract higher rates than the ½% stamp duty charge that is levied on the purchase of shares. Thus, for example, SDLT of 3% is charged where the total consideration paid for 'commercial' land and property exceeds £250,000 – the cost rises to 4% where the consideration exceeds £500,000 (but see 12.17).

No stamp tax is now payable on intellectual property, goodwill or the transfer of book debts – see 12.19.

BASIC OVERVIEW OF SHARE PURCHASE

Increased commercial exposure

12.15   In contrast to an asset-based acquisition, a purchase of shares carries the risk of taking over the target company's undiscovered or contingent liabilities. Carefully drawn warranties and indemnities are therefore required to reduce the purchaser's potential financial exposure. Clearly, it is often preferable to identify and quantify the potential risk by conducting an appropriate due diligence investigation beforehand (see 12.2–12.3).

Tax benefits

12.16   Although no immediate tax relief can be claimed for the cost of the shares purchased, in many cases the shares are now likely to qualify as a 'substantial shareholding' under *TCGA 1992, Sch 7AC*. Consequently, a subsequent disposal of the shares may benefit from the valuable Substantial Shareholdings Exemption (SSE), enabling them to be sold completely free of tax (see 3.40).

If the company has unrelieved tax losses they will remain within the company for the indirect benefit of the purchaser, subject to the potential application of certain anti-avoidance rules (see 12.56).

Potentially lower stamp duty costs

12.17   A share acquisition often attracts a lower stamp duty liability due to the lower rate of ½% payable on the purchase price of shares (the ½% charge arises irrespective of the amount paid for the shares).

The extent of any saving would depend on the 'make-up' of the target company's underlying assets (including any value referable to goodwill) and the amount of its debts and liabilities. This is because the ½% stamp duty charge on shares is, in effect, based on the *net* value of the company (ie its *total* assets (including goodwill) *less* debts/liabilities). There may be cases where the stamp duty charge would be greater than the 'comparable' SDLT charge (which is confined to the *full* value of the *property*). For example, consider a company that is being sold for £10 million that has various trading properties worth around £1 million. In this case, the stamp duty cost to the purchaser would be £50,000 (ie ½% of £10 million). However, if the company's trade and assets were purchased instead, the SDLT payable on the properties would be about £40,000 (ie 4% of £1 million).

TRADE AND ASSET PURCHASE – DETAILED ASPECTS

Sale and purchase agreement

12.18   The agreement for an asset purchase should identify precisely the assets and liabilities which will be taken over. This could comprise:

(*a*)   freehold/leasehold premises;

(*b*)   plant, machinery and vehicles;

(*c*)   leasing, hire purchase and other agreements;

(*d*)   intellectual property, trade marks, designs and know-how;

(*e*)   goodwill;

(*f*)   stock and work-in-progress;

(*g*)   debtors and creditors;

(*h*)   benefit of contracts;

(*i*)   employees (particularly key personnel);

(*j*)   business accounts and records.

12.19   Trade debtors, etc can be assigned without any stamp tax implications.

Depending on the nature of the business, there may be a need to assign contracts and leases which may create practical difficulties, for example, the target company may have non-assignable contracts and third-party consents may not be readily obtainable.

Fewer warranties tend to be required on an asset sale covering such areas as the particular assets (and liabilities) transferred, the previous conduct of the company's trade, key customers and suppliers, etc, assignment of trade debts and exemption from stamp duty.

Transfer of Undertakings rule for employees

12.19A Employees will normally be transferred automatically on an asset and trade sale under the *Transfer of Undertakings (Protection of Employment) Regulations 2006*, commonly referred to as the TUPE provisions. Broadly, the sale will be treated as a 'relevant transfer' under the TUPE rules since it will fall to be treated as the 'transfer of an economic entity which retains its identity' in the purchaser's hands.

The TUPE rules mean that the purchaser acquires all the employees' previous employment history and obligations. The selling company must provide the purchaser with 'relevant employee information' in relation to all the employees – which will include (for each employee):

– Identity and age;

– Details of employment that the employee is obliged to give the employee (under s1 ERA 1996);

– Information of any disciplinary procedures taken against an employee or any grievance procedure taken by an employee taking place within the previous two years.

Where there is a large workforce, the gathering of this information is likely to prove a fairly onerous process. There are significant penalties for non-compliance with these rules.

The selling company is also obliged to inform its employees about the proposed sale of the business and 'consult' with them (through appropriate employee representatives) with a view to seeking agreement.

Allocation of purchase consideration

12.20 The purchaser's primary objectives will be to maximise any 'immediate' tax deductions and minimise SDLT. For both corporate tax and SDLT purposes it is important to include the 'breakdown' of the total purchase price against the various assets in the purchase contract. (An apportionment of the consideration must be made for SDLT/stamp duty purposes – see 12.24.) If the apportionment of the price is stipulated in the purchase agreement, the parties cannot argue about it after the contract has been signed. As a general rule, HMRC are unlikely to interfere with any arm's length transaction between unconnected parties, unless it is clearly artificial (for example, see *EV Booth (Holdings) Ltd v Buckwell* [1980] STC 578). In any deal, there is usually a parameter of values of each asset which can be substantiated commercially

However, it is important to note that HMRC have the statutory power to re-allocate or apportion the consideration on a just and reasonable basis. For example, see *CAA 2001, s 562* (capital allowances); *TCGA 1992, s 52(4)*

(capital gains); and *CTA 2009, s 165(3)* (unconnected purchase of trading stock). Where there is a large disparity between the contract values and the subsequent fair values attributed to assets in the statutory accounts (under FRS 7 – see below), there is growing evidence that HMRC are seeking to apply the 'FRS 7' fair values as a 'just and reasonable' amount.

The purchase of goodwill and other intangible assets is dealt with under *CTA 2009, Part 8*, which is generally based on the amounts amortised in the accounts in accordance with GAAP. In practice, this means that these amounts will generally be derived from the fair values adopted in the accounts under FRS 7 (which may not necessarily reflect the amounts stipulated in the sale and purchase agreement). Indeed, *CTA 2009, s 856 (3)* states that where assets are acquired together, than any amount allocated to goodwill and intangibles in accordance with GAAP must be used for tax purposes. If there is no such apportionment, *CTA 2009, s 856 (4)* imposes a 'just and reasonable' allocation (see 12.48).

Stamp duty land tax (SDLT) on property included in trade and asset purchases

Overview of SDLT

12.21 The purchaser is liable to pay:

- stamp duty land tax (SDLT) on the purchase of UK land and property [*FA 2003, s 121*]; and

- stamp duty on any purchase of shares.

SDLT is charged on all UK land and property transactions. SDLT is effectively a mandatory tax since it does not rely on the existence of a legal document or the legal completion of a land transaction. Thus, for example, it is no longer possible to avoid duty by 'resting on contract' [*FA 2003, s 42*]. Non-UK property is not within the charge to SDLT, although it may be subject to a similar tax in the overseas jurisdiction.

Basic charge to SDLT

12.22 Under the SDLT legislation, a 'land transaction' represents an 'acquisition' of a 'chargeable interest' (*FA 2003, s 43*). This means that tax is payable not only on a normal land purchase but also on the creation, release, surrender, or variation of a chargeable land interest. This clearly includes the grant of a lease, which is subject to special rules (see below). SDLT is also charged on the value of any fixtures substantially attached to the land under land law. Items that retain their character as chattels and moveable property will not be charged to SDLT.

Broadly, SDLT is payable on the 'completion' of a land transaction by the purchaser (*FA 2003, s 42*). However, the SDLT charge is brought forward where a land transaction is 'substantially performed', such as where a substantial (90%) amount of the consideration is paid (which includes the first 'rent' payment on a lease) or where the purchaser takes possession (for example, occupation).

The purchaser (broadly the person acquiring the relevant land interest) (*FA 2003, s 43(4), (5)*) must submit their 'self-assessed' land transaction return (SDLT 1) and pay the relevant SDLT within 30 days from the 'effective date', ie normally when the contract is completed or substantially performed [*FA 2003, ss 77* and *86*]. (An acquisition of a freehold interest does not have to be notified where the consideration is less than £40,000 – such transactions are self-certified.)

Care is clearly required to ensure that the SDLT return contains accurate figures for chargeable consideration or where relevant, market value and so on. Such returns are subject to SDLT enquiry with the normal tax-related penalties for 'careless' errors (see 4.57 to 4.62). Certain SDLT avoidance schemes involving commercial property worth at least £5 million may need to be disclosed to HMRC (see 1.16).

SDLT rates

12.23 SDLT (at the appropriate rate) is applied to the chargeable consideration for the relevant land transaction. Different tax rate scales apply to residential property and non-residential or 'mixed-use' property.

In the context of a trade and asset acquisition, the property will normally be of a 'commercial' (non-residential) nature. However, for completeness, residential property is defined in *FA 2003, s 116* and includes buildings that are used or suitable for use as dwellings, their accompanying gardens and grounds, and residential accommodation for school pupils and students (other than those in higher education). Residential property situated in a disadvantaged area is exempt provided it is sold for less than £150,000 (see 12.27). There is no longer any 'disadvantaged area' exemption for commercial properties.

Certain buildings, such as hospitals, hotels or 'care' homes, are effectively deemed to be non-residential. The transfer of six or more dwellings in a *single* transaction is also regarded as 'non-residential' for all SDLT purposes [*FA 2003, s 116(7)*].

SDLT rates are applied on the so-called 'slab system' – thus, where the consideration exceeds the relevant threshold, the higher rate of SDLT is applied to the total amount. The application of a nil or lower rate of SDLT also depends on the relevant land transaction *not* being part of a linked transaction. Broadly, linked transactions are those made as part of a single scheme or arrangement between the *same* seller and purchaser (or their 'connected' parties). If the transaction is linked (such as on a trade acquisition), the rate of SDLT is fixed by reference to the *total* consideration for all the linked chargeable land transactions [*FA 2003, s 55(4)*].

The current relevant rates are shown below.

Non-residential property or mixed-use property		Residential property	
Chargeable consideration	*Rate*	*Chargeable consideration*	*Rate*
Up to £150,000	Nil	Up to £125,000*+	Nil
£150,001 – £250,000	1%	£125,000 – £250,000	1%
£250,001 – £500,000	3%	£250,001 – £500,000	3%
More than £500,000	4%	More than £500,000**	4%

* The nil rate threshold was temporarily increased from £125,000 to £175,000 on 3 September 2008 to 31 December 2009.

+ From 25 March 2010 to 25 March 2012, the SDLT threshold is £250,000 for 'first time' buyers. Purchases below this amount will not incur any SDLT provided the purchaser is buying 'first time' (i.e. they have never owned a house or flat before)

** From April 2011, an SDLT rate of 5% applies to residential property purchases of £1 million plus (for one year).

Chargeable consideration

12.24   SDLT is levied on the 'chargeable consideration', which includes money or money's worth. Importantly, where the purchaser assumes an existing liability of the seller/transferor (such as an existing property mortgage), this forms part of the chargeable consideration for these purposes.

The chargeable consideration will include any VAT that is payable on the property, although in many cases VAT 'transfer of going concern' relief should enable the property to be transferred on a 'VAT-free' basis. However, this is not the case where VAT becomes chargeable following an option to tax being made *after* the 'effective date' of the transaction for SDLT.

On a trade and asset purchase, the properties purchased will be 'linked', and therefore the rate of SDLT will be based on the *total* 'chargeable consideration' (ie the amount paid for all the UK properties).

The SDLT treatment of deferred consideration depends on whether it is:

● contingent; or

● uncertain or unascertained.

Contingent consideration (ie a fixed amount that is payable or ceases to be payable if some future event occurs) is initially brought into account for SDLT purposes on the basis that it will be payable – the contingency is therefore disregarded. Where the deferred consideration is uncertain or unascertainable, the SDLT return (and hence the SDLT payable) is initially based on a 'reasonable estimate' of that future consideration. The purchaser can elect to defer the payment of the SDLT where at least one tranche of any contingent or uncertain consideration is payable six months after the effective transaction date (*FA 2003, s 90*).

The original SDLT liability is subsequently adjusted when the circumstances surrounding the contingency are resolved or where the (initial) unascertainable consideration becomes determined. This is done by making a further SDLT return within the normal 30-day period.

Allocation of asset values and valuation issues

12.25 The seller's and purchaser's agreed allocation of the total consideration between the various assets must be specified on the Stamp Taxes form – the apportionment must be made on a 'just and reasonable' basis. (Professional advisers should note the Court of Appeal decision in *Saunders v Edwards* [1987] 1 WLR 1116 which held that a solicitor involved in making a blatantly 'artificial' allocation was guilty of professional misconduct.) The total consideration for the assets must agree to the various constituent elements (broadly) between cash, the issue of shares or loan notes, and the assumption of liabilities.

HMRC set out its practice with regard to goodwill valuations relating to trade-related properties in April 2009. It is reasonably clear from HMRC's note that it intends to seek to attribute a greater value to the property element in the sale and purchase of a business than previously. (Cynics would argue is that HMRC is simply trying to collect more SDLT!). Where a business is sold as a going concern the sale price generally reflects the combined value of the tangible assets and goodwill. HMRC argue that the combination of both tangible and intangible assets often enables substantial value to be realised and that in the past inadequate value has been attributed to property assets.

For tax purposes (especially SDLT), HMRC concludes that property-related businesses are invariably sold with property rights and it is necessary to recognise the contribution that each asset makes to the combined value of the business. It therefore follows (according to HMRC), that a property from which a successful business trades must have some goodwill of its own. Many tax advisers do not agree with this proposition – they take the view that goodwill attaches to the business and that the property value is independent of this.

Property values are largely determined by their location. Property values can generally be reliably estimated by expert valuers based on local property valuation databases, and these are normally derived from the inherent characteristics of the property and its location. However, just because a business trades successfully from a particular location, it does not necessarily follow that the successful trading increases the value of the property. If a hotel or pub is situated in a place where a profitable trade can be expected, that particular 'location' will influence its value and will be reflected in the property valuation.

Goodwill is often difficult to value. However, where there is a third party sale, the value of goodwill should be ascertainable under GAAP since it has an agreed basis of calculation being the *excess* of the consideration paid for a business over the fair value of its net tangible assets (see 12.48). HMRC can therefore expect their reasoning in this area to be challenged.

Calculation of SDLT on trade and assets purchase

12.26

Example 1

SDLT payable on a trade and asset purchase

On 30 June 2011, Bonds plc purchased the trade and assets (including goodwill) of Billy Ltd's successful computer game software design and development business for a total consideration of £4,100,550.

The sale and purchase agreement allocated the consideration as follows:

	£
Freehold property (including immovable fittings and fixtures)	1,200,000
Goodwill	2,500,000
Computer and office equipment	580,000
Debtors	270,670
Creditors	(450,120)
Cash consideration	4,100,550

A SDLT liability of £48,000 (ie 4% × £1,200,000) only arises on the freehold property (including the immovable fixtures). No duty arises on the other assets.

Bonds plc would obtain corporate tax relief on the amount paid for goodwill based on the amount amortised in its accounts each year (see 12.48). Capital allowances would also be claimed on the computer and office equipment.

Disadvantaged area relief for residential property

12.27   New or old *residential* property situated in a designated 'disadvantaged' area is exempt from SDLT provided the sale consideration does not exceed £150,000 (*FA 2003, Sch 6, para 8*). Where several residential properties are acquired on the same transaction, the exemption is unlikely to apply – they will be 'linked transactions', so the £150,000 limit operates by reference to the amount paid for *all* the properties (see 12.23). Currently, there are around 2,000 designated 'disadvantaged areas' in the UK. These can be checked in advance of any proposed transaction on the HMRC Stamp Taxes website – *www.hmrc.gov.uk/so/pcode_search.htm* – the search is made on a 'post code' basis.

For pre-16 March 2005 deals, non-residential (for example, commercial) properties situated in a disadvantaged area were *completely exempt* from the charge to SDLT, regardless of the amount of the consideration.

Leases

Basic principles

12.28   Some 'trade and asset' deals involve the seller leasing the business property to the purchaser (as opposed to an outright sale). The SDLT legislation defines a 'lease' as:

- an interest or right in or over land for a term of years (whether fixed or periodic); or

- a tenancy at will.or other interest or right in or over land terminable by notice at any time.

[FA 2003, Sch 17A, para 1 (as introduced by the Stamp Duty and Stamp Duty Land Tax (Variation of the Finance Act 2003) (No 2) Regulations 2003 (SI 2003 No 2816)).]

A lease does not include a 'licence to use or occupy land'. Such licences do not attract SDLT (s 48(2)(b)). However, a licence only provides a 'non-exclusive' right of occupation, which does not give the occupier any legal protection. A legal document may be 'drawn up' as a 'licence', but if it effectively grants an exclusive right of possession to the occupier, it will be treated as a lease (Street v Mountford [1985] 2 All ER 289, HL).

Put simply, the SDLT payable on the grant of a lease is broadly based on 1% of the net present value (NPV) of the total rent payable under the terms of the lease (known as 'the relevant rental value'). The methodology here is to discount each separate rent payment back to its present day value, using a discount rate of 3.5% per year. The total of these discounted rent payments are then found to give the relevant rental value for the lease transaction.

No SDLT liability arises on commercial property where relevant rental value does not exceed £150,000. Similarly, residential properties are exempt where relevant rental value is no more than £125,000 (between 3 September 2008 and 31 December 2009, the limit was £175,000).

For leases only, the SDLT calculation follows the 'slice' system so that SDLT is only levied on the amount falling within the relevant 1% band. Thus, where the relevant rental value exceeds these thresholds, SDLT is charged at 1% on the excess amount only (£125,000 for residential property and £150,000 for non-residential/commercial property) – see Example 2 below.

HMRC must be notified about the grant of all leases (that exceed seven years or more) or lease assignments on the land transaction return SDLT1. Notification is required for leases of less than seven years duration, where they carry an SDLT liability.

HMRC's Stamp Taxes website provides a simple 'lease calculator' which automatically computes the SDLT on lease rentals.

Worked example of SDLT liability on lease

12.29

Example 2

SDLT payable on lease

In January 2011, The Zola Trading Co Ltd granted a four-year lease of an industrial unit to Upson Ltd. The lease provided for a yearly rent of £160,000 over the four year lease term. The SDLT would be calculated as follows:

Year	Rent (£)	Discount f actor @ 3.5%	NPV £
2011	160,000	0.9661835	154,589
2012	160,000	0.9335107	149,362
2013	160,000	0.9019427	144,311
2014	160,000	0.8714423	139,431
NPV of rent payable under the lease			£587,693

The SDLT payable by Upson Ltd on the grant of the lease is £4,376 calculated as follows:

			£
First	£150,000	@ 0%	–
Next	£437,693	@ 1%	4,376
	£587,693		4,376

Special lease provisions

12.30   In practice, property leases can be structured in a variety of ways. The NPV calculation for fairly 'simple' leases with a specified rent for a fixed period should be relatively straightforward.

If it is possible for a lease to end before its fixed term (for example, under a 'break' or 'forfeiture' clause), this is disregarded in ascertaining the lease period. Such provisions cannot therefore be used as a device to shorten the lease period for the purposes of the NPV calculation. Any option to renew the lease is also ignored (*FA 2003, Sch 17A, para 2*). Thus, where a ten-year lease gives the lessee the option to extend the term for a further four years, it is still treated as a ten-year lease for working out the NPV of the lease rents.

Other lease agreements may be more difficult to interpret in terms of calculating the NPV of the rents. For example, a lease may contain a formula for calculating the rent (which may be based on the turnover of the lessee's business or increased annually in line with the retail prices index (RPI)). *FA 2003, Schs 5* and *17A* lay down the detailed rules for determining the 'rent' payable over the lease (including rent reviews) and the term of the lease in special situations.

Lease premiums

12.31   A separate SDLT charge arises on lease premiums received on the grant of the lease, which is calculated under the normal SDLT rules (*FA 2003, Sch 5, para 9(1), (4)*) (see 12.24). The lease premium would be treated as 'chargeable consideration' and taxed at the relevant main rate based on the so-called 'slab system'. Thus, where the chargeable consideration (lease premium) exceeds the relevant threshold, the *higher rate* of SDLT is applied to the total amount.

Where a lease is granted for both a premium *and* an annual rent, a special 'anti-avoidance' rule applies to prevent the respective values being manipulated to reduce SDLT. For example, to minimise SDLT, a lease could be granted for a higher initial premium (which might fall within the zero-rate band) but at a lower annual rent.

The rule for commercial properties is that where the (average) annual rent exceeds £1,000 (£600 per year before 12 March 2008), the relevant 'zero-rate' band for taxing the lease premium does *not* apply. The amount falling entirely within the 'nil-rate' band is therefore taxed at 1% (*FA 2003, Sch 5, para 9(2)*).

VAT and the transfer of going concern (TOGC) provisions

Basic TOGC conditions

12.32   The transfer of the trade should not be subject to VAT, as the transfer of going concern (TOGC) provisions in *art 5* of the *VAT (Special Provisions) Order 1995, SI 1995 No 1268* should apply

One of the key requirements is that the assets are as part of the transfer of a business as a going concern. (The relevant conditions for TOGC relief are summarised in 15.16.) Given the relatively subjective nature of this test, it is perhaps not surprising that TOGC relief cases regularly appear before VAT Tribunals!

Where the purchaser acquires the goodwill and all the assets of an existing trade (together with its workforce), these requirements will normally be satisfied. In the ECJ case, *Zita Modes Sárl v Administration de l'enregistrement et des domains, C-497/01* [2003] All ER (D) 411, it was held that the purchaser does not need to have pursued the same kind of business as the seller before the transfer, but must intend to carry that business on after the transfer (as opposed to liquidating the assets).

The VAT treatment of some deals may be less clear-cut. In these cases, TOGC relief would only be justified where, in substance and taking all relevant factors into account, the purchaser acquires the activities of a 'going concern' that can be continued. While statements made in the sale and purchase contract to the effect that the parties regard the transaction as a TOGC may be helpful, they are not conclusive. The transfer of goodwill and business name would be good 'indicators' of a TOGC. Other persuasive indicators would include the transfer of customer lists, transfer of contracts, business premises, transfer of plant and equipment, substantial stock, staff and the provision of a restrictive covenant. However, in *Associated Fleet Services 17255*, it was held that a business was capable of being transferred as a going concern even where no employees were being transferred across.

HMRC indicate that there should not be any significant break in the trading pattern before or immediately after the transfer.

It is important to identify any property falling within the Capital Goods Scheme (CGS) that is transferred under a TOGC – typically property (including refurbishments) that have been acquired in the past ten years costing more than £250,000 (excluding VAT) where VAT was suffered on the purchase price. In such cases, the CGS history will pass to the purchaser.

Unfortunately, HMRC are no longer prepared to give 'informal' TOGC rulings in the vast majority of 'routine' cases (but a ruling may be sought for complex cases in accordance with VAT Notice 700/6).

VAT status of purchaser

12.33 The fact that a 'new company' purchaser does not have a VAT registration number (or has not taken steps to register for VAT) at the time of the purchase does not prevent it from being a TOGC. Assuming the other conditions are met, a trade purchase will qualify as a TOGC where the taxable turnover exceeds the VAT registration threshold. A business is currently obliged to register for VAT if its taxable turnover in the previous 12 months exceeds £73,000 (*and the seller's 'historic' turnover is counted for this purpose*), or is expected to exceed £73,000 in the next month alone.

Property rental businesses

12.34 The default VAT provisions treat sales of land and property as exempt from VAT, but there are numerous exceptions to this rule which treat the supply as standard or zero rated. Many property letting businesses will be subject to an option to tax election, so that the sale of the property would be standard rated. However, on a sale of the property letting business, the TOGC rules should operate so that the supply is not subject to VAT provided the purchaser notifies HMRC that it elects to opt to tax the property before the transfer (or any earlier tax point for VAT, for example, the receipt of cash consideration). These rules also apply to property that has been occupied by the seller for trading purposes in the relatively rare cases where an option to tax has previously been made. The TOGC rule would not apply where the property letting business ceases after the transfer – for example, where the property is acquired by the tenant so that it becomes owner-occupied. Following the *FA 2004* anti-avoidance rules, the purchaser also has an additional statutory obligation to tell the seller that they have made the option and that it will not be disapplied (under the rules in *VATA 1983, Sch 10, para 2*). If the seller does not receive this notification from the purchaser, the TOGC treatment may be invalidated. Since the onus is on the seller to apply the correct VAT treatment, a prudent seller will generally ask for written evidence that the purchaser's option to tax has been made by the relevant date (such as a copy of the notification letter) and confirmation that the purchaser's option to tax will not be disapplied.

While it is possible for the purchaser to retain the seller's VAT registration number (by completing Form VAT 68), this is not usually recommended as the purchaser would then inherit any potential VAT liabilities of the previous owner.

Incorrectly charged VAT

12.35   Where VAT has been incorrectly charged by the seller (because it has subsequently been found that the transaction should have been treated as a TOGC), the seller should cancel any VAT invoice by issuing an appropriate credit note (refunding the VAT). If this is not done, HMRC can still collect the relevant VAT from the seller, but the purchaser will not be able to reclaim it (as a TOGC is not a taxable supply). However, HMRC may permit the purported 'input VAT' to be recovered if they are satisfied that the seller has accounted for and *paid* it to them (*VAT Notice 700/9/02, para 2.2* and *Internal Guidance V1-10, Chapter 2, para 3.2*).

VAT recovery on legal and professional costs

12.36   Where the TOGC rules apply, VAT will still be payable on legal and professional costs relating to the transaction. Assuming the purchaser is 'fully taxable' for VAT purposes (for example, where the assets being purchased are subsequently used for the purposes of making taxable supplies), such VAT can be reclaimed in full.

The same VAT treatment applies to costs relating to advice sought by the company when raising finance for any proposed business purchase. These are a general business expense for VAT and recoverable in line with the purchaser's VAT recovery rate. Similar treatment applies to share issue costs (since the share issue is *not* an exempt supply for VAT purposes) following the ruling in *Kretztechnic AG v Finanzamt Linz (C-465/03)*. The ECJ held that an issue of new shares does not constitute a transaction within the scope of Art 2(1), Sixth Council Directive (77/388/EEC). The issuing company therefore has the right to deduct the VAT on expenses relating to the share issue (provided all the company's supplies are taxable for VAT).

If the transfer of assets does not fall within the TOGC rules, the seller should account for VAT on the purchase price. The purchaser's recovery of this VAT as well as VAT incurred on other acquisition costs (such as professional costs) would depend on the VAT status of the underlying business. Thus, for example, the VAT would be fully recoverable if the transferred business is fully taxable but only partly recoverable on the transfer of a partly exempt business.

Corporate tax relief on borrowing costs

12.37   In many cases, the purchasing company will need to borrow from a bank or other lending institution to finance the purchase of the trade and assets. In such cases, the interest incurred on the borrowing would normally be deductible as a trading expense under the loan relationship rules [*CTA 2009, s 297(3)*]. If the interest is 'substantial', immediate relief will only be given provided the purchasing company has sufficient tax 'capacity' (ie taxable profits) to absorb the interest costs, although any excess interest 'loss' could be surrendered under the group relief provisions.

Any related borrowing costs, such as loan arrangement or guarantee fees, would also qualify for relief as a trading expense. The tax relief is based on the amount charged in the accounts. In such cases, the borrowing costs are normally 'capitalised' (and shown as a reduction against the loan) in the accounts – with the amounts being 'expensed' over the life of the loan.

New trade or expansion of existing trade

12.38 The integration of the acquired trade with the purchaser's existing business may be treated as merely expanding its own trade or the commencement of a new trade (for example, see *Cannon Industries Ltd v Edwards* (1965) 42 TC 625 and *George Humphries & Co v Cook* (1934) 19 TC 121). If the acquisition is treated as an extension of the purchaser's existing trade, there are no adverse consequences and any unused trading losses of the purchaser's existing trade may effectively be offset against the profits of the 'new' trade.

On the other hand, if HMRC successfully argued that a new trade had commenced, any unused trading losses of the existing business could not be offset against future profits of the merged business. This is because under *CTA 2010, s 45 (ICTA 1988, s 393(1))* the losses can only be set off against future profits of the *same* trade. It may be possible to avoid this problem by treating the acquisition as a separate trade and preparing tax computations for the two trades.

The increased profits arising from the trade acquisition may cause the company to be liable to pay its corporation tax in instalments (subject to the 'one year' period of grace where the profits are less than £10 million (reduced for associated companies) (see 4.41)).

CORPORATE TAX TREATMENT OF ASSETS PURCHASED

Buildings

12.39 Industrial, hotel and agricultural buildings allowances were completely abolished from 31 March 2011 and hence no relief will normally be available for expenditure incurred on buildings. However, purchasers must not overlook the opportunity to identify the 'plant and machinery' element in the relevant buildings and agree an amount that could justifiably be allocated to it (see also 12.43). .

Relief could be claimed on industrial, hotel and agricultural buildings purchased before 31 March 2011 but only up to 31 March 2011. Broadly, annual allowances were given based on the amount to which the seller would have been entitled (since, from 21 March 2007, there was no balancing adjustment). This means that the purchaser's annual WDA for the year to 31 March 2010 will be what the seller would have been entitled to had he not disposed of the property (ie 2% of the seller's original cost(s)). The WDA rate for the year to 31 March 2011 would be just 1% on the seller cost(s).

If the seller's WDAs are based on 'second-hand' building rates, these WDAs will be scaled down on the same basis. This would mean 75% of the WDA (that would have been available to the seller if the building had not been sold) is given in the year to 31 March 2009, 50% of the seller's WDA in the year to 31 March 2010, and finally 25% of the seller's WDA in the year to 31 March 2011.

For tax treatment of fixtures attached to buildings, see 4.20 and 12.43.

Before 21 March 2007, the annual allowance would generally have been the original construction cost (or purchase price, if lower) spread over the remaining period of the 25-year tax life of the building (50 years for pre-6 November 1962 buildings) [*CAA 2001, s 311*].

In certain cases, relief can be claimed on commercial buildings situated in a 'qualifying' enterprise zone. 100% enterprise zone initial allowances can be claimed on industrial/commercial buildings purchased unused or within two years of first use. (The expenditure must be incurred within ten years of the site being designated within an enterprise zone.) Almost all the original enterprise zones are now time-expired.

If the purchasing company or group has made capital gains on qualifying assets, either within one year before or three years after the date of acquisition, the expenditure on the freehold/leasehold property can be used to roll over these gains [*TCGA 1992, s 152*]. (Goodwill gains can no longer be rolled over against property acquisitions – see 12.13).

Plant and machinery

Overview

12.40 Currently, expenditure on plant and machinery may attract plant and machinery capital allowances. However the first £100,000 (£50,000 before 1 April 2010 and proposed to be £25,000 from April 2012) may be eligible for the 100% annual investment allowance (AIA), giving an immediate write-off of the expenditure (although the amount of relief depends on other qualifying expenditure already incurred by the company). If the acquiring company is a member of a group, this will depend on how much of the AIA annual limit has been 'used-up' by other group members. Certain assets do not qualify for AIAs including cars and integral features [*CAA 2001, s 38B*].

Unfortunately, the temporary FYAs of 40% (available to all companies) for the one year to 31 March 2010 has come to an end.

The definition of 'plant' extends beyond industrial plant and can include central heating, moveable office partitions, computers, special electrical installations and so on (see 4.11). Specific types of plant and equipment which meet certain energy-saving performance criteria rank for special 100% FYAs.

12.41 FYAs are not available on certain assets, such as cars, long life assets, assets for leasing. The balance of plant and machinery expenditure not attracting AIAs (or FYAs) generally qualifies for the 'default' 20% WDA, which is calculated on a reducing balance basis, except where the plant is treated as 'long life' [*CAA 2001, ss 11(4)* and *15(1)(a)*].

The qualifying expenditure is added to the purchaser's existing pool, with 20% being claimed on the total balance (see 4.29). Before 1 April 2008, the WDA rate was 25% with a hybrid-rate applying to accounting periods straddling 1 April 2008 (see 4.30).

For a detailed discussion of plant and machinery capital allowances generally see 4.15–4.32. A detailed discussion on the capital allowance rules before April 2008 is provided in the 2007/08 edition of this book.

12.42

Example 3

Calculation of plant and machinery allowances on asset purchase

Curbishley Ltd (a singleton company) is a manufacturer of specialised car components and draws up accounts to 31 March 2011. On 20 October 2010, it acquired the trade and assets of a competitor business for £1,750,000 (excluding cars). No other plant was purchased during the year.

For the year ended 31 March 2011, it will be able to claim:

- AIAs of £100,000 (which attract a 100% allowance)

- 20% WDAs on the balance of £1,650,000 (£1,750,000 – £100,000) = £1,650,000 × 20% = £330,000

This leaves £1,320,000 (£1,650,000 less £330,000) to be carried forward in the pool to be claimed as WDAs in future years.

In the year ended 31 March 2012, WDAs of £264,000 (£1,320,000 × 20%) would be claimed, leaving a balance of £1,056,000 to qualify for WDAs of 18% (the post-31 March 2012 rate) in the following year and so on.

With a WDA of 18% (computed on a reducing balance basis), it will take 12 years to obtain tax relief for nearly 90% of the expenditure.

Fixtures and integral features

12.43   Fixtures can often represent a significant part of an industrial or commercial building. Special rules are required because (in law) any fixture attached to a building becomes the property of the freeholder. The capital allowances legislation therefore contains a number of special provisions that treat the fixtures as belonging to the company, etc that incurred the expenditure.

Determining whether an item is a fixture essentially depends on its degree of annexation to the land and the purpose of its attachment – the greater the degree of attachment, the more likely it will be that the item is a fixture. As a general rule, the court will generally consider the item to be a fixture where it is placed on or attached to the land with the intention of becoming an integral part of, or a permanent and substantial improvement to, the land's architectural design and structure. More obvious items include alarm systems, air-conditioning, lifts, escalators, and 'deeply embedded' heavy plant and machinery.

12.44   When a building is purchased or a leasehold interest is assigned, it is likely to contain various fixtures upon which plant and machinery allowances can be claimed (see 4.14–4.17 and 12.34). There can often be difficulties in determining the part of the total purchase consideration that relates to the fixtures. The contract allocation should be based on a 'just and reasonable' apportionment' otherwise it could be challenged by HMRC (see *Fitton v Gilders & Heaton* [1955] 36 TC 233 and *CAA 2001, s 562*). The 'just and reasonable' amount included in the contract (which cannot exceed the amount on which the seller originally claimed capital allowances) will be used for the seller's disposal value and the purchaser's capital allowances claim.

However, there is an important exception which overrides this rule – and one that is often adopted in practice. The parties to the contract can make a joint election under *CAA 2001, s 198* to agree the price that is being paid for the fixtures. Section 198 elections which fix the consideration paid for the fixtures are negotiated between the parties. There is an in-built tension in that sellers will generally prefer their disposal value to be as low as possible and the purchase would like to maximise it.

The elected value cannot exceed the *lower* of the amount on which the seller claimed capital allowances or the total sale price of the property. As a general observation, section 198 elections tend to favour the seller since the agreed elected value tends to be lower than the amount that would have applied on a 'just and reasonable' allocation. Many elections are based on the (notional) 'tax written down value' of the fixtures or even £1 – which would invariably be in the seller's favour. Following the introduction of 'integral features' into the capital allowances code, *s 198* elections should specify amounts for both integral features (see below and 4.24) and other fixtures.

It is advisable for a detailed list of the specific plant and machinery 'fixtures' to be attached to the election rather than a general statement that it applies to 'all the plant and machinery fixtures within the building'. The election should also be agreed within the sale and purchase agreement.

12.45   A pro-forma specimen election is provided below:

Election under Section 198 of the Capital Allowances Act 2001	
We the Seller and the Buyer wish to elect (under the Sale And Purchase Agreement) and Section 198 of the Capital Allowances Act 2001, as follows:	
Seller's Name and address	Hurst Retail Ltd Sirs Road Chadwell Heath RM 66 1GH
Seller's tax district and reference :	North West Lancashire – 449 – 19571 97210
Buyer's name and address :	Moore Properties 6 Wembley Way Wembley NW 108 6BM
Buyer's Tax District :	East London 1 – 623 – 19641 96706
Property :	Irons Warehouse, Irons Trading Estate, 11 Green Street, Upton Park, E13 9AZ
Title number :	WH 194158
Interest :	Freehold
Date of exchange :	12 April 2010
Date of completion :	12 April 2010
Total price :	Five hundred and sixty six pounds only (£560,000) (exclusive of VAT)
Plant and machinery in respect :	See attached schedule of which election is made
Part of total price to be attributed to plant and machinery fixtures :	Two Hundred Pounds (£200,000) (exclusive of VAT)
Signed	Signed ....
Name	Name ....
For and on behalf of the Seller	For and on behalf of the Buyer

Section 198 elections can only be made where the seller is required to bring in a disposal value for capital allowance purposes [*CAA 2001, s 196(1)*]. Hence, it is not possible to make an election where the seller is a property trader/developer, pension fund or a charity. Furthermore, the election only applies to fixtures and does not extend to chattels.

Where the seller did not previously claim capital allowances on all eligible fixtures, the purchaser's allowances may be based on their replacement value under *CAA 2001, s 562*.

Since April 2008, a 10% WDA on fixtures that are 'integral' to a building – known as integral features – can be claimed and go into a separate 10% pool (and do not attract WDAs via the main pool). Integral features include lifts, cold water and heating systems (see 4.24).

However, in the Budget 2011, the Government announced that there will be a further series on designated enterprise zones located in Liverpool City Region; The Black Country; Nottingham; Nottinghamshire, Derby and Derbyshire; Western England (including Bristol); London; Greater Manchester; Leeds City Region; Sheffield City Region; North Eastern; Greater Birmingham and Solihull; and Tees Valley. In certain limited areas, where there is a strong element in manufacturing, enhanced capital allowances will be available.

Goodwill and intangibles

Scope of corporate intangibles regime

12.46 Expenditure on goodwill and all other types of intangible fixed assets attract relief under *CTA 2009, Part 8* (previously referred to as the *FA 2002, Sch 29* tax regime). These rules only apply to goodwill/intangibles acquired (from an unrelated third party) or internally created *after 31 March 2002*. (This means that the 'old' capital gains treatment will still apply for goodwill and intangible fixed assets acquired from a 'connected' seller who held them at 31 March 2002).

Under the corporate intangibles regime, companies can obtain a tax deduction for purchased goodwill and other intangible fixed assets (which include intellectual property (IP), brands, names, logos, customer lists, copyrights, registered designs, commercial formats, and so on).

Before April 2002, the capital cost of most intangible types of fixed asset, such as purchased goodwill and intellectual property, did not attract any tax relief against trading profits.

Importance of FRS 10 and timing of relief

12.47 For the vast majority of owner managed companies, the timing of the tax relief for intangible fixed assets will generally follow the rules in Financial Reporting Standard (FRS) 10, which deals with goodwill and other intangibles, including IP. FRS 10 requires such assets to be amortised or written off against profits based on the useful working life of the asset.

In particular, goodwill purchased with a trade is capitalised and amortised, although usually not over a period exceeding 20 years. However, where circumstances justify, its useful life may be extended beyond 20 years (or even indefinitely, which would mean no amortisation!)

The accounts' carrying value of the goodwill is subject to impairment reviews to confirm that it is worth at least that amount. Impairment reviews are generally made where there are adverse changes in the company's commercial and economic environment indicating that an impairment may have occurred. Broadly, if the recoverable amount of the goodwill is less than its carrying value, the reduction in value is charged against profits as an impairment write-off. (For these purposes, the recoverable amount is defined as the lower of the net realisable value or value in use (ie the present value of the future cash flows obtainable from the continued use of the goodwill).

The tax treatment of the purchase of goodwill (and any other intangible fixed asset) is governed by the corporate intangibles regime. The acquiring company can claim tax relief on its acquisition of goodwill and intangibles, which is based on the amounts amortised or impairments charged in the acquiring company's statutory accounts (subject to certain exceptions).

12.48 Goodwill will invariably be acquired as part of the acquisition of a successful business. In such cases, the amounts allocated to the relevant assets acquired as part of the business purchase are subject to FRS 7. Broadly, this requires the acquiring company to reflect the acquired assets at their *fair market value* – which may not necessarily be the amount reflected in the sale and purchase agreement.

Under GAAP, goodwill is generally defined as the difference between the purchase price and the fair value of the identifiable assets and liabilities acquired. It will therefore be the balancing figure out of the purchase consideration after accounting for the revised 'fair value' of the assets acquired.

Given that the corporate tax deductions for goodwill and other intangible assets follows the accounting treatment, they will generally reflect the 'fair value' amounts reflected in the accounts under GAAP (see *CTA 2009, s 856*) (see 12.20). Thus, where (old) goodwill is being sold by the seller (ie goodwill held at 1 April 2002), it is possible for the disposal to be taxed by reference to the 'contract' value (in the seller's hands) with the purchaser obtaining intangibles tax relief based on the goodwill reported in the accounts after applying the FRS 7 'fair value' process. HMRC accept that this is the correct analysis for goodwill and other intangibles.

The accounting treatment adopted will therefore influence both the amount and the timing of the tax relief for the purchased goodwill or other intangible asset, based on the amount amortised (or impaired) in the accounts. However, this general rule is subject to certain exceptions. It may not apply where, for example, roll-over relief is claimed under the intangibles regime, where the amortisation is based on the reduced tax cost (see 12.50).

Furthermore, as an alternative to the accounts amortisation, companies can elect to claim tax relief at the rate of 4% (straight line) of the original goodwill/ intangible asset cost per year. The election must be made within two years of the end of the accounting period in which the asset is acquired [*CTA 2009, ss 730–731*]. An election would be beneficial where, for example, the goodwill is amortised in the accounts over a longer period than 25 years or where it is not amortised at all (for example, where the company has adopted International Financial Reporting Standard 3, which requires that goodwill is *not* subject to amortisation but is regularly tested for impairment with appropriate write-downs being made.

Example 4

Calculation of corporate tax deduction on intangible fixed assets on asset and trade purchase

On 31 December 2010, Shilton's Pharmaceuticals Co Ltd acquired the trade and assets (including goodwill) of Banks plc's pharmaceutical and herbal remedy business.

The allocation of the purchase consideration in the sale agreement was as follows:

	£
Freehold property	1,500,000
Plant and equipment	1,100,000
Goodwill	500,000
Patent rights	800,000
Know-how	500,000
Trade debtors (net of trade creditors and other liabilities)	200,000
Net consideration, satisfied in cash	£4,600,000

The above amounts were also reflected in the company's accounts (since they approximated to the fair values of the assets).

Based on the company's amortisation policy for intangible fixed assets (and ignoring any future impairment write-offs), it should be able to claim an annual trading tax deduction (starting with the accounting period to 31 December 2010) on the intangible fixed assets purchased from Banks plc as follows:

	Capital cost	Amortisation period	Annual write-off
	£	£	£
Goodwill	500,000	5 years	100,000
Patent rights	800,000	10 years	80,000
Know-how	500,000	4 years	125,000
Total	1,800,000		305,000

Example 5

Fair value allocation of asset values under FRS 7 and inter-action with FA 2002, Sch 29 tax deduction rules

In July 2010, Ashton Bio Ltd acquired a biotech business from Dean plc for £12 million. Dean plc had carried on its biotech business since 2000.

The allocation of the consideration given for the various assets acquired (in the sale and purchase agreement) and the subsequent fair values adopted in Ashton Bio Ltd's accounts under FRS 7 are summarised as follows:

	Sale and purchase agreement	FRS 7 fair values in company's accounts
	£	£
Freehold property	3,400,000	2,800,000
Computers and scientific equipment	2,300,000	2,500,000
Goodwill	3,600,000	4,000,000
Trade debtors (net of trade creditors)	2,700,000	2,700,000
Net consideration	£12,000,000	£12,000,000

Dean plc's disposal of goodwill will be reported as a capital gain (with the proceeds being £3,600,000 – ie the amount reflected in the sale and purchase agreement).

The acquisition of goodwill by Ashton Bio Ltd is eligible for relief under the corporate intangibles regime [*CTA 2009, Part 8*]. Thus, the future tax deductions (on the amortisation in the accounts) will be based on the £4,000,000 FRS 7 fair value, which is assumed to be a 'reasonable' amount.

Although normally based on the expenditure allocated in the sale and purchase agreement, HMRC might also contend the capital allowances for the expenditure on computers and scientific equipment should be based on the FRS7 fair value (under the 'just and reasonable' rule in *CA 2001, s 562*).

Negative goodwill

12.49   In the current economic climate we have seen an increasing number of 'distressed' business sales. In many cases, such transactions will give rise to 'negative goodwill' in the hands of the purchaser. This is because, when the acquired assets are 'fair valued' under FRS 7 in the acquiring company's books, the aggregate fair value of the acquired assets *exceeds* the consideration paid for the business. The balancing excess amount is treated as *negative goodwill,* which is akin to a discount on the fair value of the assets acquired.

Under FRS 10, the acquiring company will match the negative goodwill with the fair value of the non-monetary assets (such as trading stock and fixed assets) purchased. The negative goodwill credit is then released to profit and loss account over the period in which these assets are recovered through use (depreciation) or sale – so it would often be on a weighted pro-rata basis to the periods in which stock and plant depreciated.

From a tax viewpoint, any negative goodwill credit is only taxable under the intangibles regime where it relates to a relevant (identifiable) intangible asset within *CTA 2009, Part 8* (which is relatively rare (but see also 12.52).

Profits on sale of 'new' goodwill and IP

12.50   Any profits on the *sale* of (post-31 March 2002) goodwill and IP will be treated as income rather than capital gains [*CTA 2009, ss 735–736*]. However, the tax can be deferred under an 'intangibles' style roll-over relief, provided the proceeds are reinvested into other new regime IP assets, including goodwill, within the normal roll-over 'reinvestment window' starting one year before and ending three years after the gain arises [*CTA 2009, ss 754–763*]. Qualifying reinvestment in goodwill and intangibles by a 75% fellow-group company can also be counted for these purposes (*CTA 2009, ss 777–779*)

In contrast to the capital gains roll-over rules, the 'intangibles' roll-over regime effectively brings back into charge an appropriate part of the 'rolled-over' credit over the life of the new asset. This is because the tax base cost of the new 'replacement' asset(s) is effectively reduced by the gain/profit that has been rolled-over against it, as illustrated in Example 6 below. Thus, where intangibles regime roll-over relief has been claimed there will be a difference between the accounts cost and tax cost of the goodwill/intangible assets.

12.51 Under special transitional rules, *capital gains* on 'old-regime' goodwill can only qualify for the intangibles roll-over relief. Such gains must therefore be rolled-over against acquisitions of goodwill and other intangible fixed assets.

Example 6

Effect of intangibles roll-over relief

On 2 January 2009, Green Ltd purchased the trade and assets of Claret & Blue Ltd. This included the purchase of know-how for £1,000,000, which was to be amortised over ten years.

Green Ltd elected to roll-over a previous gain of £400,000 which arose on the sale of goodwill in August 2008 against the purchase of the above know-how. The goodwill was in respect of its 'London' trading division.

Green Ltd draws up its accounts to 31 December each year.

The tax effects of the roll-over claim for 2010 to 2012 are illustrated below:

		Tax deduction		
		2010	2011	2012
	£	£	£	£
No roll-over claim				
Know-how – cost	1,000,000	100,000	100,000	100,000
With roll-over claim				
Know-how – cost	1,000,000			
Less: Goodwill gain rolled-over	(400,000)			
Adjusted tax cost	600,000	60,000	60,000	60,000

The effect of the roll-over relief claim is to reduce the annual tax write-off in respect of the know-how by £40,000 (effectively this part of the goodwill 'gain' is being taxed each year).

Trading stock

12.52 *Unconnected seller* – The purchase of trading stock is relieved as a trading expense, as and when the stock is realised. Where the stock is acquired on from an unconnected seller, the purchaser generally brings in the amount paid for the stock. HMRC would only be able to challenge the amount allocated to the purchase of stock if it is so artificial as to fall outside the protection of *CTA 2009, s 165(3)* (*Moore v R J Mackenzie & Sons* (1972) 48 TC 196).

In 'distress' sale cases (see 12.42A), the amount paid for stock (as allocated in the split of the consideration under the sale & purchase agreement) is often below the fair value amount that is debited to trading stock in the accounts in accordance with FRS 7. For example, as part of a trade and asset purchase, the amount allocated to stock in the sale and purchase agreement might be (say) £520,000 but the FRS 7 fair value booked in the acquirer's accounts is £750,000. The accounting profit would therefore be determined after deducting the £750,000 when the trading stock is realised whereas the amount agreed with the seller for the purchase of the stock was £520,000 under the sale and purchase agreement. The better view, based on the decided cases such as *Stanton v Drayton Commercial Investment Co Ltd* [1982] STC 585, is that the profit should be based on the amount allocated to trading stock in the sale and purchase agreement and therefore an adjustment is required. (Note – while *CTA 2009, s 46* says GAAP applies when determining accounts profits, this is subject to any adjustment required by *law* (which can be interpreted to include common law established by judges).)

12.52A *Connected seller* – If the stock is purchased from a *connected* party (who is subject to UK-UK transfer pricing), the seller will have had to bring it in at its market value for tax purposes (*CTA 2009, s 162(2)*). In such cases, the purchaser can claim a compensating adjustment to 'uplift' the value of the stock to market value under *TIOPA 2010, ss 147–217 (ICTA 1988, Sch 28AA)*. The purchaser therefore gets additional tax relief in the period of acquisition (even where the stock remains unsold at the end of its accounting period).

If the transfer pricing rules do *not* apply, *CTA 2009, s 166(1a)* applies to treat the stock as being sold at its market value. However, this is subject to the special *CTA 2009 s 167* election which enables both parties to substitute the *higher* of the actual sale price or book value. In practice, the election normally enables the purchaser to acquire the stock at its actual transfer value for tax purposes. The election must be made within two years of the end of the seller's CTAP.

SHARE PURCHASE – DETAILED ANALYSIS

Purchaser's business and tax risks

12.53 A purchase of shares does not produce any cessation of trade problems for the company – the business continues in its existing form albeit under new ownership.

The purchaser, however, will inherit the target's previous history and any previous tax problems. Normally, the risk can be minimised by obtaining appropriate warranties and indemnities from the seller (see 12.62–12.75).

Use of hive-downs

CTA 2010, Part 22, Chapter 1 succession of trade rules for capital allowances and tax losses

12.54 If there is considerable risk, for example, a large contingent liability, the purchaser may require the seller to hive the trade down first into a newly formed subsidiary. The subsidiary would then be acquired as a clean company with the unwanted liabilities remaining behind in the transferor company.

It is recommended that the trade and assets are transferred under a hive-down agreement. This will detail the relevant assets (and liabilities) that are being transferred to the subsidiary and the allocation of the agreed purchase consideration between the assets. The purchase consideration is often left outstanding on inter-company loan account, with the purchaser subsequently injecting sufficient cash into the company (typically on loan) for it to be repaid.

A hive-down of the trade and assets to the 'new' subsidiary should fall within the mandatory 'succession of trade' conditions of *CTA 2010, ss 938–948 (ICTA 1988, s 343)*. This broadly requires the trade to have been carried on under the same (at least) 75% common ownership both before *and* after the hive-down – the post-hive down ownership test would be met by ownership of the subsidiary's shares.

The succession of trade rules enables:

- The transferor company's capital allowance assets (such as plant and machinery) to be transferred to the subsidiary at their tax written down value (thus, avoiding any balancing adjustment for the transferor), irrespective of the actual transfer price placed on the assets in the hive-down agreement.

- Any unused tax losses relating to the trade to be transferred to the subsidiary for offset against its future trading profits. The tax losses can only be transferred in full provided the *transferor* company broadly remains solvent immediately after the hive-down. The losses transferred are restricted, if the transferor's balance sheet is left with net 'relevant liabilities' (ie an excess of relevant liabilities over relevant assets (including the purchase consideration for the trade and assets hived-down)). In such cases, the amount of trading tax losses transferred is reduced by the 'net relevant liabilities'.

To ensure the beneficial provisions of *CTA 2010, ss 938–948 (ICTA 1988, s 343)* apply, care must be taken that no binding contract or similar arrangement to sell the subsidiary company is made *before* the hive-down takes place. This would cause the holding company (ie the transferor) to lose beneficial ownership of the subsidiary *before* the hive-down, thus breaking the post-hive-down '75% ownership condition' (see *Wood Preservation Ltd v Prior* [1969] 45 TC 112*)*.

A further requirement is that the subsidiary must be carrying on the trade for a suitable period *after* the hive-down, whilst it is still under (at least) the 75% ownership of the 'transferor' holding company. The Special Commissioners decision in *Barkers of Malton v HMRC* [2008] UKSPC 689 demonstrates the risks of failing to satisfy this test (see 13.62).

Trading stock

12.54A   Care should be taken with the tax treatment of trading stock sold to the new subsidiary. This will be a connected party transfer within *CTA 2009, s 166*. Although it is normal to place a 'sale value' on the stock in the hive-down agreement, the deemed 'market value' rule applies for tax purposes (see 12.52A). However, the transferor and subsidiary can make a joint election (within two years of the hive-down date) for (broadly) the stock to be treated as sold at its actual sale value. Unfortunately, this option is not open to large companies subject to transfer pricing rules (see 4.11). in such cases, the stock must go across at 'market value' under these rules which take priority [*CTA 2009, s 161*].

Intra-group transfers for CGT and intangibles and degrouping charges

12.54B   Although protection is initially available for CGT chargeable assets, which are transferred across for tax purposes on a no gain/no loss basis under *TCGA 1992, s 171*, the gain would effectively be 'clawed-back' as a *TCGA 1992, s 179* degrouping charge. Similarly, any post-March 2002 goodwill (or other intangibles) included in the hive-down are also transferred on a tax-neutral basis (under *CTA 2009, ss 775 and 776*), which is again subject to an intangibles degrouping charge under *CTA 2009, s 780*.

In both cases, when the subsidiary is sold, any goodwill transferred on the hive-down is treated as having been sold and immediately reacquired at its market value (*at the time of the original intra-group transfer*). However, in the case of a distressed business, the value of the goodwill is likely to be negligible or very small, so no material tax charge should arise.

It is possible that a degrouping charge may arise on any land or property (based on its value at hive-down). An SDLT cost may also be incurred (see 12.54C below).

Even where a degrouping charge arises, these can be mitigated under:

- *TCGA 1992, s 179A*, by reallocating the *s 179* gain to another group company, which may enable it to be sheltered, for example, by capital losses or a unused non-trade loan relationship deficit brought forward in another group company

- *TCGA 1992, s 179B*, by rolling the degrouping gain over against qualifying reinvestment by other group members in chargeable 'business' assets, such as a new factory or fixed plant and machinery. It is not possible to roll-over the gain against goodwill (since that is dealt with under the intangibles regime).

There are similar rules for reallocating and rolling over degrouping charges on (post-March 2002) goodwill and other intangible assets [*CTA 2009, ss 791 and 792*].

SDLT issues

12.54C Any land and property (or shares) transferred as part of the 'hive-down' may not be available for SDLT (or stamp duty) intra-group transfer relief. Broadly speaking, intra-group relief is denied where there are arrangements for the subsidiary to leave the group, as will invariably the case when the hive down takes place. [*FA 2003, Sch 7, para 2; FA 1927, s 27(3)(c)*]. However, even if the 'arrangements' rule can be side-stepped, any SDLT/stamp duty relief would be clawed-back under *FA 2003, Sch 7, para 4* (or *FA 2002, s 111*) when the subsidiary leaves the group (within three years).

Base cost of shares

12.55 The consideration given for the shares, together with other allowable costs of acquisition, will establish the purchaser's base cost for the future capital gains purposes. However, in future, this will often be a relatively unimportant issue as the ultimate gain on the sale of the shares is likely to be completely exempt under the Substantial Shareholdings Exemption.

If the purchaser issues shares or loan notes, the market value of the shares/loan notes will be treated as the consideration given. This will normally be the value attributed to the transaction where the parties are at arm's length (*Stanton v Drayton Commercial Investment Co Ltd* [1982] STC 585).

As a general rule, all legal and professional fees relating to the acquisition of shares will be disallowed as a capital cost (although relief is given for the related costs of borrowing to finance the acquisition – see 12.37). Stamp duty at ½% is payable on the acquisition of shares. All such costs incurred in connection with the acquisition of shares will form part of the capital gains' base cost of the shares.

Future use of trading losses

12.56   A share purchase may be particularly desirable if the target company has accumulated (tax-adjusted) trading losses which may be available for offset against future taxable profits of the target company. This can also be achieved where an asset-purchase is restructured as a hive-down, followed by the purchase of a new 'clean' company. However, the carry over of tax losses into the new subsidiary can be restricted where the transferor company is technically insolvent after the hive-down (see 12.54).

However, there are important anti-avoidance rules which prevent the carry-forward of trading losses where there is a change in the ownership of a company, such as where a company is sold. These rules prevent the trading losses being carried forward where there is a major change in the nature or conduct of the company's trade/business within a three year period either side of the sale, etc [*CTA 2010, ss 673* and *674 (ICTA 1988, s 768)*]. The acquisition of unused tax losses can be a very valuable asset, in many cases sheltering a number of years of future trading profits from corporation tax. Thus, where the acquired company has substantial trading losses it is essential that the operation of the target company is carefully managed to avoid any forfeiture of the losses. The purchaser should seek an appropriate warranty from the seller that there has been no prior major change in the trade in the three years before the acquisition (and also any losses denied as a result of a 'pre-acquisition' act are covered by the tax indemnity) (see 12.70). Given the vulnerability of unused tax losses under *CTA 2010, ss 673* and *674 (ICTA 1988, s 768)*, it is best to ensure that any payment for them as part of the purchase consideration is deferred until such time as the offset of the losses is effectively 'agreed' by HMRC – for example, when the enquiry period for the CT600 return has passed.

After the acquisition, the purchaser has control and must ensure that any (sometimes inevitable) changes to the acquired company's trading activities of the company are carefully kept outside the range of the *ss 673* and *674* 'radar'. SP 10/91 indicates that, when determining whether a 'major change' had occurred, HMRC would look at the extent of changes in a company's business premises, the identity of its suppliers, management or staff, its methods of manufacture or the pricing or purchase policies. A major change in one factor would be decisive. (It has been held that 'major' means something more than 'significant' but less than 'fundamental' (*Purchase (Insp of Taxes) v Tesco Stores Ltd* [1984] STC 304).)

Helpfully, HMRC would not generally seek to argue major changes had occurred simply to increase operating efficiency and to keep pace with developing technology. Further, it would not seek to apply *ss 673* and *674* where a company seeks to rationalise its product range or changes its products provide this does not constitute a 'major change' in the type of products etc dealt with.

Some of the examples that SP 10/91 puts forward as triggering a 'major change in the nature of the trade' include a saloon car dealership switching to tractors and a public house converting to a discotheque! In *Willis v Peeters Picture Frames Ltd* [1983] STC 453, a group which manufactured and sold picture frame mouldings acquired a loss-making company operating in the same field. Although the acquired loss-company continued manufacturing it changed its selling methods from mainly wholesale on the open market to wholesale among group distribution companies. However, the Court of Appeal held these changes were not sufficient to constitute a major change in the company's trade.

Many tax advisers consider that the rules in *CTA 2010, ss 673* and *674 (ICTA 1988, s 768)* can be broken by transferring the trade from the acquired company (with the tax losses) to another member of the acquirer's group.

Capital losses and pre-entry loss rules

12.57   Any unused capital losses in the target company would effectively be 'ring-fenced' under the pre-entry loss rules in *TCGA 1992, Sch 7A* (and are also subject to further anti-avoidance rules introduced by *FA 2006 [TCGA 1992, s 184A].* These rules were introduced to prevent 'capital loss' buying, ie where the acquiring company sheltered its own capital gains by routing the disposal of assets through the purchased 'capital loss' company. Such pre-entry capital losses can only be deducted against gains arising on assets owned by the target company at the date of acquisition or on gains realised on assets subsequently acquired from third parties.

Similar restrictions apply to the pre-acquisition element of a capital loss realised on a subsequent disposal of any assets held by the target company on acquisition.

Tax relief for borrowing costs

12.58   Interest incurred on borrowing to finance the acquisition of shares will normally be treated as a non-trading debit under the loan relationship rules. As a non-trading debit, it will initially be offset against any loan relationship income (such as interest receivable) of the same accounting period. A claim can be made to offset any net non-trading *debit* for the period in a number of ways, for example, against the company's current taxable profits, or by surrender to fellow group companies under the group relief rules (see 4.4(*d*) for further details).

Other costs incurred in relation to debt financing (such as loan arrangement fees) would generally be accounted for in accordance with FRS 4, thus, such costs will be 'debited' to the balance sheet as a deduction from the relevant debt/loan and then written off in the accounts over the life of the debt (see

12.37). Under the loan relationship regime, relief will therefore only be given for the amount written-off against the company's profit and loss account for the relevant period.

VAT recovery on acquisition costs

12.59 An acquisition of shares is treated as a business activity for VAT purposes. The recovery of input tax on costs associated with the acquisition is based on the purchaser's VAT status and is regarded as a business overhead.

If the purchasing company is fully taxable for VAT purposes, then all the input tax is recoverable. If the company is partially exempt, the input tax would be restricted.

If shares are issued as part of the consideration, the input VAT on the related professional costs may now be recoverable (following the ECJ ruling in *Kretztechnic AG* (see 11.16A)). Before the *Kretztechnic AG* ruling, the issue of shares was treated as an exempt supply leading to a potential restriction in the relevant input tax. However, in *Southampton Leisure Holdings plc v Customs and Excise Comrs* [2002] V & DR 235; [2002] STI 1523, the Tribunal held, on the particular facts, that the majority of the professional costs related to the purchase of shares (in a share for share exchange deal), and therefore the related VAT was residual input tax.

It is not uncommon for the purchasing company to 'pick-up' costs incurred by the bank or venture capital provider. In such cases, the related VAT would not be recoverable since the services have not been provided to the purchaser.

Integration with existing activities

12.60 Once acquired, the purchaser will need to decide how the company will be integrated with its existing operations. The acquired company may be left as a separate subsidiary company, in which case the various reliefs available to groups will apply (see 4.39). This would also create an additional 'associated company' for corporation tax purposes and may, therefore, lead to an increase in tax liability for the 'group' members (see 3.20).

Alternatively, the trade of the target company may be hived-up and integrated with the purchaser's existing trade or kept separate on a divisionalised basis (see 3.30).

Payment of interest and dividends within the group

12.61 Payments of annual interest, patent royalties and so on are now made on a 'gross' basis (ie without deducting tax) where the recipient is a

UK resident company (or UK branch) (although this rule is vulnerable to a challenge as being discriminatory under EU law). Thus, such payments can be made between group companies without any tax being withheld.

Tax relief for the interest will generally be deductible under the loan relationship (LR) provisions based on the amount charged in the accounts. It will be relieved as a trading deduction where the loan was borrowed to finance trading activity or capital investment within the trade. In other cases, the interest is deducted as a non-trading debit for LR purposes.

The recipient group company is normally taxed on the interest receivable (as a non-trade credit, assuming the loan was not made in the course of a lending trade).

Dividends can flow up the group without any material tax consequences. The dividend income is generally 'tax-free' in the hands of the recipient group company.

The tax treatment of dividends was changed by the *FA 2009* which (from July 2009) introduced a new corporate tax exemption for dividends and other distributions in *CTA 2009, s 931A(1)*, which covers the majority of dividends (irrespective of whether they are paid from a UK or overseas resident company). There are certain limited exceptions to this rule which mainly apply to dividends from companies resident in overseas tax-havens!

PROTECTING THE PURCHASER

'Caveat emptor' principle and due diligence

12.62   The legal principle of *caveat emptor* (let the buyer beware) is predominant in the context of a 'share' purchase of a company. The company retains responsibility for all liabilities and actions and therefore the purchasing company will inherit all these problems, subject to any express agreement with the seller in the contract.

The purchaser should therefore ensure that its inherited liabilities are limited to those which were known at the time of acquisition and hence were fully reflected in the price paid for the company. In many cases, a full due diligence investigation will be conducted by their accountants. This should give the purchaser the necessary assurances about the operation of the business, the value of its assets, its tax position and particularly the full extent of its liabilities. If a limited due diligence investigation is considered appropriate, this should concentrate on those areas where the purchaser perceives the greatest potential problems. For example, in the case of a manufacturing company, this may be the condition, age and realisable value of the stock, potential future costs of cleaning 'contaminated' industrial land and so on.

Warranties and indemnities

12.63   In some cases, a full investigation by the purchaser's accountants may not be justifiable or practicable, particularly if there is time pressure to complete the deal. The prospective purchaser must therefore seek protection under the sale agreement, by means of obtaining adequate warranties and indemnities. The purchaser will normally do the first draft of the agreement to place the full burden on the seller. The seller will aim to make the purchaser aware of all relevant facts through the disclosure letter.

12.64   A *warranty* is a contractual representation made by the seller(s) (or warrantor(s)). It is a factual statement about any relevant aspect of the target company, such as the conduct of its trade, its assets, its financial position, tax matters and so on. If the warranty is subsequently shown to be incorrect, the seller(s) will be in breach of contract and would therefore be liable to pay contractual damages to the purchaser.

On the other hand, an indemnity refers to an agreement to compensate (normally) the purchaser for the loss caused by a particular event. In practice, indemnities are often confined to giving protection against historic tax liabilities (in the tax indemnity or tax covenant). However, they can in some cases be extended to commercial matters. Indemnities tend to provide a simpler and more effective mechanism of recovery than warranties.

Principal functions of warranties and tax indemnity

12.65   The basic aim of warranties and the tax deed of indemnity (or tax covenant) should be to allocate the financial risks between the purchaser and seller. However, warranties and, to a lesser extent, indemnities play a vital role in forcing the seller to think and make disclosure about relevant items and events. Such draft 'information seeking' warranties can then be used to draw up specific warranties applicable to the precise circumstances.

The warranties will appear in the sale agreement between the sellers and purchasers (often accounting for about two-thirds of the agreement!). A separate tax deed of indemnity (or tax covenant) should be given in favour of the purchaser, thus enabling any indemnity payments to be treated as adjusting the purchase consideration (see 12.74 – ESC D33).

WARRANTIES

The use of warranties to obtain information

12.66   One of the main purposes of drafting comprehensive warranties is to flush out all relevant information about the target company (or group) through disclosure by the seller in a disclosure letter. The purchaser normally prepares the first draft of the sale and purchase agreement with comprehensive tax and commercial warranties. The seller must carefully consider the full implications of each warranty statement and provide all relevant facts and qualifications on the warranties through the disclosure letter (any warranty considered irrelevant may be deleted from the sale agreement).

The disclosure letter

12.67   The disclosure letter will qualify or modify various warranties. The production of a clear and comprehensive disclosure letter is a vital exercise for the seller. The purchaser will not be able to make any claim for an incorrect or breached warranty where the seller has restricted it by providing full details in the disclosure letter.

The enquiries and analysis involved in the preparation of the disclosure letter will concentrate the seller's mind on any potential problems within the target company or group. The danger for the seller is the possibility of innocent non-disclosure. It is reasonable for a seller to require that any information obtained in the purchaser's due diligence investigation is deemed to be disclosed.

Purchasers can suffer a deluge of very late disclosures involving mountains of paperwork, which could put them at a disadvantage. They should therefore insist that draft disclosures and supporting documentation are produced at an early stage to allow time to consider their significance.

Obviously, any disclosure of a significant liability or problem of which the purchaser was previously unaware is likely to lead to the terms of the transaction being renegotiated. The purchaser may request a reduction in price or require a specific indemnity or retention (see below).

Damages for breach of warranties

12.68   The warranties also enable the purchaser to claim damages for misrepresentation or breach of contract to compensate for the loss. If a warranty is breached or proved to be untrue, the purchaser can be compensated for the 'loss' suffered in consequence. The measure of damages is the amount that could reasonably have been expected to arise at the date of the contract (ie to place the purchaser in the same position had the warranty been true). This would normally be less than the full amount of the loss or additional liability since the purchaser would have discounted the price for remoteness, etc.

A court may decide the amount of damages after hearing expert evidence which can be a costly and time-consuming exercise. In such cases, the purchaser is often encouraged to compromise even where there is a strong case. However, the use of a 'liquidated damages' clause in the sale agreement provides a practical formula for calculating the 'loss' and avoids court involvement.

Normal limitations on warranty claims

12.69   It is normal for warranty claims to be limited to a specific figure. This will often be the total sale consideration but the amount will depend on the circumstances of each case, such as where a substantial part of the consideration is to be satisfied by shares in the acquiring company.

De minimis limits will be established to avoid trivial claims. The seller will also impose other appropriate restrictions, such as limiting the period within which a warranty claim can be made, for example, one to two years from the date of completion for commercial warranties and six to seven years for tax warranties.

THE TAX INDEMNITY/TAX COVENANT

Role of the tax indemnity

12.70   The current legal practice is to have a tax deed of indemnity or tax covenant supplementing the warranties. A tax indemnity is given by the covenanter(s) (the seller(s) – generally jointly and severally if more than one) to the purchaser under which they will indemnify the *full* amount of any *relevant tax liability* which subsequently arises in the target company or group.

The tax indemnity is more direct and provides the purchaser with a convenient method of recovering money from the seller. In contrast with warranties, purchasers do not have to prove their loss and have no inherent duty to mitigate their losses under common law. Sellers are therefore exposed to a potentially greater liability under the indemnity.

Tax liabilities covered by indemnity

12.71   The tax indemnity would cover all relevant taxes, such as corporation tax, PAYE, NICs, VAT, stamp duty, overseas taxes and so on. Broadly, the tax indemnity would cover any tax on profits or events arising on or before the last statutory accounts date and tax on disposals, dividends, etc since then up to the date of completion. The indemnity invariably 'picks-up' taxable events arising on completion, enabling it to cover such tax liabilities as the capital gains degrouping charge (under *TCGA 1992, s 179*) and the stamp duty land tax degrouping charge (under *FA 2003, Sch 7, para 9*).

The primary objective of the tax indemnity is to protect the purchaser against any unprovided *pre-acquisition* tax liabilities. The cancellation or forfeiture of any tax relief or losses will often be counted as a 'deemed' tax liability for the purposes of a claim under the indemnity. Where the withdrawal of any tax relief, etc gives rise to a tax liability, the claim would be the amount of that liability. The loss of *future* tax reliefs (against a pre-sale tax charge or event) is a more difficult area. The extent to which it should be indemnified is a matter for negotiation, particularly if the price paid by the purchaser does not reflect such reliefs.

Generally, the purchaser will also seek to be indemnified against all costs, interest on overdue tax and tax penalties which may arise on the tax liabilities covered by the indemnity.

Typical 'seller protection' provisions

12.72   The seller(s) should seek to limit their liability under the tax indemnity by inserting appropriate 'exclusions' or 'carve-outs' from it. From the seller's perspective it would be reasonable to *exclude* from the indemnity any tax liability which:

- is covered by a provision or reserve in the last accounts or (where relevant) completion accounts – the purchaser should only be covered for unanticipated tax liabilities;

- arises from transactions carried out in the ordinary course of the business after the date of the last accounts;

- would not have arisen but for a voluntary act or omission by the purchaser or the target company post-completion;

- arises as a result of a retrospective increase in tax rates or a change in legislation;

- can be recovered or reclaimed by the purchaser or the target company from someone else (including insurance); and

- has been 'compensated' by an over-provision' that has been determined on other tax items in the last accounts or completion accounts.

If the target company pays its tax in instalments, certain adjustments may be required to the tax indemnity. For example, the seller may not wish to pay the additional tax and interest which arises due to an event taking place after completion, even if it arises in the normal course of trade.

The seller's liability under the tax indemnity is also usually covered by the same restrictions on claims as used for warranties (see above). However, purchasers generally resist accepting disclosures, etc against the indemnity.

Control of target's tax affairs

12.73   The 'purchaser' would normally deal with the target company's tax affairs after completion. However, the seller(s) will seek to have some control over the tax affairs for the pre-sale periods to limit their liability under the warranties and/or tax indemnity.

The seller(s) therefore normally require appropriate terms in the tax indemnity giving them the ability to handle and negotiate with HMRC in relation to any pre-sale tax liability. This should ensure that any such liabilities are vigorously contested and defended. On the other hand, the purchaser will not want the previous owner to have the ability to dictate the target's tax affairs after the take-over. Thus, a reasonable position to take in the tax indemnity would require the seller to be properly advised in the event of any potential tax appeal case, for example, by using tax counsel of appropriate experience.

CGT TREATMENT OF INDEMNITY PAYMENTS

12.74   Until the introduction of ESC D33 (on 19 December 1988, revised in November 2001) the target company itself was often a party to the deed. It is now best practice to avoid the target company being treated as a party to the deed.

Under ESC D33, any payment made under a tax deed by the seller to the *purchaser* is regarded as an adjustment of the purchase price under *TCGA 1992, s 49*. Consequently, the payment does not give rise to a taxable receipt in the purchaser's hands. The concession also requires that the indemnity payment is made under the terms of the contract for sale. The indemnity should preferably be in the form of a schedule attached to the sale agreement. However, HMRC are prepared to accept the use of a separate tax deed (as still used by some lawyers) provided the covenant is part of the overall terms of the sale agreement (see *Capital Gains Manual*, CG13042).

On the other hand, where an indemnity payment is made to the target company, this would normally be treated as a capital sum derived from an asset, namely the right to bring a legal action, following the doctrine laid down in *Zim Properties Ltd v Procter* [1985] STC 90.

Despite the protection given in ESC D33, purchasers usually require all payments under the tax deed to be 'grossed up' so as to give them the same post-tax receipt (in the unlikely event of the payments being taxed). As the tax indemnity aims *fully* to reimburse the purchaser for the unprovided tax liability, this is a difficult argument to resist. In practice, the seller generally agrees to the 'gross-up' clause provided the purchaser does everything possible to mitigate the risk that the 'gross up' will apply. Thus, the seller will insist that the tax indemnity is only given to the purchaser and that all payments are made to the purchaser, so as to fall within the terms of ESC D33.

RETENTION AGAINST WARRANTY/INDEMNITY CLAIMS

12.75   It is not inconceivable that the seller may become insolvent, be liquidated or simply vanish. Thus, if the seller or warrantor is not available or has no financial resources, any claim for compensation under the warranties will be fruitless. It may therefore be appropriate for the purchaser to negotiate for a certain portion of the sale consideration to be 'retained' (as security for the payment of funds due on a breach of warranty). The retention monies will usually be held by one or both parties' solicitors in an 'escrow' account.

FRANCHISING

Advantages of franchising

12.76   There is no reason why a family or owner-managed company should not expand its business by offering a franchise. This involves franchisees running 'clones' of the franchisor's established business, under licence and in return for an initial fee and ongoing fees. A brand name is used and this is the main difference as compared with networking.

The advantage of using franchising as a means of expansion is that this expansion is achieved through someone else's funds. Furthermore, the franchisees do the managing and are likely to show more commitment than an employee who is used to expand the company's own business.

Faster growth should be achieved by the franchisor, with a higher return on capital, and indeed there are few disadvantages as far as a franchisor is concerned in the early years.

At a later stage, successful franchisees could create problems as they might well need convincing that they would not be better off withdrawing from the franchise agreement and starting up on their own in the same line of business. Furthermore, at some point, the franchisor might well feel that more money could be made by opening 'company-owned' sites under an established name and reputation.

Choosing a franchisee

12.77   Great care is needed when choosing a franchisee. There is a potential risk factor as far as confidentiality is concerned and, all things considered, choosing a franchisee is more important than choosing an employee. Franchisees will have their own ideas about how to run the business but nevertheless they are using the company's name so control is needed.

Tax treatment

12.78   When looking at tax considerations for a franchisor, it is important to determine the legal nature of all receipts under the terms of the franchise agreement. The fee the company receives for granting the franchise is capital expenditure by the franchisee, but is likely to be a revenue receipt of the franchisor. The franchisee would be able to obtain tax relief on the 'amortised' capital payment – see 12.46–12.48.

The franchisee will obtain a trading deduction on their management service fees in the normal way.

PLANNING CHECKLIST – EXPANDING THE COMPANY'S ACTIVITIES AND STRUCTURING BUSINESS ACQUISITIONS

Company

- A trade and asset purchase usually provides increased tax relief on acquired assets, particularly as goodwill and other intellectual property assets can now be amortised on a tax-deductible basis – the purchase price should ideally be weighted in favour of tax allowable assets.

- On a trade and asset deal, it is particularly important to agree the individual amounts paid for each type of asset (especially fixtures included within a building).

- Where the purchase of a business is subject to fair value adjustments under FRS 7, this will influence the amount of goodwill and intangibles that can be written off for tax purposes under GAAP. Remember that the amounts allocated in the sale contract would not affect the tax relief for goodwill intangibles where an FRS7 fair value adjustment is subsequently made for those assets in the accounts.

- The purchase of commercial property frequently entails a considerable stamp duty land tax cost.

- Share purchases are often seen as beneficial as they provide 'succession of trade ' in the target company and retention of any unused tax losses. Careful management of the target company's trade is generally required to avoid the 'major change in the nature of trade' anti-avoidance rules in *CTA 2010, ss 673* and *674*, which can deny the availability of the tax losses against the target's post-acquisition profits.

- Integration of the 'target' trade with the acquirers should be structured to avoid prejudicing any unrelieved tax losses.

Working shareholders

- The shareholders of the acquiring company need to limit their commercial exposure on a corporate acquisition by obtaining carefully structured warranties and tax indemnities. Full disclosure

---

can generally be obtained on all material items affecting the target company. These commercial risks can also be reduced by a 'risk-based' due diligence exercise before the deal proceeds.

- Obtain non-competition covenants from sellers.

Other employees

- Rationalisation of workforce can lead to high redundancy and compensation costs (employment contracts are automatically transferred on asset purchases).

Non-working shareholders

- Require controlling/working shareholders to protect their position. May need a shareholder's agreement to protect their interests.

Chapter 13

Reorganising Shares and Trading Activities (Including Share Buy-backs)

INTRODUCTION

13.1 Developments in the life of a family or owner-managed company may make it necessary for the company to change its structure by including new shareholders or to increase or decrease the number of shares in existence. An existing shareholder may wish to give shares to the next generation as part of succession or capital tax planning. The directors or shareholders may decide to provide a valuable 'key' manager or new manager with shares as an incentive and to foster a sense of proprietorship.

13.2 The mechanics of providing shares, whether through a new issue or by a transfer from an existing shareholder, may involve a CGT liability. However, in most cases, business asset hold-over gift relief should be available to 'defer' the tax liability (provided the fairly stringent 'trading' company requirement can be satisfied) (see 13.15 and 13.27).

If shares are made available to an existing or new employee or director for less than full consideration, the employee will suffer an 'employment income' tax charge on the 'profit' element, unless it can be demonstrated that the shares do not derive from their employment or prospective employment. This can normally be demonstrated if the employee is a member of the (close) family (see 13.31).

Where employees or directors receive shares carrying 'restricted rights', these may also be vulnerable to certain income tax charges. However, it is possible to minimise their impact by making a joint election with the employing company within 14 days of the share issue/award (see Chapter 8 (especially 8.14 and 8.32) and 13.33 and 13.34).

13.3 The ability of a company to buy in its own shares means that the shareholders can look to the company itself as a willing buyer for their shares. This provides a useful 'exit' route in a number of situations. For example, where the controlling shareholder wishes to realise the value of his shares and, at the same time, make way for the next line of management. A buy-in can also be used to buy out a dissident or uninterested shareholder. The company law and tax aspects of an own share purchase are covered at 13.41–13.57.

13.4   Some family businesses eventually develop to the stage where various activities or trades are run by different members of the family. If the shareholders each have different aspirations and requirements regarding the running of their divisions this may lead to a need to separate out the various trades. The trades could be transferred to new companies so that they can be run independently by the relevant shareholders. This can be achieved by a reconstruction or demerger the mechanics and tax implications are discussed at 13.57A–13.95 below.

GIFT OF SHARES – MARRIED COUPLES (AND CIVIL PARTNERSHIPS)

Inter-spousal transfers

13.5   Where shares are transferred between a husband and wife (or between civil partners – see 13.8) who are living together during the year of assessment in which the disposal takes place, no CGT liability arises. A husband and wife (or civil partners) are not considered to be living together if they are separated by court order or by deed of separation or they are separated in circumstances that are likely to prove to be permanent [*ITA 2007, s 1011*].

The inter-spousal transfer is treated as a disposal for such a consideration as will result in no gain or loss to the transferor spouse [*TCGA 1992, s 58*]. For a post-5 April 2008 transfer, this means that the transferee spouse will acquire the transferred shares at the transferor's original CGT base cost. Since indexation ceased to be available for all disposals after 5 April 2008, this cannot be carried across as part of the transferee's deemed base cost (see 13.6). The transferred shares would be treated as an acquisition of shares by the transferee spouse (and will form part of their share pool). On a subsequent disposal, the transferee spouse is treated as acquiring the shares at the same time as the transferor.

Pre-6 April 2008 inter-spousal transfers

13.6   When taper relief was introduced on 6 April 1998, the previous indexation regime for individuals and trusts was retained but was frozen at April 1998. This meant that for intra-spousal transfers, the transferee spouse automatically inherited the transferor spouse's indexed base cost (ie the transferor's base cost plus the accrued indexation thereon). Under the old taper relief regime, the transferred asset (such as shares) would be deemed to have been held from the 'transferor-spouse's' acquisition date (Tax Bulletin, Issue 52, April 2001).

Some individuals decided to 'bank' their CGT indexation before it disappeared on 6 April 2008. One popular way of doing this was for married couples to transfer the relevant asset between themselves, which HMRC confirmed was acceptable tax planning ahead of the new CGT regime. This would have triggered a deemed 'no gain/no loss' consideration for the transfer, enabling the recipient spouse to carry forward the accrued indexation as part of the asset's base cost. The *Finance Act 2008* confirms that, where the transferor held the asset at March 1982, the recipient spouse's future base cost (on a pre-6 April 2008 intra-spouse transfer) would equate to March 1982 value of the asset plus the related indexation (being 104.7% of that value) [*TCGA 1992 s 35A*].

A special 'indexation' restriction applies where the transferee spouse subsequently realises a capital loss on an asset acquired on a (post-29 November 1993) inter-spousal transfer. In such cases, any indexation built into the transferee's capital loss (including that 'inherited' from the transferor spouse), will be deducted to give a no gain/no loss result [*TCGA 1992, s 56(2)*]. No such restriction arises where the transferee's disposal gives rise to a capital gain.

Shares held in joint names

13.7   It is helpful to note that where close company shares are held in joint names by a married couple, the joint holding is treated as held individually by the husband and wife. For CGT purposes, the joint shareholding would be taxed in accordance with its beneficial ownership. This would normally be a 50:50 split, although it is possible for the couple's beneficial interests in the shares to be held in different proportions as tenants in common.

Transfers between civil partners

13.8   Since 5 December 2005, single-sex couples registered as civil partners have been able to enjoy the same tax breaks as married couples. Consequently, the transfer of shares between members of a civil partnership is treated as a no gain/no loss disposal. The CGT mechanics of the transfer are dealt with in the same way as explained in 13.5 and 13.6.

GIFTS OF SHARES – FAMILY MEMBERS, EMPLOYEES, ETC

Basic CGT treatment

13.9   A straightforward gift or 'undervalue' transfer of shares from an existing shareholder to another family member or close friend, etc will invariably represent a disposal at market value for CGT purposes. This will apply whether the parties to the transaction are connected or not [*TCGA 1992, ss 17, 18*]. In such cases, it is often possible for the parties to hold-over the gain under *TCGA 1992, s 165* (see 13.14).

A deemed 'market value' disposal also arises where shares are gifted or transferred at an undervalue to a director or an employee in recognition of their services provided to the company [*TCGA 1992, s 17(1)*] (see 13.31). This rule applies where the shares are simply transferred without an option (and for share options exercised before 10 April 2003).

However, where existing shares are acquired on the exercise of an option, then *TCGA 1992, s 144ZA* disapplies the 'market value' rule to the acquisition of the shares. In practical terms, this means that the transferor (for example, the owner-manager or an employee benefit trust) has disposal proceeds equal to the amount actually received on the exercise of the share option (plus any amount received for the grant of the option). Similarly, the transferee employee's/director's base cost is the actual consideration paid for the shares, increased by any amount charged as 'employment income' under *TCGA 1992, ss 119A* and *120* (see 13.32). (Note that the 'actual consideration' rule imposed on option shares is not affected by *TCGA 1992, ss 144ZB–144ZD* introduced by the *F(No2)A 2005*. These provisions are broadly aimed at most 'non-commercial options', but specifically exclude share options [*TCGA 1992, s 144ZB(2)(a)*].

13.10 Where the director/employee acquires 'new' shares through a share issue, *TCGA 1992, ss 17(2)* and *149A* collectively treat the shares as being acquired for the actual amount paid (once again, subject to any increase under *TCGA 1992, ss 119A* and *120* for any 'employment income' charges).

If the disposal is to a connected person and a loss results, that loss is only available for set-off against future gains from a disposal to the same person [*TCGA 1992, s 18(3)*].

Special CGT valuation rules for consecutive disposals to connected persons

13.11 Where the gift/transfer is part of a series of disposals made to the same person or a connected person (within *TCGA 1992, s 286*) over a six-year period, the CGT anti-avoidance rules in *TCGA 1992, s 19* may apply. These provisions seek to circumvent the potential 'valuation' advantage that may be gained by fragmenting the disposal of a significant shareholding into a number of smaller minority holdings. Because of the sizeable valuation discounts often applied to small minority shareholdings, the aggregate CGT valuations would often be much less than the valuation that would have applied to a disposal of an equivalent larger holding. (For a detailed discussion on relevant share valuation principles, see 14.49 to 14.62.)

Although the application of *TCGA 1992, s 19* can often be overlooked in practice, HMRC can seek to apply it where the above conditions are satisfied. In such cases, HMRC will aggregate the various disposals to the same person/ connected persons and calculate the value of the aggregated shareholding (as if it were a single holding). The CGT valuation of each previous relevant disposal will then be increased as a pro-rata proportion of the 'aggregate' valuation (ie replacing the original 'discounted' disposal value).

Clearly, HMRC are unlikely to invoke these rules where the previous transfers were subject to CGT hold-over claims.

Example 1

Application of s19 TCGA 1992 to series of prior transfers to connected persons

Mr Busby formed Babes Ltd in May 1968 holding all the 1,000 shares in the company.

In recent years, Mr Busby has transferred some of his shareholding to his children as follows:

Date	Transferee	Relationship to Mr Busby	No of shares
May 2008	Georgie	Son	300 shares
August 2007	Nobby	Daughter	250 shares

In June 2011, Mr Busby transferred 200 shares out his remaining holding in Babes Ltd to Bobby (his youngest son).

The current share valuations of holdings in Busby Ltd are as follows:

Holding	Value per share
75%	£250
50%	£200
20%	£40

Mr Busby's CGT consideration on the shareholding gifted to Bobby (who is connected with him) would be based on its market value. However, this is part of a series of transactions with connected persons within the previous six years under *TCGA 1992, s 19*. Thus, the value of the shares used for this purpose would be that applicable to a 75% holding. (75% represents 750 shares made up of 300 shares to Georgie, 250 shares to Nobby and the current gift of 200 shares to Bobby.) The deemed market value consideration for the transfer to Bobby would therefore be £50,000 (ie 200 shares × £250 per share). Because *TCGA 1992, s 19* applies, the 200 shares are not valued in isolation (ie at £40 per share).

The gift to Bobby also triggers a revision of the prior share valuations under *TCGA 1992 s 19*. Thus, the 300 shares to Georgie and 250 shares to Nobby should be based on a 75% value in May 2008 and August 2007 respectively.

Inheritance tax treatment – potentially exempt transfers

13.12 The gift or transfer at undervalue of shares by an existing shareholder to an individual qualifies as a potentially exempt transfer for IHT purposes [*IHTA 1984, s 3A*]. Where the recipient of the shares is an (unrelated) employee/director, it is usually possible to demonstrate that the relevant shares are being transferred to them for valid commercial reasons (without any intention 'to confer a gratuitous benefit'). Thus, where the recipient is considered vital to the company's future, there should be a strong argument for exempting the transaction under *IHTA 1984, s 18* (see 17.6), although of course the employee would still suffer an employment income charge if the shares were gifted or acquired at under-value.

In cases where the transaction is treated as a PET (for example, where there is a familial connection), any IHT liability should generally be avoided. The transferor will either survive the 'seven year' period or, if the PET crystallises, business property relief (BPR) should be available (provided the recipient still retains the shares and the company continues to be a qualifying company) (see 17.10 and 17.22).

A gift or transfer at undervalue to an interest in possession or accumulation and maintenance trust was potentially exempt before the *Finance Act 2006* IHT trust regime. Since 23 March 2006, such trusts are regarded as 'relevant property' trusts and hence transfers to them are chargeable. However, since most owner-managed trading companies will qualify for IHT BPR, it should still be possible to transfer their shares into a trust without any immediate IHT charge. Shares that do not attract BPR will, however, incur a 20% IHT 'entry' charge on any value transferred in excess of the available IHT nil rate band (see Chapter 17).

Legal formalities

13.13 The transfer of shares by way of gift would be valid when the transferor had executed a share (stock) transfer form and the transfer and certificate is delivered to the transferee (*Re Rose* [1952] Ch 499). However, in

Pennington v Crampton [2004] EWCA Civ 819, a gift was also held to be valid where the transferor had clearly intended to make an immediate gift of the shares, but (due to her death) the share transfer form/share certificate had not been delivered. In such cases, the use of the share transfer form was sufficient to transfer the beneficial interest in the shares.

BUSINESS ASSET HOLD-OVER RELIEF

Basic conditions for hold-over relief

13.14   A non-arm's length transfer of unquoted shares in a trading company will normally be eligible for business asset hold-over gift relief under *TCGA 1992, s 165*. However, hold-over relief is not available in the following two cases:

- where shares are transferred to a company ([*TCGA 1992, s 165(3)*]; and

- where an individual transfers shares to a 'settlor-interested trust' (ie broadly where the individual transferring the shares or their spouse/civil partner is an actual or discretionary beneficiary of the relevant trust). Since 6 April 2006, the 'settlor-interest' trust definition includes the settlor's dependent children [*TCGA 1992, s 169B*].

13.15   To qualify, the shares in question must be unquoted shares in a trading company or holding company of a trading group. In broad terms, s 165 hold-over relief will therefore only be available provided at least 80% of the company's/group's activities are trading. This is because the legislation only permits up to 20% of the total activities to be of a 'non-trading' nature without prejudicing the relief [*TCGA 1992, s 165(8)*]. When determining whether a 'trading group' exists, any intra-group transactions are effectively ignored (For full details of the 'trading company and 'holding company of a trading group' definitions see 15.36–15.39.)

Hold-over relief can also be claimed for quoted shares in a personal trading company/holding company of a trading group [*TCGA 1992, s 165(2)*]. A personal company is one in which the individual transferor exercises at least 5% of the voting rights [*TCGA 1992, Sch 6, para 1(2)*].

Where shares in a 'non-trading' or investment company are gifted, hold-over relief cannot be claimed and therefore the transferor will suffer a CGT liability based on their market value [*TCGA 1992, s 165(2)(b)*].

Procedure for making hold-over election

13.16   The transferor and transferee must jointly elect for hold-over relief, except where the transfer is made to trustees, in which case only the transferor makes the claim [*TCGA 1992, s 165(1)(b)*]. Under self-assessment, the hold-over election must be made on the prescribed form on help sheet IR 295 which should preferably be submitted with the transferor's tax return. However, the claim can be made at any time up to the fifth anniversary of 31 January following the tax year in which the gift or transfer is made.

Mechanics of hold-over relief

13.17 Where the shares are gifted such that they are transferred for no consideration or are transferred at an undervalue, hold-over relief for gifts of business assets will be available [*TCGA 1992, s 165*]. This will have the effect of eliminating the transferor's chargeable gain – see Example 2 below.

The gain will in turn be deducted from the transferee's deemed market value acquisition cost [*TCGA 1992, s 17*]. The held-over gain will therefore become chargeable if and when the transferee subsequently makes a disposal of the gifted shares. In effect, the transferee will inherit the transferor's original base cost. (See 2010/11 and earlier editions of the book for treatment of pre-6 April 2008 gifts.)

Example 2

Business asset hold-over relief on pure gift

On 1 June 2011, Brian Clough gave his son, Nigel, 30% of the shares in the family company, Cloughies Breakfast Foods Ltd, which he incorporated in August 1987.

The value of the shares transferred on 1 June 2011 has been agreed by HMRC – Shares & Asset Valuation at £60,000. Brian wishes to eliminate his gain by claiming s165 hold-over relief. .

	£
Consideration = MV	60,000
Less Part disposal cost (say)	(2,500)
Capital gain	57,500
Less TCGA 1992, s 165 relief	(57,500)
Chargeable gain	£ –

Nigel's CGT base cost will be £2,500 (ie MV of £60,000 less gain held over of £57,500). This is effectively the 'cost' of the shares transferred.

Dispensation from formal share valuation

13.18   It will be appreciated that the computational effect of a full hold-over claim can be computed without reference to the market value of the shares (see 13.17)). Consequently, HMRC will in most cases permit a hold-over claim to be made without the need to prepare a computation of the chargeable gain or to agree a formal valuation of the gifted shares. This helpful concessionary treatment (provided by SP 8/92), must be claimed in writing on form IR 295 (see 13.16), by both the transferor and the transferee. Both parties must confirm they are satisfied that the (estimated) value of the shares exceeds the original base cost and also provide full relevant details of the shares transferred, including the date of their acquisition and the allowable expenditure.

HMRC will generally require proper valuations to be prepared where the hold-over relief is restricted in some way (see 13.20).

Shares sold at an under-value

13.19 If the shares are sold at an under-value for an amount exceeding the transferor's base cost or deemed March 1982 base value, the gain eligible for hold-over relief will be restricted by the amount of the excess consideration (the concessionary treatment under SP 8/92 is not available) [*TCGA 1992, s 165(7)*].

The excess of the actual consideration received by the transferor shareholder over their base cost, therefore, becomes chargeable. Under the pre-23 June 2010 regime, the s 165 hold-over relief is considered by HMRC to take priority over ER, so that any remaining chargeable gain becomes eligible for ER gains reduction.

From 23 June 2010, the ER 10% CGT rate is simply applied to the residual gain.

Since the hold-over restriction only applies where shares are sold for more than their base cost, it is therefore possible for shares to be sold at their original base cost or rebased March 1982 value without incurring a capital gain, provided a hold-over election is made.

Example 3

Hold-over relief where actual consideration received

In Example 2, if Nigel had provided some actual consideration, of say £20,000, Brian's held-over gain would be restricted by £17,500 which is the amount by which the actual cash received £20,000 exceeds the base cost of £2,500:

	£	£
Indexed gain (as Example 2 above)		57,500
Less TCGA 1992, s 165 relief:		
Gain	57,500	
Less Amount restricted	(17,500)	(40,000)
Chargeable gain		17,500
Less: Annual exemption		(10,600)
Taxable gain		6,900
Assuming Brian makes an ER claim –		
ER – CGT @ 10%		£690

Nigel's CGT base cost would then be £20,000 (ie £60,000 less held-over gain of £40,000), which represents the amount he paid.

Restriction in hold-over gain for company's non-business assets

13.20 There are a number of potential traps which may restrict the amount of hold-over relief and therefore create unexpected tax liabilities. It should perhaps be reiterated first that, given the stringent 'trading company' definition, the shares would only be eligible for s 165 hold-over relief in the first place provided the relevant company's non-trading assets/activities did not breach the 20% test (see 13.15).

The most important restriction is where a personal company (ie broadly one in which the individual transferor has at least 5% of the voting rights) holds chargeable non-trading/investment assets when the shares are transferred. It is therefore necessary to examine the company's balance sheet before any transfer of shares is made. In such cases, the held-over gain is limited by reference to the following formula:

$$\text{Relevant gain} \times \frac{\text{Market value of chargeable business assets}}{\text{Market value of chargeable assets}}$$

The above restriction means that a chargeable gain will arise (reduced by any claimed ER) to the extent that the value of the company's chargeable assets (for CGT purposes) reflects non-trading or investment assets. Note that any surplus cash funds held by the company do not affect this calculation since they are a chargeable asset for CGT purposes [*TCGA 1992, Sch 7, para 7*].

13.21 The current market value of the company's goodwill does not appear on its balance sheet, but must still be counted as a chargeable (business) asset. Goodwill represents the difference between the value of a business as a whole and the aggregate of the fair value of its identifiable net assets (see FRS10 and 12.47). The goodwill value can, therefore, normally be derived by valuing the company/business first – this will usually be based on a 'multiple of earnings'– and then deducting the value of the company's tangible net assets. Clearly, where a restriction is required due to the presence of chargeable 'investment' assets, the inclusion of goodwill will have a beneficial effect on the chargeable business asset/chargeable asset calculation. However, note that post-31 March 2002 goodwill is dealt with under the intangibles regime (and hence is no longer a chargeable asset for these purposes).

A similar 'consolidated' chargeable assets calculation is required for shares in a holding company of a trading group. Broadly, this would bring in the chargeable business assets and chargeable assets for each group member (ignoring the investments in its 51% subsidiaries). If a subsidiary is not wholly owned, only the relevant percentage of the chargeable assets/chargeable business assets is included.

Entrepreneurs' relief (ER) – interaction with hold-over relief on pre-22 June 2010 gifts etc

13.22 Since 6 April 2008, qualifying disposals of shares (which would include a gift or undervalue transfer of shares) are eligible for ER.

In HMRC's view, relief under *TCGA 1992, s165* is deducted in priority to the pre-22 June 2010 ER gains reduction (*TCGA 1992, s 169N(a)* applies ER to the 'relevant gains'). *Section 165N(5)(a)* treats these 'relevant gains' as those computed in accordance with the relevant rules in *TCGA 1992* in fixing the amount of the chargeable gain. HMRC take the view that this wording is sufficient for roll-over/hold-over reliefs, such as those in *TCGA 1992, s 165* to take priority over any claim made for ER. Thus, where s 165 hold-over relief is taken, this would 'trump' any ER claim. (It is worth stating that the legislation is not entirely clear on this point and it is possible to arrive at an alternative interpretation of the order of offset!)

Where the s 165 hold-over claim is restricted – for example, because the transferee gives actual consideration exceeding the transferor's base cost (see 13.19) – then any residual chargeable gain may be subject to an ER claim – see Example 4.

However, ER ceased to be given as a 4/9ths reduction in the gain from 23 June 2010, so this interaction point is no longer relevant for gifts made from that date. From 23 June 2010, ER is simply given by taxing any residual gain (after deducting any hold-over relief etc) at a 10% rate.

Example 4

Business asset hold-over relief – Interaction with ER

Edwards Ltd is a property developer and qualifies a trading company for s 165 relief purposes. Duncan has owned the entire share capital of Edwards Ltd since February 1958.

In May 2010, as part of Duncan's succession planning, he sells 30% of his shareholding to his son, Matt, for £300,000. This was at an 'under-value, since the valuation of the gifted shares in May 2010 was agreed with HMRC Shares & Asset Valuation at £800,000.

The 'part-disposal' March 1982 valuation (based on a controlling holding) was also agreed with HM Shares & Asset Valuation at £150,000.

Duncan's CGT computation (reflecting his claim for ER) is as follows:

		£
Market value consideration		800,000
Less Relevant March 1982 value		(150,000)
Capital gain		650,000
Less: *s 165* hold-over relief		
Gain	650,000	
Less: Amount restricted under *s 165(7)*		
(£300,000 less £150,000)	(150,000)	(500,000)
Chargeable gain		150,000
Less: ER – £150,000 × 4/9		(66,667)
Chargeable gain after ER		83,333
Less: Annual exemption		(10,100)
Taxable gain		£ 73,233
CGT @ 18% (pre-23 June 2010 gain)		£ 13,182

Matt's CGT base cost (with *s 165* relief) is £300,000 (£800,000 less £500,000) which equates to the amount he paid for the shares.

ISSUE OF NEW SHARES

Value shifting charge

13.23　A controlling shareholder might be tempted to procure an issue of shares to a prospective shareholder in order to avoid a direct disposal out of their holding. However, where new shares are issued for less than full consideration, a deemed CGT charge may arise under the value shifting legislation in *TCGA 1992, s 29*. Broadly speaking, a deemed disposal will arise where:

(a)　a controlling shareholder exercises control; and

(b)　as a result, value passes out of shares owned (or rights over the company exercisable) by them (and/or someone connected with them under *TCGA 1992, s 286*); and

(c)　this value passes into other shares in or rights over the company [*TCGA 1992, s 29(2)*].

13.24　A deemed CGT charge can also occur where a group of shareholders exercise control in concert to cause value to be shifted out of their shares into other shares (see *W Floor v Davis* [1979] STC 379). These rules apply even if there is no intention of tax avoidance.

13.25　Controlling shareholders may therefore be subject to a value-shifting charge where they procure an issue of shares to others which causes their own shares to depreciate in value. In such cases, the shares acquired by the allottees are likely to be worth more than the cash subscription price they paid for them. A deemed CGT charge would also catch any value flowing out of the controlling shareholder's holding where there is a variation in the rights attaching to their shareholding or other shares. It is now fairly well settled that *TCGA 1992, s 29* cannot apply where a person transfers value from one class of shares into another class of shares owned by them. This means that individuals cannot make a disposal or a shift of value to themselves – see article in British Tax Review 1977 by Andrew Park (at page 113) and Taxation (14 January 1999, page 347). Where rights are altered or restrictions are removed over employment-related shares and their value is increased this may be taxed under the wide-ranging provisions of *ITEPA 2003*.

13.26　Clearly, where shares are issued to an employee/director at an undervalue, they will be subject to an employment income tax charge in accordance with the general principles established in *Weight v Salmon* 19 TC 174 (see 8.10 and 13.29–13.35). It should not be forgotten that the company would normally be able to claim a corporate tax deduction for the amount taxed as employment income (see 8.86).

In some cases, shares in a private company might be classified as 'restricted securities' under the current 'employment-related' securities regime. In this context, it is debateable whether shares are 'restricted' simply because they are subject to the standard pre-emption provisions normally found in a private company's Articles. However, given the potential tax risks in this area, advisers take the view that it is best to assume they are 'restricted' and ensure that protective s 431 elections are made in all cases (see below).

Where shares issued to employees/directors are subject to more substantive restrictions, they will almost certainly be 'restricted securities'. The employee/director will still suffer an employment income tax charge to the extent they pay less than market value for their shares. However, 'restricted securities' are particularly vulnerable to further income tax charges on subsequent future events (such as on a sale of the shareholding or lifting of restrictions, etc). It is usually possible to completely or partially eliminate these potential income tax charges provided a joint election is made between the employee and the company. It is generally recommended that such elections are always made, since there is always a risk that HMRC may (retrospectively) contend that the relevant shares were restricted (see 8.13–8.37 for further commentary).

Availability of hold-over election

13.27   Although *TCGA 1992, s 29* creates a deemed disposal by the controlling shareholder without deeming a corresponding acquisition by the 'beneficiary', in practice, HMRC will accept a business asset hold-over relief claim under *TCGA 1992, s 165*. A hold-over election should therefore prevent a value-shifting charge crystallising in most cases.

Example 5

Effect of value shift on issue of shares

Alan owned the entire 1,000 £1 issued ordinary shares in Mullery Ltd. His shareholding was worth some £150,000 in March 1982 and is currently worth £600,000 – the company has authorised share capital of 5,000 £1 ordinary shares.

In August 2011, Alan arranged for the company to issue 800 £1 shares at par to a valued manager, Alf. This depreciated the value of Alan's holding to £250,000.

Since Alan has control of the company and had exercised it so that value shifted out of his shares into those held by Alf, Alan would be treated as making a part disposal of his shares at market value under *TCGA 1992, s 29(1)*.

It is assumed that £100,000 would be paid for the shares if the parties had been dealing at arm's length (given the relatively minor restrictions in the company's Articles, this would also equate to the unrestricted value).

Alan makes a TCGA 1992, s 165 hold-over election on the gain arising:

2011/12 – August 2011 disposal	£
Deemed consideration (MV):	100,000
Less March 1982 base value (part disposal)	
$£150,000 \times \dfrac{£100,000}{£100,000 + £20,000}$	(42,857)
Chargeable gain	57,143
Less TCGA 1992, s 165 relief	(57,143)
Taxable gain	–

Inheritance tax issues

13.28   The IHT legislation contains similar provisions for value passing out of someone's estate as a result of the alteration of share rights in an unquoted close company. The IHT provisions examine the diminution in value to the donor's estate. Thus, where the alteration reduces the value of the donor's shareholding, this will be treated as a transfer of value by the relevant shareholders, subject to the exemption for non-gratuitous transfers and business property relief, etc (see 17.6 and 17.18) [*IHTA 1984, ss 10, 103*]. It is important to note that the IHT value shifting transfer is a chargeable transfer for IHT purposes and does not qualify as a potentially exempt transfer [*IHTA 1984, s 98(3)*].

EMPLOYMENT INCOME TAX CHARGES FOR DIRECTORS AND EMPLOYEES

Income tax charge under *Weight v Salmon* principle

13.29   An income tax charge will arise on the director or employee where they have received shares either as a gift or at a reduced price. This employment income charge arises on the amount of the undervalue element (based on the money's worth of the shares) in accordance with the general principles established in *Weight v Salmon* [1935] 19 TC 174, since this amount represents earnings within *ITEPA 2003, s 62*.

In practice, it is normally very difficult to refute an employment income tax charge where shares are being transferred to a director or employee. The best 'litmus' test is to ask the question 'would the shares have been made available on these terms to the individual if they were not a director or employee of the company?' If the answer is 'no', the shares will be treated as a benefit derived from the employment. Usually, the only realistic chance of avoiding the 'benefit' of shares being taxed as earnings is where shares are gifted to a member of the family, as this would characterise the transfer of the shares as a personal gift in the context of a family relationship (see also 13.31).

Companies should ensure that they 'pick-up' and claim the appropriate tax relief on all employee share awards, options and other taxable events (see 8.86).

Restricted or unrestricted shares

13.30 The basic *ITEPA 2003, s 62* earnings tax charge applies irrespective of whether the shares are 'unrestricted' or 'restricted'. However, if the shares are 'restricted', the 'value' of the shares would reflect the relevant restrictions based on the 'money's worth' principle (see 14.41). This basic tax charge may need to be increased further by making an election to be taxed on the market value of the shares ignoring the relevant restrictions (see 13.34).

However, where a director/employee is provided with shares that do not impose any further special restrictions, they are unlikely to be 'restricted securities' under *ITEPA 2003, Pt 7, Ch 2*. However, there are some uncertainties about whether the standard restrictions imposed by the Articles of Association of most private companies are sufficient to make the shares 'restricted' (see also 13.26). These provisions would normally include the usual pre-emption provisions on share transfers, the board veto on share transfers, compulsory fair valuation, etc. Such rights are treated as an inherent characteristic of the shares (rather than employee specific provisions). HMRC currently consider that these conditions are likely to be sufficient to make the share 'restricted'. However, it is debatable whether they create the necessary reduction in the value of the shares to bring them within the 'restricted security' definition in *ITEPA 2003, s 423(1)(b)*.

Nevertheless, given the potential tax risks in this area, advisers invariably treat most private company shares as restricted in practice, ensuring that protective s 431 elections are made (see 8.17, 8.32 and 13.34).

Example 6

Calculation of employment income charge under Weight v Salmon principle

Alf subscribed for 800 £1 ordinary shares in Mullery Ltd at par when those shares were worth £100,000 (see Example 5). As Alf is an employee of the company, he is subject to an employment income tax charge on the 'undervalue' element, as follows:

	£
Market value of shares	100,000
Less Actual price paid 800 × £1	(800)
Taxable amount	99,200

Although it is considered that the standard Table A restrictions should not cause the shares issued to Alf to be treated as 'restricted securities' (since the unrestricted and restricted value would virtually be the same), a protective *ITEPA 2003, s 431* election should still be made (see 13.34).

Alf's CGT base cost should be £100,000 (see 13.39).

Employment-related and restricted securities regimes

Scope of restricted securities legislation

13.31   Shares issued or transferred to directors or employees may be subject to a charge under the *ITEPA 2003, Pt 7 (ss 417–484)*. See Chapter 8 for a further analysis of the 'employment-related securities' regime. The most important aspect of this legislation is probably the 'restricted securities' regime.

In the context of a family or owner-managed company, shares issued to a director or employee are caught where:

(a)   they constitute 'restricted securities'; and

(b)   the shares are acquired by reason of the individual's current, former or prospective directorship or employment; and

(c)   the shares are acquired for less than their market value ignoring the relevant personal/employee specific restrictions.

Restricted securities are widely defined for these purposes, but include shares and interests in shares carrying restrictions. In essence, the market value of such shares must be less as a result of the relevant restrictions (see 8.15 and 13.32).

Shares, etc are not caught by the 'employment-related securities' regime where the right or opportunity is made in the normal course of the domestic, family or personal relationships of that person (*ITEPA 2003, s 421B(1)–(3)*). Owner-managers should therefore normally be able to 'safely' gift or transfer shares to their spouse or children without the shares attracting any 'restricted securities' tax charge in the recipient's hands. HMRC have confirmed that where shares are provided in a company controlled by an individual or their family, and the shares or option has been procured by them, this will meet the *ITEPA 2003, s 421B* 'exemption'. In such cases, it is necessary to show that there is a demonstrable relationship between the individual/family and the employee and no element of 'remuneration' reward is intended.

Where a private company is not 'family-controlled' with perhaps a wide spread of shareholders, there might be cases where shares are (for example) treated as being awarded to a wife by reason of her husband's employment rather than because of a close family relationship.

The 'restricted securities' regime potentially applies to shares issued under the Enterprise Management Incentives (EMI) scheme, but it does not generally apply to shares issued under the other types of Approved Share Scheme (but see 8.20 for the extended scope of the regime from 18 June 2004).

Relevant restrictions

13.32 Director/employee shareholdings are frequently subject to 'restrictions'. These would include requirements for the director/employee to sell their shares back to the company at their nominal or par value on leaving or certain events giving rise to a forfeiture of the shares.

HMRC now seem to take the view that shares issued subject to the standard Table A conditions might be sufficient to make them 'restricted', although the point is debateable (see 13.30). The legislation is really aimed at employee specific restrictions. However, in practice, advisers still recommend that *ITEPA 2003, s 431* elections are generally made to avoid any risk (see 8.32 and 13.34).

Employment income tax charges

13.33 Broadly speaking, employment income tax charges only arise under the restricted securities legislation where the director/employee acquires the shares for less than their full market value (calculated on the basis that any additional personal/employee restrictions are ignored). This is the known as the 'unrestricted value' of the shares and provided the employee pays this amount, any future growth in the shares normally falls within the CGT regime.

It is always advisable to make a protective *ITEPA 2003, s 431* election to avoid any risk of incurring an income tax liability on a subsequent chargeable event, for example, when the shares are sold. This ensures that if there is any subsequent valuation challenge from HMRC, any income tax risk is isolated to the difference between the unrestricted value and the amount paid when the shares were acquired (see 13.34 below).

Election to be taxed on initial unrestricted value of shares

13.34 There is a valuable 'escape' provision in ITEPA 2003, s 431(1), (2) which enables the director or employee to enter into an election with the 'employer' effectively to be taxed 'up-front' by reference to the (unrestricted) market value of the shares. An election is likely to be beneficial in the vast majority of cases and particularly where the shares are expected to increase in value. For 'standard' ordinary shares, there is unlikely to be any material difference between their unrestricted and restricted value. (Importantly, *s 431(1)* elections are now deemed to have been made for 'full value' EMI options, thus obviating the need to make actual elections where the EMI shares are acquired at their 'date of grant' market value (see 8.61–8.62).) Pro-forma elections can be obtained from the HMRC website under www.hmrc.gov.uk/shareschemes/s431-1-pe.rtf.

The election must be made within 14 days of the receipt of the shares (which fits in with the PAYE timetable).

Reporting obligations

13.35   HMRC require details of (unapproved scheme) shares or securities acquired by directors or employees to be reported on the (wide ranging) IR Form 42. The reporting requirements apply to share awards, the grant and exercise of share options, as well as any chargeable events under *ITEPA 2003, Pt 7* (see 8.14–8.37). Details must be given even where no income tax arises, for example, where an employee acquires shares at their market value.

PAYE and NIC on share benefits – readily convertible assets (RCAs)

13.36   Employment-related income tax liabilities must be accounted for under PAYE if the shares are 'readily convertible assets' within *ITEPA 2003, s 702*. Class 1 NICs are also levied on the 'taxable' benefit of shares and unapproved share option exercises where the relevant shares are 'readily convertible assets'.

Any employment income liability arising on shares in a (private) family or owner-managed company would often be dealt with in the recipient's self-assessment return. However, private company shares may fall within the PAYE (and NIC) regime if 'arrangements exist' now or at some future date which enable the recipient director/employee to realise an amount similar to the cost of the shares. This would include situations where there is an impending sale of the company or where employees are able to sell their shares to an employee trust. A formal or informal understanding that employees will be able to realise the value of their shares in due course may also be caught.

Since 16 April 2003, the RCAs definition was extended to include shares or share option exercises that would not be eligible for a corporation tax deduction under *CTA 2009, Part 12* (previously referred to as the *FA 2003, Sch 23* regime (see 8.86)). Notably, this would include shares in a subsidiary of an unlisted company (*CTA 2009, s 1008(1), condition 2(b)*).

Where shares are RCAs, the company is liable to account for PAYE and NIC on the 19th of the tax month following that in which the shares, etc were received. For example, the PAYE and NIC on shares (that constitute RCAs) acquired by an employee on (say) 10 September 2011 would be due on 19 October 2011.

If the PAYE tax is not recovered from the employee/director within 90 days after the shares have been provided, a further income tax charge will arise on the director or employee under *ITEPA 2003, s 222*.

The director/employee would generally make a cash reimbursement of the tax. The company could also recover the PAYE from any other cash payment made to the director/employee in the remainder of the tax month after conversion. This recovery charge can also be avoided if the company makes a beneficial interest-free loan (properly documented at that time) to the employee/director to enable them to reimburse the PAYE tax.

Where the shares are subject to PAYE, the employing company will need to estimate their value. This valuation can be submitted to the Shares Valuation (PAYE Valuations) at Fitzroy House, Castle Meadow Road, Nottingham NG2 1BD, for their confirmation that it is reasonable for PAYE purposes. Full details of the transaction must be given, specifying that the value is being checked for PAYE purposes.

Shares which are not RCAs

13.37   Where the shares do not constitute RCAs, any taxable benefit arising on the shares must be returned as a benefit on the employee's personal tax return at a proper valuation, which may have to be agreed with HMRC – Shares and Asset Valuation. The employing company will have returned the relevant share award/option details on the Form 42 (which provides HMRC with a useful cross-check!).

It should be noted that HMRC – Shares and Asset Valuation also enable shares to be valued for employment income tax purposes using the fast-track Post Transaction Valuation Check procedure enabling the value to be agreed (hopefully) before the filing deadline for the recipient employee's tax return (see 14.46).

Use of Enterprise Management Incentives schemes and approved Company Share Option Plans

13.38   The potential tax charges under the 'restricted securities' legislation can be avoided by granting 'full value' share options under the Enterprise Management Incentives (EMI) scheme (see 8.48). However, following the

Finance Act 2008 restrictions, which prevent EMI options being granted by companies with more than 250 employees, this may not always be possible.

For post-18 June 2004 EMI options, the legislation automatically deems an *ITEPA 2003* election as having been made when the shares are acquired (provided the options are not 'discounted' – ie they are being acquired for at least their market value at the date of grant). For earlier EMI options, it was usually possible to elect for the EMI option shares (assuming the option is granted at market value at the 'grant' date) to be effectively taken outside the restricted securities regime (see 8.48).

Similarly, shares acquired on the exercise of an approved Company Share Option Plan (CSOP) do not generally create any employment tax charge. In such cases. the employee/director is required to pay the market value of the shares (based on when the option is granted) when they exercise their CSOP option.

CGT treatment for transferor/transferee employee

Direct acquisition of shares

13.39   Where shares have been gifted (or sold at an undervalue) by an existing shareholder to a director/employee, it is likely that they will be required to enter into a hold-over election under *TCGA 1992, s 165*. This means that the recipient's deemed CGT market value base cost will be reduced by the transferor shareholder's 'held-over' gain. However, the recipient director/employee will be subject to an employment income tax charge on the market value of the shares (less any amount paid for them). As the amount treated as employment income is now added to the director's/employee's CGT base cost under *TCGA 1992, s 120(5A)*, this should effectively restore their base cost to market value (thus eliminating any potential 'double tax' charge).

Where an employee/director acquires new shares on subscription, HMRC will normally treat them as having been acquired at market value. Although the shares have been acquired without a corresponding disposal, the view appears to be that full market value has been given by reference to the employee's/ director's duties (so that the potential restriction in *TCGA 1992, s 17(2)* to actual consideration does not apply). This understanding is confirmed in the Capital Gains Manual, para 56356. The 'market value' CGT base cost will therefore generally equate to the amount which is taxed as employment income plus the subscription price.

A 'market value' base cost may also be obtained if the share issue is subject to a 'value shifting' charge under *TCGA 1992, s 29*, subject to the impact of any *TCGA 1992, s 165* hold-over election – see 13.24–13.27.

The resultant CGT base cost is broadly the same where a director/employee acquires restricted securities (see 13.31) or convertible securities. *TCGA 1992, s 149AA* prescribes that the transferee's base cost of the restricted securities is made up of the actual consideration given by the employee and the amount which is treated as employment income.

Where an employee benefit trust transfers shares to directors or employees, by concession, HMRC do not seek to base the trust's CGT proceeds on the strict 'market value' rule where the recipient employees are subject to a full income tax charge on the shares. The trust is therefore taxed on the actual consideration given (ESC D35). This beneficial treatment does not apply where the employees are existing '5% shareholders'.

Shares acquired on exercise of options

13.40 Following the surprising decision in *Mansworth v Jelley* [2003] STC 53 (see 8.28), the *FA 2003* effectively reinstated from 10 April 2003 the previously accepted analysis of shares acquired under a share option. This introduced *TCGA 1992, s 144ZA* which prescribes that the recipient director/employee is treated as acquiring their option shares for an amount equal to:

(a)   the actual amount received on the exercise of the share option; and

(b)   any amount paid for the option itself.

TCGA 1992, s 149A prevents the 'market value' rule from applying to the actual grant of the option. Similar rules apply to the acquisition of restricted securities. See 8.28 for a further discussion of base cost issues arising from the *Mansworth v Jelley* case.

On the exercise of an unapproved share option, the 'recipient' director/employee is subject to an income tax charge under *ITEPA 2003, s 476*. Similar tax charges arise on discounted EMI or non-qualifying CSOP options. In those special cases where the relevant shares constitute 'readily convertible assets' (see 8.38 and 13.36), PAYE and NIC liabilities will arise.

Before 16 April 2003, options that were capable of being exercised more than ten years (seven years for options pre-6 April 1998 grants) after the date they were granted were subject to a tax charge at the grant date. This was based on the value of the option less any amount paid for the grant.

The director/employee's CGT base cost would be increased by any amount which has been taxed as employment income under *TCGA 1992, ss 119A, 120* and *149AA*.

Where relevant, the transferee would be treated as disposing of the shares for the combined amounts in (a) and (b) above.

PURCHASE OF OWN SHARES (POS)

Advantages of a share buy-back

13.41 The use of the company as a willing buyer for the purchase of its own shares (POS) can provide a useful and tax-efficient exit route for its shareholders. Such arrangements have played an invaluable role in owner-managed business succession planning. A typical scenario would be where the controlling shareholder wishes to retire from the business and hand over the reins of control to the incumbent management team. The team may represent the next generation of the proprietor's family and/or an established group of respected key managers. A direct purchase of the proprietor's shares by the family members/management team is unlikely to be practical since they are unlikely to have sufficient funds. Furthermore, any borrowing they made to finance the share purchase would have to be repaid from additional taxed income extracted from the company (for example, by way of bonuses or dividends), which is likely to be an expensive option.

A more efficient solution would be for the company to buy-back the proprietor's shares. The purchase consideration is satisfied by the company – any additional borrowing required would be within the company and repaid out of its trading cash flows. Since the proprietor's shares are cancelled on the buy-back the remaining shareholders (ie the management team) will then have control of the company.

Broadly speaking, under a POS, cash leaves the company to pay for the purchased shares with the remaining shareholders owning a larger slice of the smaller 'cake'. The immediate cancellation of the shares bought back, increases the relative percentage ownership for the remaining shareholders since they would then have a 'larger' share of the company 'cake'.

A buy-back can also be used on the death of a shareholder where his personal representatives or beneficiaries do not wish to keep the shares. A typical arrangement in most owner-managed companies is for all shareholdings to be subject to put and call options, which become exercisable on the shareholder's death. Appropriate life or 'key-man' insurance is put in place by the company to provide the necessary funds for it to purchase the shares. This has a number of benefits. The existing shareholders avoid losing control to a 'disinterested' widow/widower and it provides a mechanism for the estate to receive cash for the deceased's shareholding – particularly helpful where the estate is illiquid and the main asset is the shares!).

Legal requirements and stamp duty

13.42 It is vital that the POS arrangements follow the legal requirements laid down in *Companies Act 2006, Part 18* (which are effective from 1 October

2008). Broadly the *Companies Act 2006* restates most of the requirements contained in the predecessor *Companies Act 1985* and changes others – see earlier editions of this book for relevant *CA 1985* references.

One of the key requirements for a private company is that the purchased shares are cancelled by the company (see Table 1 below). Furthermore, the company must make an immediate 'payment' to acquire the relevant shares. The term 'payment' is normally taken to mean 'satisfied in cash' and HMRC will treat any POS as invalid if the consideration for the shares is satisfied by the transfer of a 'non-cash' asset. However, this appears to be at odds with the obiter comments made by Justice Andrew Park (now Sir Andrew Park) in *BDG Roof-Bond Ltd v Douglas* (2000) BCC 770 (a 'non-tax' case) in which he stated that the word 'payment' in *CA 1985, s 159(3)* (the predecessor to *CA 2006, s 691*) was not limited to the payment of money but could also include the 'transfer of assets'.

Failure to comply with all the relevant rules would mean that the purported acquisition of the shares by the company is void and therefore legally unenforceable [*CA 2006, s 658(2)*]. This would mean that the relevant shares would not be cancelled and therefore still retained by the seller (Company Taxation Manual, para CTM17505). In such cases, the company's payment to the purported 'seller' shareholder is likely to be treated as a loan, which might produce a liability under *CTA 2010, s 455* [*ICTA 1988, s 419*] (see 2.57).

HMRC have stated that they will only consider a clearance application for a transaction which appears to be a valid POS (Tax Bulletin, Issue 21). Consequently, such arrangements must be carefully planned in advance. In particular, the company will need to have built up a sufficient level of retained profits to satisfy the intended buy-back consideration. Under company law, the purchase price must be met out of distributable profits. Although it is also possible to use the proceeds of a fresh issue of shares, the 'premium' or profit element paid on the buy-back (which will often be a substantial part of the proceeds) must be from the distributable reserves [*CA 2006, s 692(2)*].

It may be possible for the seller-shareholders to retain a 'special share' to enable them to share in any 'uplift' in value if the company is subsequently sold in the medium term. Such rights cannot be structured as deferred consideration for the shares, since the relevant consideration on repurchased shares must be paid in full on completion. Thus, the special shares retained by the seller would contain rights similar to an 'anti-embarrassment' clause on a normal company sale, although care would need to be taken to ensure the widely drawn '30% post-buy-back' connection test is not broken (see 'Table 2' conditions for shareholder – (4)).

The *Finance Act 1986, s 66* provides that ½% stamp duty is payable on the 'purchase' consideration paid by the company (charged on the return (form G169) which must be delivered to the Registrar of Companies within 28 days of the purchase).

Summary of legal conditions

13.43   The main legal requirements for a POS by a private company are summarised in Table 1 below. A Board meeting would be held to report on the proposed POS and call the Extraordinary General Meeting (EGM) to pass the necessary special resolution. It is possible to obtain consent to short notice provided the contract is made available for at least 15 days (as noted in Table 1(4)). The contract for the purchase must be approved in advance, although the company may enter into the contract provided the shareholders authorise the contract terms by a special resolution [*CA 2006, s 693, s 694(2)*]. If the contract is not approved, the company cannot purchase the relevant shares and the contract lapses.

The company must make a return to the Registrar of Companies within 28 days of the POS , stating the number of shares purchased, their nominal value, and the transaction date [*CA 2006, s 707*].

Note that failure to satisfy the relevant legal conditions could make the transaction void and legally unenforceable.

Table 1

Company law requirements for POS by a private company

1.   The relevant shares must be fully paid up.

2.   The consideration for the shares must be paid for on purchase [*CA 2006, s 691(2)*]. Payment must therefore be made on completion of the transaction and it is not possible for payment(s) to be made on a deferred basis (but see 13.55 and 13.56 below for possible alternative structures.)

3.   CA 2006 does not require a company to have express power in its Articles of Association to POS although its articles may restrict or prohibit a POS [*CA 2006, s 690*].

4.   The contract for the ('off-market') share repurchase must be available at the EGM and approved by special resolution of the company's shareholders. (From a practical viewpoint, it is sensible for the shareholders whose shares are being repurchased not to vote as this avoids any possibility of the approval being rendered invalid under *CA 2006, s 695(2)*.)

    For the resolution to be valid, the contract must have been available at the company's registered office for at least 15 days before the General Meeting. The resolution must be filed with the Registrar of Companies within 15 days of the EGM.

5. It would appear that the 'share repurchase' resolution could be passed by a written resolution (but not signed by the shareholder whose shares are being repurchased). In such cases, the contract must be produced to each shareholder at or before the time the resolution is produced for their signature.

6. There is no limit to the number of shares which may be purchased back, although at least one irredeemable share must be held after the purchase.

7. The purchased shares are immediately cancelled on redemption/ repurchase [*CA 2006, s 706(b)*]. (Under the *Companies (Acquisition of Own Shares) (Treasury Shares) Regulations 2003 (SI 2003/1116)* only 'listed' companies can hold repurchased shares in 'treasury' for future sale or transfer to employees through an employee share scheme.)

8. The shares to be purchased can be bought by the company:

    (a) out of its distributable profits; or

    (b) out of the proceeds of a fresh issue of shares; or

    (c) out of capital, provided all distributable profits are used first.

    However, any payment made out of the proceeds of a fresh issue cannot 'frank' any premium (effectively the seller's 'profit' element) made on the shares bought-back.

9. A capital redemption reserve (which is non-distributable) must be set up to the extent that shares are purchased from distributable reserves – the amount transferred being equal to the nominal value of the shares purchased. This facilitates the maintenance of the company's capital base.

10. Where the shares are purchased out of capital this requires, inter alia, a special resolution, a statutory declaration of solvency by the directors (accompanied by a 'concurring' auditor's report) and publicity in the London Gazette and a national newspaper.

11. The share repurchase contract must be retained at the registered office for ten years.

DISTRIBUTION TREATMENT

Calculation of distribution

13.44 Under basic principles, a POS is treated as an income distribution under *CTA 2010, s 1000 [ICTA 1988, s 209(2)(b)]*. The income distribution is the amount by which the sale consideration exceeds the original subscription price of the repurchased shares (including any premium paid) (see *CTA 2010,* *ss 1024–1026* [*ICTA 1988, s 211*] and Company Taxation Manual CT 17510). Thus, if the seller originally acquired the shares 'second-hand', it is necessary to look back to the price paid by the original subscriber.

The POS distribution is grossed up for the 10% tax credit (being one-ninth of the distribution). For post-5 April 2010 buy-backs, this is then taxed at the seller's 'dividend' tax rate(s), depending on the level of their total income (with the distribution treated as the top slice of their income), as follows:

Total taxable income (including buy-back distribution)	Tax rate applied to gross distribution (including tax credit)	Effective tax rate on net distribution
Below basic rate income threshold – £37,400	10% (covered by 10% tax credit)	0%
Between basic rate threshold and £150,000	32.5% (less 10% tax credit) = 22.5%	25%
Above £150,000	42.5% (less 10% tax credit)	36.1%

Sellers generally wish to avoid paying the 'penal' 36.1% or even the 25% effective tax rates and will seek to consider ways of structuring their POS within the CGT regime (see 13.46).

However, there will be cases where the consideration for the POS is sufficiently low with the selling shareholder only being a 'basic-rate' taxpayer. Here it will generally be beneficial for the seller to receive their proceeds as a 'income' distribution since it will effectively be received 'tax-free' (the 10% tax liability being completely offset by the 10% tax credit).

If the shares being purchased were originally acquired in exchange for shares on a prior takeover, the original subscription price (the new consideration given) would be the full market value of the shares 'sold' on the prior share exchange. (It is not the nominal value of the shares issued in exchange.) However, since the shares will have a lower base value (for CGT purposes under the 'new for old' reorganisation rules), this means that part of the POS proceeds will be charged to CGT.

Example 7

Buy-back taxed as distribution

In July 2011, Mr Cole sold his 200 £1 ordinary shares in Ashley Ltd back to the company for £200,000. He originally subscribed for the 200 £1 shares at par on the incorporation of the company in December 2007.

As Ashley has held his shares for less than five years, the transaction cannot benefit from the CGT treatment (see 13.46 below and Table 2 – 'seller shareholder' condition 1).The share 'buy-back' transaction would therefore be taxed as a distribution, taxed at Ashley's marginal dividend tax rate, as follows:

	£
Amount received	200,000
Less Subscription price	(200)
Net distribution	199,800
Tax credit (1/9)	22,200
Gross distribution	222,000
Tax at 42.5%	94,350
Less Tax credit	(22,200)
Tax liability	72,150

The tax liability represents 36.111% of the net distribution (£199,800).

CGT treatment of 'income' distribution buy-back

13.45 Although the POS 'distribution' is subject to income tax, the seller also makes a disposal for CGT purposes. However, *TCGA 1992, s 37(1)* excludes from the taxable consideration any amount which has been charged to income tax (thus avoiding any 'double tax' problem).

The net income distribution is therefore eliminated from the CGT consideration which would then equate to the original amount paid for the shares. In most cases, this will give a neutral CGT result, but if the seller-shareholder has a higher base cost, for example, 31 March 1982 rebasing value or actual 'second-hand' purchase consideration, they would establish an allowable capital loss. This loss would be freely available as it is not restricted by the 'connected party' loss rules in *TCGA 1992, s 18*. This is because the company does not acquire the shares on a buy-back transaction which is a prerequisite for *TCGA 1992, s 18* to apply – for private companies, company law currently requires them to be cancelled [*CA 2006, s 706(b)*].

FA 2003, s 195(2) confirms that shares bought back by the company are not treated as 'acquired' for tax purposes (this rule was introduced following the changes to company law enabling listed companies to hold the purchased shares in treasury (see 13.43, Table 1(5)).

If the seller was the original subscriber, it might be possible to make a claim for share loss relief, which would provide an income tax offset for the capital loss under ITA 2007, s131 (see 16.26–16.29). One potential stumbling block is the requirement for an arm's length disposal in ITA 2007, s 131(3)(a), which may be more difficult to sustain on a 'buy-back' sale by a controlling shareholder. However, if successful, a s 131 claim could be used to reduce the income tax charge on the distribution itself!

CAPITAL GAINS TREATMENT

Requirements for CGT treatment

13.46 CTA 2010, s 1033 [ICTA 1988, s 219] et seq effectively imposes mandatory CGT treatment for the POS if the relevant conditions are satisfied. Strictly, the legislation prevents the 'income' element from being treated as a distribution for tax purposes. This means that the shareholder's entire return is a capital gains receipt. For CGT treatment to apply, the purchasing company must be a trading company, which in this context means wholly or mainly trading (*CTA 2010, s 1048(1)*, [*ICTA 1988, s 229(1)*]. This is less stringent than the 'trading' test used for Entrepreneurs' Relief (ER) or under the pre-6 April 2008 business taper relief). It may therefore be possible for the company to pass the 'trading' hurdle for s 1033 with the shareholder's gain not being eligible for ER (where, for example, the company's non-trading activities exceed HMRC's 20% de minimis rule). The 'trading company' requirement means that any POS by an investment company will always be taxed as an income distribution.

The POS must be for the benefit of the company's or group's trade; this often means that the shareholder must sell his shares, although he may retain a small sentimental stake (of no more than 5%) [*CTA 2010, s 1033(2) (ICTA 1988, s 219(1)(a))* and *SP 2/82*].

Many share buy-backs are sensibly used to arrange for the current owner-manager to retire and make way for new management, which is normally acceptable as satisfying the 'trade benefit' test (see SP 2/82, para 2). However, where the funding of the share repurchase is prejudicial to the trade, this test is unlikely to be satisfied, as demonstrated by the Special Commissioner's decision in *Allum & Allum v Marsh* [2005] (SSCD) 191. In this case, all the company's shares were owned by a married couple except one, which was owned by their son. As they wished to retire from the business and leave their son in control, this was achieved by the company purchasing their entire shareholding. However, the share re-purchase was funded by the sale of the company's trading premises. The sale proceeds also funded the repayment of the directors' loan and voluntary 'ex-gratia' payments of £30,000 each(!). The company's operations were reduced considerably following the sale of the premises and the loss of the directors' financial support and services, all of which were linked to the share buy-back. Consequently, it was held that the shares had not been purchased wholly or mainly for the benefit of the trade, but to facilitate the directors' retirement.

The main conditions for CGT treatment are summarised in Table 2 below:

Table 2

Main conditions for CTA 2010 s 1033 capital treatment

Conditions for company	*Statutory references (all to CTA 2010)*
1. The company must be an unquoted trading company or an unquoted holding company of a trading group (shares quoted on the AIM are treated as unquoted for this purpose).	*s 1033 (1)*
2. The purchase must be made wholly or mainly for the purpose of benefiting the company's trade (or the trade of any of its 75% subsidiaries).	
'For the purpose of benefiting a trade' is sensibly interpreted in IR SP 2/82. HMRC would normally wish to see the seller giving up his entire interest in the company, although the retention of a minimal 'sentimental' stake may be allowed. Furthermore, to ensure the 'trade benefit' test is satisfied, any existing directorship with the company must be severed and a director should not normally continue to act for the company in a consultancy capacity (see SP 2/82).	*s 1033(2)*
3. The POS must not form part of a scheme or arrangement to enable the owner to participate in the profits of the company without receiving a dividend or to avoid tax.	*s 1033 (2)(b)*
4. Conditions 2 and 3 above do not apply to certain cases involving personal representatives of a deceased shareholder. This is where 'all or almost all' (see IR SP 2/82, para 6) the payment (excluding the CGT paid thereon) is applied by them in discharging the IHT liability of the deceased shareholder within two years of death. However, they must also show that the IHT liability could not otherwise have been satisfied without causing undue hardship.	
Also, in such cases, the conditions required to be satisfied by the seller shareholder (see below) are ignored.	*s 1033 (3)*

Conditions for shareholder	*Statutory references (all to CTA 2010)*
1. The seller must be resident and ordinarily resident in the UK in the tax year of purchase.	*s 1034*
2. The shares must have been owned by the seller for at least five years before the date of sale.	
If the seller inherited the shares, the period of ownership of the deceased shareholder/personal representatives can also be counted and the ownership requirement is reduced to three years.	*ss 1035 and 1036*
3. The seller must dispose of all their shares. If they do not, their proportionate shareholding (including associates – see below) must be substantially reduced, although HMRC would not normally accept that this benefits the trade (see condition 2 for company above).	*s 1037*
4. The seller must *not* be 'connected' with the company immediately after the purchase (and there must be no scheme or arrangements in place that would enable them or their associates to have disqualifying interests in the company).	*s 1042*
For these purposes, the seller would be connected with the company if they (together with their associates (see below)) possess or are entitled to acquire more than 30% of:	
(*a*) the issued ordinary share capital; (or)	
(*b*) the loan capital and issued share capital; (or)	
(*c*) the voting power of the company.	*s 1062(2)*
For this purpose, loan capital includes any money borrowed by the company and any debt for capital assets acquired by the company [*CTA 2010, s 1063*].	
The interests of associates must therefore be added to the seller's for the purposes of the 'connection test'. In the context of a POS, the 'associate' test is narrower.It will include an individual's spouse (or civil partner), any trust created by them (or in which they may benefit); and their minor children. However, the definition excludes, for example, adult children, brothers and parents. In this context, shares held by other family members must be beneficially held by them (see *Preston Meats Ltd v Hammond* [2005] (SSCD) 90).	*ss 1063(4), 1059 and 1060*

Optimising the seller's tax position

13.47   In many cases, the seller should effectively be able to choose the tax treatment of the sale of the shares back to the company. Assuming the relevant *CTA 2010, s 1033 [ICTA 1988, s 219]* conditions for CGT treatment can be satisfied (see above), the seller can either opt for distribution (see 13.36) or capital gains treatment. Unfortunately, this cannot be done by simple election.

In the majority of cases, ER should be available on the seller's capital gain, which should enable them to benefit from a CGT rate of 10% on up to the current ER lifetime threshold of £10 million (or, if less, their unrelieved ER gains allowance). (See 15.34 for pre-6 April 2011 ER gains limits.) In such cases, the seller will invariably prefer CGT treatment since their tax charge will be just 10% (and well below the effective 36.1%/25% rates that would operate on most 'income' buy-back distributions). If the seller does *not* qualify for ER, CGT treatment should be beneficial if they would otherwise suffer the 'top' 36.1% rate under the distribution regime. (See earlier editions for CGT taper relief treatment of pre-6 April 2008 buy-backs.)

The detailed qualifying conditions for ER and the relevant computational rules are reviewed in 15.33–15.39. However, even though ER only requires the seller to satisfy the 'personal company' and 'employee/director' requirements throughout the one year before the buy-back disposal, the seller must have held the shares for a minimum of five years (three years, if inherited) to secure the necessary capital gains treatment on a share buy-back (see Table 2 at 13.46 – conditions for shareholder (2)).

13.47A   If the seller has built up their shareholding over a period of years, the 'five year' holding requirement is tested by taking the earlier share acquisitions before the later ones (ie on an FIFO basis), which is preferential to the seller. If the 'five year' test is satisfied (and CGT treatment is available), the normal CGT rules will apply for the purpose of computing allowable base costs etc (see 14.64).

13.47B   A 'capital gains' buy-back has become the standard 'route' given the lower tax charge that will often be available to the 'outgoing' shareholder. An example of the comparatively low tax cost which may be available on a share repurchase from a retiring shareholder in 2011/12 is shown in Example 8 below:

Example 8

CGT structured POS exit in 2011/12

Michael wishes to retire as a full-time working director of Owen Ltd in January 2012 and has ensured that the company has built up sufficient reserves and funds to enable his 75% shareholding to be sold back to the company for £600,000. (Michael started the company in 1972 and his shareholding was worth £75,000 in March 1982)

After the buy-in, the company will be controlled by his two adult sons who have effectively managed the business in recent years and currently hold the remaining 25% of its shares.

Michael qualifies for ER and wishes to claim it against his capital gain on the share buy-back in 2011/12 , which is projected as follows:

	£
Sale proceeds	600,000
Less March 1982 value of shareholding	(75,000)
	525,000
Less Annual exemption	(10,600)
Taxable gain	514,400
ER CGT @ 10%	£51,440

POS from trustee sellers

Where POS proceeds are 'capital' in the hands of the trust

13.48 Under established trust law principles, the sale proceeds received on a POS transaction by trustees will generally be on 'capital' account. However, where the normal 'distribution' treatment applies, the 'distribution' element would fall to be taxed as income in the trustee's hands (despite its capital nature).

Since the amount is capital under trust law, the proceeds of the POS are not normally payable to income beneficiaries (under an interest in possession trust). *ITTOIA 2005, s 383* makes it clear that 'dividends and other distributions are to be treated as income', even though they might be regarded as capital in law.

The basic position is that the trustees would be liable to the 10% dividend 'basic rate' tax (which will be fully extinguished by the 10% tax credit carried with the dividend). However, ITA 2007 s 481(3) also provides that the amount of the 'qualifying distribution' is subject to the 'dividend trust rate' (currently 42.5% of the grossed-up distribution) in the trustees' hands. This special charging provision is needed since otherwise the POS distribution would not be caught by the normal 'additional rate' charging provisions in *ITA 2007, s 479* which only apply to (broadly) accumulated *income* or *income* payable at the discretion of the trustees. (For special tax rules which apply on a POS from trustees, see also 17.80). The trustees also make a disposal for CGT purposes, but the CGT consequences will normally be 'neutral' (see 13.45).

On the other hand, if the CTA 2010 s1033 'no-distribution' treatment applies, the POS proceeds received by the trustees are taxed as a capital gain in the normal way – see 13.46 and Table 2 above. HMRC have also confirmed (see *HMRC Trusts Settlements and Estates Manual* 3205) that where the conditions in *CTA 2010, s 1033* apply, *ITA 2007, s 482* (the special rates for trustees) will not apply.

Settlor interested trusts

A potential difficulty arises with shares sold by the trustees of a settlor-interested trust (see 17.44). Where the POS is treated as an income distribution, this would be taxed in the settlor's hands. However, there would be no *TCGA 1992, s 37* reduction against the capital gain since this is only given to 'the person making the disposal' (ie the trustees).

Consequently, the trustees would also suffer a capital gain (based on the same sale proceeds). (The 'settlor-interested' UK trust gain rules were abolished on 6 April 2008 so that the gain would be taxed on the trustees.) HMRC have confirmed (albeit under the pre-6 April 2008 regime) that they would apply *TMA 1970, s 32* to eliminate the capital gain in such cases. (*TMA 1970, s 32* broadly enables HMRC to reduce all or part of a tax charge if they are satisfied the taxpayer has suffered tax more than once for the same transaction.)

POS from corporate sellers

13.49   Because of the many limitations in the capital gains POS rules in *CTA 2010, ss 1033–1048*, a POS from a corporate seller will often be treated as a distribution. The net taxable distribution is (broadly) calculated as the excess of the POS consideration less the 'repayment of capital (broadly, the amount that was subscribed for the shares when they were first issued).

Where the POS is from a corporate seller, HMRC have long held the view (see SP4/89 and *Strand Options and Futures Ltd v Vojak 76 TC 220 (CA)* that the *TCGA 1992, s 37(1)* exclusion of 'income' distributions from CGT proceeds does not apply. Thus, there will still be a capital gain s calculation based on the full sale proceeds. HMRC's view under SP4/89 was that distributions were *not* charged to corporation tax. Since 1 July 2009, most distributions are still not subject to corporation tax under the modified rules in CTA 2009, Part 9A and the same principles still apply. However, in most cases, the POS gain should be exempt under the SSE rules (see 3.40).

HMRC clearance for CGT-based treatment

13.50   Typically, the seller is likely to seek CGT treatment for their 'buy-back' transaction. They (or more likely their advisers) must ensure that all the detailed 'CGT' conditions will be satisfied and that they are considered when arranging the financing of the purchase consideration.

Advantage should always be taken of the advance clearance procedure in *CTA 2010, s 1044 [ICTA 1988, s 225]* under which the company can obtain assurance from HMRC that the contemplated transaction qualifies for desired tax treatment.

A 'capital gain' share repurchase by a close company could potentially be subject to an income tax charge under the 'Transaction in Securities' (TiS) provisions in *ITA 2007, s 698*. The TiS rules were radically changed from 6 April 2010, becoming more targeted in scope. A key element was the introduction of a 'fundamental change of ownership' exemption. Broadly, this enables the seller to be exempt from the TiS legislation provided they (and/or their associates) do not retain more than 25% of the company's shares after the buy-in and for throughout the following two years (see 15.73 and 15.74 for further commentary). Consequently, there should be no need to seek an *ITA 2007, s 701* clearance in such cases.

In any event, as with all buy-back transactions, it must be ensured that the seller does not remain connected under the 30% rule (see Table 2 – conditions for shareholder (4)) as well as the relevant TiS exemption.

In difficult or uncertain cases, advance clearance should be obtained under *ITA 2007, s 701*) on the basis that the buy-back is being undertaken for 'non-tax avoidance' reasons to remove any doubt. A single clearance application should be made under both *CTA 2010, s 1044* and *ITA 2007, s 701* (see 15.72).

The company must also submit details of the buy-back transaction to HMRC within 60 days of the buy-back transaction where *s 1033* 'capital' treatment applies. In practice, only a short letter is usually necessary with a copy of the prior clearance application and HMRC's *s 1044* clearance letter.

Breaking the CGT conditions to obtain distribution treatment

13.51   There may be situations where the seller will obtain more advantageous tax treatment by having their buy-back treated as a distribution (although they are now likely to be relatively rare). For example, they may have substantial 'income' losses which can be relieved against the income distribution or their buy-back proceeds may be small enough to be taxed entirely within their basic-rate band. It is important to remember that in such cases, CGT treatment will be automatically applied where the relevant conditions in *CTA 2010, s 1033* are satisfied – ie the CGT treatment is not optional.

If distribution treatment is required, then one of the CGT conditions must be deliberately broken to disapply the automatic CGT treatment. It may therefore be necessary to engineer a deliberate breach of (at least) one of these conditions. Some comments on the main methods used are given below:

(a)   *CTA 2010, s 1034(2)* states that if the shares are held through a nominee, the nominee must be a UK resident. This rule could therefore be broken by transferring the shares to a non-resident nominee. The transfer to a nominee would not involve any disposal for CGT purposes (see TCGA 1992, s 60). This route may be vulnerable to a challenge by HMRC under the dicta in *Furniss v Dawson* [1984] STC 153;

(b)   it may be possible for the seller to immediately lend back some of his proceeds to the company to break the 'connected with company' test in CTA 2010, s1042(1). The aim here is to ensure that the buy-back proceeds are immediately lent back to the company as a loan exceeding 30% of the combined share and loan capital (HMRC treat an ordinary loan as loan capital). This is probably the most 'popular' route for ensuring distribution treatment. In many cases, an immediate loan back to the company of only a small amount would break this condition;

(c)   a transfer of shares to/from a spouse (or civil partner) prior to the share purchase or a termination payment to the seller will usually be regarded as an arrangement to avoid tax. It has been reported that clearance for capital treatment is invariably refused in such cases (see, for example, Taxation, 23 July 1998, page 456);

(d)   it might be possible to put forward the argument to HMRC that the buy-in was not for the purposes of the trade, but to provide cash for the shareholder.

13.52   Sufficient certainty can be obtained in advance about the efficiency of the arrangements to provide a distribution treatment by invoking the 'negative clearance' procedure in *CTA 2010 s 1044(3)*. This requires HMRC to confirm within 30 days they are satisfied that the purchase falls outside *CTA 2010, s 1044(3)*.

Tax comparison between CGT and income distribution treatment

13.53   A comprehensive example illustrating the tax effects of a proposed buy-in under *CTA 2010, s 1033* and as a distribution is provided below.

Example 9

Capital gains v distribution treatment for POS

Mr Ramsey is the controlling shareholder of Wembley Ltd, a company which he formed in July 1966. Mr Ramsey is 67 years old and would like to retire from the company in December 2011. He owns 700 of the issued £1 ordinary shares. His two sons, Ron and Terry own the remaining 300 shares between them.

Mr Ramsey needs to realise the value of his shares as he has no other major assets. He has agreed with his sons that control of the company should remain in the hands of his family and outside shareholders should not be brought in. However, his sons cannot personally afford to buy him out. Mr Ramsey has been advised that all these objectives can be satisfied by Wembley Ltd purchasing his shares. His shares will then be immediately cancelled, leaving the company under the control of Ron and Terry, without any direct personal cost to them. The company's auditors have determined that Mr Ramsey's shares should be sold at their fair value of £700,000. Mr Ramsey pays tax at the top income tax rates.

Mr Ramsey subscribed for his 700 £1 ordinary shares at par in July 1966 and they were worth around £60,000 in March 1982. Prima facie, Mr Ramsey and Wembley Ltd would be able to satisfy the conditions for capital treatment in *CTA 2010, s 1033* (see Table 2 at 13.46).

Tax implications for Mr Ramsey

CGT treatment can be expected to apply to the proposed POS of Mr Ramsey's shares and he would make an ER claim to reduce his CGT liability. If the POS takes place in December 2010, Mr Ramsey's expected CGT liability would be calculated as follows:

December 2011 – CGT disposal	£
Sale proceeds	700,000
Less March 1982 value	(60,000)
Chargeable gain	640,000
Less Annual exemption	(10,600)
Taxable gain	629,400
ER CGT @ 10%	£62,940

However, if Mr Ramsey's POS was treated as a distribution, a tax liability of £252,525 would arise, calculated as follows:

December 2011 – Distribution	£
Amount received	700,000
Less Amount subscribed on issue	(700)
Net distribution	699,300
Add Tax credit (10/90)	77,700
Gross distribution	777,000
Income tax thereon £777,000 × (42.5% – 10%)	£252,525

The net distribution is effectively taxed at 36.111% (ie £699,300 × 36.111% = £252,525).

The CGT route reduces Mr Ramsey's tax liability by a considerable £189,585 (£252,525 less £62,940) and undoubtedly this would be more favourable.

It should be noted that if the POS was treated as a distribution for tax purposes, this would not prevent a disposal arising for CGT purposes. However, *TCGA 1992, s 31* prevents double taxation by eliminating the element of the consideration taxed as distribution 'income' from the charge to CGT. This means that the seller is normally treated as selling his shares for an amount equal to the subscription price and therefore no gain arises. However, a loss may arise if March 1982 rebasing applies (see below) or where shares were purchased for an amount exceeding the subscription price.

As March 1982 rebasing applies, Mr Ramsey will also have a capital loss under the distribution route, as demonstrated below:

	£
Sale proceeds	700,000
Less Taxed as 'distribution' income	(699,300)
CGT proceeds	700
Less March 1982 value	(60,000)
Capital loss	(59,300)

HMRC accept that where a company buys in its own shares there is no acquisition by the company as those shares are immediately cancelled under *CA 2006, s 706 [CA 1985, s 160(4))]*. (Even though listed companies are now able to acquire and hold repurchased shares in 'treasury', the tax rules still treat such shares as having been cancelled.) Consequently, the capital loss restriction on disposals to connected persons in *TCGA 1992, s 18(3)* does not apply so the capital loss is freely available. It may be possible to relieve the capital loss against the individual's income (including the distribution) under the share loss relief rules *ITA 2007, s 131*. The relief under *CTA 2007, s 131* can only be used where, inter alia, the loss was incurred 'by way of a bargain at arm's length'. Relief may therefore be claimed by a minority shareholder, but HMRC might be difficult where the POS is from a controlling shareholder.

Tax consequences for Wembley Ltd

If the POS is treated as 'capital' under *CTA 2010, s 1033*, Wembley Ltd would be treated as having made a capital payment on which no tax relief is available – it would not be a distribution.

If the CGT rules are not brought into play, Wembley Ltd would be treated as having made a distribution.

Conclusion

It would clearly be beneficial for Mr Ramsey's POS to be treated as a capital gain as it gives him a much lower tax liability. Care must therefore be taken to ensure that the necessary pre-conditions for CGT treatment (see 13.39) are fully satisfied.

BUY-BACKS – FINANCING ISSUES AND PROBLEMS

Company law requirements

13.54   Company law requires that payment for the purchased shares be made on completion [*CA 2006, s 691*]. The company will therefore need sufficient cash or borrowing resources (bank or venture capital) to finance the purchase price. There must also be sufficient distributable reserves at the time of the buy-back.

The company may not be able to satisfy the repurchase price immediately out of its financial resources and/or retained reserves, particularly as commercial prudence would dictate having a buffer of cash and reserves to meet contingencies, etc.

Phased buy-back of shares

13.55 In such cases, the company could agree to buy back the relevant shares in successive stages, conditional upon future distributable profits and cash being available.

However, if the shareholder requires CGT treatment, a phased share buy-back programme must pass the 'substantial reduction' test (and also satisfy the 30% 'connection' test in relation to the shares held after each buy-back 'tranche'). This means that after each tranche of shares is bought back, the seller's fractional interest must not exceed 75% of his pre buy-in fractional interest (taking into account that the repurchased shares are immediately cancelled). This test must be satisfied after each share repurchase (*CTA 2010, s 1037* [*ICTA 1988, s 221*]).

The minimum number of shares that need to be repurchased to satisfy the test can be computed as follows:

$$\text{Minimum number} = \frac{nx}{4x - 3n}$$

Where: n = the number of shares comprised in the seller's holding (including associates)

$\times$ = company's issued share capital

HMRC will expect to see an agreed programme for buying out (all) the shares so that the shares buy-back satisfies the 'benefit of trade' test.

Care is required with the legal mechanics of the phased buy-back – an unconditional contract to buy back all the shares (albeit over a period of time), creates a CGT disposal at the date of the contract [*TCGA 1992, s 28*], which would mean paying all the CGT 'up-front'. In such cases, it may be better to use put and call options to defer the CGT liabilities for each subsequent buy-back. This puts beyond any doubt that the CGT only becomes payable as and when each option is exercised.

In the exceptional cases where the shareholder requires distribution treatment, a conditional contract to buy the shares in separate tranches works well (there is no need, for example, to satisfy the 'substantial reduction' test). As an alternative, it may be appropriate for the seller to lend part of the 'buy-back' consideration back to the company on interest bearing loan account to be drawn down as the company's cash flow permits. This may cause the seller to fail the 'connection' test (where the loan-back exceeds 30% of the company's combined share and loan capital) – see 13.46, Table 2 – conditions for shareholder (4). Thus, the scope for using a seller 'loan-back' is often limited where CGT treatment is required.

Example 11

Phased share buy-back programme

Mr Tevez holds 20,000 of the 100,000 £1 ordinary shares in City Ltd. He has agreed that the company will buy back all 20,000 of his ordinary shares over two years, in two equal tranches, for a total consideration of £400,000, starting from 31 December 2011, conditional on there being sufficient reserves and cash.

Mr Tevez has substantial capital losses and therefore requires CGT treatment. Therefore, amongst other things, the 'substantial reduction' test must be satisfied after the first 10,000 £1 ordinary shares are purchased.

The POS programme is as follows:

	Share Capital					
	Mr Tevez	Others	Total	CRR	P&L a/c	Cash
	£'000	£'000	£'000	£'000	£'000	£'000
Balances at 1 Jan 2011	20	80	100	–	470	300
Cash flow						70
Post tax profit					80	
Dec 2011 buy-in	(10)		(10)	10	(200)	(200)
Balances at 31 Dec 2011	10	80	90	10	350	170
Cash flow						100
Post-tax profit					120	
Dec 2012 buy-in	(10)		(10)	10	(200)	(200)
Balances at 31 Dec 2012	–	80	80	20	270	70

Notes:

1. An amount equal to the nominal value of the shares bought back must be transferred (from the profit and loss account) to a non-distributable capital redemption reserve (CRR).

2. The 'substantial reduction' test for the December 2011 buy-in is satisfied as Mr Tevez's holding is reduced by at least 25%.

	Before	After
Mr Tevez's holding	20/100 = 20%	10/90 = 11.1%
Proportionate shareholding is reduced by 44.5% ((20% – 11.1%)/20%)		

3. Mr Tevez would be eligible to claim ER on his CGT disposals.

Multiple completion route

13.56 In practice, HMRC is also prepared to allow CGT treatment (assuming all the other conditions are met) on an unconditional multiple completion contract to buy back the shares. This was also confirmed in the ICEAW Technical Release 745. Broadly, this involves the seller contracting to sell their shares back to the company, but with the legal completion of the buy-back subsequently taking place in tranches, as illustrated below:

Multiple completion share buy-back

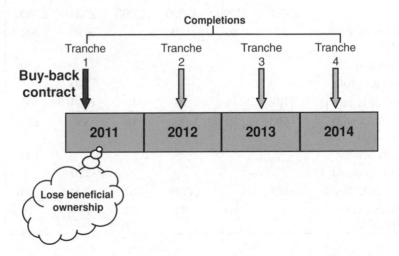

Under the multiple completion route, the selling-shareholder must give up their beneficial interest in the repurchased shares on entering into the contract and therefore the 'substantial reduction' test does not apply. Thus, the seller cannot subsequently take dividends or exercise voting rights over the shares. However, for CGT purposes, the disposal of the entire beneficial interest in the shareholding takes place at the date of the contract [*TCGA 1992, s 28*].

The seller therefore needs to ensure that they have sufficient cash resources to be able to pay the full CGT liability by the 31 January following the tax year in which the buy back contract is made.

The writer has successfully obtained tax clearance from HMRC for a number of multiple completion share buy-backs. However, sometimes, the HMRC clearance team may not readily appreciate the legal effect of the POS. For example, I was made aware of a case where HMRC were indicating a refusal to grant clearance on the basis that until completion, the voting rights which are under the multiple completion contract remain with the seller and hence they would remain connected with the company under *CTA 2010, s 1062(2)* (c) if the voting rights exceed the 30% limit. However, eventually, HMRC finally accepted that the remaining voting rights on the shares could be removed under the contract, which would prevent the '30% connection' test from applying. Alternatively, HMRC have also accepted a reclassification of the shares into different classes prior to the POS between voting and non-voting shares.

The multiple completion POS contract needs to be carefully worded and contain appropriate protection for the seller.

REDUCTION OF SHARE CAPITAL UNDER THE COMPANIES ACT 2009

13.57 Since 1 October 2009, private companies can reduce their share capital by special resolution without any need to go to court [*CA 2006, s 64*]. A share capital reduction must be supported by a solvency statement from the directors made within 15 days of the special resolution that each of the directors is of the view that there are no grounds for the company being unable to pay its debts and that any winding-up of the company within 12 months would be a solvent liquidation.

Some companies may use the reduction in share capital procedure to eliminate a 'profit and loss account' deficit. The company will simply reduce its share capital (with each shareholders holding being reduced on a pro-rata basis) with a corresponding credit being made to the profit and loss account. As far as the shareholders are concerned, their shareholding interest should not alter. Furthermore, since no payment is involved, the reduction of the share capital will fall within the capital gains reorganisation rules in *TCGA 1992, s 126*. The elimination of part of the shares will not therefore involve any disposal [*TCGA 1992, s 127*] and the shareholder's CGT base cost will simply be represented by fewer shares – ie the base cost of the retained shares will increase.

The 'return of capital' provisions are also use to facilitate a demerger without triggering a 'distribution' income tax charge (see 13.93A).

COMPANY PARTITIONS AND DEMERGERS

Partitioning company between shareholders

13.57A Many owner-managed or family businesses develop to the stage where different members of the owner-managers/family team become responsible for separate parts of the business. Sometimes, the owner-managers may subsequently have a fundamental disagreement about the direction of the business or simply find that they 'cannot work together'. In such cases, they may decide to 'partition' the company so that each shareholder takes over the relevant part of the business.

A 'split' of a company's or group's businesses may also be driven by a number of other reasons, such as:

- commercial risk management – because of the different levels of business risk inherent in various types of trade, the shareholders may decide to retain the 'higher' risk ones in separate legal entities;

- differing financing requirements of each trade – only certain businesses may have the ability to attract wider forms of financial support (such as venture capital) or it may be that it would be easier to raise finance for one of the businesses if it were not so closely associated with the other; and

- plans to sell off defined parts of the business – a demerger may be used where there is an intention to sell one or more of the businesses carried on by a company/group but retain the others. In such cases, it is likely that a 'non-statutory' type of demerger would be needed to separate the relevant businesses before the sale.

It may also be attractive to separate both trading and investment businesses to optimise the tax reliefs obtainable under Entrepreneurs' Relief (see 15.33) or the Substantial Shareholdings Exemption (SSE) (see 3.40).

A company or group partition exercise would broadly entail the relevant company transferring the trade and assets of the relevant businesses (or shareholdings in its trading subsidiaries) to separate shareholder groups. Without special relieving provisions, this could trigger significant tax liabilities for both the company and the shareholders.

However, it should normally be possible to split or demerge the relevant business units on a 'tax-neutral' basis, apart from perhaps a stamp duty or stamp duty land tax (SDLT) cost (see 13.58), by 'partitioning' the company under a 'non-statutory' type of demerger or one of the permitted statutory demerger schemes. For company partitions made after 19 May 2005, a demerged business engaged in property letting or property investment is likely to attract a full SDLT charge (since 'acquisition' relief is no longer given is such cases) (see 13.70).

Generally speaking, the legal and other costs of advising on company demergers would mainly be disallowed. The disallowance would be on the grounds that the expenditure is of a 'capital' nature or is not incurred wholly and exclusively for the purposes of the company's trade (the demerger transaction being incidental to a change of ownership of a trade, etc) (*Kealy v O'Mara (Limerick) Ltd* [1942] 2 ITC 265).

Non-statutory v statutory demergers

13.58 In essence, a demerger involves the division of a company or group into two or more companies or groups, with the ultimate share ownership being maintained or separated:

- a non-statutory demerger necessitates winding up the company and distributing the relevant 'business' and assets or subsidiaries to new companies owned by some or all of the shareholders, using the procedure laid down in the *Insolvency Act 1986, s 110*. This is covered at 13.59–13.79;

- a statutory demerger entails distributing one or more trading subsidiaries directly to all or some of the shareholders, or one or more trades or trading subsidiaries to new companies owned by some or all of the shareholders under the statutory code in *CTA 2010, Chapter 5 [ICTA 1988, s 213]*. A statutory demerger avoids winding the company up, but the legislation contains numerous restrictions, for example, there must not be any 'intention' to sell the demerged company. Statutory demergers are dealt with at 13.80–13.95.

Non-statutory demerger under IA 1986, s 110

13.59 In many cases, a non-statutory form of demerger must be used since it may not be possible to satisfy all of the various tax and legal conditions for a statutory demerger. Non-statutory demergers are commonly used in the following cases:

- Where an investment business (such as property letting) is being demerged (the statutory demerger legislation only allows the splitting of trades).

- If there is an intention to sell off one or more of the demerged businesses (this is not permitted under the statutory demerger legislation).

- Where the company has insufficient distributable reserves to declare a dividend in specie equal to the underlying book value of the assets/or subsidiary transferred [*CA 2006, s 846; CA 1985, s 276*] enables any unrealised profit, recognised in the accounts ie, the difference between the market value and book value of the asset, to be treated as realised for this purpose (see 13.96)).

Under a non-statutory demerger, the company is wound-up and the relevant 'business' and assets or subsidiaries are distributed to new companies owned by the shareholders, using the procedure laid down in *IA 1986, s 110*.

The detailed procedure and tax consequences of a company partition under an *IA 1986, s 110* scheme will be explained through the use of a comprehensive case study example, as below (Example 12).

Example 12

Company partition scheme

13.60   Barnes (Transport & Haulage) Ltd carries on two separate businesses which are considered to be of similar value. The shares in Barnes (Transport & Haulage) Ltd have always been owned equally by John Barnes and Paul Barnes, two brothers, since the company was incorporated in 1975. John runs the transport and warehouse business and the haulage business is managed by Paul. It has now been decided that the two businesses would be better operated if John and Paul owned their respective businesses, to develop as they wish. The company's tax advisers have recommended that (for a number of reasons, including the lack of sufficient distributable profits) the demerger should be effected by a reconstruction under *IA 1986, s 110*.

Key steps in *IA 1986, s 110* reconstruction

13.61   The various steps would be as follows:

(a)   Barnes (Transport & Haulage) Ltd is formally liquidated by the shareholders passing a special resolution – it is not possible to use the 'informal' dissolution procedure in *CA 1985, s 652* using ESC C16 to carry out this type of reconstruction;

(b)   the share capital of Barnes (Transport & Haulage) Ltd would be converted into two classes of ordinary shares – 'A' and 'B' shares split according to the respective values of each trade – in this case of similar value. If the businesses were of unequal value, they could be equalised through the apportionment of liabilities and/or an equalisation payment – although any payment would be chargeable to CGT on the recipient shareholder;

(c)   John will form 'Barnes Transport Ltd' to take over the transport and warehouse business and Paul will form 'Barnes Haulage Ltd' to take over the haulage business;

(d)   under *IA 1986, s 110*, a scheme of reconstruction takes place under which the liquidator:

(i)   transfers the transport and warehouse business to Barnes Transport Ltd which, in turn, issues shares to John as consideration;

(ii)   transfers the haulage trade to Barnes Haulage Ltd which, in turn, issues shares to Paul as consideration.

Using a special purpose 'liquidation' vehicle

13.62 It may well be that the original company or holding company of a group would have problems in transferring contracts, licences or leases. The shareholders may also feel that the legal announcement of the liquidation (which is completely tax driven) may be misinterpreted by its customers and other business contacts, etc. If the liquidation of the original company is likely to involve such commercial difficulties, then it normally is possible to use a 'special purpose' holding company. This 'new' company can acquire the original company by means of a 'tax-free' share for share exchange under *TCGA 1992, s 135*. (This transaction would be included as part of the combined *TCGA 1992, s 138* clearance application (see 13.79).)

As this should involve a 'mirror-image' exchange of shares, the stamp duty exemption in *FA 1986, s 77* should normally apply to the acquisition of the original company by the new holding company.

The 'clean' holding company is then liquidated but the liquidation transfers must be made from this company. This may include 'hiving-up' one or more businesses from the original company and the new 'interposed' holding company distributing these businesses and the original company's shares to the new companies.

In such cases, it is vital for the newly formed holding company to carry on the relevant businesses for an appropriate period before their onward distribution, to ensure that the requirements of the relevant tax 'reconstruction' reliefs (including *CTA 2010, Part 2, Chapter 1*) (*ICTA 1988, s 343*), and any VAT transfer of going concern relief (see 12.32)) can be fully satisfied. The holding company should actually carry on the business(es) for an appropriate 'short' period (with the transactions being booked in its accounts).

The importance of ensuring that the trade is actually carried on for a meaningful period was underlined by the recent decision in *Barkers of Malton v HMRC* [2008] UKSPC 689. In this case a trade was hived down to a subsidiary at 9 am (with the trade being carried on by the holding company as undisclosed agent for its subsidiary). The subsidiary then sold the hived-down trade an hour and a half later! The Tribunal found that the requirements of (what was) *ICTA 1988, s 343* had not been satisfied. Simply owning the trade for one hour and a half was not enough. No transactions had been recorded during that period and the reliance on agency was insufficient. This decision gives a clear warning to those who adopt a casual approach in this area!

Basis of split and valuations

13.63 Each separate shareholder group will want to ensure that they get their 'fair' share of the partitioned businesses/companies. This will generally involve obtaining professional valuations and negotiations being conducted on an arm's length basis. HMRC will also wish to ensure that the division of the businesses/companies gives each shareholder/shareholder grouping their appropriate share of the distributing company and that no value shift occurs between the shareholders.

The value of the businesses/companies allocated to each shareholder is typically based on the value of their proportionate shareholding in the distributing company (based as a percentage of the total share capital with no minority discount (since it is effectively a sale!)).

Provided the partition has been negotiated on an arm's length basis, HMRC will not insist on a precise split of value. For these purposes, assets and liabilities should be valued and divided at the time the partition takes place, with some form of 'completion accounts' being drawn up.

In many cases, the allocation of the net asset values between each business/company may not reflect the value fairly attributable to the relevant 'post-partition' shareholder groups. The allocation will therefore require adjusting to bring the values into line with the underlying shareholder entitlements. For example, creditors/loans of one business can be allocated to another or cash balances may be allocated to one of the businesses and a bank overdraft to another. HMRC generally accept that such arrangements may be required to arrive at the proper allocation of values, but these should be disclosed in the advance clearance application (see 13.79).

In more extreme cases, one group of shareholders may need to pay some form of compensatory 'equality' payment to another. This will generally be treated as a capital sum derived from the shares under *TCGA 1992, s 22*, and will thus be subject to CGT in the hands of the recipient shareholders.

Barnes (Transport & Haulage) Ltd – diagram of transactions

13.64 The various transactions are illustrated diagrammatically.

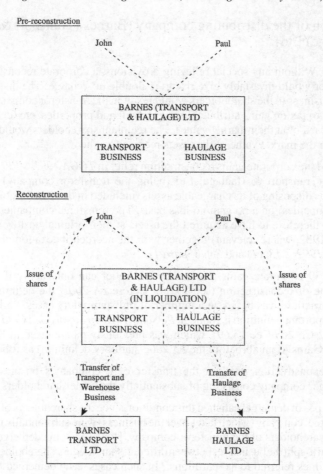

The position will therefore end up as follows:

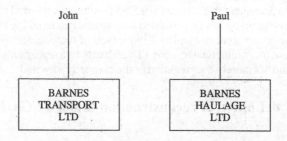

Position of the distributing company (Barnes (Transport & Haulage) Ltd)

13.65 Without any special relieving provisions, a corporate reconstruction/ demerger would invariably give rise to a 'double tax' charge. The distribution of the business to the shareholders would result in the transferor company being charged to tax on gains attributable to goodwill and properties, etc (deemed to be disposed of at their market value). The recipient shareholders would also be taxed on the market value of the assets received by them.

Provided the corporate gains reconstruction relief in *TCGA 1992, s 139* applies, Barnes (Transport & Haulage) Ltd (being the transferor company) will be treated as disposing of its chargeable assets (included in the transfers to the two new companies) on a no gain/no loss basis. The transferee companies will be deemed therefore to have acquired the assets at their original cost (rebased to March 1982, where relevant) together with the accrued indexation allowance [*TCGA 1992, s 139(1)* and *Sch 3, para 1*].

The s 139 corporate gains 'reconstruction' relief can only apply if there is a scheme of reconstruction (see 13.66). Before *FA 2002*, the definition of a 'reconstruction' was based on a number of old stamp duty cases. Perhaps the most important definition is found in *Re South African Supply and Cold Storage* [1904] 2 Ch 268 (see 13.69), which was previously paraphrased in HMRC's Capital Gains Manual (before the *FA 2002* statutory definition) as follows:

'A reconstruction involves the transfer of a company's business … to another company consisting of substantially the same shareholders.'

Many types of demerger satisfied this condition since the shareholders of the new 'transferee' company (which takes over the business) were substantially the same as the shareholders of the transferor company. However, some demergers were designed to split the businesses between different shareholders/shareholder groups – sometimes referred to as 'partitions'. In such cases, each demerged business would be carried on by a different shareholder or group of shareholders and would not therefore meet the requirement that (substantially) the same shareholders should carry it on. However, the Inland Revenue used to operate a generous concession in Statement of Practice (SP) 5/85 (sometimes referred to as a 'press release reconstruction'), which permitted a company's undertaking to be divided into two or more companies owned by different sets of shareholders, provided this was carried out for commercial reasons. (There had to be a segregation of trades or businesses and not merely a segregation of the company's assets.)

Statutory definition of reconstruction under *TCGA 1992, Sch 5AA*

13.66 SP 5/85 had no statutory basis and was successfully challenged by the taxpayer in *Kersley (Morgan's Executors) v Fellows* [2001] STC 1409.

Somewhat unusually the taxpayer did not want the CGT reorganisation treatment applied by *TCGA 1992, s 136* since this gave a lower base cost for the transferred assets. The Revenue responded in *FA 2002* by introducing a statutory definition of a 'scheme of reconstruction' (within *TCGA 1992, Sch 5AA*) which applies from 17 April 2002. This effectively codified the Revenue's existing practice (hitherto applied by SP 5/85) on a statutory basis, so that there was no opting out. Among other things, the new statutory definition encompassed a partition of a business between different shareholders, as in the case of *Barnes (Transport & Haulage) Ltd*.

SP 5/85 and the old case law definitions of reconstruction are now replaced by the statutory regime in *TCGA 1992, Sch 5AA* for the various capital gains reliefs. However, the old case law precedents (see 13.69) still apply for stamp duty and stamp duty land tax.

Under the *FA 2002* statutory definition a 'scheme of reconstruction' must satisfy the following key elements:

- only the ordinary shareholders of the relevant business must receive ordinary shares under the scheme (via a new issue of shares), ie no one else must be entitled to the new share issue [*TCGA 1992, Sch 5AA, para 2*];

- the proportionate interests of the shareholders both before and after the reconstruction must remain the same [*TCGA 1992, Sch 5AA, para 3*]. (It is generally necessary to carry out a preparatory reorganisation of the distributing company's share capital to create separate classes of share. In such cases, the 'equality of entitlement' condition is tested after the completion of the share reorganisation [*TCGA 1992, Sch 5AA, para 6*]; and

- the business previously carried on by the 'original' company or companies must subsequently be carried on by one or more successor companies [*TCGA 1992, Sch 5AA, para 4*].

Alternatively, the scheme must be carried out under a compromise or arrangement under *CA 2006, s 895 (CA 1985, s 425* or equivalent provision) [*TCGA 1992, Sch 5AA, para 5*].

The statutory reconstruction rules still enable a partition of the business between different groups of shareholders to qualify as a reconstruction for capital gains purposes. As far as Barnes (Transport & Haulage) Ltd is concerned, the proposed partition scheme should satisfy these conditions:

- both John and Paul receive shares in their Barnes Transport Ltd and Barnes Haulage Ltd respectively;

- their proportionate interests in the business remain the same after the reconstruction (ie there is no value shift), even though they have each taken over a separate part of the original business;

- the two successor companies (Barnes Transport Ltd and Barnes Haulage Ltd) will carry on the business previously carried on by Barnes (Transport & Haulage) Ltd.

Other key conditions for *TCGA 1992, s 139* relief

13.67   The operation of the 'no gain/no loss' rule in *TCGA 1992, s 139* for the transfer of chargeable assets on a reconstruction requires a number of other conditions to be satisfied:

(a)   the scheme must involve the transfer of the whole or part of one company's business to another company;

(b)   the scheme must be effected for bona fide commercial purposes and not for the avoidance of corporation tax, CGT or income tax – advance clearance can be obtained from HMRC to confirm that this condition is satisfied [*TCGA 1992, s 139(5)*];

(c)   both the transferor and transferee companies must be UK resident (or within the charge to UK corporation tax) at the time of transfer [*TCGA 1992, s 139(1)*]; and

(d)   the transferor must not receive any part of the consideration for the transfer other than the assumption of its liabilities by the transferee companies [*TCGA 1992, s 139(1)(c)*].

The 'reconstruction' transactions contemplated by Barnes (Transport & Haulage) Ltd and its shareholders should therefore enable capital gains to be deferred at the company level.

Reconstruction relief for post-31 March 2002 intangibles

13.67A   Any (post-31 March 2002) intangible fixed assets included in a reconstruction would also be transferred on a tax neutral basis – thus effectively being transferred at their original cost [CTA 2009 s 818,]. The conditions for intangibles reconstruction relief are virtually the same as those for *TCGA 1992, s 139* relief in 13.66 and 13.67 above, which includes satisfying the genuine commercial purpose test in *CTA 2009, s 831*). Certainty can be obtained by the transferee by obtaining an appropriate tax clearance from HMRC under *CTA 2009, ss 831(2) and 832.*

Corporate reconstruction transfers involving shares in 51% subsidiaries

13.68   Some types of *Insolvency Act 1986, s 110* reconstructions will involve the liquidator distributing shares in 51% subsidiaries. In such cases, the shares in the 51% subsidiary are treated as a 'business' (under *TCGA 1992, Sch 5AA,* *para 4(3)*. Consequently, the transfer of the shares will qualify for *TCGA 1992, s 139* corporate gains reconstruction relief. On the other hand, minority shareholdings (even if they trade in the same industry) will not be treated as part of the business of the transferor company (see *Baytrust Holdings Ltd v CIR* [1971] 1 WLR 1333). In such cases, it should be noted that any *TCGA 1992, s 139* relief will always take precedence over any entitlement to the corporate Substantial Shareholdings Exemption (see 3.32 and 3.33) (*TCGA 1992, Sch 7AC, para 6(1)(a)*).

Where shares in a 51% subsidiary are transferred under *TCGA 1992, s 139* on a 'no gain/no loss' basis, this may trigger a degrouping event under *TCGA 1992, s 179*. Since 19 July 2011 (the date of Royal Assent for FA 2011), any *TCGA 1992 s 179* degrouping gain (on chargeable gains) will be added to the sale proceeds of the disposing company for capital gains purposes (*TCGA 1992, s179 (3D)*). HMRC have confirmed that where a degrouping gain is attributed to the disposing company's proceeds on a *TCGA 1992, s 139* transfer it is effectively 'exempted' under the no gain/no loss 'deemed consideration' rule. This beneficial rule can also be invoked on post-31 March 2011 transfers by making an 'early commencement' election under *FA 2011, Sch 10, para 9(5)*.

The effective 'degrouping' exemption under a *TCGA 1992, s 139* no gain/ no loss transfer is only available for chargeable 'capital gains' assets. It will not therefore apply where a degrouping charge arises under the corporate intangibles relief (*CTA 2009, s 775 and s 776*). In such cases, the taxable intangibles degrouping profit will still be deemed to arise in the 'degrouped' subsidiary.

It should be noted that *s 139* reconstruction relief will always take precedence over any entitlement to the Substantial Shareholdings Exemption (SSE) [*TCGA 1992, Sch 7AC*].

Interaction of Substantial Shareholdings Exemption rules with post-demerger companies

13.68A   Where, as a result of a group reorganisation, a company acquires a subsidiary which is subsequently to be sold, the deemed period of ownership is extended where those shares were acquired under a no gain/no loss transfer [TCGA 1992, Sch 7AC, para 10]. In situations where the acquiring company is a pre-existing trading company this is straightforward. However, where the shares are acquired by a new company as a result of a distribution in specie under TCGA 1992, s 139 the question arises as to whether the extension of the holding period in para 10 also deems the holding company to have been trading for an extended period.

It is fairly clear from para 10 that this does not go so far as to deem the investing company to have been trading for the period prior to the *s 139* transfer, since *para 10(1)* only applies for the purposes of *Pt 2* of *TCGA 1992, Sch 7AC* which deals with the substantial shareholding period.

This point needs to be borne in mind where a sale of a subsidiary is contemplated following a s 110 reconstruction (ie where it is not possible to sell the new company itself).

Basic stamp duty land tax (SDLT) and stamp duty issues

13.69   In the case of a 'partition', stamp duty land tax (SDLT) is charged on the value of land and property transferred (see 12.21–12.32), while stamp duty would be levied on the value of shares in companies that are transferred to the new companies as part of the reconstruction exercise. It is worth noting that the transfer of goodwill and debts no longer attract any stamp duty costs, which is beneficial for many partition exercises.

It should be noted that where there is a 'pure reconstruction' with 'mirror image' shareholdings before and after the transfer, it may be possible to satisfy the strict conditions of *FA 2003, Sch 7, Part 2* and *FA 1986, s 75* to secure complete exemption from SDLT and stamp duty respectively. The *FA 2003, Sch 7, para 7* reconstruction relief applies to all 'chargeable transactions' including property sales and the grant, surrender or assignment of leases. As will often be the case, the consideration for the acquisition must consist of the issue of (non-redeemable) shares in the acquiring company or the assumption/ discharge of the transferor's liabilities. Both the stamp duty and SDLT reliefs require the transaction to be carried out for genuine commercial reasons and not mainly for tax avoidance.

The complete exemption from SDLT is only given where post-transfer each shareholder holds the same shareholding interest (or as nearly as may be the same proportion) as they did previously in the transferor. .

For stamp duty and SDLT purposes, there is no statutory definition of a 'reconstruction'. (The *TCGA 1992, Sch 5AA* definition (see 13.66) only applies for the purpose of the various capital gains 'reconstruction' reliefs – it does not apply to stamp taxes). For both stamp duty and SDLT, special conditions must be satisfied and guidance must also be sought from case law. Probably the most authoritative definition of a 'reconstruction' comes from Buckley J in an old stamp duty case (*Re South African Supply and Cold Storage Co Ltd (1904) 2 Ch 268*):

> 'What does 'reconstruction' mean? To my mind it means this. An undertaking of some definite kind is being carried on, and the conclusion is arrived at that it is not desirable to kill that undertaking, but that it is desirable to preserve it in some form, and to do so, not by selling it to an outsider who shall carry it on – that would be a mere sale – but in some altered form to continue the undertaking in such a manner as that the persons now carrying it on will substantially continue to carry it on. It involves, I think, that substantially

the same business shall be carried on and substantially the same persons shall carry it on. But it does not involve that all the assets shall pass to the new company or resuscitated company, or that all the shareholders of the old company shall be shareholders in the new company or resuscitated company. Substantially, the business and the persons interested must be the same.'

The proposed split of the business carried on by Barnes (Transport & Haulage) Ltd, with its two trades being transferred to different shareholders, would not meet the specific 'mirror image' shareholding requirements in the stamp taxes legislation. (The SDLT exemption will not therefore apply to the property transfers included in the reconstruction undertaken by *Barnes (Barnes (Transport & Haulage) Ltd* in Example 12 at 13.60). it will therefore be appreciated that company partitions will often involve an SDLT and/or stamp duty cost.

Where SDLT 'reconstruction' relief is not available, it will sometimes be possible to claim a reduced SDLT rate of ½% under the 'transfer of undertakings' or 'acquisition' relief in *FA 2003, Sch 7 para 8*. SDLT acquisition relief is only given where the consideration for the acquisition is satisfied by the issue of non-redeemable shares to the transferor company or all/any of its shareholders, provided the transaction is undertaken for genuine commercial reasons and not mainly for tax avoidance. In such cases, the acquiring company is permitted to satisfy part of the consideration by assuming or discharging the transferor company's liabilities. (Although a limited amount of cash consideration may also be given, this would prevent the corporate capital gains reconstruction relief being given (see 13.67 (d)).) However, see 13.70 for the important exclusion for property dealing or property investment businesses.

Where shares are transferred on a partition, they would normally carry a normal stamp duty liability of ½% (without the need to invoke the relieving provisions 'transfer of undertakings' reduced rate relief in *FA 1986, s 76*). (See 13.69 in 2003/04 edition of this book for stamp duty treatment of pre-1 December 2003 partitions.)

SDLT problems for property investment/dealing businesses

13.70 Unfortunately, following the *Finance (No 2) Act 2005*, there is now likely to be a significant SDLT liability where the partition includes a (mainly) property letting or property dealing business. In broad terms, since 20 May 2005, the (½%) acquisition relief is only available if the business being acquired is wholly or mainly a trade (but not a property dealing trade). It should be emphasised that this restriction does not apply to the SDLT reconstruction relief, which may still exempt property-related investment businesses.

FA 2003, Sch 7, para 8(5A) now effectively blocks acquisition relief for properties comprised in a property investment business (not a trade) or property dealing business, thus exposing them to the full SDLT rates. This means that, in practice, the acquiring company would only obtain the benefit of such relief for properties used in a trade or possibly where the trade being transferred has a 'small' property letting activity.

SDLT clawback charges

13.71 SDLT reconstruction or acquisition relief claimed on properties (see 13.69) would be 'clawed-back' where control of the acquiring company changes hands within three years after the relevant reconstruction/acquisition transfer. The claw-back only operates if the acquiring company still retains the relevant properties when it changes ownership. The primary purpose of the claw-back charge is to prevent the relevant SDLT reliefs being exploited to transfer property to third parties through the use of special company vehicles.

For these purposes, control of the acquirer would change where it becomes controlled by a different person or group of persons (using the wide 'control' test in *CTA 2010, ss 450* and *451 [ICTA 1988, s 416]* (see 3.19)). Specific exemptions prevent the claw-back charge being triggered where the company changes ownership in certain specific cases. This would include a stamp duty exempt intra-group transfer of the company's shares or where it comes under the control of a new holding company by virtue of a stamp duty free transfer under *FA 1986, s 77*.

Where the SDLT relief is clawed-back, the SDLT liability is effectively computed based on the market value of the retained property/properties using the prevailing SDLT rates at the date of the original reconstruction/acquisition transfer, ie the SDLT that would have been paid if no relief had been given (less any actual SDLT paid under the acquisition relief).

'Capital allowance' assets and tax losses

13.72 The reconstruction provisions do not prevent the normal corporation tax consequences of a cessation of trade unless the succession provisions of *CTA 2010, s 948 [ICTA 1988, s 343]* can be brought into play. If the succession provisions apply, this will enable any trading losses and the tax written-down value of plant, industrial buildings, etc, to be carried over into the transferee company.

In the worked example 12 (at 13.60), the common 75% beneficial ownership test required for a succession of trade transfer within *CTA 2010, Part 22, Chapter 1 [ICTA 1988, s 343]*, may not be satisfied after the reconstruction. Before the transfer, each trade is owned equally by John and Paul whereas after the transfer, each trade is owned separately by John and Paul. However, there is a fairly strong argument for saying that as 'associates' (brothers), John and Paul are regarded as one person [*CTA 2010, s 941(7)(8)*] which would then enable the succession of trade rules to apply, but HMRC might resist this approach.

Where it is important to obtain *CTA 2010, Part 22, Chapter 1* relief, for example, where one of the transferred trades has substantial tax losses, consideration should be given to hiving down the relevant trades to new wholly-owned subsidiaries under *CTA 2010, Part 22, Chapter 1* first. The liquidator would then distribute these subsidiaries in specie to the new companies under the protection of *TCGA 1992, s 139* (the subsidiaries would be regarded as businesses).

However, since 19 July 2011 (or, by election, 1 April 2011), any *TCGA 1992, s 179* degrouping charge in respect of the chargeable assets previously transferred under TCGA 1992, s 171 on the hive-down will effectively be exempted under the deemed 'no gain/no loss' corporate gains reconstruction rule in *TCGA 1992, s 139* (see 13.68). This useful relief does not apply to *CTA 2009, s 780*-type degrouping charges arising under the intangibles regime (ie on goodwill and other IP assets created or acquired after 31 March 2002). Consequently, a taxable intangibles profit will crystallise within the distributed subsidiary.

The statutory demerger code offers a specific exemption for all types of degrouping charge (see 13.89). The possibility of implementing a statutory demerger should therefore be considered where an *Insolvency Act 1986, s 110* reconstruction is likely to involve a material degrouping tax charge. The tax costs of the various demerger routes must therefore be compared to determine the best way of structuring the transactions. If the trade succession provisions in *CTA 2010, Part 22, Chapter 1* do not apply, it may still be possible for plant to be transferred at tax written-down values (thus avoiding a balancing charge) provided there is common 51% control at shareholder level by electing under *CAA 2001, s 266*. (Industrial buildings are no longer subject to any balancing adjustment – see 15.10.)

Transfer of trading stock

13.73   Where trading stock is 'sold' on a reconstruction, the consideration is reflected in the shares issued by the 'new' successor company. Since full consideration has been given, this would strictly mean that the trading stock passes at its market value and it is not therefore possible to make an election for it to be transferred at original cost/book value under *CTA 2009, s 167*. However, in practice, since no consideration actually passes directly to the transferor company (the stock is distributed in specie), HMRC generally accept a transfer at book value provided the same amount is used by both companies (provided a competent *CTA 2009, s 167* election is made to disapply the deemed market value rule, which would invariably be the case).

However, where the 'UK to UK' transfer pricing rules apply to the distributing company, the stock is treated as being transferred at its market value (since the transfer pricing rules take precedence under *CTA 2009, s 161*).

VAT – transfer of going concern relief

13.74   The transfer of the trade and assets transferred would normally qualify as a 'transfer of a going concern' (TOGC) for VAT purposes and hence the value of the transferred assets (such as plant, trading stock, etc) would not be subject to VAT [*VAT (Special Provisions) Order 1995, art 5*].

Where land and property is transferred (which has been subject to an option to tax election), the transferee company will also need to elect before the transfer is made to enable the property to be transferred 'VAT-free' under the TOGC rules. The transferor must therefore be satisfied that the transferee company has opted to tax (see also 12.32).

Position of shareholders (John and Paul)

13.75   Potentially, where shareholders of an existing company receive shares in another company on a reconstruction, this would be regarded as an income distribution, being an indirect transfer by the company to its members. This is why it is essential for the disposing company in the worked example 11 (at 13.60) – Barnes (Transport & Haulage) Ltd in this case – to be liquidated before the reconstruction exercise. Amounts received during the course of a winding up do not constitute an income distribution (see 16.11) [*CTA 2010, s 1030*].

The value of the shares acquired by John and Paul would therefore fall to be treated as a capital distribution [*TCGA 1992, s 122(1),(5)*]. However, John and Paul will be protected from any CGT liabilities under *TCGA 1992, s 136* provided the shares are issued as part of the arrangements for a scheme of 'reconstruction'. Here again, this scheme would satisfy the various requirements of *TCGA 1992, Sch 5AA* (see 13.66).

Under *TCGA 1992, ss 136* and *127*, John and Paul will be treated as making no disposal for CGT purposes as regards their shares in Barnes (Transport & Haulage) Ltd with the result that the shares they acquire in their respective new companies – Barnes Transport Ltd and Barnes Haulage Ltd – will be treated as the same asset acquired at the same time as their old shares. If the original shares are retained, they will be regarded as having been cancelled and replaced by a new issue – the original base cost will then have to be apportioned between the various shareholdings.

Main requirements for *TCGA 1992, s 136* relief

13.76   *TCGA 1992, s 136* requires the following conditions to be satisfied:

(a)   there must be an arrangement between the disposing company and its shareholders;

(b)   the shareholders must receive shares (and/or debentures) in the 'new' company in respect of and in proportion to their shares in the disposing company – these shares must either be retained or cancelled [*TCGA 1992, s 136(1)(b)*];

(c)   the reconstruction must be effected for bona fide commercial reasons and not for the avoidance of tax. The advance clearance procedure in *TCGA 1992, s 138* is used to confirm that HMRC are satisfied that this is the case [*TCGA 1992, s 137(1)*].

HMRC will normally accept the pre-reconstruction period as counting towards the 'one year' ER qualifying period where *TCGA 1992, s 127* applies, although this treatment is not strictly available under the CGT legislation (see CGT entrepreneurs' relief and share for share exchange note issued by CIOT Technical Department – 26 May 2010). This would be very beneficial where a new recipient/successor company is sold within one year of the reconstruction. However, the relevant shareholder would also have to satisfy the ER conditions in the transferor/distributing company for the appropriate (pre-reconstruction) period.

Position of recipient companies (Barnes Transport Ltd and Barnes Haulage Ltd)

13.77   The new companies will acquire the relevant chargeable assets at the transferor's base cost (rebased to March 1982, if appropriate) with accrued indexation allowance [*TCGA 1992, s 139*]. It should be noted that the de-grouping charge in *TCGA 1992, s 179* cannot apply in this situation as the chargeable assets are not transferred to a 'group' company.

Planning a company partition and relevant tax clearances

13.78   Each partition exercise will be underpinned by various generic tax principles and reliefs. In practice, each tends to have its own unique issues and challenges. It is not always possible to implement a corporate reconstruction without any tax cost, for example, a partition may involve SDLT or stamp duty liabilities. There will also be a whole panoply of legal, accounting, and commercial issues, which may have a direct bearing on the structure of the particular reconstruction exercise.

To obtain certainty in advance that HMRC is satisfied that transaction(s) are being made for genuine commercial reasons (rather than mainly for tax avoidance), a 'combined' tax clearance application should be submitted under the various sections mentioned below (see 15.46 for relevant details).

•   *TCGA 1992, s 138* for the shareholders' CGT reconstruction relief (see 13.63), and any prior share exchange (see 13.62).

- *TCGA 1992, s 139(5)* for the corporate gains reconstruction relief (see 13.67) and/or *CTA 2009, ss 831(2)* and *832* for intangibles reconstruction relief (see 13.67A).

- *ITA 2007, s 701* – Transaction in Securities (TiS) legislation – (see 15.48).

13.79 A considerable relaxation was made to the TiS rules on 6 April 2010 through the introduction of the 'fundamental change of ownership' exemption. Since common ownership is generally maintained on a 'reconstruction', this relief is unlikely to apply and it is still necessary to seek an *ITA 2007, s 701* clearance.

PERMITTED TYPES OF STATUTORY DEMERGER

13.80 A 'non-statutory' demerger scheme requires the transferor company to be liquidated to avoid the shareholders being subject to tax on an income distribution. This may not always be feasible or desirable.

As will be seen, it is not necessary for all the existing shareholders to take shares in the demerged businesses or companies. Each business carried on by a company or group can be passed to a different shareholder or different shareholder 'groupings'. Thus, if the various tax and legal conditions had been achievable, it would have been possible to demerge the two businesses carried on by Barnes (Transport & Haulage) Ltd (see Example 12 at 13.60) by way of a statutory demerger. This could be achieved without having to liquidate Barnes (Transport & Haulage) Ltd, with a simple demerger distribution of one of the trades.

The statutory demerger rules in *CTA 2010, Chapter 5* [*ICTA 1988, s 213*] permit three types of demerger, without the need for liquidation. It achieves this by treating a qualifying demerger distribution as an 'exempt' distribution and therefore there is no income tax charge in the shareholder's hands. Each statutory demerger takes the form of a distribution in specie of one or more trades or shares in one or more 75% subsidiaries:

Type 1 *(Direct demerger)* — The direct distribution by a company of shares in a 75% subsidiary (or subsidiaries) to *all or any* of its members (*CTA 2010, s 1076*).

Type 2 *(Indirect demerger)* — The transfer of a company's trade or trades to one or more 'transferee' companies in consideration for the issue of shares in those companies to *all or any* of the members of the distributing company. (*CTA 2010, s 1076*) This is known as an 'indirect' distribution.

Type 3 *(Indirect demerger)* — The transfer of shares in a 75% subsidiary (or subsidiaries) to one or more 'transferee' companies in consideration for the issue of shares in the companies to *all or any* of the members of the distributing company. *CTA 2010, s 1076,*) This is known as an 'indirect' distribution.

However, many contemplated demergers will be unable to satisfy the numerous pre-conditions, commonly the prohibition on demergers in contemplation of a sale and the use of a demerger to separate trades from investment businesses. In such cases, a non-statutory 'liquidation' demerger will normally have to be used instead (see 13.59).

STATUTORY DEMERGER RELIEFS FOR SHAREHOLDERS

Exempt distribution rule

13.81 Provided the various qualifying conditions are met, the shares received direct or the 'consideration' shares received for the transfer will not rank as an income distribution in the shareholders' hands. The distribution is termed an 'exempt distribution' and does not, therefore, give rise to an income tax liability in the (individual/ trustee) shareholder's hands [*CTA 2010, s 1075*].

Although this exemption does not prevent the 'distribution' falling within the capital gains regime, the CGT reconstruction reliefs will invariably be available to prevent any tax charge arising (see 13.82 and 13.83 below).

Type 1 – Direct demerger

13.82 On a Type 1 'direct' demerger, the distribution is not treated as a capital distribution, which would have created a part disposal for CGT purposes.

Although SSE may potentially apply to exempt the distributing company (see 13.86) from the gain for corporation tax (*TCGA 1992, s 139* will not normally apply here since the distribution will usually be to individual shareholders), this does not mean that the shareholders will acquire the shares at their market value under general principles. This is because there is a specific rule in *TCGA 1992, s 192(2)* which treats the shares in the distributed subsidiary as received in a 'new for old' reorganisation for CGT purposes. Thus, the shares in the subsidiary are related back to their shareholding in the distributing company under the deemed application of *TCGA 1992, s 127*. (The shares in the distributed subsidiary would therefore be deemed to be acquired by the recipient shareholders at the time of the 'original' shareholding at their pro-rata base cost of the original shares (based on the respective market values of the distributing and subsidiary company/companies).

Type 2 and 3 – Indirect demergers

13.83 A Type 2 or 3 demerger should usually qualify as a scheme of reconstruction within *TCGA 1992, Sch 5AA* (see 13.66). (Because of the restrictions imposed by the statutory demerger rules, shares in a 75% (as opposed to a 51%) subsidiary must be transferred under a Type 3 demerger – this is treated as a transfer of a business under the 'reconstruction' rules.)

The issue of shares in the new recipient companies as part of the demerger should fall within *TCGA 1992, s 136* (see 13.75). This means the 'new for old' reorganisation relief rules would apply) [*TCGA 1992, s 127*].

STATUTORY DEMERGER RELIEFS FOR DISTRIBUTING COMPANY

Exempt distribution

13.84 The distributing company is treated as having made an 'exempt distribution'. An 'exempt distribution' under the statutory demerger rules does not give rise to any shadow ACT where this is relevant (see 9.9) [*CTA 2010, s 1075*].

Treatment of disposal under a Type 1 direct demerger and application of SSE

13.85 A Type 1 demerger does not qualify for *TCGA 1992, s 139* relief (as the assets are not transferred to a company). However, many Type 1 demergers should be exempt under the Substantial Shareholding Exemption (SSE) (see 3.40), assuming the relevant conditions are satisfied.

Of course, if the demerger disposal does not qualify for the SSE, a chargeable gain will be triggered on the disposal of the demerged subsidiary's shares, based on their market value. In such cases, it may be possible to mitigate the gain, for example, by paying a pre-sale dividend or transferring assets out at an undervalue (preferably at original cost to avoid creating a value shifting charge under *TCGA 1992, s 32*).

A Type 1 demerger is likely to be particularly attractive if it qualifies for the SSE as it is also normally exempt from stamp duty.

13.86 The shares must actually be distributed 'in specie'. This avoids the pre-existing 'debt' stamp duty trap. Any prior declaration of a dividend equal to the value of the subsidiary creates a debt (within *SA 1891, s 57*) and thus gives rise to stamp duty (at 0.5%) when it is then satisfied by the transfer of the shares.

Section 139 Reconstruction relief for corporate gains on indirect demergers

13.87   Under general principles, capital gains would normally arise by reference to the market value of the assets being transferred [*TCGA 1992, s 17*]. However, Type 2 and 3 (indirect-type) demergers will usually qualify for 'reconstruction' relief under *TCGA 1992, s 139* to prevent capital gains being generated on the transfer of the relevant assets. Such distributions will generally meet all the relevant conditions for *s 139* relief – for example, the trade/shares in a 75% subsidiary will be transferred to another UK company for no consideration (except for the assumption of liabilities).

Although shares in a subsidiary are treated as a business for the general 'reconstruction' rule in *TCGA 1992, Sch 5AA, para 4(3)* (see 13.67), the actual demerger conditions are more restrictive. The relevant provisions require the demerger to consist of shares in a 75% subsidiary.

The SSE (see 3.40 and 13.86) could potentially apply to the disposal of a qualifying shareholding, such as on a Type 3 demerger. However, where the disposal falls within the *TCGA 1992, s 139* corporate reconstruction provisions (providing 'no gain/no loss' disposal treatment), these will take precedence over the SSE [*TCGA 1992, Sch 7AC, para 6(1)(a)*].

Degrouping charge exemption

13.88   In a Type 1 and Type 3 demerger, a de-grouping charge could arise under *TCGA 1992, s 179* in consequence of assets transferred intra-group to the demerging company within the previous six years. However, a specific exemption is given for any de-grouping charge [*TCGA 1992, s 192(3)*]. Similar protection is given from the degrouping charge under the intangible fixed assets regime (see 12.46–12.51).

No protection is available for SDLT degrouping charges. An SDLT clawback charge may arise where property has previously been transferred to a subsidiary (under the SDLT intra-group transfer exemption) which subsequently leaves the group via a demerger within three years of the original transfer (provided it still retains the property) (see 13.69).

Other relieving provisions

13.89   The statutory demerger provisions do not offer a complete tax-free basis for demergers. They mainly prevent the demerger distribution from being taxed in the shareholders' hands. Reliance must, therefore, be placed on the other corporate 'succession' or reorganisation legislation to obtain exemption or carry-over of various tax reliefs.

Any unused trading tax losses may be vulnerable under *CTA 2010, ss 673* and *674 [ICTA 1988, s 768]* (see 12.56) where the demerger of the shares to a group of shareholders triggers a 'change of ownership', although such cases are looked at sympathetically (see SP 13/80).

STATUTORY DEMERGER CONDITIONS

Summary of main conditions

13.90 A demerger will only qualify for the 'exempt distribution' treatment and the special reliefs mentioned above if it satisfies all the relevant conditions. These conditions are more onerous than for a non-statutory demerger by liquidation and reference must always be made to the detailed legislation in each case.

The main conditions for a qualifying demerger are summarised below:

(a) all companies participating in the demerger transaction (the 'relevant companies') must be resident in the UK or an EU member state [*CTA 2010, s 1081(1)*];

(b) the distributing company must be a trading company or member of a trading group [*CTA 2010, s 1081(2)*]. After the demerger, the distributing company must remain a trading company or member of a trading group [*CTA 2010, s 1082 (2)* or *1083(2)*]. For these purposes, the 'trading company' and 'trading group' requirements are based on the less stringent 'wholly or mainly' trading test.

However, this condition need not be met where the distributing company is a 75% subsidiary of another company or where it is wound up after the demerger of two or more 75% subsidiaries without there being any net assets available for distribution (other than to cover liquidation costs, etc) [*CTA 2010, s 1082 (3), (4)*];

(c) at the time of its distribution, a demerged 75% subsidiary must be a trading company or member of a trading group [*CTA 2010, s 1081(2)(b)*];

(d) the distribution must be made wholly or mainly for the benefit of some or all of the trading activities formerly carried on by the company/group [*CTA 2010, s 1081(3)*];

(e) the distribution must not form part of a scheme or arrangement for:

    (i) the avoidance of tax, stamp duty or SDLT [*CTA 2010, s 1081(5))*];

    (ii) the making of a 'chargeable payment' (see 13.92 and 13.93 below) [*CTA 2010, s 1081(5)*];

    (iii) the transfer of control of the demerged company to persons other than members of the distributing company (such as on a subsequent sale of the company) [*CTA 2010, s 1081(5)(d)*].

(iv) the cessation or sale of a trade after the demerger distribution [*CTA 2010, s 1081(5)(e)(f)*].

There are further pre-conditions for each type of demerger [*CTA 2010, ss 1082 and 1083*].

Statutory demerger tax clearances

13.91 Advance clearance can be obtained from HMRC to confirm that they are satisfied that the demerger has been carried out for bona fide commercial reasons and not for the avoidance of tax [*CTA 2010, s 1091 (ICTA 1988, s 215)*]. Indeed, tax clearances under *TCGA 1992, s 138* for the shareholders' CGT reconstruction relief; *TCGA 1992, s 139(5)* for the corporate gains reconstruction relief and *ITA 2007, s 701* (transaction in securities legislation) will also be necessary (see 13.79). A single combined tax clearance application covering all the above sections should be made – see 15.46 for details.

Chargeable payments

13.92 Any 'non-commercial' payment (broadly representing the value of the demerged assets/shares) made to shareholders within five years of the demerger is taxed as income. The payment is not an allowable deduction for corporation tax purposes.

A chargeable payment would also lead to a withdrawal of the degrouping charges exemption (but not the other 'demerger' and 'reconstruction' reliefs).

The chargeable payments rules are very widely drawn and it is normally advisable to seek advance clearance from HMRC under *CTA 2010, s 1092* that any contemplated 'payment' would not be caught.

Practical case involving chargeable payments and subsequent sale

13.93 In practice, probably the most important restriction is the one that denies statutory demerger treatment where it is intended to sell the demerged company. In some cases it may be necessary to demonstrate to HMRC that at the time the demerger was executed there was no intention to sell the demerged company.

In a recent practical case in which the author advised, HMRC were sceptical about the directors' plans where shortly after the demerger of a subsidiary, the directors received an 'unsolicited' offer from a large corporate group to acquire 100% of the recently demerged company. This potential purchaser had demonstrated sound strategic reasons for seeking the acquisition. The offer was received just a few months after the demerger had been completed. A satisfactory demerger clearance had been obtained from HMRC, following an application which cited genuine commercial reasons for the demerger (which included the need to cater for different management styles and responsibilities over two distinct trades as well as key issues surrounding finance, risk and ease of administration).

After considerable discussions, the shareholders agreed to sell the company for a substantial amount payable over a period of three years, dependent upon achievement of certain targets.

Because of the earlier 'statutory demerger', the purchaser had obvious concerns that the payment of the purchase consideration could be regarded as a chargeable payment given the relatively wide scope of *CTA 2010, ss 1088 and 1089*. This included any payment motivated by tax avoidance reasons which is made to a shareholder of the demerged company. If the amount were considered to be a 'chargeable payment', it would be taxed as income and would also nullify any degrouping charge protection (see 13.67C), although the other demerger reliefs remain undisturbed.

For various reasons, the purchaser insisted that confirmation from HMRC was sought under *CTA 2010, s 1092* [*ICTA 1988, s 215(2)*] that the sale consideration (including the deferred payments) was being paid for genuine commercial reasons and would not be treated as a chargeable payment. After making considerable enquires into the offer letter and negotiations surrounding the sale, HMRC were satisfied that there was no intention to sell the demerged company at the time of the demerger. HMRC accepted that the sale proceeds were not chargeable payments, and therefore fell to be treated as a normal capital gain.

Key VAT issues on demergers

13.93A If there is a direct 'statutory' demerger distribution of shares in a 75% subsidiary (see 13.82), there is no consideration, so there should be no supply for VAT purposes. Contrastingly, on an 'indirect' type of demerger, the transferee company issues its shares in consideration for the transfer of the business or shares in a subsidiary company, thus creating a supply for VAT purposes.

In the context of a demerger, HMRC are likely to contend that the vast majority of the legal, professional and other relevant costs relate to exempt supplies of the transfer of the demerged companies. Thus, the input tax directly related to these costs will fall to be irrecoverable (subject to the possible application of the VAT grouping and partial exemption deminimis rules).

To the extent that the costs can be allocated to the issue of shares, it may be possible to reclaim the related input VAT. The ECJ in *Kretztechnic AG v Finanzamt Linz* (C-465/03) ruled that the issue of shares did not create any supply for VAT purposes (see 12.59). Consequently, provided the issuing company only makes taxable supplies, the 'share issue' input tax can be fully deducted as a general business overhead.

If the demerger involves the transfer of a business/assets as a going concern (see 13.74), the input VAT on the related legal and professional costs should be recoverable under the 'general business overheads' rules. Thus, if the company is 'fully taxable' for VAT, this will enable it to recover all the VAT.

RETURN OF CAPITAL DEMERGERS

13.93B The *Companies Act 2006* enables private companies to reduce their share capital without having to seek 'court permission', provided certain statutory safeguards are complied with (see 13.57).

A demerger can therefore be structured as a return of capital, which means that the shareholders do not suffer any income tax charge under the distribution legislation. This is achieved by ensuring that the demerged companies represent a 'repayment of capital' on their shares. It is therefore usually necessary to 'interpose' a new holding company under a share for share exchange so that it can reflect the market value of the group's subsidiaries. Since the legal analysis is that the shareholders have 'subscribed' for the new shares in the holding company at a full 'market value' consideration, this should provide sufficient 'capital' to 'frank' the demerger distribution under company law principles.

From a tax perspective, the demerged company/companies will not create a taxable distribution since the amount received will represent a repayment of capital (*CTA 2010, s 1000(1)B(a)*).

COMPANIES ACT REQUIREMENTS – DEMERGER DISTRIBUTIONS AND OTHER INTRA-GROUP TRANSFERS

Legality of demerger and other reorganisation transfers

13.94 The company law implications must always be considered when structuring a statutory demerger. The *Companies Act 2006* seeks to provide certainty on the treatment of demerger distributions and other 'pre-reorganisation' asset transfers to fellow group companies. Such demergers and other transfers must satisfy certain legal requirements; otherwise the transaction may be set-aside and negate all or part of the intended demerger or reorganisation.

The 'Aveling Barford' case

13.95 The case of *Aveling Barford Ltd v Perion Ltd* [1989] BCLC 677 created a number of uncertainties in relation to the commercial price at which assets should be transferred, and still remains good law for companies that have negative reserves.

Broadly, Aveling Barford (which was in financial difficulties and had negative reserves of around £18m) sold a large site to Perion (which was effectively a commonly controlled company). The sale was completed in February 1987 at an agreed price of £350,000, although the property was worth considerably more. Later, in August 1987, the site was sold for some £1,560,000.

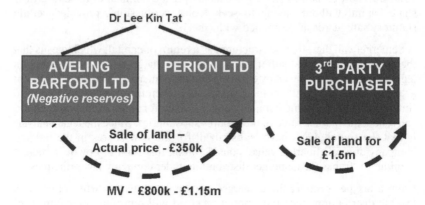

Mr Justice Hoffmann held that the sale at undervalue to Perion was a breach of the director's fiduciary duty. Furthermore, the grossly undervalued sale enabled Perion to realise a profit. Perion was controlled and 'introduced' by its sole beneficial shareholder. It therefore followed that the transaction was a 'dressed-up' distribution. Since Aveling Barford had a deficit on its reserves, this meant there was an unauthorised return of capital, which was ultra vires (and the transaction was incapable of being ratified by shareholders).

The Aveling Barford decision made clear that where a company has negative reserves, a transfer at below book value is an unlawful distribution. Its implication where a company has positive reserves were less clear. Before the *CA 2006*, it was generally thought that where transfer took place at book value, there should be no legal distribution, although there was some doubt since there was often an 'undervalue' element in the transfer. Some thought that a company required sufficient reserves to cover any excess of market value over sale price. However, a transfer at market value could never create an unlawful return of capital.

For further detailed discussion on the legal issues surrounding distributions and dividends, see 9.2 to 9.7.

It should be appreciated that the *Companies Act* concepts of a distribution are different from those that apply for tax purposes. Broadly, the main tax distribution rules are set out in *CTA 2010, s 1000* [*ICTA 1988, s 209*]. As a general rule, a 'tax' distribution on the transfer of assets to a shareholder will arise to the extent that the market value of the assets transferred exceeds any consideration paid/given by the shareholder.

Companies Act 2006 requirements

13.96 The *Companies Act 2006* now makes clear the measure of any distribution for assets for company law purposes. *CA 2006, s 845* provides that, where a company has distributable reserves, the measure of any distribution is based on the book value of the asset (ie broadly the amount at which it is stated in the accounts). The general principles are:

- where the transfer consideration (TC) of an asset is at least equal to its book value (BV), there is no distribution;

- where the TC of an asset is less than its BV, the distribution is the excess of BV over TC.

Thus, where a company has realised profits, assets can be transferred at their book value without creating a distribution (although, of course, this is likely to create a distribution for tax purposes under *CTA 2010, s 1000*).

Similarly, where a company is about to undertake a statutory demerger distribution, it must have sufficient distributable profits to cover the carrying book value of the subsidiary/assets being 'demerged'. In such cases there is no TC and therefore the distribution amount under company law (but not for tax purposes) is simply the BV of the net assets or the shares in the 75% subsidiaries.

For these purposes, revaluation surpluses that have been booked in the accounts can be treated as realised profits under *CA 2006, s 846*. This will typically apply where properties have been subject to a prior revaluation. In such cases, the revaluation surplus can effectively be applied as part of the 'distributable profits' for the purpose of the in-specie distribution of the property.

The principles in Aveling Barford (see 13.95) remain relevant for companies that have no distributable profits. In such cases, where assets are transferred at an undervaluation, this will be an unlawful distribution.

Directors should also be mindful of their fiduciary duties. In some cases, it may therefore be prudent to transfer the assets at their full market value. If the transferring company went into liquidation or administration, transfers at 'market value' would not be vulnerable to being overturned under 'two year' rule in *Insolvency Act 1986, s 238*.

PLANNING CHECKLIST – REORGANISING SHARES AND TRADING ACTIVITIES (INCLUDING SHARE BUY-BACKS)

Company

- Several businesses can normally be partitioned without tax cost amongst different shareholders under a non-statutory 'liquidation' demerger or a statutory demerger.

- A partition exercise may be helpful where a company or group has a mixture of both trading and investment businesses. The partition of a property letting or property dealing business is likely to be charged at full SDLT rates, but pure reconstructions remain unaffected. This type of partition may also be driven by the desire to reduce the business risk attaching to certain trades within the existing company or group.

- The transfer of shares in a 51% controlled subsidiary would be sufficient to ensure the transfer of a business for the purpose of the reconstruction rules, but a 75% subsidiary is needed to facilitate a statutory demerger

- Following the *FA 2011* changes to the capital gains degrouping rules, a *TCGA 1992, s 139* reconstruction transfer of shares in a (75%) subsidiary enables any degrouping gains to be exempted under the deemed 'no gain/no loss' consideration rule. The Substantial Shareholdings Exemption may apply to direct demerger distributions of '75%' trading subsidiaries (and should also be exempt from stamp duty).

- Statutory demergers avoid a liquidation but can only be carried out where the distributing company has sufficient distributable reserves to execute a demerger distribution equivalent to the 'carrying cost' (per the accounts) of the assets/shares transferred. Such demergers cannot be implemented where there are plans to sell the demerged company. In such cases, it may be possible to use a liquidation-based 'non-statutory demerger' (provided this is done well ahead of any prospective sale).

Working shareholders

- In many cases, shares awarded or option shares exercised in private companies are only subject to the standard *Companies Act Table A* condition. There still remains some uncertainty about whether such shares would be regarded as 'restricted securities'. However, even where the relevant shares are unlikely to be 'restricted', it is still generally prudent to make a 'defence' *ITEPA 2003, s 431* election.

- Where shares are subject to substantive restrictions on transfer or forfeiture, etc (that reduce their value), they are likely to constitute 'restricted securities'. In such cases, the recipient director/ employee would suffer an employment income tax charge on the restricted value of the shares (less any amount paid for them). However, it will normally be beneficial for them to make an election under *ITEPA 2003, s 431* to be taxed on the 'unrestricted value' of the shares up-front (and/or pay that amount for the shares).

- Shares can normally be transferred or trades moved to different companies via a reconstruction or demerger, without any immediate tax costs.

- Funds can be extracted from the company on the shareholder's retirement in a capital gains-efficient manner by arranging for the company to buy back the shares. To obtain CGT treatment, it is important to demonstrate that any buy-back motivated by retirement benefits the ongoing trade of the company.

- Capital gains tax treatment on a share buy-back is generally only available where the shares have been held for at least five years. In many cases, the outgoing shareholder will be able to reduce their CGT liability by claiming the lower ER 10% rate.

Other employees

- Where shares are awarded or share options are exercised (at less than their money's worth), they may constitute 'restricted securities'. In such cases, it will normally be advisable to make an election under ITEPA 2003, s 431 to be taxed on the initial 'unrestricted value' of the shares.

- They can look to the company to buy their shares where they wish to cease their involvement with the company. The value paid for their shares often depends on whether they are classed as a 'good' leaver (for example, ill-health or have reached retirement age) or 'bad' leaver.

Non-working shareholders

- Non-working shareholders may not be able to benefit from ER on a share buy-back unless they hold an office with the company (such as being a non-executive director)

- Non-working shareholders must participate in a corporate reconstruction.

Chapter 14

Valuing a Family or Owner-Managed Company

INTRODUCTION

14.1   Share valuations are required in a variety of situations. Commercial valuations fix the price at which shares in unquoted companies should change hands in actual transactions or where a valuation is sought for the purposes of a divorce settlement or financing arrangement. Tax legislation also requires shares to be valued in various circumstances giving rise to the need for fiscal or tax-based valuations. This chapter discusses commercial and tax based valuations. It will be seen that although similar concepts apply to both these types of valuation, there are marked differences in approach.

COMMERCIAL VALUATIONS

14.2   Commercial share valuations determine the price to be paid for the shares where, for example:

(*a*)   the shareholders wish to sell the company or a prospective purchaser wishes to make an offer for the company;

(*b*)   a shareholder is retiring and is required to sell his shares to the other shareholders or back to the company under an own share purchase (see 13.31–13.56).

The price will essentially be negotiated, based on all the relevant circumstances at that time.

14.3   A commercial value inevitably reflects the circumstances of both the vendor and the purchaser in that it seeks to arrive at a negotiated value reflecting what the vendor is giving up and what the purchaser acquires as a result of the acquisition.

VALUATIONS REQUIRED UNDER THE COMPANY'S ARTICLES OF ASSOCIATION

14.4   The Articles of Association for the vast majority of private companies will contain pre-emption provisions restricting the shareholder's ability to transfer their shares. Typically, any shareholder proposing to transfer their shares (other than to a member of their family or family trust) is obliged to offer them first to the other shareholders or the directors or to someone nominated by the directors. These provisions will need to be examined carefully where the shareholder wishes to dispose of their shares on 'retirement', etc.

The Articles will also provide a mechanism for fixing the price (value) and often requires the amount to be determined by the company's auditors. The Articles may, for example, require the shares to be valued on a discounted minority basis or on a full pro-rata one. A full pro-rata value would normally be such proportion of the (full 'control') value of the entire equity shares as the relevant shares (being valued) bear to the total number of issued equity shares.

Alternatively, the transferor may be required to state the price required for their shares and this will be used provided the directors agree it. In some cases, the Articles may provide a formula to be used by the auditor or other professional 'valuer'. A requirement to value the shares at their 'fair' value differs from the 'market value' basis in so far as it is presumed to be *fair to both parties* to the transaction.

Such share valuations are often based on a straight pro-rata proportion of the company's value. The Law Commission report on 'Shareholder Remedies' (Law Com No 246) proposed that the company's shareholders should be able to elect for the valuation to be discounted for minority shareholdings. A 'fair value' basis may also be relevant where a company purchases its own shares. The value placed on the vendor's shares may need to reflect some of the increase in value accruing to the other shareholders (resulting from the increase in their proportionate holdings following the 'buy-in').

VALUE OF COMPANY

Gathering empirical data of similar deals, etc

14.5   Where the shareholders are seeking to sell the entire company, they will require an indication of how much the company is worth. The capitalised earnings basis (ie applying an appropriate multiple to the sustainable profits of the business) is the principal determinant of value. Empirical evidence of prices at which similar/comparable businesses have recently changed hands will provide a very important guide. Details of recent disposals can be obtained from a wide variety of sources, including:

- The Financial Times (historical statistics);

- Reuters Investor (www.reuters.co.uk);

- Acquisitions Monthly;

- Investors Chronicle;

- CORPFIN and similar databases; and

- industry trade press.

The general economic climate, the state of the particular industry in which the company trades and its particular position within it will also influence the valuation.

In many ways, a company is worth what somebody is prepared to pay for it. Consequently, the 'price' can also reflect the prospective purchaser's rationale for acquiring the business, for example, to achieve increased market share, economies of scale and so on. An attempt should be made to quantify the financial benefits (such as post-acquisition synergies, etc) accruing to the purchaser.

Capitalised earnings model

14.6   The commercial valuation of a company or business is essentially a matter for negotiation between the vendor and the purchaser. The basic approach is to determine what the company or business can earn or realise. The majority of company and business valuations are based on earnings. A capitalised earnings valuation requires an estimate of the business's future maintainable earnings and the application of an appropriate rate of return or price/earnings (P/E) multiple.

Standard industry methods

14.7   It should be noted that certain industries have well established 'benchmark' valuation methods. For example hotels (price per room), advertising agencies (multiple of billings), professional firms (multiple of fee income), radio stations (multiple of hours listened), etc. These valuations are geared to the fact that the purchaser is willing to pay for turnover or market share and that profitability and margins are relatively similar within a given industry sector.

Discounted cash flow basis

14.8   Some would argue that the value of a controlling interest should be based on discounted cash flow (DCF) as the purchaser/investor is ultimately only interested in cash generation (which is not affected by accounting policies). This approach would require details of the forecast cash flows over a substantial period of time, which would then be discounted at an appropriate interest rate – the interest rate would reflect the time value of money and the investor's perception of the risk inherent in the investment. The sum of the discounted cash flows would give the net present value of the investment.

A DCF valuation may be used for new business ventures where there is no track record or trading history – such as e-commerce business applications, or where the business has an erratic cashflow profile.

Although this is a theoretically defensible approach, in practice the purchaser/investor often has insufficient details to perform this type of calculation.

MAINTAINABLE EARNINGS

14.9

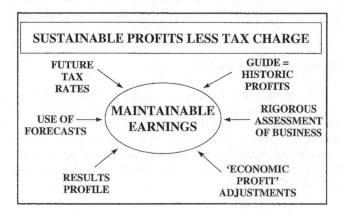

Determining the sustainable profits

14.10 The principal determinant of business valuations is usually the capitalised earnings basis. Historic profits are generally taken as a starting point for determining a company's *maintainable or sustainable profits* as they are based on actual trading results and provide readily ascertainable (and audited) figures.

Maintainable earnings represent the maintainable profits after deducting the appropriate future tax charge (and any preference dividend). Historical profits will only provide a guide to the business's future maintainable earnings. A rigorous assessment of the company's reported accounting profits will be required to quantify the adjustments needed to arrive at the true sustainable economic profit of the business.

Potential items that may require adjustment are:

- any exceptional or non-recurring items – such as the loss of a major customer or substantial bad debt write off, profits or/and losses on the sale of fixed assets, investments, etc;

- income and expenses relating to discontinued or new operations and products;

- departures from generally accepted accounting principles (GAAP);

- excessive directors' remuneration and benefits, pension contributions and so on, which reflect returns to the directors in their capacity as owner-shareholders – this 'excess' element is effectively a 'quasi-dividend', as this would not be paid to an arm's length management team (conversely, if the directors extract 'their' profits wholly or substantially as dividends the profits will need to be adjusted to reflect the commercial costs for their management or other roles in the business);

- business transactions that are not conducted on arm's length terms, such as the benefit of an interest-free loan from a controlling shareholder or fellow group company.

Indicators of future sustainable profits

14.11   It is important to remember that the historical profits are being used as a guide to the business's *future* profit levels. As a general rule, if the adjusted profits reflect a stable position, it will often be appropriate to use the last reported results as a basis for the future maintainable profits. Where the trading history is volatile, a 'judgemental' average may be used. Weighted averages should not be applied as a matter of course, as their theoretical justification is weak. The valuer may be required to exercise a commercial judgement to evaluate the business's prospective profits.

Forecasts or projections may be used as a guide provided it is recognised that they are based on certain assumptions and are potentially unreliable (vendors clearly have a 'vested' interest in suggesting high future profits!). Future trading plans (such as the impact of new products) and market conditions must also be 'factored' into the estimate of future maintainable profits. The performance of the general economy also tends to have a significant bearing on the company's future profitability.

Clearly, an assessment of future earnings is likely to be made when valuing a company with potential high growth but with no historic track record such as an online gambling business – the current volatility in this sector should, however, dictate a degree of cautious prudence in estimating earnings and prospective/exit multiples.

Dealing with surplus assets

14.12 As the earnings basis values a company's ability to generate earnings, income from 'surplus' assets and investments that are not required for generating the operating trading profits must be *excluded* from the maintainable 'earnings' figure. The vendor may often be required or wish to extract 'surplus' assets (often of a 'private' nature) before the company is sold. In appropriate cases, the market value of surplus assets is then added to the earnings-based figure to arrive at the total valuation of the company.

Future tax rate

14.13 Once the maintainable profits have been determined an appropriate future tax rate is applied to arrive at the maintainable earnings. The main corporate tax rate is normally used (26% for the year ended 31 March 2012, reducing 1% each year to 23% for the year ended 31 March 2015)) unless the company is likely to benefit from the small profits rate or there are substantial relievable tax losses, etc.

PRICE/EARNINGS (P/E) MULTIPLE OR RATE OF RETURN

14.14

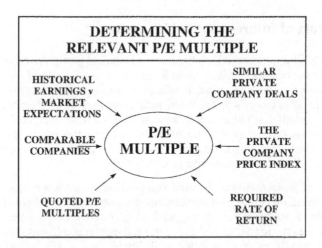

The investor's required rate of return

14.15 The amount that an investor is willing to pay for an investment is based on their required rate of return. If the investor's rate of return is not known, then it can be determined from comparable recent deals in the market.

The rate of return comprises the 'risk-free' rate (such as that earned on gilts) plus the 'risk premium' (based on the risk inherent in the investment, for example, the uncertainty of whether future earnings will be achieved, uncertain trading conditions). This is invariably difficult to quantify and largely depends on the individual investor's attitude to risk. The conceptual relationship between the rate of return required and the varying degrees of investment risk is illustrated graphically below.

The primary company/business valuation model (ignoring future growth in earnings) is as follows:

$$\text{value} = \frac{\text{Maintainable earnings}}{\text{Required rate of return}}$$

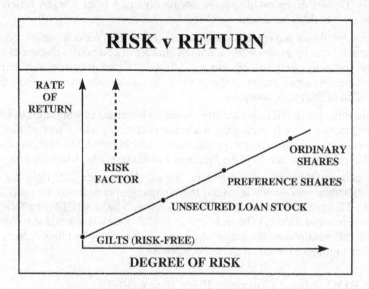

Price/earnings (P/E) multiples

14.16 More typically, business/company valuations are determined by using the P/E ratio or multiple (*which is the reciprocal of the rate of return or earnings yield*). The P/E multiple is then *multiplied* by the maintainable earnings. It should be noted that the published P/E ratios of publicly traded companies are generally derived from the prices obtained from transactions in very small holdings, although at times the market price may be heavily influenced by institutional investors, speculators and potential takeover bids.

The P/E multiple is calculated as:

$$\frac{\text{Price per share}}{\text{Net earnings per share}}$$

Earnings per share is defined in FRS 14, 'Earnings Per Share'. Broadly, it represents the profits attributable to each ordinary share, based on the (consolidated) net profit/loss after deducting taxation and, where appropriate, minority interests and preference dividends. The P/E ratio can be thought of as the number of years earnings per share represented by the share price.

Selecting an appropriate P/E multiple

14.17   Considerable judgement is required when selecting an appropriate P/E ratio or multiple. Clearly, empirical evidence of prices at which similar or comparable businesses have changed hands will provide a very important guide. Details of recent disposals can be obtained from a wide variety of sources – see 14.5 for details.

If such details are not readily available, published P/Es for comparable quoted companies can be used – select a limited number of companies that are closest to the company being valued. Since published P/Es are based on transactions involving very small minority stakes, they may need to be increased to reflect the value of the entire company.

On the other hand, P/E ratios are often based on historical earnings figures while share prices generally anticipate market expectations. The effect of this lag between (low) historical earnings and share prices based on future expectations can be quite pronounced and the P/E ratio would need to be discounted for this.

If a comparable company cannot be found, the average P/E ratio for the industrial/business sector in which the company operates may be used as a guide. This can be found in the FT Actuaries Share Indices (FTASI) published in the Financial Times. (The industry sector P/E index is a weighted average of the P/E multiples of the major companies in the sector and thus reflects the market's rating of the larger quoted companies.)

The BDO Private Company Price Index (PCPI)

14.18   The BDO Private Company Price Index (PCPI) is especially useful when valuing private companies. The PCPI is the arithmetical mean of the P/E ratios achieved on actual private company sales completed in the relevant quarter period where sufficient information has been disclosed. BDO also track the average P/E ratios of deals involving a private equity buyer – known as the Private Equity Price Index (PEPI).

It should be noted that as private companies are often owner-managed, their reported or published profits may be lower than they would be after they are sold. This means that it might sometimes give misleading information, since it does not take into account the 'inside information' on which the actual sale price is based.

For example, the owner-managers may have remunerated themselves generously. Very often, private companies also tend to incur expenses that would not continue to be paid post-sale. On this basis, the PCPI may be slightly overstated. On the other hand, some companies' profits may be overstated because the owner-managers may have rewarded themselves via large dividends (rather than bonuses). All these differences would have been adjusted in arriving at the amount paid for the company but may not be apparent from the publicly available profit data used to calculate the sale price. In fact in *Elliott v Planet Organic Ltd* [2000] BCC 610 (at p 615), the PCPI was referred to as a 'flimsy guide' but it was still followed by the court!

The PCPI is often regarded as the most authoritative source on private company valuations by leading accountancy firms and HMRC's Shares & Asset Valuation team.

The table below provides a useful quarterly comparison between:

* the P/E ratios (based on a four-month rolling average) for the Financial Times non-financial (listed) companies (FTNFs) (FT non-financial companies excludes property and insurance companies); and

* the PCPI; and

* the PEPI.

Table – BDO – Comparative FTNFs, and PEPI P/E multiples from Q1 2008 to Q2 2011

Quarter	FT Non-Financials P/E (four month moving average)	PCPI	PEPI
March 2008	12.8	13.2	12.9
June 2008	12.4	11.3	11.1
Sept 2008	11.0	11.5	11.2
Dec 2008	9.0	11.5	11.6
March 2009	8.5	10.1	10.4
June 2009	9.3	11.1	11.8
Sept 2009	12.4	11.7	12.3
Dec 2009	15.1	11.9	12.0
March 2010	14.8	12.0	13.3
June 2010	12.5	12.1	11.3
Sept 2010	12.6	10.7	13.0
Dec 2010	12.5	12.0	11.2
March 2011	12.1	9.0	10.8
June 2011	11.9	10.8	10.8

The table (for the quarter to June 2011) shows that private companies are being sold (on average) for 10.8 times their historical post-tax profits. The corresponding four monthly average figure P/E for the FT Non-Financials is 11.9 .

Where companies are being sold to private equity buyers, the average exit multiple is 10.8 times their historic post-tax profits.

The PCPI and PEPI are both average measures and should be used in that context. Many other factors will also influence the particular valuation.

The above table shows the 'discount' between the market valuations of (non-financial) 'quoted' and private companies. This enables private companies to be valued using the methodologies used to value public companies. The latest figures show that market prices are gradually recovering from their low point during the depth of the slump in 2008. Sellers' price expectations have marginally improved, although some potential buyers will probably look for some form of earn-out based on future performance, given that the trading conditions are still relatively fragile.The overall trend is that quoted P/E multiples must still be appropriately discounted in arriving at a suitable multiple for an unquoted company (bearing in mind that unquoted companies are often smaller and their shares are not readily marketable).

Another factor that needs to be recognised is that the prices (and hence P/E multiples) of quoted companies are invariably determined from market transactions of small minority shareholders. Thus, in a takeover scenario, the price would be substantially increased to reflect a 'bid' premium.

EBITDA multiples

14.19 EBITDA (earnings before interest, tax, depreciation, and amortisation) is another commonly used valuation tool, particularly in the US and Europe. The EBITDA multiple values a company independently of its financing structure and tax position, enabling (arguably) more meaningful comparisons to be made between companies. When the EBITDA multiple is applied to a company's sustainable earnings (before interest and taxation and depreciation), this produces the so-called 'enterprise value'.

When the company's debt is deducted from (or the net cash is added to) the enterprise value, this gives a value for the company's equity shares.

Many valuers will simply 'add back' interest costs and depreciation charges to arrive at a maintainable EBITDA figure to which an appropriate EBITDA multiple is applied. It is not always easy to obtain published EBITDA data. However, it should often be possible to derive estimated EBITDA information from published p/e data, which can be appropriately adjusted (reduced) to 'add-back' the effect of taxation, depreciation, and interest costs.

NET ASSET VALUATIONS

Basic net asset valuation principles

14.20   A valuation based on 'net assets' is not a true method of determining a going concern value for a trading company. A net asset based valuation will involve calculating the total *current* value of assets less current and long-term liabilities (properties, etc, may therefore need to be revalued). Net asset valuations are inherently subjective, for example, estimating the value of used plant and equipment can be difficult. Such valuations also ignore goodwill, unless purchased goodwill is recorded in accordance with GAAP.

Use of net asset valuations

14.21   A net asset value can be viewed as a prudent method of valuation, as it ignores the risks inherent with future earnings, etc. Companies with poor profits or large losses may have a going concern ('earnings') valuation which is less than their net asset backing.

In certain situations, the company may only have a 'value' on a liquidation. Winding-up valuations should recognise the 'break-up' value of the assets and the closure costs.

A more common situation is one where the going concern value is less than the 'net asset' value, but where it is still worthwhile for the business to continue. This shortfall in net asset value is known as 'negative goodwill'.

Net asset values are really only directly applicable:

- for companies with quality assets, such as property investment and hotel businesses;

- where the company's assets are being 'under-utilised' (ie the profits do not provide an adequate return on the assets);

- where the business is making substantial losses and there is a strong likelihood of liquidation/'break-up'.

Validation check on 'goodwill'

14.22   After computing an earnings based valuation, further comfort is usually obtained by computing a net asset valuation. A net asset valuation is based on the company's balance sheet values, adjusted to reflect the current market value of properties, intellectual property and possible stock write-downs, etc.

The difference between the earnings based valuation and the net asset value of the company represents the goodwill valuation. The purchaser will then ask whether the amount effectively being paid for goodwill is appropriate, given the nature of the business and the current economic climate.

Special considerations

14.23 The basis of valuation will primarily depend on the vendor's reason for selling and the purchaser's rationale for making the acquisition. In practice, the skill is to determine the correct basis of valuation. In certain cases, the valuation would also need to reflect the benefits of synergy with the purchaser's existing business, the costs of merging with the purchaser's existing business, etc (see 14.28–14.30).

If a company is loss making, the value will be based on the future perception of the business and its prospects for recovery, (ie is it only a temporary downturn or will the company cease to exist?). In the latter case, a break-up value of the assets would be appropriate with adjustments to reflect the forced sale value of assets, irrecoverable debts and termination costs, etc.

14.24 There is likely to be difficulty in assessing the maintainable earnings of companies with little or no track record. Forecast profits are likely to be used as a basis for valuation, but a purchaser would need to be comfortable with the underlying assumptions. In practice, a purchaser is likely to make part of the sale price contingent on profit warranties or value the business in 'hindsight' by using an earn-out (see 15.57).

Example 1

Valuation of company – case study

Cottee Ltd operates a chain of retail outlets selling high quality hi-fi and multi-media equipment. The retail outlets are situated in a number of 'affluent' towns. The company also provides a complete sound and media support facility for conferences and corporate events, which contributes healthy margins to the company's overall results.

It is necessary to value the company in September 2011 to gauge the price that could be expected on a future sale of the company. The most appropriate basis of valuing the company is by reference to its earning capacity.

Recent trading history

The recent results of Cottee Ltd (all audited) are summarised as follows:

	Year ended 30 September		
	2009	2010	2011
	£'000	£'000	£'000
Turnover	840	760	790
Profits before directors' remuneration	320	266	340
Directors' remuneration	(90)	(95)	(141)
Trading profit before interest	230	171	199
Interest	(10)	(8)	(7)
Profit before taxation	220	163	192
Taxation	(52)	(41)	(43)
Profit after taxation	168	122	149
Effective tax rate	23%	25%	22%

Maintainable earnings

14.25 Based on discussions with the company's management, the year ended 30 September 2010 was the worst trading period in recent years, reflecting the impact of the recession and the slowdown in consumer spending on 'luxury goods', such as hi-fi equipment. However, the year to 30 September 2011 shows a marginal improvement indicating that the worst may be over. Given that current trading conditions look reasonably stable, it would be prudent to estimate maintainable (*pre-tax*) profits at around £200,000.

The accounts would then be analysed for any unusual items, etc and for adherence to standard accounting policies, which give rise to the following adjustments.

Example 2

Maintainable earnings computation

	£'000	£'000
Maintainable profits		
Estimated to be		200
Adjustments		
Reduction in depreciation charge (company's rates more prudent than the norm)		25
Excessive directors' remuneration (based on prevailing industry rates for two directors) (£141,000 – £100,000)		41
		266
Less Taxation (£286,000 × (say) future rate of 21%)		(56)
MAINTAINABLE EARNINGS		210

Selecting an appropriate P/E ratio

14.26 The assessment of an appropriate P/E ratio is obviously a subjective exercise, and there are many factors that need to be considered.

A survey of recent comparable transactions revealed that a small hi-fi discount stores chain retailer had sold out in December 2010 on a multiple of 6.

The 'exit' multiples for the majority of *smaller* unquoted companies have historically stood at a 20% to 30% discount to (non-financial) quoted companies.

On 16 September 2011 , the majority of the quoted P/Es in the general retailers section fell within the range of 5 to 15 based on historic results. The FTSE Actuaries All Shares P/E index for the general retailers sector was 9.46 . The FTSE 350 stood at 8.60 .

When valuing smaller owner-managed companies, it is accepted that a discount should be applied against comparable publicly quoted companies (see comments in 14.17).

In September 2011, the general outlook for the UK economy remained bleak, with GDP growth forecasts being revised to just 1.1% for 2011 and 1.3% for 2012. This shows that the recovery continues to be weak.

A reasonable degree of caution must therefore be exercised in the 'valuation' judgment as there is still some way to go before the economy stabilises.

Cottee Ltd is a relatively small company and, based on all the above data , a P/E ratio of 5 is considered appropriate.

Example 3

Value of Cottee Ltd

Maintainable earnings (per 14.25):	£210,000
P/E (per 14.26):	5
Value of the whole of the issued share capital of Cottee Limited £210,000 × 5 =	£1,050,000

Given the limited information available, on 27 September 2011 , the shares could be valued in the range of £900,000 and £1,100,000.

Quasi-partnership valuations

14.27 Many companies are incorporated on the principle of a 'quasi-partnership', which can often have a significant impact on their share valuations. In such cases, the articles or shareholding agreement will usually provide that the shares are subject to pre-emption transfers at the pro-rata value (of the company) without any minority discount being applied.

This principle was affirmed (by the Privy Council) in *CVC/Opportunity Equity Partners Ltd v Demarco Almeida* [2002] 2 BCLC 108, which involved an 'unfair prejudice' action brought by a minority shareholder. Applying the dicta in the important case of *Ebrahimi v Westbourne Galleries* [1973] AC 360, Lord Millett highlighted the main characteristics of a 'quasi-partnership' company, which include:

- a business association formed or continued on the basis of a personal relationship of mutual trust and confidence;

- an understanding or agreement that all or some of the shareholders should participate in the management of the business; and

- restrictions on the transfer of shares so that a member cannot realise their stake if they were excluded from the business.

In essence, the shareholders have used a corporate vehicle to carry on a business that could easily have been run by them as a partnership. A quasi-partnership valuation may be appropriate where a member has been unfairly prejudiced and brings a successful action under *CA 2006, s 994*. Where the courts find that a quasi-partnership exists, it may require the relevant member's shares to be purchased at a pro-rata value of the company (ie based on a notional sale) without being reduced by any minority discount (see also *Re Bird Precision Bellows Ltd* [1984] 3 All ER 444). Shares in 'husband and wife' companies are often dealt with in a similar way in divorce cases.

PURCHASER VALUATION ISSUES

Purchaser 'pricing' issues

14.28 A prospective purchaser will normally seek an assessment of the target business's future earnings stream. This will entail a detailed assessment of the post-acquisition earnings of the target business after adjusting for the financial impact of proposed changes. For example, the earnings could reflect the anticipated cost savings of fewer directors/managers being required after the acquisition and certain other economies of scale. Further adjustments may be necessary to reflect different financing structures and judgment about future trading conditions, etc (see 14.29–14.30). As a general rule, the purchaser should not pay more than the acquisition is worth to *them*.

The purchase price – the amount that is required for the deal to be accepted by the vendor(s) – should be less than the 'synergy value' to the purchaser. Synergy value represents the net present value of cash flows that will flow from the synergy and improvements that are made post-acquisition.

Synergy value

14.29 Synergy value will reflect:

- cost savings, such as job cuts, economies of scale, reducing duplication of facilities, etc;

- reduced funding costs (resulting from the pooling of working capital finance resources and cash surpluses);

- tax benefits.

Earnings multiple valuation

14.30 In practice, many purchasers will use the normal earnings multiple approach to evaluate whether the price they are being asked to pay for the business is sensible. The purchaser's view of prospective earnings will be adjusted to reflect the structure and operations of the company/business post-acquisition. Thus, the earnings could reflect the anticipated cost savings of fewer directors/managers being required and certain other economies of scale. Further adjustments may be necessary to reflect different financing structures and the purchaser's judgment about future trading conditions, etc.

Using an earn-out to resolve the 'price-gap'

14.31   Negotiations for the sale of a company often reveal a gap between the vendor's asking price (often based on 'next years' profits!) and the purchaser's view of its value, which is generally based on the company's most recent audited accounts and often a cynical view of its projected profits.

The 'earn-out' type deal evolved to reconcile this 'price gap', enabling the company to be sold for an amount which depended on its future results and enabling both parties to strike a deal which they might otherwise have been unable to achieve.

A typical earn-out scenario is where the target business has been built up and still relies upon the technical ability or creative flair of its few owner-managers. The purchaser can ensure that the value of the business is preserved and enhanced by retaining the vendor's services during the earn-out period, secured by an appropriate service agreement. During this period, the vendor will concentrate on enhancing the company's profitability.

Earn-out deals are commonly used on the sale of 'service' type businesses. In such cases, there is typically no strong 'asset-backed' balance sheet and the purchaser will also have concerns about the business retaining its key personnel post-completion.

If the vendor is successful, they will obtain large 'earn-out' payments, thus increasing the total consideration for the sale of their shares. However, 'earn-outs' often pose particular tax problems for the vendor which must be addressed (see 15.57–15.60).

FISCAL OR TAX-BASED VALUATIONS

Why fiscal valuations are required

14.32   Fiscal or tax-based valuations are required by the tax legislation in various situations, for example:

(*a*)   shares held at 31 March 1982 must be valued at that date for rebasing purposes;

(*b*)   shares transferred otherwise than at arm's length must be valued (although if hold-over relief can be claimed both parties can elect to dispense with the valuation (see (13.18));

(c)   determining the value of shares chargeable to inheritance tax on death or by reason of a lifetime transfer becoming chargeable on a death within seven years;

(d)   determining the taxable employment income arising on shares (including restricted securities) made available to employees (see Chapter 8 and 13.29–13.36), or to ensure that no such benefit arises when shares are made available under a formal approved employee share scheme;

(e)   determining the value of shares which are the subject of options granted under an Enterprise Management Incentive (EMI) scheme, an approved Company Share Option Plan (CSOP) or an unapproved share plan (see Chapter 8).

Arm's length and connected party share transfers

14.33   Shares transferred otherwise than at arm's length are deemed to be transferred at their open market value. This will always be the case where shares are sold or gifted to a connected person (*TCGA 1992, s 18*). Shares passing between unconnected persons are treated as being by way of a bargain at arm's length, unless exceptionally, there is donative intent. This was considered in *Bullivant Holdings Ltd v CIR* [1998] STC 905. The High Court upheld the Special Commissioner's decision that the amount paid for two 25% shareholdings acquired from two unconnected individuals was a full and fair price, even though it appeared to be very low based on the relevant facts. Nevertheless, the evidence supported that the deal was struck by the parties at arm's length.

It is possible that the commercial price agreed on a sale of shares between unconnected parties may differ from the open market value arrived at for tax purposes. The actual conditions and information on which the sale is based will be different from the hypothetical assumptions and case law which govern the determination of market value for tax purposes.

If the actual consideration for a sale of shares appears to be considerably different from their market value, it is important that sufficient evidence is retained, such as documentary evidence of real negotiations between the parties showing they each took separate legal and commercial advice. This can then be used to demonstrate to HMRC (if a challenge was made) that the transaction was freely negotiated and no gratuitous benefit was intended.

BASIC VALUATION CONCEPTS

Open market value

14.34   The statutory rules for determining market value are deceptively simple. In *TCGA 1992, s 272(1)* and *IHTA 1984, s 160(1)*, the market value is the price which those assets/the property might reasonably be expected to fetch if sold in the open market. There is of course no open market for unquoted shares. A considerable body of case law and practice has therefore been built up over the last hundred or so years to provide the conceptual framework for valuing unquoted shares. Although valuations are carried out on an academic basis, it must always be remembered that share valuation is an art not a science; or 'intelligent guesswork' as Mr Justice Dankwerts called it in *Holt v CIR* [1953] 1 WLR 1488.

The value of a share is therefore what the valuer can successfully argue it to be. The tax or taxes on which the valuation turns will have a bearing on the situation. For example, if the shares are being valued for March 1982 rebasing purposes, as high a value as possible will be negotiated. If the same shares were being valued on death for IHT, a (much) lower value is likely to be argued for.

Hypothetical sale

14.35   The main principles were succinctly summarised by Mr Plowman J in *Re Lynall (deceased)* (1971) 47 TC 375. Unquoted shares are to be valued on the basis of a hypothetical sale, based on a price that could be reasonably expected to be paid:

(*a*)   by a hypothetical willing purchaser;

(*b*)   to a hypothetical willing vendor;

(*c*)   in the open market.

The value has to be the best price that could be obtained by the vendor (whose actual identity is irrelevant) in an arm's length bargain in the open market. To put it another way, we have to imagine that the shares are being offered for sale to the whole world and the value is the best price obtainable from the competing bids. For this purpose, the restrictions on the transfer of shares normally found in most Articles of Association are disregarded in the hypothetical open market, although the purchaser is deemed to take the shares subject to those restrictions.

This concept of the hypothetical purchaser was addressed in *Grays Timber Products Ltd v CIR* [2010] UKSC4, which considered whether shares with enhanced rights on a sale should be taken into account when arriving at their market value. (Although this was for determining whether the shares were sold for more than their market value under *ITEPA 2003, s 446X*, the same CGT valuation principles applied.) A key finding in the judgement was that if these rights are personal to a shareholder they would be of no value to the hypothetical purchaser'. This is because such rights would be extinguished on sale and thus cannot be transmitted to the purchaser. Thus, it followed that no purchaser would ever pay for them.

This followed the principle established in *CIR v Crossman* [1937] AC 26 which requires the hypothetical purchaser to step into the seller's shoes' in the sense that he acquires the same property but does not take on the seller's personal characteristics (see also 8.36).

Grays Timber Products was decided on its own special facts. The problems created by the ruling can be overcome by providing the enhanced rights in the articles to a particular class of shares (since they would be transferable to a (hypothetical) purchaser.

Although the same valuation rules generally apply for both CGT and IHT, there is a fundamental difference between the computational approach. For CGT purposes, the valuation normally relates to the shares that are being disposed of (subject to the special rules in *TCGA 1992, s 19* – see 13.11). IHT valuations will normally seek to establish the loss to the transferor's estate, and will therefore involve valuing the transferor's shareholding both before and after the transfer (as opposed to the actual holding being transferred) (see 17.5). In most cases, this will mean that the value of the shares transferred for CGT and IHT purposes will differ. Where CGT hold-over relief is claimed under either *TCGA 1992, s 165* or *260* an election can be made to avoid a formal valuation of the shares (see 13.18).

Deemed information standards

14.36 The hypothetical willing purchaser is assumed to be reasonably prudent and will therefore obtain all information that would be reasonably required (see *TCGA 1992, s 273(3)* and *IHTA 1984, s 168*). According to *HMRC's Share Valuation Manual (Chapter II)*, regard must be had to the 'information that is reasonably available to the purchaser of the particular shareholding being acquired'. This would depend on such things as

- the physical availability of the information (it must actually be available although may not be published); and

- the influence of the potential purchaser (either in terms of voting power or the cost/size of the investment.

The relevant details required would largely depend on the size of the shareholding and the amount of capital invested. For example, a prudent hypothetical purchaser acquiring a controlling interest would certainly require detailed knowledge about the relevant company. This would include the company's historic and current year financial accounts, budgets and forecasts, details of remuneration paid to directors, arrangements with major customers and suppliers and so on.

On the other hand, less information would be available to a purchaser of a minority stake (eg published information only), unless a 'significant' sum was being invested.

A greater amount of information is therefore required as the size of the relevant shareholding and 'weight of money' invested increases. For example, in *Administrators of the Estate of Caton (deceased) v Couch* [1995] STC (SCD) 34, [1997] STC 970, it was accepted that a hypothetical purchaser considering an investment of £1,000,000, representing only a minority holding of

14.02%, would have required access to confidential management information. Consequently, the purchaser would have reasonably required details as well as up-to-date information from management accounts and budget forecasts. Relevant details about the sale prospects were taken into account in the valuation process and the potential sale value was discounted by 50% (reflecting the fact that no formal offer had been made).

HMRC Shares & Asset Valuation (SAV) take the view that, if the shareholding is small (ie less than 5%) and large sums of money are not involved, a prospective purchaser would only have access to published information. In *Clark (executor of Clark, deceased) v Green* [1995] STC (SCD) 99, a small minority holding of 3% (agreed to be worth over £168,000) was held to be of insufficient size or outlay for a prospective purchaser to have reasonably required information about a possible sale, but did reasonably require unpublished management accounts regarding the recently completed financial year.

Shareholder rights and voting power

14.37   The valuation will primarily be influenced by the relative size of the shareholding. Majority/controlling shareholdings confer greater rights and power than minority/non-controlling shareholdings and are therefore worth more per share. It is usually helpful to allocate the shares being valued into one of the following categories.

Voting power	Rights of shareholder
90% or more	Can accept offer to sell shares in company and can give purchaser compulsory power to acquire remaining shares. Enjoys total control of company.
75%–89.9%	Has effective control of the company. Has requisite votes to pass a special resolution and can put the company into liquidation or sell it as a going concern.
50.1%–74.9%	Enjoys day to day control (but cannot pass special resolution).
50%	May have shared control or a deadlock situation. Can block an ordinary resolution regarding normal business requirements. Value would depend on spread of other shareholdings.
25.1%–49.9%	Influential minority – has right to block a special resolution (which requires 25% of the votes). Value would depend on spread of other shareholdings.
10.1%–25%	Small minority, but cannot be bought out by majority.
Up to 10%	Small minority liable to forced sale on a takeover under compulsory purchase legislation.

Comparison between majority and minority shareholders

14.38 Majority shareholders (having more than 50% of votes) can pass an ordinary resolution. They therefore enjoy practical command of the company, being able to decide the company's dividend policy, level of directors' remuneration and can often determine whether the company should be sold, floated, or wound up. A control holding will therefore be based on the value of the entire company. In the case of a going concern, the value will be based on the company's underlying profitability and hence the earnings basis of valuation is normally used for trading companies (see 14.9–14.17).

In contrast, minority shareholders are relatively impotent. They do not have control and the value of their holding would be primarily determined by the rights in the company's Articles of Association, the size of their own holding and the spread of other shareholdings. Frequently the Articles will impose a restriction on the right to transfer shares, subject to the Board's discretion. The minority shareholder will therefore be locked in and would not usually have any effective sanction against the Board of Directors. The restricted rights of a minority shareholder therefore produce a much lower valuation.

As dividends generally constitute the return for the minority shareholder, such holdings may be valued on a dividend yield basis, particularly where the taxpayer wishes to establish a low valuation. However, many unquoted companies do not pay dividends even though there are sufficient earnings to do so or their dividend payment record may be erratic. In such cases, the preferred approach would be to value the holdings on an earnings yield basis, although a lower (ie discounted) P/E ratio would be applied than for a control holding. The level of discount varies according to the size of the holding and the spread of the other shareholdings (for example, a 40% shareholding may give practical control if the remaining shares are spread amongst ten shareholders).

Valuation discounts

14.39 There are no published formulae for discounts and HMRC – (Share and Assets Valuation (SAV)) usually succeed if the negotiations turn on the level of discount to be applied. Generally, discounts of between 45%–75% are sought by the Revenue for small minority holdings. For example, in *Administrators of the Estate of Caton (deceased) v Couch* [1995] STC (SCD) 34, [1997] STC 970, discounts of 60% to 70% were considered appropriate for a 14.02% holding in an unquoted trading company.

Where a shareholder holds 50% of the shares, but also has a casting vote as chairman, this does not give control in the context of a fiscal valuation of shares. A sale of the shares only is being placed in the hypothetical open market, and these do not carry control without the chairman's contract that gives the vital casting vote. A 50% shareholding is therefore treated as a 'dead-lock' holding and would often be subject to a 25% discount (subject to the size of the other holdings).

Lower discounts of 30 to 40% are normally applied for larger minority holdings of up to 49% (see SAV Manual). However, the level of discount will vary according to the circumstances of each case, such as the spread of the other shareholdings – it is generally a matter of negotiation. Use of the earnings basis avoids calculating notional dividends, which are less easy to support in negotiations with the Revenue. Earnings based valuations have become popular when valuing minority shareholdings for March 1982 rebasing purposes as this generally enables higher values to be negotiated with the Revenue.

EMPLOYEE SHARE VALUATIONS FOR EMPLOYMENT INCOME PURPOSES

Unrestricted shares

14.40 Where (non-restricted) shares are awarded to a director or employee at an undervalue, they are taxable as earnings under the *Weight v Salmon* (1935) 19 TC 174 principle. The value is based on the money or 'money's worth' that could be realised in the open market by the recipient employee. This focuses on the subjective benefit to the employee, the value being based on the employee's 'own' information or knowledge about the company's affairs – there is no 'deemed' information standard. (This may mean that employees with holdings of the same size may each have a different valuation, according to their 'personal' knowledge.) The inherent rights and restrictions attaching to the individual's shares such as under the Articles of Association would also be taken into account.

Unrestricted and restricted valuation bases

14.41 Where the shares are restricted (for example, they are subject to certain employee specific restrictions, such as the requirement to sell the shares at a reduced price on leaving), the CGT 'market value' basis must be used – see 14.34–14.36 (*ITEPA 2003, s 421(1)*). Inside information available to a director/employee purchaser is ignored for CGT (and IHT) based valuations – remember, it is an imaginary purchaser. Of course, this is where the (academic) assumptions upon which fiscal valuations are based differ from transactions in the real world.

In the vast majority of cases, an *ITEPA 2003, s 431* election will be made to base the tax charge on the 'unrestricted' market value of the shares (or UMV) (see 8.32). This will ensure that any subsequent growth in the value of the shares falls within the CGT regime. Consequently, the shares would be valued using normal CGT criteria, but would ignore the effect of any personal or employee specific restrictions relating to the shares. CGT valuation principles reflect the normal 'pre-emption' restrictions imposed on all shareholders by the articles (since the hypothetical purchaser takes the shares subject to those provisions). Based on recent experience with Shares Valuation, this may represent about 25% to 30% of the normal discount for a small minority holding. Much of that discount is likely to reflect the lack of marketability of the shares.

Where a 'restricted value' of the shares is required, this would necessarily reflect the detrimental impact of employee specific restrictions.

- *Specific restrictions on transfer* – A typical discount of between 2% to 4% per each year (of restriction) would be applied to the unrestricted market value, subject to an overriding total limit of 10% to 15% .

- *Forfeiture conditions* – These generally require the employee to sell their shares on 'leaving' for an amount that is less than their market value and may have a material impact on the fiscal share value in the case of a (increasingly) profitable company. The discount applied to the unrestricted value would be influenced by such factors as the length of the forfeiture period and the difference between the transfer price given on leaving and initial unrestricted value. Likely discounts would range between 10% to 20% of the unrestricted value.

- *Non-voting restrictions* – Traditionally, a discount of up to about 10% is often applied when valuing small holdings of non-voting shares (as compared with the equivalent voting shareholding). The unrestricted value of shares carrying temporary restrictions on voting would probably be discounted by 1% of every year of restriction (up to an overall limit of 10%).

- *Dividend restrictions* – This usually requires looking at the dividends likely to be paid by the company over the period of restriction. The total potential dividends are then discounted to their net present value, with a further discount being applied for the 'risk' element (recognising the financial and 'dividend-paying' prospects of the company and the period of restriction).

The 'risk discounted' net present value of the likely dividends forgone would then be deducted from the unrestricted value of the shares (and may also be expressed as a discount percentage of that unrestricted value).

HMRC now appear to contend that the standard pre-emption restrictions that invariably apply to private company shares would be sufficient to make them 'restricted'. However, it is debatable whether such 'restrictions' cause the share to have a lower valuation (as required by *ITEPA 2003, s 421*). In such cases, *s 431* elections are usually made on a protective basis to cover any 'valuation' risk.

Other employee share tax charges

14.42   For the purposes of computing the other various tax charges under the 'employment-related' securities legislation (in *ITEPA 2003, Pt 7, Chs*

2–5), such as on the exercise of unapproved share options, all relevant share valuations are subject to the statutory 'open market' basis of valuation that applies for CGT [*TCGA 1992, ss 272–273*] (see 14.34). The application of the 'market value' rules was tested in *Grays Timber Products Ltd v CIR* [2010] UKSC4 (see 14.35).

EMI and other approved share schemes

14.43   Valuations prepared to determine the market value of shares at the date of an EMI option grant have always followed the CGT valuation basis [*ITEPA 2003, Sch 5, para 55*]. Given that EMI valuations are typically 'minority-based', the hypothetical purchaser would only have access to publicly available information, such as the last published accounts, information on the company's website, press comments and so on (see 14.36). Such valuations should therefore ignore employee 'insider information'. However, in practice, (SAV) often request this information (such as the latest management accounts and budgets) and seek to take this data into account in agreeing share valuations at the grant date (see 8.19).

If the EMI option shares are 'restricted', the £120,000 limit on the market value over shares under EMI options will be based on the *unrestricted* market value of the shares (UMV), which is their value ignoring the effect of restrictions. However, under the EMI rules, employees will need to pay an option exercise price at least equal to the actual market value of the shares at the date of grant (i.e. the value taking into account the restrictions). Provided this is done, then an ITEPA 2003 s 431(1) election is specially deemed to have been made, thus ensuring that no part of any subsequent gain is subject to income tax.

However, where the option exercise price is 'discounted' (i.e. it is below the actual market value of the shares the 'grant date', then an actual s 431(1) election will be needed.

In theory, the CGT based value gives the UMV (which must then be discounted to reflect any restrictions).

The same valuation concepts also apply for determining the market value of shares under approved company share option and share incentive plans.

DEALING WITH HMRC – SHARES & ASSET VALUATION TEAM

Referral of valuations to HMRC – Shares & Asset Valuation team (SAV)

14.44   It is important to appreciate that Inspectors of Taxes and Examiners at the Capital Taxes Office must refer all share valuations and goodwill valuations to HMRC Share & Asset Valuation (referred to as 'SAV'). Where a share valuation is included on the tax return, the taxpayer must tick the CGT schedule on the self-assessment tax return to indicate that an 'estimated value' has been used. Any tax return incorporating a share valuation will be referred to SAV, unless the Inspector is able to resolve the matter by reference to a file held locally or there is little or no tax at stake.

The HMRC *Enquiry Handbook* indicates that SA tax returns including CGT valuations, estimates, etc may be taken up for review and these cases may lead to 'aspect' enquiries (where the Inspector only enquires into one or two specific aspects of the tax return).

Valuation 'aspect' enquiries

14.45 Where SAV wishes to challenge a valuation, it instructs the local Inspector to issue a notice of enquiry under *TMA 1970, s 9A*. The matter is then taken out of the local Inspector's hands. The SAV Examiner would send their individually tailored enquiries to the taxpayer or taxpayer's agent. While the share valuation is being negotiated, the taxpayer's tax return remains open, but HMRC will not enquire into unrelated matters once the normal enquiry period (of 12 months from the filing date) has passed (Statement of Practice 1/99).

Following the decision in *Langham v Veltema* [2004] STC 544, it is important to ensure that HMRC cannot subsequently raise 'discovery' assessments due to insufficient details being shown about the use of an 'un-agreed' share valuation. It is therefore recommended that tax returns should provide a note to the effect that the valuation may be incorrect. Clearly, this would not be necessary where the valuation has already been agreed by (SAV) under the post-transaction valuation check system (see 14.46).

Post-transaction valuation check procedure

14.46 A head start can be made in agreeing valuations by making use of SAV's 'Post Transaction Valuation Check Procedure'. This enables valuations to be sent to the tax office (soon) *after* the relevant transaction on form CG34 *before* the filing date for the SA return. If submitted early enough, this should considerably accelerate the negotiation and agreement of share valuations. SAV have indicated that it will give such cases priority attention (to avoid the need to issue *TMA 1970, s 9A* notices). A further benefit is that the maximum additional tax exposure (on the basis of SAV's alternate value) would be highlighted at an early stage.

Under the 'fast-track' system, the local district send the form CG34 to SAV which should either accept the value or put forward an acceptable alternative within 56 days. If SAV are unable to agree the valuation, they will enter into negotiations with the view to agreeing a value before the SA return filing deadline.

There will be cases where the value is submitted too late or where the valuation is complex which cannot realistically be settled before the SA return is submitted. In such cases, the SA tax return must still be submitted before the deadline with the taxpayer's proposed share valuation. If the share valuation is not agreed by nine months *after* the filing date for the tax return, the local inspector will be asked to issue a (protective) *TMA 1970, s 9A* notice. Where the final agreed valuation differs from the taxpayer's (estimated) valuation incorporated in the tax return, the taxpayer is invited to make an amendment to his self-assessment liability under *TMA 1970, s 28A*.

Share valuation reports

14.47   The writer's preferred approach is to submit a realistic share valuation report to SAV at the outset. The report would clearly set out all the relevant background information and the principles upon which the share valuation is based.

The main items covered in the report would be:

(*a*)   the purpose of valuation indicating which tax or taxes are involved;

(*b*)   the date on which the shares are being valued (this is critical as information which cannot be established at that date is not admissible);

(*c*)   the statutory principles upon which the value is based;

(*d*)   financial and trading background, this would include a summary of past results, trends, profit forecasts, shape of the company's order book, state of the industry in which the company operates, economic background and other factors affecting the valuation;

(*e*)   a clearly reasoned valuation, showing detailed calculations and the reasons for the various steps.

14.48   HMRC's Share Valuation examiners should not be underestimated – they have considerable experience and expertise and are armed with an extensive database. Examiners will always consider realistic valuation submissions carefully. It is unwise to submit an unrealistic valuation in anticipation of SAV starting from the opposite side, with a view to meeting somewhere in the middle. This approach usually signals a weakness to SAV which makes it easier for them to commence negotiations on very strong ground and the taxpayer will often find it very difficult to recover from this position.

The case of *Denekamp v Pearce* [1998] STC 1120 provides a useful reminder that all the relevant valuations and points must be presented in any appeal before the Special Commissioner. In this case, the taxpayer's attempt to persuade the High Court to include goodwill in his 31 March 1982 valuation was doomed to fail. This was not presented in his evidence before the Special Commissioner who gave a proper conclusion in the light of the evidence placed before him and the court could not subsequently intervene.

Fiscal share valuation techniques

14.49   Share valuations are normally based on one of the following methods (or sometimes a *weighted* combination of two or all three of them):

(i)   *Earnings (capitalised earnings) basis*

Maintainable earnings per share × P/E ratio.

(ii)   *Net assets basis*

Balance sheet value of net assets (after deducting liabilities), adjusted to reflect current open market value of assets (divided by number of shares in issue).

(iii)   *Dividend yield basis*

$$\frac{\text{Gross dividend }\%}{\text{Required gross dividend yield}} \times \text{Nominal value per share}$$

Earnings basis – majority shareholdings

14.50   On the basis that a company's profits provide an acceptable return from the assets employed, SAV will invariably value majority shareholdings by reference to the company's future maintainable earnings. The earnings basis was discussed in 14.9–14.17 and the same considerations apply where shares are valued for fiscal reasons.

14.51   The general approach is to look at the company's profit record for the last three years although a longer period may be necessary if the trade is cyclical. The profit record is used to give a guide to the company's future performance and various adjustments may therefore be required to reflect reasonable directors' remuneration and pension contributions. The SAV manual indicates that 'evidence suggests that a pension of up to 20% of the total directors' remuneration package is reasonable' (see also 14.10). A 'notional' tax charge is then applied to arrive at the maintainable or sustainable earnings.

The information assumed to be available to a prospective purchaser would be based on the size of the shareholding and the value of the transaction. For a controlling interest (of 50% or more) the purchaser would be deemed to have access to all the available financial information, including the possibility of a future sale, management accounts and the order book, etc (*Administrators of the Estate of Caton (deceased) v Couch SpC* [1995] SSCD 34; [1997] STC 970).

Hindsight information which becomes available after the date on which the value is being determined cannot be used to influence the valuation.

P/E multiples

14.52   The P/E multiple applied to the maintainable earnings is *best* assessed by looking at the ratios of comparable *unquoted* companies, ideally based on recent known company sales/takeovers.

If comparable reported transactions cannot be found, the P/E multiple for an appropriate comparable quoted company or industry sector is normally used (see 14.17) – HMRC's (SAV) manual discourages the use of *quoted* P/E multiples for valuing majority shareholdings. The P/E multiple for the quoted company/sector will usually need to be discounted to reflect the differences in prospects, size of company, geographical coverage, profitability, quality of management as compared with the unquoted company being valued.

Valuation discounts – majority holdings

14.53   Unless the company is wholly-owned, the value would be discounted to reflect the size of the controlling interest, which would normally be in the following regions:

Voting power	Discount %
99%–75%	5%–10%
below 75%	15%–20%

Earnings basis – minority holdings

14.54   Non-controlling shareholdings may also be valued on an earnings basis. A purchaser of an influential minority stake would be expected to have similar information but in less detail. The details provided for a small minority (5%–25%) would be dictated by the transaction value, ranging from full disclosure to the basic information contained in the published accounts, etc. For small minority holdings, 'excess' director's remuneration and pension contributions should *not* be added back to profits as such shareholders would not be able to influence the level of director's remuneration, etc. In the case of non-influential minority holdings, published accounts are only assumed to be available when signed. Valuation discounts normally sought for minority holdings by SAV are set out in 14.39.

Example 4

Valuation of controlling interest on earnings basis

Hunter's Butchers Ltd has carried on a long established family business of retail butchers and manufacturers of meat based products. Mr Hunter, who owns 80 of the company's 100 £1 ordinary shares, has received an offer for the company. He acquired his shareholding in 1971 on the death of his father and wishes to estimate the March 1982 value of the holding to compute his likely CGT liability.

The company's pre-tax profits for the three years to 31 December 1981 (adjusted for excessive director's remuneration) were as follows:

	£'000
y/e 31/12/79	238
y/e 31/12/80	207
y/e 31/12/81	382

Prospects for the business were good in March 1982 and management accounts showed increased monthly profits to that date. A supportable figure of maintainable profits would be £400,000.

The company's tax charge between 1979 and 1981 ranged between 25% and 30%, as a result of stock relief claims. It would therefore be appropriate to apply a tax charge of 30%.

Maintainable earnings:	£'000
Maintainable pre-tax profits	400
Less Tax at 30%	(120)
Maintainable earnings	280
Relevant P/E's for the food sector at 31 March 1982 were:	
Food manufacturing (average)	7.85
Food retailing (average)	13.77

Given that a 'control' holding is being valued, a P/E of 10 could prudently be taken.

Valuation of company:

= Maintainable earnings × P/E ratio

= £280,000 × 10

= £2,800,000

Value per share:

£2,800,000 × 100 = £28,000 per share

Value of Mr Hunter's 80 shares at 31 March 1982:

Discounted by 10%

£28,000 × 90% = £25,200 per share.

£25,200 × 80 shares = £2,016,000

NET ASSETS BASIS

When net asset valuations may be appropriate

14.55   Asset based valuations are adopted where:

- the company has substantial asset backing (such as property and investment companies);

- the company is about to go into liquidation; or

- a purchaser is likely to strip the assets out of the company and wind it up (usually if the assets are underutilised).

For example, in *Cash & Carry v Inspector* [1998] STC (SCD) 46 the trading results of a cash and carry business deteriorated steadily from 1978 to a loss making position in 1982. In this case, the company's shares were valued on a net assets basis, uplifted to reflect the market value of its property.

Furthermore, although a going concern value will normally be calculated by reference to earnings, it is always worthwhile valuing the business on an asset basis as a cross check. Material differences may need to be explained or investigated. Normally, the capitalised earnings basis should exceed the value of the tangible net assets with the difference being the goodwill element – is the goodwill figure reasonable in the circumstances? However, if the asset value exceeds the earnings basis, this could indicate that the earnings have been under-capitalised.

Going concern valuation

14.56   There are various types of asset based valuations. If the company is being valued as a going concern, then the open market value of its assets at the valuation date would be taken. The book value of the assets may therefore require adjustment. Although the balance sheet may fairly reflect the value of stock, debtors and possibly plant, a revaluation adjustment may be required in the case of land and buildings.

Break-up basis

14.57   If a 'break-up' basis of valuation is applicable (ie the value that would be realised on a liquidation), then the realisable value of the assets will be taken. The Revenue's Share Valuation manual suggests that a further reduction of between 10% and 30% of the net asset value may not be unreasonable for the asset stripper's profit.

14.58   The closure would also involve redundancy payments and other termination costs (for example, cancellation of lease agreements, etc), costs of liquidation and tax charges arising on the disposal of assets. For these reasons, the break-up value of the business is much lower than either a going concern or 'balance sheet' value.

Example 5

Net asset valuation

An extract from the balance sheet of Hunter's Butchers Ltd at 31 March 1982 (see Example 4 at 14.54), together with estimated market value, shows:

	Net book value	Market value
	£'000	£'000
Freehold shop premises	430	700
Leasehold shop premises	210	250
Processing Unit and Warehouse	100	450
Net current assets	980	
	1,720	

Current value of net assets

	£'000
Current market values of	
Freehold shops	700
Leasehold shops	250
Processing Unit and Warehouse	450
Net current assets	980
	£2,380

Value per share

$$= \frac{\text{Net asset value}}{\text{Number of shares}}$$

= £2,380,000 × 100

= £23,800 per share (before discount applicable to relevant shareholding).

SAV may seek a discount against this value to take account of the contingent CGT in the asset values. At 31 March 1982, this would be a maximum of 28% of the gain inherent in the shops and warehouse, reduced to reflect the remote probability of the tax becoming payable.

DIVIDEND YIELD BASIS

When a dividend yield basis should be used

14.59   A small minority shareholder's return will be based on the company's dividend policy. If the company has a reliable track record of dividends which are either constant or show a steady increase or decrease, a dividend yield basis may be used. If the company is about to go into liquidation, a break up asset basis would be used with a significant discount for lack of control, etc.

An earnings based value can be used for an influential minority shareholder, particularly where the other shares are thinly spread and he is able to exert some degree of influence. It is important to remember that a fiscal valuation can take no account of the personal qualities or actual influence of the individual shareholder on dividend policy, etc. The transaction is assumed to be an imaginary one in the assumed open market between a hypothetical willing vendor and hypothetical willing purchaser.

An earnings valuation may also be more appropriate if the company's dividends widely fluctuate or it does not pay dividends. Although it is possible to assume a notional dividend (based on an appropriate 'dividend cover', etc), this is very subjective.

In the writer's view, it is better to adopt an earnings valuation which can be argued with greater certainty (particularly if a March 1982 rebasing value is sought), although a greater discount would be required to reflect the impotence of a small minority holding.

Dividend yield formulae

14.60   A dividend yield is calculated as follows:

$$\frac{\text{Nominal value of shares} \times \text{Dividend (as \% of nominal value)}}{\text{Value of share}} = \text{Dividend yield}$$

Thus, to calculate the value of the shares, the formula becomes:

$$\frac{\text{Nominal value of shares} \times \text{Dividend (as \% of nominal value)}}{\text{Dividend yield}} = \text{Value per share}$$

Required dividend yield

14.61   The starting point is to determine the required dividend yield. In practice, SAV will normally start by applying the dividend yield from a comparable quoted company. It is usually difficult to find a true comparison particularly for small family businesses who typically carry on a limited range of activities (quoted companies often have a diverse spread). Consequently, the average dividend yield from the most comparable sector of the Financial Times Actuaries Shares Indices is normally taken. This average yield would then be increased to recognise the increased risk associated with investment in unquoted companies, such as the lack of marketability of the shares, smaller size, and limited activities. SAV suggest that the yield on quoted shares should be uplifted by between 10% and 30% for the lack of quotation and normal restrictions on transfer.However, in *Administrators of the Estate of Caton (deceased) v Couch* SpC [1995] SSCD 34, a yield of three times that of quoted shares was accepted, even though it was considered to be on the high side. However, if the unquoted company has features which reduce risk to an investor, such as high asset backing, quality products, enjoys a niche market, a high level of dividend cover, etc, then the required yield should be adjusted downwards.

14.62   An alternative approach which is sometimes taken in practice is to take a risk free rate of return (for example, the yield on medium term gilts) and then add a premium for the degree of risk associated with the investment. This would give the investor's required rate of return. Some valuers *double* the relevant income yield on medium-term gilts, which is then adjusted to reflect a normal 'dividend-cover' of between three and four times and the reliability of dividend payments.

Example 6

Value of shares on a dividend yield basis

Frank owns 50 £1 shares (representing a 5% holding) in Lampard's Electricals Ltd which trades as a retailer of electrical goods.

SAV have agreed that the 5% holding can be valued on a dividend yield basis as follows:

Net dividend per share	= £2.00
Dividend percentage*	= $\dfrac{£2 \times}{£1}$ 100 = 200%
Comparable quoted dividend yield	= 6%
Adjustment for:	
Non-marketability, reduced size of company, etc	4%
High asset backing	(2%)
Dividend yield	8%
Value per share	
$\dfrac{\text{Dividend percentage} \times \text{Nominal value per share}}{\text{Dividend yield}}$ =	Value per share
$\dfrac{200\% \times £1}{8\%}$ =	£25 per share

*Following the abolition of repayable tax credits on dividends, the dividend is based on the *net* dividend (ie the percentage dividend is not grossed up for the 1/9 tax credit).

MARCH 1982 REBASING VALUATIONS

Basic approach

14.63   The valuation of shares at 31 March 1982 is often required for the purposes of CGT rebasing. The March 1982 rebasing legislation assumes that the shareholder has notionally sold and reacquired their shareholding at its market value at 31 March 1982. Each shareholder is looked at separately for rebasing purposes, which often gives an unfair result for minority shareholders (see below).

Individual or trustee shareholders selling shares they held at March 1982 can only deduct the March 1982 value of those shares (without any indexation allowance).

The value of a controlling interest held at March 1982 will be based on the value of the company at March 1982, with a small discount if the company is not wholly owned (see 14.53). The notional acquisition at March 1982 is based on the proportion of the shares held at that date.

Share pooling rules

14.64   Since 6 April 2008, individual/trustee shareholders must pool all the shares (of the same class) they hold in each company for CGT purposes. This means that all shares acquired at different times in the same company are now treated as a single asset, regardless of when they were actually acquired. It should be noted that for all CGT purposes, any rights or bonus issues are strictly allocated to the original share acquisition (as opposed to the actual date of the rights or bonus issue).

Under these rules, share sales are first identified with any shares purchased on the 'same day' and within the next 30 days (designed to counter 'bed and breakfasting' arrangements). After that, they will then be identified with the single share pool (which will frequently be the case for owner-managed companies).

For summary of pre-6 April 2008 share identification rules, see 2010/11 and earlier editions of this book.

14.65   The market value of any shares held at 31 March 1982 will form part of this pooled holding. Where shares of the same class in a company have been acquired at different times (before 1 April 1982), ESC D44 provides they are treated as a 'single holding' for the purposes of a rebasing valuation at 31 March 1982.

Following the introduction of share pooling, the March 1982 rebasing value will only be fully accessed when the vendor sells all their shares. Where the vendor only sells/transfers part of their holding, the March 1982 value will simply be a component of the average base cost of the part-disposal.

Example 7

Part disposal of mixed share pool

In June 2011, Alan sold 400 out of the 2,000 ordinary shares he held in Toon Scorers Ltd.

Alan held 1,250 shares at 31 March 1982 which have an agreed value of £60 per share.

The other 750 shares were acquired in October 2006 by way of a gift from his brother, Kevin, under the protection of a *TCGA 1992, s 165* hold-over relief claim – which gave Alan a 'net' base value of £67,500.

Holding	Number	Base cost/value
		£
March 1982 holding	1,250	75,000
October 2006 – Gift from Kevin (with s 165 relief)	750	67,500
Balance at June 2011	2,000	142,500
June 2011 – Disposal (400/2,000 × £142,500)	(400)	(28,500)

Alan will be able to deduct £28,500 as his part-disposal base cost against his June 2011 disposal proceeds.

Part disposal valuations

14.66 Where there is a part disposal of shares from a majority holding, the deductible March 1982 base value would be a pro-rata proportion of the value of the shares held in March 1982 (not the March 1982 value of the shares being sold), as illustrated in the example below.

Example 8

Part disposal of (March 1982) majority holding

In October 2011, Malcolm sold 200 out of the 700 shares he held in Macdonald's Foods Limited, a successful foods company. Malcolm's sale consideration was £600,000 (net of disposal costs).

The company had an issued share capital of 1,000 £1 shares. Malcolm's 700 shares were acquired by him at par in 1975.

Malcolm has been managing director of the company since it started trading in 1979.

The relevant share valuations at March 1982 were:

Holding	Value per share
%	£
100	300
70	250
25	100

657

As Malcolm held a 70% interest at 31 March 1982, he would be entitled to value his March 1982 holding at £250 per share for all CGT disposals. He would also be entitled to claim the 10% Entrepreneurs' relief CGT rate on his chargeable gain (see 15.33–15.34).

His CGT would be calculated as follows:

	£
Sale proceeds	600,000
Less Part disposal – March 1982 base value	
200 shares × £250 per share (70% majority value)	(50,000)
Chargeable gain	550,000
Less: Annual exemption	(10,600)
Taxable gain at ER rate	539,400
ER CGT rate @ 10%	£53,940

Fragmented March 1982 shareholdings

14.68   Each shareholding is looked at separately when valuing shares at March 1982 – there is no aggregation principle. This rule works rather unfairly in the context of a family company where shareholdings are fragmented amongst different members of the family.

A minority holding at March 1982 would be discounted to reflect the shareholders' inability to control, restrictions on transfer, and reliance on the directors for his dividend income. This means, for example, that a 25% holding would be worth substantially less than 25% of the value of the entire company.

On a sale of the entire company, each shareholder will have a pro-rata share of the proceeds (which will generally reflect the value of the whole company). However, the March 1982 value of a minority shareholding would not be a pro-rata share of the March 1982 value of the company. Thus, a minority shareholder is bound to have a disproportionately large gain, even if the value of the company has kept pace with inflation since March 1982.

14.69   Some comfort can be derived from *Hawkings-Byass v Sassen* [1996] STC (SCD) 319. Here, the Special Commissioners considered that multinationals and the two existing rival family 'shareholder' groups would be prepared to pay a premium to acquire certain minority holdings (18.16%, 11.09%, and 9.09%) in a trading company. They therefore fell to be regarded as 'special purchasers' in determining the 31 March 1982 value of these shareholdings. It was accepted that the shares could be valued as a pro-rata value of the entire company (based on its assets and turnover), but with a one-third reduction to reflect the inherent uncertainties of such bids, such as the ability of the rival family groups to raise the finance. However, a 20% premium uplift was given on this value to arrive at the value of the 18.16% holding.

In some cases, it may be possible to argue that the shareholdings should be valued on a (higher) 'quasi-partnership' basis which would mean taking a simple 'pro-rata' valuation of the entire company (see 14.27). This basis is only likely to apply where it can be demonstrated that one or more of the other shareholders would be 'special purchasers' prepared to pay a pro-rata basis.

Example 9

Valuing minority shareholding at 31 March 1982

In September 2011, Lineker Sports Clothes Ltd was sold for £1,000,000. The company had an issued share capital of 1,000 shares, which had always been held equally by five shareholders (each holding 200 shares).

Based on the sale price, the following statistics can be derived:

Net earnings (ie post tax)	£80,000
Net earnings per share	£80
P/E ratio	12.5

The value of each individual's shareholding at 31 March 1982 is computed along the following lines:

Maintainable net earnings at March 1982 (say)	£20,000
Net earnings per share	£20

The FT Actuaries Textiles Sector P/E at 31 March 1982 was 13.42. After adjusting for non-marketability, minority holding, etc, a P/E ratio of 6.0 is taken for a 20% holding. The value per share is therefore £120 (ie £20 × 6).

Each shareholder receives proceeds of £200,000, but will only have a deductible March 1982 base value of £24,000, ie £120 per share × 200 shares.

Husband and wife shareholdings at 31 March 1982

14.70 Where a company is controlled jointly by a husband and wife, although each separately has a minority holding, their shares must still be valued in isolation (there is no equivalent of the 'related property' rule which applies for IHT (see 17.8)). However, if the couple own shares in the same company (of the same class) at 31 March 1982 and the wife subsequently transfers her shares to her husband, those shares can be treated as held by him at 31 March 1982 for the purposes of the rebasing valuation. The same rule applies if the husband transfers shares to his wife (see *TCGA 1992, Sch 3, para 1* and SP5/89).

The mandatory 31 March 1982 share valuation will automatically apply to the entire March 1982 holding (ie including those originally held by the transferee spouse and those subsequently transferred). This concession provides a valuable tax saving opportunity where the sale of a 'husband and wife' company is contemplated. By arranging a transfer of shares from one spouse to the other, the recipient spouse may be able to substantially increase their March 1982 valuation by switching it on to a controlling basis. The transfer of shares should be executed before a purchaser is found to avoid the risk of HMRC countering the advantage under the *Furniss v Dawson* principle (*Furniss v Dawson* [1984] 1 All ER 530). (See the decision in *R v CIR, ex p Kaye* [1992] STC 581.) However, the impact on the shareholders' ER entitlement would also have to be considered.

Example 10

Valuation at March 1982 – aggregation of spouse's holding

The March 1982 valuations for the shares in Hughes Builders Ltd were as follows:

	Shares	March 1982 value per share	March 1982 Valuation
		£	£
Mr Hughes	40	120	4,800
Mrs Hughes	40	120	4,800
Mr Emilyn	20	30	600
	100		

However, if prior to a sale of the company, Mr Hughes transferred, say, 36 shares to Mrs Hughes, she would then have 76% holding. This holding (valued on an earnings basis) might be worth, say, £700 per share. Mrs Hughes' total base value would then be increased to £53,200 (76 × £700 per share).

Mr Hughes will be entitled to keep the original March 1982 valuation for the four shares he retains.

Valuing shares by reference to size of transferor's March 1982 holding

14.71 Where shares held at 31 March 1982 are subsequently transferred between husband and wife, ESC D44 enables the *transferee* spouse to elect for their valuation to be calculated by reference to the size of the *transferor's* holding. This will often enable a higher March 1982 valuation to be obtained (due to the lower 'valuation' discounts applied to larger shareholdings) (see Example 11 below). The election must be made within 12 months of the 31 January in the tax year following that in which the shares are sold, or such later time as permitted by HMRC.

Example 11

Application of ESC D44

Mariner's (Boats and Leisure) Ltd was incorporated in 1976 with 100 £1 ordinary shares, which were held as follows:

Mr Mariner	80
Mrs Mariner	20

Mr Mariner transferred a further ten shares to his wife in May 2009.

On a subsequent sale, Mrs Mariner can elect under ESC D44 to compute her March 1982 valuation as 30/80ths of the value of an 80% shareholding in the company at that date (rather than a 30% holding in isolation at 31 March 1982).

KEY MARCH 1982 REBASING ISSUES

Main basic principles

14.72 It is useful to highlight some of the main principles affecting March 1982 share valuations:

(*a*) It is not possible to index back to March 1982 from the ultimate sale price. On the other hand, the use of foresight is permissible and should be used to demonstrate that the trading prospects and future growth, etc were rosy before March 1982.

(*b*)   If there are any arm's length transfers of any shares within a year of March 1982, these may provide very persuasive evidence of a high March 1982 valuation.

If, on the other hand, low valuations have previously been established with SAV for CGT or capital transfer tax purposes close to March 1982, they should be distinguished, by reference to the size of the shareholding and other circumstances. This stance is clearly easier to sustain if the original value was agreed with SAV reserving its position on a 'without prejudice' basis.

(*c*)   The size of the shareholding will influence the level of financial and other information deemed to be available to a prospective purchaser at 31 March 1982. Controlling shareholders have full access to in-house information, such as management's accounts, forecasts, etc leading up to March 1982. On the other hand, minority holdings of 'low value' shares may only be entitled to those published accounts which are signed before 31 March 1982. This may mean, for example, that if the accounts to 31 December 1981 were not available at 31 March 1982, only the 31 December 1980 and previous year's accounts could be taken.

(*d*)   The maintainable profits are normally determined from the last three years audited accounts, adjusted for excessive director's remuneration, etc. The general recession in the early 1980s meant that most companies experienced a decline in profits between 1979 and 1982. This trend may work to the advantage of a minority shareholder bearing in mind the information standards mentioned in (*c*) above. On the other hand, this may be detrimental to controlling valuations which are based on up-to-date information.

(*e*)   Many companies did not pay the headline corporation tax rate in the early 1980s, due to the availability of 100% capital allowances and stock relief. This can be used to substantiate a lower or even a nil tax charge, thus increasing the maintainable earnings. (Note, however that P/E ratios (at 31 March 1982) published in the *Investors' Chronicle* reflect a full corporation tax charge and are higher than the FTASI. A consistent approach must therefore be taken.)

(*f*)   The SAV's 'Post Transaction Valuation Checks' system (see 14.46) should be used to obtain early comfort and agreement on 31 March 1982 share valuations. This is done by completing HMRC's prescribed form CG34 *after* the relevant share transaction. In many cases, provided the form is submitted promptly, the 31 March 1982 valuation should be agreed before the 31 January deadline for the self-assessment return (IR press release 4 February 1997).

(*g*)   There is also an alternative SAV procedure for early agreement of 31 March 1982 share values (only) where this is required by a number of shareholders of the same company. The 31 March 1982 valuations for each shareholder can be submitted to SAV *after* the disposal. All shareholders with similar holdings to be valued at March 1982 must be prepared to be bound by the value agreed. For these purposes, the SAV must be provided with a full list of the shareholders, giving the size of their holdings at both 31 March 1982 and the date of disposal, and supplying details of their individual tax offices (*IR Press Release* – 18 November 1991). However, many shareholders are likely to prefer the 'fast track' system using form CG34 which enables them to agree their 31 March 1982 values on an *individual* basis.

Practical points from the Marks v Sherred case

14.73   The Special Commissioners' case of *Marks v Sherred* SpC [2004] SSCD 362 gives an interesting practical insight into the contrasting arguments surrounding a 31 March 1982 valuation of shares. The relevant shareholding being valued was a 66% holding in Ross Marks Ltd, a domestic electronics import and sale business. Both sides agreed that the correct basis of valuation was to use the capitalised earnings basis (see 14.50–14.54).

The taxpayer's expert witness based her calculation on the last available accounts to *31 March 1981* (which showed turnover of around £1.5 million and pre-tax profits of £160,000). However, in the next year (US$/£) exchange rate movements and increased overheads had adversely affected profits. Consequently, she recalculated the figures to smooth out the effects of the exchange fluctuations by reference to the average for the previous three years, which gave net maintainable earnings of £190,000. Using a P/E multiple of 11, this valued the shares at £1,050,000.

The Revenue expert decided that a hypothetical purchaser would be more heavily influenced by the current trading and adverse exchange position at the time as the company paid for almost all its stock in US dollars (and it did not hedge its dollar position). He also considered that a purchaser would require sight of the 1982 books. On the other hand, he thought that a purchaser would seek to make savings on the existing high levels of directors' remuneration and entertaining. These findings produced maintainable earnings of £85,000, and based on a multiple of 10, gave a valuation of £561,000.

14.74   Following *Caton v Couch SpC* [1995] SSCD 34 (see 14.51), the Commissioner agreed with the Revenue's expert that a purchaser would insist on seeing even confidential information, and so would look at all possible current trading data leading up to the purchase. At March 1982, the exchange rate was $1.82 to the £ (which was considerably less than the 'smoothed' rate of $2.13 to the £ used by the taxpayer's expert). The company would have to acquire products based on current conditions although a purchaser would seek to cut costs. Another relevant factor was that the company was contemplating moving part of its manufacturing to the UK to reduce its exchange risk. Furthermore, if the business was basically sound, a prudent purchaser would not be unduly influenced by one bad year (1982).

Having weighed up all these factors, the Commissioner valued the shares at £633,000 (by applying a multiple of 10 to net maintainable earnings of £95,510).

PLANNING CHECKLIST – VALUING A FAMILY OR OWNER-MANAGED COMPANY

Company

- Maintainable earnings are normally used to value a business as a going concern – the maintainable earnings must reflect the likely future circumstances of the business and therefore historic results may need to be adjusted.

Working shareholders

- Commercial valuations of the entire company/business are based on a full knowledge of its prospects, trading results, conditions, etc.

- Minority share valuations required under the Articles are frequently discounted (unless a 'quasi-partnership' basis is appropriate).

- Fiscal valuations are only based on details that would reasonably be relevant to the size of the relevant 'stake' in the company (other gleaned information is ignored).

- It is often possible to support a robust 'favourable' 31 March 1982 share valuation with a carefully structured business case.

Other employees

- 'Unrestricted' shares are valued on a 'money's worth' principle which reflects the employee's personal knowledge about the company's affairs.

- Restricted shares (that are subject to employee-specific conditions) are valued on a CGT 'open market' basis, therefore taking into account only details that would be relevant to a hypothetical purchaser. However, somewhat incongruously, HMRC – SAV often seek to take interim management accounts and budgets into account.

- Shares in an approved share option or EMI scheme are valued according to CGT 'open market' principles.

Non-working shareholders

- 'Minority' share values are heavily discounted – this is good news where tax is payable, but bad news for March 1982 rebasing deduction purposes.

- Consider transferring shares to/from spouse to increase size of holding for March 1982 rebasing valuation retrospectively.

Chapter 15

Selling the Owner-Managed Business or Company

GROOMING A BUSINESS FOR SALE

15.1   At present economic activity remains cautious. However, there is plenty of evidence to demonstrate that buyers are keen to purchase 'smaller' owner managed businesses that have survived the economic downturn and are well positioned to take advantage of opportunities over the next years. Indeed, many buyers and investors with readily available cash or access to relatively cheap finance have been quick to make acquisitions whilst sale prices still remain relatively attractive.

Owner-managers must plan for the sale of their company well in advance. To obtain the best possible price, the owner manager should seek to maximise the company's earnings. For example, they might need to consider whether is it possible to lift margins or postpone expenditure with a long term payback (for example an advertising campaign). The timing of any planned exit will depend on a number of factors. These would include market trends (there are likely to be more potential buyers in a growing market), the general level of mergers and acquisitions activity within the relevant market/industry sector, and the future prospects within it.

To stand a realistic chance of obtaining the best price, the owner manager will need to demonstrate that the underlying performance of the business is strong, preferably showing an improving trend. Many prospective purchasers will also wish to ensure that the business has a dedicated and committed management team. Other important factors would include a tightly-controlled business, strong brand image and market profile, proven ability to attract a wide range of 'desirable' customers, and a clean 'tax profile'. The identification of these (and other key issues) should take place well in advance (in some cases up to two years) to enable the required improvements to take place in the business well before it is put up for sale. In some cases, it may be necessary to 'clean-up' the company by eliminating shareholder loans and personal use of company assets.

Recent empirical evidence suggests that the majority of owner-managers who have built up successful companies expect to sell them on and start again, indicating the emergence of the so-called serial entrepreneur. A large majority of owners hope and expect that they would be able to sell their business on to trade or financial acquirers in the next two to three years, after which they intend to repeat the exercise. Obtaining the 'right' price was regarded as the biggest priority when selling, with job security for staff also being considered a principal consideration.

POSSIBLE SALE ROUTES AND STRUCTURES

15.2 Many company sales are made to 'trade' buyers – which can be a competitor, an overseas buyer wishing to obtain a 'foothold' in the relevant sector in the UK, or a company seeking to enter into a new market via acquisition. Depending on the relevant factors, the purchaser may be willing to pay a premium to enter into the owner manager's market. One important area will be to ensure that the seller's management team remain committed to the deal. If key managers hold shares this will provide a degree of incentive. In some cases, it may be desirable to award one-off bonuses as a 'sweetener'

The owner-manager may wish to sell to their existing senior management team under a management buy-out (MBO). Some owner managers look on an MBO as a reward for loyalty and support to management for their role in developing the business. In many cases the management team may not be able to assemble sufficient financial resources to buy the business. Private equity funding will often be used to help to bride the gap. For these reasons, the price obtained under an MBO deal is generally lower than the owner manager can expect to receive under a trade sale. Furthermore, many trade buyers will often be prepared to pay a premium (see 14.28).

There are two main sale structures. Owner managers may either secure the sale of the trade and assets out of the company or they can sell their shares in the company. Each method gives rise to different commercial, tax and legal consequences, which therefore influences the way in which the transaction is structured.

Generally, the sellers prefer to sell their shares, whereas the purchaser will often prefer to buy assets (unless the stamp duty land tax cost is prohibitive – see 12.17), but there will be situations where one party requires the opposite route. In the writer's experience, there are often one or two key factors which will dictate the manner in which the business is to be sold. Although this is a matter of negotiation between the two parties, in some cases one of the parties will have the 'upper hand' in imposing the structure of the deal.

This chapter focuses on the tax implications and strategies for the seller. The purchaser's position is considered in detail in Chapter 12.

BASIC CGT RULES

Date of disposal

15.3   The sale of the company's assets or shares will involve a disposal for CGT purposes. A disposal is recognised for CGT at the time an unconditional contract is entered into, and not the date of completion. In *Jerome v Kelly* [2004] STC 887, the House of Lords reinforced the view that this provision only dealt with the timing of the disposal. It does not go as far as saying that this is when the disposal is made (ie when an asset is transferred on completion). The date of disposal under a conditional contract arises when the relevant condition precedent is satisfied or waived [*TCGA 1992, s 28*].

On an asset sale, the company's corporation tax accounting period ends on the date the trade and assets are sold, representing the cessation of trade for the seller company. A company (liable to corporation tax at the main rate) pays its tax on the profits of the 'asset sale' period under the quarterly instalment basis. A company's tax is paid in instalments starting six months and 13 days from the start of the accounting period and ending on a date which is three months and 14 days after the end of the accounting period (see 4.48). Interim instalments are payable every three months, as the length of the company's accounting period allows. All other companies (ie those paying the small profits' rate of tax or benefiting from marginal relief) will pay the tax on an asset sale within nine months after the end of the corporation tax accounting period (see 15.6 for illustration on an asset sale).

Under self-assessment, individuals are liable to pay their CGT on 31 January following the year of assessment. Where an individual anticipates selling their shares shortly before the end of the tax year, consideration should be given to deferring the date of disposal until after 5 April, as this will delay the payment of the tax by one year. (Prior to 6 April 2008, in some cases, this may also have secured additional taper relief – see 15.22.)

Consideration

15.3A   In most cases, it will be reasonably straightforward to ascertain the consideration received for the disposal of the shares or other business assets. However, in some situations, the precise legal drafting of the obligations placed on the purchaser might be construed as additional 'consideration' received by the seller. For example, in *Spectros International plc v Madden* (1997) STC 114, the sale agreement required the purchaser to pay $20,001,000 million, of which $20,000,000 million should be used to clear the target company's bank overdraft (which had been used to pay a pre-sale dividend) and $1,000 for the target company's common stock (ie shares). The court had little difficulty in rejecting the seller's contention that the company's common stock had been sold for $1,000. Justice Lightman held that, on a true construction of the agreement, the 'consideration' paid for the common stock was $20,001,000 since the seller could direct how the amount should be applied. He added that it if the parties had intended to sell the common stock for $1,000, the sale agreement could easily have been worded to achieve this. It is therefore important to ensure that any obligation to clear a company's indebtedness is dealt with as a 'subsidiary' term of the contract rather than forming part of the main 'consideration' clause.

Similarly, in *Collins v Revenue and Customs Commissioners* [2009] EWHC 284 (Ch), part of the stated consideration for the purchase of shares consisted of making a payment to the target company to fund a contribution to the seller's pension scheme. This was found to be treated as part of the seller's sale consideration for CGT. Once again, the precise legal wording of the sale contract was unhelpful to the seller. However, the courts follow the clear wording of the specific agreement and will not attempt to redraft it to obtain a better tax result. In the *Collins* case, the target company could have made the pension contribution before the shares were sold, with an appropriate reduction being made in the consideration for the shares to reflect this.

Deferred consideration

15.4 If a fixed part of the consideration is deferred, this must initially be included in the CGT consideration, without any discount for the delay in receipt or the fact that it may not be paid (see 15.57–15.67 for the treatment of variable 'earn-out' consideration). The same rule applies even if the deferred element of the consideration is conditional upon a specified event. The original CGT liability will only be revised if the taxpayer can satisfy the Inspector that part of the consideration has proved irrecoverable [*TCGA 1992, s 48*].

The requirement to bring the full amount of the deferred consideration into the original CGT computation and pay tax on it can often give rise to cash-flow difficulties. Thus, provided the sale consideration is payable over a period exceeding 18 months, HMRC may allow the seller to pay the tax in instalments. This instalment relief must be claimed by the seller [*TCGA 1992, s 280*]. Generally, HMRC will look for CGT instalments equivalent to 50% of each deferred tranche of sale proceeds until the CGT is fully paid. The instalment period cannot exceed eight years.

In *Collins v Revenue and Customs Commissioners* [2009] EWHC 284 (Ch) the deferred consideration included further payments based on future turnover, which was therefore variable in nature. The actual amount received was lower than expected and the taxpayer sought a partial refund of the original CGT. However, it was held that the (unascertainable) deferred consideration fell to be taxed in accordance with the principles in *Marren v Ingles* (1980) STC 500 (see 15.58), and thus the *TCGA 1992, s 48* refund mechanism was not available.

On a share sale, it is often preferable to obtain a tax deferral by securing the issue of a loan note from the acquiring company for the deferred consideration (see 15.49–15.56).

SALE OF ASSETS AND TRADE

Legal overview

15.5   The starting point in framing any agreement for the sale of the trade and assets is to identify precisely the assets and liabilities which will be taken over. This may also involve the assignment of leases and novation of trading contracts. Employees will be transferred under the *Transfer of Undertakings (Protection of Employment) Regulations 1981*.

The legal documentation for an asset sale is likely to contain fewer warranties than under a share sale. Most sale agreements will require the seller to covenant that he will not compete with the business being sold within a reasonable time scale and/or defined geographical limits (although unreasonable 'non-compete' covenants are unlikely to be upheld by the courts).

General tax consequences

15.6   Under this method, the company will sell the trade, together with its various trading assets. This will inevitably create a cessation of the trade for tax purposes, which will bring an end to the accounting period for corporation tax purposes, unless the company is continuing another trade [*CTA 2009, s10(1) (d)(e) (ICTA 1988, s 12(3)(c))*]. The termination of the accounting period will accelerate the payment of tax liabilities. For example, take a company that does not pay tax at the main rate and normally produces accounts to 31 December each year. It sells its trade and assets on 31 August 2011 thus creating a corporation tax accounting period (CTAP) of eight months to 31 August 2011. The tax for this period would, therefore, fall due on 1 June 2012 (ie nine months following 31 August 2011).

Any unrelieved trading losses will effectively be lost when the seller company ceases to trade [*CTA 2010, s 45(4) (ICTA 1988, s 393(1))*]. Where there are substantial trading losses that would otherwise go unrelieved, the company should seek to allocate more of the sale consideration (on a commercially justifiable basis) to those assets giving rise to a trading receipt, such as trading stock, plant and *CTA 2009, Part 8* regime intangibles. If the seller company is part of a group, it may be possible to shelter the taxable profits on sale by way of group relief (see 4.39).

Capital gains may arise on the disposal of property and (provided it was held by the company on 1 April 2002) on goodwill (see 15.12). Under the *corporate* capital gains regime, indexation relief continues to be given in full. Since 21 March 2007, disposals of industrial buildings (and hotels/agricultural buildings) no longer trigger a balancing adjustment – the purchaser of the building effectively 'stands in the shoes' of the seller and can continue to claim IBAs on the same transitional basis as the seller would have done (until the 31 March 2011 abolition date) (see 15.11).

The sale of 'new' goodwill and any other intangible fixed assets (acquired or created by the seller company *after 31 March 2002*) generally gives rise to a taxable trading receipt.

Potential double tax charge

15.7 Probably the main disadvantage of an asset sale is the potential double charge to tax. This is further exacerbated by the lower CGT rates that are often secured on share sales (where Entrepreneurs' relief (ER) is available).

The proceeds for the sale of the business will be subject to corporation tax. If the seller needs the cash from the sale of the business, a further tax liability will be suffered on the extraction of the net proceeds from the company. The manner in which the cash is extracted will influence the tax liability (see Chapter 2).

Apportionment of sale consideration

15.8 The tax payable by the company would depend upon the nature of each asset and the consideration that has been attributed to each one. In this context, it is important to achieve a sensible allocation of the total price paid for the business amongst the various individual assets and this should be specified in the sale agreement. For example, if the company has unused trading losses which would be lost on cessation, it may be possible to absorb them by allocating higher values to assets that would produce additional trading receipts, such as trading stock or plant and machinery which would produce a balancing charge.

In some cases, it may be possible to save tax by placing a realistic value on the business' books and records, with the tenable argument that the value of each valuable individual file, book, etc is below the £6,000 chattel exemption in *TCGA 1992, s 262*. Given the wide range of the underlying books, files and computer records, it would be difficult for HMRC to argue that the books and records are a 'set of articles'. (If they were treated as a 'set', this would negate the 'capital gains' benefit of each individual item being below £6,000.)

Provided the seller and purchaser have negotiated the price at arm's length and the allocation has been specified in the sale agreement, HMRC are unlikely to challenge the apportionment of the total price. However, it should be noted that HMRC have a statutory power to re-apportion the consideration on a 'just and reasonable' basis for virtually all types of asset. This authority is given for the purposes of computing chargeable gains; capital allowances and corresponding balancing adjustments; and the tax on the sale of trading stock (on cessation). For relevant legislation, see *TCGA 1992, s 52(4)*; *CAA 2001, s 562*; *CTA 2009, s165(3)*. In *EV Booth (Holdings) Ltd v Buckwell* [1980] STC 578, it was held that a *party* to a sale could not resile from the apportionment in the contract for CGT purposes. Justice Browne-Wilkinson also went on to say, by way of obiter, that the Inland Revenue might be able to look through the apportionment in some cases. In practice, HMRC is only likely to challenge the split of the consideration in arm's length deals where the allocated prices are blatantly unrealistic. HMRC (Stamp Taxes) will also generally accept any 'sensible' allocation for SDLT purposes (see 12.25).

A slightly different approach is taken goodwill and other intangible fixed assets under *CTA 2009, Pt 8*. Since this is an accounts-based regime, *CTA 2009, s 856(3)* states that the amounts allocated in the accounts under GAAP, must be used for the intangibles legislation in *CTA 2009, Pt 8* (see 12.47 and 12.48).

The detailed considerations that might apply in relation to the main categories of asset are set out in 15.10–15.18 below. Many of these factors will also influence the manner in which the price is apportioned.

Optimising seller's indexation allowance(s)

15.9   On a corporate trade and asset sale, it is particularly important to recognise that the indexation allowance (which is still available to companies) cannot create or increase a capital loss. If the intended apportionment of the sale price gives rise to a restriction of indexation allowance on one or more assets (thus giving a 'nil' gain), yet one or more of the other assets show capital gains, the allocation should be adjusted. If the price of each 'indexation-restricted' asset is increased, this will reduce or eliminate the wasted indexation allowance. As far as possible, the broad rule of thumb must be to ensure that each asset is sold for an amount at least equal to its CGT base cost and the accrued indexation thereon (see Example 1 below).

Example 1

Minimising loss of indexation relief on asset sale

Upson Ltd is negotiating the sale of its hi-fi retail business as a going concern, involving the sale of its trade and assets. The company purchased the business in March 1994.

Both parties have agreed a price of £500,000 for the retail premises and goodwill (with stock being purchased at book value). The draft sale agreement has apportioned the price as follows:

	£
Retail premises	350,000
Goodwill	150,000

The net capital gain based on the above apportionment would be:

	Sale Price	Cost	Indexation @ (say) 75%	Capital Gain
	£	£	£	£
Goodwill	150,000	(20,000)	(15,000)	115,000
Retail premises	350,000	(250,000)	(100,000)*	–
	500,000			115,000

* £250,000 × 75% = £187,500 but restricted to £100,000 to produce no gain. Indexation relief of £87,500 is therefore 'wasted'.

A more sensible apportionment (assuming the figures could be justified) would be:

	£
Retail premises	440,000
Goodwill	60,000

This would reduce the chargeable gain to £27,500 as shown below:

	Sale Price	Cost	Indexation at 75%	Capital Gain
	£	£	£	£
Goodwill	60,000	(20,000)	(15,000)	25,000
Retail premises	440,000	(250,000)	(187,500)	2,500
	500,000			27,500

Property

15.10 The disposal of freehold or leasehold property may give rise to a capital gain or loss. The seller may wish to retain the property and grant a lease to the purchaser instead. Any premium received on the grant will represent a 'part-disposal' for capital gains purposes, with an appropriate A/A + B apportionment of base cost.

If a 'short' lease is granted, part of the premium will be taxed as property business *income [CTA 2009, s 217 (ICTA 1988, s 34)]*. The amount taxed is computed by reference to the following formula:

$$P \times \frac{(50 - Y)}{50}$$

Where   P = the amount of the premium; and

Y = the number of complete years of the lease (except the first year).

If the property was owned at 31 March 1982, its value at that date can be deducted as the base cost in arriving at the capital gain. With indexation based thereon currently running at about 190% (for a corporate seller), the capital gain may be small or nil, given the trend in property values over the period. Stamp duty land tax will be payable by the purchaser on the acquisition of the freehold/leasehold interest or the grant of a lease (see 12.21).

Where a leasehold interest which has less than 50 years to run is being sold, the deductible base cost is restricted by a 'depreciation' adjustment, *TCGA 1992, Sch 8* and a disposal at book value may therefore produce a taxable gain.

Where the property has been occupied and used for the purposes of the trade, it may be possible to roll-over any capital gain against the acquisition of qualifying re-investment expenditure. This may be useful if the company or group has other trading activities or is likely to begin a new trading venture in the near future [*TCGA 1992, s 152* and *s 175*]. It is not possible to roll over 'property' gains against acquisitions of goodwill and other intangibles [*TCGA 1992, s 156ZA*].

Gains on assets owned *personally* by a shareholder may also be rolled over in this way provided the old and the new assets are used in the shareholder's *same* 'personal company' [*TCGA 1992, s 157*]. For these purposes, a personal company is one in which the individual holds at least 5% of the voting rights. A claim for roll-over relief was denied by the Special Commissioners in *Boparan v HMRC* [2007] (SpC 587), where 'personally-owned' chicken breeding farms and feed mills were let to a 100% *subsidiary* company. Since Mr Boparan (the shareholder) did not directly exercise the voting rights of the subsidiary, it was not his 'personal company'. It was not sufficient that control of the subsidiary could effectively be achieved on a 'look-through' basis by virtue of Mr Boparan's ownership of the holding company's shares. Had the assets been let to the holding company instead or had Mr Boparan had a minimum 5% direct equity voting stake in the subsidiary, his roll-over relief claim would have been successful.

Industrial buildings or hotels

15.11   The seller may have claimed industrial buildings allowances (IBAs) or hotel buildings allowances ('HBAs'). However, these allowances were completely abolished on 1 April 2011, and thus there is no clawback of previous allowances.

Before 1 April 2011 'abolition date', any (post-20 March 2007) disposal of an industrial building or qualifying hotel did *not* trigger any balancing adjustment. In such cases, the legislation deemed the post-sale residue of qualifying expenditure to be the same as the pre-sale residue. This meant that the purchaser took over the seller's unrelieved qualifying expenditure (and claimed IBAs on the same basis as the seller would have done under the transitional phase-out rates until 31 March 2011). .

Goodwill

Tax treatment of pre- and post-1 April 2002 goodwill and intangibles

15.12   Goodwill or other intangible fixed assets are subject to two distinct tax regimes depending on whether the relevant asset was acquired or originated before 1 April 2002 or afterwards.

If the seller held the goodwill or intangible asset on 31 March 2002, it will fall within the capital gains regime. In many cases, the goodwill will be internally created by the seller over the period of its trading. There is no question of any apportionment being made since CTA 2009, s884 states that if the company was in business before April 2002, then its entire goodwill will be taxed under the capital gains rules. The same treatment applies if the selling company had acquired the trading goodwill from a related party that owned it before 1 April 2002. This would apply, for example, on a prior intra-group transfer where the transferor group company carried out the relevant trade before April 2002.

Where goodwill is taxed as a *capital gain* and the selling company was trading in *March 1982*, the March 1982 value of the goodwill can be deducted as the base cost. If the company can show it was generating substantial profits prior to March 1982, this will be particularly beneficial. The goodwill valuation for March 1982 may be derived from the March 1982 rebasing value of the 'company' – ie it would be based on an appropriate earnings multiple after deducting the value of the company's tangible net assets at 31 March 1982 – see 14.6, 14.9–14.18 and 14.21.)

Where the selling company only commenced trading (or purchased the goodwill/intangible asset from an 'unrelated' party) after 31 March 2002, the profit or loss on disposal falls within the 'income' regime in *Part 8* of the *CTA 2009* (previously referred to as the *FA 2002, Sch 29* regime). The taxable profit or tax loss will usually be the amount reported in the accounts, which would be based on the sales proceeds less the amortised cost per the accounts (there is no indexation relief).

These key principles are illustrated below:

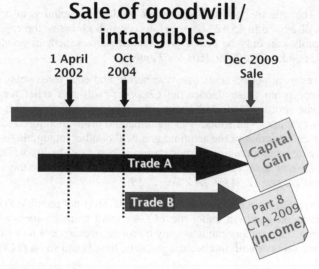

Sale of goodwill/ intangibles

Trade A was carried on before April 2002 and therefore the sale would be taxed as a capital gain.

Trade B started in October 2004 and therefore the profit on sale would be taxed as (trading) income under CTA 2009, Part 8

Know-how

15.13 On a sale of 'old' *capital gains* regime goodwill (see 15.12), there may still be advantages in allocating part of its disposal value to know-how owned by the company – for example to offset against unused trading losses brought forward.

Know-how is defined in *CTA 2009, s 176(1)* and *CAA 2001, s 452(2)* and includes industrial information about manufacturing and processing. However, the sale of know-how on a disposal of the trade is treated as a sale of *goodwill unless* a joint election is made between the seller and purchaser within two years following the sale [*CTA 2009, s 178)*]. It is therefore vital to ensure that a joint election is made where the transaction is to be treated as a sale of know-how and this should ideally be signed before the sale contract or be a binding condition of the contract.

Provided the appropriate election is made, the seller company can treat the know-how profit as a trading receipt.

The *purchaser* will generally be able to obtain tax relief on the know-how (based on the amount written off each year under GAAP) under *CTA 2009, Part 8*.

Roll-over relief for capital gain/income profit

15.14   The sale of goodwill will either produce a capital gain or income profit (as discussed in 15.12 above). However, in both cases, the capital gain/income profit can only be rolled-over against reinvestment in goodwill and intangibles under *CTA 2009, Part 8, Chapter 7*.

The reinvestment period starts one year before and ends three years after the gain/income profit arose. Under the *Chapter 7* roll-over relief regime, the gain/income profit is deducted against the reinvestment expenditure for the intangibles regime. The rolled-over gain/income profit therefore reduces the future tax amortisation of the acquired goodwill or other intangible fixed asset. (In such cases, the intangibles amortisation is based on the tax written down value of the new asset rather than the carrying value debited in the accounts) (see also 12.50 and 12.51) [*CTA 2009, s 758*].

It is important to recognise that (since April 2002) it is not possible to roll-over capital gains on goodwill under the *TCGA* capital gains business asset roll-over regime. These gains can now only be rolled-over against new qualifying expenditure on goodwill, intellectual property, brands and so on [*TCGA 1992, s 156ZA*].

For these purposes, the gain/income profit is deemed to be reinvested as the last component of the reinvestment expenditure. Thus, if the qualifying expenditure on the acquired goodwill/other intangible asset is less than the proceeds arising on the sale, it is only possible to roll-over the amount by which the reinvestment expenditure exceeds the original cost of the old asset, as shown in Example 2 below.

Example 2

Roll-over of capital gain on goodwill under the intangibles regime

The Moore Group Ltd has operated a number of different leisure-based businesses for many years.

In July 2010, it sold its chain of night clubs. As part of this deal, it received £2,000,000 for the related goodwill which generated a capital gain of £2,000,000. (Since the company started the trade, there was no base cost for goodwill).

In January 2012, it decided to purchase a small advertising business paying £1,500,000 for the goodwill (including the client lists).

The company will only be able to claim partial roll-over relief on the capital gain of £2,000,000 because it has only spent £1,500,000 of the July 2010 sale proceeds.

	£
Expenditure on goodwill/client lists (Jan 2012)	1,500,000
Less: Base cost of Night Club business goodwill	(–)
Amount available for roll-over relief	1,500,000

Following the claim for roll-over, the tax written-down value of the new goodwill/client lists is reduced to nil as follows:

	£
Goodwill/client lists – cost	1,500,000
Less: Intangibles roll-over relief	(1,500,000)
Tax written down value	–

This means that there is no tax deductible 'amortisation' (since the tax written down value has been fully extinguished by the roll-over claim).

Plant and machinery

Balancing adjustments on sale

15.15   In practice, plant often tends to be sold at its net book value. As the company is ceasing to trade, this will give rise to a taxable balancing charge, where the proceeds exceed the tax written down value (TWDV) of the plant. (A balancing allowance arises if the TWDV exceeds the sale proceeds.) If the company wishes to minimise the balancing charge, it may prefer to sell the plant at TWDV. Provided the purchaser can claim capital allowances on the plant, HMRC cannot substitute market value [*CAA 2001, s 61(2) Table* (Disposal event 1)].

Many buildings contain fixtures (eg some parts of the electrical system, lifts, etc), upon which plant and machinery allowances would normally have been claimed. Where the building is sold, part of the sale proceeds should be ascribed to the 'fixtures'. The amount allocated to the capital allowances 'pool' by the seller will be the lower of the 'just and reasonable' apportionment or the original cost.

However, to obtain certainty on the allocated proceeds both the seller and purchaser can make an election under *CAA 2001, s 198* to agree this amount for their respective tax purposes. (The election must contain various details, including the agreed amount, the parties to the election and their tax district references and details of the relevant fixtures and property – see 12.44 and 12.45.)

Capital gains treatment and chattels exemption

15.16   It should not be forgotten that plant (used for trading purposes) will qualify as a chargeable asset for CGT purposes. Thus, if the plant is sold for an amount in excess of its indexed base cost, a capital gain will arise, although where the consideration for an individual item of plant is less than £6,000, the gain is not taxable [*TCGA 1992, s 262*]. Where the seller company is disposing of a large number of individual items of plant which qualify for the £6,000 chattel exemption, it will often be advantageous to specify the consideration allocated to each item in the sale agreement. This documentary evidence would be used to the claim for the chattels exemption in the event on an HMRC enquiry (see also 15.8 – sale of books and records).

Capital gains arising on the sale of *fixed* plant and machinery would be eligible for capital gains roll-over relief in the normal way.

Loss restriction for capital allowances claimed

15.17   Plant is usually sold below its original cost (for example, at net book value), producing a loss. Because of a special rule, the base cost for CGT purposes must be restricted by the net capital allowances claimed on the asset, being the difference between cost and proceeds [*TCGA 1992, s 41(1), (2)*]. This will invariably produce no gain or loss. If the other assets cannot take full advantage of indexation (for example, if there is no base cost), the seller's overall tax position may be enhanced by selling plant for an amount at least equal to the cost plus accrued indexation. In such cases, the sale proceeds would be restricted to cost when computing the balancing adjustment for capital allowance purposes.

Trading stock and work in progress

15.18   Any profit arising on the sale of trading stock and work in progress will be treated as a trading receipt. Where the trading stock and work in progress is sold to another UK trader, HMRC generally accepts the price agreed between the two parties [*CTA 2009, ss 162, 165 (and s 163)*]. However, *CTA 2009, s 165(3)* requires the amount allocated to stock on a 'cessation' sale to be computed on a just and reasonable basis. Nevertheless, in most cases, there should still be some scope for flexing the price at which the stock is sold in order to achieve the desired tax position.

If trading stock is sold to a *connected person* on cessation, the transfer is deemed to be at market value. This deemed 'market-value' treatment could be displaced by a joint election to treat the transfer as being made at the higher of the actual sales price or book value. (The election can only be made if both these amounts are less than market value.) [*CTA 2009, ss 166 and 167*].

However, if the *transfer pricing regime* applies to the sale (see 4.11–4.12), the implied 'market price' will apply to the seller (and no election is possible) [*CTA 2009, s 162(2)*]. The purchaser should of course be able to make a compensating adjustment under *ICTA 1988, Sch 28AA, para 6*.

VAT – transfer of going concern relief

15.19   In the vast majority of asset and trade sales, VAT will not be chargeable on the sale of the assets, as the transaction will be treated as a non-supply under *VAT (Special Provisions) Order 1995, art 5* (see also 12.32 for detailed commentary).

HMRC is no longer prepared to give an informal ruling as to whether a particular trade and asset sale constitutes a transfer of a going concern (in relation to straightforward deals). The onus will therefore be on the seller company to satisfy itself that no VAT should be charged. Where the seller treats the sale as a transfer of a going concern for VAT purposes, it should obtain protection by ensuring that the sale price in the contract is exclusive of VAT. Furthermore, the seller should have a contractual right to subsequently raise a VAT invoice if HMRC subsequently considers that VAT should have been charged on the sale.

Pre-liquidation dividends versus capital distributions

15.20   Once the trade has been sold, the individual shareholders will often wish to extract the proceeds from the company.

If the proceeds are extracted by way of dividend before the company is liquidated [see *CTA 2010, s 1030*]; the cash received is taxed at the shareholder's marginal tax rate(s). For 2011/12, these are summarised as follows:

Total taxable income (including gross dividend income	Tax rate applied to gross dividend	Effective tax rate on the net dividend payment
Up to basic rate threshold – £35,000	10% less 10% tax credit = NIL	0%
£35,000 to £150,000	32.5% less 10% tax credit = 22.5%	25%
£150,000 plus	42.5% less 10% tax credit = 32.5%	36.1%

Nevertheless, it will generally be more efficient to distribute the net proceeds as a capital distribution (after the company has been placed into liquidation).

In many cases, shareholders should be able to qualify for Entrepreneurs' Relief (ER) on such capital distributions (up to their current £10 million or lower unused ER gains limit). Any excess gains above the ER limit will be taxed at the top CGT rate of 28%. (Prior to 23 June 2010, the normal flat 18% CGT rate would apply.)

A more detailed discussion on determining the best method of extracting surpluses prior to or on a winding-up or dissolution is given in 16.15–16.24.

Example 3

Sale of trade and assets

In April 2011 , Mr Tevez was approached by City plc to acquire the assets and undertaking of his profitable haulage business, The Carlos Transport Ltd (TCT Ltd). He incorporated the company in 1976 with £100 share capital and his shares were worth £1 million at 31 March 1982.

City plc has offered a total consideration of £4.45 million for the business.

TCT Ltd normally makes up accounts to 31 March each year. Its current summarised balance sheet (together with the relevant tax written down values (TWDV)) is as follows:

	£'000	
Warehouse property	410	
Lorry fleet	550	(TWDV = £385,000)
Debtors	390	
Bank overdraft	(200)	
Creditors	(400)	
	750	

The trading 'goodwill' was worth £480,000 at 31 March 1982. The warehouse was purchased in May 1999 at a cost of £410,000. .

The prospective purchaser's accountants have performed a brief acquisition review and have supplied the following tentative valuations for the assets to be taken over:

	£'000
Warehouse property	1,200
Lorry fleet	550
Goodwill (balance)	2,700
	4,450

Mr Tevez draws an annual salary of £200,000 from the company. He has not previously used any part of his ER.

The net amount that could be paid to Mr Tevez on the basis of the above deal is computed below.

Tax liabilities on sale of TCT Ltd's assets

TCT Ltd's tax liability on the sale of the relevant assets in (say) June 2011 is computed as follows:

Chargeable gains

	Warehouse	*Goodwill*	*Total*
	£'000	*£'000*	*£'000*
Sale proceeds (net of disposal costs)	1,200	2,700	
Less Cost/March 1982 value	(410)	(480)	
Indexation at (say) 42%/196%	(172)	(941)*	
Gain	618	1,279	1,897

* As the goodwill was held by TCT Ltd on 1 April 2002, it is treated as a 'capital gains' disposal

Balancing charge on lorry fleet**

	£'000
Eligible cost/proceeds	550
Less TWDV	(385)
Balancing charge	165
Taxable profit on sale of assets	2,062
Tax thereon @ 26%	536

** There is no clawback of IBAs on the warehouse.

Capital gains arising on capital distribution

TCT Ltd's distributable reserves upon completion would be as follows:

	£'000	*£'000*
Per current balance sheet		750
Book profit on disposal:		
Warehouse (£1,200,000 – £410,000)	790	
Goodwill	2,700	3,490
Liquidation and other realisation costs (say)		(34)
Tax on disposal		(536)
Available to distribute		£3,670

Assume all the reserves were distributed as a capital distribution on liquidation in (say) January 2012. Mr Tevez would qualify for ER (on the capital distribution *TCGA 1992, s 169(5)* (condition B)) since:

- he has satisfied the relevant employee/shareholding tests (for at least 12 months) before the trade ceased (ie when the trade was sold in June 2011);

- the capital distribution was made within three years of the June 2011 'cessation' date.

With ER, the 'net proceeds' available to Mr Tevez would be £3,404,000 computed thus:

	£'000
Capital distribution	3,670
Less March 1982 value	(1,000)
Chargeable gain	2,670
Less Annual exemption	(11)
Taxable gain	2,659
ER CGT @ 10%	266
Post-tax proceeds	£3,404

A pre-liquidation dividend in 2011/12 (on which tax would be payable at effective rates of 36.1%) would have been clearly disadvantageous.

SALE OF SHARES

Advantages of share sale

15.21   Some of the key tax advantages of selling shares are summarised below:

(a)   the avoidance of the double tax charge, as the seller receives the proceeds directly (see 15.7);

(b)   most owner managers should be able to secure an ER CGT rate of 10% on (up to) their first £10 million of eligible gains, with the balance being taxed at 28% (see 15.34 for details of pre-6 April 2011 ER limits and CGT rates). The ER regime is covered in detail in 15.33 to 14.42);

(c)   the ability to defer the capital gain on disposal where the acquiring company is able to satisfy the sale consideration through the issue of shares or loan stock;

(*d*)   the seller could avoid CGT by emigrating for the requisite five year period;

(*e*)   the seller may be in a position to obtain EIS CGT deferral relief (by reinvesting the proceeds in shares of a qualifying EIS company);

(*f*)   a share sale may enable some value to be received for the company's tax losses (which could not be transferred to purchaser on an asset sale) (see 15.6).

15.22   As a sale of shares constitutes a 'transaction in securities' or TiS, the anti-avoidance rules in (what is now) *ITA 2007, s 684* are potentially applicable. However, an important exclusion to the TiS rules was introduced by the *FA 2010*. Broadly, if there is a fundamental change in ownership of the company within *ITA 2007, s 686*, the seller will be exempt from the TiS rules. The fundamental change in ownership rule is tested in relation to each seller of the company. In broad terms, the exemption would generally operate where the company is being sold to a third party (ie where there is no connection with any of the sellers) – see 15.74 for further details. HMRC introduced this important 'let-out' to avoid the need to seek advance clearance on 'clean' straightforward sales.

Although the exemption is certainly useful, some sellers may still wish to seek the comfort of a clearance where they are nervous about the application of the TiS rules to some aspect of the transaction. Furthermore, advance tax clearances may still be required for other purposes – for example, where part of the sale consideration is being satisfied in the form of shares or loan notes (see 15.45).

Where the 'fundamental change in ownership' exemption is not available, sellers will need to gain HMRC's acceptance that the transaction is being undertaken for genuine commercial purposes and not tax avoidance by seeking clearance under *ITA 2007, s 701*. (see 15.72 – 15.79).

Selling shares under the Entrepreneurs' Relief (ER) regime

15.23   Most owner managers are likely to qualify for Entrepreneurs' relief (ER) on selling their companies, which effectively delivers a 10% CGT rate on their 'exit' gains up to overall 'lifetime' ER gains limit of £10 million. Any gains in excess of the £10 million ER threshold are taxed at the main CGT rate of 28%.

The £10 million ER threshold has applied since 6 April 2011 (for details of earlier CGT rates and ER limits – see 15.34).

If the owner manager's share sale gain is likely to exceed £10 million, it may be possible to increase the ER capacity by transferring part of their shareholding to other 'suitable' family members. ER is discussed extensively in 15.33–15.42.

For 'very small' share sales, some sellers may pay CGT at the lower 18% CGT rate (to the extent their gain falls within their unused 'basic rate' band for income tax purposes. The 18% CGT rate is unlikely to apply very often!

Sales by trustees and personal representatives will always be liable to CGT at the 28% rate (except in the rare cases where trustees are able to claim the 10% ER CGT rate (see 15.35).

Legal and commercial aspects

15.24 As a purchaser of shares will effectively inherit all the company's liabilities and problems, a share sale agreement usually includes extensive warranties and indemnities given by the seller, except perhaps in the case of a management buy-out. The function of warranties and indemnities is discussed in 12.63–12.73.

Company law can also impinge heavily on share sales. A careful check should be made to ensure that all pre-sale and related transactions fall within the company's articles and objects clause in its Memorandum of Association.

A well advised purchaser may seek to negotiate a reduction in the 'consideration' price for the company's shares to allow for the contingent tax inherent in the value of the company's assets (the amount of the discount would depend on the likelihood and timing of the assets being sold). In practice, this point is often taken in connection with property development companies where the properties are likely to be sold in the short to medium term. On the other hand, the seller shareholders of a trading company would normally resist this stance.

Apportionment of the sale consideration

15.25 The sale consideration, the form in which it is taken (for example, cash, and/or loan notes and/or shares in the acquirer), and the apportionment between the seller shareholders will invariably be laid down in the sale and purchase agreement. In many case, sellers may be given a free choice as to the form in which they receive their sale consideration and there is no tax rule which requires them all to take the same proportion in (say) cash and shares in the acquiring company.

In some cases, each seller's sale consideration entitlement may not reflect their proportionate shareholding. Some sellers may receive an amount that is more than their pro-rata entitlement based on their shareholding. This may be in accordance with special rights laid down in the Articles of Association or shareholders' agreement. It may also be possible that different shareholders manage to secure different amounts from the purchaser.

However, HMRC are beginning to look more closely at such situations and may seek to impose an employment income tax charge on shareholders who receive more than their entitlement based on a straight pro-rata split of their shareholdings. The argument is that they have disposed of their shares for more than their market value and hence the excess falls to be taxed under *ITEPA 2003, Chapter 3D, Part 7* – see 8.35 for further discussion.

The impact of 'financial assistance'

15.26 The *Companies Act 2006* repeals the provisions in *CA 1985, ss 151–158* and thus abolished the statutory prohibition on the provision of financial assistance for the purchase of shares in a private company from 1 October 2008 (see earlier editions of this book for pre-1 October 2008 position)

However, directors entering into a transaction that involves providing 'assistance' for the purchase of 'their' company's shares must still consider the interests of its creditors and minority shareholders. They must also check to ensure that the company has the relevant legal capacity to provide financial assistance under its articles – many lenders now insist on a specific provision empowering the company to provide financial assistance.

Any financial assistance provided must be consistent with the directors' duty to act in good faith and must be likely to promote the success of the company for the general benefit of its shareholders. The directors should provide detailed board minutes to reflect their reasoning for giving the assistance. They would also need to examine the effect on the company's cash flow and net asset position, and ensure the assistance would not create any financial problems.

Clearly, if the company is struggling financially and there is a risk of insolvency, the provision of assistance is unlikely to be in the best interests of the company's creditors. Furthermore, the directors may liable for wrongful or fraudulent trading or the assistance might be set aside under the Insolvency Act 1986 provisions dealing with transactions at undervalue or 'preferences'.

15.27 The common law restrictions evolving from the ruling in *Trevor v Whitworth* [1887] cannot generally be invoked following the removal of the statutory restriction (see *Fifth Commencement Order of the Companies Act 2006, Sch 4, para 54*). However, the common law principles can still apply to unlawful reductions in capital. Thus, where the company has insufficient distributable reserves, these rules can still be invoked to set aside loans or gifts made by the company to facilitate the purchase of its shares (see 13.95).

A private company can still not give assistance for the purpose of the acquisition of shares in its *public* parent company.

MAIN CGT RULES FOR SHARE SALES

Date of disposal

15.28   The seller will normally generate a capital gain when they sell their shares. A disposal of an asset will be recognised for CGT purposes when an unconditional contract is executed for its sale *(TCGA 1992, s 28(1))*. (The contract date is therefore likely to be particularly important for transactions that straddled the change in the CGT regime on 23 June 2010 since this will determine the relevant CGT rate(s) and ER treatment.)

The case of *Thompson v Salah* (1971) 47 TC 559 provides authority for the proposition that a (prior) oral contract can create a disposal for CGT purposes (except in relation to land) even though it may be unenforceable.

In the case of a conditional contract, the date of disposal is deferred until the relevant condition precedent is satisfied (or waived) *(TCGA 1992, s 28(2))*. A condition precedent refers to an event which is outside the control of the contracting parties – for example obtaining satisfactory tax clearances or relevant regulatory approval etc.

On the other hand, a 'condition subsequent' is merely a term of the contract required to be fulfilled by one of the parties and does not create a conditional contract for CGT. For example, in *Eastham v Leigh London & Provincial Properties* 46 TC 687, one party to the contract covenanted to build an office block and the other party agreed to grant a lease if the office block was completed. It was held that the requirement to build the office block was a condition subsequent being a term of the contract that had to be fulfilled to carry out the contract.

Cash consideration is immediately chargeable to CGT in the tax year of disposal (TCGA 1992, s 28). Tax must be paid on any fixed (ie ascertainable) deferred consideration, even it if is conditional, although the HMRC will refund the tax when it is satisfied that the conditional amount will not be paid. Instalment relief may be available for the tax payments, given the difficulty of paying the tax before the full cash proceeds are received (TCGA 1992, ss 48 and 280).

Historically, fixed deferred consideration has been structured through the use of loan notes as this enabled the relevant CGT to be deferred. However, sellers will now (usually) have to make an election to tax the 'loan note' consideration 'up-front' to benefit from the 10% ER CGT rate on this part of the consideration (see 15.49).

Calculation of capital gain

15.29 In broad terms, under the post-FA 2008 CGT regime, an *individual's/ trustee's* capital gain is simply calculated as the amount by which the sale proceeds (net of allowable incidental costs of disposal) exceeds the amount they originally paid for the shares – often referred to as the 'base cost'.

For individuals/trustees, March 1982 rebasing is compulsory for shares held at 31 March 1982.

The detailed treatment of owner managed company sales under the pre-6 April 2008 regime (including the taper relief rules) is covered in the *2007/08* and earlier editions of this book.)

Example 4

CGT computation for sale of shares

In September 2011, Cristiano sold his 100% shareholding in Ronaldo Ltd for a cash consideration of £4 million (net of legal and professional costs).

Cristiano originally acquired his shareholding in June 1994 for £100,000. Ronaldo Ltd has always been a trading company.

Assuming he claims ER, his CGT liability will be computed as follows:

	£
Net sale proceeds	4,000,000
Less: Acquisition cost (June 1994)	(100,000)
Chargeable gain	3,900,000
Less: Annual exemption	(10,600)
Taxable gain	3,889,400
ER CGT @ 10%	£ 388,940

Pooling of shares

15.30 From 6 April 2008, all shares in a particular company (of the same class) are generally treated as a single 'pooled' asset, regardless of when they were actually acquired. (Following the abolition of taper relief, it is no longer necessary to have special share identification rules.)

This means that where a part disposal of shares occurs, the base cost for each share sold will be based at the average cost of the pooled shares.

Example 5

CGT computation for part disposal of shares

In August 2011, George sold 400 of his 2,000 shares in Best Winger Ltd for £1,500,000 (net of transaction costs). George was neither a director nor an employee of Best Winger Ltd and did not therefore qualify for ER.

He previously acquired his shares as follows:

	Number of shares	£
May 1996 – Purchase	1,500	150,000
June 2007 – On death of founder shareholder – MV	500	1,200,000

George's capital gain would be calculated as follows:

Share Pool

	Number	CGT cost £
May 1996 – Purchase	1,500	150,000
June 2007 – Inherited on death of founder (MV)	500	1,200,000
	2,000	1,350,000
August 2011 – Disposal (£1,350,000 × 400/2,000)	(400)	(270,000)
Balances c/fwd	1,600	1,080,000

CGT computation

	£
Net sale proceeds	1,500,000
Less: Part-disposal cost (from pool)	(270,000)
Capital gain (subject to annual exemption)	1,230,000

Capital losses and the annual exemption

15.31   Sellers will generate a capital loss where their deductible base cost/value exceeds the related sale proceeds. Capital losses arising from 'unacceptable' tax planning (in HMRC's view) may be challenged under the general capital loss anti-avoidance rule (in *TCGA 1992, s 16A*) introduced from 6 December 2006 by the *FA 2007*. Broadly, these provisions prevent losses being allowed for CGT purposes where they arise from arrangements (mainly) designed to secure a tax advantage.

15.32 Special rules prevent the annual exemption being wasted by the use of brought forward losses. For these purposes, the legislation applies the concept of 'adjusted net gains', being the total chargeable gains for the year less the capital losses for the *same* tax year. Provided the adjusted net gains for the year do not exceed the annual exemption, any allowable losses brought forward are ignored and can be carried forward in full. If the adjusted net gains for the year exceed the annual exemption, the amount of brought forward capital losses which may be deducted is restricted to the 'excess' amount only. Capital losses brought forward are, therefore, only used to reduce the adjusted net gains down to the annual exempt amount.

ENTREPRENEURS' RELIEF (ER)

Main qualifying conditions

15.33 For normal share sales the following conditions must be satisfied throughout the one year before the disposal (*TCGA 1992, s 169I(1)(2)(c), (5), (6)*). The seller shareholder must:

- hold shares in a trading company or holding company of a trading group (see 15.36–15.38); and

- be a director or employee of that company (or fellow group company) and it must be their 'personal company' – ie they must own at least 5% of the *ordinary* share capital (carrying at least 5% of the voting rights).

Most owner-managers should have little difficulty in satisfying the relevant tests. The 'director/employee' requirement should not be that onerous, since there is no requirement to work on a 'full time' basis – part-time working would therefore suffice.

The 5% 'shareholding/votes' test must be satisfied by the individual seller alone (for example, there is no attribution of spouses' or relatives' shares). Individual vendors are required to own at least 5% of the *ordinary shares* throughout the relevant period (but see 15.44A for treatment where there has been a recent share exchange). Ordinary shares are widely defined in *CTA 2010, s 1119* to include *all* shares other than *fixed rate* preference shares (ie shares which only have a right to dividends at a fixed rate and no other rights to share in the profits of a company).

Where companies have private-equity investment, this is likely to substantially increase the 'ordinary share' capital and hence may dilute many small minority holdings below the required 5%.

The exercise of employee share options shortly before a sale will also dilute existing shareholdings and must be factored into the potential ER availability for 'minority' shareholders.

The ER conditions are more restrictive than those which applied to the (pre-6 April 2008) business taper regime. For example, a large number of minority and employee shareholders will be unable to meet the conditions necessary to secure ER. They will therefore suffer a significantly higher CGT rate of 28% or 18 % (compared with their typical rate of 10% under the pre-6 April 2008 taper regime).

Trustees can also claim ER in certain special cases where their trust has one or more beneficiaries holding an 'interest in possession' (see 15.35).

ER must be claimed (broadly) 22 months after the end of the relevant tax year in which the share sale is made. Thus, for example, an ER claim on a qualifying gain in 2011/12 must be made by 31 January 2014. Once claimed, ER is applied to the complete eligible gain (up to the maximum £10 million cumulative threshold – see 15.34 for pre-23 June 2010 ER limits) – it cannot be restricted in any way.

However, some flexibility could be provided by selling shares in separate tranches, with an ER election being made against specific disposals.

Basic mechanics of ER

15.34 ER is modelled on the old 'retirement relief' regime, although there is no minimum age requirement (and there is no need to retire!). The shares only need to be held on a qualifying basis for at least one year to obtain ER.

The *Finance (No 2) Act 2010* radically changed the way in which ER is given. For qualifying disposals after 22 June 2010, the gain is simply taxed at an ER CGT rate of 10%. Gains in excess of the current £10 million ER limit are taxed at the top CGT rate of 28%.

Example 6

Calculation of 'post-22 June' 2010 ER

	£000	£000	£000
Eligible gain	1,000	2,000	5,000
ER CGT @ 10%*	100	200	500

* Ignoring annual exemption

Before 23 June 2010, ER chargeable gains were reduced by 4/9ths. Since all gains (including ER gains) were taxed at a flat rate of 18%, the 4/9ths ER reduction resulted in a chargeable balance of 5/9ths taxed at 18%, which produced an effective CGT rate of 10% (ie 5/9 × 18%).

The previous ER gains limits were:

6 April 2008 to 5 April 2010	£1 million
6 April 2010 to 22 June 2010	£2 million
23 June 2010 to 5 April 2011	£5 million

The ER gains allowance is given to both husband and wife, separately, which may be an important consideration when structuring shareholdings.

Example 7

Computation of pre-23 June 2010 ER

	£000	£000	£000
Eligible gain	1,000	2,000	5,000
Less: ER – (4/9ths reduction)	(444)	(888)	(888)
Taxable gain	556	1,112	4,112
CGT @ 18%	100	200	740

*Ignores annual exemption and assumes lifetime limit of £2 million.

ER disposals by trustees

15.35   Trustees can also claim ER in certain special cases where their trust has one or more 'qualifying' beneficiaries holding an *interest in possession* over the entire trust fund or part of the trust (eg a 'sub-fund) which contains the relevant shares) (*TCGA 1992, s169J*). Thus, this relief only applies to those trusts where (broadly) the beneficiary/beneficiaries enjoy(s) an immediate entitlement to the trust income as it arises (see 17.43). However, the trustees do *not* have their own separate ER gains allowance. They merely have the opportunity to benefit from the beneficiary's unused ER allowance (who must give their consent to the 'surrender'). There are special rules to deal with cases where there is more than one qualifying beneficiary (see *TCGA 1992, s 169O*).

The main trust conditions are directed at the 'qualifying beneficiary' rather than the trustees. Thus, the trustees can make a claim for ER provided the *qualifying beneficiary*

- is a director or employee of the company (or any fellow-group company), *and*

- holds at least 5% of the ordinary shares in the company (carrying at least 5% of the voting rights) in their own right.

There is no minimum shareholding condition for the trustees. These 'trust' conditions must be satisfied throughout a period of *one year* ending within the *three years* before the sale. The company must also be a trading company or a holding company of a trading group (see 15.36–15.38) throughout this period.

The conditions mean that to facilitate a potential ER claim by a trust, the (qualifying) beneficiary must have a personal holding of at least 5% of the shares (carrying at least 5% of the votes). The qualifying beneficiary effectively assigns to the trustees all or part of their unused ER allowance (by entering into a joint election). Therefore, if the beneficiary has used all their £10 million allowance, this will preclude any ER claim by the trustees. (*TCGA 1992, s 169N(8)* makes clear that where the trust sells the relevant shares on the same day as the beneficiary (in their own right), the beneficiary is deemed to sell theirs first.)

Any decision for a beneficiary to surrender part of their ER allowance to the trust is not straightforward. For example, if they expect to use their unused ER allowance in the future, they are unlikely to consent. Furthermore, if the beneficiary is not entitled to receive a capital appointment/advancement from the trust, they may not be willing to give up their unused relief (unless perhaps the trustees agreed to make a compensatory payment!)

Trading company/group test

15.36   The ER 'trading company/group' test is virtually the same as the one that previously applied for business asset taper relief and is therefore relatively stringent (*TCGA 1992, s 165A*). One of the key requirements for ER on a straightforward company share sale is that the seller must hold their shares in a trading company or a holding company of a trading group throughout the 12 months before the disposal date.

For ER purposes, a trading company qualifies if it carries on trading activities and its activities do not include 'substantial' *non-trading* activities (see 15.37). The trade must be conducted on a 'commercial basis' with the view to the realisation of profits.

A company will qualify for ER where it carries on activities:

- in the course of, or for the purposes of, its trade;

- for the purposes of a trade it is *preparing* to carry on;

- *with a view* to its:

  (i)   acquiring or starting to carry on a trade;

  (ii) acquiring a significant (ie 51%) interest in the share capital of

      –   another trading company; or

      –   a holding company of a trading group company (see 15.38); or

      –   a qualifying shareholding in a joint-venture company (see 15.39).

  provided that this is actually done as soon as 'reasonably practicable in the circumstances' [*TCGA 1992, s 165A(4), (5), (6)*].

A property letting business of furnished holiday lettings (within *CTA 2010, s 65*) counts as a trade [*TCGA 1992, s 241(3))*].

Since the ER 'trading company' test is virtually the same as the one that applied for (pre-6 April 2008) 'business taper', previous HMRC statements and practices for business taper should also be followed for ER. For example, HMRC indicated that where a company sets aside funds and receives investment income, this will *not* prevent it from being engaged 'wholly' in trading. However, in such cases, the investment must be closely related or integral to the trading business or represent a 'short-term' deposit of funds to meet known future trading liabilities. Furthermore, where a company temporarily holds funds pending their onward distribution to its shareholders, these can normally be counted as a trading activity (*IR Tax Bulletin*, Issue 62, December 2002).

Potential risk areas that are likely to be regarded as 'non-trading' include investment property let to third parties; 'portfolio shareholdings; loans to directors/shareholders and 'non-group' companies, and possibly 'excessive' cash balances (but see also 15.37).

To ensure the availability of ER, a prudent approach should be adopted. This would require, for example, any potentially 'tainted' non-trading activities being transferred to a separate company or being retained in the (proprietor) shareholder's personal ownership.

De minimis test for non-trading activities

15.37 A company is permitted to have non-trading activities for ER provided they do not have any *substantial* effect on the company's activities. HMRC interpret 'substantial' as more than 20%. Thus a 20% benchmark is effectively applied to a range of potential measures to determine whether a company's 'non-trading' activities represent more than 20% of its business. Under self-assessment, it is up to the taxpayer to decide whether the *de minimis* threshold is satisfied (see *Taxline,* March 1999).

All or some of the measures mentioned below would be considered, depending on the facts of the particular case:

● turnover;

● the asset-base, including the value of non-trade assets, such as investments;

● expenses;

● time spent by management and employees.

Thus, for example, the turnover/sales income from non-trading activities would be compared with the total turnover generated by the company and so on. It may be necessary to build up the correct picture over time and this may involve striking a balance between all these factors (*IR Tax Bulletin,* Issue 62, December 2002). There is also a view that the profit and loss account provides a better measure of 'activity' than a balance sheet, and therefore more weight should be given to a company's turnover, income and employee costs.

Although the 20% *de minimis* rule has been adopted by HMRC as their interpretation of 'substantial', it should not be taken as a definitive statutory test. Although HMRC invariably analyse the most difficult cases in practice by applying this methodology, it should not unduly restrict the meaning of 'substantial', which was intended to be an absolute test rather than a relative one (see 3.33A). If any appeal is taken to the Commissioners on this point it is likely that they would form a qualitative assessment on whether any nontrading activities were 'substantial'.

In less 'clear-cut' cases, the principles established in *Farmer (executors of Farmer decd) v CIR* [1999] STC (SCD) 321 (an IHT case on Business Property Relief (BPR) may also be usefully applied to support a company's 'trading' status. In *Farmer,* the Special Commissioner required the whole business to be looked at 'in the round' and all relevant factors had to be considered in determining its qualifying status for BPR. The fact that the property lettings were more profitable than the farming business was not considered to be conclusive – 'the overall context of the business, the capital employed, the time spent by the employees and consultants, and the levels of turnover' all supported the finding that the business mainly consisted of farming. (The judgment in *Farmer* was recently approved of and followed by the Upper Tier Tax Tribunal in *CIR v Andrew Michael Bandler (As executor of the will of the late fourth Earl of Balfour)* [2010] UKUT 200 (TCC).)

Areas where there may be difficulties include companies carrying large cash balances. In the author's experience, such cash balances would have to be shown to be required for working capital or the future requirements of the trade. Clearly, it would be helpful if the company prepared contemporaneous evidence to substantiate this, such as board minutes or formal business plans. In one particular case in which the author was involved, the Inspector was satisfied that a substantial cash balance was required to enable the business to strike profitable deals (as it was able to pay cash 'on the nail!'). Similarly, large cash deposits that are required to carry on the trade would be accepted as being for trading purposes, for example travel agents normally need to keep a fixed level of cash on deposit for bonding requirements. A payment received from a large contract may be held on deposit, etc to meet a future trading requirement (such as the payment of a trade liability or investment for future expansion of the trade (see *ICAEW Tax Faculty, Taxline*, November 2004)).

On the other hand, if the cash is clearly surplus to the current or future needs of the business, it may be prudent for it to be 'extracted' by the shareholders to avoid the potential loss of ER. However, there is a strong view that any surplus cash would have to be actively 'managed' before it was considered to be a 'non-trading' activity of the business. This follows the thinking in *Jowett v O'Neill and Brennan Construction* [1998] STC 482 (see 3.27) which ruled that the mere holding of surplus funds in a bank account does not amount to an activity in any case. Applying that principle, the holding of 'non-managed' surplus cash would be completely ignored.

In summary HMRC tends to accept that cash generated from trading activities should not necessarily prejudice a company's 'trading' status. However, if cash balances are applied and managed as 'investment' assets then HMRC will treat them as 'non-trading' items.

Holding company of a trading group

15.38   To qualify as a holding company of a trading group, a two-stage test must be satisfied:

(a)   the company must be a holding company – ie a company that has one or more 51% subsidiaries (*TCGA 1992, s 165A(2)*);

(b)   the group must be a trading group, ie when looking at all its activities together, it must carry on trading activities (as defined in 15.36), although 'insubstantial' non-trading activities within the 20% *de minimis* rule noted in 15.37 are permitted (*TCGA 1992, s 165A(7)*).

The statutory definition looks at 'all the activities of the group' *taken together*. This means that all intra-group activities are ignored – thus the letting of property by one (51%) group member to another would be disregarded when looking at the level of non-trading activities. However, this 'netting-off' does not apply to transactions with qualifying joint venture companies (see 15.39).

Provided these criteria can be satisfied, the parent company's shareholders will be able to claim ER, despite the fact that the company might be treated as an investment company for corporation tax purposes.

Investments in joint ventures

15.39   On general principles, substantial investments in 'joint-venture' companies could prejudice a company's/group's 'trading' status for ER purposes (unless they fall within the 20% *de minimis* rule for 'non-trading activities' (see 15.37).

However, there are beneficial rules in *TCGA 1992, s 165A* which enable certain qualifying investments in 'joint venture' companies (defined in *TCGA 1992, s 165A(145)*) to be treated as part of a company's/group's trading activities. A shareholding in a 'joint-venture company' (JVC) qualifies for 'trading' treatment provided the participating company (or group) holds at least 10% of its ordinary shares and:

(*a*)   the joint-venture company is a trading company or holding company of a trading group (see 15.36–15.38); and

(*b*)   at least 75% of the joint-venture company's equity share capital is held by five or fewer participating shareholders (irrespective of their tax residence status)

Where the equity investment in the JVC qualifies, an appropriate part of its trading activities are attributed to the 'investee' trading company or group. Thus, for example, where a holding company of a trading group holds 40% in a qualifying JVC, it is deemed to be carrying on 40% of the JVCs trading activities.

Where various group members each hold a shareholding in the same JVC, all these shareholdings are aggregated and treated as a single shareholding for the purpose of the above tests. If the JVC is itself a holding company of a group, the legislation looks at the activities of its group as a whole, enabling intra-group activities to be ignored.

Example 8

ER – Holding company of a trading group (with joint venture shareholding)

The structure of the Banks Ltd group (showing the ordinary shares held) is as follows:

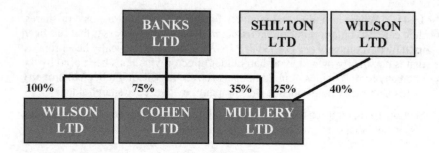

As 51% + subsidiaries, both Wilson Ltd and Cohen Ltd will form part of the Banks Ltd 'trading group' for ER purposes.

However, although Mullery Ltd is not a 51% subsidiary, it should be a qualifying JVC (since it is a trading company, at least 10% of its ordinary share capital is held by Banks Ltd, and at least 75% of its share capital is held by no more than 5 companies). This means that the Mullery Ltd shares are not treated as an investment by Banks Ltd. Instead, Banks Ltd is treated as carrying on 35% of the trading activities carried on by Mullery Ltd.

Taking all these facts together, Banks Ltd qualifies as a holding company of a trading group.

Dealing with risk and informal HMRC clearances

15.40   In certain cases, shareholders may have doubts as to whether their company satisfies the relatively stringent criteria to be a qualifying 'trading company or holding company of a trading group' for the purposes of ER. For example, a company or group may hold substantial cash investments giving rise to a real concern as to whether any 'excess' element falls within HMRC's 20% de minimis rule (see 15.37).

Some degree of certainty can be obtained from HMRC under the 'non-statutory' business clearance procedure (introduced from April 2008). HMRC have indicated they are willing to accept applications in cases of genuine uncertainty on issues affecting shareholders' ER entitlement (provided this is commercially significant). It is therefore possible, for example, to obtain a ruling from HMRC as to whether a company qualifies as a 'trading company' or 'trading group' for ER purposes. HMRC have indicated a target date of 28 days for replying.

ER on associated disposals of personally held property

15.41 Where an individual qualifies for the relief on the disposal of shares, they can also obtain relief on an *associated* disposal of an asset that has been used by the company (*TCGA 1992, s 169K*). This would typically be a property that is personally owned by a shareholder/director which has been used by the company for its business, but it might also cover the sale of intellectual property that is personally held (outside the company) by the seller shareholder.

Section 169K requires the following conditions to be satisfied for a qualifying 'associated disposal' (in the context of an ER-related share sale within *TCGA 1992, s 169K(2)(b)*):

- The seller shareholder must make the 'associated disposal' as part of their 'withdrawal from participation' in the business carried on by the company or by a member of the trading group [*TCGA 1992, s 169K(3)*]. It is understood that HMRC will interpret this in the same way as it did for the 'old' corresponding 'retirement relief' associated disposal condition. Thus, the 'withdrawal from participation' test can be met by simply selling part of the shareholding – a single share will apparently suffice!

- Throughout the *one-year* period (normally) prior to the sale of the shares, the relevant property has been used for the purposes of the company's trade [*TCGA 1992, s 169K(4)*].

The conditions for associated disposal relief are therefore quite restrictive in terms of timing. For example, the sale of the property some time before the share sale would not qualify (since it would *not* have been used for the purposes of the company's trade up to the date of the share sale).

15.42 The ER on an associated disposal can be also scaled down on a 'just and reasonable' basis (under *TCGA 1992, s 169P*) to reflect cases where (amongst other things):

- the property has only been *partly* used for the purposes of the company's trade throughout the seller's period of ownership;

- a rent has been charged (*after 5 April 2008*) by the 'seller' to the company for its use of the property.

The restriction is generally calibrated from the date the property was first acquired, with an important exception being made for the receipt of rent. In this context, rent is defined as 'any form of consideration given for the use of the asset'.

In making the 'just and reasonable' restriction for rent, any period before 6 April 2008 is ignored (*TCGA 1992, s 169S*). This makes sense since, under the pre-6 April 2008 taper regime, the payment of rent did not affect the availability of business taper on personally held property let to trading companies. Thus, where the owner-manager had previously charged a commercial rental for the property before 6 April 2008, this would not restrict their 'associated disposal' ER. However, continuing to charge a rent after 5 April 2008 will lead to a 'just and reasonable' restriction in the gain (potentially) qualifying for ER. Thus, where a full market rent has been charged throughout the (post-5 April 2008) period of ownership, the gain would not qualify for associated disposal relief. HMRC would effectively regard the asset as a non-eligible *investment* one.

STRUCTURING THE CONSIDERATION FOR A SHARE SALE

Types of consideration

15.43   Sellers may sell their shares for:

(*a*)   a cash consideration;

(*b*)   shares in the acquiring company;

(*c*)   loan notes issued by the acquiring company;

(*d*)   a mixture of the above.

The consideration may be paid immediately on completion or on a deferred basis. Deferred consideration can either be structured as fixed (see 15.4) or variable, for example, depending on the future profits under a so-called earn-out arrangement (see 15.61). There is much to be said for receiving all the consideration up-front as a guaranteed amount, despite the fact that it will attract an immediate tax liability.

Consideration satisfied in shares

Basic share exchange rules

15.44   Where sellers of a private company receive shares in the acquiring company in exchange for their shares, the CGT liability on the disposal can usually be deferred under *TCGA 1992, s 135* provided:

(*a*)   the acquiring company ends up with more than 25% of the target company's ordinary shares (or the greater part of the voting power in the target company); and (*b*)   HMRC are satisfied that the transaction was undertaken for commercial reasons and not for tax avoidance (see 15.45) [*TCGA 1992, s 137*].

It is usually advisable to obtain advance clearance on this point from HMRC under *TCGA 1992, s 138*. If only part of the consideration is satisfied in shares, then only a pro-rata portion of the gain can be 'rolled-over'. Thus, if the consideration consists of a mixture of cash and shares in the acquiring company, then *TCGA 1992, s 128(3)* will come into play to treat the cash received as a disposal of an interest in the shares. In computing the capital gain on the cash 'element', the base cost of the original shareholding would be apportioned on a pro-rata basis (ie cost multiplied by cash consideration/ total consideration (being cash plus the market value of the new consideration shares). The balance of the original base cost would be attributed to the new shares in the acquirer.

Strictly, the CGT reorganisation rules provide that the 'new' shares received by the seller in the acquiring company are treated as having been acquired at the same time and for the same amount as his old shareholding [*TCGA 1992, s 127*]. Thus, if the original shares were held at 31 March 1982, the base cost of the new 'consideration' shares will be the 31 March 1982 value of the old shares.

Where the seller receives both shares and cash (as discussed above), the new shares would only carry part of the original base cost (deemed to be acquired at the same time as the original shares).

Where ER is potentially available on the sale, it is possible to make a special election to disapply the 'no disposal' rule. This enables ER to be claimed against the consideration received as shares in the acquirer (see 15.47).

Example 9

Sale consideration satisfied in shares

In July 2011, Mr Beckham sold all his 51% shareholding in Galaxy Ltd to Freekicks plc for £5,000,000, which was satisfied in the form of 500,000 new ordinary £1 shares (worth £10 each) in Freekicks plc.

Mr Beckham originally acquired his Galaxy Ltd shares for £100,000 in May 1993. Going forward, his new shareholding in Freekicks plc represented about 20% of its share capital (carrying commensurate voting rights). Mr Beckham will also continue to act as Operations Director for Galaxy Ltd.

Assuming the necessary TCGA 1992, s 138 clearance is obtained; Mr Beckham's share exchange will not give rise to any disposal for CGT purposes. He will be treated as having acquired his 500,000 £1 Freekicks plc shares in May 1993 for £100,000, ie 20p each.

He probably will not wish to make an election under *TCGA 1992, s169Q* (see 15.47) since he is likely to benefit from ER on a subsequent sale of his Freekicks plc shares. Based on current facts, he should qualify for ER since he now holds around 20% of the ordinary shares in Freekicks plc and is a director of Galaxy Ltd (a fellow-group company of Freekicks plc).

Share exchanges and the ER 'personal company' test

15.44A   On a close reading of the ER 'personal company' definition in *TCGA 1992, s 169S(3)* and *TCGA 1992, s 135* share exchange legislation, it is difficult to come to the conclusion that the 'look through' CGT reorganisation provisions can treat the pre-share exchange period as counting towards the minimum one year 'personal company' condition for ER purposes. Thus, where a sale of the 'new' shares takes place within one year of a share exchange, it would appear that the sale could not qualify for ER.

The CIOT Technical department put this problem to HMRC in 2010 and obtained confirmation from HMRC's Capital Gains Technical Group that (provided no *TCGA 1992, s 169Q* election has been made – see 15.47 below), the pre-share exchange period would count towards the one year personal company test provided the relevant ER conditions were satisfied in relation to the previous shareholding. This practice would appear to be in the nature of an HMRC concession since the legislation does not provide for it.

The genuine commercial purpose/no tax avoidance test

15.45   The seller only receives their CGT deferral under *TCGA 1992, s 135* where they take shares and/or loan notes wholly/partly as consideration for their original shares provided the transaction has been structured for genuine commercial purposes and not mainly driven by tax avoidance motives [*TCGA 1992, s 137*].

The seller can obtain certainty on this point by applying for advance clearance under *TCGA 1992, s 138* to confirm HMRC is satisfied that the 'commercial purpose/no tax avoidance' test has been met. It should be noted that a clearance under *TCGA 1992, s 138* will not necessarily guarantee that the other preconditions for s 135 relief have been met, as HMRC invariably points out by way of caveat in their clearance letter.

However, the 'commercial purpose/tax avoidance' test in *TCGA 1992, s 137* does not apply to 'minority' shareholders who hold no more than 5% of the target company's shares. The rationale for this useful rule is that such shareholders are unlikely to have any say in how the transaction is structured – they are effectively deemed to be acting commercially.

Issues arising from the *Snell* case

15.46 HMRC will almost certainly deny clearance where they consider the taxpayer has taken shares/loan notes with the view to becoming non-resident (enabling to avoid a UK CGT charge on their sale consideration). This was demonstrated in the recent case of *Snell v HMRC* [2007] STC 1279. In December 1996, Mr Snell agreed to sell his shares for a total consideration of around £7.3 million of which approximately £6.6 million were taken in the form of loan notes. Mr Snell left the UK on 2 April 1997 and subsequently became non-UK resident. The Revenue sought to deny the deferral of the gain attributable to the loan notes on the grounds that *TCGA 1992, s 137* applied since one of the main purposes of Mr Snell taking loan notes was to avoid CGT. (A *s 138* clearance was *not* sought.)

The High Court concurred and concluded that the main purpose of the arrangements (ie the taking of the loan notes with the view to their redemption whilst non-resident) was for the avoidance of CGT. Thus, *TCGA 1992, s 137* applied to prevent the operation of *TCGA 1992, s 135* and Mr Snell had a CGT disposal when he received the loan notes. In reaching their decision, the High Court placed particular significance on the Special Commissioners' findings of fact. It was very important to consider what was in Mr Snell's mind at the time he agreed to take loan note. This was largely based on contemporaneous documentary evidence, which looked at such things as information memorandums and reports by the taxpayer's advisers. Although there were obvious difficulties in considering Mr Snell's 'purpose' (given that this took place a long time ago), the Special Commissioners concluded that, on the balance of probability, Mr Snell was much more likely to have dictated that he wanted a loan note 'in the expectation that it would be redeemed when he was non-resident'.

Special election to obtain ER on share exchange

Effect of election

15.47 Because the 'reorganisation' rule provides there is no CGT disposal, the seller would normally be unable to claim ER on the value of the acquirer's shares received as part of their sale consideration. This would be unfortunate if the seller was unable to claim ER on a later sale of their 'consideration' shares – for example, because they did not possess the requisite 5% shareholding in the acquiring company.

The ER legislation recognises this problem and provides that the seller can make a special election (under *TCGA 1992, s 169Q*) to opt out of the normal share-for-share exchange treatment. By making a s 169Q election the seller is treated as having made a normal CGT disposal with the value of the acquirer's shares being reflected as all/part of their overall sale consideration. In such cases, the benefit of the ER would be reflected in the (higher) market value base cost of the shares in the acquiring company.

Example 10

Effect of special ER election on share exchanges

Martin has been a 'management' shareholder since June 2000 and holds 10% of the equity share capital of Peters Ltd (a successful music publishing and recording company). He acquired his 10,000 £1 shares at par but was subject to an employment income tax charge on their full market value of £20,000 (which was therefore his base cost).

In July 2011 Peters Ltd was taken over by Boleyn plc. As part of this transaction, Martin received sale consideration of £600,000, which was satisfied as follows:

	£
Cash	200,000
Shares in Boleyn plc, valued at	400,000

Martin's shares in Boleyn plc represent a 3% shareholding (with commensurate voting rights). He is therefore unlikely to qualify for ER on a subsequent sale of these shares. However, by making a TCGA 1992 s 169Q election, he could benefit from ER on the *total* consideration received on the July 2011 sale, as shown below:

		£
Sale consideration	Cash	200,000
	Boleyn plc shares	400,000
		600,000
Less: Base cost		(20,000)
		580,000
Less: Annual exemption		(10,600)
Taxable gain		569,400)
ER CGT @ 10%		£56,940

Martin's base cost of his Boleyn plc shares would be their full market value of £400,000 (as opposed to £13,333 (4/6 × £20,000), being the pro-rata original cost of his Peters Ltd shares if the reorganisation rules had applied).

Deciding whether to make a s 169Q election

15.48   The *s 169Q* election is made on an 'all or nothing' basis. Thus, for example, it is not possible to restrict its application to gains of up to the (current) £10 million ER limit. Such elections must be made within 22 months after the end of the tax year in which the sale occurs.

The potential consequences of making a *s 169Q* election should always be considered when structuring any deal. Because the reorganisation rule is disapplied, the seller would generally incur a CGT liability on the 'ER-relieved' gain. The seller would therefore need to ensure they had sufficient cash consideration to fund the tax liability. Furthermore, the timing of any future tax liability (when the higher base cost comes into play) must also be considered.

Clearly, such an election would not be appropriate where the 'cash' element of a company share sale produced chargeable gains exceeding the ER limit of £10 million.

LOAN NOTE CONSIDERATION – QCBS VERSUS NON-QCBS

QCB v non-QCBs

15.49   In many deals, the seller may agree to accept deferred payment for part of the sale consideration by taking loan notes in the acquiring company. As a general rule, where the purchaser satisfies part of the consideration by issuing loan notes, an appropriate part of the seller's gain is deferred until the loan note is redeemed for payment. The precise mechanics of the deferral depends on the tax status of the loan note, as this varies between Qualifying Corporate Bonds (QCBs) (see 15.50) and non-QCBs (see 15.54)

These CGT deferral rules are subject to HMRC being satisfied that the loan note has been issued for genuine commercial reasons and not mainly to avoid tax (*TCGA 1992, s 137*) (see 15.45). The seller would normally apply for a *TCGA 1992, s 138* clearance to seek advance confirmation of this point from HMRC.

QCBs

15.50   Broadly, most non-convertible loan notes will represent Qualifying Corporate Bonds (QCBs). Where the acquiring company satisfies the consideration by the issue of QCB loan notes, no immediate CGT liability arises. A *TCGA 1992, s 138* clearance should be obtained to ensure that HMRC is satisfied that the loan note has been issued for a bona fide commercial purpose and not for tax avoidance (see 15.47 for 'combined' tax clearance procedure). However, the capital gain (or loss) based on the *deemed* disposal of the shares at the time of the exchange is held-over and will become payable (or allowable) when the QCB is either paid or redeemed. Effectively, the seller's tax position is frozen at the date of the exchange with the payment of the CGT being postponed on an interest-free basis [*TCGA 1992, s 116(10), (11)*].

For *post-5 April 2008* redemptions, any taper relief that would have accrued on the held-over gain is lost. *Section 116(10)* only holds over the chargeable gain, which is before taper relief [*TCGA 1992, s 2A(2)*]. Thus, where the gain becomes charged on a (post-5 April 2008) redemption no taper relief will be applied. However, in certain cases, it may be possible to claim transitional ER against the pre-6 April 2008 gain (see 15.52)

QCB gains and ER – sales between 6 April 2008 and 22 June 2010

15.51   Under the pre-23 June 2010 regime, where QCBs were received on a share sale, any available ER is deducted in arriving at the gain held over under TCGA 1992, s 116(10).

Thus, provided the seller qualifies for ER and it is claimed, the 4/9ths ER reduction is applied against the QCB gain. For the purposes of ER, TCGA 1992 s 169R then calculates the deferred QCB gain as though it arose at the time of the original share sale with the 4/9ths reduction. This reduced amount then becomes chargeable under TCGA 1992, s 116(10)(b) when the QCB is redeemed/encashed. Consequently any encashment before 23 June 2010 is taxed at 18% (effective rate – 10%) and from 23 June 2010, if the 28% rate applies, the effective rate is 15.55% (5/9ths 28%).

For details of transitional ER that may be available on pre-6 April 2008 QCB gains, see 15.52.

QCB gains and ER – sales after 23 June 2010

15.51A   The *Finance (No 2) Act 2010* made an unwelcome change to the way ER is dealt with on QCB gains held-over from 23 June 2010. This follows the change in ER to a straight 10% CGT charge. In such cases, any available ER is no longer factored into the held-over gain, so that the 'gross' gain is postponed.

If the seller wishes to claim ER on their QCB gain, they must make a special election under *TCGA 1992, s 169R*. This treats the QCB gain as being a chargeable disposal at the time of the share sale (ie the original shares are treated as sold for the QCB consideration), against which the ER CGT 10% rate can be claimed. By making an election, the normal QCB hold-over rules in *TCGA 1992, s 116(10)* do not apply. The *TCGA 1992, s 169R* election must be made by the 31 January following the tax year of the share sale.

This change therefore gives rise to a dilemma for sellers – should they elect under *TCGA 1992, s 169R* and pay 10% ER CGT 'up-front' on the share gain or defer their share gain under *TCGA 1992 s 116(10)* and (probably) pay CGT at 28% on the full held-over gain on redemption (with no ER)?

If the seller wishes to tax the QCB gain up-front to obtain a low ER CGT 10% rate, they would need to ensure that the deal structure provides sufficient cash funds to pay the CGT liability on the 31 January following the tax year of the sale. Where the *TCGA 1992, s 169R* election is made, there is no QCB hold-over and thus the redemption does not trigger any taxable gain. See Example 11 below.

Example 11

Treatment of QCB gains and ER (post-22 June 2010 share sale)

In May 2011, Joe sold his 40% shareholding in Magic Cole Ltd to Blues plc for £4,000,000 of which:

–   £500,000 was paid in cash on completion: and

–   £3,500,000 was satisfied by the issue of a QCB loan note (bearing interest at 9%, bank guaranteed and redeemable after 12 months)

Joe subscribed for his 40,000 £1 shares in Blues Ltd at par in May 2002.

Joe's CGT position is as follows:

2011/12 – CGT on cash consideration

Cash			£
Sale consideration	– Cash		500,000
Less: Base cost	£40,000 ×	$\frac{£500,000}{(£500,000 + £3,500,000)}$	(5,000)
Capital gain			495,000
Less: Annual exemption			(10,600)
Taxable gain			484,400
ER CGT @ 10%			£48,440

If Joe does *not* make an election under TCGA 1992, s169R, all the QCB gain is held-over (without the benefit of ER).

Postponed QCB gain

		£
QCB consideration		3,500,000
Less: Base cost	£40,000 less £5,000 used against in 2011/12 disposal	(35,000)
Postponed gain		3,465,000

The postponed gain is likely to become taxable on redemption at 28%, being £970,200 (ignoring the annual exemption).

2011/12 – Taxable QCB gain at ER CGT rate

If Joe makes an election under *TCGA 1992, s 169R* for the QCB consideration to be taxable in 2011/12 , he can obtain a 10% ER CGT rate on the QCB gain.

	£
QCB consideration	3,500,000
Less: Base cost	(35,000)
Capital gain	3,465,000
ER CGT @ 10%	346,500

An election to benefit from ER would give Joe a substantial tax saving provided he can manage the acceleration of his tax liability.

Transitional ER for pre-6 April 2008 QCBs

15.52   Special rules apply to QCB loan notes that were acquired as consideration for a pre-5 April 2008 share sale. Taper relief ceases to be relevant where QCB gains are crystallised under the new CGT regime. However, the benefit of any indexation allowance that was built into the held-over gain is retained on a post-5 April 2008 redemption.

After strong representations, HMRC considered that it would be inequitable to grant no form of transitional relief in such cases. There are therefore special rules which enable ER to be claimed against the QCB gain becoming chargeable on a post-5 April 2008 redemption (*FA 2008, Sch 3, para 7*). Clearly, the QCB holder must have unused ER available to offset against the crystallised gain.

However, relief is only given provided the seller would have been entitled to ER on the original pre-6 April 2008 share sale (on the assumption that the ER legislation had been in force at that time).

FA 2008, Sch 3, para 7, provides for 'transitional' ER to be claimed on pre-6 April 2008 share sale gains which have been held-over under the EIS CGT deferral regime. In such cases, the seller can claim ER when the deferred gain crystallises after 5 April 2008 ER is only available where the seller would have been able to satisfy the relevant ER conditions at the time of the original share sale (assuming the ER legislation was then in force). The transitional rules are quite complex and the application of ER depends on when the first 'disposal' of the QCB takes place – known as the 'first relevant disposal'. This would be when part or all of the loan note is encashed/redeemed (see *FA 2008, Sch 3, para 7(2)*).

Where the 'first relevant disposal' took place before 23 June 2010, the 'transitional' ER on the entire postponed gain is claimed and calculated at that point (with the prevailing £1 million/£2 million gains limit (see 15.34) being applied, depending on whether this is before 5 April 2010 or between 6 April 2010 and 22 June 2010). An appropriate part of this postponed gain is then charged under *TCGA 1992 s 116(10)* (reflecting the ER reduction) at the prevailing CGT rate.

Example 12

Treatment of (pre-6 April 2008) postponed QCB gains

Scott had been a 40% shareholder director of Captain Ltd until May 2007 when the company was sold to Icelandsson Ltd. As part of the deal, Scott received a QCB loan note of (say) £600,000 which carried a postponed gain of £500,000.

Since Scott would have qualified for ER in May 2007 (on the assumption that the ER legislation had been in force), he is entitled to claim the ER against the postponed gain on his 'first relevant disposal' after 6 April 2008. Thus, when £250,000 of the loan note was repaid in May 2010, Scott's chargeable ER postponed gain would be £138,889 – calculated as follows:

First relevant disposal = May 2010	
	£
Full Postponed gain	500,000
Less: ER 4/9ths	(222,222)
Post-ER gain	277,778
Taxable in May 2010	
£277,778 × (£250,000(encashed)/£500,000)	£138,889

On the other hand, if Scott's first relevant disposal took place after 22 June 2010, the new ER CGT 10% rate would apply to the postponed gain crystallising on the redemption (with the prevailing ER gains limit being applied).

Bad debt relief issues with QCBs

15.53 A serious disadvantage with QCB loan notes is that no bad debt relief is available if the acquiring company is unable to pay (since a QCB is not a chargeable asset for CGT purposes).

However, when the loan note is redeemed for little or no value (for example, by the liquidator), the original gain would still be taxed in full. In these dire circumstances, HMRC (by concession) permit the worthless loan note to be 'gifted' to a charity under *TCGA 1992, s 257* without triggering the held over gain (see Revenue Interpretation RI 23). However, it would be prudent not to rely on this and it is therefore always advisable to seek commercial bank guarantees for the loan notes which means the seller will always get their money, and so the lack of 'bad debt' relief with QCBs ceases to be a problem.

Non-QCBs

Common non-QCB terms

15.54 Different rules apply where the purchaser issues non-QCBs.

The terms of such loan notes are designed to fall outside the definition of a QCB in *TCGA 1992, s 117*. Thus, common types of non-QCBs would include loan notes which:

- are convertible into shares in the acquiring company;

- carry the right to subscribe for further shares or loan notes (see, for example, *Businessman v Inspector of Taxes* [2003] STC (SCD) 403); and

- contain the right of repayment in a foreign currency at a spot rate prior to redemption.

In such cases, the possibility of the loan note generating an exchange gain which might be a 'deep gain' (when viewed at the outset) was considered sufficient for it to be treated as a Relevant Discounted Security (RDS) (within what is now *CTA 2010, Chapter 8, Part 5*). Unless the holder's potential gain was appropriately 'capped', this could cause the (purported non-QCB) loan note to be a QCB. However, HMRC confirmed that they would not seek to apply the RDS rules in this way.

Some useful commentary on the use of 'foreign currency conversion' clauses to create non-QCB loan notes was provided in *Harding v HMRC* [2008] EWCA Civ 1164. In this case, the taxpayer's loan notes contained an option for redemption in various foreign currencies so that they fell outside the QCB definition in s117(1)(b) TCGA 1992 (which requires a *QCB loan note* to be 'expressed in sterling and in respect of which no provision is made for conversion into, or redemption in, a currency other than sterling'.

Although the main tax issue arising in *Harding* has now been dealt with by amending legislation, HMRC did accept that a right to redeem a loan note in a foreign currency would be sufficient to make it a non-QCB, even where there was a 'cap and collar' mechanism to reduce the foreign currency risk (in this case, the potential foreign currency exposure on redemption was limited to two per cent).

Basic CGT treatment

15.55   Where a debenture (ie any written acknowledgement of a debt) is received in exchange for shares/debentures under the CGT reorganisation rules, this is automatically deemed to be a security for CGT purposes under *TCGA 1992, s 251(6)*. It is not therefore necessary for the debenture to constitute a (debt on a) security under normal principles (ie it does not necessarily have to be 'marketable', readily transferable and so on).

Since non-QCB loan notes represent a security, where they are received in exchange for shares, this is treated as a share reorganisation under *TCGA 1992, s 127* (by virtue of the share exchange rules in *TCGA 1992, s 135*) (see 15.44). The appropriate part of the seller's original base cost in the target company's shares is therefore treated as given for the non-QCB security at the original acquisition date(s). (Non-QCBs were often used under the taper relief regime to extend the seller's taper relief period, but these taper relief issues cease to be relevant after 5 April 2008.)

Since the CGT deferral for non-QCBs is governed by the CGT reorganisation rules in *TCGA 1992, s 127*, ER may potentially be claimed on the value of the sale consideration received as a non-QCB (assuming the relevant ER conditions are satisfied) by making a TCGA 1992, s 169Q election (*TCGA 1992, s 169Q(1)*). By making this special election, the value of the non-QCB consideration is brought into the seller's CGT computation at the date of the sale (as explained in 15.47). (Following the change in the treatment of ER on QCB gains, the QCB treatment now operates in a similar way to non-QCBs.) Before structuring any deal or deciding whether an election would be beneficial, the relevant factors in 15.48 should be considered.

15.56   Where the seller is unable to obtain a commercial bank guarantee for the loan note, many feel that a non-QCB would be a more prudent alternative to a QCB. This avoids the QCB-type risk of triggering a CGT charge on the cancellation of the loan note (for example, where the acquiring company becomes insolvent – see 15.53).

The CGT reorganisation treatment also means that automatic 'bad debt' relief is obtained, as any gain or loss on the ultimate redemption of the non-QCB loan note is calculated by reference to the amount actually repaid (rather than the original sale value). Therefore, little or no gain would arise where the holder is forced to accept minimal redemption proceeds (because, for example, the acquiring company has become insolvent).

The benefits of a 'non-QCB' loan note would not, of course, be realised if the seller elects to tax it 'up-front to 'lock-in' to the 10% ER CGT rate (see 15.55 above).

EARN-OUT DEALS

Background to earn-outs

15.57   Earn-outs fulfil a useful function by reconciling the so-called 'price gap' that often exists between a seller and purchaser. Many sellers believe that they are selling their business ahead of its maximum profit potential. Consequently, they will want to negotiate a price for the business that reflects its future earnings potential. On the other hand, most prudent purchasers will only be willing to agree a deal based on future (increased) profits when they are actually 'delivered' by the business. Thus, by incorporating an 'earn-out' arrangement as part of the pricing mechanism for the purchase of the shares, the seller's and purchaser's objectives can be satisfied.

An earn-out deal typically involves the seller receiving a fixed sum on completion, with further sums being paid over the next two or three years, calculated on a formula based on the actual results of the business over this period. The seller usually continues to be employed in the business during the earn-out period in a key management, technical or sales position. Thus, through their efforts during the 'earn-out' period, sellers have the incentive to increase their disposal consideration, thereby ensuring that the purchaser's acquisition is successful.

However, a number of tax issues should carefully be thought through before the earn-out consideration clauses are agreed, otherwise the seller may have some undesirable or indeed unintended tax charges – these are discussed in 15.58 to 15.71. Furthermore, care must also be taken to avoid the risk of HMRC characterising all or some of the earn-out payments as an 'employment' bonus, since this would trigger PAYE and NIC charges (see 15.69).

The *Marren v Ingles* dicta

15.58   The tax treatment of an earn-out transaction is largely based on the decision in *Marren v Ingles* [1980] STC 500. Consequently, where a taxpayer sells an asset (the original or main asset) with a right to receive a future unquantifiable sum (for example, a formula based earn-out), the value of that right is included as part of the CGT consideration received for the original asset. Consequently, to the extent that ER is available, the gain enhanced by the value of that right (included as consideration) would qualify for ER in the usual way.

It was further held that the taxpayer acquires, as an entirely separate asset, a 'right' or 'chose in action'. Thus, as and when the earn-out payments are received, further (deemed) CGT disposals arise in respect of the earn-out right itself under *TCGA 1992, s 22* (representing capital sums derived from the right to receive the earn-out and not the disposal of shares).

Even where the seller has ER available after the original share sale, 'earn-out' gains can never qualify for the relief. As they effectively relate to a (part) disposal of the *earn-out right*, they do not meet the 'disposal of shares' requirement for ER (see 15.33). Thus, gains arising on earn-out payments made after 22 June 2010 would invariably be taxed at 28% (18% between 6 April 2008 and 22 June 2010).

If the deferred consideration can be readily ascertained at the date of the sale, this is taxed under *TCGA 1992, s 48* (and the *'Marren v Ingles'* principles do *not* apply).

Election to carry back capital loss on earn-out payments

15.59   One of the main potential problems arising from the *Marren v Ingles* treatment is the risk of being taxed on an unrealised gain, ie the seller would suffer tax on the value of the right (when their shares are sold). In an extreme case, if the earn-out falls (well) below expectation, this could result in a capital loss arising on the disposal of the right in a subsequent tax year. Before the *Finance Act 2003* introduced a special relief, any such capital loss could not be carried back to reduce the seller's original capital gain. This meant that the seller would suffer tax on an amount that exceeded his overall economic gain from the earn-out transaction.

Under *TCGA 1992, ss 279A–279D* capital losses arising on *earn-out rights* (arising after 9 April 2003) can be carried back against the gain on the original sale of the shares (which includes the original value of the earn-out right). This special capital loss carry back rule is only available to individual and trustee sellers (companies do not benefit from this facility).

An individual or trustee seller can make an election under *TCGA 1992, s 279A*, provided broadly:

● the right was acquired as full/partial consideration for the sale of another asset;

● the right is a *Marren v Ingles* right to 'unascertainable' consideration (such as in the case of an 'earn-out');

● when the right was acquired, there was no corresponding disposal of it (for example, where it arose from the contract for the sale of shares); and

- the disposal of the original asset (such as shares) was made in an earlier tax year.

Where an election is made under *TCGA 1992, s 279A*, any allowable capital loss arising on the disposal of the (earn-out) right can be 'carried back' and set-off against the gain arising on the sale of the original asset (for example, the shares).

A *s 279A* election is irrevocable and must specify:

- the relevant capital loss;

- the right disposed of;

- the tax year in which the right was disposed of;

- the tax year in which the right was acquired; and

- the original asset(s).

The election must be made by the first anniversary of the 31 January next following the tax year of loss. Each loss must be the subject of a separate election.

Structuring as a bonus arrangement

15.60   Occasionally some cash earn-out transactions have been structured as a 'bonus' arrangement to avoid the undesirable tax effects of the *Marren v Ingles* dicta. This broadly involves providing for a 'profit-based' bonus under the seller's director's service agreement which replaces the earn-out in the sale agreement. The bonus would only be taxable as earnings when *received*. This may also suit the purchaser as the bonus would be deductible against the target company's trading profits (which may outweigh the inherent employer's NIC cost). However, since CGT rates are still much lower than income tax rates, most sellers are likely to prefer the traditional 'earn-out' route.

Even though a significant part of the earn-out may be taxed 'up-front', it is likely to be taxed at a much lower rate than the 40%/50% PAYE income tax on a bonus. However, HMRC might seek to challenge certain 'earn-out' deals (with the view to taxing them as employment income). This is likely to be the case where they consider that the substance of the 'earn out' arrangement is to provide a reward for services as an employee/director as opposed to consideration for the sale of shares (see also 15.71).

Quoted company purchasers also tend to prefer the earn-out route to avoid potentially substantial bonuses having a detrimental impact on their earnings. They may seek to satisfy the earn-out in shares or loan notes, which would enable the seller's CGT on the earn-out to be deferred (see 15.62–15.67).

Worked example of cash-based earn-out

15.61 The CGT treatment of a (cash) earn-out transaction is explained in Example 13 below.

Example 13

CGT treatment of share sale on a 'cash' earn-out basis

Tony formed Cottee Ltd in July 1985 subscribing for the entire share capital of 50,000 £1 ordinary shares at par.

On 5 January 2012, Tony sold all his shares in Cottee Ltd on an earn-out basis. The sale contract provided for:

- initial cash consideration of £500,000 (net of disposal costs) to be paid on completion; and

- a deferred earn-out consideration based on the 'defined earn-out' profits for the three years ending 31 December 2014, payable in cash six months following the end of each relevant accounting period.

Tony also entered into a three-year director's service agreement, under which he would continue as managing director of the business during the three year earn-out period.

Technical overview

Tony's earn-out consideration is 'unascertainable' at the date of disposal (5 January 2012). Under the rules established in *Marren v Ingles,* he is treated as selling his shares for an initial cash consideration (£500,000), plus the value at that date of the right to receive the earn-out consideration (which is agreed by HMRC – Shares Valuation at £1,120,000). Tony is eligible for ER and therefore is able to claim relief on the share sale.

When the earn-out payments are made on 30 June 2013 and 2014 (relating to the years ended 31 December 2012 and 2013), they will trigger a part-disposal of the right /chose in action. In each case, the actual earn-out payment is taxed after deducting the part disposal cost of the right [*TCGA 1992, s 22(1)*]. ER cannot be claimed on these 'earn-out' gains – since they do not relate to a sale of shares. The gains would (after deducting any annual exemption) be taxed at the top CGT rate of 28%.

The base value of the right is apportioned between each part disposal by applying the A/A+B formula in *TCGA 1992, s 42*. It is necessary to compute the residual value of the right (ie B) at the date of each part disposal – the value of the residual right at 30 June 2013 and 30 June 2014 is agreed at £1,100,000 and £900,000 respectively.

The earn-out (for the year ended 31 December 2014) payable on 30 June 2015 will represent the final disposal of the right under *TCGA 1992, s 22(1)* with the residual base value of the right being applied against the earn-out consideration.

CGT computations – 2011/12–2015/16

The relevant capital gains which arise on the 'earn-out' sale are calculated as follows:

2011/12

	£
Consideration (Sale of shares – Jan 2012)	
(£500,000 + value of right £1,120,000)	1,620,000
Less Base cost (July 1985)	(50,000)
Chargeable gain	1,570,000
Less: Annual exemption	(10,600)
Taxable gain	1,559,400
ER CGT @ 10%	£155,940

2013/14

Assuming the earn-out consideration for the year ended 31 December 2012 is £650,000, a part disposal of the right will arise on its receipt on 30 June 2013.

	£
Consideration	650,000
Less Part disposal of right	
$£1,120,000 \times \dfrac{£650,000}{(£650,000 + £1,100,000)}$	(416,000)
Chargeable gain (before annual exemption)	234,000

2014/15

Assuming the earn-out consideration for the year ended 31 December 2013 is £936,000, a part disposal of the right will arise on its receipt on 30 June 2014.

		£
Consideration		936,000
Less Part disposal cost of right		
Initial value of right	1,120,000	
Used in 2013/14	(416,000)	
Balance available	704,000	
£704,000 × $\dfrac{£936,000}{(£936,000 + £900,000)}$		(358,902)
Chargeable gain (before annual exemption)		577,098

2015/16

Assuming the earn-out consideration for the year ended 31 December 2014 is £980,000, the final disposal of the right will arise when it is received on 30 June 2015.

		£
Earn-out consideration		980,000
Less Base cost of residual right		
Initial value of right	1,120,000	
Used in 2013/14	(416,000)	
Used in 2014/15	(358,902)	
		(345,098)
Chargeable gain (before annual exemption)		634,902

Optimising ER on earn-outs

Valuing the earn-out right

15.61A Until relatively recently sellers often preferred to avoid incurring the initial CGT charge on the value of the right, since this was an *unrealised* gain. This is relatively easy to achieve in practice since the seller can negotiate with the purchaser to structure the earn-out so that it can only be satisfied by the issue of actual loan notes in the purchasing company. This would bring the earn-out consideration within the automatic deferral rule in *TCGA 1992, s 138A* (see 15.62 below).

In essence, the *Marren v Ingles* treatment fragments the share sale into (at least) two different CGT disposals, being:

- The share sale itself ;and

- The part-disposals/disposal of the earn-out rights (which are triggered when the earn-out payments are received).

Under the current CGT regime, this means that:

- With an ER gains limit of £10 million, there is far more ER 'headroom' now on the amount of the earn-out right attracting the 10% ER CGT rate as part of the share sale consideration.

- Currently, there is an 18% differential between the 10% ER CGT rate on the initial value of the earn-out right (taxed as part of the share sale consideration) and 28% CGT rate that applies to gains on the actual earn-out payments (although this could be more if CGT rates were to rise in later years!).

Thus, assuming that there is sufficient scope within the seller's overall 'deal' value, there is perhaps some sense in placing a more realistic (!) initial value on the earn-out right. This valuation now becomes an important factor in 'splitting' the overall CGT charge on the deal between the ER CGT 10% rate (on the share sale) and the 28% rate on earn-out gains. Thus, provided it can be substantiated under valuation principles, the higher the value of the earn-out right that can be agreed with HMRC, the greater the amount of tax that can be saved at 28%.

Some will point to the fact that this will lead to a higher *up-front* CGT charge. However, given the prevailing level of interest rates, the 18% tax saving should significantly outweigh the 'interest cost' of accelerating part of the tax charge.

Using a 'profit warranty' approach

15.61B In some cases, it might be possible to maximise the value of the 'earn-out' consideration taxed at the ER CGT rate of 10% by structuring the share sale for the maximum possible deferred consideration value.

In such cases, the deferred consideration should be *ascertainable,* and should not therefore be subject to the *Marren v Ingles* computation basis. Instead the full deal value will be taxable under the 'fixed' deferred consideration rule in *TCGA 1992, s 48* (see 15.4). This has the benefit of bringing in the full deferred amount *without any discount* for risk and contingency, which often substantially reduces the value of the earn-out right under the *Marren v Ingles* rules.

Under the *ascertainable* deferred consideration route, effect is given to the 'earn-out' arrangement by providing that any under-performance against the maximum profit/earnings etc. is 'clawed-back' by a series of 'profit-warranties'. Since such deals are typically based on a multiple of earnings, it should be possible to define the warranty damages in terms of an appropriate multiple of the profit 'shortfall'. Careful drafting of the profit warranty clauses is clearly required to ensure that this route is effective.

The subsequent warranty payments would therefore *reduce* the original maximum deferred consideration under *TCGA 1992, s 49(2)*. In this way, the seller should pay the 10% ER CGT rate on the entire deal value (up to the available ER gains limit).

Earn-outs satisfied in shares or loan notes

TCGA 1992, s 138A treatment

15.62   Many earn-outs are structured so that all or part of the seller's earn-out can only be satisfied by shares or loan notes in the purchasing company. In such cases, a corresponding part of the capital gain on the future earn-out right (which would otherwise be taxed under the principles in Marren v Ingles – see 15.58) can effectively be deferred under *TCGA 1992, s 138A*. However, a large number of sellers are now likely to 'opt-out' of the *TCGA 1992, s138A* deferral route to maximise their ER (see 15.67A below).

Where shares are sold on an earn-out basis (that can only be satisfied by shares and/or loan notes), this right is automatically deemed to be a security. This has two consequences:

- the seller avoids the 'up-front' tax charge based on the value of the right;

- the seller is treated as exchanging his original shares (normally partly) in exchange for a deemed (non-QCB) security (representing the earn-out right).

This effectively provides 'paper-for-paper' treatment for the subsequent earn-out right.

15.63   If the seller has any option to take part of the earn-out in cash, the deferral relief offered by *s 138A* will not be available. However, it is possible to have an earn-out agreement which is structured so that an identifiable part is satisfied in shares/debentures and the remainder is satisfied in cash. In such cases, s 138A relief would be available on the 'shares/debentures' earn-out element but an initial tax charge would arise on the cash element.

The deferral relief in *TCGA 1992, s 138A* can only operate if the share exchange rules in *TCGA 1992, s 135* would apply but for the intermediate earn-out right, ie assuming the earn-out right is shares or debentures issued by the acquiring company [*TCGA 1992, s 138A(2)*]. Consequently, the detailed requirements of *TCGA 1992, s 135* must be fulfilled (see 15.44).

Deemed non-QCB treatment under s 138A

15.64 *TCGA 1992, s 138A(3)(a)* provides that the earn-out right is deemed to be a security issued by the acquiring company and is not to be treated as a qualifying corporate bond ('QCB'). By treating the earn-out right as a deemed security, this enables the gain attributable to the earn-out right to be deferred until the shares or loan notes received under the earn-out are subsequently sold or redeemed (see 15.66 below).

An illustrative diagram showing the mechanics of a typical earn-out transaction satisfied in shares and/or in loan notes is shown below.

Earn-out deals – shares/loan notes (using TCGA 1992, s 138A)

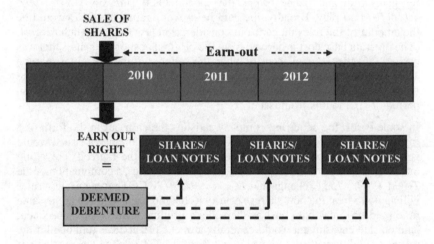

Apportionment of base costs

15.65 The base cost of the seller's deemed security is derived from the base value of their old shares in the target company. Typically, the seller will receive some initial consideration (received on completion), which may be cash or actual shares/loan notes or a combination of both, in addition to the earn-out consideration to be satisfied in the form of shares or loan notes.

The initial cash consideration is subject to an immediate CGT charge as a 'part disposal' in respect of the seller's shares in the target company under *TCGA 1992, s 128(3)*. The base cost of the seller's old shares may need to be apportioned in three ways:

(*a*) initial cash consideration – to be used in the part disposal calculation under *TCGA 1992, s 128(3), (4)*;

(*b*)   initial shares/loan notes – to form the base cost of those new shares or, in the case of QCBs, to be used to calculate the gain/loss at the date of the exchange under *TCGA 1992, s 116(10)*;

(*c*)   deemed *s 138A* security – subsequently to form the base cost for the future shares/loan notes.

Dealing with actual QCBs/shares issued as earn-out consideration

15.66   Where the earn-out consideration is satisfied in the form of a QCB loan note, this will be dealt with under the 'corporate security' conversion/ exchange rules in *TCGA 1992, s 132*. This treats the event as a CGT reorganisation and hence brings the special QCB rules in *TCGA 1992, s 116(10)* into play. Broadly, the gain held-over against the QCB would be the amount of the relevant earn-out consideration less the pro-rata base cost. (The pro-rata base cost is derived from the original cost of the shares that was carried into the deemed security when the seller sold their original shares.) The postponed gain would generally be taxed at the prevailing 28% CGT rate when the QCB is finally encashed – HMRC permit a minimum redemption period of six months from issue.

In some cases, the acquiring company satisfies the earn-out in the form of a fresh issue of its shares (or a non-QCB). The number of shares issued would generally depend on the earn-out consideration and the (agreed) prevailing market price/value of the acquirer's shares. In such cases, a combination of the *TCGA 1992, s 132* exchange and *TCGA 1992, s 127* CGT reorganisation rules will apply to treat the new shares/security as having been acquired at the same time (and pro-rata) base cost as the seller's original shares. Any subsequent gain on sale/encashment would generally attract CGT at 28%. (although if the relevant conditions were satisfied, the lower ER CGT rate may be available if the consideration shares were held for at least a year (see 15.33)).

The deemed 'earn-out' security and ER

15.67   The ER legislation does not contain any special rules to assist with earn-out transactions. However, ER is capable of applying to securities, since *TCGA 1992, s 169I(2)(c)* states that a 'disposal ... consisting of ... shares in or securities of a company' is a qualifying disposal for ER. As the deemed non-QCB treatment prescribed by s 138A applies for all the purposes of the TCGA 1992, the deemed non-QCBs could potentially attract ER.

In many cases, the deemed non-QCB will be 'exchanged' for actual QCB loan notes within *TCGA 1992, s 132*, with the relevant earn-out gain being captured and held-over under *TCGA 1992, s 116(10)*. Where the 'earn-out' QCBs are issued after 22 June 2010, this will follow the rules in 15.51A. Where (exceptionally) ER is available, the benefit of the 10% ER CGT rate can only be obtained by making a *TCGA 1992, s 169R* election to tax the QCB at the date of its issue (following the determination of the relevant earn-out payment). In the absence of a *TCGA 1992, s 169R* election, the 'earn-out' gain will be deferred in the normal way until the QCB is redeemed, which would then be generally be subject to the 28% main CGT rate. Given that the relatively short period until such QCBs are redeemed, it will generally be beneficial to elect if the ER can be claimed. (The treatment of ER on deferred QCB gains before 23 June 2010 is different – see 15.51.)

ER will only be available in those (rare) cases where, throughout the 12 months prior to the 'disposal' event, the seller:

- holds shares in a *trading company* or *holding company of a trading group* which is their 'personal company'; and

- they are a director or employee of that company/fellow group company.

In most cases, the seller is unlikely to be able to meet the 'personal company' requirement since this requires them to hold at least 5% of the ordinary share capital (carrying at least 5% of the voting rights) of the 'acquiring company'. This means that, unless the seller also holds at least 5% of the *voting ordinary shares* in the purchasing company post-sale, they would not be able to apply ER to their 'earn-out' loan notes.

Opting out of deemed TCGA 1992, s 138A deferral treatment

15.67A With a current ER gains limit of £10 million and the 18% CGT gap between the 10% ER and 28% main CGT rate, there will be many sellers who are likely to elect to disapply the automatic *TCGA 1992 s 138A* deferral in order to 'lock-into' a 10% ER CGT rate on the value of the earn-out right. By making an election under *TCGA 1992, s 138A(2A)*, the seller effectively opts to tax the earn-out on a *Marren v Ingles* basis (see 15.58). The right would then be taxed at 10% (if and to the extent there is unused ER) and the excess of the actual earn-out consideration over the initial value of the right would usually be taxed at 28%. Broadly, *s 138A(2A)* 'opt-out' elections must be made within 22 months from the end of the tax year in which the original share sale is made.

Worked example of earn-out satisfied in loan notes (under TCGA 1992, s 138A)

15.68 The CGT treatment of an earn-out transaction satisfied by QCB loan notes is illustrated in Example 14 below.

Example 14

CGT treatment of earn-out satisfied in (QCB) loan notes

Harry formed Hammers Ltd in September 1987 subscribing for the entire share capital of 40,000 £1 ordinary shares at par. On 7 July 2011, he sold all his Hammers Ltd shares to Pompey plc. The sale contract provided for:

- an initial cash consideration of £5.5 million (net of disposal costs) to be paid on completion; and

- a deferred earn-out consideration based on the 'defined earn-out' profits for the two years ending 30 June 2013, which was to be satisfied in the form of Pompey plc loan notes (that would be issued when the accounts for the relevant years (and the earn-out profits) were approved). The maximum earn-out consideration for the year ending 30 June 2012 and 30 June 2013 is £2.4 million and £3.6 million respectively.

The earn-out right has been valued at £3 million (in July 2011).

Harry would also continue as managing director of Hammers Ltd during the earn-out period.

Assume the *actual* earn-out consideration is (say) £1.8 million and £2.5 million for the year ended 30 June 2012 and 30 June 2013 respectively. The actual Pompey plc 'earn-out' loan notes are received in October after the relevant year-end and redeemed in the following May. (The CGT on the earn-out consideration would be taxed when the loan notes are encashed.)

CGT computations – 2011/12–2014/15

Harry's earn-out transaction automatically qualifies for *TCGA 1992, s 138A* relief, since the right to the earn-out can only be satisfied in the form of Pompey plc loan notes. His capital gain on the share sale (for 2011/12) would therefore only be computed by reference to the initial cash consideration.

The right to the 'earn-out' loan notes would be treated as a 'deemed non-QCB security' under *s 138A* and therefore qualifies for 'paper-for-paper' relief under *TCGA 1992, s 135*. (The deductible base cost is apportioned between the cash and earn-out elements of the consideration.)

The relevant CGT computations are as follows:

2011/12

Sale – July 2011	£
Consideration –	5,500,000
Less Apportioned base cost	
$£40,000 \times \dfrac{£5,500,000}{(£5,500,000 + £3,000,000^*)}$	(25,882)
Chargeable gain	5,474,118
Less: Annual exemption	(10,600)
Taxable gain	5,463,518
CGT liability	
ER CGT @ 10% – £5,463,518 @ 10%	546,351
* Value of earn-out right	

TCGA 1992, s 138A treats the earn-out right as a deemed non-QCB. When the earn-out figures are determined and the actual QCBs are issued for these amounts, the relevant gains are computed and held-over under *TCGA 1992, s 110(16)*. These gains crystallise when the QCBs are encashed in the following May.

2013/14

Earn-out – May 2013	£
Earn-out proceeds	1,800,000
Less Apportioned base cost	
$£14,118^* \times \dfrac{£1,800,000}{(£1,800,000 + £2,000,000^{**})}$	(6,688)
QCB chargeable gain crystallising	1,793,312
* Residual base cost = £40,000 less £25,882 (used in 2011/12) ** Value of residual earn-out right	

2014/15

Earn-out – May 2014	£
Earn-out proceeds	2,500,000
Less Residual base cost (£14,118 less £6,688 used in 2013/14)	(7,430)
QCB chargeable gain crystallising	2,492,570

Note: QCB gains would be taxed at the prevailing CGT rate in the year of redemption (likely to be around 28%). However, if Harry makes an election under *TCGA 1992, s 138A*, a large part of the deal value would be taxed at 10%.

Potential income tax and NIC charge on earn-outs satisfied by loan notes/shares

15.69 The introduction of the complex 'employment-related' securities regime in *Finance Act 2003* created some uncertainties in relation to the tax treatment of earn-outs satisfied by loan notes and/or shares in the acquirer. HMRC consider that such a right effectively falls within the definition of a 'securities option' within *ITEPA 2003, s 420(8)*. Interestingly, where the purchaser has the choice of satisfying the earn-out in cash *or* shares/loan notes, this will *not* be a 'securities option'. However, the *TCGA 1992, s 138A* deferral will not be available here and so the strict *Marren v Ingles* basis will apply (*TCGA 1992, s 138A(1)(d)*).

Where the 'right' is obtained *by reason of employment or prospective employment* (as defined in*ITEPA 2003, s 47*), the receipt of the 'earn-out' loan notes or shares would be subject to both income tax and National Insurance Contributions (NICs). However, HMRC have confirmed that where an earn-out fully represents consideration for the sale of the target company's shares (as it will normally do), then the income tax/NIC charges under *Pt 7, Ch 5* of *ITEPA 2003* would *not* apply.

15.70 On the other hand, where all or part of an earn-out relates to value provided to an employee as a reward for services over a performance period, this 'earnings' element would suffer an income tax and NIC charge under *Chapter 5*.

The following key factors would generally determine whether an earn-out is further sale consideration rather than earnings:

- the sale agreement shows that the earn-out is part of the valuable consideration given for the target company's shares and the value received from the earn-out reflects the value actually received for those shares;

- it would also be helpful to demonstrate the genuine commercial nature of the earn-out as consideration for the target's shares in any advance clearance made under *ITA 2007, s 701* and *TCGA 1992, s 138* (see 15.77);

- where the seller continues to be employed in the business, the earn-out does not reflect 'compensation' for receiving less than the full remuneration for their continuing employment;

- clearly, there should not be any *personal* performance targets incorporated in the earn-out;

- furthermore, the earn-out must not be conditional on future employment beyond a reasonable 'hand-over' period to protect the value of the business being sold.

15.71 Clearly, the above points should be considered when drafting the sale documentation. Any evidence that future bonuses were reclassified or 'commuted' into purchase consideration would indicate that the earn-out was, at least partly, earnings rather than consideration for the disposal of securities.

Where the earn-out is partly deferred consideration for the target's shares and partly a reward for services or an inducement to continue working for the business, then a 'just and reasonable' apportionment of the value would be made.

POTENTIAL SCOPE OF TRANSACTIONS IN SECURITIES LEGISLATION

15.72 It is important to appreciate that the 'Transactions in Securities' (TiS) anti-avoidance rules (as they apply for income tax purposes) in *ITA 2007, s 684* can potentially apply to counter the tax advantage obtained by selling family or owner-managed (ie 'close') companies in such a way as not to suffer income tax.

Most owner managed and family company sales will potentially fall within the TiS provisions by virtue of *ITA 2007, s 685*. This legislation broadly applies (amongst other things) where a seller receives 'relevant consideration' in connection with the distribution of assets of a close company as defined in *CTA 2010, s 439 (ICTA 1988, s 414) [ITA 2007, s 989]* (see 1.3). In other words, the seller has received consideration on a sale of a company that could have been taken as a dividend.

Given the ability to enjoy capital gains at lower tax rates, HMRC can use *s 684* as a weapon to counter any deals which appear to be structured to give the shareholder(s) an 'income tax advantage' rather than being (mainly) commercially driven.

Whilst all owner managed company sales will fall within the ambit of TiS, the vast majority are now effectively exempted under the 'fundamental change of ownership' rules (see 15.73 below). The revised TiS provisions now focus on the intended target, which is to catch cases where the seller purports to enjoy sale proceeds as a lowly taxed capital gain yet retains a sizeable interest in the business after the sale, such as on a sale to a 'connected' company.

See earlier editions of this book for details of the pre-24 March 2010 TiS regime.

The revised TiS regime (from 24 March 2010)

15.73 *FA 2010* substantially relaxes the application of *s 684* by introducing a 'carve-out' exemption for sales to unconnected third parties, which applies from 24 March 2010. This represents a fundamental and significant shift in HMRC's approach. The new exemption provides greater clarity and certainty and carefully targets the application of the TiS rules to transactions which are *mainly* motivated towards obtaining a tax advantage.

The refocused TiS legislation should only catch those who enter into a relevant transaction with a tax avoidance objective.

From 24 March 2010, the TiS legislation will apply where all the following conditions are met

- The shareholder must be a party to a TiS (or two or more TiSs);

- Broadly, they must receive relevant (non-income taxable) consideration in connection with the distribution, transfer or realisation of assets of a close company;

- The shareholder cannot take advantage of the 'fundamental change of ownership' exclusion (see 15.74);

- The shareholder's main purpose (or one of the main purposes) of the TiS/ TiSs is to obtain an income tax advantage *and* an income tax advantage must actually be obtained (see 15.75).

A key component of the revised TiS regime is 'the fundamental change in ownership' exclusion rule, since sales which meet the relevant conditions are completely exempt from the TiS legislation.

The application of the 'fundamental change of ownership' rule

15.74 The ambit of the TiS provisions is very wide and includes sales of shares as well as the issue or sale of securities. In the context of a company sale, the application of the TiS legislation is applied to each seller. However, from 24 March 2010, a (new) *s 686* provides a valuable exemption to the seller where the 'fundamental change of ownership' test is met. This applies where the seller holds shares in the target company and *after the sale and throughout the two year period following the sale*

- at least 75% of the Target company's ordinary shares are held by third parties who are *unconnected* with the relevant selling shareholder

- those shares held by the 'unconnected' third parties carry at least an entitlement to 75% of the distributions which may be made by the company

- those shares also carry at least 75% of the voting rights

The 75% rule is based on historic HMRC practice prior to the *FA 2010* changes which was to grant *ITA 2007, s 701* clearance to those sellers where a 75% change in ownership took place. The two year period test ensures that the change of ownership is sufficiently permanent.

Looked at in another way, a seller cannot be connected with any more than 25% of the purchasing shareholders in the two years following the sale.

The *ITA 2007, s 993* 'connected person' definition applies here. Importantly, this would include a company controlled by the seller or the seller together with those connected with them. A seller's spouse/civil partner, brothers, sisters, parents and children as well as the trustees of any settlement created by them are also connected for s 993 purposes. In practice, this is likely to catch sales made to a company controlled by the seller or together with members of their family.

Example 15

Section 686 fundamental change of ownership exemption

Mr Redknapp sells his 100% holding in shares in Pompey Ltd in June 2010. He will satisfy the 'fundamental change of ownership' rule provided he is not connected with 75% of Pompey's shareholders at any time in the two years to June 2012).

15.74A The 'fundamental change of ownership' exemption should easily be satisfied on a 'clean' exit where the seller is completely unconnected with the purchaser, as will invariably be the case for commercial 'trade' sales. Historically, such cases would normally have received clearance under *ITA 2007, s 701*, but the post-23 March 2010 'fundamental change of ownership' carve-out now removes such cases from the ambit of the TiS rules and obviates the need to obtain advance clearance under *ITA 2007, s 701*. HMRC expect a considerable reduction in the number of applications made under the new regime. The view is that sellers can rely on the *FA 2010* exemption and do not need to apply for clearance!

Under the *FA 2010* regime, the previous genuine commercial purpose test has been 'dropped' as the intention is that such cases should invariably be covered by the 'fundamental change of ownership' rule. There will, of course, be cases where, for example, the seller retains an equity interest in the business going forward which does not meet the 'fundamental change of ownership' test. These situations will therefore be tested for a tax-avoidance motive – ie where the main purpose or one of the main purposes is to obtain an 'income tax advantage' (see above) and HMRC would decide each case on its own merits.

The advance clearance procedure in *ITA 2007 s 701* is still retained for sellers. In general, applications are now likely to be made where the seller is not confident they can rely on the fundamental change of ownership 'let-out'. This might be the case where there is some 'continuing' shareholder connection, for example, where a company is being sold to a 'connected' or related company or in certain secondary MBO transactions. In such cases, the seller will need to obtain certainty before proceeding that HMRC does not consider tax avoidance to be one of the main drivers behind the deal. Based on experience, it is likely that many cases which fail to satisfy the 'fundamental change of ownership' exemption would be denied clearance under *ITA 2007, s 701* since HMRC often suspect that the sale is being engineered to extract cash at low CGT rates. On the other hand, HMRC generally have no issue where the sale to the 'related' purchaser is structured as a share for share exchange (without any material cash consideration).

Determining whether the relevant transactions are carried out for tax avoidance reasons is a subjective matter which looks at the overall intention and motives of the directors, shareholders, and (in some cases) the professional advisers.

Obtaining an income tax advantage

15.75 Section 687 provides a revised definition of an 'income tax advantage' for these purposes. In broad terms, an 'income tax advantage' is obtained where the income tax that would arise if the relevant 'sale proceeds' were a qualifying distribution *exceeds* the CGT liability on the same amount. The comparative calculation only looks at the available profits that could have been distributed to the relevant shareholder. Thus any sale proceeds in excess of the maximum dividend that could have been paid to the seller (based on the company's distributable profits) are ignored. Given the large differential between income tax and CGT rates (especially with ER) an income tax advantage would be enjoyed by the vast majority of sellers.

Retained equity interests, the Cleary case and secondary MBOs

15.76 In recent years, HMRC has taken particular interest in the potential application of *s 684* to secondary buy-outs. Typically, in such cases, an existing venture capitalist wishes to realise their investment and a new 'replacement' investor is found. The new investor will form a new company (Newco), funded by a mixture of debt and shares. Newco will then purchase the target company, buying-out its existing venture capitalist and management shareholders.

In many deals, the management shareholders receive Newco shares, as well as cash and loan notes. These deal structures are often viewed by HMRC as falling within *CIR v Cleary 44 TC 399*.

Following the introduction of the 'fundamental change of ownership' exemption from 24 March 2010, those involved in secondary MBO deals are likely to be exempt from the TiS legislation. Where a seller has a 'clean' exit they will satisfy the 'fundamental change of ownership' exemption. Similarly, each 'continuing' management shareholder' would normally be able to show they are not 'connected' with Newco post-sale (since they would each typically have a minority interest and would not be related to their co-shareholders).

It is helpful to look at the leading *Cleary* case since this demonstrates the main principles used by HMRC in their application of the TiS legislation. The case involved two sisters who needed some cash and one of 'their' companies, Gleeson Development Co Ltd (Development had substantial cash funds. Consequently, they sold M J Glesson Ltd (Glesson) (in which they each held 50% of the shares) to Development. The shares in Gleeson were sold for their true market value of £121,000.

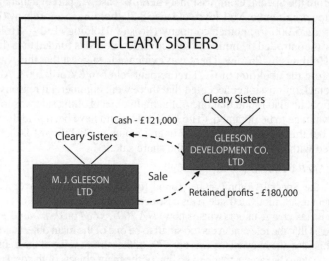

THE CLEARY SISTERS

However, the Revenue issued a counteraction notice (under what is now *ITA 2007, s 684*) charging the entire £121,000 proceeds to income tax. The Revenue considered that the three preconditions for the legislation to apply were satisfied, namely:

- The sale of the shares was a TIS

- The sale fell within the prescribed condition in what was *ITA 2007, s 689* (under the pre-26 March TiS legislation). The company was under the control of five persons or less and the sisters had received consideration that would have been available for distribution by way of dividend (had it not been applied in acquiring the shares in Gleeson).

- There was a tax advantage – income tax had been avoided.

The House of Lords agreed with the Revenue – the sale of the shares had come within the strict wording of (what is now) *ITA 2007, s 701*. The Cleary sisters lost their case on the basis that the capital sum represented amounts that could otherwise have been paid out as (taxable) dividends.

It is perhaps worth observing that the *Cleary* case would still be caught by the revised *FA 2010* TiS legislation. In particular, the sisters would not have satisfied the 'fundamental change of ownership' rules since they remained connected with Gleeson through their control of Development.

15.77 In recent years, the TiS rules have been also held to apply in the following cases: cases summarised below would also be caught under the revised TiS rules.

Lloyd v HMRC [2008] SpC 672

HMRC succeeded in applying (what is now) *ITA 2007, s 684* to 'internal' share sales before the Special Commissioners in *Lloyd* case. As part of a management succession programme, Mr Lloyd sold his 38.2% holding in a company (Prosaw Ltd) for £275,000 to another company (Prosaw Holdings Ltd – 'Holdings') which was controlled by him. The sale consideration was funded by a dividend paid to Holdings by Prosaw. There was evidence to suggest that this was being done before the abolition of CGT retirement relief in 6 April 2003. Although the Special Commissioner accepted that there were commercial reasons for the transaction, he also found that one of the main objects of the sale was to enable a tax advantage to be obtained. (The £275,000 could have been paid directly by Prosaw but this would have resulted in an income tax liability of £62,357 – as compared with the £6,392 CGT on the share sale.)

Snell & Snell v HMRC [2008] SpC 699

In *Snell*, the Special Commissioner found for HMRC in a similar (apparently) 'retirement relief' motivated sale. This case demonstrates that any attempt to escape the income tax charge under (what is now) *ITA 2007, s 684* on *de minimis* grounds, on the basis that the relevant tax is too small to be one of the main objects, may well fail. In this case, the relevant tax was only 7% of the current value of the transaction. This was held to be large enough to be one of the main objects of the deal.

Grogan v HMRC [2011] STC 1

Mr Grogan was a director and majority shareholder in Nigel Grogan Ltd (NGL), which operated three car dealerships. In February 2003, NGL sold two of its dealerships and was in negotiations to sell the other one. Subsequently, NGL contributed £633,000 to a qualifying employee share ownership trust (QUEST and obtained a corporation tax deduction under *FA 1989, s 67*. In December 2003, the QUEST acquired 15,750 NGL shares from Mr Grogan for £630,000.

HMRC contended that these transactions were caught by the TiS rules on the grounds that the company's contribution to the QUEST and its subsequent acquisition of Mr Grogan's NGL shares was motivated by tax avoidance. It was contended that the QUEST had no real commercial purpose since, as at December 2003, NGL's only employees were Mr Grogan and his secretary. Furthermore, Mr Grogan's advisers' promotional material had emphasised the tax advantages and their fees for setting up the QUEST was calculated by reference to the total tax savings.

Although the tax deduction for the QUEST was based on specific statute, the Upper Tribunal agreed that the 'wider scheme' of the arrangements had to be considered. It was held that they were motivated by tax avoidance and thus the TiS rules applied.

Example 16

Application of ITA 2007, s 684 on partial 'exit'/MBO

Goran City (Plastics) Ltd has traded for many years as a plastics injection moulder. Mr Sven (the founding shareholder) has 80% of the ordinary share capital, having passed 20% to the company's management team in 1998.

In June 2010, Mr Sven entered into an MBO transaction with his management team under which they acquired a substantial interest in the company, but with Mr Sven retaining a (controlling) 51% stake in the business going forward.

Goran City (Plastics) Ltd has distributable reserves of some £7 million at the time of the deal.

The management team therefore set up a Newco to acquire the entire share capital of Goran City (Plastics) Ltd for a total consideration of £10 million, which is satisfied as follows:

	Sven	Management Team	Total
Shares in Goran City (Plastics) Ltd	*80%*	*20%*	*100%*
Consideration	*£'m*	*£'m*	*£'m*
– Cash	5.92	–	5.92
– Shares in Newco Ltd	2.08	2.00	4.08
	8.00	2.00	10.00

The shares received by Mr Sven and the management team in Newco should be treated as a share for share exchange within *TCGA 1992, s 135* (see 15.44).

HMRC will take the view that the cash of £5.92m is being taken by Mr Sven to obtain an 'income tax advantage' since the income tax payable on a deemed dividend of that amount would (considerably) exceed the corresponding CGT on the same amount.

It is almost certain that HMRC would refuse a *s 701* clearance for Mr Sven since it falls within the TiS rules above. He is clearly connected with Newco after the sale since he has a controlling interest in it and would not be exempted under the 'fundamental change of ownership' rule. HMRC would probably enquire why he did not take all his sale consideration in the form of shares in Newco!

Ultimately, unless Mr Sven changed the terms of the MBO before proceeding – for example, by agreeing to take £8 million in the form of Newco shares – he is very likely to be subject to a *s 698* counteraction notice, which would tax the £5.92m as a 'dividend'. (Goran City (Plastics) Ltd has sufficient reserves to be able to pay a dividend of £5.92m to Sven so no restriction in the counteraction assessment would be given). The assessment on the £5.92 million would be at an effective rate of 36.1%!

Clearance applications under ITA 2007, s 701

15.78 *Section 684* is broadly designed to prevent shareholders from effectively receiving the value of the company's reserves (which could otherwise have been paid out as dividends) in an income tax-free form. The sellers' equity interest in the target company (before the sale) and, where appropriate, any 'continuing' interest held through the purchasing company should be set out in the application.

Experience suggests that clearance is likely to be refused where the potential seller is effectively retaining a 'substantial' economic interest in the business post-sale (either personally and/or through 'related parties'). Problems in obtaining *s 701* clearance have typically been encountered on share sales to 'connected' companies, employee benefit trusts, and pension funds and so on.

From 24 March 2010, sellers who wish to obtain certainty that their share sale does not offend the tax avoidance rule should apply for advance clearance under *ITA 2007, s 701*. HMRC do not expect those meeting the 'fundamental change of ownership' exemption to apply for advance clearance, although some sellers may still want the comfort of a clearance, even where they qualify for the relief! In some cases, tax clearances may indeed be required for other aspects of the transaction.

The clearance application should clearly explain the commercial reasons for the sale and why the transaction is *not* being carried out for tax reasons. (A *single* advance clearance application should be made to cover all relevant 'tax clearance' requirements (for example, covering both *ITA 2007, s 684* and *TCGA 1992, s 138* (see 15.49)). HMRC have a statutory obligation to respond within 30 days. If their reply contains queries or a request for further information, this must be dealt with within 30 days (or, at HMRC's discretion, a longer period) [*ITA 2007, s 701(2)(3)*].

The relevant contact and address details for *non-market* sensitive clearance applications are:

H M Revenue & Customs
Clearance & Counteraction Team,
Anti-Avoidance Group
First Floor
22 Kingsway
London WC2B 6NR

Market sensitive clearances should be sent to the Team Leader at the same address.

It is possible to send clearance applications by email to *reconstructions@ hmrc.gsi.gov.uk* (although information about market/price sensitive matters or well known individuals should not be sent by email).

The clearance application team may be telephoned on 020 7438 7474 (but they do not generally like constant chasing!).

Deciding *not* to apply for clearance exposes the taxpayer to a lengthy 'waiting' period since s698 counteraction assessments are outside the scope of the self-assessment regime and can be raised at any time within six years following the end of the relevant tax year.

Processing of clearance applications and dealing with 'refusals'

15.78A The clearance team generally aim to divide clearance applications according to their perceived tax risk:

- 'low-risk' cases, which should be turned around within seven days; and

- 'high-risk' cases, which would require a review by at least one other Inspector and may take up to the full 'statutory' 30 days to reply.

Clearances are often refused where the commercial rationale for a transaction has not been clearly stated. It should also be noted that the refusal to grant a *s 701* clearance does not necessarily mean that HMRC will raise a *s 684* counter-action assessment. In practice, the sellers have a choice. Either they must go through with the transaction (and the worrying uncertainty of a *s 684* liability) or they may try to discuss the situation with the clearance inspector. In the vast majority of cases, the clearance team may reserve their position until the transaction proceeds.

Section 698 counteraction assessments

15.79 TiS legislation falls outside the self-assessment regime, HMRC must raise the necessary assessment to counteract the 'tax advantage'. *Section 684* tax is not subject to self-assessment – it is up to HMRC to raise the necessary assessment to counteract the 'tax advantage'. It has been confirmed that the six year time limit for raising a *s 698* counteraction assessment will continue (and is not currently within the *FA 2008* reduction in the 'discovery' assessment window to four years). The 'normal' one year enquiry end from the relevant 31 January date under self assessment does not apply.

If a *s 698* assessment is raised, the sellers can then lodge an appeal against it within 30 days, stating the reasons for the disagreement. If the issues cannot be resolved, any appeal must now be made to the First-tier Tribunal (which replaces the former *s 704* Tribunal process). There is also a statutory right to request an internal review of HMRC's decision without resort to the First-tier Tribunal.

The *s 698* notice counters the 'income tax advantage' obtained by the seller and thus will look at the amount of the sale proceeds that could have been extracted as a distribution from the relevant company. HMRC will look at the level of the target company's (and the purchaser's) reserves at the relevant point (see Examples 16 above and Example 17 below). For these purposes, the reserves would not always be measured at the date of sale, but HMRC could, for example, take the level of reserves when 'consideration' loan notes are redeemed.

In the context of a group, HMRC will argue that the retained reserves of the subsidiaries are available to be distributed to the parent company and can therefore be counted.

The assessed amount is then taxed at the seller's effective dividend tax rate – 25%, or 36.1% where the dividend falls in their £150,000 plus taxable income bracket. (These rates take into account the 10% tax credit given in calculating the tax). For pre-6 April 2010 transactions, an effective rate of 25% normally applied.

Where a 'continuing' seller shareholder takes loan notes, this is generally regarded as deferred cash consideration (thus representing an amount received 'in respect of future receipts of the company' within *ITA 2007, s 685(4)(b)*.

Where *s 701* clearance has been refused, HMRC has generally applied a 'wait and see' test to look at the distributable reserves of the issuing company when the loan notes are redeemed (However, in some cases, the author has seen HMRC seeking to levy *s 684* tax on loan notes at the time of issue). In such cases, HMRC may be prepared to give clearance if the loan notes cannot be repaid until the management shareholder leaves (or the acquiring company is sold) or if non-redeemable preference shares are taken instead.

Example 17

Computation of s 698 counteraction assessment

Mr O'Neil was involved in a management buy-out in June 2010. He sold his 10% shareholding in the original 'Target' company for a cash consideration of £800,000 and shares in the acquiring company (Newco). These consideration shares in Newco gave him an effective 51% equity stake in the business going forward.

HMRC refused the company's *s 701* clearance in respect of Mr O' Neil, although he did obtain *TCGA 1992, s 135* share exchange relief for the shares issued by Newco.

After negotiations with Mr O' Neil's advisers in summer 2010, *a s 698* counteraction notice (based on a qualifying distribution) of £600,000 was agreed. This produces the following tax liability:

	£
Deemed qualifying distribution	600,000
Add: Tax Credit (1/9)	66,667
Gross dividend	666,667
Income tax @ 42.5% 283,334	
Less: Tax credit	(66,667)
Tax payable	216,667

Mr O'Neil's June 2010 capital gain would be adjusted to be based on sale proceeds of £200,000 (£800,000 less net amount taxed under *s 698* of £600,000).

ENTERPRISE INVESTMENT SCHEME – CGT DEFERRAL RELIEF (IN RELATION TO SHARE SALES)

Basic rules and qualifying conditions

15.80   Sellers planning to purchase shares in other 'qualifying' non-quoted trading companies may be able to defer all or part of their 'share sale' gain under the Enterprise Investment Scheme (EIS) CGT deferral regime. The relief is available to both individuals and trustees. Although gains on any type of asset are capable of being deferred under the EIS deferral rules, the comments here are confined to its use in relation to OMB share sales.

Sellers *cannot* defer their gains by investing in a Venture Capital Trust (VCT).

15.81   The EIS CGT deferral rules in *TCGA 1992, Sch 5B* provide that all or part of the gain (for example on a share sale) can be deferred by investing in one or more qualifying EIS companies within one year before or up to three years after the gain arises. This reinvestment period may be extended at HMRC's discretion. The seller must subscribe *wholly in cash* for eligible shares in a Qualifying Company (Qualco) and be UK resident at that time.

Eligible shares are, broadly speaking, irredeemable shares which do not contain any preferential rights to dividends, to assets on a winding-up or redemption (*TCGA 1992, Sch 5B, para 1* and *19; ITA 2007, s 173(2)*). If the investment is made within the year before, the shares must be retained by the seller when the gain is made.

Key EIS CGT deferral conditions

15.82   EIS CGT deferral relief is only given if:

- the individual's share subscription is used to finance a 'qualifying business activity' (broadly a qualifying trade or research and development activity) by the company or its qualifying 90% subsidiary as defined for EIS purposes – see 11.40 [*TCGA 1992, Sch 5B, para 1, TA 2007, ss 179 and 189–199*];

- the entire share issue proceeds are applied for the qualifying trade within the two year period required by *ITA 2007, s 175*, which starts from when the shares were issued (or, if later, when the trade began). (Before 22 April 2009, at least 80% of the share subscription monies had to be spent on the trade within 12 months of the share issue/trade commencing, with the balance being employed within the following 12 months) – see 11.33);

- the investee company is a qualifying company (Qualco) (see 11.40 and 15.85);

- the share issue is made for bona fide commercial purposes and not for tax avoidance.

Relief will be withdrawn if any of the above pre-conditions are subsequently breached.

For shares issued after 19 July 2007, investors can only claim EIS CGT deferral relief provided the total amount invested in the company under the various venture capital schemes during the previous 12 months ending on the day of the relevant EIS issue does not exceed £2 million (£10 million from 6 April 2012, assuming EU State Aid approval is granted). The £2 million/£10 million limit is tested on a 'rolling basis' and 'EIS' investment breaching the limit is disallowed in full. (*TCGA 1992, Sch 5B, para 1(2)(da) (7)*). The relevant risk/venture capital schemes comprise EIS, (CVS – withdrawn 1 April 2010), and VCT investment in the company *(ITA 2007, s 173A)*.

Reinvestment in 'own' company

15.83   It is possible for sellers to reinvest in their 'own' company as there is no 'connection' test for the CGT deferral relief. (However, EIS income tax relief and CGT exemption on disposals carry further restrictions, for example, the investor's equity interest cannot exceed 30%, see 11.34.) The seller can be a passive shareholder of Qualco if they wish. However, many investors will want a directorship to monitor and control their investment risk. In such cases, the level of their remuneration should be kept to a modest amount in the first three years to ensure that this does not jeopardise the relief.

Reinvestment in original company (or group company)

15.84   No CGT deferral relief is given against the share subscription in the company in which the original gain was made or any fellow group company.

It is, however, possible for an individual to 'reinvest' in the same trade through a *new company* which is used to acquire the trade or acquire the shares of the original company as a subsidiary.

If the *shares* are purchased, Newco would be a member of the same group as the original company, but provided this was done *after* the 'EIS CGT deferral' shares were issued, the legislation would not be breached (*TCGA 1992, Sch 5B, para 10*). Arguably, the share subscription moneys would not be employed for trading purposes. However, following the *FA 2004*, it is no longer necessary to hive-up the trade. This is because the acquisition of shares in a trading company now counts as a qualifying use of the subscription monies (*Taxline*, November 2004).

Before the *FA 2004* changes, the Revenue denied deferral relief where the monies were used to acquire *shares*, unless the trade was hived-up to the new company immediately after the acquisition (see *Taxline*, April 1999, page 5). Clearly, HMRC accept that share issue proceeds are applied for trading purposes where an *existing trade is acquired*.

Qualifying company

15.85   An investee company's share issue will only qualify for CGT deferral relief if its *gross* assets (per its balance sheet under GAAP):

- do not exceed £7 million *before* the relevant shares are issued; and

- do not exceed £8 million *after* the relevant shares are issued.

For shares issued after 6 April 2012, the asset limits are £15 million before the relevant shares were issued and £16 million after. (These limits also applied to pre-6 April 2006 shares.)

If the investee company has qualifying subsidiaries, the 'gross assets' test is computed on an aggregate 'group' basis (see 11.40 (c)).

For shares issued after 5 April 2007, the company must also be within the overall £2 million limit (£10 million from 6 April 2012) for 'venture capital' shares (see 15.82 and 11.30).

From 19 July 2007, the company must also comply with the EIS employee requirement. It must have no more than 50 (equivalent) full time employees when the shares are issued. However, the company's workforce can subsequently exceed 50 full time employees without triggering any clawback of the relief. (The above limits are under sympathetic review by Government in consultation with interested parties and we *may* see an increase in:

The employee limit increases to 250 employees from 6 April 2012 (assuming EU State Aid approval given).

The company must also meet the following qualifying conditions when the share investment is made and throughout the relevant three year period (otherwise the relief will be clawed back):

(*a*)   Qualco must usually be an unquoted company (not necessarily UK resident) which:

   (i)   exists wholly for the purpose of carrying on one or more qualifying trades. For these purposes, certain 'incidental purposes' which have no significant effect on the trade are ignored. In practice, HMRC will disregard any non-qualifying 'excluded activities' (see (*b*) below) if they represent less than 20% of the company's total activities (this 20% *de minimis* test may be measured by reference to a combination of factors, including turnover, net profits, capital employed and managerial and director time spent on each activity) [*ITA 2007, s 181(2)(a)*]; or

   (ii) is a parent company of a qualifying trading group, which means that the group's activities (taken together as a single business) substantially represent qualifying trades. The 'substantial' test in (i) above is applied on a group basis [*ITA 2007, s 181*].

   Although there is no UK residence requirement for Qualco, the share subscription monies test in *ITA 2007, ss 175* and *179* required that the trade of the company (or subsidiary) must be carried on wholly or mainly (ie more than 50%) in the UK. However, The *Finance (No 2) Act 2010* now enables companies with overseas trades to qualify provided they also operate a permanent establishment in the UK);

(*b*)   a *qualifying trade* is any trade *except* the excluded activities (outlined in *ITA 2007, s 192*) which can be summarised as follows:

   (i) land, commodities or share dealing;

   (ii) dealing in goods otherwise than in the ordinary course of a wholesale or retail distribution trade;

   (iii) banking, insurance, money lending and other financial services;

   (iv) oil extraction activities;

   (v)   leasing (including letting assets on hire) or receiving royalties or licence fees. However, a trade will qualify if the licence fees or royalties, etc substantially derive from *internally created* intellectual property, such as patents, trade marks, registered designs, etc which fall to be treated as an intangible asset under GAAP (see also 11.43 and 11.44);

   (vi) legal and accountancy services;

   (vii) property development;

   (viii) farming and market gardening;

   (ix) forestry and timber production;

   (x)   operating or managing hotels, guest houses, nursing homes and

738

      residential care homes (but only where the operator/manager has an interest in or occupies the relevant establishment);

(xi)   provision of administration services, etc to a commonly controlled company which carries on one of the above trades

(xii)   shipbuilding, coal production/extraction, and steel production (from 6 April 2008 onwards – these were added to comply with the European Commissions State Aid for risk capital (SACR) guidelines).

The general aim of the above exclusions is to prevent perceived 'lower risk' activities attracting relief. However, most wholesale and manufacturing trades will qualify for relief. The qualifying company conditions for EIS CGT deferral relief is largely based on the EIS rules – see further commentary in 11.40 to 11.44). Reference must always be made to the detailed legislation to determine whether a particular company will qualify.

Advance clearance procedure

15.86   HMRC operate a formal advance clearance procedure to confirm whether a potential investee company satisfies the relevant conditions for being a Qualco and whether the rules for the share issue are met. The clearance application should be made to the

Small Company Enterprise Centre,
HM Revenue and Customs,
1st Floor,
Ferrers House,
Castle Meadow Road,
Nottingham, NG2 1BB.

The company completes form EIS 1 after the relevant EIS share issue (giving details of the shares issued etc). HMRC will then authorise the company to issue the EIS 3 (1998) certificates to the investors (which incorporates a claim for the CGT deferral relief).

Operation of EIS CGT deferral relief

15.87   Sellers must make a claim to defer a specified amount of their gain by matching it against the investment expenditure on the relevant EIS shares. The amount specified for deferral may be all or part of the gain, thus giving complete flexibility in the amount of relief taken. (If there has been a previous EIS deferral claim against the shares, the gain is matched against the 'unmatched' part of the EIS share subscription.)

Before 23 June 2010, sellers could claim an ER reduction of 4/9ths against their postponed gain under the EIS CGT deferral regime, which is strictly brought in when the gain crystallises. Since there are no special transitional rules, if the ER relieved postponed gain crystallises after 22 June 2010 (see 15.88), it is likely to be charged at the top CGT rate of 28%. This means that the post-ER gain is effectively taxed at 15.55% (ie $100 \times 5/9 \times 28\%$).

FA 2008, Sch 3, para 8, provides for 'transitional' ER to be claimed on *pre-6 April 2008* share sale gains which have been held-over under the EIS CGT deferral regime. In such cases, the seller can claim ER when the deferred gain crystallises after 5 April 2008 ER is only available where the seller would have been able to satisfy the relevant ER conditions at the time of the original share sale (assuming the ER legislation was then in force). These rules operate in much the same way as the transitional rules for pre-6 April 2008 QCB gains and thus the precise treatment depends on whether the (first) chargeable event occurs before 23 June 2010 or after 22 June 2010 (see 15.52).

From *23 June 2010*, ER is simply given as a 10% CGT rate (rather than a 4/9ths reduction in gain). This has important implications since it is no longer possible for gains to be deferred under the EIS CGT deferral provisions with the benefit of ER. Those with ER-eligible gains now have to forgo any deferral of their gains to enjoy the ER CGT rate of 10%. On the other hand, if they wish to defer their gain, they cannot claim ER.

The maximum amount of EIS CGT deferral relief is therefore the lower of:

- the chargeable gain on the shares (for pre-22 June 2010 gains only after deducting any available ER)

- the amount subscribed for shares in the qualifying EIS company.

Example 18

EIS CGT deferral relief claim on share sale

In May 2010, Mr Owen received £650,000 on the sale of his controlling shareholding in Kop Ltd. Having made a claim for ER (pre-23 June 2010 rules), he realised a taxable gain of £305,556 on the share sale, calculated as follows:

	£
Net sale proceeds	650,000
Less: Original cost (Feb 1987)	(100,000)
Chargeable gain	550,000
Less: ER – £550,000 × 4/9ths	(244,444)
Taxable gain	305,556

In December 2011, Mr Owen set up his own retail company, Magpies Ltd, subscribing for 500,000 £1 ordinary shares (representing the entire share capital).

As Magpies Ltd is a Qualco (and all the other relevant conditions are satisfied), Mr Owen makes an EIS CGT deferral claim under *TCGA 1992, Sch 5B* in respect of his Kop Ltd gain. The calculation of his optimum deferral claim should take account of his unused annual exemption.

Mr Owen's optimum claim is calculated as follows:

	£
Capital gain – (May 2010)	305,556
Less: EIS CGT deferral claim (balance)	(295,456)
	10,100
Less: Annual exemption (2010/11)	(10,100)
Taxable gain	–

(Note – if Mr Owen's Kop Ltd share gain arose after 22 June 2010, he could not factor ER into his deferral claim. He would either claim ER CGT at 10% (with no deferral) or opt to postpone his gross gain under the EIS deferral rules).

Mr Owen's CGT base cost of his Magpies Ltd shares is £500,000 – the deferred gain of £295,456 does *not* reduce his base cost.

If Mr Owen sold his Magpies Ltd shares in, say, June 2013, the crystallised gain of £295,456 (including ER reduction) on the shares in Kop Ltd would (subject to any annual exemption) be taxed at the prevailing CGT rate(s), which might be 28%

Mr Owen cannot claim any EIS income tax relief or capital gains exemption on the sale of his shares in Magpies Ltd as he is clearly 'connected' with the company.

Clawback of relief

15.88   The (EIS CGT) deferred gain is effectively 'held-over', but does not reduce the base cost of the 'reinvestment' EIS shares.

However, *TCGA 1992, Sch 5B, paras 3* and *13* provide that the deferred gain will crystallise (and be taxed at the CGT rate in the year of clawback):

- on the sale or transfer of the relevant EIS shares at any time (except on the transfer to a spouse or civil partner);

- where the individual (or their spouse who has acquired the EIS shares) becomes non-resident within three years (five years for shares issued before 6 April 2000) of the share issue (except in certain cases where 'full time' employment is taken abroad);

- where the relevant EIS shares cease to be 'eligible shares' (for example, as a result of the company ceasing to be a Qualco) within the relevant period of three years following the share issue (or, if later, the commencement of trade) (see *Taxation*, 18 February 1999, page 486);

- if the individual (or, in some cases, another person) '*receives value*' from the investee company (as defined in *TCGA 1992, Sch 5B, para 13*) within the period of restriction, ie the one year before and three years following the share issue (or, if later, when the trade started). Insignificant receipts of value are ignored for this purpose (see 11.38). (For shares issued before 5 April 2001, different relevant periods applied.)

The 'receipt of value' rules *exclude* the receipt of reasonable director's remuneration and dividends representing a normal return on *those* shares.

For post-16 March 2004 share issues, a more liberal regime also applies on loans repaid to investors. Before then, the EIS CGT deferral relief was often denied on shares issued within the 12 months following the repayment of a loan account. This generally prevented relief being given where an individual's loan account is wholly or partly capitalised for shares (presumably on the basis that it does not represent 'new' money) [*TCGA 1992, Sch 5B, para 13(2)(b) (i), (7)(i)*].

From 17 March 2004, where a loan account is wholly or partly repaid in these circumstances, this will not prevent a CGT deferral relief claim provided the repayment is not linked to the subsequent share issue. This welcome change recognises the commercial reality of many situations where a company seeks emergency funding (see also 11.39).

Any company share buy-back within the period of restriction after the share subscription will also result in the shares ceasing to be eligible shares, since a share buy-back is treated as 'value received by other persons' under *TCGA 1992, Sch 5B, para 14*.

PRE-SALE TAX PLANNING STRATEGIES

Application of the *Furniss v Dawson* doctrine

15.89   In addition to the various tax structuring principles already outlined in this chapter in connection with company share sales, there are a number of other pre-sale strategies that may provide a useful reduction in the seller's tax liability.

Certain tax planning techniques may be vulnerable to challenge by HMRC under the '*Furniss v Dawson*' doctrine (see 1.10). The key 'tax avoidance' cases have established that the '*Furniss v Dawson*' principle can only apply where an intermediate tax planning step has been inserted at a time when the ultimate transaction has reached 'the point of no return'. As a general rule, this would be when there is no practical likelihood that the subsequent (sale) transaction would not happen.

Negotiations for the sale of shares in an unquoted company can often be prolonged and it is not unknown for a transaction to be aborted shortly before a sale was to take place. The implementation of a pre-sale tax mitigation strategy should therefore normally be effective, even if it takes place (say) only two to three weeks before the sale agreement is executed.

Pre-sale dividend

15.90   Individual/trustee sellers now generally pay CGT at rates varying between 10% and 28%. As a general rule, it will not therefore be efficient to extract a pre-sale dividend for tax mitigation purposes. (For similar reasons, pre-sale stock (or scrip) dividend alternatives are no longer recommended.)

Nevertheless, there will be cases where the purchaser will require the seller to extract any 'surplus' cash balances held by the company before completion.

In many cases, the most practicable method would be for the seller to declare an appropriate cash dividend (although it would be subject to an average effective rate of 25% to 36.1% (before 6 April 2010, 25% tax charge).

Alternatively, it may be possible for the purchaser to pay a 'grossed-up' amount for the shares to reflect the cash. A corporate purchaser should be able to access the cash after the acquisition without any tax cost. This would usually be preferable for the seller as they would maximise their tax-efficient capital gains (subject to the possible application of the corporate TiS rules in *CTA 2010, s 733* (and particularly *s 735*)).

Ex-gratia/termination payments

15.91   Many shareholder-directors are strongly tempted by the prospect of a £30,000 tax-free ex-gratia/termination payment prior to the sale. By arranging for a corresponding deduction in the share price, this would save them CGT at their effective rate. However, where such payments coincide with the sale of shares in a family or owner-managed company, the Inspector's almost automatic reaction is to disallow the payment. This is normally on the basis that the payment is either a distribution or part of the consideration for the sale of the shares, which would deny the benefit of the £30,000 tax-free exemption in the individual's hands (*James Snook & Co Ltd v Blasdale* (1952) 33 TC 244) (see also 5.27).

In special circumstances, it might be possible to argue that the termination payment was made for valid commercial reasons unconnected with the sale. It will be necessary to demonstrate that all shareholders received full market value for the shares and the termination payment was an independent transaction.

15.92 It is vital that the making of any ex-gratia payment should not be in the agreement for the sale of the shares and a Board resolution should be passed indicating that the payment is considered to be in the interests of the company.

Further dangers arise when the recipient of a termination payment is at or approaching retirement age. The official view is that such payments represent an 'unapproved pension benefit' which should be taxed as employment income.

Pension contributions

15.93 The scope for making 'one-off' company pension contributions has now been considerably restricted and incurring a penal tax charge can become a trap for the unwary! Company contributions are subject to the *FA 2011* £50,000 annual allowance 'input' rules.

Pension contributions made as part of a 'termination package' are not counted as a termination payment provided the amount is paid to an approved pension scheme [*ITEPA 2003, s 408*].

Inter-spousal transfers and ER

15.94 Proprietors' spouses often hold shares in owner-managed companies to benefit from the spreading of dividends for income tax purposes.

Although the ER lifetime gains limit is now at a very generous £10 million (see 15.34), some owner managers (particularly those anticipating extremely large gains) may still wish to transfer a suitable shareholding to their spouse to enable them to benefit from ER in their own right.

Care must be taken to ensure that the recipient spouse is able to meet the necessary ER conditions in their own right. Thus, they will need to be a (genuine) director/employee (although not necessarily working full-time), and hold at least 5% of the ordinary shares/voting rights (see 15.33). The recipient spouse would need to meet these conditions for a minimum of one year before the relevant share sale. The spouse's ER holding period runs from when they actually acquired the shares from the transferor spouse.

Maximising CGT base value at March 1982

15.95 Where the seller held the shares at March 1982, they will be able to deduct the March 1982 value of the shares, together with indexation relief from the sale proceeds. While this may provide a significant relief for a controlling shareholder of a company which was profitable in 1982, a minority shareholder will typically have a low March 1982 base value (as the shares will be discounted for lack of control, etc (see 14.38, 14.39 and 14.68)).

15.96 This can be a problem in 'husband and wife' owned companies, if neither have control. However, by concession, it is possible to boost the March 1982 value by arranging for one spouse to transfer sufficient shares to give the other control before the onward sale of the company (see 14.69).

BECOMING NON-RESIDENT

Overview

15.97 Perhaps the most radical step contemplated by many sellers (and achieved by few!) is to establish non-resident status in order to avoid paying UK capital gains tax on the sale of their company. While this has always been possible with careful planning (and a certain willingness to give up the often overlooked pleasantries of living in the UK!), the *Finance Act 1998* added further difficulties with the 'five year' absence rule.

Prospective sellers will often pay ER CGT at 10% with owners of investment companies attracting a 28% tax rate on exit. At these relatively reasonable rates, many will seriously question whether they are willing to endure the inevitable personal and economic upheaval of emigrating for five years to avoid this tax, although, of course, their decision would ultimately depend on the *absolute* amount of tax potentially payable. Following the *Gaines-Cooper* case, sellers can only realistically shed their 'UK residence' status by demonstrating they have left the UK permanently. In practice, this increasingly difficult requirement is only likely to be achieved by those selling their company with a view to retiring abroad or those that wish to emigrate for good!

Five-year non-resident rule

15.98 Sellers leaving the UK who have been tax resident in the UK for at least four out of the last seven years *before the tax year of departure*, must now be prepared to go abroad for at least five complete tax years. (The five year rule does *not* apply to assets acquired by the taxpayer after the date of departure or in any intervening year when the taxpayer was non-resident [*TCGA 1992, s 10A(3)(a)*].The concessional 'split year' residence basis (ESC D2) does not generally apply for CGT (unless, exceptionally, the individual has only been a 'short term' UK resident – see 15.101).

Thus, if the shares are sold after the date of departure, but in the same tax year, then the gain will be taxed in that year under normal rules.To escape

CGT using the 'five year' absence rule, the seller must be commercially able to finalise the sale negotiations and complete the sale contract after they leave the UK (also requiring an 'understanding' purchaser). Great care must also be taken to prevent a binding contract being created before the end of the tax year of departure – hence, any communications between the parties and heads of agreement, etc must clearly be stated as being 'subject to contract'.

In the vast majority of cases, an individual seller must ensure that he is neither resident nor ordinarily resident for at least the five complete tax years *after* the tax year of departure. In practice, this means that the seller must leave the UK before the tax year of disposal and ideally remain absent from the UK throughout the tax year in which the shares are sold. (An individual will always be regarded as tax resident in the UK if he spends more than 183 days here The seller must also avoid being treated as resident and ordinarily resident in (at least) the following four tax years. For someone who has lived in the UK all their life, the recent Supreme Court decision in *R (on the application of Davies, James & Gaines-Cooper) v HMRC* [2011] UKSC 47, demonstrates the difficulty of shedding 'ordinary residence' status. Mr Gaines-Cooper had established a base in the Seychelles and spent less than 91 days a year in the UK on average. However, the Supreme Court upheld the previous Court of Appeal ruling. The Supreme Court concluded that Mr Gaines-Cooper had remained ordinarily resident in the UK because it had remained 'the centre of gravity of his life and interests'. HMRC also received judicial support for their view that the so-called '91-day' test only applied where the taxpayer was able to demonstrate first that they had 'permanently and indefinitely' left the UK (based on its prior guidance in IR20). Sellers who wish to claim they have broken their UK residency now have a higher burden of proof imposed on them.

Currently, those sellers wishing to demonstrate they have ceased to be 'resident/ordinarily resident' in the UK, both in the tax year of the share sale (and the following four years), will need to demonstrate they have left here on a permanent basis. They can expect careful scrutiny from HMRC which will investigate the claim by building up a full and complete picture of their lifestyle and habits. Amongst the many factors taken into account, HMRC will wish to compare the pattern of presence in the UK compared with that achieved overseas (rather than a simple 'day' count).

HMRC's current practice is now firmly enshrined in HMRC6. This shows taxpayers who claim to have left the UK 'permanently or indefinitely' must demonstrate a clear break from their former social and family ties within the UK. For example, if a seller's spouse and children remain here, it shows that they did not intend to leave the UK permanently (and cannot therefore mechanically rely on simply satisfying the average 91 days test over a four year period!).

Following the *Gaines-Cooper* case and HMRC's current stance, if an owner manager wishes to avoid CGT on a sale of their company by shedding their CGT residence status, they should ensure:

- They have acquired permanent residence for tax purposes in another jurisdiction

- Their existing UK home has been sold or let-out on a long lease

- Their wife and children accompany them and their children obtain their education abroad

- Any employment takes place overseas

- Membership of UK based clubs and organisations, UK directorships etc have been reduced to the minimum possible

As part of the tax planning, the seller should take appropriate professional advice about the tax position overseas. There is no point in emigrating to avoid UK CGT if a substantial tax liability arises in the destination country. In some cases, it might be necessary to take a long holiday elsewhere to avoid being resident in the destination country for the year, especially if a material tax liability is likely to arise there. The most desirable destinations are tax-havens or those that do not tax capital gains.

Proposed statutory residence test (SRT)

In June 2011, the Government announced its proposals for introducing a statutory residence test (SRT) for tax purposes to provide greater clarity and certainty, given the highly complex case-law driven principles.

The SRT proposals are currently being finalised but it seems clear that those who retain close connections with the UK will continue to be treated as UK resident under the proposed SRT. Thus, for those with more complicated affairs, the SRT would take into account both the amount of time they spend in the UK and the other connections they have with the UK (see Part C below). Once someone has become resident and built up connections with the UK, they would have to scale back their ties to the UK significantly and/or spend far less time here before they can 'sever' their UK residence status.

The SRT is broken down into three alternative parts.

Part A – Conclusive non-residence

An individual will *not* be UK resident in the UK for a tax year if they:

- were not resident in the UK in all of the previous three tax years; and

- they are present in the UK for fewer than 45 days in the current tax year;

or

- were resident in the UK in one or more of the previous three tax years; and

- they are present in the UK for fewer than 10 days in the current tax year;

or

- leave the UK to carry out full-time work abroad provided; and

- they are present in the UK for fewer than 90 days in the tax year; and

- no more than 20 days are spent working in the UK in the tax year.

Part B: Conclusive residence

Provided Part A of the SRT does not apply, an individual will be *conclusively resident* for the tax year under Part B if they meet *any* of the following conditions:

- are present in the UK for 183 days or more in a tax year; or

- have only one UK home (or have two or more homes and all of these are in the UK);or

- carry out full-time work in the UK.

Where an individual does not meet *any* of the Part B conditions, they would have to consider Part C of the test.

Part C: Other connection factors and day counting

This is aimed at those with more complicated affairs and reflects the principle that the more time someone spends in the UK, they will need to have to minimal connections with the UK to be non-resident here.

In the context of company sales, it is probably only necessary to consider Part C (ii) (which deals with those who were UK resident in one or more of the previous three tax years (called 'leavers'). In these cases, the following 'connection factors' may be relevant to an individual's residence status where, at some time in the relevant tax year, they have

- a UK resident family;

- substantive UK employment (including self-employment);

- accessible accommodation in the UK;

- spent 90 days or more in the UK in either of the previous two tax years;

- spent more days in the UK in the tax year than in any other single country

These connection factors in Part C are combined with days spent in the UK to determine residence status as follows:

Days spent in UK	Impact of connection factors on residence status
Fewer than 10 days	Always non-resident
10 – 44 days	Resident if individual has at least four factors (otherwise not resident)
45– 89 days	Resident if individual has three factors or more (otherwise not resident)
90 – 111 days	Resident if individual has two factors or more (otherwise not resident)
120 – 182 days	Resident if individual at least one factor (otherwise not resident)
183 days or more	Always UK resident

The proposed SRT is expected to apply from 6 April 2013 and these rules are highly relevant for those wishing to ensure they become non-resident prior to a sale of their company from 2013/14 onwards.

CGT entry charge

15.99 If the individual seller of an owner managed company becomes resident during the 'five year' period, the capital gain on the share sale (realised whilst non-resident) will be taxed in the tax year of return to the UK (similarly, relief will be given for any capital loss realised on the shares) – these rules, of course, apply to gains and losses arising on any chargeable assets held before departure which are realised during a non-resident period of less than five years.

In computing the UK CGT on the entry charge, credit would be given for any overseas tax incurred on the gain in the usual way. The legislation was amended in F(No.2)A 2005 to ensure that the CGT entry charge cannot be prevented by the terms of any double tax treaty provision. A diagrammatic illustration of the rule is shown below.

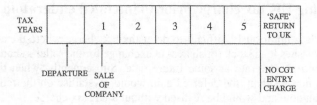

'Five year' non-resident rule

The disruption caused by leaving the UK on a 'permanent' basis and spending at least five years away from it, is only likely to appeal to those selling out at the end of their business career.

Dividend strip whilst non-resident

15.100 There are other potential solutions which are not based on the 'five year' non-resident period imposed by the CGT regime. For example, if the owner-manager's company has substantial reserves, it may be appropriate for the seller to emigrate for a shorter period (at least one complete tax year) with a view to extracting a dividend from the company whilst non-resident. As the 'seller' would be a non-UK resident, there should be no further UK income tax liability in respect of the dividend. This opportunity is unlikely to be available for much longer.

If the seller is resident in a non-treaty country, he is treated as receiving the dividend net of the dividend ordinary rate of 10% [ITTOIA 2005, s 399]. FA 1995, s 128 will prevent any dividend higher rate liability. Treaty country resident shareholders generally receive the benefit of the 10% tax credit, but would invariably be liable to tax in that overseas country.

Short-term UK residents

15.101 In the comparatively rare event that an individual seller has only been UK tax resident for less than four years out of the last seven tax years before the year of departure, they will be able to avoid a UK CGT charge on selling the shares by either:

(*a*)   going abroad under a full-time contract of employment spanning at least one tax year; or

(*b*)   leaving the UK before the tax year of disposal and going abroad for at least three tax years (so as to be neither resident nor ordinarily resident in the UK in the tax year of disposal). Return visits may be made back to the UK within the limits mentioned in 15.99. The individual should also sell their UK residence or let it so that it is not available to them.

Deferring UK tax charge prior to intended emigration

15.102 It is notoriously difficult to defer the tax charge where the acquiring company issues loan stock (or shares) in exchange for the seller's shares where they intend to emigrate at some future date. Subsequently, when the seller becomes non-resident, the deferred gain would crystallise on the redemption of the loan note and would be realised without a UK tax charge.

TCGA 1992, s 138 clearance applications are invariably refused where the issue of loan notes is purely designed to avoid tax as opposed to being dictated by the purchaser's commercial requirements – see the recent case of *Snell v HMRC* [2006] EWHC 3350 (Ch) which confirms HMRC's view on this point (see 15.46). It should be noted that if the seller has indicated an intention to emigrate after the sale, this must be fully disclosed in the, *s 138* clearance application otherwise any tax clearance could not be relied on.

Non-domiciled sellers

15.103   The *Finance Act 2008* made radical changes to the taxation of non-domiciled individuals. Such individuals must now make a special claim (under *ITTOIA 2005, s 809B*) if they wish to continue using the 'remittance basis' for taxing their foreign income and capital gains (unless their unremitted income/gains are less than £2,000). Overseas income and gains will be treated as remitted if the proceeds are remitted to the UK in any form (and the post-5 April 2008 regime widens the scope of remittances that are 'taxable'). Where a 'remittance-basis' election is made, the individual cannot benefit from the normal personal allowances and the CGT annual exemption.

However, the remittance basis will *not* be available to those who have been UK tax resident for seven out of nine tax years before the relevant tax year, unless they pay an annual charge of £30,000 (subject to the £2,000 de minimis rule). (This increases to £50,000 from 6 April 2012. The increase only applies to those who have been UK tax resident for 12 out of the last 14 years.) The £30,000 (£50,000)will offset the tax arising on the actual remittance of funds, provided it is paid direct to HMRC.

Subject to these constraints, it still remains possible for a non-domiciled seller to defer (and possibly avoid tax altogether) by setting up the 'right' structure when the company is first incorporated. Typically, this would entail establishing a foreign incorporated company (which would be UK tax resident on the grounds of being centrally managed and controlled here). The foreign company's shares would be regarded as non-UK assets (and hence, when sold, CGT would only be payable on a remittance basis). Alternatively, if a UK company is used, some or all of the shares can be placed in a non-resident trust while their value is relatively low.

USE OF NON-RESIDENT TRUSTS AND STRUCTURES

Non-resident trusts

15.104   Penal anti-avoidance legislation now significantly frustrates any tax advantages of using non-resident trusts and underlying non-resident companies have all but gone! One major problem is that a deemed 'market value' disposal would arise on the emigration of an existing UK trust or direct transfer of shares to a non-resident trust [*TCGA 1992, ss 17(1)* and *80*]. After 5 April 1999, pre-19 March 1991 non-resident trusts are also subject to the settlor-charge (in the same way as post-18 March 1991 trusts) where the settlor and immediate members of their family can benefit under the trust.

Non-domiciled settlers

15.104A   Despite the changes made in the *FA 2008*, overseas trusts may still prove to be effective CGT shelters for *non-domiciled* individuals. For example, overseas trusts created by non-domiciliaries are not subject to the settlor charge under *TCGA 1992, s 86* (see 17.57). However, gains arising in such trusts would be taxed when the trust makes a capital payment to its UK resident beneficiaries. Before 6 April 2008 the capital payments regime only applied to UK domiciled beneficiaries. Since 6 April 2008, capital payments to non-domiciled beneficiaries are also caught, subject to the special transitional rules. These broadly ensure that only gains arising after 6 April 2008 can be matched with a capital payment. For these purposes, a rebasing election can be made to exclude the pre-6 April 2008 element of a gain from being taxed under these rules.

Non-domiciled individuals can still retain gains in their overseas trust without them being taxed in the UK (and it may be possible for them to extract them on a subsequent emigration).

Transferring shares into overseas structures

15.105   It is not possible to gift or transfer at an undervalue, shares to a *company* (regardless of its residence status) under the protection of a *TCGA 1992, s 165* business asset hold-over election. Consequently, the transfer of shares into any form of overseas corporate structure will now produce a tax liability on what is essentially an unrealised gain. This also thwarts a pre-sale transfer of shares into an 'offshore bond' structure (which used to be set up by a number of leading merchant banks and insurance companies).

Whilst the use of offshore corporate and offshore bond structures can still be used in 'start-up' situations, where there is no pregnant gain in the shares, their future role must surely be of limited application in view of the reasonably palatable CGT rates which now prevail. Very few are now likely to incur the costs and additional risks associated with overseas structures.

INHERITANCE TAX ISSUES POST-SALE

15.106   Sensible tax planning is a vital integral part of securing a successful sale of an owner managed company. For many owner managers this is their one big chance to get the maximum financial return for many years hard work. However, an often overlooked area is the seller's inheritance tax profile post-sale.

Before the sale, the value of the company would normally have been outside the IHT net (due to the availability of 100% business property relief (see 17.17). However, the after tax sale consideration will *not* be protected from IHT and is therefore potentially exposed to a 40% IHT charge on death. Given that many owner managers tend to sell their companies at or near retirement age, this potential IHT problem cannot be easily solved. In such cases, the use of Discounted Gift Interest Trusts ('DGTs') may prove a helpful solution (see 17.4 for a detailed review).

PLANNING CHECKLIST – SELLING THE OWNER-MANAGED BUSINESS OR COMPANY

Company

- The corporate tax liability on asset sales may be reduced by sensible allocation of disposal proceeds – avoid creating 'wasted' indexation losses.

Working shareholders

- A share sale is generally preferred as this avoids a double tax charge.

- Where shareholders allocate their sale consideration on a basis which is *not* proportionate to their shareholdings, there is a risk that those receiving more than their pro-rata entitlement (who are directors/ employees) may be exposed to an employment income tax charge on the 'excess' amount.

- Where the seller meets the post-23 March 2010 'fundamental change of ownership' requirements under the Transaction in Securities rules, there is no legislative need to obtain clearance under *ITA 2007, s 701*. This exemption will often be satisfied on sales to 'unconnected' companies. However, where consideration is taken in shares and/or loan notes, a *TCGA 1992 s 138* clearance would still be necessary.

- Sellers that do not clearly meet the 'fundamental change of ownership' TiS test (for example, where the acquiring company is connected with them) should apply for advance clearance under *ITA 2007, s 701* (and, where appropriate, *TCGA 1992, s 138*) and allow sufficient time to do so (allowing for the 'statutory' 30-day response period). HMRC will look at each case on its merits but often find that one of the motivating reasons for the sale is to generate tax-friendly capital gains on the proceeds if this is the case the *ITA 2007, s 701* clearance would be denied.

- Owner-managers should claim ER wherever possible (since it reduces their effective CGT rate to 10% on up to £10 million of share sale gains). In some cases, owner-managers might consider transferring sufficient shares to their spouse to increase the available ER (with the spouse being eligible for ER in their own right).

- If there is a genuine uncertainty about whether the company/group meets the stringent 'trading' status test for ER, it may be desirable to seek a non-statutory business clearance from HMRC to remove any doubts on this point.

- Sellers who are receiving shares as part of their sale consideration (and have unused ER) should consider making the special TCGA 1992, s169Q election to benefit from ER on the consideration satisfied in the form of shares in the acquirer.

- Sellers who have deferred QCB gains on pre-23 June 2010 sales will invariably have a 28% CGT tax liability when they redeem their loan notes. If ER had been claimed on the postponed gain, the effective rate would be 15.55%.

- Where a seller is given QCB consideration on a post-22 June 2010 share sale, they can only access the 10% ER CGT rate if they make an election under TCGA 1992, s169R to tax the QCB consideration on the share sale date. If they wish to take advantage of the QCB deferral, it is not possible to claim ER and therefore the postponed CGT gain is likely to be taxed at 28% (without any ER).

- Earn-out transactions should be carefully analysed and planned for to ensure that the intended CGT position is obtained. With an ER gains limit of £10 million, there may be some CGT advantages in structuring a cash-based earn-out which will enable the seller to 'lock-in' some of the earn-out value at the 10% ER CGT rate. In contrast, any gains on the subsequent earn-out payments are likely to be taxed at 28%.

- Where the earn-out is to be satisfied in the form of shares/loan notes in the acquiring company, the value of the earn-out right is not taxed 'up-front'. This effectively means that the entire value of the earn-out is likely to be taxed at the main 28% CGT rate. In many cases, sellers are now likely to prefer to elect out of the automatic TCGA 1992 s 138A deferral to increase the amount taxable at the (much) lower 10% ER rate. .

- Ensure that earn-out are structured to minimise any risk of them being subject to income tax under the *ITEPA 2003* 'employment-related' securities regime.

- A pre-sale dividend is generally likely to increase the seller's overall tax liability and should usually be avoided (consider adding potential dividend to extract 'surplus' cash to the sale price).

- If a seller wishes to avoid CGT by ceasing their UK 'resident/ ordinarily resident' status, this must be carefully implemented. Following the *Gaines Cooper* case, it is essential to show that they have left the UK on a permanent and indefinite basis, evidenced by ceasing their social and family ties with the UK. In any event, they must also be able to demonstrate that their 'non-resident' status lasts for at least five complete tax years.

- The seller shareholders can limit their exposure under the warranties and indemnities by disclosing all relevant details in the relevant disclosure letter.

- A post-liquidation capital distribution is likely to be a better method of extracting the post-tax profits arising from an asset sale (as opposed to a 'pre-liquidation' income dividend).

- Watch out for potential IHT exposure on the post-tax proceeds from a company sale. Consider the use of Discounted Gift Trusts as a means of sheltering the future IHT liability.

Other employees

- A share sale provides them with the opportunity to realise a gain from an employee incentive scheme share.

- Employees holding at least 5% of the ordinary shares/votes should be able to enjoy the (lower) ER CGT 10% rate on sale.

- Employment contracts will continue to run on both asset or share sales.

Non-working shareholders

- They should resist giving warranties and indemnities (as the running of the company is outside their control).

- Their individual tax position may be prejudiced by structure of deal – must analyse early as changes can sometimes be made.

Chapter 16

Winding-Up, Administration of Companies, and Disincorporation

BACKGROUND

16.1   The shareholders of a family or owner-managed company may decide to wind it up voluntarily, perhaps following a sale of the assets and trade or a planned closure of the business. In such cases, there will often be a surplus available for distribution to the shareholders after the interests of the creditors have been satisfied. It will be essential to ensure that the surplus funds are distributed in a tax-efficient manner (see 16.15–16.32). Where a company is wound-up voluntarily, there may be time to implement appropriate corporate tax planning measures to increase the amount ultimately available to the company's shareholders.

In some cases, the existing shareholder(s) may simply wish to 'disincorporate'. This would normally entail winding the company up and transferring its trade and assets to the shareholder(s). The shareholders would then continue to carry on the trade through a sole trader or partnership structure (see 16.33–16.43).

16.2   An insolvent company may be put into administration. An administrator will often be appointed by a key creditor seeking to enforce its security under a floating charge. However, an administrator can also be appointed by the company, its directors or by the court. The process of administration often enables a company to be rescued, which might involve the trade being sold on as a going concern (see 16.44 – 16.46).

If a company is wound-up by a receiver or creditor, then its shareholders are likely to lose most if not all of their capital stake. It will then be necessary to consider what tax relief can be claimed in respect of their shares (see 16.47–16.52) and any irrecoverable shareholder loans (see 16.53–16.58). Where the company is insolvent, the actions of the receiver/liquidator will be dictated by commercial requirements but, where possible, these should be conducted on the most tax efficient basis to enhance the amount available for both creditors and shareholders. However, there is no point in planning to reduce tax liabilities that are never going to be paid due to insufficiency of funds.

CONSEQUENCES FOR THE COMPANY

Pension provision

16.3 Before the company ceases trading the proprietors'/directors' pension provision should be considered. Unless full provision has already been made, there may be some scope for making 'top-up' payments to an approved pension scheme, subject to the relevant £50,000 annual allowance restrictions. Provided the pension contributions are paid in the final corporation tax accounting period (CTAP) (ie up to cessation of trade), a trading deduction can normally be claimed with no spreading of contributions. This will also reduce the funds remaining for distribution and hence the shareholder's exposure to tax.

Where a company has not made any pension provision for its proprietors/ directors, it may be possible for the company to enter into a Hancock Annuity arrangement. The company would purchase an annuity from an insurance company before the trade ceases. Following the case of *Hancock v General Reversionary & Investment Co Ltd* (1918) 7 TC 358, the purchase of an annuity to fund a future pension was held to be deductible against profits – it was not a capital payment. The insurance company would then be responsible for paying the pension.

HMRC have confirmed that 'Hancock' annuities can still be purchased post-A Day as long as they comply with the new pension rules (see Chapter 10). A specially purchased Hancock annuity for a retiring employee would normally be set up through a registered scheme in the same way as any other pension scheme, especially if a tax-free lump sum is to be provided. Tax relief for the employer contribution is subject to the 'wholly and exclusively' rule. (It also possible for the company to purchase a Hancock annuity through a registered scheme.)

Under a Hancock-type arrangement, all benefits will have vested, so it does not have to satisfy the annual allowance rules (see 10.21). The lifetime allowance (see 10.28) does apply. If the retiring employee is over 75 or has exhausted their lifetime allowance, then benefits could be provided by an employer-financed retirement benefit scheme.

Termination of CTAP and closure costs

16.4 The company's trade will usually have ceased before it is wound-up and this will have a number of important tax consequences.

The cessation of the company's trade will bring about a termination of the company's current CTAP [*CTA 2009, s 10 (d)–(f)*]. Generally, this will accelerate the date on which the company pays its tax liability. Companies which do not pay their tax in instalments, must pay the corporation tax for the final CTAP within nine months following the end of that period. For other companies, the final instalment date is effectively brought forward, being due three months and 14 days after the end of the CTAP (see also 15.6).

Any unprovided expenses incurred after the cessation of trade (known as 'post-cessation' expenses) can only be offset against post-cessation receipts (see 16.9), which reduces the prospect of obtaining relief [*CTA 2009, ss 196 and 197*].

In drawing up the tax computation to cessation, particular care must therefore be taken to ensure that specific provisions are made for all known trade expenses that have been incurred up to the date of cessation. This will include provisions for warranty claims and bad and 'impaired' trading and loan relationship debts.

HMRC will disallow any expenses incurred in connection with the cessation of trade. However, following the Privy Council's decision in *Commissioner of Inland Revenue v Cosmotron Manufacturing Co Ltd* [1997] STC 1134, HMRC will normally allow relief for contractual redundancy or severance payments made on cessation of trade. The rationale is that the payment is made under a pre-existing contractual or statutory obligation incurred as a consequence of the employees being employed for the purposes of the trade (Tax Bulletin, Issue 39, February 1999).

Termination payments that do not qualify under the above principle, such as ex-gratia payments, can be specifically relieved under the statutory trading deduction rules. Specific statutory relief is given for statutory redundancy payments and any additional redundancy payments (up to three times the amount of the statutory redundancy payments). Such payments are treated as paid on the date of cessation if they are paid after the trade ceases [*CTA 2009, s 74(4)*]. See 5.22–5.27 for income tax treatment of termination payments in the recipient employee's hands.

Sale of plant etc.

16.5   The cessation of trade will give rise to a deemed disposal of plant and machinery for capital allowance purposes, resulting in a balancing adjustment [*CAA 2001, s 61(2), Table, item 6*]. If the plant is sold either before or shortly after the trade ceases, the disposal value will generally be the net disposal proceeds [*CAA 2001, s 61(2)*, Table, item 1].

The sale of industrial and agricultural buildings or hotels no longer gives rise to any balancing charges/allowances (see 12.39).

Capital gains on property sale

16.6   The sale of the company's chargeable assets may also produce capital gains, giving rise to a significant tax liability. Broadly, the disposal of a property, etc is recognised for capital gains purposes when an unconditional contract for the sale is made [*TCGA 1992, s 28*]. If the company has significant trading losses in the final CTAP, the company should enter into the sale contract for the property on or before it closes down the trade (although completion can take place afterwards). This would enable any gain on the property sale to be sheltered by the current trading losses that might otherwise be forfeited on cessation.

Inevitably, there will be situations where it is not possible to sell the property until some time after the trade has ceased so that any gain cannot be offset by the trading losses generated in the final CTAP to cessation. Furthermore, the gain might be taxed at the full corporation tax rate if the company becomes a close investment holding company (see 16.10). In these cases, it may be beneficial to crystallise the gain before the trade ceases by arranging for the property to be sold to the owner-manager and then possibly licensed back to the company. The sale of the property would attract SDLT (see 12.21).

Where appropriate, it might be possible for the property to be distributed in specie to the owner-manager. This would be treated as a distribution, taxable at the current effective rates of 25% or 36.1% (depending on the owner manager's taxable income). The in-specie distribution would also give rise to a capital gains disposal, based on its market value (see 9.8)

An in-specie distribution of the property would generally be exempt from SDLT, although SDLT would apply to any mortgage or loan taken with the property (since this represents actual consideration).

Sale of trading stock

16.7   Where the company's trading stock and work in progress is sold to an unconnected UK trader, the actual sale proceeds will be credited in the trading account for tax purposes. In such cases, HMRC would not normally be able to impute a market value for tax purposes (see 15.15) [*CTA 2009, ss 162–165*].

Relief for trading losses

16.8   The liquidator or administrator must consider how to make best use of any remaining tax adjusted trading losses. Trading losses can only be carried forward for offset against profits of the same trade [*CTA 2010, s 45, (ICTA 1988, s 393(1))*]. Consequently, any unrelieved tax losses cannot normally be carried forward beyond the date of cessation except where they can be offset against post-cessation receipts (see 16.9).

The main reliefs which are likely to be relevant for (tax adjusted) trading losses are as follows:

(a) the offset of trading losses for the final CTAP to cessation against the company's total profits (before charitable donations relief) of that period [*CTA 2010, s 37(3)(a), (ICTA 1988, s 393A(1)(a))*] (see 4.33);

(b) the offset of any remaining trading losses by carrying them back against the total profits (before charitable donations relief) for the previous year [*CTA 2010, s 37(3)(b) (ICTA 1988, s 393A(1)(b))*];

(c) tax adjusted trading losses arising in the final 12 months before cessation of trade can be carried back against the company's total profits against the CTAPs falling within the three previous years on a LIFO basis [*CTA 2010, ss 37(3)* and *39 (ICTA 1988, s 393A(2A), (2B))*]. (Since this is a terminal loss claim, it is not subject to the general £50,000 'offset restriction' for the earliest two years under the temporary extended carry-back rules in the *FA 2009* (see 4.35).) See example 1 for detailed terminal loss computation.

A company's CTAP terminates on cessation of trade – if an earlier CTAP straddles and ends in the final 12-month period, any trading loss for that CTAP is time apportioned and added to the terminal trading loss claim.

Example 1

Terminal loss relief

Capello Ltd normally prepares accounts to 31 December each year. The company ceased trading on 30 April 2012, having sold its trade and assets under a distress sale to a competitor company. However, in the four months to 30 April 2012, it made a tax-adjusted trading loss of £78,500.

During the year ended 31 December 2011, Capello Ltd also suffered a trading loss (tax-adjusted) of £240,000.

Capello Ltd's terminal loss claim is computed as follows:

Computation of terminal loss – 12 months to 30 April 2012

	£
4 months to 30 April 2012	78,500
8 months to 31 December 2011	
8/12 × £240,000	160,000
Total loss	238,500

Relief for terminal loss

	2008	2009	2010
Trading profits	180,400	140,730	80,470
Non-trade LR interest	640	420	–
Total profits	181,040	141,150	80,470
Less: Terminal loss relief			
8 months to 31/12/11 – £160,000 loss*		(79,530)	(80,470)
4 months to 30/04/12			
–£78,500 loss**		(61,620)	
PCTCT	181,040	Nil	Nil

*The loss for the 8 months to 31 December 2011 can be carried back against the total profits of CTAPs covering the three years to 31 December 2010 (i.e. prior to the loss making CTAP). The loss is fully offset against 2010 and 2009.

The remaining loss of £80,000 (£240,000 less £160,000) for the 12 months to 31 December 2011 cannot be relieved.

** The loss for the 4 months to 30 April 2012 can be carried back against the total profits of CTAPs covering the three years to 31 December 2011 (ie prior to the loss making CTAP). In this case only £61,620 of the £78,500 loss can be relieved against the 2009 profits, leaving unrelieved losses of £16,880.

Post-trading receipts and election to carry back to cessation date

16.9   Income receipts arising after a company has ceased to trade are assessable as 'non-trading' post-cessation receipts [*CTA 2009, ss 190–192*]. These would include the write-back of excessive provisions (upon which tax relief was originally claimed) and the unanticipated recovery of a bad debt that had been provided against or written-off [*CTA 2009, s 192*] and the release of trading liabilities after the trade has ceased [*CTA 2009, s 193*].

Post-cessation expenses can normally be deducted against post-cessation receipts. However, *CTA 2009, s 198* provides that a special election can be made for post-cessation receipts received within six years of the trade ceasing (i.e. the final trading CTAP) to be carried back to the cessation date. This election is likely to be beneficial if the company has unused trading losses (which would invariably be forfeited on cessation). The election must be made within two years of the end of the CTAP in which the amount is received. By bringing the 'receipt' into account on the last day of trading, the company would often be able to shelter the tax on it by carried forward trading losses under *CTA 2010, s 45 (ICTA 1988 s 393(1))* or current year losses under *CTA 2010, s 37(3)(a)(ICTA 1988 s 393A(1)(a))* (see 16.8 (a) above). Even where there are no losses, there will also be cases where a lower company tax rate applies in the earlier 'cessation' period.

It is unlikely that an election to carry-back would be made if this increased the tax but if this is the case, *CTA 2009, s 200* deals with the relevant mechanics.

Even though the facility for making a carry-back election exists, it appears that relief for a post-cessation receipt could also be obtained by the offset of trading losses carried forward beyond the cessation date. This is based on HMRC's Business Income Manual (at BIM 80535) which indicates that what was *ICTA 1988, s 105* (now *CTA 2009, s 196*) permits the (exceptional) carry forward of unrelieved losses of the discontinued business enabling them to be offset against post-cessation receipts.

Close investment holding company (CIC) status

16.10   Where a close company ceases to carry on a trade or property investment business, it will usually be treated as a close investment holding company (CIC) [*CTA 2010, s 34 (ICTA 1988, s 13A)*] (see 4.44–4.47). A CIC cannot benefit from the small profits rate of corporation tax nor can it claim small profits marginal relief, irrespective of the level of its profits. In such cases, the company's post-cessation income and gains would be taxed at the main corporation tax rate – 28% to 31 March 2011, then 26% for the year ended 31 March 2012, and then decreasing by 1% each year over the next three years.

If the company is not a CIC throughout the CTAP which ends on the commencement of its winding up, it will not be treated as a CIC for the next CTAP [*CTA 2010, s 34(5) (ICTA 1988, s 13A(4))*]. However, where the company has ceased trading for a short period before it is wound up, this exemption is unlikely to apply. The company will normally have already become a CIC before it goes into liquidation.

Pre-liquidation tax liabilities

16.11   The liquidator will need to take account of pre-liquidation tax liabilities as either preferential or ordinary claims [*IA 1986, ss 175, 386*]. Broadly, preferential creditors have the right to repayment of their debts ahead of the unsecured creditors.

Preferential creditors are confined to liabilities broadly representing unpaid employee remuneration, etc for the four months before the winding-up. Notably, unpaid VAT, PAYE and NIC liabilities are no longer preferred creditors.

Furthermore, assessed taxes do not count as preferred debts, so any unpaid pre-liquidation corporation tax would rank as an unsecured creditor. Corporation tax arising during the liquidation is, however, normally treated as a liquidation expense (*Re Toshoku Finance UK plc, Kahn (liquidators of Toshoku Finance UK plc) v CIR* [2002] STC 368).

A practical approach will normally be required by the liquidator of the insolvent company when dealing with the company's tax affairs. He must inform HMRC of his appointment and determine the outstanding corporation tax position. Where the company is insolvent or has substantial brought forward tax losses, HMRC may be prepared to agree a 'nil liability' position without the need to submit detailed tax computations (but a CT600 must be submitted). However, if the liquidator wishes to agree an amount of trading losses for the purposes of a loss relief claim (see 16.8), HMRC will require sufficiently detailed computations and accounts to agree the amount of the loss.

Post-liquidation tax liabilities

16.12 The commencement of a winding-up terminates the company's current CTAP and a new accounting period will begin. (A winding-up normally starts when the resolution is passed or the petition is presented to place the company into liquidation [*CTA 2009, s 12(7)*].) Each successive CTAP will last for 12 months, with the final CTAP ending on the date the winding-up is completed [*CTA 2009, s 12*]. Similar rules apply where a company goes into administration (see 16.44).

Corporation tax liabilities which arise during the course of the winding-up are treated as an expense or disbursement of the liquidation (see *Re Beni-Felkai Mining Co Ltd* (1933) 18 TC 632). In most cases, the only taxable income received during the winding-up period is interest receivable on realised funds. However, interest received from HMRC on overpaid corporation tax (in the company's final 'winding-up' CTAP) is exempt from tax where the amount is less than £2,000 [*CTA 2010, s 633 (ICTA 1988, s 342 (3A))*].

As a necessary disbursement of the liquidation, the tax liabilities must (together with any overdue tax) be met in priority to the claims of all creditors and the liquidator's remuneration. However, where appropriate, the liquidator can apply to the court for an Order of Priority to be made to ensure that his remuneration and expenses can be dealt with equitably.

Legal formalities

Members' voluntary liquidation

16.13 The shareholders of a solvent company can proceed to wind-up the company voluntarily. Generally, a special resolution of the shareholders is required to place the company in voluntary liquidation. Before this is done, the directors need to make a statutory declaration of solvency. After having made a full inquiry, the directors must declare that the company will be able to pay its debts within 12 months following the commencement of the winding-up.

A member's voluntary liquidation must be dealt with by a licensed insolvency practitioner. Under a liquidation, a company can generally be restored to the Register within a period of six years after the winding-up has been completed (although claims for death or serious injury can be made at any time) [*CA 2006, s 1030*]. Before 1 October 2009, the 'restoration-window' was limited to two years [*CA 1985, s 651*]. Such an order can be brought by a member or creditor or any other interested person. A creditor who surfaces after the company has been liquidated has six years to put the company back on the register and even then can only overturn distributions made if the liquidator did not take proper steps to contact creditors. Quite often, the costs of a formal voluntary liquidation may seem relatively high compared to the value of the company's assets.

Dissolution under *CA 2006, s 1000*

16.14   A solvent company may be dissolved as a result of the company's name being struck off the register by the Registrar of Companies under *Companies Act 2006, s 1000* (*Companies Act 1985, s 652* prior to 1 October 2009). This route is sometimes preferred to a liquidation since it generally costs less! HMRC are prepared to treat a dissolution under *CA 2006, s 1000* as a 'winding-up' for tax purposes under ESC C16 (see 16.16). However, *CA 2006, s 1003* imposes additional stringent requirements on the directors such as the need to notify all shareholders, employees, creditors, etc with tough penalties for non-compliance. Furthermore, it is necessary to wait at least three months after the trade has ceased before an application can be made.

Where a dissolution is used, it is vital that any remaining assets must first be stripped out of the company, otherwise they will pass to the Crown under the 'bona vacantia' rule in *CA 2006, s 1012* [*CA 2005, s 654*].

In the past, the strict legal position was that a company could not repay its share capital (and other non-distributable reserves) to shareholders on a dissolution. This meant that any share capital, etc, would fall to be treated as 'vacant goods' and would therefore pass to the Crown. However, if the company sought to repay 'small' amounts of share capital, there was comfort from The Office of the Treasury Solicitor, which indicated that it would not seek to recover unauthorised distributions of less than £4,000. However, the Treasury Solicitor announced as from 14 October 2011 that this concession would no longr apply, with immediate effect.

The reason for this is that *CA 2006, s 654* now enables private companies to reduce their share capital to, say,, £1 by special resolution and should provide a solution to the potential 'bona vacantia' problem. By going through the relevant procedure, a company can now effectively repay its share capital. The resolution for reducing share capital must be supported by a solvency statement (signed by each of the company's directors) indicating that the company is able to repay its debts as they fall due both at that time and for the next 12 months – this should not be a problem when a company is being dissolved after all its debts have been repaid. The reduction of share capital will create a corresponding increase in the company's distributable reserves (since it is treated as a realised profit (The Companies (Reduction of Share Capital Order) 2008). This would mean that the company could then distribute the relevant amount to the shareholders. From a tax analysis, the share capital repaid should represent a return of the original share subscription.

As with liquidations, a dissolved company can generally be restored by a court order within six years from the publication of the striking off notice in the Gazette [*CA 2006, s 1030*]. Any member or creditor who 'feels aggrieved' can apply to the court for such an order. It would therefore be possible for a creditor to come forward at any time during the six year period to overturn a transfer of assets to the members. Where there is a claim for damages against the company for personal injury, the 'restoration' period is unlimited.

The normal six year period under *CA 2006* is much shorter than the 20-year period that applied under the older rules under *CA 1985, s 653*.

DEALING WITH SURPLUS AVAILABLE TO SHAREHOLDERS

Capital distributions

16.15 Where a company has surplus funds (ie after its creditors have been paid), it is necessary to decide how these can be extracted for the shareholders' benefit in the most tax efficient manner.

Distributions made in the course of dissolving or winding-up the company are treated as 'capital distributions' and are therefore chargeable to CGT [*TCGA 1992, s 122*]. Where an in-specie capital distribution is made, the recipient is taxed on the market value of the asset (*TCGA 1992, s 122(5)(b)*) (see 16.24). A distribution made to shareholders during the course of the winding-up does not count as an 'income' distribution for tax purposes and therefore no tax credit is available to the recipient shareholder [*CTA 2010, s 1030 (ICTA 1988, s 209(1))*].

A shareholder is treated as making a disposal of an interest in the relevant shares for CGT purposes when they become entitled to receive the capital distribution from the company [*TCGA 1992, s 122(1)*]. The commencement of the liquidation does not trigger any deemed disposal for the shareholder.

Capital distributions under ESC C16

16.16   Under ESC C16, HMRC will treat a distribution made prior to a dissolution as having been made under a formal winding-up, and therefore as a capital payment (and hence liable to CGT in the recipient's hands as opposed to being taxed as an income distribution).

Certain assurances must be given to the Inspector beforehand. Normally, the Inspector will require that any remaining tax liabilities are paid and also confirm that, once the assets have been distributed, the company will request the Registrar of Companies to strike the company off the register (see 16.14). Although ESC 16 merely requires the company and its shareholders to agree to pay any corporation tax, in practice, HMRC insist that it is actually paid otherwise they will object to the 'striking-off' application. Under current applications for ESC C16 treatment, inspectors now appear to insist on the formal signatures of both the company secretary (on behalf of the company) and all the shareholders (as opposed to the company's agents) (see Taxation, 25 July 2002, page 453).

In applying ESC C16, HMRC will also wish to ensure that the relevant company is not subject to an HMRC investigation; and

- potentially 'caught' by the Transactions in Securities anti-avoidance provisions (see 16.27–16.30A), such as where it plans to sell or transfer its assets/trade to another company owned by all or some of the existing shareholders (see HMRC CTM36875).

It is always recommend that HMRC approval for ESC C16 is obtained before any distributions are made as part of the dissolution process.

In the past, a company could not distribute its share capital and other non-distributable reserves under the 'dissolution/striking off' procedure. Thus, unless the amounts involved were relatively small, a formal winding-up was normally recommended (see 16.13). However, it may now be possible for a company to take advantage of the useful Companies Act 2006 provisions to reduce and return capital to shareholders (see 16.14). The Treasury Solicitor's office confirmed in November 2011 that no action will be taken by them to recover share capital under the 'bona vacantia' rule.

HMRC are planning to legislate ESC C16 as part of their on-going process of legislating many of its extra-statutory concessions (following the House of Lords' ruling in *R v HMRC ex p Wilkinson* [2006] STC 270, which raised concerns about the validity of certain ESCs and the extent of HMRC's discretion to make and apply them. ESC C16 is to be put on to a statutory basis from 1 March 2012. However the statutory relief is less generous!

The proposed 'new' *CTA 2010, s 1030A* would apply to distributions made in anticipation of the company being dissolved and exempt them from income tax (hence CGT treatment will apply) provided:

- the company has collected (or will collect) any amounts due and pays any liabilities owing, and

- the total distributions do not exceed £25,000.

Many will appreciate that the £25,000 distribution limit is very low and will force company 'closure' exercises to proceed via a formal liquidation after 1 March 2012 (see 16.13).

CGT on capital distributions

16.17   In many cases, capital distributions made should be entitled to Entrepreneurs' Relief (ER) (see 16.18). Such capital distributions no longer carry any indexation allowance or taper relief entitlement.

ER enables the gain arising on the capital distribution to be taxed at 10% up to the current £10 million (£5 million between 23 June 2010 and 5 April 2011) lifetime limit with the remaining gains being taxed at the 'higher' CGT rate of 28%. (This limit is calculated on a 'cumulative' lifetime basis for multiple ER claims).

For 2011/12, where ER is not available, gains may be taxed at 28% or 18% (where and to the extent that the shareholder's total taxable income and taxable gains including the capital distribution for the year fall below the £35,000 basic income tax rate threshold).

See earlier editions of this book for treatment of pre-23 June 2010 capital distributions.

Entrepreneurs' Relief on capital distributions

Qualifying conditions for ER

16.18   Capital distributions made during a winding-up (or distributions treated as capital under the concessionary ESC C16 treatment) may be eligible for ER, since they are treated as a disposal of an interest in shares under *TCGA 1992, s 122* (*TCGA 1992, s 169I(2)(c)*).

ER can be claimed in such cases provided the conditions in *TCGA 1992, s 169I(7)*, are satisfied:

1   The company must be a trading company (or holding company of a trading group) in the one year before it ceases to trade (or ceases its 'holding company of a trading group' status).

2   Throughout the one year before the company ceases to trade (or be a qualifying holding company), the recipient shareholder is required to have:

    –   held at least 5% of the ordinary share capital (carrying at least 5% of the voting rights), and

–   served as a director or employee of the company (or fellow group company).

3   The relevant capital distribution must be made within three years after the date the trade ceases (or the company ceases to be a qualifying holding company). HMRC have no discretion to extend this 'three-year' period.

The mechanics for claiming ER are covered in 15.30.

Planning considerations

16.19   These special ER rules are based around the date the company ceases to trade (or loses its qualifying 'holding company' status without becoming a trading company).

Particular care must be taken to ensure that the company is in a position to pay a capital distribution within the three years after it has ceased to trade. The liquidator must therefore endeavour to realise the company's assets within this time-frame.

Example 2

Calculation of taxable gain on capital distribution

Ferdinand Ltd ceased trading on 30 May 2011 after selling its trade and assets. The company was then immediately wound up with a capital distribution of £850,000 being paid on completion of the winding up on December 2011.

Mr Rio incorporated Ferdinand Ltd in March 1975 with 100,000 £1 ordinary shares and his shareholding was worth £200,000 at 31 March 1982. (He is a higher rate taxpayer.)

Mr Rio's capital gain on the capital distribution would be calculated as follows:

	£
Capital distribution	850,000
Less: March 1982 value	(200,000)
Chargeable gain	650,000
Less; Annual exemption	(10,600)
Taxable gain	639,400
ER CGT @ 10%	63,940

* Mr Rio has been a director of Ferdinand Ltd holding 100% of the shares and voting rights in the 12 months before the trade ceased on 30 May 2011. He therefore qualifies and claims ER on the capital distribution which is made within three years of the company's trade ceasing.

Multiple capital distributions

16.20   If a shareholder receives more than one capital distribution, all but the last one will be treated as a part disposal in respect of the shares. The normal

$$\frac{A}{A + B}$$

part disposal formula in *TCGA 1992, s 42* will be used to apportion the base cost of the shares where:

A = the amount of the interim capital distribution

B = the residual share value at the date of the interim distribution.

16.21   In practice, a relatively relaxed approach is taken with regard to agreeing interim valuations of shares (for the purpose of calculating 'B') where the liquidation is expected to be completed within two years of the first distribution (SP/D3). For example, if all the distributions are made before the CGT is calculated, HMRC will normally agree that the residual share value at the date of any interim distribution equals the total amount of subsequent distributions, without any discount for the delay in the receipt of the subsequent payments.

16.22   Depending on the amounts involved it may be beneficial to phase the timing of the capital distributions over as many tax years as possible. This will enable the shareholders to benefit from more than one annual exemption. Although all parties may be anxious to conclude the liquidation as quickly as possible, by timing the liquidation shortly before the start of the tax year, it may be possible to pay capital distributions over three separate tax years (but paid over a period of only (say) 18 months). Where there are a number of shareholders, the benefits from using multiple annual exemptions may be considerable.

Example 3

Tax treatment of multiple capital distributions

Brooking Ltd went into liquidation on 1 June 2011 , having ceased trading on 6 April 2011 . After the trade ceased, the company leased out its trading premises on a short lease until the property was sold during the liquidation.

Mr Brooking formed the company in September 1997, subscribing for all the 20,000 ordinary £1 shares at par.

The liquidator made the following distributions to Mr Brooking from the residual profits and initial capital.

	£	£
6 July 2011	45,000	
31 March 2012 (final)	24,000	

Entrepreneurs' Relief is available and claimed by Mr Brooking on the capital distributions (which are made within three years of the company ceasing to trade).

Mr Brooking's CGT computations would be as follows:	£	£
2011/12:		
6 July 2011		
Capital distribution	45,000	
Less Part disposal cost		
$£20,000 \times \dfrac{£45,000}{(£45,000 + £24,000)}$	(13,044)	
Chargeable gain		31,956
31 March 2012		
Final capital distribution	24,000	
Less Cost: £20,000 less £13,044 used in July 2011	(6,956)	
Chargeable gain		17,044
Total chargeable gains		49,000
Less: Annual exemption		(10,600)
Taxable gain		38,400
ER CGT @ 10%		£3,840

Small capital distributions

16.23 'Small' interim distributions are deducted against the shareholder's base cost, thus effectively postponing any gain [*TCGA 1992, s 122(2)*]. For these purposes, a distribution not exceeding £3,000 is always taken as small.

In all other cases, the distribution is accepted as 'small' provided it does not exceed 5% of the value of the relevant shareholding at the relevant date. However, HMRC do not insist on deducting the small proceeds against the cost where it is beneficial for the shareholder to crystallise a capital gain, for example, if it can be covered by an otherwise unused annual CGT exemption (Tax Bulletin, Issue 27, February 1997).

Where the capital distribution exceeds the allowable CGT base cost, the 'small proceeds' rule does not apply. Instead, the shareholder can elect to offset the capital distribution against his base cost [*TCGA 1992, s 122(4)*]. Once the base cost has been fully used, the balance of proceeds and any subsequent distributions will be fully chargeable to CGT.

Distributions in specie

16.24 If a liquidator distributes assets to the shareholders in lieu of their entitlement to a cash distribution, this will still constitute a capital distribution for tax purposes [*TCGA 1992, s 122(5)*]. In specie capital distributions can still rank for ER in the usual way (see 16.18).

Capital distributions of assets are always treated as a transaction at market value because the shareholders are connected with the company [*TCGA 1992, s 17(1)(a)*].

In contrast to a capital distribution for cash, a distribution in specie involves two disposals – one by the company in respect of the asset disposed of (which would be relieved by indexation relief) and one by the shareholder in respect of his shares. The value of the capital distribution may qualify for ER (see 16.18). In specie distributions of shares or property should be exempt from stamp duty/ stamp duty land tax – (see 9.7)

As there is no tax credit available on a capital distribution, this gives rise to an acute form of the 'double charge' effect, as shown in Example 4 below.

Example 4

Tax charges on an in-specie capital distribution

Johnny owned the entire share capital of Budgie Byrne Ltd, which went into voluntary liquidation on 1 October 2010 following a sale of its business in July 2010 . The company still holds the freehold factory that is leased to the purchaser of the business, which is currently worth £1,200,000 (and was purchased in September 2000 for £600,000.)

In December 2010 , the factory is distributed to Johnny. This triggers a capital gains disposal for the company and a capital distribution in Johnny's hands under *TCGA 1992, s 122.*

The part-disposal cost of the shares is calculated as £40,000 (since the company still has further amounts which it needs to distribute).

Disposal by company

	£
Market value of property	1,200,000
Less: Base cost	(600,000)
Less: Indexation relief £600,000 × 0.333	(199,800)
Chargeable gain	400,200
CT @ 28%	£112,056

The company would be a CIC from 1 October 2010 and thus pays corporation tax at around 27% (see 16.10).

CGT disposal for Johnny (2010/11)

	£
Capital distribution*	1,200,000
Less: Part disposal cost	(40,000)
Capital gain	1,160,000
Less; Annual exemption	(10,100)
Taxable gain	1,149,900
ER CGT @ 10%	£114,990

The in-specie distribution of the factory is not charged to SDLT (since there is no consideration – *FA 2003, Sch 3, para 1*).

PRE-LIQUIDATION/DISSOLUTION DIVIDEND VERSUS CAPITAL DISTRIBUTION

Benefits of CGT treatment

16.25 Most capital distributions received by owner managers should be eligible for ER, although care is needed to ensure that the relevant conditions are satisfied in the 12 months before the trade ceases (see 16.14). There is an added advantage in that payments paid out up to three years after the cessation of trade will still qualify for ER. Provided the shareholder has not previously used any ER relief, they will pay an ER CGT rate of 10% on gains (up to the post-5 April 2011 ER limit of £10 million), with 28% CGT applying to any excess (see 16.17).

Certain groups of shareholders will not benefit from ER (such as small minority shareholders holding less than 5% of the voting equity and 'non-working' passive shareholders). Broadly, since 23 June 2010, they will pay CGT at 28% or at the lower 18% rate (but only to the extent their taxable capital distribution/other gains, together with their taxable income falls within their basic income tax rate threshold).

(See previous editions of this book for pre-23 June 2010 treatment of capital distributions and ER.)

In contrast, pre-liquidation dividends received by a higher rate taxpayer would be subject to income tax at much higher income tax rates. Consequently, subject to the exception noted in 16.26 below, it will generally be preferable to wait until the company is wound-up before extracting its retained profits as a capital distribution (which is taxed at a lower rate). Similarly, where the company is being dissolved (see 16.14), distributions should be made under ESC C16 to obtain 'capital' treatment.

Dividends taxed at basic rate

16.26   There may be some cases where it would be advantageous to extract the company's reserves as a (pre-liquidation) income distribution. For example, if the amounts to be distributed (perhaps over several years) could be paid within the shareholders' 'basic rate' income tax bands no further tax would arise on their dividends (due to the availability of the 10% tax credit – see 9.11). Such planning must be considered and implemented before the company is wound-up, since income dividends can only be paid before it is placed into liquidation.

LIQUIDATION AND *ITA 2007, S 684* ISSUES

Phoenix company arrangements

16.27   The availability of an effective 10% ER CGT rate may tempt some owner-managers to retain profits in their companies with the view to subsequently liquidating them and extracting the reserves as a capital payment. With a current ER gains limit of £10 million, very significant sums can now be extracted in this way at a very modest tax rate, which is much lower than the effective rates of 25%/36.1% currently suffered on income distributions.

16.28 The business could subsequently be carried on under identical or similar ownership via a new company – often called a 'phoenix company'. There may of course be tax charges and stamp duty land tax arising on the transfer of the assets to the new company.

However, such planning aspirations are fraught with a number of technical difficulties. HMRC may be able to argue that the accumulated profits give rise to 'non-trading' assets on the company's balance sheet. If the 'surplus' cash reserves have been retained over a lengthy period before a subsequent 'capital' distribution to the shareholders, the argument would run that they are never going to be required for a trading purpose. HMRC are likely to adopt a far more stringent approach to surplus cash in such cases as opposed to where cash is built up within a 'continuing' trading company. If HMRC succeeded on this point, the company would not qualify as a trading company. In such cases, the benefit of ER would be denied and the benefits of obtaining a capital gains receipt would then be reduced.

Section 684 and the Joiner case

16.29 It has been firmly established that the Transactions in Securities (TiS) legislation in *ITA 2007, ss 684* and *689* (previously *ICTA 1988, s 703)* can apply where a company (with retained profits) is liquidated with its business being sold to another company under the same or substantially similar ownership. This is broadly what happened in *CIR v Joiner* [1975] STC 601, where the House of Lords held that the TiS legislation applied where a shareholder's agreement varied the shareholders' rights before the company was liquidated. This enabled the company's main (75%) shareholder to continue to carry on the trade in a new company after liquidation, having extracted the old company's distributable reserves as capital (rather than income). HMRC will therefore generally seek to apply the Joiner principles to 'phoenix' arrangements where shareholders extract the company's reserves as a capital distribution on liquidation and carry on the existing trade through another company (see 16.29). This view is also supported in HMRC's Inspector's Manual (at IM4524 and IM4519). However, it is also worth noting that HMRC were unable to persuade the Lower Tax Tribunal to apply TiS to a liquidation, based on its own special facts, in *Ebsworth v HMRC* [2009] UKFTT 199 (TC), (see 16.30A).

Ordinary liquidation should not be a TiS

16.30 The Joiner case also concluded that simply putting a company into liquidation was not sufficient (by itself) to be a TiS. The Revenue subsequently issued a statement that s 684 would not be applied to an 'ordinary liquidation' (in line with assurances given by the minister when the TiS legislation was enacted (Hansard, 25 May 1960, Col 5 11). This effectively means a genuine winding-up of a company, whether it comes to an end or its business is taken over by another entity that is under substantially different control, is unlikely to be vulnerable to a challenge. On the other hand, HMRC are likely to challenge the transfer of a business to another 'commonly controlled' company in the course of a winding-up, as indicated at CTM 36850 (see 15.48–15.50). HMRC might take a similar stance where the shareholder(s) seek(s) to 'disincorporate' their company to enable them to continue to carry on the trade as a sole trade or partnership, although arguably *ITA 2007, s 684* should not be in point (see 16.43).

In contrast, HMRC are likely to accept cases where the businesses are being transferred as part of a genuine reconstruction operation within *TCGA 1992, ss 136* and *139* using s 110 of Insolvency Act 1986 (see 13.59–13.62).

HMRC's defeat in the 'Ebsworth v HMRC' liquidation case

16.30A HMRC's approach to the application of the TiS rules to liquidations was tested in the recent case of *Ebsworth v HMRC* [2009] FTT 199 (TC). Mr Ebsworth held 51% of the shares in Business Systems Applications and Solutions (BSAS), with his wife owning the remaining 49%. BSAS operated two divisions, one highly profitable landline telecommunications network division and the other not very profitable division that supplied telephone handsets (which was worth very little). Mr and Mrs Ebsworth separated in 1998, although they both continued to run BSAS. The profitable network division ceased in 2001, with a substantial compensation payment being made to cancel the main trading contract.

Mr Ebsworth then set up a new company – BSAS 2 and the not so profitable handset supply division was transferred to it for a nominal amount. BSAS 2 also entered into a fresh agreement for the telecommunications network business. Mrs Ebsworth 'wanted out' from BSAS after the main trade ceased, and so BSAS was liquidated and capital distributions were made to Mr and Mrs Ebsworth. However, although the liquidation itself was not a TiS, HMRC contended that the creation of the new company (the issue of shares) created a TiS. Furthermore, the receipt of capital sums on the liquidation of BSAS rather than dividends contravened the TiS legislation, and a counteraction assessment was raised on Mr Ebsworth. (No counteraction was made against Mrs Ebsworth, since she was making a 'clean' exit and played no part in BSAS 2.)

Although the Tribunal stressed that its decision was based on the individual facts, HMRC lost on all points. It is worth considering Judge Shipwright's conclusions in some detail.

- There was no tax advantage – Mr Ebsworth would only achieve a tax advantage if this was shown by comparing his CGT on the capital distribution with a 'comparable' income distribution. HMRC sought to argue that the proper 'comparator' in this case was that BSAS should have purchased Mrs Ebsworth's shares (under a POS) with a dividend then being paid to Mr Ebsworth. However, the Tribunal held that HMRC had not established that a POS was either 'commercially or legally viable' or that this would give Mrs Ebsworth the required 'capital' treatment (under what was previously *ICTA 1988, s 219*) (see 13.46). Judge Shipwright found that HMRC did not satisfy their burden of proof on this issue, commenting that 'It would have helped if HMRC were clear what it was they thought was the proper comparator rather than changing their views during the hearing'. He concluded that the simplest and most commercially desirable route would have been to wind-up BSAS and for Mr Ebsworth to purchase Mrs Ebsworth's share of the 'handset supply' division. This would have enabled both shareholders to obtain capital distributions on the liquidation of BSAS so there was no tax advantage in relation to the transactions actually carried out.

- If Judge Shipwright was wrong on the tax advantage point, it did not arise from the combination of the liquidation and TiS. Judge Shipwright held that the only TiSs here were the issue of shares by BSAS 2 and the transfer of Mrs Ebsworth's shares in that company to Mr Ebsworth and these had no impact on the 'alleged' tax advantage. Although HMRC contended that BSAS could not have been wound-up without the transfer of the trades, Judge Shipwright considered that its activities could have been distributed to the shareholders in specie with Mrs Ebsworth transferring her part of the business to her husband. These would have been capital transactions and thus this would have been a normal liquidation of BSAS (see 16.30) having no connection with BSAS 2. Thus, any 'alleged tax advantage (assuming there to be one) did not arise from the TiS.

- The transactions were carried out for bona fide commercial purposes and not for tax avoidance purposes. Judge Shipwright concluded fairly briefly that the 'predominant motive was to bring the business and personal ties [of Mr and Mrs Ebsworth] to an end' The liquidation was required by Mrs Ebsworth 'so as to provide a clean break with the previous phase of her life' and this was no tax scheme. He therefore held that even if there was a tax advantage arising under a TiS, the so-called 'escape clause' precluded any TiS assessment. The fact that Mr Ebsworth sought tax advice (with his wife) did not of itself mean that tax avoidance was a main objective of the transactions. (Note that the commercial purpose test has been dropped from 1 April 2010 with a 'fundamental change of ownership' exemption applying instead).

Clearly Mr Ebsworth's case was helped by him being an 'honest, open and helpful' witness, which assisted the judge in establishing the motives behind the relevant transactions. The Ebsworth ruling also provides an important reminder that seeking tax advice does not necessarily mean that tax avoidance is a main driver for the implemented deal structure!

ER ON ASSOCIATED DISPOSALS OF PERSONALLY HELD PROPERTY

Conditions for associated disposal relief

16.31 Some owner-manager's prefer to hold the company's trading premises personally (away from the clutches of the company's creditors). In such cases, it is likely they may wish to sell the property to a third party at the same time or shortly after the company has ceased trading.

There are special rules which extend the availability of ER to mitigate the gain arising on such disposals (known as 'associated disposals') where the shareholder makes a qualifying disposal for ER [*TCGA 1992, s 169K (1) (2)*]. In the context of a disposal arising on a capital distribution, the vendor-shareholder must meet the conditions summarised in 16.18.

Furthermore, to obtain ER under the 'associated disposal' rules, two additional conditions must be satisfied:

- The associated disposal must be made as part of the 'withdrawal from participation' in the company. In HMRC's view, this is taken to mean the individual reducing their shareholding in the company. Since a capital distribution creates a disposal of an interest in the relevant company's shares, this test should normally be met [*TCGA 1992, s 169K (3)*]. Broadly, HMRC would expect the associated disposal to be triggered by the liquidation/dissolution of the company (giving rise to the shareholder's exit).

- The property (or other personally owned asset) disposed of must have been used in the company's trade throughout the one year before it ceased trading [*TCGA 1992, s 169K(4)*]. It is therefore important to ensure that the property etc is used in the trade right up to the cessation of that trade.

Restrictions on gain qualifying for associated disposal ER

16.32 As a general rule, associated disposal relief only comes into play if the shareholder has unused ER remaining after calculating their taxable gains on the capital distributions. Associated disposal relief is relatively restrictive and the gain on the associated disposal qualifying for relief may be restricted under *TCGA 1992, s 169P*. The main areas in which relief may be restricted and the basis on which this is done is summarised:

Circumstances	TCGA 1992 reference	Restriction to relief
Property only used for the purposes of the company's business for only part of the period of ownership.	S 169(4)(a)	Relief restricted to period of business use only.
Only part of the property is used for the purposes of the company's business.	S 169(4)(b)	Relief is given on a pro-rata basis for the time that it was used for business purposes.
Company pays rent to shareholder for using the asset.	S 169(4)(d)	No relief is available if a full market rent was received. Partial relief is available where the rent paid was less than the full market rent. For these purposes, no account is taken of rent relating to a pre-6 April 2008 period (*FA 2008, Sch 3, para 6*)

Any restriction of the gain qualifying for associated disposal relief is made on a 'just and reasonable basis' by reference to the full ownership period of the relevant asset (subject to the special 'transitional' rule noted above which prevents any pre-6 April 2008 rent payments restricting relief). However, where the shareholder continues to charge a full commercial rent to the company for its use of 'their' asset after 6 April 2008, HMRC will deny relief completely (since it is regarded as an investment asset as opposed to a trading one).

The restriction in respect of rental income is likely to cause particular difficulties to individuals who borrowed to acquire a commercial property and let it to their company. They will generally wish to charge a rent to the company to fund their personal loan interest payments.

DISINCORPORATION OF THE BUSINESS

Corporate v partnership/sole trader structure

16.33   The choice of trading medium invariably depends on a whole range of tax and commercial factors. The recent changes in both corporate and personal tax rates will have affected the relative tax costs between company and partnership/LLP/sole trader formats.

However, for those at the smaller end of the business spectrum, the fiscal 'scales' may now be tipping in favour of running very small businesses as a sole trader (or partnership/LLP). A number of proprietors will have found that trading through a company is 'not all it was cracked up to be' – for example, paying substantial amounts of tax on company cars, operating PAYE on their own 'drawings', additional accountancy fees, Companies Act compliance and reporting, and so on. A number of small businesses may therefore consider disentangling themselves from a company structure by 'disincorporation'. This envisages that the trade carried on by the company will be transferred to its shareholder(s), who would then continue to carry on the trade as a sole trader or partnership/LLP.

Planning a disincorporation

16.34   Unfortunately, the process of 'disincorporating' a business does not have any CGT relieving provisions. Despite the continuity of ownership, the current tax rules do not facilitate the transfer of the company's assets (including goodwill) on a 'tax-neutral' basis. However, in July 2011, the Office of Tax Simplification published a consultative document in July 2011 outlining proposals for a form of capital gains roll-over/hold-over relief to facilitate a broadly 'tax-neutral' disincorporation. It remains to be seen whether these proposals are taken forward by the Government.

Undere the current tax regime, the potential tax charges and events which arise on a disincorporation would be similar to those which would occur on any 'third-party' sale of a company's business and assets (see 15.46). Consequently, there may be some tax to pay on getting the trade and assets out of the company into the shareholder's hands, enabling them to continue to carry on the business as a sole trader/partnership although it should normally be possible to avoid any clawback of capital allowances. However, for the smaller 'one-man-band' type business, disincorporation may be implemented with minimal tax costs, especially where there is little or no 'freely transferable' goodwill (see 16.42 below).

Legal mechanics and basic tax treatment

16.35   From a company law viewpoint, the disincorporation of a business can be implemented either as:

- a members' voluntary winding-up – this can only be used where the company being liquidated is solvent; or

- a simple dissolution.

Where a formal liquidation is used, the trade and assets will be transferred to the new unincorporated business, owned by the shareholder(s). The liquidator will pay off the creditors and distribute the surplus to the shareholder(s) – see 16.13. The distribution to the shareholder(s) should be a capital one under *TCGA 1992, s 122* (see 16.15), although there is a possibility (albeit a small one) that HMRC may tax the amount as income under the 'Transaction in Securities' anti-avoidance provisions now contained in *ITA 2007, Part 13, Chapter 1* (see *16.43*).

Where a 'dissolution' process is used, the company will first transfer its trade and assets to the unincorporated business. Liabilities can either be settled by the company or assigned to the successor business (provided agreement is obtained from the relevant creditors). The company will then be dissolved under *CA 2006, s 1000* (formerly *CA 1985, s 652*). A dissolution therefore involves fewer legal formalities and minimises costs (see 16.14). Under ESC C16, HMRC is normally prepared to treat a shareholder distribution prior to the dissolution as having been made under a formal winding-up – see 16.16. The distribution should therefore be treated as a capital distribution for the shareholder, subject again to the small risk of HMRC making a counteraction under *ITA 2007, Part 13, Chapter 1* (see *16.43*).

Inevitably, a disincorporation will normally involve a classical 'double tax' charge, since the tax suffered by the shareholder on the capital distribution creates a further tax liability on the appreciation in the value of the company's chargeable assets which has already been taxed in the company.

Disincorporation case study

16.36 The various mechanics and tax consequences of a disincorporation are illustrated through the following case study:

Example 5

Mark has run his small bed and breakfast business since 1991 through his 100% owned company, Noble's Towers Ltd. He would now like to run the business as a sole trader, since this is more appropriate to its future scale of activities. The disincorporation takes place on 30 June 2011, when the company trade is transferred to Mark and Noble's Towers Ltd is wound up.

The balance sheet at 30 June 2011 (reflecting the trading profits to date) is as follows:

	Note	£'000	Book value £'000	Market value £'000
Freehold property	1		120	240
Goodwill	2		–	20
Fittings, plant and equipment	3			
Cost		20		
Less: Depreciation	4	(8)	12	15
Stock	4		10	12
Debtors			7	
Bank overdraft			(4)	
Creditors	5		(9)	
Represented by share capital (£100) and reserves			£136	

Notes:

1 The freehold property has not been subject to depreciation – and represents the cost of the premises when it was acquired in March 1992.

2 The goodwill value is considered to represent 'free' goodwill (and is not attributable to the premises or Mark personally!).

3 The tax written down value of the plant etc on 1 January 2011 was £9,000.

4 Stock and plant etc are transferred at their book values.

5 No tax provision has been made in the above figures.

In the six months to 30 June 2011, the tax adjusted trading profit (before making any cessation adjustments) was £40,000.

Main corporation tax consequences

Deemed consideration of trade

16.37 There is a deemed cessation of trade for corporation tax purposes on its transfer to Mark (even though the actual trade is continuing under different ownership) [*CTA 2009, s 41*].

Termination of corporation tax accounting period

The cessation of trade automatically brings to an end the current corporation tax accounting period (CTAP) of Noble's Towers Ltd. The company will therefore have a six-month CTAP to 30 June 2011 [*CTA 2009, s 10(1)(e)*].

Unused trading losses

If Noble's Towers Ltd had any unused trading losses, these would effectively be lost on the disincorporation since they cannot be carried forward beyond the deemed cessation of trade [*CTA 2010, s 45, (ICTA 1988, s 393(1))*]. There is no provision for their transfer to the unincorporated successor business.

If the company had a current year trading loss in the final CTAP, this could be offset against any other corporation tax profits, including chargeable gains of the current and preceding one year [*CTA 2010, s 37 (ICTA 1988, s 393A(1))*]. However, any current trading loss could not be matched against chargeable assets transferred/distributed to the shareholders during the course of the winding-up/dissolution, since these would arise in the subsequent CTAP (see below). In such cases, a sale of the chargeable assets to the shareholders at open market value before 'cessation' should be considered to achieve the appropriate loss offset.

The possibility of making a terminal loss relief claim should only be considered after all other forms of loss relief have been exhausted [*CTA 2010, ss 37 and 39 (ICTA 1988, s 393(2), (2A))*]. (See also 16.8).

Transfer of closing trading stock

As Noble's Towers Ltd (the transferor company) is 'connected' with Mark (see *CTA 2009, s 168*), who will continue to carry on the trade, the deemed 'market value' rule in *CTA 2009, s 166* will apply to the transfer of closing stock. (Based on the facts of the case study, the amount of stock held by the company's 'bed and breakfast' trade is relatively small, so this is not a material issue here).

However, in most cases, it should be possible for the parties to make a joint election under *CTA 2009, s 167* to transfer the stock at its actual transfer value (or, if higher, the book value). In the unlikely event of the company being subject to UK-to-UK transfer pricing, the stock must be transferred at an arm's length market value [*CTA 2009, s 162(2)*].

Capital allowances: plant and machinery

The normal 'capital allowance' cessation rules apply. No writing-down allowances are given in the final basis period and a balancing adjustment is calculated [*CAA 2001, s 61* and *Table, Item 6*]. The balancing adjustment will generally be computed by reference to the actual transfer value.

However, if both parties make an election under *CAA 2001, s 266* the cessation rules will not apply and the plant can be transferred at its tax written down value [*CAA 2001, s 267*]. In this context, an election to transfer the plant at its tax written down value may not be advantageous if the 'disincorporated' company is going to have unrelieved trading losses. In such cases, the balancing charge can be used to absorb the loss, thus increasing the tax value of the plant for the successor business.

VAT

Assuming the business is VAT registered, the general rule is that where a trade ceases, the 'registered person' is deemed to make a taxable supply of all the goods then held by the business. However, since the business will be transferred to the shareholder(s) who will continue to carry it on as a sole trader/partnership, there should be no VAT levied on the transfer (by virtue of the 'transfer of going concern' provisions in *VAT (Special Provisions) Order 1995, art 5* (see also 12.32). It may be considered appropriate to elect to continue to use the business's existing VAT registration number (on form VAT 68), particularly as the history of the business will be well-known to the shareholder(s).

Capital gains on transfer of assets to Mark

16.38   The company is likely to trigger capital gains where assets are transferred to the shareholders as part of the disincorporation process. The chargeable assets of the company (including goodwill) are deemed to be disposed of at market value for tax purposes [*TCGA 1992, s 17*].

The capital gains likely to arise in Noble's Towers Ltd are summarised as follows:

Goodwill (transferred with trade on 30 June 2011)	£'000
Market value	20
Less: Base cost/indexation	(–)
Chargeable gain	20

The property would (probably) be distributed in specie during the winding-up to avoid SDLT. However, this will still trigger a chargeable gain in the subsequent CTAP by reference to the property's market value (note – companies can still claim indexation relief):

Freehold Property – in-specie distribution:	£'000
Market value	240
Less: Base cost	(120)
Indexation – £120,000 × (say) 75%	(90)
Chargeable gain	30

Corporation tax computations

16.39   The corporation tax computations covering the CTAP to 30 June 2011 (when the trade and assets (except property) are transferred to Mark) and the subsequent CTAP (say) to 31 October 2011 (when the winding up is completed) are set out below.

Provided the appropriate tax elections are made in relation to trading stock (under *CTA 2010, s 167*) and plant [*CAA 2001, s 266*], the corporation tax computation for the six months to 30 June 2011 would be as follows:

CTAP – 6 months to 30 June 2011

	£'000
Tax adjusted trading profit (no cessation adjustments)	40
Chargeable gains on sale of Goodwill (see 16.29)	20
Taxable profits	60
Corporation tax liability @ (say) 20.5%	£12.3

CTAP – four months to 31 October 2011

	£'000
Chargeable gain on property (see 16.38) = Taxable profits	30
Corporation tax liability @ 20%	£3.6

The additional corporation tax arising from the assets transferred as part of the disincorporation is relatively modest and is likely to be an acceptable cost of getting the business into Mark's hands for him to carry it on as a sole trader. However, not all disincorporation exercises will be as simple or as inexpensive. Where property is held within the company and/or there is clearly significant business goodwill, the 'double-tax' costs may make it very costly, possibly persuading those involved to maintain the corporate 'status-quo' – see 16.41 and 16.42 for a further discussion of the relevant issues relating to property and goodwill respectively).

Tax liabilities arising on shareholders

16.40   The company will be wound-up or dissolved as part of the disincorporation and the amounts/assets distributed will normally represent a capital distribution in the hands of the shareholder(s). The amount will therefore be subject to CGT (provided HMRC do not successfully invoke the Transaction in Securities anti-avoidance legislation – see 16.30).

Based on the case study, the computation of the likely capital distribution and estimated CGT thereon payable by Mark is set out below:

Estimated capital distribution

	£'000	£'000
Net reserves at 30 June 2011 (before disincorporation)		136
Realisations:		
Goodwill – surplus on transfer		20
Freehold property – surplus on distribution in specie – £240,000 less £120,000		120
		276
Less: Corporation tax liabilities – say £12,300 + £6,000 (say)	(18)	
Liquidator's fees and other costs (say)	(10)	(28)
Surplus available to distribute		£248
Satisfied by		
Distribution *in specie* – market value of property		240
Distribution in specie – other net assets		8
		£248

Estimated CGT

Based on the above capital distributions Mark's estimated CGT liability (ignoring his negligible base cost) with the benefit of the 10% ER CGT rate would be around £24,000 calculated as follows:

	£'000
Capital distributions	
Cash	8
Market value of property	240
Total amount	248
Less: Annual exemption	(10)
	238
CGT liability @ (say) 10% ER CGT rate	£24

Given that only minimal cash is being extracted, Mark is likely to have a very good chance of obtaining clearance under *ITA 2007, s 701*.

Dealing with property on disincorporation

16.41 In those cases where the shareholder personally holds the trading premises and has granted the company a (non-exclusive) licence to occupy it, no further action is normally required.

However, where the property is owned by the company, the CGT cost of 'disincorporating' may prove to be prohibitive, particularly if a substantial capital gain is likely to arise. If the decision to disincorporate has been made and the tax cost of transferring the property is manageable, then it may often be preferable to 'distribute' it to the shareholders in specie during the winding-up. This will normally avoid any SDLT charge (see *FA 2003, Sch 3, para 1*) and ranks as a capital distribution in the shareholder's hands. However, any assumption of a property loan/mortgage by the shareholders would represent 'consideration' for the transfer, with a consequent SDLT charge.

If the property is sold to the shareholders on or just before the trade ceases (this may be done, for example, to access trading losses that might otherwise remain unused), then SDLT will be payable at the relevant rate (see 12.23).

There is no longer any clawback of IBAs previously claimed on the disposal of properties.

Treatment of goodwill

16.42 The business goodwill invariably follows the transfer of the trade on disincorporation and may therefore generate a significant capital gain, depending on the market value agreed with HMRC. (However, where the business was established after 31 March 2002, the gain will be treated as a taxable (trading) credit under the Intangibles regime in *CTA 2009, Part 8*.)

Given HMRC's recent stance with regard to goodwill valuations on business incorporations (where the trader has opted to sell goodwill to the newly incorporated company at its full market value), it will be interesting to see whether the same approach is adopted on a disincorporation! For many small businesses, HMRC have typically contended that the value of transferable goodwill is low or insignificant. This is because, HMRC argue, that most if not all of the goodwill attaches to the proprietor personally and so is not capable of being transferred. (The over-analytical approach adopted by HMRC in relation to goodwill was recently questioned by the Special Commissioner in Balloon Promotions (SpC 524)). It is, however, likely that many very small 'one-man-band' type businesses will have minimal goodwill which should facilitate a relatively easy disincorporation.

On the other hand, there will be a number of businesses which have built up significant 'free' goodwill attributable to the reputation built up by the business, its name, and trade connections and so on. Any potential uncertainty surrounding the value of goodwill in these cases must be carefully factored into the tax cost likely to arise on the disincorporation. Agreeing the value of goodwill with HMRC – Shares and Asset Valuation could well turn out to be a protracted process and may be uncertain. In some cases the CGT involved may well make the disincorporation unacceptable.

Disincorporation and the 'Transactions in Securities' Rules

16.43 The Transaction in Securities (TiS) provisions now contained (for income tax purposes) in *ITA 2007, Part 13, Chapter 1* must always be considered in relation to transactions involving the company's shareholders. Following the House of Lord's decision *in IRC v Laird Group plc* [2002] STC 722, the better view is that (by itself) the winding-up and the distribution of the company's assets by a liquidator would not fall within the ambit of the TiS legislation.

On the other hand, *CIR v Joiner* [1975] STC 657 considered that these provisions would apply where a company's shareholders continue to carry on the trade in a new company after liquidation, having extracted the old company's distributable reserves as capital (rather than income) (see also 16.29).

Even though the trade is being transferred into personal ownership (rather than a commonly-owned company), it is probably prudent to assume that HMRC could seek to counteract the 'tax advantage' from the liquidation/dissolution (ie extracting the reserves in an income tax-free form as a capital receipt) under *ITA 2007, s 684*. However, provided it can be demonstrated that the disincorporation was not motivated by obtaining an income tax advantage, it should escape any TiS assessment.

The practical application of *ITA 2007, Part 13, Chapter 1* clearly depends on HMRC's interpretation of the facts in each case. For example, HMRC is likely to challenge those cases where they suspect the shareholders have only 'disincorporated' to extract the company's reserves at a beneficial CGT rate (possibly assisted by ER).

On the other hand, where all (or substantially all) of the company's funds need to be re-invested in the successor sole trade/partnership business, a more benign approach is likely to be taken. The overall tax costs of the 'disincorporation' may also be an important factor in HMRC's deliberations.

The shareholders will need to obtain certainty on the tax treatment of the capital distribution and should therefore apply for advance clearance under *ITA 2007, s 701* to confirm that HMRC agrees there is no tax avoidance motive.

COMPANIES IN ADMINISTRATION

Purpose of administration and role of administrator

16.44   Where a company is struggling and looks unlikely to be able to pay its creditors as they fall due, the directors have the option of petitioning for an administration order. The administration option is generally pursued to rescue the company's business and achieve a higher realisation of value than under a formal liquidation.

Once a company is in administration it is protected from any winding-up orders and creditors are prevented from taking any action to enforce their debt.

An insolvency practitioner is appointed to run the company and their role is to rescue the business wherever possible and achieve the best possible deal for the company's creditors.

An application for an administration order is often subject to the bank's consent (since it will typically have a floating charge under its loan/debenture). The banks must be given five days' notice in which they may appoint their own administrative receiver.

An administrator acts as an officer of the court (irrespective of whether they have been appointed by the court) [*Insolvency Act 1986, Sch B1, para 5*]. The administrator is the proper officer of the company for tax purposes under *TMA 1970, s 108*.

Tax implications of administration

16.45 For corporation tax purposes, a new CTAP commences and ends on the cessation of the administration. Subject to this the normal CTAP rules will apply – thus typically, once a CTAP starts on the commencement of the administration, the CTAPs will follow the normal 12-month statutory accounting periods whilst the company is in administration [*CTA 2009, s 10(1) and (2)*].

Companies will continue to trade during the administration period, and hence close companies should not normally be subject to the CIC rules in *CTA 2010, s 34* (previously *ICTA 1988, s 13A*) (see 4.37 to 4.40). Thus, where applicable, the small profits rate (or marginal relief) can still be claimed.

In contrast with formal liquidations, the appointment of an administrator does not generally disturb existing group or shareholder relationships for tax purposes, although HMRC appear to take view that the ability to surrender losses to companies 'above' or in 'parallel with the company that is administration may be restricted – see below.

Associated company test – this test is important as it may influence such things as the rate of corporation tax paid by a company (see 3.13 to 3.19) or whether the company is subject to the quarterly instalment payment rules (see 4.41). Where a company is in administration, this does not affect the existing shareholder's or shareholders' control. The *CTA 2010, ss 450* and 451 (previously *ICTA 1988, s 416*) control test is very wide. Thus, a company in administration will still be treated as 'associated' with other (active) companies where all the companies are commonly controlled by the same shareholder or group of shareholders (including their close relatives etc) (see 3.19).

Group relief – HMRC contends that companies in administration fall within the 'arrangements' anti-avoidance rule in *CTA 2010, s 154* (previously *ICTA 1988, s 410*). The argument is that the administrator is able to 'control' the company's affairs within the meaning of *CTA 2010, s 1124* (previously *ICTA 1988, s 840*).

The main principles are best illustrated by looking at the following group structure. Geoff Ltd is 100% owned by Bobby Ltd, although it is currently in administration.

HMRC would contend that the affairs of Geoff Ltd (which is in administration) are conducted in accordance with the wishes of the administrator for *CTA 2010 s 1124* (previously *ICTA 1988, s 840)* purposes (even though its shares are still 100% beneficially owned by Bobby Ltd. This means that current trade losses generated by Geoff Ltd cannot be surrendered to Bobby Ltd (or indeed any other subsidiaries that are directly owned by Bobby Ltd). However, there are a number of reasons why this view is not accepted by many tax practitioners!

On the other hand, the group relief relationships with companies below Geoff Ltd (such as Martin Ltd) remain unaffected since Geoff Ltd still controls them for group relief purposes.

PRE-PACKAGED ADMINISTRATIONS

16.46   In a large number of cases, a 'pre-pack' or pre-packaged insolvency sale will be negotiated to sell the business and its assets as it is placed into administration. Typically, this will be to a new (phoenix) company that includes the directors of the original company (in administration). A pre-pack will often be used by the directors or shareholders of a distressed business to free the company from the burden of unmanageable debt.

The original company would then be wound-up or dissolved. This may mean that some or all of the company's unsecured debts remain unpaid.

Despite adverse comments in the press, pre-packs have been successful in achieving a rapid recovery of the company and preserving the value of the business. Pre-packs normally protect the workforce which transfers into the purchaser under TUPE. The administrator has to show that the pre-pack deal was in the best interests of the company's creditors and achieves proper value for its shareholders. In many cases, the distressed business will have been 'marketed' for sale in the months leading up to the administration, with no buyers willing to pay a price sufficient to discharge all or a sufficient part of the bank debt. Furthermore, the proposed administrator will have carried out appropriate valuations of the business.

RELIEF FOR SHAREHOLDERS OF INSOLVENT COMPANIES

Negligible value claim

16.47   Where the shares are worthless, a shareholder can make a 'negligible value' claim. There is no specified form for making the claim, but it should clearly identify the shareholding which is being claimed as becoming of negligible value, the date on which the capital loss is deemed to arise (see below), and that the claim is being made under *TCGA 1992, s 24(2)*.

HMRC should accept a 'negligible value' claim where the shares are 'worth next to nothing' (see Capital Gains Manual CG 13124). This will enable the shareholder to be treated as disposing of their holding for no or virtually no consideration. (Where a capital loss is deemed to arise before 6 April 2008, any available indexation cannot be used to increase or create a capital loss.)

The deemed disposal does not take place until the claim is made – the claim does not have to be made at the earliest opportunity. [*TCGA 1992, s 24(2)(a)*]. However, some flexibility is given in establishing the tax year in which the capital loss arises since there is a limited 'retrospection' period. *TCGA 1992, s 24(2)(b)* permits a negligible value 'capital loss' claim to be backdated to an earlier date specified in the claim, which must be within two years before the start of the tax year in which the claim is made. Importantly, a 'backdated' claim can only be made if the shares were (held by the claimant and) also worthless at that earlier date.

The tax rules do not specify any particular form for the claim. Claims for the current year could be made by letter to HMRC. Retrospective claims for the prior years could be made on the tax return, by an amendment to the return if possible or by letter.

Sometimes, negligible value claims are refused because HMRC successfully show that the shareholder's base cost is substantially less than the amount paid for the shares. This is often the case where the shares have been subscribed for shortly before the date of the negligible value claim and are deemed to have been acquired at a (low) market value (either by way of the 'non arm's length bargain rule' in *TCGA 1992, s 17(2)* or on a share reorganisation within *TCGA 1992, s 128(2)*) (see 16.42). Genuine capital loss claims would not be affected by the general Targeted Anti-Avoidance Rule or TAAR in *TCGA 1992, s16A*, which are primarily aimed at arrangements that are intended to avoid tax – typically from marketed avoidance schemes.

It is perhaps worth noting that the Inspector has the discretion to accept certain types of negligible value where the claim is free from any doubt or difficulty (such as the need to agree share valuations). These are for capital losses of under £100,000 on shares in UK unquoted companies that, at the date of the claim or any earlier specified date:

- were in an insolvent liquidation; or

- had ceased trading with no assets.

16.48   If a shareholder does not make a negligible value claim, their capital loss will then be deemed to arise when the company is finally dissolved. In practice, this would be when the liquidation is completed or when the company is finally dissolved – a disposal arises for CGT purposes when the shares are finally extinguished [*TCGA 1992, s 24(1)*].

Example 6

Backdated negligible value claim

Mr Cohen's company, Craven Cottage Ltd, went into liquidation in July 2005. The liquidation was completed in July 2011 without Mr Cohen receiving any distributions from the liquidator.

Mr Cohen formed the company in June 1987 subscribing for 10,000 £1 ordinary shares.

A negligible value claim is made in January 2012, which backdated the deemed disposal of his shares to March 2011 (ie 2010/11).

The calculation of the allowable loss arising in 2010/11 is as follows:

	£
Capital distribution	–
Less Cost	(10,000)
Allowable loss	(10,000)

Share loss relief (Income tax relief for capital losses on shares)

Application of *ITA 2007, s 131* relief to companies in liquidation

16.49   In certain circumstances, shareholders may be able to make a share loss relief claim under *ITA 2007, s 131* for a capital loss incurred on their ordinary shares. This will enable them to offset the capital loss against their other taxable income. Relief for the capital loss can be claimed against the shareholder's other income of the tax year of the loss and/or the previous tax year. Income tax relief is particularly valuable, as capital losses cannot be relieved unless and until the shareholder makes a capital gain.

In relation to liquidations, income tax relief can be claimed in respect of a capital loss arising on:

● a capital distribution during a winding-up;

● the cancellation (extinction) of the shares under *TCGA 1992, s 24(1)*; or

● a negligible value claim under *TCGA 1992, s 24(2)* [*ITA 2007, s 131(3)*].

In many cases, it may be beneficial to establish that a deemed capital loss has arisen by making a negligible value claim. This treats the shares as having been disposed of and immediately reacquired at their negligible value (see 16.41).

As far as timing is concerned, the deemed capital loss can be specified to arise at the date of the claim or at any time within the two years before the start of the tax year in which the claim was made (provided the shares were also 'negligible' at that time). Where s 131 is claimed for a deemed 'negligible value' loss, a clear claim must also be made under *TCGA 1992, s 24(2)*. This was confirmed by the Special Commissioner's decision in *Marks v McNally* (2004) SSCD 503, where a share loss relief claim was denied because of the failure to show unambiguously that the capital loss was being claimed under *TCGA 1992, s 24(2)*.

Section 131 relief is also available for a capital loss arising on the dissolution of the company where the shares are effectively extinguished normally without any capital distribution being received [*ITA 2007, s131(3)(c)*].

'Subscriber share' requirement

16.50   Shareholders can only obtain share loss relief (against their taxable income) if they originally subscribed for the shares. Shares acquired on a no gain/no loss basis from a spouse who originally subscribed for the shares also qualify. However, it is not possible to claim relief for shares acquired 'second-hand'.

Special identification rules deal with cases where the claimant shareholder has a 'mixed' shareholding – ie where the shareholder has 'subscriber' shares qualifying for s 131 relief and other shares acquired by purchase, gift, etc. However, these are unlikely to be necessary on a liquidation since all the shares would generally be treated as disposed of at the same time.

Where the shareholding is made up of BES shares, EIS 'income tax' relief shares and EIS 'CGT deferral' shares, these 'subscription' shares are broadly identified on a FIFO basis.

Detailed conditions for s 131 relief

16.51   The 'insolvent' company must also satisfy numerous conditions. For shares issued after 5 April 1998, s 131 relief is only available if the company is a qualifying (unquoted) company for EIS purposes. A qualifying trading company must be trading or a holding company of a trading group and more than one half of its trade must have been carried on in the UK. Furthermore, any 'non-qualifying EIS' activities (see 11.26) must broadly be less than 20% of the total business).

If the company was 'trading' at the date of disposal, it must have traded for at least six years up to the disposal date or, if less, throughout its active existence.

Where the company is not trading at the disposal date, it must have ceased trading within the previous three years and not commenced any non-qualifying activity (such as property investment). Furthermore, before it ceased trading the company must also have satisfied the requirement to trade for at least six years (or, if less, throughout any shorter period of its active existence).

Slightly different rules apply to pre-6 April 1998 share issues but in many cases the differences will not be relevant.

16.52   Section 131 relief for disposals (or deemed 'negligible value' disposals) is claimed against the shareholder's income for the tax year of the disposal and/or the previous tax year. Where a claim is made for both years, the claim must specify the year against which the *s 131* deduction is to be claimed first. Otherwise, the claim must specify the relevant year being claimed [*ITA 2007, s 132*]. Under self-assessment, any carry back claim is treated as a claim for the later year. The relief is calculated as the reduction in the previous year's tax liability as a result of the claim. The consequent reduction in the previous year's tax liability is treated as an additional 'payment on account' of the later year [*TMA 1970, Sch 1B, para 2*].

The claim must be made within 12 months after the 31 January following the tax year in which the loss is incurred [*ITA 2007, s 132(4)*].

RELIEF FOR SHAREHOLDER LOANS

Capital loss relief for irrecoverable loans

Outline of *TCGA 1992, s 253* relief

16.53   Generally, a simple debt is outside the scope of CGT and therefore if it becomes irrecoverable, relief would not be available for the creditor's loss. However, an individual shareholder (or indeed any other individual lender) can make a claim under *TCGA 1992, s 253* to obtain a capital loss equal to the principal element of their irrecoverable loan (which can include credit balances on current accounts). Corporate lenders generally obtain relief under the loan relationship regime unless they are 'connected' with the borrowing company (see 4.10).

The claimant will receive a capital loss equal to the amount that the Inspector has agreed is irrecoverable. The capital loss cannot be offset against income under *ITA 2007, s 131* (as it does not relate to shares).

The capital loss on an irrecoverable loan arises when the claim is made. However, it is also possible to establish the loss at an earlier time, being within the two previous tax years before the start of the tax year in which the claim is made, provided the loan was also irrecoverable at that earlier date [*TCGA 1992, s 253(3), (3A)*].

Conditions for s 253 relief

16.54   To make a competent claim under *TCGA 1992, s 253*, a number of conditions must be satisfied, the most important of which are:

(a)   the loan must be irrecoverable and the claimant must not have assigned their right of recovery;

(b)   the amount lent must have been used wholly for the purposes of a trade (which can include capital expenditure and trade setting-up costs) carried on by a UK resident company. This trade application test is also satisfied where the borrowing company has lent the monies to another 'fellow' group company for use in its trade. The fellow group company must be a trading company (see 15.30–15.31) and be part of a 75% group relationship. Relief is also available where the borrowed amount is used to repay a loan that would have qualified.

The relief is not therefore available for loans to investment companies or to purchase 'investment' assets;

(c)   the loan must not constitute a 'debt on security' (broadly, a debt on security represents a loan held as an investment which is both marketable and produces a return or profit to the holder) [*TCGA 1992, s 253(1), (3)*].

In judging whether a loan has become 'irrecoverable' at the date of the claim (or earlier date), HMRC are likely to examine the prospects of its recovery based on relevant balance sheets and other information. The Inspector would seek to determine whether there is a reasonable likelihood of the loan (or part of it) being repaid, having regard to the borrowing company's current and probable future financial position.

In practice, where the borrower is insolvent and has ceased trading and it is clear that the loan (or part of it) would not be repaid, a s 253 claim would usually be accepted for the relevant amount. On the other hand, relief may be denied where the borrowing company is still trading (albeit making losses). Similarly, if the borrower was in a parlous state when the loan was made, the Inspector may refuse the claim on the grounds that the loan had not become irrecoverable as required by *TCGA 1992, s 253(3)(a)*.

In *Crosby (Trustees) v Broadhurst* [2004] STC (SCD) 348, the Special Commissioners agreed that relief was available on an irrecoverable loan that had (as part of the terms of the borrowing company's sale) been waived before the formal claim was submitted to the Inspector. They did not accept the Inspector's view that the loan had to be in existence at the time the claim was made.

Any subsequent recovery of part or all of the debt will be treated as a chargeable gain arising at the date of repayment. Capital loss relief cannot normally be claimed on intra-group loans under *TCGA 1992, s 253* (but see 16.55).

Guarantee payments

16.55   Where an individual shareholder has provided a personal guarantee which is called in by the lender, they will be able to claim capital loss relief on any payment made under the guarantee. Claims for guarantee payments made by an individual must be made before the fifth anniversary of the 31 January following the tax year in which the payment is made.

Capital loss relief may also be available where a group company makes a payment under a guarantee in relation to a borrowing by a fellow group company. The claim must be made within six years of the accounting period end in which the payment is made. The group guarantor company would become entitled to the rights of the original lender and can therefore claim capital loss relief if it is prevented from claiming a deduction under the loan relationship legislation (see 16.58) [*TCGA 1992, s 253(3), (4)(c)*].

Example 7

Capital loss relief for irrecoverable loan

Wright Ltd has traded profitably for a number of years. However, the company has experienced a downturn in trading during the last three years. In May 2006, Mr Billy, the controlling shareholder, had to make a cash injection of £80,000 to the company to ease its ailing finances. However, in December 2011, the company's bankers called in the receiver and the company was subsequently wound-up. No part of Mr Billy's loan account was repaid.

Mr Billy can therefore claim under *TCGA 1992, s 253* for the £80,000 to be treated as an allowable loss for CGT purposes.

If Mr Billy realises a capital gain of, say, £50,000 in 2011/12, he should be able to relieve it with his capital loss on the loan, provided he makes the claim by 5 April 2014. To do this, Mr Billy must be able to satisfy the Inspector that the full amount of the loan (or substantially all of it) was irrecoverable by 5 April 2012.

CONVERTING LOANS INTO NEW SHARES

16.56 Given the potential advantages of income tax relief by making a claim under *ITA 2007, s 131*, shareholders may be tempted to 'capitalise' their loans by subscribing for further shares. However, if the company is insolvent, the amount subscribed for the new shares is unlikely to be (fully) reflected as part of the shareholder's CGT base cost.

Where the shares are issued in satisfaction of the debt, *TCGA 1992, s 251(3)* deems the shares not to be acquired at a greater amount than their market value. Where the company is distressed or insolvent, this will typically be a low or of negligible value. Under *TCGA 1992, s 17(1)* (which may also be in point) the shares will deemed to be acquired at their (negligible) market value where the amount subscribed is greater than market value.

Alternatively, the capitalisation of the loan for new shares may constitute a 'reorganisation' for CGT purposes. This would be the case where, for example, all the existing shareholders subscribe for additional shares in proportion to their existing holdings. (This test might be satisfied where a company is owned by a single shareholder who has also advanced a loan to the company, which they now wish to capitalise.) On a 'reorganisation', *TCGA 1992, s 128(2)* effectively provides where the amount subscribed was not by way of an arm's length bargain, that this amount will only be reflected in the shareholder's base cost to the extent that the relevant shareholding increases in value.

Debt conversions were examined by the Special Commissioner in *Fletcher v HMRC* [2008] SpC 711. In this case, the company capitalised a loan made to it by issuing new 'B' ordinary shares (which had minimal rights). The company subsequently went into liquidation and the B shareholder made a negligible value claim for the capital loss on the B shares.

HMRC argued that the shares had no base cost and thus no loss arose (since the B shares had no value when the loan was capitalised applying the market value rule in *TCGA 1992, s 251(3)*).

However, the Special Commissioner found that the CGT reorganisation rules in *TCGA 1992, s 126* must apply on the authority of *Dunstan v Young, Austen and Young Ltd* [1989] STC 69 (although this point had not been made by the taxpayer's representative!). Applying this case, the Commissioner concluded that an increase in share capital could be a 'reorganisation' even if it did not come within the precise wording of s 126(2), provided the existing shareholders acquired the new shares because they were existing shareholders and this was in proportion to their existing holdings.

The Special Commissioner held that the face value of the debt (£50,000) could be added to the shareholder's original base cost under *TCGA 1992, s 128*. He decided that the potential restriction in *TCGA 1992, s 128(2)* proviso was not in point. (This restriction operates where the consideration was given by way of a non-arm's length bargain). Since the B shares were treated as acquired on a reorganisation, there was no acquisition for CGT purposes [*TCGA 1992, s 127*] and *TCGA 1992, s 251(3)* was not in point

Many consider that the decision in Fletcher to be a lucky escape for the taxpayer. Where an owner-managed company is insolvent or distressed, there will be normally be difficulties in securing a (full) CGT base cost. In such cases, it will normally be disadvantageous to substitute share capital for shareholder loans. Instead, the shareholder should seek to claim capital loss relief for his irrecoverable loan under *TCGA 1992, s 253* (see 16.53–16.54) since if it is 'converted' into shares there is unlikely to be any form of tax relief!

Example 8

Capitalising debt and 'market value' rule

In recent years, Mr Carrick has lent £250,000 to his friend's company, Ace Ltd, to assist it through a difficult period.

Unfortunately, it has now been decided that the company would cease trading and Mr Carrick has been invited to 'capitalise' his loan with the £250,000 being used to subscribe for new ordinary shares in Ace Ltd.

Ace Ltd's summary balance sheets (before and after the proposed capitalisation of Mr Carrick's debt) is shown below:

	Before proposed capitalisation of loan	After proposed capitalisation of loan
	£	£
Net assets	50,000	50,000
Mr Carrick loan	(240,000)	-
	(190,000)	50,000
Represented by		
Share capital	10,000	250,000
Profit and loss	(200,000)	(200,000)
	(190,000)	50,000

However, Mr Carrick will not obtain a full CGT base cost for his shares, since the value of the company has only increased by about £50,000 (due to its prior insolvent position). Although Mr Carrick 'paid' £250,000 for his shares, his base cost will only be about £50,000.

Losses incurred on Qualifying Corporate Bonds (QCBs)

16.57 In some cases, the shareholder may hold a loan note evidencing the debt. This will invariably constitute a Qualifying Corporate Bond (QCB) and represent a 'debt on security'. However, exceptionally, provided the loan was made before 17 March 1998, an allowable capital loss can still be claimed for the irrecoverable part of the debt under the provisions of *TCGA 1992, s 254* for CGT loss relief.

However, to qualify the QCB must comply with the 'qualifying loan' rules and the funds concerned must have been lent wholly for the purposes of a trade carried on by the borrower. It follows that if the holder received the QCB as consideration for the acquisition of shares relief will not be available [*TCGA 1992, ss 253, 254*].

No CGT loss relief is available for QCB loans made after 16 March 1998.

Loans made by companies

16.58   Capital loss relief under *TCGA 1992, s 253* is not available where the lender is able to claim a deduction under the loan relationship rules [*TCGA 1992, s 253(3)(a)*]. In many cases, a corporate lender should be able to claim a 'non-trading' loan relationship deduction for an impairment loss on a 'non-trading' loan (ie where the loan is effectively written off or provided against as an irrecoverable bad debt). A trading deduction would only be available where the loan was made in the course of a trade.

However, if the borrower is a connected person, such as a fellow group member or a 'parallel' company under common control, then it is not generally possible to claim a tax allowable impairment loss [*CTA 2009, s 354*]. In this context, *CTA 2009, s 355* provides a mechanism for a lending company to obtain relief only on amounts arising after it ceases to be 'connected' with the borrower which subsequently become subject to an impairment 'write-off' after. This means that amounts remaining outstanding when the borrower goes into liquidation cannot be relieved (*CTA 2009, s 355(2)*). It should be noted that GAAP usually requires impairment of debts that are not expected to be recovered. Hence the lender is likely to have already impaired most, if not all, of the loan balance prior to the commencement of liquidation etc. when the companies were connected within *CAA 2009, s 354*. Relief will only be available on such amounts that remain 'unimpaired'.

The legislation works by preventing any tax deduction being taken for impairment losses that were denied relief whilst the companies were 'connected'. It is helpful to understand why the 'connection' test in *CTA 2009, s 466* would be broken where the 'connected party' debtor goes into insolvent liquidation or administration. In broad terms, *CTA 2009, s 472* provides that a person has control of a company for this purpose if they are able to conduct the company's affairs in accordance with their wishes through holding the requisite shares, voting power or powers conferred by the Articles of Association or any other documents (such as a shareholders' agreement). Where the borrowing company goes into liquidation or administration, this 'control' nexus is likely to be broken since the liquidator/administrator would take over the management of the company's affairs. Thus, for example, a parent company would lose its ability to control the affairs of its insolvent subsidiary and hence would no longer 'control' the company within *CTA 2009, s 472*.

Exceptionally, where the lending company is able to deduct an impairment loss for amounts becoming impaired post-liquidation, it should be allowed as a non-trading (or trading) deduction.

PLANNING CHECKLIST – WINDING UP THE FAMILY OR OWNER-MANAGED COMPANY

Company

- Company must pay appropriate pension contributions before trade ceases.

- Specific provision should be made for all known costs and expenses in the final tax computation.

- It is possible to elect for post-cessation receipts to be carried-back as a 'trade receipt' to the last day of trading. This would be useful if the company has unused trading losses which can be used to shelter them.

- If an insolvent company wishes to claim relief for trading losses, it must produce appropriate accounts and tax computations to enable HMRC to agree the amount of the loss claimed.

- Where a distressed company goes into administration, it still remains the beneficial owner of its assets for tax purposes. Thus, where relevant, it is still counted as an associated company. However, special rules may prevent group relief being obtained in certain cases.

Working shareholders

- It will normally be more tax efficient to extract surplus reserves by way of a capital distribution.

- In many cases, ER should be available to reduce the shareholder's CGT liability on their capital distributions (up to the £10 million threshold). The relevant ER shareholder and 'trading company' conditions must be satisfied in the year before the trade ceases. Where these tests are met, capital distributions only obtain ER where they are paid within three years of the trade ceasing.

- Beware of arrangements that purport to secure a materially lower CGT liability on (large) capital distributions where the business is being sold to another company under the same or substantially the same ownership. Although it is by no means certain that HMRC could

---

successfully apply the TiS rules in *ITA 2007, s 684* (as demonstrated by the recent First Tribunal ruling in the 'Ebsworth' case), the risk of a s 684 counteraction should always be assessed. For example, if HMRC can show that tax avoidance was a main driver, the distributed profits are likely to be subject to an effective income tax charge of 25%/36.1% of the amount received.

- Associated disposal ER relief may be available to reduce the shareholder's CGT liability on the sale of personally-held property used in the company's business. However, this must take place as part of the shareholder's liquidation exit. Only rent charged for the use of the property after 5 April 2008 would restrict the gain qualifying for ER.

- In certain situations, it may be appropriate to maximise use of the annual CGT exemptions by phasing capital distributions over more than one year.

- Where the shareholders wish to disincorporate and continue to carry the trade on through an unincorporated business, they should consider the potential CGT costs of doing so – particularly, if the company holds valuable property and/or has substantial 'transferable' goodwill. On the other hand, a 'one-man-band' type company may be disincorporated at an acceptable tax cost.

- If the company's trading property is to be acquired by the shareholder(s), consider transferring it by way of a distribution in specie rather than a sale – this is likely to save SDLT.

- Capital losses on worthless shares can be triggered up to two years earlier by making a negligible value claim.

- Capital loss relief can be claimed on shareholder-loans that become irrecoverable. If the company is insolvent, any capitalisation of loan accounts into shares often leads to a loss of capital loss relief.

Other employees

- The cessation of the trade may provide an opportunity to enjoy up to £30,000 in tax-free redundancy/termination payments.

Non-working shareholders

- May also benefit from capital distributions (possibly on a 'staggered' basis – see above).

- Negligible value claims can be used to trigger earlier relief for capital losses (as indicated above).

Chapter 17

Succession Planning and Passing on the Family or Owner-Managed Company

INTRODUCTION

17.1   Owners of most family or owner-managed companies either seek to pass the business on to the next generation or sell it to a third party, perhaps by means of management buy-out or straight sale. This chapter examines the tax and commercial implications of handing the business down to the next generation. In some cases, the business will be handed on to the children for little or no consideration. Alternatively, the retiring shareholder may seek payment for their shares, perhaps by arranging a sale of their shareholding back to the company.

17.2   The current capital tax regime is probably as favourable as it is ever going to be in terms of providing for succession in the family or owner-managed company. When Capital Transfer Tax (the predecessor of IHT) was introduced in 1974, there was no relief for family or owner-managed businesses. Following the *Finance Act 1996* changes, all shareholdings in unquoted *trading* companies are completely exempt from IHT. On the other hand, shareholdings in family *investment* companies will be fully chargeable to IHT.

17.3   March 1982 rebasing and business asset hold-over relief for unquoted (trading company) shares (see 13.14) usually make CGT on lifetime transfers of shares a manageable problem, although the recipient will inherit the deferred CGT liability in the shares. However, the availability of a tax-free CGT uplift on death combined with the 100% IHT exemption often makes it attractive to retain the shares until death.

RELEVANT INHERITANCE TAX PRINCIPLES

Chargeable transfers, the cumulation principle and the nil rate band

17.4   It is helpful to begin with a brief review of the IHT system, particularly as it applies to gifts of unquoted shares. The IHT tax regime taxes certain lifetime

803

transfers of capital and estates transferred on death and also on transfers into and out of trusts. Transfers to spouses and civil partners are exempt.

IHT is payable by UK domiciled (or deemed domiciled) individuals on their worldwide assets and is calculated on the cumulation principle. Broadly speaking, individuals who are non-UK domiciled (under the general law) who have been living in the UK for 17 out of the last 20 tax years, are regarded as deemed domiciled for IHT purposes and hence fully chargeable to IHT [*IHTA 1984, s 267*].

Each chargeable transfer is added to the total amount of prior chargeable transfers within the previous seven years to determine the rate of IHT.

In recent years many more estates are being drawn into the IHT 'net'. Currently, HMRC's annual receipts from IHT are in the region of £3.5 billion to £4 billion. However, the *FA 2008* changes which enable a surviving spouse to benefit from an additional nil rate band (unused by their deceased spouse) should alleviate the future IHT liability for many 'middle class' families. However, the Conservative's party plan to raise the IHT threshold to £1 million has now been put on hold as part of the Con/Lib coalition agreement, so this is unlikely to be implemented in the medium term.

For 2011/12, the IHT rates on chargeable *lifetime* transfers are as follows:

Chargeable transfers within previous 7 years	*Rate*
Up to £325,000 (the nil rate band)	Nil
£325,000 plus	20%

Notes:

(a) The nil rate band is 'frozen' at £325,000 from 2011/12 to 2014/15

(b) Since 22 March 2006, chargeable lifetime transfers mainly comprise transfers to companies and most types of trust (such as interest in possession trusts and discretionary trusts)

(c) Where a surviving spouse or civil partner dies after 8 October 2007, a claim can be made to transfer the unused nil rate band of a pre-deceasing spouse/civil partner (see 17.15).

The nil rate bands for chargeable transfers made in earlier years (since March 1992) were as follows:

	Nil rate band
	£
10 March 1992 – 5 April 1995	150,000
6 April 1995 – 5 April 1996	154,000
6 April 1996 – 5 April 1997	200,000
6 April 1997 – 5 April 1998	215,000

6 April 1998 – 5 April 1999	223,000
6 April 1999 – 5 April 2000	231,000
6 April 2000 – 5 April 2001	234,000
6 April 2001 – 5 April 2002	242,000
6 April 2002 – 5 April 2003	250,000
6 April 2003 – 5 April 2004	255,000
6 April 2004 – 5 April 2005	263,000
6 April 2005 – 5 April 2006	275,000
6 April 2006 – 5 April 2007	285,000
6 April 2007 – 5 April 2008	300,000
6 April 2008 – 5 April 2009	312,000
6 April 2009 – 5 April 2011	325,000

'Loss to donor' principle

17.5   IHT is based on the 'loss to donor' principle. The measure of the value transferred is the reduction in the value of the donor's estate [*IHTA 1984, s 3(1)*]. In relation to a transfer of shares, the transfer of value for IHT purposes would be computed as follows:

Value of shareholding before the gift	X
Less Value of shareholding after the gift	X
Transfer of value for IHT purposes	X

Since the donor is primarily liable for the IHT, the loss to their estate will also include the IHT on the chargeable transfer (see 17.7).

The 'diminution in value' principle can mean that the 'transfer of value' for IHT purposes may *exceed* the value of the shares actually transferred. This would certainly be the case where a controlling shareholder transfers a small minority stake out of his holding, but thereby loses control – the value of a controlling holding would be worth considerably more than the value of a non-controlling holding (discounted to reflect the lack of influence). This principle is illustrated in Example 1 at 17.7.

Commercial and arm's length transactions

17.6   Commercial transactions are excluded from being a transfer of value under *IHTA 1984, s 10* where, broadly, they do not confer any gratuitous benefit and were made on an arm's length basis between unconnected persons. If the transfer is to a connected person, it must be shown that a similar deal would have been struck between unconnected parties. A sale of unquoted shares must also be at a freely negotiated price or at a price expected to result from free negotiations. Difficulties may arise where shares are sold for an amount which does not reflect the loss to the donor's estate.

For example, a controlling shareholder may sell some shares (out of his controlling holding) to various key employees of the company at what is considered to be a fair price – the actual minority value. This would be reasonable given their wish to retain key employees who are vital to the future success of the company and the fact that the employees are unlikely to pay more than the actual value of the shares purchased. If the shares gifted cause the transferor's shareholding to cross a critical valuation threshold (see 14.36–14.39 and Example 1 below), there would be a transfer of value but it would be contended that the transaction was not intended to confer any gratuitous benefit. HMRC might accept this argument based on the relevant supporting facts, but they would only need to consider this if the donor died within the relevant seven years and crystallised the tax (the transfers would be PETs).

Computing IHT on a lifetime chargeable transfer

17.7   Since the IHT on a lifetime chargeable transfer is the primary liability of the transferor, the loss to his estate will also include the tax. Consequently, unless the transferee agrees to bear the tax, the net transfer will have to be 'grossed up' by the tax.

Example 1

Computing transfer of value

Keegan (Investments) Ltd is an unquoted investment company.

The shareholdings in Keegan (Investments) Ltd, together with their respective values were as follows:

	Number of shares	*Value per share*
Mr Keegan	51	£14,000
Mr Macdonald	30	£5,000
Mr Waddle	19	£2,000

In May 2011, Mr Keegan transferred 21 of his shares to a discretionary trust for the benefit of his family, leaving him with 30 shares.

The transfer of value for IHT purposes would be:

	£
Value of Mr Keegan's shareholding before the transfer –	714,000
51 shares × £14,000 per share	
Less Value of Mr Keegan's shareholding after the transfer –	(150,000)
30 shares × £5,000 per share	
Transfer of value	564,000

Note: For CGT purposes, the value of the shares transferred would be £2,000 per share (being the value of a 21% holding). However, CGT hold-over relief would be available on a transfer to a discretionary trust under *TCGA 1992, s 260,* provided it is not a settlor-interested trust (TCGA 1992, s169B). Broadly speaking, this means that neither Mr Keegan, nor his wife, nor his dependant children are discretionary beneficiaries of the trust – see 17.45.

Related property

17.8   The related property rules prevent an individual fragmenting their shareholding by transferring some of their shares to a spouse, civil partner, or certain 'exempt' trusts [*IHTA 1984, s 161*]. The related property provisions require the transferor's shares *and* those held by their spouse, etc ('related property') to be valued as a single asset (based on the degree of control, etc).

Shares held by other members of the family and family trusts are not aggregated as related property and in some cases it may therefore be beneficial to spread the shareholdings along these lines.

The effect of the related property rules is illustrated below.

Example 2

Impact of related property on valuation

Assume that prior to Mr Keegan's transfer to a discretionary trust (in Example 1), the shareholdings were held as follows:

Mr Keegan	30
Mrs Keegan	21
Other shareholders	49
	100

In measuring the value of the 21 shares transferred, Mr Keegan would be deemed to hold 51 shares before and 30 shares after the transfer *for IHT valuation purposes*. Thus, the transfer of value would be computed as follows:

	£
Value of Mr Keegan's shareholding before the transfer:	420,000
30 shares × £14,000 per share (based on 51% valuation)	
Less Value of Mr Keegan's shareholding after the transfer:	(45,000)
9 shares × £5,000 per share (based on 30% valuation)	
Transfer of value	375,000

Main exemptions

17.9   Certain exemptions are available against the transfer of value in arriving at the chargeable transfer for IHT purposes. The most important are:

(*a*)   the spouse exemption, under which transfers made to a (UK) domiciled spouse are completely exempt from IHT. If the donee spouse is non-UK domiciled, the spouse exemption is limited to gifts of £55,000 [*IHTA 1984, s 18*]. Since 5 December 2005, the spouse exemption also extends to gifts made to a civil partner. (The Civil Partnership Act 2004 enables 'single-sex' couples to enter into a civil partnership. For tax purposes, civil couples are treated in the same way as married couples);

A special rule applies on a post-8 October 2007 death of a surviving spouse. The surviving spouse's estate may claim the benefit of the proportion of the 'unused' nil rate band on the first death [*IHTA 1984, s 8A*] (see 17.15).

(*b*)   annual exemption – £3,000 per annum, although one year's unused exemption can be carried forward to the next year [*IHTA 1984, s 19*];

(*c*)   small gifts exemption – £250 per donee each year – this is often useful for small presents! [*IHTA 1984, s 20*];

(*d*)   normal expenditure out of income – This is a potentially generous exemption since it is not subject to any monetary limit and depends on the donor's circumstances. The gifts must form part of the donor's normal expenditure so that they are left with sufficient income to maintain their standard of living [*IHTA 1984, s 21*]. The expenditure must form part of a regular pattern of payments (for example, this might include life insurance premiums paid for the benefit of another, school fees for grandchildren, or covenanted payments). The relief is only available if the donor meets the expenditure from their surplus net income (after income tax). Thus, expenditure made out of one-off receipts, such as inheritances or capital proceeds from the sale of investments would not count.

In determining whether the expenditure is 'normal', each case is judged on its own facts, looking very closely at the transferor's standard of living and the pattern of giving. See, for example, *Bennett v CIR* [1995] STC 54, where it was stated that a pattern of gifts is intended to remain in place for more than a nominal period and for a sufficient period (barring unforeseen circumstances) fairly to be regarded as a regular feature of the transferor's annual expenditure.

The 'normal expenditure out of income' exemption is generally claimed by the deceased's executors. Hence, the donor should retain contemporaneous documentary evidence during their lifetime to support their reliance on this relief. Schedule IHT 403 (included in the IHT return account IHT 400) provides a helpful template for recording income and expenditure for the purposes of the exemption.

Business property relief (BPR) provides a very valuable relief for the majority of owner-managed or family companies and careful vigilance is required to ensure that it is not jeopardised or wasted. BPR is covered extensively in 17.19–17.33.

Potentially exempt transfers (PETs)

17.10   Following the *FA 2006* changes (which apply from 22 March 2006), only outright gifts of shares or other assets to *individuals* will qualify as potentially exempt transfers (PETs) [*IHTA 1984, s 3A(1A)*]. From that date, where an individual transfers shares, cash or other property to *any trust* (subject to very narrow exceptions) this is treated as a *chargeable transfer* (and does not fall within the PET rules).

Before 22 March 2006, most lifetime transfers were treated as potentially exempt transfers (PETs). Thus, for example, the transfer of shares, etc to an individual, an interest in possession trust, or an accumulation and maintenance trust would have been a PET [*IHTA 1984, s 3A(1)*].

A PET becomes permanently exempt from IHT, provided the donor survives seven years from the date of the transfer. After seven years, the gifted shares would be excluded from the donor's estate (subject to the gift with reservation of benefit rules (see below) and cannot therefore be taken into account in computing the tax on the donor's subsequent 'chargeable' gifts and taxable estate held on death [*IHTA 1984, s 3A(4), (5)*].

However, if the donor dies within seven years of transferring the shares (under a PET), the value of those shares at the date of the original gift is included in their chargeable estate on death. However, any IHT crystallising on a PET made more than three years before the donor's death is eligible for a tapered reduction. This reduces the relevant IHT on a sliding scale between 20% and 80% (see 17.11 below).

When making a material PET, it may be considered appropriate to take out a (declining) term insurance policy to fund the IHT in the event of the PET failing within seven years. Such policies provide for a lump sum only if the insured dies within a specified period or before a specified age – no payment is therefore made if the insured survives the relevant period – and are, therefore, one of the cheapest forms of insurance.

A PET has the beneficial effect of freezing the value of the gifted shares. Any subsequent appreciation in value would escape IHT. If the asset has reduced in value (which might be the case in the current economic climate) the taxpayer may claim that the reduced value be used for the purposes of the calculation of the tax payable [*IHTA 1984, s 131*]. BPR (see 17.18) may be available to eliminate or reduce the IHT liability on a PET of unquoted shares becoming chargeable. However, there would be no BPR if the transferee has disposed of the gifted shares before the transferor's death [*IHTA 1984, s 113A(1), (2)*]. This would mean that the tax on the crystallised PET on the original gift of the shares is calculated without regard to BPR.

The broad aim of the IHT regime is to restrict effective lifetime gifts to those cases where the donor is content to enjoy no further use or occupation of the property gifted and survives the 'seven year' period.

Special anti-avoidance rules in *FA 1986, s 102* therefore apply to gifts made where the donor reserves a benefit (known as a gift with reservation of benefit or GROB) – see also 17.50 and 17.66. These prevent effective transfers being made for IHT purposes (after 17 March 1986) where the donor is still able to enjoy any benefit from the gifted property. Consequently, if the donor subsequently dies whilst still preserving some benefit or use from the property, it will be treated as part of their chargeable estate on death. However, if the donor ceases to benefit from the property during their lifetime, they will be treated as making a PET of the property at that time.

The legislation contains detailed provisions that block planning arrangements designed to side-step the GROB rules (see *FA 1986, ss 102–102C*), which has been supplemented by the charge on pre-owned assets, which operates from 6 April 2005 (see 17.78–17.87).

IHT crystallising on a PET

17.11 The calculation of IHT on the PET becoming chargeable involves adding the value of the PET to the total *chargeable* transfers made within the seven years before the PET. The PET (after any available annual exemption, etc) is treated as the 'top slice' for the purpose of calculating the relevant IHT (which will be at the 'death rate' of 40% after the donor's nil rate band has been used).

IHT taper relief is available where the PET occurred more than three years before the donor's death, discounting the amount of IHT payable by the following rates:

Period before death	Reduction in IHT
3–4 years	20%
4–5 years	40%
5–6 years	60%
6–7 years	80%

This procedure is repeated for subsequent PETs. The tax on the PET crystallising on the donor's death would normally be borne by the donee (who can provide for the tax by taking out a decreasing term assurance policy – see 17.10). As the tax is payable by the donee, the tax is calculated on the value of the PET only – there is no 'grossing up'.

Types of lifetime chargeable transfers

17.12   Following the changes introduced by *Sch 20* to the *Finance Act 2006*, we now have a much wider range of lifetime transfers that are immediately chargeable to IHT (subject to the nil rate band, etc). The main types of chargeable transfer will include transfers to:

- an interest in possession trust;
- a discretionary trust; or
- a company.

Such transfers are not PETs. Before 22 March 2006, chargeable transfers mainly comprised of those made to a discretionary trust or a company – transfers to interest in possession trusts were previously treated as PETs (see 17.10).

Treatment of lifetime chargeable transfers

17.13   Chargeable transfers are subject to a lifetime IHT charge of 20% if the value transferred (reduced by any IHT business property relief (BPR) etc)) exceeds the transferor's available nil rate band – this is the amount of the current nil rate band (see 17.4) after allowing for any chargeable transfers made in the previous seven years.

Additional IHT may become payable if the donor does not survive seven years. The tax is calculated on a similar basis to a PET becoming chargeable (see 17.11). The IHT on the original transfer is re-calculated using the *current* death rates (ie 40% after the nil rate band has been used). If the chargeable transfer was made more than three years from the date of death, this may be eligible for a taper relief reduction (based on the sliding scale in 17.11).

Credit is then given for tax paid on the original transfer (however, no repayment can be made if the lifetime IHT is higher).

Example 3

Computing IHT on lifetime chargeable transfers

Following on from Example 1, the IHT payable on the transfer to the discretionary trust by Mr Keegan in May 2011 (assuming there were no prior chargeable transfers in the previous seven years and the trustees paid the tax) would be as follows:

	£
Transfer of value	564,000
Less Annual exemption (2011/12)	(3,000)
Annual exemption (unused 2010/11 c/fwd)	(3,000)
Chargeable transfer	558,000

Note: No BPR is available as the company is an investment company.

IHT thereon	£
on first £325,000 @ 0%	–
on next £233,000 @ 20%	46,600
	46,600

If Mr Keegan died in August 2014 (just over three years later), the additional tax payable by the trustees (*with the frozen nil rate band of £325,000 and current IHT rates*) would be:

	£
On first £325,000 @ 0%	–
On next £233,000 @ 40%	93,200
	93,200
Less Taper reduction @ 20%	(18,640)
	75,560
Less Tax already paid re May 2011 transfer	(46,600)
Additional tax	27,960

TRANSFERS ON DEATH

Calculation of chargeable estate on death

17.14 On death, the total value of the individual's estate (after deducting allowable liabilities and funeral expenses) is chargeable to IHT [*IHTA 1984, ss 5(1)* and *172*]. The individual's estate also includes the value of any gifted assets over which they retained a benefit (under the so-called 'gift with reservation of benefit' or GROB rules – see 17.45 and 17.60). Business property relief (BPR) and agricultural property relief may be claimed against qualifying assets, and is given as a reduction in the relevant asset entering into the value of the chargeable estate on death (see 17.19).

Various exemptions may also be claimed for assets passing to a spouse, charity, etc.

The transfer on death is effectively treated as the individual's final transfer, which is equal to the value of their estate before death. The IHT payable must therefore take into account the total chargeable transfers (including PETs which crystallise on death – see 17.10 and 17.11) made within the previous seven years.

Once the available nil rate band has been used, IHT would be payable at the rate of 40%. However, from 9 October 2007, the *unused* IHT nil rate band of a pre-deceasing spouse/civil partner can also be claimed by the executors of the surviving spouse/civil partner (effectively increasing the amount sheltered from IHT on the second death) (see 17.15 below).

The IHT return on death (and calculation of tax) is made by the personal representatives on form IHT 400 (previously IHT 200). HMRC do not need precise asset valuations where the assets pass to an 'exempt' beneficiary, such as a surviving spouse. In most cases, a reduced IHT account can be made where the gross value of property passing to chargeable beneficiaries (together with the value of transfers made in the prior seven years) is below the nil rate band. Very small estates are exempt from making IHT returns.

Transferable nil rate band from predeceased spouse

17.15 The *Finance Act 2008* enables a surviving spouse or civil partner to benefit from any unused nil rate band of their pre-deceasing spouse/civil partner. This rule only applies where a surviving spouse/civil partner dies after 8 October 2007 [*IHTA 1984, s8B*].

The survivor's personal representatives will normally make the formal claim for the unused nil rate band of their pre-deceasing spouse/civil partner (which is made using form IHT 402 (previously IHT 216), and delivered with the form IHT 400 (see 17.14)). The claim for the unused nil rate band should be accompanied by:

- A copy of the pre-deceased's will (if any) and any deed of variation

- The death certificate

- The marriage/civil partnership certificate

- A copy of the grant of representation (or confirmation in Scotland)

HMRC appear to accept that complete information may not be available for deaths that occurred many years ago and give Inspectors some discretion in deciding whether the claim is valid (see *IHT Manual 43004 and 43008*). For deaths after 8 October 2007 (ie when the transferable nil rate band rules came into force), additional details are required to those above, including a copy of the pre-deceased's IHT 400 (previously IHT 200) or reduced account form IHT 205 (form C5 in Scotland) or full details of assets in the estate (including values) – HMRC have indicated that such information should be retained from the 'first death' and, as a practical measure, it would be sensible to keep all this information together with a copy of the survivor's will.

The date of the predeceased spouse's/civil partner's death is irrelevant, but it is necessary to calculate the amount of their nil rate band that remains unused. Thus, if all their estate previously went to the surviving spouse, then their entire nil rate band would remain unused. However, in other cases, the unused percentage of the predeceased's nil rate band must be determined.

The statutory calculation of the available (i.e. unused) nil-rate band claimable is summarised as follows:

1   The unused nil-rate band on first death

$= M - VT$

Where:

M = Maximum nil rate band available to pre-deceased's estate (including any additional amounts that might be claimable from any spouse/civil partner that the pre-deceased survived (on an earlier marriage or civil partnership))

VT = Value actually transferred on first death (as a chargeable transfer) or nil if no value transferred

2   Specified percentage

$= (E / NRBMD) \times 100$

Where:

$E = M - VT$ (ie the unused nil rate band on first death)

$NRBMD$ = Maximum nil rate band available on first death

3   Claimable nil rate band by survivor's personal representatives = Prevailing nil rate band at time of survivor's death × Specified Percentage (in 2)

The 'transferred' nil rate band of the predeceased can only be used against the IHT payable on the surviving spouse's/civil partner's death – it cannot be applied on a lifetime chargeable transfer. Thus, the transferred nil rate band may be used to shelter the IHT on the survivor's free estate (including any property treated as a gift with reservation of benefit (see 17.10) and a qualifying interest in possession held by them (ie on a pre-22 March 2006 trust – see 17.76). It can also be used against a failed PET (see 17.11), which takes priority over the IHT on the estate on death.

Example 4

Claim for pre-deceased spouse's unused nil rate band

Kathy died on 1 November 2011 leaving an estate of £1,500,000. Her husband, Martin, had died in June 1993.

Under his will, Martin had left chargeable legacies of £30,000 to his children with the residue passing to Kathy.

Kathy's executors can claim to use Martin's unused nil rate band, which would be calculated as follows

1	*Martin's unused nil rate band*	
	M (Nil rate band at June 1993) =	£150,000
	VT (Value transferred) =	£30,000
	Therefore: M – VT =	£150,000 – £30,000
	=	£120,000
2	*Specified percentage*	
	E = M – VT =	£120,000 (in 1 above)
	NRBMD (Maximum nil rate band	
	in June 1993 =	£150,000
	(E / NRBMD) × 100 =	(£120,000 / £150,000) × 100
	=	80%
3	*Claimable unused nil rate band*	
	Nil rate band in November 2011 =	£325,000
	Therefore – £325,000 × 80% =	£260,000

Kathy's executor's can therefore claim Martin's unused nil rate band of £260,000 to use against Kathy's chargeable estate (as well her own nil rate band).

Note; If Martin had not made any chargeable legacies, the executors would have been able to claim an additional £325,000 instead (ie 100% of the 'November 2011' nil rate band)

Business property relief (BPR)

17.16 If the shareholder retains all or some of their shareholding until death, the shares would normally be excluded from their chargeable estate due to the availability of 100% business property relief (BPR) (see 17.19–17.33 for detailed coverage). The shares should always be specifically transferred under the will (otherwise the benefit of the BPR reduction in IHT would effectively be spread across the entire estate).

The prospect of obtaining 100% BPR from IHT combined with a tax-free uplift in base value for CGT purposes will often discourage the controlling shareholder from transferring their shares before death. Given the controlling shareholder's natural reluctance to give up his shares, this stance is understandable. Clearly, it is not possible to 'guarantee' that the 100% BPR will be available on the owner manager's death. That said, most tax pundits expect unquoted trading company shares to remain exempt from IHT for the foreseeable future.

Valuation of shares

17.17 It is important to appreciate that, for CGT purposes, the shares will effectively be rebased to their market value at the date of death [*TCGA 1992, s 62*]. Consequently, any capital gain in the shares will be 'washed out' on death; similarly there will be no relief for any loss.

The value 'ascertained' for IHT purposes on death would usually be taken as the CGT base value [*TCGA 1992, s 274*]. However, the related property rules may therefore apply to give a higher base value for IHT purposes. However, if the shares are completely exempt from IHT, due to the availability of 100% BPR or otherwise, the value would not need to be 'ascertained' for IHT. This means that the value for the shares cannot be agreed until a subsequent disposal takes place. Furthermore, HMRC – Shares Valuation are then likely to take the view that the shares should be valued in isolation under the normal CGT rules in *TCGA 1992, s 272*, without regard to related property (*HMRC Interpretations, RI110 (April 1995) Inheritance Tax – valuation of assets at the date of death*).

Deeds of Variation

17.18   In broad terms, a Deed of Variation (DOV) is a formal written instruction from a beneficiary to the personal representatives, to redirect property passing to them under a will/intestacy to another. Jointly-owned assets passing by survivorship can also be redirected under a DOV.

A DOV is therefore a gift and under general IHT principles this would be treated as a 'transfer of value' by the original 'transferor' beneficiary (or beneficiaries). However, *IHTA 1984, s 142(1)* provides that the assets redirected under the DOV are instead treated as made by the deceased for all IHT purposes (as opposed to a transfer of value by the beneficiary or beneficiaries).

The parties to the DOV must include the original beneficiary (including anyone disadvantaged by the variation) and the personal representatives, where the variation leads to an IHT liability/increase in an IHT liability. Although there is no requirement for any new beneficiaries to be party to the DOV, it is usual to make them party to the DOV by confirming acceptance of the gift. Similarly, where a DOV is used to create a new trust, the trustees are normally invited to join in to confirm their acceptance of the trust.

The favourable IHT treatment of a DOV is only available where the conditions in *IHTA 1984, s 142(2)* are satisfied. The variation must be in writing and there must be no consideration given between the parties (other than the surrender of benefit by the original beneficiary/beneficiaries). It is therefore important to ensure that legal costs involved in the drafting and implementation must be borne by the original beneficiary/beneficiaries. Furthermore, there must be no 'reciprocal arrangements' between the parties so that any benefit flowing from the DOV subsequently passes back to the original beneficiary/beneficiaries under some other arrangements.

The DOV is only effective if it is made within two years of the date of death and it must contain an irrevocable statement by the parties whose interests are varied that they intend the variation to have that effect [*IHTA 1984, s 142(1)*]. The personal representatives' consent is also required where additional IHT is payable.

A DOV can be beneficial in a number of situations. For example, a DOV may be used to ensure that ensure that maximum benefit is taken of the deceased's nil rate band or perhaps enabling BPR to be claimed on shares that would otherwise have passed to the surviving spouse. In many cases, this might be achieved by redirecting the relevant assets to a discretionary trust.

Similar beneficial treatment applies for CGT purposes [*TCGA 1992, s 62*], although it is not necessary to invoke both relieving provisions. However, from 6 April 2006 special deeming rules were introduced for CGT (and income tax) purposes where property becomes held on trust as a result of a DOV. In such cases, the person 'giving-up' their entitlement as legatee, etc is treated as providing the property for the trust. However, where the property was already comprised in a trust under the will and the DOV re-directs it into another trust, then the deceased is treated as the settlor [*TCGA 1992, s 68C*]. This follows the previous treatment that applied for CGT, based on the ruling in *Marshall v Kerr* [1994] STC 638.

BUSINESS PROPERTY RELIEF FOR THE FAMILY OR OWNER-MANAGED COMPANY

100% relief for qualifying shareholdings

17.19 100% business property relief (BPR) applies to *all* unquoted shareholdings (including non-voting ordinary or preference shares) in trading companies. (Shares in AIM companies are 'unquoted' for this purpose and hence rank for 100% BPR.) Unquoted shares are completely exempt from IHT, both on a lifetime transfer and on death. BPR operates by reducing the value transferred – in this case to nil [*IHTA 1984, s 104(1)*].

The relevant shareholding must be held for at least two years prior to the transfer/death to qualify for the relief [*IHTA 1984, ss 106, 107*]. Where shares are acquired on the *death* (as opposed to a lifetime transfer) of a spouse, their period of ownership also counts towards the two-year minimum ownership period [*IHTA 1984, s 108(b)*]. Where the two-year period is not satisfied, relief may still be available under the special rules for replacement business property [*IHTA 1984, s 107*], or successive transfers made within two years [*IHTA 1984, s 109*].

BPR is available to both working and passive shareholders – it is not necessary for the shareholder to be a director or work full time (for further potential restrictions, see 17.25–17.34).

Securities in unquoted trading companies may also qualify for 100% relief, provided the special 'control' conditions in [*IHTA 1994, s 105(1)(b)*] are satisfied.

It may be possible to defer any IHT liability on shares that do not qualify for 100% BPR (for example, shares in a family *investment* company) and certain other assets by electing to pay it over ten years in equal instalments (see 17.74). The IHT can be deferred on an interest-free basis for most business assets (see *IHTA 1984, ss 227, 228, 233* and *234* for detailed conditions).

50% relief for business property owned by a controlling shareholder

17.20 Where the owner-manager personally holds property or plant and machinery outside the company which are used in the company's trade, then BPR of 50% is available on these assets on a chargeable lifetime transfer or on death (see also 17.106). However, the shareholder only qualifies for this relief if they control the company. For these purposes, related property, such as shares held by a spouse (see 17.8), is also taken into account in determining whether the transferor has the necessary control.

The Special Commissioners' decision in *Walkers Executors v CIR* [2001] STC (SCD) 86 may be helpful in cases where only 50% of the shares are held. In this case, the shareholder was chairman of the board of directors and beneficially owned only 50% of the company's ordinary shares. Under the company's Articles of Association, the chairman was entitled to a casting vote at a general meeting of the shareholders. The combination of the 50% shareholding and the casting vote was held to be sufficient to secure control and thus 50% BPR was given on property owned by the (deceased) shareholder which had been used in the company's business. Companies that adopt Table A of the *Companies Act 1985* are likely to provide for a chairman to be appointed [*s l 91*] and for them to have a casting vote [*s l 88*]. However, relief may not be secured in those cases which provide for a 'rotation' of the casting vote, as the chairman may die at the 'wrong' time!

Loan accounts

17.21 Family and owner-managed companies are often financed by loans from shareholders (which can be repaid more readily). However, loans, debts, directors' current account balances, etc do *not* qualify for BPR. In appropriate circumstances, it may therefore be beneficial to 'capitalise' such loans as preference or ordinary shares, taking care that the rights, etc attaching to the new shares do not create any unintended shift in the balance between the company's existing shareholdings.

Planning with rights issues of shares

17.22 In appropriate cases, a rights issue of shares can be used to access BPR where an owner manager personally holds substantial cash but is unlikely to meet the two year BPR ownership period before death – ie they are in 'poor health and unlikely to live very long.

Such planning relies on the special rules in *IHTA 1984, s107(4)*, which provide that unlisted shares which are 'acquired' under a CGT reorganisation within *TCGA 1992, ss 126–136* (such as on a rights issue) are identified with shares already held by the owner manager. Thus, a right issue of shares would be treated as held for the same period as the owner manager's existing shares. These 'new' shares would therefore invariably qualify for BPR immediately after they were issued (since they would be deemed to have satisfied the 'two year ownership' test).

An attempt to use this type of planning failed in *The Executors of Mrs Mary Dugan-Chapman & Anor v HMRC* [2008] SpC 666. However, this was only because of a failure to implement the rights issue correctly, which requires an offer to all the company's shareholders in proportion to their existing shareholdings.

In this case, Mrs Chapman, who was recently widowed and had failing health, was advised by Counsel to capitalise her £300,000 loan account by subscribing for further shares under a rights issue in the family trading company. HMRC accepted that BPR was available on these 300,000 £1 shares. However, documentation was also prepared for a further share subscription of £1,000,000 by Mrs Chapman. She subscribed for the shares (through an attorney) but died two days later. However, because there was no offer to the other shareholders at the time of this subscription, it was not a rights issue. Consequently, since the shares did not fall within the special provisions in IHTA 1984, s107(4), the Special Commissioner held that BPR was not available on Mrs Chapman's subsequent £1,000,000 share subscription. Following this decision, the 'Chapman family' took a successful negligence claim against the lawyers on the grounds that, had the planning been executed properly, BPR would have been available (see *Vinton v Fladgate Fielder* [2010] EWHC 904 (Ch).

BPR on a PET of shares becoming chargeable

17.23   Where a PET of shares (see 17.10) becomes chargeable on the donor's death (within seven years of the gift), BPR will only be available on the 'failed PET' if the *donee* has retained the shares until the donor's death and the shares still qualify for relief at that point [*IHTA 1984, s 113A*].

There is a potential BPR trap where a PET subsequently becomes chargeable in relation to shares transferred to an accumulation and maintenance (A&M) trust before 22 March 2006. (It is no longer possible to make a PET on transfers to a trust following the *FA 2006* changes – see 17.64.) Where the settlor of the A&M trust dies within seven years, the PET will crystallise and become chargeable (see 17.11). Clearly, the original donee on such a transfer would have been the trustees. However, the beneficiaries of such trusts often acquire the right to (their share of) the income from their 18th or 25th birthday. Where an interest in possession has vested before 22 March 2006 in a pre-*FA 2006* A&M trust, HMRC – Capital Taxes take the view that the beneficiary then 'owns the property for IHT purposes and not the trustees'. Applying this analysis, HMRC's view is BPR relief will *not* be available against the 'failed' PET (see *ICAEW Tax Faculty Taxline,* January 2003, Point 13).

Binding contract for sale of shares

17.24   No BPR is available if a binding contract for the sale of the relevant business property has been entered into at the date of transfer (IHTA 1984, s113). The question of whether a 'binding contract for sale' exists at the date of the relevant transfer is a question of fact, which will be determined by the precise circumstances of each case. Private company shareholders should therefore be aware of agreements which *require* their executors to sell their shares to the remaining shareholders if they die before retirement. This is fatal as HMRC regard this as a binding contract for sale and therefore deny BPR (SP12/80).

The basic rationale behind this rule is to prevent the transferor from obtaining BPR where they enter into a binding agreement to sell their relevant business property and then make an immediate transfer of it. In effect, the transfer becomes one of all or part of the proceeds of sale.

HMRC will look very carefully at the availability of BPR in cases where an actual sale or flotation of a company takes place shortly after a transfer of the shares.

No BPR restriction applies where the business (or interest in a business) is sold to a company wholly or mainly in exchange for shares *or* the sale is part of a reconstruction or amalgamation transaction.

The 'binding contract for sale' restriction may (exceptionally) catch certain buy and sell agreements which are sometimes entered into by shareholder-directors of owner managed companies. Typically, these agreements are triggered where one of the shareholders dies before retirement and gives the surviving shareholders the right to purchase the deceased shareholder's shares (from funds provided by life assurance policies).

In most cases, if the company's articles simply require the personal representatives of the deceased shareholder to *offer* to sell the shares back to the company or other shareholders (without any legal obligation by them to purchase the shares), this will not constitute a binding contract for sale. On the other hand, such agreements will cause BPR to be denied where the deceased's shares pass to their personal representatives and

- the personal representatives are required to sell the shares to the other shareholders; and

- the other shareholders must buy them (SP12/80).

In practice, the potential denial of BPR is normally avoided by using 'put and call' options (see 17.48) which give the deceased's personal representatives an *option* to sell the deceased's shares and the remaining shareholders (or the company) the *option* to buy the same shares (out of the proceeds of an appropriate life insurance policy – see 17.36). Either party can, therefore, ensure that the shares are transferred without the risk of losing BPR (as there is no binding contract for sale). From a CGT perspective, it may be desirable to have successive (and different) exercise periods for the put and the call option.

Mortgaging shares

17.25   If shares (or other BPR-eligible assets) are mortgaged, BPR would only be available on the *net* value (ie after deducting the mortgage). (*IHTA 1984,* *s 162(4)* provides that, where assets are encumbered, this reduces the value of the relevant asset for IHT purposes.) Thus, it is sensible to ensure as far as possible that any charges or mortgages are given against non-business assets.

BPR QUALIFICATION ISSUES AND TESTS

Qualifying and non-qualifying activities

17.26 BPR relief is primarily focused on trading companies and groups. However, the statutory qualification for BPR is framed in a 'negative' way. Broadly, as far as companies are concerned, 100% BPR is available on any shareholding provided the company's business *does not* consist *wholly or mainly* of;

— dealing in shares and securities or land and buildings: or

— making or holding investments (subject to very limited exceptions) [*IHTA 1984, s 105(3)*].

For these purposes, 'mainly' is taken to mean more than 50% (see 17.26). Additionally, shares do not rank for BPR where a company's business consists *wholly or mainly* of dealing in securities, stocks, shares, or land or buildings. Property development should however qualify as a trading activity (see 17.29).

BPR is therefore determined on an 'all or nothing' basis, which means that the relevant shares either fully qualify or they do not. Relief will therefore be completely denied if the company is an 'investment company', which wholly or mainly makes or holds investments, even if it carries on a 'small' trade [*IHTA 1984, s 105(3)*]. Similarly, it is possible for shares to qualify for 100% BPR in full where the company is predominantly trading even though it also carries on (say) a modest property rental business (subject to any reduction for 'excepted assets' – see 17.32).

The exclusion for 'investment companies' does not apply to qualifying holding companies (see 17.31–17.32).

It is important to remember that BPR is available if the company carries on a qualifying *business* which has a wider meaning than trade. This point was applied successfully by the taxpayer in *Phillips and others (Executors of Rhoda Phillips Deceased) v HMRC* [2006] STC (SCD) 639 where HMRC had argued that the shares in a company that made loans to other family companies did *not* qualify for BPR. This was on the basis that the company's business was that of 'making or holding investments' under *IHTA 1984, s 105(3)*. However, the Special Commissioner took the view that the company did *not* make or hold investments. He decided that BPR was available since the company was '… in the business of making loans and not in the business of investing in loans'. The loans were therefore a finance facility (money lending) rather than investments.

Various problems can arise in practice, for instance, with companies which carry on qualifying and non-qualifying activities, for example, a company which builds houses and receives rental income from a number of properties. The various caravan park and other property letting cases heard by the Special Commissioners in recent years show that the question of determining whether a business consists mainly in the making of investments is not always an easy one to decide (see 17.31).

The BPR regime does not contain any territorial limitation. Thus, for example,

–   if an owner managed company opens up a branch in an overseas location through which it carries on a business there, or

–   sets-up an overseas 'trading' company (as a fellow-group company);

these will be treated as qualifying business activities for BPR purposes.

100% BPR can also be claimed on shares directly held in an overseas-registered and/or overseas resident company.

BPR will not be available if a company is in liquidation at the relevant time, except where the company is being wound-up for the purposes of a reconstruction under which the trade or businesses are continuing [*IHTA 1984, s 105(5)*] (see 13.57A).

Applying the 'mainly' test

17.27   HMRC's Capital Tax Office (CTO) generally look at the relevant turnover, profit and underlying asset values for each activity and 'mainly' is interpreted for this purpose as being over 50%. HMRC Share Valuation Manual para 27570 indicates that the preponderant activities of the business, its assets and sources of income and gains, will be reviewed over a reasonable period before the relevant transfer. The fact that the business profits have been assessed as trading income is not determinative of, or even relevant to, this point (see *Furness v CIR* [1999] STC (SCD) 232).

The issue of whether an 'investment' business is carried on is a question of fact and degree, to be determined by reference to the specific features of each case. Although the activities of the business should be tested at the date of the transfer/death, the courts and HMRC tend to look at the position that has been established over the last two to three years.

In this context, the important ruling in *Farmer (executors of Farmer deceased) v CIR* [1999] STC (SCD) 321 may be particularly helpful. In *Farmer* a large part of the business comprised lettings of farm buildings (22 tenancies) and static caravans. The capital employed in the letting business was £1.25 million compared to £2.25 million on the rest of the farm, although the rents received exceeded the farming profits. The Special Commissioner found that a wide variety of factors should be examined over a period of several years, including time employed on managing the various activities (divisions), turnover, expenditure, levels of staffing, and capital employed together with profits earned. Having regard to all the criteria, it was then 'necessary to stand back and consider in the round whether the business consisted mainly of making or holding investments'. Based on this, it was held that all the evidence supported the conclusion that the business consisted 'mainly of farming'. The fact that the letting activity was more profitable than the rest of the business was not conclusive.

The approach in *Farmer* was followed by the Court of Appeal in the leading case of *CIR v George [2004] STC 147*, which involved a caravan park operator. The main activities included providing pitches for 'residential caravans, utility services, the sale and storage of caravans, and the provision of a club/bar (open to all). However, it was concluded that the business should be viewed in 'in the round'- it was an active family business and the holding of investments was only one component of it. Thus, the business was not mainly that of making or holding investments.

If the *predominant* activity is qualifying, then BPR is given on the *entire value* of the company's shares, subject to any restriction for 'excepted assets' (see 17.32). Where the company predominantly carries on a non-qualifying activity (for example, property letting), no BPR is given, ie it is an 'all or nothing' test.

HMRC informal clearance procedure for BPR

17.28   HMRC operate a non-statutory clearance procedure which enables business owners to obtain confirmation that their shares will qualify for BPR before (or after) making a transfer of value. When applying for clearance, owner-managers must demonstrate the commercial significance of the transaction in relation to the business itself and the material uncertainty over the application of the BPR exemption. HMRC will not consider 'hypothetical cases' – ie a commercially significant transfer must be contemplated and there must be a potential IHT charge (in the absence of BPR). HMRC will endeavour to reply within 28 days. To assist in making a clearance application, HMRC provide a very helpful checklist (which is available on their website at www. hmrc.gov.uk/cap/Checklist.pdf,

Informal clearances on a company's BPR status will generally remain valid for six months. HMRC have given assurance that it will consider itself bound by the advice given where the taxpayer reasonably relies on the advice, having fully disclosed all relevant facts.

'Qualifying' holding companies

17.29   Group holding companies can often benefit from the protection of the 'holding company' exception in *IHTA 1984, s 105(4)(b)*. Holding companies and subsidiaries are as defined in the *Companies Act 2006 [IHTA 1984 s 103(2)]*.

Broadly speaking, a holding company would either be:

- a member of the subsidiary and be able to control its board of directors; or
- hold more than 50% of its equity share capital.

Whilst holding companies generally make and hold investments, the BPR prohibition does *not* apply where the relevant company's business is *wholly or mainly* acting as the holding company of one or more subsidiaries whose business is *not* an excluded one (broadly an investment business). In essence, the test is that the group must be mainly carrying on trading activities.

Thus, it is possible for shares in a holding company to qualify for BPR, even if it holds shares in some 'investment' subsidiaries. However, when calculating the amount of the transferor's BPR, the value of any 'investment' subsidiary must be *excluded* from the value of the holding company's shares – effectively reducing the value qualifying for relief. In such cases, it might be possible to improve the BPR position by transferring an investment business to another group company without disturbing the qualifying 'trading' or 'holding' company status of the recipient group company. For example, if it can be shown that a company is mainly a trading company, any 'secondary' investment business activity/assets will also effectively qualify for BPR.

Intra-group letting of property is effectively ignored and does not count as an investment activity for this purpose provided the letting is to group companies which would themselves qualify for BPR [*IHTA 1984, s 111(2)(b)*].

Example 5

BPR on holding company structures

(a) Structure 1

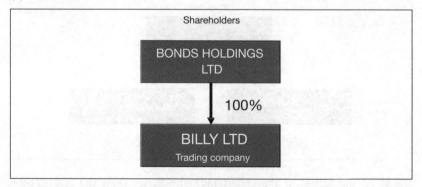

100% BPR should be available to the individual shareholders of Bonds Holdings Ltd since it is a qualifying holding company within *IHTA 1984 s 105 (4)(b)* (ie its business is a holding company of (at least) one 'trading' subsidiary (Billy Ltd).

(b) Structure 2

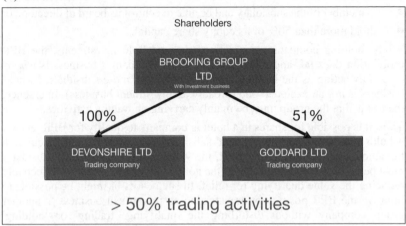

Brooking Group Ltd carries on an investment business and holds shares in two trading subsidiaries (Devonshire Ltd and Goddard Ltd).

The individual shareholders of Brooking Group Ltd should qualify for BPR since the company appears to be *mainly* a qualifying holding company within *IHTA 1984 s 105 (4)(b*. This should be the case where the combined value of its trading subsidiaries effectively exceeds the value of the investment business operated within Brooking Group Ltd itself. The value of the investment business is effectively sheltered by BPR and there is no *IHTA 1984 s 111* restriction (since the investment business is *not* within a subsidiary).

(c) Structure 3

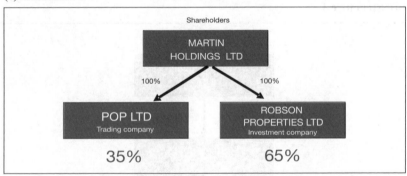

Based on the values of the underlying subsidiaries (Pop Ltd and Robson Properties Ltd), Martin Holdings Ltd is mainly carrying the business of holding shares in investment (as opposed to trading) subsidiaries. Thus, on the facts, Martin Holdings Ltd appears to be *mainly* an investment company (rather than a holding company of a 'trading group').

The shareholders of Martin Holdings Ltd would not qualify for any BPR (even on the 'trading' element within the group).

However, the BPR position for the shareholders might be improved by using a *IA 1986, s 110* reconstruction to separate the trading and investment activities so that they are held separately by the shareholders (through two new companies) (see 13.57A). BPR would then be available on the 'trading' element within Pop Ltd).

Property development companies

17.30   Some BPR claims for 'property development' company shares may give rise to difficulties, largely due to the often blurred distinction between 'non-eligible' dealing (see 17.25) and 'eligible' development activities. As a general rule, development involves changing the character of the land or changing/improving a building – but sometimes it is difficult to determine how much work is required for it to be treated as 'development'. Sometimes land acquired with the object of development may have to be sold on due to planning difficulties, but this does not necessarily mean property dealing, especially if the business clearly carries on other development work/activities.

In the current economic climate many property development companies may have to temporarily let property that was originally intended for development. The existence of rental income does not necessarily point towards an 'investment' activity as demonstrated in *DWC Piercy's Executors v HMRC* (2008) SpC 687. The Special Commissioner had to determine whether a company qualified for BPR (or whether it was mainly holding or making investments). HMRC had denied BPR as the company received substantial amounts of rental income from its retained land bank and it was therefore considered to be carrying on the business of making or holding investments.

Historically the company had developed and sold 256 flats but then switched to small community shopping centre developments. One particular development ran into difficulty regarding planning permission due to uncertainties regarding a rail-link. It was therefore forced to build some short term industrial workshops with the intention of replacing these when residential development became feasible. It was held that the land still continued to be held as trading stock (even though it produced a rental income) and there was nothing to demonstrate that it had been appropriated as an investment. The company's shares therefore qualified for BPR.

Brown's Executors v CIR – excess cash deposits – a helpful case on future intentions

17.31   Where a company holds excess 'cash deposits', it may still be possible to argue that its shares qualify for BPR on the grounds that the cash is required for future business purposes. This was demonstrated in *Brown's Executors v CIR* [1996] STC (SCD) 277, which involved a company that carried on a nightclub business. The club was sold in 1985 and the sale proceeds were invested on short-term bank deposits. The directors subsequently investigated the possibility of buying another nightclub and were still looking in November 1986 when Mr Brown died holding a significant shareholding. The Special Commissioners rejected the Inland Revenue's contention that the company was an investment company as it only held cash on deposit. They accepted the executor's argument that the company had not changed the nature of its business at the date of Mr Brown's death as it was actively seeking a new club and the funds on short term deposit were held for this purpose. Thus, BPR relief was given on Mr Brown's shares.

Decided cases on investment businesses

17.32   The following activities have *not* qualified for BPR on the grounds that they constituted 'investment' business:

- lettings of industrial units on three-year leases (*Martin (executors of Moore, deceased) v CIR* [1995] STC (SCD) 5);

- letting furnished flats on assured shorthold tenancies (*Burkinyoung (executor of Burkinyoung, deceased) v CIR* [1995] STC (SCD) 29);

- owning and managing a caravan park, including the receipt of pitch fees for caravans – from short and long-term residents – and letting of chalets (*Hall (executors of Hall, deceased) v CIR* [1997] STC (SCD) 126; *Powell (personal representatives of Pearce, deceased) v CIR* [1997] STC (SCD) 181; and *Weston (executor of Weston, deceased) v CIR* [2000] STC (SCD) 30).

In contrast, a caravan park operator successfully claimed BPR in *Furness v CIR* [1999] STC (SCD) 232 – based on the facts, particularly the net profit from caravan sales having consistently exceeded caravan pitch rentals, the business was not mainly the holding of investments.

BPR restriction for excepted assets

17.33   A close review of the company's activities and assets is necessary to ensure that the shareholder's BPR is not restricted by the 'excepted assets' rule. BPR is reduced to the extent that the value of the shares reflects any 'excepted assets' held by the company [*IHTA 1984, s 112*]. Broadly, this is an anti-avoidance provision aimed at preventing 'taxable' personal assets being 'sheltered' from IHT by being held within a BPR-eligible company – this might include holiday villas and other 'private' assets that are held within the company for the owner-manager's private use. The excepted assets restriction will also prevent BPR being given on 'excess' cash reserves being built up within a company.

An asset is an 'excepted asset' if it was *not* used wholly or mainly for business purposes in the previous two years *unless* it is required for *future use* in the business [*IHTA 1984, s 112(2)*]. HMRC will generally seek to examine the accounts and other relevant documentation to establish whether the company's assets were being used by the business at the time of death/ chargeable transfer. It is likely that large cash balances may be queried by HMRC on the grounds that they may not be required for future business use. There will, of course, be seasonal trades which generate a large cash balance at particular times of the year. In such cases, it should be possible to show that the cash was required to meet significant expenditure on re-stocking etc after the date of death.

Other cases will be less clear-cut, such as the circumstances in *Barclays Bank Trust Co Ltd v CIR* [1998] STC (SCD) 125. Here, the Inland Revenue accepted that £150,000 of a cash balance of £450,000 was needed for future use in the business, so that the remaining £300,000 constituted an 'excepted asset'. On the relevant facts, the Special Commissioner ruled on the relevant facts that the £300,000 was not required for business purposes. The fact that an asset *might* be required for the business at any time in the future did not prevent it being counted as an 'excepted asset'. The *IHTA 1984, s 112(2) (b)* 'required' test did not extend to the possibility that the money might be required should a suitable opportunity present itself after 'two, three or seven years time'. No clear evidence was presented which showed that the money would be used for a clear business purpose or project (such as here when the company invested £355,000 in a import 'venture' some seven years after the relevant death)

Where the company has passed the *mainly* 'trading' test but includes a combination of both trading and investment activities, investments which form part of an investment business will *not* be treated as excepted assets. As a result, where a trading company has over time accumulated a number of investments, the entire value of its shares will qualify for BPR provided it remains predominantly a trading company and the investments are managed as a business (see 17.26).

Other assets which are likely to be excluded from BPR as excepted assets include assets used personally by the shareholder, such as holiday homes, yachts, private jets, where there is little or no business use.

Assets used for investment business

17.34   Leading counsel, Kevin Prosser QC, considers that assets used in a 'secondary' investment business can be required for *business* purposes, as well as those used for trading purposes. It is therefore possible to present an argument that cash is required for the future use of an investment business. However, the mere holding of cash on deposit does not constitute an investment business (see *Taxation*, 25 June 1998, page 325).

The 'excepted assets' restriction works by excluding the part of the value of the shares transferred which is attributable to the excepted asset. This is very much a question of negotiation and would, for example, depend on whether the valuation of the shares was based on earnings or assets.

Worked example of BPR on chargeable estate on death

17.35

Example 6

Calculation of IHT on death and BPR

Mr Matthews dies on 26 February 2012, leaving an estate summarised as follows:

(*a*)   family home valued at £200,000;

(*b*)   personal chattels worth £40,000;

(*c*)   200 ordinary shares in Stanley Ltd (representing a 20% interest) valued by HMRC – Share Valuation at £860,000. Stanley Ltd manufactures sportswear;

(*d*)   the entire share capital (1,000 ordinary shares) in Matthews Ltd valued by HMRC – Share Valuation at £1,200,000;

   Matthews Ltd trades as a retailer of sports merchandise through a chain of shops – HMRC – Capital Taxes has successfully contended that £350,000 of the share value relates to substantial (permanent) cash deposits which are not required for working capital or the purposes of the business;

(*e*)   bank balances and a portfolio of investments valued for IHT purposes at £560,000.

Mr Matthews had made no gifts within the previous seven years.

Under Mr Matthews' will, the family home, personal chattels, bank balance and investments pass to Mr Matthews' wife. The shares in Stanley Ltd and Matthews Ltd pass to his son, who is a managing director of Matthews Ltd.

Mr Matthews' chargeable estate for IHT purposes is as follows:

		£	£
(a)	Family home		200,000
(b)	Personal chattels		40,000
(c)	Shares in Stanley Ltd	860,000	
	Less BPR (100%)	(860,000)	–
(d)	Shares in Matthews Ltd	1,200,000	
	Less Excepted assets	(350,000)	350,000
		850,000	
	Less BPR (100%)	(850,000)	–
(e)	Bank balances and investments		560,000
			1,150,000
	Less Spouse exemption (a), (b) and (e)		
	(£200,000 + £40,000 + £560,000)		(800,000)
	Chargeable estate		350,000
	IHT payable		
	On £325,000 @ 0%		–
	On £25,000 @ 40%		10,000
			£10,000

SUCCESSION ISSUES FOR THE OWNER MANAGER

Importance of succession planning

17.36 The owner manager must really consider their basic objectives for the future development and running of the business before embarking on any serious capital tax planning. Empirical evidence shows that the chances of the family business surviving beyond the first generation are not that great. The probability of a first generation of a family-owned business successfully passing to the second generation is about 30% and the odds of the second generation switching the business to the third are as little as 10%. However, there is a belief that these prospects improve by using a trust to hold shares in the company. Furthermore, a trust can protect the shares against potentially damaging events, such as divorce, insolvency, or incapacity of family members (see 17.53)

In the context of an owner-managed business, 'succession planning' can perhaps be best described as prudent and considered strategies which will help protect the business from *unnecessary* deterioration arising from future (possibly unexpected) events. Clearly, it is important to provide for the continuity of the business and its management in the event of the owner-manager's death, disability or pre-determined retirement plans.

However, most owner-managers tend to avoid confronting the 'succession planning' issue. For many, *their* business is *their* life – it often defines them as a 'successful person' – and they are reluctant to give up the control and the financial security that goes with it. Furthermore, they seldom wish to face the emotional issues that are likely to be involved in transferring the business to the next generation. But 'ducking the succession issue' will not be in the best long term interests of the business, and in some cases may lead to its sudden demise. Having a proper strategy in place for succession will help to maintain/build the value of the company and provides security for its employees.

The reasons why many owner-managers find it difficult to hand-over the 'reins of control' are varied, but typically entail such factors as the fear of retirement, the potential threat to their identity, or perhaps the inability to make a choice amongst their children. Although these are all understandable reasons, owner-managers have a real responsibility to have a mechanism in place for passing-over the management and/or ownership of their company over a period of time.

Every owner manager should develop and produce a *written* succession plan, which should be reviewed and updated at regular intervals. Part of this exercise will entail assessing the skills and future potential of their successors. Where appropriate, training and development plans should also be put in place and the owner-manager should involve the family members and employees in their thinking.

In some cases, there will not be a natural 'family' successor willing to take over. It is important to reach this conclusion as early as possible. This will give the owner-manager the necessary time to realise their investment, possibly by selling their shares to a third party trade purchaser or an incumbent management buy-out team.

Keyman insurance

17.37   A keyman insurance policy may be taken out to provide a much needed cash sum for the company in the event of the owner-manager's or another 'key' shareholders' death. Care must be taken to evidence that the primary purpose of the keyman insurance is to provide the funds to enable the owner manager's shares to be acquired on death.

In the unfortunate event of a pay-out, HMRC will invariably look at the reason why the key-man insurance policy was established. Based on the author's experience in several cases(!), provided it can be shown that the proceeds were intended to finance the purchase of the shares from the deceased's estate, they should be exempt from tax as a capital sum. (In *Greycon v Klaentschi* [2003] STC 370 it was held that where a key-man policy is taken out for a capital purpose, the proceeds are themselves capital). It is not sufficient simply to state that none of the premiums were previously deducted for corporation tax. Evidence on the underlying purpose is the key. If it is lacking, this may lead HMRC to conclude that the proceeds were intended to cover a 'shortfall' in profits in the event of a death and should therefore be subject to corporation tax (see *Williams Executors v CIR* 26 TC 23).

Typically, on death, the company may use the relevant funds to buy-back the owner-manager's/key shareholder's shares on death, often providing much needed cash for their spouse and other dependants. For BPR reasons, the deceased's shares will often be subject to 'put and call' options, enabling the estate to sell (put) the shares or the company to buy (call for) them (this avoids creating a binding contract which would deny BPR – see 17.23).

In some cases, the remaining shareholders themselves will undertake to purchase the deceased's shares. Such arrangements are covered by a shareholders' 'protection insurance' policy. This would be taken out on the life of each shareholder written into trust for the benefit of the other shareholders.

Key-man policies are also invariably required by banks and other lenders, so the established purpose is to facilitate the company's borrowing. Again, this must be carefully documented and should characterise any payment as 'exempt' capital.

Succession planning options

17.38   Once the commercial decisions have been taken, the relevant capital tax planning strategies can be implemented to meet those objectives.

The owner manager will usually need to keep their options open (for example, their children may be too young to express any leanings or interest towards the business). The tax planning approach must be 'tailored' to the owner-manager's personal circumstances. It is usually unwise for proprietors to commit themselves to any particular course of action too early on.

For instance, the owner-manager will (naturally) be reluctant to transfer any shares until they have decided that the shares will pass to the next generation and a sale has been ruled out. The unexpected may happen, for example, premature ill-health or a fantastic offer to buy the company which cannot be turned down! All such eventualities must be catered for as far as it is practically possible. The main options available to the owner-manager are discussed below.

Allocation of shares between family members

17.39   Ideally, capital tax planning should be considered when the company is incorporated, as the shares will then be of minimal value.

Fragmenting the company's shareholdings amongst different members of the family, including family trusts, will have a beneficial effect on share value and perhaps more importantly will enable future appreciation in value to accrue outside the donor's estate. However, proprietors will invariably want to be in control of their own destiny and be able to exercise leadership. Consequently, they (perhaps together with their spouse) will normally require at least a 51% shareholding.

If there is a possibility that the company may be sold in the future, the proprietor is likely to retain a substantial proportion of the shares. At this stage, the proprietor's children are likely to be very young (or not even born) and they will not know whether the children will be interested and sufficiently competent to work in the company. Flexibility and effective control can be retained by placing some shares in an appropriate family trust, for example, a discretionary trust (see 17.54).

Transfer of shares to next generation

17.40   For the existing family company, the passing of shares and ultimately control to the next generation clearly depends upon whether the proprietor's children (or other members of the family) are interested in developing the business. Perhaps more importantly, the proprietor's children should also demonstrate that they have the necessary commercial acumen and expertise to develop the business (entrepreneurial parents do not always have entrepreneurial children!).

Certain members of the family may not wish to play an active role in the business. If this is the case, the controlling shareholder could take out a life insurance policy (as early as possible) with a view to providing a cash sum on death for these 'non-active' members. This would enable the appropriate degree of balance to be struck with the shares passed on to the family members involved in the business. The proprietor may also need to take pre-emptive action to minimise the risk of losing key managers or employees who may feel that they were being 'passed-over' or neglected.

Obtaining financial independence

17.41   Most proprietors are financially dependent on their company and they are, therefore, likely to seek to maintain control of it to secure their future income in retirement. They may not trust their children to provide them with a consultancy fee or an 'unfunded' pension from the company.

This is why pension planning remains an important part of succession planning (pension planning is considered in Chapter 10). Owner managers should aim to build up a healthy pension and adequate savings over their working life from dividends and remuneration from their companies. They can then be financially secure and independent in retirement, enabling them to surrender control.

The owner manager may also be able to unlock capital from the company through a purchase of own shares with their gain usually benefiting from the favourable CGT rates (see 13.41–13.43). The retention of trading property held outside the company might be used to provide rental income during retirement.

No succession route available

17.42 If the proprietor does not have a natural successor in the family, they may wish to sell their shares to a key employee, manager or management team. Soundings would need to be taken early on to see whether the employees/ managers were interested in acquiring the company and if so, whether they could raise some personal finance and obtain the required bank/institutional borrowing. It is also possible to structure a management buy-out through a company purchase of own shares (along the lines indicated in Examples 8 and 9 in Chapter 13).

Planning for a 'trade' sale

17.43 If the proprietor plans to realise his investment in the company via a 'trade' sale of his shares to a third party, this must be planned at an early stage. (The various implications of selling the owner-managed company were dealt with in Chapter 15.) In the writer's experience, the process of selling the family business can take several years before the 'right' deal is struck. Advance planning reduces the cost and disruption to the business and gives time to rectify any weaknesses in the business, thus enhancing its value. It is often found that the value of the business is heavily dependent on its controlling shareholders. In such cases, the purchaser may (not unreasonably) require them to work in the business for the next two or three years to hand over their expertise and contacts, etc perhaps using an 'earn-out' arrangement (see 15.58–15.67).

17.44 Owner managers are now likely to realise 'exit' gains at 10% (with the benefit of Entrepreneur's relief on the first £10 million), with any excess gains being taxed at the 'top' CGT rate of 28%. However, in some cases, it may be possible to increase the ER even further by fragmenting shareholdings to 'qualifying' family members (see 15.33–15.42).

It must be recognised that a sale of the company completely changes the owner-managers IHT profile. Before the sale, 100% BPR would normally be available to exempt the value of their shareholding from IHT but after the sale, the entire post-CGT consideration would potentially be exposed to IHT at 40%. Given that many owner managers tend to sell out when they approach retirement age, normal IHT solutions may not be effective. A number of owner managers are now opting to use Discounted Gift Trusts (DGT) to remove substantial post-sale cash from their chargeable estate whilst ensuring a future income stream (see 17.44).

Alternatively, the proceeds realised on the sale of the company could be reinvested in IHT exempt or favoured assets (for example, woodlands or investments on AIM).

Use of Discounted Gift Trusts (DGTs)

17.45 Discounted Gift Trusts (DGTs) are essentially financial products which are available from a number of reputable providers. An outline of how a DGT works is given below.

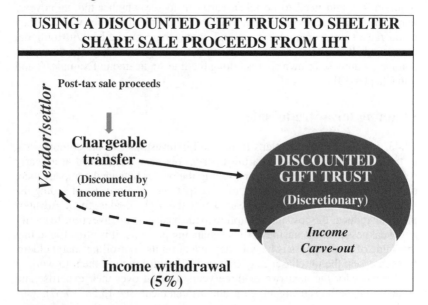

The use of a DGT and its related tax analysis (in relation to post-sale IHT planning) can briefly be summarised as follows:

- The owner manager would acquire a bond, which would be written into trust – this can be either an absolute (bare) trust (see 17.54 and 17.66) or a discretionary trust (17.54 and 17.79), although discretionary trusts provide greater flexibility.

- A DGT will provide the individual with a future income stream – for the rest of their life (or until the fund is exhausted). The income is calculated using the annual 5% 'tax-free' withdrawal facility (A lower or higher percentage can be taken but, if higher, there would potentially be income tax payable on the excess. Income tax would also potentially be payable if the 5% withdrawals last for more than 20 years.

- The 'carved-out' income stream is a return of capital and 'discounts' the value transferred into the trust. These retained rights are assumed to have been sold on the open market for IHT purposes and represents the value of property not being gifted.

  The fund required to produce the income stream is actuarially calculated and its value immediately falls outside the individual's estate liable to IHT. (However, if the individual does not spend their income stream, this will increase the value of their estate again.)

- HMRC have published tables (which can be found on HMRCs website) to ensure consistency of approach in calculating the income (annuity) stream – the value of the future income would be the reduction given in calculating the transfer of value for IHT purposes. HMRC have made it clear for many years that someone over 90 was not entitled to any discount. The ruling in *Bower & Anor v Revenue & Customs* [2009] STC 510 demonstrates that only a 'nominal' discount will be given where the taxpayer is 'uninsurable' due to very old age – the taxpayer in Bower was a 90 year-old lady.

For a transfer into a discretionary trust, the 'discount' reduces the chargeable transfer. In many cases, this will bring the transfer within the individual's nil rate band (see 17.4). Provided the settlor has not made any chargeable transfers within the previous seven years, this will avoid any immediate lifetime IHT charge. From an IHT viewpoint, HMRC have confirmed that this type of 'carve-out' (where the settlor's rights are clearly defined) does not give rise to any gift with reservation of benefit under s102 FA 1986 (see 17.66). After seven years, the individual's nil rate band is refreshed and the value of the CLT is outside their estate.

Where a discretionary trust is used, the value of the DGT at the ten-year anniversary would not be liable to any ten-year charge provided it falls below the nil rate band (at that time). Amounts remaining in the DGT on the settlor's death pass to their beneficiaries under the terms of the trust.

Where a DGT is written as an absolute trust, the 'discount' reduces the value of the PET.

In summary, provided the taxpayer is 'insurable', a DGT can provide a beneficial shelter from IHT, with any investment growth occurring outside the taxpayer's estate. With care, it should be possible to create a DGT with no immediate IHT cost.

PASSING SHARES TO THE NEXT GENERATION

Lifetime transfers

17.46 If the owner-manager wishes to transfer shares to their children or other members of the family, this can basically be done in one of two ways. Shares could be transferred, perhaps on a phased basis, as they approach retirement. Such transfers to individuals will qualify as PETs for IHT purposes and CGT business asset hold-over relief should normally be available (see 13.9).

The effect of a hold-over election is to pass on the contingent CGT liability to the transferee shareholder(s). As the transfer is a PET, if the donor dies within seven years of gifting the shares, an IHT charge will arise (subject to the availability of BPR).

When the transfer is made it is important that the controlling shareholder has not reserved any benefit (such as very favourable employment rights or benefits) in relation to the shares gifted as they would then be regarded as remaining in their estate for IHT purposes [*FA 1986, s 102*]. Any continuing remuneration drawn as a director will be disregarded by HMRC as long as it is 'reasonable'. However, where the former owner manager wishes to remain as a director it is desirable for him to enter into an appropriate service agreement, which would be binding on the company and viewed by the company as being in its interests. Ideally, this decision should be taken by an independent Board evidencing that the service contract is for the company's benefit. Any pension arrangements and benefits in kind should be written into the contract.

The IHT transfer of value (based on the 'diminution in value' principle) may differ from the value used for CGT purposes (see 17.5 and 17.7). For CGT, the value of the shareholding actually transferred is taken. Frequently, it will not be necessary to value the shares transferred if both parties agree to dispense with submitting a market value when making a hold-over election (see 13.16).

Value freezing schemes

17.47 As it is now relatively easy to transfer ownership of a family trading company, the use of value freezing or value shifting schemes has declined in popularity. Such schemes might be considered if the proprietor does not wish to transfer his shareholding or where the company's activities restrict the availability of business asset hold-over relief.

There are many scheme variations, all involving various tax and valuation complications, so specialist professional advice should always be obtained. Generally, they would involve a bonus issue of new shares (which only participate in future growth and profits) which would be placed in the children's hands or the use of a parallel company for placing genuine *new* business.

Passing shares on death

17.48 The owner manager could retain their shares (or most of them) until death. Normally, the shares would pass to the children, etc free of IHT due to the availability of 100% BPR. It may be considered inappropriate for the children to take the shares directly outright, for example, if they are too young. In such cases, a suitable trust vehicle could be used (see 17.54).

If the most desirable distribution of the estate is not clear at the time of the will, it is possible to use a discretionary will trust. Under *IHTA 1984, s 144*, capital distributions made from the trust within two years of death are treated as made under the will. For example, a discretionary will trust could be created for the benefit of the surviving spouse and the children. This would ensure that the income and capital would remain available to the spouse if required.

It might be considered preferable for IHT exempt shares to be passed to the children, etc at this stage, for example, if they are managing the business or perhaps to protect against any adverse changes in capital tax. Furthermore, the surviving spouse (or civil partner) can take the *chargeable assets* free of IHT anyway under the spouse exemption.

17.49 The children will inherit the shares at their market value at the date of death for CGT purposes (and do not therefore take over any contingent CGT liability in the shares which would have occurred had the shares been transferred before death). The combination of absolute exemption from IHT and CGT rebasing to probate value is particularly beneficial. Indeed, this favourable tax treatment provides a persuasive argument for holding on to the shares until death.

This, of course, assumes that the 100% BPR exemption will remain intact (see 17.19). Consequently, if the family wish to sell the shares shortly after the death, there will be no clawback of BPR and there should be little or no CGT due to the deemed 'market value' base cost established on death. In such cases, where 100% BPR is available, it will normally be necessary to agree the probate value of the shares afterwards (see 17.17).

It should not be forgotten that the owner manager may be under some moral pressure to pass at least some of the shares to their children *before* death to motivate them and maintain management morale.

There, will of course, be many cases where the owner-manager's shares have to be acquired by the company or the remaining shareholders, with appropriate key-man' or shareholder protection insurance being in place to fund the purchase (see 17.36 for detailed commentary).

DRAWING UP A WILL AND RELATED PLANNING ISSUES

The will

17.50 It is important to get the basic aspects right, such as ensuring that a will is properly drawn up and is regularly reviewed to take account of changing circumstances. Where an individual has assets in an overseas country or countries (for example, a holiday villa in Portugal or Spain), it will normally be advisable to make concurrent 'overseas' wills to deal (only) with the relevant assets in those jurisdictions.

The main will would cover the English assets, and should exclude the overseas assets and make reference to the overseas will(s). It is important to avoid the trap of any subsequent overseas will accidentally revoking the main English one!

Destination of shares and other assets

17.51 It is important to ensure business property relief (BPR) and agricultural property relief (APR) entitlements are maximised. For example, where possible the 'BPR eligible and other relievable assets' should not be left to the surviving spouse. In many cases, the shares, etc should be left directly to the children or possibly through an appropriate will trust (with the surviving spouse being included as one of the beneficiaries) (see 17.45). In such cases, the will should contain a specific 'gift' of the shares to the children/will trust. There will, of course, be situations where the shares are subject to 'put and call' options enabling the shares to be purchased by the company or the existing shareholders (see 17.36).

It is possible for the 'chargeable' part of the estate to be left to the surviving spouse (or civil partner) on a flexible interest in possession trust (see 17.54). Wide powers would be given to trustees to terminate that interest to enable the surviving spouse to benefit in a different capacity. Provided the life interest trust is created under a will (or intestacy) *and* that interest in possession 'kicks-in' on the testator's death, that will trust – strictly known as an immediate post-death interest trust (IPDI) – will rank for special treatment under *IHTA 1984, s 49A*. In broad terms, the IPDI is treated as a pre-22 March 2006 life interest trust (see 17.77). Consequently, the property passing into an IPDI for the surviving spouse/civil partner will benefit from the spouse exemption (see 17.9).

An IPDI trust gives the surviving spouse access to income which may make them feel more comfortable with making PETs to reduce the value of their estate. Using an IPDI, the trustees (which may include the spouse) could subsequently decide to terminate the spouse's interest over part of the assets. Such assets could, for example, be appointed on a discretionary trust (for the children's/spouse's benefit) within the spouse's unused nil rate band. The surviving spouse is *deemed* to make a transfer of value within *IHTA 1984, s 52* on the termination of their interest in possession. However, where this occurs after 21 March 2006, this is also regarded as a 'gift' [*IHTA 1984, s 102ZA*]. This means that the GROB rules would apply where the surviving spouse continues to benefit from the trust property – this would be the case, for example, where the spouse is able to benefit from a discretionary trust (see 17.10 and 17.66). (The deemed disposal should not be caught by the POA rules (see 17.111).)

IPDI trusts (see 17.77) can also be used to protect significant capital assets for the ultimate benefit of the deceased's children. For example, the surviving spouse could be given a life interest in the property which terminates on her death or remarriage. Such trusts are frequently used in 'second' marriages, since they enable the surviving spouse to enjoy the same quality of life. However, on the spouse's death, the underlying assets would pass to the deceased's own children rather than their 'step-children (unless that is desired as well). Furthermore, an IPDI trust can avoid assets being potentially diverted away from the 'bloodline' children in the event of the surviving spouse marrying again.

Since October 2007, the ability to transfer nil rate bands from a pre-deceased spouse/civil partner means that it is no longer necessary to equalise estates between married couples/civil partners. Until these changes, it was generally sensible for couples with assets in excess of the nil rate band to have a nil rate band will trust. With transferable nil rate bands, couples with relatively simple affairs may feel this is unnecessary. However, there still will be cases where a nil rate band will trust is advisable – for example, where someone had remarried and has children from a prior marriage. A will trust would ensure that they have access to assets post-death (where the (later) surviving spouse is still alive). If the surviving spouse is in business, a will trust can offer some protection from creditors (as opposed to an outright transfer of assets). Some also consider that a discretionary trust provides certainty of using the nil rate band (since legislation is always susceptible to change!).

Life policies and death-in-service pension payments

17.52   In some cases, it may be considered appropriate to nominate (at the discretion of the pension fund trustees) the tax-free 'death-in-service' amount of a pension policy in favour of a family discretionary trust (perhaps including the surviving spouse). This would ensure that the funds remain outside their estate on death but the trust could be given powers to make lend money to them on an interest-free basis.

In certain cases, any tax-free death-in-service benefit could be used to purchase, from the deceased's surviving spouse illiquid assets that have been left to her, such as shares in the family or owner-managed company.

Appropriate life insurance arrangements should also be in place to cover potential IHT liabilities which cannot be mitigated by planning. Life insurance premiums can normally be paid for the benefit of the other members of the family free of IHT, usually under the 'normal expenditure out of income' rule or annual exemption (see 17.9) – the benefits of the policy should be held in trust for the beneficiaries so that they do not form part of the individual's estate.

Some life policies are written in trust for the spouse/partner and/or children or are taken out to provide funds to pay off loans or mortgages.

Dealing with the family home and other properties

17.53 In many cases, the family home represents a significant part of the estate. If property, such as the home, is jointly owned, it is important to establish whether it is owned as a joint tenancy or as tenants in common.

Where property is held under a *joint tenancy*, each joint tenant owns the whole of the property and hence, on death, the entire asset will pass to the surviving owner. In such cases, the will or intestacy rules are irrelevant and there is no need to obtain a grant of probate since legal title passes on the production of a death certificate. A joint tenancy is therefore likely to be appropriate for a married couple where they are confident that the survivor will provide for their children in the second death.

If property is held as tenants in common, each party owns their relevant interest – typically on a 50%–50% basis. Thus, when one of the owner's dies, their share of the property will pass according to their will (or under the rules of intestacy). (A joint tenancy can be 'converted' to ownership as tenants in common by a deed of severance (the Land Registry will also need to be informed)).

This would enable their share to be passed directly to the children. However, this stratagem requires complete trust in the children. Since they would own a share in the house, they could force a sale of the home or the value of their share could be taken into account if they got divorced. Such problems could be avoided by the will providing for the share in the home to be passed into a (nil-rate band) discretionary trust, with the children as beneficiaries but, say, a trusted friend or other family member acting as a trustee.

Where the family home is held as tenants in common, the will can still provide for the deceased's share of the home to be left to the surviving spouse (or co-habiting partner). This would clearly attract IHT on the survivor's death. Similarly, if the surviving spouse or partner is given a right to occupy it for life, this again would fall to be treated as part of their chargeable estate for IHT purposes – since the right is given under a will, this would be an IPDI and thus, exceptionally, the underlying property would be treated as part of the survivor's estate on death. It is not possible for the surviving spouse/partner to gift the house to (say) their children, with the survivor continuing to occupy it. This would clearly be caught by the gift with reservation rules (see 17.95) except where a commercial rent was paid.

In appropriate cases, it may be desirable to leave the home to the surviving spouse, leaving (say) cash to a 'nil rate' band discretionary trust for the surviving spouse/children, etc. If the surviving spouse requires the cash post-death, they may be able to arrange for the trustees to lend it to them with a proper charge being made on the house (thus reducing the value of their potential estate). Specialist advice must be taken before implementing this and similar arrangements and must avoid the potential traps highlighted in the case of *Phizackerley v R&CC* [2007] STC (SCD) 328.

The ability to pass on any unused 'nil rate' band on the death of the first spouse to be used in the estate of the survivor should now ease some of the problems in passing down the family home (see 17.15) [*IHTA 1984, s 8A*].

USE OF TRUSTS

Benefits of using trusts

17.54   Trusts can be used to shift value and future capital growth outside the proprietor's estate. Trusts can be a more flexible and helpful method of transferring shares or other assets than an outright absolute gift. Many proprietors are sceptical about the use of trusts and it will be necessary to dispel their fears. It is worth pointing out that trusts have been in existence for hundreds of years and are widely used (whatever HMRC might think!) to protect family assets (including shares in the family/owner-managed company). Understandably, many parents are nervous about their children marrying 'fortune hunters' or having direct control of family assets where they are considered too young to handle them responsibly or make decisions affecting them. Furthermore, trusts are particularly efficient vehicles for holding shares in family/owner managed companies to facilitate succession planning and control the destination of assets from beyond the grave.

It is helpful to begin with the leading definition of a trust provided by Sir Arthur Underhill:

> 'A trust is an equitable obligation, binding a person (who is called a Trustee) to deal with property over which he has control (which is called trust property) for the benefit of persons (who are called the Beneficiaries or the *cestuis que trust*) of whom he may himself be one and any one of whom may enforce the obligation.'

The trustees do not therefore personally own the trust property, just the legal interest in it in a fiduciary capacity. They hold the trust property on behalf of the beneficiaries, who may be named or ascertained by description in the trust deed. The trustees will generally make decisions over the trust assets acting in the best interests of the beneficiaries as a whole.

These beneficiaries have the beneficial ownership of the property, as prescribed by the terms of the trust deed. The individual creating the trust is usually referred to as the 'settlor'. In most cases, it will be necessary to register the trust deed with HMRC.

Trusts can either be created during the settlor's lifetime (by a formal trust deed) or by will (a 'Will Trust'), which is treated as written at the date of the settlor's death. In the case of lifetime trusts, settlors can appoint themselves and possibly their spouses as trustees. This enables them to retain the decision making and control over the trust. Although trustees have a duty to act in the interest of the beneficiaries, this should normally coincide with the proprietor's own wishes. The courts generally impose an onerous duty of care on trustees.

In some cases, the settlor may wish to appoint a 'protector' of the trust (for example, a close family friend) to 'watch over' the trustees. A protector would have certain powers, such as the ability to appoint and dismiss trustees.

The property transferred into the trust (such as the shares) will be set aside for either specified individuals or a nominated class of individuals until a given age or event.

Trusts also enable the underlying income and capital value of the settled shares to be protected where the children are too young to handle capital properly or if there are concerns about the children's spouses or partners. By transferring shares into trust, the owner-manager can defer his decision as to which children, grandchildren (or anyone else) should inherit and what stake they should have in the company. Such difficult decisions may not become clear until much later on and may often involve a degree of conflict – for example, family values which generally entail equality of treatment may be at odds with the need to reward those who are the top 'family' contributors to the success of the business. Furthermore, as the children grow up, the owner manager will often find that only some of the children will seek involvement and responsibility in the business.

If a trust entitles the settlor or their spouse/civil partner to potentially benefit from the trust, it will not be effective for income tax purposes and indeed would be treated as a gift with reservation of benefit for IHT (see 17.95). To avoid such problems, the trust deed must be drafted to irrevocably exclude the settlor or their spouse/civil partner from benefit. It is worth noting that since 6 April 2008, *capital gains* of (UK) settlor-interested trusts are taxable on the trustees (and not the settlor, as was the case previously) (see 17.62).

Despite the best efforts of the courts, trusts continue to play a valuable role in protecting assets on divorce or marriage breakdown. Where this is a key consideration, owner managers should *exclude* their spouse (or spouses of their children) from the class of beneficiaries at the outset. If the spouse is to be a beneficiary of a trust, it is possible to provide power to irrevocably remove them at a later date should this become necessary.

Main types of trust

17.55   The main types of trust can be summarised as follows:

Bare trusts (or simple trusts) – With such trusts, the beneficial owner of the property is fully entitled to both the income and capital of the property, although the property is held in the trustee's name. In such cases, the trustee effectively holds the property as a nominee. A bare trust can be created or arise in a number of different circumstances. For example, property may be held by parents as bare trustees for their minor children simply because the children cannot legally hold property or give valid receipt for money until they reach the age of majority. Similarly, where under the terms of a trust a beneficiary becomes 'absolutely entitled as against the trustee(s)', the trustee(s) will hold the property as a bare trustee pending the legal transfer of the trust property to that beneficiary (see 17.66 and 17.67).

Interest in possession (or life interest) trusts – These trusts give one or more beneficiaries the right to the income (or enjoyment of the trust property) for a defined period, often for life. (This is a concept of trust law – *FA 2006* has not changed the characteristics of such a trust – merely its IHT consequences.) Such trusts are often referred to as life interest or fixed interest trusts. An interest in possession trust is often used where the settlor wishes to give an immediate benefit of income to a beneficiary but intends the capital to be gifted to someone else (see 17.68). Such trusts might be used, for example, to give a child an income stream but deferring the entitlement to the actual capital until later on in life. The settlor must ensure that they do not retain any benefit from the trust property as the assets would be treated as remaining in their estate for IHT purposes and the trust would also be 'transparent' for income tax purposes (see 17.60).

Discretionary trusts – Under a discretionary trust, the income and capital is to be paid out at the trustees' discretion. The trustees may decide to retain the income and accumulate it for future use. Thus, the beneficiaries only have a hope or expectation of income or capital – they are not entitled to it as of right (see 17.79). (Employee share ownership trusts are a specialised form of discretionary trust (see 8.82).)

Given their potential power, the choice of trustees for a discretionary trust is very important. Settlors (ie the individuals creating the trust) are normally advised to leave a 'letter of wishes' with the trustees, even where they start off by being one of the trustees.

The letter of wishes sets out the settlor's present and future intentions for the trust property. The letter is sent to the trustees on a 'private and confidential' basis, and records the settlor's reasons for the trust and their motives. It may give suggestions on how discretions might be exercised in the light of potential future circumstances. Although the expression of wishes should give some assistance to the trustees as to the settlor's insight, it must not become a series of instructions.

Accumulation and maintenance trusts – A&M trusts used to be a very popular trust vehicle for holding assets for children and grandchildren (aged under 25). Such trusts were effectively a product of a specific beneficial IHT regime, which was abolished on 22 March 2006. There are many A&M trusts in existence where their terms were amended before 6 April 2008 to take advantage of special transitional IHT 'protection' (see 17.96–17.105).

Special types of FA 2006 trusts – As part of a radical 'shake up' of the IHT trust regime in *FA 2006*, the government introduced a number of specialised rules to alleviate the potentially disadvantageous IHT effects on many existing trusts. These rules have effectively created a number of special trust regimes, which include:

- immediate post-death interests ('IPDIs') (see 17.77);

- transitional serial interest ('TSIs') (see 17.78);

- age 18 to 25 trusts (see 17.102); and

- bereaved minor trusts (see 17.105).

NON-RESIDENT TRUSTS

OVERVIEW

17.56 Given the wide-ranging anti-avoidance legislation that applies to non-resident trusts, the vast majority of owner-managers are now likely to use *UK resident* trust vehicles as part of their estate/succession planning. It should be noted that the coverage of trusts in this chapter is mainly confined to *UK resident* trusts. However, given that *non-resident* trusts may have been set up historically (possibly hysterically!) by some owner-managers, it is helpful briefly to highlight some of their potential CGT issues.

The vast majority of tax planning opportunities that used to be provided by non-resident trusts have now been negated by stringent tax legislation, although *non-UK domiciled* individuals were safeguarded from these provisions until 5 April 2008. The *FA 2008* considerably lessened the appeal of such trusts for non-UK domiciled individuals as well!

The residence test for trusts changed on 6 April 2007 – so that a trust will *not* be resident in the UK for a tax year if either:

- *all* the trustees are non-UK resident; *or*

- the settlor was either non-UK resident *or* non-UK domiciled when they created the trust and there is at least one non-UK resident trustee.

The key anti-avoidance provisions for non-resident trusts are set out below.

Exit charge on migration

17.57   Where a UK trust becomes non-resident (by switching entirely to non-resident trustees) it is subject to an 'exit' charge under *TCGA 1992, s 80*. (A number of recent European Union cases have questioned the validity of tax 'exit' charges imposed on migration but it is unsafe to rely on them in planning!) The 'exit charge' is computed by reference to a deemed disposal (and reacquisition) of all the trust's assets (including any shares held in an owner-managed company) at their market value. Assets that remain within the charge to UK tax are not subject to the exit charge. The trustees are taxed on the resultant gain(s).

The UK settlor charge

17.58   A (UK resident and domiciled) *settlor* is taxed on capital gains made by a 'non-resident' trust in which they have an interest [*TCGA 1992, s 86*]. Trust gains attributed to a settlor for *2010/11* are taxed at 18% (irrespective of whether they arise before/after 23 June 2010). From 2011/12 onwards, they will normally be taxed at the main 28% CGT rate.

A very wide 'settlor-interest' definition applies for non-resident trusts. Settlors are treated as having an interest in an overseas trust if any interest (even discretionary) is held by them, their spouse/civil partner, their children (and their spouses), or a company controlled by them and their spouses/children. For *post-16 March 1998* trusts, the inclusion of grandchildren as beneficiaries will also be caught by this rule. Where the beneficiaries of the trust only consist of friends and other relatives (such as the settlor's parents), the 'settlor charge' would *not* apply.

The UK beneficiaries charge

17.59   If the non-resident trust gains are *not* taxed on the settlor (under the above rules), they are then counted as 'trust gains' – which are calculated under the normal CGT rules. These trust gains are then subject to CGT when they are distributed as a capital payment to a UK resident (and UK domiciled) beneficiary [*TCGA 1992, s 87*]. From 6 April 2008 capital payments are also taxed on *non-UK domiciled* but resident beneficiaries, unless they can be sheltered by claiming the remittance basis (which frequently involves paying the £30,000 annual 'toll-charge').

There are special rules for matching *s 87* trust gains to capital payments on a 'beneficiary-by-beneficiary' basis. Broadly, trust gains are allocated to the recipient beneficiary up to the amount of any capital payment(s) made to them.

The gains are apportioned to beneficiaries in the proportion of the capital payments they have received from the trust in the same or any earlier tax year. Any excess gains (often known as 'stock-piled gains') are carried forward to match with any subsequent capital payments. From 6 April 2008, capital payments are matched with prior trust gains on a LIFO (last-in first-out basis). Hence the payments would be matched to more recent gains before earlier ones (Before 6 April 2008, the reverse FIFO rule applied, with earlier gains being matched in priority.)

Similarly, any excess capital payments would be matched with any trust gains made in later years, restricted where appropriate to the trust gain. The matched amounts would be taxed on the relevant beneficiaries.

In 2010/11 (when the CGT rate increased to 28% on 23 June 2011), the 28% CGT rate will normally apply to 'matched' 'matched' capital payments received after 23 June 2010. Pre-23 June 2010 'matched' capital payments would be taxed at the 'old' main 18% rate. The normal 28% CGT rate applies from 2011/12.If the gains are not promptly distributed, the CGT is increased by the supplementary charge [*TCGA 1992, s 91*]. The trust must distribute any gains within the same or following tax year to *avoid* the supplementary charge.

The charge is calculated by applying 10% to the *CGT* for each year starting from 1 December following the tax year in which the gain arose until 30 November after the tax year the (matched) capital payment is made. The charge is effectively limited to a maximum of 60% of the tax.

For post-22 June 2010, distributions, this would generally mean that cash can be repatriated to UK beneficiaries at a maximum tax cost of 44.8% (CGT at 28% plus maximum supplementary charge thereon – 60% × 28%). Those who had the foresight to distribute their 'historic' trust gains before 23 June 2010 at a maximum combined cost of 28.4% cost will have felt rather relieved!

Where the beneficiary has their own gains, the allocated trust gain attracting the supplementary charge can be treated as being taxed as the *lowest* amount.

Example 7

Allocating non-resident trust gains to beneficiaries (including supplementary charge)

Mr Matty (UK resident and domiciled) set up 'his' company (Etherington Ltd) in 1990. At that time, 20% of the shareholding was placed in 'his' non-resident discretionary trust. The beneficiaries of the trust comprised his father (Matthew), long time girlfriend/partner (Matilda) and any future children.

The entire share capital of Etherington Ltd was sold for £2 million in 2006/07. The capital gain arising in the non-resident trust (after taking account of incidental disposal costs and taper relief at 75%) was £96,000.

In May 2011, the trustees made a capital payment of £10,000 to Matthew and £40,000 to Matilda. On 1 June 2011, Matilda had realised a chargeable gain of £18,000 in her own right. She was a higher rate taxpayer for 2011/12.

Attributed trust gains	Matthew	Matilda	Total
	£	£	£
Trust gains b/fwd			96,000
2011/12 – Apportioned gain	10,000	40,000	(50,000)
Trust gains c/fwd (to be matched with future capital payments)			46,000

Matilda's CGT position for 2011/12,

	£
Allocated trust gain*	40,000
Less: Annual exemption	(10,600)
	29,400
Own gain	18,000
Total chargeable gains	47,400
CGT thereon	
Total CGT	47,400 @ 28% £13,272

*Trust gain is treated as the lowest part of Matilda's trust gains

Supplementary charge

Matilda would also have to pay a supplementary charge of 40% on the 'trust' CGT, computed as follows:

Relevant period – 1 December 2007 to 30 November 2012	= 5 years
Therefore: 5 × 10%	= 50%
CGT on trust gain (= lowest part)	
29,400 @ 28%	£8,332
Supplementary charge = £8,232 × 50%	£4,116

Matilda will therefore have to pay a total amount of £12,348 (£8,232 + £4,116) in respect of their trust gains.

Non-domiciled settlors/beneficiaries

17.60 Whilst being UK resident, *non-UK domiciliaries* enjoy complete protection from the CGT charges that apply to UK settlor-interested trusts (see

17.60); together with *gains arising before 6 April 2008* distributed to resident UK beneficiaries (see 17.58). Non-resident trusts will remain effective tax-shelters for non-domiciliaries since gains can still be realised by the trust without any CGT arising on them. A charge will only arise when a 'matched' capital payment is received by a UK resident and non-domiciled beneficiary (subject to the 'remittance basis user' rules).

Interestingly, HMRC announced in March 2009 that it will no longer process forms DOM1 which were used to obtain a formal 'ruling' on an individual's domicile status. In future, individuals will have to decide their own domicile status when submitting their tax returns, which HMRC could challenge under the normal enquiry process.

From 6 April 2008 distributions of 'matched' gains arising from that date to UK resident but non-UK domiciled beneficiaries are taxable. The 'matched' trust gains are treated as foreign chargeable gains (irrespective of whether the gains arise in foreign or UK-situs assets held by the trust). If the payment is *received offshore* and not brought to the UK a CGT charge may be avoided if the non-domiciliary is a 'remittance basis user' (ie in the majority of cases, has elected to pay the annual £30,000 remittance basis charge).

In those cases, where a CGT charge arises on a *non-domiciled* beneficiary, the trustees can opt to apply rebasing on their pre-6 April 2008 trust assets. This effectively means that the relevant assets are 'rebased' at 6 April 2008, enabling the charge to apply only on the post-6 April 2008 element of the 'distributed' gain.

Transferring an *existing* (valuable) shareholding into a non-resident trust would generally be unattractive as this would trigger a 'dry' tax charge. CGT would be levied on a deemed 'market value' disposal of the shares and it is not possible to hold-over gains on a transfer to a *non-resident* trust (see *TCGA 1992, ss 166* and *261* and *13.14*).

On the other hand, it would be possible for a *non-domiciled* owner-manager to set up a company with (say) some of the shares held in a non-resident discretionary trust (in which they benefit) and potentially escape a CGT charge on a subsequent sale of the company. Any capital gain on the shares sold by the trust would *not* be imputed to the owner-manager after 5 April 2008 (see *TCGA 1992, s 86(1)(c)*). However, any gain distributed to the owner-manager would be taxed in the UK unless they were a remittance basis user and the gain was not remitted to the UK. Obviously, specialist advice is required for such planning, with particular care being taken to ensure that the trust properly operates as a non-resident trust.

Having said that, many non-domiciled owner-managers may not wish to enter into such complex arrangements, especially if they are reasonably confident of obtaining the relatively low 10% ER CGT rate.

SETTLOR-INTERESTED TRUSTS

Income tax

17.60A If the settlor (*or their spouse/civil partner*) has an interest, even if it is of a discretionary nature, in their trust, the income arising in the trust will be taxed on the settlor (even though the income is retained within the trust) (*ITTOIA 2005, ss 624* and *625* (previously *ICTA 1988, s 660A*)).

Although the settlor suffers income tax on the trust income, the trustees would initially incur an income tax liability as recipients of the income at the relevant rates appropriate to the type of trust (see 17.69 for interest in possession trusts; see 17.81 for discretionary trusts).

The settlor records the relevant income on their personal tax return (on Form SA 107 Trusts). They can deduct the tax paid by the trust on the relevant income against their personal income tax due on the trust income, which may result in a refund or further payment. The trustees should provide the settlor with a statement showing the amount of tax they have incurred on the income.

This so-called 'settlor-interested' settlement rule also applies where there is no formal trust vehicle. In recent years, HMRC have attempted to use these provisions challenge the use of 'income-splitting' which involved the payment of tax-efficient dividends to spouses. Whilst the House of Lords found these arrangements to constitute a settlement, the settlor was exempted under the 'outright gifts' exemption in (what is now) *ITTOIA 2005, s 626*, so the dividends were taxed on the spouse (as intended) – see 9.23 to 9.27 for further commentary.

Parental settlements

17.60B Special anti-avoidance rules also apply to income *paid out* of or made available by trusts created for the benefit of the settlor's unmarried children aged under 18. Such income is deemed to be the settlor's (subject to a *de minimis* limit of £100 for each child every year) [*ITTOIA 2005, s 629*]. (See 17.76 for treatment of bare trusts for minor children).

However, income arising in a discretionary or accumulation and maintenance trust created for the benefit of the *settlor's* children would *not* be taxed on the settlor whilst it is retained by the trust (as the income does not belong to the child. In these cases, the parent is only liable to tax under *ITTOIA 2005, s 629* when the trust pays the income out to the child or applies it for their benefit (for example, by paying their school fees).

There is no equivalent rule for CGT and any capital gains arising in the trust therefore belong to the child, who can set their own annual CGT exemption against them. In the case of a bare trust, the child will be able to call for the capital when they reach their 18th birthday.

However, if the trust is properly established by another 'family' member, for example, a grandparent, then any income paid out of the trust can be treated as that of the children (and hence covered by their personal allowances, etc). However, the legislation prevents the use of reciprocal arrangements – for example, if Bobby sets up a trust for the benefit of Hayden's children, with Hayden doing the same for Bobby's children – in such cases, both trusts would be caught by the parent-settlement rules (*ITTOIA 2005, s 620(3)(c)* previously *ICTA 1988, s 660G(2)*). A will trust created for the benefit of the settlor's children would *not* be caught (see also 17.66).

Capital gains of settlor-interested trust

17.60C   From 6 April 2008, capital gains arising in a settlor-interested trust (ie one in which the settlor or their spouse is able to benefit (even if only potentially) ceased to be subject to any special deeming rules. Thus, gains arising in such trusts are now taxed in the trust in the normal way. This was a simplification measure following the alignment of the trust CGT rate with the then 'personal' 18% CGT rate. It is therefore no longer possible for a settlor to offset their personal losses against gains arising in a UK settlor-interested trust. A settlor charge still applies to *non-resident* trust gains which are within the very widely defined 'settlor interest' rules (see 17.57).

All post-22 June 2010 trust gains are taxed at 28%. CGT at the 'old' 18% rate applies to pre-23 June 2010 gains.

Before 6 April 2008, settlor-interested trust gains were imputed to the settlor [old *TCGA 1992, s 77(2)*].

IHT

17.60D   Under the *FA 2006* IHT trust regime, the transfer of property to an interest in possession trust is a chargeable transfer. This analysis still applies where the *settlor* is entitled to the interest in possession. Thus, the settlor would make a chargeable transfer where they passed assets to an interest in possession trust for their benefit. Furthermore, since the settlor continued to benefit from the transferred assets, this would also be a gift with reservation of benefit (GROB) for IHT purposes (see 17.95) with the asset remaining in their estate on a subsequent death (provided they retained their interest in the trust). A GROB does not invalidate the IHT status of the transaction as a chargeable transfer.

The IHT treatment of interests in possession contrasts sharply with the pre-22 March 2006 position which used to treat the life tenants of such trusts as owning the underlying capital supporting the income for IHT purposes. This meant that if the *settlor* was entitled to the interest in possession, ie the income of the trust, there was no transfer of value – the settlor's estate did not suffer a reduction as they were deemed to own the capital value of the trust fund.

Where the settlor retains an interest as a *discretionary* beneficiary, this will also be treated as a GROB and remain as part of their chargeable estate (unless and until the interest is released). However, this does not prevent the trust being 'relevant property' under the IHT trust regime, and hence subject to exit and ten-year charges.

Once again, a chargeable transfer arises for IHT when assets are transferred into the trust. A CGT charge may also be triggered, bearing in mind that hold-over relief (under *TCGA 1992, s 165 or 260*) is no longer available in such cases.

If the settlor dies whilst retaining an interest in the trust, the property will be included as part of their taxable estate on death [*IHTA 1984, s 102(3)*]. The *Inheritance Tax (Double Charges Relief) Regulations, SI 1987/1130* may apply to provide relief where the relevant assets have been subject to a double charge, due to the operation of the GROB rules.

CREATING THE TRUST – TAX IMPLICATIONS

Basic CGT rules

17.61   The tax implications of creating a trust (by transferring cash or assets) generally depends on the nature of the property being transferred and the type of trust.

The transfer of property to a trust is a disposal for CGT purposes, even if the settlor retains some interest as a beneficiary or is a trustee of the trust [*TCGA 1992, s 70*]. This disposal is deemed to take place at market value (obviously, a cash payment has no CGT effect).

Where the transfer of an asset to any trust produces an allowable loss, this loss can only be used against gains on future disposals to the same trustees [*TCGA 1992, s 18(3)*] – they are 'connected' with the settlor under *TCGA 1992, s 286(3)(a)*.

CGT hold-over reliefs

17.62   Capital assets transferred to a relevant property trust (eg interest in possession or discretionary trusts) after 21 March 2006 are treated as chargeable transfers for IHT purposes (see 17.64).

This means that CGT hold-over relief under *TCGA 1992, s 260* is potentially available to shelter the settlor's capital gain. However, hold-over relief is now denied where the relevant trust is a 'settlor-interested' one. The definition of a settlor-interested trust was substantially widened from 6 April 2006. This wider definition effectively means that hold-over relief would now be denied where the trust's beneficiaries include the settlor's minor (unmarried) children. In such cases, a 'dry' CGT charge may therefore arise on the transfer (see 17.63).

On the other hand, where the trust is not a 'settlor-interested' one, the settlor will normally be able to hold-over the gains under *TCGA 1992 s 260* (see 13.19–13.21 and 17.63). (This is because the disposal of assets to the trust will be treated as a chargeable transfer for IHT purposes, even if it falls within the 'nil rate band'. Even where the assets transferred constitute eligible business assets for the purposes of *TCGA 1992, s 165*, the hold-over relief under *TCGA 1992, s 260* takes precedence).

Pre-22 March 2006 transfers to an interest in possession or accumulation and maintenance (A&M) trust were PETs. Thus, it was only possible previously to claim CGT hold-over relief for business assets (such as shares in an unlisted trading company) under *TCGA 1992, s 165*. Any *TCGA 1992, s 165* hold-over claim would have been subject to a restriction where the shares are in a company that owns chargeable *investment* assets (for example, let property or shares in non-subsidiaries) at the transfer date (see 13.19–13.21). As with *s 260* relief, no *s 165* relief can be claimed on post-9 December 2003 transfers to 'settlor-interested' trusts (see 17.63).

A pre-22 March 2006 transfer of *investment* assets (such as shares in a property investment company) to an interest in possession or A&M trust may have produced a CGT liability (since no form of hold-over relief used to be available in such cases).

Transfers of assets to discretionary trusts (before 22 March 2006) still obtained CGT protection using *s 260* hold-over relief (see above). Once again, no relief was available for post-9 December 2003 transfers to a settlor-interested trust (see 17.63).

For both types of hold-over relief, the settlor must make the formal election (not the trustees) by using the prescribed HMRC form IR 295 [*TCGA 1992, ss 165(1)(b)* and *260(1)(b)*]. The trustees effectively acquire the asset at its original base cost (ie market value less the held-over gain). This will include indexation where the disposal occurred between 31 March 1982 and 6 April 2008. However, it is possible to avoid computing the proper market value of the asset if both parties agree to invoke the 'valuation dispensation' in SP8/92 (see 13.13).

Hold-over relief restriction for settlor-interested trusts

17.63 CGT hold-over relief under *TCGA 1992, s 165 or s 260* cannot be claimed where the settlor or their spouse/civil partner has an 'interest' in the trust, even where they are a *potential* beneficiary [*TCGA 1992, s 169C*]. (A 'separated' spouse or widow or widower can be included without prejudicing the relief.)

Since 6 April 2006, the concept of a 'settlor-interested' trust is now extended to include cases where the settlor's minor unmarried children (including step-children) are able to benefit under the trust. This restriction therefore prevents any CGT hold-over relief being claimed on family trusts that benefit the settlor's minor children! (It is possible, however, to prevent the settlor's children from benefiting under a trust whilst they remain under-18 –this type of clause would prevent the trust being a settlor-interested one)

The hold-over restriction also applies where there are 'arrangements' under which a settlor or their spouse could obtain an interest in the trust.

Furthermore, no hold-over relief is given or, where appropriate, any relief previously claimed is clawed-back if any of the above 'settlor-interested criteria' are satisfied within the relevant 'clawback period' (However, relief is not denied or clawed-back where the trust subsequently becomes 'settlor-interested' as a result of the post-5 April 2006 widening of the definition to include dependent children.). The 'clawback period' starts from the date of the transfer into trust and ends six years after the end of the tax year in which the transfer was made [*TCGA 1992, s 169B*]. In such cases, the gain would be computed on the basis that the hold-over claim was never made with the trustees having acquired the shares at their market value.

Basic IHT rules

17.64 FA 2006 provides that the transfer of assets to virtually *any* type of trust during the settlor's lifetime (*after 21 March 2006*) is a *chargeable* transfer for IHT purposes (unless the trust qualifies as a disabled trust). Relevant property trusts include both interests in possession created after 21 March 2006 and discretionary trusts.

Where shares in a qualifying trading company are transferred to a trust, 100% business property relief (BPR) (see 17.18) would normally be available to exempt the transfer from any IHT. However, if the value transferred is not protected by any relief, then the value transferred (in excess of the available nil rate band) will suffer IHT at 20%. In many cases, settlor's will not wish to incur the 'upfront' lifetime IHT charge of 20%, which would normally be involved when creating a substantial trust.

Many settlors are generally unwilling to incur a lifetime IHT charge of 20% and if the value to be transferred exceeds their available nil rate band, will look for ways in which the IHT can be mitigated. It may be possible to shelter the IHT liability under the 100% BPR or 100% Agricultural Property Relief provisions. Where such reliefs are not available, it may be possible to reduce the value transferred into the trust by selling the assets at an under-value. Provided the assets are sold for no more than their original cost, the CGT on the gain (based on market value) can still be held-over. Typically, the settlor can leave any sale proceeds due to them as outstanding on a loan account due from the trust.

It might also be possible for the settlor's spouse to also make a trust in their own right (using their nil rate band) – effectively doubling-up the nil rate bands available. However, any assets passed to the spouse must be made without any stipulation as to their use, otherwise the 'transferor' could still be considered as the 'real' settlor.

Before 22 March 2006, the transfer of assets to an *interest in possession* or *A&M* trust was a potentially exempt transfer (PET). No IHT liability would therefore arise provided the settlor survived for seven years (see 17.10) [*IHTA 1984, s 3A*]. However, where the settlor died within the seven year survivorship period, IHT could still be avoided if BPR was available – see 17.22 for detailed conditions.

The *FA 2006* changes did not alter the treatment of assets transferred to a *discretionary trust*. These have always created a *chargeable* transfer, incurring a 20% IHT charge on the value transferred after the settlor's available nil rate band was exhausted (subject to the annual exemption and any other available reliefs, such as BPR (see 17.19)).

Powers of trustees

17.65   As the main trust asset is likely to be shares in a family or owner-managed company, the trustees should have complete discretion in dealings with the trust assets. The trust deed should normally give the trustees appropriate powers and have regard to the *Trustee Act 2000*.

The trustees will also generally have a power to appoint income or capital to a nominated beneficiary and possibly a power of advancement enabling them to make a payment or distribution of capital to a beneficiary before they would normally become entitled to it under the trust deed.

BARE TRUSTS

Tax implications

17.66   As the trust property is, in effect, held by the trustee in a 'nominee' capacity, the income and capital gains of the bare trust are taxed on the underlying beneficial owners. A bare trust can be as simple as a bank account being held in the trustees' name. The tax legislation requires the relevant income and capital gains to be reported on the beneficiary's (ie the beneficial owner's) tax return, unless the income falls to be treated as the settlor's under the 'parental settlement' rules (see below).

Bare trusts have not been affected by the radical changes that were made to the IHT regime for trusts by *FA 2006*. Consequently, bare trusts may be preferred to more traditional trust vehicles. The transfer of assets to a bare trust is effectively treated as being made to the beneficial owner and would therefore be counted as a potentially exempt transfer for IHT purposes (ie completely exempt from IHT if the donor survives the 'seven year' period). Similarly, the settlor may have a capital gain on any chargeable assets transferred.

From an IHT perspective, property held by a bare trustee is treated as part of the beneficial owner's estate. This point has now been confirmed by HMRC following advice from leading tax counsel. Thus, a lifetime gift for a minor absolutely (irrespective of whether the provisions of *Trustee Act 1925, s 31* are excluded), will be treated as a PET (see 17.10). Furthermore, an absolute trust of this nature is not a settlement for IHT purposes and does not therefore come within the 'relevant property' trust regime.

Bare Trusts for minor children

17.67   Bare trusts have tended to be a useful IHT planning device to give cash to children or grandchildren. It is common for bare trusts to hold funds on behalf of minor beneficiaries – the adult trustees would hold the funds until the beneficiary is old enough to give a valid receipt. Once the beneficiary reaches their 18th birthday, they can insist that their share of the trusts assets is transferred into their own name (this is not a taxable event since there is no change in beneficial ownership).

Child beneficiaries would be able to use their annual CGT exemption against gains made by the 'bare trust'. However, in certain cases, income arising from bare trusts created by parents in favour of their children would be taxed on the parents under the 'parental settlement' rules in *ITTOIA 2005, s 629* (previously *ICTA 1988, s 660B*) (see 17.60). This is because the law was changed on 9 March 1999. Before that date, the income of a bare trust created by a parent for the benefit of their (minor unmarried) child was taxable in the child's hands (ie escaping the parental settlement provision) unless it was paid out to or for the child's benefit. This is still the case for income arising on funds, etc transferred to a bare trust before 9 March 1999. However, income from *parental* bare trusts created (or on *amounts added to an existing bare trust*) after 8 March 1999 would be taxed in the parent's hands under *ITTOIA 2005, s 629(1)(b)* unless it was below the £100 per child exemption.

INTEREST IN POSSESSION/LIFE INTEREST TRUSTS

Creation of trust

17.68   An interest in possession (or life interest) trust is now treated as a 'relevant property trust'. Consequently, a post-21 March 2006 transfer of shares, etc to such trusts will be treated as a chargeable transfer. This means that IHT will only be avoided where the transfer is sheltered by 100% business property relief, or some other relief (see 17.9), or the transferor's available nil rate band. The spouse exemption is *not* available where the life tenant of the trust is the settlor's spouse.

Any amount transferred in excess of the nil rate band will be taxed at 20%. The amount transferred forms part of the settlor's cumulative chargeable transfers for computing IHT on subsequent gifts and transfers. The ongoing IHT treatment of an interest in possession trust is summarised in 17.72.

HMRC's view is that the same IHT treatment applies where assets are added to an existing interest in possession trust created before 22 March 2006 – the addition is effectively treated as a separate trust and creates an immediate chargeable transfer. The added property becomes 'relevant property' and will therefore need to be separately identified for future IHT calculations.

The disposal is deemed to take place at market value for CGT purposes. Although hold-over relief under *TCGA 1992, s 260* is potentially available (see 13.19–13.21 and 17.62), this will not be the case where the trust is a *settlor-interested* one. The wider definition of a 'settlor-interested' trust which applies from 6 April 2006 is likely to deny hold-over relief in many cases. (Naturally enough, the definition catches trusts that benefit their settlor (and/or spouse) but now also the settlor's minor (unmarried) children.)

The IHT treatment of transfers into an interest in possession trust is completely different to that which applied before 22 March 2006. Under the pre-*FA 2006* regime, the transfer was treated as a PET (see 17.10). The IHT treatment of transfers to interest in possession trusts before 22 March 2006 is covered in 17.75.

Taxation of income

17.69   Under an interest in possession/life interest trust, the beneficiary/ beneficiaries (life tenant(s)) have the right to receive the trust income as it arises, usually for life, but it can be for a fixed period. The capital would then normally vest in someone else (the 'remainderman').

The *current* rates of income tax payable by the *trustees* of an interest in possession trust are as follows:

Income	Rate	Notes
Gross dividends and other distribution income	Dividend ordinary rate of 10%	*This tax is completely offset by the 10% tax credit carried on dividends, thus there is no further tax liability*

Income	Rate	Notes
Distribution on a company purchase of own shares (grossed-up)	32.5% (from 6 April 2004)	*This special rate is imposed by ITA 2007 s 481(3) (previously ICTA 1988, s 686A). After the 10% tax credit on distributions, the net rate is 22.5% (effective rate is 25% on the net distribution)*
Savings income	Basic rate of 20%	*This will normally be offset by the basic rate tax deducted at source from savings income*
Other income (such as property income, etc)	Basic rate of 20%	

These trusts are not therefore generally exposed to the high income tax rates imposed on discretionary trusts (see 17.81). No personal allowance is given in computing the trust's taxable income. Similarly, there is no relief for any trust expenses, which are therefore met out of post-tax income.

17.70   As the income (net of any 'income-related' expenses) must be paid out to the beneficiary/beneficiaries, the 'net' income is taxed in their hands at their normal income tax rates (and would therefore, where appropriate, suffer additional and top rates of income tax). Many trusts mandate dividend and other income directly to the beneficiaries. Trustees can elect to pass their tax liability to a beneficiary who receives the income direct. Thus, a dividend would be taxed at the dividend ordinary rate applicable in the hands of the beneficiary – as with individuals, the tax credit is non-repayable [*ITTOIA 2005, s 397(3)*].

The beneficiary of the trust is provided with a form R185 (trust income) showing the net amount of income and the tax deemed to be deducted. The income is taxed at the relevant income tax rates in the beneficiary's hands.

CGT on trust gains

17.71   Although the life tenant has no right to the capital, the trustees could be given power to pay capital to them or they may become entitled to capital on reaching a specified age.

Since 23 June 2010, trusts pay CGT at 28% on their gains (pre-23 June 2010 gains were taxed at 18%; pre-6 April 2008 gains were taxed at 40%) [*TCGA 1992, s 4*]. (Before 6 April 2008 gains of settlor-interested trusts were taxed in the settlor's hands but this anti-avoidance rule was removed on 6 April 2008 (see 17.55).)

Trusts enjoy an annual exemption equal to one-half of the individual exemption, ie £5,300 (= 1/2 × £10,600) for 2011/12 [*TCGA 1992, Sch 1*]. However, to counter the potential fragmentation of trust assets, if the settlor has created more than one trust (after 6 June 1978), the trust exemption is shared equally between the trusts, subject to a minimum exemption of one-fifth of the normal trust annual exemption. For example, for two trusts created by the same settlor, the annual exemption is £2,525 (£5,050 × 1/2).

Many CGT reliefs can be claimed by the trust in relevant circumstances.

CGT Entrepreneurs' relief for interest in possession trusts

17.71A In limited circumstances trustees may share the life tenant's lifetime Entrepreneurs' relief (ER) allowance to reduce the CGT rate on a disposal of shares to 10% (see 15.32). The relief is only available if a qualifying 'interest in possession' beneficiary is a director or employee of the company (or fellow 'group' company) and holds personally at least 5% of the ordinary share capital and voting rights of the company.

As any relief claimed by the trustees reduces that potentially available to the beneficiary on a future disposal, a joint election by the trustees and the beneficiary must be made. Since the beneficiary may have no right to benefit from the capital of the trust, it may not be in his best interests to make the election.

IHT treatment of post-21 March 2006 life interest trusts

17.72 Under the *FA 2006* rules, a post-21 March 2006 interest in possession trust is *not* treated as if the life tenant had owned the underlying trust assets, as was previously the case. (Such trusts are sometimes referred to as 'non-estate IIPs'.) Hence, the assets of the trust will not therefore be aggregated with the life tenant's estate on death. The death of the life tenant will therefore largely be irrelevant for IHT purposes.

As a relevant property trust, the trust will be liable to the normal 'exit' charge when property leaves the trust (see 17.74) and a 'ten-year' charge on every ten year anniversary (see 17.74). Because of the way in which these charges are calculated, where an interest in possession trust is set-up within the transferor's nil rate band, it will not incur any exit charges during the first ten years.

Pre-22 March 2006 interest in possession trusts (or estate IIPs) remain subject to the pre-*FA 2006* regime, which broadly treats the beneficiary as owning the underlying capital of the trust, as explained at 17.75. (For IHT treatment where an existing interest-in possession terminates before 6 October 2008 in favour of another such interest, see 17.76).

Exit charge on capital distributions/property leaving the trust during first ten years

17.73 Under the *FA 2006* regime, interest in possession trusts created after 21 March 2006 are subject to an IHT exit charge when the property leaves the trust, typically by way of a capital distribution to a beneficiary. From a CGT perspective, there is no uplift to market value on the death of the life tenant of a new interest in possession trust. However, as property leaving the trust is a chargeable transfer for IHT purposes, CGT hold-over relief should be available under *TCGA 1992, s 260*.

Where the trust assets are subsequently appointed on discretionary trusts, this is effectively a 'non-event' for IHT purposes and hence no 'exit' charge arises. (This is because discretionary and post-21 March 2006 interest in possession trusts fall within the same 'relevant property' trust regime.)

The exit charge is calculated using an effective IHT rate, which is applied to the property leaving the trust. The calculation of the effective IHT rate on an exit event is summarised in Table 1 below. In essence, the trust rate is derived from a deemed transfer by the settlor at the time of the exit charge

Table 1 – Computation of exit charge during first ten years

(a) Take the value of the hypothetical transfer into the trust by the settlor – this is the value actually transferred into the trust (and any additions made to the trust before the relevant capital distribution and the initial value of any 'related' settlement (see *IHTA 1984, s 62*)).

(b) The IHT liability on the total notional value transferred (in (a)) is found by applying the lifetime rate of 20% to that value (reduced by any prevailing 'nil rate' band available to the settlor). The effective rate is the IHT calculated as a percentage of the total notional transfer. The effective rate is then time apportioned by applying the fraction $q/40$ where:

(c) The effective rate is then time apportioned by applying the fraction $q/40$ where:

$q =$ the number of complete quarters between the start of the trust and the day before the distribution (special pro-rata rules apply for added-property)

$40 =$ the number of complete quarters in the ten-year period

(d) The actual IHT rate to apply to the capital distribution is found by taking 30% of the apportioned effective rate in (c).

(e) If 100% business property relief (BPR) applied on the original transfer into the trust it cannot be used to reduce the value of the shares initially received by the trust – the trustees will not have held them for the requisite two years. However, once the shares have been held for the relevant 'two-year' period, 100% BPR can be applied against the value of the shares subject to a distribution or exit charge.

(f) No exit charge arises within the first three months of the start of the trust (or a subsequent ten-year charge).

(g) If the trustees pay the tax, the value of the property leaving the trust has to be 'grossed up' for the relevant IHT.

Note – Many trusts will be set up within the settlor's nil rate band and hence the calculation in (a) above will be nil. This means that no exit charge will generally arise during the first ten years.

Example 8

Calculation of IHT on capital distribution (during first ten years)

On 20 November 2009 Mr Magnusson transferred a 30% shareholding in his property investment company, Magnusson Properties Ltd, to The Magnusson Trust. The trust was primarily for the benefit of his son, Terry (aged 22), who was entitled to the income of the trust. (Note, the gain on the transfer of the shares was held-over under *TCGA 1992, s 260*. Hold-over relief is available since the trust was *not* a settlor-interested one – Mr Magnusson's son is over 18 years old.)

The value of the shares settled into the trust was agreed with HMRC – Shares Valuation at £450,000. At the time of the transfer, Mr Magnusson had made chargeable transfers of £200,000 within the previous seven years.

Assume that on (say) 5 September 2011, the trustees advanced capital of £100,000 to Terry (exercising their power under the trust deed).

The IHT payable on the exit charge would be £758, calculated as follows:

5 September 2011 – capital distribution of £100,000	£
Value of hypothetical chargeable transfer	
Value of 30% shareholding at 20 November 2009*	450,000
Total of previous chargeable transfers	200,000
Aggregate chargeable transfer	650,000
IHT at lifetime (half-death) rates	
First £325,000 × 0%	–
Next £325,000 × 20%	65,000
	65,000
Less: Tax on previous chargeable transfers	–

Tax on assumed chargeable transfer	<u>65,000</u>
Effective rate:	
£65,000/£450,000 × 100	<u>14.4444%</u>
No business property relief is available since Magnusson Properties Ltd is an investment company	
Number of complete quarters between start (Nov 2009) and exit (Sept 2011)	7
Rate chargeable:	
14.4444% (effective rate) × 7/40 × 30%	0.7583%
IHT payable:	
£100,000 × 0.7583%	<u>£758</u>

First ten-year (or periodic) charge

17.74 Interest in possession trusts set up after 21 March 2006 are 'relevant property' trusts and are therefore subject to a ten-year anniversary (or periodic) charge. The ten year anniversary is taken from when the trust started. Where the trust is created under a will, the date of the testator's death is treated as the commencement date.

IHTA 1984, ss 64–66 provides for the calculation of the ten-year charge, which is summarised in Table 2 below. See Example 9 for calculation of a ten-year charge.

Table 2 – Computation of ten-year charge

(a) Compute the chargeable amount – this is based on the value of the trust property immediately before the ten-year anniversary. The trust property includes the capital and the accumulated income of the trust and is reduced by its liabilities. Where the trust property includes shares in an owner-managed company, they are likely to qualify for 100% business property relief (after two years) which can be deducted in arriving at the chargeable amount.

(b) Calculate the actual rate of tax to apply to the value of the trust in (a). This is 30% of the effective IHT payable on a notional transfer consisting of:

– the chargeable amount in (a)

– the value of any related-settlement at commencement;

  –   the value at commencement of any other property in the settlement which is not relevant property

  –   the total chargeable transfers made by the ettler of the trust within the seven years before they created the trust;

  –   the total of any capital distributions that have been subject to an exit charge within the last ten years (before the relevant anniversary).

The actual tax is calculated by reference to the prevailing nil rate band at the relevant ten-year anniversary.

(c)   100% BPR is available provided the trustees satisfy the relevant BPR conditions at the relevant ten-year anniversary date.

(d)   If the value of the other trust assets falls within the nil rate band, there will be no ten-year charge (ie those not qualifying for BPR).

(e)   The ten-year charge is payable by the trustees (but there is no 'grossing-up').

(f)   Where some of the property was not relevant property for the whole of the 10 year period there are special rules to time apportion the charge.

Notes

(1)   In many cases, trusts will be established within the settlor's nil rate band. Provided the settlor has no prior chargeable transfers (as will often be the case), the ten year charge will frequently simplify to an IHT rate of 6% (ie 30% × lifetime charge of 20% (in b)) being applied to the current value of the trust assets (*after deducting the prevailing nil rate band*).

(2)   If qualifying shares are retained in the trust, they will often attract 100% BPR and hence would be exempted from the taxable value of the trust assets.

IHT treatment of pre-22 March 2006 life interest trusts

17.75   The *FA 2006* retains the pre-existing IHT treatment for existing interest in possession trusts (ie those trusts established before Budget day 2006) whilst the present interest continues. Under the pre-*FA 2006* regime, life tenants of such trusts are treated as owning the underlying capital of the trust for IHT purposes, even if they are never entitled to receive it [*IHTA 1984, s 49(1)*]. Thus, where a life tenant of an interest in possession trust dies, their IHT liability is calculated by adding their part of the trust fund to their personal estate. The IHT relating to the trust capital is paid by the trustees out of the trust funds.

As a result of the rules in 17.76, any increase in the value of the chargeable assets up to the date of death generally escapes liability to CGT [*TCGA 1992, s 72(1), (1A)*]. Where a life interest under an existing IIP terminates after 21 March 2006, this will either be:

- a PET, if the settlement comes to an end at that time so the life tenant is treated as making a gift to another individual under *IHTA 1984, s 3A (1A) (c)-(i)* (see 17.10); or

- a chargeable transfer, if the settlement continues – this will generally be a 'relevant property' trust and the life tenant is treated as making a chargeable transfer when the interest is terminated (see 17.64). Furthermore, the life tenant is treated as making a *gift* of the 'no longer possessed' property. This means that there will be a GROB where they retain an interest in or have continuing enjoyment in that property (see 17.95)

CGT on termination of pre-22 March 2006 life interest

17.76   The underlying assets of a pre-22 March 2006 interest in possession (or a TSI) are effectively rebased for capital gains purposes, where that interest terminates on the life tenant's death and the assets pass to the individual(s) becoming absolutely entitled. In such cases, there will be a deemed disposal and reacquisition by the trustees of the shares/other assets at their market value [*TCGA 1992, ss 71–73*]. The deemed disposal does not give rise to any chargeable gain (or allowable loss). Nevertheless, CGT will crystallise on any held-over gain claimed [*TCGA 1992, s 74*] when the shares, etc were originally transferred into the trust. Where the interest terminates before 6 April 2008, taper relief may reduce the tax on the crystallised gain (based on the trustee's holding period). (Under the pre-6 April 2008 rules, if the original transfer into trust took place between 1 April 1982 and 5 April 1988, the held-over gain can be halved under the transitional rebasing rules in *TCGA 1992, Sch 4, para 2*.)

Where the shares qualify as a business asset under *TCGA 1992, s 165(2)(b)* (which will often be the case for a trading company), then the crystallised held-over gain can be the subject of a further hold-over claim under *TCGA 1992, s 165* (see 13.19–13.21).

Where a life interest ends (other than on the death of a life tenant, for example, on their re-marriage) with the property remaining in trust, there is no CGT effect.

Protected 'immediate post-death interest' (IPDI) trusts created by will

17.77   The pre-*FA 2006* IHT treatment of interest in possession trusts will continue where the life interest is created through the settlor's will or intestacy – referred to an immediate post-death interest (IPDI) trust. In such cases, the life interest commences *immediately* on death. HMRC accept that this test is met where the interest in possession takes effect on death by virtue of the special 'reading back' provisions for deeds of variation (see 17.18) or survivorship clauses (*IHTA 1984, s 92*)

The 'immediate post-death interest' (IPDI) is taxed under the old regime. This means that the life tenant is treated as owning the underlying capital of the trust under *IHTA 1984, s 49A*. It will therefore be included in the life tenant's estate for IHT purposes on their death (see 17.76). Whilst the IPDI continues it will not be treated as a 'relevant property' trust – the life interest is not subject to any exit or periodic charges.

The testator would be eligible for the spouse/civil partner exemption where an IPDI is granted in favour of the testator's spouse (or civil partner) (see also 17.50).

Transitional serial interest (TSIs) trusts

17.78 *IHTA 1984, s 49C* provides special protection for existing life interests (at 22 March 2006) that come to an end between 6 April 2006 and 5 October 2008. These rules apply to pre-22 March 2006 life interest trusts that terminate before 6 October 2008 and on that event, another interest in possession is created.

DISCRETIONARY TRUSTS

Flexibility of discretionary trusts

17.79 Discretionary trusts probably give the greatest flexibility for estate and IHT planning and largely remain unaffected by the *FA 2006* IHT trust changes. The income (for example, dividends on the shares) and often the capital would be held by the trustees to be dealt with at their discretion. The trustees (normally including the proprietor) will usually have the power to accumulate the income arising in the trust (normally) during the first 21 years and decide which interest each of the children will have in the trust's assets at a later date.

These features should help to make genuine discretionary trusts relatively safe from divorce claims (unless perhaps where there is a regular pattern of income being paid out or where the trust has been formed to 'frustrate' such claims). The beneficiaries are entirely reliant on the trustees' discretion being exercised in their favour. Hence, where there are concerns or fears about their children's marriages or other long-term relationships, parents may prefer to place the company's shares in a discretionary trust rather than give them directly to their children.

Following the *FA 2006* abolition of the beneficial statutory regime for accumulation and maintenance trusts (see 17.96), discretionary trusts generally play an important role in planning for grandchildren – for example, to provide for school fees. The trustees can assess and monitor the needs of each grandchild and the lump sum(s) transferred into the trust will reduce the value of the grandparent-donor's estate for IHT. Alternatively, outright gifts can be made within the donor's annual £3,000 exemption (see 17.9) each academic year.

Income tax payable by discretionary trusts

Self-assessment return

17.80 The trustees are returning the trust's income (and capital gains) on the trust self-assessment return form (SA 900) and paying the relevant income tax under the normal self-assessment timetable. Two equal annual payments on account are made on 31 January (during the tax year) and 31 July (following the end of the tax year). These 'on account' payments are normally based on the trust's income tax liability for the previous year. Where the trust's tax liability for the relevant tax year exceeds the two payments on account, a further balancing payment is due on the 31 January (following the end of the tax year). Similarly, if too much tax has been paid on account, then a repayment is due from HMRC.

Example 9

Income tax SA payments by trust

The Pardew Discretionary Trust made the following tax payments on account of its income tax liability for 2011/12.

31 January 2012 – *(50% of 2010/11 liability of £24,000)*	£12,000
31 July 2012 – *(50% of 2010/11 liability of £24,000)*	£12,000

The trust's 2011/12 self-assessment return was completed in January 2013 and the tax liability for 2011/12 was calculated as £27,500. Thus, the total payment due to HMRC by 31 January 2013 would be £17,250, calculated as follows:

Balancing payment due for 2011/12 – *(£27,500 less payments on account of £24,000)*	£3,500
1st payment on account for 2012/13 – *(50% of 2011/12 liability of £27,500)*	£13,750
Total income tax payable	£17,250

RELEVANT TAX RATES

17.81 Since income may be accumulated within discretionary trusts, they are subject to special rules. It is perhaps unfortunate that the former Labour Government sought to unduly penalise many discretionary and accumulation and maintenance trusts. The post-5 April 2010 penal 'top' income tax rates apply to such trusts irrespective of their income levels (subject to the paltry £1,000 standard rate band!). Trusts do not have any upper income threshold before these rates apply.

The current relevant trust rates (on income above the £1,000 standard trust rate band) are:

Income	Trust rates
Dividends and distributions	42.5% (the 'dividend trust rate)
All other income	50% (the 'trust rate')

The standard trust rate applied to the first £1,000 income (since 2006/07) is the one which an individual taxpayer would pay on the relevant type of income (*ITA 2007, s 491*). This means a basic rate of 20% on property or trading income, or savings income, and 10% on dividend income, with the appropriate special tax rate being applied in that sequence. Where the settlor has created more than one trust, the available standard rate band is shared equally between the trusts subject to a minimum of £200 for each trust [*IHTA 2007, s 492*].

Currently income (other than dividend income) above the £1,000 standard rate band is taxed at the trust rate of 50%. Thus (ignoring trust expenses), the trust will pay extra tax of 30% on income already taxed at 20%. The net rate on gross dividend income is 32.5% (42.5% less the 10% tax credit) – this corresponds to an effective rate of 36.11% on the cash dividends received. Trust management expenses can be deducted against trust income taxable at the normal trust rate (50%) and dividend trust rate (42.5%) (see 17.83).

In the face of the penal income tax rates, the trustees could consider granting (temporary) revocable interests in possession to improve the level of post-tax distributions to beneficiaries (see 17.69). Once the appropriate income has been distributed to the relevant beneficiary/beneficiaries, the life interest can be revoked thus retaining the discretionary nature of the trust. In some cases, it may even be appropriate to convert the discretionary trust to an interest in possession trust (which now involves no IHT difficulty since both 'trusts' remain within the 'relevant property' regime for trusts).

In *Howell v Trippier* [2004] STC 1245, the Court of Appeal held that a stock dividend was chargeable at (what is now) the dividend trust rate. The trustees argued that the stock dividend (representing shares worth some £15 million) represented capital for trust law purposes and was *not* 'income which is to be accumulated or payable at the discretion of the trustees' which was taxable under (what is now *IHT 2007, s 479*) but this analysis was rejected.

When the income is distributed to the beneficiaries, credit is given for the tax suffered by the trust, thus avoiding double taxation (see 17.86).

Trusts with only a small amount of income (ie below the £1,000 'standard trust rate' band) are likely to avoid payment of the normal trust rate on their income. Their standard rate liability would generally be covered by tax deducted at source/dividend tax credits).

Special rules apply to qualifying trusts with vulnerable beneficiaries (ie defined disabled persons and certain minors). By making an appropriate election, trustees (and the beneficiary) can elect to compute their income tax liability by reference to the individual beneficiary's personal allowances and basic rate band (see *FA 2005, ss 23–45* and *Sch 1*).

Trust rates for 2009/10 and 2008/09

17.82   The trust tax rates for 2009/10 and 2008/09 can be summarised as follows:

		2009/10 and 2008/09
Trust rate on 'non-dividend' income	*Standard trust rate on income up to £1,000**	10%
	1st – Non-savings income	20%
	2nd – Savings income	20%
	Income above £1,000	40%
Dividend trust rate	3rd – *Standard trust rate on income up to £1,000**	10%
	Income above £1,000	32.5%
		(22.5% after deducting 10% tax credit)

* Special trust rate is applied to income in the order specified above.

Deduction of trust management expenses

17.83 Trustees can deduct trust management expenses that are properly chargeable to income in calculating their taxable income at the 50% trust rate or 42.5% dividend trust rates (but *not* in calculating income taxable at the special *lower* trust rates). This means that the income applied in paying trust expenses would suffer the relevant lower rates of tax.

The expenses of managing a trust can be deducted against the relevant trust income provided they are properly chargeable from trust income. Following the *ITA 2007*, HMRC accepts that trust expenses from 6 April 2007 are deductible from trust income on an accruals basis.

Based on the leading precedent set by *Carver v Duncan* and *Bosanquet v Allen* [1985] STC 356, HMRC's view is that where an expense benefits the entire trust fund, then it should be charged to 'capital' and thus disallowed (even where the expense is recurrent). This was confirmed in *Trustees Of Peter Clay Discretionary Trust v R&CC* [2009] STC 928 which considered the treatment of management expenses incurred by a large discretionary trust. Before the Court of Appeal hearing, HMRC agreed that it was possible for the following expenses to be apportioned (generally on a time-spent basis)

- Executive trustee fees' (charged on a time-spent basis)
- Bank charges
- Custodian fees
- Professional fees for accountancy and administration

Amounts apportioned to income could be deducted by the trust. For example, the time spent by an executive trustee in exercising their judgment in relation to 'income' matters could be properly apportioned to and deducted against income.

The Court of Appeal therefore only had to rule on the treatment of the investment management fees and the non-executive trustee fees':

- Investment management fees were, on the facts, properly chargeable to capital. Once the trustees had decided to accumulate the income, those monies were regarded as capital. Thus, investment advice relating to income that was to be accumulated was for the benefit of the entire trust fund, since the advice determined the best way to make the income into capital

- *Fixed* fees of non-executive trustees could be apportioned between income and capital where adequate records were kept of the time spent on each part. However, the difficulty in this case was that no such records were maintained. It was therefore difficult for the trustees to establish the time spent addressing matters that were exclusively for the benefit of income.

Trust management expenses should therefore be apportioned between income and capital based on the proportion of the work performed on each element – as well as being required for tax purposes there is also the need to protect the interest of different classes of beneficiaries. Where fixed fees are charged the trustees should ask the service-provider to keep and log appropriate time sheets to support an 'income/capital' split of the fixed fee.

In practice, HMRC will generally allow, for example, the cost of maintaining accounting records and preparing tax returns and certificates (with appropriate apportionment being made between income and capital). On the other hand, expenses relating to changing trustees or seeking investment advice would be classified as capital and would not be admissible deductions. Although investment management charges may be levied on a regular basis, they clearly relate to capital as confirmed by *Carver v Duncan* [1985] STC 928

Trust management expenses (chargeable against income) are deductible in calculating the trustee's 'additional' income tax (but not their 'lower/basic' rate) (see Example 10 at 17.86). For these purposes, the expenses are matched with the different sources of income in the following order:

(*a*) Distribution and stock dividend income;

(*b*) Foreign dividends;

(*c*) Savings income (for example, bank and building society interest);

(*d*) Other income (for example, property and trading income).

Income distributed to beneficiaries

17.84 Where income is paid out to the beneficiaries, each beneficiary is given a form R185 (trust income) showing the net amount and the tax credit – the gross amount is the income multiplied by 100/50 (before 6 April 2010 – 100/60).

However, since the trustees are deemed to have suffered the 50% tax on their distributions, they have to ensure that they have suffered this tax (in the current or previous tax year) and account for it under *ITA 2007, s 496*. The trustees' *s 496* liability is calculated as follows:

Income tax due under *s 494*

Trust distributions × 50/100	A
Less: Trustees tax pool available for the year (ie tax pool b/fwd + tax paid by trust for the relevant tax year)	(B)
Trustees' *s 496* tax liability	X

The trustees' tax pool broadly represents the income tax incurred by the trust at the trust rate or dividend trust rate (and, from 6 April 2005, the tax paid at the lower standard rates of 20% or 22%). Non-repayable dividend tax credits do not enter the pool, which makes the receipt and distribution of dividend income very costly – see 17.85.

Where tax paid in previous tax years has not been used to 'frank' the tax on payments to beneficiaries, the 'excess' amount is carried forward as the trustees' tax pool to the following tax year.

Each beneficiary's share of income is subsequently reported on their personal tax return (using the information supplied on their R185 on 'form SA 107', with credit being given for the 50% (before 6 April 2010 – 40%) tax that is deemed to have been suffered. Thus, if a beneficiary's income tax liability on their trust distribution is less than the 50% tax deducted at source, an appropriate tax repayment will be made. The deemed 50% deduction applies, irrespective of the underlying tax rate suffered by the trust.

DISTRIBUTION OF POST-5 APRIL 2010 DIVIDEND INCOME

17.85   However, since dividends do not carry a *repayable* tax credit, the tax credit cannot be included in the trustees' tax pool . This means, that distributions paid to beneficiaries out of *dividend* income received by the trust will suffer an additional layer of tax (unless the trustees already have a sufficient pool of 'tax paid' to make up for the lack of dividend tax credits) as shown below:

	£
Dividend (2011/12)	90
Tax credit (1/9)	10
Gross dividend	100
Tax payable by trust	
Dividend tax @ 42.5%	42.50
Less: Tax credit	(10.00)
Tax paid to HMRC	32.50
Maximum distribution to beneficiary	
Net dividend (= cash)	90.00
Less: Total tax @ 50%	(45.00)
Amount distributed to beneficiary	45.00
Breakdown of tax	
Tax on dividend (see above)	32.50
s 496 additional tax on distribution (£45 less £32.50)	12.50
	45.00
Overall effective rate on net cash dividend	**50%**
(£45/£90 × 100%)	
Overall effective rate on gross dividend	**45%**
(£45/£100 × 100%)	

If dividends are continually paid out to beneficiaries, the trustees' pool of tax credits will eventually become depleted, leading to additional tax payable by the trust on the distributions paid out.

Of course, this problem should not arise if little or no (dividend) income is paid out to beneficiaries or funds are paid out as a genuine capital distribution.

In some cases, it may be appropriate for the shares held by the discretionary trust to be redesignated as a separate class of shares (although continuing to rank *pari passu* with the other shares, which would avoid any 'value-shifting' charge). This would build in additional flexibility with regard to future dividend payments enabling, for example, different levels of dividend to be paid out. Indeed, in some cases, assuming there are no problems under the 'settlement' rules, it may be more efficient for a separate class of shares to be held directly by those 'family' shareholders (who have little or no other income) to enable 'tax-free' dividends to be paid within their basic rate bands.

Many discretionary trusts will have been created to hold shares and similar investments, normally due to the availability of CGT hold-over relief under *TCGA 1992, s 260*. However, an interest in possession trust is a more tax efficient vehicle for holding shares and receiving dividends (since there it does not suffer any additional income tax charge).

Where a discretionary trust receives substantial dividend income, there may be a case for converting it into an interest in possession trust (provided there is no conflict with the settlor's intentions and so on). Since both are 'relevant property' trusts under the *FA 2006* regime, this can be done without triggering any IHT exit charges.

Worked example of trustee's income tax liability

Example 10

Calculation of income tax payable by discretionary trust

17.86   The Venables Discretionary Trust has the following income and expenses for 2011/12.

	£
Bank interest (net)	5,200
UK dividends	19,000
Trust expenses	(2,800)

The trustee's income tax liability for 2011/12 is calculated as follows:

	Gross	Tax Credit
	£	£
UK dividends ((£19,000 – £2,800 expenses) = £16,200 × 100/90)	18,000	1,800
Bank interest (£5,200 × 100/80)	6,500	1,300
	24,500	3,100

Tax	£	£
Special lower rate (on bank interest) – £1,000 @ 20%		200
On balance of trust income after expenses (£24,500 less £1,000)		
Dividend income – £18,000 @ 42.5%		7,650
Bank interest – £5,500 @ 50%		2,750
		10,600
Less tax credits		(3,100)
Tax payable		7,500

Assume that £1,700 is included in the trustee's tax credit pool brought forward at 6 April 2011.

The trustees' available pool of tax credits is:

	£
Tax pool b/fwd	1,700
Tax liability for year (£10,600 less *non-repayable* dividend tax credit of £1,800)	8,800
Available tax pool under s497	10,500

The trustees' make a distribution of £20,000 to a beneficiary on 31 December 2011 , which is grossed up at 50% – £40,000 (£20,000 × 100/50), with a tax credit of £20,000.

The trustees would be liable to pay an additional liability for 2011/12 under *ITA 2007, s 496* of £9,500, calculated as follows:

	£
Tax deducted from distribution (£20,000 × 50%)	20,000
Available tax pool for year	(10,500)
Additional liability for 2010/11	9,500

CGT payable by discretionary trust

17.87   Discretionary trusts are subject to CGT at the rate of 28%. (Between 6 April 2008 and 22 June 2010, gains were taxed at 18% and at 40% before 6 April 2008.) The capital gains are computed with the normal trust exemption in the same way as a life interest/interest in possession trust.

Where chargeable assets are distributed to a beneficiary (or the beneficiary otherwise becomes absolutely entitled to the relevant assets), a deemed disposal at market value arises under *TCGA 1992, s 71*. Capital gains arising on the distribution of assets to beneficiaries can normally be held over under *TCGA 1992, s 260* (since this is a chargeable transfer for IHT purposes, even if it is at 'nil rate') – see 17.62. It should be noted that *TCGA 1992, s 260* relief takes precedence over *TCGA 1992, s 165* relief (*TCGA 1992, s 165(3)(d)*). Since the disposal is being made from the trust, the trustees must jointly elect with the recipient beneficiary to hold-over the gain.

However, no *TCGA 1992, s 260* hold-over relief is available for assets distributed within the first three months of the trust's life or within the three months following a 'ten-year' anniversary charge. Nevertheless, if the asset transferred is a qualifying business asset, such as shares in an unquoted trading company, it will usually be possible to claim hold-over relief under *TCGA 1992, s 165* instead.

IHT/CGT on assets transferred to discretionary trust

17.88   The broad objective of the IHT regime is to treat a discretionary trust (and, following *FA 2006*, most other trusts) as though it were a separate individual. The underlying capital of the trust is not attributed to the beneficiary or beneficiaries. IHT is therefore collected from the trust as though a gift of the property held by it had been made every generation. However, given the need to collect the tax at more regular intervals, each discretionary trust is currently subject to IHT when property leaves the trust and also there is a periodic charge every ten years (at a maximum rate of 6%).

The general view is that these tax costs represent a reasonable toll-charge to pay for the privilege of keeping property in a separate trust as opposed to remaining in an individual's taxable estate. However, in practice, most trusts have tended to pay only modest amounts of IHT or nothing at all. This is largely due to the operation of the 'nil rate' band and/or important reliefs (such as business property relief or agricultural property relief).

17.89   A gift of assets into a discretionary trust has always been a *chargeable transfer* and is not a PET – the same IHT treatment therefore applies both before and after the *FA 2006* changes. Consequently, to avoid a 20% IHT charge, the value transferred should normally be kept within the transferor's nil rate band (allowing for annual exemptions) and any available business property relief (BPR) – see 17.16–17.33.

If the value of the asset exceeds the transferor's available nil rate band, they could consider reducing the amount of the chargeable transfer by *selling* the asset to the trustees at an under-value, leaving the consideration unpaid (and secured by a charge or formal loan note.

In most cases, BPR will apply (where the shares have been owned for the requisite 'two-year' period) to avoid any IHT chargeable transfer on the transfer of shares in a private family or owner-managed company.

If the shares do not qualify for BPR, for example, if the company (mainly) carries on an investment business (see 17.26), then a lifetime IHT charge at 20% can only be avoided if the relevant value transferred (see 17.4) is broadly within the transferor's available nil rate band, preferably allowing some 'headroom' for agreeing the share value(s) with the HMRC Shares Valuation team.

CGT hold-over relief will normally be available (under *TCGA 1992, s 260*) for the transfer of shares, etc to a discretionary trust, except where relief is denied under the 'settlor-interested' rule (see 17.62). It should be noted that hold-over relief under *TCGA 1992, s 260* takes priority over any *TCGA 1992, s 165* hold-over claim for CGT (see 17.87). However, if the transferor has sold the asset to the trustees at an under-value, there may be a chargeable gain on the 'realised' amount (ie the excess of the actual consideration over the transferor's base cost) due to the restriction in hold-over relief under *TCGA 1992, s260(5)* (see also 13.17). This restriction would not operate if the asset is sold for no more than the transferor's original CGT base cost.

17.90   Before 17 April 2002, it was possible to reduce the value of the chargeable transfer by using a special form of discretionary trust, often called a *'Melville'* type trust after the name of the case that established the legal precedent. Such trusts typically *include the settlor* as a potential beneficiary and give them the right to direct the trustees to transfer all or part of the trust property to them. Based on the decision in *Melville v CIR* [2001] STC 1271, this arrangement enabled the value of the settlor's retained right (for the trustees to return all or part of the trust property to them) to be taken into account as 'valuable' property for IHT purposes. Hence, the 'diminution in value' of the settlor's estate (see 17.5) was substantially reduced. It will be appreciated that this enabled *TCGA 1992, s 260* hold-over relief to be claimed on a substantial transfer of investment assets, such as shares and loan notes held in a listed plc which were not eligible for BPR. From 17 April 2002, *FA 2002* effectively blocked the '*Melville*' trust arrangement and subsequent legislation has also blocked similar variants of the scheme.

Capital distributions from 'nil rate band' trusts

17.91   If the shares were originally transferred within the nil rate band, then no IHT arises on a subsequent appointment of the shares to the beneficiaries (or to another trust) within the *first ten years*. The position where the transfer of shares to the trust was made under the protection of BPR is dealt with in 17.73.

Calculating IHT on capital distributions (during first ten years)

17.92   A distribution or exit IHT charge arises on assets (such as shares) or cash distributed to beneficiaries. This is based on a notional transfer of the value of the shares (and any other property in the trust) *immediately after the trust started*, computed at one-half of the death rate ie 20% (taking into account the transferor's nil rate band). That amount is then multiplied by 3/10 × q/40 (where q is the number of complete quarters between the start of the trust and the day before the distribution).

No IHT charge arises on property distributed within the *first three months* of the creation of the trust (or ten-year charge).

The detailed computational rules for exit charges (during the first ten years) are covered in 17.73. See 17.94 for calculation of IHT on capital distributions made after a ten year charge.

Ten-year or periodic charge

17.93   A discretionary trust is subject to a periodic IHT charge every ten years, which is broadly 30% of the rate applicable to a deemed transfer of the current value of the property held in the trust (taking into account the settlor's total lifetime transfers within the seven years prior to the creation of the trust) [*IHTA 1984, s 66*]. If the relevant trust property had not been held in the trust throughout the ten-year period, the effective rate is reduced by 1/40th for each complete quarter (three months) before the property was transferred into the trust. See 17.74 for detailed rules for calculating the ten-year charge.

The maximum ten-yearly charge is 6% (being 30% × 20%), but is usually lower. This is generally considered to be an acceptable price to pay for the privilege of placing the shares and other assets outside the settlor's and beneficiaries' estates.

Example 11

Calculation of a ten-year anniversary charge

The Pompey Family 2001 discretionary trust was set up on 24 June 2001 by Mr Pompey for the benefit of his children and grandchildren.

On that date, Mr Pompey transferred a 49% shareholding in the Fratton Park Property Investment Company Ltd to the trust. Mr Pompey had previously made several PETs, but no chargeable transfers.

The ten-yearly charge for the trust falls to be calculated on 24 June 2011.

Following negotiations with HMRC's Shares Valuation team, the value of a 49% holding at 24 June 2011 is finally agreed at £870,000. This represented the entire value of the trust.

Calculation of the ten-yearly charge

	£
Value of assumed chargeable transfer	
Value of 49% shareholding at 24 June 2011	870,000
Total of previous chargeable transfers	–
Aggregate chargeable transfer	
IHT at lifetime (half-death) rates	870,000
First £325,000 × 0%	–
Next £545,000 × 20%	109,000
	109,000
Less: Tax on previous chargeable transfers	–
Tax on assumed chargeable transfer	109,000
Effective rate:	
£109,000/£870,000 × 100	12.52874%
Rate chargeable:	
12.52874% × 3/10	3.758621%
IHT payable:	
£870,000 × 3.758621%	£32,700

No BPR is available as the company does not qualify as a trading company for BPR purposes (see 17.74). However, it is possible for the trustees to pay the IHT of £32,700 in ten equal instalments. This is because broadly the underlying trust property represents shares in an unquoted company, the value transferred exceeds £20,000 and the shareholding is more than 10% [*IHTA 1984, ss 227(1) (c), (2)(b)* and *228(1)(d),(3)*].

Calculating IHT on capital distributions after a ten-year charge

17.94   Exit charges on capital distributions made after a ten year charge are based on the effective IHT rate at the last ten-year anniversary. However, the rate must be recalculated by reference to the nil rate band prevailing at the time of the distribution.

Gifts with reservation of benefit (GROB) rule

17.95   The gift with reservation of benefit rules will apply if the settlor is able to benefit directly or indirectly from the gifted shares, ie as an actual or potential beneficiary (*Law Society Gazette*, letter of 10 December 1986). On the other hand, if the settlor retains a reversionary interest (ie has an interest subject to some prior right), this is not treated as a reserved benefit (Inland Revenue letter of 18 May 1987).

If a benefit has been reserved, the shares would be treated as remaining within the proprietor's estate for IHT purposes (although BPR may be available). However, this does not alter the IHT status of the original chargeable transfer – any potential 'double' IHT charge is mitigated by the *IHT (Double Charges Relief) Regulations (SI 1987 No 1130), regs 5* and *8 [FA 1986, s 102]*. The GROB rules only operate for IHT purposes and do not affect the operation of any other taxes – for example, a disposal will arise for CGT purposes in the normal way.

The continued receipt of (favourable) remuneration from the company via arrangements made prior to a gift of shares by a proprietor/trustee might be regarded as a reservation of benefit. However, HMRC accept that this will not be the case where the remuneration received is 'reasonable' (see also 17.45).

ACCUMULATION AND MAINTENANCE TRUSTS

Abolition of the favourable IHT regime for pre-22 March 2006 A&M trusts

17.96   Accumulation and maintenance (A&M) trusts are trusts that were specially created to fall within the privileged IHT treatment. In some ways, it is better to think of A&M trusts in terms of a favoured IHT regime rather than a particular type of trust. A&M trusts were primarily intended for minor children and enabled shares or other assets to be retained within a beneficial IHT regime for a relatively long time.

Although akin to a discretionary trust, such trusts did not incur any ten-year anniversary charge or exit charges. Furthermore, the transfer of assets to an A&M trust was a PET. However, the A&M's tax privileges were effectively withdrawn by *FA 2006* [*FA 2006, Sch 20, paras 2, 3*]. This means that it is likely that few, if any, new A&M trusts will be created – any new A&M trust would be subject to the normal IHT 'relevant property' regime and any assets transferred into them would be chargeable.

Under special transitional rules, the *FA 2006* regime permits *existing* A&M trusts to retain their IHT advantages until 6 April 2008 (see 17.99 below). At that point, the property held within the trust will be subject to the normal 'relevant property' rules (see 17.64). Any new trusts set up for the children/ grandchildren of a family are now likely to be framed as a discretionary trust, with powers to accumulate the income or apply if for the children's education and/or maintenance.

Pre-22 March 2006 A&M trusts – qualifying conditions

17.97   To obtain (and retain) the beneficial A&M trust treatment, the trusts had to be carefully drafted to meet the necessary conditions in *IHTA 1984, s 71*. The main requirements were as follows:

- one or more of the young beneficiaries *must* either become absolutely entitled to their share of the trust property or have the right to the interest in possession from it by age 25 at the latest, although it can be as early as their 18th birthday;

- no interest in possession must subsist and the trust's income must either be accumulated or distributed for the maintenance, education or other benefit of the trust's beneficiary or beneficiaries; and

- all the beneficiaries must have a common grandparent (*or* not more than 25 years must have elapsed since the settlement was made).

If there was any possibility of the conditions being breached, the trust would not benefit from the beneficial IHT rules for A&M trusts – the normal discretionary trust rules would then apply.

Many settlors felt that it was prudent to give the beneficiaries only the right to the income from age 18 or 25, preferring to delay the release of capital until a later date. Where capital assets were appointed subsequent to the beneficiary/ beneficiaries having the right to the income, then it was not be possible to obtain hold-over relief unless the assets qualified as business assets under *TCGA 1992, s 165*, for example, shares in an unquoted trading company (see below).

The trust income may be accumulated during the relevant accumulation period, generally up to 21 years, although it may be applied for the general maintenance and education (for example, school fees) of the beneficiaries.

Creation of A&M trusts under pre-FA 2006 regime

17.98   Under the pre-*FA 2006* rules, a transfer of shares to an A&M trust would have been a PET for IHT purposes, and therefore completely exempt from IHT provided the donor survived the 'seven year' period (see 17.10). As this was not a chargeable transfer for IHT purposes, CGT hold-over relief could only be claimed under *TCGA 1992, s 165* (since *TCGA 1992, s 260* relief was not available).

It was therefore normally possible to transfer shares in most family and owner-managed companies with the benefit of hold-over relief. On the other hand, capital gains were likely to arise where *non-business* assets, such as a portfolio of quoted investments or non-agricultural land, were transferred to an A&M trust.

Treatment of existing A&M trusts (post-21 March 2006)

17.99   A&M trusts were a popular vehicle for holding shares in the family company or other family assets for the benefit of the (minor) children or grandchildren of the family. The assets could be sheltered from IHT for a relatively long period. Furthermore, it was not necessary for the children/ grandchildren to acquire the assets absolutely by their 25th birthday. They frequently only became entitled to an interest in possession at that age (as was permitted under the *IHTA 1984, s 71* rules (see 17.97)).

FA 2006 enabled the existing 'A&M' treatment to remain until 6 April 2008 (or earlier) for those trusts subsisting at 22 March 2006. This gave time for settlors to rearrange their affairs! Such trusts could enter the regime before 6 April 2008 where, for example, an interest in possession vested before then. Having considered the settlor's intentions and the needs of the beneficiaries, some trustees decided to 'break' their trust before 6 April 2008 by appointing the assets outright to the beneficiaries (where this was possible under the terms of the trust deed).

In other cases, the trustees generally had to apply to the court to break-up the trust. Any assets appointed out before 6 April 2008 (provided no earlier IIP subsisted) were free of IHT and would be available for CGT hold-over relief (see 17.100).

Any assets held within an A&M trust at 6 April 2008 will have entered the normal 'relevant property' trust regime (see 17.101) *except* where:

- the terms of the trust were amended to provide that assets will go to the beneficiary/beneficiaries absolutely on their 18th birthday (ie are given the capital outright) [*FA 2006, Sch 20, para 3(1), (2)*]; or

- the trust then qualifies as an allowable 'Age 18 to 25' trust (see 17.70).

Relatively few existing A&M trusts permitted property to pass outright on (or before) the beneficiary reaching the age of 18. They will therefore have needed amending by 6 April 2008 if they were to continue to benefit from the favourable A&M trust rules. Where a beneficiary becomes absolutely entitled to their share of the trust's assets on their 18th birthday this will *not* be subject to an exit charge (but see 17.102).

IHT advantages for 'protected' A&M trusts

17.100   Existing A&M trusts enjoy considerable IHT advantages whilst they are still subject to the pre-*FA 2006* regime (but see 17.99 above). Since they are not treated as a 'relevant property' trust, existing A&M trusts are *not* subject to either the normal ten-year or exit charges.

Capital payments or distributions to a beneficiary (for example, when the beneficiary becomes absolutely entitled to the trust assets) do not give rise to any IHT liability. However, there may be problems in securing CGT hold-over relief where the 'distributed' asset does not attract hold-over relief under *TCGA 1992, s 165*. Whilst *TCGA 1992, s 260(2)(d)* provides a CGT hold-over mechanism for assets transferred out of an existing A&M trust, it is fairly restrictive. This is because the relief is only available where the beneficiary has *not already* become entitled to an interest in possession before 22 March 2006. In the majority of cases, the beneficiary will already have become entitled to receive the income of the trust (this automatically occurs under the *Trustee Act 1925, s 31* unless the trust deed expressly or impliedly excludes it). Thus, where capital assets are appropriated after the beneficiary has previously obtained an interest in possession, hold-over relief is only available where the asset qualifies as a business asset within *TCGA 1992, s 165* (see 13.9). However, where the interest in possession arose after 21 March 2006 the assets became relevant property at that stage and *s 260* CGT holdover relief is available on a distribution, albeit with an IHT exit charge.

Existing A&M trusts entering the 'relevant property' regime at 6 April 2008

17.101   Where an existing A&M trust has become subject to the normal 'relevant property' rules on 6 April 2008, it will become subject to (amongst other things) ten-year anniversary charges and exit charges (see 17.73 and 17.54).

The ten-year anniversary charge is computed from the date the trust was created [*IHTA 1984, s 61(1)*] but the IHT rate only reflects the period between 6 April 2008 and the relevant ten year anniversary date. This means that the tax rate is reduced for each complete quarter from the start of the trust (or, if this was more than ten years ago, the last 'notional' ten-year date) and 6 April 2008.

THE FA 2006 'AGE 18 TO 25' TRUST REGIME

Background to the 'Age 18 to 25' IHT trust regime

17.102 The thrust of the original Budget 2006 proposals (particularly in relation to A&M trusts) was to encourage the passing of assets to beneficiaries on their 18th birthday! These plans met with considerable criticism – parents and trustees were aghast at the idea of capital assets passing to 'spendthrift' children at such a young age! The government response was to introduce a compromise solution for those who did not want to release capital outright at 18. In June 2006, amendments were therefore made to the original Finance Bill 2006 permitting existing A&M trusts to become (so-called) 'Age 18 to 25 trusts'. Such trusts offer partial protection by giving a lower exit charge on assets passing out to a beneficiary after their 18th birthday (provided they vest by the age of 25) and by exempting them from the normal 'ten-year charge'.

Basic section 71D conditions

17.103 Assets held within an existing A&M trust can be held on an 'Age 18 to 25 trust' (or *s 71D* trust) where the terms of the trust deed are amended so that the assets pass absolutely to beneficiaries on (or before) their 25th birthday.

In broad terms, *IHTA 1984, s 71D(3)* applies the 'Age 18 to 25' trust regime to an existing A&M trust at 6 April 2008 where:

- the trust holds assets for a beneficiary who has *not* at that time reached the age of 25;

- the beneficiary will become absolutely entitled to the assets (not just an interest in possession) at or before the age of 25 (together with all the trust income that has been accumulated for their benefit).

Under the 'Age 18 to 25' trust regime, a reduced 'exit' charge applies after the beneficiary's 18th birthday, when the beneficiary:

- becomes absolutely entitled to the trust property;

- has assets applied for their benefit; or

- dies.

The calculation of the 'exit' charge follows the principles in 17.73, but the effective rate is only based on the period after the beneficiary's 18th birthday. This will therefore be a maximum period of seven years – producing a maximum rate of 4.2% (ie 6% × 7/10).

Income and capital gains of A&M trusts

17.104   Income tax liabilities of A&M trusts are calculated in the same way as those of general discretionary trusts – the rules set out in 17.80–17.81 will therefore apply.

Income currently paid to or for the benefit of the 'young' beneficiaries is deemed to have suffered tax of 40% (50% after 6 April 2010). In the case of payments to grandchildren, their personal allowances may completely 'shelter' the payments received from the trust, enabling them to reclaim the 40%/50% tax deducted at source. The repayment claim would normally be made by the parent or guardian. This advantage cannot be obtained on payments to the settlor's *minor children*, as this income is deemed to be the settlor's under the parent-settlement rules in *ITTOIA 2005, s 629*.

Since 23 June 2010, trusts will pay CGT at 28% on their gains (after deducting the trust annual exemption). (Between 6 April 2008 and 23 June 2010, a flat CGT rate of 18% applies.) See 17.71 for further details.

Bereaved minor trust

17.105   This type of Will trust is likely to be used where a testator has young children. If they die while their children are under 18, the testator can provide for them using a bereaved minor trust (without giving them an immediate entitlement to income). This type of trust effectively retains the IHT advantages of the pre-*FA 2006* A&M trust regime (see 17.97), but the assets must vest when the beneficiaries reach 18 (see *IHTA 1984, ss 71A-71C*).

ASSETS HELD OUTSIDE THE COMPANY

BPR entitlement

17.106   It is not uncommon for the company's trading property to be owned by the controlling shareholder with the property being let to the company. However, this is detrimental for IHT purposes. BPR of only 50% is available for land, buildings, machinery or plant used in the company's trade, but held outside the company where the owner of the asset is a controlling shareholder. This means that the owner must be in a position to exercise the majority of the voting rights ('related property' shareholdings are also counted for this purpose) [*IHTA 1984, ss 104(1)(b)* and *105(1)(d)*]. If the proprietor is also a first named trustee of a discretionary trust which holds shares in the company, these may also be taken into account on the grounds that (as first named trustee), he would have control of the voting rights (see *Taxation Practitioner*, November 1994).

Thus, where the company's trading property is held outside the company by the proprietor, there is a strong incentive for them to retain a controlling shareholding. It may, of course, be possible for the proprietor to increase the relief on the property to 100% by transferring it to the company by way of gift (under a *TCGA 1992, s 165* business asset hold-over election). 100% BPR will then be available on the value of the shares, which will have been uplifted by the value of the property. This course of action would have to be weighed against the potential commercial disadvantages, such as exposing the property to claims by the company's creditors.

However, if the value of the property was held by the company and was therefore reflected in the value of the company's shares, 100% BPR would be available.

17.107 If the trading property is held by a non-controlling shareholder, no BPR would be available. The property would then be fully chargeable to IHT, even if it was used for the purposes of the company's trade.

17.108 If the property is held by an elderly member of the family (perhaps the founder or founder's widow) and is particularly valuable, consideration might be given to transferring some additional shares to them so as to give a controlling holding, particularly if the shares and property will revert to the next generation on their death. Obviously, a considerable element of trust is required here!

Gifting or selling trading property to the company

17.109 Where it is feasible (and much would depend on the disposition of any other shareholdings), the property could be gifted to the company, with hold-over relief being claimed under *TCGA 1992, s 165*. It should be noted that a gift to a company cannot qualify as a PET (*IHTA 1984, s 3A*), but, if the company is wholly-owned by the transferor, there will be no reduction in value of their estate. However, any gift of property would normally incur an SDLT charge by reference to the market value of the property.

17.110 If the shareholdings are fragmented, then careful consideration will need to be exercised to ascertain the value of the transfer (particularly bearing in mind the discount attaching to minority shareholdings). Alternatively, a transfer of value or gift could probably be avoided by transferring the property in exchange for shares (as there would be no 'donative intent'). However, a

CGT liability might arise – business asset gift hold-over relief would not be available as full consideration would be received in shares. SDLT may also arise on the property.

PRE-OWNED ASSETS – INCOME TAX CHARGE

Outline of pre-owned assets (POA) charge

17.111 From 2005/06 onwards, an income tax charge on certain pre-owned assets (POAs) may be levied in appropriate cases. Given that the POA rules may potentially impact on certain transactions undertaken by owner-managers, the relevant rules are briefly examined here. The pre-owned asset legislation (in *FA 2004, s 84* and *Sch 15*) is primarily aimed at a number of IHT avoidance arrangements that broadly enable individuals to dispose of their assets (for IHT purposes) whilst retaining the ability to use or have access to them. Such arrangements would generally be structured to avoid the gift with reservation of benefit (or GROB) rules (see 17.10 and 17.95). However, given its wide-ranging nature, the POA legislation could also affect many innocent transactions, sometimes in an unsuspected manner.

POA charge on land

Basic charge on land

17.112 In broad terms, the basic POA charge on land applies where the individual (the chargeable person) currently *occupies* the relevant land and (since 18 March 1986) they had either:

(a) disposed of the relevant land or other property (with someone else using any sale proceeds from a subsequent sale of that other property to acquire the relevant land, unless the original disposal of the land/other property was via an excluded transaction (see 17.114)) (known as the *'disposal condition'*); or

(b) gifted someone else directly/indirectly with part of the consideration (other than via an excluded transaction – see 17.114) to acquire the relevant land interest (known as the *'contribution condition'*). Importantly, no POA charge applies where a gift of cash is made more than seven years before the first time the POA charge applies (being the later of 6 April 2005 and the date of the occupation).

One of the main pre-conditions is that the chargeable person is in 'occupation' of the relevant land, which is construed widely. For example, it covers actual occupation of the property, using it for storage purposes, and having exclusive access to the property and using it from time to time. On the other hand, it would not cover limited use of a former residence (for example, social visits, short-term stays (less than one month a year), or social visits). A landlord would not be regarded as being in occupation of property from which they receive rental income (see para 4.6, *'Pre-Owned Assets – Technical Guidance Notes'* March 2005).

Practical application of POA rules

17.113 Although the scope of the POA rules seems potentially wide, in practice, many cases should escape a POA charge either because they involve an 'excluded transaction' (see 17.114) or are covered by one of the exemptions (see 17.115). Thus, for example, (say) David gifts his house to his son Brooklyn and continues to live in that property, this would be caught by the 'disposal condition' above. However, since the house will remain in David's estate under the gift with reservation of benefit rules (see 17.10 and 17.82), the arrangements will therefore be exempt from the POA charge. Similarly, if David *sold* the house (for full consideration) to Brooklyn, there would be no POA liability (since it would be an 'excluded transaction' – see 17.114).

The POA rules are primarily aimed at arrangements that seek to 'side-step' the gift with reservation of benefit (GROB) rules. As a general rule, the GROB provisions do not contain any tracing mechanism for outright gifts of cash. Thus, for example, in March 1999, Victoria made an outright cash gift of £300,000 to her daughter, Romeo. Three years later, in June 2002, Romeo spent £250,000 on purchasing a bungalow for her mother to live in (on a 'rent-free' basis). Provided the gift was not made conditional in some way, there should be no direct linkage between the benefit of Victoria's rent-free enjoyment of the bungalow and her prior cash gift. Consequently, it should not be caught by the GROB rules. However, from 6 April 2005, a POA charge will be levied on Victoria's occupation since the 'contribution condition' is satisfied. The POA charge would be based on the value of the bungalow at 5 April 2005 (see 17.117).

On the other hand, if Victoria had gifted the cash in (say) February 1998, she would be exempted from the POA charge under the 'seven year' rule (since the outright cash gift would have been made more than seven years before Victoria met the contribution condition on 6 April 2005). No POA charge therefore arises where cash gifts were made before 6 April 1998.

POA rules should not apply to genuine co-ownership arrangements. Provided a reasonable (say 50%) share in the family home is gifted to the donee (as a tenant in common) who also lives at home (for example, an adult child), then the PET should not be treated as a GROB because of the rules in *FA 1986, s 102B*. HMRC would expect to see living expenses being split on a reasonable basis or borne by the donor. The key point is that the donee(s) must not pay more than their fair share of the expenses. The POA charge does not apply because *FA 2004, Sch 15, para 11(5)(c)* prevents exemption where the occupation would be treated as a GROB but for *FA 1986, s 102B*. Such arrangements may also be useful for holiday homes.

It should not be overlooked that where children own the family home, a significant CGT liability may arise on its subsequent sale (as they would not normally benefit from any principal private residence relief under *TCGA 1992, s 222*). Where individuals retain the family home in their estate, IHT may be payable on it (often on the death of the surviving spouse), but the beneficiaries would obtain the benefit of a CGT-free uplift to market value.

Excluded transactions

17.114   *FA 2004, Sch 15, para 10* excludes a wide range of transactions from the POA charge, the main ones being where:

- the chargeable person disposes of their whole interest in property to an 'unconnected' third party on an arm's length basis or to a connected person on comparable arm's length terms;

- transfers to an individual's spouse (or by court order to their former spouse) made on an outright basis or to an interest in possession trust for the spouse's/former spouse's benefit. From 5 December 2005, this 'exclusion' rule also applies to transfers to a civil partner (see 17.9);

- outright gifts made within the annual IHT exemption of £3,000, and dispositions falling within the IHT family maintenance exemption.

As noted in 17.112, the provision of consideration for someone else's acquisition of property is an excluded transaction if this is by way of an outright gift of money made at least seven years before the later of 6 April 2005 or the occupation of the land.

Main exemptions

17.115   Key exemptions from the POA charge include cases where:

- the total taxable amount for the tax year does not exceed £5,000 (note that the £5,000 is not an exempt band, so that an annual rental value of (say) £5,100 would be fully subject to a POA charge); or

- the asset still forms part of the taxpayer's estate for IHT purposes either under general rules (but watch *FA 2006, s 80* exception) or on the basis that the asset is caught by the gift with 'reservation of benefit' rules – see 17.10 and 17.95) [*FA 2004, Sch 15, para 11*].

Election to bring assets within IHT regime

17.116   A number of taxpayers have used certain sophisticated arrangements (such as the home loan and double trust schemes) to take their 'homes' outside the charge to IHT. They are now likely to be vulnerable to an annual POA income tax charge.

Some may wish to avoid the POA charge, but would find it difficult (or very expensive) to carry out the necessary unravelling of such schemes, especially where trusts have been used. The legislation caters for this by providing an option to elect out of the POA regime by bringing the value of the property within the charge to IHT instead. This is achieved by treating the transactions as a GROB whilst the 'chargeable person' continues to occupy the property on a rent-free/low rent basis. This election should have been made by 31 January 2007 at the latest (or if the POA charge first applies after 2005/06, the deadline is 31 January in the tax year after the first tax year of charge). There is a concern that taxpayers have not made such elections because they were unaware of the requirement to do so. However, *FA 2007* gives HMRC the power to accept late elections in certain cases, particularly where the taxpayer did not previously know about their election obligation!

Where the property is able to qualify for some form of IHT relief/exemption, it would be beneficial to elect; other cases are likely to be less 'clear-cut' [*FA 2004, Sch 15, paras 21 and 22*].

Calculation of POA charge on land

17.117 The appropriate rental value for land is calculated (under *FA 2004, Sch 15, para 4*) as:

$$\frac{(R \times DV)}{V}$$

less any rent paid by the chargeable person (under a legal obligation, for example, lease agreement)

Where: $R =$ Annual rental value (assuming standard landlord's repairing lease)

$DV =$ Under the disposal condition, the value of the interest in the land disposed of by the chargeable person (or, where appropriate, the land value that can reasonably be attributable to the property sold by the chargeable person).

Under the contribution condition, the land value that can reasonably be attributed to the consideration provided by the chargeable person

$V =$ Value of the entire relevant land

The relevant values are taken on 6 April for the relevant tax year (unless the POA charge applies from a later date in the year). Once an initial valuation is made, subsequent valuations only have to be carried out every five years.

17.118

Example 10

Calculation of taxable amount under POA regime

In December 2001, Harry gifted shares (worth around £70,000) in Redknapp Management Ltd to his son, Jamie. In April 2008, these shares were sold for some £100,000. Jamie used these proceeds towards the purchase of a bungalow for £150,000, which was then occupied by his father as a main residence on a 'rent-free' basis. The annual rental value of the bungalow in 2011/12 is £16,000.

In this case, the shares are 'other property' that was sold by Jamie with the proceeds being used to buy an interest in land (the bungalow) to be occupied by his father. The 'disposal condition' (see 17.112) is therefore satisfied.

Harry will have an annual POA charge for 2011/12, calculated as follows:

$$£16,000 \times (£100,000/£150,000) = £10,667$$

POA rules for chattels

17.119   Similar rules apply to those who benefit from having free or low cost enjoyment of chattels (such as valuable paintings or ornaments) that they *formerly* owned. Unless the prior disposal qualifies for one of the exemptions/exclusions (see 17.114 and 7.115), a POA income tax charge would arise where either the 'disposal condition' or 'contribution condition' (see 17.112) was satisfied in relation to the relevant chattels [*FA 2004, Sch 15, paras 6* and *7*].

The calculation of the POA charge for chattels is calculated in a slightly different manner in that the official rate of interest is applied to the value of the chattels (as determined along the lines shown in 17.118). Any amount paid for the use or enjoyment of the chattels is deducted in arriving at the taxable amount.

POA rules for intangible property in which settlor retains interest

17.120   The POA rules also catch intangible property (which includes cash) that is transferred to a trust (after 17 March 1986) where the settlor would be taxed on the income of that property under *ITTOIA 2005, s 624* (previously *ICTA 1988, s 660A*). (However, the POA charge does not extend to cases where the trust is settlor-interested only because their spouse is able to benefit.)

In such cases, the POA tax charge is determined by applying the official rate of interest (see 7.54) to the value of the relevant intangible property. This value is then reduced by any income tax or CGT payable in respect of that property (under one of the 'settlor-interested' trust rules). Only the exemptions outlined in 17.115 apply to relevant intangible property.

Certain types of specialised insurance-based products are available to mitigate IHT in an efficient way. HMRC have confirmed that gift and loan trusts and discounted gift trusts (see 17.44) do not normally attract any POA income tax charge.

In the context of owner-managed companies, it is common for shareholders to take out life insurance policies to provide funds on their death to enable their shares to be purchased by their fellow shareholders/the company. Provided a shareholder is not a beneficiary of their own policy, it will not attract any POA charge.

PLANNING CHECKLIST

SUCCESSION PLANNING AND PASSING ON THE FAMILY OR OWNER-MANAGED COMPANY

Company

- Investment companies or trading companies that hold significant investments frequently involve material capital tax liabilities for the shareholders.

Working shareholders

- Succession planning options should be kept open to deal with changes in personal circumstances and tax law.

- Consider benefits of retaining shares in the family/owner-managed company to obtain complete exemption from IHT on death (donees also inherit shares at market value for CGT).

- Consider sensible will drafting to maximise use of available nil rate band and business property relief (BPR). In many cases, it would be beneficial to leave shares and other assets qualifying for BPR via a will discretionary trust (which could include the surviving spouse as one of the beneficiaries).

- Lifetime transfers to next generation (which may be necessary to preserve management morale, etc) are usually tax-free, but donee takes on deferred CGT liability.

- It is not possible to hold-over gains on transfers into trust in which the settlor, their spouse, or dependent children have an actual or discretionary interest.

- Owner managers who sell their companies (where, for example, there is no succession path) must consider their increased IHT exposure (since they will cease to hold exempt 'business property') and their realisation proceeds will be potentially chargeable to IHT at 40%. They may wish to consider the use of Discounted Gift Trusts as a means of sheltering part of this IHT liability.

- Trusts are particularly efficient since they can be used to retain control over shares, but enable value and future growth in shares to be transferred outside shareholder's estate.

- Discretionary trusts may offer a degree of protection for assets against subsequent divorce claims brought (for example) by the spouses of the owner-manager's children. They also offer a degree of flexibility and are a particularly useful vehicle for holding at least part of the shareholding in an owner-managed company. With the benefit of business property relief, any IHT charges should be minimal.

- Dividends received by discretionary trusts are generally liable to a trust dividend effective rate of 36.1% (once the trust income exceeds £1,000!). Because the 10% tax credit carried with dividends is not repayable this cannot be built into the trustees' tax pool to frank the onward distribution of the income to the beneficiaries, leading to an overall effective tax rate of 50%. Trustees may wish to consider granting revocable life interests/interests in possession to beneficiaries before they receive substantial dividends, since the dividends would then only be taxed at the beneficiaries' marginal tax rate. These interests can subsequently be revoked without any IHT consequences.

- In most cases, discretionary trusts will now be used to hold shares for the future benefit of the owner-manager's children and/or grandchildren (but watch 'hold-over' relief restriction where settlor's *minor* children benefit from the trust).

- Interest in possession trusts tend to be used where the settlor wishes to provide an automatic right to income (but wishes to protect the underlying capital assets from their potentially 'wastrel' children). However, following *FA 2006*, such trusts are now exposed to exit and ten-year IHT charges (subject to any exemption conferred by business property relief or the settlor's nil rate band). However, the CGT savings that may be available from claiming hold-over relief (irrespective of the type of asset) may well outweigh any IHT exit charges).

- Watch out for the potential application of the gift with reservation of benefit rules and the pre-owned assets income tax charge for certain family arrangements, particularly those involving the gifting of property that is subsequently occupied by the donor and certain settlor-interested trusts.

Other employees

- Key employees should be involved in succession planning or they may become disenchanted and leave.

- If there is strong second-tier management, consider an MBO if there is no obvious succession route.

Non-working shareholders

- Similar considerations apply as for working shareholders.

Index